Dean Acheson

Also by Robert L. Beisner

Twelve against Empire: The Anti-Imperialists, 1898–1900

From the Old Diplomacy to the New, 1865–1900

Arms at Rest: Peacemaking and Peacekeeping in American History
(co-edited with Joan R. Challinor)

American Foreign Relations since 1600: A Guide to the Literature
(Kurt W. Hanson, assistant editor)

Dean Acheson

A Life in the Cold War

ROBERT L. BEISNER

OXFORD
UNIVERSITY PRESS

OXFORD

UNIVERSITY PRESS

Oxford University Press, Inc., publishes works that further
Oxford University's objective of excellence
in research, scholarship, and education.

Oxford   New York
Auckland   Cape Town   Dar es Salaam   Hong Kong   Karachi
Kuala Lumpur   Madrid   Melbourne   Mexico City   Nairobi
New Delhi   Shanghai   Taipei   Toronto

With offices in
Argentina   Austria   Brazil   Chile   Czech Republic   France   Greece
Guatemala   Hungary   Italy   Japan   Poland   Portugal   Singapore
South Korea   Switzerland   Thailand   Turkey   Ukraine   Vietnam

Copyright © 2006 by Robert L. Beisner

Published by Oxford University Press, Inc.
198 Madison Avenue, New York, NY 10016

www.oup.com

First issued as an Oxford University Press paperback, 2009

Oxford is a registered trademark of Oxford University Press

Library of Congress Cataloging-in-Publication Data
Beisner, Robert L.
Dean Acheson : a life in the Cold War / Robert L. Beisner.
p. cm.
ISBN: 978-0-19-504578-9; 978-0-19-538248-8 (pbk.)
1. Acheson, Dean, 1893-1971.
2. Statesmen—United States—Biography.
3. United States—Foreign relations—1945-1953.
4. Cold War.   I. Title.
E748.A15B45   2006
973.918092—dc22
[B]   2006010820

Printed in the United States of America
on acid-free paper

To Valerie

CONTENTS

PART III

PART IV

PART V

PART VI

PART VII

ACKNOWLEDGMENTS

In one of his novels, Cormac McCarthy writes that knowledge comes from "borrowing and every fact a debt." I have certainly borrowed from numerous secondary sources, but those are properly credited in footnotes. Less obvious because not flagged in that conventional way are the many debts I owe to those who read all or parts of the manuscript. I owe the most to a group of talented friends who were generous and intrepid enough to read either all or virtually all of it: Kurt W. Hanson, Robert Kagan, Walter LaFeber, Melvyn P. Leffler, Wilson D. Miscamble, Anna K. Nelson, Chester J. Pach, Jr., and Sara Wilson. None hesitated to object when they thought I had erred or gone astray and cannot be indicted for the times I ignored their suggestions.

Others who read and critiqued substantial parts of the manuscript include Eduard M. Mark on the early cold war and McCarthyism; Howard Jones on the Truman Doctrine; Lawrence S. Kaplan, Frank Ninkovich, and Marc Trachtenberg on the early cold war, European diplomacy, NATO, and NSC-68; Warren I. Cohen on China; Michael H. Hunt on China and Indochina; Gary R. Hess and Michael M. Sheng on China, Indochina, and the Korean War; James I. Matray, William W. Stueck, Jr., and Heath Twichell, Jr., on the Korean War; George C. Herring, Jr., and Robert J. McMahon on Southeast Asia; Robert Griffith, John Earl Haynes, and Arthur M. Schlesinger, Jr., on Alger Hiss and McCarthyism; Andrew J. Rotter on India and Indochina; Peter L. Hahn and Linda Wills Qaimmaqami on the Middle East; Marc S. Gallicchio on Japan; Roger V. Dingman on Japan and the Korean War; Thomas Borstelmann and Thomas J. Noer on Africa; James F. Goode on the Middle East and Africa; and

Philip Brenner, Nick Cullather, Michael L. Krenn, Stephen G. Rabe, Stephen M. Streeter, and Christopher Welch on Latin America. Nor are any of these good people responsible for any of my errors.

Before writing came research, magnificently aided by Dianne Schaefer, who, among other things, screened the *New York Times* for the period covered in this book. In addition, both Laurie Bryant and Angie Blake found documents I had missed earlier, some at that most remarkable institution, the Truman Library in Independence, Missouri.

Librarians and research professionals were unfailingly helpful, both when I visited their institutions and when I telephoned or wrote with further inquiries. Particularly helpful were Dennis Bilger, Carol Briley, Benedict Zobrist, and Pauline Testerman at the Truman Library; Regina Greenwell, Claudia Anderson, Linda Hanson, Michael Parrish, and John Wilson at the Lyndon Baines Johnson Library in Austin, Texas; Robert Parks at the Roosevelt Library in Hyde Park, New York; and William J. Maher at the University of Illinois Archives. The staff of the American University Library was also invaluable to me, especially Rolliette Gooding, Mary Evangeliste, and Andrea Paredes-Herrera, who steadily supplied me with works borrowed from other libraries. I also thank the staff of the Yale University Library and, for providing illustrations, Marquette University and *Stars and Stripes*.

For leading me to particular documents and providing other helpful information, I also want to thank Senate historian Mary Baumann and state department historians Vicki Futscher, David Patterson, and Chris Tudda. Walt LaFeber and Arnold Offner generously gave me copies of documents from their own research in the Truman-Acheson era. Other vital documents came from Chris Welch, Bruce Craig, and Denis Smith. Key pieces of information came from Eileen Findlay, John Fousek, Elisabeth Griffith, George D. Moffett, and Stephen A. Schuker. Robin Barr listened to recordings with me to help characterize the tenor of Acheson's voice. Byrna Campbell and Christine Conroy photoduplicated and mailed numerous manuscript packages to my readers and publisher.

Throughout, I was the beneficiary of the extraordinary patience and good editorial judgment of Oxford's Sheldon Meyer and Peter Ginna. From her Oxford office, Laura Stickney was a great help as we moved from manuscript to finished book. Joellyn Ausanka expertly oversaw the entire production process; Aly Mostel was in charge of ideas about marketing; and Patterson Lamb helped through her thorough and sensitive copy-editing.

Even when they were not directly involved (or cared much about Dean Acheson), family members helped me enormously in keeping up the energy and commitment needed as I researched, wrote, and rewrote this book, and so I want to thank my children, John Beisner, Katharine Beisner, Signe Allen Linscott, and John Allen. Several marriages occurred during the gestation of my book, and three wonderful grandchildren appeared, too, Jack and Judd Linscott and Ruby

Ahlquist. Unfortunately, my parents, to whom I owed decades of extraordinary love and support, both died as the Acheson project neared its end, but the memory of Al and Charlene Beisner lives with me every day.

Finally, I thank my wonderful wife of thirty years, Valerie French. I am grateful to her not only on general principles but for her acute perceptions of Dean Acheson. She repeatedly offered on-target responses to my often inchoately formed notions of what Acheson did and what he stood for. In all seriousness, I think she often doubted I would ever complete this book, but I overheard her tell others that that didn't matter, because she could tell I was having a wonderful time researching and writing anyway. She is a fine historian and teacher herself, but she is the dedicatee of this book because she is simply a stunningly fine and generous person.

DEFINITIONS OF ACRONYMS
AND ABBREVIATIONS

AEC	Atomic Energy Commission
ANZUS	Australia, New Zealand, United States Security Treaty
Aramco	Arabian American Oil Company
CCP	Chinese Communist Party
CFM	Council of Foreign Ministers
CHINCOM	Coordinating Committee (for regulating western trade with People's Republic of China)
CIA	Central Intelligence Agency
CIG	Central Intelligence Group
CoCom	Coordinating Committee (for regulating western trade with Soviet bloc)
DOD	Department of Defense
ECA	Economic Cooperation Administration
EDC	European Defense Community
ERP	European Recovery Program
EUR	Europe (State Department division)
FBI	Federal Bureau of Investigation
FE	Far East (State Department division)
FRG	Federal Republic of Germany (West)
FSO	Foreign Service Officer
GAC	General Advisory Committee (Atomic Energy Commission)
GATT	General Agreement on Tariffs and Trade
GDP	Gross Domestic Product

GDR	German Democratic Republic (East)
GOP	Grand Old Party (Republican Party)
HST	Harry S Truman
HUAC	House Un-American Activities Committee
IMF	International Monetary Fund
JCS	Joint Chiefs of Staff
KGB	Based on Russian-language acronym for Soviet Security Agency
KMT	Kuomintang (Chinese Nationalist Party)
MDAP	Mutual Defense Assistance Program
NAACP	National Association for the Advancement of Colored People
NASA	National Aeronautics and Space Administration
NATO	North Atlantic Treaty Organization
NE	Near East (State Department division)
NSC	National Security Council
NSC-68	National Security Council Paper Number 68
NSC-81	National Security Council Paper Number 81
OSS	Office of Strategic Services
PINCHER	First post-World War II war plan against Soviet Union, 1946
PPS	Policy Planning Staff (State Department)
PRC	People's Republic of China
ROK	Republic of Korea (South Korea)
SAC	Strategic Air Command
SCAP	Supreme Commander Allied Powers (Japan)
SEATO	Southeast Asia Treaty Organization
SHAPE	Supreme Headquarters, Allied Powers, Europe
STEM	Special Technical and Economic Missions
SWNCC	State-War-Navy Coordinating Committee
TAPLINE	Trans-Arabian Pipeline
TCC	Temporary Council Committee ("Wise Men")
UK	United Kingdom
UN	United Nations
UNESCO	United Nations Educational, Scientific, and Cultural Organization
UNRRA	United Nations Relief and Rehabilitation Administration
USSR	Union of Soviet Socialist Republics
VFW	Veterans of Foreign Wars
VOA	Voice of America

Dean Acheson

1

INTRODUCTION
"THE SHINIEST FISH THAT
EVER CAME OUT OF THE SEA"

In the immediate aftermath of World War II, leaders of the victors had little sense of where they now stood. At first, it was unclear if new quarrels among the allies were transitory or the first round of a new conflict. It became clear soon enough. With the United States armed with nuclear weapons and the Soviet Union about to develop its own, with European empires crumbling and sharp disputes erupting in Iran, Greece, and Germany, tensions between east and west worsened. By 1950, armies again fired on one another, in Asia, thousands of miles from Washington and Moscow. The cold war was well under way, to last nearly a half century.

Some of the most significant milestones of the cold war occurred while Harry S Truman was president. Even many of his greatest admirers considered him an ordinary man, a true John Q. Citizen, but in scholars' rankings of presidents, he typically stands behind only Abraham Lincoln, George Washington, Franklin D. Roosevelt, Thomas Jefferson, Andrew Jackson, Theodore Roosevelt, and Woodrow Wilson. Underlying Truman's rating is admiration for the palpable courage with which he made some of the most important decisions in American history. He might have been less honored had he served in easier times, but he did not, and his large decisions tumbled one after another from the desk displaying the little sign saying, "The buck stops here."[1]

Dean G. Acheson was far from ordinary. As one of his law partners put it, he was "the shiniest fish that ever came out of the sea,"[2] uniting a pungent personality to a mind so keen his opponents scurried from its sweep. A slower and less forceful man would almost certainly have made a lesser record than Acheson, who became one of the greatest and most consequential secretaries of state in American history. His years in the state department confirm that individuals count in history.

Because the president was the responsible party, the subject of any sentence summarizing U.S. foreign policy in Acheson's era must be *Truman*. But scrutiny of the evidence highlights Acheson's highly visible influence, first as under secretary (1945–47) and then secretary of state (1949–53). His fingerprints— whole hand and footprints—are all over the president's diplomacy and national security policies. The link between the two men critically shaped the reputation of each. Truman's high standing rests on the shoulders of Acheson's achievements, but the president made those possible with gifts of trust and autonomy greatly expanding Acheson's reach. This does not mean they always agreed, and some of Acheson's most trying and absorbing moments came when they did not.

Knowing when those moments were likely to come requires knowing the men. The Truman in this book can be found, unfiltered, in the archival and public record, but I have also benefited from many biographers' and historians' studies. Regarding Acheson, I have only briefly replowed the ground of his early years that James Chace tilled in his biography, or of the post-secretarial years described in a book by Douglas Brinkley. Here, Acheson enters the state department at age forty-seven in Chapter 2. Noteworthy episodes of his retirement years appear in Chapter 36.[3]

In between is a comprehensive narrative and analysis of Acheson's years as a major American policymaker. I pay close attention to how he made policy, how he led others in the state department, and how he managed his relationship with Truman, all necessary to understand the policies he conducted in his years at the tiller. There is little mystery about what he believed in and wanted to do, for only the thinnest space appears between the Acheson who made public statements and the man who engaged in exchanges with other diplomats, between what he told Congress in testimony on the Hill and what he whispered to another foreign minister. Forthrightness was one of his most outstanding traits. Both he and Truman were likely to speak their minds.

While there is much here about other nations and their policies, this book is about a maker of the foreign policy of the *United States* and based mostly on its records, though I have examined many studies written from other states' vantage points. Because Acheson's core strategy was to increase western strength before approaching a negotiating table with the communists, negotiations make fewer appearances in the pages ahead than might be expected. By Acheson's design, and because Josef Stalin had meager interest in discussions for his own reasons, much of the following recounts U.S. relations with the United Kingdom, France, and the nascent new state in West Germany. An adept negotiator, Acheson practiced virtually all his "diplomacy" with allies rather than enemies.

The disparity between time spent talking to Britons and haggling with Russians is clear in his superb memoir, *Present at the Creation: My Years in the*

State Department.[4] The voice in this engaging Pulitzer Prize–winning memoir is vigorous and self-assured. The same is true of the Acheson appearing in the official documentary record. At the Truman Library in Independence, Missouri, I examined much of that record, along with over a hundred oral histories. I have also relied heavily on the official compilation of state department records, *Foreign Relations of the United States*. Acheson's personal correspondence at the Yale University Library was also invaluable, especially for his retirement years. Another extraordinary source is the four microfilm reels of "Princeton Seminars," tape-recorded sessions held at the Institute for Advanced Study in Princeton in 1953–54, with the assistance of Acheson's friend, J. Robert Oppenheimer. At Princeton, intending to marshal material for his memoirs, Acheson and colleagues exchanged memories of their work just past.

As the cliché has it, this large body of evidence for Acheson's diplomacy allows him to "speak for himself." Like all historians and biographers, however, I have made judgments about which sources best represent his "voice" and hope I have done so fairly and accurately. In finding meaning in the data and explaining and interpreting his actions, I sometimes add my own voice, not intending to mask my view of those actions.

There is little point for historians to write books and articles if their colleagues do not read and use them. Besides numerous biographies and memoirs, I have consulted thousands of secondary works. Many were essential as I fleshed out my narrative and formed my analyses. Acheson has thus far been fortunate in those writing about him, and among the most important works I have relied on are full studies of Acheson by Gaddis Smith, David McLellan, and James Chace, along with numerous monographs on particular facets of his record. I have found these, and many other works, highly useful, even when disagreeing with their interpretations, and have fully credited them in the footnotes.[5]

As I neared completion of this book, I coincidentally used some down time by reading Herman Melville's *Moby-Dick* for the first time. There I found the following passage: "Out of the trunk the branches grow; out of them, the twigs. So, in productive subjects, grow the chapters." So it has been with this book. Generalizations unsupported by details, or a mere "profile," are inadequate to an understanding of the productive Acheson. The only way to understand what he did and who he was in all their complexity, is to show him at work over time. I have tried to do this. The result is a book much shorter than it once was, longer than originally planned, but no longer than Acheson's place in the history of American diplomacy warrants.

Part I

2

RARE MEAT:
ADDING REACH TO POWER

Before the State Department

On 11 April 1893, when Dean Gooderham Acheson was born in Middletown, Connecticut, around thirty miles south of Hartford, Grover Cleveland was president. When Acheson finished his undergraduate education at Yale, Woodrow Wilson was in the White House. In between, insulated from depression and war, young Acheson lived a mostly charmed life, wrapped in a mother's love and steeled for later tests by a father's rigor. His mother, born Eleanor Gooderham, was the daughter of a wealthy banker and distiller in Toronto, where she met Dean's father, E. (Edward) Campion Acheson, a Scottish-Irish immigrant who became an Episcopal clergyman, Middletown's rector, and Bishop of the Connecticut Diocese. Son of a professional soldier who fought in the Crimean War, Edward distinguished himself in combat in the 1883 Riel Rebellion and fighting Indians in 1885. After this University of Toronto graduate married Miss Gooderham, they moved to Connecticut, where Dean, his younger brother Edward, and sister Margot lived their early days.[1]

The stylish and soldierly mien in the adult Dean that many called aristocratic drew on both parents. Though the Achesons of Middletown were not wealthy, they were attended daily by two servants and a governess and lived in a large house provided by distiller Gooderham. Tall and striking like her son, Dean's mother was a staunch anglophile who talked and dressed the part while focusing her energies on Middletown society. She indulged her children, who "adored her uncritically," surely in part because she was "a crack shot" with a .22

rifle she kept at her desk. "How dearly I love you and how necessary you are to my happiness," Acheson wrote her at thirteen. All his life he fed on her nurturing approval. The Right Reverend father, while sporadically fun loving, was erect and distant. Given to hyperbole in the pulpit, he would roar, "I believe in one God!" over an accompanying drum roll and the heads of cowed parishioners. When Dean as a college student argued with him over politics, the often stern and uncommunicative pastor banished him from the home for a year. But both father and mother supplied models of tolerance, good works, and democratic sentiment. A hospitable woman and efficient manager, Eleanor organized World War I Red Cross efforts and a local service of home nurses. Edward mixed comfortably with all manner of people, preached a theology of "hope and redemption," and defended workers' rights from the pulpit. When he discovered a Jewish shop-keeper needing religious education for his sons but stranded in a town with no synagogue, he brought them to Holy Trinity—"I'll teach them your religion. The Old Testament is good enough for me." The boys joined Dean in the choir.[2]

Acheson often waxed nostalgic about the fun and mischief of a sunny child-hood in a golden age. But there was school, too. Educated at first by a governess, in local schools, and at nearby Pomfret Academy, Acheson found himself sent to Groton prep school in Massachusetts in 1905, five years after Franklin Delano Roosevelt had left this breeder of statesmen. Although Acheson later persuaded himself of the school's value and sent his own son there, at the time he did not flourish, academically or socially. Groton was stuffy, and he was rascally. It had rules, and he was stiff-backed and smart-alecky. He performed poorly at his lessons. The Middletown youngster formed a lifelong friendship with the slightly older W. Averell Harriman, who mentored him in rowing, but Groton's master, Endicott Peabody, found Acheson immature. He wrote on his report card: "Irresponsible, forgets books, doesn't remember lessons, makes excuses." He was nearly expelled. When Peabody summoned his mother to confess he had failed "to make a Groton boy out of Dean," in riposte she said she wanted him educated, not made a "Groton boy." "Oh, we can educate him," said Peabody. "Then," she insisted, with Acheson's own later flair for getting his way, "I suggest you do it." He hung in to graduate in 1911 with a 68 average, last in a class of twenty-four. Later he spoke or wrote of Groton with evident crossness, entirely omitting it from the informal volume of memoirs (*Morning and Noon*) covering his early years.[3]

After graduating, he escaped for a summer working shoulder to shoulder with immigrants building railroads in far northern Canada, becoming adept with saws, axes, and other practical tools. The other laborers reinforced his father's preference for the "common man," helping fit his son for the roughhouse of American politics and sparing him much of the snootiness common among mid-century American diplomats. The summer had revived his "sense of freedom amidst uncoerced order" and recaptured "a priceless possession, joy in life. Never again was I to lose it or doubt it."[4]

"From the time of my first trip to New Haven, Yale was the college I wanted to attend," he later said. He had such a wonderful time there his friends thought he had much more money than actually filled his pockets. He was too busy partying, making friends, and rowing (with Harriman again) to hit a book. Sister Margot at Wellesley introduced him to her roommate, Alice Stanley, whom he later married, partly for "her dark bun and her dreamy Impressionist beauty." At Yale, he took on the stylish ways that later so infuriated his foes. Selected for Scroll and Key (just beneath Skull and Bones in cachet), he also joined Delta Kappa Epsilon, partied and rented a house with fellow DKE Cole Porter, and befriended other large talents-in-progress and future colleagues, including William C. Bullitt, Robert Lovett, and poet Archibald MacLeish. Acheson, "Archie" recalled, seemed "the typical son of an Episcopal bishop—gay, graceful, gallant." Lapsing from his father's views about the "common man," he also seemed "snobby," MacLeish thought, and not a little arrogant. Still, his peers selected him the "fifth most witty and tenth 'sportiest' in the class." A roommate recalled: "I don't remember seeing Dean study, although he must have. He was always ready for a good time, for a new experience." Acheson would later blame his neglect of studies, and even some of his superciliousness, on his rejection of Yale's archaic pedagogy, "learning things that were meaningless. You memorized more facts about subjects you had already memorized in school. There was no point in it—Greek, chemistry, biology—all those subjects had either been learned enough or they were not worth continuing."[5]

After a whirlwind, post-graduation trip to Japan, he moved to Harvard Law School, along with Bullitt, Porter, and MacLeish. Bullitt dropped out, and Porter, with whom Acheson shared a Cambridge house, was soon expelled before switching permanently to Broadway. Another year of merriment followed before Acheson fell under the spell of Felix Frankfurter. First discovering his own great intellectual powers, he became one of Frankfurter's all-time favorite students. Acheson made "a tremendous discovery," he recalled, of the "power of thought." The charmer was charmed by the law's unforgiving demand for logic and reason. "Not only did I become aware of this wonderful mechanism, the brain, but I became aware of an unlimited mass of material that was lying about the world waiting to be stuffed into the brain." The law would give him a way to think, to analyze and solve problems, and a means to personal advancement. In 1918, he graduated fifth in his class. Frankfurter had been his inspiration and now became a lifelong friend.[6]

In the summer of 1917, the threat of war with Mexico sent Acheson to train with a national guard unit (the Yale Battery) in the Poconos. He served in a Brooklyn Navy Yard naval auxiliary unit during World War I. In the meantime, on 5 May 1917, he married Alice Stanley, with Margot standing in as "best man." A talented painter interested in politics, Alice played a conventional role as spouse to a rising male professional. Central in giving Acheson a stable and predictable life, Alice, in MacLeish's words, was "a continually steadying breeze blowing from a fixed corner." While she awaited the birth of their first child with her in-laws (David, who would be followed by Jane and Mary), Dean returned to Harvard Law for graduate studies. He quickly abandoned these when Frankfurter nabbed him a job as clerk (then called "secretary") to new Supreme Court Justice Louis D. Brandeis. When the family moved to Washington in June 1919, Dean found his city of destiny and two more of his heroes, Brandeis and his colleague Oliver Wendell Holmes, Jr. That three jurists were his heroes, two of them Jews, argues for a deep legal-intellectual bias and immunity to some common contemporary prejudices. Brandeis and Holmes's intellectual rigor and skepticism greatly appealed to him, as did Holmes's astringent sense of duty. Writing briefs, making arguments, and testing them against Brandeis's mind immeasurably sharpened his own, while he honed his wit amid the caustic dialogues at Holmes's afternoon teas.

In 1921, he left Brandeis for the growing law firm of Covington, Burling and Rublee. His first successful assignment came with a team that won a case for Norway against the U.S. government before the Permanent Court of Arbitration at The Hague. He soon had a weighty caseload, mainly representing corporations and foreign governments. At twenty-eight, he had already placed himself amazingly well, the protégé of Frankfurter, Brandeis, and Holmes. As David S. McLellan writes, he had "what every young man longs for—a sense of destiny— the knowledge that one has been tested and that the gods have looked favorably." Compared to the stimulus of public office, however, day-to-day lawyering always threatened to bore him. Clients often vexed him. Still, he found outlet and achieved reputation in appellate venues, especially the U.S. Court of Appeals and the Supreme Court itself.[7]

Paid little at first, Acheson managed in 1922 to buy a bare-bones house on P Street in Georgetown, which he and Alice gradually enlarged. Two years later, they acquired a farm north of D.C. in Sandy Spring, Maryland, for relaxation and relief from Washington's frightful summers. The Achesons were enjoying themselves. At both homes, they hosted their friends, businessmen, judges, other attorneys, and those from the liberal left—MacLeish, writers Stuart Chase and Sinclair Lewis, the old muckraker Norman Hapgood, assorted La Follettes, and union leader John L. Lewis. Acheson helped Lucy Madeira find funds for her school for girls and joined its board of trustees in 1933. He thrived, discussing law, literature, and politics with smart people in a city that never bored him. He had already figured out that the center of American power was shifting from New York to Washington, and he was an ambitious man.[8]

The connections of his firm, in which he was a partner by 1926, led Acheson to growing involvement in the Democratic Party. Republican protectionism and his own pro-labor views, drawn from his father, Frankfurter, and Brandeis, secured his loyalty to the party. Being a Democrat then did little to boost a young Washington attorney's career, but respect for his firm and his Brandeis-Holmes lineage did. Acheson aspired for appointive office but seemed never to have considered going into electoral politics, a decision reinforced by living in the voteless District of Columbia. In 1932, with Democrats having a new chance to take national power for the first time in his adulthood, the thirty-nine-year-old Acheson participated in the Democratic convention on the fringes of Franklin Roosevelt's circle. He barnstormed for him in the Maryland suburbs and after the election helped draft his legislative program. Washington already knew him as "an international lawyer with a dazzling wit and a budding future," and he thought he deserved to become solicitor general in the justice department. Despite the backing of Frankfurter, who had himself turned it down, he did not get the job, possibly because his father as Episcopal Bishop of Connecticut had refused to sanction Attorney General Homer Cummings's most recent marriage. A bitter Acheson and his wife left the city for a long automobile trip.[9]

But he was closer to "the flypaper of taking part in government" than he thought. When he returned from vacation, he found an offer from Secretary of the Treasury William Woodin to become under secretary, though he was no economist. When the formal offer arrived on 19 May 1933, he quickly accepted. When Woodin fell gravely ill, Acheson as acting secretary found himself in the center of a noisy dispute with FDR—an "unequal encounter"—over currency policy. The president had decided to try raising incomes and creating jobs by deliberately stirring inflation, asserting his authority to raise the government price for gold, set by Congress at $20.67, to as high as $40. Many doubted the legality of this devaluation, but others thought it justified, including the attorney general. It was Acheson's job to make the purchases, for, as Drew Pearson noted in his column, Acheson was now the "virtual Secretary of the Treasury." His friend, New York banker James P. Warburg, was dismayed, and Brandeis reinforced Acheson's own view that the scheme was not only illegal, but would slash the value of government bonds held by both banks and individuals. Looking "scarlet"-faced and "like a thunder cloud," he went to see the president. The encounter was one of the most dreadful moments in a long career. Strenuously arguing against the maneuver, he demanded FDR give him written purchase instructions. It was easy enough for him to order people around, he told FDR, since he would incur no liability by putting *his* signature on the paper. No, *he* "would be the boy on the burning deck," as he later put it, "and there would be very few companions around." FDR erupted: "That will do!" Acheson executed the orders but still detested the policy. After rumors reached Roosevelt that Acheson was spreading stories about the gold policy, on 27 October he called a meeting at which he stormed that anyone refusing to support the inflation plan should get out of the administration. Briefly out of sickbed, Woodin told Acheson that FDR wanted to fire him; Woodin too would resign if that happened. "You'd better resign gracefully yourself," he concluded. FDR wrote asking for Acheson's resignation and then announced his departure to the press before his victim received the letter. It was only November 1933, and Acheson had been cashiered. *Then*—before FDR learned someone else had probably spread the irritating tales—Acheson wrote a gracious resignation letter, thanking FDR for his "many marks of kindness." Woodin's resignation quickly followed (because of his health), and Henry Morgenthau, Jr., became the new treasury secretary.[10]

Acheson recalled the blowup with FDR two decades later at one of his Princeton seminars. The incident "made very deep impressions" on him, and his dissatisfaction with his own performance strongly influenced how he arranged relations with "his" president. "It wasn't that what I had done was wrong," he said, but he had overlooked "the problems of the President, partly because I was young and shy [!] and wasn't on the inside." Overreacting to his offended feelings and wounded pride, he had caused a "public embarrassment" for FDR, particularly embarrassing because, after the inflationary policies failed, people gossiped about how Acheson had been right after all. What he should have done was declare his disagreement, resign, go on vacation, and drop "out of the picture without making any great crisis or fuss about the thing." He had learned the necessity of helping presidents protect their prestige, and when he became secretary of state, he was "quite determined" to avoid any fights with Truman. If they *did* fight, he would be sure no one else knew about it. And he would be alert to what a president needed to do instead of to his own reasons for not doing it.[11]

After his lopsided encounter with FDR, Acheson returned to what had become Covington, Burling, Rublee, Acheson, and Shorb. This was one of the first firms to grow prosperous guiding clients through the growing forest of New Deal regulations, but he quickly grew restive in his corporate regimen. Accustomed to the "French cuisine" and "rare meat" of political power, Frankfurter observed, Acheson found it "painful to return to the hardtack of the law." Nor was it enough to be a trustee of the new Brookings Institution or, after 1936, a senior fellow of the Yale Corporation, or to spend evenings reading about the history of Victorian Britain. The Treasury debacle still stung—and his father blamed him for it—despite how his sound financial views attracted clients, and he was eager to make amends. Rebuffing advances from conservatives, he attacked the Supreme Court assault on the New Deal and heaped praise on Secretary of State Cordell Hull's reciprocal trade agreements. Even though Acheson fought Roosevelt's attempt to purge Millard Tydings, a conservative Maryland Democrat, from the Senate in 1938, FDR, who also harbored misgivings about their clash, was forgiving. He was already telling others that Acheson knew "how a gentleman resigns." In 1939, the administration enlisted Acheson to work on a committee concerned with helping citizens running afoul of new federal regulations. The same year, after Acheson represented Frankfurter in successful and widely noted confirmation hearings for a seat on the high court, FDR offered him a place on the District of Columbia Federal Court of Appeals. Acheson declined the appointment, saying he "was too young for a life sentence to such sedentary confinement." Nor did he want to become the justice department's first assistant attorney general for civil rights.[12]

Going back to government would be fine, but he wanted to be in the middle of the action. In private life as a healthy, prospering, and well-connected gentleman still in his mid-forties, he lacked none of the accoutrements of success. Partner in a flourishing firm, a regular at the Supreme Court, he counted some of its justices as close friends. In practicing international law, he acquired influential new friends in Europe with whom he would reconnect during and after World War II. With three grown or growing children, Dean and Alice lived comfortably in Georgetown, which the New Deal had made a fashionable district. On weekends, they often took to their country digs (now the stylish "Harewood," even with its eighteenth-century buildings unheated until the 1940s). Alice painted. Dean created wood cabinets at his lathe and raised dahlias. They took nearly annual vacations in Murray Bay, Quebec. Acheson might even have resigned himself to remaining a civilian.[13]

Then on 1 September 1939, the Nazis attacked Poland, radically changing Acheson's life. The war returned him to public office in 1941, where he stayed until January 1953, except for eighteen months in 1947–48. His immediate response to the war was internationalist and interventionist. As a second-level bureaucrat, he would find in the war opportunities to serve, wield influence, and exercise power. In the war he would develop many of the views that later underlay his work as secretary of state. Hitler and Nazis aside, he came to believe the conflict grew out of the general international discord created by nationalistic, protectionist, and overly managed economies. In the course of the war, he would form strong impressions of all the important belligerents and of how to accomplish large objectives. Dismayed by the chaos in the state department, and its low status under FDR, he would also display a notable capacity for getting his way with superiors and genius for commanding the loyalty of subordinates. His wartime assignments would focus first on economics, then congressional relations, a job that would leave him deeply ambivalent about the federal legislature and public opinion.

In the State Department during World War II

In November 1939, three months after the war began in Europe, university overseer Acheson addressed Yale students in a speech that foreshadowed many of his later views. The breakdown of civility embodied in the "totalitarian military state" and the war itself, he told them, stemmed from the derangement of the international economy and final breakdown of vital banking and diplomatic mechanisms centered in the United Kingdom. Long before Britain and France came under attack, he dismissed what he later called the "autohypnotic trance" of American isolationists. It was impossible for the United States to hide from dangerous world events, and isolationism would cause it to be encircled with hostile fascist and hypernationalist regimes menacing to fundamental American interests and values. Thus encircled, the nation would be forced into actions that eroded its liberal economy and free polity, ending the "American experiment."

Acheson wanted the United States to send arms to those already fighting the Axis powers. It should also move quickly to increase its own military strength, both to defend against attacks from any quarter and to gain enough "striking power" to take the offensive. With the same faith in action that made him comfortable as a New Dealer, he also thought Americans should take the lead in creating a new international order, abandoning protectionism and other policies that stifled an open world economy. It was essential to avert the chains of economic smashup that led to totalitarianism and war. Though without the Soviet Union in mind, by 1939 he had already identified the key lineaments of an assertive strategy for countering dangerous powers, whoever they might be. The United States must amass military and economic strength. It must extend the "reach" of its power by pushing its security frontier as far as possible from its own borders. Like a "boxer," it must "add reach to power." His bare mention of Asia in his Yale speech also presaged his Eurocentric impulses. And he peppered his address with evidence of his preference for the practical over the metaphysical and speculative. It was a waste of time, he asserted, to worry about distinctions between defensive and offensive weapons in rebuilding U.S. military power, for on matters of security, "you can be wrong only once." The "judgment of nature upon error," he said, quoting Holmes's maxim, "is death."[14]

He later said that in 1940, FDR just "sat on his hands" while France collapsed and Britain came under air attack, but Roosevelt was certainly preferable to the isolationists. Acheson joined the Committee to Defend America by Aiding the Allies to push the president forward. No longer concerned about FDR's aptitude for playing fast and loose with the law, he also threw himself into finding a way to bypass Congress in the destroyer-bases deal, which allowed the president to send World War I destroyers to Britain in exchange for the right to build bases on British territories in the western hemisphere. He wrote campaign speeches for FDR's 1940 reelection campaign and in a radio broadcast called on Republican candidate Wendell Willkie to remove his "stage overalls" so the country could "have a real look at him"; without them, "we see clearly that he is not the man who is needed to guide America in the next four years."[15]

Early in 1941, after Acheson helped draft legislation for lend-lease, the reelected president's imaginative plan for sending U.S. aid to putative allies, Cordell Hull asked him to join the administration in the state department. On 1 February 1941, Brandeis administered the oath to a new assistant secretary of state for economic affairs. Acheson had returned to the diet of rare meat so abruptly taken from him in 1933.

No sooner had he taken office than he exploited some committee assignments to intrude deeply into the Asian conflict he had neglected at Yale. With FDR's tacit approval, treasury secretary Morgenthau pushed Hull to take a harder line against Japan. Having purportedly told a colleague the United States should "get into the war—*in order* to speed up our defense program," Acheson wanted Hull to be even more aggressive than Morgenthau asked, but most department officials backed the secretary's caution. Acheson could make his own moves, however, operating from the interagency Foreign Funds Control Committee. This body had authority over foreign assets in the United States, with a potential to block purchases of war products made in the United States. Through his department proxy, Under Secretary Sumner Welles,[16] FDR gave a vague nod in late July 1941 when the department, following on action Acheson and others had already taken, announced a freeze on Japanese assets held in the United States. This restricted Tokyo's ability to buy petroleum. FDR later claimed he only wanted to bring Japan "to its senses, not its knees," but in August he looked the other way when two additional committees refused to release Japanese funds for otherwise authorized export licenses. Officials never expressly informed Tokyo it could not buy petroleum but, in a decisive stroke, also never told it how *to* make purchases. With Welles's implicit support, Acheson had made an end-run around Hull and the department's Far Eastern Division. The ban on oil sales soon gained acceptance as a fait accompli, reversible only on pain of looking weak in the face of Japanese belligerence. The rest is familiar. Instead of moderating its behavior, Tokyo pushed into Indochina and prepared to attack the oil-rich Dutch East Indies. It also started planning a preemptive assault on Pearl Harbor.[17]

All this was wonderful rare meat indeed, but at times Acheson felt he dined alone. He had grave doubts about Roosevelt and about the department and his immediate boss, Cordell Hull. Most of Acheson's comments about FDR are disparaging—and retrospective, probably shaped by his later admiration for Harry Truman. The 1933 clash left an ineradicable image of a cavalier and superficial chief executive, eventually a powerful war leader but earlier unready for crisis and interested only in Latin America. Bereft of any strategic vision, he failed to identify mounting threats to U.S. security. This left policy to Hull's "moralistic, pacifist, and laissez faire preachments," backed by congressional isolationists and the country at large. Roosevelt struck Acheson as someone who thought he was "apart from mankind," not unlike the "Queen of Rumania" and other continental monarchs. Remarking on FDR's habit of patronizing and jollying subordinates, Acheson commented that it was "not gratifying to receive the easy greeting which milord might give a promising stable boy and pull one's forelock in return." He neither believed FDR had "hidden depths" nor succumbed to his charm.

He was especially critical of FDR's treatment of the state department, even though he agreed with much of the presidential indictment. Roosevelt sneered at the department's conservatism and incompetence and deliberately used his own ad hoc agents to circumvent its professionals. The result was a neglected, disorderly agency, brought to its lowest status in the history of the republic during the war. A probably apocryphal story said FDR gibed after Pearl Harbor that State "was neutral in this war," and he "hoped it would at least remain that way." He was hardly its only critic. "The faded and moth-eaten tradition of Victorian diplomacy," said writer Robert Bendiner, "seeps out of every cranny" of the "antiquated" nineteenth-century Victorian pile that housed State. There, next to the White House, officials operated from "a code of elegant cynicism" and "tactical shrewdness" that were irrelevant "beyond the horizons of the chessboard." Acheson was fond of the building itself, with its "great, high ceilings, little swing doors, fans on the top of the ceiling, spittoons on the floor," but he considered the agency inside somnolent, with neither premeditated strategies nor any other ideas. It could only react to external events of the moment. Immobilized in addition by divisions among encrusted geographic baronies, the department Acheson knew was utterly unprepared for war.[18]

Welles's privileged position deepened Hull's bitterness amid a series of explosive internecine mêlées. With FDR's amused sufferance, the "slow, circuitous, cautious" Hull made matters worse by focusing on stopping future wars with free trade and a successor to the dead League of Nations. Sunday mornings, he gathered his assistants to mull over the latest cables in a habit Acheson thought violated the Eighth Amendment ban on "cruel and unusual punishment." In wintertime, his office was so warm it left Acheson "half-fainting" and feeling "detached" from his "own body." Hull would inevitably summon an assistant, "an excellent Foreign Service Officer, Cecil Gray, known as 'Joe.'"

When he appeared, Mr. Hull would say, "Joe, look at that thermometer."
"Joe" would do so, and report: "Eighty, Mr. Secretary."
"I thought so," Mr. Hull would say. "Let's have some heat."

With the suspicious Hull simmering in his sauna over sundry "slights and grievances," State's influence leaked into oblivion. Some of the key actors would later serve Acheson as secretary of state. The chief player was FDR's medium, the sartorially splendid and formal Welles, with whom Acheson maintained cool but good relations. A class ahead of him at Groton, Welles once apologized for laughing at one of Alice's remarks: "Pardon me. You amused me." Other assistant secretaries included the gifted Adolf A. Berle, Jr., another FDR man and Acheson's only dedicated enemy. Acheson's own assistants included Donald Hiss (Alger Hiss's brother), later a close friend and law partner; Adrian (Butch) Fisher, soon to navigate bombers over Europe before becoming Secretary Acheson's legal adviser; and Edward G. (Eddie) Miller, Jr., who later became a law partner of John Foster Dulles before serving as Acheson's assistant secretary for inter-American affairs. Acheson's personal secretary was Barbara Evans, who stayed with him, in and out of government, for the rest of his life. *New York Times* reporter James Reston wrote that FDR without Marguerite (Missy) LeHand and Acheson without Evans "would have been as helpless as children."

FDR had wanted Acheson back in the government, considering him "the ablest lawyer in Washington." Outsiders, however, considered Acheson a Hull man. In fact, he sidestepped Hull's combat with Welles, which ended in the latter's forced resignation in 1943 over a past homosexual indiscretion. Berle, whose name rhymed with "surly" (*Time*'s apt touch), ballooned his dislike of

Acheson's connection to Frankfurter into a brief against him as a dangerous, pro-British, pro-Soviet liberal. David Acheson claims it was only the threat that Berle might write a biography of Acheson that prompted his father to write his own memoirs.[19]

Compared to the great endeavor of defeating the Axis, some of Acheson's first assignments seemed trifling. But to a man of ambition, they could all be of value. He armored himself against opponents and informed himself about the corps of career foreign service officers (FSOs) on various foreign service boards. Though it took "inordinate" time, he also learned how to scuffle with other agencies. He used his economic portfolio in defending Hull's authority, not always with success, but he seldom left even victorious opponents unscathed. Morgenthau's second-in-command, Harry Dexter White, called Acheson "a throat-slitter of a very vicious kind." In a 1944 controversy that illustrated Acheson's power to attract subordinates' devotion, he defended a young assistant, Eugene V. Rostow, against a rampaging Patrick J. Hurley. A onetime general and secretary of war periodically used by FDR, and a man Acheson said attracted trouble "like a cloud of flies around a steer," Hurley went on the warpath when Rostow called his plans to remake Iran in the American image so much "messianic globaloney." When Hurley stormed into the state department to berate Rostow, Acheson let him know that *he* was responsible for anything emerging from his office and "that how I conducted the internal affairs" of that office was none of his business. Unaware of Rostow's discharge from the army for serious back ailments, Hurley jeered, "If you were a real man, you'd have a uniform on now." Acheson threw himself between them and then refused to talk to Hurley until he behaved himself.[20]

Hurley was a nuisance, but Leo Pasvolsky, the Russian immigrant and economist who ran the Division of Special Research, drove Acheson half crazy with his myriad planning committees aimed at transforming the postwar world along liberal economic and democratic lines. Acheson was cold to many of these enthusiasms, anyway, but had to chair Pasvolsky's Subcommittee on Economic Policy, sit on the Reconstruction Subcommittee, and supervise the work of eight other committees. He attended seventy meetings of the Policy Committee and forty-four of the Post-War Programs Committee. Reams of reports and recommendations streamed from the committees, all rendered nugatory by State's impotence. He could not "remember one of the meetings," Acheson claimed. It was a "singularly sterile" project "uninspired by gifts either of insight or prophecy."[21]

In contrast, Acheson did relish most of his economic work, even when results were disappointing. Exercising export licensing powers to wage economic war evolved into an only marginally successful effort to block German trade with neutrals. Among the prime quarries were Spain and Switzerland, the latter, Acheson recalled, proving to be the very "cube of stubbornness." One of his more winning efforts came in 1944, when Washington sent tank fuel to Spanish dictator Francisco Franco as the price to end Spanish sales of strategic minerals to Hitler. Protecting historic ties to Spain and Portugal, Britain resisted more effective forays against them, and allied military action after the Normandy invasion rather than diplomatic-economic pressure finally stopped Sweden's ball bearing shipments to Germany. Swiss sales to the Third Reich ended only with the interposition of allied armies between the two countries, and Switzerland long remained singularly uncooperative in turning over Nazi gold looted from occupied Europe. "Finally," Acheson jabbed in his memoirs, "in April 1945, the Swiss surrendered—only a month before General Jodl did." He later concluded that the campaign against the neutrals "accomplished almost nothing."[22]

Acheson was also in the thick of 1943 talks leading to formation of UNRRA, the United Nations Relief and Rehabilitation Administration. There he first made friends with Jean Monnet, the Frenchman who did so much to promote postwar European unity, and Oliver Franks, the Briton who later became ambassador to Washington. Acheson saw his work founding UNRRA, which used some $4 billion to help people in countries liberated from the Nazis, as that of "John the Baptist of the Marshall Plan." The experience reinforced his view that preventing a new war required Europeans to abandon their über nationalist struggles against one another in favor of unity and cooperation. It took only another intellectual step or two for him to conclude, early in the cold war, that maintaining a "multilateralist" economy was a pivotal tactic in immunizing western Europe from the Soviet Union's sinister designs.[23]

He had the primary responsibility of negotiating the gritty details of lend-lease agreements with both the Soviets and the British. Although, as we shall see, he would be comparatively patient with Moscow in the first year after the war, three years of haggling with its diplomats had already left him with a sour taste for Russians themselves. They were "clumsy and difficult," trussed by hidebound instructions, and lacked a "feel for the possible." Much more rode on the British negotiations. As early as 1933, the UK embassy had viewed the "intelligent, energetic and humorous" Acheson as friendly to British interests. Thus, the British must have been taken aback when he used lend-lease talks to push for an end to their "imperial preference" system, which favored Britain's colonies and dominions in trade. Most American officials—Hull most aggressively—disliked this system, and Acheson particularly saw it as another example of the nationalist and restrictive economic behavior that had caused the war. He was resisted by Ambassador Lord Halifax, who considered Americans "very crude and semi-educated," and Acheson's primary British interlocutor, economist John Maynard Keynes. The latter succeeded in causing Acheson to reduce his pressure out of concern for the likely economic plight the UK would face after the war. Postwar U.S. interests, Acheson became convinced, would be far better served by a strong than a weakened United Kingdom, and it seemed especially important to preserve its ability to act in the Middle East and Asia. Acheson failed, however, to impart this vision to the treasury department, which demanded yet more liberal postwar trade rules and payment for the basing of U.S. troops on British territories. Treasury's chiefs, Morgenthau and White, he thought, wanted World War II to end with both enemies and allies "prostrate—enemies by military action, allies by bankruptcy." He was still trying to help protect British dollar reserves from Treasury depredations when Truman wrecked the effort by abruptly cutting off lend-lease in August 1945.[24]

"A Low Life but a Merry One"

Ill, tired, annoyed with Roosevelt, Hull resigned in November 1944. The forty-four-year-old Edward R. Stettinius, Jr., who had succeeded Welles as under secretary, took Hull's place. A former General Motors and U. S. Steel executive and lend-lease administrator, Stettinius came from central casting: tall, handsome, youthful, and silver-haired. Acheson thought he had "comparatively modest equipment" and called him "Snow White." Appointed because he would accept state department subservience, he adopted the United Nations negotiations as a personal project. But he also wanted his own team and in the "Christmas surprise" staged a purge. Replacing him as under secretary was the veteran foreign service officer, Joseph C. Grew, ambassador to Japan when Admiral Yamamoto struck Pearl Harbor. Stettinius dispatched Acheson nemesis Berle to Brazil and other assistant secretaries to private life. Among the newcomers were Nelson A. Rockefeller (briefly) for Latin America, career man James Clement Dunn for Europe, and Acheson's old friend MacLeish for cultural affairs. With no policy significance visible in these moves and the department recently exceeding its norm in chaos, commentators jeered at the reorganized team as "a bevy of tycoons surrounding" a "poet." A displeased FDR remarked that the versifier was "the only liberal in the bunch, which is topheavy with Old Dealers." Others too thought the changes had yanked the department from left to right.[25]

Acheson thought he was out of work, for his economic post went to the multilateralist seer and former Texas cotton factor, six-foot-six William L. Clayton. Summoned by Grew, yet another Groton alumnus, Acheson thought "Joe had the solemn and portentous look of an eminent physician about to impart grim news." Expecting a refusal, Grew offered Acheson Christmas leftovers, assistant secretary for congressional relations and international conferences. Acheson accepted, not wanting to depart in a "general housecleaning." But he was not happy and, having already sat for confirmation hearings in 1941, refused to join the rest of the new team before the Senate Committee on Foreign Relations. When the confirmation show moved to a mass swearing-in and rally at Constitution Hall, "complete with United States Marine Band," he grudgingly joined but again broke unanimity by wearing a light rather than a dark suit. When the beaming Stettinius completed his introductions by turning "last, but by no means least" to Acheson, "an evil spirit" prompted him to utter at the microphone: "These little pigs went to market/But this little pig stayed home."

Stettinius lasted six months, leaving in a general exodus of New Dealers from Truman's government. But Acheson threw himself into his new posting with verve. For someone reputed to scorn Congress, he demonstrated a surprising skill with senators and representatives. For eight months, he used his office as "a first-class law firm," writing speeches for congressmen and making them look good to their constituents by feeding them department information. In return, he expected them to look to him only when they wanted the department's help.[26]

While he lobbied for the department on the Hill, his daughter Mary took leave as an army cryptanalyst to convalesce from tuberculosis at Lake Saranac. Acheson tried speeding her recovery with a stream of cheerful letters, merrily exaggerating the fun he was having and waxing sarcastic about his new skill at backslapping. On 22 May 1945, he wrote: "At lunch at the Capitol I was asked to sit at a table with [Congresswoman] Jesse Sumner of Illinois, the worst of the rabble rousing isolationists." They "got along famously," raising doubts about whether he had "any principles at all." May 26: "This life is amusing but not calculated to engage or extend all those faculties which when used to the full give one the sense of the good life." June 7: "My poor aching feet! The badge of a statesman lobbying on Capitol Hill. . . . This is a low life but a merry one." June 13: "Bob Taft and I had it out in the Committee for two hours. He was rude; I was polite, but put fish hooks in his pants." June 21: In a lunch at the Senate, "a real Texas ham was offered and whiskey. I am getting to be a real politician." June 25: "This business of talking to everyone and attending meetings all day is a shiftless way of conducting oneself." Some congressional barons and baronets emerged from their transactions holding Acheson's chits, sometimes the other way around, but his enthusiasm was only for Mary's benefit. Soon, he seemed only to be hanging on, waiting for the right moment to leave or get a better position.[27]

Morgenthau and White bore the brunt of defending the historic Bretton Woods agreements of July 1945, but Acheson, who had insisted the U.S. delegation include members of Congress, provided major help in gaining congressional approval of these accords. The agreements had emerged from an international conference in the sylvan White Mountains of New Hampshire. At the conference, the U.S. government promoted what turned out to be remarkably durable institutions for organizing and stabilizing postwar economies. The International Monetary Fund (IMF) would regulate currencies, while the International Bank for Reconstruction and Development (World Bank) would finance loans to war-crippled and undeveloped economies. Treasury, represented by Harry White (who was passing information to the Soviet Union), dominated the conclave. From the World Bank committee run by Keynes, Acheson protected State's interests, resisted White's urge to bankrupt London, and fought off Soviet efforts to use a developmental institution for large war reconstruction loans. Moscow's role became moot in December 1945, when it backed out of a system it claimed was hostile to socialist principles.

Working with Keynes reinforced Acheson's view, drawn from many evenings of his reading, that the nineteenth-century international economy owed its fluidity to liberal lending by London banks. "Oh, heck with it," he told an assistant. "Trade isn't important. Money is the important thing to make the international economy work the way you want it to work." In defending the agreements in Congress in October 1944, he reiterated his fears of a return to thirties-style economic combat. This would lead to "a shrinking international trade, lower levels of living, and hostility between nations," with each country "trying to climb to some sort of security over the backs of its neighbors." Peace—and "free enterprise"—depended on a general expansion of worldwide production, trade, and consumption. The IMF and World Bank would help this come about, just as the United Nations would help order political relations between states. "To construct a peace there must be one peace—an economic peace as well as a political and military peace." Acheson predicted that recovery from the devastation of the war would generate huge demands for American goods from societies unable to pay for them, at least in the short run. Grants and credits would have to fill the gap, but ultimately world prosperity required wholesale changes in liberalizing trade and investment practices, including making national currencies convertible.[28] After the war, the United States would have a market rather than production problem, caused by other nations' eroded purchasing power. Since it would be impossible to absorb all American production domestically, the United States must act to stimulate international trade. The bleak alternative was a controlled, autarkic economy, which "would completely change our Constitution, our relations to property, human liberty, our very conception of law."[29]

Acheson's large concern at the time was that nations would be struck by new economic crises. These would stir forces of the "right and left," dragging Washington and Moscow into conflict almost against their will. Americans, he said in a February 1945 radio broadcast, lived "right smack in the middle" of the world and would be drawn into future wars just as in 1941. Preventing such wars required opening the world "to a busy, energetic life," free from "bullies going around and beating people up and taking things away from them." The task then facing Americans, he would say in his memoirs, was "just a bit less formidable than that described in the first chapter of Genesis. That was to create a world out of chaos; ours, to create half a world, a free half, out of the same material without blowing the whole to pieces in the process." This prose evokes images of a world divided between the "free" and the "unfree," but when Acheson defended Bretton Woods before Congress, he saw it otherwise, thinking to keep the peace mainly by advancing economic recovery and avoiding commercial warfare. British recovery, vital to European stability, was essential. When Truman rashly canceled lend-lease shipments in August 1945, Acheson wrote later, he "knocked the financial bottom out of the whole allied military position."[30]

A desperate London, bitter about Truman's reneging on FDR's hints he would use lend-lease to finance postwar reconstruction, did not yet realize the grisly truth about its coming economic straits. Clement Attlee's new Labor government, taking over from Churchill, did know it needed help simply to buy necessities and avoid even more severe rationing than imposed during the war. Short of dollars for goods available almost exclusively in the United States, Britain also owed billions of pounds sterling to Commonwealth nations. Unaided, it might hunker down for an extended siege of austerity, using every device of economic management the Americans deplored. Given its past financial supremacy, even an unconditional dollar grant would seem humiliating. What it received instead was a loan of $3.75 billion based on mortifying conditions. In the negotiations, held in Washington, a skinflint U.S. treasury seized the chance to demand open trade and currency convertibility. London accepted Washington's sour terms in the first week of December 1945, with Acheson, joining late in the talks, signing for the United States. The House of Commons assented a week later. American approval came harder, the Senate not passing the necessary bill until April 1946, the House not until July. The president signed the loan legislation on 15 July 1946.[31]

Again a key spokesman in gaining public and congressional approval, Acheson shared none of the common *Schadenfreude* about Britain's predicament. Instead, he questioned the ability of a whipped UK to serve U.S. interests. "He knew," recalled Franks, his country "couldn't afford to tear this unrent fabric of [the] free world into shreds." Remembering Keynes's forecast that Britain might revert to bilateral trade, if not protectionism, Acheson in a speech on 3 January 1946 made the case for helping a nation that "had been almost the lungs of world trade." The reason was not altruism, but "to enable us to keep the kind of world we want," that is, one that was open and liberal, both economically and politically. Thinking legislators were best moved by appeals to self-interest, he hit hard on how expanded markets for U.S. goods would result from an end to exclusionary trade policies and prevention of "the division of the world into warring economic blocs." The world economy, he told them, was worse than Washington had realized. "Destruction is more complete, hunger more acute, exhaustion more widespread." He wrote Truman at the end of April: "I cannot overstate the urgency." Dismayed by legislators' tepid reactions, he reportedly told Secretary of Commerce Henry Wallace he had never seen "such stupendous ignorance in his life." With distaste but with an eye for the future, he noticed when the loan finally passed that congressional yawns over economic analysis had given way to huzzas when members thought they were saving Britain from the "communists."[32]

FDR was dead by this time, and the new president, Harry Truman, seemed confused by foreign affairs. He had no agenda and little understanding of what he faced. In his first weeks in office, friction grew with the Soviets, first arousing more nervousness than hostility in Washington. Attitudes toward Stalin's regime ran from unruffled to outraged. In April 1945, Truman probably shared his predecessor's vague hope of a satisfactory relationship with the Soviets. Not privy to FDR's ad hoc decision-making process, Truman leaned on inherited advisers, themselves of several minds about how to work with the prickly Russians. Secretary of War Henry L. Stimson counseled cautious cooperation. Harry Hopkins was wed to warm ties with Moscow, as were Wallace and Joseph E. Davies, the former ambassador to the Union of Soviet Socialist Republics (USSR). Partly because James F. (Jimmy) Byrnes claimed he knew what had happened at Yalta the previous February, the president named this South Carolinian to be secretary of state in July 1945. A sixty-six-year-old former senator, Supreme Court justice, and director of economic stabilization, Byrnes thought he deserved the vice-presidential nomination Truman received in 1944. As FDR's proper heir, he first endorsed the Hopkins-Wallace line on Moscow. But Truman listened also to Harriman, the current ambassador to the Soviet Union, when he rushed home with advice to get tough with Moscow. Truman was receiving similar advice from congressional conservatives and his chief of staff, Admiral William D. Leahy. Though trying his best, the president veered from A to Z. In a rough meeting shortly after his ascension, he had a strenuous argument about Poland with Foreign Minister Vyacheslav Molotov. Perhaps worried he had been too tough, he asked the Russophile Davies: "Did I do right?"[33]

Acheson's first reaction to the suddenly elevated Missourian was decidedly positive. Within twenty days of Roosevelt's death, Acheson thought Truman was doing "an excellent job." After a meeting two days into his presidency, Acheson had left thinking Truman was "straight-forward, decisive, simple, entirely honest." He was undoubtedly limited in "his judgment and wisdom" by inexperience. But he seemed a quick learner who would "inspire confidence."[34]

While Truman was trying to master events and the war was nearing its climax, fierce arguments over Asia were breaking out through the state department. These pitted "Chinese hands" against Grew's "Japan crowd," which pushed to end the Pacific war by allowing retention of key Japanese imperial institutions, at least the person of the emperor. Though not one of the principals, Acheson equated Grew's preference for sparing Hirohito with appeasement, a view he later confessed was "quite wrong." The end came as a shock. Horrified by the news of the 6 August bombing of Hiroshima, he wrote his daughter: "The news of the atomic bomb is the most frightening yet. If we can't work out some sort of organization of great powers, we shall be gone geese for fair."[35]

Dismay at the department's condition deepened his pessimism. Discarding his jaunty tone, he wrote Mary while Stettinius was still secretary: "I am getting full of years and venom in the Department." With one foot already out the door and with Grew giving him "the most acute pain," Acheson expected to "get fired" any minute for being too candid. Just before his death, FDR had finally agreed to make him solicitor general, but a preoccupied Truman, who hardly knew him, ignored the ready-to-sign commission. In June 1945, Acheson turned down an offer to head the Foreign Economic Administration. Earning $9,000 as an assistant secretary, he pondered a move to improve his fortune. When Stettinius resigned on 27 June, Acheson thought he would be "gone soon" but for appearance's sake did not want to "hurry mounting the tumbril." He was unenthusiastic about Byrnes's appointment four days later, but it hardly mattered, for the new secretary would surely ask him to leave. He told Mary he would "probably die of boredom" in private life, but Grew was "tired, worried, and very out-to-lunch," and the "poor old Department," now leaderless with Truman and Byrnes at a conference in Germany, would suffer through yet another reorganization. Almost no one noticed when Acheson resigned, two days after the news of Hiroshima. When Truman returned from the three-power Potsdam summit, he routinely accepted the letter of resignation. The Achesons left to visit Mary at Lake Saranac. No sooner had they arrived than Byrnes called, saying the president had erred and wanted him back immediately to succeed Grew. On 14 August, the day Japan surrendered, Acheson was back in the capital, delivered by army plane from upstate New York. After a desultory conversation with Byrnes, he accepted the assignment as number two man and resumed his holiday. Truman announced Grew's resignation and Acheson's appointment on the 16th.[36]

At first a recess appointee, Acheson was sworn in on 27 August 1945. TRB of the *New Republic* applauded the appointment of State's leading progressive. The *New York Times* saw him as a friend of Russia and Britain but got almost everything else wrong, especially calling him Byrnes's protégé and predicting he would clean out "the 'striped pants' type of diplomat" disliked by Truman. Acheson never figured out why Truman first accepted his resignation, unless he was simply late to notice he needed to replace Grew, who was leaving regardless. But he did figure out the impact of his new job, writing in his memoirs: "The whole course of my life was completely changed." In late September, the Senate took up his nomination, which sparked a debate echoing earlier controversies over Asia and foreshadowing others. Republican conservatives fell on him for his recent public reprimand of five-star general Douglas MacArthur. As the Supreme Commander Allied Powers (SCAP) in Japan, MacArthur ran the U.S. occupation from the pinnacle of his brow. Long considered a prima donna, he had announced the occupation was going so swimmingly U.S. troops could return home. Both military and diplomatic officials muttered at this presumptuousness, and in a press conference on 19 September, Acheson repudiated the Tokyo declaration, saying the United States would not be rushed in enforcing a rigorous peace and teaching the Japanese a few lessons. He added that MacArthur had failed to consult Washington, where policy was "fixed by a committee of top war-state-navy officials." This refusal to kowtow to MacArthur in language a reporter described as "positively fiery" attracted attention. MacArthur retreated, but congressional Republicans would not let the matter rest. Senator Kenneth Wherry of Nebraska, who became an ardent enemy and favored object of Acheson's loathing, wailed that he had "blighted" MacArthur's name and found twelve colleagues to support a resolution recommitting the nomination. An "angry and bitter" debate ended anticlimactically with a vote of sixty-nine to Wherry's one for confirmation. Informed of the tally, Acheson's caretaker at Harewood Farm exclaimed, "hardly worthwhile for the other fella to run!" Ordered to check with the Pentagon in the future, MacArthur wrote a friend that Acheson's attack had been directed by Truman, who was "starting out to fool the people just like Roosevelt did." Acheson would later write: "If we could have seen into the future, we might have recognized this skirmish as the beginning of a struggle leading to the relief of General MacArthur from his command on April 11, 1951."[37]

Byrnes ostensibly wanted his new subaltern to reorganize the department in line with recent recommendations from the bureau of the budget. In reality, he cared not a whit about such things, undercutting most of what Acheson did attempt. Acheson took a shot at sinking the encrusted battleships of veteran FSOs moored in regional and country offices, but this mainly led to a further flight of the "Japan crowd" in favor of those preferring a Sino-centered Asian policy, a thoroughly Rooseveltian idea. Acheson's appointment of old China hand John Carter Vincent to head the office of Far Eastern affairs prompted wholesale resignations of Grew partisans.

Generally, American foreign policy continued lurching from pillar to post, treating first Britain and then Russia as the obstacle to postwar stability. With Byrnes mostly in Europe, Acheson frequently handled major policy issues as acting secretary but lacked clear instructions and was hamstrung by the nimble obstructionism of careerists. He also felt squeezed like "the ham in the sandwich" between Byrnes and Truman, to both of whom he owed "complete loyalty." The continuing disarray diminished his pleasure in his new powers. FDR's key men were either bailing out or being tossed out of the administration, and the uniformed services savaged one another over shrinking budget dollars. The department itself was disorganized and disheartened. When military chieftains requested guidance on strategic priorities so they could slap together some kind of war plan, the diplomats waffled or took refuge in platitudes. In this leadership vacuum, control of important decisions gravitated to army generals in the field: MacArthur in Japan, Lucius D. Clay in Germany, and John R. Hodge in Korea. Perforce, Acheson moved cautiously.[38]

Byrnes was vainglorious and cavalier about orderly decision making. He ignored Acheson for a "tight little coterie" headed by State's counselor, Ben Cohen, nominally Acheson's subordinate. The "Department went on without Byrnes and Byrnes went on without the Department," leaving Acheson so equivocally placed, he submitted a letter of resignation in April 1946 for Byrnes to use whenever he liked. Truman's own displeasure grew when Byrnes ignored a recent U.S.-British-Canadian agreement to discuss nuclear issues only among themselves and impulsively told Molotov that Washington and Moscow might work out a cooperative arrangement. When this overture leaked, it caused outrage in the Senate Atomic Energy Committee and among those who considered the bomb America's "secret weapon." It also made Truman look unable to control his own secretary of state and, on the president's orders, Acheson sent Byrnes a cable that jerked him into line. A similar dither less than two weeks later required

Acheson to mediate between Truman and Senator Arthur H. Vandenberg, with the powerful Michigan Republican virtually dictating a presidential statement on nuclear policy. Acheson blamed Byrnes but grew dispirited by the direction of policy, on which he tended to be closer to Byrnes. Truman's shambling attempts to restore order were a further discouragement.[39]

On nuclear matters, Washington now also blasted British hopes, which had rested on promises from FDR to continue wartime sharing of nuclear resources and know-how. Each time Truman tried mollifying London, senators pounced, so he did nothing for months at a time. Robust Senate Democrats, led by Connecticut's Brien McMahon, rushed into the void. Considering the administration too loose-lipped with other countries and too tight-lipped with Congress, legislators passed the McMahon Act in the summer of 1946. This established the Atomic Energy Commission, asserted civilian control over nuclear energy and weapons, and imposed narrow limits on information sharing with allies. Cooperation with London continued in the division of uranium supplies, but this also became more difficult in May 1947, when Congress first learned from Acheson, the unhappy messenger, about additional FDR promises to Britain, including consulting with London before ever using an atomic bomb. This being incompatible with the McMahon Act, Truman abandoned the promise. A January 1948 modus vivendi gave the United States two-thirds of Britain's uranium ore stockpile and a two-year monopoly on uranium acquired by the Anglo-American combine in the Belgian Congo. A disillusioned British government decided to develop their own bomb.[40]

Union Station

As Acheson's days as under secretary continued, the Truman administration looked doomed. Truman's firing of Wallace in September 1946 was typical. As early as July, Wallace had written the president, sharply criticizing his Russian policy. On 12 September, six days after Byrnes used a speech to signal a sharp, arguably anti-Soviet turn in German policy, Wallace used a speech of his own to contend that the "tougher" the United States became, "the tougher the Russians will get." State department officials sought unsuccessfully to alter a draft of the speech, but Truman quietly rubber-stamped Wallace's words. After the president claimed in a press conference that the speech was "exactly in line" with the secretary of state's diplomacy, Byrnes wired from Europe that Truman could not have two foreign policies and would have to choose between them. The president temporized, holding a meeting with Wallace on the 19th from which the commerce secretary emerged to tell reporters, "Everything's lovely." At this, Byrnes asked Truman to let him resign, but on the 20th, Truman cashiered Wallace instead. Acheson, casting for trout in the Canadian Rockies, witnessed none of this charade, but the sound of Wallace's head rolling echoed over long distances.[41]

Almost unnoticed, Byrnes's absences and slack oversight gave Acheson an opportunity to work closely with Truman, who despite his errors attracted the under secretary's growing admiration. Once Truman came to trust Acheson and talk to him regularly, proximity began translating into influence. Under Byrnes's successor, George Marshall, Acheson became the most commanding number two man in State's history. Byrnes and Marshall were constantly away at international conferences, Byrnes spending 350 of 562 days as secretary abroad, with wags quipping that "Washington fiddles while Byrnes roams." Marshall too was absent 228 of 633 days through mid-October 1948. Acting secretary Acheson was at Truman's side, briefing him four or five times weekly and even more often by telephone. He discreetly tutored him in foreign policy, hoping he would see the wisdom of relying on the department. This was an uphill battle, for Truman like FDR was full of mistrust, telling his diary the "smart boys in the State Department, as usual, are against the best interests of the US." He called them "striped-pants boys" in an August 1946 letter to First Lady Bess Truman. The department as a whole aside, Acheson's assiduous effort to keep Truman informed and out of trouble increased his own power. Conspicuous exhibitions of loyalty did not hurt, either. He defended Truman against the New Deal crowd at Georgetown soirées and unavailingly chided Byrnes for calling him "Harry."[42]

Acheson later described the event that sealed this alliance. In November 1946, Truman was in Independence, Missouri, to vote in the fall elections. Democrats lost both houses of Congress for the first time since 1929, and defeated party members blamed Truman's unpopularity—caused by inflation, disappointment with world tensions, and evidence of his incapacity. Democratic survivors distanced themselves. A new Republican Congress would be keen to do more damage. Thus burdened, Truman boarded the train with Bess and daughter Margaret to return to Washington. "It had for years been a Cabinet custom," Acheson wrote, "to meet President Roosevelt's private car on his return from happier elections and escort him to the White House." Acheson may have guessed he would be alone at Union Station in greeting Truman but later claimed it had never occurred to him "that after defeat the President would be left to creep unnoticed back to the capital. So I met his train. To my surprise and horror, I was alone on the platform where his car was brought in, except for the station master and a reporter or two. What the President expected, I do not know." Nor do we, but what Truman did was take Acheson to the White House to talk about post-election strategy. He would not ignore such manifest fidelity.[43]

3

PATTERNS OF PERIL:
JOINING THE COLD WARRIORS

"It Is Absolutely Unthinkable that We Should Fight Russia"

The relationship between President Truman and Dean Acheson was significant because of how both men acted early in the cold war's history. Eventually the president trusted Acheson and often followed his counsel to the letter. More than anyone else at the time, Acheson translated viewpoints into actions based on large strategies. With a formidable penchant for generalization and synthesis, his intellectual and persuasive powers usually outmatched those of others in the administration. Truman, however, would become a dedicated cold warrior before Acheson, who for a year or so after World War II remained less worried about Soviet machinations than the state of war-broken societies. He was not among those crowding around the new president to urge an end to kid-gloves treatment of Moscow. Through his two stints as under secretary, however, his view underwent a fundamental shift. From believing conventional diplomacy capable of handling friction with the Soviet Union, he came to oppose virtually any communication with it. Once convinced the Soviets posed a serious and unconventional threat, he acted tirelessly to apply countermeasures against it. His shift formed an important dividing line in the early cold war and helped turn it into a deep freeze, so its timing is significant. Why did he become a cold war militant? When did he change in comparison to others? Even a quick glance identifies the moment as sometime between August 1945, when he hoped for future U.S.-Soviet cooperation, and the Greek-Turkish crisis of February 1947, but when exactly, and why?[1]

In the aftermath of the war, State's European desk officers grew increasingly skeptical of Soviet intentions and behavior but without swaying Acheson. He also seemed agnostic about the Jeremiahs descending on Truman, chief among them Averell Harriman, whom he described in May 1945 as "ferocious about the Rouskis." Acheson wanted to be firm with the Russians, who he agreed were "behaving badly" and trying "to dominate Europe and elsewhere." Unlike his friend Harriman, however, he did not want to "beat them" with "any stick" he could find. The great powers, he thought, might unite on common ground, or at least not divide. Acheson supported generous UNRRA aid to the Soviets and wanted them included as a most-favored-nation trading partner. In mid-1946, he still considered a large reconstruction loan to Moscow a real possibility. In January of that year, he said in a speech that "it is absolutely unthinkable that we should fight Russia." Instead of finding reasons to draw the line against the Soviet Union, he worried about how events in Germany and Iran might kindle east-west disputes and how signs of U.S.-British solidarity in the Middle East might arouse Soviet suspicions. As late as August 1946, as the White House prepared its notoriously alarmist "Clifford-Elsey Report" on the "Soviet threat," he made the mild and philosophical observation that U.S.-Soviet differences arose from nothing more than diverse national approaches to foreign policy.[2]

Yet by January 1947 he marched resolutely in Washington's vanguard against the Soviet Union, a change he explained in his memoirs as a response to Soviet actions in Poland in 1945 and Stalin's announcement, in a February 1946 speech, of an anti-western "offensive." Stalin, Acheson continued in 1969, had begun the "cold war," which reached "its crescendo in Korea and the 'hate America' campaign of the early 1950s." Fifteen years before publication of his memoirs, he indirectly offered a different explanation in a letter to Truman. There he attributed aggressive Soviet behavior to a historic error committed by the United States of wholesale military demobilization in 1945–46. All along, he implied in both ex post facto accounts, he had accurately gauged Soviet conduct and shifted his own views when it changed for the worse. Hence, he held mild views of the USSR at first and became combative against it when conditions changed.[3]

Contemporary evidence, however, says that his relatively complacent early mood (punctuated by short spikes of suspicion) held until August–September 1946, when in a sharp and decisive turn an accommodating Acheson became militant.

Like many, including Truman, Acheson had been torn in interpreting Moscow's behavior. His potential as a cold warrior surfaced in a November 1945 speech before a Madison Square Garden gathering of the National Council of American-Soviet Friendship marking the twenty-eighth anniversary of the founding of the USSR and twelfth of U.S.-Soviet diplomatic ties. The Garden, Acheson later recalled, was packed and the audience "vociferous" as it was informed of greetings from U.S. leaders, including the president. Before

Acheson took the stage, the assemblage passed resolutions celebrating Stalin and heard speeches from various crowd-warmers, including former ambassador to Moscow Joseph E. Davies, Hewlett Johnson (Britain's "Red" Dean of Canterbury), and singer and Communist Party member Paul Robeson. Acheson rose feeling "like a bartender announcing that the last drink before closing time would be cambric tea." Much that he said was closer to the prevailing mood than he later wished to remember. After expressing sympathy for the Soviet war experience and describing factors encouraging good U.S.-Soviet ties, however, he turned to those that did not, starting with Moscow's failure to respect the rights of its neighbors. The U.S. government, he said, deplored the movement from "persuasion and firmness" to "coercion, where a knock on the door at night strikes terror into men and women." The chances for a U.S.-Soviet conflict would increase if either nation pursued its interests unilaterally without regard to the United Nations (UN) and other international organizations. Although they were not mentioned in contemporary newspaper accounts, Acheson wrote that "boos and catcalls" greeted his peroration rejecting both excessive optimism and pessimism about future U.S.-Soviet ties. "When I finished," he recalled, "protest drowned out even polite applause." Whisked by a policeman from the Garden, he escaped to a friend's house for a "quiet scotch." He had shown his colors, but those "who took their red straight, without a chaser of white and blue, were not mollified."[4]

Other glimpses of latent cold war aggressiveness appear in contemporary state department documents, many drafted by subordinates but signed "ACHESON" as acting secretary of state. While ambiguous in identifying his views, they seem to show him as immune to the kind of "popular front" sentimentality promoted by Davies and other pro-Moscow partisans. As acting secretary in September 1945, Acheson successfully urged keeping troops in Czechoslovakia to buttress the U.S. position there until a mutual withdrawal of U.S. and Soviet troops occurred in November. Although opposed to sending more military aid to Chiang Kai-shek's Nationalist regime in China, he also expressed resignation at having to back Chiang in case General George Marshall's attempt to mediate the Nationalist-Communist dispute failed. While insisting Washington was not picking a fight, in 1946 he wanted to keep American forces in Korea until Koreans themselves created "a self-governing and democratic" state, preferably in concord with the Soviets.[5]

A confrontation over Iran in 1945–46 formed a major milestone in the developing cold war ("Iran I," with an iteration coming later in 1946). Balancing Acheson's wish to warn the USSR off dangerous action was his unruffled translation of its behavior. The Big Three powers had all sent forces to protect Iran from Nazi influence in the war and to guard oil supplies and lend-lease routes to Russia. They were supposed to leave six months after the war ended, with the Soviet withdrawal scheduled for early March 1946. Washington grew concerned on realizing the Soviets were using the interregnum to establish puppet regimes in Kurdistan and Azerbaijan, provinces on its borders in which the USSR could exploit indigenous separatism. Years later, Vyacheslav Molotov recalled seeing Stalin examine a postwar map of the USSR in 1945. Noting its new borders and smiling about the new order of things in many areas of the map, he punched at the southern Caucasus and muttered: "But I don't like our border right here!" But then he "went too far," Molotov said, trying to take a slice of Azerbaijan.[6]

In November 1945, Soviet-backed Azerbaijanis rose against the Iranian government of Reza Shah Pahlavi. When Byrnes went to Moscow in December for a meeting of the Council of Foreign Ministers (CFM), Acheson urged him to express Washington's concern, citing 1930s "appeasement" analogies, but Byrnes shrugged off his view that this was a test case for "a small state victim of large state aggression." On 5 March 1946, Byrnes belatedly responded to Iran's appeals for help with a protest Moscow never bothered to answer. Despite thinking the situation might soon disintegrate, Acheson held to his temperate views. Moscow might cause troubles for a long time, but its gradual advances in civilization would make things better. On 18 March, the UN Security Council put the issue on its agenda, and Iran dispatched an emissary to the USSR. With both the Americans and British backing Iran, Moscow folded its cards. Molotov announced a settlement and plans for prompt Soviet withdrawal, which took place in April. Moscow had already "poisoned the Persians' mood," Nikita Khrushchev said later, but as soon as "the smell of gunpowder was in the air and we had either to fight or to leave," Stalin said, "We must leave before it's too late."[7]

This episode reveals little about Acheson's transition. When tensions recurred after Iran reneged on forming a joint oil company with the USSR, he interpreted Moscow's reaction as that of a conventional, if unreliable, great power patiently making another effort to achieve advantage. He may even have seen in the sequence of crisis, strong U.S. reaction, and Soviet retreat a sign that Russians would listen to reason. He hinted at this view when he looked back in a 1948 speech at the War College. In the "row over Azerbaijan," he and his colleagues had thought the Russians "will set up this puppet government, they will subsidize it, it will be stronger than anything else around there." Instead the puppet Azerbaijanis "skipped into Russia" after the firing of a "half dozen shots." The regime "collapsed overnight, and the Russians did nothing about it. I would have bet a thousand to one that such a thing would not happen, and I was just as wrong as I could be."[8]

The Acheson-Lilienthal Plan

On nuclear issues, Acheson had long stood apart from the growing anti-Soviet consensus in Washington. He advocated sharing information on nuclear energy and weapons with Moscow and worked hard to create a workable system of international weapons control through the "Acheson-Lilienthal Plan." However unrealistic this plan appears in retrospect, his role in its evolution underscores how much his views changed from 1945 and early 1946 to 1947, when he led the way in developing the Truman Doctrine.

Anxious about nuclear weapons from Hiroshima forward, he hoped to control and even abolish their use, forestalling a deadly arms race. Already thinking Stalin's physicists and engineers were probably no more than a few years behind the United States, he joined outgoing Secretary of War Henry L. Stimson's bid to exchange nuclear information with the USSR. Since development of a Soviet bomb was inevitable, trying to guard U.S. "secrets" would only arouse Moscow's suspicions. On 21 September 1945, Stimson's seventy-eighth birthday, Truman devoted a cabinet meeting exclusively to the issue. Already identified as an ally by Stimson, Acheson attended in Byrnes's absence. Stimson proposed nothing more radical than sharing "basic scientific data," not the engineering steps to create a bomb, something Stalin had already concluded the western powers would hold to their chest. Stimson had written the president to argue that refusing to share information while wearing the bomb "ostentatiously on our hip" could only generate hostility. He elaborated on this view in the cabinet session. In the ensuing discussion, which Acheson considered muddled and imprecise, Stimson drew fire from several cabinet members, especially Secretary of the Navy James V. Forrestal, who saw the bomb as U.S. "property" and the Russians as untrustworthy and "essentially Oriental in their thinking." Stimson's strongest support came from Acheson and commerce secretary Henry Wallace. Though noncommittal, Truman seemed friendly to Stimson's views and ended the meeting by asking those interested to give him their views in writing.[9]

Prepped by bomb designer and friend, J. Robert Oppenheimer, Acheson made a powerful case for Stimson's views in a memo sent to Truman on 25 September, just as the *New York Times*, probably through Forrestal's leak, headlined that Wallace wanted to "reveal the secret of the atomic bomb to Russia." Acheson branded continuing secrecy as "futile and dangerous" and urged a cooperative quest for the international controls needed "to prevent a race toward mutual destruction." Part of his urgency came from his bleak conclusion that a defense against future Russian bombs was impossible—and that engineers could soon strap nuclear weapons to rockets, endangering "vast areas" of the earth. Since nuclear war could destroy civilization itself, a supposed edge in a nuclear arms race was "nothing compared with not having the race." Letting things drift would lead only to an armed truce, and American values ruled out preemptive war. Thinking it would be folly to depend on the UN, Acheson wanted the public prepared for direct U.S.-Soviet (and British) negotiations on the bomb. The parties should seek agreement on exchanging information and collaborating in developing peaceful uses of nuclear power. All sides should renounce further weapons development and subscribe to a credible inspection system to enforce the ban. But unbeknownst to Acheson, espionage at Los Alamos had already given Moscow essential bomb design information. As he wrote, even richer data were being lifted from the Manhattan Project for transit to Soviet physicists.[10]

Appearing to accept Acheson's ideas, Truman put him to work with White House staff members to write a special congressional message. But the message that emerged on 3 October diverged sharply from Acheson's premises and, seen in connection with other, later Truman statements, represented a defeat. The president mentioned only the UK and Canada in references to international cooperation and implicitly encouraged belief in a U.S.-owned nuclear "secret." In an impromptu news conference in which he described bomb-assembly knowledge as an American secret, he added that the Russians would "have to do it on their own hook" if they hoped to "catch up with us." In an aggressive Navy Day speech on 27 October 1945, he declared the bomb a "sacred trust" too valuable to share with a "lawless world." And in November, even as Truman was slashing military budgets, he urged Congress to keep the United States safe through "the only kind of strength an aggressor understands—military power."[11]

Early in 1946, Acheson received another chance when Byrnes asked him to devise an international control plan. Acheson first established a committee and then, to inform committee members (and minimize the army's influence over a foreign policy issue), he also formed an advisory committee. He packed the latter with scientists and the science-minded, led by Oppenheimer and another friend, David E. Lilienthal, chairman of the Tennessee Valley Authority and later the first head of the Atomic Energy Commission. The primary committee included Harvard president James B. Conant and presidential adviser Vannevar Bush, former assistant war secretary John J. McCloy, and the director of the Manhattan Project, General Leslie R. Groves. Significantly, only Groves had not been associated with Stimson. Through discussions at the gracious Dumbarton Oaks estate in Georgetown, Acheson sought both enlightenment and to recoup his losses. He also wanted to assert state department control and educate Truman and Byrnes, neither one of whom, he told Lilienthal, had an understanding of what was involved in "the most serious cloud hanging over the world." Oppenheimer conducted evening seminars, tutoring Acheson and McCloy by using "a borrowed blackboard on which he drew little figures representing electrons, neutrons, and protons, bombarding one another, chasing one another about, dividing and generally carrying on in unpredictable ways." When the physicist decided it was hopeless to instruct men who really thought atomic particles were "little men," Acheson said he and McCloy "admitted nothing."[12]

By early March, a draft emerged that Acheson thought "brilliant and profound." Mostly Oppenheimer's work, it became the gist of the Acheson-Lilienthal Plan. The plan proposed creating an International Atomic Development Authority that would own all uranium mines and other nuclear materials and control all hazardous activities, leaving individual states to pursue peaceful use of nuclear technology on their own. Eventually, all nuclear weapons would be handed to the Authority. To gain Soviet support, the plan downplayed inspections, which the authors thought could not provide foolproof protection in any case. In Acheson's altered view, they would do more damage to comity than they were worth. The committee also rejected sanctions against violators, thinking such institutional tinkering ineffective. Serious violations would signal the plan's failure, anyway. During the plan's first stages, the United States could retain its (small) stockpile of bombs and presumably make more. On 25 March 1946, Acheson privately outlined the plan in Congress and on a radio broadcast touted it as a means to prevent conflict with the Soviets. The current—and temporary—edge in U.S. superiority should be used to build "a lasting peace through international agreement."[13]

This was a daring scheme, considering that it arose amid rising tension over Iran, sensational stories about Russian spy rings in Canada, and escalating rhetoric in both Moscow and Washington. Although he called the plan dangerous, nuclear physicist Edward Teller also said it was "bold," "ingenious," and "basically sound." Right-wing newspapers attacked it as a giveaway to the USSR, but in fact the plan would protect the U.S. nuclear monopoly while under negotiation. Stalin was indifferent, for he wanted his own bombs. He would surely have rejected an even more generous scheme, for the Acheson-Lilienthal Plan would expose the internal workings of his regime and ban Soviet production of weapons while Washington kept its own supply. He would be forced to rely on the goodwill of the Americans, who, for all he knew, might later abandon the plan for renewed production.[14]

Any chance of Soviet acceptance fell to naught when Truman and Byrnes named Bernard M. Baruch to manage the proposal in the United Nations. As U.S. representative on the UN Atomic Energy Commission, this seventy-five-year-old financier and sage, whose reputation Acheson viewed as "without foundation in fact and entirely self-propagated," immediately sharpened the plan's edges, the better to prick the Soviets. Some old Acheson-Baruch business exacerbated relations between the Baruch circle and the Acheson-Lilienthal group. Although they had briefly worked together during Acheson's 1933 Treasury stint, years of mutual suspicion had followed, and Acheson's original sponsor, Felix Frankfurter, loathed Baruch.[15]

Tacitly against Truman's wishes, Acheson battled for his original ideas through the spring of 1946, including leaking details of his own plan before Baruch saw them. Retaliating, Baruch added automatic punishments for any state violating the Authority's rules and a ban on use of the Security Council veto to escape discipline. When the Acheson and Baruch groups met, Acheson argued that attempting to find the right instrument of control at the dawn of nuclear history was like "trying to devise a cowcatcher without ever having seen a locomotive." Though he failed to make a dent in Baruch's sanctions, he continued the fight. The old financier, who accused Acheson of taping their telephone conversations, staged a showdown. Carrying in his pocket the support of army chief Dwight Eisenhower and White House chief of staff William Leahy, he told

Acheson to "find another messenger boy" and Byrnes that he had to choose between his plan and Acheson's. Truman caved in to all his important demands on 7 June, after which Byrnes confessed to Acheson: "This is the worst mistake I have ever made. But we can't fire him now."[16]

Truman's submission to Baruch may have been influenced by Byrnes's bruising experience with Molotov ("hammer-man" in Russian) in the London CFM meeting of January 1946. An increasingly glum Byrnes wanted to delay any steps toward nuclear cooperation. Even the retired Stimson had left Acheson's corner. Acheson was excluded from Anglo-American-Canadian nuclear discussions in Washington. The three governments agreed on a united position in the UN against the Soviets, exactly what Acheson had opposed. Thoroughly outflanked and outnumbered, he swallowed hard and boarded Baruch's bandwagon. On 14 June, the U.S. delegation tabled the "Baruch Plan" at the United Nations. The Soviets claimed to want general disarmament first and refused acceptance of any international controls until the United States destroyed its nuclear arsenal. Oppenheimer considered these demands negotiable, knowing Washington would have to sacrifice only nine bombs. But Truman was flatly unwilling to abandon nuclear arms for the United States—or expose the scanty size of its armory.[17]

After lengthy discussion, the UN Atomic Energy Commission backed Baruch's plan, 10–0, with the Soviets and Poles abstaining. The plan then languished in the Security Council, where Moscow's veto was intact. By the time his plan was pronounced dead, Baruch had resigned, using the same timing, observed John Hersey, that always allowed him to sell stock "near the top of the market." Afterward he and Acheson made tart observations about each other. Baruch wrote the *New York Times*'s Arthur Krock in 1949 that Acheson would do "anything to win a case." Much later, Acheson again condemned Baruch's insistence on the "swift and sure" punishment of violators, "very dangerous words that added nothing to a treaty and were almost certain to wreck any possibility" of Soviet acceptance. Renunciation of the veto, in Acheson's view, was utterly implausible, for only that provision had made the UN possible in the first place. Baruch had taken the Acheson-Lilienthal Plan and "balled it up." This was true enough but probably irrelevant, because Stalin would never have given up his own atomic program.[18]

Stalin, Kennan, and Churchill

That Acheson in the name of arms control flew in the face of new gusts of cold war passions in Washington raises questions about how this enterprising man viewed his career prospects. When he did become a cold warrior, was it to return to the inside of the political consensus? The question itself is too simplistic but suggests the need for further examination of the events that influenced him, and how they did. While Acheson was working on the nuclear control plan in

September 1945, Igor Gouzenko, a clerk at the Soviet embassy in Ottawa, defected to the Royal Mounted Police. The combustible secrets he turned over exposed an ambitious Soviet espionage campaign against Canada, the United States, and Britain. At first unknown to the public, Gouzenko's revelations were crucial in moving some U.S. figures toward a hard line—but not Acheson. He continued working for his plan, and with considerable passion, as late as June 1946. Nor did he stop because the Soviets abandoned the Bretton Woods agreements or because Byrnes had an increasingly rough time in negotiations with them.

Many American officials joined the cold war camp between 9 February 1946, when Stalin delivered an important "election" speech, and 5 March, when Winston Churchill gave his "iron curtain" address at Westminster College in Fulton, Missouri. Between these two events, on 22 February, chargé d'affaires George F. Kennan in Moscow sent his "Long Telegram" to the state department. All were markers in the breakup of the wartime coalition, but Acheson did not make his own turn until the late summer of 1946.

Stalin gave his speech to four thousand party, government, and military officials at Moscow's Bolshoi Theatre. In what was mostly an economic disquisition, he proposed another series of five-year plans and called on workers and consumers to make yet another round of sacrifices. Some Americans took the hints of national mobilization as Stalin's groundwork for a possible war between the communist and capitalist worlds, even though he asserted that a far more likely conflict would be that between the "imperialist" governments of the United States and the United Kingdom. Many in the United States, however, read in the speech a rude rejection of the wartime alliance. At the least, it seemed to signal an end to an open postwar world. More frenetically, Supreme Court Justice William O. Douglas called it a "Declaration of World War III." The administration, said columnist Walter Lippmann, must buckle down for a contest of power. With public exposure of the spy ring in Canada breaking two weeks later, prominent Americans stepped forward with dark announcements of coming hostility, including Byrnes and Republican Party (GOP) leaders John Foster Dulles and Arthur Vandenberg. Some writers have suggested these reactions were nearly universal, Truman biographer David McCullough writing: "Washington was stunned."[19]

Acheson took the speech in stride. Calmness also prevailed at the *Washington Post*, *Time*, *Newsweek*, and *Business Week*, which described Lippmann as "berserk." Truman laughingly told an audience, "Well, you know we always have to demagogue a little, before elections." Although Acheson would repeatedly characterize the speech later as the announcement of a cold war offensive, his contemporary response was quite different. When Paul H. Nitze, then a mid-level official, ran to him with his own scarifying analysis, Acheson told him he was "just seeing mirages" and "hobgoblins under the bed." A state department aide urged Byrnes to make the speech "required reading for everyone in the

Department" and asked Kennan, the foreign service's first and foremost Soviet expert, to offer an analysis. He was altogether eager to do so.[20]

He complied in the "Long Telegram," a snapshot of Washington's paradigm shift in the winter of 1946: what had once been tolerable Russian behavior was now provocative. Kennan's five thousand words chilled and thrilled Washington, giving people new keys for decoding their anxieties. The Soviets were unremittingly hostile to the west, Kennan explained, the result of internal factors—historical and ideological—rather than of anything the United States had done. If not conventionally expansionist, Soviet policy was deeply malignant. Americans should not expect armed aggression from this patient regime but a long, harsh political struggle. While others reacted to the telegram with increasing combativeness toward the Kremlin, Acheson did not, partly, perhaps, because he had read the fine print, that is, Kennan's judgment that the Soviets were "still by far the weaker force." The optimum response to Soviet belligerence, Kennan wrote, was clear thinking and the courage to stick "to our own methods and conceptions of human society." Acheson paid the cable little mind. Later he pointed to its strengths and weaknesses. Kennan's "recommendations—to be of good heart, to look to our own social and economic health, to present a good face to the world, all of which the Government was trying to do—were of no help." His historical analysis, he judged, years after he and Kennan had clashed, "might or might not have been sound, but his predictions and warnings could not have been better."[21]

Then came the visit of Churchill, now leader of the Tory opposition. The British took fright more quickly than their American cousins, for many of Stalin's apparent challenges targeted their spheres of influence in the Middle East and the Mediterranean. They worried that the economic recovery had stalled. From London, the French looked demoralized, the Germans sullen, and the Americans restless to go home. American power would be vital to save Europe from Russian power and from alien ideas. Truman joined Churchill by rail to Fulton, Missouri, the two whiling their time at poker while the president sipped at his bourbon and the former prime minister at his Scotch. A few hours before Churchill delivered his speech at Westminster College on 5 March 1946, Truman read it and said it would "do nothing but good." In the speech itself, Churchill called for a "special" Anglo-American relationship and declared his satisfaction with the U.S. nuclear monopoly. With his trademark flamboyance and rumbling voice, he described an "iron curtain" falling across Europe, from "Stettin in the Baltic to Trieste in the Adriatic." Moscow menaced "all the capitals of the ancient states of Central and Eastern Europe." After genuflecting to the wartime comradeship with the Soviets, he warned against appeasing them now, artfully linking their threat to that of the Nazis. Stripped of camouflage, he had called Stalin a new Hitler and asked a nuclear-armed America to join Britain in halting Soviet aggression.[22]

At a time when polls reported 71 percent of Americans condemning Soviet actions, U.S.-UK leaders had to be surprised by the stir the Westminster speech caused. Many lauded the former prime minister's effort, but others leaped on him as a warmonger. Alarmed yet again, Lippmann called the speech an "almost catastrophic blunder." Three senators jointly condemned Churchill's infatuation with "the roll of the drums and flutter of the flag of empire." Stalin angrily denounced Churchill and then, recalled Khrushchev, "became obsessed with shoring up our defenses against the West." British Foreign Minister Ernest Bevin privately decided it was imperative to repair relations with Moscow. In a prevaricating press conference, Truman asserted that in a free country Churchill could say anything he wanted. About the content of the speech, he barked, "No comment." Hurrying into the woodwork, Byrnes abruptly ordered Acheson to cancel plans to host a New York dinner honoring Churchill. Acheson's own reaction is something of a mystery. He does not mention the speech in his memoirs, and bailing out of the New York dinner was not his idea. On the evening of the oration, he and Alice hosted a dinner that included Wallace, Soviet specialist Charles E. Bohlen, and Australian ambassador Richard Casey. Wallace remembered his tablemates thinking Washington "should run the risk of immediate war with Russia by a very hardboiled stand." This may have been the product of his own excitable nature and passionate opposition to anti-Soviet views. Whatever Acheson actually thought, he was still riskily spending political capital on the Acheson-Lilienthal Plan and still hoping to prevent a rupture in U.S.-Soviet relations. He was not advocating an Anglo-American alliance.[23]

Instead of joining the Churchill chorus, Acheson, with Will Clayton, was pushing Byrnes to use an upcoming CFM meeting in Paris to present a plan for a great power settlement on Germany, Austria, and the minor Axis powers. Acheson's intent was to halt the drift toward conflict and unite the Europeans in the task of economic recovery. He and Clayton also wanted Byrnes to underline U.S. determination to stay in Europe. Otherwise, European fear of isolation might lead to the formation of an anti-Soviet alliance, then a troublesome prospect to Acheson. Equally worrisome was the possibility that Moscow would simply wait for American withdrawal before making its own dangerous moves. Byrnes listened politely but instead went about his business in the incremental way he liked. Truman, meanwhile, reacted to rumors of an intended communist coup in France with orders for a military alert, which Acheson tried in vain to reverse. The Acheson-Clayton plan got nowhere but demonstrates that as late as the spring of 1946, Acheson still hoped for a settlement that avoided the division of Europe.[24]

Turkey

A Soviet-Turkish conflict arose in August 1946 that pushed Acheson over the edge, ending his hopes for U.S.-Soviet cooperation. In March 1945, the Soviet Union had denounced existing treaties with Turkey and hinted at territorial claims against it. Now, in a note on 7 August, it insisted on a role in defending and fortifying the Turkish straits and Dardanelles in contravention of the Montreux Convention of 1936. If Turkey gave in, Soviet troops would end up on its soil, but since Moscow had been belaboring its neighbor for a year without dire results and this time said nothing about territory, the gravity with which Washington met these latest demands requires explanation, especially considering that they were plausibly consistent with promises Churchill had made during the war. Timing accounted for some of the knitted brows in the U.S. capital: the Soviets and their clients seemed up to no good in too many places at the same time. Moscow's note coincided with a U.S. plane being forced down over Yugoslav territory. But Belgrade responded to a sharp note from Acheson on 15 August by proclaiming its innocence and swiftly releasing the crew members. On the same day, Acheson joined military leaders in a White House meeting that marked the decisive moment of his evolution toward a hard-line view of the contest with the Soviet Union.

What prompted such urgent concern? As recently as January 1946, Washington barely had a policy for this region, which seemed less than a critical U.S. interest, and embryonic war plans ruled out defending the area. But with Soviet pressure increasing on both Turkey and Iran, Pentagon attitudes changed significantly, first out of growing concern at the erosion of Britain's ability to maintain its traditional influence in the region. Military leaders now developed a preliminary war plan for the area, code-named PINCHER, which underlay the administration's reaction to the new Russian note. Decisions emerged from the State-War-Navy Coordinating Committee (SWNCC), which in Byrnes's absence met in Acheson's office the day before the White House meeting of 15 August. SWNCC's conclusions rested on a broad geopolitical analysis of Soviet conduct. Five months earlier, the administration had already come close to thinking Turkey worth a fight, if that seemed necessary to halt the disintegration of Britain's position. There was growing—and shocked—recognition in Washington that the British were no longer able to take command in a region where they had traditionally held preponderant outside power. Consequently, an outmatched Turkey was now the sole obstacle to any Soviet effort to dominate the eastern Mediterranean and North Africa, which the SWNCC conferees thought must be protected for "*global reasons.*" Otherwise, "other bulwarks in Western Europe and the Far East" would crumble at a fast rate. The only real deterrent was to convince Moscow that hostile action against Turkey would "result in a war with the United States."[25]

At the White House on the 15th, Acheson and Forrestal spearheaded the diplomatic-military group urging Truman to take the toughest steps yet in the cold war. These steps, they told him, could conceivably lead to war. In trying to place a naval base in the Black Sea straits, the Soviets aimed at domination of Turkey itself. Soviet success, Acheson said in a foreshadowing of the domino theory, would endanger "the whole Near and Middle East." Greece would fall to Soviet domination, cutting Britain's lines to India. The region might be "cut off from the Western world," encouraging the Soviets to act in India and China as well. Although Acheson thought it was time to resist Soviet aggression "by all means at our disposal," for now he wanted only a firm note to Moscow and the dispatch of a naval task force to the eastern Mediterranean. Quickly agreeing, Truman said, "We might as well find out whether the Russians were bent on world conquest now as in five or ten years." When Acheson asked if he fully understood what he was ordering, Truman laughed, opened a desk drawer, took out a "great big map" of the region, and "gave us a ten-minute lecture on the strategic importance" of the area.

On 17 August, the state department urged Turkey in a note to hold on and published the note on the 21st. On 19 August, Acheson handed another note for Moscow to the chargé of the Soviet embassy, explaining that the U.S. government firmly believed "Turkey should continue to be primarily responsible for the defense of the Straits." Washington, he pointedly added, would appeal to the UN Security Council in response to any acts of aggression. A new U.S. aircraft carrier, *Franklin D. Roosevelt*, moved into the Mediterranean, joined by cruisers, destroyers, and other vessels.[26]

Despite some worst-case thinking, Acheson and his colleagues neither wanted nor expected war. To give Stalin a chance to back down, to reassure west European friends, and to avoid frightening the American public, they acted quietly and mostly secretly, concerned that the American people might not support such strong measures. Acheson thought a firm but cool demonstration of willingness to risk war would prevent it. Blustering would make war more likely. The best way to deal with the Soviets, he told Lilienthal, was to act firmly "and say little." Emphasizing restraint, Truman conspicuously left for a vacation cruise on 16 August, and Acheson downplayed the crisis in conversation with Britain's ambassador. The administration was acting "with restraint and seriousness," he said, "doing everything in our power to bring about a peaceful solution of the matter." None of the naval actions was remotely threatening; no ships steamed to the straits or any Turkish port. The United States was signaling its confidence in Moscow's wish to act with the same restraint.[27]

Nonetheless, Eduard Mark's research reveals "heretofore unsuspected" war preparations, including orders to the air force to plan strategic air operations within twenty days. Secret planning continued through the end of October 1946. By the first of that month, a full carrier task force had reached the eastern Mediterranean. Air Force planners finished plans for conventional bombing of Soviet oil installations in October and another plan, for a full-scale nuclear attack on the USSR, in December. Perhaps, as some historians contend, Washington blew this crisis out of proportion, but Molotov's reminiscences and other recently disclosed records point to a genuine threat. According to Molotov, Stalin had an ongoing interest in the Dardanelles and in areas where the Armenian, Azerbaijani, and Georgian peoples straddled Turkish and Soviet territory. As his polite requests of wartime allies to gain a role in the straits had failed in 1945, he resumed his campaign unilaterally in 1946, convinced the Anglo-American capitalist-imperialist powers were too busy watching each other to act against him. When his peremptory demands proved unavailing, Molotov recalled, Stalin ordered him: "'Go ahead, press them for joint possession!' Me: 'They won't allow it.' 'Demand it!'" Molotov did as ordered, as Soviet naval units maneuvered in the Black Sea and troops patrolled along the Turkish border. This Soviet pressure, Molotov later conceded, inopportunely threw a "bad scare" into the Turks and would probably have provoked a severe western reaction had Stalin not retreated. The Soviet leader did not want war, especially with the United States, but probably hoped to make large gains through acts of intimidation.[28]

What Washington most feared was that such bullying might lead to world war through misjudgment of western determination. The big difference between how the United States reacted to Soviet noises over Turkey in March and in August 1946 was that in the latter case, intelligence reports suggested that the Kremlin was willing to use military force to seize territory beyond what it had gained in the war—gains Washington had accepted, if halfheartedly. This perception of grave danger arose gradually. Few U.S. officials thought the small crisis in March raised prospects of Soviet aggression, and when Truman met with Pentagon leaders in June 1946, no one then believed war was near. But in the same month, in a meeting with military planners, Kennan expressed worry that Soviet underestimation of "American strength" raised the odds of war.[29]

The sense of emergency in August was real and ebbed only in October. During this period, officials reacted to a series of intelligence reports, sometimes misinterpreting them. Some seemed quite sinister, even after Moscow dropped its demands on Turkey. The new Central Intelligence Group (CIG), precursor to the Central Intelligence Agency (CIA), thought the gravest danger of war lay in a collision of Soviet and British interests in the Middle East. Signs of increased Russian military activity in the Balkans, Czech Communist Party forecasts of the "complete liberation" of European peoples, Soviet violations of the Potsdam accords in Germany, and separatist agitation in Turkey stimulated by the Kremlin's agents seemed to confirm the danger. In early September, Washington learned that the Soviets had put a stop to their postwar military demobilization. Most disturbing of all was evidence of Soviet troops pouring into Bulgaria and Romania, where they were 600,000 strong. The CIG saw in the flurry of movements "an intensive war of nerves" intended to test the seriousness of the U.S. commitment to Europe. As anti-American propaganda grew more virulent, information indicated that Molotov still planned to tighten the screws on Turkey, even at the risk of war, and Moscow did issue public declarations in support of Bulgarian claims on Turkish territory. The spell of alarming intelligence climaxed in mid-October with new accounts of Soviet military preparations. At a minimum, all the reports pointed to a major Soviet campaign to browbeat Turkey and at the maximum to invade it. Still certain Stalin did not want war with the United States, policymakers feared he might bring it on anyway by misjudging U.S. resolve. A Soviet attack followed by western retaliation could willy-nilly cause World War III.

Informed by his agents of U.S. determination to protect Turkey, Stalin on 24 September suddenly dialed down the crisis, indirectly confirming Americans' fears of a Soviet miscalculation. Moscow now sent a reassuring note to Ankara and after another round of exchanges dropped all its demands in late October, definitively ending the crisis. Whatever his first intentions, Stalin may have taken fright at what he had provoked, falling back in the face of U.S. resolve. In contrast, U.S. officials, including Acheson, became both more concerned about Soviet intentions and more confident they could counter them. In November, Acheson told the U.S. ambassador in Ankara that the United States had shown the USSR that resistance to aggression would go beyond "words."[30]

The man who fought against unilateralism on nuclear development and chided Paul Nitze for his panic at Stalin's election speech had vanished. The Dean Acheson who replaced him is the one familiar to historians: profoundly suspicious of the Soviet Union, tough as nails in policy prescriptions, and quick to interpret particular events within large strategic frameworks.

A narrative alone of how he reacted to these events is not the same as an explanation of why they seemed so important. Acheson was more likely to be alarmed by actions than words. He shrugged off Stalin's speech and Kennan's Long Telegram, and perhaps Churchill's speech, but the intelligence reports about Soviet behavior worried him as nothing else since 1945. After the first Soviet note to Turkey, he briefly feared world war. It is possible, as Deborah Welch Larson suggests, that in an epiphany he grasped the full strategic significance of this Soviet pressure on the straits. Since effective defense of Soviet territory would require control of distant approaches to the straits as well, the logic of Moscow's demands pointed to military penetration beyond the straits to the Aegean. The Pentagon had argued for a year that Moscow's real goal was domination of the whole eastern Mediterranean. But it seems unlikely that a Pentagon strategy paper or two would have such a singular impact on Acheson.

More likely, he viewed Soviet misconduct from a fresh geopolitical perspective. But why would this particular episode so change his perspective? Pentagon anxiety was not new. Nor was the straits issue. Acheson was already familiar with the instability and importance of the region. But formerly he had considered these cases piecemeal. Now he looked at the whole, as if Truman had unfolded one of his maps so he could see the larger picture. Turkey, juxtaposed with Yugoslavia, Iran, and Greece, highlighted the interlocked connections between the straits, the Mediterranean, and regions beyond. The Turkish episode no longer looked like a Soviet probe but part of a dangerous strategic campaign, and because of U.S. demobilization, it occurred when Washington was nearly powerless to act militarily. Where Acheson had earlier seen unrelated dots on a canvas, he now saw patterns of peril. Instead of seeing Soviet actions as specific and situational, he saw them turning into a grab for hegemony. Instead of viewing the Soviet Union as a troublesome but "normal" nation-state, he saw a regime contemptuous of accepted principles of international conduct.[31]

Acheson's memoirs capture this new outlook. Events once appearing discrete now appeared to be part of the same package. Acheson writes of the USSR "simultaneously" contriving conspiracies in Turkey, Yugoslavia, and Greece. He fills the gaps between the dots, tracing the Turkish affair directly to a Kremlin plan: "The Russian *offensive* moved to the northern border of Greece, the eastern provinces of Turkey, and northern Iran. The autumn would witness Soviet fire increasingly *concentrated* there." A series of cold war moments had so combined to produce in Acheson a cold war outlook. Noticing the shift, James Reston in the *New York Times* observed that Acheson had formerly held an undoctrinaire but "liberal" view of the Soviet Union, but "when the facts seemed to him to merit a change," he "switched with the facts." Acheson would have said he had seen the facts from a new or different angle. The advocate of conciliatory links to the USSR disappeared, never to return.[32]

When and Why Acheson Became a Cold Warrior

With the Turkish crisis, Acheson moved tightly within the cold war consensus and back into synchronous orbit with Truman. The *U.S. News and World Report* would later say he had remembered his 1933 clash with FDR and "swung with" prevailing opinion. This was too cynical by half, considering his lifelong willingness to defy conventional wisdom. But it calls to mind the need for another glance at the role of expediency. Acheson certainly felt the gales of anti-communist fear blowing through Washington. Despite his phlegmatic reactions to the bombastic Clifford-Elsey Report, Stalin's speech, and Kennan's telegram, he knew by the time of the Turkish crisis that Truman's view of the Russians was fast becoming more rigid. Wallace's dismissal six weeks after the Soviet note to Ankara was another straw in the wind.[33]

Far more important than career anxieties was the fact that recent events had cast such a harsh light on Britain's sudden inability to manage a crisis in its old area of influence. One reason Acheson had earlier seemed relatively complacent about the Soviet threat may have been that he implicitly assumed that Britain, as a stout pillar of the postwar order, would assume the responsibility for tasks the United States was unready to take on. It was extremely disturbing, not only to Acheson, to discover through 1946 and 1947 that the British were now out of the business of world management. Despite all his economic negotiations with them, Acheson had not fully grasped how far the war had drained London's power, and it must have come as a shock when Ankara looked to Washington instead for help. Britain's quick decline helped propel him from a comparatively expansive view of U.S. responsibility to believing in the *necessity* of American leadership. At least in this case, Washington had to shoulder the obligation of a first-responder's intervention in the hope it could also rally declining powers back to the game.³⁴

No wonder the Turkish affair seemed more dangerous than the Iranian fracas of 1945! It was now *America's* job to protect western interests. The apparent threat to Turkey and environs dissolved Acheson's lingering complacency about postwar dangers. It elevated his view of Washington's responsibilities. It stiffened his view of the USSR as a hostile and menacing state. "Civilization" might in the long term reduce its menace, but now he saw the risks of making policy on such an abstract supposition. He chose the clarity of conflict over the scanty prospects of cooperation.

His evolution is portrayed graphically below. The pre–cold warrior appears in *italics*, the militant in **bold** print:

February 1945	*Says chief purpose of great powers should be to prevent war*
September 1945	*Urges more generous UNRRA aid to USSR*
September 1945	**Opposes withdrawal of U.S. troops from Czechoslovakia**
September 1945	*Advocates sharing nuclear information with USSR*
November 1945	*Deplores U.S.-UK-Canadian "combine" in nuclear talks*
December 1945	**Favors warning to USSR on Iran**
December 1945	**Agrees on support for Chiang if Marshall mission fails**
January 1946	*Says war between U.S. and USSR unthinkable*
January 1946	*Worries at appearance of Anglo-American, anti-Soviet combine in Middle East*
January–March 1946	*Sees no "cold war" issues in UK loan or international trade issues*
January 1946	*Directs Acheson-Lilienthal Plan*
February 1946	*Acts indifferently to Stalin election speech*
February 1946	*Reacts little to Kennan's Long Telegram*
March 1946	*State Department dissociates Acheson from Churchill's iron curtain speech*
March 1946	*Defends Acheson-Lilienthal Plan in congressional testimony*
April 1946	*Favors settlement with USSR leaving Europe undivided*
April 1946	*Protests Baruch's changes to Acheson-Lilienthal Plan*
May 1946	*Opposes contingency plan for armed intervention in France*
June 1946	*Attempts to salvage Acheson-Lilienthal Plan*
August 1946	*Responds mildly to Clifford-Elsey Report query on Soviet violations of international agreements*
August 1946	**Responds strongly to crisis in Turkey over Soviet note on straits**
August 1946	**Responds strongly to Yugoslav shootdown of U.S. plane**

A few more events discussed below complete the picture:

September–October 1946	**Displays heightened concern about USSR activities and intentions in Iran**
October 1946	**Urges Kennan to make more "hard-line" speeches**
November 1946	**Says United States will back Iran if necessary against USSR**
December 1946	**Gives strongly anti-communist and anti-USSR policy guidance on Indochina**

The pattern shows Acheson was not a pioneer in adopting a cold war view of relations with the Soviet Union. From the fall of 1945 to the late spring of 1946, he fought for a plan of nuclear cooperation to forestall conflict with the USSR. In the spring of 1946, he joined a concerted effort to stir Byrnes into negotiating a broad European settlement with the Russians. Only that August, when Soviet machinations over Turkey no longer looked like customary nation-state behavior but a threat to western geopolitical interests, did he think chances of normal east-west relations too slender to champion.

When Kennan publicly attacked Wallace two months after the Turkish episode, Acheson prodded him to spread the word by putting more speeches on his schedule. Though not disappearing, Acheson's nuanced views of the links between economics and national security grew paler in his own statements. He was now more focused on national power and military strength. In December 1946, when fighting erupted between French forces and guerrillas in Vietnam, he told a department official visiting Indochina to keep in mind that rebel leader Ho Chi Minh had a long record as an "agent" of "international communism" and expressed concern that the fight might end in establishing a "communist-dominated, Moscow-oriented" regime.

"Iran II" further illustrates his shift. "Iran I" arose during his "cooperative" phase of policy thinking, but "II" came to a head during the crisis over neighboring Turkey, and he responded quite differently. When Iran's prime minister, Ahmad Qavam, made overtures to Moscow rather than seize the chance to reestablish control over Azerbaijan, Acheson ordered the U.S. ambassador to warn that this was an excellent way to lose Iranian independence—but he also promised a $10 million credit to help. In "Iran I," he hoped for a solution allowing Moscow to save face as it retreated. *This* time he hurried to seal a U.S. advantage, pledging "unqualified support" in November when Qavam asked for reassurances of backing in the UN. Then Qavam expelled pro-Soviet members of his cabinet and reoccupied Azerbaijan, ending the life of the puppet "autonomous" republic. At a Washington dinner, Acheson promised more aid in a toast to Iran's ambassador. Since the British and Russians had jostled for influence in the neighborhood for decades, Iran's appeal to Washington undoubtedly sharpened Acheson's awareness of waning British influence. And rather than reacting to the nonviolent denouement in Azerbaijan with optimism, he remained suspicious. Since Moscow had "found a soft spot turning into a hard spot," it backed off, but it would now "probe somewhere else." This thinking was analogous to Kennan's depiction of Soviet expansion as a toy car, stopping only when it ran up against a greater force.[35]

As the Turkish crisis neared an end in early September, a *Times* headline read: "U.S. Must Wage Long Fight For Peace, Acheson Holds. Believes We Should Intervene Abroad Because Wars Cannot Be Isolated." To prevent future wars, he told Reston, the United States must stand guard around the world. It was too hazardous to stand aside. Lamenting public ignorance of the complexity and intractability of problems facing Washington, he warned that it would take "years" to achieve "dependable security." Sharing a New York platform with Baruch in October, he made a sweeping commitment to human rights, democracy, free elections, aid for weak and endangered nations, and expanded trade, while warning again that progress would come slowly. In private, he bluntly described the USSR as the chief barrier to U.S. goals. It was not a traditional nation-state but a malevolent force with objectives almost impossible to accommodate short of surrender. Within the department in November 1946, he said the United States had a choice. It could either support the UN in trying "to draw the Soviet Union towards an accommodation," or "lick the hell out of them in 10 to 15 years." In principle, Washington was committed to the former, but "practical men" had to be ready "to adopt the latter course." He had also shifted his outlook on the primarily humanitarian UNRRA. On 9 December, he announced that Washington would oppose giving any further UNRRA aid to countries that were rearming or using food as political weapons. To make the point clear, he told UNRRA director Fiorello La Guardia to publicly identify the offenders: Byelorussia, Ukraine, Yugoslavia, Czechoslovakia, Poland, and Albania. Though China had once bored him, Acheson now wanted to maintain a U.S. military presence to deter "some other country from interfering" there. Before, he did not care if U.S. aid buttressed socialism in Poland. Now he warned Warsaw it would receive no more help if it "joined" its economy "to the closed economic system of the Soviet Union."[36]

By early 1947, he was making barely disguised, public attacks on the USSR. He had given up on nuclear cooperation. The state department, he told journalist Louis Fischer in January, was "busy" countering one Soviet move after another: "They throw bricks into the window and we push a newspaper in that hole and try quickly to plug another hole." In testimony on the Hill in February, he called Soviet foreign policy "aggressive and expanding." When Moscow protested, he drafted the note rejecting the protest, though he used narrow grounds to avoid a public quarrel. An alert Arthur Krock described Acheson's star as rising. Acheson told his own staff to be more aggressive: "One week must be lend-lease week and we must stress the fact that Russia hasn't settled. . . . Next week we will pick another problem and keep on the offensive about it." When London directly asked Washington to take over its duties in Greece and Turkey, he quickly seized leadership for the department. Detecting this new energy, the *Times* on 23 February 1947 reported dramatically altered U.S.-Soviet atmospherics. Within six weeks, Washington had barraged Moscow with five different "formal notes." It had protested Soviet failure to pay lend-lease bills. It criticized delays in handing over Manchurian territory to the Chinese government. It ripped into Moscow for conducting rigged elections in Poland. It objected to restrictions on U.S. reporters in Moscow. From this time forward—to the end of his life—Acheson barely budged from this altered outlook on the Soviet Union. He had become the very model of an American cold warrior.[37]

4

ROME AND CARTHAGE:
THE TRUMAN DOCTRINE

Marshall at the Helm

Taking Acheson into the early months of 1947 leaps ahead of his state department story. The department remained a mess in 1946 and would stay that way until Truman put George Marshall in charge. Though serving only seven months under Marshall, Acheson had far greater influence and power than before and played a central role in forming the Truman Doctrine and Marshall Plan, two of the most revolutionary acts in the history of American foreign policy.

Jimmy Byrnes's days were numbered as soon as he made too obvious he thought *he* should be president. Truman did not act hastily, for he could not be seen running through secretaries of state like middle-inning relief pitchers. He still had many days of puzzlement in foreign affairs and needed a prominent figure heading the state department. On probation until Truman found a replacement, Byrnes clashed with the White House in late 1945 by switching to conciliatory tactics toward the Soviets just as Truman headed the other way. He got into serious trouble at the Moscow Council of Foreign Ministers in December by ignoring Truman's nuclear policies, not keeping him informed, and, in the president's view, "babying" the Russians. By mid-1946, Washington was awash with leaks about Byrnes's disagreements with Truman and neglect of his own department. These came on top of stories about Truman's flubbing of the Churchill and Wallace speeches. Complaints about diplomatic disarray became part of the "mess in Washington" that swept Republicans into control of Congress in November. Compounding Acheson's delicate spot between president and secretary, Truman told him in the summer he had already asked Marshall to succeed the South Carolinian. Acheson admired the general but found Truman's subterfuge dismaying.[1]

In the meantime, Acheson became tightly connected to Marshall's effort to mediate the civil war in China. Since Japan's defeat, Chiang Kai-shek's Kuomintang (KMT) regime and the Chinese Communist Party (CCP) had resumed their armed contest for power. Truman asked the just-retired Marshall as his personal representative to go to China and try mediating an end to the civil war. Marshall dutifully agreed but insisted his communications go to Acheson through military channels rather than the state department's Far East division. Acheson would transmit them when appropriate to Truman. Although this put Acheson in yet another bureaucratic squeeze, it also brought him closer to both Marshall and Truman. Marshall's increasing disgust with the KMT government would shape Acheson's own approach to China as secretary of state.[2]

Though with no enthusiasm, General Marshall thought the United States would have to stick with Chiang if the mediation failed, but for a while he hoped for success. Briefly, Chiang and Mao Zedong acted agreeably, neither wishing to appear the spoiler. They ostensibly consented to a cease-fire and unification of their armies. The Soviets were behaving well, too, pulling troops out of Manchuria by the spring of 1946. But when the Chinese civil war resumed that summer, Marshall finally gave up. He returned home early in 1947, having abandoned hope for a coalition government. This was sensible enough, since neither Chiang nor Mao really intended to cooperate with the other. But Washington now had a bankrupt policy on its hands—limited support for a tottering regime in which it did not believe. The consequences would come on Acheson's rather than Marshall's watch.[3]

Truman and Byrnes apparently agreed on a date for Marshall's succession just before his return, but the announcement came prematurely on 8 January 1947 because of another press leak. Two weeks later, Marshall asked Acheson to stay on as under secretary. Eager to repair his fortunes, Acheson had banked on leaving with Byrnes but agreed to stay until the end of June.[4]

It was an eventful decision for Acheson. In the memories of state department professionals, the Marshall-Acheson interval that followed set off a golden, two-year heyday for the state department, which—through the Truman Doctrine, the Marshall Plan, and the North Atlantic Treaty Organization (NATO)—made a remarkable comeback from its pitiable condition under FDR. With Truman's benign and sometimes uninformed support, Marshall and Acheson carried out this restoration. Accustomed to orderly staff work, Marshall knew how he wanted the department run and would not tolerate State's habitual fecklessness. But it would be up to a chief of staff to end the disorder. That was Acheson. Marshall wanted him to organize the flow of paper and monitor the offices and divisions, keeping Marshall abreast of vital issues without bothering him about things others could handle. Because this was largely how Acheson also conceived the department's operations, he flourished.

Marshall, Acheson, and the State Department: Organizing for Glory

Acheson and Marshall developed easy communications with one another, a slight surprise given the general's reserve and monumental reputation. George Catlett Marshall was a national icon, a five-star general and career officer from the Virginia Military Institute who had planned America's victories while selflessly giving Dwight D. Eisenhower the command at Normandy he coveted for himself. Roosevelt wanted him nearby, and Marshall almost never said no to presidents. Sixty-four at war's end, he retired as chief of staff in November 1945 only to have Truman send him to China. Then he became secretary of state. Truman could not believe his luck in having such a man working for him, or Acheson in having such a man to work for.

Marshall was formal, grave, even cold, no one to trifle with. He called everyone by his last name: "What do you have for me today, Acheson?" To "all of us," Acheson recalled, "he was always 'General Marshall,'" a title fitting him "as though he had been baptized with it." Acheson never heard anyone but Marshall's wife call him "George." Here were the same stoicism and dignity Acheson admired in Justice Holmes. After Acheson spent six weeks working with Marshall, David Lilienthal found him "bubbling over with his enthusiasm, rapture almost." One reason for this happiness was Marshall's large grant of authority to Acheson—"greater powers than ever in the administration of the department," observed the *Times*. Marshall, thought Lilienthal, "would have been completely sunk" without Acheson. In turn, working with Marshall had made "a new man of Dean."[5]

Marshall referred to Acheson as "my deputy chief of staff." He told him to vet everything rising to Marshall's level unless he "chose to decide the matter himself." Down was the same as up: everything from Marshall to Acheson and onward, with "no other channel." When Marshall asked why he was smiling at these instructions, Acheson replied that the rate of "heart attacks in the Department was due for a sharp increase." The "system could not work quite as he described it," but Acheson "would try to approximate it." Marshall also wanted Acheson's "complete and brutal candor" since he "had no feelings" himself "except those" he reserved "for Mrs. Marshall." Acheson probably also heard Marshall's standard preachment on morale. "Gentlemen, enlisted men may be entitled to morale problems, but officers are not." High-level officials should "take care of their own morale. No one is taking care of my morale." He did so himself by leaving State daily at four o'clock.[6]

Dismayed to discover a lack of long-range planning capabilities after returning from the Moscow CFM in late April 1947, Marshall established the policy planning staff (PPS), headed by George F. Kennan. Truman, Marshall, Acheson, and Kennan comprised a remarkable team of policymakers, but as PPS veteran Louis J. Halle remarked, they were not "made of bronze but of flesh," which is why someone invented administration in the first place. Acheson now reinvented the department according to Marshall's wishes. "The beneficent passage of time and rules of retirement," as Acheson later put it, produced a happy excuse to bring in new blood. Marshall imported Colonel Carlisle Humelsine from the Pentagon to run a central secretariat that would keep right and left hands on speaking terms, sparing the secretary of trivia while subordinates decided what to recommend to him. Acheson urged Marshall to delegate less than he preferred, so he could personally shape policies before they solidified. When Marshall asked if any internal decisions were urgent, Acheson mentioned moving to recently built quarters in Foggy Bottom, vacated when the war department moved to the Pentagon. The move would allow the White House to take State's old home for executive offices. The state department could consolidate its 3,200 employees (up from 900 in 1939), strewn through seventeen other buildings. Marshall wondered why they hadn't already moved. "Tradition," replied Acheson, to which Marshall barked: "Move!"[7]

Acheson's favorite administrative instrument was the "9:30 meeting," a conclave he first used to oversee the department when Secretary Byrnes was out of the city. Byrnes chaired it a few times, but when he lost interest in such tidiness, Acheson resumed control. Early in 1947, the 9:30 meeting took the shape it would hold through Acheson's years at State. He and his chief line officers gathered nearly every morning, not to make policy but to "assign responsibility for new matters as they arose; to follow and guide work in progress; to assign additional help when needed; to reassign when necessary; and, when ready for action, to present proposals to the president for necessary decisions, authority, and means." Those attending called it the "prayer meeting." Pressure to join came from those not attending, swelling the group's size. "Only continuous pruning saved it," Acheson recalled. Here he kept order, stayed informed, and gained "excellent insight into my colleagues." One reason for the rise in department morale was his gratifying habit of going directly to subordinates for help and information. One of the assistants said Acheson "would frequently telephone, having seen a copy of an incoming cable, and ask about it, make suggestions about it. It was his practice always to have a desk officer come to his office when he was seeing a foreign visitor." The Olympian Marshall, who preferred everything in writing, gave Acheson free rein to indulge his own love of talk as a source of information and aid to decision making.[8]

Virtually every problem the 9:30 group considered inspired calls from someone to go to the United Nations. Americans seemed to be believers in the UN, hoping it would immunize their nation from excessive involvement. Now and then, Acheson would bow to this vision with platitudinous pro-UN utterances—but not often. He "never attached any real importance or significance to the U.N. at all," remembered Clark Clifford. Acheson had described the new organization's limitations to Harvard alumni in a 1946 speech. Worried whether the American people would respond as needed to the new tests facing the country, he disparaged their faith in taking "a powder" for international "headaches" and threw cold water on their faith in the UN. Merely a collection of states, at best it could be no more than the sum of its parts. Even in the "Arab proverb, the ass that went to Mecca remained an ass." What was essential to achieve peace was "the continued moral, military and economic power of the United States," not the UN.[9]

Present at the Creation: The Truman Doctrine

The Truman Doctrine, said the president in his memoirs, was "the turning point in America's foreign policy," and Acheson was its architect. The Truman Doctrine was also the culmination of months of evolving policy ideas and product of the state department's growing confidence. Already the government had acted more boldly in world affairs than anyone expected from an administration headed by Harry Truman, floating a huge loan for Great Britain, warning the Soviets off Iran and Turkey, and taking the first steps toward a separate West German state. Whatever the real intent of Josef Stalin's probing, U.S. officials took it seriously. And they saw in his retreat in Iran and Turkey evidence that exerting U.S. strength worked. With conservative Republicans now controlling Congress, veterans of the British loan knew they were more likely to get what they wanted by using anti-communist arguments rather than nuanced economic appeals.[10]

Regardless of the GOP gains, energy and optimism about making a difference suffused the state department. At the heart of its day-to-day operations, Acheson led Washington's charge against the USSR. Suspicions mounted as it launched a barbed anti-American propaganda campaign, rejected the Baruch Plan, and shilly-shallied in sterile talks over Germany and Austria. Distrust of the Russians and rising assurance among U.S. policymakers fed a growing impulse toward interventionism. There was no doubt how they would react in case of a new call for help against the communists.

Britain's emergency plea for the United States to take over its responsibilities in Greece and Turkey is a familiar part of cold war lore. As Nazi troops left Greece to fight the resurgent Red Army, civil strife erupted between a British-backed conservative regime and a guerrilla coalition led by communists. War raged off and on through 1945. Britain planned elections and a plebiscite on whether Greece's exiled king could return. The 31 March 1946 election resulted in large conservative majorities because of a leftist boycott, and the plebiscite six months later restored King George II to his throne. With help from communist Albania, Bulgaria, and Yugoslavia, insurgents sought victory by arms. The Athens government, corrupt, covetous of neighbors' territory, and intolerant of opposition, sought the same. At first, Acheson shared the general distaste of a democratic country for this quite undemocratic regime. He winced, too, at bolstering British imperial outposts in the region. In January 1946, when he notified Athens that Washington had approved a $25 million loan, he stipulated that additional help would depend on the government's making significant reforms. In August, he privately described Greek premier Constantine Tsaldaris as a "weak, pleasant, but silly man" who headed an expansionist and spendthrift government. As months passed, with a royalist majority in parliament and the king on his throne, armed resistance grew and the government's behavior seemed no more satisfactory. As late as 21 October, Acheson was complaining to Felix Frankfurter about supporting this "reactionary regime."[11]

Gradually at first and then with a rush, after the Turkish crisis Americans turned 180 degrees in their view of Greece. Truman's decisive support for Turkey, Acheson would write, became the foundation for going ahead in Greece too. They seemed strategically connected. Officials now stifled criticism of Athens and soon actively sought ways to help it. Washington agreed to London's proposal to continue shipping military supplies to Turkey, Greece, and Iran, with the understanding that Americans would step in if necessary. On 24 September 1946, Byrnes described supporting both Turkey and Greece as vital, and a new dollar credit quickly went to Athens. By then, Secretary of the Navy James Forrestal had the carrier USS *Franklin D. Roosevelt* showing the flag in Athens's port of Piraeus. On 30 September, he announced establishment of a permanent U.S. fleet in the Mediterranean.[12]

Groundwork for the Truman Doctrine was long coming. Months before the emergency leading to it, Loy Henderson of the office of Near Eastern and African affairs told the Greek ambassador that the administration considered his country's "integrity" vital. Acheson told the U.S. ambassador in Athens, Lincoln MacVeagh, a Groton classmate and aficionado of the classics, that a major international "crisis" revolving around Greece might be forthcoming. MacVeagh in turn pressed the Athens government to be less repressive. A temporary spate of faith in British resourcefulness caused a pullback in early November 1946, complete with recommendations that Athens rely on Britain. MacVeagh's SOS's on Soviet aggressiveness soon punctured this complacency. As a special mission gathered information in Greece, Byrnes in mid-December told fellow cabinet members that Turkey and Greece were U.S. "outposts." Also raising Washington's sense of crisis was awareness of the imminent shutdown of UNRRA aid to Greece and CIA estimates that it was "losing its fight against starvation, inflation." With the Greek Communist Party in February 1947 deciding on all-out war, a torrent of frantic cables hit Washington. Mark Ethridge, on a UN inspection team in Greece, described the Soviets as expecting it to fall like a "ripe plum"; after being stopped in Iran and Turkey, they were out "for the kill." MacVeagh wanted a public declaration against "foreign encroachment" threatening Greece's "independence and integrity." As state department officials darted from meeting to meeting looking for a Greek fix, on 20 February another urgent cable from MacVeagh urged Marshall to ask Congress for a large new loan to Greece.[13]

Unlike in Greece, there was no immediate threat to Turkey by the end of 1946, but U.S. officials linked the two nations in their larger strategic concerns, current crisis or not. Near the end of the earlier Turkish crisis that had so aroused Acheson, he had pointedly declared that Washington's stand on the Dardanelles demonstrated its "direct interest in any question that might develop a threat to world peace." Greece's vulnerability at first lowered policymakers' willingness to take any risks over neighboring Turkey, but in early January 1947, they had information pointing to renewed Soviet territorial ambitions along its borders. This was followed by another urgent cable, this one from Walter Bedell Smith, Eisenhower's wartime aide, serving as ambassador in Moscow: "Turkey has little hope of independent survival unless it is assured of solid long term American and British support."[14]

In exchange for other considerations, Stalin during the war had promised Winston Churchill to leave Greece alone. He only kept his bargain in part, avoiding direct intervention to minimize his own risks. But he both prodded Yugoslavia to help its "Greek comrades" and promised his own help to appear more militant than Tito. Greek insurgents actually received arms from neighboring satellite states, who, with the exception of Yugoslavia, could hardly have acted without Stalin's say-so. In any case, with the stakes so high, Washington was determined that Moscow not profit *either* in Greece or Turkey. As Acheson recalled in 1953, the USSR was using a "pincer" movement from both sides of the straits, and if it won on either side, it would have victory on the other too. Soviet domination of Turkey and Greece in turn would cause countries farther to the east, like Iran, to collapse. "If France went communist," his 1953 recollection continued, "Italy and Greece were through; if Italy went communist, Greece was through; and if Greece went communist Turkey was in trouble; and if they all went communist Iran was in trouble."[15]

On Friday, 21 February 1947, as Marshall traveled to make a speech at Princeton University, the first secretary of the British embassy urgently requested a meeting with Henderson. In six weeks, the UK would have to abandon its commitments in Greece, he told him. Britain hoped the U.S. response would rise to the level of the situation's "extreme urgency." Henderson promptly went to Acheson. The department was already primed to do *something* in Greece, for as Acheson told his friend and Canadian ambassador, Hume Wrong, policymakers knew "drastic American action" was necessary, and they knew Britain's strength was rapidly fading. Suffering from a terrible winter, its economic recovery still lagged despite the U.S. loan. During the war, the UK had lost "two-thirds of its exports, one-fourth of its merchant marine, one-half of its overseas investments, and one-fourth of its financial reserves," as historian Bruce Kuniholm reports, and staggered under 15.5 percent unemployment. Prime Minister Clement Attlee's government had just announced an end to British rule in India and

Burma. It was about to surrender its mandate over Palestine. Despite all this, the timing and totality of Britain's bailing out of Greece came as a huge shock. "They were pulling out," said George C. McGhee, Acheson's special assistant for economic affairs. "They didn't ask us; they told us."[16]

Acheson was ready to act. As he later recalled, the United States in 1945 had not yet "donned the imperial purpose of world leadership," but two years later he was personally ready for such tailoring. A hard-line view of the world situation was now part of his standard repertoire, and everything in his personal makeup dictated strong, immediate action. He knew this crisis offered the state department a chance to lead in a way that had long eluded it. After telling Truman by telephone of Britain's message, he set key advisers working to produce concrete proposals before he told either the president or Marshall what he was doing, confident of their support. Only hours before the British request, Marshall, in response to Henderson's warning that the left might overthrow the Greek government with the loss of the "whole Near and Middle East," had asked him for aid proposals to deal with the threat. With Henderson in the lead, Acheson's cadre worked through an adrenaline-charged weekend amid the clutter of packing boxes marking the department's imminent move to Foggy Bottom. The Pentagon contributed with estimates of Greek needs and of what it could quickly ship from inventory. By Sunday, 23 February, Acheson's platoon had nearly finished the memorandum Marshall would need to ask for urgent assistance to Greece. Underlying it was a broad assumption of U.S. readiness to make large financial and political commitments to both Greece and Turkey. At home, Acheson made a few revisions, and then he and Henderson "drank a martini or two toward the confusion of our enemies."[17]

Those involved would long consider the period from the moment of Britain's appeal to formation of the Marshall Plan as a brief season of daring and wisdom when the United States forsook isolationism and assumed leadership of the west in the cold war. Once Truman and Acheson signaled that the United States must lead, Paul Nitze remembered, "the whole atmosphere in Washington changed overnight." Scholarly scrutiny has stripped some Herculean features from this view, but the rapidity of the administration's response remains striking.[18]

So, too, was the foreclosure of alternatives, which has drawn far less attention. No one who had an important say in the matter hesitated to take over Britain's forsaken responsibilities. Almost no one thought the British were pulling a fast one. Acheson told Marshall they were "wholly sincere" and the situation "as critical as they state," leaving Washington with the biggest decision it had "faced since the war." No one proposed sending armed forces; the aid package that became the Truman Doctrine substituted for more forcible action. Although Marshall was headed for talks in Moscow, no one recommended he try to settle the crisis through persuasion of Stalin. No one proposed belaboring Marshal Josip Broz Tito, who was doing far more than Stalin to nourish the

Greek insurgents. No one asked the Pentagon for advice, only for supply figures. Acheson brushed aside vagrant thoughts of invoking the United Nations. And no one spoke with congressional leaders until key decisions were already made.[19]

The congressional matter would quickly become critical, for the administration would have to ask legislators for new money and authority for this emergency, and early 1947 was an inauspicious time to do it. The November elections had administered a stinging rebuke to Truman, leaving Congress for the first time in a generation under the control of Republicans, who clamored to cut income taxes by a fifth and Truman's budget by a sixth. They did not seem eager to help either Britain or, more to the point, Truman. Few Democrats were much friendlier. Flying a new and expensive European initiative into such hostile winds would prove difficult, maybe impossible.[20]

The recommendations Acheson took first to Marshall and then Truman were strong but scalable downward if they insisted. He personally wanted action that reached beyond Greece, but as Clifford noted, he was "wise in the ways of Washington" and first wanted to see if Marshall, Truman, and Congress would follow. Distracted and "agitated," he told journalist Louis Fischer during a Metropolitan Club lunch on 24 February that "only two powers" remained. "The British are finished. They are through. And the trouble is that this hits us too soon before we are ready for it. We are having a lot of trouble getting money out of Congress." "If the Near East and France go communist," he told Fischer, "I fear very much for this country and for the world." Marshall quickly approved the weekend memorandum. The crisis having roused what Nitze called Truman's "normal fighting spirit," so did he on the 26th. Congress was next, and the president quickly scheduled a meeting with a handful of its leaders for the next day.[21]

Truman, Marshall, and Acheson represented the administration at this meeting, held in "unusual secrecy." Arthur Vandenberg, chairman of the Senate Foreign Relations Committee, headed the Republican group. Key Democrats included House Minority Leader Sam Rayburn and Senator Tom Connally, ranking member of the Foreign Relations Committee. The meeting went indifferently at first. Truman asked Marshall to lay out the issues for the congressional leaders. Though Marshall said "we are faced with the first crisis of a series which might extend Soviet domination to Europe, the Middle East and Asia," his sober presentation, read from a prepared text, fell flat. Listeners grumbled about costs and pulling British chestnuts out of the fire. According to state department official Joseph M. Jones, Acheson then leaned over to Marshall and quietly asked: "Is this a private fight or can anyone get into it?"[22]

Gaining the floor, Acheson resolved to eliminate the trivia blocking the big picture. With his memory still fresh of Vandenberg and Rayburn being more worried about communism in Britain than its economy during debate on the loan, he attached U.S. action now to an "openly anti-Communist" rationale. His recollection of this White House meeting is heroic but probably accurate as he brought the legislative plenipotentiaries around. With no time for a "measured appraisal," he resorted to a stark view of the U.S. predicament. The United States and the Soviet Union now stood like Rome and Carthage, he said, "divided by an unbridgeable ideological chasm." The Soviets were aggressively pitting "dictatorship and absolute conformity" against "democracy and individual liberty," squeezing one of the world's most delicate nodal points—Iran, Turkey, and Greece. A breakthrough would "open three continents to Soviet penetration." Speaking for ten to fifteen minutes "as a fervent advocate" rather than a judge, Jones recalled, Acheson insisted not on the need to save anyone's chestnuts but to protect U.S. security and "freedom itself." Both would have "a poor chance of survival" if the Soviets succeeded. Invoking various metaphors, he spoke of rottenness spreading from one apple to another, with "the corruption of Greece" infecting Iran and points east, an infection that would extend "to Africa through Asia Minor and Egypt, and to Europe through Italy and France, already threatened by the strongest domestic Communist parties in Western Europe." Taking a low-cost gamble, the "eager and ruthless" communists had no need to win every throw of the dice. Just one winning toss would be an "immense" victory, and "we and we alone were in a position to break up the play."

After a long silence, Vandenberg, the Senate's most influential member in foreign policy, turned to Truman to say: "Mr. President, if you will say that to the Congress and the country, I will support you and I believe that most of its members will do the same."[23]

Vandenberg had worried, as had others, that the administration's foreign policy had been moving step by step without a clear strategy for the whole journey. Acheson had relieved such worries with this vigorous portrayal of the threat and needed response. According to Hume Wrong, the well-placed Canadian ambassador, he had fed critics' hunger for a "broad and imaginative initiative." "Bold action" would overcome lingering isolationist opinion and free the United States to "execute her full responsibilities as the strongest Power in the world." Foreign policy, Vandenberg told Wrong, would now change "from top to bottom." The people would rise to boldness like a "trout to a fly," not to "step into Britain's boots, muddied by imperialism," but to "pursue a vigorous 100% American foreign policy, which would combat on a world scale the spread of Communism." Vandenberg, too, though Acheson did not know it, thought Greece "could collapse fifty times over" before the United Nations could "hope to handle a situation of this nature."[24]

There was still work to do. Greece and Turkey had to *ask* for help, and Truman had to ask Congress. For the first, the state department gave the Greek and Turkish embassies drafts of the requests they should make. Responding to Henderson's spur, both governments speedily made the needed requests, the Greeks astutely emphasizing war damage and humanitarian needs rather than a contest with communism. Despite Acheson's ideological appeal at the White House, he wanted any presidential address to Congress to avoid explicit condemnation of the USSR or of "communism." It would be preferable to appear altruistic—and innocent of dividing the wartime alliance. But the temptation to use black-versus-white rhetoric was great. Eventually, thought columnist Joseph Alsop, Truman must pose foreign policy issues in terms of "the survival or nonsurvival of this country."[25]

The Speech

Only after the White House meeting did Truman decide to address Congress personally. How to cast his speech preoccupied the state department for over a week, the president having turned the work over to State while he made a flying visit to Mexico. White House staff would also have a large say in deciding on a final text. With Marshall still abroad, Acheson took charge of both the speech and necessary draft legislation. On 28 February, he handed out assignments in what Jones considered a "masterful" display of leadership. Henderson and Jack Hickerson, then director of the office of European affairs, would draw up necessary legislation, recruit people to go to Greece, and coordinate with the Pentagon. Francis Russell of the office of public affairs received the mandate for the message itself but delegated the drafting to Jones. The president, Acheson told the assistants gathered in his office, should speak of waging a "global struggle between freedom and totalitarianism," emphasizing the protection of "individual liberty" and of "democracy everywhere in the world." Helping Greece and Turkey was not "a matter of vague do-goodism" but action to protect "our whole way of life." The Soviet Union should not be mentioned in the speech. When he was done, the staff was aflame with enthusiasm, aware they had a central role to play in a major turning point in U.S. history. Jones felt inspired by "the spectacle of the government of the United States operating at its very finest, efficiently and effectively."[26]

For security reasons, the speechwriters worked separately from one another. As his scribes labored, Acheson briefed reporters and kept Marshall informed. "Everyone knew," he remembered, "that the State Department was facing its last clear chance to get a job done." Jones did most of the writing, drawing information and ideas from Acheson. They discussed and edited numerous drafts, "sentence by sentence." On 6 March, Acheson looked through the window toward the White House and said, "If F.D.R. were alive I think I know what he'd do. He would make a statement of global policy but confine his request for money right now to Greece and Turkey." He sent the latest version to the White House on the 7th, in time for Truman's return from Mexico. On his way home, the president had foreshadowed the speech to come in an emphatically ideological address at Baylor University drafted in the state department. Back in the White House, he approved State's draft, scheduled the speech for 12 March, and announced his plans to cabinet members. Acheson told them Greece left much to be desired as an object of U.S. solicitude, but the spread of Stalinist rule had to be stopped somewhere. It might be necessary later to help many other countries, even Hungary, where embers of freedom still burned. Truman said he faced "a decision more serious than had ever confronted any President." The United States would now go "into European politics," requiring "the greatest selling job ever." At this point, state department officials responsible for UN matters had not been consulted.[27]

Before its delivery, several officials challenged the thrust of the speech. Kennan strongly objected to its ideological and universalist character, and for including Turkey. Marshall, goaded by Charles E. Bohlen, entered similar but mild objections from Paris. But neither Kennan nor Marshall possessed Acheson's grasp of Truman's political needs. Thus, the two-ways-of-life emphasis held, even when congressional liberals "raised Ned" with Acheson about supporting British "imperialism." With Marshall's long-distance backing, Acheson deleted a section, inserted at the behest of treasury secretary John Snyder, on the challenge of communism to capitalism. This struck Acheson as gratuitously provocative and bound to offend Britain's Labor government. In any case, the issue was not socioeconomic systems but whether countries remained "free to work out their destinies in their own way." He also axed geopolitical passages from Forrestal on the threat to Middle Eastern natural resources.

The most vociferous attack on State's draft came from Truman's aide George M. Elsey, who thought it unnecessarily hostile to the Soviet Union and premature. Truman might need a truly "All-out" speech later to rally the people to even more far-reaching policies. With barely a nod from Acheson, however, Clifford parried these objections, telling Elsey the state department draft was exactly what Truman needed to start a campaign to convince Americans of the urgency of the Greek-Turkish situation. Acheson privately told Robert Oppenheimer the speech would signal that "we were entering an adversary relationship" with Moscow. As White House staffers dotted i's and crossed t's, they noticed the complete omission of reference to the UN. This was Acheson's intention. The United Nations was slow, incapable of doing the necessary job, and subject to a Soviet veto, but the White House added innocuous language about the UN in the final and, by one student's careful count, ninth draft. No one, Jones observed, had evaded the government's central purpose, with the atypical result that editing had strengthened rather than weakened the message. "Fast, brave, and clean," Jones wrote, the administration had entered diplomatic "adulthood."[28]

Truman previewed the speech for a large group of congressional leaders two days before its delivery. Reacting coolly, they made no pledges to rally to Truman's standard. GOP conservatives still doubted British motives and remained eager to cut rather than increase spending. Liberals squirmed at propping up a "reactionary" Greek regime. There seemed no guarantees that the bid for public support would succeed.

On 12 March 1947, in the House of Representatives, Acheson took the secretary of state's seat, Marshall being still absent in Paris. Truman delivered this historic speech in a dogged and sturdy rhythm, spitting out words with almost violent syncopation. He immediately had the legislators' attention. He requested $250 million ($2.2 billion in 2005 dollars) in aid to help Greece defeat "a military minority" and create a "healthy democracy." Mentioning "Communists" only once, alluding to but never naming the USSR, he made mostly ideological arguments. Because undermining "free" nations endangered U.S. security, it was essential to "help free peoples to maintain their free institutions and their national integrity against aggressive movements that seek to impose upon them totalitarian regimes." The world was split between "alternative ways of life." One was based on majority will and "free institutions," the other on "the will of a minority forcibly imposed upon the majority." The Truman "doctrine" was that U.S. policy must "support free peoples who are resisting attempted subjugation by armed minorities or by outside pressures." The alternative was that Greece might fall. Turkey, for which he requested $150 million, would also suffer grave consequences. "Confusion and disorder might well spread throughout the entire Middle East," with reverberations imperiling European recovery. Only the United States, not the UN, was "in a position to extend help of the kind that is required." The "free peoples of the world," he told Congress, "look to us for support in maintaining their freedoms."[29]

The speech only obliquely revealed the administration's strategic rationale. Not wanting to provoke a warlike stampede of public opinion, its authors were less than candid about their anti-Soviet inspiration. For decades, critics have deplored the ideological cast of the speech. Facets of the address were certainly oversimplified, but the critics fail to appreciate the foundations of Truman's cold war leadership. He was doing more than seeking public applause. He wanted the public to understand that Greece and Turkey represented large issues and that the days of reacting to random emergencies were over, succeeded by a design to defend vital principles. The Truman Doctrine speech, therefore, marked what Frank Ninkovich has called "a high moment of speaking seriously about fundamentals." While Acheson and others soon spread the word that Truman did not intend to leap into the breach every time a government felt threatened from the left, they did nothing to discourage the belief that he was now the steward of a coherent foreign policy.[30]

At first, Walter Lippmann was cheered, writing that "with all the world watching, our ideals and professions will be put severely to the test." But he quickly had second thoughts, criticizing the administration for excessive zeal and neglect of the United Nations. His home newspaper, however, the *New York Herald Tribune*, praised Truman for buttressing western confidence by offering an alternative to communism. He had inaugurated a new era, said the *New York Times*, by moving beyond the "epoch of isolation" to an era of "American responsibility." What the press mostly missed was the administration's new determination to control events and to play rough if necessary. Critics in the center and right remained skeptical that Truman would follow through; those from the left feared he would. The president and his subalterns still had plenty of selling to do.[31]

Mobilizing Support

Many senators and representatives had sat on their hands during Truman's speech, and many remained cool afterward. Senator Robert Taft disliked the division of the world "into zones of political influence, Communist and anti-Communist." Others worried that the administration could not guarantee that the governments it tried to encourage, including Greece, would be receptive. The day before Truman's speech, Acheson sought to reassure Athens that the United States would not take over Britain's old sphere of influence policy or supply only stopgap help. To block aggression by "armed minorities" and "outside pressures," Washington would stay the course. But he also put Greece on notice to expect close supervision of U.S. aid and that it was not aimed simply at helping the current government.[32]

To mobilize public opinion, Truman mostly relied on Acheson, Forrestal, and Secretary of the Army Robert Patterson. In a move that was tactically shrewd but had regrettable results for civil liberties, the president ten days after his speech challenged resistant conservatives by creating a "loyalty" program to identify and eject communists from the U.S. government. With the loyalty program and Truman Doctrine in hand, he essentially asked conservatives: Do you want to help me stop communism or not? Those who had criticized the administration "for not standing up to the Russians," James Reston claimed, now had to stand behind Truman. But, he added, conservatives and liberals alike resented all the responsibility being loaded on them. "Bewildered" by the large choice of "accepting or rejecting world leadership," they bemoaned having to face the choice at all. As promised, Vandenberg was positively disposed but he was irritated, too, harping on the failure to anticipate the crisis and give Congress enough time and information to act. He was also irritated that Truman had made his $400 million request on the eve of a debate on his nomination of the liberal Lilienthal to head the Atomic Energy Commission. What Vandenberg really wanted, Acheson thought, was more stroking, for he never stopped trading on his "prior history of isolationism."[33]

It was Acheson's job to assuage fears, calm ruffled feathers, and bolster congressmen's courage. He started by invoking the high principle of bipartisanship. Years later, he defined this to mean "politics stops at the seaboard, and anybody who denies that postulate is 'a son of a bitch and a crook and not a true patriot.'" Far more persuasive in 1947, he toiled for hours to win over mainline Republicans, giving them one-on-one consultations, working the Capitol cloakrooms, and repeatedly testifying in both open and closed committee sessions. His most crucial testimony came on Thursday and Friday, 20–21 March, first in the House and then in executive session in the Senate. Cross from the bright lights and dim congressmen on the 20th, he became "somewhat acid," observed a reporter. "He didn't exactly tell the committee to go to hell, but his attitude in some instances bespoke it." After a good night's sleep, he became good-natured and "exceedingly self-possessed," speaking in a "warm and calm" voice. He spent much time saying what the Truman Doctrine was *not*. It was not an extension of the Monroe Doctrine, not a call to rescue the British, and not, he insisted disingenuously, a case of "stepping into" Britain's "shoes." With tongue in cheek, he also said it did not aim at Moscow but at "the forces of disintegration."[34]

Truman and Acheson saw the new policy as doctrinal but did not want to terrify Congress by saying so. Knowing they could not promise aid to all comers, Acheson worked to discourage such thoughts. Washington could not help every "free" regime, he said. Not intending to set a pattern, it would consider situations case by case. Chiang Kai-shek's partisans were riled at his view that help was necessary for Greece but not China. When asked at a press conference on 13 March about the distinction, he responded: "Is that a question which is asked to try to lure me into trouble, or are you really looking for information?" Some asked, what about helping in eastern Europe? No, he answered, it "would be silly" to try acting "within the Russian area of physical force." But however much he shaved too-large expectations, perceptive observers grasped the large drift of this ambitious new doctrine. Greece's fate, said the *New York Times*, summarizing Acheson's statements, would "determine in large measure the future of all Europe" and "deeply affect the power balance between Russia and America." Republican Senator H. Alexander Smith of New Jersey wondered about the alternative of settling the Greek matter by negotiating with Moscow. Shaking his head, Acheson said one could not "sit down with the Russians and solve questions." When Smith repeated the question, he got the same reply: "You cannot sit down with them."[35]

This was intriguing, for the USSR appeared recently to have moderated its conduct, a perception closely held in the administration. Acheson knew it was making concessions in the Yugoslav-Italian dispute over Trieste and reducing the size of its armies in eastern Europe. He knew of reports suggesting that Stalin, perhaps shaken by the Turkish episode, wanted to relax western vigilance by creating a "temporary breathing space." But whenever the Kremlin showed weakness or hesitation, it was always his impulse to press harder yet. War, he believed, was far more likely to result from excessive caution than strong action, such as the Truman Doctrine. When directly asked on the Hill if the Doctrine would lead to war, he told the muted hearing room, "I was going to say—no possibility it would lead to war." After a pause, he added, "I don't think it could lead to war. By strengthening the forces of democracy and freedom, you do a great deal to eliminate the friction between the big powers." "In other words," Vandenberg remarked, "I think what you are saying is that wherever we find free peoples having difficulty in the maintenance of free institutions, and difficulty in defending against aggressive movements that seek to impose upon them totalitarian regimes, we do not necessarily react in the same way each time, but we propose to react." Acheson replied: "That, I think, is correct." This is what Joseph Jones called Acheson's "test of practicability," both defining and limiting "the global implications of the Truman Doctrine."[36]

Cajolery of individual members of Congress, and especially the courting of Vandenberg, produced dividends. Acheson's wooing of Vandenberg required a final buss: giving him some meaningless words about the UN to put the senator's "brand" on the Doctrine. It took the form of an innocuous amendment that would end U.S. aid to Greece and Turkey once the UN demonstrated it could take over. As we have seen, this was hypocrisy on Vandenberg's part, and Acheson gave a fitting response by allowing the amendment. It was "a cheap price" for Vandenberg's "patronage." More straightforward lobbying gained the endorsement of others, including New York Governor Thomas Dewey, widely expected to be the next president. State department polls and surveys of media, prominent individuals, and organizations reported broad backing crossing ideological and party lines. What neither the president nor the department recognized, however, was that the people who now offered support because they feared communism and the USSR might, in more fearful conditions, sweep control from the government's hands with demands for more militant action.

For now, supportive public opinion helped move the "Act to Provide for Assistance to Greece and Turkey" through Congress, if slowly. In early May, the House approved the bill, 287–107, the Senate by a 67–23 margin, with decisive GOP majorities voting "yea." Truman signed the bill on 22 May 1947. Moscow's reaction was subdued. At Washington's first signal it planned to rescue Greece, a Soviet UN delegate asked Ethridge, "What does this mean?" "It means," the American responded, "that you can't do it." Smiling, the Russian replied, "I quite understand, Mr. Ethridge."[37]

The Outcome in Greece

About half of Truman Doctrine aid for Greece went for military purposes, with the first shipments unloaded at Piraeus on 1 August 1947. Truman's personal representative was soon considered the "Most Powerful Man in Greece," and before long U.S. officials were looking over the shoulders of Greek politicians and bookkeepers. United States army officers directed the fighting. Mostly ignoring acts of repression by the Athens government, Washington oversaw the victorious end of the civil war in 1949.

The withdrawal of external communist support was as vital as Truman Doctrine aid. Moscow had endorsed the proclamation of a provisional communist government on Christmas Eve 1947, but after vigorous U.S. warnings, neither Stalin nor any other communist government formally recognized it. In

January 1948, sparking the Soviet-Yugoslav split, Stalin ordered Tito to cease efforts to expand his influence in Greece and Albania, so as not to "provoke our former allies." He told a delegation of satellite-state communists the Americans would never let the Greek rebels win. Tito ended direct aid to the Greeks in February. Even more important, under heavy U.S. pressure in July 1949, he closed the border to Greek rebels, to whom he had taken a dislike for their support of Stalin. Without a refuge, the insurgents faced a pounding by a greatly enlarged Greek army using the aggressive tactics and growing firepower supplied by the Americans. By October 1949 the war was virtually over. American aid barely touched some of the social and political pathologies behind the strife, but it saved Greece for the west in a now ongoing cold war.[38]

In 1947, few Americans realized what a historic milestone the Truman Doctrine would become. Critics were already concerned that its open-ended invitation to intervention would make altogether too much history. Instead of sounding the tocsin for an unlimited "ideological crusade," Lippmann wrote, the administration should have made narrow promises to back Greece and Turkey against pressures from the USSR, which Truman should have named. Since people all over the world, he continued, could read their "own fears and hopes" into this open-ended policy, it was likely to "act as incitement and inducement to civil strife in countries where national cooperation is delicate and precarious." Not taking well to this critique, Acheson shortly thereafter argued fiercely with its author at a dinner party, accusing Lippmann of sabotaging U.S. policy. Both emerged badly bruised and suspicious of the other. The next morning Lippmann suffered such a terrible nicotine headache, he became a nonsmoker for life.[39]

One reason for Acheson's anger at Lippmann may have been his conviction that the administration in fact had acted quite reasonably. Though Acheson did not yet have a clearly defined, overall strategy for dealing with the Soviet Union, no more than Lippmann did he want to contest every spot on the globe, one reason for eluding Chiang Kai-shek's embrace. He did not think the current conflict with the Soviets heralded the Day of Armageddon. He was aware of both America's limited resources and the public's limited taste for interventionism. But he was also sure that Lippmann's idea of asking Congress to help two faraway Mediterranean countries for meager reasons would have laid a gigantic egg, leaving Truman helpless to offer any aid. Acheson sought a middle path between an uninhibited globalism and a minimalist standard to which the American people would surely not rally. He was willing to alarm them enough to gain their support. He was equally willing to calm fears of universalism by specifying where the United States would fly into the breach, and where it would not.[40]

His concern in the spring of 1947 was not that the United States had promised too much. It was rather that, in reacting to a string of isolated crises, the administration would be unable to persuade the people that the health of all western Europe was a vital concern. The Truman Doctrine pointed where they should follow to prevent "the piecemeal murder of independent nations." But an even broader approach was necessary to counter serial attacks on western societies, a strategy Acheson in March 1947 knew Washington had not yet formed. He was becoming increasingly aware that many European societies critical to U.S. security that were still stumbling toward economic reconstruction looked acutely vulnerable to radicals enamored of Moscow, whether the Soviets did anything or not. As much as he had stiffened in his view of the USSR, he still believed that internally induced disorders in western Europe endangered American security. In either case, regardless of the rhetorical flights with which it was announced and that gave it enduring power, the Truman Doctrine in its concrete application was a stopgap measure. The United States needed something more basic that reached beyond a single emergency, and Acheson would spend his last few months as Marshall's under secretary helping discover it.[41]

5

THE MARSHALL PLAN AND
RETURN TO PRIVATE LIFE

The European Crisis

The Truman Doctrine did not give the administration the power to cope with what Acheson now realized was a great European crisis—a crisis of economy, society, polity, and confidence. Everyone had misjudged the difficulties of reestablishing productive capitalist economies. Postwar planners knew helping Europe would be necessary, but Americans thus far had failed to meet the gaping deficits now exposed. The bleak winter of 1946–47, succeeding a drought and followed by another, threatened to overwhelm people doing battle with the decay around them. Wrecked merchant ships barricaded harbors, and broken bridges and railroads impeded the simplest commercial traffic. Ragged men and women picked at debris looking for their next meal. Britain was bankrupt. Winston Churchill described the continent as "a rubble heap, a charnel house, a breeding ground of pestilence and hate."[1]

This malaise was more daunting than the Greek crisis. By mid-1946, the gains from U.S. aid had been disappointing. The expiring UNRRA was unpopular in Congress, which also noticed that loans to Britain and France had disappeared like rain into sand. Neither nation could even feed itself yet. The Export-Import Bank was short of funds and the World Bank not yet open for business. The UK had not lived up to promises to make sterling convertible. Acheson was acutely sensitive to London's financial vulnerability and to how much a sinking British economy could damage U.S. interests worldwide. With quick fixes failing to produce recovery, American officials feared the combination of east-west tensions and economic stagnation might doom hopes for an era of security, rooted in a regime of democracy, capitalism, and multilateral trading.[2]

Washington's anxiety was still not really focused on the Soviet Union. The state department remained concerned that the Europeans would resort to illiberal means to prevent a smashup. Social misery would boost the appeal of communists, as in Italy and in France, where they had won 26 percent of the parliamentary vote in October 1945 and a plurality a year later. In the spring of 1947, the Paris government included a communist defense minister. Communists also held major positions in governing coalitions in Italy and Belgium. Europeans had neither dollars nor exports to pay for urgently needed U.S. goods. An emergency turned into a grave crisis when the worst winter of the century strapped western Europe for heating fuel and exposed an acute coal shortage. Governments hoarded hard currencies and moved toward schemes of control and protection: quotas, higher tariffs, bilateral trade, currency manipulation, and state planning. Another round of cutthroat rivalry could spawn yet more regimentation. The 1930s depression and World War II had already damaged the reputation of liberal capitalism, and a turn toward *dirigisme* would open the gates for communists or other authoritarians. A world of ministerially managed economies and trade might push the United States out of its own ideological orbit. The limited state and individual freedom would give way to a government regulating the economy and nearly everything else. A fragmented world of such states would compel permanent maintenance of large armies as protection against aggression and internal controls against domestic subversion. Acheson's prime concern was not about U.S. export markets (between 1945 and 1950 exports counted for only 3.6 percent to 6.5 percent of gross domestic product [GDP]), but about what kind of polity Americans would be forced into in an authoritarian, autarkic international economy.[3]

To alleviate these socioeconomic problems, Acheson had repeatedly urged more liberal U.S. trade policies on Congress. If U.S. tariffs were lower, Europeans would have a better chance to earn dollars for their exports. This might temporarily hurt U.S. companies, but the alternative was worse. Restrictionist policies in Europe combined with the "dollar gap"—the shortage of dollar reserves needed to buy American goods—would pull down U.S. exports. Larger issues than the operation of economies were involved. Continued failure in western Europe would open the door to radicals of all stripes. Lacking better possibilities and looking to restore their own shattered economies, Germans and Japanese might try eluding the control of their western occupiers to make deals with the Soviet Union. The movement of such potentially massive resources into the Soviet column would be the equivalent of losing the war just won. Such a calamity would make it even more likely the United States would have to join others in a controlled economy, burdensome defense spending, and restricted liberties.[4]

The administration was becoming more open to a "large" policy that leapfrogged the piecemeal requests so irritating to Congress. A major reason was Secretary of State George Marshall's disappointment with the Moscow Council of Foreign Ministers, which overlapped with development of the Truman Doctrine in Washington. Despite Marshall's readiness to compromise on reparations shipments from the western zones of Germany to the Soviet Union, negotiators argued about a German peace treaty from 10 March to 24 April 1947 without reaching a settlement. The standoff gravely disillusioned the British and caused the French to abandon old hopes of a mediating role between the Soviets and Anglo-Saxons. Most important, it exhausted Marshall's hopes. Stalin's nonchalant remark that a settlement could take a long time convinced the secretary of state the Kremlin simply wanted time to exploit European misery. He told British Foreign Minister Ernest Bevin the Soviets were "just fooling," and when he returned home informed the president the Russians were uninterested in any German settlement the United States might find acceptable. In Berlin on his way home, he instructed General Lucius Clay, head of U.S. forces in Germany, to begin talks to combine the U.S. and UK occupation zones into a separate, self-sufficient economic unit. In a radio broadcast in the United States, he blamed the deadlock on the Soviet Union's insistence on a centralized German government "adapted to the seizure of absolute control." Meantime, he added, the European "patient sinks while the doctors deliberate."[5]

Without knowing Stalin's intentions, Marshall was seeing their application. The Soviet ruler had never thought the chances were good that the Americans and British would agree to four-power controls over a centralized Germany. Thus, immediately after the war he began work to carve out an eastern zone for a Soviet sphere of influence. He harbored faint but real hopes that, without provoking a war, Moscow might still dominate all of Germany. The western powers reacted accordingly, and as early as the summer of 1946, London and Washington were beginning to peel off from the wartime coalition on German issues. Partly to *avoid* contentious differences with the Russians, they began inching toward formation of a separate West German state.[6]

Though the connection was not yet obvious in 1946, the shambles in which the war had left the German economy was the key postwar fact that led to the Marshall Plan. German textile, steel, and chemical production stood at about 20 percent of prewar levels. The anthracite coal needed to heat homes and run factories throughout Europe stood at 41 percent (an early draft of the Marshall Plan was titled, "Coal for Europe"). As early as May 1946, Acheson wanted more coal dug in the German pits "to help recovery in France and other Western European countries." States to the west also needed to trade with Germany, whose foreign commerce had plummeted 80 percent from prewar levels. Hypothetically, the victors could just take what they wanted and call it "reparations," but this seemed deeply offensive when Germans were starving by the thousands and dying in their frozen beds of hypothermia.

Because of the state department's long-standing avoidance of "operations," it was the U.S. army's task to enforce discipline and deprivation in the American occupation zone of Germany. Already losing its relish for vengeance, the army fought any measures that would leave Germans even more threadbare. General Clay, Washington's occupation proconsul, warned they were unlikely to cooperate on only a thousand calories a day when communists were offering fifteen hundred. The impoverishment must end if Germany was to help jump-start the rest of Europe's economy. But with equally compelling logic, State held that it was even more important to raise the living standards of Germany's recent victims. Thus, any solution for German misery must both lighten the U.S. army's burdens and satisfy Germany's neighbors. It must also maintain control over Germany and block Soviet expansionist designs. The continent was like an empty bathtub with toy boats foundered on the bottom. To float any of them, Washington would have to raise the whole fleet.[7]

Altruistic and Practical Impulses

As antagonism toward the USSR grew, so did the determination of U.S. and British officials to integrate German resources within a western security orbit. With Moscow's designs in mind, some Americans had long thought this the proper course. As the Soviets stripped capital equipment from the east, Averell Harriman called the USSR "a vacuum into which all movable goods would be sucked." In December 1946, the U.S. and UK governments agreed to unite their zones into a consolidated economic unit. Although the French were not yet part of this "Bizonia," its creation was a large step toward fracturing the World War II alliance. The future of Germany, said the *New York Times* in March 1947, would "determine in large measure the future of all Europe" and "deeply affect the power balance between Russia and America."[8]

The impetus for the Truman Doctrine came from the eastern Mediterranean, but for the Marshall Plan it came from the continuing European economic crisis, from growing east-west tensions, and from Germany's predicaments. No one planned the transit from Truman Doctrine to Marshall Plan, and though they sought greater strategic clarity as spring approached in 1947, Truman and the state department did not think they were following a road leading to a harsh, militarized cold war policy. The officials drafting cables headed to Greece worked in the same offices as those discussing the dollar gap, European fuel shortages, and the influence of communists in Italy and France. The administration still needed to glue all this together, and while working on the Truman Doctrine speech, Acheson formed an interagency group to canvass other areas needing "analogous financial, technical and military aid." This was the first bureaucratic step toward the Marshall Plan. On 13 March, a day after Truman's address to Congress, former president Herbert Hoover, who had publicly urged swift rehabilitation of the German economy to relieve U.S.

taxpayers and stimulate European recovery, pressed Acheson to lift ceilings on its production.[9]

That so many U.S. officials were working simultaneously on related issues indicates why it is futile to try identifying a single author of the Marshall Plan, a label Truman insisted on. The president himself could rightfully claim parentage since he gave the green light to the surge of plans and took responsibility for the outcome; the same was true of Marshall. The evangelical Will Clayton deserves credit as well. So does James Forrestal for helping put in Marshall's mind that only the resource-rich United States could be "a catalyst in the restoration of the world economy." In 1948, Walt Rostow identified Acheson as the Plan's "inventor," while in 1973, state department official Elbridge Durbrow said Acheson and Charles Bohlen dreamed up the plan. Months after Marshall gave the speech announcing what would be called the Marshall Plan on 5 June 1947, the *Times* identified its origins in a speech Acheson gave in Mississippi a month earlier. Besides Acheson himself, Bohlen, George Kennan, and Loy Henderson all worked on the Mississippi speech. Arthur Krock described that speech as Acheson's throwing "a forward pass" to Marshall, who "caught and ran" with it. The actual *planning* of the "Marshall Plan" came mainly from Kennan in the policy planning staff, working under Marshall's orders to "avoid trivia" in finding a way to save Europe.[10]

In the weeks Marshall was abroad, Acheson and those around him had in effect pushed U.S. policy in a tougher direction than the secretary of state favored before he left. On Marshall's return, Acheson, already working on his Mississippi speech, told him how much the "atmosphere" had changed in his absence. Acheson realized that the decisions to revitalize western Europe and enlist German resources in the enterprise might magnify tension with the USSR. But he was confident, as he told David Lilienthal in June 1947, that unless they were "absolutely out of their minds the Politburo will carefully avoid war." With equal confidence, Forrestal wrote privately that "as long as we can outproduce the world, can control the sea and can strike inland with the atomic bomb, we can assume certain risks otherwise unacceptable in an effort to restore world trade, to restore the balance of power—military power—and to eliminate some of the conditions which breed war."[11]

More than confidence would be necessary to persuade a skeptical Congress to pass the largest foreign aid bill yet. James Reston was reporting members as "bewildered," "grim," and "resentful" about Truman's expectations of them. The speech Acheson was planning to deliver early in May before farmers, merchants, and their families at the Delta Council in Cleveland, Mississippi, would add to those expectations. Besides influencing Congress, and public opinion, Acheson hoped to set the stage for a broad declaration of policy. As Truman remarked, the Mississippi speech would be the "prologue" to the Marshall Plan. Acheson made sure as he planned the address that he had

Truman's approval. "I am going to throw up a ball and it's going to have to come down somewhere," he told him. Truman told him to go ahead.[12]

Joseph M. Jones, who drafted the Truman Doctrine speech, was Acheson's writer for his Mississippi outing. On 9 April, they first met to discuss what Acheson wanted for the Delta Council speech and several others coming up. His primary purpose in all of them, he told Jones, was to lay out a "more comprehensive" foreign policy that would rest on both altruistic and practical impulses. While advancing the cause of democracy, he wanted to disarm criticisms of administration globalism and also to hold UN enthusiasts at bay. The Mississippi speech should leaven American philanthropy with the yeast of self-interest, emphasizing that stabilizing European economies would strengthen U.S. security and expand its trade. But Americans would have to practice what they preached by lowering trade barriers. He also told Jones he wanted language for a groundbreaking discussion of converting Germany from despised enemy to partner in Europe's recovery.[13]

His first spring speech, on 18 April 1947 for the American Society of Newspaper Editors, was a meaty synthesis of where the administration was going after two years of improvising. Anticipating the title of his state department memoirs, published in 1969, he quoted Sir Willmott Lewis, longtime Washington correspondent for *The Times* of London: "We have chaos but not enough to make a world." In the center of the "chaos," was the struggle between the United States and the Soviet Union. Giving what was then unusual public expression of Washington's antagonism to Moscow, he described the east-west conflict as the greatest since the eras of "Athens and Sparta and Rome and Carthage." The conflict was fundamentally about ideas, setting a nation that believed in "the worth of the individual, the preservation of individual rights and individual enterprise" against a "police state" that exercised "rigid control and discipline over the individual." Drawing from Kennan's thinking, he insisted that Soviet enmity was self-generated rather than a response to anything the United States had done or failed to do. Moscow's virulent anti-American propaganda only demonstrated its dependence on fictional enemies to justify tyrannical rule. Stalin and his minions had joined historically disagreeable Russian manners to communist discipline in a campaign to "subjugate" their closest neighbors. They would expand farther west if they could, using local communist parties. The Soviets might not want war, he told the editors, but they would "outsit the democracies" and "probe wherever there is weakness." None of this, however, was cause for despair. Communism was not the wave of the future, and the Soviets, who often acted stupidly, were vulnerable to potential restiveness in their satellite empire. Building progressive, healthy societies was the best response to communist belligerence, a task that would take years and require steady nerves. Part of the task was holding on to the world's great "workshops," in which he tacitly included Germany and Japan. The United States was always ready to negotiate with Moscow, but not for the sake of talking. Instead of a phony east-west "settlement," the United States would use its strength to build barriers against further Soviet expansion.[14]

From the first, officials thinking about a comprehensive recovery program debated the wisdom of offering participation to the Soviet bloc. Thus, shortly before his Mississippi trip, Acheson asked Durbrow, just back from Moscow, whether his "Soviet clients" would join such a plan. Durbrow thought not. "I agree with you," Acheson replied. Beginning to prepare public opinion, he tried to distract European journalists from Henry Wallace's criticisms of U.S. policy. He also briefed Reston, who was happy to act as Acheson's "transmission belt." Then he was off to delta country in the president's plane to deliver "the curtain raiser for General Marshall's historic proposal." The Marshall Plan "germinated" among many officials, Clark Clifford recalled, and "flowered" in Mississippi.[15]

Acheson's plane landed on a field outside Cleveland, where, as described by *New Yorker* writer Philip Hamburger, a greeting committee took the under secretary "to the schoolhouse for a fried-chicken lunch and then to the school gymnasium, where several hundred farmers, in galluses, were awaiting his talk." Sweltering in humid delta heat, Acheson took off his jacket and rolled up his sleeves. Putting aside the Jones text, he ad-libbed, dramatizing the imminent European disaster and crystallizing the link between economics and security— the short "distance from food and fuel either to peace or to anarchy." Unless the United States acted quickly, Europeans would probably fall into "hopeless-ness and despair," endangering democracy and national independence, since "hopeless and hungry people often resort to desperate measures." Though he recommended only emergency help, he also hinted at broader actions and a new willingness to divide the world between allies and enemies. With Moscow doing all it could to frustrate recovery, American resources were needed to create stability, promote freedom, reinforce "liberal trading policies," and support "the authority of the United Nations." Precisely two years after VE-Day, he urged pushing "ahead with the reconstruction of those two great workshops of Europe and Asia—Germany and Japan—upon which the ultimate recovery of the two continents so largely depends." The west could not wait for a four-power accord. Instead, he implied, it should go ahead in commandeering German and Japanese resources, even at the cost of greater tension with the Soviet Union. As with the Truman Doctrine, the administration was acting to help "free peoples who are seeking to preserve their independence and democratic institutions and human freedoms against totalitarian pressures."[16]

Reston's *Times* captured the speech's immediate newsworthiness in the headline, "GERMANY-JAPAN AID LINKED BY ACHESON." As hoped, the British reacted favorably. Laced amid generally positive press comment were some criticisms, including *Times* columnist Anne O'Hare McCormick's dis-approval of Acheson's apparent surrender of hope for east-west understanding.

Old friend James P. Warburg, a student of Germany and financier, applauded Acheson in a letter for abandoning the crusading tone of the Truman Doctrine but insisted that only cooperation with Moscow would produce recovery. Truman had "scared the hell out of me," he went on, while warning Acheson that exaggerated ideological markers would attract isolationists and extreme nationalists to the administration while alienating "puzzled and reluctant liberals and progressives." Acheson, who in office rarely wrote revealing letters to anyone outside his family, did not reply.[17]

Kennan, in the meantime, had indeed avoided trivia in racing to come up with a plan for Marshall. On 23 May, he recommended starting with a bang by unplugging a single economic "bottleneck" like coal. He also told his superiors that "communist activities" were not the main problem. Four days later, the under secretary for European affairs, Will Clayton, just returned from a European visit, pleaded for decisive action, arguing that it was vital to "make a strong spiritual appeal to the American people" to make the necessary sacrifices to "save Europe from starvation and chaos." The fact that the continent was "steadily deteriorating" as millions were "slowly starving" would inevitably shape Europe's political future. Washington needed no more studies but, to prevent the economic, social, and political disintegration of Europe, should find a way to spend $6–7 billion a year for three years to save the situation. He added two essential conditions. The governments of western Europe must themselves create a plan Washington could pay for, and then, *"The United States must run this show."* Clayton's zeal galvanized the administration, and within a week, a draft of Marshall's historic speech at Harvard was ready.[18]

European leaders' edginess over the militancy of the Truman Doctrine underlined the need for the administration to decide on the relationship between any new aid program and communist states. Not wanting blame for the rupture between east and west on Washington's back, the state department suggested counting the USSR and its satrapies as possible aid recipients if they agreed to abandon the "near-exclusive Soviet orientation of their economies." Moscow should contribute as well as receive aid and be required to act in concert with western Europe and allow scrutiny of its use of aid—all of which guaranteed a rebuff. If Stalin unexpectedly accepted, policymakers expected Congress to kill the whole idea. Nonetheless, as Acheson recalled six years after the event, it seemed essential to take the gamble of inviting Soviet participation to avoid the stigma of dividing Europe. Marshall's solution was to be "vague," leaving it to the west Europeans to decide whether to invite the Russians and their dependents. His advisers were certain the communist regimes would never agree to the "disclosure" requirements. If the Kremlin had been "wise," Acheson thought, they would have joined the program to sabotage it. Instead, Stalin would reject the Marshall Plan and then raise the iron curtain even higher.[19]

With Bohlen's help, Marshall finished his speech, which, like Acheson's in Mississippi, highlighted the collective participation of Europe and the need to draw on Americans' altruism and practicality. While the Truman Doctrine underlined U.S. combativeness and military aid, the Marshall Plan would underline cooperation and economic assistance. On 5 June at Harvard, fellow honorary degree recipient T. S. Eliot listened as Marshall spoke. Almost no one had seen his speech before its delivery, and Acheson had to "pry" a text from the secretary's military aide "at almost the last moment over the telephone." Marshall's delivery was so subdued, the speech might have escaped wide transatlantic notice had Acheson not prompted British reporters in advance to pay attention. In response to Europe's plight, Marshall declared the United States ready to be generous if the Europeans designed plans to which it could respond. The design must be cooperative and integrated, for Washington would not write checks for a series of national shopping lists. "Our policy," he insisted, "is directed not against any country or doctrine but against hunger, poverty, desperation, and chaos. Its purpose should be the revival of a working economy in the world so as to permit the emergence of political and social conditions in which free institutions can exist." Those who were constructive would meet a generous response. Those hoping "to block the recovery" of others or seeking "to perpetuate human misery" for political gain would "encounter the opposition of the United States."[20]

The Europeans reacted as hoped. Bevin said Marshall had thrown "a life-line to sinking men" and that the "generosity" of the plan that followed was "beyond our belief." After discussions on 17–18 June in Paris, Bevin and French Foreign Minister Georges Bidault issued invitations for a comprehensive meeting, to begin on 12 July. At those meetings, the west Europeans emerged with a plan and, Bevin said, the "birth of the Western bloc." The Soviets at first participated but then played into Washington's hands by walking out, after which Stalin strong-armed the departure of Czechoslovakia and Poland, both eager to participate. Czech Foreign Minister Jan Masaryk was crushed by the walkout. The plan of the remaining sixteen states, completed on 23 September, asked for $27 billion. Over time, the U.S. government pared the request to $17 billion and eventually paid out $13 billion. This was approximately 4.5 percent of the gross national product and 15 percent of the federal budget—$113 billion in 2005 dollars.[21]

The Campaign for Approval

Approval of the Marshall Plan required a strenuous campaign. Acheson played a major role, first in government and then out, for by his original agreement with Marshall, he left the administration on 30 June 1947. Shortly afterward, he repeated his familiar views in support of the Marshall Plan on the Hill. He also joined the executive board of the Citizens' Committee for the Marshall Plan, which sent him on the campaign trail. Federal law barred the state department from overt lobbying, so the Committee acted in its place, using open-sesame ties with Acheson's old colleagues. Partisans of the Marshall Plan worried that congressmen's insistence on their financial prerogatives might defeat or dilute it.

In illustration, Acheson's successor as under secretary, Robert Lovett, noted in August that about a hundred were scheduled for a junket to Europe to remind everyone they controlled the purse strings.[22]

Acheson's speaking campaign took him all over the country and before a national radio audience. In one sortie, the Committee sent him to San Francisco, Portland, and Spokane in the west, and Duluth and Minneapolis in the midwest. Everywhere, he urged Americans to see their interest in keeping goods and resources flowing to Europeans, despite their current inability to pay cash for them. They were working heroically to overcome terrible weather, coal shortages, crop failures, and sharply rising prices for imports. Withholding aid would be ruinous, sapping "the strength and the institutions of the free, of the democratic peoples of Europe." This in turn would "bring disaster to hundreds of millions in Africa, in Asia, in South America, in North America" whose prosperity depended on trade with Europe. After making "between twenty and thirty" statements in a ten-day period, he said he could keep it up "almost in my sleep," adjusting the presentation "for any group from the first year in the kindergarten, up or down." After first emphasizing the restoration of European prosperity, in San Francisco in November 1947 he spoke of the Marshall Plan's role in restoring the balance of power. It would be "of incalculable importance" to U.S. security. Claiming ignorance of the reasons for Soviet obstructionism, he quipped that the line, "I know how to handle the Russians," ranked with "Liquor doesn't affect me" among the most notable "last words of famous men." Whatever their reasons, the Soviets' break from the wartime coalition had made the Marshall Plan necessary. As he campaigned, he continued drawing a sharp line between the former alliance and current, cold war, conditions.[23]

On 19 November, Truman sent enabling legislation for the Marshall Plan to Congress. Europe's economic tailspin had continued unabated. A cataclysmic run on the pound forced London to break the terms of its U.S. loan by suspending currency convertibility, and in October, the president had summoned a special congressional session to advance emergency help to Britain, France, Italy, and Austria. This brought little relief, but evidence of Washington's seriousness encouraged west European governments. Their own growing irritation with local communists, not U.S. pressure as critics alleged, caused the French and Italian governments to complete a process begun earlier of rinsing communist parties out of their coalitions. The Italians also promulgated austere deflationary policies recommended in Washington.[24]

Everywhere he went, citizen Acheson urged boldness. He spent two days in January 1948 testifying at the House of Representatives, where he argued that once the Marshall Plan succeeded in stabilizing European economies, the realists in the Kremlin would probably accept the inevitable, improving chances for better U.S.-Soviet relations. On the other hand, if Congress timidly slashed the funds requested by the president, recovery would slip out of Europe's grasp, resulting in financial collapse, disintegration of the middle classes, and coups leading to the same kind of "closed economic system which now extends from Poland to the Pacific." Americans should be sympathetic rather than impatient with the Europeans who, despite a frightful decline in living standards, were doing their best. What would the administration do, he was asked, if leftists staged an insurrection in a nation receiving Marshall aid. After jibing, "I should suppose that, like sin, we would be against it," he soberly added that if the Europeans succumbed, "our institutions would be under very great strain to maintain the liberties and freedom which we have, in a system in which we would have to devote so much of our time in dealing with fears."[25]

Congress loitered until communists staged a coup against the quasi-democratic Czech government on 25 February 1948, which brought months of debate to a halt. The House passed the necessary legislation by a 318–75 vote, the Senate by voice vote. Truman signed the Plan into law as the European Recovery Program (ERP) on 3 April 1948.

Quelling Fears and Nourishing Hopes: The Significance of the Marshall Plan

The Marshall Plan was Janus-faced. It was a pacific program for socioeconomic problems and a money gun aimed at Soviet domination of Europe. The European Recovery Program rested on the assumption that European distresses rose from economic dislocation rather than Soviet military threats. Its application was reminiscent of U.S. efforts in the 1920s to assuage postwar dislocations, but this time Washington's leaders would not rely on the mysterious working of market forces. They demanded that Marshall Plan recipients unite on a common plan, restrain domestic spending, reduce restrictive trade practices, and generally cooperate with one another. American technocrats scrutinized their budgets with an eye to advancing American preferences. The ERP would work by promoting multilateral trade, establishing stable prices for products and commodities, and restoring agricultural, extractive, and industrial production. Politics, intellectual failures, and human cussedness caused anomalies in the execution. Treating western Europe as a separate economic unit, for example, violated multilateralist principles, and deflationary policies designed to achieve price stability caused credit shortages and a withering of private investment.

Ironies abounded in the ERP. It became necessary mainly because Washington had failed to help enough earlier. Although U.S. leaders believed European economic recovery would reduce tension with the Soviet Union, fears of communist subversion rose with the levels of continental disorganization. In the eyes of Congress, the Marshall Plan was about combating communism, making the ERP, as John S. Hill writes, "a means of carrying on the struggle" rather than easing or muffling it. Contradicting the Plan's idealism were the large dollops of aid sent to colonial areas for production of products needed to earn American purchasers' dollars or of substitutions for U.S. imports to *save* dollars.

Either way, the ERP propped up European imperialism, greatly complicating efforts to convince indigenous nationalists that Washington was their friend. Acheson was typical in being frustrated by this neo-colonialist complicity and in failing to escape it.[26]

The Marshall Plan was nonetheless one of the grand successes in the history of American foreign policy. Merely the "doing of it," Acheson wrote, broadcast "an image" of the country to be proud of. "It was the soundest diplomacy because it created confidence inspired by good faith—and by good works." The Marshall Plan formed a transatlantic conduit for the dispatch of U.S. goods to the ailing Europeans. It countered the production shortfalls that gave the clamorous left and Soviet sirens their power to push Europe in harmful directions. Washington's demand for cooperation in deciding on the makeup and distribution of aid gave a huge push to European integration. Insisting that Nation X could benefit only through the rehabilitation of Nation Y went far to build Europeans' confidence in their collective selves. The Marshall Plan, writes its historian Michael J. Hogan, helped create a supranational market that "could absorb German power, boost productivity, raise living standards, lower prices, and thus set the stage for security and recovery on the Continent and for a fully multilateral system of world trade."[27]

American generosity made the Marshall Plan succeed. As an act of one nation-state to assist others, it was unparalleled and magnanimous. What made this liberality so exquisite was its perfect fit with U.S. interests. As French economist François Perroux wrote: "The perfectly sincere desire to spread prosperity does not exclude the notion of doing so with increased dividends." The Plan appealed to Americans' idealism and their self-interest. It satisfied philanthropic impulses, concern about recession, and anxiety about communist expansion. It succeeded because of the unity and insight of the American foreign policy establishment. It worked because gifted European statesmen responded shrewdly and imaginatively. It worked because Americans and Europeans together created effective institutions to implement it. It carried the day because its recipients were talented and eager to resuscitate economies they already knew how to run. Europe, said one U.S. official, was "a camel ready for water." Finally, the Marshall Plan succeeded because it was audacious. Leaders slashed through minutiae to achieve large purposes, the opposite of Acheson's definition of a failure, when people met "big, bold, demanding problems with half measures, timorous and cramped."[28]

This does not mean the Marshall Plan met all its goals, especially that of closing the seemingly endless "dollar gap," which still had life in it. Only massive U.S. purchases abroad during the Korean War, just as the Marshall Plan ended, finally rested fears about reestablishing steady European economic growth. Moreover, though it went far to restore confidence, it did not make its recipients feel militarily secure. Instead of concentrating foursquare on economic development and uniting in self-defense, they obsessed, fearfully but indecisively, about the Soviet Union. Although the west faced an intolerable military imbalance in Europe, U.S. policymakers had hoped the Marshall Plan would be enough to restore Europeans' optimism about the future. But it was *not* enough—and thus, NATO. One of NATO's key functions, Acheson would decide as secretary of state, was therapeutic, to provide a blanket of military security under which Europeans felt safe to do what was necessary to restore their economies and societies. This is not to say that *deficiencies* of the Marshall Plan made NATO necessary, but that nothing short of a U.S. commitment to defend western Europe would generate the confidence needed for economic recovery.

British historian Alan S. Milward thinks the Marshall Plan did not work nearly this well and belittles its impact. The economic disturbances of 1946–47, he contends, were mere bumps on a road to rapid recovery. The ERP partly hindered a lasting recovery and certainly "did not save West Europe from economic collapse." Acheson's contemporaries had their own worries about the program's efficacy. The British Labor government rejected U.S. criticisms of their highly regulated economy and Commonwealth trading system and showed no enthusiasm for "integration." Germany, the key to west European recovery, barely benefited at first because of the Berlin blockade.

Milward's estimate is nevertheless unconvincing. As Charles S. Maier has noted, perhaps U.S. aid by sheer dollar count was marginally significant—some 10 percent to 20 percent of capital invested in the Plan's first years—but this was exactly the margin that freed private, domestic funds to flow into productive investment. The ERP also broke trade bottlenecks and eased the burden of hard currency payments, spurring Europeans to accumulate their own investment capital. Marshall aid was "like the lubricant in an engine—not the fuel—allowing a machine to run that would otherwise buckle and bind." The combined national product of recipient countries, Diane B. Kunz points out, jumped by a third over prewar levels and by 17 percent in the program's first two years. The dollar gap persisted, but the Plan "quelled the fears and nourished the hopes of leaders and public alike." It also, Kunz adds, "supplied an idealism previously lacking in American foreign policy." Linked to the integration of West Germany, the impetus toward European unity, and the development of NATO, the Marshall Plan created a formidable alliance that outlasted the cold war.[29]

It also helped make the cold war chillier than it had been. In the summer of 1947, Moscow forced trade "agreements" on its satellites, forming "Comecon," a kind of backhanded answer to Marshall. In September, Stalin established the Cominform, an international organization of communist parties (for now excluding the East Germans). His current heir apparent, Andrei Zhdanov, proclaimed the inexorable conflict between the "two camps" of "socialism" and "capitalism." A prominent Yugoslav communist, Milovan Djilas, denigrated his French and Italian brethren for their revolutionary timidity. Instructed from Moscow, French communists set off immense strikes and demonstrations, hoping to obliterate the economy and pull down the government. In December 1947,

Stalin ordered more help sent to Greek communists. He grew more serious about collectivizing economies throughout his east European empire, where his servants also purged their governments of those inadequately enthusiastic about the USSR. The most shocking responses to the Marshall Plan came in the first six months of 1948: the communist coup in Czechoslovakia, the expulsion of Yugoslavia from the Cominform, and the onset of the Berlin blockade. Although these events caused a fright in the west, astute observers noticed their defensive character and chalked them up as signs that the Marshall Plan was already succeeding. Stalin was hunkering down, and his crackdown in the east further fueled the cold war. Well before the announcement of the Marshall Plan, and certainly before it took shape, he had isolated the Soviet Union diplomatically and economically, a colossal strategic error.[30]

"An Insidious and Seductive Drug"

When he heard of Acheson's intention to resign, James Reston thought it bad news that the state department was losing an able, experienced servant because of inadequate compensation. It was paradoxical for a man to leave when he had never been "happier" at work. As Marshall's No. 2, Reston wrote on 12 May 1947, Acheson's "authority and prestige" were at their peak, and his influence had grown "immeasurably on Capitol Hill." Even if he called Acheson "at ten in the morning," commented Senator Arthur Vandenberg, "and asked him to deliver the Washington Monument to my office by noon, he would somehow manage to treat this as a proper request and deliver it." Widely known as the "Number One Number Two Man," Acheson now would have no number at all. On 28 May, the Senate had confirmed Robert Lovett as his successor. A fifty-one-year-old Republican banker, former assistant secretary of war, and hypochondriac, Lovett was an old friend, one of the key men, along with Acheson, who provided continuity in Washington's postwar international security establishment. Acheson introduced him to Vandenberg with the comment, "I've known Bob since Yale and I hope you will be agreeable to accept his services." Vandenberg welcomed him with the hope that "God have mercy on your soul." Through May and June, Lovett apprenticed with Acheson, working side by side. "On Tuesday, July 1, 1947," Acheson wrote, Lovett "merely moved to the chair at the desk, thoroughly familiar with what was going across it."[31]

A private citizen again, Acheson felt the need to replenish his bank account. He had started married life without independent capital and gained only modest earnings in the interwar years by later law firm standards. He had served in government for seven years, most of the time at less than $10,000 a year. He turned down a large offer for his memoirs, partly because he had left all his documents behind in the department, Reston later reporting that "the use of public documents for private ends" was something on which Acheson held "strong views." After a Canadian vacation, he returned to his firm and was soon practicing before the Supreme Court. He won a case for some Japanese-Americans stripped of their property in California but lost DuPont's attempt to retain control of General Motors. "Our poor clients triumphed," he recalled, "and our rich client met defeat."[32]

But the law could never satisfy Acheson's love of public policy or quench his furnace of ambition. In a letter he wrote his daughter Jane shortly before resigning, he said he felt "very sad and somewhat panic stricken to be going back to the Union Trust Bldg." In government, he had gained a "sureness of touch" and discovered others were ready "to let me drive." He missed being in the center of action. Though only fifty-four, he could entertain few hopes of returning, for few expected a renewal of the Democratic lease on the White House. Later reflecting on this 1947–48 interregnum, he commented that a public career was "not only a powerful stimulant but a habit-forming one." It was "an insidious and seductive drug." Government service gave him a chance to exercise "vital powers . . . along lines of excellence." That was now gone, along with the claim to command. Adjusting to "shrinkage in the scope for action" left him feeling "the flatness of life."[33]

Truman tried to keep him distracted. He had him take over the late Fiorello La Guardia's post as head of the U.S. section of the Permanent American-Canadian Defense Board. He appointed him vice-chairman of the Hoover Commission, which was designing ways to improve the workings of the federal government. (The commission would urge the state department to consolidate diplomats serving abroad and career officials at home into a single diplomatic corps. Acheson's attempt as secretary of state to implement the idea encountered heavy resistance from Foggy Bottom denizens not eager to go to Pakistan and then flagged when McCarthyites damaged the morale of foreign service officers.) Acheson and Hoover became friends, and a year or two later, when Acheson overtook the former president on a Manhattan sidewalk, he called out that "it would greatly improve my financial and social standing if I might be seen walking with you." "Anything I can do," answered Hoover, "short of a loan." Truman also wanted Acheson to run the Economic Cooperation Administration (ECA), the agency administering the Marshall Plan, but both men probably knew a GOP Congress would not accept a retired State official and partisan Democrat to boot. As Acheson predicted (and recommended), the office went to automobile executive Paul G. Hoffman. Luckily for Acheson, this left him free to become secretary of state in 1949. In 1947–48, meanwhile, he dined on what was available, defending the Marshall Plan, practicing law, and working with Hoover. With no inkling of his large future, he also spoke out more often and more openly about America's place in the world.[34]

The Views of a Private Citizen

Acheson never claimed to join the minority of one to anticipate Truman's stunning November triumph. His days in government apparently over, he felt freer to speak his mind and did so in a series of speeches. The most notable came in April 1948 at Oberlin College as part of his Marshall Plan canvass, and two others in September of 1948, off the record at the National War College and publicly before the Michigan bar association in Ann Arbor. At Oberlin, his account of cold war origins changed yet again, with far more emphasis on Soviet culpability and with a deliberate appeal to his listeners' "passions." The United States, he urged them to recognize, confronted a state for whom "evil" practices were the norm. Now interpreting Stalin's 1946 election speech as a declaration of war, he identified Iran, Greece, Czechoslovakia, Hungary, and the rest of eastern Europe as targets of "Russian aggression." Under such pressure, a host of free nations "might give way to authoritarian control," producing a communist "system extending from the Atlantic to the Pacific, controlling the Mediterranean and with outposts in Africa." The very success of efforts to meet this threat, he warned, could provoke the frustrated Kremlin to violence. War was a "terrible" possibility, but compromising fundamental principles was "worse." "Past experience," however, taught him the Soviets would eventually accept "the facts as they are" if the United States acted vigorously and wisely. In short, the west could solve its own "crisis" without resort to negotiating with the Soviets.[35]

The National War College speech was an extended essay on the constraints of policymaking set in the context of Acheson's concern that the public habitually hoped for easy triumphs and simple solutions. It was part of his persistent efforts to elevate popular understanding of hard issues, the better to make intelligent policies. Unlike the deeply antidemocratic George Kennan, Acheson was a political animal who knew that Congress, the press, and the people were all inescapable parts of making foreign policy and permanent constraints on policymakers. Traditional American attitudes, he told his War College audience, also inhibited those with the responsibility for conducting U.S. policy. One such was that the United States had no legitimate concern about the "internal affairs" of other nations. In Acheson's view, this false (and "realist") proposition contributed to the U.S. failure to confront the evil of either Nazi Germany or communist Russia in a timely fashion. It was not an "internal" affair when communist parties seized power in decent societies by exploiting their weaknesses. The United States could not have salvaged Greece from communist expansion without ignoring the chimera of nonintervention in the "internal" affairs of others.

Journalists' assumption that they had a right to get their stories, come what may, was also a damaging attitude. The "irrepressible conflict" between reporters and policymakers explained why "diplomats become diplomaniacs." This reportorial presumption flew in the face of the compelling need at times to act with secrecy. When the preliminaries of vital negotiations were paraded across the front pages, governments lost their chance to explore alternatives without fear of being crucified for their flexibility. The time to reveal basic information about negotiations was when they were complete, and then, he implied, the informed public should rally to the government standard.

A man with great tolerance for ambiguity, comfortable with lack of closure, Acheson in his War College speech exposed a tangy impatience with his fellow citizens' demands for victory and certainty. Because "every problem has every kind of a drawback on one side, and every advantage is balanced by a drawback," it was impossible to find solutions free of ragged edges. Officials simply had to deal with the inevitable difficulties of diplomacy. They must not "slink from problems" but "do the very best they can in meeting them and get on."[36]

He returned to the theme of constraints in Ann Arbor. Referring to the growing hubbub about "communists in government," he warned that it was "dangerous" to expect to control all circumstances and "silly to paint the other person's conduct in deep black and your own in pure white." He came close to doing so himself when he charged that no legitimate grievances justified Soviet conduct. In abandoning the wartime alliance, Moscow had acted like a "fire department" that began "cutting the hoses and lighting more fires." He remained confident, nonetheless, that steady, patient statecraft and the timely application of pressure, rather than persuasion and sweet reason, would check the worst the Soviet Union could throw at the west.[37]

"I'm Going to Have a Highball for Breakfast"

Acheson's speech making for the Marshall Plan had just begun when his former ally on nuclear weapons control, Henry A. Wallace, threw his hat in the ring against Truman as a member of the Progressive Party. The Republicans nominated Thomas E. Dewey for a second run at the presidency at the end of June 1948. With southerners walking out because of a civil rights plank in the party platform, Truman accepted the Democratic nomination on 15 July. Acheson signed a statement of the Americans for Democratic Action urging New Deal Democrats to oppose Wallace and vote for Truman.[38]

On 2 November, Acheson stayed up all night with a law partner to hear the election returns, getting drunker as the trickling results began to signify the greatest electoral upset in American history. By early morning, he was "overjoyed and quite drunk." Catching a morning train for New York, he announced at Union Station: "I'm going to do something I've never done. I'm going to have a highball for breakfast," and thence toasted the president.[39]

Marshall was ill and planning to step down. He was like "a four-engine bomber going only on one engine," Acheson said in 1947. Truman would have to find a fourth secretary of state. Right after the election, Vandenberg heard *he* would be appointed in a show of bipartisanship. In mid-November, Acheson predicted one of three men would get the job—Ambassador Averell Harriman in Britain, former budget director Lewis Douglas, or Supreme Court Justice William O. Douglas—and "bet" on the first. About two weeks later, however, Truman summoned Acheson and "without preliminary said that he wished me to become Secretary of State." "You know," the president said, "twenty guys would

make a better Secretary of State than you, but I don't know them. I know you."
After talking to Alice, Acheson agreed the next day, but Truman's decision went
unannounced until 7 January 1949, and the ongoing speculation gave Acheson "a
useful lesson in modesty," since his name was not "in the forefront." Truman had
picked him, Acheson thought, because he knew "I was as loyal to him as anybody
he could find in the United States, whether he was in the White House or not."
"And he could count 100 per cent on my doing nothing which would be contrary
to his interests or policies."[40]

When Truman made his announcement, Reston wrote that Vice-President-
Elect Alben W. Barkley had been "decisive" in the choice. Because Acheson was
"brilliant and outspoken," Reston expected "fireworks" to light up his confirmation hearings. Although some, like journalist Elmer Davis, considered Acheson
a "left-of-center liberal," Reston expected his attacks on the Russians to draw fire
from liberals. Acheson, he wrote in praising the nomination, had "suffered under
the Byrnes policy of being told nothing, and under the Marshall system of being
expected to do everything." Now he would "take hold of his job quicker and stay
the course longer than any of his predecessors since Mr. Hull." A *Times* editorial
quoted Truman to say Acheson was a man of "prodigious industry." Hoover
proudly expressed pleasure at his colleague's appointment. Columnist Joseph
Alsop wired congratulations from Paris: "THE DUBIOUS FUTURE LOOKS
AT LEAST LESS DUBIOUS TONIGHT. LOVE TO ALICE." Europeans,
reports said, were disappointed Harriman had not gotten the nod. The British
embassy in Washington described Acheson as "a man of high character and
standing" but "essentially a lawyer" who would likely be a compromiser.
Communist sympathizers in Europe were unhappy. The Soviet-licensed *Berliner
Zeitung* called Acheson Wall Street's man, and Rome's *Repubblica d'Italia* considered him a "zealot of the so-called strong policy toward Russia and an
inflamed anti-Communist."[41]

His credentials vouched for or denounced, Acheson began daily briefings.
His interlocutor was the same Lovett he had readied for the under secretary job
in 1947. But no one could have prepared him for what lay ahead.

Part II

6

THE INNER AND OUTER ACHESON

Acheson's most conspicuous personal qualities—intellectual brilliance, moral courage, and elegant style—usually served him well as secretary of state, but not always, for these properties are not the norm in any society, let alone a popular democracy, where they are as likely to be resented as much as admired. By 1949, Acheson had buffed these qualities to such a high gleam, they bordered on the prodigious, and they often stirred indignation. The fact is, his personality was so glaring, it is nearly impossible to imagine his being appointed to high office in our own times. In *his* time, he had offended, or overpowered, enough people to guarantee at least some tension in his confirmation hearings.

On 13 January 1949, those hearings began in a room jammed with spectators. Bitter at Truman's reelection and thinking Acheson reeked of unorthodoxy, Republicans hoped to stir trouble. His old detractor Adolf Berle disappointed them with a telegram minimizing their past differences. In a warning of dark days to come, however, Acheson was forced to explain repeatedly that Donald rather than Alger Hiss had reported to him in the wartime state department. In executive session testimony described in Chapter 17, he went on at length about Alger. Otherwise, senators seemed interested only in "Russia" and internal security. Styles Bridges of New Hampshire accused Acheson's brother, Ted, a George Washington University professor, of being "soft" on communism. Others demanded to know why Acheson's law firm had so many dealings with Poland. Acheson understood the needs of the day and put on an eye-catching display of deference. He would urge his law firm to take his name off its title. He would omit "no step" to sweep out department communists. Committee chair Tom Connally finally gave him a soft pitch by referring to Moscow's anger in 1947 when Acheson accused it of expansionism. Using words Senator Arthur Vandenberg wrote for him, he denounced communism as a "fatal" doctrine "to a free society and to human rights and fundamental freedom." The insurgent Acheson, however, made a brief appearance in executive session on the 14th, when he strongly suggested he would no more exert himself to save Chiang Kai-shek's hide than Marshall did.[1]

Senate confirmation came later that day by a vote of 83 to 6. All the "no" votes came from Republicans, including Nebraska's Kenneth Wherry, who had cast the only "nay" against him as under secretary in 1945. Acheson took his oath of office a week later. He went to work on transitional trivia and met his staff. Soon he was working on Marshall's half-finished legacy, the treaty forming the North Atlantic Treaty Organization.

In Your Face

For his readers in the *Manchester Guardian*, Alistair Cooke described the fifty-five-year-old Acheson as a "six-foot-two Velasquez grandee who has submitted, with a twinkling eye, to his present reincarnation in fine tweeds as a Connecticut Yankee." He had "one of the most creative political minds of his time." His "vivacity, his smiling irony, his sleek tailoring are readily admired by snobs and by homesick Europeans who like to have their diplomats that way." His "enormous industry" and "democratic passion" accounted for "his long forbearance with Congressmen who think as hounds do, by padding off in the direction of suspicious smells." Some who disliked him were put off by his very appearance. By the 1950s, his erect 6' 1" frame (Cooke gave him an extra inch) had filled out to 175 pounds. Steel blue, "merry, searching eyes" and a "wolfish" grin balanced his "military bearing." His graying, slightly wavy hair came to a sharp widow's peak in the center of a broad forehead. He spoke with the rounded, plummy accent of the Connecticut Valley. He commonly wore glasses but only out of camera range. Cartoonists lavished attention on his hawk nose, capacious ears, and especially his reddish-gray guardsman's mustache and eyebrows. This remarkable mustache, which he first sported at Yale and which linked him to his father, reached its pointed ends just beyond the extremities of his mouth. The equally remarkable dark and bushy brows undulated northward. When he smiled, his large teeth flashed just below the trimmed mustache. Watching him testify before a House committee in 1949, Arthur Krock called him "the brilliant, handsome, lean and reasonably young Mr. Acheson."[2]

Some people are headlights, and some reflectors. Acheson was a headlight, and his mustache and tailored wrappings were part of his exhibit of power and spirit. Philip Hamburger in a brilliant *New Yorker* profile believed the mustache had "a personality of its own" and an "enormously fond" owner. As a young man, Acheson's mustache had been "large, unruly, and reasonably aggressive." It was "pushy." Having once looked ready "to climb his cheeks, like a vine seeking the sunlight," it had recently received permission to be "at peace with itself, quietly aware of its responsibilities." It still hinted at "the unpredictable," the "adornment of a man who has conquered not only himself but his mustache." When he exercised his "art of thinking," which he did "with some violence," he pulled at and groomed it into its "well-tailored" look. When he left home in the morning, he took "a sharp look up and down the street from his front door," then almost leapt "down a flight of stone steps to the street" while managing to keep himself and mustache "in perfect harmony." David Acheson considered the mustache his father's "chief vanity," regularly treated with "Pinaud's mustache wax" to secure its "ends against gravity." In short, as James Reston detected, it was "a triumph of policy planning." It became such a symbol that when right-wingers attacked Acheson in 1950, Averell Harriman implored him to shave it—in vain. Hamburger thought it betrayed Acheson's "uncertainty," but it more likely reflected his insistence on saying, "I am what I am!"[3]

Acheson's clothing, another expression of power, aroused critics to apoplexy. He was a "dude, a fashionplate," recalled David. Almost too elegant in Hamburger's view, he favored white-striped, double-breasted Farnsworth Reed suits, shoes shined to a mirror, and "blue-and-white candy-striped shirts with stiff white collars." In a daily "bravura" performance, he showed boutonnières, pocket handkerchiefs, and snowy cuffs bolted with gold monogrammed cuff links. Socks were gartered. He avoided the "solecism" of striped ties on a striped shirt. Sporty at Yale, tweedy at his first Supreme Court appearance, he was stylish as secretary of state, with ties bulging slightly from snug vests. An assortment of black homburgs, even panamas, crowned his head. Young David McCullough saw Acheson emerge from a New Haven clothing store looking "like a strapping handsome actor all dressed up to play the part of Dean Acheson." If the eyebrows betrayed an intermittently toxic temper, his clothes displayed the man who told irreverent stories while taking five minutes to make a perfect martini.[4]

The wardrobe too was a subject of policy. Alice Acheson admitted to keeping Dean's home peaceful but not his clothes, except for an occasional "flashy" vest or tie she would buy him. "No," she remarked. "He would not have anyone choose his clothes." His clothing, David observed, was "the skin he put on to reflect the personality beneath—crisp, harmonious, bold but not quite flamboyant, a challenge to perfection in the last detail." On the farm, he sat for dinner in "outrageous" fashion, in summers in "a pleated cotton wedding shirt from Mexico or the islands, lime green slacks, no socks, sandals or Mexican *huaraches* on the feet, an orange sash around the waist falling to the knee." There, among family, his "*outré* dress" released him from the need to conform to public conventions. Family members vied with one another to see how far he would go in wearing their gifts, but there were no limits: "Green Belgian shoes, pink elephant socks," and boxers flecked with "red ants." None "produced any response from Dad but delight."[5]

Hamburger's view that there was a large "discrepancy between the outer Acheson and the inner Acheson" is mistaken, but his description of both is deft. Outside, Acheson was "an austere, tall, slim, long-legged, and outrageously mustached fashion plate, a parody of the diplomatic virtues." Inside was a man with "a quick wit and a skeptical mind, impatient with procedural form, self-analytical to an advanced degree, and a taskmaster who will accept from himself nothing less than what he considers perfection." As he shifted "from foot to foot" at required functions, a "perverse devil deep inside him" would lead him to play the role of "Acheson." At a recent "particularly humid gathering of people who concern themselves with foreign affairs,

> the outer Acheson pulled noncommittally at his mustache, raised and lowered his thick eyebrows in a manner that could signify everything or nothing, engaged in talk so small as to be almost invisible, and bowed from the waist with punctilio. Not until a stranger in striped trousers approached him and said fatuously, "Mr. Acheson, you must be proud indeed of your achievements in life" did the outer Acheson send forth a hurry call for the inner Acheson. "Sir," replied the Secretary, dipping into his gag file, "all that I know I learned at my mother's knee, and other low joints."[6]

If the press invariably had him "dapper," "debonair," or "jaunty," that was how he wanted it. Byron's "finish'd gentleman from top to toe," Acheson refused to take cover, especially when at the center of the public eye. In a press conference two months after his confirmation, he deliberately pointed to his sartorial reputation by noting that the Custom Tailors Guild rated him the nation's best-dressed man, undoubtedly beating out Adolphe Menjou. What both David Acheson and Hamburger miss in Acheson's style is its truculence. Clothes and mustache were more than a dandy's embellishments. They were the in-your-face equipage of a man who demanded acceptance on his own terms, the rebel against paternal authority, the Groton scamp, and the sub-cabinet officer who defied an imperious Franklin Roosevelt. He could act correctly and put on a show of deference. He could lavish exaggerated compliments on the remarks of slow-witted congressmen. But his inner self would eventually insist on moments of truth that scraped the skin of convention. "This is me," his fabulous mustache and suits declared, "whether you like it or not."[7]

An Imaginative and Vehement Man

High office compelled some changes in Acheson's daily habits. He wrote few private letters until he left government. He had time to read only summaries of daily newspapers. Weather permitting, he continued his mile-and-a-half morning treks to work, usually in tandem with Justice Frankfurter. As they walked, they debated literature and philosophy but rarely policy or politics. Acheson strode vigorously down the sidewalk while the diminutive jurist scurried to keep up, their hats bobbing up and down, "the incarnation of Law and the Constitution," observed French statesman Jean Monnet during a Washington visit. Acheson's workload permitting, he would lunch at the Metropolitan Club. He stayed home nights more than before, subtracting rather than multiplying social appearances. To screen out needless dinners and receptions, he required "an appointments secretary with a Southern accent, a heart of ice, and a will of iron." He took an unlisted phone number and entertained mainly at hotels. When he could, he weekended at his farm: "I try to see that the Secretary has a proper weekend—without interruptions," explained Alice.[8]

Whether in Georgetown or Harewood, he sought the balanced life, but tilted toward vivid. He wanted dash in his automobiles and drove to the farm in his favorite, a blue Chrysler convertible. He enjoyed being a country squire, complete with horses and Herefords to tend and tenants to supervise. He had complex views on clearing woods to produce a "deer park" and sent family members out to hack at the brush. "Group activity" was all-important, preferably "frequent, instructive, outdoors, vigorous, and (if possible) fun." At Christmas, he would lift his eggnog and enthusiastically sing carols in a "full-throated" baritone. To celebrate the rites of spring, he would put some Stravinsky on the record player, flip a handkerchief from his pocket, and do a dance of "a poor little crocus shivering through the cold and wind and finally blossoming with the spring." All year long, he doted on his daughters, admitting when one married that "the father of the bride is a pitiable creature." When one of Archibald MacLeish's daughters married, he brought "a Revolutionary War sword to cut the cake with."[9]

Acheson's recreational and sensory pastimes ranged from refined to Philistine. He quit smoking both pipe and cigarettes while secretary of state. Except for a fondness for seafood, he was a meat-and-potatoes man at dinner. A connoisseur of cocktails, he favored old-fashioneds before becoming a devotee in the fifties of the dry martini. He was a fan of his wife's landscapes but when confronting obscure contemporary art, he might exclaim, "Who do they think they're kidding?" He enjoyed Handel, Brahms, and Grieg, but only duty would send him to a concert hall. His abrupt exits from boring theatrical productions mortified the family. Movies and musicals were all right if red-blooded, or if Myrna Loy showed up. He liked Tarzan, *The Thin Man*, and "blood and thunder" films but was "intensely" bored by "introspective" Swedish movies. Musical comedies amused him, especially Cole Porter's, "but he required crispness, style, pace, and melody of a high order, or he started looking for the exit." Acheson appeared as a character in Irving Berlin's *Call Me Madam* (1953), with Ethel Merman belting out the line, "Hey, Dean where the hell is Lichtenburg?" His commitment to reason was laser-like, but his leisure reading was eclectic. On his nightstand lay Thucydides, Shakespeare, Twain, Dickens, Smollett, Trollope, and Vernon Louis Parrington. He had once read French, but the skill faded. Trying to speak it reduced him "to panic"; listening, a Frenchman would look like "a mastiff trying to overlook the impertinences of a fox terrier." He did not travel for travel's sake, though he vacationed several times in Britain and France in the thirties. He never set foot in the Soviet Union, saw China and Japan only as a young man, and visited Latin America once in a short official visit to Brazil. In the 1960s, he managed landfall in Southeast Asia as an attorney for Cambodia. But he loved going to the mountains to cast for fish and eventually took annual vacations and "went native" in Antigua. After brief enthusiasms for riding and handball, he played tennis, shot skeet, paddled around the swimming pool, and, mentored by German leader Konrad Adenauer, took to bocce, the Italian lawn-bowling game. Not a great fan of the national pastime, he turned down tickets for the World Series opener in 1950.[10]

When the fools on the Hill got him down, he put on khakis and shirtsleeves and made furniture in a little shop near Alice's studio. Working at his lathe "demanded complete absorption or you lost a finger." Churning out hutches and tables for friends helped him keep his "sense of proportion and sanity." A finished table, Alice remarked, "stands or falls," unlike a foreign policy, so he did not have to "wait twenty-five years to see how the thing comes out." He also cultivated dahlias and developed an "intoxicating" relationship with gladiolus, planting "nearly sixty to seventy yards" of numerous varieties. He filled the house with them and gave them away "by the basketful." Eventually, he created the "white garden," a two-by-thirty-yard bed featuring anything white, from lilies and daisies to snapdragons. He ushered guests to the garden and asked, "What do you think of that?"

Gardening reinforced organic views of life and foreign policy, and gardening metaphors punctuated his talk. Statesmen grew policies from seeds of oppor-tunity, using intellectual nutrients. A good policy might take years to ripen, and often the best thing was to step back and let it grow. Truman, he said, was the "head gardener." Both woodworking and tilling the garden demanded orderly habits, discipline, and hard work—and, as a White House staffer noted, "Acheson never disappeared when it was time to work."[11]

The same man inhabited home and office. The squire of Harewood smoothed relations with diplomats and a good many members of Congress. When he ran into toughs immune to his charm, he "fell back on exquisite manners as a defense." As Washington grew more tempestuous, he beguiled those willing to be affected, but many were not. He was "an intellectual artist," wrote Reston, a "man of fierce personal loyalties and distastes and strong convictions. He is both idealistic and cynical, puritanical and Rabelaisian, grave and witty, short-tempered and patient." He was also "ambitious, persevering and orderly," with "more style than a new Cadillac." Smiling at an Acheson attempt to portray himself as "a simple country boy," Reston recorded the Washington suspicion "that he doesn't precisely make his suspenders out of plow lines, or his shirts out of feed sacks."[12]

Acheson's impish sense of humor charmed some and irritated others, espec-ially in Congress. He took his job seriously but not himself and enjoyed making people laugh. He curbed his talent for mimicry in public but not his wit. On the radio during the war, he announced that UNRRA would distribute $2 billion in aid, a half billion less than mentioned in his prepared text. When a reporter asked what had happened to the missing five hundred million, he replied: "A split-second decision after a Martini." Intricate jokes demanded full attention. Asked why Republicans seemed so intent to intervene in Asia but not Europe, Acheson, "displaying that talent for erudite and sober-faced wit for which he is respected and feared," responded that "one of the sound rules of ancient justice was that the wise thing for a court to do was to observe the limits of its jurisdiction." A chronic ironist, he loved needling Washington's growing platoons of irony police. Having alluded to a "distinguished statesman" who thought Washington could have rescued Chiang Kai-shek had it given him "sincere aid" in time, he commented: "I was interested to observe the introduction of the word 'sincere,' which, of course, raises all possibilities of argument: Was the aid given with tongue in cheek? Was it insincere?"[13]

Irony and wit were only part of what drew other men to Acheson as friends. As John Maynard Keynes said of someone else, Acheson "was skeptical of most things, except those that chiefly matter, affection and reason." Oliver Franks, the ambassador from Britain who worked closely with him, viewed Acheson as a "romantic" of "quite astounding" loyalty. State department aides remembered him as kind, even sweet. German specialist Perry Laukhuff recalled him as "very kind and very—well an admirable man, in every respect." Thomas D. Cabot, claiming Acheson did "suffer fools gladly," admired his gentle treatment of a naïve young officer (namely, Cabot). Charges that Acheson was a snob, Cabot insisted, were false, a misconstrual of his meticulous dress and speech. Reston, a chronicler of his arrogance, detected a "very strong character" underneath Acheson's lordly manner. The objects of Acheson's admiration said much about his own values. He particularly esteemed those who sacrificed their own comfort to make better futures for their countries: thus his high regard for Truman and Henry Stimson and his pleasure in working with Marshall and French Foreign Minister Robert Schuman. He was extremely fond of men of ordinary upbringing, light learning, plain speech, and tough character—like Britain's Foreign Minister Ernest Bevin, and again Harry S Truman. He indulged a patronizing fondness for such Senator Claghorns as Arthur Vandenberg and Tom Connally.[14]

Scoffing at the popular image of Acheson as an anglophile, Franks described him as "a pure American type of a rather rare species." Franks once negotiated with Acheson in the middle of a "large plowed field" at Harewood—"Now, we cannot be overheard or bugged," the secretary explained—and could probably take his measure as well as any foreigner. In his view, Acheson melded "an 18th century style of personal taste with the moral conscience and austerity of a 17th century puritan." He carried on a "far from ostentatious" life in Georgetown; on the farm, it was "downright austere." Rooted in New England, he took "pride in doing hard, pioneering things" and in this way was "profoundly American."

Acheson, he judged, believed that "being a gentleman is not a matter of who you are born, or of how much money or what class, but of the style in which you conduct your living." Acheson's style, however, commonly brought charges of aloofness, which clandestinely dismayed him. In a 1955 letter he recounted to Truman how he had run into a group of men digging away with picks and shovels on Manhattan's East 38th Street. One looked up, smiled, and exclaimed: "For the love of God, if it ain't Dean Acheson. I seen you on the Dave Garroway show yesterday morning." None of the men, he wrote, "seemed to be dismayed by the cold exterior."[15]

"No harpooner is worth a straw who ain't pretty sharkish," wrote Melville, and Acheson was the state department's harpooner. His astringent view of mankind emerged from what he identified as the same "stern morality" that made him read books clear through with "no peeking at the end." This same inner moral voice forbade displays of "distress, shock or disappointment." He was "excellent company" and a fine raconteur, recalled his ambassador to France, David K. E. Bruce, but could also "be severe against anyone whom he distrusted, or even whom he disliked." He did *not* "suffer fools lightly." The antidote to an imperfect world, he thought, was strength and yet more strength. But because evil and perverse behavior was a predictable part of the mixed menu of life, he had reason to tell those around him to brighten up—and get to work. Human misconduct *could* make his temper flare; Congressman Walter Judd said, "If you prick him a little sometimes his face gets red." Normally, however, he could wait out bad behavior, for he enjoyed "nearly inexhaustible" patience. This was possibly a product of his father's trout fishing lessons but surely reinforced by having to watch helplessly as his daughter Mary struggled with tuberculosis. What was most likely to make him *impatient* was whining over the human condition. He equally disliked responding to defeats with self-destructive pique. "I do not believe," he wrote Schuman in 1952, "that the way to solve a difficult question is to inject one which is presently insoluble." Hugely confident himself, he found it hard to abide those who were not. They would probably be of little use in the long haul of the cold war.[16]

Strength, patience, toughness, confidence—all contributed to Acheson's power as a leader. An enameled confidence and near immunity to indecision fortified him for cold war tensions, political attacks, and Truman's occasional lack of good sense, ordeals that could dismantle less self-possessed men. At a time when events challenged isolationist traditions, he was an activist, an ambitious man who sought responsibility, exulted in tough decisions, loved exercising power, and believed there was "no better or fuller life for a man of spirit" than public service. Like Ulysses Grant, he might have thought that he was "a verb instead of a personal pronoun." In 1957, he wrote a neighbor about the "old Greek conception of happiness"; it was the opportunity to exercise "vital powers along lines of excellence, in a life affording them scope." To Acheson, the link between "the power of decision" and responsibility was "exhilarating." Scornful of officials who awaited pressure from below before acting, he and his decisive president would lead without prior call. "Life is action," declared Holmes.[17]

Honesty, courage, and loyalty to subordinates made Acheson a powerful leader within the department. In contentious moments, he was likely to be both blunt and zestful. For a high official, he was amazingly willing to take risks and pick fights. A young admirer probably had Acheson in mind in saying that all the great men he had known had "contempt for dull, grey, prudent policy." At home or abroad, Acheson would challenge clients or other powerful men. A judge said he was a "stern critic of younger lawyers" and not "easily manipulated by a client." Near the end of Acheson's life, TV commentator Eric Sevareid mentioned an upcoming magazine article in which Acheson would brand the joint chiefs of staff as foolish and misinformed, prompting him to remark: "You're making me seem a little blunter than I usually am." When Sevareid persisted, Acheson added: "Dear me, I'm always in trouble."[18]

David thought his father's "Wild Ulster streak" made him "imaginative, vehement, an effective advocate, not averse to risk, and a larger-than-life person." Acheson admired irreverence, and he lived irreverently. "Discretion meant absolutely nothing" to him, and he enjoyed shocking others. "I'm not a candidate for office," he said, "and I won't live like a nervous, stuffed shirt lawyer." His courage in facing down critics, Franks thought, was like "a blade of steel." His audacity, his "moral courage" bordering on "recklessness," as a former colleague described it, also engendered many of his worst problems. Among men of tepid personalities, he burned hot, causing foes to wilt in humiliation or blaze back in anger. He was often gratuitously forthright, telling reporters in 1946 that Americans who swallowed current criticisms of U.S. policy did not "deserve their reputation for native shrewdness and common sense." "In a city with large egos," writes Clark Clifford, "he was the most self-confident man I ever encountered." He did not mind "making enemies," MacLeish adds, "and had almost no tolerance for what he felt was inferior intellect or stupid questioning." He "positively exuded an attitude that made other people feel belittled and scorned," said Clifford.[19]

Here we enter the territory of his notorious defect of character, usually called "arrogance." He was *not* always patient, and Marshall thought he had to "let fly against something" every few months to prevent explosion. He would erupt in anger, complete with "rich, imaginative cursing." "The Lord's name was not merely taken in vain," writes David, "but summoned to work ruin in ingenious ways on inanimate objects that failed to behave as Dad thought they should." Not all his English "came from Groton and Yale." He rarely struck directly at a person but at his stupidity, which seemed like "willful defiance." He was so disgusted by intellectual shoddiness that he would stick "a long needle" into the offender, leaving Washington full of wounded people waiting to hit back. Acheson's arrogance was the glare of his huge supply of self-confidence. At worst, it produced behavior that was deeply offensive. At its least objectionable, it took the form of showing off, as in a press conference episode when he mistook a man for a Russian journalist. "I will respond to the question," he was saying, "if one may call it a question, by the representative of Tass . . ." The reporter angrily broke in: "The Secretary should know that I do not represent Tass, but the Information Service of the People's Republic of Poland," whereupon Acheson immediately countered: "I stand corrected: Demi-Tass."[20]

Friends in the Fourth Estate shook their heads at this aggressiveness, which had probably been part of him since he noticed he could tame his ornery and lazy childhood pony with "a fast punch in the nose." Elmer Davis wrote that he never heard Acheson say: "That is a stupid question." But he often looked as if he thought it, "and to look it can be more withering—and more unfortunate, if you happen to look it at a member of a congressional committee." It was not his "fault that he looks like, and indeed is, a Superior Person," but it was "very annoying" to congressmen. Reston, who described Acheson as "smarter than most of his colleagues in the Truman cabinet, but not smart enough to hide it," wrote in 1950 that he was "a provocative, even a belligerent man" who focused on other people's "weaknesses rather than their strengths and possibilities." He lacked the gift "to foresee how his public remarks will look in tomorrow morning's newspapers." He periodically tried to curb himself, once after a tongue-lashing from Marshall for "antagonizing" rather than "managing" people. A few years earlier, Reston thought Acheson had begun to "go easy on the brilliant phrase" and in public to stop such phrases "somewhere between the top of his head and the sound of his voice." But the impulse would not be permanently downed. Shortly after Acheson became secretary, Reston wrote him privately to say that satire was "fun" but had "a limited future." Two months later, he thought he saw improvement in Acheson's congressional testimony on NATO. "Mr. Acheson has always had a good fast ball," he wrote, "but he has often lacked control. He has a tendency to scorn fools, which is dangerous on Capitol Hill. He has a tendency to knock curved-ball questions out of the park, which is not popular in these parts." But today "he was a model witness," answering "flabby" questions "as if they were the most penetrating and original queries of the day." He had finally made "concessions to popular prejudice." He "has trimmed his mustache, an unruly ornament in the past. He has curbed his tongue. And today he appeared in a blue and white tie that must have satisfied the Congressional passion for the picturesque." But such self-restraint would not last.[21]

Sectors for Thought and Action

Acheson shared little in the life of the mind with President Truman apart from an interest in history, which they approached quite differently. The autodidact president had piled up bushels of historical narrative saddled with hoary and whiggish interpretations. He used history the way he played the piano—by ear and from memory. "I'm not a scholar," he once told the Achesons. "I know I read the wrong books, but I read a lot, and I suppose I get some good ones now and then." Nor was Acheson a sophisticated historian, but while Truman's history came from the grand old library books he pillaged in his youth, Acheson was attuned to contemporary analysis and read with a sharply trained eye, what one would expect after Groton, Yale, and Harvard Law. The only president since Grover Cleveland who never attended a baccalaureate college, Truman was certainly smart. He would score high in "experiential learning"—farming, commanding Battery D, running a store, managing a county, winning elections, and getting along with Boss Pendergast. But he had neither schooling nor experience in foreign affairs. Acheson did and he had Truman's ear.[22]

We need to know more about the mind of a man who had a president's ear— how his mind worked, what he believed in, and why. As an old man, Acheson's normal mind-set differed little from earlier but was sharpened to the point of caricature. Working through untold crises had whittled to a sharp point his mistrust of ideological fantasists. At the end, his sense of a drag on hope had degenerated into crabby cynicism. His bent for bluntness had taken him beyond civility to churlishness.

Even in his last years, his mind worked at a horsepower few could match. Though not an original thinker, he worked adeptly with the ideas at hand, adapting them for his own and national ends. His intellectual speed and facility with language often left opponents nursing defense wounds like paper cuts. Razor sharp in his logic, he moved quickly to the core of issues. Urging a junior Covington, Burling attorney to reduce his planned four-point case to one or two, he told him, "You soar a lot better than you pounce." Despite frequent lapses into the passive voice, he wrote clearly and often colorfully, and one of his ambassadors, Ellis O. Briggs, recalled a "fountain of memorable phrases." With what Lewis Douglas called a "queer ability to help untie knots and snarls," he analyzed and explained such snoozers as international currency transactions with words known to any literate American and did so without sacrificing complexity or subtlety. U. Alexis Johnson, who helped him prepare for the 1951 hearings on General Douglas MacArthur's dismissal, said he "could instantly weave a very eloquent presentation out of my rather pedestrian dates, facts and talking points." An ally in the invention of the International Monetary Fund was impressed that Acheson "could read a memorandum on economics, expound it, and even dress it up with stories to amuse his hearers." He did all his writing in longhand and then gave it to women like Barbara Evans to type. In retirement, he found a new vocation as a writer, publishing a stream of books and articles, from memoirs and polemics to gentle recollections of deceased friends and short stories. When arguing a case, he zeroed in on the problem at hand, turned it on one side and another, and moved to a solution. He opened a 1947 radio broadcast on "What Should We Do for Europe Now?" with the crisp injunction: "Tonight's question is our No. 1 problem. To decide it right will take the most sober, hard-headed, and orderly thought, so it's essential that we begin with the fundamentals and do

not confuse ourselves by discussing all aspects of the problem at the same time."
"His mind," Franks observed, "has a lucid, penetrating and compelling intellectual quality which can sweep all before it." He was "the greatest persuader,
I think, that has ever been."[23]

The thinking of this middle-class, Anglo-Canadian-American resembled
that of many successful late-Victorian males. Though not an anglophile and
believing the first half of the twentieth century had exhausted the old Britannic
order, Acheson's mind and personality bore the stamp of that order. He was a
child of the nineteenth century, he said in 1961, and described the pre-World
War I era as "the days of man's innocency," a "stable and predictable" time when
British and American men "believed themselves moving on the great current of
Progress to the reign of universal peace and universal law." If mildly virtuous
and hard working, only the "hazards" of disease, alcohol, and "the lottery of
marriage" would hold them back from success. Much had changed since then, but
Acheson still cast his anchor in the temperate sea of his youth, where verities of
reason, order, and moderation reigned, or so it seemed. This did much to shape
the politics of a man who never strayed far from the center. A youthful partisan of
Teddy Roosevelt's Bull Moose campaign, his liberalism came from his father's
bias for the working man and his ties to Frankfurter and Brandeis. He became
loyal to FDR's New Deal and Truman's Fair Deal. A strong conservative streak
may have come from nostalgia for Victorian equilibrium but owed more to his
practice of corporate law, memories of Roosevelt's monetary unorthodoxy, and
his belief that conservatives and practical men outthought radicals and theoreticians. He distrusted academics who, "strictly channeled into one discipline,"
wanted "to run them all." He called career reformers "Christers" and in his old
age turned to the right.[24]

Generally, he took ideas seriously, but he distrusted the theoretical and what
his friend Noël Annan called "the pulverising style of German professors."
Steering clear of dogma or intellectual speculation, he made choices based on
general propositions about life. The limits of humans impressed him more than
their powers. He accepted the "natural aim of man to achieve an impossible
ideal," but emphasized *impossible*. He was incredulous when someone would
forecast exact results of a policy. It was simply not in human nature to be sure of
results, a truth he repeatedly illustrated by quoting the local judge who said:
"This Court is often in error but never in doubt." Never having doubts was
to miss one of the joys of life, for the world, as he told National Defense
University students in 1949, was marked by "complexity" and "confusion." The
"more difficult a situation is, the more challenge there is to our powers, the more
keenness there is in life."[25]

Human imperfection was not the only reason to dislike dogma and distrust
the overly certain. Acheson also viewed "facts" themselves as indeterminate and
mutable. Their significance depended on who looked at them and from where.
While uncertain what the "facts" were, he knew policymakers had to work with

them anyway, never knowing for sure either what they were or what they meant. "What are the facts?" he asked on television with Sevareid. They were interpretations "of a very limited segment of data that one gets," and no one knew what other data existed. "The poet says things are not what they seem. The great trouble is sometimes they are what they seem. The question is are they or aren't they what they seem?" This is why foreign policy was "an art and not a science."

In his 1948 War College speech, he had stressed the inevitability of making mistakes in response to elusive "facts." Perhaps *only* artists could conduct foreign policy, because they understood the impossibility of simply making policies and carrying them out as long as other people in other countries were trying to do the same. The department had a mountain of facts on Spanish neutrality in World War II, for example, but "the truth was never what we thought it was." At best, officials might foresee problems only "dimly" while overlooking the greatest problems of all. This was not an excuse to be fearful or irresolute, or to adopt a quietist resignation, or to accept the worst the world offered. Discovering their own "limitations" allowed policymakers to discover the "elements" of their own "power." An unadvertised existentialist, Acheson believed one must simply press forward and do one's best. Solving problems did not mean evading difficulty. Since "you cannot avoid difficulty," you must "make the best decision you can to meet that situation and not slink from it." People with responsibility "don't slink from problems" but "do the very best they can in meeting them and get on."[26]

Being a lawyer also shaped Acheson's thinking and work habits but not necessarily in expected ways. When an assistant put a paper in front of him, he might ask: "By what authority do I sign this?" A legal education and experience had something to do with his enthronement of logic and ability to pick out the significant from the immaterial. In making the case for his policies, he acted as a litigator. As a negotiator, he usually refused discussions until opponents offered to settle.

But he was not "legalistic" or a hairsplitter and often urged others not to quibble over minutiae. He would not place international law on a pedestal above the reach of truly vital national interests. If not for himself, he often considered the legal profession a poor preparation for diplomats, especially if a prior commitment to defending clients' narrow interests caused them to miss the sweep of the issues facing them. When he came to know Schuman, he concluded it made a large difference between being trained in Anglo-Saxon and continental law. Harvard Law had left Acheson with a "spurious desire for the specific," in which Schuman was little interested. The more he tried to pin Schuman down to specifics, the less he achieved and the more he annoyed his French partner. Schuman would have "flunked" out of Harvard in three weeks. "His ideas were too big and too broad and too vague for this specific kind of thing."[27]

Acheson's faith in reason sometimes betrayed him. He was baffled by the hostile reaction to the 1949 *China White Paper*, a closely reasoned but misguided brief defending policy in China. He would later confess Frankfurter had told him "that intellectually I was a frustrated schoolteacher, persisting against over-whelming evidence to the contrary in the belief that the human mind could be moved by facts and reason." His own mastery of reason was a source of his arrogance and of his most withering displays of superiority. He usually reserved these for the muddle-headed. Observing these, Franks thought Acheson's "sheer lucidness could be overwhelming," propelling him beyond what the argument of the moment was even about.[28]

His own intellectual model was Oliver Wendell Holmes, Jr., who inspired a case of idolatry. From "the first moment I saw Justice Holmes I succumbed to hero worship," he wrote in retirement: He "was and is my chalice." Holmes's stinging language and social *hauteur* matched some of Acheson's own. But as an intellectual rather than social mentor, his pragmatism and skepticism were more important. Acheson must have quoted, cited, or referred to Holmes in three-quarters of his speeches, essays, and appearances before Congress. Writing Truman ("Dear Boss") in 1961 about President John Kennedy's difficulties getting good military advice, he commented: "As Holmes said, every day we must make decisions on imperfect knowledge." Countering a friend's views in 1963, he wrote: "As Holmes said, 'Deep seated principles cannot be argued about. You cannot argue a man into liking a glass of beer.'" In a 1948 speech, he quoted a favorite Holmesianism: "The chief end of man is to frame general propositions, and no general proposition is worth a damn." "My hero, Mr. Justice Holmes, said," Acheson wrote in another letter, "General principles do not decide concrete cases."[29]

Practicality dominated his own mental habits. He favored the concrete over the abstract, disliking introspection and speculative discussion. Solving riddles was fun, but he cared nothing for their nature, for according to a law partner, "he was not a man to wander into the penumbra of thought." When U.S. diplomacy met difficulties, he would simply say, "We are in bad shape." If he was a "realist" as historians and political scientists use the word, it was because of this ante-rior and habitual practicality. Experience, he thought, based on the best "facts" available, was the best source for discovering wise action. He constantly quoted Marshall's admonition to his staffers: "Don't fight the problem! Decide it!" Policymakers were usually "confronted by a condition and not a theory," he thought. A "poor idea" won in an argument against "no ideas," but he was not fussy where the ideas came from. Being practical did not mean he did not have strong beliefs, but he disliked heating up the diplomatic atmosphere with them. Searching for "the absolute" and universalist "doctrines," he told students at the National Defense University in 1949, was a human failing and common source of trouble. The unconditional surrender policy in World War II had been one example, delaying Japan's capitulation. So was the view that American and Soviet "systems" could not "exist in the same world," or the corollary "that one is good and one is evil, and good and evil cannot exist in the world." This was simply silly. "Good and evil have existed in this world since Adam and Eve went out of the

Garden of Eden." Searching for unreachable absolutes might cause the United States to stretch for goals "too great for our powers, and to enter on courses the end of which we cannot see."[30]

Until old age changed him, pragmatism rarely degenerated into cynicism. When an assistant dismissed a proposal because "we just couldn't get that accepted on the Hill," recalled one, Acheson would say: "Well, now, to hell with that. Let's first consider what we ought to do, what the right thing is to do, and reach a decision on that. Then we'll come back and look at it again in terms of expediency and practical objections and see to what extent we have to modify it." It was his job, anyway, not theirs, to decide when it was time to be expedient. His skill at letting matters rest and returning to them later came from his matter-of-factness and a nice sense of timing. Good policy might result from nothing more exotic than tidily revisiting earlier decisions and not going off half-cocked. "Proper timing," he thought, "is all important and it is as important to know when to sit and wait as it is to know when to push ahead." He would sometimes tell an overexcited aide, "Don't just do something; stand there!" Behind patience, and behind timing, must lie strength, in which he believed deeply, saying: "Charm never made a rooster."[31]

Acheson was not religious but would not discuss this "personal and sacred matter" when ordinary citizens inquired about it. He never talked "about God," wrote David, or "about any theological issue." Mysticism, whatever its source, was beyond his ken. With the omnipresence of evil in mind, he thought God probably did not exist; even worse, as in *King Lear*, gods were around to "kill us for their sport." But he was "*thoroughly* impregnated" with the Book of Common Prayer, which he was wont to quote in negotiations. Asking allies' forgiveness for a Washington blunder, he intoned, "Our sins are grievous and abhorrent to us and we repent thoroughly of them." Schuman commented: "Ah, yes, we have something like that in the Roman Catholic liturgy, too." Bevin countered: "Well, I wouldn't know anything about that, I'm a bush Baptist, and we don't have anything like that." "What in the world," Acheson asked, "is a *bush* Baptist?" "I don't know," said Bevin, "why don't you ask your President? 'e's probably one, too."

Acheson lived according to a code, not a theology, especially the stoic's code of Holmes and Brandeis. Brandeis, he said, thought a great "end in life" was to triumph over "weaknesses and fears and laziness." Acheson's own code, Frankfurter believed, of "loyalty, essential truth," and "not pretending to be better than you really are," made him feel "meaningful and organic," "civilized and free." For Acheson, stoicism was mainly about duty. He quoted an old partner as saying of an obligation, not "I have to do it" but "I have it to do." And he might have to do it alone, for Acheson thought "all really great decisions are made by yourself." To live right meant sticking to stout principles of behavior and style, to be independent and trustworthy, hardworking, honorable, and courageous. And to the devil with those who didn't like it![32]

Despite some practical differences, Acheson thought the same of *national* honor and decency. For all his flirtation with relativism, he never doubted his ability to tell the difference between good and bad behavior. He rarely condemned communists for their beliefs but constantly affixed moralistic labels on their conduct. "To deal truthfully, honorably, and courageously," he thought, "is better than to practice duplicity, conspiracy, and treachery." Correct action (behavior) inspired correct, and effective, thought. Ideals did not decide a nation's actions, but the other way around. Worthy objectives emerged from decent and civil action. Man, Holmes said, was "born to act," and "to act is to affirm the worth of an end, and to persist in affirming the worth of an end is to make an ideal." Method and morality were linked. "There should be no bullying," Acheson wrote, "no advantage taken of the hardship of others to drive political bargains, no lying or boasting in our propaganda or our dealings with others, no sanctimonious lecturing of others on their faults, no consciousness of our own effortless righteousness, or the thanking of God that we are not as other men." Acheson's intellectual and moral principles would not answer all the questions he would face, or cope with all the obstacles to policymaking. Success as a steward of the nation's foreign policy would also require the sagacious management of a ministry and cultivation of a strong-minded president. His stoic and austere code would take him a long way in meeting these requirements.[33]

7

ACHESON, THE PRESIDENT, AND THE STATE DEPARTMENT

Introduction

It had not been so long since all the employees of the state department could pose together on the front steps in annual pictures. By January 1949, however, five times as many people worked in its new building at Foggy Bottom as in the old State-War-Navy headquarters on Pennsylvania Avenue. The department employed a little over 600 people in the early 1920s, nearly 1,000 by the eve of World War II, and almost 6,000 by 1948. In 1947, it had approximately 12,000 Americans working abroad; in 1950, the figure was nearly 16,000. From 1938 to 1948, the staff of the office of the secretary of state rose from 21 to 186 and workers in the geographic and political offices from 112 to 318. The United States was served by 737 career diplomats in 1936, 1,217 in 1950. Around the world in 1951, the department ran 59 embassies, 14 legations, and 196 consular offices, and people on the State payroll helped run the occupation regimes in Germany and Japan. Department appropriations rose from $2.6 to $33.7 million from 1938 to 1948, money that paid for a rising tide of communications—by 1950, 25,000 incoming and outgoing telegrams and 250,000 memos and other official messages.[1]

Acheson put his own stamp on this organization. He brought to management a forceful temperament, robust intellect, and strategic imagination. Though he largely inherited his staff, he added his own people, shifted veterans to new tasks he wanted done, and inspirited foreign service officers with his leadership. A key reason for his achievements was the close connection he forged with President

Truman, reviving State's lost supremacy in foreign affairs. Ironically, he had barely completed rescuing State from the crypt to which Roosevelt's contempt had consigned it than Joseph McCarthy's defamatory campaign and controversies over China and Korea returned it there.

In a presidential government, the state department could never have a monopoly over foreign policy, but FDR had reduced its role below normal. Acheson as secretary of state would continue efforts he started as under secretary to restore its standing. To do so required putting a stop to the poaching of other agencies, and new competitors had arrived with the National Security Act of 1947, which created the Central Intelligence Agency and National Security Council. Secretaries of state, Acheson thought, must have a "killer instinct" in Washington, "where some of the methods would have aroused the envy of the Borgias."[2]

Above all, Acheson had to maintain a close and trusting connection to President Truman. A cardinal event that boosted the president's regard for him was the meeting of the Paris Council of Foreign Ministers in the spring of 1949. There, Acheson not only carried the day for U.S. policy but kept Truman meticulously informed in a way he had never before experienced. Armed with Truman's lavish praise for the effort, Acheson's reputation rose dramatically in the cabinet and among staff members in the White House. This translated into power across the bureaucracy, putting legal tender into Acheson's hands and those of his aides. Thereafter, when he made strong policy statements, officials in other departments, realizing the statements almost surely had the president's blessing, were less likely to challenge Acheson. He remained ever vigilant. In September 1950, for instance, he told White House staffers he would not permit their efforts to "clear" department speeches. In Europe, he routinely opposed attempts of Marshall Plan administrators to speak for U.S. foreign policy.[3]

"My President . . . A Great Chief"

Even when they disagreed, Truman knew Acheson would carry out his directives, allowing him to "go to bed without worrying." If Truman wanted special information, Acheson turned State "upside down in a hurry" to get it. He showed up at the White House to help write presidential messages. "I remember situations," recalled a young Richard Neustadt from Truman's staff, "in which Dean Acheson, who had a very good sense of timing, would come in, take off his coat, sit down, and join the roundtable till the end." His loyalty to the president and resolve to keep State on top in U.S. foreign policy, said an adviser, created "a bright hiatus in the State Department relationship with the White House." Noticing how he relied on Acheson, Loy Henderson said Truman was finally "playing the game according to the rules."[4]

The diminution of state department authority has usually resulted from presidents protecting their own freedom of action, and Acheson protected his own authority by making sure he did not act against Truman's. One of his most important achievements was to penetrate Truman's protective screen. Since 1945, Acheson had acted to engender trust in the president and hold him close to the department. He prepared himself thoroughly for their meetings. He anticipated Truman's needs and offered advice when he thought it welcome. He always granted the president the respect due him. More carefully than Marshall, he gave Truman a chance "to influence policy before it congealed into flat alternatives." Wanting to march to the same music as the president and at the same cadence, he "never did anything without touching base with Truman," reported Charles Bohlen. He tried to keep bureaucratic fights from landing on Truman's desk. He sharpened the quality of information, counsel, and decisions he offered him. His unstinting public loyalty to an uncertain, often unpopular chief executive produced deep gratitude and loyalty in return. Shortly before Acheson had left government in 1947, Truman wrote him: "With you and our incomparable Secretary, the General, over there I don't have a worry in the world." When Marshall died in 1959, Truman wrote again: "Do you suppose any President of the United States ever had two such men with him as you and the General? In my study of the history of the Presidency I haven't found a single case like it."[5]

This may understate Truman's own agency and initiative in foreign policy. One of his assistants, Charles Murphy, said he was "his own chief of staff in the foreign policy field." Clark Clifford considered him generally responsible for the direction of American policy but not its "complexities." He had a "black and white" view of a world of good and bad men, "and, by God, he was going to see to it that the men in the white hats prevailed." Acheson, however, thought presidential support for his own work would be more effective if Truman did grasp the complexities. Sloppy or disingenuous thinking elicited some of his sharpest criticisms of the president. On the other hand, Acheson could grow irritable when Truman exercised his mind independently. He always worried when Truman went off alone to meetings like that on Wake Island with General Douglas MacArthur in 1950, the "sort of lethal" thing "Chiefs of State get into." All summits were probably a bad idea, because Acheson could not predict or control how Truman might behave.[6]

At times, Truman opposed Acheson's wishes or was slow to act on them. He might opt for the position of one of Acheson's competitors or even try to hoodwink the department altogether. These outbreaks of independence usually involved China or the Middle East, and almost never Europe or NATO. Their biggest unacknowledged conflict, in which, as we will see in Chapter 14, Acheson acted indirectly to frustrate the president's ends, came over defense budgeting. And in one case in 1952, as described in Chapter 33, Truman attempted outright bamboozlement of Acheson in Guatemala. On other occasions, he gave into Acheson's recommendations only after first offering resistance. Acheson occasionally enlisted Murphy to persuade Truman to get aboard, only, as Murphy recalled, to have the same problem "crop up again in maybe a different form." Truman would finally sign the necessary orders, "but he really didn't agree."[7]

Both men guarded their differences from the public, but they left Acheson frustrated. Aware of his superiority in intellectual power and, perhaps, worldly wisdom, he sometimes acted like a smooth attorney getting his client to act in the *lawyer's* best interests. After retirement in 1953, he was schoolmasterish in advising Truman on his memoirs and current politics. Earlier, while they were in office, the president's limitations could infuriate him. He once said Truman was "like a boy you tell not to stick peanuts up his nose, and the minute you turn around, there he is sticking peanuts up his nose." "Do you see these gray hairs?" he asked, when a friend praised the president's spontaneity. "That's Truman's spontaneity." He admired Truman's decisiveness, saying "it doesn't take him a hundred years to read something and make up his mind," but he also worried that his penchant for not looking back would lead to reckless, unthought-through commitments. He discreetly kept a close watch, not only to keep State's place of privilege but to guard against blunders.[8]

Probably no modern secretary of state had more leeway to act on his own. There seems little doubt that Acheson's praise of Truman as free of "imperiousness" reflected his own ability to dominate policy. Applauding the president's understanding of his job, including the wisdom to defer to the state department, was consistent with Acheson's remaining in charge. So was advising Truman not to get "too immersed in manure and weed-killer." Acheson's loyalty and coaching certainly raised Truman's confidence in foreign affairs but also elevated the authority of the brilliant entrepreneur at his side. If the results were good, both men gained reasons to praise the other. Truman lauded Acheson as part of his gifted entourage, while Acheson bowed to a president wise enough to understand when to take charge and when to leave matters to his secretary. With each profiting from the other, the two men's partnership had much to do with the success and clarity of Truman's foreign policy.[9]

Acheson may have occasionally conned Truman, but his respect and admiration for him were genuine. Had he mainly viewed him as someone to manipulate, he would never have asked him to read so many department papers, which the president did, studying into the night. Acheson dedicated *Present at the Creation*, "To Harry S. Truman, 'The captain with the mighty heart.'" He said of Truman's policies: "All of them were dangerous. All required rare capacity to decide and act. All of them were decided rightly and vigorously followed through." This language contains both exaggeration and self-congratulation, but Acheson meant it when he wrote his daughter in January 1950 that "one could not ask for a commander with more directness, understanding and courage." To appreciate Truman, he thought, one had to be "wired for spirit," as was the animated Acheson.[10]

Over time, mutual respect became deep friendship. Truman biographer David McCullough remarks that "Harry Truman never had such a friend before." They *really* were buddies," remembered State's Jack Hickerson. "My President," Acheson would fondly insist. "He was my President." Secretary of the Treasury John W. Snyder, a hard-drinking St. Louis banker Truman had first met at a 1928 army reserve camp, relished his Missouri connection to the president. He distinguished between the president's friendship with Acheson and with his poker-playing, bourbon-drinking companions. Acheson rarely appeared socially at the White House and never took such liberties as going to the White House and on "up to Mr. Truman's bedroom." "And yet," Snyder said, Truman considered Acheson "one of his very, very good friends." A naval aide to the president, Admiral Robert L. Dennison, thought the Truman and Acheson families were "the closest of friends, and background be damned."

Acheson had never had such a friend, either. What especially moved him was Truman's "tender nature, a deeply loving and tender nature." When Acheson was traveling during Mary Acheson's bouts with tuberculosis, Truman would phone the hospital, hear from Alice how Mary was doing, and telephone Acheson daily on her condition. "Well," recalled Acheson, "this is the kind of person that one can adore." Though repeatedly misspelling his secretary of state's last name ("Atcheson"), Truman reciprocated such feelings. After Acheson appeared at National Airport in 1949 as the Truman family embarked on a Key West vacation, the president wrote him: "You always do the right thing. I'm still a farm boy and when the Secretary of State of the greatest republic comes to the airport to see me off I can't help but swell up a little bit." Wondrously, both the supercilious secretary of state and the gruff politico were sentimentalists![11]

There were many other similarities between the border state haberdasher and mustachioed Connecticut lawyer. They both grew up in "small towns," wrote Philip Hamburger, in "a relatively carefree and easygoing America." They were both left of center but "lodged there in a conservative way." Like Acheson, writes McCullough, Truman experienced "his first youthful brush with the 'real world' working with a railroad crew." Both pretended to special knowledge in architecture, enjoyed reading history, and kept going back to Mark Twain. "If Acheson was a fashion plate," McCullough adds, "so, of course, was Truman," with his hats, double-breasted suits, and Key West shirts. They both hit the sidewalks for morning walks, "enjoyed a convivial drink, a good story," and adored their daughters. Acheson's assistant, Lucius Battle, said they were both gutsy, courageous, and salty. They were also both devoted to the gospel of hard work. Orderly men, they detested the chaos of FDR's cavalier approach to administration. They emphatically preferred making rather than avoiding decisions. "Both men," writes Alonzo Hamby, "demanded movement and accepted gambles." And they both shared their generation's belief that the time had come to lead in constructing a world order in which their nation could prosper.[12]

They were also alike in being clear about the other one's role. Acheson never mistook himself for the chief executive, and Truman "never thought he was the

Secretary." Acheson could be "deferential" yet candid, but Truman was "the President of the United States, and you don't say rude things to him—you say blunt things to him. Sometimes he doesn't like it. That's natural, but he comes back, and you argue the thing out. But that's your duty. You don't tell him only what he wants to hear. That would be bad for him and for everyone else." Acheson claimed he wanted Truman to "listen to everybody who has anything to say on foreign affairs" but to look to him for ultimate guidance. At least once, he lectured Truman on his proper role. The occasion, in 1950, was a difference of opinion on the appointment of an ambassador to London. Acheson wanted a skilled representative who could earn British confidence and not "go gabbing around the place." Truman wanted a friendly former dairy company executive, James Bruce, just returned from Buenos Aires. Acheson said Bruce had "many virtues, but he wasn't up to this task." Too bad, said Truman, he was already "committed." Acheson retorted that he was committed instead to his presidential oath to "faithfully perform the duties" of his office. Appointing Bruce would not measure up. Just as Acheson wondered if he had gone too far, Truman said, "I think you are quite right; I think you are absolutely right. What do you suggest?"[13]

Not only did Truman and Acheson hide their disagreements from the public, they skillfully created an image of unity and resolve. The secretary of state, Acheson once wrote, can "always speak effectively if he speaks for the President, knows what he is talking about, and is telling the truth," but it is not that simple, as they knew. They also had to stay on the same page, and they usually did this in a way that enhanced each man's position. They choreographed little duets, echoing each other on particular issues in press conferences. When the administration announced it would build the hydrogen bomb in February 1950, reporters first drew comments from Acheson. When they asked Truman the next day, he said the secretary "spoke for the State Department," which spoke for his foreign policy. As Acheson described the process, Truman would "say, 'The Secretary of State, after consultation with me, has stated our position' and that is all there is to it." Thus, they foiled hopes of putting "a screwdriver in between the President and me." When someone tried stirring dissension, Truman and Acheson "smothered the fire." James Reston also noticed how carefully Acheson avoided upstaging Truman or grabbing "headlines away from" him.[14]

When Acheson came under public attack, Truman forcefully (and often) defended him. In a press conference on 30 March 1950, he protested that he had already been "perfectly clear that I think Dean Acheson is—and will go down in history as one of the great Secretaries of State." Since Truman was then sinking in the polls, it is especially remarkable that he defiantly embraced Acheson rather than distancing himself. Whatever Acheson's liabilities, Truman may have understood that he represented a largely successful foreign policy, which the wounded president needed. In December 1951, after a year of grave difficulties in Korea, Reston observed that Acheson was "closer than ever" to Truman and "likely" to enjoy "more authority over foreign affairs than ever before." The presidential-secretarial "bond" grew "stronger each passing month," noted Reston's colleague, Cabell Phillips; Acheson's "unflinching" loyalty to Truman had resulted in his receiving more "latitude" than any of his predecessors. After Truman saw Acheson off at the airport for a European trip in 1952, Acheson commented: "That's what gets me through." Truman's official calendar, which probably omits unscheduled meetings, shows Acheson meeting Truman at airports, at the White House, at cabinet and other meetings, at dinners, and at Acheson's home and farm 536 times—122 as under secretary, 8 as a private citizen, and 406 times as secretary of state.[15]

If Acheson worked hard for Truman, the converse was also true. Despite fears he might be exploiting the president's work ethic, Acheson sometimes gave him 150 pages to read overnight, and the president would do it, as part of his 5:30 A.M. to 11:00 P.M. workday. They regularly met together on Mondays and Thursdays for a thirty- to sixty-minute lunch. Acheson would go over the day's events and find out what was on Truman's mind. They talked on the telephone almost daily, and sometimes they met that frequently as well. Acheson could directly ring Truman's line whenever he wanted. They sat side by side at cabinet meetings (usually Friday mornings) and, once Truman began attending, at Wednesday National Security Council (NSC) sessions. Truman often held lunches with members after Friday cabinet meetings, too, and Acheson often spoke to him again *after* lunch. When he returned to Foggy Bottom, he would relate presidential wishes to Barbara Evans and Battle, or Battle might pop his head in Acheson's door and ask, "What happened?"[16]

It was vital for both men that Acheson keep Truman well informed. To do so while Acheson was overseas, he developed a routine communications system. He sent a full dispatch of the day's talks to the department with a summary for the president he could pull out of his desk to show congressmen. He also sent personally dictated analyses and solicited Truman's suggestions. These documents made Truman "feel present at the scene and participating." When Acheson's aides wrote a first draft, they had to get it right. One longtime foreign service officer, J. Graham Parsons, recalled the time he produced a "rather dry, factual and highly summarized" account that went up the chain to Acheson. It came back with his blue pencil marks: "No, no, no I don't want this sort of thing. This is a personal message from me to the President. I want it written in a very informal style. It want it very full, I don't want any detail left out that could conceivably be of interest to him."[17]

Leadership and Esprit de Corps

Acheson once said that nobody had been able to run the state department in a century and a half, and one of his first tasks was to refigure it in line with proposals from the Hoover Commission he had vice-chaired. He directed his under secretary to carry out the changes. By the autumn of 1949, these and other changes were in effect, including a new layer of deputy under secretaries for day-to-day administration and new offices for economic affairs, public affairs, and intelligence. Legislation gave the secretary of state broader authority over all department personnel and FSOs. Along with opportune solvents of mandatory retirements, these allowed Acheson to move against some encrusted fiefdoms, if at the cost of some resentment among old-timers. "Control" and "policy" were now more centralized and execution decentralized, something like the military's division between operations and staff.[18]

The department had enjoyed "an *esprit de corps* that has never been surpassed" when Acheson was under secretary, according to Joseph M. Jones. Now Acheson thought the state department "without doubt the best foreign office" in the world and worked to keep it, and its reputation, that way. He estimated that he spent a sixth of his time testifying before congressional committees (214 times), made countless speeches, talked endlessly to reporters, and encouraged aides to do the same. But by 1950, he also had to defend himself, the department, and its personnel against the McCarthyite onslaught, which began in force in 1950. Understandably, some officers, instead of fighting back against McCarthyism, drew in their heads, and eventually collective courage ebbed. Intellectual daring came to seem incompatible with job security, let alone advancement. Those pounding his associates, Acheson said, were "fools and self-seeking blackguards, touted by the press." He often interposed his own body to take "many of the hits" aimed at assistants or reduced their exposure by shipping them to less visible posts. He often tossed reports from the department's own "security" monitors in the wastebasket. By January 1953, however, his own influence diminished and energy abated after years under attack, he could or would not protect a few of the most vulnerable targets and allowed them to fall.[19]

Even when under savage criticism, Acheson and State dominated the making of foreign policy. Acheson avoided the errors of his predecessors. He did not reprise Cordell Hull's meandering and confusing meetings. Unlike Marshall, he did not wait at the top of the decision-making ladder but joined deliberations on lower rungs so he could know what options were available to him and shape them before they solidified. His engagement, energy, and zest for work fired up those around him. Marshall commanded, but Acheson led, through what he called "guidance and influence." While establishing core policies, he inspired others to take the initiative in the belief that "the springs of policy bubble up" more often than "down." To keep the springs effervescent meant leading with confidence and with hands on—and showing, as he put it, that he "was never afraid of making a slip." The clearer it was that he took responsibility for his subordinates and their work, the more creatively they worked for him. Taking full responsibility, in short, protected his aides while amplifying his own authority. "Whatever actions are taken by the Department I'm responsible for," he announced in a 1951 press conference, "and that's all anybody needs to know," whether they want "to heave a brick or not."[20]

He managed the department day-to-day through openness, engagement, and clear assignments of responsibility. He used the department secretariat to keep things orderly, but officers could "go around that" to higher-ups. He tackled issues early, encouraged fresh thinking from subordinates, paid personal attention to them and their arguments as recommendations moved upward, and raised questions throughout. He insisted his people not waste time on choices he knew Truman would not accept. As the process percolated, if he did not yet know Truman's position, he gave assistants the chance to move in possibly contrary directions, but he would rein them in if necessary once the president had spoken—and tell them why.[21]

His commitment to free discussion accounted for much of his assistants' enthusiasm and their loyalty to him. He liked "to talk with the experts," recalled one. He would sit around the table to see where his aides were going, prodding them with good-natured cross-examination. "It was a delight to work with him." Acheson thought such sessions the very "oil of government," allowing him to hear grievances while "preserving *amour propre*." They also afforded opportunities to "exercise authority over detail." Although he might have broad strategies in mind, most specific actions, he believed, "arose from specific incidents." Subordinates usually had the first crack at these, and one function of an open channel was to steer them away from ideas neither he nor the president would accept. In discharging policy, he gave aides wide leeway. If they needed help, he kept his door open, but he did not "look over their shoulders." After naming Jack K. McFall assistant secretary for congressional relations, he told him he had found the "man for the job" and now expected him to do it; he would let him know if he disliked the results. "But unless you come to me and ask for suggestions or help or counsel or advice," he told McFall, "you'll be left on your own to do your job and if you do it right you'll remain."[22]

Acheson not only strove to protect his people from McCarthy's depredations but congressional harassment generally. While the Founders did not intend executive-congressional relations to be "restful," he wrote in 1956, Congress should stay out of the executive branch's "internal processes." In practice, this meant shielding subordinates from the unequal struggle against solons staring at them from their high perches. The lower the official, the higher Acheson tried to erect the shield. He would disclose who had labored on policies "that went sour" only if they were presidential appointees who knew how to take care of themselves. Otherwise, he simply defied the questioners so they could not victimize the vulnerable. Thus, in 1950 when the department came under fire because it had prepared its diplomats for Chiang's fall by arguing Formosa's strategic insignificance, Acheson refused to hand over "the names of his juniors" who wrote the offending document.[23]

Acheson valued discussion, as already noted, but only if it led to solutions. Before the Korean War crowded his schedule, he liked dropping in Wednesday afternoons to policy planning staff (PPS) meetings. He would enter the PPS conference room, kick the door shut, and talk shop on all kinds of issues. The only rule was that no one could take notes. He did not mind if conflicts arose on the way to a decision, for it was better to sharpen than stifle differences if he wanted to give Truman insight into a problem. He also wanted advisers to know the reasoning behind his own decisions. His enjoyment of talk was one reason so many people had easy access to him. He wanted assistants to argue for their own ideas "vigorously," recalled Paul Nitze, making him "sheer joy" to work with. H. Freeman (Doc) Matthews, a deputy under secretary, noted the absence of any "rigid" lines blocking chances to see Acheson. He was "not afraid of his staff," said an Asian specialist. He also opened the door of the department generally to the outside world, welcoming the involvement of academics, businessmen, labor leaders, and even peace activists. His personal channel would close only when he knew he was about to go against advisers' counsel. Then, Nitze remembered, "he would shut the door on us."[24]

The most important reason for all the talk in the Acheson state department was to clarify his own thinking. He could not think unless people were arguing, he told a European diplomat. In what was still a clubby department, its leader, whom Reston considered "strictly a smoky-room diplomat," moved from one smoke-filled room to another to chart the paths to policy. Before the 9:30 "prayer meetings," he skimmed through new cables in a black leather logbook, taking notes on a legal pad. He did his homework so well, Reston wrote, he was always "mentally at the head of the table." Others were ready, too, or had to explain why. The prime task at 9:30 was not to make decisions but catch up on what needed doing and decide who should do it. Acheson sat at the head of the table, with Bohlen, Philip Jessup, and others along the sides. Documents circulated. Once the talk started, Acheson mainly listened, remembered Laukhuff, "leaning far back in his red leather chair" until he sprang forward to take some penciled notes. Even a junior officer like Laukhuff felt free to challenge barons like Bohlen. Once the group reached agreement, Acheson would break his silence with a recap that, said one participant, was like "a fine judge charging a jury." He did not end meetings inconclusively, like Hull, and his habit of summary animated his staff and readied him for decision.[25]

He also used the meeting to gather information for Truman, assiduously keeping him abreast of problems and choices. He was acutely aware of how Byrnes had torpedoed himself by neglecting the president. Truman still looked at the department with narrowed eyes, and his suspicions had boiled to a fury in 1948 when it resisted his decision to recognize Israel. Acheson did not quibble when Truman vetoed a department proposal but would send a clear message to aides that they were not to grumble, either—or leak their dissatisfaction to reporters. As one of Acheson's assistants, Fisher Howe, put it, the secretary "protected the Foreign Service from Truman, and protected Truman from the Foreign Service." Such fealty put even more chips on the lieutenant's table. After Acheson had been in office ten months, Truman told him the department's public image had "improved." It was now a "vigorous and united organization," completely supportive of "the administration"—that is, him. The department had "never been in better condition," he said shortly afterward.[26]

"Foggy Bottom" had all the character, Reston wrote, of "a Fifth Avenue showroom." Acheson's headquarters was on the fifth floor of this modernist saltine box. It "looked exactly like the second-class dining room on the Europa," he thought. Alice redecorated the huge room, pulling down contemporary art and putting up American primitives borrowed from the National Gallery. Worried about Latin American visitors, her husband took the Mexican War scenes back down. He reached the office around 9:15, either by limousine or via his morning ramble with Felix Frankfurter. He oversaw the writing of dispatches with care. Looking at a draft cable to Konrad Adenauer, he said, "Oh, no, that won't do at all, that's not right," scribbled something on his own pad, and gave it back with the instruction, "Now, tidy it up and send it off, I don't want to see it again." He typically headed home by seven o'clock. According to a delicious but apocryphal story, he had three trays on his desk, "In," "Out," and "Too Hard." With visiting dignitaries, he was "invariably good-humored, sympathetic, brief, and cryptic." At one such empty meeting, a visiting European politician "entered ceremoniously, bowed ceremoniously, shook hands ceremoniously, and said, 'Mr. Secretary, what of the future?' 'What of it?' I said, and the man shook hands and left." Acheson had lost only forty-five seconds, but the visitor had met with the secretary of state.[27]

Deciding how to spend his time was difficult, especially because of the heavy volume of unavoidable reading. But he needed "relaxed unhurried talk" and "quiet," too. He might take lunch alone to read, or round up some assistants for some talk. He might enter the cafeteria and sit at an empty table—or find an empty chair at an otherwise full table. His energy was likely to flag at dusk. As soon as possible, he went home, now fitted with a scrambler telephone. Security regulations forbade taking classified documents with him, but he found other work to do until about midnight. Then he would "drink a whiskey, read for five minutes, and sleep like a log until the alarm rings."[28]

Co-Conspirators

Although Acheson was a political appointee, unlike Hull and Byrnes he entered his job knowing the department's inner mechanisms and its workers' foibles. However much he enjoyed working with careerists, he knew "no man looks bad in his own cables" and viewed many with a gimlet eye. He thought they did too much hunch playing instead of making judgments based on evidence. He was determined they understand that he, not they, controlled policy in the name of the president. At the time of his appointment, some European observers considered him an opponent of career officers.[29]

He certainly was not a great friend of women in the foreign service or diplomacy generally. Vijayalakshmi (Nan) Pandit, Prime Minister Jawaharlal Nehru's sister and ambassador to Washington, said Acheson "found it difficult to accept me as my country's official representative." "Why do pretty women want to be like men?" she says Acheson asked her. While Truman named the first woman ambassador in 1949 (Eugenie Anderson), none held truly important posts while Acheson was secretary. Inside the department, the most prominent were Dorothy Fosdick on the PPS and Ruth (Ma) Shipley, the hard-liner who virtually owned the passport office from 1928 to 1955. Shipley, said a British observer, was "not only above reproach but beyond intimidation." At Acheson's side from 1941 until he died was his incomparable secretary, Barbara Evans. In 1946–48, she had shuttled between State and Covington, Burling, Rublee, Acheson, and Shorb. In the department, she was "a tower of strength," Nitze recalled, "fully prepared to correct him when she thought his memory had slipped or he was simply wrong." She was also an intrepid gatekeeper. Columnist Joseph Alsop once wrote that she had been "incomparably rude" to him, a person for whom "butter would not melt." Early in Acheson's term, Delia Kuhn of the office of public affairs was important to him as a speechwriter and came up with the phrase, "Point Four."[30]

African-Americans did little better than women in Acheson's department. The cafeteria he used had been segregated as recently as the outset of World War II. Ralph Bunche, the grandson of a slave, worked at the UN and won the Nobel Peace Prize in 1950 for his efforts to keep the peace between Jews and Arabs in Palestine, but he turned down a State assistant secretaryship because, he told Truman, he never intended to live again "in a segregated city like Washington." A handful of blacks entered the foreign service in the Truman years but were still in a tiny minority. The department upgraded Edward Dudley in Liberia from minister to ambassador in 1949. Chicago attorney Edith Sampson became an alternate UN delegate in 1950. She toured Europe in 1951–52, praising U.S. race relations and denouncing communism. Foundation executive Channing Tobias, an officer in the National Association for the Advancement of Colored People (NAACP), joined the UN delegation in 1951. In April 1951, when an African-American group asked Acheson why more blacks were not in the foreign service, he said he had no power to change the admissions policies of the elite universities from which the service drew so many of its members. By the end of the Truman administration, a combination of internal and external pressures broke the habit of sending blacks only to "Negro circuit" posts centering on Liberia. If still mostly in subordinate positions, African-Americans now found postings worldwide.[31]

As already noted, Acheson's personal assistant was Lucius D. (Luke) Battle, a law school graduate and former navy lieutenant. Acheson plucked him from the Canadian desk. Officially titled "Foreign Affairs specialist on the Executive

Secretariat," the thirty-one-year-old, "tall, good-looking Floridian" became the equivalent of Britain's "private secretary to the Minister." Acheson wanted him available at all times and thus to stay single, but he caved in after meeting Battle's intended and suffering the censure of Barbara Evans, whom Battle considered State's "ultimate conscience." Battle was undaunted when Acheson warned that standing guard against "senior officers" demanding to see the secretary might blight his career. He became Acheson's shadow. After 9:30 meetings, officials who far outranked him huddled around Battle's appointment book, but few complained. Gaining "access" to Acheson was not difficult—and Battle arranged it. It was Battle who saw to the "daily telegram" to Truman when Acheson was in Europe. Soon Acheson took him along everywhere in Washington, including the White House. Both Achesons treated him like a second son, one who could argue with the secretary of state, which he did, sometimes over the contents of ill-humored letters. "I dictate the letters," Acheson said, and "Luke tears them up."[32]

Acheson did not get his own under secretary, selected by Truman after long discussions. Anticipating extensive travel, Acheson wanted someone who had Truman's confidence and who would "be absolutely square with me and wouldn't be playing any game of his own." Truman's choice was forty-three-year-old James Webb, director of the budget since 1946. A Horatio Alger figure, Webb went from a rural southern boyhood to a state university, to the Marines, to a congressman's staff, to law school, and then to business, making millions at the Sperry Gyroscope Company and other firms. Then he rejoined the Marines, making major in the war. He knew the federal city, congressmen liked him, he had a flair for administrative organization, and he had the president's trust. Acheson viewed him as the man to do the reorganizing work while staying out of policymaking. He would help keep the circuits to Truman open. His foreign policy inexperience was a plus.

Always interested in science—later becoming the first director of the national aeronautics and space administration—Webb sent science attachés to U.S. embassies. As he worked on the flow chart, department professionals, who sniffed at this outsider, sometimes undermined his work, especially his attempts to institute "foreign policy indicators" comparable to the economic indicators he had established at the budget bureau. Eventually, Acheson also found him hard to take. Webb seemed insensitive and irritated Acheson by repeatedly citing the "flavor" of his thinking. Not much happier, Webb developed terrible migraines and left the department in 1952, succeeded by David K. E. Bruce.[33]

Webb's reorganization had also produced a new set of regional offices. Among the assistant secretaries heading them were Edward G. (Eddie) Miller, Jr., in inter-American affairs,[34] George W. Perkins in European and Canadian affairs, W. Walton Butterworth in East Asian and Pacific affairs, and George Crews McGhee in Near Eastern and South Asian affairs.[35] Because China policies aroused such controversy, Butterworth's bureau turned into a hot seat, and he soon wanted to get off it. In 1950, he happily escaped to Sweden as ambassador. The China country desk was another center of woe. "It wasn't a good assignment," recalled one of its holders, Arthur R. Ringwalt. Acheson watched the regional and country officers carefully, always concerned they might construe "their" region or nation as deserving preferential status. Other important subordinates early in his tenure were John E. Peurifoy in internal security; John D. Hickerson, covering the United Nations; and, in legislative affairs, first Ernest A. Gross and then McFall.[36]

An important and nearly invisible department official was Carlisle Humelsine, who in 1947 came to State with Marshall from the war department to become deputy under secretary for administration. As "the traffic policeman" for the executive secretariat, this Pennsylvania Dutch administrator regulated the flow of information to and from Foggy Bottom. The department's deputy under secretary, fifty-year-old Doc Matthews, ran an office that became the "differential joint of the State Department; everything went through it." Acheson's legal adviser, thirty-five-year-old Adrian S. (Butch) Fisher, backstopped Acheson on all kinds of issues. A burly Tennessean who played football at Princeton, clerked for Brandeis, and navigated bombers in the war, his overriding task was to keep Acheson out of trouble. Public opinion and the Voice of America were the bailiwicks of forty-year-old Edward Barrett, formerly with *Newsweek* and the Office of War Information. He had to sell department policies without violating the 1947 Smith-Mundt Act, which barred spending to influence Congress. Ernest Gross, who came to State from an army post, moved from legal adviser to congressional relations and finally to the United Nations. Onetime Amherst statistician Willard Thorp, formerly at Dun & Bradstreet, stayed in the assistant secretaryship for economic and business affairs he had held since 1946.[37]

Though Perkins headed European affairs, Acheson often worked more closely with Henry A. Byroade, director of German affairs. Born in 1913, a West Pointer with an advanced engineering degree from Cornell, he was the youngest general to emerge from the war. The rank was temporary and Acheson called him "Colonel." An assistant to Marshall in China, Byroade was loaned "at a cocktail party" in 1949 to the state department by the secretary of the army. He helped ease the transition from defense to state department control of German policy. Because of his military background, sleek dress, and reputation as a "ladies' man" with "playboy instincts," he cut a colorful swath at Foggy Bottom but gained Acheson's admiration as a shrewd analyst. In 1952, he became assistant secretary for Near Eastern and South Asian affairs. When he wondered why someone originally tutored on Asia and recently focused on Germany received the Middle Eastern brief, Acheson told him no one who knew anything about the Middle East wanted the post "because of the Arab-Israeli problem and that's why we want you!"[38]

Byroade inherited the Middle Eastern portfolio from George McGhee. A Texan and Rhodes Scholar with a physics doctorate from Oxford, McGhee was an oil geologist by training and millionaire by marriage. He had helped coordinate aid to Greece and Turkey and labored with Dean Rusk on the Palestine refugee problem. Though deeply involved with Acheson, he never won his confidence. This was partly because, with his "impregnable self-assurance and sharp tongue," he gave "convulsions" to the British, who referred to him as "that infant prodigy." "Too full of energy and too much the man of action," according to a countryman, he was also not "too well-liked" in the department either. Years later, Acheson admitted he felt "churlish" in admitting that McGhee had always bored him. He had "ability without great insight."[39]

But Acheson delighted in Eddie Miller, the thirty-eight-year-old New Yorker who ran Latin American affairs. A native of San Juan, Puerto Rico, who grew up in Cuba, he had a Harvard law degree and was fluent in Spanish, Portuguese, and French. A former law partner of John Foster Dulles and friend of Nelson Rockefeller, he came to know Acheson in the wartime state department, helping him massage hemispheric delegates at Bretton Woods. Since Acheson had little interest in Latin America and saw no paramount national security issues there, he turned it all over to Miller.[40]

The Soviet Union was technically Perkins's responsibility, but Acheson took command from the first. On tap for advice were the fabled experts, Bohlen and George Kennan. Born to the purple and a Harvard graduate, Bohlen might have received Acheson's confidence on the strength of his expulsion from St. Paul's School (New Hampshire) for defiance of authority, if not for being a pioneer Soviet specialist. But this was not to be. Acheson partly indicated why in a 1960 letter describing the Soviet experts as "dangerous" counselors; they peddled "uncommunicable" hunches that "must be accepted by those who have not the same occult power of divination." Bohlen, he wrote, had essentially told him, "Dean, you came to this field too late to be able to get the feel of it." Acheson's ties with Bohlen and Kennan are important to understand, since so many historians have suggested that one secretary of state after another under Truman merely executed their ideas, but Acheson knew otherwise. So did Frank Pace, Jr., who had no axe to grind. A former budget director who became secretary of the army, in the 1970s he interrupted an interviewer who kept asking about Kennan's and Bohlen's ideas. "No, no," Pace expostulated. The key policymaker was Acheson, who was "a clear, incisive, and in fact, brilliant thinker." Of course, the specialists contributed, but Acheson laid down the "essential pattern of that period."[41]

Of Kennan's soulmate, Acheson said simply, "I can't run foreign policy out of Chip Bohlen's restaurant," but he had no more tangled or troublesome association than with Kennan. Though in the foreign service since 1926, he was eleven years Acheson's junior. A native of Milwaukee, a Princeton graduate, a lifelong skeptic about democracy, his claim to singular expertise was not his only bothersome trait in Acheson's eyes. His pedantic susceptibilities and proclivity to angst affronted Acheson's practicality and distaste for introversion. His sensitivity and emotionalism hoisted bile to Acheson's gorge. A 1933 fitness report on the young diplomat singled out what taxed Acheson's patience, faulting Kennan for an emotional approach to "intellectual concepts" and for veering from "idealistic" to "hopelessly cynical."[42]

Already known for the Long Telegram and "Mr. X" article, Kennan still headed the policy planning staff when Acheson became secretary. Though a key contributor to the Marshall Plan, he would oppose NATO and deplore the key cold war strategy paper, NSC-68. German rearmament horrified him. His public reputation, which depended partly on his stylistic skills, annoyed Acheson, who was amazed that a "footnote of the Truman presidency" would "masquerade as an important policymaker." A lone ranger, Kennan personally wrote most of the PPS reports. Contrary to reports, he could not walk directly into Marshall's office, but Robert Lovett as under secretary had kept the door unofficially open for him. That now changed. Webb was suspicious of Kennan, and Acheson began chafing at the impressionable Kremlinologist's close proximity. In March and April 1949, while Kennan traveled on a mission to Germany, Acheson replaced him on the NSC committee covering that subject. He made no objection that September when Webb began screening Kennan's PPS papers through country desks, depriving him, as Kennan instantly realized, of "direct access" to Acheson and letting "operational" offices veto his papers. With remarkable insight, he also realized Acheson probably considered him interesting but someone he could not take "seriously" because he "lacked foundation in the daily grind of operational routine." Soon afterward, Nitze took over the policy planning staff. Kennan soldiered on in the immaterial role of "counselor" before taking a sabbatical at Robert Oppenheimer's Institute for Advanced Study at Princeton.[43]

It is a common myth that Acheson forced Kennan out of the department, but his departure was self-propelled. Kennan grasped that it was not his person that made Acheson querulous but his advice. Acheson paid no attention to his argument for delaying a Japanese peace treaty. After flirting with Kennan's advice on Germany, Acheson rejected it. In 1950, he suppressed Kennan's report on Latin America because of its gloomy remarks about the flawed character of Latin Americans and their governments. Many years later, Acheson would even take a hammer to Kennan's celebrated and seductive prose; it had "a sort of sad lyrical beauty about it which drugs the mind" but, in Acheson's case, only briefly. To evaluate Kennan's memoranda "calmly," he claimed to have reread them with "verbs and adjectives omitted." As Holmes imagined Shakespeare saying of himself, "I have written five thousand lines of pure gold and a good deal of padding," Acheson thought, in Kennan's case, it was "mostly the padding which has survived. His reputation has outrun his professional performance." Matthews thought Acheson probably just "got tired of hearing all of George's wails. George could never really be satisfied with anything." Webb noted piquantly that Kennan "had never lived in a democracy" and was always complaining about having to cater to Congress.[44]

But, far more than Acheson would let on, especially in later years, Kennan also commanded his respect. He repeatedly drew on his ideas, perceptions, and experience, which had encompassed posts in eastern and central Europe, Portugal, and the Soviet Union. Even when they clashed, Acheson knew he had a worthy foe, one who could also be a great friend in times of grave need. That Acheson often rejected Kennan's counsel did not mean he did not want to hear it. He asked Kennan to delay exiting from government at the outset of the Korean War and gratefully accepted his help at the time of China's intervention. He repeatedly praised him before others. Testifying in the Senate in 1949 at a time Kennan was thinking of leaving, he dilated on his industrious acquisition of foreign language skills. If he did leave, Acheson wanted him to go to Yale to save him from Harvard's clutches, but what he really wanted was for him to stay "the rest of his public life in the State Department." When Kennan actually left, Acheson told a National War College audience it filled him with "despair" to lose someone with such a rare "sweetness of nature." "You did me too much honor," Kennan wrote him after witnessing these remarks. When liberals attacked Kennan in 1951, Acheson invaded their clubhouse to defend him at the annual dinner of the Americans for Democratic Action. But their relationship deteriorated over time. Fosdick could not help "feeling sorry for Dean," because he found it impossible "to deal with Kennan toward the end." Battle was sad, too: "They admired each other enormously but there was just not a meshing either of goals or of thought processes."[45]

Ironically, Acheson as under secretary had vetoed Kennan's choice of the sharp-tongued Nitze as an economic specialist for the PPS. Kennan should get a deep thinker, not "a Wall Street operator." Now, Acheson came to admire him and enjoy his company. Forty-one in 1949, Nitze was a Republican (and former and future Democrat). He had grown up in the neighborhood of the University of Chicago, where his father was a linguistics professor. Educated first at the university's schools and at Hotchkiss, Paul joined Bohlen's party circle at Harvard. The millions he made afterward on Wall Street freed him for public service. As a culmination of several wartime assignments, he directed the U.S. strategic bombing survey and later worked on the Marshall Plan in Europe. By 1949 he had impressed Acheson more than once, and he was the secretary's choice to replace Kennan on the policy planning staff.

Nitze took over on 1 January 1950, in time to take the lead on the famed national security council paper, NSC-68, which advocated pulling out all stops in the cold war. Before long, he became a virtual alter ego of Acheson. The two collaborated especially well on military issues, Nitze helping pilot Acheson's evolving views on nuclear strategy. "Most of my time," Nitze recalled happily, "was devoted to being with Dean Acheson." They met every morning and through the day. Nitze could speak with authority for him in and out of the department. They would descend on the Metropolitan Club, where Nitze held a prized membership, for spirited lunches, and the two men dined, politicked, and talked economics and national security until Acheson died. "The happiest and most productive years of my life," Nitze then said, "were those from 1947 to January 1953, when I was among those working closely with Dean creating the modern world."[46]

Acheson had a more mixed relationship with Dean Rusk. A Georgian, born in modest circumstances in 1909, he had been a Rhodes Scholar at Oxford. After taking an MA in Germany, he taught political science at California's Mills College. In World War II, he was an army colonel on the staff of Chiang's American tormentor, General Joseph Stilwell, before becoming one of Marshall's protégés. In 1949, he moved to the state department as deputy under secretary, running the UN affairs office. Advising both Acheson and Webb, he coordinated business between regional and "functional" offices and worked as a liaison to the defense department. Heavy involvement in Middle Eastern affairs showed a willingness to take on "sticky problems" others preferred avoiding. The most celebrated such act came in March 1950 when he took a voluntary demotion to what Acheson called "the dirtiest job" in the department, as assistant secretary in the troubled Asian office. It was, Acheson said, "a very magnanimous thing to do." But Rusk's reputation for courage coexisted oddly with whispers about lack of spine. He was "a man of impeccable integrity," said a subordinate, John F. Melby, but he "kept his own counsel" and "never stood up and voted for anything or anyone." Having heard the whispers himself, Rusk boasted to be in the small minority of people who were "close friends of both Dean Acheson and John Foster Dulles." Late in 1951, he resigned to head the Rockefeller Foundation. Acheson's recommendation was instrumental when John Kennedy named Rusk secretary of state in 1961, but his former boss soon became a sharp critic.[47]

At first, Acheson was especially close to Philip Jessup, one of his "closest friends," who served as ambassador at large. Fifty-two in 1949, Jessup was a distinguished international lawyer from New York's blue line of success: Hamilton College, Yale for law, and Columbia for the doctorate. A prominent Presbyterian layman and fixture of the Columbia law faculty, he had written books on Elihu Root and international law. He had also been a prominent member of the America First Committee. During the war he rediscovered his internationalism and served with UNRRA and as a delegate at Bretton Woods. He joined the UN delegation afterward, to which he returned following his Washington assignments. A big man, his secretary called Jessup "the large ambassador." His big *trouble* while with Acheson originated in his loyalty to Alger Hiss, by then gone from the state department and ensconced as president of the Carnegie Endowment for International Peace. As a director of the Endowment, Jessup testified to his probity at both Hiss perjury trials, first in writing, then in person. Consequently, Acheson remarked, McCarthy gave him a "shellacking" in an attack that only intensified Acheson's (and Truman's) resolve to keep him on.[48]

Two other men associated with the department warrant mention. The first was Acheson's successor, the Republican Dulles, the grandson of one secretary of state (John Watson Foster) and nephew of another (Robert Lansing). His own involvement with foreign affairs went back to the Versailles conference. Already a periodic veteran of Democratic administrations, in 1950 he returned as a special adviser at Rusk's urging to help check conservative attacks on China policy, a move coinciding with the Teflon-like Rusk's transfer to the Far Eastern office. Acheson agreed but was unenthusiastic, for he had probably considered Dulles untrustworthy ever since he refused to endorse FDR's destroyer deal with Britain in 1940. He was also a "notorious leaker to the press." As it turned out, Dulles labored successfully in negotiating the 1951 Japanese peace treaty. When a new election neared, he cut loose and embittered both Truman and Acheson with his harsh campaign criticisms. Another Republican serving under Acheson was Warren R. Austin, ambassador to the United Nations. A seventy-two-year-old former Vermont senator, he had been in the post since 1947. Someone in the department, probably Jessup, thought he should "go." But he was allowed to stay, probably because Acheson thought nothing important would happen in the UN anyway.[49]

While many of those who worked for him were proudly apolitical, Acheson made no bones about being a Democrat working for a Democratic president. As proof that there was no alternative to being "political," he estimated spending about "80 percent" of his time shoring up domestic support for his policies. His supple "responsiveness to American public opinion," Ambassador Oliver Franks told London, guaranteed a reduction in friction between the White House and Foggy Bottom.

Some of the professionals who wanted to keep their skirts clear of politics were ambassadors. Acheson was personally appalled at the thought of being an ambassador, but he appreciated them for doing the "donkey's work" of diplomacy's "daily grind." Of all those serving while he was secretary of state—a list would include Kennan, McGhee, Bruce, Robert Murphy, Claude G. Bowers, Chester Bowles, Jefferson Caffery, Lewis W. Douglas, James C. Dunn, and Henry F. Grady—he was closest to Loy Henderson, ambassador to India and Iran. With ties dating to World War II, their collaboration culminated in their work on the Truman Doctrine. A year older than Acheson, this Ozarks native, pastor's son, graduate of Northwestern University, and former Red Cross official was another early Soviet specialist. He had watched Moscow from Latvia before FDR recognized the USSR in 1933 and then witnessed Stalin's Moscow show trials. Because Roosevelt disliked Henderson's anti-Soviet views, which drew complaints from the Soviet ambassador, he banished him to Iraq.[50]

Another Acheson favorite was John J. McCloy, who was effectively an ambassador while serving as U.S. high commissioner for Germany. McCloy agreed in May 1949 to leave the World Bank to take this post as part of the state department's takeover of responsibilities in Germany from the army. He enjoyed direct access to Truman but worked intimately with Acheson when the United States moved toward German rearmament in 1950 and often assisted Acheson in his sometimes contentious relations with the military and the defense department.

Acheson loved working with most of these men, but even when they rubbed him the wrong way, he vigorously defended them if they came under attack, especially from McCarthyites. Elsewhere in the administration, cabinet heads sought cover from anti-communist bedlam, but Acheson went public with spiky denunciations of Joseph McCarthy and his ilk. Before an audience of newspaper editors in April 1950, he ripped into McCarthy's "vicious" charges and defended the "victims" in an extraordinary and ironical profile of U.S. policymakers, whom he described as his "co-conspirators."[51]

A "Killer Instinct"

In the National Security Act in 1947, Congress not only created the new defense department, first called the "national military establishment," but also formed the joint chiefs of staff (JCS) to head the military chain of command. To replace the wartime Office of Strategic Services (OSS), the act established the Central Intelligence Agency (CIA). Another of its creations was the National Security Council (NSC), aimed at making sure the president was advised by a consolidated group of government leaders most concerned with the diplomatic, military, and financial facets of "security." Acheson was unenthusiastic about both the NSC and CIA and had "the gravest forebodings" about the latter. He warned Truman that, given its congressional design, no one "would be in a position" to know what it did or "to control it."

Acheson's most likely competitor in this forest of new agencies was the defense department, but from the outset he enjoyed several advantages. First was a president with an amateur historian's views of cabinet government who "never" doubted State's rank as "the senior department." The second was a lack of unity in the Pentagon complex, exacerbated by the search for postwar roles and Truman's unrelenting budget cuts. Acheson, too, bewailed these cuts but was careful not to adopt a dog in any of the internecine fights they set off. A third advantage, executed through Nitze and other advisers (who were instructed to develop channels to strategic planners), was making sure the state department showed up at interagency committees armed with the best paper and clearest arguments. In developing NSC-68, Nitze circumvented defense secretary Louis Johnson's obstructionism with informal get-togethers with JCS staff members. These sessions then continued throughout the Korean War.[52]

Marshall (with Lovett as under secretary) took over from Johnson in the summer of 1950, by which time Acheson had grown contemptuous of how the military was organized and of the advice it proffered. The design of the defense department, he wrote in 1971, "suggests the work of a madman with a sense of humor, a knowledge of history and a lively civilian fear of a too efficient military organization, like the old German General Staff." He blamed James Forrestal and writers of the National Security Act. The individual uniformed services were uncontrollable and backed by patrons in Congress. The joint chiefs, he thought, could not coordinate their thinking and hardly knew what they wanted, a problem he again traced to the power of the individual services. Thus, the defense department could not lead until the JCS allowed it, and the chiefs themselves did not "know what they think until they hear what they say." Once they had said something, it was as if the Pope had spoken. In NSC meetings, the chiefs often uttered views the defense secretary had never heard, let alone shared. The saving grace was that Truman would accept Acheson's views, if for no other reason than that the Pentagon's were "so silly." Both president and secretary seemed to look down on the generals and admirals and tried confining them to their own "bailiwick."[53]

Acheson's personal contest with Johnson raised bureaucratic tensions through much of 1949 and 1950. A native West Virginian born in 1891, the bald, square-shouldered, 250-pounder was an aggressive and usually aggrieved man. A World War I infantry captain, he commanded and helped found the American Legion, organized the influential Steptoe and Johnson law firm, and served as an assistant secretary of war under Roosevelt. When Forrestal, the first defense secretary, committed suicide, Truman gave the post to Johnson, his chief fundraiser in the 1948 campaign. Johnson followed the president's budget-cutting orders, slashing left and right with minimal attention to the sensitivities of the beribboned generals and admirals. He was also, according to Joe Alsop, a "practiced liar, without a scruple I was able to discover." With aspirations to succeed Truman, this dedicated cabalist continuously tried to displace Acheson at the president's right hand. Offering a "blank wall" to offers of cooperation, he fought Acheson over NATO, China, Formosa, Germany, the defense budget, and the writing of NSC-68, especially in NSC meetings. At times, the two men were not on speaking terms, and in August 1950, according to Acheson, his behavior "passed beyond the peculiar to the impossible" as he openly schemed to have Acheson fired and Averell Harriman put in his place. Sick of the catfights and needing stronger department of defense (DOD) leadership in Korea, Truman cashiered Johnson instead.

In fact, the struggle was not simply an issue of Johnson, whom Acheson considered at the least neurotic. Johnson or no Johnson, institutional flaws guaranteed conflict. The Pentagon, writes Anna K. Nelson, "had a 'not for State Department Distribution' category in its mail distribution system, while the State Department had a top-secret summary of political events that was specifically circulated to State Department officers only." The chiefs sent missions abroad without telling State. When he succeeded Johnson, Marshall signaled his rejection of "military"-vs.-"civilian" thinking by sitting on Acheson's side of the table in interdepartmental meetings, but the problems continued anyway. Little improved even after Acheson's good friend Lovett succeeded

Marshall in 1951. With Lovett, Acheson wrote, "you would get millions of words but no information, and we were completely, totally, absolutely frustrated."[54]

Questions of international finance often brought tangles with the treasury department, which Acheson found "the hardest thing to penetrate." When British dollar reserves slipped, Treasury donned its green eyeshade and cracked the creditor's whip. In contrast, the state department wanted to open U.S. coffers wide enough to help an ally gain the strength to help withstand any Soviet challenges. Acheson now dealt with Secretary John Snyder rather than the wartime team of Henry Morgenthau and Harry Dexter White. Appointed secretary in 1946 at fifty-one, Snyder seldom had direct run-ins with Acheson, who could usually be confident that on issues related to NATO allies, Truman would follow his lead.[55]

But he could not be confident about controlling foreign aid programs. Out of the same suspicion that blocked Truman when he wanted Acheson to run the Marshall Plan, Congress began prying all aid programs from the state department. The department itself seemed unready to manage them, with its traditional emphasis on the political over the economic and making over executing policy. Career FSOs and almost all political officers scorned economic specialists. The same syndrome delayed State's assumption of responsibility for Germany and, combined with continuing congressional mistrust, led in time to the loss of control over information and arms control programs. In January 1949, when Truman proposed a technical aid program for underdeveloped areas of the world (Point Four), a surprised Acheson, unenthusiastic but unwilling to lose control of the program, succeeded in holding on to it. But when Congress in 1951 established the Mutual Security Agency to consolidate military and economic aid programs, it put Point Four under its aegis, too.[56]

At the outset, Truman distrusted the National Security Council. He suspected it of being a Republican-invented Trojan horse that would strip him of his rightful authority in foreign affairs, though he was somewhat mollified in 1949 when new legislation added the vice-president and joint chiefs to the council and subtracted the service secretaries. After attending its first meeting in September 1947, however, he absented himself from over 80 percent of its sessions into 1950, partly because Webb as budget director worried the council might force him into unwise decisions. After the outbreak of the Korean War, Truman attended regularly.

Forrestal was certain Acheson would try to "castrate" the NSC, and he did share his misgivings about it with Truman at the time of its founding. Webb and Kennan, too, thought the chiefs would try to convert it into a "super agency over foreign policy." Acheson's main concern was to keep it in its place. He wanted no foreign body invading the bloodstream of *his* policy organs. He also disliked how the process of producing policy papers forced him to make artificial, thumbs-up or down judgments. Over time, however, he mainly considered the National Security Council a nuisance and waste of time. It was then staffed by officers drawn from other departments, including State's PPS, and its executive secretary, Admiral Sidney W. Souers, was reassuringly self-effacing, "objective," and no bureaucratic imperialist. Acheson trusted to his relationship with Truman to beat off any trouble in the NSC. Once the president began showing up for meetings, Acheson also attended faithfully, mainly to repel Pentagon threats to state department objectives.[57]

The President Again

Acheson's association with the NSC was just one thread of many connecting Foggy Bottom to the White House. Truman had a small and protective staff that included virtually no foreign policy specialists. Agencies formally part of the presidency were also part of the "White House," including the national security resources board, bureau of the budget, and the NSC. Because it was mainly his job to assure smooth workings with this group, Webb met regularly with Souers and his successor, James (Jimmy) Lay, Jr., with Louis Johnson, and with CIA Director Roscoe H. Hillenkoetter to smooth the National Security Council process.[58]

Acheson's careful tending of the ties to the White House was part of his non-stop campaign to counter Truman's dogged mistrust of the department. As late as January 1952, Truman still described State as "a peculiar organization, made up principally of extremely bright people who made tremendous college marks" but were "clannish and snooty." He sometimes felt, he said, like "firing the whole bunch." A couple of levels below Acheson, Truman wrote Representative Maury Maverick, officials had not awakened to the fact that the age of British supremacy was over and "that we are the leader now." As he toiled to overcome these prejudices, Acheson also knew *Truman* knew he could not run foreign policy from the Oval Office. "The administrative tasks of the great departments of government" were beyond the capacity of the White House. Truman knew that "the buck stopped with him," but also that "neither he nor the White House staff was the Secretary of State, or Defense, or Treasury, or any other." Despite lingering doubts about the department, Acheson's performance at the 1949 Paris talks, he later recalled, had "a very helpful effect on relations between the State Department and the White House."[59]

His tender treatment of the president did not extend to his staff. "Don't ever tell me that I must do something because the White House says so," he told Battle. "If the President says so, that's a different thing." As for Truman's military aide, Harry Vaughan, "I don't ever want to hear anything he thinks about anything." When Rusk became secretary of state, Acheson told him, "Never let anybody get between you and the President." Most of Truman's staff, however, worked well with Acheson. Finding Matt Connelly "cordial, simple, and gracious," he was more likely to tangle with George Elsey, Clark Clifford's successor, who skirmished with him over the Truman Doctrine speech. Not a bit timid, Elsey through 1950–51 wondered if McCarthyite attacks had made Acheson damaged goods and a liability for the president.[60]

If anyone was more protective of Truman than Elsey, it was Acheson himself. William Bundy claimed his father-in-law thought the "presidency had a halo around it," but it was the Missourian he esteemed. "A great chief," he would sigh after a telephone conversation. He made decisions "as straight as fence posts" and had a profound capacity "to understand complex questions and to decide," one of the "rarest qualities possessed by man." He did not "care a hoot what Congress, Schlesinger or any other historian would say." He always asked, "Is this the right thing to do?" If the answer was yes, he did it, "however unpopular it may have seemed." The American system, Acheson thought, often threw men into the presidency unprepared in foreign affairs, forcing them to learn on the job. Truman "caught hold quickly, perhaps in 18 months," a better performance, he wrote in 1965, than those of Roosevelt, Eisenhower, Kennedy, or Johnson. When Admiral Dennison asked why he had never written a book on Truman, he replied: "Well, I have such a high regard for him, and I am so fond of him, that I feel I could not possibly be objective."[61]

He was not reluctant to express those feelings directly to the "boss." On 12 April 1951, the sixth anniversary of FDR's death, two days after the firing of General Douglas MacArthur, Congress rang with calls to impeach Truman. Acheson wrote him:

> Six years ago today the world descended on your shoulders. Six years ago tomorrow I went to work for you in a meeting in the Cabinet room. You were facing the first of more trials than any President has ever faced—except possibly Lincoln. Others have faced war with its terrible choices. But you have faced, and met, these without the unity that war brings—in fact, with almost the reverse, the apathy which the end of war brings.
>
> To me that meeting began the affection for a man and devotion to a chief which has been, and is, my life.
>
> The times ahead will be rough. You are sailing the ship and I am signed on. We have always spoken the truth to one another and always shall.
>
> As this seventh year begins I send you my loyalty and profound respect.
>
> Dean Acheson[62]

8

KEEPING THE AMERICANS IN,
THE RUSSIANS OUT, AND
THE GERMANS DOWN, 1949

The event in 1949 that assured Acheson's place as Truman's primary guide and adviser in foreign policy was not the conclusion of the North Atlantic alliance in April. Instead, it was the four-power discussion of Germany in May and June at the Council of Foreign Ministers (CFM) in Paris. Acheson's success at the CFM session greatly solidified his authority in the administration and his leadership in foreign affairs. The measure he took of the Soviets' intentions in Paris reinforced his view that there was really no point in talking to them. The conference also sealed his conversion to the view that the west could not risk losing the western occupation zones of Germany but must integrate them into the west, making West Germany part of the western alliance. Finally, it marked a further evolution of Acheson's overall cold war strategy. He not only wanted the west to be strong enough to *contain* the Kremlin. To win the cold war, he thought the west must have *superior* strength. Continuing discord with Moscow, he came to believe, was less risky than ongoing negotiations with it.

Germany was at the heart of these developments. In January 1949, Acheson did not yet have settled views on the remnants of Hitler's state, but with the president's approval he would soon choose policies that remained intact for two generations. Rather than risk the unpredictable outcome in the unlikely event the Soviet Union permitted Germany's reunification as a neutral state, Acheson, hesitantly at first, drove to pull western Germany into an American, and western, sphere of influence, or what Acheson would soon call a "situation of strength."

This strategy was risky business. Trying to fold Germany within the alliance could possibly rupture it instead. The fresh memory of Nazi horrors caused the

French especially to quail at Germany's resuscitation. To persuade the European allies to accept that rebirth, Washington found it necessary to commit its own power to their defense. It did so by joining in the formation of NATO, which expressly defended its members from Soviet aggression and at the same time implicitly protected them from a reborn Germany. Reassured by U.S. pledges, France and Britain joined the United States in rejecting Soviet attempts to restore four-power control of Germany at the Paris conference.

NATO: "Worse than Original Sin"

American foreign policy leaders had gradually concluded that a restored and neutral Germany, loitering in the heart of Europe, vulnerable to Soviet intimidation or blandishments, would be unacceptable. They joined with the British and French to combine their German occupation zones, at first with economic recovery in mind but also with increasing suspicions of Moscow's objectives. The decision to settle the future of the western zones unilaterally culminated in the "London Program" of 4 June 1948. This integrated their sectors into a single economic unit eligible for Marshall aid, with continuing international controls over Germany's industrial district along the Ruhr River. "London" called for a constituent assembly to form a provisional government as a first step to restoring West German sovereignty. The west then introduced a stronger currency in its zones, further consolidating them economically and isolating them from Soviet influence.

Stalin felt beleaguered, given the blow of the Marshall Plan, expulsion of communists from western governments, restiveness in Yugoslavia, hints of a western military alliance, and the removal of Ruhr reparations from his grasp. He countered by blocking access to Berlin. He might thereby squelch the London Program or at least rid the city of western influence. Avoiding a military face-off, Truman with strong British backing relieved the city via airlift. From his law office, Acheson thought Stalin was acting defensively rather than aggressively. The blockade, he wrote Truman years later, began as a response to the west's "economic threat" and then grew into an attempt to "get us out of Berlin altogether." The Soviets had "blundered into" the crisis.[1]

Stalin may have acted defensively, but his actions in Berlin and Czechoslovakia exposed the nakedness of western defenses. "All the Russians need to get to the Channel," Under Secretary of State Robert Lovett thought after the Czech coup, was "shoes." The west seemed to be doing well enough politically, but apart from U.S. nuclear possibilities, not militarily. In central Europe, more than thirty Soviet divisions faced a dozen disorganized and ill-trained western counterparts fattening on occupation duty. Nearer to the Soviet Union than the Americans, Europeans grew worried first. In Brussels, on 17 March 1948, Britain, France, and the Benelux states (Belgium, Netherlands, and Luxembourg) formed the Western Union and pledged to defend one another from external attack.[2]

Paris hoped the Brussels pact would protect it from both German and Soviet dangers but wanted something better, while Britain chiefly feared Moscow. With Britain's Ernest Bevin leading, both countries pressed Washington for a security alliance. Bevin was an important NATO pioneer, but the Americans transformed his idea of an Atlantic alliance linked to the Western Union into a single, grand pact. American, British, and Canadian officials in 1948 followed formation of the Union with secret discussions at the Pentagon. Though still without the wherewithal, U.S. military leaders hoped in case of war to hold at the Rhine instead of first abandoning the continent, then liberating it. As diplomats and generals conferred, the state department quietly consulted with leading members of Congress. This led on 11 June 1948 to passage of the Vandenberg Resolution. Named for Michigan Republican Arthur Vandenberg, this put the seal of Senate approval on U.S. membership in a regional collective security alliance.

The pace now quickened. In early July 1948, shortly after the start of the Berlin blockade, further negotiations began in Washington, termed the Exploratory Talks on Security. These led nine months later to the establishment of the North Atlantic Treaty, the third leg, after the Truman Doctrine and Marshall Plan, of the revolutionary tripod now forming the basis of U.S. foreign policy. Since 1778, the United States had never offered an advance commitment to assist another nation in a future war. The fifty-year-old Texan, Jack Hickerson, one of State's driving forces behind NATO, said he did not "care whether entangling alliances have been considered worse than original sin since George Washington's time." It was essential to form "a military alliance with Western Europe" and "do it quickly." George Kennan and Charles Bohlen ranged from lukewarm to hostile to the idea. Lovett was supposedly keeping Congress informed. The Washington discussions were not far from completion when Acheson became secretary of state.[3]

Of the major initiatives in Europe in the Truman era, only the birth of NATO found Acheson absent at the moment of conception. "He was present only on the sixth, the last day of creation," recalled a Canadian, "but that was a particularly busy day." Although he fumbled at first, his vigor and expansive view of U.S. policy energized the secret discussions, following the cautious and fatigued Marshall. As Acheson entered the talks, it was not yet clear what the alliance would mean for the United States. Some officials feared that with a military alliance in hand, Europeans would neglect the critical business of economic recovery, undermining the Marshall Plan. *Without* an alliance, Europeans worried the Yanks would again leave them to their own devices to confront an embittered Germany and resurgent Russia. From the first, NATO carried a heavy burden of expectations. It was supposed to deter Soviet aggression. By thus boosting Europeans' confidence, it should stimulate economic recovery. It would give France a way to allow West Germany a place within the "west." It would allow Britain to preserve its straddle between Europe and the Atlantic "community." It would prevent a reprise of American isolationism. As Lord Ismay, its first secretary-general, declared, NATO would "keep the Americans in, the Russians out, and the Germans down."[4] When a senator asked him if NATO would protect its European members against a West Germany gone bad as well as the Soviet Union, Acheson responded: "Yes. It works in all directions."

Economics had much to do with Washington's first backing of NATO. American policymakers thought the Marshall Plan would counter the dread and pessimism inhibiting reconstruction, but now it appeared as if military guarantees were also necessary. With the menacing Russian bear nearby, with no shield against its tanks and artillery tubes, west Europeans found it hard to summon faith in either recovery or their own resilience. Acheson told senators in April 1949 that only the United States, by raising such a shield, could "promote full economic recovery through removing the drag of a sense of insecurity." NATO, therefore, like the Marshall Plan, embodied therapeutic purposes. As Acheson told the Portuguese foreign minister, NATO could make Europeans think "the difficult task of reconstruction is worthwhile." But its primary end was military deterrence. As Acheson later remarked, Americans now understood their "defense line" lay across the Atlantic. Real military dangers, he said in 1949, justified taking steps "completely outside our history."[5]

Just a week after taking office, Acheson spent a Saturday morning with Hickerson and others to catch up. Because of breaking events elsewhere, however, he did not give full attention to NATO until 3 February 1949. Negotiations had been mostly secret, and the administration had done little to prepare the public for this extraordinary treaty. Acheson was taken aback to discover simmering resentments in the Senate. It turned out that Lovett had supplied only sketchy briefings, and only Vandenberg had seen any treaty language. Democrats again controlled Congress, and Tom Connally of Texas had not only replaced Vandenberg at the head of the Foreign Relations Committee but was chafing at not being paid Vandenberg-like deference.

As Acheson began mending fences, he broke others. His first session with ambassadors of prospective NATO partners—then the UK, France, Canada, and the Benelux states—came on 8 February. Poorly briefed and cutting a wide swath for a newcomer, he tried to torpedo Article 2, a Canadian project to infuse the alliance with social, economic, and cultural purposes. Congress would reject such an airy attempt to fulfill "every worthy aspiration that ever occurred to any human being," he explained in a schoolmasterly mien. Other countries also opposed the article, but Acheson shocked everyone with his "linguistic vandalism" against a text Marshall and Lovett had approved after weeks of tugging and pulling. Ottawa appealed over Acheson's head to Truman while Hickerson and his assistant Theodore Achilles drafted a substitute they hoped Acheson and skeptical senators would accept. Hickerson, Achilles, and Canadian ambassador Hume Wrong cornered Acheson at home, down with the flu. Surrounding his bedside, they "beat the poor sick man over the head." Acheson retreated but never surrendered his doubts about Canadian political judgment, later telling

Canada's foreign minister, Lester Pearson, that his people were "moralistic" and "interfering." In his memoirs, he scoffed at "the plane of high principle upon which the Department of External Affairs prefers to rest Canada's more mundane interests."[6]

In mid-February came a spate of critical Senate speeches. In an "*opéra bouffe*" tirade, Connally bellowed that the treaty incorporated an unacceptably "automatic" system for U.S. intervention in European wars. Piling on, Vandenberg said each alliance state must decide what it meant to respond to an attack. The British groaned at this "deplorable" rash of isolationism. Now fully alert to Lovett's failures as senatorial masseur, Acheson warned the two plaintiffs that France would destroy the treaty if Washington reneged on the solemn guarantees of collective defense.[7]

On 16 February, he opened a back channel to British Ambassador Sir Oliver Franks, who would become his "friend and confessor." Once holding Adam Smith's chair of moral philosophy at the University of Glasgow, Franks, also a clergyman's son, had risen rapidly in the wartime British government. He had a mind for international economics and a reputation for unflappability first earned when a *Luftwaffe* raid sent him dashing into the street in his pajamas but "carrying his briefcase." Acheson and Franks had worked together in war-related conferences. A good friend of Bevin, the forty-three-year-old Franks was named ambassador in 1948. In the ambassadorial corps, only Wrong, whose father had attended the University of Toronto with Acheson's father, might have been friendlier than Franks to Acheson. Impressed by his intellectual creativity, Acheson swiftly incorporated Franks into his informal policymaking council. They frequently dined together in secret and officially reported their get-togethers only by mutual consent. Franks could see Acheson whenever he liked, a privilege enjoyed by no other envoy. Acheson met with him more than all other foreign ambassadors combined and consulted him, he told British journalist Henry Brandon, "on problems that have nothing to do with Anglo-American relations." "If you write this," he added, "I'll cut your throat." Franks, meanwhile, cultivated the U.S. press and spread the word about his worthy country in visits to all forty-eight states. Britain, in his view, should be a U.S. partner rather than part of "the European queue."[8]

Putting aside a treaty draft already vetted by subordinates, Acheson emerged with new proposals after his first clandestine meeting with Franks. The nub of their discussion concerned the "pledge" in Article 5. The continental states wanted this to be as automatic as possible, but senators joined the administration and United Kingdom in wanting a little wiggle room on the commitment to battle. Since only Congress could declare war for the United States, Acheson looked for words that would unite senators and both groups of NATO states. In a White House meeting on the 17th, Truman supported a meaningful military pledge and, at Acheson's request, gained Connally's backing. Acheson's cylinders were now moving in harmony. On 18 February, he gained the support of the full Foreign Relations Committee. As finally adopted, signatories promised in Article 5 "that an armed attack against one or more of them in Europe or North America shall be considered an attack against them all." In such a case, "each of them, in exercise of the right of individual or collective self-defense recognized by Article 51 of the Charter of the United Nations, will assist the Party or Parties so attacked by taking forthwith, individually, and in concert with the other Parties, such action as it deems necessary, including the use of armed force, to restore and maintain the security of the North Atlantic area." Mollified by "the use of armed force" and especially by "forthwith," the continental states swallowed "as it deems necessary." French ambassador Henri Bonnet wanted even more automaticity, and France would long try converting "forthwith" into "automatically" by making sure U.S. troops were stationed in the path of any Soviet attack. Paris worked from the theory that four Americans "and a corporal" on the front lines would guarantee its safety.[9]

Deciding on NATO members beyond the original core did not come easily. In the absence of malicious Soviet conduct, Norway had hoped to join a neutralist Scandinavian Pact led by Sweden. But Oslo's complacency vanished after the Czech coup and sudden gusts of hostile propaganda and accusatory diplomatic notes from Moscow. With the proviso it could ban "foreign" bases on its territory, Norway now joined the others, a significant addition given its command of North Atlantic sea lanes and air routes. Bonnet threatened to veto Norwegian membership without an invitation to Italy, hoping that including a Mediterranean state would smooth the way to shoehorning French North Africa into the alliance. A group in the state department headed by Hickerson had long favored Italian membership, but Truman and Acheson did not. Because Britain too was mildly opposed, and the Benelux states were ready to follow the U.S. lead, Acheson's reluctance left France isolated—and angry. Acheson gave way only when Bonnet played his trump card, a threat to block formation of a new West German state or even NATO itself unless Rome was invited. His tactics infuriated nearly all the negotiators, but after long discussions with Truman and key senators, Acheson agreed to "swallow" Italy on 2 March 1949, by which time he no longer saw a compelling argument against its membership. Wanting to avoid anything looking like western disunity, he now also worried that an "unattached" Italy might succumb to its own powerful communist movement. Thus, as E. Timothy Smith notes, an alliance fashioned to stop external aggression admitted Italy for fear of its loss to internal subversion.[10]

On 8 March, the state department officially invited Rome to join. It unilaterally added invitations to Denmark, Iceland, and Portugal, which incited grumbling at Whitehall about not being consulted, but historic British ties with Portugal had much to do with its inclusion, along with its ownership of the offshore Azores. Though not a separate state, Algeria made its way into the alliance as an integral part of metropolitan France, but not other parts of North Africa or any other European colonies. Denmark's invitation stemmed from the need to encompass Greenland and supply bases for the Scandinavian flank. Iceland's membership underlined the pact's "Atlantic" character, but others knocked on the door in vain. Ireland's insistence that Washington pressure the UK to free the Northern Counties kept it out. Sweden overreached by demanding receipt of U.S. armaments, rejecting Article 5's "pledge," and insisting simultaneously on forming its own "Nordic Pact." The rebuff to Sweden led to the enlistment of Iceland, Norway, and Denmark. Soon, Turkey and Greece would harangue Acheson for a place. These the joint chiefs opposed for two years. NATO membership for West Germany would await the Eisenhower administration, but Article 6's coverage of attacks against occupation forces wrapped its territory into the alliance from the outset.[11]

Getting all this approved involved shuttling between ambassadors and Senate tycoons. Acheson—"I was like a circus performer riding two horses"— used the worries of one to pressure the other. In time, Achilles thought, every Foreign Relations Committee member knew the treaty "by heart and had a vested interest in it." Acheson took their views seriously, limiting the treaty to a twenty-year term over French objections at their suggestion. Vandenberg loved the courtesies lavished on him, declaring NATO the first treaty in U.S. history to be "concluded with the *advice* and consent of the Senate." On 9 March 1949, Acheson concluded that "all debris had been cleared away," and senators were ready to ratify.[12]

Moscow began blustering about the same time, flaying the pact in notes to western ministries as a violation of the UN Charter, Yalta and Potsdam agreements, and existing Soviet treaties with Britain and France. It uselessly withdrew from the World Health Organization, closed consulates in Italy and Iran, clamped down on lingering exports of chrome and manganese to the United States, accused U.S. reporters of espionage, and jammed Voice of America (VOA) broadcasts. Accusing Washington of Nazi-like aggression, *Pravda* said a Soviet military buildup would answer its "sabre rattling." Soviet troops maneuvered along the Norwegian, Yugoslav, and Iranian borders, and state department analysts saw a "remote possibility" of a coup against Finland. But violence remained confined to rhetoric. Stalin personally was apparently indifferent to what he took as a toothless league, probably understanding its defensive character and lack of threat to the USSR.[13]

To prepare the public and foreclose further dithering among the allies, the U.S. government released the treaty text on 18 March. In press conference and radio broadcast, Acheson underlined the pact's capacity to improve western morale and military strength. Rather than distinguishing between the legal and moral commitments established by the treaty, he insisted they were equivalent. He allayed concerns that the alliance would enlarge incidents into wars with the remark, "You don't take a sledge hammer to kill a fly," but he also held that the treaty probably covered internal subversion. As to complaints that treaty makers had overlooked the UN, he blamed Moscow for its ineffectiveness. Mixing realpolitik and idealism, he said the treaty would prevent "a single aggressive, unfriendly power" from controlling Europe and would defend "western civilization." With fingers crossed, he claimed Article 2 would spread "tolerance, restraint, and freedom." Alluding to those not included in the pact, he warned that the United States would be concerned about threats to the peace wherever they occurred but with equal emphasis declared NATO's purposes pacific: democracies did not "plan aggressive wars." The people, he urged, should be patient and realistic, for making a stable peace would be a "continuous and hard" effort.[14]

The signing ceremony came on "a bright and pleasant spring day" in Washington, 4 April 1949. Truman, who believed "there would have been no NATO" without him, insisted that Acheson sign for the United States. The marine band struck up appropriate refrains from *Porgy and Bess*, including "Bess, you is my women now" and, apropos NATO's actual armed strength, "I've Got Plenty of Nothin." Asked what language foreign ministers would use in their brief statements, Pearson offered, "North American English with a French accent." Acheson rode back to Foggy Bottom with Hickerson, remarking: "Well, Jack, I think this treaty is going to work. If it works, for generations there will be arguments in the United States as to who more than anybody else is responsible for it, but if it doesn't work, there will be no damn doubt, you did it."

What he meant by "working" did not then encompass what lay in the near future, for Washington in 1949 thought money and arms would be the main U.S. contribution to defending western Europe. Ultimately, NATO became the chief western bulwark against the Soviet Union and communism. NATO, with the European Coal and Steel Community, would supply the institutions making possible a Franco-German rapprochement and help prevent the rise of a new fascist or *revanchist* German government. The alliance also did much to force Britain against all its instincts to continuous involvement with the continent. And it was the emblem for Americans' molting of the consolations of isolationism.[15]

A Divided Germany in a Divided Europe

With the London Program, the western allies had acted to reduce the humiliations of occupation and prepare the western zones of Germany for rebirth as a new and almost fully sovereign state. Signs were not all auspicious, however. Early in 1949, the German economic recovery had stalled, and, with the blockade still under way, the allies wrangled over dismantling industries of the former *Reich*. Washington wanted a halt to tearing down German factories and for the Germans to sustain themselves without heavy reliance on U.S. taxes. "We were voting money to go into Germany to help to build it up," one official recalled, while the British and French "were taking machinery out." The French, said another, wanted "every brick, every place, torn down and powdered into dust." With one eye on future German commercial competition and the other glancing covetously on the dismantled equipment, Paris and London found Washington's newfound beneficence irritating.

When Acheson took office, the American with the most decided ideas about Germany's future was Kennan. In September 1948, he had asked citizen Acheson to join department talks on a new Kennan plan. According to what came to be called Program or Plan "A," all foreign forces would withdraw from a reunified Germany as a way to get the Soviets to evacuate central Europe. The State hierarchy did not support the idea, because it risked loss of western control over the former Nazi state. Acheson, however, had few independent thoughts about Germany and was intrigued. He would not definitively abandon "A" until May 1949.[16]

A few large points about German policy were already clear. The Truman administration had already reversed FDR's expectation that the United States would only temporarily stay in Europe after the war. It had decided western European economic recovery would fail without a strong German contribution. Unlike in the 1920s, the United States would act to prevent this war-prone state from wrecking the international order. Recalling Soviet-German pacts of 1922 (Rapallo) and 1939 (Hitler-Stalin), U.S. officials were determined to block another such pact by integrating Germany's western zones within a web of transatlantic institutions spun under American leadership. What all this meant in detail was yet unclear. Acheson understood that thinking of Europe "without a Germany is to think about a body without a heart," but the awkwardness with which Washington approached Germany in the spring of 1949 mocks any picture of a conscious process of empire building in Europe. Stalin, too, was less clear-sighted than once thought, but, as Norman M. Naimark writes, the Soviets and their own German accessories already planned the "permanent Sovietization" of the east. Stalin was not likely to reverse this process. Without definitively admitting the fact, both east and west were finding advantage for themselves in splitting Hitler's state.[17]

A meeting of the Council of Foreign Ministers (CFM) in Paris, the price paid for ending the Berlin blockade, compelled the state department to clarify U.S. intentions in Germany. If haltingly, it first opted for integration over punishment, as Washington was also doing in Japan and Italy. It was better to discard wartime passions to enlist the help of former enemies against a new adversary. By 1949, policymakers had completely rejected the "Morgenthau Plan," the former treasury secretary's design to strip Germany of its industrial power. American officials had concluded, without publicly advertising the fact, that a divided Germany best served U.S. and west European security. They would still talk of reunification to placate German public opinion, but "as long as the continent remained cut in two," Bohlen told Bonnet, allowing a reunified Germany was "inconceivable." Behind this view was the fear—not apparently shared by Kennan—either that a reunified Germany would again march against both the east and west or drift into the Soviet orbit, tipping the balance of power against the west. Acheson was in the course of discovering—as had Marshall—that a divided Germany looked better than any other outcome.[18]

His path to a clear point of view was angular. He listened to everybody and read their papers. In 1946, he had hoped to prevent a rupture of the wartime alliance over Germany. Without drawing conclusions about the nation's future, in 1947 he favored enlisting its industry to restart the European economy. Examining Plan A in 1948, he reacted positively to Soviet interest in discussing Germany anew. In 1949 he would abandon that view. His 1953 recollection that the Soviets were planning a giant "pincer movement" from Iran to Germany was more dramatic than his occasionally muddled contemporary impressions. An even later recollection about fearing a revived German "nationalism," however, matched what he actually thought in 1949, one reason he remained provisionally open to negotiating the issue with Moscow.[19]

Just as Acheson was taking office, Stalin hinted he was ready to end the blockade in exchange for a new session of the CFM. With East Germany bleeding from the western counterblockade, he turned from driving West Berlin's protectors out of the city to blocking a new West German state. Philip Jessup from the UN delegation was soon holding secret parlays with the Soviets' Jacob Malik. By March, with American confidence growing that Stalin played a weak hand, Bohlen advised rejecting any offers of "olive leaves" that had "hooks" in them, James Webb pushed for protecting the U.S. "position of advantage," and Jessup himself wanted to lead "from strength."

Acheson detailed Jessup's negotiations with British foreign minister Ernest Bevin and his French counterpart Robert Schuman on their arrival in Washington to finish the NATO discussions. He had never met either man and took immediately to both. Bevin seemed a little rattled, suspicious of Stalin, and wary of a new CFM. Eager to snatch the peace issue from Moscow, Acheson reminded him they had already agreed to a conference if the blockade ended. That Stalin was promising to lift the blockade beforehand demonstrated his diminishing bargaining power. On 4 May, agreement was reached to lift the blockade and schedule a CFM meeting in Paris later in the month. Although he was clear in his mind that Stalin acted from weakness, Acheson was still far from clear about a German strategy. Straight out of Plan A, he had talked to Bevin about relaxing "the Berlin situation" through "a sort of peripheral withdrawal from Germany."[20]

With his own views still unsettled, Acheson found it frustrating to discover three different departmental offices wrangling over the German issue. It was "a mess," he told James Reston. Some officials wanted to put down the Germans, others to accommodate them, yet others, somehow, both. Fearing they might yet slalom out of control, Kennan after an inspection trip fretted about the mismatch between Germans' national and democratic values. In 1945, Washington had signed on to a "four D's" policy—Denazification, Demilitarization, Decentralization, and Decartelization—but by 1949 had largely backed away from all but demilitarization. The intrusive denazification campaign aroused nationalist resentment, and decartelization (or dismantlement) looked both economically and politically unwise. In 1950, the commitment to demilitarization would also flag.[21]

The Americans wanted to dismantle dismantlement because it burdened the German economy, thus increasing the drain on the U.S. treasury, retarding the effects of the Marshall Plan, and slowing European economic recovery. Britain and France, however wanted to keep Germany denatured and protect their own industries; they especially wanted permanent limits on German steel production. French obstructionism seemed especially irritating to the United States, and General Lucius Clay, heading the U.S. occupation authority, thought Paris was deliberately trying to "retard German recovery" at American expense. In March, Acheson informed the French government that Americans would tolerate limiting only industries essential for war making. And he told Bevin that if the British were so worried the Soviets would overrun or co-opt Germany, his country should stop hampering the revival of "German life." Ambassador Lewis Douglas in London was supposed to lead the way in negotiating an end to dismantlement, but he was unable to find agreement. This left it to Acheson, whose long-term views were still in flux, to find a settlement when Schuman and Bevin came to Washington. Hoping for a reasonable compromise, he urged the army to silence its anti-French tirades. He asked Kennan, as chair of an NSC "steering group," to come up with a clearer strategy for him within two weeks.[22]

This returned the "A" plan to center stage. Kennan disliked how Washington clung to the London Program—"like a mother to a child"—because it lent plausibility to Moscow's cynical claims of western encirclement and, thus, powered its instinct for repression. Until free elections reestablished a united nation, he wanted foreign troops to leave all of central Europe except small watchdog forces garrisoned in enclaves just inside Germany's borders. Department critics were certain this would produce a dangerously powerful and unrestrained state. They were far more comfortable sticking to the idea of a separate West German state. Trying to meet such criticisms, Kennan muddied his own proposals, insisting they would not permit Germany to reemerge as an independent military power and positing some kind of European union as a precondition for reunification. But he did not want Washington meddling in the process, preferring a restrained, even passive U.S. role on all European issues.[23]

A unified allied posture on Germany grew more elusive as it became more important. One reason was the increasingly murky thinking on Germany in the state department. Acheson's frustration mounted as he waded through "reams and reams of paper" displaying the precious erudition of "extreme experts on a small sub-division of one small problem." He knew none of it would help him make specific decisions. Treading water, he pondered whether he was dealing with the Germans who were the cosmopolitan soul-descendants of Goethe or Wagner's nationalist offspring. In either case, he was not inclined, a là Kennan, to voluntarily relinquish the western hold on Germany. Probably trying to let Kennan down easily, in early March, he claimed to regret the breakdown of four-power concord on Germany and said he "he was sorry" to learn that Kennan, too, now accepted the idea of a West German state. In fact, he no longer saw how Kennan's ideas could work. Acting director of the office of German and Austrian affairs, Robert D. Murphy, just returned from Germany, where had had advised Clay, reminded Acheson of Marshall's strong backing of the London Program. Acheson decided to send Kennan to Germany for a firsthand look but have Murphy run the steering group. He thereby tacitly gave up on reunification. He still worried, however, how to reply should Moscow at the CFM propose something resembling Plan A. He would keep his mind open until Kennan's return.[24]

In Kennan's absence, Acheson warned his assistants he "knew very little about Germany and wanted to make sure he was carefully briefed." Murphy leapt into this breach with a 10,000-word memorandum. General Eisenhower's political adviser in the war, the fifty-four-year-old Murphy, who had been in the foreign service since the twenties, agreed with Kennan on many points. A Franco-German rapprochement could supply the needed pan-European frame-work both he and Kennan wanted as the basis for creating a German state. A "partial" Germany, Murphy advised Acheson, would better serve western inter-ests than a united Germany of "uncertain orientation" and vulnerable to Soviet control. If prospering, it would also cause grief for the Russians in their eastern European empire. Thus, in Murphy's view, Washington should use its "nego-tiating power" to gain "the predominant voice" on German issues. It should take the lead in blocking any effort at the CFM to frustrate the London Program. Assuming a Soviet rejection of a chance to join the Program, Acheson should seek "a *modus vivendi*" allowing two Germanys to coexist and trade with one another. Plan A, he contended, driving a stake through its heart, would "provide a fertile field for the rebirth of aggressive German nationalism and permit a rapproche-ment with the Soviet bloc." Dangling "between East and West," Germans might revert from habit to "extreme authoritarian rule," which was the "heart of the German problem." This paper moved Acheson farther down the road to a separate west German state, but not all the way. His vacillations were not over.[25]

Acheson's conversion to a cold war stand on the USSR was now nearly three years past, but he had not quite yet reached the conviction that the United States held the higher hand in the cold war and should use its superiority to push the Soviets even harder rather than to find agreement with them. This transitional state accounts for a kind of temporizing on Germany. What he *was* clear about already, as were Kennan (returned from his tour) and Murphy, was the need to conciliate "good" Germans by preemptively closing down the occupation (with-out a complete withdrawal of troops) instead of doing so later under pressure. On 31 March, Acheson took these and other ideas to Truman. He gained the presi-dent's approval to work for a simpler and less restrictive occupation regime and to take the next steps in establishing a new West German government, overseen by a civilian "Allied High Commission" that would still exercise some "reserved" powers. If Acheson could gain Big Three unity on these terms before the CFM, the allies might hazard negotiating different arrangements with the Soviets should it seem advisable. Yet even as he acquired Truman's endorsement of this approach, Acheson was having his conversation with Bevin about a "peripheral withdrawal from Germany." In fact, Acheson felt rushed to judgment—partly by the army's eagerness to shed the burden of occupation—and had not wanted to meet Bevin and Schuman so early. What he considered premature discussions with Bevin and Schuman would short-circuit his chance to find fresh ideas for any possible four-power concord.[26]

Worries about the popular mood in Germany complicated deliberations. Clay's new adviser, James Riddleberger, reported successful communist exploitation of nationalist and neutralist moods and blamed western indecision for this "political deterioration." Moved by this urgent mood, Acheson, Bevin, and Schuman discarded all their experts' technical papers and, at Acheson's insistence, focused on essentials. The "Washington Agreements" resulted, modifying the London Program and simplifying occupation rules. The three foreign ministers agreed to jettison dozens of "reserved" powers but retain overall "supreme authority" and first responsibility over "select" areas, a euphemism for foreign policy and war crimes. At the CFM, they would invite Moscow to accept the same formula for the eastern zone. Acheson thought he and his partners had produced "almost prodigies of agreement," and on 7 April, a cheerful Bevin praised him to the president. But Germans were angry about the reserved powers. So was Clay, about to give way to a civilian high commissioner. Acheson had wanted to go even further but accepted compromises in the name of unity. With the Marshall Plan, NATO, and Washington Agreements, he claimed, the west had successfully substituted strength for weakness.[27]

Germany now became a state department show. John J. McCloy left the World Bank to become high commissioner and to administer Germany's ECA funding. The fifty-four-year-old World War I infantry veteran accepted the position after Truman agreed he could have direct access to the White House. Acheson's and McCloy's careers had recently moved in parallel. McCloy entered government service in 1940 after a fabled career in finance. A few months before Acheson joined State under Cordell Hull, McCloy started working for Henry Stimson in the war department (acquiring a fierce wish to punish Germany). Acheson treasured McCloy, a classmate at Harvard Law and old fishing partner, and expected him to have the vitality necessary for his new assignment: "He never tires, never flags. His mind stays fresh, imaginative, and vigorous throughout a whole night of complex negotiation. Physically he bounces. Jack McCloy has been known to wear to tatters two pairs of socks during a tennis match." His posting, remarked a Foggy Bottom official, "heralded the beginning of a restoration of true diplomatic relations with a truly independent West Germany."[28]

Preparing for the CFM

Some pessimism crept into allied ranks despite McCloy's bounce. West German socialists were thinking they could get better terms. With Chiang Kai-shek's Chinese government collapsing, Bevin wanted "Bonn in his pocket" before talking to the Russians and thought Jessup's blockade negotiations "dangerous." Acheson went into deep submersion to prepare for his first meeting as secretary with the Soviets. In the six weeks before the Paris sessions convened on 23 May, he spent many evenings in solitary study. He also worked intensively with advisers (eight times between 5 and 16 May), often into the night. It was like getting ready for a Supreme Court plea. Truman offered no personal advice and, had it not been for Acheson, would have been singularly uninformed about Germany. Assiduously, Acheson tried to correct this, sitting down with the president through seventeen meetings and at least five telephone conversations about Germany. He also sent flurries of messages across the Atlantic. Kennan played little role and did not attend the Paris conference. Nonetheless, with Acheson still occasionally feeling "all confused about the German business," as late as mid-April echoes of Program A bounced off his office walls. Increasingly, however, he saw the advantages of a separate west German state dependent on the United States. Keeping it "split," said Jessup, would contain its potential for mischief. The industries of the Ruhr basin would add to the sum of western power in checking the Soviets.[29]

The U.S. goal in Germany, Acheson said in a radio broadcast, was a nation "integrated into a new common structure of the free peoples of Europe." Though a four-power accord on a unified Germany was welcome, the United States would not wait indefinitely for it. He also condemned Moscow's continuing efforts to paralyze Europe by blocking any German solution not guaranteeing "virtual Soviet control." Columnist Anne O'Hare McCormick speculated that Acheson could speak "with such authority and confidence" only because the Big Three were already agreed. On which he might have commented, "I only *wish*." The situation was still fluid. A worried Bevin cabled that Stalin still aimed at "a heavily centralised totalitarian state, controlled by the Communists," with its economy piped into that of the Soviet Union and its satellites.[30]

In ending the Berlin blockade, Stalin was tacitly admitting he could not block the London Program. On 8 May, the western military governors and a West German parliamentary council approved the Basic Law[31] establishing the Federal Republic of Germany (FRG). The U.S. chargé in Moscow gleefully listed all the problems the Kremlin now faced, from a defiant Yugoslavia to another possible "Tito" in China. Now the new FRG might shake Stalin's control in East Germany. But, he added, he might yet turn the tables on the west. A show of conciliation in Paris might divide the allies, "disorient" public opinion, and kill popular willingness to proceed with NATO and plans for "military preparedness." Amid the uncertainty, Acheson, partly because of Jessup's urging, was still open to Kennan's ideas and in effect still considering both *x* and *non-x*—full integration of the FRG into the western orbit versus restoration of a united Germany. Early in May, State sent a Kennan-like outline to the Pentagon, which responded sharply. Clay lashed at it as "suicidal to our objectives." Program A's ninth life was near its end, despite Kennan's renewed efforts to promote it and Acheson's tenacious sympathies.[32]

On 11 May, just as Stalin pulled down the barriers around West Berlin, Acheson sent a White House-approved sketch of his current thinking to Bevin and Schuman. Most of its contents were unremarkable, including Acheson's lack of reverence for the idea of German reunification. While a true European peace would ultimately require pulling Soviet troops behind the Russian marshes, people should not hold their breath waiting for this event—or remove western forces to accomplish it. The removal of all troops from Germany would be tantamount to relinquishing hopes of adding West German to west European strength. Alluding to Kennan's thinking, he remarked that only if Moscow agreed to move its armies out of eastern Europe altogether would he consider redirecting allied forces from Germany's center to its port cities. He would always be willing to compromise on the margin but not make concessions from fear or domestic criticism. Nor were any concessions dependent on "Soviet goodwill" reliable. The best outcome in Paris might be a modest modus vivendi on Germany and Berlin. But he also accompanied his message with instructions to Jessup and Bohlen, about to embark for preparatory meetings, to tell the allies that "Program A" was still worth discussion.[33]

Kennan's plan did not have *ten* lives. On 12 May, the press leak of a simplified version of Plan A, underscoring withdrawal of U.S. forces from Europe, killed it. Reston published the story, probably getting his information from the Pentagon or an opponent of Kennan's views at Foggy Bottom. Already abroad, Bohlen reported the leak had raised "a good deal of hell in Europe." Shocked Europeans who thought NATO meant an end to American isolationism wondered if they had been scammed. Jessup tried extinguishing the fury with denials Washington had ever endorsed Kennan's plan. The Pentagon pointed out that a "mutual withdrawal" meant Moscow would retreat 300 miles but Washington up to 3,000. It also opposed regrouping troops within Germany. In assailing the plan on the 14th, new defense secretary Louis Johnson quoted JCS Chairman Omar Bradley. Defending western Europe, Bradley held, required U.S. troops to be near the site of a likely Russian attack, not hanging on the continent by their fingernails where Soviet columns could push them into the sea. The Germans would "throw up their hands and quit," Clay cabled, if the west adopted Kennan's plan. In Kennan's own words, the leak had administered his plan a "spectacular *coup de grace*" and brought Acheson's flirtation to a full stop.

Besides ending his own irresolution, the uproar took Acheson off the hook. Now he kept his eyes on the main prize, West Germany. With Russia no longer contained by Germany and Japan, he hypothesized to senators, NATO might some day need to add West Germany to reestablish a military balance of power. This speculation was part of a series of briefings on the CFM for Truman and reporters as well as senators. At best, he told these various parties, the conference would produce "propaganda exchanges" and, perhaps, new deputies' committees for any follow-up negotiations. The Soviets would probably try to score propaganda points in Paris but do nothing risking their grip on East Germany. In turn, the west should keep its gains in West Germany. The creation of a "strong West German government" would have to precede any regrouping of troops. And any future reunification would have to be an extension of the fait accompli of the Big Three in West Germany. He told the NSC to stay out of his hair while he was in Paris.[34]

Acheson's public statements usually closely followed what he said in private. If the Russians did nothing but spout propaganda in Paris, he told a few regular reporters in an off-the-record session, his delegation would simply demonstrate to world opinion the futility of trying to talk to them and then "pack up our marbles and come home." Washington would go "full steam" ahead with the new West German government "come hell or high water." It would insulate the FRG from the Soviets' eastern "stooges," keep troops around as long as needed, and demand stout preconditions for reunification, which he did not consider an "end in itself." If reunification meant pushing "freedom as far east as possible," then "fine; if not, to hell with it." Only agreements that *confirmed* "an existing situation" were worth negotiating. He told senators virtually the same on 19 May 1949, emphasizing the difficulty of ever achieving a stable Europe "with Russian troops 100 miles from Hamburg." He also rejected notions of recreating a German army as "quite insane" and "colossally foolish."[35]

The prospect of a long struggle with the Soviets did not particularly bother Acheson. He had recently warned the public the contest would not lift like a headache because its causes were not "removable." They were "manageable." Some senators yearned for more optimism, hoping Acheson could locate and press the cold war's STOP button. When Vandenberg realized instead that he *intended* to elicit negative responses from the Soviets, he asked if this meant that for "all intents and purposes that there is a permanent cold war." Acheson demurred at "permanent" and suggested that one could "get further" toward a cold war settlement after the west developed "more strength." The Michigan senator mused to reporters: "One thing is sure—if there ever was any suspicion about his being pro-Russian it is all different now. As a matter of fact he is so *totally* anti-Soviet and is going to be so *completely* tough that I really doubt whether there is any chance *at all* for a Paris agreement."[36]

Until the moment he flew to Europe, Acheson was receiving last-minute reports and recommendations. Jessup's preparatory group agreed to feel out the Russians before revealing western conditions for "German unity." Kennan sent a last-ditch threnody on Program A's fate, grumbling that the "logic" of his program was "broken" and warning that "some day" the United States would "pay bitterly" for not making getting "the Russians out of the Eastern Zone" its first priority. As he often did when he failed to get his way, he now wanted the United States to drop the whole business. Let the Europeans handle Germany on their own. Acheson appeared to ignore the memo but probably not its tone.[37]

Paris: "All Fleas and No Dog"

Acheson's ultimate rejection of Plan A is doubly significant. What is obvious— that it took him some time to square away his thinking about Germany—is certainly important. Far more so, however, is that his eventual decision marked a further evolution of his approach to the cold war. In 1946, over Turkey, he abandoned assumptions about working with the Soviets for a hard line against them. Now, because of his deep immersion in the German issue (and his nego- tiating experience to come in Paris), he moved further. He rejected Kennan's preference for chancy diplomatic maneuvers. Implicitly, he even rejected his notions of "containment." Instead, he decided that *strength*—of all varieties, moral, political, economic, and military—was the key to winning the cold war. He wanted the west not just to be strong enough to hold off the Soviets but to achieve paramount power. Because of such strength, whenever it occurred, the cold war would end on western terms, not through negotiations, but because the Soviets finally acknowledged, recognized, and decided to live with what the United States and its allies had wrought.

In May 1949, as the U.S. party flew across the Atlantic on Truman's DC-6, *Independence*, Acheson was probably as unsettled as anyone on board. However remote the chance, if the Soviets offered to unify and neutralize Germany, all Washington's actions in Europe since the Truman Doctrine could be imperiled. As Melvyn P. Leffler writes, a unified Germany "might maneuver between East and West," working each against the other in a "scheme to gain its preponderant position." It might even join the anti-western bloc. Even Kennan would say in June that if Germany and Russia ever arranged "a happy marriage," the United States "might as well fold up." Acheson also had worries about British resolve. Bevin might still covet a chance to mediate between the Americans and the Russians. As it turned out, he opted forthrightly for western cohesion in reaction to what Paul Nitze called Soviet Foreign Minister Andrei Vyshinsky's "extreme, assertive, and nasty" polemics, which produced a profound revulsion in all three western delegations. When Acheson went to the Paris talks, it was his first visit to Europe in eleven years. When he left, he was convinced east-west talks would accomplish nothing and that it was vital to keep West Germany on the side of the west.[38]

In the City of Light, Acheson, along with U.S. delegate John Foster Dulles and Luke Battle, enjoyed the hospitality of the U.S. embassy, hosted by Ambassador David K. E. Bruce, formerly Marshall Plan administrator in France. First came two days of intensive talks with Schuman and Bevin. Quarrels would sporadically sour allied relations while Acheson was secretary of state, especially when the British or French felt acutely dependent on the Americans. But more often, allied foreign ministers would trust and rely on Acheson, who came to symbolize for them Washington's commitment to defend Europe. He embodied the U.S. willingness to link its interests to those of its European allies. They drew courage from his aplomb and intellectual verve. They knew he spoke for Truman and that he would defend strong transatlantic ties to Congress and the American people. The western European nations joined Acheson's long list of satisfied clients, impressed by his candor and freedom from personal or national pride. He tactfully muffled disputes between France and the UK and rarely took sides between them. Seeing Europe's problems through a strategic vision, he strove to end the cycles of wars that threatened U.S. security and to use new institutions to transform old enemies into associates in the conflict with the USSR. "His sense of gravity" while "dealing with other nations," writes David McLellan, "inspired his highest skills and instincts." Though ready to act alone, he knew that quarterbacks with blockers won more games than those who scrambled on their own.[39]

Acheson once told Nitze, "We must talk to people outside the United States to clarify our own mind, and only the British are intellectually close enough to us to fulfill this function." One of Bevin's successors, Sir Anthony Eden, offered Acheson the ultimate compliment: "I would never hesitate," he wrote, "to go tiger-hunting with him." His 1949 partners tapped deeply into Acheson's pleasure in friendship with other accomplished men. Bevin, who had disliked Jimmy Byrnes and found George Marshall forbidding, grew fond of their successor. Now sixty-eight, the orphaned son of an unknown father and servant mother, Bevin had started as a truck driver before becoming a renowned trade union leader. Short, beefy, with "streaked black and white hair," he had a flattened nose, fleshy lips, and piercing eyes behind horn-rimmed glasses. Overweight with a short neck "not naturally adapted to star-gazing," he rolled rather than walked. He ignored the chain of ailments that soon killed him—"angina pectoris, cardiac failure, arteriosclerosis, sinusitis, enlarged liver, damaged kidneys, high blood pressure"—slept little and poorly, shunned exercise, and zestfully smoked, ate, and drank everything forbidden by his doctors, one of whom found "not a sound organ in his body, apart from his feet." Acheson thought his physique matched "his inside—he was solid, squared away to the world, somewhat pugnacious, powerful, slow. He had the general good nature of a man of his build, with curious flashes of temper and anger, which would flare up with quite a good deal of violence, and then disappear." Prime Minister Clement Attlee gave him as much room to act on his own as foreign secretary as cabinet government allows. Truman disliked him, an "English John L. Lewis." He thought he lacked couth and resented Bevin's past accusations that Truman had played politics over Israel. But Acheson thought they were kindred types, both self-educated and omnivorous readers. Bevin last sat at a school desk at ten but had a corner on "the market for common sense." Acheson admired his energy and sense of honor. Bevin "was an earthy, vigorous, strong, affectionate person, that you just had to like, and he stood with you," a "great person." Sure of his values, deeply immersed in British history, he "knew his mind" but was "subject to education" and willing to compromise. "Ernie" and "Me lad" became chums. When congressional Republicans demanded Acheson's head in 1950, "Ernie" bucked him up: "Don't give it a thought, me lad. If those blokes don't want yer, there's plenty as does."[40]

The "Mr. Acheson—M. Schuman" connection was not anything like "Ernie" and "Me lad," for only in his capacity for warm affection was the sixty-three-year-old Schuman like Bevin. Acheson described this tall, bald, stooped, long-nosed, soft-spoken foreign minister as "shy, ascetic," and "very solitary." He had a "habit of sinking chin in collar to peer over the top of his spectacles." Unlike the bawdy Bevin, his sense of humor was "almost furtive." He was "formal, dignified, and gravely courteous." A prime minister in 1947–48 (Acheson sometimes called him "M. le President"), he worked hard to learn English and eventually handled it on his own in informal settings but usually relied on interpreters in official meetings. Born in Luxembourg, educated in Alsace, he soldiered under the German flag in World War I. Technically becoming "French" only at thirty-two, he was not a nationalist; in conversation, he called the French "they." Like Abraham Lincoln from the borderlands, he believed in union and "in reconciliation after strife." Different intellectual styles sometimes complicated the Acheson-Schuman tie, as did France's shaky coalition governments and the refractory French foreign office, which required Schuman constantly "to watch his flanks and rear and his communications with Paris." But Acheson almost thought of Bevin and Schuman as one. They had both emerged from Europe's "tragic" century and agreed on "the menace of communism" and Soviet "imperialism." Both wanted a transatlantic alliance to "maintain a balance of power and, with it, peace."[41]

In one of his recurrent appearances at the National War College, Acheson remarked on the need to "respect our opponents" and remember "for a long, long period of time they will continue to believe as they do." The Soviet delegate in Paris was not likely to inspire such respect. Short like Bevin but slenderer, the sixty-six-year-old, Polish-born Vyshinsky had begun his career in the law. A Menshevik at the time of the Soviet revolution, he became an arrow in Stalin's quiver but never part of his inner circle. Vyshinsky had been recruited by Stalin from the middle class, and Georges Bidault of France commented, "every day he made up with his zeal for his unworthy origins." From chief prosecutor in the purge trials of 1936–38, he became deputy foreign minister and then foreign minister before Vyacheslav Molotov returned to that post in 1953. "High-coloured, voluble and satanic-looking," Vyshinsky punctuated a genial and unpolemical mien with staccato bursts of propaganda. Acheson compared him to "a criminal lawyer who gets hired by a gang to spring them after they have been arrested" but found his witty tongue an intermittent source of amusement. "Unscrupulous," he did not "really believe the Soviet line in diplomacy." A "natural blackguard," he was "cultivated and amusing"—and "vain." He was far less adroit than Acheson had anticipated. Though "a master of vindictive denigration," he was predictable, "long-winded and boring."[42]

The western foreign ministers reviewed their positions and tactics before meeting Vyshinsky. Already in harmony on essentials, they agreed on steps to stimulate the FRG economy and on parrying any effort by Vyshinsky to seize a share of the Ruhr's riches. They united on the German-Polish border, on still divided Austria, and, should there be no larger agreement forthcoming, on elements of a four-power modus vivendi. They did *not* reach full accord about troops, for even now Acheson was a carrier of Kennan's virus. While his partners worried about any reduction of western forces, he countered that they could not keep them there forever and would eventually have to offer incentives for a Soviet withdrawal. His hopes of a mutual withdrawal faded, however, when Bohlen repeated the Soviet high commissioner's remark that the Russians would hang on to their garrison, since "the Germans hate us."[43]

The conference convened just as the FRG's "Basic Law" went into effect. Formal sessions were held in the Grand Salon of the Palais Rose, a pink-pilastered Edwardian mansion. The ministers could gaze at the ceiling, where "satyrs pursued nymphs through clouds without gaining on them even through the double translation of Vishinsky's longest speeches." Or they could gaze at the gardens, which "soothed and refreshed spirits tortured by the excruciating boredom" inflicted by the repetitious meetings. Beginning in mid-afternoon, sessions regularly lasted into early morning hours. Surrounding each foreign minister were aides who looked, recalled one, "as though butter would not melt in their mouths." Throngs of officials balanced "papers on their knees." On 24 May, Vyshinsky proposed achieving German reunification through a revived Allied Control Council and restoring four-power rule of Berlin using the military committee called the *Kommandatura*. He wanted new reparations deliveries and partial control of the Ruhr basin. The Big Three promptly denounced such attempts to turn the clock back to a system, Acheson retorted, that had "failed so disastrously in the past." Nor would they allow the poverty of the Soviet-controlled zone to dilute West German recovery, which, Acheson cracked, would be like "asking a paralyzed person who was three-quarters recovered to go back to complete paralysis." Though he told Truman it had been a "completely sterile" session, American reporters detected a western propaganda victory. Acheson had put the onus of a divided Germany squarely on Soviet shoulders. As the westerners proposed expansion of Germany's freedom, Vyshinsky sought to return it to its blackest moment of defeat. Acheson quickly concluded the Soviets were intent to offer only Potsdam redux. "Almost with a swagger," said the *Times*, he drew sharp lines between western openness and Soviet concealment. Truman told the cabinet: "It looks like Dean has got Mr. Vyshinsky on the run."[44]

Bevin's many years as a union leader had bred bottomless distrust of communists of any variety, especially after their cynical actions in the Spanish civil war. They were like breakaway trade unionists, whom he hated almost as much. On Saturday, 28 May, he presented the west's counterproposal: no more Soviet reparations and no more Soviet-run companies. East Germany could be absorbed within Bonn's constitution, reunifying society and state, currency and economic life, everything to be confirmed in free elections with only Nazis ineligible to participate. Remaining four-power controls would be exercised through majority rather than unanimous votes. Vyshinsky genially promised to study the allied document. Based on intelligence sources, however, Acheson expected a rejection, which Vyshinsky confirmed at the beginning of the second week when he denounced the Basic Law as a western-dictated, "secret, undemocratic document." Acheson cabled home that Moscow was uninterested in reunification and probably hoped only for a modus vivendi to "increase east-west trade."[45]

Reducing the number of people in the conference room—Acheson's suggestion—improved nothing. Bevin urged meeting both in the mornings and afternoons, to which the Russian countered, what about afternoons and evenings? Bevin retorted that Vyshinsky obviously never slept if his long-winded speeches were to be trusted. When Vyshinsky replied that at least he "did not sleep during the meetings," Bevin urged him to try it as "a very restful practice." Stalemated on 4 June, the allies tried drawing Vyshinsky out at dinner, only to have him say the food "was too good to be spoiled by business talk." Meanwhile, Acheson was scoring points in the press at home, called the conference's "dominant figure" by Anne O'Hare McCormick, but with no sign of a breakthrough, the *Times* on 5 June shifted the daily CFM story to the left side of its front page.[46]

As the conference plodded toward its inconclusive end, Canadian observers described Acheson as the west's leader. Heartened by the Senate Foreign Relations Committee's unanimous vote for NATO, he looked for ways to end the conference. When Vyshinsky applauded an agreement on the innocuous first and last paragraphs of the U.S. proposal on Berlin but approved none of the ten interceding paragraphs, Acheson quipped, "it was like agreeing on the whiskers and the tail of some creature without knowing whether we had an animal, a fish, or a bird in between." Futile arguments about currency convinced him that "fear of a united Germany" lay at the bottom of Vyshinsky's tactics. The more fearful the Soviets seemed, the more the Americans' assurance mounted. On 10 June, Vyshinsky abandoned any pretense at negotiations in favor of a wave of propaganda broadsides. With slightly less heat, the Big Three responded in kind. Acheson urged that deputies work on Germany while the principals looked for an escape from the occupation and division of Austria. These talks failed, too. His efforts to find a modus vivendi on east-west trade or stabilized four-power control of Berlin also collapsed. The Russians, he wired the president, would remain unbending about the east but had surrendered hope for influence in the west. At the most, he thought Vyshinsky wanted to avoid isolating the Soviet Union altogether through a breakdown in relations.[47]

Two barren meetings on 12 June 1949 left Acheson irritated "almost beyond the bounds of passion." With an act of will, he controlled his temper, despite feeling his "blood going up the back" of his neck. Sick of Vyshinsky's proverbs, he started inventing his own, usually claiming Indian tribal tradition for inspiration. In one case, he remarked that "to use an old Indian expression," the Soviet proposal for a German peace treaty was "as full of propaganda as a dog is of fleas, though in this case it was all fleas and no dog." This led quickly to farce:

> Vyshinsky: "Well, I am now quoting the scriptures, and 'one must not try to catch fleas, lest a camel slip through your fingers.'"
> Bevin: "You are quoting what?"
> Vyshinsky: "That's in the Scriptures."
> Bevin: "It's not in the King James version of the Scriptures."
> Vyshinsky: "Oh no, our Scriptures were written by Saint Vladimir."

As they laughingly debated St. Vladimir's knowledge of fleas, translators in three languages scurried to keep up. Vyshinsky, Acheson decided, knew he was "in bad shape." The Russian's unbending proposals also dashed brief hopes for an Austrian settlement and German modus vivendi. Real security against a new crisis, Acheson cabled Webb at midnight of the 14th, lay not in the Paris or other talks, but in NATO and the Mutual Defense Assistance Program (MDAP) that would accompany it. "An illusory agreement" would be "worse than none." Satisfied with Acheson's work, Truman let it go at that.[48]

The conferees in rushing to adjourn agreed to maintain the status quo on the blockade, vaguely talked about a new CFM conclave without scheduling one, and named committees to work on language of an Austrian peace treaty. They had already reached accord on Austria's boundaries, protection of Slovene and Croat minorities, and a waiver on war reparations. At home, Webb was unhappy with some of Acheson's concessions on Austria, raising the secretary's hackles by comparing them to FDR's bargain on China at Yalta. Later events justified Webb's skepticism. Soviet obstructionism mounted, probably spurred by resentment of western gains in Germany and distrust of Tito. When Stalin died, the powers quickly reached an Austrian peace treaty, concluded in 1955.

On 20 June 1949, the last day of the conference, delegates exchanged a "round of compliments," marveled yet again at the decorations of the Palais de Marbre Rose, blinked at the photographers' flashbulbs, "drank a last glass of champagne" and parted, "hoping," Acheson later wrote, "not to meet again soon." By midnight, the Americans were over the Atlantic in the *Independence*.[49]

Appraising the Palais Rose Meetings

"Well done!" Truman told Acheson, meeting him at the airport. Fortified by Truman's public remarks about their close communications, Acheson was ebullient. At a press conference on 23 June 1949, a reporter asked if the CFM had been a success or failure. "Do we always have to use dichotomies?" he asked back. Then he said all such conferences were like pressure gauges, measuring actions already taken. Vyshinsky's inflexibility signaled a USSR on the defensive, desperate to preserve its hold on East Germany. The "failure" of the CFM, in contrast, marked the growing strength of the allies and their progress toward bringing the FRG into the democratic fold. "What did not happen," he insisted, another blockade, was more significant than what did. A week later, Vyshinsky baldly claimed the Marshall Plan had failed and that the Soviet Union had prevented the west from dividing Germany. What Stalin and his servants actually believed is hard to know. In 1948, Stalin had told a Yugoslav official, "The West will make Western Germany their own, and we shall turn Eastern Germany into our own state." For several years, however, he lurched back and forth between minimalist hopes and ambitious visions of a united Germany under Soviet influence. At no time, however, writes Vojtech Mastny, did he show a "readiness to entertain a German settlement on terms other than his own."[50]

Liberals criticized Acheson for not patching up the wartime relationship with Moscow. If this bothered him, it is not noticeable, for he was basking in Truman's praise. He was thoroughly content with the outcome of the CFM, believing non-events better than bad agreements. There may have been no east-west "settlement," but the west had created NATO, sponsored a new west German state, and stared down Stalin's blockade. The Truman administration was playing an extremely vigorous role in Europe and meeting almost no domestic resistance in doing so. Bevin and Schuman had taken to Acheson as point man of a new and spirited U.S. American strategic leadership.

Acheson thought the Palais Rose meetings were a positive marker in the cold war and with Bohlen at his side took this message to an executive session of the Senate Foreign Relations Committee on 23 June. Blending analysis and amusing anecdotes, he summarized western strategy and narrated conference highlights, emphasizing evidence that Moscow now dealt from weakness. He saw no reason to convene another meeting of the CFM. Germany's future would be determined by the Marshall Plan, NATO, and MDAP, the "Rock of Gibraltar" of European security. He communicated three key themes to senators. Security lay in strength rather than negotiations. Quick approval of MDAP was essential to form practical NATO military power. And the west held the strategic initiative. As Bohlen put it, the Soviets were "battening down the hatches," because "the tide is running against them."[51]

The Paris meetings were a turning point in Acheson's career. Truman's unmistakable approval of his performance greatly strengthened his role as Washington's foreign policy leader, an authority he would use to act on his conviction that Moscow had no interest in easing east-west differences. He would favor discussions over the green baize of the negotiating table only if the allies first established enough military, political, and economic strength to compel realistic Soviet behavior. He did not yet use the phrase, but creating "situations of strength" was at the core of his strategy. It is possible that pursuit of this strategy resulted in lost opportunities at least to check Moscow's temperature at other conferences. But there is no sign that lack of such talks caused the United States to miss a chance to end the cold war, except on terms only the Kremlin would have found agreeable.[52]

Acheson would often look back on the Paris conclave. Robust western countermoves, he remarked in July 1953, had caused the Russians to pull down the blockade, proof that "power talks." The CFM had strengthened his ties with Schuman and Bevin. It convinced their governments, he wrote Truman in 1953, "of the true situation," clearing the path "to meet the ensuing danger and hardships with a common appreciation of the facts." It educated the American people and the Washington bureaucracy that words were futile in dealings with the Soviet Union. It taught his colleagues the merits of "organized work"—they could "outwork any" other ministry. It had improved State's reputation at the White House, as well as his own. Power, steadfastness, and western unity stood at the center of Acheson's European record in 1949. Western strength had stymied the Russians in both Berlin and Paris. "It seemed to us," he reflected, "that power was an important factor in dealing with the Soviet Union." Skill in mobilizing and using power was the key to winning the cold war.[53]

9

STRATEGY IN EUROPE: BACKING THE WEST, PROBING THE EAST

Strategy: Pulling Our Socks Up

Since Acheson's viewpoint would change little after the 1949 conference in Paris, the beginning of this chapter, which concerns both western and eastern Europe, is a fitting place to refresh the picture of his view of America's place in the "vast external realm" of international affairs.

His formative adult years, from 1914 to 1945, had been an epoch of disorder, insecurity, and violence unprecedented in modern times. Two world wars had radically changed the "realm" in which he was born. That world, dominated from London, collapsed in the destruction that followed, leaving an increasingly uncongenial realm and a vacuum of leadership. Acheson described the cold war era that dawned as a "terrifyingly" harsh time built on the "unbridgeable conflict" between "two communities with antithetical conceptions of decency."

He had no doubt the United States should seize the leader's role and do so in the service of high ideals. Belief in freedom was the ideological foundation of a strategy to create an "environment in which the American experiment of life can prosper," for domestic and foreign realms were inseparable. It had become imperative to defend a civilization built on liberty against one founded in tyranny, and how societies organized themselves was at the root of the matter. Economic systems based on liberal principles, Acheson thought, led to democracy, while those seeking guaranteed results through state planning and iron curtains generated authoritarian and externally aggressive states. Neither communism nor socialism endangered the United States. The Soviet *state* did, transformed by Marxism-Leninism into a leviathan ruled by men who felt secure only when others, within and beyond Soviet borders, did their bidding. In contrast, Acheson said in a 1950 speech, "we are children of freedom" who "cannot be safe except in an environment of freedom." If Soviet expansionism turned the world into an armed camp, if every American "had to have a number and a duty," they would lose what their society stood for. They would live a "regimented" existence "under the most rigid orders and most rigid discipline." Defending a free "experiment of life" was to defend U.S. "interests."[1]

Acheson's emphasis on values, and his clarity about what in the American order was imperiled by the "external realm," distinguishes him from most other twentieth-century U.S. statesmen, including those who mostly reacted to quotidian events. It also sets him apart from a Henry Kissinger, claiming to scorn ideology. Acheson's general belief that the United States could be secure only in a free international environment is vaguely Wilsonian, but his practicality and toughness would have made him an odd partner to Woodrow Wilson, and he expressly denied any such link.

That there was any similarity to Wilson, however, challenges the wisdom of calling Acheson a realist, or, for that matter, a pragmatist. Acheson's pragmatism was a category of opportunism, and he rarely quibbled about how to reach strategic targets, but steadfastness about large objectives accompanied suppleness about the small ways of reaching them. His tactics could be as flexible as success demanded (one reason he preferred experience to theory in his counselors). He could be consistent or inconsistent, globalistic or nonglobalistic, whatever worked. He told senators in 1949 that if it was best for U.S. interests "to do one thing in one country and another thing in another country, then *that* is the consistency upon which I propose to advise the president." The point was to do what he could to allow American liberty to "survive and flourish." He used words with premeditation, and one of his favorites, *flourish*, reveals the expansive ends served by his elastic tactics. He was quite forthright, however, in his unsqueamish readiness to exercise power. Unabashedly believing in its bold use, he liked Benjamin Disraeli's question, "What is the usefulness of power if you don't make people do what they don't like?" Its proper use, he wrote Truman in 1956, was essential in an international jungle "where the judgment of nature upon error is death." In the cold war, there were no "rules, no umpire, no prizes for good boys, no dunce caps for bad boys." "Good intentions" in the fight with the Soviets were "not worth a damn; moral principles are traps; weakness and indecision are fatal." "Spiritual values" were well and good, but, he noted in 1954, "common sense and a little organization and a gun or two around in a critical moment" were essential.[2]

Europe was at the center of Acheson's strategic vision, the home of necessary allies and supranationalist institutions he hoped would magnify NATO beyond the sum of its parts. A presence in Europe—pushing the U.S. defense line to the Rhine, as a common phrase had it—served also to distance American citizens from the fields of greatest peril. Though he could be quite stern with allies, his greatest achievements involved cooperating with them, and he believed that protecting a congenial environment from "predators" required "common action with like-minded states." Immune to strains of anti-Europeanism that influenced even FDR, he described western Europe as the "very keystone in the arch" of U.S. defense and the source of nearly all its ideas "in government, philosophy, morals and ethics." Values shared with Europeans were vital to U.S. security, but so were shared resources, for, as he noted in 1961, between them the United States and western Europe accounted for "twice the population and three times the productive capacity of the Soviet Union, an ample base for military defense and economic development."[3]

Protecting a "way of life" and practicing realpolitik were not antagonistic. A military assault on a kindred Europe would threaten the balance of power on which U.S. security rested. Because the collapse of the Soviet Union in 1991 so exposed its weaknesses, critics have concluded that Acheson's generation must have inflated its menace to guarantee U.S. superiority and justify arms spending. Considering postwar American economic dominance, the U.S. edge in nuclear armaments, and, after 1947, Washington's growing confidence about besting the Soviets in Europe, the criticism is plausible. But it overlooks the ability to feel fear and confidence simultaneously. Even a confident Acheson viewed Moscow as a menace. It was adept at manipulating and intimidating others. Its provocative behavior might spawn a war no one wanted. The looming threat of Soviet aggression might generate the protracted mobilization Acheson feared would corrode republican principles and institutions. These were not trivial worries.

Acheson's harsh view of the Soviet Union involved both its communist system (viewed by the state department as "quackery") and its behavior, but especially the latter, and about even this, his rhetoric was seldom inflamed. Moscow, he told newspaper editors, threatened "the very basis of our civilization" and the "safety of the free world" through its actions. It sowed "suspicion and misinformation," stockpiled weapons "far beyond any requirement of defense," used international communist parties as instruments of "direct and indirect aggression," and used violence to impose its will on others. Gaining power as a "conspiracy," Soviet leaders' danger to others stemmed from their demands for complete security at home and ideologically driven hopes for revolution abroad. He later wrote that their threat to Europe was "singularly like that which Islam had posed centuries before, with its combination of ideological zeal and fighting power," but he was far more concerned about the fighting power. Shorn of Marxism-Leninism, he said in 1947, "Stalin is no different from Peter the Great or Ivan the Terrible."

Communist ideology had transformed the Soviet regime into an inexorable force, like a river. "You can dam it up, you can put it to useful purposes, you can defeat it, but you can't argue with it." Soviet diplomats—never "housebroken"— equated negotiations with war. The American concept of negotiations, he would later claim, was rooted in New England horse trading, while the communist idea was "war by other means" with no interest in a "common result." Communists would simply consume one concession before demanding another. They treated U.S. diplomats in Moscow like "criminals" and jailed or hanged any of their own citizens who talked to them.

But none of this meant that war was inevitable. Good and evil—part of the "theater of the human spirit itself"—could exist concurrently. Acheson worried when Truman or others exaggerated Soviet ideas over actions. In 1949, he urged Clark Clifford to strip the inaugural speech of passages emphasizing "an ideological conflict" that could end only with "the triumph of one ideology over the other" through war. Truman should focus on what communists "do" rather than what they "*think* to themselves."[4]

In Acheson's view, Kremlin leaders knew a major war would shake their own power, and protecting that power was their top concern. He nonetheless increasingly worried about not being sufficiently vigilant. While George Kennan essentially thought the United States and the USSR were in a kind of stable balance, Acheson thought it was unstable. Moreover, as became increasingly clear, he was not satisfied with a mere balance but hoped to tip the balance in the west's decided favor. Until that time came, a crisis might paralyze western Europe in fear of what Moscow might do and might tumble the United States into an unpremeditated—and losing—war. Thus, at the time of the 1949 Paris CFM, he believed, on the one hand, that Moscow thought a life-or-death war between communism and capitalism would inevitably come, and, on the other, that the Soviets were currently in a defensive crouch. Even at the time of the first Soviet nuclear test in August 1949, when he thought the USSR would remain content with a war of nerves, biding its time while seeking openings to "grease the wheels of economic and social confusion abroad," he also feared that any appearance of western weakness might cause Soviet leaders to miscalculate.

The result could be war, and Acheson wanted enough military strength to fight that war. As we will see in later chapters, he never believed nuclear weapons were enough for such a fight, and in any case, the U.S. nuclear arsenal was tiny in 1949. Worse, American ground forces were a shadow of those that fought at Normandy and Okinawa. Allies were neither strong nor united on basic issues. The American people might "tire or become confused." Over the years, he vacillated about whether democracies were at a disadvantage in a contest with an authoritarian regime, but some of his more pessimistic moments came in 1949–50. In any case, that he and his colleagues then felt militarily vulnerable is certain.[5]

Feelings of vulnerability coexisted with ambitions to *win* and, he said in March 1949, American security concerns ranged beyond "boundaries and frontiers." Any threat to the peace *anywhere* was a direct U.S. concern. Having broad interests did not mean the United States must act truculently, but in this new era it must certainly lead. Acheson did not blanch at this expansion of responsibility.

His personality, sharp elbows, and vision of American interests all moved him toward activism, but he was concerned the public and Congress would not follow. And, he told House members in February 1949, the United Nations was "utterly worthless to create that environment which we want." Only a "powerful group" of democratic countries could.[6]

The first step in strengthening the west was actually to put together the various parts of power the west needed to project. This would add reach to power and thus have the further virtue of distancing the United States from the scenes of antagonism. A "balance of power" had historically been an excellent "international sheriff," but Acheson aimed to accumulate *more* strength than the other side, certainly enough to deter the USSR from foolish action and, he hoped, enough to defeat it if deterrence failed.

But he avoided commitments that outreached available strength, which partly explains his unease with the notion of "containment," a word he rarely used. Instead, he pointed to its flaws. Containment, strictly speaking, put the United States in a defensive posture and left its foes free to attack when and where they chose. It committed Washington to an indiscriminate defense of everything on this side of the containment line. In 1953, when China threatened Chiang's control of the offshore island of Quemoy, Acheson chided Truman for publicly declaring that "whenever and wherever we are challenged by the Communists we must meet the challenge." "You cannot mean this," he wrote. The struggle with Moscow was "a dangerous business which requires lots of sense and coolness in making decisions of where and how." Late in life, he described containment as merely "one man's" (Kennan's) view "of what he thought was going on." It had never been Acheson's intent to "oppose the Soviet Union whatever it did." He preferred to range *overall* strength against the other side's strength and eliminate important areas of weakness. With strength enough, the west could cope with any danger. Strength would convince Moscow not to push too far. Military muscle would reassure western Europe. Manpower and materiel would flesh out NATO's paper skeleton. Vigor would induce Konrad Adenauer's Germans to join the west and frustrate Russian hopes of intimidating its neighbors and their temptations to seize western strong points. He left unstated but clearly believed that growing *U.S.* strength increased its influence with allies, clearly not a component of a strategy of containment. He also left unsaid that with enough strength, the United States was more likely to get what it wanted in any international situation, in other words to practice what international relations theorists would call coercive diplomacy.[7]

In 1948 congressional testimony, only the precise words, "situations of strength," were missing as Acheson identified "areas of weakness or vacuums of strength" as a major *cause* of international friction. Removing them (or filling the vacuums), therefore, was the proper way to improve relations with the Soviets. Danger came from letting weakness fester rather than "pressing forward resolutely to restore strength." Had there ever been something called the

"Acheson Doctrine," this would have been it. Throughout the world, amassing "greatly increased strength" removed Moscow's temptation to "fish" in "troubled waters," improving chances to settle the cold war. But precisely because it was the work done to build situations of strength that expanded "the areas of possible agreement," he denied that *negotiations* could end the east-west conflict. Instead, a settlement would come when, in the absence of available troubled waters, Moscow stowed its fishing gear. Occasionally, like Kennan, Acheson hinted this would happen only after a change in the Soviet regime itself, when the "Russian people," as he put it in February 1950, "can examine themselves and criticize themselves and examine the course of their government and criticize that government."[8]

As chief architect of the new western house of security, Acheson simultaneously constructed foundation, inner rooms, and roof alike, using the Marshall Plan, NATO, and Mutual Defense Assistance Program. Such a house could withstand Soviet efforts to bulldoze postwar debris into forms harmful to western interests. Putting strength at the center of strategy required reversing the annihilation of German and Japanese power, which had released pressure traditionally containing Russian power. It meant reversing America's postwar demobilization. And it required repudiating isolationists who wanted to "pull down the blinds and sit in the parlor with a loaded shotgun, waiting." He too wanted a shotgun but was not content to wait in the parlor. Instead, he would amass more guns and friends to shoulder them. Together, they would patrol the west's acreage, ready to shoot trespassers. There would be no over-the-fence conversations until enough guns and ammunition were in stock. Even then, talks would aim at warning off hostile trespassers, not at passing the time with them. Conversation was appropriate with friends, not criminals. The United States would be open to negotiations only from strength, not to make bargains, but to gain Moscow's acceptance of the western buildup of economic, political, and military power; the talks would codify the situations of strength. First invoking this idiom in February 1950, he asserted that Washington's objective was to "create strength instead of weakness which exists in many quarters," eventually giving the Soviets chances to "recognize facts." Thus, the west could resolve cold war dangers through its own actions while ignoring the untrustworthy Russians. Many years later, on being asked if having both sides bent on negotiating only "from superior strength" didn't guarantee no talks at all, he commented: "That's a good argument for a high-school debate, but not much help for making foreign policy."[9]

There were other reasons to avoid negotiations. Talks and the prospect of talks would arouse cries of appeasement from the American right and sap support for foreign aid and rearmament on the left. They could stir messy contention among allies. The Kremlin would take western willingness to talk as a sign of weakness. Acheson rejected a Stalin-Truman summit as part of the Berlin settlement and in the months after the 1949 Paris CFM sessions discouraged his ambassador in Moscow, Alan Kirk, from even meeting Stalin. Since divisions between east and west were so "grave and basic," he told him, nothing short of "a basic change" of Soviet attitudes would justify discussions. The following year, British observers noted that Truman and Acheson always "worried" that signs of Soviet reasonableness would cause "Congress to weaken its support for the Administration's foreign policy."[10]

Early in 1949, Acheson was mostly confident about the success of western strategy. Communists trying to exploit misery had been "forced into retreat," he told senators in February. Stalin's retreat on Berlin signified "the first fruits of a policy of firmness." In April, he saw the Marshall Plan, NATO, and Washington accords on Germany as changing the international atmosphere by putting "strength into what previously had been a vacuum of weakness in Western Europe." Then in Paris, the west put the Soviets "on their heels." Not counting the atomic bomb, a summer 1949 intelligence report viewed the west as "definitely" militarily stronger than the east.

Then came the first Soviet atomic test in the autumn. With Kirk telling Acheson that Stalin, a healthy Georgian likely to "live a long time," thoroughly dominated the Kremlin, Washington's effervescence after the CFM meeting fizzled. The economy had slipped into its first postwar recession, slowing the allies' recovery as well, already punished by Britain's bleeding economy. With the culmination of the communists' successful takeover of China nearing, Acheson told reporters the Asian situation was "bad." Congress was in a narrow, xenophobic mood. "We must realize," he told them, "that the U.S. is in a helluva fix today" and needed allies. News of the Soviet atomic bomb, he observed later, left U.S. leaders realizing "we have now got to pull our socks up, and be in for a long matching of strength and power with the Soviet Union." There would be no magic solutions. The west had to get "into a position of power" and change "the power relationship" with the USSR.[11]

The Second and Third Pillars

Back from Paris, Acheson found an overflowing "in" tray, headed by getting NATO ratified. In doing so, he laid a mine in testimony that would explode in 1951, when Truman first sent nonoccupation army divisions to Europe. The statement that later snagged him was his answer to Iowa Republican Senator Bourke Hickenlooper, who asked if Washington would have to send "substantial numbers of troops" to Europe "more or less" permanently. Later claiming he was referring only to legal obligations, Acheson gave "a clear and absolute 'No.'" The ratification process rolled over this bump, however, with bipartisan boosts from Thomas E. Dewey and John Foster Dulles. Although fading in health and influence, Arthur Vandenberg fought off GOP reservations, and on 21 July the treaty passed muster, untainted by killer amendments, by a vote of 82–13.[12]

The administration failed to anticipate the struggle facing it in gaining approval for NATO's Siamese twin, the Mutual Defense Assistance Program (MDAP). The Democratic Congress was in a foul mood, restive about costs, allies' alleged lack of self-reliance, and the future role of U.S. forces in Europe. Lawmakers even feared that robust U.S. policies would provoke a war with the Soviets. Less than a decade since the heyday of isolationism, the administration had already asked Congress to approve the British loan, Truman Doctrine, Marshall Plan, and a tradition-shattering alliance. Now it was supposed to buy the alliance's weapons to boot, which the administration had informally promised its NATO partners. Without the arms program, NATO would remain a set of promises on paper. West Europeans alone could not defend themselves but with the meat and potatoes of MDAP could go far in that direction. To deflect accusations of "imperialism," as well as congressional *amour propre*, the administration arranged for allies to ask for the aid rather than offer it outright. Immediately after signing the Atlantic treaty, they did.

The fight for MDAP—which Acheson called the third "pillar" of U.S. European policy, after the Marshall Plan and NATO—was bruising and began inauspiciously. The U.S. military, its wartime bloom bleached white by Truman's budget cutting, wanted a buildup of its own but loyally testified for the program. The administration's own fumbles caused the worst problems. Concerned to get NATO approved first, Acheson from Paris had approved delaying the request for MDAP. Against his advice, Truman chose this moment to start a factious brawl in demanding congressional repeal of the Republicans' favorite achievement of the 80th Congress, the Taft-Hartley labor act. An irked Vandenberg told Acheson and his legislative affairs assistant, Ernest A. Gross, that Congress's view of MDAP was "damned bad." State might have to choose between MDAP and Truman's technical aid program, Point Four. Both Vandenberg and Democrat Tom Connally were pessimistic about early approval of arms aid.[13]

Truman waited until 25 July, amid blistering summer heat and four days after NATO ratification, to ask for the military aid, specifying $1.4 billion. Opponents, inadequately briefed by either State or the White House, immediately ran a buzzsaw through the request. Acheson had barely read the text. Now he discovered it included an incendiary grant of presidential authority to decide when, where, and how to spend the money. Nor had the administration said how the billions would be connected to strategy. Finally, no one considered the reaction to excluding the embattled Chinese Nationalists from the aid list. Except for the weather, every problem was self-inflicted. Opponents paraded before seventeen intense Senate committee hearings. Despite earlier warnings about the erosion of bipartisanship, Vandenberg shocked Acheson on 2 August by accusing Truman in executive session of attempting a power grab through a "warlord bill" that would make him "the top military dictator of all time." A furious Acheson, who blamed aides for failing to spot defects "even a child would have picked up," gained Truman's approval for a hasty rewriting of the bill, cutting back the discretionary powers, erasing an emergency slush fund, and restricting aid to NATO allies, Greece and Turkey, and the non-European trio of Iran, South Korea, and the Philippines.[14]

On 16 August, the House fell into what Acheson called "one of its berserk moods," rolling over Speaker Sam Rayburn to slash the fund in half, stunning everyone. The paroxysm seemed to spend opponents' fury, however, for now Truman rallied supporters in a speech, and the House "awoke from its spree a trifle ashamed." Legislators finally asked why the administration wanted the bill in the first place. Because the aid was essential, officials answered. In light of Europeans' inability to defend themselves, Acheson said in testimony, Washington must relieve their "morbid and pervasive" feelings of insecurity. Economic aid had failed to instill a "sense of security and faith in the future," which depended on "a firm belief in the ability of the free nations to defend themselves." MDAP could not match every Russian soldier or gun but could persuade Moscow that attacking would be folly. At the least, MDAP would allow the Europeans to clog invasion routes until the United States responded, either with a replay of the recent war's continental counterattack or by pulling the nuclear trigger. The Kremlin might consider attacking "an organism with a soft shell" but not countries hardened with arms and confident about using them. When asked why *ground* forces were so important in light of the U.S. nuclear armory, Acheson pointedly noted that the latter had not prevented either the Czech coup or the Berlin blockade. They could not reliably avert an attack on western Europe.[15]

The vote following this hard struggle was anticlimactic. The legislation passed at the end of September 1949, 223–109 in the House and by a voice vote in the Senate, but only after news of the Russian atomic explosion. "An ill wind blows some good," Acheson quipped. Truman signed the bill on 6 October despite conditions attached by Congress. Two were most important. Congress would not actually appropriate any but token funds until NATO produced a concrete defense plan worth the cash. And the allies would have to show they were serious about cooperation, or integration. Congress also forced the administration to swallow $50 million for "the general area of China" (see Chapter 11). Overlooking the administration's own errors, Acheson believed the causes of this outbreak of restiveness were a wave of budgetary conservatism, pressure from Chiang's partisans, widespread "unwillingness to face and accept the responsibilities of power," and especially the "bitter resentment" of the GOP over Truman's 1948 electoral victory. Still, the administration had again gained most of what it wanted, this time an extraordinary authority to grant allies the sinews of military power that might prevent a new war. Uncertainty remained about strategic objectives and how to reach them. But the third pillar now stood next to the Marshall Plan and NATO.[16]

"String, Chewing Gum, and Safety Pins"

In the early months of the Atlantic pact, Acheson had to slap at Mediterranean mosquitoes buzzing for attention. He brushed off Greece's demand for NATO membership with the insinuation it was being ungrateful for past favors. When Italy wanted a seat on newly formed NATO executive committees, he reminded Hitler's former accomplices they still lacked the other allies' "full confidence."

The most pressing problem, however, was to come up with the strategic plan demanded by Congress. Acheson considered the demand absurd, since no forces were yet in being, but he went through the motions to liberate the escrowed funding. In effect, the state department and joint chiefs, winking broadly, scratched a few bromides on a tablecloth and called it the Medium Term Defense Plan. Acheson considered it "incomprehensible" and "out of all relation to reality." Little more than a vague outline of the division of labor, it held Washington responsible for certain bombing targets, London for various naval tasks, and so forth. But Congress was appeased, so the money could flow.[17]

In discussions of the alliance's future, participants eventually glanced at the gorilla in the room, Germany. At first, NATO was an empty vessel into which one could pour both hopes and fears, and Germany embodied both. Paris's *Le Monde* said German rearmament was "lodged in the Atlantic Pact like an embryo in an egg," contradicting Robert Schuman's flat assertion that Germany would remain disarmed. Schuman told the National Assembly that letting Germany into NATO was "inconceivable." Not yet committed to any other position, Acheson was resolved at a minimum to keep West Germany on the side of the west. In a world chess match, it would be pleasant to have East Asian rooks and Middle Eastern bishops, but compared to Europe's queen, they were nothing. Germany's industrial strength was essential in peace, and its military prowess might be vital in war. Acheson would repulse every future Soviet bid to talk about Germany. That he mistrusted Stalin hardly mattered, for he preferred the status quo anyway.

Elections in August for a new West German government opened the way for waves of voters' criticisms of remaining occupation and dismantlement controls. Just settled in as high commissioner, John McCloy warned the Germans to remember how much others still mistrusted them. Acheson winced at the resentful rhetoric of the campaign, which ended on 14 August with Christian Democrats taking 139 Bundestag seats to the Social Democrats' 131. Putting on a good face, he called the results "a victory for moderation and common sense" and dismissed anti-occupation rhetoric as a "release of long pent-up emotions after 16 years of dictatorship and military rule." But he too posted a warning, reminding the people of the Federal Republic they were "privileged to live under the jurisdiction of freedom-loving nations" and should take care not to "alienate Western sympathies."[18]

Unchastened, the new Bundestag in Bonn vociferously attacked the dismantling policy; then, on 15 September, it chose Konrad Adenauer as the first federal chancellor by the narrowest possible vote. His coalition government was in business five days later, operating under new rules set in the Washington Agreements hammered out by Acheson, Bevin, and Schuman. Though this new Federal Republic of Germany was not yet truly sovereign, western powers quickly recognized it. On 7 October, the other shoe dropped, with the USSR protesting establishment of the government. On the 12th, it announced formation of the German Democratic Republic (GDR) in the east, which Acheson publicly stigmatized as "an illegal and undemocratic instrument of 'Soviet masters.'" But he surely agreed with the U.S. chargé in Moscow that its formation was a sign of Soviet "weakness."[19]

Adenauer provoked a brief flurry three days after taking office by remarking in a press conference that Bonn should be in NATO. He denied having rearmament in mind, but he had made his point—Germans would not forever stand mute and unarmed while others planned Europe's defense. London told Washington it was thinking about Germany as part of both the Western Union and NATO but not until "the end of the road." Rearmament was flitting through American minds, too, spurred by a rising congressional chorus for Germans to do their share; a Texas Democrat called for twenty-five divisions under U.S. command. Men in the Pentagon murmured to one another that defending Europe without the Germans was impossible. But in mid-November, in one of their first-Acheson, then-Truman, press conference games, both denied anyone was measuring Germans for new uniforms.[20]

German pressure against the dismantling program played Acheson's game, for he also wanted sharp reductions in a scheme he considered obsolete and stupid. Despite Americans' dislike of Bonn's lack of contrition, they feared further dismantlement would cause even more dangerous alienation of West Germany from the west. McCloy warned against making the interwar mistake, when the west hastily gave up "to the wrong government things we had long begrudged to a better one." When Bevin and Schuman came to Washington in September 1949, Acheson had urged them to drop a bad policy voluntarily rather than abandon it later under pressure. When they demurred, he warned further that "nobody likes to be occupied," certainly not enough to embrace the goals of the occupiers. On 5 October, forty-four senators demanded an end to dismantlement. When McCloy told a German reporter it was a "lost cause," Acheson moaned that he just could not "keep his mouth shut," but, in fact, the high commissioner was also playing his game, for Acheson was trying simultaneously to placate allies, eliminate dismantlement, and advance European unity. Bevin came around on dismantlement in late October, and the matter rested there until new meetings in November.[21]

A constructive approach to the Germans seemed essential at a time NATO, as Acheson later put it, was "held together with string, chewing gum and safety pins." In 1949, however, he still had hopes the British and French would take the lead in integrating the FRG with the western coalition. As his doubts mounted they could or would do the job, his conviction grew that the transatlantic "partnership" was *not* one of equals. Determined to prevent the partnership from succumbing to "brakes" exerted by its weakest member, he concluded that the United States, with the alliance's strongest "engine," must blaze the path. There could be "no substitute for strength at the center," he would say in 1951. American economic and military strength at the center would "breed strength at the periphery of our associations." The United States had already assumed de facto responsibility for Europeans' economic well-being, financing a fourth of western Europe's imports and devoting a sixth of the 1950 federal budget to foreign aid. Now it must lead militarily.[22]

When the Marshall Plan came to its scheduled end in 1953, Acheson feared, "the whole structure of the Western World could fall apart" unless its leaders faced up to taking "the necessary action." Despite his readiness to lead, he knew he had to do so through Washington's chief allies. The flies in the ointment were British resistance to integration and French to normalization with Germany. London wanted to stand apart from the continent and forge a special relationship with Washington. Paris, fearing such a condominium would expose it to a restored Germany, began haltingly to think of strengthening its security through webs of mutual interest spun around its neighbors. First seeing "integration" as a defense *against* Germany, it would soon envision Germany as part of the web itself.[23]

How Acheson worked through this issue late in 1949 makes calling him an anglophile laughable. Sometimes he seemed like one. Sometimes he seemed like a francophile, or a germanophile. In fact, he was an Americanophile using what worked. Although often irritated by UK detachment from the continent, at times the British choice seemed best for U.S. interests as well. He did not care a fig that Bevin worked for a socialist government or care much more about London's protective attitude toward its ties to the Commonwealth sterling trading bloc. The point was to strengthen Britain as an ally. Since politics took precedence over economics, he worked to increase U.S. sterling imports while averting his eyes when the British discriminated against American exporters. On the other hand, because of Britain's diffidence toward "Europe," he sought to place the mantle of continental leadership on France's shoulders. He placated Paris, flattered and reassured it, hoping to reinforce its best impulses. France must lead in Europe, he told Schuman and Bevin in September 1949, for the United States was "too far away." Ultimately, "there must be a solution of Franco-German troubles under French leadership."[24]

Since French "intransigence" was responsible for prolonging Germany's postwar humiliation, it would require enlightened French leadership to solve the problem. Acheson prodded Schuman to press hard on European integration, and the French foreign minister appeared to detect the sotto voce warnings imbedded in Acheson's increasingly warm tributes to Paris: If France did not rise to his partnership challenge, he would look to West Germany itself. In September, Schuman asked fellow cabinet ministers: "What about Germany? What do I have to do to meet the responsibility put upon me?" Acheson was delighted at Schuman's enhanced role in a new French coalition but warned again in late October 1949 that the Germans would get out of hand unless their "resources and energies" were freed to support Europe's security and welfare. To stifle dangerous nationalist impulses, "France and France alone" must bring Bonn into Western Europe through liberalized trade rules and "supranational institutions." This might be France's "last chance" for European leadership.[25]

Bevin pulled back in distaste when offered even a sip of the new French elixir of integration. He avoided any steps compromising Britain's role as "a world power and not merely a European power." Many Americans, on the other hand, especially those in Congress reluctant to spend more on wastrel Europeans, regarded "integration" as a panacea. Acheson could see both sides. He could sympathize with the UK, partly out of respect for what Oliver Franks called the "deep rootedness of nationalism," and his suspicion of trusts and cartels was also deeply rooted. He vigorously opposed integration evangelist Paul Hoffman's wish to slash Marshall aid to countries insufficiently integrative in spirit. Thus, while encouraging the French, he sometimes commiserated with the British. His ultimate embrace of integration was mostly about wanting to solidify France's place in the anti-Moscow alliance.[26]

Steps toward integration did little to solve current trade issues. Allies had warned Acheson they needed to sell more goods to the U.S. market, or to the Soviet bloc—or show up again on Capitol Hill with their begging bowls. Britain's economic malaise was the most tenacious. With gold and dollar reserves again plummeting, Clement Attlee's government asked for yet more help. The treasury department, Acheson worried, would react instinctively by hammering at protectionist and socialist practices and punishing British aversion to European integration. Congress was a worry, too. London would have to accept the domestic pain of currency devaluation if it hoped again to dip into U.S. coffers. Devaluation would cause another hit to Britain's living standards and ability to buy U.S. goods, but it would make British exports more attractive to American consumers. The only permanent solution to the British illness, Acheson told everyone, was for Americans to buy more goods from the UK. Congressional pressure to "Buy-US" was misdirected, even a form of "fanaticism." It was crucial to U.S. policy in Europe to act generously to improve the health of the entire sterling trading area. It was imperative for Americans to realize how much they needed their allies, not just vice versa. The United States could not just start "popping" nuclear weapons "over the North Pole" but must cooperate with others. After extensive briefings from department economic adviser Herbert Feis, Acheson took to the hustings in a modest education campaign to eliminate the lopsided U.S. trade balance. He told the National Trade Council in early

November that the so-called favorable U.S. balance of trade left other nations chronically dependent on emergency assistance, the long-term solution to which was the expansion of American imports. The United States must lower tariffs, eliminate agricultural surpluses, end "Buy American" programs, and abolish discriminatory regulations against food and drug imports. Gibing at the protectionists, he claimed to have heard that corpses in coffins were "dutiable as an article of merchandise."[27]

This campaign came after a September 1949 Anglo-American-Canadian financial summit in Washington. Acheson expected the British to show up "frightened and rather exhausted." They were also ill, or at least Bevin and Chancellor of the Exchequer Stafford Cripps were. New elections loomed at home. Knowing Truman and Congress would react badly otherwise, Acheson had warned Bevin he must show up with a constructive plan, for otherwise Treasury and the ECA would do their best to expose the sterling economies to the cold shower of dollar competition. Acheson and Secretary of the Treasury John Snyder agreed to hold off anything but pleasantries until they heard what the British had to offer. Acheson hoped for the best, but, he told Franks, the conference might resemble one of those "rare, inevitable but difficult evenings when husband and wife" had to reexamine their marriage, "all too dreadful for anything" but necessary. As the summit opened, the Americans "sat around grave, but not saying a word," Franks recounted, until "we British made up our minds what to do." Bevin had already made up his mind to devalue the pound but not how much. Once he announced the intent to devalue, "the dam broke." The International Monetary Fund offered short-term help to the sterling bloc, and the administration promised to accept a modest UK role in European integration and make further efforts to lower tariffs against British imports.[28]

An announcement on 18 September of Britain's 30 percent devaluation spurred a round of similar devaluations in western Europe, but France and the Low Countries were unhappy at signs of Anglo-Saxon collusion and Washington's apparent endorsement of Britain's aloofness from Europe. Schuman's unease was intensified when a column by the Alsop brothers parsed an Acheson statement to mean French leadership on the continent would give both the Americans and British excuses to shrug off their European duties. In New York for UN sessions, Acheson disowned the column in talks with Schuman. The Frenchman nonetheless warned him against any Anglo-American attempt to force an understanding between France and Germany. He *wanted* such an understanding, but he also wanted help to achieve it. Carefully measuring his words, Acheson described the Marshall Plan, NATO, and MDAP as signs of "the increasing association of the United States with the Atlantic Community" and of its "deep concern" with Europe. Acheson did not grasp that the more the United States accepted responsibility for western European security, the more the Europeans were tempted to shirk their own responsibilities.[29]

Standoff in Moscow's Sphere of Influence

Except for Yugoslavia, Acheson considered eastern Europe a secondary theater in the cold war, though as time passed, he also grew convinced that a satisfactory end to the east-west conflict demanded an end to Soviet domination of the area. For now, it was too dangerous to meddle in the satellite states and too tempting to leave them alone. But he and Truman were always clear the region was not worth a war. Because of its ancillary role, Acheson's record in eastern Europe is best examined here in its entirety.

His comparative indifference to eastern Europe followed traditional American inattention, except for Wilson's paternalistic work at Versailles founding the successor states to the Austro-Hungarian Empire. Habits of policy by passive resistance, as in Roosevelt's nonrecognition of Soviet control of the Baltic states, persisted in Truman's tacit refusal to acknowledge Moscow's rule in the satellites. Equally reminiscent of FDR, however, was Truman's de facto acquiescence. But U.S. policymakers could not ignore the area, either, for satellite regimes bordered on such loci of western strategy as Germany, Greece, and Turkey. Potential satellite discontent also offered chances to stir up trouble in the Soviet empire, though few arose. Yugoslav issues often commanded Acheson's attention, but he looked to subordinates to deal with the rest of eastern Europe.[30]

Truman eschewed, high-stakes gambles, but his penchant for bluster made him wish for a fiercer policy. Spurning Acheson's selections, in 1949 he demanded "tough guys" as new ambassadors to Czechoslovakia and Hungary. Feeling this presidential nudge in the back, the state department that autumn looked for ways to stir the pot in the satellite states. The time was ripe, said the policy planning staff, to challenge the Soviets' "predominant influence," or at least seize the moral high ground and rattle Stalin's nerves. By 1950, Acheson had become aggressive enough about eastern Europe to irritate risk-averse allies. In 1951 and 1952, he routinely pronounced the departure of Soviet armies from eastern Europe a sine qua non of an east-west accord. In retirement, he touchily defended himself against criticisms of "realists" for not accepting the Soviet sphere of influence. The "forces of nationalism in the satellites" were real, he wrote sharply to historian Norman A. Graebner in 1959, three years after anti-Soviet uprisings in Poland and Hungary. What Graebner and Kennan identified as "'the new realities' escapes me." One could not turn the clock back to the 1930s, but the situation of the people of eastern Europe was not final, as "events in Poland and Hungary showed."[31]

Relations with the most noxious Soviet chattels were execrable and in the winter and spring of 1949–50 grew even worse in a wave of harassment of U.S. diplomats and show trials of American civilians seized by secret police. Despite such provocations, Acheson counseled restraint. He wanted Washington to appear the mature party and open to better relations. It should reserve severe reprisals for more serious incidents that might follow. But as harassment of U.S. citizens, diplomats, and local nationals working at U.S. diplomatic posts intensified, he approved some sharp ripostes. In the summer of 1949, Washington blocked UN membership for Albania, Romania, Hungary, and Bulgaria. In September, Acheson denounced Bucharest's refusal to carry out human rights provisions in the Romanian peace treaty. In February 1950, Washington suspended relations with Bulgaria. The state department imposed severe restrictions on travel rights of Eastern bloc diplomats in the United States. NATO allies preferred a softer approach, partly from trade concerns, but Washington was ready to act alone. It denounced violations of human rights and military buildups that went beyond limits prescribed in 1946 peace treaties. In February 1949, when Hungary arrested and imprisoned Cardinal Jozsef Mindszenty, Acheson condemned its "conscienceless attack upon religious and personal freedom." Repression and internal purges left several bloc regimes badly disorganized in 1950 and 1951. Their shaky temper may have resulted partly from taunting broadcasts by the Voice of America. With little faith in such devices, Acheson instead resorted to harsher diplomacy. In the first five months of 1950, Washington not only suspended relations with Bulgaria, but froze all the assets held in the United States by Bulgaria, Romania, and Hungary, and slapped sharp travel restrictions on the Romanian UN delegation. That summer, Acheson attacked the "ruthless domination" of Hungary by "tyrannical forces." Prague's harassment of Americans escalated after three Czech pilots escaped with their planes to West Germany and then received U.S. asylum. Acheson in response ripped into Czechoslovakia in 1951 for its "nihilism, fraudulence," and "servility."[32]

On the Adriatic was gnomish Albania, where Washington tried real mischief with ghastly consequences. Like the Yugoslavs, and with their help, the Albanians liberated themselves from the Nazis and created a communist state on their own. Also like Yugoslavia, Albania openly aided the Greek communists, Washington's reason for refusing diplomatic relations with Tirana. Acheson and Bevin discussed Albania during the 1949 Washington financial talks, considering the possibility of inciting "a serious revolution." Though Acheson knew the effort might exacerbate Yugoslav-Greek conflicts, he and Bevin vaguely agreed to try overthrowing the Albanian government if the opportunity arose. In June 1949, the CIA had established the Free Europe Committee to stimulate resistance east of the iron curtain, and State officials talked quietly with the "Albanian National Committee." In December, the NSC wanted to go "on the offensive," with Albania as the first target. Americans were latecomers to this game, for British operatives had been parachuting into Albania from Malta since 1946. With fresh dedication, Britons and Americans now sent waves of émigré Albanians into the tiny state, only to have all their stratagems come a cropper. The émigrés ignored security fundamentals, and British spy Kim Philby spirited one covert plan after another to the communists. Most agents were swiftly caught and executed. Acheson had subscribed to these efforts partly to keep the Soviets from using Albanian naval bases to blockade Yugoslavia. By late 1950, however, he was disgusted with the Albanian venture. Never enamored of covert escapades, he also scotched a separate CIA-related plan for Greece to seize a slice of Albania.[33]

Nothing of the sort was contemplated for Finland. Instead, Washington donned kid gloves in approaching a state trying to hang on to independence yet acknowledge the inescapability of Soviet influence. Acheson sought not to affront Moscow over Finland. When U.S. officials in 1945–46 approved $35 million in Export-Import Bank credits, they hoped the action would not ruffle Russian feathers. Worrying in both 1948 and 1949 about a possible Czech-like coup in Finland, Americans were careful to avoid handing Moscow any pretense to act. Washington assured Helsinki at the time of NATO's founding that no one planned to disturb Finland's "special position." Such caution continued to the end of the Truman presidency. Conspicuously large loans to Finland, explained Llewellyn Thompson of State's European division in June 1949, would alarm the Russians. Accordingly, the department stated six months later, Washington should avoid any action sparking Soviet "counter-measures" that would reduce "Finland's freedom of action and access to the west." Acheson in 1950 opposed as "dangerous" Truman's musings about trying to put a crimp on cozy Soviet-Finnish ties. The key, the NSC held in early 1952, was to avoid action provoking "drastic Soviet measures inimical to Finnish independence." Thus, as Jussi Hanhimäki has demonstrated, Acheson's state department deliberately sought to "limit US influence" in Finland, both to reduce tensions with the Soviets and make life easier for the Finns.[34]

Equivocal Success in Yugoslavia

After the United States became the world's first country to recognize Yugoslavia in 1919, the two nations amicably separated for a quarter of a century, when the Balkan state returned to Washington's consciousness as an aggressive communist enemy. Bordering on Italy and Greece, it seemed eager to do combat against the west, and its rebellion against Stalin in 1948 was a response to his efforts to curb Yugoslav zeal and belligerence. Acheson disliked mollycoddling a communist dictator but approved giving economic and military aid to consolidate Josip Tito's break with the Cominform. Discretion was essential, however, and U.S. help was so contrived to avoid directly challenging Soviet prestige. Tito should not appear to look like a U.S. stable boy, for intelligence reports constantly detected signs Moscow might send the Red Army from any of three neighboring satellite states to quash him. Administration policies on Yugoslavia drew fire from congressional conservatives who thought "Communists belonged to a genus without subordinate species." Nonetheless, along with the strenuous U.S. counterattack in Korea, the U.S. interest in Tito may have saved him from a

Soviet assault. In time, the administration would make Yugoslavia a silent partner to NATO. Then in the late fifties, Tito reverted to his antiwestern preferences while still avoiding Soviet rule.[35]

Acheson had first dismissed chances of a Soviet-Yugoslav break as "rubbish," and U.S. tardiness in spotting Tito's rebellion was partly the fault of incompetent diplomatic representation. Department professionals widely viewed U.S. ambassador, Richard C. Patterson, Jr., a former RKO-NBC executive and heavy contributor to Truman's campaigns, as a vainglorious "idiot." He seldom actually appeared in Belgrade during his 1944–46 incumbency, but he wanted a major general's commission so "he could wear the uniform and go hunting with Tito." He also once proposed dragging Tito to the United States "for a month of indoctrination." As ex-ambassador, he denounced Tito in speeches just as the latter wandered off the Soviet reservation.[36]

If a little slowly, the administration at Kennan's urging came around to exploit the Tito-Stalin split. Acheson's endorsement of the strategy on becoming secretary of state was another example of his willingness to follow Kennan's advice in specific cases. The very existence of an independent communist state seemed momentous. Acheson knew he could not ask Tito for blatantly pro-western actions and assumed he would have to "sit on the fence." Some liberalization of the Yugoslav regime would be nice, but actions that worried the Kremlin would be far nicer. Early in 1949, however, Washington began to focus on how to turn Tito's break with Moscow against the Greek rebels he was supporting. When Patterson's successor, Cavendish W. Cannon, advised letting Tito "maintain himself as orthodox but prosperous Communist," Acheson agreed, but he also thought his economic troubles made him vulnerable to pressure. Washington should quietly offer Yugoslavia relaxed trade controls, including controls on weaponry, and allow it to borrow from private lenders or the World Bank, but Acheson wanted a return on these carrots in Greece. So Cavendish told Tito in February: U.S. economic aid to Yugoslavia hinged on an end to Tito's helping the Greek rebels.

It took months, but in mid-summer of 1949, Tito publicly attacked the Greek insurrectionists as tools of Soviet aggression and cut off their access to Yugoslav sanctuaries. Within days, the state department began squeezing Secretary of Defense Johnson and Commerce Secretary Charles Sawyer for approval to sell Tito a steel mill. This set off one of the first of Acheson's fights with Johnson, who threatened to have Truman reverse State's recommendation. Acheson returned fire with both barrels, while Truman stayed out of the fight. Both Johnson and Sawyer gave way after Acheson insisted that U.S. approval of a Yugoslav purchasing license would signal to other satellites the advantage of defying "Kremlin orders." Sawyer wrote later: "Dean Acheson is a very persuasive person."[37]

Dividends came quickly. Party backbiting rose in satellite states. Yugoslavia and Italy made a trade agreement and worked to settle the Trieste boundary dispute. Discreetly encouraging the Soviet-Yugoslav split he considered "worth hundreds of B-36's," Acheson still wondered about new eruptions of Tito's communist hormones, knowing he still thought capitalists were "bad" people and that he did not go "to bed with our thumb in his mouth." Worse, Acheson feared that if Tito thumbed "his nose" at Moscow, the Kremlin would send its armies after him. That he hoped to prevent, even though it would remove "the last bit of the fig leaf" from the Soviet empire. In case Moscow did attack, Acheson was acutely aware the United States could only "raise hell" but not "send in the B-36's." He did not want a Yugoslav crisis to land in the United Nations, either, where U.S. backing would stamp Tito as an ally of "imperialists." Advised from Belgrade of Russian determination "one way or another to liquidate the Tito regime," he simply hoped the marshal could hang on and that Washington could help him do so with the kinds of assistance that would not foment a Soviet assault.[38]

Even if Tito fell, Acheson advised Truman, Stalin's chance to see how vigorously Washington had acted in his behalf might deter bullying of the western European nations more vital to U.S. security. Seeing the "Tito heresy" as possibly "the deciding factor in the cold war," Charles Bohlen wanted to go "the limit" to help Yugoslavia. Averell Harriman seconded the sentiment, thinking it might determine "victory or defeat in the cold war. If Tito is No. 1 business for Stalin, it should be No. 1 business for us." The United States should even send weapons if Tito asked, European adviser George Perkins added, even though he saw no prospects that Titoism would spread elsewhere. Early in November, Washington sent Tito another $13 million credit.[39]

Late in 1949, U.S. officials still expected Stalin to sweep away their effort, perhaps through war the following summer. What did Acheson think Washington had achieved? The perils of a growing commitment to "our son-of-a-bitch" Tito were obvious. Short of a pledge to go to war, what might deter Moscow? Distracted at the end of the year by a fierce struggle for control of China policy, he may have avoided such questions. Having already broken the Yugoslav link to the Greek communists, he stuck to what seemed to be working. Tito was also starting to open up his economy and make improvements in civil liberties that would distinguish his regime from other communist states. Still mulishly independent, he shouted that his people would "go naked" before bowing to imperialist pressures, and his recognition of Ho Chi Minh's North Vietnamese government in February 1950 caused muttering in the department about cutting off aid. Acheson reacted coolly. Except for delaying a public announcement of a new loan, he stayed on course, saying it was reasonable to expect Tito to display his communist bona fides now and then, as in his recognition of Ho. It was more than reasonable for the United States to support his effort to remain independent "under very severe pressure" and was in Washington's interest. Another Export-Import Bank credit of $20 million soon followed. By May, the CIA was discounting the likelihood of a Soviet military attack. Acheson told the Yugoslav ambassador on 19 June 1950, on the eve of the Korean War, that assistance was granted "not for sentimental reasons but simply because it is in the interest of the US, as of Yugoslavia, that the latter continue to maintain its independence."[40]

Optimism faded later. Just before war struck Korea, U.S. officials were fretting about possible Soviet military actions all over the world, including Yugoslavia. With the beginning of the war, they then grew anxious that Stalin was actually drawing attention to Korea so he could strike Tito. Tito's reactions to the new war were of great interest to Washington, too. After a few unfriendly UN votes, Belgrade turned around, condemning North Korean aggression and joining the pro-U.S. majority in other important Korea-related resolutions.

Truman's forceful rejoinder in Korea and the accompanying U.S. military buildup stunned Stalin. A Hungarian general later claimed that U.S. action "nipped Stalin's pet project in the bud." By January 1951, Acheson thought a proxy attack of satellite forces was far more likely than a Soviet assault that could cause a general war. He told senators the administration would "quickly and effectively" supply arms to Tito if necessary. Though loath to make "a great public fuss" about it, he considered Yugoslavia's security a "major strategic" matter. In February, he warned that an invasion of Yugoslavia would represent aggression that could "strain to the breaking point the fabric of world peace." In June 1951 came an agreement for accelerated shipments of arms to Belgrade.[41]

Once he gave up on "Titoism" spreading elsewhere (including China), Acheson found Tito an increasingly annoying accessory. He wrangled over NATO defense planning, complained about not getting enough military help, and protested the absence of concrete promises of help against a Soviet attack. Still, Acheson thought backing Yugoslav independence strengthened morale in Italy and Greece and fortified the west in the Mediterranean and Middle East. With Truman's full support, military and economic aid (mostly loans) continued, $36 million in 1949, $20 million in 1950, and a $60 million 1951 Mutual Defense Assistance grant in 1951. A $38 million grant for famine relief late in 1950 engendered warm feelings for Americans in Yugoslavia.

American policy irritated enemy and ally alike. Washington's consultations with a Yugoslav military mission on long-range strategy in the spring of 1951 surely alarmed Moscow. And allies frowned when the United States took a conspicuously neutral stance on the Trieste issue, forcing Italy to a compromise settlement in 1954. Acheson never expected much from Tito in return. Pleased at any sign of a leavened authoritarianism, as in Tito's release in December 1951 of an imprisoned Catholic cardinal, Acheson considered such measures the lucky by-products of a policy justified for other reasons. Mostly he ignored what Tito did domestically. Thus, he did not respond when a Catholic bishop upbraided him about harsh treatment of religious groups in Yugoslavia.[42]

In 1952, Yugoslavia began retreating from Uncle Sam's anomalous embrace, a process that quickened after Stalin died. Acheson's reservations about Tito mounted when he made new anti-American speeches and broke diplomatic relations with the Vatican. Far more alarming, however, was the combustible GOP campaign rhetoric about liberating the satellites, a "prescription for disaster." Equally irritating to Acheson, as soon as they gained office, Eisenhower and Dulles breathlessly courted Tito, pushing him toward formal NATO membership and urging him to lead in removing the shackles from eastern Europe's "captive peoples." Instead, he hurried his rapprochement with Stalin's successors.[43]

Washington's support of Yugoslav autonomy was a success. Even after the Yugoslav-Soviet rapprochement, the Kremlin could never again count on Tito's fealty. American policies helped remove hostile pressure on Greece and Italy, still recovering from war and civil war. It may have prevented the positioning of Soviet naval bases on the Adriatic and Mediterranean. These were low-risk achievements, for Acheson did *not* consider Yugoslavia, or all of eastern Europe, as an area of weakness (which it was) that must be converted into an area of strength. Thus, the United States would *not* have forcibly intervened had the Red Army invaded Tito's stiff-necked republic. Giving Tito running room and nuisance value was important, but it was not central to the contest with the Soviet Union. Germany was worth a war. So, too, Acheson would decide, was Korea, but not Yugoslavia or its satellite neighbors.

10

LOOKING FOR CHANCES
IN CHINA, 1949

Introduction: Acheson's Effort and Failure in Asia

Dean Acheson inherited a thick Asian diplomatic record that added up to something like a strategy. General Douglas MacArthur, following Washington's instructions, was reforming the Japanese state, George Marshall had vainly attempted mediating the Chinese civil war, and the army was overseeing the creation of a state in South Korea. Washington had supervised the advent of Philippine independence. After first accepting continuation of Dutch imperialism in Indonesia, it moved to end it. It had urged Britain to resolve the festering dispute between India and Pakistan over Kashmir. And it was beginning to give Paris unwelcome advice about reestablishing order in Indochina.

Acheson had no idea in January 1949 how much pain Asia would cause him or how important it would become in U.S. foreign policy. He had bigger fish to fry in Europe. For several years, he had viewed Japan as primary in this secondary theater but like others did not anticipate the large troubles lying ahead in China, Korea, and Indochina. Nor did he realize what a nettlesome friend the Philippines would be. On China, he followed Marshall in his disdain for Chiang Kai-shek's Nationalists, who appeared to be breathing their last. Marshall worried more about what Moscow might do in China than what its own communists might do. Also like Marshall, Acheson hoped to forge an accommodation with the communists but from the first reserved the right to choose hostility over amity. No sooner had he begun to define a China policy than it was disputed at every turn: the Hill, the White House, the Pentagon, and even within Foggy

Bottom. Seeking broad support, he offered a documentary rationale in the *China White Paper*, which to his bewilderment generated more opposition instead. By January 1950, he had stalemated the military and barely held a restive Truman to his side, but his strategy was foundering, partly because he underestimated Mao's anti-imperialist zeal. Ironically, the Chinese leader preferred worse to better relations with the "beautiful imperialist."[1]

Through 1947 and 1948, U.S. officials forecast further weakening of the Nationalist forces in China but also doubted Mao's ability to control the whole country. In any case, few expected China to pose a threat to the west. Early postwar contingency plans did not consider it in a regional but world context, as part of World War III, in which the main prizes would be western Europe and the Middle East. Demobilization and budget scarcity having turned their army into a near nullity, U.S. generals were anxious to pull troops from Korea and had no plans for using force on the Asian mainland. Should the large conflagration come, they wanted to deny Formosa to the Soviets and use it for launching raids against them. It was, MacArthur said, an "unsinkable aircraft carrier." For its industrial potential and strategic location, generals and diplomats alike agreed on the necessity of holding Japan.[2]

President Truman never knew or learned much about Asia. Not a page in two volumes of his memoirs treats a series of important 1949 events—arguments over Formosa, the founding of the People's Republic of China (PRC), or the festering controversy over recognizing Mao's government. Occasionally, when he must have felt particularly vulnerable politically, the president suddenly intervened with belligerent outbursts about the Chinese communists. Otherwise, he is virtually absent from the archival record of U.S.-Chinese relations. But for all his ignorance, he "knew," first, that Chiang was a corrupt bungler and, second, that he, Truman, would pay the piper if Washington did anything to cause Chiang's Kuomintang (KMT) regime to fall. As he told the cabinet in 1948, he hoped not to deal "the final blow to the Government of the Generalissimo." Just before Acheson took office, Truman also told the cabinet he opposed "making any deals with a Communist regime."[3]

The joint chiefs, more than the state department, worried about Chiang's descending prospects. But they shared State's Europeanist focus and did not want to expend military resources in either Formosa or China. MacArthur agreed, though he rejected Eurocentric definitions of U.S. security. The state department's greatest worry about a communist takeover of China concerned its effect on Japan and international commercial markets, especially how Europeans would react to the loss of China as a customer. These concerns were more about its neighbors than China itself. Following wartime habits, the United States still gave aid—now having run to billions—to the KMT regime, much of it either dribbled away by grafters or, in the form of weapons, picked up by Mao's soldiers when Chiang's soldiers abandoned them in battleground routs. Chiang absconded with the rest of the U.S. cash when he fled to Formosa in 1949. His military and political errors over the years had left him contemptible in the eyes of most U.S. officials. When Acheson took office, they expected his fugitive regime to collapse and had no plans to rescue it. Most of Acheson's advisers wanted to cut Chinese losses quickly and, if possible, gracefully.[4]

Acheson's personal views on Asia were inchoate when he took office, just as they were on Germany. In January 1949, according to his memoirs, "Chiang was in the last stages of collapse," and "I arrived just in time to have him collapse on me." As late as 6 October 1949, he remarked that "he had not yet formulated a policy" for East Asia. It was "a blank sheet of paper" on which someone would write "the future." At first he did not consider this region an important area of weakness to convert into a situation of strength—except for Japan, which, in light of China's likely unavailability as a western partner, would become vital in fulfilling U.S. objectives. With some knowledge of the economic workings of Japan's 1930s empire, he also wanted to restart its productive motors, first to spare Americans the costs of occupation and then for larger purposes. His top priority was preventing the loss of Japan's economic potential to the USSR, which would ruinously shift the world balance of power against the west. He also had some general understanding of the surges of nationalism and social unrest sweeping through Asia. Ideally, he hoped to accommodate indigenous nationalism, not prop up the remnants of European colonialism. Borrowing a metaphor from the policy planning staff, early in 1950 he described U.S. interests in Asia as centered "at each end of the crescent or semicircle" that ranged from Japan to India.[5]

American dominance in Japan helped account for his complacency about Chiang's likely fall in China. But this sanguinity also reflected an optimism about Asia in general, the main source of which was ignorance. Many months would pass before officials grew alarmed about French struggles in Indochina. The British, they thought, still had the subcontinent in hand, as the Americans did the Philippines. No one lost sleep over Australia or New Zealand. Washington had no sense yet of the deadly outcome of its competition with Moscow in Korea. China's becoming communist, many policymakers thought, would give something of a hit to U.S. prestige but not add dangerously to Soviet power. In fact, it had been Marshall's belief that a communist China would become a sinkhole for Soviet resources.

Acheson's tendency to see Asia as a blank sheet suggests how little connection he had to any non-Europeans, and a few of his remarks about Asians make one wonder if he had donned a pith helmet to make them. In a harsh moment, Dean Rusk said Acheson "did not give a damn about the little red-yellow-black people in various parts of the world," and Asian specialist Edwin W. Martin heard him say things about Indochinese that he "wouldn't want to repeat." Acheson traveled to Europe eleven times as secretary of state but never made an Asian landfall. Nor did he pretend to special insight, having told interlocutors at his confirmation that China was beyond *anyone's* "experience or knowledge." China, if not Asia as a whole, became an intermittent source of tension between Acheson and Truman, but it was not because either one knew more than the other.[6]

Both men, according to many scholars writing in the 1960s and 1970s, were responsible for a "lost chance" to reach a decent accommodation with Mao's communists. Yet this is precisely what Acheson tried to do in what became a politically damaging and eventually insolvent effort. Documents unavailable to writers of the "lost chance" thesis now reveal its indefensibility. They show instead that Mao (Acheson's contemporary, born in 1893), his Chinese Communist Party (CCP), and the PRC were determinedly hostile to the United States and pro-Soviet. As early as 1945, writes Michael M. Sheng, they saw the world in terms of an "American-led capitalist camp and the Soviet-led socialist camp," and associated themselves with the latter. If not yet by treaty, Mao and Stalin had effectively become allies by the summer of 1946. Mao enthusiastically endorsed the September 1947 Cominform declaration dividing the world into democratic and imperialist factions. A powerful and sentimental attraction to communism's mother state intensified his ideological reflexes. He expected only malevolence and intervention from Americans. He would welcome their blandishments only for tactical reasons and would make friendly gestures only to "confuse" them.[7]

Acheson entered office with a small paper trail of his own on China. As under secretary, he had backed arms to Chiang while disapproving their use in the civil war. He had momentarily favored keeping U.S. troops in China to deter "predatory" Soviet designs but, influenced by Marshall, gave it up as a lost cause by 1947. What he now hoped for—all still faithful to Marshall's example—was to extricate Washington from both the civil war and Chiang, find an accommodation with the communists, and persuade Mao to act independently of Stalin. More concerned about Russian plans than the fate of China itself, he sought a Sino-American understanding to block a Sino-Russian collaboration harmful to western interests, especially in Japan. He was trying less to establish a position of strength in China than to keep Moscow from doing the same. His "policy" rested on three legs: indifference to Formosa, adaptation to the CCP, and prevention of a Sino-Soviet union. Any of the three could collapse under the weight of domestic politics or international events over which neither the United States nor Acheson had control.

Seeming at first unaware of these risks, he grew more openly scornful of Chiang Kai-shek. Himself the cause of the KMT fiasco, Chiang was too dumb to avoid standing "in front of a locomotive." Only an impossibly extravagant commitment of resources could conceivably save his rule. The communists, Acheson held, enjoyed broad support, while Chiang had repeatedly squandered U.S. aid and spurned its counsel. The Pentagon, too, rejected thoughts of intervention and considered the Nationalists unworthy of American sacrifices, encouraging Acheson to believe Washington might quietly walk away from Chiang while working something out with his successors. Despite already visible signs of CCP antagonism, State was anticipating the transition, closing posts attached to the KMT and evacuating diplomats' families. "We would do business with the new government," Martin recalled; "We all expected to do it."[8]

Acheson harbored no sentimental ideas about the Chinese communists. The intent of his effort to make an accommodation with them was utilitarian. How to implement his design was a large problem. For a starter, Washington would need diplomatic ties. Acheson, a traditionalist about diplomatic recognition, thought it should automatically follow Mao's control of the landscape. An ambassador on the scene could explain to Mao the differences between Washington's benign purposes and Moscow's selfish aims. At a minimum, a U.S. envoy could keep his ear to the ground. If necessary, he might help boost the fortunes of Chinese opposed to both the CCP and KMT. Washington, not Moscow, could offer attractive trade benefits, access to the international market, even grants and loans. It and it alone could help China restore economic ties with Japan. As Chiang's regime crumbled, state department officials nudged American businessmen, educators, and missionaries to hang on to their mainland contacts. When Acheson's gestures to the CCP met with rebuffs, he would switch to low-grade threats but with the same end of bringing the communists around.[9]

He also had to find a way around Formosa. Ruled from China, 115 miles away, since the seventeenth century, Formosa had fallen to Japanese control in the 1890s. The anti-Axis coalition had promised its return to China after the war, and Acheson thought executing this pledge would be a good sign of amicable U.S. intentions. As the Nationalists dug in on the island and more Americans rose to their defense, he considered a miscellany of schemes to neutralize Chiang: an autonomous Formosa governed by indigenous non-KMT leaders, a UN-sponsored plebiscite on Formosa's future, or a temporary UN trusteeship. These outraged both Mao and Chiang's followers, who agreed on the indivisibility of Formosa and the mainland. The best outcome, Acheson probably thought but could not say, was a quick communist takeover, which would preempt Chiang's entrenchment and stifle his partisans in the United States. Had Mao seized the island in 1949, an adviser would recall, "there never would have been a Formosa problem." Finally, Acheson needed time to find a path through Washington's bureaucratic minefields, but he turned out to be wrong in thinking that time would improve the political setting in his favor.[10]

In fact, time repeatedly worked against him. When he wanted to avoid the subject, China would not stay on the back burner. Partly because of the anti-communist rhetoric the administration used to gain support for European policies, it now faced excited demands for action on Formosa and China. Congressmen, businessmen, editors, clerics, and other members of the "China Lobby" pounced on every sign of apathy about Asian communism. They wanted Chiang's redoubt defended and the Generalissimo given a chance to retake the mainland. Sharing like impulses, feeling the Lobby's breath on his neck, Truman reacted to communist outrages in China like a dog to an insolent cat. Acheson could never predict when he might suddenly demand more militancy. Moreover, while sympathies for accommodation were common among FSOs serving in China, several key officials in the department disliked Acheson's sangfroid in the face of the Nationalist collapse, including Rusk, Philip Jessup, John Paton Davies, and George Kennan. The Pentagon's gut instinct was to save Formosa without using any of its own resources. The British shared Acheson's preferences but followed their own timetable toward normalization. Acheson zigzagged through this thicket for over a year. At the very end of 1949, he seemed to gain a victory over the military while holding Truman to his side in favor of disengagement from the Kuomintang. But it was a near thing and did not last. He was ingenious in distracting his critics and in stalling when the quick collapse of Formosa did not come about. But he was eventually stymied, mainly by domestic pressure, and lost the China contest. In 1950, the rise of McCarthyism and war in Korea left his original China strategy in tatters.

In a way, his risky attempt to carry out this strategy never mattered, for the CCP's profound hostility precluded acceptance of U.S. overtures. He had greatly misreckoned the anti-colonial, anti-capitalist, and anti-white fury in China and much of Asia. Chasms of culture, historical understanding, and ideology separated all U.S. officials from the Chinese revolutionaries. Acheson presumed that if he could only make himself clear, Beijing would see reason and meet him halfway. But to Mao, it was already clear from U.S. bankrolling of Chiang that Washington was a deadly and untrustworthy enemy. Like Truman, he too "knew" the enemy, which had plans "for enslaving the world, to run Europe, Asia, and other parts of the world like wild beasts." The Americans would try destroying the Chinese communists, not befriend them. As Acheson became secretary of state, CCP leaders were "more certain than ever before," writes historian Shu Guang Zhang, "that the United States was likely to challenge their victory."[11]

Acheson never dreamed of an Asian war until he was blindsided by a conflict in Korea that put the quietus on his China venture. Oddly, he would choose his most unfamiliar diplomatic ground, Asia, on which to take his greatest political risks. There, his persuasive powers left enemies unmoved and were irrelevant to allies. With respect to Asia, too, he was unduly confident he could ignore unhappy members of Congress. He heard their rumbles without listening to them. Consequently, his past lordliness toward them would rebound brutally.

Tito or Lenin under the Dust?

Americans were unclear about what was actually happening in China. As their position disintegrated in January 1949, the Nationalists began a "mass exodus" from Nanjing to Canton, asking foreign embassies to trail along. (The final move to Formosa was months away.) Perhaps screening their real intentions, the Soviets complied. Western powers, however, sent subordinates to Canton while keeping their top people in Nanjing on the Yangtze, ready to deal with the communists when they crossed the river. American diplomats were ready to act either in Nanjing or Canton, but the state department often found their reports perplexing.

Acheson had not yet revealed his intentions. His advisers looked for chinks large enough to fit wedges between Mao and Stalin. Some thought the Russians were uneasy at Mao's victories and pressing him to make a war-ending deal. Another viewed Andrei Vyshinsky's ascent from a Moscow sickbed to bid adieu to the KMT ambassador a sign of Soviet support for the Nationalists. But in fact, Stalin's high-level assistant, Anastas Mikoyan, was in China telling the CCP to repel friendly U.S. overtures. Zhou Enlai, the communist diplomatic specialist, issued a "Directive on Diplomatic Work" equating "non-recognition" with freedom from the imperialists. The Moscow embassy told Acheson on 3 February the Soviets were foursquare behind Mao, condemning Chiang and the KMT as American stooges. A Soviet publication described the triumph of China's "democratic forces" and the "bankruptcy" of "Wall Street's" plans for aggression.[12]

Acheson was tangled in contention over China and Formosa policy through his entire first year as secretary of state. He could generally afford to ignore views on Europe that might spring up in the national security council because of his rapidly advancing confidence about what he was doing there. But Asia was another matter, and the struggle over China and Formosa was almost entirely played out in the NSC. The military chieftains were not admirers of Chiang, but they wanted Formosa safe for bases in case of war with the Soviet Union. Considering his newness in office, Acheson countered this position with notable ardor in a meeting on 3 February 1949. Arguing that it was unimportant either to retain such bases or deny them to the Soviets, he demanded the JCS fish or cut bait. If they would not say outright that Formosa was a vital interest, worthy of military defense, he wanted them to get out of the way of better ideas. Refusing to obscure the stakes, as he understood them, he also told them diplomatic and economic measures alone would probably not hold Formosa. He gave way on continuing trickles of economic aid to the Nationalists but rightly insisted they would not silence administration critics. His own department, he allowed, was "split down the middle" on aid to the KMT, but he personally favored delaying scheduled aid shipments so they would not fall into Mao's hands.

Foggy Bottom was united, however, in regarding China as a secondary issue and Chiang's regime unsalvageable. Keeping in mind the daunting task Mao would face in transforming a "fiction" into a "nation," Acheson thought a full reappraisal of U.S. policy must await a chance to inspect what was "left" after a KMT collapse. For now, he was intrigued by certain halfway options, especially a "spontaneous" movement for Formosan independence led by forces opposed to both the KMT and CCP. The 3 February NSC meeting ended with promises of more concrete JCS suggestions and further examination of options by the state department. Acheson urged Truman to "suspend" military aid to Nationalists still on the mainland (including shipments already at sea) after consulting with congressional leaders. Cutting a fine line, Truman delayed *new* shipments instead when, four days later, he received a query from fifty-plus Republican House members asking about the aid.[13]

Truman asked Acheson to respond somehow to the congressmen's letter. They agreed that a candid account of the current situation would "pull the rug out from under" Chiang, leaving "us in a worse hole than ever." Acheson could give a "false impression of activity" to obscure his tactic of "judicious leaving alone," or he could lay "down the facts as he saw them and take the political consequences and criticisms." He preferred the latter, and a face-to-face meeting. He would repeat what he had already told members in executive testimony, that Chiang's losses came not from supply shortages but his own incompetence and corruption. At the House panel, he had already angered KMT partisans by saying the proper course with a half-collapsed house was to "wait until what is falling down falls and some of the brick, dust, and smoke clears away and you see what is left." Washington could not "furnish" China with a government or "bring competence where competence does not exist."[14]

His longhand notes for the meeting, held on 24 February after just a month in office, reveal the rationalist at work, for he assumed that, as reasonable people, the House Republicans would infer the wisdom of government policy from the information and arguments he gave them. Rationalists often underestimate the power of emotions, and he was dumbfounded when his clear exposition of Chiang's wrong choices, strategic errors, and incompetence outraged his audience. Now, he told them, it would be the communists' problem to create an actual state in a vacuum of infrastructure or "resources." An ignorant and inert semi-nation could not threaten important U.S. interests. He could not tell them "what the next step is until some of the dust & smoke of the disaster clear away & we can see foundations on which to build." The Republicans stormed out of the meeting, having heard only that Truman and Acheson planned to wait for the dust to "settle" while Mao's armies slaughtered the last hopes of an anti-communist China. The "whole business," Acheson recalled, "went off on a phrase" so that "our policy was labelled a dust settling policy," and "we were do-nothings." Both houses of Congress soon rang with maledictions on Truman, Acheson, and state department "leftists."[15]

Meanwhile, the U.S. ambassador in China, John Leighton Stuart, was sending agonized dispatches home. One in late January 1949 described the CCP as "convinced Marxians of Leninist persuasion" and hostile to the United States. Shortly thereafter, he helplessly proposed "an attitude of quiet and watchful reserve" while China's "ancient" government decayed. A report from the head of the U.S. military aid mission, General David Barr, said nothing would stop the communists from crossing the Yangtze and seizing the whole country. Citing Barr, Acheson on 10 February dismissed advice from Canton to buttress Chiang with public statements. China's anti-communist forces were "bankrupt."[16]

If China policy was not already incoherent, it became so on 3 March 1949 when the NSC adopted three mutually contradictory papers. Resuming his argument with the military, Acheson gained some points while swallowing others, hard-line provisions he probably hoped never to execute. One of the papers, NSC-41, assembled by Walton Butterworth at Acheson's request, backed continued trade with China except in militarily significant goods. Supposing Beijing's needs would make it susceptible to economic pressure and inducements but unaware its leaders had already decided against trade with capitalists unless the Soviet bloc could not satisfy their needs, Acheson and Butterworth contended that trade would separate the CCP from the Soviets and restore much-needed outlets for Japan. In contrast, economic warfare would harm Japan and drive the Chinese into "complete subservience to the USSR."

Virtually every imaginable position appeared in NSC-34/2, an umbrella under which each agency could pursue its own objectives. It advocated driving a wedge between the Soviet and Chinese communists, though Acheson granted this might take twenty to twenty-five years to accomplish. It proposed ending military aid to the KMT while continuing to recognize the regime, even as the United States identified, nourished, and brought about a new "revolution" on the mainland. A third paper sponsored by the state department opposed Pentagon suggestions for naval maneuvers off Formosa that would lash the United States more tightly to Chiang's corpse. This would infuriate nationalists in China whose anger State wanted to direct instead at the USSR.

The NSC "decisions" of 3 March could not disguise a series of developing quarrels. Acheson and the state department objected to covert operations against the mainland at a time millions of Chinese "wanted peace at any price." They also dissented from the chiefs' contention that the United States faced "the prospect of strategic impotence on the continent of Asia." Acheson criticized the chiefs for remaining silent on whether Washington should take "overt military action" on Formosa and refusing to acknowledge how much anti-U.S. sentiment military intervention would cause. Knowing the debate would continue, he asked the JCS for workable plans *in case* military intervention seemed unavoidable. But he also insisted on "disciplined cooperation within the Government"—in short, an end to public expressions of "zeal with regard to Formosa."[17]

He probably accepted the tougher parts of the 34/2 mishmash simply because their adoption might lull Truman and the Pentagon long enough to allow for the fall of Formosa. Asking the chiefs for more planning was an excellent way to keep them buried in paper. The demand for "discipline" might conceal efforts to protect Formosa from Mao, making him more amenable to an accommodation. Regardless, the meeting settled nothing. Only the state department believed in keeping avenues of trade with China open. Acheson had already sent Livingston Merchant on a secret mission to discover whether indigenous elements might seize control in Formosa, but Merchant concluded they were "disunited, politically illiterate, imperfectly organized," and unreliable. Still, Acheson wrote Senator Tom Connally, head of the Foreign Relations Committee, to oppose new aid for Chiang. Adding to Chinese "suffering," he said, would arouse "deep resentment against the United States."[18]

Against long odds, Acheson kept pushing in the face of dogged opponents, unruly events, and his own ignorance of CCP motives. Field reports remained ambiguous. "American observers" expected a rebellion against Chiang in Formosa. This could be good news for Acheson but bad, too, for Mao would see a U.S. hand in anything keeping the island out of reach. Stuart cabled on 22 March that the CCP was "far more Communist than Chinese" and "tools" of the Soviets, but four days later "old China hand" O. Edmund Clubb, running the Beijing consulate, said Zhou favored a pro-U.S. foreign policy. This was probably disinformation aimed at keeping the Americans off balance. Mao was just then disparaging the value of diplomatic recognition by the west while urging a new party plenum to seize every chance to exhibit loyalty to the Soviet Union. Acheson did not know it, but it was already far too late to drive a "wedge" between the Soviets and Chinese.[19]

A perfect weather vane to the gusts of the Chinese revolution, Ambassador Stuart in March and April suggested some risky ways to accommodate the CCP. This son of missionaries had been born in China and returned there, after schooling at Hampden-Sydney College and the Union Theological Seminary, for a career of educational and Christian good works. Now in his early seventies, as president of Beijing's Yenching University, he had taught many of the communist leaders. Acheson knew his past connections with FDR and Henry R. Luce, Time-Life magnate and China devotee, had made him resistant to Foggy Bottom authority, as had his terrible wartime experiences of arrest and detention by the Japanese. An Indian diplomat considered the fervent Stuart (named ambassador during Marshall's failed mediation) a "minor Mahatma," forever "surprised at the villainy of the world." He was more interested in alleviating the agony of his beloved Chinese people than advancing U.S. interests. Although wary of his altruism, Butterworth pointed out that his fluency in Chinese and acquaintance with "all factions" made him a natural to reach out to the new regime. His history at Yenching put him in "the traditional position of the teacher vis à vis the pupil in his relationships with many Chinese."[20]

A week after the NSC standoff, Stuart asked for discretionary authority to explore differences with communist leaders once they crossed the Yangtze. Brashly citing his own résumé, he said the communists knew he supported Chinese independence, democracy, and "closer American-Chinese relations." If he could ease their suspicions, American "democratic influences" might still work their way even in a "communist dominated China," modifying its intolerance and raising hopes of "stability in Eastern Asia and elsewhere." Acheson took twenty-seven days to respond, agreeing to the request but with little optimism about the outcome. Then, the missionary-diplomat had a brutal encounter with the first of

Mao's soldiers to dash across the river. Oblivious to his repute, they beat up his staff, seized embassy property, and barged into his bedroom at 6:30 in the morning. This was hardly the homage expected by the old teacher. With fallen spirits, he reported communists' growing "hostility." At his own suggestion, on 22 April Acheson ordered him to come home once the CCP forces were ensconced in Nanjing. Acheson also banned him from visiting the KMT centers of Canton and Taipei en route to Washington. Having previously swung from naivete about the Nationalists to gullibility about the CCP, Stuart now ruefully admitted his tardiness in realizing the communists' vicious extremism and ideological piety. As he waited for an opportune moment to leave, Washington's confidence in Stuart crashed.[21]

Stuart's problems did not deflect Acheson from still wanting to wait for the dust to settle, especially, as he told NSC colleagues on 2 April, considering the far greater salience of Europe and NATO. In China, "since the house appeared to be falling down there was not much to be done until it had come down." He could not make plans for Asia until he could examine the wreckage. He told Ernest Bevin two days later Chiang was "washed up" and that Washington would now "pursue a more realistic policy." Trying to defuse GOP pressure by stretching the deadline to use funds already appropriated for Chiang, he told Truman some of the pro-Chiang pressure was coming from Americans still buying and selling in China. Reports from China itself, however, still warranted caution, including signs that no "third force" was likely to show up as an alternative to the KMT or CCP.[22]

Apart from the fact that Mao had no interest in a reconciliation with the Americans, Acheson never recognized the error of thinking the Chinese needed the Americans more than vice versa, or that time was on his, not Mao's, side. He also thought Washington could patiently sit high in the saddle as the potential donor of diplomatic recognition. In mid-May, he sent a long message on the subject to Stuart. Some historians have read this dispatch as a commitment against recognition, but Acheson was actually trying to keep the door open for various possibilities. He wanted Stuart's answers to three questions. First, would recognition prompt the "Commies"[23] to behave better toward Americans and their property, or would "they become more haughty and arbitrary"? Would recognition best protect U.S. interests? And would the Chinese communists immediately demand de jure recognition? That, Acheson believed, required demonstrating effective control of China, maintenance of internal order, and acceptance of the nation's international "obligations." Acheson left this word undefined, but he may have had in mind a series of past U.S. agreements with the KMT government. *Withholding* recognition, he commented, would work as a "political weapon" only in "extreme cases." Clearly flexible about the terms of recognition, he disapproved offering it hastily, even though he would shortly intimate in a press conference that it might come soon. His wish to keep a "common front" with Britain might force the issue.[24]

Domestic pressures threatened to knock him off course, including so-far minor resistance in the department. Marshall Plan administrators did not want to give up on Chiang. With ratification of NATO still pending, Congress was the most probable obstacle. In April, Republican Senator Styles Bridges charged Acheson with sabotaging the Nationalists, and William Knowland, California's "Senator for Taiwan," lambasted the administration's "do-nothing" policy. Briefing Bridges, Knowland, and Republican floor leader, Kenneth Wherry, Acheson showed them cable traffic to illustrate the need to keep Nationalist "carpetbaggers" out of Formosa so Formosans had a chance to determine "their own future." With unmerited confidence, he thought the senators had been "very appreciative of the talk."[25]

Acheson took for granted that Mao wanted U.S. recognition, but (though some historians disagree) in reality he was set on rebuffing new ties with Washington. Chinese sources shape Sheng's conclusion that the ideologically driven CCP thought Acheson wanted an embassy to "subvert the new order from within." Thus, nonrecognition was "exactly what the CCP wanted." Mao had told a Soviet visitor in February his first task was to eliminate the trash and lice now contaminating the "family house" of China. Only then would he welcome "guests"; meanwhile, "true friends" could handle a broom. Some of the reports transmitted to Acheson hinted at this impulse. "Arrogant" CCP leaders, Stuart advised at the end of April, would probably entertain recognition only on their on terms. Mao had "no idea of emulating Tito," said the Canton office, "but aspires to be an Asian Lenin." Acheson's alternatives further narrowed when 300,000 Nationalist troops moved suddenly to Formosa, ending any possibility of an anti-Chiang coup on the island.[26]

On 2 June 1949, while Acheson was at the meeting of the CFM in Paris, Clubb reported he had been informed through a "reliable intermediary" about an apparent démarche from a "very nervous and worried" Zhou. Purportedly part of a liberal group fighting radicals to achieve good relations with the United States and eager for economic help, "Zhou" hinted that friendly gestures would keep the CCP from Moscow's embrace. It was a genuine contact, Clubb thought, but he urged great caution, for he did not believe this was an outbreak of Titoism. More likely, the Chinese wanted both their "Soviet political bread" and some "American economic cake." Any reply, Clubb wrote, should be tough: "So long as Communist China is run for political benefit USSR let it pay on barrel head for what it receives." The disillusioned Stuart was even more skeptical, calling Mao the Russians' junior disciple and reporting that Nanjing shops spilled over with books by "Soviet pontiffs." On the 14th, Acting Secretary James Webb approved a cautious answer if Clubb could find a go-between with better credentials. The reply must include a protest against hostile propaganda and mistreatment of U.S. officials and inform Zhou that Washington wanted "deeds," not "friendly sentiments." Truman further braced Webb two days later with an injunction against "any softening toward the Communists." Meanwhile, Clubb reported a speech in which Mao had warned against trucking with "imperialistic elements and their running dogs" or accepting diplomatic relations with those still preserving ties with "Chinese reactionaries." By this time, Zhou's spoor had vanished, no fresh intermediary had darkened Clubb's door, and Washington dropped the matter. On 24 June, a Mao-inspired article urged vigilance against U.S. and British diplomatic wiles. Today, Chinese historians almost uniformly dismiss the "*démarche*" as phony, probably a case of communist disinformation. As U.S. interest faded, the CIA predicted it could do nothing to change the "Soviet orientation" of the CCP.[27]

On the plane home from Paris, Acheson worked on China, not European issues, preparing to face aides who had become restive about his policy. He was willing to wait out Mao on recognition, thinking delay would block any effort to play one western state "off against another." Acheson was playing for time, but events again narrowed his maneuvering room when Chiang declared a blockade of mainland ports. The department pronounced the blockade illegal, but Truman ordered nothing be done to frustrate its effectiveness. Sixteen Republican and six Democratic senators urged the president on 24 June to bar diplomatic recognition, and on the same day the archon of bipartisanship, Senator Arthur Vandenberg, publicly dissociated himself from administration policy. Chargé Foy Kohler in Moscow, reporting that Mao was "not for sale," anticipated the approach Acheson would take when he finally gave up on normal ties with the Chinese, a coercive version of the "wedge" policy. Giving Mao the cold shoulder would make him fully dependent on Moscow, exposing its utter inability to stimulate Chinese industrialization. Only then, Kohler thought, would the CCP consider taking a path "independent" of its "Soviet teachers."[28]

In yet another lurch, Stuart detected a new communist overture, receiving a visit on 28 June 1949 from former student Huang Hua, "Mao's trusted agent" and head of the CCP office of alien affairs. Responding to Stuart's request, Huang on behalf of Mao and Zhou invited him to Yenching graduation ceremonies, an opening for discussions. In his report to Acheson, Stuart evenhandedly listed the pros and cons of accepting. On one hand was a chance to bolster the "liberal anti-Soviet" group within the CCP and demonstrate Washington's receptivity to a new day in China. On the other, acceptance might confuse the American public and irritate European allies expecting to maintain a common front. It would also greatly enhance CCP "prestige" and look like a harbinger of U.S. recognition. Despite the balanced tone of his cable, Stuart on his own had already virtually packed his bag.[29]

Was this encounter yet another piece of disinformation? For years, historians considered it a genuine bid by Beijing's "liberals" and the U.S. rebuff a deplorable choice confirming all Mao's suspicions. Recently opened records instead make clear that the communists were simply taking core samples in a U.S. policy landscape they barely understood. Why, they wondered, was Stuart still in

Nanjing? Could they do something to prevent an armed U.S. intervention or seizure of Formosa? Contacting Stuart to get some answers was tactical.

Most of Acheson's advisers urged extreme caution. Butterworth thought Stuart should decline any invitation unless he could also gain the freedom of Angus Ward, a U.S. consul in Manchuria detained by Mao's troops. There was also the possible domestic reaction of which Acheson would have to be the judge. The secretary of state decided against it, laconically telling Stuart the judgment came from the "highest level" and, by way of explanation, listing the negatives from Stuart's own earlier cable. Though "lost chance" gospelers are surely wrong to consider this snub a disastrous mistake, it is at least conceivable that discussions in Beijing might have marginally lessened CCP mistrust. It is frustrating, therefore, that the reasons for Acheson's decision are so murky. He probably had *one* reason, that is, that Truman had said absolutely no. The consul general in Shanghai, John M. Cabot, regretted the decision, blaming two Truman fears—one of public opinion at home, the other of the prospect of Mao luring Stuart to Beijing "to humiliate him." Doubts in Washington about Stuart may have played a role, too. Years later, Merchant described him as "a dear man, a saint really, as innocent of politics as a newborn babe," but also ungovernable. "If the Secretary of State told him to leave Nanking, he would accept this as a serious suggestion that he should give thought to."[30]

Probably, if not certainly, Stuart's flaws paled in significance compared to Mao's purposes. As this episode was playing out, Mao denounced the United States as the world's last "imperialistic Power," a nation intending "to enslave the world" and arm Chiang "for the slaughter of millions of Chinese people." In the cold war, he declared, China would "lean to the side of the Soviet Union." These fulminations must have reinforced Truman and Acheson in believing they had done well to say no to Stuart. Acheson had told senators to expect such a proclamation and coached the president on how to respond. Coached or not, Truman hit the roof, on 11 July ordering Stuart to visit Chiang in Canton. It took Acheson nine days to reverse the order, backed by Stuart himself. When the ambassador finally left China, Mao scorched him in an article, "Farewell, Leighton Stuart," saying he symbolized China's defeat of U.S. "aggression." In faraway Moscow, Stalin told Mao's second in command, the visiting Liu Shao-chi, China should seek the overthrow of governments in India, Burma, Indonesia, and the Philippines. Then they could try Japan.[31]

"No Matter Who Is Hurt, Tell the Truth": The China White Paper

In the summer of 1949, Acheson acted to blunt rising criticism of the administration's Asian policies. First, he established the Jessup Commission of consultants, purportedly for a policy review but in reality to chew up time and give him cover. Then, the department published the *White Paper* to preempt more aggressive policies sought by the congressional China bloc and defense secretary Louis

Johnson. The commission had little long-term significance, and the *White Paper* project miscarried badly. Hindsight reveals a surrealistic story: Acheson first harbors schemes for normalization Mao would have gleefully rebuffed; then he moves just far enough to antagonize congressional conservatives, frustrate the Pentagon, irritate colleagues, and test Truman's patience; finally, he issues the *White Paper* to buttress his position, which only undermines it.

Most of the news from China itself remained discouraging, especially the communist abuse of U.S. diplomats. In November of 1948, Zhou had found numerous ways to affront diplomats, including classifying them as private citizens, hoping to provoke their voluntary exit, especially of Americans. Reporting in July 1949 from Shanghai on the detention, arrests, and beating of consuls, Cabot said no Americans were "now safe in China." He urged their prompt removal so the United States could "sit with dignity on the sidelines" while the Russians were "sucked into" China's economic disaster. Everyone but Stuart quit Nanjing in the next two weeks. Officials and businessmen from Britain and other countries tarried. Acheson carped at British "business interests" for trying to make deals with Mao's agents.[32]

On 1 July, before the CCP formed a government, Acheson wrote Senator Tom Connally promising to consult with the Foreign Relations Committee when the subject of recognition arose. In retrospect, he thought the abuse of foreigners made recognition "impossible," but in 1949 he still hoped Mao would restrain his zealots. Thus, with his hopes for normalization still alive, he acted to thicken his armor against conservatives by forming the consultants' commission and asking it to recommend the outlines of a viable policy. Jessup headed it, joined by Republicans Everett Case, president of Colgate University, and Raymond Fosdick, former president of the Rockefeller Foundation. Their instructions were to leave no stone unturned in halting "the spread of totalitarian communism in Asia." Its real agenda was to outflank Defense Secretary Johnson's new committee aimed at hardening policy toward China and Formosa. After filing a preliminary and sympathetic report, Jessup, knowing his friend's need for time, embarked on a long inspection trip, taking a slow boat to visit fourteen Asian countries from December 1949 to March 1950.[33]

More venturous, and misguided, was the attempt to win over public opinion with the *China White Paper*, a thousand-page compendium documenting Sino-American relations in the twentieth century. Originating in 1948, this project's original enthusiasts were Kennan and Davies, with Butterworth prophetically worrying it might stir new support for Chiang. Truman and Marshall scotched publication, fearful of appearing to write off the Nationalists. But officers continued to compile documents and write a narrative. Acheson took up the idea in the spring of 1949, convincing Truman over JCS objections that publication would inform the public and neutralize critics.

However negative the outcome, more than a half century later one cannot help applauding Butterworth's instructions that the work be "straight, no matter who is hurt; tell the truth." Further, Acheson urged editors to make sure they avoided defending "their own actions." Ironically, it was John Stewart Service, then under investigation for bad-mouthing the KMT, who insisted on sections detailing Chiang's early achievements. China specialist John Melby, who wrote some chapters and edited others, also drafted Acheson's fifteen-page "letter of transmittal" to the president. Melby and Butterworth occasionally hauled the manuscript to Harewood on weekends. There Acheson went "over the whole thing himself" in the old engraver's workshop he used as a study, making "changes and suggestions." Davies may have been responsible for the shrewish approach to the communists in the letter of transmittal, but Jessup gave the document his approval. Acheson "wanted it both ways," Service recalled. Thus, the *White Paper* said the department "hadn't done anything to push Chiang Kai-shek" and that it "wasn't so stupid that it didn't know what was going on."[34]

Truman—and Marshall—insisted on reading "all" of it. Jitters about appearing to shove Chiang into his grave caused repeated stays of publication. In early July, Acheson promised Truman to fix shortcomings spotted by Clark Clifford, but he ignored Pentagon objections to the very idea of publication and gave the military only a week to review it. Stuart was ordered to leave China *before* publication, arrive afterward, and then keep silent about the *White Paper*. On 5 August 1949, shortly after appointment of "consultants" Case and Fosdick, *United States Relations with China: With Special Reference to the Period 1944–1949, Based on the Files of the Department of State* appeared for public consumption.

Knowing few would plow through the body of the book, Acheson used the letter of transmittal to summarize this "frank record of an extremely complicated and most unhappy period in the life of a great country." In a mostly defensive text, "Acheson" wrote that among the key factors in the imminent communist victory was the Nationalist leaders' expectation that the United States would "win the war for them." Against U.S. advice, Chiang in 1946 had launched ill-advised offensives with fatal consequences. Washington had nonetheless backed him with billions in military equipment now lost to the communists through the Nationalists' own "ineptitude" and loss of "the will to fight."

This lawyer-like indictment seemed intolerably cruel to Chiang's admirers. They were even more outraged at the disavowals of administration responsibility. The statement that only a "colossal" all-out "commitment of our armies" could have saved the Nationalists was undoubtedly accurate but was also like waving a red flag at the China Lobby. In language critics branded hostile and defeatist, Acheson concluded that the "unfortunate but inescapable fact is that the ominous result of the civil war in China was beyond the control of the government of the United States." Nothing it did, could do, or could have done would have made a significant difference. The communists' victory "was the product of internal Chinese forces."[35]

Egged on by Davies, Acheson also hoped eviscerating the Chinese communists in the letter of transmittal would neuter conservative criticisms. This put him in the remarkable position of trying to divide Chinese from Russian communists by describing the former as fanatics subservient to the latter. He urged the people of China to condemn this betrayal, hinted at UN punishment, and predicted that "ultimately the profound civilization and the democratic individualism of China will reassert themselves and she will throw off the foreign yoke." He was giving Mao a choice between fealty to the Soviets and acceptance of a nebulous promise of friendship with the Americans—*on top* of hundreds of pages documenting a decade of Chiang's canny manipulation of Washington. Unsurprisingly, Mao issued an acidulous riposte in the Chinese press. The only policy the Americans had, he wrote, was to "make trouble, fail, make trouble again," and fail yet again "till their doom." His commentary coincided with the arrival in China of the first of hundreds of Soviet military and economic experts.[36]

Acheson had told Truman to prepare himself for "a renewed storm of attack," but neither anticipated the fury galvanized by the *Paper*. Acheson's memoirs reek with chagrin about the fate of his intended public relations coup. He had run into "immediate, unexpected, and acute trouble" because the *Paper* was "unpalatable to believers in American omnipotence, to whom every goal unattained is explicable only by incompetence or treason." Aides were as baffled as their boss as they fought for better media spin. In a 5 August press conference, Acheson tried to blunt all the faultfinding. In an opening statement, he promised to review all the department's Asian policies in cooperation with Jessup's committee, the military, NSC, and Congress. Once he opened the floor for questions, reporters hammered him with queries that, he wrote later, exposed how little they knew about "these things." He gave them snappish answers.[37]

Vandenberg attacked the *Paper*. So did Representative Walter Judd, former medical missionary and China bloc stalwart from Minnesota, who charged Acheson with following the Truman Doctrine in Europe but the "Henry Wallace" line in China. Though short-lived, the broader public reaction was also unfriendly. According to Gallup, most of the 64 percent of the people who knew of the publication were angry. The China Lobby issued a thousand-page-plus rebuttal on 22 August, and for three days the Walter Lippmann column slashed at Acheson's apologia. If Chiang was so hopeless, Lippmann demanded to know, why did the administration stick with him so long and give him $3 billion? The *Times* called the state department publication "a sorry record of well-meaning mistakes." Asked in a press conference if he had changed his policy, a prickly president said, "We have never been favorable to the Communists." The department announced on 16 August it had no plan to withdraw recognition from Chiang, and Acheson tried diverting Congress's attention to Southeast Asia. The flurries of criticism, he said later, helped convince him he must make his points "clearer than truth" in the future. For now, he fell into a brief gloom. He told Bevin it would be salutary for Mao to discover "by bitter experience" the miseries of alliance with the USSR.[38]

Though he seemed briefly to let others run China policy, Acheson was only lurking, awaiting another chance to distance Washington from Taipei, if not to establish normal relations with the communists. On 26 August, he unburdened himself in a remarkable off-the-record session with twenty-five reporters to whom he described East Asian policy as a "blotch" on the map and the *White Paper* as "an honest baring of the bosom." Since Chiang had absconded to Formosa with his pockets stuffed with money, China had "dissolved into its primitive and elemental units." It would be "madness" to pour more money into the Nationalist regime. He would not "be bullied by Congress or public opinion" into emptying the U.S. treasury for the Nationalists, he told the reporters, and "if they want another Secretary of State they can have it."[39]

Four years later, he called the *White Paper* a "giant firecracker," but it was more like an albatross around the administration's neck, where it hung for three more years. Even those who were favorably inclined noticed that *White Paper* editors had omitted embarrassing documents, especially those revealing wartime flirtations with the CCP. Melby called the letter of transmittal an "inflammatory and stupid," committee-written monstrosity that Acheson had signed out of carelessness or excessive optimism. Certainly his normal political skills had fled him in this case. It was bad judgment to kick the Nationalists while they were down, especially when the only alternative he offered was to watch the dust settle. "All of us," recalled Service, "failed to foresee the venom and public hysteria of the ensuing McCarthy period." Instead of paving the way to a more intelligent China policy, the *China White Paper* had made such a change seem less plausible than ever. Acheson, however, had not yet given up the idea.[40]

11

NEITHER WOOD NOR IVORY:
CHECKMATED IN CHINA, 1949–1950

Introduction

Acheson once remarked that chess masters played with "wood or ivory" pieces, but "in the game we play, they are alive, people move on their own; it's the human character." The Chinese proved the truth of this by moving around the board without regard for his wishes. Mao Zedong's imminent victory in the summer of 1949 put the issue of diplomatic recognition in the foreground, but Acheson had become wary following attacks on the *White Paper* and some turbulence within the administration itself. Truman's hatred of the Chinese communists tended to cancel out his contempt for Chiang Kai-shek and the Nationalists. Acheson sought purchase while being crisscrossed by divergent presidential, military, and state department views. His objectives, however, remained constant. He hoped Washington could adjust to the new Chinese realities, untie its strategy from the long romance with Chiang, and encourage Chinese independence of Moscow. Hoping to focus on Europe, in a surge of confidence near the end of the year he staged a showdown with the Pentagon for Truman's loyalty. The "win" he gained would quickly vanish.[1]

This summary exaggerates the clarity of the story. One could excuse outsiders for seeing bureaucratic tangles, ignorance, and improvisation as the main themes of China policymaking. In late August 1949, ten days after a department announcement denying plans to withdraw recognition from the Nationalists, Formosan ambassador Wellington Koo came away from meeting Dean Rusk convinced Washington would soon recognize the communists, but the same

Rusk five days later led a department discussion on rescuing Formosa. Acheson was keeping his counsel, aware of thinning support for his own predilections. Public opinion offered ambivalent guidance. In May, 43 percent of Americans saw the Nationalists as a "lost cause" yet rejected U.S.-Chinese communist trade by a 46–20 margin. In the autumn, two-thirds of those with an opinion opposed recognizing Mao's regime. Americans appeared to want no entanglement with either side.[2]

With Mao himself thinking he could seize Formosa "next summer," in July 1949, Acheson launched a Formosa policy review. His attitude may have rested in part on an assumption that defending Formosa would be harder than it actually was. Considering the activist administration approach to Europe, many considered the refusal to back Chiang anomalous, but Acheson was not likely to change his mind because of "pressure." On the contrary, he nodded tacitly when Thomas E. Dewey suggested having publisher Henry Luce nudge Chiang into exile. He and the chiefs were in brief agreement in rejecting George Kennan's startling idea of seizing Formosa, a là Teddy Roosevelt, and holding a UN plebiscite on its "ultimate disposition." He did accept Kennan's idea for the CIA to assist KMT troops stranded on the mainland. "In a matey sort of way," he exchanged views with Ernest Bevin. He probably hoped that if London joined Washington in restricting Chinese trade, Truman in turn might agree to move toward accommodation and recognition. Bevin became agreeable in the autumn to clamping down on selling strategic goods to China if Washington saw to it that Japan and the Philippines did the same.

It is plausible, as some have argued, that Acheson had already turned against accommodation, with his exchanges with Bevin presumably being part of an effort to flush out a military commitment to defend Formosa in case Truman so demanded.[3] More likely, however, he was simply trying to find middle ground between hawks in the administration and Bevin's commerce-driven policy of accommodation. During their September financial discussions in Washington, he urged Bevin to delay recognizing a communist government on grounds that it would not reduce Soviet influence but would demoralize other friends in Asia. When Bevin made clear he would not join him in a tough line, Acheson expressed hope they could at least stick together on broad objectives.[4]

The proclamation on 1 October 1949 of the People's Republic of China sent shock waves through the United States, already rattled by the Soviet atomic explosion. American diplomats returned home as ordered. When Mao officially asked for foreign recognition, Moscow promptly complied and broke its ties with Chiang. London hinted at de facto recognition, irritating Acheson, especially when he had to learn of it from the French government. Truman still tacitly backed Chiang's illegal blockade and bombing of the coast along Shanghai. Alluding to the 1917–33 period in which Washington did not recognize the USSR, he told James Webb there was "no hurry whatever" about recognizing the PRC.[5]

Politics at home, Acheson hinted to Bevin, would dictate terms for U.S. recognition. It might be "a strong card in keeping China out of Russian hands," but the department could not even consider recognition until the communists actually controlled China. Making his requirements plainer, he told Bevin and Schuman it was of the "gravest importance" the CCP first control "all of China." "We do not want to recognize them and thus acknowledge that they have won the war. We want events to dictate this."[6]

The China Round Table, 6–8 October 1949

Shortly after Acheson had described U.S. terms to Bevin and Schuman, the department sponsored a three-day forum on China. Though Acheson did not attend, the forum gave him potential backing if he pushed harder for normal Sino-U.S. ties. Part of the same review producing the Jessup Commission, this "round-table discussion" brought in twenty-five outside "consultants" for advice—scholars, businessmen, and political and diplomatic figures. Looking over the guest list, Kennan remarked that it seemed "stacked somewhat in the Department's favor." Jessup chaired the meeting, sometimes spelled by "consultant" Raymond Fosdick. Acheson hoped, hosts told the guests, that they might turn on the green light he needed to push forward. As it turned out, they did reinforce his own views, most favoring "quick recognition," which participants thought would benefit American commerce, influence "the Chinese people," and undermine pro-Soviet CCP leaders.[7]

Besides Jessup, others from the department present included Kennan, Walton Butterworth, and Ambassador Leighton Stuart. Kennan discounted both China's potential to make trouble for the United States and popular views shaping policy. Given China's primitive economy, Butterworth argued, efforts at economic warfare would fail to "strike at her vitals." Briefing officers strongly implied that the stakes were much higher in Southeast Asia than China. Research officer Cora DuBois—an anthropologist and student of Franz Boas and Ruth Benedict—worried about China's opportunity to exploit a "whole host of evils" in Indochina, including poverty, "racial discrimination," and police repression. Given the dangers, she lamented the department's dearth of Asian experts and their condescending dismissal by department hierarchs as "specialists." Virtually all department speakers underestimated PRC capabilities while depicting its internal problems as overwhelming. It would take years for the PRC to establish order or create a productive nation. Formosa, said the CIA, could "indefinitely" repel amphibious attacks against it.[8]

Kennan had been right about the guests, most of whom read recent history through the lenses of the *White Paper*. Although divided on whether the Nationalists were "finished," they overwhelmingly favored coming to terms with the communists. While some merely favored keeping up trade and fashioning "reasonably friendly" ties to the new regime, Lawrence K. Rosinger of the American Institute of Pacific Relations and author of three books on China urged final disentanglement from Chiang and prompt recognition of the CCP. Most worried about how a vulgarized ideological debate within the United States would block intelligent policymaking. Already singed by China, George Marshall (now president of the Red Cross) urged great caution in moving toward recognition. On the other hand, Nathaniel Peffer, Columbia political scientist, *White Paper* contributor, and onetime Stuart adviser, scorned such timidity. It would leave the government "hog-tied against its better judgment." Just inaugurating a legendary career as gatekeeper for Chinese studies in the United States, the forty-two-year-old Sinologist John King Fairbank of Harvard University harshly criticized the *White Paper* for its anti-communism and urged the administration to align itself with Asia's progressive forces. Owen Lattimore, then forty-nine, a department consultant and soon to become a prime target of Joseph McCarthy, had written nearly a dozen books on Asia. Decrying anti-communism, he urged bold U.S. action to bolster Asian economies. Peffer ripped into efforts at containing, sabotaging, or ostracizing the PRC, which would simply lead all Asian nationalists to say: "Well, you see the Russians are right, the Americans are just imperialists." Halfhearted harassment of the Beijing regime would be "God's gift to Mr. Stalin."[9]

But the Round Table was no uncontested anti-Chiang feast. At thirty-nine already sporting a formidable reputation in strategic studies, Yale military strategist Bernard Brodie challenged the idea that China was already "lost" and wondered how to inspire Nationalist armies to block a further CCP takeover. Republican politician and University of Pennsylvania president Harold Stassen vigorously dissented from the forum consensus, pointing to charts proving Chiang's continuing viability. Washington should ignore cries of "imperialism" and intervene in every possible way to save the Nationalist mainland regime. And then, Stassen argued, the United States should retain Formosa as a military bastion in the defense of America's Asian "perimeter."[10]

Acheson never mobilized the many Round Table supporters behind his own preferred China policy. He was listening far more closely to Truman, who loathed the Chinese communists, than to liberal academics, who were far less impressed by current political restraints than Acheson. If the day ever came when Chiang vanished as a pole of attraction for conservatives, he could draw on the professors and bankers who supported an opening to the PRC, but for now he may well have deemed the Round Table's most isolated member its most important. Stassen, a former governor and a moderate Republican, had unequivocally signaled how his kind would react should State grow too venturous. Acheson knew he was not home free.

Improvisation

In October, Truman began giving way to his hard-line impulses as an observant Acheson improvised. In closed Senate testimony on 12 October, he used sharp condemnations of the USSR and PRC as cover for opposing a gift of arms to

KMT soldiers left on the mainland. Aware now of Mao's lack of interest in recognition, he said the CCP had turned the issue upside down, resorting to the "ancient" Middle Kingdom view that *it* would choose whether to recognize "outside barbarians." But he still refused to rule out recognition. When Congress inserted dollars for the KMT into a European arms bill, Acheson and his Democratic allies fought back. After several weeks of parrying, they managed to divert Chiang's designated money into a $75 million fund in Section 303 of the Mutual Defense Assistance Act, which the president could spend anywhere he liked in the "general area of China." Truman used nearly all of it in Indochina. Though a nice finesse of China bloc pressure, "Section 303" funds propelled Washington into weighty new liabilities on China's southern flank.[11]

Acheson would more likely succeed at his purposes if he could slow friends' accommodation of the PRC. He advised Jawaharlal Nehru during a visit to the United States against early recognition and complained to Bevin about hints at British recognition. A restive Truman, having grumbled to Acheson on 17 October that London was not playing "squarely," told reporters off the record two days later he hoped he would "not have to recognize" the Chinese. But he allowed Acheson to tack further in that direction. In late October 1949, Acheson told Jessup and consultants Case and Fosdick he wanted to avoid closer ties with any reactionary Asian regimes. Good policy demanded staying on the right side of Asian nationalism and using "more brains and fewer dollars." Still looking for a politically acceptable approach, he considered coupling recognition of China with a stern attitude toward it, perhaps even trying to stimulate unrest within its borders. Or something like the reverse, de facto conciliation but no recognition. Both were consistent with advice from Ambassador Alan G. Kirk in Moscow to distinguish recognizing China from dealing with it.[12]

Events in China finally dashed Acheson's hopes of extending recognition. Egged on by Soviet advisers but guided by Zhou Enlai, Chinese authorities in October and November 1948 had arrested, interrogated, and beaten American diplomats. The most notable victim was Angus Ward, the consul in Mukden (Shenyang), Manchuria, whose official capacity the communists rejected. But only in 1949 did his case raise political heat at home. The state department's condemnation of China as "illiterate in the language of international diplomacy and decency" only confirmed Mao's resolve to force westerners out. In June 1949, shortly after Zhou's purported démarche, China charged Ward with conspiring against the revolution and "world peace." After nearly a year in captivity, during which he and his staff were beaten, half frozen, and nearly starved, they were formally arrested on 24 October and then tried and condemned.

Truman understandably seethed. Acheson was discouraged but remained calm. The Chinese used the Ward case to prove their loyalty to Moscow and willingness to isolate themselves from the west. In any case, as Acheson later recalled, the Ward outrage killed any thoughts of recognition. The department blamed Beijing's refusal to "recognize international obligations," adding that formal relations with the Formosa government would continue. Truman wanted an airborne rescue of Ward and twice pushed Webb for either a blockade or military intervention. Acheson put a halt to the aerial operation, and General Omar Bradley and the chiefs told Truman military action would cause a war without necessarily getting Ward out. Acheson announced on 16 November 1949 that recognition was out of the question until the release of Ward and his party. On 10 December, China finally deported the sixteen Americans, eleven non-Chinese aliens, four cats, and three dogs. Almost all needed immediate medical attention.[13]

The publicized brutality against Ward left Truman vulnerable as well as angry, further pushing the situation toward a point of no good options, at least in Acheson's view. Trying to "overthrow" the PRC through harassment would not work. A Titoist solution required the Chinese first to stop actively abusing Americans, but he saw no chance of that. On the other side, the Chinese considered U.S. legal protests as a screen for imperialist designs, and Mao remained eager to get the Americans out of town. As Truman fumed, Acheson treaded water, though still looking for openings to a moderate policy. This would not be easy, for Truman was unpredictable as well as furious. In mid-November, two weeks after he told Webb that Formosa would soon fall, he pushed for strong action on the Ward case. He also hoped the United States could somehow keep Britain from recognizing the communists. Acheson swerved in Truman's rhythm. He remained opposed to Chiang's "blockade" and passed word to him not to expect a forcible U.S. defense of Formosa, but he also beat State's drum of outrage over Ward.[14]

If recognition ever came about, Acheson wanted it to stand on firm ground. He asked the Moscow embassy's opinion of whether Washington had benefited from recognizing the Soviet Union in 1933. The department prepared a long memorandum on U.S. interests in China, most carrying price tags: private property and investments ($100–200 million); trade ($100–125 million annually); diplomatic "establishments" and property ($11.8 million); money owed to the U.S. government ($799.5 million). "Influence" was of incalculable value, and despite recent reversals still "one of our most valuable assets." Acheson seemed to accept the historical myths perpetuated in the report, which lauded selfless American educators and missionaries, whom it assumed Chinese had seen as generous and unexploitative. This kind of influence could not be lightly surrendered.[15]

This reckoning of interests could justify a soft as well as hard policy, and another memorandum from the Chinese affairs office supplied even more wiggle room with flexible definitions of the "minimum standards of international conduct" required to warrant recognition. Still improvising in crablike motions, Acheson also sounded harsh notes, telling Bevin and Schuman that recognition would be a "stab in the back" of non-communists holding out in China. On the other hand, despite the Ward case, in late October he inched back toward moderation, probably because of a recent challenge from the combative defense secretary, Louis Johnson. Having promised Madame Chiang to reverse

Acheson's policies, Johnson tried to get Truman to back a definitive declaration against recognition and an operation to rescue the Formosa bastion. Johnson had the support of the joint chiefs of staff, KMT lobbyists, MacArthur in Japan, and many congressional Republicans. Acheson retaliated, armed with opinions from the "consultants," especially their view that recognition would put severe pressure on relations between "Peiping and Moscow."[16] Washington should hold the door open for diplomatic relations, show the people of China the American "interest in their independence and welfare," and maintain business and philanthropic activities in China. Both the consultants and Acheson opposed trying "to detach Formosa," either through military force or a contrived UN trusteeship.[17]

Acheson had to draw Truman away from the Johnson temptation and bring him around to the consultants' views. Thus, in November 1949, amid the uproars over the Ward affair and Mao's demands for a seat in the UN, Acheson brought the consultants and Truman together for the first time. Afterward, Truman told him the meeting had given him a better understanding of why the communists won in China. Acheson explained to him that the United States could choose either to harass China and try "to overthrow" the government or—as he and the consultants preferred—try detaching it "from subservience to Moscow." If this failed, the United States could always return to a tougher policy. Truman gave guarded assent, after which, on 18 November, Acheson told his representatives in Taipei it would be impossible to help the KMT succeed, short of "some kind of spiritual regeneration" of Chiang's coterie, which Washington "cannot supply."[18]

He exuded confidence in a press conference on 30 November. Asked if Washington had "lost face" over China, this western rationalist dismissed the premise as "a particularly foolish Oriental conception which suddenly seems to have seized the American mind." The same day he held a spirited colloquy with New Jersey Republican Alexander Smith. Once a Princeton history professor (hired by Woodrow Wilson), Smith seemed eager to play a constructive role. He had sought out Acheson after visiting Formosa. The two men quickly disagreed. Citing "military authorities," Senator Smith wanted strong measures to prevent Formosa's fall. Acheson replied that the defense establishment was not of one mind on the subject and refused to rule out recognition. Having promised not to play politics on the issue, Smith immediately went public with his criticisms. Later in December, he called for U.S. occupation of Formosa. Acheson was still far from having the domestic support he needed for normalizing relations with the PRC.[19]

The Struggle to Control China Policy

In early December 1949, Acheson used the inner sanctum of the NSC to gain full control over policy toward China, Formosa, and East Asia generally. The prospects were not auspicious. The episode with Smith evinced rising unrest about Acheson's policies, even among his own assistants. MacArthur in Japan was touting the need to hold Formosa. Influenced by Johnson's competition with Acheson, the department of defense remained unwilling to commit force to Formosa's defense but adamant about keeping it from the communists. The chiefs wanted to use Section 303 money to finance advisers and equipment for Chiang.

The showdown occurred over a new policy paper, 48/2. Acheson emerged with what he soon realized was a meaningless victory, for by June 1950, McCarthyism and the Korean War had overwhelmed all chances for a moderate line. The Chinese themselves hardened their anti-Americanism and embraced Moscow more tightly just as Acheson tried again for accommodation. In Washington, no one guessed how closely Russian and Chinese communists were cooperating to frustrate his objectives. Worried about an Anglo-American intervention against their revolution, the CCP staged a "disinformation" campaign hinting at goodwill for Americans and disagreements with the Soviets, aimed, writes Sheng, at disorienting the Americans during "the last stage" of Mao's struggle to control the mainland. Meanwhile, Moscow received Chinese intelligence reports on Acheson's efforts to put his wedge strategy in place.[20]

Acheson monitored a fresh flow of news about Sino-Soviet friction through this fog of disinformation. Reports of extensive Russian involvement in Mongolia, Xinjiang province, and Manchuria buttressed hopes of scoring anti-Soviet propaganda points. From Beijing, O. Edmund Clubb thought the Chinese were beginning to realize "what imperialism is really like." Hoping Beijing would come under the control of China's own "independent devils" rather than Moscow's "stooges," Acheson would soon arrange for American journalists to broadcast gossip about Soviet covetousness. Some Sino-Soviet tension was real. An adviser told Stalin that Mao was not a real "Marxist" and might accede to pressures from the pro-U.S. "bourgeoisie." After the rupture with the USSR in the 1960s, Mao admitted the Soviets had turned the northern reaches of the country into a "sphere of influence." For now, however, Acheson was discovering that the communists were more united than divided.[21]

On 8 December 1949, the Nationalists officially moved to Formosa, where U.S. intelligence thought they could last little more than a year before a communist takeover. Still content to go slowly on recognition, Acheson told India's ambassador, Vijayalakshmi Pandit, that governments offering early recognition would gain neither "benefits," "gratitude," nor influence in China. He urged caution, reciting the obstacles to recognition, including the PRC's self-image as "a new state unfettered by the past." Although conceding that others might feel compelled to act independently, he resumed his effort to decelerate British momentum toward recognition. With Britain's ambassador, Oliver Franks, on 8 December, he invoked his recent epiphany that the PRC was a "revolutionary" rather than "evolutionary regime," which denied responsibility for standard international obligations. He took the news calmly that London might recognize China "before the year was out" but told Franks he expected advance notice. Truman, through Acheson, also advised the UK against hasty action. Diplomatic reports said that governments' recognition of the PRC would weaken U.S. influence throughout Asia; some even feared a Sino-Japanese rapprochement once Tokyo regained freedom of action. On Christmas Eve, the state department learned that British recognition would come on 6 January. Clubb chimed in from Beijing that Washington should follow suit.[22]

Acheson lobbied for support, especially among such Republicans as John Foster Dulles and Senator Arthur Vandenberg. Dulles urged "somehow" taking over Formosa and making a "show piece of it" but had nothing to say when Acheson quietly asked exactly how to do that. He took Governor Dewey home after a Gridiron Club dinner to talk into the wee hours about China. Canvassing U.S. embassies about the likely results of offering "early" recognition, he also considered either delaying recognition until many others offered it or delaying "indefinitely." The department informed diplomats in Asian posts that Formosa would "fall" soon and instructed them to minimize the likely strategic consequences. After talking to Acheson on 22 December, James Reston thought he seemed poised for success. "After one or two brushes with the pro-Chiang Kai-shek forces," he had concluded they were afraid of grabbing "this porcupine" too firmly. But Acheson had also told Reston it would take him "a long time to produce any very tangible results."

So it was that he approached a climactic end-of-the-year NSC meeting, scheduled because Truman had complained of NSC-41's obsolescence. The meeting bolstered Johnson's hope to land a knockout blow against Acheson. The secretary of state's own short-term goal was to block a Johnson raid on "303" funds for Chiang's military. His long-range objective was to break the chains to Chiang.[23]

The contest culminated in two meetings on 29 December 1949. At Acheson's request, state department officers and the joint chiefs met in his office at 11 A.M. Alongside Acheson were Rusk, Butterworth, and Livingston Merchant. Acheson wanted to know the meaning of an ambiguous paper the chiefs had submitted for the scheduled afternoon NSC meeting, which seemed to advocate a quasi-intervention to protect Formosa in one breath and deny the island was worth the use of force in another. The state department, he explained, had tried various peaceful means to hold Formosa, but time was running out on a policy doomed to "ultimate failure." General Omar Bradley, chairman of the chiefs, deflected Acheson's request for clarification. After endorsing an army suggestion to spend "303" funds to give Chiang enough weaponry to defend Formosa on his own, Bradley claimed he had no wish to interfere in decisions about the dissemination of U.S. aid.

Acheson and his men had resolved not to let the military off lightly. Butterworth and Rusk needled the chiefs on their reasoning, and then Acheson weighed in sharply, insisting on a clear distinction between checking communism in Asia generally and the singular Formosa case. Mao now ruled China because of Chiang's failures and because the communists had capitalized on the "long-smoldering agrarian revolution." Beyond China's borders, Washington should support economic development and indigenous nationalist forces, a task eased by the removal of the "dead hand of European colonialism." But the United States would fail in such an effort if it remained hamstrung by Chiang. With some patience—he had "6 or 12 years" in mind, not "6 or 12 months"—the United States might still drive a wedge between the USSR and the PRC, exploiting the fact that "Mao is not a true satellite" and "came to power by his own efforts."

None of this was possible if the chiefs kept "toying with the mousetrap," urging halfway measures too weak to protect Formosa but strong enough to alienate Asian peoples. It would be different if Formosa was actually essential to U.S. security, but the chiefs themselves had denied this. Bradley's reply appealed to a dichotomy that always infuriated Acheson, saying that while the secretary's "reasoning was political," he was only "giving the military view." Perhaps, Bradley added provocatively, State wanted to surrender Formosa "for political reasons." Acheson tacitly confirmed the statement without rising to Bradley's bait. With an eye on the afternoon NSC session, Bradley then repeated that the chiefs "recognized that political considerations might override their views."[24]

Truman chaired the afternoon meeting but, typically, was virtually silent until the end. Bradley repeated Defense's views and Acheson again challenged the chiefs' equivocations. He thought Moscow's land grabs and unrealistic prescriptions for agricultural collectivization would diminish its influence in China. The United States should stay out of Formosa, redirecting Chinese "xenophobia" toward the Soviets, but the chiefs' proposal to subsidize "armed attacks" against a regime other nations would soon recognize would cause all of Asia to identify Washington as the regional patron of reactionaries. In the big picture, "Formosa, though important to the U.S., was not vital." Bradley grudgingly admitted the chiefs might have gone "too far"; perhaps it made political sense to drop the KMT government. Pressing, Acheson declared it time to permanently extricate the United States from the Chinese civil war. Truman had heard enough. He "approved" Acheson's recommendations "for political reasons."[25]

With the formal adoption of NSC-48/2, the administration was committed to continuing to recognize the KMT regime on Formosa until its situation was "clarified" (a euphemism for a communist takeover), and nonrecognition of the PRC would continue until U.S. interests dictated otherwise. Washington would not put its "prestige" on the line to oppose other nations' recognition of Beijing, though it would still caution them against "hasty" action. Nothing would be done to help dissidents on the Chinese mainland unless they first showed their willingness to act on their own. Whenever opportunities arose, the United States would act to exploit rifts between Moscow and Beijing and those between "the Stalinists and other elements in China." "Covert means" of stirring up trouble were sanctioned as long as scrupulous care was given to avoid any actual "appearance of intervention." Semi-normal trade with China remained acceptable, but not any traffic in strategic goods that would end up in the USSR. The NSC paper, of course, did not openly advocate a speedy communist takeover of Formosa to sweep the mess from Acheson's plate. But it did declare that only large military action could keep Formosa out of communist hands—and disapproved such action. One reason for this disapproval was the current imbalance between Washington's "global obligations" and available military resources. Second, other Asian nations, from the Philippines to Japan, claimed a higher priority for U.S. security than Formosa. Acheson himself now had a reduced faith in a wedge policy, but he found it useful to have the policy sanctioned as a prophylactic against the chiefs' impulse to discover military solutions where none existed.[26]

As Acheson was forcing this face-off, Mao was inviting himself to Moscow. He arrived 16 December 1949 to a welcoming fanfare and stayed eight weeks. Amid strenuous talks, Stalin urged him to give the Americans no "pretext to intervene" in Formosa. Mao pressed for a firm security alliance to succeed the 1945 Soviet agreement with Chiang. As they parlayed, Acheson, still command-ing broad press support, engineered leaks to Reston and C. L. Sulzberger of the *Times*. Reston used an article to applaud efforts to widen the growing Soviet-Chinese "breach" rather than seize Formosa. But a new surge of dissent against Acheson arose, too. Senator William Knowland demanded a military mission to Formosa and released a letter from Herbert Hoover favoring a U.S. naval shield for Formosa and Hainan, off the coast of Indochina. Senator Robert Taft joined the chorus, as did Vandenberg in tacitly approving a GOP "gloves-off" sally against Acheson and the state department. Then MacArthur's Tokyo head-quarters leaked the recent "policy information paper" preparing U.S. diplomats for Formosa's fall. Opponents fell on this with what Acheson called "delighted unbelief," causing Congress to "burst into uproar." The onslaught led him to write Archibald and Ada MacLeish that "Formosa is the subject which seems to draw out the boys like a red haired girl on the beach. It appears that what you want most is what you ain't got."[27]

While Beijing viewed this American uproar as a screen for an imminent invasion of Formosa, Acheson in fact now wanted Truman to go public with an authoritative statement ending the commitment to Chiang Kai-shek. He sent the president a draft on 4 January 1950. Johnson, Clark Clifford, and others persuaded Truman against issuing it, only to have Acheson turn him around in an evening telephone conversation. At his morning press conference on the 5th, Truman would announce that the United States had "no desire to obtain special rights or privileges or to establish military bases on Formosa or to detach Formosa from China." Washington would send no military aid to Chiang or continue any involvement "in the civil conflict in China." Truman was uneasy and probably felt harried by Acheson. Shortly before the press session, he read the text over the telephone to Johnson and Bradley. At the general's request—and without telling Acheson—Truman deleted the line, "or to detach Formosa from China" and added "at this time" to the passage about staying out of the "civil conflict." But the press secretary had already distributed the unamended version to reporters.[28]

After the press conference, Truman belatedly asked Acheson to use his own afternoon press conference to reinforce another Bradley stylistic intervention, that "in the event of war, we might have to recapture bases on Formosa." Reporters clamored for an explanation of the differences between Truman's prepared text and actual statement. Annoyed, Acheson told them he was dedicated to be "clear to the most perverse intelligence" before loosing arrows against the culture of "leak and counterleak, gossip and countergossip." Calling for a halt to conjectures "highly prejudicial" to U.S. interests, he denied that detachment from Chiang was anything new. Reciting only legalistic formulations, he said nothing about the strategy underlying the presidential announcement. Sneering at all the "amateur military strategy" he had recently heard, he shamelessly denied any conflict with Johnson and loyally defended Truman's emendations. The president, he told the press, was simply declaring the obvious, that the United States must retain freedom of action "in the unlikely and unhappy event that our forces might be attacked in the Far East." None of this satisfied the China bloc. Predictably, it also aroused new baying in Beijing.[29]

After Truman's press conference but before his own, Acheson talked privately to Senators Knowland and Smith. He knew Knowland was a lost cause but hoped to gain ground with Smith, putatively subbing for the ill Vandenberg as superintendent of bipartisanship. He acknowledged that U.S.-Chinese relations were at their "nadir," like those with the USSR in 1918, but he found encouragement in the likelihood of future Sino-Soviet tensions. Urging the senators to accept the imminent Nationalist smashup, he contended that seizing Formosa would violate the principle of self-determination and cause "revulsion" among Asian states Washington needed as friends. After Acheson defended the notorious guidance paper as "just one of hundreds of similar papers constantly being issued" on prospective events, Knowland figuratively spat at its "spirit of defeatism." Knowland warned he would go to the people against Acheson's "fatal policy," and Smith accused him of endangering "a bipartisan foreign policy." A department notetaker concluded: "Courteous but restrained goodbyes were offered by those present."[30]

Criticism gained more steam with reports of MacArthur's flat assertion, contrary to state department views, that Formosa was defensible. In the Senate, Knowland lashed out, asking why Truman and Acheson had "less concern for human liberty in Asia" than in Europe and "no concern for the 400,000,000 people of China who have been dragged behind the Iron Curtain." Were they drawing "a color line on freedom"?

Bad news overwhelmed opinion polls showing 63 percent support for Truman's 5 January statement. India had recognized the People's Republic of China on 30 December, followed by Pakistan on 4 January. The day after Truman's announcement, London issued its long anticipated de jure recognition. (China reacted coldly and did not exchange ambassadors with the UK until 1972.) Ceylon extended recognition the same day, as did NATO partner Norway. Within two weeks, Denmark, Sweden, Finland, Switzerland, Israel, and Afghanistan followed. By midyear over twenty states had recognized the PRC, all severing ties with Taipei.[31]

On the very day it received British recognition, the PRC seized a group of western properties in Beijing, including barracks serving as a U.S. consulate. It also announced plans to confiscate all U.S. diplomatic property obtained in supposedly shady deals with Chiang. The state department promptly threatened to withdraw all remaining U.S. officials. When China went ahead, Acheson on 14 January 1950 announced the withdrawal of all department personnel, partly to avoid incidents that would further inflame relations. Knowland pounced on this "surrender on the installment plan" and demanded that those "responsible" resign. A chortling Mao in Moscow said the U.S. withdrawal was "extremely favourable for us" and told Molotov his government had deliberately ignored Acheson's apparent wish for good relations to force Americans out of the country. Mao needed time to establish order, and it was best to postpone any grant of "legal rights" to Americans in China. Acheson was threatening China "with exactly that which we are trying to accomplish." Mao had indeed gotten what he wanted—the Americans out of China.[32]

Acheson must have realized his recent NSC victory was illusory. The Canadian ambassador wrote Ottawa that the seizure of properties made U.S. recognition of the PRC "a dead issue." Had Truman and politics allowed, it might have been better to offer recognition at the time other nations did. But, of course, this assumes that the Chinese communists would have welcomed recognition, which they did not. As it was, Acheson's struggle in the NSC had *not* produced a clean break from Formosa or opened the door to relations with the PRC. On the positive side, polls showed over 70 percent of Americans (of those paying attention) opposed further aid to Chiang, and State's own pulse-takers found "*impressive*" support for Acheson's China policy in the media and among independent organizations. Possibly still hoping to outwait his opponents, Acheson had no way to know how soon events would explode the remnants of his medley of unrealized goals and half-aborted strategies. Until the middle of June 1950, he still fought for control, trimming his sails as Republicans stormed, the chiefs sulked, and Truman teetered on the edge of belligerence. Eventually, war in Korea and the wintry Chinese intervention destroyed all room for maneuver. The administration then went on the defensive in East Asia until the day Dwight Eisenhower became president.[33]

By January 1950, chances for constructive relations between the United States and the People's Republic of China were less than minimal. Political pressures at home and Mao's enthusiasm for the USSR abroad were mainly responsible. The United States would emerge from its isolation on the recognition issue only in 1979. The best Acheson might do was turn to the negative version of a wedge policy. This amounted to little more than waiting while the Chinese learned how little they would profit by tying their fortunes to the Soviets, a policy, in short, that would not come to fruition while Acheson was secretary of state. After the Chinese intervention in Korea, his original preference of diplomatic recognition became the third rail of U.S. foreign policy. His own willingness to defy conventional wisdom also had limits. Acheson was not about to fall on his sword for impossible goals in Asia if it meant sacrificing his objectives in Europe. Accommodation with China would have to come later.

Looking Back

Through occasional letters, the 1953–55 Princeton seminars, and especially a 1955 visit to Missouri to help Truman prepare his memoirs, Acheson reconstructed his China experience. Insisting that everyone involved only gradually learned what they needed to know, he denied having ever "thought the Chinese Communists were agrarian reformers," the indictment of left-wing diplomats by realists and the right. But he admitted in 1955 that he "didn't know as much about Communism as I do now." His experiences from 1945 through 1951 left him thinking of China as vast and uncontrollable. In the end, Chiang's defeat was the climax of a "century-old battle between the peasants and the land lords." Had Chiang not overreached after World War II in trying to wipe out the communists, it was possible that China, like Germany and Korea, would have remained divided, with the Russians ruling Manchuria, the communists the north, and Chiang's KMT the south. This arrangement might have been advantageous to the United States, but it was a moot question. The administration could only have pursued such an end in the spirit of realpolitik and would have caught "hell" for trying. The most remarkable thing about this comment is Acheson's apparent belief that, had it tried, the United States might somehow have succeeded in manipulating all the other parties involved to achieve such a three-way split![34]

Eventually, the communists forged a nation, an outcome Acheson did understand was beyond U.S. capacity to prevent. Even the old "China" was not "a satellite," and Washington could not tell Chiang what to do. Combining forces with the million-plus Japanese soldiers still present at war's end to defeat the CCP would have been abhorrently "Machiavellian." Mediation had been unavailing. The utterly "fanciful" idea of conquering and reforming China would have taken millions of troops and decades to accomplish at a cost of "God knows how much money." Even if it worked, Americans would have become hated colonialists just like the French in Indochina, for nobody wanted others to govern them; he shuddered to think of "damned Americans" riding around "in Cadillacs" telling impoverished Chinese how to organize their future. The administration had followed the wisest course in trying to deal with the victorious communists after a pause to let the nation-building process begin (a later version of waiting for the dust to settle), but it had not "come off." The only other possibility "was to sit on our tail and do nothing, and that we would not do."

Most of his postmortems blamed historical forces beyond anyone's control. Not a true "nation," China was "a geographical expression," as Napoleon had said of Italy. It was boundless and ungovernable. Acheson also assigned blame to the Chinese communists' own execrable behavior. In 1950 he had told UN Secretary-General Trygve Lie that Mao's regime was "an improvisation that scarcely knew what it was doing" or understood its impact on world affairs. Its ill treatment of Americans had made any accommodation virtually impossible.[35] In 1957, when Hans Morgenthau wrote Acheson saying the administration had ruined its chances by bowing to public opinion, he replied that the fault lay rather with the Chinese for refusing to "honor" international obligations, seizing U.S. property, and abusing individual Americans. Their enthusiasm for North Korea's attack on South Korea killed the last shred of hope for recognition. He could not "see any point at which it can be said that the Truman Administration was wrong in not recognizing the Chinese Communists," he wrote, and sharply disagreed they had "failed to do so through fear of public opinion."[36]

In fact, in another moment he *did* blame public opinion, if indirectly, for McCarthyism fed on popular and sentimental views of China. The problem was not communists in the state department but "holy rollers" who hated them. Americans had fallen victim to a national love affair with Cathay, fed by generations of missionaries coming home with their tales of noble service and grateful response, tales he had heard in Yale church basements. Thus was created the myth that America had "protected" China "from the rest of the world." Americans were as emotional about China as about Ireland and Israel (prompting Truman to interject: "And he points to me"). Whenever they thought about China, he concluded, "blood rushes to their ears."

For himself, Acheson knew "China" had been harder than Europe, where he could work "with good stuff, solid stuff." It was not so difficult to help "people who were willing, who had the will to be helped." Chiang would not cooperate, and the United States could not force him to wisdom. Moscow wanted to isolate the PRC from "the rest of the world." The Chinese communists were obdurate. Acheson said he could never understand why they slammed the door shut every time he opened it, but, even aside from Mao's ideological commitment, it is abundantly clear that the Chinese leader viewed slamming the door as the suitable response to *Washington's* commitment to Chiang. Acheson also never grasped how much the Chinese communists despised capitalism and imperialism, both embodied by the United States. Acheson, like his countrymen in other towns, had spent too many evenings in church basements hearing about Yale-in-China.

The fact remains that he put up a good fight for the only possible sensible policy at the time—shedding the commitment to Chiang and trying to forge a relationship with the new regime in Beijing. It was not his own shortcomings that primarily blocked achievement of these goals, but the fright put into Truman by embittered Republicans using China to savage a Democratic administration. That plus the intractable hostility of the Chinese themselves.[37]

12

OTHER EARLY ENCOUNTERS WITH ASIA AND THE MIDDLE EAST

Japanese Power Point

During the Truman administration, a great deal of drama occurred in China and Korea, both of which officials first approached with little understanding. With the exception of Japan, this was even more the case elsewhere in Asia and certainly so in the Middle East, where American diplomacy before 1945 was close to virginal. Lack of experience in these areas reflected limited prewar conceptions of America's international interests, views challenged by World War II and its aftermath. Equally important in causing Americans to approach much of Asia and all the Middle East with uncertainty was Britain's traditionally leading role in these areas. But as London's postwar decline became evident, Washington moved into its place, if at first with little grace.

Japan was an exception. The United States had been contending with the Japanese for nearly a century. Nor was Japan particularly a British stomping ground. So it was that here the United States determinedly took the lead, with results that seemed far more important than anything occurring in China or Korea. George Kennan, who opposed integrating the western occupation zones of Germany within the western alliance, was among the first to propose doing exactly that with Japan—and to advocate tying the U.S. future in Asia to Japan rather than China. In the first months after World War II, Dean Acheson had been on the other, Sino-centered side, and helped sweep some of Joseph Grew's old "Japan crowd" out of the department. Soon thereafter, he switched sides and, following Kennan's path, saw western control of Japan as vital in the competition with the Soviet Union. Located strategically off the Eurasian land mass, Japan could become a great position of strength, not for its military prowess (now deliberately minimized), but its economic potential. As Canadian officials noted, if a demilitarized Japan were cut loose, the Soviets and Chinese "could be expected to exercise a good deal of military pressure" against it. This did not happen. Instead, in the Asian analogue to U.S. policy in Germany, Washington co-opted Japan as part of the bastions being thrown up to oppose the Soviet Union. The swift integration of two great wartime enemies on the side of the west was one of U.S. foreign policy's greatest accomplishments.[1]

In the case of both Germany and Japan, Acheson as under secretary had supported the shift from punishment-plus-reform to stabilization. Long bewailed by critics, the mutation in Japan seemed a geopolitical necessity, especially once FDR's hopes for China did not pan out. At war's end, Washington had briskly established its dominance over Japan's future, determined not to invite the kind of trouble being generated by the division of Germany. The United States rebuffed Moscow's effort to gain its own Japanese occupation area. Stalin seemed to accept this at Potsdam but by October 1945 was grumbling about Americans treating the USSR like a "piece of furniture." Neither would General Douglas MacArthur brook any interference from the Russians, or for that matter from the British and Australians. Russian protests waned after Washington recognized the Romanian and Bulgarian governments in December 1945.[2]

The state department mainly watched as MacArthur reformed the Japanese land system, dissolved the *zaibatsu* cartels, introduced female suffrage, wrote a democratic constitution, and disarmed Japan, presumably permanently. Fearing that a disordered and poverty-stricken Japan would slip from its control and wanting to speed up recovery, in 1947 Washington put this radicalism aside in the "reverse course," reinforced by cold war thinking after Stalin's crackdown in eastern Europe. MacArthur, always seen in Washington as a loose cannon, demanded a quick peace treaty and an early end to the occupation. His reasons were ostensibly to liberate Japan's economy and arrest growing anti-Americanism, but he also had an interest in getting home so he could run for president. The state department briefly got on his peace treaty bandwagon but jumped off again in the face of resistance from Russians, Chinese Nationalists, and others. It then looked for outlets for Japan's goods and sources for its raw materials, increasingly in the colonial areas of Southeast Asia. With the KMT sliding into oblivion, the Pentagon worried about an unarmed Japan in easy reach of the Soviets. The chiefs wanted no treaty before Japan was economically viable and safely pro-American.

A visiting Kennan bearded MacArthur in his Tokyo den, vigorously putting the administration's new view to him, and with his hopes for the presidency gone, MacArthur cooperatively pulled back his reforms. He halted reparations deliveries to Japan's wartime victims, rehabilitated disgraced wartime figures, invited crackdowns on leftist labor unions, and urged Japanese leaders to think about rearmament. If seemingly lackadaisical about China, Acheson was urgent about Japan from his first day as secretary of state. "Japs," he told U.S. diplomats in telegraphese in April 1949, "will either move toward sound friendly relationships with non-communist powers or into association communist power system in Asia." In the Paris Council of Foreign Ministers, he had repelled Vyshinsky's attempt to butt in and planned for an American-dominated peace treaty process. Unlike the military, he wanted it done sooner rather than later.[3]

Many years later, Japan's power and western orientation have a look of inevitability, but few thought that in 1949. Its history of militarism, imperialism, and friction with the United States made the future seem chancy. Few thought Japan trustworthy only four years after Okinawa and Iwo Jima. Its utter destruction in the war, Acheson believed, had shattered the traditional East Asian balance of power and made it more vulnerable to Soviet pressures. With a Soviet-influenced communist party, Japan could succumb either to duress or to honeyed appeals from Stalin or Mao. Following the state department direction of the last couple of years, in December 1949, Acheson rejected the notion of Japanese neutrality as "illusory in the context of East-West tensions." His unqualified inclusion of Japan inside the U.S. defense perimeter in his National Press Club speech in January 1950 (described in Chapter 19) evinced a historic commitment in U.S. policy.[4]

Since at least 1947, Acheson had believed that drawing out the occupation might dangerously stir the pots of anti-Americanism. Better, he thought, to bring Japan quickly into Washington's security net in a nonpunitive settlement. Beforehand, however, the defense department wanted various assurances, including guaranteed access to Japanese military bases. Ironically, the military chiefs feared an early peace treaty would provoke a violent Soviet reaction they could not yet meet. Even after a peace treaty—when Japan would again be sovereign—the U.S. military, as Acheson later put it, not only wanted complete control over their own forces but the "power to take over" Japan itself "in case of crisis." He believed such demands would not only alienate the Japanese but confound broader U.S. purposes in Asia. Ironically, however, other Asians indirectly held similar views, wanting more severe punishment of Japan. With State and the Pentagon at loggerheads, Acheson would eventually have to kick the dispute upstairs for presidential decision in a rare case of forcing Truman to choose between key cabinet members. After prolonged deliberations and concessions to the Pentagon (described in Chapter 27), Truman would finally decide in Acheson's favor.[5]

Under Acheson, the state department consistently pushed for a quick peace and rapid economic recovery, a popular goal that drew support from such conservatives as Democratic Senator Pat McCarran of Nevada, who wanted to lift the burden of occupation from American taxpayers. In the name of recovery, the department supported continuing trade with China, except in strategic goods, and renewed commerce with Indochina. By the spring of 1949, MacArthur was pushing a position peculiarly his own, a settlement supervised by the United Nations and negotiated with the Soviets that would leave Japan neutral—an Asian "Switzerland." But consistent with State's push toward recovery (the department ignored his notions of neutrality), in July and August 1949 MacArthur moved to end the *zaibatsu* breakup. Ingratiatingly inviting Acheson to Tokyo, in September he urged him to take up the peace treaty. Acheson was happy for his support, though MacArthur's ambition to chair a peace conference was not in his playbook. Acheson stipulated the need to retain U.S. bases but tried to convince MacArthur's nominal superiors across the Potomac that Soviet aggression against Japan was far less likely than an interminable occupation that estranged Japan's people and enlivened its communists. Trying to help, Ernest Bevin promised to start lining up Commonwealth backing for a peace treaty. Support also came from the China Round Table. Several participants blamed the more radical of MacArthur's economic reforms for sabotaging recovery—one quipped that the United States was "putting the cartel before the hearse"—and advocated a benign revival of Japan's co-prosperity sphere of the 1930s.[6]

Even with a draft treaty in hand, in December Acheson moaned to Bevin and Oliver Franks that unnamed problems with the Pentagon prevented him from moving ahead. The feuding Louis Johnson was one obstacle, but more important was opposition from the uniforms to any significant changes in their dominant status in Japan. Since Acheson had already agreed to maintain U.S. forces and bases and to encourage development of Japanese armed forces, he was incensed at the chiefs' stubbornness. Thus, what looked like an unequal fight over Japan paralleled the bloody struggle he was winning over China policy at the close of 1949. He did not want the British to know about the fight over Japan and, even to Franks, disingenuously blamed delays on the "predatory and uncooperative attitude of Soviet Russia." In the climactic NSC meeting of 29 December in which he gained his goals on China, he managed only the equivalent of a pause on Japan. Truman remarked that the United States, Britain, and "China" (Formosa) could negotiate a Japanese settlement "whether the USSR participated or not." This apparently placed him on Acheson's side but left the bureaucratic struggle unresolved. Nor had the president yet pressed the military to conform.[7]

The problem continued in the new year, as did Acheson's impatience with Pentagon recalcitrance. On Thursday, 2 February 1950, as JCS staff toured Japan, he asked if they could "stop saying once a day that we don't want a peace treaty." When he heard the same tune "on the radio again" on Friday, he wondered if "we couldn't convince the Military" to put an end to its daily anti-treaty bulletins. In Truman's presence on Saturday, he lobbied Elpidio Quirino, president of one of Japan's victims, the Philippines, for a prompt end to the occupation and a peace treaty. A little over two weeks later, he gained the president's approval to begin work on an appropriate NSC paper.[8]

A large step toward ending the bureaucratic fratricide arrived in the pious person of John Foster Dulles. In a campaign marked by speeches critical of

Truman, he had lost reelection to a Senate seat he had held briefly by appointment. Now he wooed Truman for another job, informing Luke Battle through an
intermediary of his interest. As Battle recalls, he passed the idea to James Webb,
who exclaimed with astonishment, "Have you lost your mind?" On second
thought, Webb wired the absent Acheson urging the appointment. On reading
the telegram, Acheson blurted out, "Has he lost his mind?" Then *he* recon-
sidered, asking Webb to take the idea to Truman, vacationing in Florida. Of
course, the president then exploded: "Has he lost his mind?" "Not at all a
reluctant bride," in Acheson's recollection, Dulles meanwhile sent Truman a
copy of a book he had just written that was friendly to the administration.
Others urged his appointment, too, including Dean Rusk and Senator Arthur
Vandenberg. Truman resisted, telling Acheson he "would never appoint that son
of a bitch to any office again." This was Trumanesque bluster, for he had already
authorized Acheson to go ahead. Dulles received the offer on 6 April and the next
day became another of Acheson's "consultants" on Asia.9

What exactly to do with Dulles was "a very grave problem," Acheson said,
because he was untrusted and "a notorious leaker." But since it made political
sense to have a Republican linked to Asia, where most of Washington's foreign
policy controversies originated, Acheson put him to work on a Japanese peace
treaty in the spring of 1950, aided by an Asia stalwart, the forty-five-year-old
John M. Allison. A graduate of the University of Nebraska, Allison had taught in
Japan, been interned there during the war, worked for General Motors in
Shanghai, served in the UN delegation, and now headed the office of Northeast
Asian affairs. He and Dulles sided with the JCS on the issue of Japanese rearmament, but Dulles warned the Pentagon that Japan would be "a useless ally" unless
quickly and "freely" aligned "with the West." Acheson underwrote both the
concession and the warning. As he could never do on China, he had immunized
himself and the department from partisan attack on Japan. Dulles had barely risen
from the starting blocks, however, when North Korean armies dashed across the
38th Parallel, changing almost everything about U.S. foreign policy.10

Short Subjects from the Third World

The derivation of some political phrases makes little sense. Japan was part of what
the Americans called the "free world." Presumably, the Soviet bloc formed the
"second world," though this escaped common usage, as did "first world." In 1952,
however, a French sociologist, Alfred Sauvy, came up with *tiers monde* to characterize states, mostly former European colonies, hoping to escape commitments
to the "first" or "second" worlds.11

To Acheson, this third world was mostly a mystery and source of frustration.
It eventually demanded more of his attention than he wanted to give it. He
made light of soulful cries against colonialism from the "Hallelujah section" but
grasped the impulses beneath the growing chorus of nationalism. In a speech

in October 1949, he referred to Asians' "great awakening," new national "consciousness," and refusal to accept "poverty and hunger." Nonetheless, his conviction that the kernel of U.S. security lay in the center of Europe and his penchant for sneering at peripheral states and peoples limited his sympathies. He understood little about the Muslim world, Africa, or Latin America.

Acheson did not describe Africans, Asians, or Arabs as "inferior" people, but he did call Philippines President Elpidio Quirino a "child of nature," which sounds like a division of the world between civilized and "natural." If unspoken, a sense of class and racial superiority affected how low on the totem pole he placed powerless peoples of color. So did hard calculations about what was important to U.S. policy. In executive testimony in the House in February 1949 in which he spoke of third world peoples' "noble aspiration" for independence, he forecast that it would likely result in "chaos." Third world peoples were largely illiterate and lacked "the simplest ideas of social organization." They did not know how to make schools, public health systems, or even roads. Government was a "mystery" to them, so as the former victims of imperialism, they would create "democratic forms with the austere ideas of European despotism lying underneath." Age accentuated his views, and by 1961 he wrote publicly that Latin American, Asian, and African revolutionary leaders were "wholly incompetent to manage their own affairs."[12]

Allies of the United States were still lodged in power in much of the third world, and as aware as Acheson might be of the revolutionary currents sweeping through colonies and former colonies, he was equally sensitive, if not more so, to the needs of alliance partners. In a December 1949 cable, he said U.S. policy should hew "a reasonable and moderate" line between winning the "friendship" of new nations and protecting the interests of allies. Problems that lay ahead demonstrated how much easier this was to say than do. Thus, he pushed measures to strengthen the colonial powers, but fears that communists would exploit the needs of emerging peoples, combined with a sometimes stinging contempt for imperialist and puffed-chest European attitudes, drew him away from those powers. He did so, however, for reasons of state, not from the kind of idealism practiced by Eleanor Roosevelt, a member of his UN delegation, or Chester Bowles, one of his ambassadors to India. Both believed, he snorted, in "the right of everybody to do what they want to do in their own part of the world." Acting on such an attitude would cause resentment in allied capitals and, in any case, favoring "liberty everywhere" was "a very emotional and shallow view" of the cold war that overlooked the vital role of political and military power.[13]

Junketing third world prime ministers and potentates often bored him, and he sometimes ignored briefing papers for their visits. He found their importunate squeezing of the U.S. treasury galling. Yet he did not worry about their socialism, or their nationalism, or protectionism. He might privately have deplored the internal arrangements of many of their states and societies, but this had little to do with his *diplomatic* treatment of them. If he sometimes did not act on it, he had an acute perception of how incrimination in European colonialism could harm U.S. interests. Except for Egypt and Iran in 1951–52, he granted subordinates in regional offices and country desks wide autonomy to protect those interests. Webb told the thirty-seven-year-old McGhee: "George, I want you to consider that you are the Secretary of State for the Middle East, South Asia and Africa." The department had no separate division for Africa until 1958.[14]

MATERIAL MEANS TO A NON-MATERIAL END: POINT FOUR

Acheson learned belatedly about the Point Four Program, Truman's best-known effort in the third world, and then helped make it a labor in vain if not a labor lost. In the last of four proposals for achieving "peace and freedom" in his 1949 inaugural speech, the president promised help for "under-developed areas" by spreading "the benefits of our scientific advances and industrial progress." Through Point Four, people would make progress "through their own efforts." One of the program's most important progenitors was Benjamin Hardy, a former agriculture department official now in the state department. He hoped to gain the loyalty of third world peoples through such homely means as digging wells and potato cellars, and his backers wanted "to move millions of people half an inch, rather than moving a few clear through the ceiling." When State gave him a deaf ear, Hardy caught the ear of the White House's George Elsey, who considered the idea an "answer to a maiden's prayer." The onetime farmer in the Oval Office liked it too. Clark Clifford saw propaganda punch in it, and Senator Brien McMahon of Connecticut called it a "peace bomb." As Acheson prepared for confirmation hearings, White House speechwriters brushed aside state department criticisms.[15]

The state department was "caught flatfooted" by Point Four, said its director in 1952–53, Stanley Andrews, who later recalled that officials simply did not know "what in the hell" Truman had in mind. First learning about Point Four as he listened to the inaugural speech "on the platform of the Capitol," Acheson scrambled for leverage. He discovered that the department had no ideas about the origins or execution of the program. At a press conference, he nimbly wrapped the idea in a broader framework, borrowing from economic adviser Herbert Feis to say it would use "material means" to advance the "non-material end" of freedom, aiding those still mired in the "ancient struggle" to gain their "bread from the soil." But, in a remark that already chipped away at its principles, Acheson implied that Point Four's test of success would be recipients' ability to attract private capital. He overrode White House staff in insisting on state department control but promised he would give high priority to this "Cinderella of the foreign aid family." Truman was doubtful but went along, Clifford remembers, "to keep the peace within the official family."[16]

In a move calculated to produce neglect, Acheson put Point Four in an "autonomous" office, adding it to the regular duties of economics assistant secretary, Willard Thorp. The state department never emphasized the program as Truman wished. Remembering that it was "very close to the heart of the President," Acheson, who apparently saw no anti-Soviet profit in Point Four, touted it just enough to keep it in his own bailiwick. Also acting to minimize its impact were Marshall Plan administrators, who viewed Truman's godchild as wrongheaded in rejecting heavy capital investment. A frustrated Elsey complained that State had to act more boldly to get Point Four "out of the mud," but conservative resistance (Robert Taft called it a "global W. P. A.") blocked appropriations until the spring of 1950. When finally ready to take off, the program found a charismatic director, Henry Bennett, but in December 1950 he was killed in a plane crash. When Andrews took over, Acheson told him: "Well, Stanley, you know about these damned country boys and the pie in the sky that you're peddling. You go ahead." The program handed out $306 million in 1952–53 before the omnibus Mutual Security Agency swallowed it, taking it away from State.[17]

Terra Incognita

Washington emerged from World War II with an expanded view of the Middle East's importance, but no one predicted the future gravity in American foreign policy of this area of Holocaust survivors, Palestinian refugees, oil sheiks, mullahs, and terrorists. The Sixth Fleet went on permanent cruise in the Mediterranean in 1946, but American generals considered the Middle East indefensible and wanted no part of it, expecting the UK to lead the way here in any war with the Russians. The U.S. military contribution would come from the air. Planes could raid Soviet cities, bases, and oil centers from bases in the Middle East, and nuclear bombers could land there after hitting the USSR from Britain.

American diplomatic officials contemplated a growing role in the region, if only because of petroleum. The United States was now an importer of oil, and its military forces obtained half its petroleum from the Middle East. More important, European economic recovery was hinged to energy, and one Marshall Plan dollar in ten paid for oil. The state department, which elevated legations in Lebanon, Syria, and Jordan to embassies in 1951, fretted about London's unpopularity and declining strength in the area, especially in Egypt, which began asking for U.S. military advisers to replace those from Britain in 1947. Britons in contrast recall this period for how the Yanks began to muscle into their old dominions. Friendly U.S.-UK relations would often depend on London's deference to a Washington on which it felt humiliatingly dependent. Acheson viewed this "unplanned, undesired, and haphazard" transfer of influence as a sign of declining European wisdom and growing inability to maintain order. As European power "waned," that of the United States "waxed." Russia, as Acheson wrote later, had great new opportunities for a movement to "warm water, to oil, and to mischief-making" because of Europe's decline, conflicts between Arabs and Jews, and the rise of nationalists in Egypt and Iran.[18]

Much of what Truman and Acheson did in the Middle East set patterns that long survived the administration, especially that of trying both to cosset Israel and to keep friendly relations with neighboring Arab states, many with oil underground. The United States also tried simultaneously to maintain close ties with the British and French who had dominated the area and with the nationalist forces opposing them. Acheson would eventually find his efforts to square these circles gravely disappointing. Though he tried mightily, he could never pull the United States free from the nexus of British colonialists, militarists, and oil producers. What he did not try mightily was to examine the likelihood of traditional, Muslim societies being attracted to communism, one of the fears largely shaping his policies. Later he would wonder bleakly if it might have been far better simply to develop overwhelming military power in the region to block Soviet seizure of oil, vital in any future war, whether or not a country or two went "communist." Behind all these concerns was Britain's decline, the consequence of which was a large expansion of responsibilities for Washington. Thrown into this unfamiliar theater, Acheson and his aides sought stability above all else, despite their intellectual recognition of the need to get on the "right" side of anti-imperialist nationalism. They quickly found that trying to maintain the status quo in an inherently explosive region made little sense. Acheson once remarked that short-term stability had its advantages—"When you step on a banana peel you have to keep from falling on your tail, you don't want to be lurching all over the place all the time"—but in Egypt and Iran especially he would realize this posture was not only clumsy but costly.[19]

Insofar as he tried wooing the Arabs, he got precious little help from Congress, which refused to approve any but trivial sums for Arab aid. Thus, the department sought private paths to economic development, which it took for granted would underwrite stability. This, along with the even more salient issue of oil, explained State's support for the Trans-Arabian Pipeline (TAPLINE). Constructed by the U.S.-owned Arabian American Oil Company (Aramco), this project, begun during the war, would move oil across the deserts of Saudi Arabia to western Europe via the Mediterranean. Thousands of workers earned wages building the pipeline, while host countries, especially Syria, took in valuable revenues. But turmoil rather than stability often accompanies economic "progress." Fellow officers murdered Syrian ruler Colonel Husni Zaim because of his pro-American cooperation, one of several Syrian coups in the era. Still, TAPLINE continued, and oil began flowing into tankers off Lebanon in December 1950. Other schemes also produced uncomfortable results, including the U.S. air base at Dhahran. This was the first key connection between the liberal American and medieval Saudi civilizations. It was also a source of fear to Moscow, for Dhahran put the heaviest Soviet industries within reach of U.S. bombers.[20]

The Americans were spreading themselves thin. At first both inexpert and aloof, Acheson said, "You know, I just don't understand what's going on in Syria at all. I just don't understand it." In time, he would take primary command over the Arab-Israeli dispute and the British conflicts with Egypt and Iran, but he never mastered the Middle East, especially its "fanatical xenophobia." When he left government, he felt "dissatisfaction with everything" he had done there.[21]

HEARTBURN IN THE HOLY LAND

Palestine was a hive of acrimony. Just as Acheson took office, a set of bilateral armistices ended the first Arab-Israeli war, in which the new Jewish homeland had established its precarious statehood. Out of both Zionist idealism and concern for the Jewish vote, Truman led the way in behalf of heavy Jewish immigration to Palestine and then in recognizing the new state. Acheson was out of government at the time of recognition. Earlier, he had managed to stay clear of mêlées between Truman and Marshall over Palestine. His sympathies, however, were with Marshall and the department professionals who opposed recognition, and he worried that the west would pay a high price for Israel's existence. When he later evaluated a draft of Truman's memoirs in 1955, he skewered Truman's depiction of Arab thinking and defended the department against his libels of anti-Semitism. His own education on Zionism had come mainly at the hands of Felix Frankfurter, but disagreements about its impact on U.S. foreign policy put it in quarantine as a subject in their conversations. In 1945, Acheson had vaguely meditated on having Brazil supply a homeland to the Jews, an idea about as valuable as UN Ambassador Warren Austin's later plea that Arabs and Jews "settle this problem in a true Christian spirit." Although an unquantifiable number of his colleagues were guilty as Truman charged, anti-Semitism was alien to Acheson, but he begrudged Israel's conflicts for their power to distract and to drain energy and resources away from more important matters. He also resented Israel, and its friends, for their power to cause disagreements between him and the president. Carefully nurturing his White House capital, he gradually brought Truman closer to department thinking. He kept him fully informed, warned him when decisions might provoke domestic counterpressures, and reassured him that he would take no vital decisions in the area without his participation. Friction still occurred, but far less than might have been.[22]

Rusk predicted that department decisions on the Middle East would "cause the President considerable heartburn," a good forecast considering that Acheson always found the Israelis more irritating than the Arabs. Bevin added to his concern with a report that the Soviets were courting Arab states. Acheson argued with Tel Aviv over its slow acceptance of Egyptian armistice proposals and refusal to consider letting 100,000-plus Palestinian refugees return within Israel's boundaries, which also bothered Truman. Both men thought the repatriation issue damaged U.S. interests, but Acheson got nowhere when he complained in the fall of 1949 to the Israeli foreign minister that the issue was upsetting the "good order and well-being of the Near East." He preferred a tougher attitude toward Israel but was also disgusted with the Arabs. Both sides were "unrealistic and intransigent." Following more pressure from Truman, Tel Aviv made a few inadequate gestures to repatriate Palestinian refugees.[23]

This was early in the development of the so-called Jewish lobby, but Webb was already telling Acheson that Israel "had more influence with US than has US with Israel." Assiduous lobbying by Tel Aviv and its friends in the United States reinforced broader popular sympathy and guilt about the Holocaust. In 1949, Israel was deliberately trying to drive a wedge between Truman and the state department on the refugee issue, mostly through White House staffer David Niles. Niles so actively represented Israeli interests that the CIA finally tattled on him for leaking secret information, which embarrassed and angered Truman. Miffed at Israel's "smear campaign," Acheson urged the president to withhold aid promised earlier and strip tax-exempt status from the United Jewish Appeal. Working together, Truman and Acheson assured a dawdling reaction to an Israeli request for an Export-Import loan, and Truman refused to back Israel on the refugee issue in various international bodies. But he remained unpredictable on matters concerning Israel. Thus, his approval in October 1949 of an NSC paper calling for a "revision" of attitudes toward Israel if it did not cooperate on the refugee issue followed by two months his forcing the release of Ex-Im funds for Israel sequestered by Acheson. Sometimes, Peter Hahn writes, "two bureaucracies," the state department and the Israeli foreign ministry, "battled for Truman's blessing." It seemed to Acheson that each time he and the president shook hands on an Israeli issue, Tel Aviv would spot Truman winking over the secretary's shoulder.[24]

With the end of the Arab-Israeli war came an end to a UN arms embargo, prompting new concern about a regional arms race. Egypt, Syria, and Israel queued up to buy U.S. arms. In September, Washington approved private arms sales for internal security and "self defense," providing they not endanger the armistice. This policy soon broke down, leading in the spring of 1950 to a major Anglo-French-American initiative treated in a later chapter.[25]

INDIA

Acheson seldom became involved in South Asia, which he considered a secondary theater. Associating the new nation of India with purveyors of pie in the sky, he found it hard to escape "from a childhood illusion that, if the world is round, the Indians must be standing on their heads—or, perhaps, vice versa." In 1952, he remarked that the country was so hot, American diplomats in New Delhi had to "pull their cots out in the yard to sleep" (not unlike the District of Columbia before the era of air conditioning). Three years before, he had told Indian Ambassador "Nan" Pandit—Prime Minister Jawaharlal Nehru's sister—he anticipated that her democratic and nationalist country would lead Asia in defeating communist "encroachment" in Asia. She thought he "knew very little, past or present" about India. Few other Washington officials did, either. After Indian independence in 1947, they mainly deplored tensions resulting from the Kashmir border dispute caused by the subcontinent's division into the states of India and Pakistan. Washington cut off arms shipments to both sides but dodged British entreaties to mediate. Britain as "senior member of the Commonwealth," Acheson told Bevin in February 1950, should lead. When a persistent London asked that someone like Marshall mediate, an amused Acheson replied that since "we had only one General Marshall," he was certain "the President would not agree."[26]

An early lowlight of U.S.-Indian relations came with Nehru's first visit to the United States in October 1949. Acheson had admitted to Bevin six months before that U.S. "thinking" about India had so far been "vague," but by August he had learned enough to tell Truman that Nehru might become the "dominant political force in Asia." Nehru's commitment to neutralism and refusal to compromise on Kashmir displeased U.S. officials, but the advent of Communist China motivated them to send aid to a nation whose biggest problem was feeding its own people. Nehru wanted cheap loans, while Acheson preferred modest Point Four programs and private investment. The administration lavished flattery on the prime minister in advance of his journey, Acheson referring to him as "a world figure" who could take the lead in Asia's "rehabilitation."[27]

Weighed down by a large chip on his shoulder, Nehru expected no fundamental sympathy or understanding from the Americans. Nor did he get it. After a warm greeting from Truman at the airport, one official recalled, things "went rapidly down hill." A speech by Acheson at a formal dinner misfired. Another cabinet minister at the dinner, garrulous and worse for wear from hard spirits, insulted Nehru's daughter (future prime minister, Indira Gandhi) with noisy jabs at "these foreigners who come over here and take our money away from us." Acheson took Nehru to the bosom of his home to talk informally, but instead of relaxing, the Indian addressed the American "as Queen Victoria said of Mr. Gladstone, as though I were a public meeting." Nehru "went through the roof" talking about Kashmir. At White House and state department discussions, he lectured instead of listened. On a department-organized "discovery of America" tour, he turned up his nose at America's moneymaking culture. Privately, he viewed Truman "a mediocre man" and Acheson "equally mediocre." Truman said he "just doesn't like white men." His hosts did a slow burn when Nehru used his tour to go over the government's head as he complained to Americans that their government had ignored India's needs. Yet in fact, his pride had prevented him from directly asking for help. Acheson considered him "one of the most difficult men" he had ever dealt with and was happy when he left.[28]

Relations with India declined, not because of the summit debacle but because of Kashmir and Washington's failure to meet India's foreign aid expectations.

Shortly after the Nehru tour, Acheson threw cold water on Ambassador Loy Henderson's idea of a $500 million aid program. The Indians would have to tough it out with loans and self-reliance. The NSC at year's end downgraded India's importance to U.S. security, and policymaking remained reactive. When Pakistani prime minister, Liaquat Ali Khan, arranged a summit in Moscow, Truman did the inevitable, inviting him to Washington in May 1950. Acheson again played the host, with even less enthusiasm.[29]

Iran

Another careerist in asking for expensive help was the *nouveau* king of Iran, Mohammed Reza Shah Pahlavi. At twenty-two, he had been placed on the Peacock Throne during the war after British and Soviet forces ousted his pro-Nazi father. Since the crises of 1945–46, Washington had paid Iran little heed, sending small-scale military missions and counting on Britain to keep things quiet. Iran would soon explode, precisely because of Britain, but foreign aid was at the top of the agenda during the Shah's November 1949 pilgrimage to Washington. Acheson had scorched Moscow in March for its "press and radio propaganda" against the Shah but privately pooh-poohed the likelihood of aggression. Congress designated Iran eligible for MDAP funds even though the Pentagon thought it could no more make efficient use of military aid than China did during the war. Agreeing, Acheson believed Iran should depend on private investment, Export-Import Bank loans, and Point Four for economic development. But the Shah wanted nothing less than a combination of Marshall Plan and MDAP.[30]

Coming a month after Nehru, this newest supplicant's descent on the capital convinced Acheson that most state visits were stupid. The Shah, he recalled in 1954, was "a very impractical young man" full of "grandiose ideas." Imagining himself a strategist, he ruminated in an "utterly fanciful" way on Iran's role in containing the USSR. (Acheson had already rebuffed his bid to join NATO.) Escorted by McGhee, the even more youthful Shah bubbled over with grandiosity. Truman, who needed little tutoring on the history of the ancients, heard all about the "long history of Iran, its ups and downs and the extent of the Persian Empire under Darius the Great." Acheson lectured *him* on making "economic and social development" his priority. "The best way to prevent war," he told him, was to immunize Iran from Soviet designs through such development. He then cited the "Chinese lesson," relating how Chiang had lost the confidence of his people and his own army after squandering millions in senseless military adventures.

Deaf to Acheson's lessons, the Shah asked for Marshall Plan aid. When Acheson told him it was only for Europe, the Shah cheekily replied that Turkey was hardly European. When Acheson told him to look to the World and Export-Import banks for help, the crestfallen monarch explained that "he could not return empty handed. Was there something more that we could do, whether in the economic or military field?" Refusing any explicit commitments, Acheson nonetheless told him he could be certain the United States would not ignore Iran "if trouble should come." Back home, Shah Pahlavi made a trade deal with Moscow and dickered for refurbished political ties as well. Annoyed, Acheson warned him that "any close relationship" with the Soviets would sour public and congressional opinion toward Iran.[31]

*   *   *   *

Apart from Japan and China (and later Korea), Acheson regarded most non-European areas of the world as insignificant and nuisances withal. Rulers like Nehru and the Shah seemed to specialize in annoying him and stealing time from doing what really mattered, which was building the western alliance against the Soviet Union. Much work remained to create situations of strength in Europe, but he was reasonably sure he knew how to do *that*. The world of uprooted Palestinians and pompous South Asian prime ministers, however, was disorderly, impenetrable, and beyond U.S. control. He wanted them to hold still, to stay in their secondary place. They usually did not.

Part III

13

WEAPONS: THE H-BOMB

The reader will recall how the 1949 meeting of the Council of Foreign Ministers in Paris boosted Acheson's optimism about his place in the administration and about the west's edge over the Soviets. The optimism about the latter was short-lived, however, and as Acheson looked back two or three years, he could see grounds for serious worry. Four years since the British loan and now well into the working of the Marshall Plan, the economies of western Europe, especially Britain's, still faltered in their paths toward recovery. The great Chinese nation had fallen into the hands of a disciple of Josef Stalin. NATO was a marvelous invention but still a shell as far as providing real defense for western Europe. Worst of all, the west could do almost nothing if the hundreds of thousands of Red Army artillery and infantrymen in the satellite states, backed by even more in the USSR, decided to attack westward.

Of course, the United States could respond by raining atomic bombs on Soviet troops and cities, but Acheson had never believed nuclear weapons could win such a war. And now, the Soviets had their own bomb. Even though the American supply of nuclear weapons greatly outnumbered Stalin's arsenal, the time was drawing quite near when Washington could expect direct retaliation should it send nuclear bombers over the Soviet Union. Whatever progress the west was making territorially, that is, in strengthening this or that country abroad against Soviet intimidation or subversion, a gigantic hole remained in the agenda of converting positions of weakness to situations of strength. Military power—the capacity either to win or deter the enemy—was a necessary foundation of statecraft, and at the moment, Acheson felt the foundation crumbling underfoot. A headline in December 1949 read:

MR. ACHESON'S TROUBLES NOW COVER THE GLOBE
Secretary of State Finds a Cause for a "Headache" Wherever He Looks on the Diplomatic Map of the World[1]

These anxieties formed the background for two secret and historic policy reviews of late 1949 and early 1950. The first led to the decision to develop a hydrogen bomb vastly more powerful than the atomic bomb dropped on Hiroshima. The second produced NSC-68, which called for a more aggressive and military-oriented approach to the cold war. President Truman told the public about the H-Bomb, but the classified NSC-68 saw the light of day only through indirect filters of policy speeches, notably Acheson's. Critics within the government fought both the H-Bomb and NSC-68. In Acheson's case, his sponsorship of the latter was an expression of his reservations about the former. In contrast, Truman decided on the bomb quickly but was extremely hesitant about supporting NSC-68. Only with the Korean War would he sign and execute it, with large and manifold consequences, from German rearmament and an exploding defense budget to deepening U.S. involvement in Indochina.

Soviet Strength, American Quandaries

Overrating himself, Vyacheslav Molotov recalled that "everything was snuggled in Stalin's fist and mine." What plans did the Americans think the Soviet ruler had in his fist? His drive for supremacy in ground forces opened the postwar arms race. Washington erred in some of its estimates, but policymakers were not simply exaggerating Soviet military capabilities to justify their own plans. While U.S. military plans and actions doubtless contributed to Stalin's belligerence, his concern about European economic and political developments was more important. The Marshall Plan and Tito's defection imperiled his grip on eastern Europe. He may have worried far less about NATO, which he understood to be defensive in aim, than the CIA's creation of the Free Europe Committee in 1949. The committee was one of his pretexts for repression and an arms buildup that doubled the size of Soviet forces to 5.8 million men. He "stepped up preparations for a war before the Americans did," writes Vojtech Mastny. Though the United States actually underestimated this mobilization, the JCS warned in February 1950 that Moscow "could invade Europe from a standing start." Rearmament created new problems for Stalin, too, for east European economies cracked under the strain, setting off mid-1950s upheavals in East Germany, Poland, and Hungary.[2]

Stalin knew about the holes in American military capabilities. Basing problems and intelligence lacunae would compromise plans for nuclear bombing attacks. American infantry had poor support from tactical air forces. Should a war come, Stalin might expect his armored divisions and nascent nuclear capability to be sufficiently intimidating to both Americans and Europeans to preclude a stalwart U.S. reaction. Washington officials knew NATO could not stop a Soviet attack without a large infantry buildup—or quick resort to American atomic attacks. In the view of U.S. policymakers, one of the greatest dangers was that European allies would be paralyzed by the fear of war. As the Dutch prime minister told Acheson in 1952, Moscow understood it had no need to "cut anyone's throat when you can put poison in his soup." Yet both east and west also understood that over time, western resources would outmatch the Soviet bloc's. A state department intelligence report judged the Soviet Union "definitely inferior" to the west for the long haul, even not counting "the atom bomb." The crucial question in 1949–50, therefore, was how to mobilize western resources to get over the hump of temporary western inferiority. Some answers would appear in NSC-68.[3]

Thinking at this time about the Soviet challenge always brought to mind the current U.S. nuclear monopoly (in Acheson's case, not reassuringly), which strongly shaped war planning. It was on Stalin's mind, too, and from the outset of the Manhattan Project, his agents were helping him make it a duopoly. In 1946, long before Truman decided to develop thermonuclear, or fusion bombs, Stalin, unknown to U.S. officials, had ordered an emergency program to develop his own. The Soviet Union's first test of a fission bomb on 29 August 1949 came considerably earlier—anywhere from one to three years—than the CIA had projected. Truman waited nearly a month to announce U.S. detection of the test. With Stalin's confidence growing, his heir apparent, Georgi Malenkov, trumpeted the failure of capitalism in a November speech. If the imperialists started a war, he warned, "the sorrow of mothers, wives, sisters and children will visit the American continent." American officials worried, writes Melvyn Leffler, that as Moscow grew bolder, "the possibilities of an accidental war would increase, and the Western alliance would falter."[4]

The Americans most confident about U.S. military prowess had the long term in mind and were usually civilians. The uniformed officers better understood the fragility of their military shield, but a fixation on World War II precedents hampered their strategic thinking. So did a tardy awareness of the revolution wrought by nuclear weapons. Complicating all planning were fierce interservice contests over Truman's defense budgets, a struggle leading early in 1949 to an "admirals' revolt" against shrinking naval resources. As the internecine struggles continued, only five U.S. army divisions stood opposite the large Soviet force standing on the berm of western Europe. They were occupation troops, not combat-ready. American defense in 1949 relied on nuclear weapons to deter that Soviet force from attacking. If deterrence failed, war plans assumed western armies would hold off the Red Army long enough for the U.S. air force to bomb the Soviet Union to oblivion.

The Atomic Energy Act of 1946 gave the president sole control of the U.S. nuclear arsenal, which as late as the spring of 1947 consisted of only seven bombs, hardly enough to supply a margin of victory. Uranium and plutonium shortages frustrated efforts of the Atomic Energy Commission (AEC) to build more. In addition, exercises in 1948 showed that strategic air command crews could not put "a weapon on target" in wartime conditions. The Strategic Air Command (SAC) was then an under-armed and under-trained "hollow threat." As General Curtis LeMay revamped it, the stockpile grew to two hundred bombs by late 1949 and three hundred by June 1950. Technical advances soon made it possible to make far smaller bombs still packing the punch of earlier models. But even when the arsenal remained tiny, the department of defense put it at the center of war planning. A 1948 plan called "Fleetwood" called for dropping the whole supply of atomic bombs on Soviet cities in the first thirty days of a war. War plans in 1949 were so ambiguous about the ability to defend western Europe, Americans could not discuss them with allies.⁵

The Harmon Committee Report in the spring of 1949 suggested that none of these plans would work. Ordered by the JCS and staffed equally by the three services, the committee reached its conclusions unanimously. It doubted SAC's assurances of piercing Soviet defenses and estimated its bombing accuracy to be less than advertised. The attack would unwind so slowly, said the report, that Soviet armies could reach the English Channel in the interval. A SAC attack might kill millions and destroy the Soviet oil industry, but it would not produce a Soviet surrender. Echoing the strategic bombing survey of World War II, the report claimed that SAC bombing would not "destroy the roots of Communism or critically weaken the power of Soviet leadership to dominate the people" but would "validate Soviet propaganda, unify the people, and increase their will to fight." (The committee did not explain how millions of deaths would increase the will to fight.)

The Harmon Report was an indirect condemnation of Truman's budgets, which had stripped conventional forces to the bone and increased dependence on nuclear weapons. Quiet cheers came from the army and navy, angry at the lopsided share of budgets the air force was harvesting. Because of its budget implications, Defense Secretary Louis Johnson, Truman's enthusiastic executor of scarcity, successfully kept the report off any Oval Office desk. Acheson, too, understood the report's significance, hoping it would make the chiefs more "responsive" to his own arguments that the key U.S. objective was to prevent rather than fight a war. The Harmon Committee itself, however, proposed to solve the problems it unearthed by building even more nuclear weapons. Thus by the fall of 1949, U.S. planning relied on them more than ever. Truman had never given any thought to the dilemmas of nuclear strategy and had no problem with such reliance, telling advisers in mid-July that since arms control schemes were futile, "we must be strongest in atomic weapons."⁶

Nuclear Anxieties

The secretary of state's job was not to decide how to use national weaponry should diplomacy fail. But because the ostensible Soviet threat affected so many diplomatic issues, Acheson made military strategy his business, especially as he came increasingly to mistrust Pentagon judgment. He had long believed the extension of U.S. defense frontiers was a key to national security. But one could establish this "reach" with ground troops on European soil, SAC bombers spanning continents, or both. Many strategic debates within Washington and with allies concerned creating the proper mix of the two.

Acheson may first have thought that the NATO alliance itself would deter any Soviet plans of attack, which would allow a military revival to proceed at a pace that did not jeopardize Europe's economic recovery. The fear of an American industrial mobilization would probably arrest Moscow long enough for the allies to form their own military deterrent. When Korea exploded these views, he had already decided that NATO's banners must boast more than vows of mutual support to impress the Russians. Equally important in pushing him toward a military solution was his concern that the allies would not muster the confidence to move forward economically and socially without the protection of armies on the ground. Regardless, the west needed ways to respond to a surprise invasion or accidental war. With the European military buildup slow in coming, Acheson and other Washington policymakers grew increasingly concerned about how to stop a Soviet assault through central Europe. At best, NATO might retard an attack, allowing the release of U.S. nuclear strikes, followed by a slogging ground war of restoration. Thus, in 1949 and early 1950, Americans foresaw World War III as a nuclear war but long, ending in a slugfest with the Red Army.

High politics drove the search for a "forward" defense. The image of a restored rather than defended Europe appalled allies. French Premier Henri Queuille said the Americans "would probably be liberating a corpse and civilization would be dead." Nor were Germans encouraged at the thought of having their territory conceded without a fight, and Konrad Adenauer feared his countrymen might prefer a deal with the USSR. To Acheson, that would mean losing the cold war. American occupation troops would have to mutate into a fighting army to meet the Russians as soon as they attacked. Ultimately, Washington would accept this burden only if the allies rebuilt their armies and came along. By 1950, it added the condition that the Germans fight alongside, an obnoxious idea in Europe, especially in France. Until the alliance could solve these problems, it was stuck with a puny, poorly trained force barely able to nick the Soviets as they rushed to the Channel. The Pentagon's plans in 1949, said a later critic, amounted to "little more than assignment to withdrawal routes." Perhaps worse, they assumed nuclear action that would devastate Germany even more than ground warfare. Ten days before war began in Korea, British General Bernard Montgomery forecast "scenes of appalling and indescribable confusion in Western Europe if we were ever attacked by the Russians."[7]

This takes us ahead of our story. Late in 1949, the admirals' revolt, Harmon Report, and Soviet atomic test caused a spate of hard thinking about nuclear weapons. Acheson's hopes for international control were long dead, and he had come to consider nuclear weapons a grim necessity, either as a war-fighting weapon or a deterrent. For them to serve as the latter, he noted in October 1949, the enemy must believe the United States would actually use nuclear weapons. Unlike George Kennan, he *wanted* Moscow to fear them, but he remained uncomfortable relying on nuclear weapons. As noted earlier, he pointed out that even with a U.S. monopoly, nuclear "deterrence" had failed to avert either the Czech coup or Berlin blockade. With the Harmon Report in mind, he had privately told senators in June the United States had too few atomic bombs to stop an invasion of western Europe.[8]

He pushed even harder for a conventional arms buildup after Moscow bared its own nuclear teeth. In all likelihood, the USSR could soon neutralize plans to respond to a Soviet invasion of western Europe with a nuclear attack on Russian targets. Who would believe, Acheson asked, that Washington would knowingly invite a nuclear reprisal by thus reacting to a *conventional* attack? Nor was "preventive war," much bruited about in 1950, a solution. It was impossible to justify, he told senators in January 1950, merely because someone said "100 years or 50 years from now we might lose a war." The real solution to Soviet nuclear power was to build situations of strength across the board, conventional as well as nuclear, economic and political as well as military.[9]

"What a Depressing World It Is": The "Super"

A request by the joint chiefs for more atomic bombs was the event that led to the decision to build the H-Bomb and to the writing of national security council paper 68. The request came in the wake of the Soviet test, the communist takeover in China, and revelations of Soviet espionage against western governments. In October, Truman appointed a special NSC committee of Acheson, Johnson, and AEC chairman David Lilienthal to assess the request and then reappointed them a month later to resolve the ongoing argument about the H-Bomb. Finally, on 31 January 1950, when Truman made his H-Bomb decision, he asked Acheson and Johnson to lead yet another special committee to review U.S. "objectives in peace and war," especially as they might be affected by the development of either American or Soviet H-Bombs. The new committee met Acheson's hope for a forum where he could push for more conventional armed strength. Secondarily, the committee offered a place for H-Bomb opponents like Lilienthal to voice their concerns.[10]

Acheson assigned Paul Nitze, now deputy to Kennan but already effectively in charge of the policy planning staff, to forge improved communications with the military's strategic planners. He needed to circumvent his attritional feud with Johnson, caused mostly by the defense secretary's envy of his ties with Truman. Acheson was not about to forfeit Truman's increasing reliance on State. He asked both Nitze and Kennan, whose stock was still on the decline, to join him in drafting appraisals of the strategic situation. Kennan exposed his growing estrangement with an anguished plea to eliminate nuclear weapons and revive arms control talks. In contrast, Acheson and Nitze sought ways to compensate for the impact of Soviet nuclear weapons on the U.S. defense posture. All three, however, opposed tying U.S. strategy too closely "to the atom bomb."[11]

The H-Bomb and strategy reviews were so intermixed that participants blended them in memory, but the H-Bomb came first. Kennan thought Moscow's behavior might hinge on Washington's, but virtually nothing the United States did, or did not do, would have blocked development of a Soviet H-Bomb. As early as 1946, Moscow's scientists were teasing out the technical problems, and Stalin ordered them to accelerate production of a hydrogen bomb immediately after the first Soviet atomic test, thus dispensing, as David Holloway writes, with "the soul-searching that took place in the United States." American scientists had lost interest in the "super-bomb" after the war. Robert Oppenheimer and others doubted its viability and moral legitimacy. Instead of going for the H-Bomb, Oppenheimer, then head of the AEC's General Advisory Committee (GAC), preferred keeping the United States "strong and healthy" and close to its "friends." This was not good enough for AEC commissioner Lewis Strauss, who in October 1949 exhorted Truman to initiate development of the H-Bomb. The ensuing review occurred in great secrecy, with committee members debating candidly and proceeding as if options were open. The prevailing secrecy also reflected the national security establishment's growing independence and a media passivity unimaginable today. Secret or not, Truman could point to the orderly process when he announced his decision in favor of development.[12]

Evidence that he was not making a snap decision was important to Truman, but he had probably decided to build the H-Bomb weeks earlier. The review committee framed the question around the wisdom of a "crash program" to build it. Resources poured into a *failed* fusion bomb project would be unavailable to current *fission* bomb production. After first wavering, concerned about using scarce dollars on deuterium and tritium rather than the plutonium needed for fission bombs, the joint chiefs decided it "would be intolerable" not to have an H-Bomb if the Soviets had one. For weeks, Acheson's mind seemed genuinely open. He chewed over several kinds of questions as the review went forward. He was concerned, for example, that deciding against H-Bomb development would shake allies' confidence in U.S. guarantees. In contrast, his greatest misgiving was that a decision in favor of a crash program would trump the conventional buildup he wanted.

Acheson's friend Oppenheimer doubted the weapon would even work, and the entire GAC had come out against a crash fusion-bomb program. Most members seemed to think that if the United States unilaterally foreswore the H-Bomb, its power of example would persuade Moscow not to build one either. After a break in secrecy led to a senator's revelation that the government planned to build a bomb a thousand times more powerful than the Nagasaki weapon, AEC opposition became more marked. Fear of the impact on fission bomb development was one reason, but that paled compared to commissioners' growing moral objections to the "Super." When informed by Lilienthal of these views, Acheson turned "quite gray" before saying: "What a depressing world it is." To help make up his own mind, he enlisted Nitze, Legal Adviser Adrian Fisher, and R. Gordon Arneson, a nuclear expert plucked from the UN delegation. He seemed genuinely unbiased to observers as he picked the brains of bomb opponents. But he finally concluded it was impossible to "say we're not going to do this thing, that we will put it in a bushel basket somewhere." The United States might not build an H-Bomb, but "certainly the Russians would, the British would, maybe even Pakistan, certainly the French."[13]

With Kennan, Nitze, Fisher, Dean Rusk, James Webb, Llewellyn Thompson, and John Paton Davies present, Acheson converted a PPS meeting on 3 November 1949 into a sounding board for his lingering doubts. Thinking no arms control measures could stop a war from "eventually" going nuclear, he mulled over negotiating an 18–24-month U.S.-Soviet moratorium on H-Bomb production. Gathering a remarkable ball of wool, he also wondered aloud about a step-by-step attempt to end the cold war altogether. The two sides might pick one tough issue after another, get the best possible resolution for each through negotiations, then take up another problem, and another, and then see "what you would have if you put them all together." This would be better than "just sitting and exchanging glassy stares." A moratorium would give time for the administration to mobilize economically and prepare the people "to do whatever is necessary," putting it in a better position for full-scale H-Bomb development if negotiations failed. This was a remarkable bit of speculation, utterly contrary to his standing assumption that there was no point in talking to the Soviets. Apparently, he was simply talking about the idea to hear how it sounded. It must have seemed dissonant, for nothing further was heard of it.

Four days later, Acheson asked Truman for more time. On 9 November, the AEC voted 3–2 against the fusion project. The president, who also wanted advice about publicizing "this matter," received a forceful letter urging H-Bomb production from Senator Brien McMahon. Head of the Joint Committee on Atomic Energy, McMahon said it was impossible to draw a moral line "between a big explosion which causes heavy damage and many smaller explosions causing equal or still greater damage."[14]

To further study the issues, near the end of November, Acheson appointed a new committee under Nitze. Most members were clearly in favor of H-Bomb development. Acheson instructed them to avoid "the ultimate moral question at this time," which should be saved for consideration in the study's conclusion. For now, he wanted them to focus on practical questions. How would developing the H-Bomb affect other ventures? How could the United States *use* such a bomb? What was its value in the face of likely retaliation? "If both sides have it, will either use it?" What would happen if the Soviets went forward and the Americans did not? Would approval provide the platform for a successful east-west "modus vivendi" to "stabilize world conditions"? He also worried that Washington's H-Bomb discussion would cause other nations to believe the United States considered war inevitable.[15]

The temperature of the debate rose, with Kennan's increasingly anti-bomb views pushing him to the fringe. Nitze wanted to go ahead with research and development but reserve a decision about production. In a career day in strategic thinking, Acheson on 20 December dictated a long memorandum to ready himself for upcoming meetings with Johnson and Lilienthal. In retrospect, his trajectory toward a "yes" stance is clear, but this memo was full of Kennan-like misgivings. He doubted the military efficacy of either nuclear or thermonuclear weapons. He questioned whether publicly declared determination to use nuclear or thermonuclear weapons would actually deter an attack in Europe. He worried that stacking up nuclear weapons might cause Europeans to renege on building conventional forces.

More broadly, he doubted *any* military strategy could alter the will of another nation. Soviet war plans might already have discounted a U.S. nuclear attack, that is, the Red Army might plunge forward regardless of what the United States threw at it. He raised doubts about the wisdom of promising to defend Europe if the result was a Soviet nuclear attack on the continental United States. But since he understood that any signs of U.S. indecision could shatter NATO, he expressed his doubts guardedly, virtually in code. He also considered the risks of pushing vigorously ahead. If the Russians mistakenly thought the west planned on war, they might strike preemptively. However improbable, such unpleasant prospects helped end his doubts. More important, so did the thought of Stalin owning the world's only superbomb. How, he asked Oppenheimer, could any president "survive a policy of not making the H-bomb"? If Moscow went ahead, Truman would be ruined when opponents discovered he had said no to H-Bomb production, and one of Acheson's self-appointed tasks was protecting the president politically.[16]

Acheson would have the swing vote on the Special Committee, since Johnson and Lilienthal had already leaped into the pro and con corners of the ring. Through late December and January, the review fell into inconclusive body punching. Lilienthal grew more depressed by the day, and Johnson tried to make Acheson look bad to the president. To compensate for dissension on China,

Acheson wanted to give the president a unanimous vote. He told Arneson after a troubled conversation with Oppenheimer, "You know, I listened as carefully as I knew how, but I don't understand what 'Oppie' was trying to say. How can you persuade a paranoid adversary to disarm 'by example'?" He was dismayed, too, at what he considered Lilienthal's unpersuasive moral arguments. With unanimity still elusive, he delayed, but, with Strauss's backing, the aggressive Johnson made an end run past the committee in mid-January by sending a JCS memo supporting the bomb directly to Truman. Already, in a *Saturday Evening Post* article, General Omar Bradley had tacitly confessed that U.S. defense plans depended on nuclear weapons. Now in the memo for Truman, the chiefs not only discarded their last reservations, they expressed derision for those entertaining moral doubts about the H-Bomb and generally disparaged civilian wisdom on "military" matters. The memo seemed to impress Truman, the more so because the JCS denied the need for a "crash" program. Acheson only learned about it when NSC Executive Secretary Admiral Sidney Souers told him on 19 January 1950 that Truman would consider the memo part of the regular process—if the Special Committee acted swiftly.[17]

On 23 January in a secret White House briefing, Acheson heard that 70 percent to 85 percent of U.S. bombers would reach their destinations in a nuclear attack on the Soviet Union, but only 50 percent to 70 percent would return to their bases. In such an attack, bombers would do lasting damage to 50 percent to 67 percent of their industrial targets. Altogether, the estimates suggested indecisive results at an extremely high cost. Four days later came news that physicist Klaus Fuchs in Britain had confessed to spying for the Russians at the Manhattan Project and in discussions of the "Super" at Los Alamos. This news deepened Washington's worries and convinced some of those involved to enlist in a cold war consensus they had formerly rejected. Theoretical physicist Marshall Rosenbluth, a former critic, now joined the U.S. project. "I thought Stalin was just a terrible son of a bitch. If he ever got the bomb before we did it could be very dangerous."[18]

On a gleaming wintry Tuesday, 31 January 1950, the Special Committee gathered for its climactic session in Acheson's old wartime quarters in the Executive Office Building office, now Admiral Souers's retreat. The principals ranged around the conference table. "Rather warily" chairing, Acheson tabled a recommendation by Arneson asking the president to instruct the AEC to decide whether the H-Bomb was technically feasible and, if so, to begin development. The AEC and Pentagon would jointly decide on the pace and scale of the effort, while a committee would conduct a review (leading to NSC-68) on the effort's strategic impact. The president should announce the H-Bomb decision to the public but otherwise embargo information on the subject. Although Lilienthal reluctantly agreed, furnishing the unanimity Acheson wanted, he expatiated on his reservations. Patiently, Acheson said that nothing in what Lilienthal had said, however reasonable, was of use to the president. Growing international tension and rising congressional pressure—dismissed by Lilienthal as an "atmosphere of excitement"—redoubled the need for strategic clarity. Acheson himself, he wrote later, could not "overcome two stubborn facts." First, the Americans might procrastinate, but the Soviets would not. Second, the public would find it intolerable on "so vital a matter" to hold back while trying to negotiate differences with a Soviet regime that had made its own H-Bomb. The committee formally decided to recommend production and then added commas and checked the spelling in Arneson's draft. Since they already had an appointment with Truman, Johnson now steered members for a walk to the White House to "get a decision."[19]

Acheson and Souers handed the recommendations to the president in the Oval Office. Truman could see at a glance he had the backing he wanted. But Acheson asked him to hear out Lilienthal, and the outgoing AEC commissioner launched into an abridged version of his objections. Truman cut him off: "Can the Russians do it?" Yes, said Lilienthal. "In that case," Truman said, in a buck-stops-here moment, "we have no choice. We'll go ahead." He signed, approved the wording of the public announcement, and ordered work on the recommended strategic reassessment. The meeting lasted seven minutes.[20]

"No Excuse for . . . Closing Their Eyes"

Acheson would no more look back than his chief. The government had a duty "to explore this thing. There was no excuse for people of responsibility closing their eyes to an area which, if discovered, might be disadvantageous to us." But if he had decided for the hydrogen bomb, he had not put away his concerns about its possible uselessness, which went for atomic bombs too. He still thought relying on them was dangerous and would erode western willingness to mobilize conventional forces. He and Nitze had plans for that.[21]

Having suffered the pain necessary to decide on the least onerous alternative, Acheson was vexed at those who disagreed, most unpalatably Lilienthal, Oppenheimer, and Kennan. All friends, they now spouted ethical objections he mocked. Lilienthal's hope to halt H-Bomb research while negotiating with the Kremlin was the untenable equivalent of staying ignorant while relying on the Soviets' "perpetual good will." Though Acheson had a soft spot for the "one half poet," Oppenheimer, on the H-Bomb he was one of the "most naïve" men Acheson knew.

He reserved his harshest criticism for Kennan, who had harried him with memos and finally took an absolute stand against the H-Bomb, saying it would be better for the Soviets alone to suffer the odium for the heinous act of building it. Better, too, Acheson claimed Kennan said, for Americans to "perish rather than be party to a course so evil as producing that weapon." Acheson says he snapped in response: "If that is your view you ought to resign from the Foreign Service and go out and preach your Quaker gospel, but don't do it within the department." Acheson's retrospective bark was worse than his contemporary bite. No evidential remnants support a story of such ill-tempered fury, but over the years his anger at Kennan's position must have grown proportional to the expanding differences between them. In part, however, Acheson's ex post facto embellishments on his exasperation in 1950 were probably less about the H-Bomb than his troubled ties to this inventive and sensitive man who had such a talent for getting under his skin.[22]

Public opinion remained a worry. Fuchs's arraignment in the UK probably aroused as much fear as support. Truman's decision provoked considerable and vocal dissent, causing him to tell Acheson that the "less said the better" about the bomb. In a staggering turnaround, McMahon now called for eradicating all nuclear weapons and making a "world-wide atomic peace" with a $50 billion "global Marshall Plan." Democratic Senator Millard Tydings of Maryland blasted Acheson for "sitting still and waiting for disaster" as he urged people to "sweat out" crises that could result in "total, incinerating war." Physicist Hans Bethe railed against the H-Bomb as "a means of extermination of whole populations," and Albert Einstein expressed horror at developing a weapon that could cause "radioactive poisoning of the atmosphere and hence annihilation of any life on earth." Americans for Democratic Action (ADA) liberals, including John Kenneth Galbraith and Arthur M. Schlesinger, Jr., bewailed the bomb's damage to America's "moral and political strength." They added what Acheson already believed, that reliance on the H-Bomb made it harder to counter non-nuclear aggression. James Reston thought the administration showed a lack of "faith in the effectiveness of international cooperation" and suffered from excessive skepticism.[23]

Acheson put on a show of confidence in a press conference on 8 February 1950. The best solution to the cold war, he said, was creating "facts" to which a "realistic" Soviet government must adjust, to build "situations which will extend the area of possible agreement, that is, to create strength instead of the weakness which exists in many quarters." That future nuclear wars might be worse than wars past simply meant Americans must have steadier nerves than before. Fortuitously speaking the day before Senator Joseph McCarthy's opening salvo in Wheeling, West Virginia, Acheson censured strident faultfinding of the government and exposure of internal divisions to others. Amid such sober circumstances, these would injure the national interest. Also criticizing those who urged the president to put his "feet under the same table" as Stalin, he insisted the administration had learned from "hard experience" that building strength was the only way to deal with the Soviets. Watching somberly as the barometer fell, the *New York Times* commented that the administration had reached a "watershed," ending "an era whose hopes and efforts had proved vain." The paper vigorously applauded Acheson for facing "hard facts."[24]

Criticism of the H-Bomb decision faded as other issues came to the fore. It helped that Eleanor Roosevelt and Bernard Baruch, from left and right, rallied to the administration. Polls showed four of five Americans wanted a bigger U.S.

bomb. But as spring neared, armed with points from Nitze, Acheson took the offensive against excessive faith in nuclear weapons. He told reporters in March 1950 the two great powers were playing with "dangerous boxes of matches." The U.S. position would deteriorate as other governments realized how unlikely it was that the United States would defend others with nuclear weapons in the face of almost certain and utterly ruinous retaliation. He told his own UN delegation in the summer that relying solely on a nuclear arm meant the United States would have to threaten "total war" against even the smallest instances of aggression. The U.S. nuclear arsenal grew to over 500 fission bombs late that year. But the Soviets, as Acheson feared, were rapidly producing the only riposte they needed—their own bombs.[25]

The effort to balance nuclear and conventional forces continued for decades. As a sponsor of both the H-Bomb and NSC-68, Acheson faced in two directions. He favored developing the H-Bomb and never called for reducing the country's nuclear armaments. But he always preferred the NSC-68's emphasis on conventional forces. At an NSC meeting in January 1951, a high official dubbed the atomic bomb Washington's "political ace." With Truman's blessing, Acheson rejoined that even threatening to use the bomb would "frighten our allies to death." It would also leave the Soviets unfazed. Nuclear weapons alone—whether "super" or not—were insufficient for western defense. Without strong armies, their existence might actually reduce American and western security.[26]

14

WORDS: NSC-68, PUBLIC OPINION,
AND TOTAL DIPLOMACY

Introduction

Usually when the two men disagreed on policy, Dean Acheson either quietly submitted to President Truman's wishes or worked hard to change his mind through persuasion and conversation, sometimes extended over many months. There were exceptions, however. At times, especially with respect to China, Truman took preemptive actions that did not necessarily reverse Acheson's goals but sharply restricted his ability to reach them. As we will see later, the president also worked behind Acheson's back in an ill-fated effort to overthrow the government of Guatemala.

The most conspicuous instance in which Acheson directly opposed the president came over defense spending. Truman brought to office a strong distaste for deficit spending and labored hard to reduce a government that had ballooned in power and (in his mind) profligacy. Congress, whether under Democratic or Republican rule, reinforced his fiscal caution. In the area of national security, this soon led to a large gap between diplomatic goals and the means to reach them, or at least the military means to back them up. Truman did not flinch at the increasingly expansive direction of his foreign policy, from the Truman Doctrine and Marshall Plan to NATO, but he seemed to think the United States could carry them out on the cheap. Having demobilized the huge World War II military machine as quickly as he could, he was extremely reluctant to build it back up, and his defense secretary, Louis Johnson, steadfastly enforced his boss's intentions.

The men at the head of the military services reacted in various ways. They fought with each other for the leavings of Truman's budgets. Trying to cope with his regime of scarcity, they looked for ways to maximize the funds they did have. Thus, they pushed the state department to withdraw U.S. forces from South Korea, and they resisted State's impulses, as in the Middle East, to further expand America's international commitments. Before long, Truman grasped one of the nasty little budgetary truths of the cold war, that expanding the number of the nation's atomic bombs was far cheaper than expanding the number of men in uniform, and the generals and admirals who headed those forces were in no position to contradict him.

If Acheson ever had a conversation in which he directly told Truman his fiscal conservatism would be the ruination of the nation's security, I have not found a record of it and doubt it ever occurred. Because Truman's insistence on curbing military spending was obviously close to his heart, Acheson chose to combat it obliquely, seizing the opportunity presented in the strategic review ordered by the president in connection with his H-Bomb decision. The result was NSC-68. This was ostensibly an impartial review of where national security stood in the early days of the nuclear age, and it *was* that. But it was far more. Acheson also understood the comparative costs of nuclear and conventional forces and believed strongly in the necessity of a large buildup of the latter—infantry, artillery, ships, and tanks. A challenge to Truman's budgets, NSC-68 exposed the gap between nuclear and conventional forces and more broadly the insolvency of current national security policy. The nation's expanding and ambitious international ends had outrun the military means to support them. Without mentioning specific spending figures, NSC-68 bluntly asserted the need to spend far more on defense. It also held that such spending would do no harm to the U.S. economy.

Harry Truman was an intelligent man, and it is clear that when he read NSC-68 he understood what Acheson was up to. As we will see below, instead of telling him something like, "Nice try, Dean, but I'm not going there," he used other methods to neutralize this challenge to his leadership. And as Acheson himself grasped, the president would have won this contest had it not been for the Korean War. The war unmasked as no bureaucratic study could do how far Truman's foreign policy had outreached his resources for carrying it out. Though not immediately, the president yielded. Now having to act, he found a rationale ready at hand—NSC-68. Acheson never publicly admitted what he had been up to, but he knew that he had "won" only through an unexpected war, a war that nearly destroyed the administration and Acheson's ability to conduct the nation's foreign policy.

Contexts

The sense of international threat and danger that made the H-Bomb seem necessary found crystallized form in the national security council paper 68 (NSC-68).

This was written in February and March 1950 and given to President Truman in April. Because Johnson participated little in a process he knew would challenge his cost cutting, Acheson could get the findings he wanted. One of the paper's purposes was to synchronize foreign and military policy, previously absent because of systemic flaws imbedded in the department of defense as structured by the National Security Act of 1947. In Acheson's view, the joint chiefs since then had come to believe they spoke for the department, and with as much infallibility as the pope. But their work was slipshod. Skimping on their homework, they typically produced "undigested" and ambiguous recommendations. Their disorderly methods gave Acheson an edge with the president, who was more likely to back State's better-prepared views than the military's "silly" presentations.[1]

Truman's miserly budgets drove the military into a corner. Under pressure since the war to reduce taxes, the president routinely sacrificed military to social spending. He had allotted the armed forces $11.8 billion (in a $39.2 billion budget) in fiscal 1947. Though the cold war had now been under way for several years, he dictated a ceiling of $13 billion for fiscal 1951. The chiefs discarded plans for small-scale warfare in favor of more affordable nuclear weapons. Even though cold war tensions were undermining the assumptions of his budgets, Truman continued to consider them adequate to protect western Europe and sustain nuclear superiority. When Korea exposed the hollowness of the U.S. military, he reluctantly released the floodgates of defense spending, finding to his surprise that the infusion of dollars invigorated the U.S. economy instead of bankrupting it.[2]

Acheson later alleged that NSC-68's purpose was to "bludgeon the mass mind of 'top government'" so it would properly execute the president's policies. But the real targets were Truman himself, his vicar Johnson at the Pentagon, and other champions of penury, including the "mice in the Budget Bureau." Truman had refused to spend an extra congressional appropriation of $800 million for the air force in October 1949. His stockpiling of atomic bombs and decision to develop the H-Bomb partly aimed at thwarting pressure for greater spending on the conventional forces Acheson thought essential. In Acheson's view, Truman's parsimony endangered national security, and NSC-68 aimed to recruit (or force) him to State's strategy of building strength. Korea did that instead. George Marshall as secretary of state had never challenged Truman on the military budget but thought it left the United States speaking "from weakness." Afterward, from his perspective as secretary of defense in 1950–51, he thought the United States had become "a very powerful country."[3]

No Holds Barred

Acheson had little time for the details of writing NSC-68. According to his own understated recollection, his duty was to give the president "communicable wisdom." What this really meant was to gain his support. He would not overwhelm him with programmatic details that others could challenge but offer him a general analysis oriented toward action.

Formal responsibility for NSC-68 belonged to a State-Defense Review Group, which consisted of eleven regulars and a few occasional participants. Six men from State joined four from Defense, including retired army General James H. Burns, serving as liaison to the state department, and Najeeb Halaby, a forthright opponent of budget stringency. Overseeing the effort in principle was NSC's James S. Lay, Jr., but Paul Nitze as the committee chair had little trouble dominating the group because of Johnson's forfeiture. Nitze's use of top-secret classification rules to control who participated left Treasury and the budget bureau in the dark. Inside the committee, secrecy encouraged candor and chances to consider the unorthodox and to preempt criticism. Nitze summoned possible detractors as short-term consultants, converting Robert Oppenheimer, James Conant, and Robert Lovett into advocates. Department critics who wanted more emphasis on economic aid than military renewal were stopped cold by Nitze's maneuvers. Two other likely critics, David Lilienthal and George Kennan, had left government.[4]

Nitze started almost nonstop work early in January 1950, gathering reams of data and opinion, including JCS predictions that the Soviet Union would have as many as 135 atomic bombs by mid-1953. Although still considering an all-out Soviet attack unlikely, he postulated in an 8 February paper that the Kremlin, in an effort to defeat the United States, was acting with a new "boldness" bordering on "recklessness." The "chance of war through miscalculation" was growing in line with new Soviet willingness to use force in areas from Berlin to Korea. Now armed with nuclear weapons, the USSR thought the time ripe to take "aggressive political action against all or most soft spots in the periphery."

Informed that congressmen's constituents demanded "bold action," the Review Group met with Lovett on 16 March searching for "Hemingway sentences" to communicate the gist of NSC-68 to the public. In Lovett's mind, the "moral conflict" in which Washington was now engaged differed from a "hot" war only in the sense that "death comes more slowly and in a different fashion." He wanted to "fight with no holds barred," using hugely enlarged intelligence services and a "Department of Dirty Tricks" run at the highest levels. A banker when not serving in Washington, he was confident that large national security expenditures would stimulate the economy. On the 20th came physicist Ernest O. Lawrence, director of the Radiation Laboratory at the University of California. Heaping scorn on the dissent of "talking" scientists, he urged a tenfold expansion of the "chicken-feed" Washington now spent on nuclear work, not precisely what Nitze wanted to hear.[5]

Primed for a briefing of the principals, Nitze called a meeting for three P.M., Wednesday, 22 March, in the PPS offices (Acheson lacked a decent conference room of his own). The host delegation included Acheson, Nitze, Dean Rusk, and Gordon Arneson. Arriving from DOD were Johnson, General Omar Bradley,

Burns, Halaby, and others. Admiral Sidney Souers headed the NSC and White House contingent. In a bizarre convulsion of bureaucratic discord, the meeting ended after fourteen minutes with Johnson exiting in a huff and General Burns sobbing. According to Acheson—in an account verified by Souers and State's notetaker—the meeting started amicably with Nitze beginning to read and summarize an already circulated paper. Johnson, whom Acheson claimed to be "mentally ill," suddenly "lunged forward with a crash of chair legs on the floor and fist on the table, scaring me out of my shoes." Johnson "shouted" that people were holding unauthorized meetings, writing papers, and summoning him to conferences "contrary to his orders." "What was this paper?" he demanded. Acheson recounted Truman's instructions, reminded Johnson he had named Burns to represent him, and said Nitze had sent a twenty-seven-page draft summary to him a week before. "But he would have none of it and, gathering General Bradley and other Defense people, stalked out of the room." As others sat in shock, Burns "put his head in his hands and wept in shame." Acheson was summoned to his own office, where he found Johnson spewing accusations against him. "This was too much. I told him since he had started to leave, to get on with it and the State Department would complete the report alone and explain why." After Acheson reported through Souers what had happened, an angry Truman told him to "carry on exactly" as before. After returning from a NATO conference in Europe, Johnson found a revised version of the paper on his desk, garnished with his own people's signatures. As Bradley recalled, the "JCS unequivocally supported NSC-68, creating a rare, awkward and ironic situation in which the three military chiefs and their chairman were more closely aligned" with the views of Acheson (an "uncompromising hawk") than of Johnson. The trapped secretary of defense signed too, and NSC-68 went to the White House on 7 April.[6]

Acheson and Nitze had also run into opposition within their own department. Under Secretary James Webb, Truman's former budget director, joined those resisting new spending, and Willard Thorp rebutted projections of Soviet economic progress. Edward Barrett from public affairs worried about starting "a gigantic armament race" and denied that its implementation required radical spending increases, a position similar to that of another assistant secretary, George Perkins, and Soviet specialist Llewellyn E. Thompson, Jr. In contrast, Charles Bohlen wanted the defense buildup but objected to the paper justifying it. Moscow's leaders, he insisted, worried more about their own power than the world outside—and had no "design" of world "domination." His protracted sniping at Nitze magnified Acheson's mistrust of "Soviet specialists." Neither he nor other critics carried the day. Acheson was the secretary of state and Nitze now his alter ego of choice.[7]

But they were not yet out of the woods. The eccentric Johnson's budget views were closer to those of Truman, who had approved nothing yet. When he gave the NSC paper to Souers for cost estimates, the president was thinking about new efforts at arms control rather than arms spending. He eluded the spot in which Acheson had put him by telling reporters he still planned to hold the line on the defense budget. With submissions for the fiscal 1951 budget a half year off, he could stall while Souers used an ad hoc NSC committee to study costs. But the breakout of war in June forced his hand, and after formal NSC approval, he signed NSC-68 on 30 September 1950. When White House assistant Charles Murphy said he now hoped Washington could "wrest the initiative from the Soviets and . . . roll them back," Acheson remarked that this was "very important and quite right."[8]

"The Stark Fact that Our Independence as a Nation May Be at Stake"

Acheson was uninvolved in the day-to-day writing of NSC-68, but his diplomacy and rhetoric thereafter acted on and sounded its themes. The paper brimmed with statistics and comparative tables on U.S. and Soviet resources and production as background for descriptions of the Soviet ideological and military threat. Nitze was ambivalent about public opinion. On one side, he seemed to think it possible to shape it enough to gain the support needed for NSC-68's ambitious goals; on the other, he thought it necessary to overcome the disabilities of a tolerant democracy confronted by a despotic foe.

As to the policies themselves, both isolationism and preventive war were wrongheaded. But current policy was also unsatisfactory. Instead, Nitze and his fellow authors advocated "a rapid build-up" of both nuclear and conventional forces as part of a general increase in western "political, economic, and military strength," with the goal of attaining "clearly superior overall power" for the United States. Since fiscal restraint must bow "to the stark fact that our independence as a nation may be at stake," NSC-68 considered it prudent to spend up to half the gross national product on national security.[9]

NSC-68 placed new emphasis on the role of ideology in the east-west conflict. As in the Civil War and World War II, the cold war was a contest between slavery and freedom. Democracy apparently had its advantages after all, for, though lethal, the Soviet Union was weakened by resting on "force, fear, and favor." The Kremlin was "animated by a fanatic faith, antithetical to" America's "idea of freedom," which permanently stood as a threat to a "slave society." The United States had never before confronted a regime "so irreconcilable with ours, so implacable in its purpose to destroy ours," or—alluding to racial and other domestic rifts—"so capable of turning to its own uses the most dangerous and divisive trends in our own society." The greatest peril from this regime would come in 1954, when its nuclear arsenal could neutralize Washington's, a temptation to war.

Even now in 1950, Nitze held, the Soviet Union could wreak horrific damage on the United States. His catalogue of risks facing Washington supplied justification for the mobilization promoted by NSC-68. The Soviets and their satellites could already overrun western Europe, except perhaps Spain and Portugal, slice into Middle Eastern oil territories, and consolidate past gains in Asia. From the air, they could attack Britain, and from the air and sea could strike Atlantic "lines of communication." They could savage all North America with atomic bombs. Moscow's nuclear capacity allowed it to neutralize American bases in the UK and frustrate amphibious invasions of a conquered Europe. Having seized the heart of western Europe, the Russians could hit Great Britain simultaneously with air and sea attacks. In a third world war, they could then proceed to invade Iberia and Scandinavia, launch more strikes at North America and Atlantic sea lanes, and stage "diversionary attacks" in the Middle East.

NSC-68 said extremely little about the details of the buildup needed to meet this challenge, nothing about numbers of troops, air wings, or naval vessels. While doubting that even a massive nuclear arsenal could deter a Soviet nuclear attack, NSC-68 with an inexplicable faith in quantities demanded more. The United States must have the capacity to deter a Soviet attack, defeat it if deterrence failed, or, in between, successfully wage non-nuclear war. It should build whatever was needed whenever the need appeared. To avoid alarming the president—and to leave less for specialists to challenge—Nitze gave no cost figures. It is likely, however, that Acheson and he had in mind a defense budget of from thirty to fifty billion dollars.[10]

Without ever saying so, NSC-68 implied that Truman's fiscal policies had harmed national security. While NSC-68's explicitly stated goals ruled out anything like conquering Russia or forcing it into "unconditional surrender," its objectives were breathtaking enough. Combining doctrines of containment and situations of strength, it aimed to frustrate Kremlin designs by "means short of war," thereby fostering "a fundamental change in the nature of the Soviet system" and accelerating its "decay." In short, Acheson and Nitze wanted to use external pressure to "reduce the power and influence of the Kremlin *inside* the Soviet Union and other areas under its control." NSC-68 advocated a large increase in the United States' capacity to conduct covert operations and the ability to wage economic, political, and psychological "warfare." The goal was first to foment and then support "unrest and revolt in selected strategic satellite countries" (or as critics of NSC-68 have said, it proposed cold war "rollback"). The United States must also have stouter programs of "internal security and civilian defense" at home. Virtually all these goals were already public currency. Acheson and Nitze were trying to push the government to go beyond declaration to "action."[11]

Acheson always knew that the strategy of building positions of strength entailed a risk of war, making it essential to handle east-west friction with care. And NSC-68 admitted the hazards of its prescriptions. Yet the risks of "making ourselves strong" were less than those of standing still. While NSC-68 agreed with Acheson's wish to avoid negotiations until the west had eliminated positions of weakness, it also spelled out the need to *appear* willing to negotiate differences. This was essential to maintain public support for the "program of building strength" and for capturing the moral high ground in the "struggle with the Soviet system."

Education in the Obvious

After publication of the long-secret NSC-68 in 1975, historians sharply criticized its ideological heat, alarmist rhetoric, and extravagant estimate of the Soviet menace. They dissected its failure to demarcate among "threats" or draw a judicious balance between ends and means. These critiques appeared after Acheson's death, but they would not have fazed him. He acknowledged in his memoirs that "we overreacted to Stalin, which in turn caused him to overreact" to U.S. policies, but he thought critics at fault in not seeing that inaction would have been worse. To the criticisms from his own shop, especially Kennan and Bohlen's claim that NSC-68 inflated Moscow's capabilities while ignoring its limited intentions, he countered brusquely that as a prudent public servant, he had no choice but to make calculations based on capabilities, since iron-curtain secrecy veiled Soviet intentions. Moscow's hostile behavior, he thought, signaled its capabilities quite nicely—and the number of Red Army divisions stationed in Germany and eastern Europe said as much about its intentions. In truth, he was unimpressed by efforts to separate "capabilities" from "intentions." Their *combination*, he remarked in 1950, "creates very grave danger to the survival of free nations and free institutions." That was good enough for him. And the criticism that he overlooked a disparity between ends and means, he said waspishly in 1951, was the typical exhalation of someone eager to "reduce our commitments."[12]

In 1953, Nitze described NSC-68 as "a fairly simple idea ponderously expressed," but he defended it for decades. Not without cause, for this allegedly extremist manifesto opposed isolationism and preventive war, sought ways to lengthen the U.S. nuclear fuse shortened by Truman's cost cutting, and favored an eventual negotiated end to the cold war. In 1950, U.S. intelligence mainly upheld Nitze and Acheson's inflated estimates of Soviet military strength. It would be hard to overstate—and NSC-68 did not—the dark nature of a regime the Czech Republic's Václav Havel said "justifiably gave the world nightmares" or that the *Russian* parliament called a "criminal enterprise" in 1991. What of the criticism that Acheson backed NSC-68 cynically, that it was all about bludgeoning "the mass mind of 'top government' "? Bludgeoning he agreed with, but, though cool to covert operations and psychological warfare, he fully agreed with NSC-68's depiction of the cold war conflict and Soviet threat and in 1953 called it "one of the great documents in our history." The United States had great advantages, but NSC-68 captured his concern it was doing too little with them. "We produce so damned much more aluminum than they do," he remarked, but "what do we do with it? We put it on the front of automobiles, we throw it all over the place." It was imperative to muster American strength. "It takes more than bare hands and a desire for peace to turn back this threat," he said a few months after NSC-68 was written.[13]

As to the language of NSC-68, he frankly stated that dramatization and magnification were necessary to push people where they should go. Faithful to Holmes's adage that "we need education in the obvious more than investigation of the obscure," he thought it essential to distill the case for the "mythical 'average American citizen,'" and he intended to do so on the hustings. For citizens with so little time to spare for understanding the "vast external realm," he would have to make his points "clear." And if "we made our points clearer than truth, we did not differ from most other educators and could hardly do otherwise." This was not like writing a "doctoral thesis. Qualification must give way to simplicity of statement, nicety and nuance to bluntness, almost brutality, in carrying home a point." Doubting Truman was yet convinced, he now launched a campaign for "total diplomacy" that he hoped would bring both president and public to his view of what must be done.[14]

Military Doubts and Dilemmas

Realization many years later that the west greatly outmatched the Soviet Union —that it was an Upper Volta with rockets—does not gainsay the authenticity of concerns in 1950. The USSR had far fewer divisions in eastern Europe in 1949–50 than Washington counted, but those in place were in prime condition. If Moscow's new atomic bombs could stay Washington's own nuclear hand, the Red Army might easily cut through the flimsy, twelve-division barrier of western occupation troops in Germany. Most officials thought passing time would make matters worse.[15]

Acheson, who in another connection explained that he preferred power to agility, elected for the risks Kennan and Bohlen abhorred. He would rather brandish strength than depend on artful "maneuver," a preference he considered a blend "of monasticism and the diplomacy of earlier centuries." Early in 1950, he and Nitze were more impressed by current western weakness than strength. They pushed MDAP funding of NATO allies, taking the "calculated risk" they could build enough force to deter a Soviet attack. Convinced the west was unready for what might come, Acheson considered many others oblivious to the present danger. As late as the 1960s, some Pentagon planners acted as if the Russian bomb did not exist, weaving elaborate scenarios without thought of the risks of retaliation. Truman himself wrote in his diary in 1952 the Soviet A-Bomb was a "phony" and said in a 1950 NSC meeting that "the USSR would blow up." The government took corrective actions only slowly. NSC-68 promoted early-warning radar, interceptors, and conventionally armed rockets to defend against Soviet bomber sorties, but they did not appear until the Eisenhower administration.[16]

Acheson's preference for armies on the ground soon led him to German rearmament, but the dilemmas imbedded in his solutions held for forty years. Officially, the United States adhered to a pledge to defend Europe—with nuclear weapons if necessary—that increasingly seemed implausible. Acheson pushed all concerned for the ground forces that would deter Soviet aggression *without* nuclear weapons. He understood that until that day came, Washington must make its threat to use nuclear weapons believable. But his doubts about the usefulness of nuclear weapons and the future U.S.-Soviet nuclear standoff never left him. In executive testimony in 1951, he told Senator Theodore Green of Rhode Island: "If you and I are standing close together and I am pointing a .38 at you and you are pointing a BB gun at me, I have a considerable advantage. But if we are standing very close together and I am pointing a .45 at you and you are pointing a .38 at me, the advantage has declined." "I do not think I should go into this any more," he ended.[17]

Resigned that the west could never match Soviet conventional forces and that any east-west ground war would soon "go nuclear," he sought the western forces that would prevent such a catastrophe. Thus, he wanted to finesse Washington's promise of a nuclear defense of Europe. The arms race continued. Moscow continued its effort to neutralize growing U.S. nuclear power, while the west tried in vain to achieve a match for the Red Army. In Truman and Acheson's time, however, the west never escaped dependence on nuclear weapons, and the policies of their successors deepened the dependence.

Backing and Filling

Acheson began unofficially publicizing the NSC-68 program before the paper was finished. In mid-February, he first spoke of "total diplomacy" in a speech. He drew on memories of World War II's mobilization to underline the contemporary struggle to protect a national way of life. The situation then and now erased lines between domestic and foreign policy and, he implied, required more discipline and less internal criticism. Tacitly answering McCarthy later in the month, he challenged citizens to "prove the superiority" of American values by supporting policies that advanced a "society of nations based on the principles of tolerance and restraint" against those who would assign a role for every man and woman from "the Kremlin."[18]

The state department acted as if Truman had already approved NSC-68. Barrett saw his public affairs job as keeping "the Soviet bear so busy scratching his own fleas that he has little time for molesting others." Others pushed for more aggressive CIA operations. Concerned in April about the growing Soviet menace to U.S. security, Acheson in an NSC meeting urged the enlargement of U.S. and allied military forces. Even at the cost of greatly expanding the share of "national income to the cold war," he wanted to undermine "the Soviet world economically and psychologically." Averell Harriman, always close to Truman, fully agreed.

By early May, Nitze and Webb were handing out department assignments for executing the "programs under NSC 68."[19]

Until the Korean War, Truman continued to work at cross-purposes with Foggy Bottom. He said no to its request that he make a big foreign policy speech in Chicago. He disallowed publication of a sanitized version of the NSC paper. He urged Johnson on 20 April to find military hardware he needed somewhere on the shelf, even if it was "rusting." He told reporters off the record on 4 May he planned an even smaller defense budget the following year. Publicly on 20 May, he said the defense budget had a "ceiling" on it. With a midterm election coming up, the *Times*'s James Reston observed, Truman was resistant to new "defense expenditures." The Pentagon also disappointed Acheson and Nitze. Instead of "the billion dollar effort" Nitze had in mind, the officers were thinking of adding another division here or squadron there. Neither Truman nor Johnson was moved by a new CIA report that supplied ammunition for mobilization. Analysts detected evidence that the Soviets were deliberately testing western resolve throughout the world. Noticing signs of "dissension and uncertainty," the Kremlin seemed to doubt "US tenacity of purpose." In May, when Acheson returned from a trip abroad, he found both Truman and Johnson throwing darts at his NSC-68 trial balloons. The president was telling advisers to question the paper's financial projections and asserted in a 1 June press conference that the world was closer to peace than in 1945. Just after Acheson urged increased defense spending at a Senate hearing, Johnson flatly contradicted him. Nitze had "a very depressing meeting" in which the "Military" rejected immediate execution of NSC-68. Acheson and Nitze felt alone in absorbing recent CIA reports of rising Soviet risk-taking. As Moscow grew more confident, said the agency somewhat obscurely, it might take actions that, while not themselves a casus belli, tied to its other aggressive acts, "might become an issue out of proportion to its actual merits and thus precipitate war." That is, it might provoke the *west* to initiate hostilities.[20]

There the matter stood when the Korean War began sixteen days after the CIA analysis. Even then, Truman tugged against implementing NSC-68. In September, the NSC adopted the paper as a statement of U.S. policy for the coming four to five years, but Truman still embargoed public discussion of the document or its costs. The military budget swelled nonetheless, from his original request of $13.5 billion for fiscal 1951 to $48.2 billion. As Acheson preferred, most of the increase went for the general buildup, not Korea. By November, Truman seemed fully on board, and Acheson was planning speeches to further educate the public. By the end of the year, Truman had informed congressional leaders of plans based on NSC-68 and summarized its essence in a national radio address. By then, with Acheson and Truman again working in harmony, European allies thought they had become *too* militant, worried that the contemplated arms buildup would endanger their social and economic recovery.[21]

Educating the Public

As Acheson would say in 1962, "an understanding of foreign policy is not simply part of the state of nature." In the months before the war, his "total diplomacy" campaign pressed his case so that both the public and Congress would achieve understanding. He was highly ambivalent about both groups. His wartime experiences with lawmakers fed a strong tendency to view them as ignoramuses. Yet he had also enjoyed bringing some of them to his views through dialogue and even enjoyed some of the attendant backslapping. Though he worried about the people's craving for quick and simplistic gratification, he knew any major ventures required popular backing. He now wanted the people to accept expansive and expensive commitments and over a long haul. The better people were informed, he said in a 1962 speech, the "more critical" they became. This required leaders to "talk with more sense," which further enhanced public understanding and the development of a "consensus." He did not worry about "world public opinion," however. It "simply does not exist on matters that concern us." In his 1950 canvass, he worked more from his optimistic than pessimistic views of the people, thinking he could persuade them to support large objectives and accept the sacrifices these entailed.[22]

Despite McCarthyism and the Korean War, the administration still reached its diplomatic and military goals with little difficulty. Even on the brink of the 1952 election, when Truman and Acheson had become lame ducks, Congress approved major treaties on Japan and Germany. In 1950, a supposedly wounded administration was well on its way toward a series of far-reaching measures, from German rearmament and expansive ventures in Iran and Egypt to deepened involvement in Indochina. Ordinary Americans heard little of how these projects started, a sign of how seldom they intruded into foreign policy at the time. Acheson, said the *U.S. News & World Report*, was "his own boss" as much as any secretary of state in history. But this would not matter, he thought, unless the administration articulated its objectives "through the press, through the radio, through the churches, through the labor unions, through the business organizations, through all the groupings of our national life." In retirement, he once more demonstrated that he was not a traditional "realist" by heaping scorn on Walter Lippmann's argument in *The Public Philosophy* on the incompatibility of diplomatic wisdom and democracy. Certainly, people were "more homo than sapiens," but he would not exchange the American public with what the "Kaiser, Mussolini, and Hitler," and the Soviets had. Despite all their shortcomings, "there is nothing better than democracies; in fact, there is nothing that we can trust half as much."[23]

He knew the state department had an "image" problem. He explained in a 1949 press conference that it was guaranteed never to win any "popularity contests" because of its lack of supportive interest groups and habit of "bringing up difficult questions from outside the borders." The department began cautious efforts to gain at least a little popularity, or persuade the public (and Truman!) to abandon prejudices about a limp and snobbish Foggy Bottom. The infant television industry might have been a big help, but concern about "live" criticism kept most State officials off shows like Lawrence Spivak's "Meet the Press." Instead, public relations mostly took the customary form of speeches. Acheson urged subordinates to spread the word on NSC-68, addressed many groups himself, and, on this issue, cooperated enthusiastically with the department's public affairs office. In March 1950, he decided to make his first key speech on the west coast. He had to get the word out "to educate the American people to the nature of the problem." "Look," he told reporters on background, "we're not utter damn fools, maybe medium damn fools."[24]

Total Diplomacy

Acheson's "total diplomacy" campaign came after weeks of rehearsing ideas in private briefings of reporters. The most important effort would be a speech on 16 March at the University of California in Berkeley. In February, he made a trial run before the Advertising Council at the White House. There he underscored both the clash between ways of life and necessity of avoiding such extremes as a "military showdown" or "preventive war." Poking some holes in the doctrine of containment, he spoke of the difficulty of knocking down every single Soviet thrust; they were neither predictable nor always susceptible to effective rejoinder. The United States, he added, should not fastidiously apply "litmus" tests to those worthy of joining the fight against Soviet aggression. Nations in danger should strengthen their own societies, reinforcing "confidence in the democratic way of life." To help them, the United States must practice "total diplomacy." All branches of government, backed by business, labor, and the media, must "agree voluntarily to concert our efforts to this one overriding task."[25]

For the administration, "total diplomacy" meant doing a far better job integrating and coordinating diplomatic, military, and economic strategy. Being "total" meant aggressively countering hostile propaganda, then centered on the communist-dominated "Stockholm Peace Appeal." "Total" meant explaining to the public why the government opposed negotiations with the Soviets. It would mean, in the upcoming Berkeley speech, defining terms for settlement should talks ever become possible. And, in an increasingly acrimonious political atmosphere, it meant resisting hysteria. The *New York Times*'s ears perked up, hearing an "Acheson doctrine" in the Advertising Council remarks.[26]

The centerpiece of his campaign was the second of two California speeches, in Berkeley on 16 March 1950, but he prefigured nearly the whole address beforehand while briefing twenty reporters in Washington. Determined to get media attention, he covered a host of issues and credited Kennan for many of his ideas. The west, he told reporters, was engaged in a "completely irreconcilable moral conflict" with the Soviet Union. This should not lead to war, but Moscow was already waging "war with all its fixings" against any society opposing it. Although the west had no plan to undermine the Soviet regime (not what NSC-68 said!), the cold war was a "struggle that must go on in the theater of the human spirit until it is resolved." The Soviets were trying "to deny us the physical environment in which to develop our own way of life"; they especially hated the United States as the only nation that could block communist expansionism. Drawing on NSC-68's analysis of risks, he admitted that the very success of western mobilization might provoke a war. If Stalin had more successes at causing "hesitation" and doubts within the western alliance, he might be tempted to "feel that the calculated risk of military probing was worth taking." This east-west struggle was a "moral" conflict, but "realists" were making U.S. policy. They did not ask the Russians to "stop being Communists" but to "make co-existence more tolerable than at present." That might be the best available in a world where "good and evil" had lived "side by side since the beginning of time."

In Berkeley, he told the journalists, he would describe the conditions for reestablishing "tolerable" relations, none of which he expected Moscow to accept, allowing Washington to continue working on strengthening the free world to the point that the Soviets would have to accept. When asked the identity of his audience, he said it was the American people, for the Kremlin already "knows all this." Did the Soviet Union's totalitarian character give it the edge in any contest of "total diplomacy"? No, he answered, for even totalitarians had trouble reaching their goals. The long term favored the United States, with its "tremendous storehouse of power."[27]

He had told Truman his speech might "relieve tension," but in this early season of McCarthyite "immolation," he preached the hard message of NSC-68. The university audience heard almost exactly what the reporters did, with the addition of his list of conditions for a cold war settlement. He left the strong implication that the Soviets had first to prove their wish for peace by permitting or carrying out each condition *before* the United States would even sit down with them. In short, these were preconditions for talks, and they were sweeping: (1) German unification (which he privately opposed) under a freely elected government; (2) withdrawal of Soviet troops from Austria; (3) an end to obstructionism against a Japanese peace treaty; (4) peaceful unification of Korea through free elections; (5) withdrawal of Soviet troops and police from the eastern European "satellite area"; (6) an end to "obstruction" in the UN; (7) cooperation in making "realistic" progress in arms control (including nuclear weapons); (8) an end to subverting other governments through use of the international communist "apparatus"; (9) decent and respectful treatment of foreign diplomats in Moscow; and (10) a halt to hostile and violent Soviet propaganda. The United States, he seemed to say, would invite Stalin to Appomattox once he had qualified for an invitation.[28]

It is impossible to know how the public reacted to this speech. The editorial pages of the *New York Times* called it a "peace" plan but summarized Acheson's demands as "an abandonment of the Communist program of world revolution and a reversal of the policies which the Soviets have pursued during and since the war." Reston wrote that if the Soviets agreed to the "about-face" Acheson demanded, they "would virtually cease to be Communists." Agreeing entirely, Moscow publications called Acheson a "fascist-minded diplomat," a "truly incorrigible liar," a "hired lackey of the warmongers" and his speech an "insolent ultimatum." Acheson always excelled at needling Soviet rulers. A quarter century later, Nikita Khrushchev called him "obstinate and aggressive" and a "political half-wit."[29]

Reston also saw in Acheson's effort an attempt to neutralize McCarthy's rampage. Acheson's speeches continued through the spring, but if they helped fight off conservatives, they did little to please the left. He later said he wanted to convince liberals "to face the long, hard years and not to distract us with the offer of short cuts and easy solutions begotten by good will out of the angels of man's better nature." But *The Progressive* jeered at the "total sterility" campaign, and *The Nation*, claiming the Soviets were offering reasonable compromises, described his policy as "so despairing as to amount to sheer nihilism." Ignoring his warnings against extremism, Democratic conservatives like Representative John McCormack of Massachusetts demanded a rupture in relations when Soviet gunners shot down a U.S. plane over the Baltic. Acheson said he "sometimes felt like a man standing on a dock with an oar, trying to get the dock to move."[30]

He tried again in a nationally broadcast address on 22 April 1950. He again warned that Soviet communism posed a threat to "the existence of our nation and our civilization that could be met only by the total application of faith, unity, strength and resourcefulness." Total diplomacy asked the people—who must have "a burning and a fighting faith" in freedom—to tell all the world "what America believes, what freedom is, what it has done for many, what it can do for all." Sensing something like NSC-68 in the background, Reston wrote that policymakers had reached a new stage. Acheson was saying that because "the cold war was here to stay," the home front must be mobilized as in World War II. American leaders had first tried the vision of "one-world," but the malevolence of the USSR had convinced them it was a "pestilence" rather than an "annoyance." Now, using a "two-worlds" vision, they fought for the Atlantic community against the Soviets and their underlings. They strove to mobilize the United States, unite western Europe, and attach West Germany to the "free world."[31]

Busy in May with conferences in Europe, on his return Acheson picked up where he had left off, thinking his campaign had just begun. A string of new speeches was already scheduled. In Dallas on 13 June, he blasted isolationism, appeasement, and preventive war, all the products of simplistic thinking. A week later, he painted a grim world picture for state governors in White Sulphur Springs, West Virginia. He had spoken "brilliantly," governors of both parties agreed, but "scared hell out of us." Less than a week later, North Korean armies rushed across the 38th parallel.[32]

North Korea's attack confirmed Acheson's warnings of how dangerous the world had become but also rendered his total diplomacy campaign immediately forgettable. The campaign mostly failed. He had not converted the president. Between Acheson's speeches, Truman was still making "we're-now-closer-to-peace-than-ever" announcements from the White House. Korea turned him around, not Acheson, whose calls for more administration "discipline" did nothing to stop Louis Johnson's guerrilla war against him and the state department. Moreover, while Acheson wanted the public focus on western Europe, now he faced the possibility the people would consider only Asia important, just as public fury with Japan after Pearl Harbor nearly overwhelmed FDR's European priorities. Finally, though Acheson had tried to smother a belligerent mood with his own measured militancy, his campaign exactly coincided with the spread of McCarthy's brushfire. In fact, Acheson's mobilization rhetoric may have helped fuel the flames of McCarthyism. In the early summer of 1950, it was an open question whether he and his policies would become captive to the zealotry he deplored.

15

REAL DIPLOMACY,
IN EUROPE, 1949–1950

Pivots for European Policy

Behind the writing of NSC-68 was the deflation of the bullishness created by the 1949 Council of Foreign Ministers meeting in Paris. Reasons for the deflation ranged from the atomic test in the USSR to the first explosions of McCarthyism in the United States. American plans for Europe again seemed stalled. European economies still dragged, hurting the U.S. economy, too, as well as its foreign policy. Acheson wondered about the allies' willingness to fight and accept West Germany in their camp. Most U.S. officials—most of the time—viewed Moscow's strength as rising rather than receding. When the UN failed to surrender Chiang Kai-shek's Security Council seat to the Chinese communist regime, the Soviets walked out of the council in protest. This move, along with Moscow's nuclear breakthrough, rattled nerves throughout the west.

Historians long ago noted how Korea shifted U.S. aid programs from an economic to a military focus, but the change had begun even earlier. As sociopolitical imagination slumped, western leaders looked to steel to brace the alliance and give NATO a more convincingly martial face. With its pared-down budget, the Pentagon had reacted sluggishly when Congress delayed Mutual Defense Assistance Program funding until NATO produced a "strategic concept." Europeans were slow off the mark, too, more concerned about domestic needs. To help, Acheson sought to expedite MDAP shipments. He also endorsed "offshore" procurement, permitting the expenditure of MDAP funds on European-manufactured hardware. With Congress increasingly hard to propitiate,

Acheson grew more earnest about converting NATO from a package of promises to a military machine. For NATO to establish a "forward" defense on the ramparts of the Soviet bloc, however, some kind of German contribution was necessary, something military officers in most western capitals quietly understood. For now, however, political leaders of the Big Three all publicly refused to consider this alternative. Acheson joined in the refusal even though he understood that a German army would reduce U.S. dependence on nuclear weapons.[1]

He was not interested in the expansion of NATO for expansion's sake, which he illustrated by rebuffing petitions by Greece and Turkey for membership. Bloodied by past wars with Russia, the Turks had pushed hard to become a charter member, but he told them a "contractual security arrangement" was then impossible. When the Greeks groused about their rejection in October 1949, he intimated that they were being ungrateful for past favors. The background for his decisions was the joint chiefs' opposition to any new members until the current slate showed it could actually defend western Europe.[2]

"Integration" rather than expansion was the watchword for European conundrums. Since the inception of the Marshall Plan, Washington had encouraged Europeans to repair their economies in concert. In that spirit, the Americans now had to overcome the allies' impulse to prevent any West German role in the alliance. To offset German power, French leaders wanted both the Americans and the British to commit to strong roles on the continent, for facing a rejuvenated Germany alone was Paris's worst dream. When it became clear Britain preferred to nurture its ties to the Commonwealth and North America, the French government saw the advantages of rapprochement with Germany, but only in a Europe-wide setting. The price the Germans would have to pay for inclusion and respect was to surrender any independent role in the heart of Europe.

Like the French, the Americans wanted strong British participation in Europe. One part of NATO's significance was that Britain's membership would help overcome its diffidence about "Europe." To lighten U.S. burdens, American policymakers also wanted the British to maintain their traditional role in South Asia and the Middle East. The price the Americans would pay was acceptance of qualified British involvement on the continent. This in turn made it essential for Paris to lead the way on Germany and thus on "integration." France was generally willing to play that role but insisted first on a sufficient revival of its own power and standing. France demanded no less than equality in any Franco-German partnership. As a consequence, the allegedly anglophilic Acheson repeatedly leagued himself with France, even as he grumbled about the costs of French cooperation, especially in Indochina.

European questions always led to Germany. Despite Acheson's misgivings about nationalistic rhetoric in West Germany's formative elections, if France refused a summons to lead and Britain remained reticent, he would look to the Germans for the strength needed against the Soviet bloc. But because the new Federal Republic could not be allowed to act alone, taking such a course would inexorably expand U.S. responsibility in Europe. These issues—Germany's role, France's leadership, and Britain's place on the continent—held center stage at a series of meetings and conferences between October 1949 and May 1950—two in Paris and others in Bonn and London.

The first Paris conclave was an off-site departmental affair, where U.S. ambassadors to area capitals thrashed out a range of issues, joined by Averell Harriman, John McCloy, and Charles Bohlen. Acheson did not attend but wanted the participants' counsel. Presiding was George Perkins, now running the European affairs office. Over the next three years, this Princeton graduate, World War I army veteran, and former businessman was usually near at hand when Acheson dealt with key European matters. Acheson had told him for this occasion that France must not be left "alone on the continent." In case the British remained standoffish, France must take the lead to avoid having Europe come under "Russian or German, or perhaps Russian-German domination." Echoing Acheson's concerns, the Paris conferees focused on how German nationalism, British parochialism, and French irresolution were causing the snail-like pace toward unity. Their host, Ambassador to France David Bruce, expressed the French resentment at U.S. toleration of Britain's "disassociation" from Europe, which stimulated French fears of having to handle the Germans alone. McCloy gave a scarifying portrait of the FRG as "plagued by economic ills, unemploy-ment," refugees, and alienated youth. Rampant German "pessimism" and "cynicism" threatened to spawn a plague-on-both-houses neutralism. To keep the Germans on an even keel, it was essential to make rapid progress toward integra-tion and restoration of their "self-respect." The conferees, Perkins told Acheson, agreed on the urgency of European integration and a major role for the Germans. Neither could occur without London's "active" help.[3]

Coloring the Wall

East Germany was also now a declared state, headed by its communist prime minister, Wilhelm Pieck. Though Stalin was unlikely to surrender control of this regime, he might have been tempted to try negotiating a reunified and disarmed Germany if he could keep it out of the west's clutches. The west at a minimum would demand withdrawal of Soviet troops from the east. Konrad Adenauer actually feared such a withdrawal, anxious that it would generate domestic pressure to conclude a deal with Moscow that left the FRG defenseless against internal subversion. A Big Three meeting was hurriedly arranged for Paris on 9-11 November 1949. Acheson's briefing papers said Stalin and Pieck were aiming to "ruin all of Germany" to give Russia a leg up in "winning the battle for Europe."[4]

Acheson had jumped at the chance when Ernest Bevin called this meeting, because the British foreign minister signaled he would now agree to a significant cutback of German dismantlement and softened terms for restoring the sovereignty of the FRG. In preparation, Acheson spent several weekends going through piles of paper, forcing cancellation of a vacation and cutting his output at the lathe to "a few wall brackets and other small knickknacks." On 30 October, he sent a pair of eloquent cables to Robert Schuman. The allies should not risk replaying the 1920s, he told him, when a humiliated generation of Germans threw over democracy for the temptations of a scheming Soviet Union. Today, *because* Germans feared the Soviet Union, they were "psychologically and politically ripe" to join an integrated western Europe, which the west should exploit with prompt and preemptive acts of "good will." Since the United States could not appropriately lead European integration, France must do it as the continent's "strongest democratic power" and the nation with the greatest stake in Germany's future. Reading between the lines of this flattery, Schuman might have seen two troublesome subterranean themes. First, that Paris by itself might have to bear the burden of German integration; second, should it fail to do so, the United States might choose Germany as the bellwether of the Atlantic alliance. Bruce thought Acheson was twisting the screws too tightly. Schuman enjoyed great prestige, but if a wave of insularity hit the French National Assembly, he warned, his role would be undermined by his liberalism, Lorraine origins, and World War I service in a German uniform.[5]

In Paris, each of the Big Three ministers had to keep an eye on his domestic front. Congress was nipping at Acheson's ankles because of the high cost of keeping Germany down and out. Bevin and Schuman's constituents preferred Germans in that posture. Acheson sought to cut back on occupation controls that annulled benefits of the Marshall Plan. Despite Bevin's recent message, he and Schuman expressed skepticism about such leniency. Hoping to strengthen Schuman in Georges Bidault's new government, Acheson remained open to compromise. Two days of secret talks left Adenauer, their Bonn partner-in-waiting, no chance to dicker. Acheson wanted Bevin to lead on occupation controls, but "Ernie" was now seriously ill, easily exhausted, and "crusty and impatient." The Big Three nonetheless quickly packaged a deal for Adenauer. They pledged to oppose recognition of the East German regime, relax shipbuilding restraints and other features of dismantlement, and extend Bonn's right to send consular and commercial officers abroad. Adenauer must continue with demilitarization, monitor certain German industries, and limit steel production. The communique gave conditional support to "the progressive integration of the German people into the European community." Adenauer agreed to the terms (the Petersberg Protocols) after brisk negotiations with the high commissioners at their Petersberg headquarters, outside Bonn. Though he had wanted more progress on dismantlement, Acheson told Truman he was encouraged by Schuman's constructive attitude on Germany and European integration. He denied press conjectures that the Big Three had talked about a German role in western defense.[6]

Before Adenauer signed the Protocols, Acheson at McCloy's urging made a three-day trip to Germany. It was the first visit by a high-ranking U.S. official in four years and the first ever by a western foreign minister. Acheson seized the opportunity to make visible the U.S. government's admiration for the West German *Bundeskanzler* (chancellor), the first large step in forming the stout postwar alliance between the Americans and Germans. In the sleepy university town of Bonn, he met President Theodor Heuss, then Adenauer. The crafty, seventy-three-year-old Adenauer had been mayor of Cologne from 1917 to 1933, when the Nazis had forced him out of politics and, near the end of the war, into a concentration camp. After the war, the British first spurned the Christian Democratic leader for his conservatism and Catholicism. Assistants had told him that as a member of the Frankfurter circle, Acheson was "a tactician and opportunist" and probably no friend of Germany. He was surprised, therefore, at Acheson's ready warmth, for the American instantly took to the German leader in "the beginning of a warm friendship." Adenauer, he observed, seemed "the human embodiment of the doctrine of the conservation of energy," for he "moved and spoke slowly, gestured sparingly, smiled briefly, and chuckled rather than laughed." His blunt acceptance of a divided Germany was surprising. The East Germans, he told Acheson, had "always looked toward Russia." He fully agreed when told the American people expected him to bury the hatchet with France. He further charmed Acheson by saying Americans were "the best Europeans" of all. Adenauer, Acheson thought, raised hopes "for a new day in Europe."

In contrast, he took an instant dislike to Adenauer's Socialist opponent, Kurt Schumacher. A native Prussian, in constant pain and crippled from World War I injuries and Nazi beatings, he too had been thrown into the camps, but Adenauer considered him a "typical East German" and thus drawn to Russia. Acheson warned the embittered Schumacher that his abrasive nationalism would block friendly relations with France, undermining U.S. acceptance of European responsibilities. He would get "short shrift" from Washington if his party tried to play east off against west or curry "favor with the voters or the Russians by baiting the occupation." Acheson viewed Adenauer as a "European" statesman but Schumacher as a poisonous, east-yearning opportunist. Adenauer sought the west's favor, while Schumacher denounced him for colluding with the occupiers of German soil. Schumacher was a "fanatic of a dangerous and pure type," and only his death in 1952 enabled Washington to work productively with his party, the party of Willy Brandt.

Adenauer drove Acheson to the Bahnhof for his return to Frankfurt. Noticing crowds of onlookers pushing against stout police lines in the dusk, Acheson caused "tantrums" in the security detail by hauling the chancellor out of the automobile for a bit of American handshaking. He "needed building up." The resulting scene, which exhilarated Acheson, gave *Der Alte* (Old Man) his first taste of "the rich wine of wild popular acclaim." Thousands swept police aside to follow the men to the train, stopping Acheson for autographs and handing him messages for Germans in the United States. The Bahnhof demonstration, in a country so recently "defeated and knocked about," strongly shaped Acheson's view of German psychological needs and convinced him the United States was the outside power best able to meet them. In the years ahead, when Acheson had to refuse Germans' requests, "they would listen" as they would not to "the French or British."[7]

A trip to Berlin completed his German education. The city's rubble-strewn destitution braced his resolve to eliminate the occupation's gratuitous humiliations. Meeting the stalwart Socialist mayor, Ernst Reuter, added to his conviction the Germans could be redoubtable allies. He also met the Soviet commandant, the square-shaped General Vasily Ivanovich Chuikov. After some minutes of pleasantries, reported the *New York Times*, Acheson offered Chuikov a farewell drink. "The hard bitten Russian general and the easy smiling diplomat drank— and it was the Russian who shook his head after drinking, not the American." Then Acheson flew home. Truman greeted him at the bottom of the ramp, hand out. "An excellent job," he said.[8]

Besides giving Acheson another prized partner, the trip stripped the bark from his wartime feelings about the Germans. Thirteen years later, he would advise Secretary of Defense Robert S. McNamara of what he had believed since 1949, "that Germany is the most important country in the world to us." Washington could shape the course of Germany as French, British, *and* Soviets could not. Germans "take on the color of the wall," Adenauer had told him, blending in with "their environment," so it was imperative to draw them away from impulses of detachment. They should be part of western Europe, where "their more liberal traditions would find strength through companionship." Acheson did not miss Adenauer's point and would work hard in helping him bring his nation inside the western environment. Armed with his friendship with the American secretary of state, Adenauer was now in a position to seek Bundestag approval of the Petersberg Protocols.[9]

With the blood of two world wars still drying, Adenauer had told Acheson he had no interest in rearmament or being part of NATO, and in November, Schuman issued an unequivocally negative statement about any German role. But the issue would not down. Two days after Schuman's statement, General Omar Bradley, head of the joint chiefs, spoke publicly of the need for German rearmament, prompting further state department denials. Acheson insisted to reporters he opposed rearming Germany with no "mental reservations," and the president "emphatically" denied interest in even a small German army. When retired General Lucius Clay went public about "a 'composite force' of French aircraft and armor, Benelux artillery, and German infantry" as the "solution to European defense," Louis Johnson disowned him. But Clay repeated his views in a Boston speech, and he and British General Bernard Montgomery published an article advocating German participation in western security. On 28 November 1950, Montgomery came out foursquare for rearmament.[10]

Acheson told French Ambassador Henri Bonnet on 1 December his department was doing everything possible "to stop" these rumors. If Bonnet had the use of a sense of humor, he might have laughed when Adenauer, having earlier told Acheson he had no interest in NATO, announced on 9 December that the allies had a choice between "a German contingent in a European army or the threat of the Soviet Union." Acheson again insisted to the press five days afterward that no one was considering "rearming" Germany, but on the 16th, the *Times* reported the JCS had examined plans to raise five German divisions for assignment to NATO command. The rumor mill never stopped until September 1950, when the administration came out forthrightly in favor of German rearmament.[11]

The Best Europeans of All—Which Europeans?

Early in 1950, U.S. policy in Europe seemed only equivocally successful. The allies had stared down the Soviets over Germany. The Marshall Plan was beginning to work, as evidenced by large increases in industrial production, trade, and growth in ordinary workers' incomes. But Acheson could not be encouraged by a growing sense of military inadequacy and European resistance to Washington's new military paradigm. Europeans were anxious at the shift of Washington's gaze to Asia, even though Acheson told Belgian Foreign Minister Paul-Henri Spaak in January 1950 that the "great issues were going to be decided" in Europe.[12]

Especially because Republicans wanted to cut foreign aid, Acheson hoped to help Europeans earn more dollars. On 16 February, in his total diplomacy campaign, he pressed for lower tariffs and creative approaches to compensate those harmed by the trade competition. He urged the president to take the lead, observing that the trade balance stood at an unsustainable 8–5 in favor of the United States. If nothing were done, the end of the Marshall Plan in 1952 would coincide with an end to European purchases in the United States, causing horrific dislocations on both sides of the Atlantic. Since economic health was vital to western strength, this would cause a sharp "shift of power from the democratic to the Soviet sphere." He urged the president to consolidate domestic and foreign economic policymaking and use his bully pulpit to persuade Congress and the people. In a speech of his own, he spoke of a "trinity" of postwar policies. The United States in the Marshall Plan had seized the European economic malaise "by the scruff of the neck." It was now attacking the problem in underdeveloped areas through Point Four. And soon it must eliminate trade barriers and close the dollar gap. Truman responded halfheartedly, naming Secretary of the Army Gordon Gray his special adviser on the dollar gap.[13]

As always, this gap was near the center of relations with Britain. Like the French, according to Julius Holmes, U.S. minister-counselor in London, the British constantly felt Washington poking them in the back to act. While Britain was "fighting a last-stand battle for survival as a world power," the United States wanted it also to act simultaneously on other pressing political, economic, and military objectives. The U.S. embassy reported that London's fits of bad temper could be explained by its consciousness of being spread thin in the special transatlantic partnership it so treasured. Whitehall particularly resented Acheson's pressure about European integration. The fatigued Attlee government faced difficult elections and, with an eye on McCarthyism, entertained doubts about American reliability and stability. Ambassador Lewis Douglas prescribed generous stroking of Oliver Franks, the UK's envoy to Washington, to Acheson. Labor's margin in the House of Commons fell from 146 to 5 votes in the February 1950 elections. From March to July, surgeries and convalescence kept Bevin hospitalized half the time, further diminishing Britain's chances to lead. However resentfully, both London and Paris wanted *Washington* to lead. "Our friends seem to demand it," Acheson remarked, "and need it and are leaving us little choice." Still, he looked once more to Schuman instead. On 8 April, he urged him to include the FRG in shaping the future of the Ruhr basin, advice that would give stimulus to the soon-to-be-unveiled Schuman Plan.[14]

Military planning now moved to the fore. Only in December 1949 had defense ministers begun designing the congressionally demanded "strategic concept," but taboo subjects and unresolved conflicts made it a nullity at birth. Having disingenuously told Congress the Europeans were doing everything possible to defend themselves, Truman and Acheson began exerting pressure for them actually to do so. Ironically, Truman's resistance to a buildup at home intensified the pressure. In turn, by March the allies were pressing the United States to adopt a more forward strategy. As a result, Washington promised to defend Europe at the Rhine instead of the Pyrenees, an objective no more workable than the "Medium Term Defense Plan" as a whole, which was adopted in March. Defending at the Rhine would be unattainable without German participation, which all plans, whether short or medium term, still ignored. Acheson later admitted they mostly resembled multinational shopping lists for American arms. They did have the merit of causing Truman to officially open the MDAP arms bazaar. But alliance dissension continued. Contrary to the promise to hold the line at the Rhine, Pentagon blueprints still bore the stamp of OFFTACKLE, focusing on a defense at the Pyrenees. Both the Americans and the British were still—quietly—assuming a posthaste retreat from West Germany if the Soviets crossed from the east. Making the disarray in strategic planning worse was the slow pace of mutual defense aid distributions. By the first week of April, only $42 million of an authorized $1.3 billion had been "obligated."[15]

The absence of Germany from these plans exposed NATO as a caucus of fabulists. It is not exactly clear what Acheson thought at this point about a German role in western defense, or, particularly, about news in January 1950 that World War II generals were advising Adenauer about the materiel needs of an army division. He consistently disavowed ideas of German rearmament until the summer of 1950, and his 1949 flirtations with Kennan's neutralization schemes point to the truthfulness of the disavowals. Truman's opposition to German rearmament gave Acheson another reason to stand with opponents. An even stronger reason was his need to persuade France to take a central role in incorporating West Germany into the alliance, broadly defined.

Nonetheless, apart from his own aggressive personality, he had reasons aplenty to envision Germans in the front lines. Among them were the Soviet atomic test, the unrealistic defense plans littering his desk, and the Europeans' tardiness in moving toward integration. His heartening personal visit with Adenauer apparently reduced his worries about inclusion of the Germans. Thus, his reiterated denials may have been an act of dissembling, the result of a pragmatic need to tack against the Germanophobic winds coming from both Paris and the White House. His campaign to convince Schuman to seize European leadership was partly a way to prepare him for including the Bonn republic in the alliance later. In any case, before Korea, he did nothing important to move Truman toward acceptance of German rearmament. Once he did move the president—in the late wartime summer of 1950—Acheson vigorously took the case to the French, ready or not.[16]

In the spring of 1950, a year after his first tuition on Germany, his absorption in the subject grew—it became "the only problem." Endless meetings, many with Henry Byroade, State's director of German affairs, dealt with "safely" adding "German strength to the West." The more interested Acheson became in this objective, the more he humored Paris. After a private dinner in early March, Franks told London that Acheson intended to help the French in Indochina as a step toward binding the Germans snugly to the western alliance. The British, too, began inching toward the same goal, prompted by an incident in which German police failed to protect British dismantlement workers from hostile demonstrators. When Adenauer claimed the troublemakers had infiltrated from the east, the UK's high commissioner saw the wisdom of letting the FRG create a 25,000-man police force—one that might well exfoliate into an army. Opposition leader Winston Churchill openly championed putting Germany in the alliance, and Attlee's cabinet virtually but unofficially agreed. Mirroring the discord in Washington, the foreign office thought the generals needed restraining and, on 4 April, the British government said it still opposed German rearmament in any form.[17]

This did nothing to deflate the growing debate in the U.S. government. McCloy bombarded Washington with a message describing Germans as "nervous, hysterical, and uncertain," while Bohlen fretted about Germans playing "the West off against the East." The joint chiefs wanted a presidential endorsement of West German participation in western military planning. Acheson still probably thought circumstances too delicate for such an endorsement. Instead, in a press conference on 5 April 1950, he repeated a "firm" U.S. commitment to German *disarmament*. Later in the month, he told McCloy to "disabuse" Adenauer from thinking he could use the "East-West situation to wring concessions from West." He intimated to Franks that before any steps could be taken toward German rearmament, the alliance must weave the FRG so tightly within

Europe-wide networks that "whether she wanted to or not Germany could not look East."

Regardless, the idea of adding German weight to NATO ranks bobbed to the surface every time Acheson pushed it under. Republicans Arthur Vandenberg and John Foster Dulles and many congressional Democrats all favored the idea. Some at State agreed, but Acheson wanted more assurance the west could rely on the Germans "in the long run." In executive testimony in May 1950, he deplored talk about German rearmament. It "frightens the French; it also makes the Germans very cocky."[18]

State department officers like their Pentagon counterparts were working on a German contingency, but Acheson and Truman stuck to their guns, Acheson even saying a new police force was an "inherent danger to democracy." From Stuttgart, McCloy declared against any "German army or air force." It was a dangerous mistake, he held, to give Germans the impression the west depended on them. In a 4 May NSC meeting, Acheson said French refusal to consider German "military participation" ruled out discussing the subject for now.[19]

France Fills the Vacuum

That spring, transatlantic cables hummed with anxiety. The French and Germans were in a scrap over the Saar, the borderland *Deutsch*-speaking territory France had occupied after both world wars. Congress sat on Truman's pleas for more MDAP funds. A string of transient scares made NATO seem pathetically wanting. The Soviets downed a U.S. plane over the Baltic, imposed a short-lived blockade of Berlin, and spewed threats against Yugoslavia. East Germany was raising a military force. A nervous Switzerland instructed its dutiful citizenry to stock supplies for war. The state department's Edward Barrett lamented the "vacuum" of "positive steps in the cold war," while Bohlen thought the Soviets were trying to appear "more interested in peace than the United States." Truman and Acheson implicitly contradicted one another in public on defense spending. Washington was "groping desperately for ideas," Franks thought.[20]

The collapse of the last shreds of bipartisanship accounted for the desperation Franks noticed. When Vandenberg sank into mortal illness, Acheson looked for a stand-in to name as a NATO consultant. He chose Republican John Sherman Cooper, a former (and future) senator. But no one even noticed. Europeans worried that the Truman administration's best intentions would be overrun by McCarthy and his ferocious friends. One of these, Styles Bridges, announced on 25 March 1950 he would begin a sustained assault on Acheson. Truman immediately chastised him in a letter for "joining the 'wolf-hounds.'" The United States had never had "a more capable and loyal public servant" than Acheson, he wrote, and only the "Politburo" would profit from Bridges' campaign. Acheson invited Bridges home for a discussion "eased with some bourbon," and Bridges received an invitation for a White House discussion with the president and secretary of state on 18 April, but "my faithful enemy," as Acheson once dubbed Bridges, still vented against him without relent. Despite these appearances, James Reston thought the war against Acheson looked worse than it was, fought by a small circle of unreconstructed opponents unable to gain new adherents.[21]

However many there were, Acheson ignored his opponents as he prepared for mid-May meetings in London of the Big Three and NATO Council. He hoped to abate Paris's growing fears of being exposed to superior German power on the continent and to overcome resistance in both London and Paris to larger defense spending. France pleaded the good fight it already waged in Indochina, while Britain blamed its dollar problems. If France and Britain were not up to the task, in due time Acheson would give West Germany a hard look as Washington's primary European partner.

Before the formal meetings in London, he flew to Paris for preliminary discussions with Schuman. There he received an immediate shock. Coal and steel were the foundation for modern war, and Schuman sprung on him a plan to pool French and German production of both. He intensified the shock by insisting Acheson keep the news to himself for at least a day, leaving the American "closeted" with information he first viewed as "the damndest cartel" he had ever heard of. But astonishment at the brilliance of Schuman's plan quickly overtook his suspicion. It illustrated half of his later remark that France always showed up at the center of the alliance's best and worst moments, and here was a moment of "the greatest inventiveness and ingenuity," integration with a vengeance. The plan had sprouted from the mind of Jean Monnet but gained cabinet approval after Schuman's adroit massaging. Once Acheson's anti-trust antennae had stopped vibrating, he realized the plan could solve a host of large problems.[22]

This was statecraft and integration by economic means and the French leadership Acheson had begged for. The quickly dubbed "Schuman Plan" might end Europe's recurrent economic problems. Even if its design failed to induce London's cooperation, British detachment would now matter less. Most vitally, it was a formula for absorbing West Germany within the alliance and ending a century of enmity between the United States' two most important continental partners. That the Schuman Plan might frustrate German rearmament while boosting French prestige seemed a negligible blemish, at least for now. As Schuman garnered cabinet consent to announce the plan, Acheson coordinated positive statements he and Truman would give in response. They issued these on 9 May 1950, when Schuman announced his plan as a way to end European wars by making them "not simply unthinkable, but materially impossible." Complementing NATO, the Schuman Plan would complete the postwar western structure against Soviet expansion. As Scott Newton notes, for the next generation France and Germany led "the continental economic community," while the "Anglo-American axis" spearheaded the offshore military alliance. Failing to grasp the plan's power to unite the continent, Moscow swiftly condemned it as a nefarious scheme concocted by Acheson to rearm Germany against peace-loving nations.[23]

With Franco-American cooperation peaking, Acheson discovered to his huge irritation on arriving in London that a team of Britons and his own assistants had proudly developed a plan to announce a "special relationship" between the United States and the United Kingdom. No doubt crimsoning as he read their paper, he observed that it inspired "two thoughts." First, he "entirely agreed" such a relationship existed. *Second*, it was "quite impossible to allow it to be known that any such paper had been drawn up or that it had been agreed to." With that, he ordered all copies destroyed. It was "dangerous" enough to talk about the connection but far worse to put it on paper. He was "shocked, horrified and overwhelmed" at the imprudence of codifying "this common law marriage." Special relationships, as Paul Nitze later put it, "can be poisonous," and Acheson wanted nothing to do with this one.[24]

The next shock came from Bevin. Sapped by illness, on hearing about the Schuman Plan, he was furious to realize Acheson already knew about it. He demanded: "'Do you know anything about this?' and I said, 'Yes, I do,' and I told him what Schuman had said to me. And then he gave me hell, and said I was a disloyal son of a bitch." Acheson thought the Labor minister felt such "rage" because joining such a "freely competitive system" for coal and steel would rob his government of grounds to run Britain "as a welfare state." But if it did not join, Britain would lose valuable markets on the continent. Bevin also resented Paris's bid to lead all of Europe. Though he quickly acquitted Acheson of treachery, he rejected the secretary's pleas to join Schuman's invention, which Acheson later called the greatest British "mistake of the postwar period." When Schuman arrived in London, he too faced a blast of Bevin's umbrage. When Acheson reminded Bevin how Britain's unilateral devaluation of the pound had inflamed the French, the king's minister saw the game was up. As the three men walked into another meeting, Schuman took Acheson's arm and murmured: "You have a large deposit in my bank." Though various obstacles delayed its formal promulgation, the Schuman Plan became the European Coal and Steel Community in 1952. Realizing the need for a broader foundation, in 1954 Paris brought forth new plans that soon led to the European Common Market. Acheson remained supportive throughout.[25]

Otherwise, military matters dominated the London meetings. Still in the embryonic stages of putting the "O" in NATO (Harriman's *bon mot*), negotiators formed a permanent NATO Council, complete with deputies to push defense plans ahead. Canadians thought Acheson's leadership in London proved beyond a doubt that, at least "morally," the United States had decided to give permanent "economic and military support" to Europe. When Bevin brandished a new strategy paper assuming German participation, Acheson said the matter was still "premature." Though a German role in western defense was "central to everything" being discussed, he later recalled, "nobody could speak about it." As a sop to German restiveness, the NATO Council told Adenauer the alliance would consider an attack against his nation an attack against all.[26]

A "Most Difficult and Hard Road"

On 19 May 1950, Acheson boarded the *H.M.S. Britannia* for a leisurely voyage home and a few crumbs of his canceled vacation. As he crossed the Atlantic, he pondered the connection between NATO's slow teething and the promotion of NSC-68. His concern was the "difficult and hard road" ahead to gain mobilization of both the United States and the allies. NATO solidarity, Reston wrote, was a "triumph for American diplomacy and Mr. Acheson's leadership," but representatives and senators in the throes of McCarthyite fantasies thought otherwise. They rebuffed Truman's idea of inviting Acheson to address a joint session of Congress. Instead, on 31 May, members gathered informally at the Library of Congress to hear his upbeat report on the London talks. His reception was cool, but the weather was not, and he soldiered on, he wrote daughter Mary, under pitiless television lights that sent the temperature spiraling past "100 degrees" in a crowded room already "steamed up with animal heat." His "collar wet," his shirt "a washrag," his suit hanging "in loose wet folds," he resisted temptations to dab his brow. Instead he sweat all "the sin of a misspent life." Afterward, the experience made him think the Constitution should provide for "two Secretaries of State, one who makes the appearances and one who is a member of the Politburo. I would choose the latter role."[27]

A few weeks before war broke out in Korea, signs of alliance malaise returned. General Montgomery churned out desolate pronouncements on the state of defenses. Allies were chagrined when Acheson appointed a little known New York lawyer, Charles Spofford, as his permanent deputy on the new NATO Council. Washington's efforts to enlist allies in a common trade embargo against the Soviet bloc mostly failed. The CIA worried that Soviet propaganda might paralyze European will. Acheson thought the Medium Term Defense Plan a "frankenstein." And Congress demanded that Europeans dig deeper in their own pockets for rearmament and pointed to Truman's meager budgets in justification.[28]

The issue of German rearmament would not rest. On 8 June, five days after newspapers said the Big Three were considering a request from Adenauer for a police force, Bradley said publicly that, from "a purely military point of view," German rearmament was desirable. Asked about this, Acheson said Bradley had only spoken theoretically. Reinforcing Acheson's caution was a McCloy cable expressing concern about "extreme countermeasures" Moscow might take against German rearmament. Truman spoke loudly and clearly on 16 June 1950 in two memoranda to Acheson. In the first, he denounced the joint chiefs "as decidedly militaristic" for wanting to rearm Germany and establish relations with Franco's Spain. In the second, he offered a history lesson. Washington should not repeat the errors that allowed Hitler to ignore the Versailles treaties while he built his lethal "war machine" that caused "the unnecessary death of millions and millions of young men of all the other European countries and the United States." He scrawled on the JCS memo: "As wrong as can be."[29]

A few days later, war erupted in Korea. By July, the same Truman wanted cost figures on implementing NSC-68. In September, he wanted German rearmament. In November, he sent an ambassador to Madrid. He knew the cold war had entered a new and dangerous stage.

16

PLUNGE INTO THE UNKNOWN: THE UNITED STATES, INDOCHINA, AND CHINA ON THE EVE OF THE KOREAN WAR

Through a Glass Darkly

Examined many years later, Dean Acheson's labors in Asia in the first half of 1950, other than in Japan, seem phantasmal. The avalanche of the Korean War soon buried efforts now difficult to unearth. Under attack by the Republican right, challenged by the Pentagon and his own aides, and sensitive to Truman's enmity toward the Chinese communists, his control of policy for East Asia was on the wane, but more freedom of action would hardly have improved the outcome. He did dominate policy toward Southeast Asia, partly because few others were paying attention. There, in recognizing Bao Dai's "national" Vietnamese government, he unfurled an American umbrella under which France waged an old-style colonial war. The Korean War deepened the commitment, and the United States plunged into the unknown in Indochina.

Democrats quarreled with Republicans and the China Lobby with the administration. State officials eager to dump Chiang clashed with his defenders, and pro-French policymakers with those trying to lift America's skirts above the debris of European colonialism. With so many sharp vectors around, a Truman-Acheson collision was not implausible. Notwithstanding the victory over the Pentagon on China policy described in Chapter 11, Acheson was circumspect, still hoping for European allies' help in Asia. In January 1950, when Commonwealth nations met in Colombo, Ceylon, to establish a regional development plan, he offered only polite benedictions. At signs that China now resolved to assume full control of Tibet, he instructed his ambassador in New Delhi to tell

Tibetans eager for help they should talk to the Indians and British. He approved aid to Burma only to supplement plans designed in London. His prime end in East Asia may have been simply not to open a new arena of Sino-U.S. conflict.[1]

Exercising restraint in Asia was a major theme of his 12 January 1950 National Press Club speech. Though sympathetic with hopes to eradicate poverty and foreign domination, he implied that Washington could be most effective standing modestly in the wings, coming on stage only if asked. This would redirect anti-colonial wrath to an expansionist USSR, where it belonged. The United States would do best playing a philanthropic and patient role rather than befriending a tyranny like Chiang's. But at the time, such doctrines seemed as dreamlike as George Kennan's preference for a similarly passive role in Europe. Anyway, Acheson's critics did not want to be patient, and his own plans grew more assertive and more dependent for realization on colonial or neo-colonial governments.[2]

By May 1950, his January goals were already compromised. Policies toward China, Formosa, Japan, and Southeast Asia became obscurely interlaced and veered toward uncertain and unwelcome ends. Historians long pointed to the Korean War as the cause of dramatic changes, but that war only reshaped changes well under way before shots were fired.

A Tail on the Battered Kite of French Colonialism

If John F. Kennedy and Lyndon Johnson first traveled down the highway of war in Vietnam, Truman and Acheson did much to survey and build it. Though aware of the hazards before him, Acheson followed the route anyway, thinking he had no choice. Like other U.S. officials, he did not fully grasp that French objectives and nationalists' hopes were irreconcilable, making the compromises he sought impossible. His strategy in Indochina would founder over time. He no more foresaw the war that would bleed American forces in Vietnam than the earlier hemorrhage in Korea. He had little interest in Indochina and, it often seemed, little respect for its peoples.

Developments during World War II made the American economy far less dependent on overseas rubber and minerals, but Southeast Asia remained a vital if potential source of raw materials and export markets for Japan, now blocked from trading with China. European allies still struggling to close the dollar gap also had much at stake in the region.

Acheson, however, usually did not have economics in mind when he picked at the Indochina scab. He was concerned instead with how defeat in Asia would vitiate France's ability to lead in Europe. Supporting Paris, he told senators on 29 March 1950, would limit U.S. involvement: "We want more [French] effort but not additional responsibility. We do not want to get into a position where the French say, 'You take over; we aren't able to go ahead on this.'" The joint chiefs worried about losing bases they counted on in a general war. The other large U.S.

concern in Indochina was Chinese expansionism. If the Chinese communists extended their revolution southward, they could destabilize all of South and Southeast Asia, shaking Japanese and Philippine faith in U.S. resolve and opening the doors for all kinds of Soviet mischief-making in a western sphere of influence. These seemed reasons enough for some degree of enmeshment in Indochina, an involvement encouraged by Britain, which was concerned about its own regional possessions. About the only identifiable person in the state department who dissented was Charlton Ogburn, a specialist in the lower ranks.[3]

Acheson solicited advice from George Kennan and the policy planning staff. The resulting paper, formally approved after the beginning of the Korean War, articulated views that shaped policy for a generation. It described Southeast Asia as a "vital segment on the line of containment, stretching from Japan southward around to the Indian Peninsula," a line now targeted by Moscow. Undoubtedly, Kennan wrote the line about U.S.-equipped French troops "being squandered in Indochina on a mission which can be justified only in terms of Gallic mystique." If Washington had accepted the Pacific Pact advocated by the Philippines, it might have found regional allies to share burdens in the region, but Acheson was dead set against this scheme, not least because India and Indonesia opposed it.[4]

Despite Ho Chi Minh's quotation from the American Declaration of Independence in proclaiming Vietnamese independence in September 1945, the U.S. government from the first considered him a dedicated communist and Stalinist lackey, a key reason it did not press the French to leave Indochina as it had the Dutch from Indonesia. As under secretary in 1946, Acheson had promised "to do anything" to help France keep Indochina out of the Soviet orbit. His task now was to solve "the colonial-nationalist conflict in a way that would satisfy nationalist aims and minimize the strain on our Western European allies." But, as he later wrote, whenever he urged the necessity of Vietnamese independence, or even autonomy, France stubbornly "balked," or, more inventively, "blackmailed us" with horrific predictions of what would happen if the United States withdrew its support. By the time Acheson became secretary of state, prospects had greatly deteriorated. Ho and his Viet Minh guerillas were making significant progress despite Paris's invention of the "French Union," into which it could stuff various colonies in an effort to impress world opinion. By 1949, Ho for two years had been a serious challenge to the very high-quality French troops Acheson would soon want assigned to NATO. By January 1950, 162,400 of France's 651,330 active military personnel served in Indochina.[5]

On 8 March 1949, Paris produced the quasi-independent state of Vietnam in the "Elysée Agreement." More quasi than independent, its head was former emperor Bao Dai, long on experience along the Riviera and short on nationalist credentials. His authority remained unclear, for Paris retained diplomatic and military powers, and the French National Assembly had yet to ratify the 8 March accord. Acheson wanted something better before offering recognition. Outgoing U.S. ambassador in Paris, Jefferson Caffery, said it was the "only non-Communist solution in sight," but Acheson correctly guessed other Asians would see Bao Dai as a puppet. But seeing no other alternatives and coming under pressure from Caffery and Dean Rusk in the department, Acheson worried himself into hesitant support of Bao Dai. He nevertheless remained reluctant to do anything that reduced the standing of the United States with other Asian governments. While he was in Paris, on 14 June 1949, a twenty-one-gun salute in Saigon marked Bao Dai's accession to office. When a cable arrived for Acheson from Washington instructing Ambassador David Bruce to tell France to do more toward granting true Vietnamese independence, Bruce exploded. Acheson backed him in dismissing this "poppycock" in favor of bland remarks about U.S. hopes for a liberal interpretation of the Elysée Agreements. Acheson told Robert Schuman and Ernest Bevin he planned to give some form of recognition to the Bao Dai regime and offer it assistance.[6]

He consistently pushed Paris to liberalize the Elysée Agreements, give the Vietnamese more independence, and find ways to broaden popular and regional acceptance of Bao Dai. Equally consistently, he chafed at the Indochina predicament and criticized French shortsightedness. He told reporters in August 1949 that colonialism was "finished" and that Washington was trying to get the French and Dutch to give it up. His doubts rose in October, when China Forum participants almost uniformly criticized involvement in France's troubled "experiment," and the junketing Nehru warned him of Bao Dai's assured failure. Acheson told senators he would not recommend recognizing Bao Dai until he gained his neighbors' support and France moved further toward liberalization. Asian consultant Raymond Fosdick in November said it would be a disaster to fly on the "battered kite" of French imperialism.[7]

If Acheson had actually demanded outright independence for Indochina as a price for U.S. backing, NATO might have splintered as it nearly did during the 1956 Suez crisis. Instead, he combined dogged entreaties that Paris do better with a modicum of passive resistance. When Emperor Bao Dai, addressing Truman as "Great and Good Friend," asked for recognition on 31 August 1949, Acheson held the president back. In September, he refused Schuman's offer of more liberal treatment of the Vietnamese regime in exchange for more aid. He thought Indochina policy needed "more brains and fewer dollars." But the premises of U.S. policy in Southeast Asia did *not* change, leaving Acheson relying on little more than hope while events kept "marching on the mainland of Asia." He felt some momentary encouragement at the end of 1949, when France officially ceded authority over Vietnam's internal affairs, and again in early February 1950, when the French National Assembly finally ratified the Elysée accords.[8]

In October 1949, thinking about Nehru's remarks, Acheson had considered taking "a closer look at Ho Chi-Minh," but this was nothing but frustration-borne vamping, like his musings about a nuclear moratorium. Cooperation with Ho would have required a complete reversal of the premises of U.S. policy. This revolutionary, who had studied in Moscow in the 1920s, had also long consorted with Mao, joining the Eighth Route Army in China in the 1930s and early 1940s. In more ways than one, he spoke Mao's language. It was immaterial that he was also a "nationalist," Acheson had said in May 1949, since the same was true of "all Stalinists in colonial areas." On 31 January 1950, Acheson said Ho was "the mortal enemy of native independence in Indochina." In October of the previous year, the CIA had forecast that when Chinese communist armies still tracking down the last of Chiang's mainland forces reached the Vietnamese border, they would give Ho aid, shifting the "balance of power" in his favor. The predicted rendezvous occurred in December and with it the flow of arms. In January, ten days after Acheson wishfully told senators Ho feared a Chinese takeover, he was actually deep in talks with Mao and Stalin in Moscow. Soon, three divisions of Mao's troops entered Vietnam, along with advisers and a quickly established officer-training school. By this time, the United States had already committed its prestige to the French cause. At dinner with the British and Canadian ambassadors in December, Acheson had delivered a "paean of praise about French achievements in Indochina."[9]

Blackmail and the Bao Dai Dilemma

During the war, FDR had talked about booting France out of Indochina, but it was just talk, and early in his presidency, Truman decided to stick with France in the east as long as it could play a leading role in the west. The issues of nuclear weapons and Indochina seem distant from each other in the abstract, but they were closely linked for Acheson. Reducing dependence on nuclear weapons meant building up the alliance's conventional forces, and France could not contribute to that goal while its men were dying in Indochina. Thus, he favored helping Paris if it would accept that Southeast Asia was more than a French issue. Viewing it as a *western* issue argued for quick movement toward independence. How to approach the problem aroused discord between department bureaus. EUR (Europe) supported France, and FE (Far East) did not. John Service recalled that "FE was anti-colonial, trying to end colonialism," but lost out to EUR, which was then "all-powerful in the Department." John Melby, another Asianist, remonstrated against further embroilment and blamed EUR officers for tolerating French "blackmail." According to Melby, the European desk officers specialized in terrifying predictions about how anything less than full support to Paris would cause communist victories in French elections and French abandonment of NATO. The joint chiefs, on the other hand, seemed united in thinking the French military on its own could not stifle the Indochinese uprising.[10]

Early in February 1950, both the Soviet and Chinese governments extended formal recognition to Ho's government. Though unsurprised by Beijing's decision, Acheson found Moscow's troublesome, for it had never recognized the Greek rebels. Moscow's action, he thought, "should remove any illusions as to the 'nationalist' nature of Ho Chi Minh's aims." When Tito recognized Ho as well, Acheson shrugged it off as a simple exercise of "Yugoslav national interests." The previous month in his Press Club speech, he had heaped more praise on France for moving toward Vietnamese "independence." He did not want to say anything that added "a feather" to Schuman's workload. Thus, immediately after Ho's recognition by Stalin and Mao, and French ratification of the Elysée Agreements, Acheson asked Truman to recognize the French-sponsored Associated States of Vietnam, Laos, and Cambodia. Recognition, he told him, would advance the cause of non-communist nationalism in Asia, encourage other states menaced by China, buttress a NATO ally, and demonstrate Washington's opposition to the communist aim of dominating Asia under the "guise of indigenous nationalism." On 3 February 1950, Truman approved, and formal recognition (in which London joined) occurred on 7 February. Acheson was more than irked when no other European or Asian state, including the Philippines, followed suit.[11]

Until France finally decamped from Indochina in 1954, U.S. policy rested on three legs—greater independence for Vietnam, further liberalization of the Vietnamese regime, and French consent for the United States to have a free hand in helping. Acheson's greatest concern was that France would abscond, leaving the United States holding the bag, which is what happened in the Eisenhower administration. In Acheson's time, the dilemmas facing U.S. policy seemed excruciating. There seemed no way to help France in Europe without also helping it in Asia, and he still had in mind keeping Indochina safe for the development of Japanese trade. In mid-February 1950, he told the French government it was not moving fast enough toward genuine independence. Moreover, while he wanted the Associated States to consider Paris a partner in resisting aggression, he also wanted them to be free to "walk out of the French Union." Since the French government vigorously disagreed, Acheson was boxed in. Washington wanted to help, but every bit it gave chipped away at U.S. bargaining power with the French, who repeatedly threatened to withdraw from Indochina absent more "long-term" aid. Blackmail, as Melby said, was the right word for this, although extortion would fit, too. But Truman and Acheson felt they could not afford to call the French bluff.[12]

France won these games without even showing its hand. At a dinner tête-à-tête with Acheson, Franks gained the impression that Washington would support Bao Dai as a sop for French acquiescence in bringing West Germany firmly into the western order. The aid would come from the Section 303 basket described in Chapter 11 for the "general area of China." But first, Acheson, wanting more information, sent off three fact-finding trips. Philip Jessup extended his travels, described earlier, to Indochina. Then at Acheson's request, Truman picked publisher R. Allen Griffin, a Republican critic from California, for an eight-week trip centering on Vietnam. Though it was part of the efforts begun the previous summer to immunize Asian policies from partisan criticism, Acheson wanted Griffin's trip unpublicized. A former ECA official in China, Griffin's main job was determining how best to use the 303 money in Indochina. Finally, John

Melby would see how to help *France* in Indochina. He would return with exhortations against further enmeshment. Reports from Jessup and Griffin would occur after the China and Indochina issues grew more intertwined and at a time of cannonading attacks against Acheson and the administration. None of the missions prevented the United States from advancing further toward its Gethsemane.[13]

"We Are Committed"

Whipped into a rage by Acheson's recent defense of Alger Hiss (see the next chapter), the secretary's detractors, now joined by Joseph McCarthy, launched an all-out assault on his Asian record in February and March of 1950. Calls came daily for Acheson's resignation. In a scoffing response, he chatted with reporters about how he had surrounded himself in the department with numerous "old-fashioned Southern Communists." Late in March, James Webb hopefully told a concerned White House that Acheson was "over the hump." With Arthur Vandenberg unavailable, the administration sought other Senate Republicans to woo. As noted earlier, Truman and Acheson met with Styles Bridges, an unlikely Vandenberg heir apparent. Subduing his pleasure at the attention, Bridges simply demanded more regular meetings with Republicans. He did not curb his criticisms.[14]

Indochina was still barely on the Republicans' radar, despite the growing U.S. commitment. Ships from the Seventh Fleet steamed into Saigon, sparking riots of Vietnamese nationalists. In the wake of a strong warning from Ogburn that Ho Chi Minh was unlikely to "wilt," Jessup returned from his journey of four months and fourteen Asian nations insisting on the strongest possible actions to "prevent Communist expansion." Washington must improve its information and propaganda programs, find qualified people to work for Bao Dai, and neutralize the influence of the overseas Chinese community. He thought the situation in East Asia "bad but not desperate." The "area cannot be written off," he added, because "we are committed." Griffin returned from his travels full of enthusiasm about using emergency economic aid to strengthen area governments. But he also warned about getting caught "between the French and Bao Dai, between the French and Ho Chi-minh, and between Bao Dai and Ho Chi-minh." Acheson could have answered that Washington was already caught. Despite his chronic misgivings, however, he would always decide the difficulties in Indochina were worth facing to help France fulfill U.S. goals in Europe. "So while we may have tried to muddle through and were certainly not successful," he wrote later, "I could not think then or later of a better course."[15]

Well before shooting started in Korea, the U.S. commitment deepened even further. Calling Southeast Asia crucial to U.S. strategy, the joint chiefs on 14 April recommended establishing a U.S. Military Advisory Group in Vietnam. Ten days later, Truman approved use of 303 funds in Indochina. As always, these additional commitments in Indochina ran parallel with doubts about their wisdom and hope that other governments would relieve Washington of its burdens. But the burdens seemed inescapable with Paris losing more officers in Indochina than the government graduated annually from its St. Cyr military academy. How, the French complained, could it do its duty in both Europe and Asia without help? In Paris talks in May, Acheson announced Washington's decision to give military aid directly for use in Indochina. Just as the Americans always harbored misgivings, the French always complained, and in this case they disliked Acheson's implication that France and the "associated states" were equals as aid recipients. Nor did they like it when he publicly announced that one of Washington's key objectives was to develop and sponsor "genuine nationalism" in the region.[16]

Back in Washington, Acheson doubtless learned the CIA view that the Soviet Union was threatening Southeast Asia to test whether the west could handle conflicts "simultaneously" in Europe and Asia. At the end of May, Ambassador Bruce, possibly "the most Francophile American ambassador to Paris since Thomas Jefferson," warned about the incompatibility of boosting "local nationalism" and supporting the French government. Acheson hardly needed instruction on the problem; he just had no solution to it. An even broader problem, he understood, was the impossibility of gaining the upper hand when operating from a position of weakness. Historical impetus lay with the rebels, not the defenders of an anachronism. The United States was trying to help from a punishing distance and had limited leverage. Nor could it keep Indochina out of communist hands without falling into France's. Acheson had warned senators early in the spring of 1950 that putting too much pressure on the French might cause them to say, " 'All right, take over the damned country. We don't want it,' and put their soldiers on ships and send them back to France."[17]

Maneuvering between China and Formosa, January–March 1950

Americans paid little attention to the fact that their government was sinking deeper into Indochina, but the erratic search for a stable policy in China and Formosa caused incessant tension. Acheson's efforts to shape, or contain, opinion led to results that defy simple description. Certainly he failed to reduce the number of those criticizing him. And, though unacknowledged, one of his critics was Truman, who might already have decided he would not recognize the People's Republic under any circumstances. "I won't recognize a bunch of bandits," he said after they seized U.S. diplomatic properties. Repeatedly, Acheson appeared to have resigned himself to the president's judgment. Then he would start talking about "normalization" again. The truth was that the administration was at a loss about what to do.[18]

Truman's statement in January 1950 ostensibly declaring neutrality in the Chinese civil war set off a rancorous Senate debate. William Knowland wanted

General Douglas MacArthur put in charge of the administration's "bankrupt" policy and a broom swept through the state department. Democrat Tom Connally fired back, wanting to know which of Chiang's admirers would send the U.S. army to rescue him and maybe set off "World War III." Robert A. Taft avoided this bait while he hammered state department leftists in what Acheson considered the first major attack on his policies as "subversive." Bridges asked why the government acted like "men in Europe" and "mice in Asia." Because of Truman's January announcement, Acheson still thought he could either defeat or outflank such critics. He told senators on 13 January that Formosa's fall was "inevitable." On the 14th, after Truman publicly suggested a joint chiefs visit to Formosa, Acheson forced a White House retraction. Three weeks later, a well-drilled president told the Philippines' President Quirino that U.S. bases in Asia would safely hem in Formosa if it fell into "the hands of the Communists."[19]

Acheson remained receptive to establishing relations with China, but since that seemed increasingly unlikely, he leaned more heavily on his coercive wedge strategy. This consisted mainly of hoping that exposure to the dangers of an excessive embrace of Moscow would shake sense in the Chinese. He seemed never to examine the singular psychological suppositions behind this hope. Given Mao's dedication to communist ideology, deference to the Soviet Union, and suspicion of American "imperialists," U.S. condemnation was far more likely to tighten than loosen the embrace. Aware of what the Americans were up to, Mao took Truman's disavowal of designs on Formosa and Acheson's Press Club speech as examples of a conspiracy to alienate him from the Soviets. A more detached observer could not be blamed for scratching his head as Acheson one day rubbed Mao's nose in his slavish dependence on Moscow and the next disclaimed any wish to menace the PRC. Within a five-day period, Acheson told Ambassador Oliver Franks he was ready to abandon Formosa and the UN's Trygve Lie that it was impossible to recognize the PRC, "an improvisation" of a government. Actually, Moscow, too, was skilled at the "wedge" game, inciting Mao to actions guaranteed to sustain Sino-American friction. The ultimate irony was that Mao *preferred* bad relations with Washington, as he underlined in mid-January 1950 by describing the exodus of U.S. diplomats from China to confederates as "extremely favorable to us."[20]

Confusion, or at least ambiguity, still reigned in U.S. policy toward the Chinese seat in the UN, too, and thus antagonized both the Chinese communists and Acheson's domestic critics. In Moscow, Andrei Vyshinsky had promised Mao the Soviets would boycott the Security Council if the western powers would not hand him Chiang's seat. Then Moscow actually moved to expel the Nationalists in January 1950. To avoid upsetting the British or defying the majority with a veto, Acheson instructed his delegation to vote "no" but proclaim it a procedural issue and thus, technically, not a veto. This was a gamble, but he accurately predicted the resolution would fail anyway. When it did, 6–3, with 3 abstentions, the Soviets bolted in a huff. Secretary-General Lie, who urgently lobbied for the

PRC's admission, later told Acheson the Russians had expected their absence to be brief, having seen U.S. criticisms of Chiang as a sign of imminent recognition of the PRC. Sticking to his equivocal line, Acheson in March ordered U.S. delegate Warren Austin to resist Chinese admission but go easy on trying "to influence others."[21]

On the nagging issue of diplomatic recognition, Washington was isolated in the world and Acheson in Washington. Formal British recognition on 6 January 1950 was soon emulated elsewhere in Europe. Acheson was supposedly waiting for the right moment, unwilling to stage a showdown with Truman or endanger his European initiatives by directly antagonizing the China bloc. Stung more than he would admit by the latter's criticisms, he reshaped his tactics, deferring recognition to a more opportune time and reassuring Senate heavyweights he would not move too far ahead of them. As if the CIA were reading his mind, it reported on 13 February that the USSR's Security Council boycott and abuses of Americans in China made "recognition of the Peiping regime increasingly difficult in the face of opposition in the US Congress and press." It did not faze his critics when Acheson told them that nonrecognition was an ineffective political tool, having no more power than a "popgun."[22]

Some of his confidence about outmaneuvering the China bloc must have rested on the lack of public attention. A February 1950 poll showed more than half of Americans had never heard of the Formosa controversy. Only 14 percent of those who knew about it wanted Formosa defended with force. Acheson could also count on the abiding incoherence in the Pentagon, which continued to worry about Formosan security while refusing to say it merited U.S. military protection. In February, the state department hectored Chiang's government for bombing raids on Shanghai. When Taipei responded by "telling us to go to hell with our protest," Acheson phoned for Livingston Merchant. Learning Merchant was out, he asked his startled assistant, Windsor Hackler, if Formosa's dismissive rejoinder gave the department "a chance to get out of Formosa and withdraw aid from the Nationalists." Hackler said "the matter was under active consideration." "Fine, fine," said Acheson, "I just wanted to be sure that you are thinking about it." To the department's surprise a few days later, Chiang announced he would reassume the KMT presidency.[23]

Although the state department had known for weeks that Mao was in Moscow, it came as a major shock when the USSR and PRC completed a treaty of alliance on 14 February 1950. This exploded hopes of loosening the Moscow-Beijing nexus with either sticks or carrots. No one would admit it, but this alliance was as disturbing as the German-Italian-Japanese (Tripartite) Pact of 1940. Through Ambassador David Bruce in Paris, a shaken Acheson persuaded *New York Times* reporter C. L. Sulzberger to print rumors of Soviet designs on Chinese territory, following which the Voice of America beamed the rumors to China as "news." In a press conference the day after the Moscow signing ceremony, Acheson asserted that China would be disillusioned by its new partner, which was capable of giving only "meager" aid to a nation verging on famine. This was a bluff, for he knew the Stalin-Mao understanding could drastically erode the western position in Asia and would seriously alarm Japan. The alliance also undermined military planning, since a war with the USSR would now sprawl throughout Eurasia. Obliged by the treaty to help the USSR militarily, China might open Manchuria to Soviet bases, further degrading the Asian balance of power. This prospect put a large question mark by Acheson's assertions of Formosa's strategic insignificance.[24]

That U.S. policy remained in disarray was confirmed in March, when the state department suddenly loosened the criteria for diplomatic recognition of the mainland. Respect for past "international obligations" fell by the wayside, and in his California speaking tour Acheson implied that only the molestation of U.S. diplomats stood in the way of normal relations. Consul General O. Edmund Clubb in Beijing, about to come home, received orders from Acheson to have informal discussions with "high" authorities about the "points of friction" between the two governments. This probe came up dry, but Acheson was in a headstrong mood and in an executive session with Senate moguls on 29 March refused to foreclose a U.S.-PRC accommodation. With amazing candor, he skewered Chiang's effort to ride "on our coat tails," using U.S. planes on terror bombing raids in an effort to start World War III. In that case, wondered Senator Henry Cabot Lodge, Jr., why didn't Washington discard him? Because, Acheson snapped, "the attitude of a large number of people in the United States and in the Congress" prevented it. He preferred a friendly Formosa but did not consider it vital to U.S. interests and said the communists would be "criminally crazy" if they did not seize it soon. In any case, none of this was worth a panic in light of Europe's far greater significance. Even "if the devil himself runs China," he concluded, "if he is an independent devil that is infinitely better than if he is a stooge of Moscow."[25]

Although he had barely left the door open to recognition, Acheson's policy was becoming more garbled as it crumbled. His mood was close to that of Clubb, who wanted China to "stew" in this "devil's broth the KMT and CCP have jointly concocted." The joint chiefs had their own incoherence problem, wanting Formosa defended but not by them. Their supposed boss, however, Secretary of Defense Louis Johnson, wanted stronger action, especially after news of the Sino-Soviet alliance, and in the months ahead repeatedly tried to sidestep Truman's edict against sending aid to Chiang. The Korean War finally seemed to settle U.S. policy toward China and Formosa—in Acheson's case, however, not yet conclusively.[26]

Inadequate Vehicles: China and Formosa to the Eve of the Korean War

As intelligent as Acheson was, when confronted by the challenge of China and Formosa, he could never put together a policy that worked, that could realistically be implemented, or, for that matter, made much sense in the real world as opposed to the circumstances he hoped for. Policies toward Mao and Chiang, and their conflicting regimes, lingered in a state of irresolution and suspended animation. Even though chances for "normal" U.S.-PRC ties were less than slight, Acheson sometimes continued to lurch in that direction. The department both lobbied to keep Beijing out of China's UN seat and refused to use its Security Council veto to that end. Disgust with Chiang still ran high, and forecasts of his imminent fall lasted through the early spring of 1950. Even as Washington continued to funnel aid to Chiang, Acheson clung to hopes of dividing China from the Soviet Union. Though now mainly relying on reproaches rather than inducements, in early April he considered sending American wheat to relieve symptoms of famine in China. The prevailing trajectory of U.S.-Chinese relations, however, veered toward conflict.[27]

On the Chinese side, attitudes were more focused and straightforward. In March, Zhou Enlai accused the Americans of trying to "cheat us again" through expansion of their influence in Asia. Clubb attributed the null result of his last-minute probe to Beijing's eagerness "to get rid of foreign influence and even foreigners," regardless of the economic cost. A fuming, low-level official finally summoned him just to say how "ridiculous" it was to think improved relations were possible while Washington still supported Chiang. Both countries sedulously fabricated self-fulfilling prophecies. China saw ghoulish American designs far more villainous than anything even dreamed of in Washington, and then responded with the kinds of hostility that fortified the hard-line camp in the United States, including Acheson's department. In mid-April, the PRC undertook a successful two-week attack on Hainan, off the Indochina coast, killing 33,000 Nationalist troops. Mao confidently unrolled his blueprints for invading Formosa. They never turned into action, however, partly because the dread of a powerful reaction by Yankee imperialists overwhelmed his view of them as weak. With muffled oars, the state department okayed large increases in nonmilitary aid to Chiang, freeing him to spend his own resources on military hardware. Those around Acheson joined him in craving an alternative to the abominated "Gimo" (department shorthand for "Generalissimo"), including a possible coup.[28]

One reason aides raised the idea of a coup was finally to win Acheson over to defend Formosa. On 28 March 1950, Rusk, who led this intradepartmental campaign, became assistant secretary for Far Eastern affairs, succeeding Walton Butterworth, who left with a sigh for the Stockholm embassy after being singed by conservatives' attacks. Vaccinated against such pathogens as a veteran of the China-Burma-India theater, the forty-one-year-old Rusk volunteered for demotion from deputy under secretary to fill Butterworth's place. Eager for the camouflage, Acheson jumped at the offer, surely aware of the price, for Rusk had always considered Formosa strategically vital. As Rusk's influence grew, Acheson's efforts to let the island drift diminished, especially since none of the conditions for his preferred course of action had come about. Chiang had already lasted longer than foreseen. The Pentagon still hoped to salvage his stronghold. Temperatures of domestic partisanship had risen instead of fallen. And Mao had tightened rather than relaxed his ties to Stalin. It was now easier for Acheson to back off, discover reasons to help Formosa, and take alarm at Beijing's threat to Indochina.[29]

He did not join Rusk's party willingly. Thomas Dewey called early in April to read him passages from a forthcoming speech. When he referred to Formosa as "the only flicker of hope for China and the Far East," Acheson said the phrase made him "very unhappy," since the real hope was "to drive a wedge between Peking and Moscow, and to reach agreement on a Japanese Peace Treaty." Dewey agreed to scratch "flicker of hope" but thought it impolitic to talk about the "wedge." With Clubb's last message at hand and the attack on Hainan under way, Acheson told Truman the only lesson to draw from the "China debacle" was that "if we are confronted with an inadequate vehicle it should be discarded or immobilized in favor of a more propitious one." But he had nothing better at hand.[30]

Through the late spring, John Foster Dulles, back in the state department, worked with Rusk and the military to change Acheson's stance. A backlash by lower-ranking desk officers against Rusk and Dulles as interlopers offered a brief respite, but Acheson had already put himself in Rusk's hands for day-to-day work, reserving only "the role of final arbiter" for himself. The public remained scarcely mindful of Asia's existence while wanting no more treasure spent on Chiang or recognition extended to the PRC. But both Congress and the JCS were pushing Acheson hard. In London in mid-May, he told an unhappy Bevin a tougher U.S. line on the PRC lay ahead, including contesting its UN seat. Yet several factors still caused him to resist the inevitable, including continued predictions of Formosa's fall. This would eliminate a major source of tension with the PRC and perhaps abrade Sino-Soviet relations. By the end of May, State was advising American citizens to leave Formosa and combing the region for a place where Chiang might find asylum.[31]

Both Truman and MacArthur favored more militancy and independently made their thoughts known on 29 May. At a White House audience for Trygve Lie, Truman said he had the "gravest difficulty" imagining renewing ties with a country that had injured U.S. officials and property in defiance of civilized international standards. In Tokyo, MacArthur wrote the JCS that Formosa in communist hands would become an "unsinkable aircraft carrier and submarine tender." Behind closed doors a day later, Rusk met with Jessup, Merchant, Paul Nitze, and the director of Chinese affairs, Philip D. Sprouse. In what a notetaker described as "this move on Rusk's part," they brainstormed at length in search of fresh ideas. Rusk, claiming that both foreign and domestic opinion disapproved of U.S. passivity on Formosa, urged using a "strong hand" to prevent Mao from seizing it. It was a suitable place to "draw the line." The group had no clear idea how to accomplish this goal but considered neutralization under UN auspices, a coup to remove Chiang, or, everything else failing, definitively sticking with him. The assistant secretary and his group presented their case to Acheson on 31 May.[32]

Records of their confrontation, if that is what it was, have not survived, but apparently a skeptical Acheson seized on the idea of a coup and probably emphasized this while offering a digest of the meeting to Truman, who was non-committal. On 6 June, Acheson told Franks that Mao could not have Formosa and that allies should not sell him any strategic goods. Even if Formosa fell, he now said, U.S. recognition of the PRC would be long in coming. "There are seeds of trouble here," cabled Franks. Rusk knew that politics were the trouble, but they worked in his favor. He told Acheson on 8 June it was "vital" to "establish our policies toward the Far East on a broad bi-partisan basis as soon as possible." Acheson's reaction is again unknown, but it must have rankled to be told to reconcile himself to the views of some of his most strident opponents.[33]

Congress's hard breathing is what Rusk probably had in mind when referring to "politics," for public opinion generally remained more permissive than restrictive. A Gallup Poll in the first week of June showed a 40 percent to 16 percent split against recognition of the PRC, but another 44 percent had no opinion. More wondrously, over a third of those polled did not know communists now ruled China. Regardless, the push for a tougher policy continued. Another MacArthur memo on the need to protect Formosa arrived in the Pentagon on 14 June, and on the 22d he sent one to the state department, too, via Dulles, then touring East Asia. On 23 June, Rusk's office told the NSC that recognizing the PRC was no longer "under active consideration." Acheson said the same to reporters and the Philippines ambassador.[34]

When the war in Korea began less than two days later, Washington still had no clear policy on China and Formosa. What Acheson might have done next in the absence of war is uncertain, but clearly, Chinese and American attitudes together had destroyed prospects for friendly relations. He had now given up on recognition, but, conveniently overlooking that U.S. aid was still going to Chiang, told reporters on 23 June that the government would still stay out of his civil war. He again disparaged the profligate Nationalist regime and gave no sign he would approve a move to rescue it.

But as soon as the Korean War began, he urgently recommended interposing the navy in the straits between Formosa and the mainland. This blocked "Gimo" from making rash attacks against the mainland amid a world crisis, but it also kept him out of Mao's reach, deeply reinserting the United States into the Chinese civil war.[35]

Early in 1950, Acheson reached none of his goals in Southeast Asia, China, or Formosa. At best, he extemporized while hoping something would turn up. Statesmen often find themselves making a virtue of inertia, and the waxing of anti-communist zeal prevented anything like a rapprochement with a communist

China. Beijing's leaders were also responsible, for they were unshakably hostile to the United States and would almost surely have rejected any overtures that did not surrender American interests. Moreover, a resolute effort to negotiate with the PRC was guaranteed to drive a wedge between Acheson and Truman. Even this speculation is moot, for, considering what the Chinese and U.S. governments wanted or would accept, Washington and Beijing by 1949–50 had nothing to offer each other. A different impasse emerged in Indochina, partly the result of the administration's international anti-communism but more of Acheson's effort to secure Europe by forging rich and rugged bonds with a key NATO ally, France. There was no sign this policy would succeed, either in Asia *or* Europe.

Acheson had gained success in Europe by identifying and bolstering positions of strength, but he found none to work with in Asia. Nothing worked as hoped. Outside of Japan, successes were small in scale and few in number. Failures stood out starkly to the naked eye, disgruntling conservatives and kindling fury among extremists. Acheson's sturdy response to this fury occasionally reached a rare standard of courage, but at other times, he needlessly poked his foes straight in the eye. Sometimes when those he called "primitives" sapped his patience and good judgment, he acted in ways even he came to regret. He accomplished little, but short of improbably joining the ranks of the revolutionaries, the United States had limited options to work with in East Asia. And Acheson made little of those he had.

17

FRIENDS IN PLACE:
ACHESON AND ALGER HISS

Fear, sometimes an undifferentiated swamp of fear, struck many Americans early in the cold war, especially after the first Soviet atomic bomb test and after the "fall" of China to the communist revolution in 1949. The most alarmed Americans thought the nation's enemies included homegrown communist agents of overseas adversaries. Many Republicans discharged pent-up political frustrations by stigmatizing the whole Democratic-New-Deal cosmos as enemies of the American system.

Scornful of his tormentors and poorly informed about Soviet espionage, Truman minimized the gravity of these accusations and derided them as the ranting of vicious partisans. A little more discreetly, Dean Acheson did the same and became his own worst enemy with a gratuitously mutinous statement about the most renowned target of the growing storm, Alger Hiss. His declaration supporting Hiss was impetuous but not impulsive, the result of hours of thought and planning. However valorous, his studied attempt to give witness was his greatest political blunder, which impaired his effectiveness and eased the election of Dwight Eisenhower in 1952. Acheson continued to conduct a capable foreign policy, but only in the teeth of incessant criticism. When he became secretary of state in 1953, John Foster Dulles promptly threw tarnished foreign service officers overboard to avert Acheson's fate. In the years ahead, many lower-ranking officers thought twice about saying anything their superiors did not want to hear. Disabled by rightist criticism, future Democratic administrations could not make any of the moves that helped wind up the cold war. Republicans immunized against anti-communist bacteria could and did.

Hiss is the center of a controversy that outlasted the cold war, even his death in 1996. The controversy's long life originated in conflicting and passionately held judgments about recent history, exacerbated for years by the absence of reliable records. While conservatives intemperately depicted Hiss's defenders as disloyal, liberals stoked their faith in his innocence with a steadfast loathing of Whittaker Chambers, J. Edgar Hoover, and Richard Nixon. Allen Weinstein's 1978 book, *Perjury: The Hiss-Chambers Case*, offered overwhelming evidence of Hiss's espionage and Communist Party membership. But rather than settle the matter, the book only stirred new passions, often directed at the author. Another storm burst in 1992, when a Russian general, Dmitri A. Volkogonov, "cleared" Hiss of charges after hastily sifting through the wrong archive of Soviet records. Despite the fact that Volkogonov quickly retracted his statement, Hiss proclaimed his own vindication, TV anchors slackly echoed him, and old anti-Nixon partisans rejoiced in yet another victory. The CIA and NSA apparently administered the coup de grâce in 1995–96 by releasing thousands of intercepts of Soviet cable traffic contained in the "Venona" project. These caused defenders of nuclear spy Julius Rosenberg to give up the ghost and unmasked other U.S. citizens as obedient agents of the Soviet Union, but Hiss defenders even contested evidence suggesting that Andrei Vyshinsky had pinned the Order of the Red Star on him in Moscow after the Yalta conference. Tony Hiss's loyal 1999 book evinced not a doubt about his father's innocence. Early in the twenty-first century, the hard right's detestation of liberalism generated new accusations of treason or near treason against past and present Democrats. Another generation may pass before the controversy breathes its last.[1]

Hiss in Brief

Once the United States became allies of the USSR in World War II, FDR called off a slender counterintelligence effort against a Soviet espionage campaign he plainly misjudged. Agents of the Federal Bureau of Investigation (FBI) could watch but seldom act as Russian operatives enlisted American communists and sympathizers to steal federal documents and industrial secrets. The most significant known result was the penetration of the Manhattan Project. It was no accident that Moscow's first bomb was a near copy of the Los Alamos device. After Moscow learned (from British spy Kim Philby) of Elizabeth Bentley's defection to the FBI in 1945, it shut down most of its U.S. network. Truman's loyalty-security program, established in March 1947, caused other spies to take cover, though the president's program mainly snared men and women guilty of bad judgment. Those actually working in the Soviet espionage apparatus— fellow travelers, party members, some full-time and others not—included Hiss (code named "Ales"), Henry Morgenthau's second-hand man at Treasury, Harry Dexter White, White House assistant Lauchlin Currie, and Laurence Duggan of the state department and UNRRA. Because many others were falsely accused, it became hard for many Americans to believe in the reality of Soviet espionage or that many of their fellow citizens willingly acted as agents for the Soviet Union. Those who did enjoyed the support of the U.S. Communist Party, which used Soviet financing to recruit agents and provide them underground cover.[2]

Hiss was the prize catch. He was a Baltimore New Dealer, in his mid-forties when the spy scandal broke. At the peak of his career, he assisted FDR at Yalta and helped develop the United Nations. Although he had grown up in a troubled family scraping to stay in the middle class, he graduated from Johns Hopkins University and Harvard Law. His actual attainments were few, but his polished style drew much admiration. Writer Murray Kempton recalled him "for a kind of distinction that had to be seen to be believed. If he were standing at the bar with the British Ambassador and you were told to give a package to the Ambassador's valet, you would give it to the Ambassador before you gave it to Alger." Another member of Felix Frankfurter's stable, Hiss had been secretary to Oliver Wendell Holmes, Jr., and served in the agricultural adjustment administration, in the justice department, and on the Senate committee (the Nye Committee) that investigated World War I "munitions makers." Then he joined the state department. In his years of contact with Acheson, he assisted in the offices of political relations (1942–43), Far Eastern affairs (1943–44), and special political affairs. Edward Stettinius was his chief sponsor.

First named by defected Soviet agent Chambers in 1939, Hiss denied everything when charges became public at 1948 hearings of the House Un-American Affairs Committee (HUAC). He had not been a communist, known Chambers, or given him classified materials for transit to Moscow, he swore. The government did not charge him with espionage because of the statute of limitations, but in December 1948, a federal grand jury indicted him for committing perjury in testimony before the grand jury. His first trial ended in a hung jury in July 1949, but the jury in a second trial convicted him in January 1950. Following failed appeals, he was imprisoned from 1951 to 1954. Many years later, it is amply clear he worked for the Soviet Union not only in the 1930s but afterward. His "devotion in adversity" to the USSR, write Allen Weinstein and Alexander Vassiliev, was "rock-solid." The "cumulative evidence" against him, adds G. Edward White, reached beyond "ambiguity."[3]

Spies, Security Inquests, and Hiss Prior to the HUAC

Soviet espionage issues first brushed Acheson's career in September 1945, when Igor Gouzenko, a twenty-three-year-old Russian cipher clerk defected in Ottawa, giving the Royal Mounties documents on Soviet espionage in Canada and the United States. The documents possibly pointed to Hiss as someone practicing a "species of espionage," setting off FBI inquiries. The Canadians first tried to smother the "affair in silence" to protect relations with Moscow. But because the documents also named British spies, Canadian Prime Minister

Mackenzie King at London's urging rushed to see Truman late in September. Already privy to a memorandum from Hoover about Chambers's 1939 identification of Hiss, Acheson was present at the White House meeting with the Canadian leader. Truman either did not know about or did not understand the Venona program and mistrusted Hoover. In any case, Washington, Ottawa, and London shortly made an implicit agreement not to confront the Soviets. Stalin learned of this passivity from another British agent, Donald Maclean, and may have taken heart from it.

After receiving updates from the FBI chief, Secretary of State Jimmy Byrnes and Acheson started quietly weeding those with suspect histories from the department. The administration was still lying low when columnist Drew Pearson broke the Gouzenko story in February 1946. The Gouzenko affair did much to make Soviet espionage a political issue and to direct unwelcome attention to the state department.[4]

Critics thought the state department had already failed on an earlier security breach in the *Amerasia* case. This centered on leaks arranged by federal officials of hundreds of classified documents to Philip J. Jaffe, editor of *Amerasia* magazine, influential among China watchers. One of the culprits was State's John Stewart Service. Having discovered the papers in an illegal raid on the journal's office in March 1945, OSS agents informed the state department, which called in the FBI. Shown a statement about the implicated pilferers, Acheson as a lawyer agreed the government had a case and urged the FBI to move ahead, as did Truman. In June, the FBI arrested Service, a career diplomat, and the others, originally for violating the Espionage Act. Service, who had already clashed with Patrick Hurley, former ambassador to China, had leaked materials of his own authorship, hoping to sway public opinion, not to help a foreign power. He was a department favorite—"Why," exclaimed one officer, he "isn't even a liberal"— and few took the case seriously. Justice department lawyers, aware that the office break-in was illegal, reduced charges to "unauthorized possession of government documents." Backstage, Currie, New Deal operator Tommy Corcoran, and State legal adviser Ben Cohen worked to keep Service free, and in July 1945, a federal grand jury voted 20–0 against indictment. (Jaffe *was* indicted and paid a $2,500 fine after pleading guilty.) Service recalled that when Under Secretary Acheson first met him, he joked: "Well, you don't look like a dangerous man." In his confirmation hearings, Acheson underscored his encouragement of the FBI. Because the government did so little about the case, Chambers reacted by being even less willing than before to talk freely to federal agents.[5]

His first reference to Hiss had come six years earlier in a visit with Adolf A. Berle, Jr., when the Nazi-Soviet pact had prompted him to talk. Journalist Isaac Don Levine arranged to have Chambers meet with Berle, a presidential pet and friend of Hoover. Contemporary author Robert Bendiner describes Berle as having "taken to playing the G-man in a small way" after FDR informally charged him to watch over security measures. "Under a magnificent old tree" on the lawn of the Woodley Park home Berle rented from Henry Stimson, Chambers spilled out information on a dozen familiar persons, including White, Currie, Duggan, Hiss, and his brother Donald Hiss, as Berle took careful notes. Berle evidently told no one except the FBI about the visit, probably because he did not believe these well-known liberals were spies, and did not at first share his notes with the bureau. Levine gave the information to Loy Henderson, too, who also kept it to himself. But he did minimize Hiss's access to sensitive material.[6]

The results of the Woodley Hill séance are mysterious. Berle said he did not tell FDR about Hiss, but two uncorroborated stories via Levine say otherwise. In one, Berle goes straight to the White House, and FDR tells him to "go jump in a lake." In the other, FDR hears the tale from gossip purveyor Walter Winchell and barks, "I don't want to hear another thing about it! . . . It isn't true." In March 1940, the Bureau told Berle it had been too busy chasing Nazis to follow up. In 1941, when he asked Acheson (just arrived at State) and Frankfurter about the Hisses, both said the allegations must be baseless, for they were fine young men. The FBI got little out of the cagey Chambers in a 1942 interrogation and only received Berle's notes in 1943. This does not add up to a cover-up, but the administration's makeshift messiness in handling the Chambers revelations would later look sinister to the conspiracy-minded. Berle himself later said he considered both Hisses habitual leakers of sensitive information but had no reason to think worse.[7]

In 1945, just as increasingly damaging rumors about him spread through the department, a Soviet agent (coincidentally) recorded Hiss's receipt of "*Soviet decorations*" for his years of help to Soviet military intelligence. When the FBI that spring told Stettinius someone was slipping documents in and out of the department for copying in New York, the abashed secretary said to Hiss, "I hope it is not you." More stoutly, Henderson told his assistants "not to discuss confidential matters" with Hiss or show him "confidential documents." Both Bureau and State security investigators returned to Chambers and also mined information from the Gouzenko and Bentley defections. Hoover himself now seized the Hiss case like a dog with a bone, telling Byrnes and Acheson he was a Soviet agent. Byrnes moved discreetly both because hearsay dominated the evidence and because he wanted to avoid giving Hiss a heads-up. He ordered him closely watched, and department security closely tracked his movements. At the least, he now had a very dubious future in the department.[8]

Hoover continued bombarding the White House and slipped unverified reports on suspected subversives to selected cabinet officers. He wanted Acheson removed to change State's "atmosphere." He grew incensed when his reports to Truman collected dust and the president named the accused White to head the International Monetary Fund. Byrnes was more responsive, advising Hiss early in 1946 to meet with Hoover to avoid being denounced as a communist. Hiss denied the charges (to one of Hoover's assistants), but Byrnes quarantined him within the department. Hoover suggested provoking his resignation, a sign that he lacked trial-quality evidence against him. In March, a Foggy Bottom security officer, Robert Bannerman, continued passing damaging information to Byrne's assistant secretary for administration, Donald Russell. Seeing how many supporters Hiss still had in the department, Russell stalled, but Bannerman kept at his probe.[9]

By then, Acheson should have reckoned Hiss radioactive, but he remained skeptical because of his confidence in the Hiss brothers' character. He would have been even more incredulous if he had seen a surreal letter Hoover gave in May 1946 to reconstruction finance corporation director, George E. Allen. It described Acheson, John McCloy, Henry Wallace, Senator Brien McMahon, and journalists Raymond Gram Swing and Marquis Childs as unwitting "pro-Soviet" enablers of an "enormous" Soviet nuclear "espionage ring in Washington." Hoover may also have had Acheson under surveillance in the summer of 1946, at a time Hiss habitually attended his 9:30 meetings. This was also near the time Acheson told House members he favored firing department communists but thought the problem "more a matter of alarm than of fact." Some of the accused were merely "New Dealers," which, he added with a smile, he did not consider "a crime."[10]

Hiss, his neck warm from the spotlight, lingered out of confidential loops and out of chances for better department jobs. As the Greek crisis deepened, Acheson told Loy Henderson and others to keep plans away from him, conceivably but not likely because Hiss might have urged UN involvement. By August 1946, the FBI and Bannerman were wiretapping Hiss's home and office phones and auditing his appointment calendar but were still unable to file charges. Everyone breathed easier when he resigned on 10 December 1946. Sponsored by an unaware Dulles, in mid-January 1947 he became president of the Carnegie Endowment for International Peace. The public was told the parting was friendly, with a "Dear Alger" letter from Byrnes and laudatory statement from Acheson.[11]

Considering its nervousness about the communist presence in the French and Italian governments, the administration found it harder to belittle the issue at home. Thus, shortly after the Truman Doctrine speech, the president established his federal security and loyalty program. Each executive branch department would have its own loyalty and security investigative boards, with appeals to a loyalty review board (only for loyalty cases) that could either affirm or overrule department decisions. Employees could be investigated based on derogatory information from any source and dismissed as disloyal or as security risks for associating with the wrong people, talking or drinking too much, acting carelessly with government records, or, as homosexuals, making themselves subject to blackmail. The secretary of state could reverse his own boards, but the higher board in turn could reverse him in loyalty cases. Accused FSOs would find little help at State's office of the legal adviser, which specialized in treaty interpretation and international law.[12]

Many came to misery within these assizes. Under Acheson, only about fifty employees were rousted from the state department and fewer than twenty dismissed outright, none for disloyalty. But morale began to plummet in the foreign service. At the time, Acheson defended the program, though in a few notable cases he voided findings of the department's own board. After he left government, he sharply criticized the whole system, writing in 1955 to accept responsibility for "what I am now convinced was a grave mistake." Talking that year to Truman in Independence, he condemned the program and took blame for insufficient zeal in resisting it: "I never really took my coat off and worked on it." In his memoirs, he gave high marks to State's board while censuring the superior loyalty review board and calling its head, former Connecticut senator, Hiram Bingham, "a wicked man." Nonetheless, it was he and the president who had countenanced a fundamental violation of legal rights by going along with "a procedure where a fellow is not confronted with the person making the charges." That was "like giving a fellow arsenic." Moreover, the system never caught real spies, who were sure to "have good references"—like Hiss, he might have added.[13]

Red Spies or Red Herring?

The Hiss case moved to its climacteric in 1948 when both private citizen Acheson and Hiss were members of the Citizens' Committee for the Marshall Plan. When Hiss was called before a federal grand jury in March, State's security head John Peurifoy reassured Dulles, head of Carnegie's board of directors, with what, by then, were amazing statements. Hiss was a conservative, he told Dulles, and even though he was mentioned in some FBI files, his loyalty was unquestioned. Most of the anti-anti-communists in the Democratic Party had left it in 1948 for the Wallace presidential campaign.

Because Truman had summoned the "do-nothing" Republican Congress for a special session, the HUAC was in full session. Now it achieved its greatest triumph in exposing Hiss. At a sensational hearing on 3 August, Chambers named former government employees he had known as communists, Soviet agents, or both, among them Alger and Donald Hiss. Donald, whom Chambers never accused of spying, flatly denied the charges while "freely" admitting he knew some of the others Chambers named in "an innocent, professional way." He had never seen Chambers in his brother's company. Alger on 5 August not only denied Chambers's accusations of party membership but demanded a chance to say so in the committee's presence.[14]

Hiss's appearance made some committee members wonder if they had made a frightful error. Truman was certain they had and at a press conference agreed with a reporter that the "spy scare" was "a red herring" to distract the public from more important matters. Dulles, however, was alarmed and spurned board member Philip Jessup's plea for a public statement of confidence in Hiss. Instead, after Nixon showed him some damning evidence, Dulles planned to oust Hiss. On

13 August, Currie, White, and Donald Hiss all paraded before the committee. Hiss fumed at Chambers's "personal attack," which he resented "very bitterly" for hurting his "family," including his octogenarian mother. "If I am lying," he challenged, "I should go to jail and if Mr. Chambers is lying he should go to jail." White drew applause for coupling his denials with a stirring declaration of his democratic credo, then died of a heart attack three days later. Another casualty came in December, after Representative Karl Mundt in the HUAC pointed the finger at Latin American specialist and Wallace adviser, Laurence Duggan. Afterward, Duggan apparently hurled himself from the sixteenth-story window of a New York office building. Though he had funneled documents to Soviet intelligence at least through 1944, callous remarks by Mundt after his death aroused a tempest of criticism. Both Berle and Sumner Welles attended Duggan's funeral.[15]

Back in August 1948, Truman was intent on disabling his critics, wondering if he could have Chambers put in a mental hospital. He prodded Attorney General Tom C. Clark to have the FBI say real communists were escaping indictment because of HUAC "meddling." But events quickly outran his stratagems. On 18 August, Dulles asked Hiss to resign but accepted a counteroffer to step down after the HUAC hearings. Hiss's position had begun to crumble the day before in a confidential encounter Nixon had arranged in New York with Chambers. Eight days later, they faced each other again, this time in an open HUAC session. Chambers testified that Hiss had been one of his close party associates in the thirties, while Hiss admitted recognizing him as someone he had known as "George Crosley." When Chambers repeated his charge on the radio, Hiss filed a slander suit. On the campaign hustings, Truman accused the HUAC of spreading "wild and false accusations," and when he won reelection, many thought Hiss might be out of the woods.

In December, however, Chambers gave Nixon microfilm copies of secret state department documents he said Hiss had passed to him in the thirties, the notorious "pumpkin papers." The stakes rose sharply, for now Chambers was saying Hiss was both a communist *and* a Soviet spy. Hiss's slander suit collapsed and some of his champions headed for cover. Chided by the *Washington Post* for trying to "suppress the whole business," on 9 December Truman doggedly reiterated that the HUAC inquiry was a "red herring." Later in the month, Hiss resigned from Carnegie, the grand jury indicted him for perjury, and Duggan committed suicide. But Hiss still had many defenders, Eleanor Roosevelt among them. She was not ready, she wrote in her column, to doubt "the word of a man, who for many years has had a good record of service to his government."[16]

"We Remain Friends"

When the case broke, Acheson had known both Hisses for years, Alger since his graduation from law school. "Donnie" (or "Donie") had been a law partner since

1947 and a "close friend." But Acheson was not close to Alger, either profession-
ally or personally. As George Ball recalled, Acheson found Alger "stuffy and
rigid," agreeing with Chambers that he lacked "a sense of humor." In 1948,
Acheson and Hiss lived nearly within shouting distance in Georgetown, Acheson
at his ivy-covered house at 2805 P Street, Hiss at 3415 Volta Place. But, despite
previous expressions of confidence, Acheson moved cautiously around Hiss and,
when accusations mounted, acted to insulate him from consequential department
discussions.[17]

Joseph Alsop witnessed this wariness during the time Acheson was out of
government. Outraged by Chambers's charges, he marched into Acheson's law
office brimming with plans for a scornful column he and his brother Stewart
would write. Acheson told him to cool it: "It's always a mistake to write about
anything that is *sub judice*." "It was perfectly obvious," Alsop wrote in an autobiographical draft, "that Dean thought that Hiss was guilty, or had been guilty,"
and the Alsops never published the intended column. Alsop thought Acheson
wanted to keep his own skirts clear. Instead, on 4 August, he gave both Hisses
complimentary help on their testimony from Covington, Burling, Acheson
and Shorb, which, of course, was Donald's firm, too. He may also have advised
Alger on the choice of an attorney. He sat in the counsel's chair for Currie at the
HUAC but told the brothers he could not represent them.[18]

What would he say about the case in his upcoming confirmation hearings?
Those who unaccountably thought him a dangerous leftist would surely ask. His
hearings lasted two days, the first open to the public on 13 January 1949, followed
by a closed session on the 14th mainly devoted to Hiss. He was confirmed 83–6,
but the friction over communists and anti-communists warned of things to come.
The first day, he was asked if he would encourage Peurifoy to remove communists from the department. In response, he vouched for Peurifoy, even claimed
credit for some of his work, and vowed he would take all necessary steps "to secure
the state department in the conduct of foreign affairs."[19] When a friend had
recently told him about Chambers's damaging testimony about Alger Hiss,
Acheson had waved it away by remarking that Chambers was probably a "crack-
pot." Now in the hearing, he said he had long waited "for the opportunity"
to speak on the issue and then read a long statement. He began by asserting,
"I should like to state to the committee that my friendship is not easily given,
and it is not easily withdrawn." Alger Hiss was a friend, and "we remain
friends."[20]

He took pains to untangle Alger and Donald. Donald had been one of his
assistants during the war, unable to do military service because of a collapsed
lung. But he had served the nation "with complete fidelity and loyalty" and was
now a law partner (which he remained for many years) and a "close and intimate"
friend. Acheson blamed the commingling of the Hisses on Berle, whose memory
had "gone badly astray." Meeting both brothers when they clerked for Holmes,
he came to know Donald well in the thirties and personally recruited him to the

state department. When Berle had cryptically asked him if "one of the Hiss brothers" had "associations which would make his presence in my office embarrassing to me and to the Department," Acheson said he would ask. If Donald said no, however, he would refuse "to change the arrangements which I had made on any such vague information as Mr. Berle had given me." And, indeed, Donald "told me that he had no such associations" and had no idea what Berle was talking about. That "closed" a matter "never referred to again by him or me." Thirty-five in 1941 (two years younger than Alger), Donald worked for Acheson until 1944, when he left the government for health reasons. Once recovered, he joined Acheson's law firm and became a partner. In the next day's executive session, Acheson compared popular "C" student Donald favorably to the "brilliant" and more "intellectual" Alger, adding that Donald was "torn to pieces emotionally" about Alger's case. As a friend, he thought the "kindest thing" to do was "just not to talk about it." Further disentangling the Hiss stories on 13 January, he noted that he had nothing to do with Alger's joining the state department, which he had done before Acheson. Nor had he assigned him to arrange the 1945 San Francisco conference on the United Nations. In response to a question from Senator Arthur Vandenberg, he refused any comment on the current legal case, "which is now before a United States court."[21]

In a lengthy colloquy behind closed doors the next day, Acheson repeatedly expressed bafflement about the Hiss case. He could not believe the man he knew would do what had been charged, yet he granted the evidence indicated otherwise. He could not resolve the contradiction. On balance, however, until he saw more compelling evidence, he could not believe Hiss was a communist, spy, or traitor. As he later recalled, he and his questioners then "tried the experiment of examining" events "on the assumption that what Chambers had said was true, and then on the assumption that it was false." Neither alternative made sense, which, even when writing his memoirs in 1969, left him thinking of the case as an unsolved "mystery."[22]

Throughout his testimony, Acheson time and again seemed first to say Hiss was innocent, then that he looked guilty, but finally that he could not believe the latter. No "theory" he considered made "any sense" of the mounting evidence against Hiss, while other factors pointed to his innocence—Chambers's self-confessed lying, Hiss's forthright denials, and the sterling reputation of his lawyers. It was "puzzling" that Hiss admitted recognizing Chambers as "Crosley" and let him use his apartment, but he still could not believe the charges against him. Thus, he would not join those "who have been throwing stones at this man when he is in serious trouble." To additional questions, he offered additional conjectures. Hiss was "a man of character" but had been acting "foolishly as a lawyer"—yet "with calm and dignity" rather than like a man "caught in a really terrible crime." If later events proved his views "unfounded," Acheson would "be glad to say so." And if Hiss lost in a fair trial, "then I should, of course, say that I would have a different attitude."

He had advised Hiss to accept the Carnegie Endowment job, not because he put any "stock" in the rumors against him, but from concern that they would never be "cleared up." Acheson told the senators he could not believe Hiss was "a liar"; if he was, "then I don't understand human nature." Perhaps, he speculated, Hiss was "protecting somebody else."[23] When Vandenberg invited Acheson to take a firmer position against Hiss, by rejoinder he vigorously declared his refusal to be a "coward" or "run for cover." No "office within the gift of anybody in the world" was worth that. But he did draw a fine line between his "very unqualified endorsement" of Donald and his "very restrained and very careful statement" about Alger. Could we assume, Vandenberg asked wearily, that if Hiss now applied for a state department job, Acheson would not take him on? "That is quite right," he answered. He again remarked in conclusion that the "theory" of Hiss's "guilt" was "incompatible with any sane conduct." It was "incredible" that, if guilty, Hiss would file his slander suit against Chambers. He just did not think Hiss was "such a fool as that."[24]

Acheson's Theory

Admirers heaped congratulations on Acheson for that part of his testimony made in public. "I have long known you were a good man," wrote James Rowe, who had worked with him on the Hoover Commission; "I am beginning to think you are a great one." Future Supreme Court judge Abe Fortas, noting how many of Hisses' friends had taken cover, thought Acheson's performance demonstrated that in the state department he would not "see our relations with other countries as black or white." Acheson responded: "What I wanted more than anything else was not to add to Alger's or Donny's troubles."[25]

To understand Acheson's ambivalence toward "Alger," we need a closer look at "Donny." In the thirties, the younger Hiss had joined the "Ware Group," a circle of young radicals, mostly communists, who worked in the agriculture department, though Donald was in the public works administration. He was secretly a Communist Party member and paid his party dues to Chambers but was under the discipline of Soviet overseers only intermittently (and ineffectively). As assistant to labor secretary Frances Perkins in 1938, he helped prevent the deportation of communist union leader Harry Bridges to his native Australia. He reluctantly agreed when the Soviets demanded he accept Acheson's invitation to the state department, but Alger vetoed agent Boris Bykov's suggestion that Donald steal State documents for copying. He probably never practiced any "spying." Though his name regularly surfaced in postwar inquiries, he escaped serious trouble because of his peripheral role, forceful denials, and Chambers's own denial that he was ever one of *his* agents. This left him with a small notoriety among Holocaust historians as a leaker of documents on the plight of European Jews. A humanitarian with a fast and loose view of official rules, he became a sieve at the division on Foreign Funds Control, dribbling secrets to more aggressive friends of European Jews at the treasury department.[26]

Acheson probably knew nothing of these irregularities. As he testified, Donald was a close friend, so close that he shared details of his executive testimony with him. More than any single factor, this close friendship probably ruled out any public disavowal of Alger. It would have been far less politically risky had Acheson simply said Hiss was innocent until proved guilty or told senators, "let's wait to see what happens in trial." This is where he seemed headed when he told senators he would gladly "say so" if Hiss's disloyalty was proved. In fact, however, he never did say so, gladly or sadly, even after Hiss's conviction.[27]

That he had doubts about Alger is clear from Alsop's story and his refusal to testify as a character witness. The puzzle is why he put those doubts aside. One piece of the puzzle was a relaxed view of 1930s radicals and disdain for their tormentors. His memoirs refer matter-of-factly to the many people "attracted by communist doctrines" who "found their way into the Government" in the depression decade. Though a middle-roader himself, he was not discomfited by unorthodox ideas and made friends across the ideological spectrum, not only with the Hisses, but with J. Robert Oppenheimer, Archibald MacLeish, Stuart Chase, Sinclair Lewis, John L. Lewis, and Harold Laski. Nor during the heyday of the wartime alliance was he aghast to find himself in the company of Soviet sympathizers. He abominated rabble-rousers of any stripe, but especially those on the right whose crusade against communism took the form of assaults on liberals. This, he wrote, was an "Attack of the Primitives" and his counterattack, the "fight with the footpads." He might have reacted differently had the accusations against Hiss come from someone other than the HUAC and FBI, which seemed opposed to just about everything he believed in. He was equally eager to vouch for his friend Oppenheimer when he was stripped of his security clearances in 1954.[28]

Other factors also may help explain his stance on Alger Hiss. It is possible that, like Berle, he thought he was only "guilty" of acts of nugatory consequence, acts that mattered little since he could no longer do any damage. It seems improbable, however, that an institution man like Acheson would sanction the transgressions with which Hiss was charged, or forgive even a friend who stole government documents and gave them to code-named intermediaries for copying and transit to Moscow. In a 1978 letter, Loy Henderson offered another explanation, that Hiss was Frankfurter's protégé, and "Acheson trusted Frankfurter's judgment." But he mostly credited his own, and his remark that any theory of Hiss's guilt belied "sane conduct" hints at his own "theory."

His judgment drew on a fusion of a pair of qualities he cherished, reason and loyalty. In some respects, this was an inharmonious combination, for one depended on thought, the other on emotion. Acheson often seemed baffled when other people or governments acted irrationally. Rather than identify the cause of "unreasonable" behavior, he sometimes simply refused to acknowledge it, as in the case of Alger Hiss. As to loyalty, like Harry Truman, Acheson would go far to avoid anything like *disloyalty*, either to Alger or, even more importantly, Donald Hiss.

Acheson, therefore, probably arrived at his judgment about as follows. It was "insane" (reasonless) to act traitorously toward the United States. If Hiss was a traitor, it was also insane to say things in his defense he knew others could expose as false. Acheson thought he could read a person and judge his character, and his own rational judgment was that the Hiss he knew would not do what his accusers charged. Besides, they were the same people who accused him, Acheson, of being a communist dupe. Knowing *that* to be untrue, it made sense to dismiss the accusations against Hiss as well. Because "Donny" was a true friend, the loyal Acheson would stick up for Alger. Finally, since Hiss might be protecting someone else (a loyal act), Acheson was left with "something else here that one does not understand."[29]

Rejecting "Counsels of Discretion and Cowardice"

Such speculation might seem beside the point had the story ended then, which seemed likely. Few criticized Acheson's public confirmation remarks, and fewer still knew what he had said behind locked doors. Soon, other espionage stories pushed the Hiss story to the back pages. In March 1949, the FBI arrested justice department employee Judith Coplon for conspiracy to commit espionage. Acheson embraced ideals of open debate by allowing visas for Russian and east European communists to attend a New York "peace" gathering, saying off the record that Americans would be better for it, even if the visitors deceived the "simple-minded." For those who disagreed, "we will bear whatever chastisement comes to us, in a philosophical and humble way." When Democrat Patrick McCarran of the Senate Subcommittee on Internal Security offered a bill to block "subversives" at the borders, Acheson opposed it on grounds that it would "drastically" harm U.S. foreign policy. Amid the opening salvos of the Korean War in 1950, the bill passed over Truman's veto.[30]

In late May 1949, just as *U.S. v. Hiss* opened in the district courthouse on New York's Foley Square, demonstrators outside the same building were jeering at police and cheering for communists being tried under the Smith Act. Hiss came fortified with support from Alsop (now lukewarm), James Reston, and Marquis Childs. Walter Lippmann also backed him, remarking to a friend, "I know Alger Hiss. He couldn't be guilty of treason." Luminaries who swore to his probity, either in person or by deposition, included Adlai Stevenson, former state department official Stanley Hornbeck, and 1924 Democratic presidential candidate John W. Davis. Acheson declined because of his "public responsibilities and duty," but with his approval, Jessup endorsed Hiss in writing and, in his second trial, personally. Most remarkably, two sitting Supreme Court justices appeared, Frankfurter as a voluntary witness and Stanley Reed, subpoenaed as a former solicitor general. This aroused speculation, wrote the observant Alistair Cooke, "about the possible shrinkage in the qualified membership of the Supreme Court, if ever this case should be appealed there." Despite all the testamentary firepower, a hung jury ended the first trial on 8 July. But on 21 January 1950, a second trial judged Hiss guilty of perjury for claiming he had never seen Chambers after 1937 or ever given him state department papers. On 25 January, one day after physicist Klaus Fuchs, a Manhattan Project veteran, confessed to espionage in Britain, the U.S. court sentenced Hiss to five years in a federal prison.[31]

The next act in this melodrama was Acheson's reaction to the sentencing, which brought him back to stage left. He was already scheduled to hold a press conference on the 25th. Now, against the wishes of all his advisers, he decided to use it to go far beyond a safe and regretful statement that most people would have accepted. Before he left the department the previous evening, he told Luke Battle he intended to declare his support of Hiss. At home, he thought for hours as he riffled through the Bible. In the morning, a worried Battle sought help from Paul Nitze and Charles Bohlen. Nitze had car-pooled with Hiss and thought he "knew him better than Dean." When Nitze entered Acheson's office, "he asked me to leave. I called Chip Bohlen," but Acheson would not see Bohlen, either. Saying he would surely be asked about Hiss, at breakfast Acheson had told Alice, "I'm going to reply that I will not forsake him." Alice responded: "What else could you say?" "Don't think this is a light matter," he went on. "This could be quite a storm and it could get me in trouble." When Alice asked if he was sure he was right, he replied: "It is what I have to do." On their morning walk Frankfurter told him not to dodge the issue.

A reporter quickly asked if Acheson wanted to comment on the Hiss case. "Edged forward in his chair," according to one account, he seemed "to count silently to ten," then said: "I think it would be highly improper for me to discuss the legal aspects or the evidence of anything to do with the case." After a pause, he returned to his "familiar, dryly ironic tone" to say he imagined his questioner had wanted to hear more. Then, "with some feeling," he went on, saying, "I should like to make it clear to you that whatever the outcome of any appeal which Mr. Hiss or his lawyers may take in this case I do not intend to turn my back upon Alger Hiss." Anyone who had worked with Hiss, he added, had on his "conscience" deciding how to view the case "in the light of his own standards and his own principles." As to his own, they were "stated on the Mount of Olives and if you are interested in seeing them you will find them in the 25th chapter of the Gospel according to St. Matthew beginning with verse 34. Have you any other questions?" Scripturally illiterate journalists hurried to an aide ready to show them verse 34: "Then shall the king say unto them on his right hand, come, ye blessed of my father, inherit the kingdom prepared for you from the foundation of the world: for I was an hungred and ye gave me meat: I was thirsty, and ye gave me drink: I was a stranger, and ye took me in: naked, and ye clothed me: I was sick, and ye visited me: I was in prison, and ye came unto me." Could reporters quote him directly? With a sigh, he replied: "As you choose."[32]

Longtime press assistant Michael McDermott escorted Acheson back to his office before asking "a favor" he had asked only once before: "May I shake your hand?" Less pleased was Nitze, who thought Acheson had jeopardized "his position as Secretary of State by supporting someone he didn't know well on an issue about which all the facts were not in." Why, he asked, had he so resolutely ignored his advisers? Because, Acheson answered, he already knew what they thought and why, but he "was determined to proceed because it was right." Anything else "would have been pusillanimous." At the White House immediately afterward, he did not precisely offer his resignation but gave Truman a chance to ask for it. Instead, the president was "wonderful." Truman, after all, had raised a ruckus by attending the funeral of Kansas City's "Boss" Tom Pendergast, "a friendless old man just out of the penitentiary." He fully approved Acheson's action. This was surely loyal, for by then Truman was convinced "that s.o.b." Hiss was "guilty as hell." The day that began in earnest talk with Alice ended at dinner, where John McCloy lifted a glass in his honor. Getting home late, Acheson wrote his daughter, Mary Bundy, again ailing at Lake Saranac: "Alger's case has been on my mind incessantly." Whatever the facts, "here is stark tragedy." It had not been "easy" to make his statement, not with that "yelping pack" at his "heels." But saying what he did had been his responsibility "above and beyond" his "desires." But there might have been a "better way," and he already wished he had found "better words and thoughts in that crowded and slightly hot and sweaty room."[33]

Acheson may have recalled that Truman a few months before had said the Sermon on the Mount supplied the philosophy of his administration, but not that Chambers had resorted to the same Christian standards in telling the grand jury why he had not accused Hiss of espionage earlier. Acheson's choice of the compassionate appeal of the Sermon did not impress his critics. While New York's *Post* and *Herald Tribune* applauded, Reston found his performance rash and mannered and was exasperated by the arch scriptural folderol. He should simply have said "that when a friend is in trouble, you don't turn your back on him." The *Times* had let Reston print the whole biblical passage, for which Acheson was grateful, but the reporter thought Acheson could have avoided the whole controversy "if he hadn't been so fancy and had merely said, 'I never kick a colleague when he's down.'" He was more charitable in private letters, saying in one that though Acheson "should have held his tongue, . . . he had guts enough to say honestly what was in his mind," a rare Washington event.[34]

Eleanor Roosevelt impaled Chambers on the spikes of her weekly column. Others simply defended and praised Acheson. James Warburg wrote to tell him he was "one of the great human beings" of his time. A triumvirate of liberal Democratic attorneys, Thurman Arnold, Paul A. Porter, and Joseph A. Rauh, Jr., in a letter to the *Washington Post*, praised his display of "compassionate sympathy" in a "Christian and democratic society." Robert Lovett offered use of a vacation house in the spring and wrote, "I pray for you—quite literally." The master of Groton praised him, too. So did Yale classmates, applauding his "guts" and promising protection from "jackals," as did Bohlen. Panjandrums on the Hill were far more critical. In the Senate, Republican William Jenner of Indiana attacked the administration as a "military dictatorship," operated by that "Communist-appeasing, Communist-protecting betrayer of America, Secretary of State Dean Acheson." Wisconsin's Joseph McCarthy referred to his statement as "fantastic" while Nixon called it "disgusting." Homer Capehart of Indiana preened himself for having voted against his confirmation. In the House, Republican Walter Judd urged Truman to "turn his back" on Acheson. Jaunty again, Acheson wrote Mary: "My goodness, what a controversial figure I have become. The Congress flies into a tantrum. The press gets all excited." A state department analysis described two-thirds of journalistic comment as negative, but he had the all-out support of New York's *Post* and *Herald Tribune* and other major papers. Some of his more anonymous supporters, Acheson wrote Mary, had restored his "faith that Walt Whitman knew more about America than some of his successors."35

His harshest critics were impervious to Whitman, not to mention the Sermon on the Mount. At the House Foreign Affairs Committee a few days after his press conference, he ran into a buzzsaw of blame named Maury Maverick, the Texas Democrat and Truman's friend. "I'm tired of hearing about you and Harvard and Yale and that you're witty. I've never heard you say anything funny," he grumbled. Laughing weakly, Acheson said it wasn't his fault he went to Yale, but Maverick interrupted, saying that if old Harold Ickes had "got caught in a whore house at 3 A.M. killing a woman, a lot of people would bail him out. But not you, you've got no friends." Anger at Acheson spawned "an extraordinary scene of ill-repressed bitterness" at a Senate appropriations subcommittee in February. Unfriendly questions elicited terse answers. Acheson said nothing at all when William Knowland hauled out old grievances about China and Formosa. When Styles Bridges asked if a friend of "a person convicted of perjury in connection with a treasonable act" should be investigated as a "security risk," Acheson, "his eyes frosty," carefully responded: "I think that would be a matter to be looked into."

Someone finally asked if he wanted to add anything to his 25 January statement. He had "no *desire* to do anything of the sort," he said, alluding to his resentment at being "harassed and misrepresented." Then he drew out a prepared statement, which he read "rapidly and with little inflection." Defiant, it did not even hint at recantation. He would stay "true to the things by which one lives." He would reject "counsels of discretion and cowardice" and spurn "the safe course" because of its "bitter and evil consequences." It was the Soviet Union, he thought, not America, where accused people's friends had to "flee from him as from the plague." The Sermon on the Mount was appropriate, because Hiss was a man "in the greatest trouble in which a man could be." No "fair mind" should read into his remarks any questioning of the courts or approval of Hiss's alleged transgressions. "But for the benefit of those who would create doubt where none existed," he concluded bitterly, "I will accept the humiliation of stating what should be obvious, that I did not and do not, condone in any way the offenses charged, whether committed by a friend or by a total stranger, and that I would never knowingly tolerate any disloyal person in the Department of State." The committee was silent. Nor did his statement end his troubles. Twice in the next three weeks, Lippmann printed columns urging his resignation—he was damaged goods. There is certainly no doubt that the outrage over Hiss diminished his effectiveness for the rest of his term as secretary of state.[36]

"Perhaps I Knocked Myself Out"

No one ever asked Acheson again about Hiss in a press conference. He never ceased asking himself. Late in 1952 he told a reporter his statement in the "awful" Hiss case "started everything," meaning the incessant attack on the whole state department. He never took blame for defending Hiss, only for how he phrased his defense and brought grief to the department and foreign service. In a Princeton seminar, he said that *I will never turn my back on Alger Hiss* was an "awful phrase." He did not give "a damn" what people thought about taking a stand, but he had been "remiss in not getting those who were in the same boat with me and saying, 'Boys, I am now going to turn the lifeboat upside down, and if you haven't got your life jackets on you are in trouble.'" Anyway, he said what he said and then "hell broke loose." In a Truman Library interview in 1955, he said his phrasing was "too quotable," but he remained impenitent on the essentials. As Alice read and sewed that night, he had pondered what to do for hours. "Then I went to bed and thought about it for another two or three hours." He ignored his counselors, because he had to do what he did, since, though Hiss was not an "intimate" friend, Donald was "one of the greatest friends" he had. In this 1955 interview, he even drew back on honoring a court decision: he had seen "juries swayed this way and that." When others were being "so holy" while they beat "a guy who's down," Acheson would refuse to "be a fellow who turns aside and pulls his skirt up" to avoid "the guy who's in the gutter." He could have stayed out of trouble but only at the cost thereafter of knowing he was a "coward," a "louse." He had made his decision alone, unaware that his wording would "be the trigger for the whole attack on the administration."[37]

He stuck to his story over the years, gradually developing an ironical pride in his troublemaking talents. On television in 1969, he told Eric Sevareid he knew reporters thought he would "run," and "I just said, I'm not going to run. I'm going to let you have it right on the jaw." But "perhaps I knocked myself out" and "got a terrible clobbering." Perhaps he "was a little grandiloquent. Perhaps it would have been better if I had said, 'I haven't anything to say about it.'" "I suppose in a way," he added, "an element of pride entered into this." In 1970, he told another interviewer there was still something about the Hiss case "which has not been clarified and perhaps never will."[38]

Certainly, pride entered into his action, both moral and intellectual. So did an unacknowledged, class-based view that his opponents—and Hiss's—were less desirable people. As Henry Luce of Time-Life once said to his employee, Whittaker Chambers, "it is the upper class that is most violent against you." But more important than pride, or class, was Acheson's tie to Donald. He never acknowledged how this affected his view of Alger's case. He never showed any awareness that it might be prudent to take a more critical look at *Donald*. Nor did he ever accept that he had allowed a personal attachment to shape his view of a serious public question—or realize that he fell on his sword for a man undeserving of such a gesture.[39]

In the years since 1950, the pervasiveness of Soviet espionage in the United States in the thirties and war years has become much clearer. That outside the Manhattan Project most of the information stolen for Moscow probably had little lasting importance is no defense for the U.S. citizens who did the stealing. Neither is the horrific record of Hoover and McCarthy in violating citizens' civil liberties. Acheson knew better than they did the need to balance security and liberty but, like many of the day's Democrats and liberals, he underestimated the gravity and menace of foreign espionage. He also ignored his own role in causing the fearful anger now pointed against him. Speaking "clearer than truth" to the people pushed some of them into the paranoia McCarthyism fed on, and his austere demand that they steel themselves for an apparently endless struggle with the USSR eroded the walls of civility, helping expose truly innocent victims of the red scare's rage.

Had Acheson listened to Battle and Nitze, he might have discovered a way to achieve his personal goals without inciting outrage. He might have announced, "I cannot comment on the legal aspects of the case," added a simple statement that he was unwilling to strike a man already down, and there ended it. But this was the aggressive man we already know. So he chose to be flagrant, to give it to someone "right on the jaw." He later described the Hiss case as "something approaching national disaster, lending, as it did, support to a widespread attack throughout the country upon confidence in government itself." Neither he, his president, nor his department could then free themselves of the burden he added to those they already bore.[40]

Coda

At least once, Acheson gave ground, on 12 March 1951, when the Supreme Court rejected Hiss's appeal. James Webb coached him on what to say if reporters asked him about the decision. A mere "no comment" might imply yet more stubbornness and stir up "more stories and antagonistic editorial comment." So Webb coached him to say: "In accordance with our judicial system, the Supreme Court has acted; this disposes of the case." Acheson had listened this time. Arriving at New York's Idlewild Airport from a Bermuda vacation on the day of the ruling, he told correspondents: "The Supreme Court is the highest court and if it acts, that disposes of the matter."[41]

18

EVIL DAYS

Flogging the China Hands

The 1950s strife over communism and anti-communism exposed Americans as their own worst enemy. "We have met the enemy, and he is us," Walt Kelly famously had Pogo say. Dean Acheson's rash defense of Alger Hiss put him in that number, too. The frenzy over communists "boring from within" coincided with a hard renewal of Soviet espionage, as station chiefs of the KGB (Moscow's secret police) in March 1950 moved toward winning over ordinary U.S. citizens. As Chinese armies poured over their American foes in Korea, the McCarthyite attack on the administration became pitiless. The biggest prize the "primitives'" wanted to bag was Acheson himself, plus anyone working for him having anything to do with Asia. Acheson himself survived and achieved most of his goals, but he paid a price in somewhat reduced effectiveness and a far higher one in personal abuse. Fighting back, he leaned precariously into the hostile winds, not "broken under fire," said one observer, but "bent considerably." He surrendered one significant hostage, John Stewart Service, and came to realize his defense of Hiss had redoubled the troubles of worthier men. His own travail led to more caustic views of his congressional foes, their media allies, and with redeeming qualifications, of the people and democracy, too.[1]

Truman wrote Acheson calling Joseph McCarthy "a pathological liar" and his partner in crime Kenneth Wherry "the blockheaded undertaker from Nebraska," but sticks and stones hurt the McCarthyites far less than those they accused. Most severely wounded were the department's "China hands," united in past China service, skepticism about Chiang Kai-shek, and the ill fortune to fall under the spotlights of red-baiters who accused them of disloyalty to the "free, God-fearing half of the world." Aspersions dated back to the war and heated up after Truman instituted his loyalty program.

Potential victims acted in different ways. When the Senate blocked his nomination to the UN delegation, Philip Jessup served anyway on a recess appointment from the president. Banished from the Chinese affairs office, Philip D. Sprouse reportedly scoured through his files, cutting "his initials off" incriminating documents. Acheson defended John Melby, who was then fired by John Foster Dulles in 1953. John Moors Cabot, armed with an "impeccable, cold roast Boston background," remained unperturbed and unscathed. Conrad E. Snow, running the department's own loyalty and security board, lit into McCarthy in speeches and got away with it. Especially as the Korean War soured, the quartet of O. Edmund Clubb, John Stewart Service, John Paton Davies, and John Carter Vincent were far less lucky.[2]

Clubb, like most FSOs in East Asia in the thirties and forties, thought the communists would come out on top in the Chinese civil war. What mainly led this native of Minnesota to grief was a 1932 incident in New York. There Whittaker Chambers saw the thirty-one-year-old diplomat passing time on a home leave in the offices of *New Masses* magazine. Though Clubb recalled Chambers as "a shifty-eyed unkempt creature," the episode put him in the soup once the ex-communist transferred it from his elephantine memory to FBI files. In 1949, Clubb was U.S. consul general in China, staying in touch with the new regime as other Americans left the country. He took over the China desk in Washington just as the McCarthyite campaign reached high gear. Though a colleague considered him "secure to the point of being boring," charges from Chambers and anonymous sources caused the department's loyalty board to find him a security (but not a loyalty) risk and suspend him in 1951.

Skeptical about the finding, Acheson summoned Nathaniel P. Davis from upstate New York retirement to review Clubb's record, promising him anonymity. When Davis, a former ambassador to Costa Rica, cleared Clubb and urged his reinstatement, Acheson reversed the loyalty board. In the heated atmosphere, however, he thought it prudent to assign Clubb to research tasks, which prompted his resignation in 1952. Acheson at least had saved his pension, and when his intervention became public, Republicans screamed in outrage and demanded the name of his consultant. In a letter, Davis praised his refusal to give it as a "characteristic" instance of sheltering his aides but released him from his promise. Clubb went quietly into retirement, only to have investigators descend on his neighborhood asking, "Did we pay our bills? Did we go to church? What did we think of Acheson?" But McCarthy never called Clubb back to his "inquisition."[3]

Service was a ghost come back to haunt Acheson, who had made light of his role in the 1945 *Amerasia* case. This time he would follow the department board and axe him in December 1951. A fly in Chiang's ointment, Service had also advised MacArthur in Japan and helped assemble the *White Paper*. Twice the department buried him in India to keep him invisible to critics, only to have its own investigative board call him back. Though it cleared him, more than once, senators considered him "extremely indiscreet," and eventually he became something of an unperson at State. Worse lay ahead after the Korean War brought new sheen to McCarthy. With criteria for dismissal reduced to "reasonable doubt," many cases were reopened in the spring of 1951. McCarthy revived charges against Service in a speech upbraiding Acheson for keeping him on; Patrick McCarran's internal security subcommittee burrowed again into the *Amerasia* case; and the government-wide Loyalty Review Board questioned Service's earlier clearance by State. With board examiners shaking their heads on learning that Service called Edward Stettinius "happy as a baboon," bad-mouthed Patrick Hurley, and praised *Amerasia*, in December 1951 they declared their "reasonable doubt" about his loyalties. He had "stepped over the line," Acheson recalled, "and if you had to find *someone*, you had to find *him*." When Acheson fired him, McCarthy crowed, "Good, good, good."

That Service was the only man Acheson dismissed outright was remarkable, considering that federal departments on average fired 6 percent of those investigated. In Service's case, Charles Bohlen, sensing Truman's itch for a sacrificial offering, blocked a letter of protest from a group of FSOs, fearing it might provoke Acheson himself to resign. But the case took a curious twist after Service appealed his dismissal. In an affidavit, Acheson said he had acted "solely as the result of the finding of the Loyalty Review Board," a procedure the courts soon pronounced invalid. This formed the basis of a 1957 Supreme Court decision negating his dismissal and ordering him rehired. As Service filed appeals (and sold steam traps for a living), Acheson supplied references for a new job, but not at State. After the 1957 decision, Dulles exiled him to the Liverpool consulate. He retired in 1962 when Secretary of State Dean Rusk failed to respond to a languid bid from Acheson to give him another chance. In 1969, the seventy-six-year-old Acheson ran into Service on the University of California campus. As they strolled together, Acheson remarked that his brother Edward, who had known Service in China, had given him "a hell of a time" about firing him. He was glad his affidavit had ultimately proved useful.[4]

John Paton Davies, Jr., endured nine loyalty board reviews before Dulles sacked him in 1954 for lack of "judgment, discretion and reliability." Born in China in 1908 to Baptist missionaries, he returned there as a fledgling diplomat after university studies, including at Yenching University when John Leighton Stuart was president. He and Service were part of the wartime Stilwell entourage that tried to prod Chiang Kai-shek into more aggressive action against the Japanese. Bookish, idealistic, and politically innocent, he led seventeen passengers who parachuted from a crippled C-54 transport above the Burma hump. As the ranking person on board (all neophytes with parachutes), he jumped first, "his attache case stuffed inside his shirt," and then led the ragged party in its month-long trek out of the jungle. The medal he won impressed none of his angry critics, who cared more about his reports on Chiang, which vibrated with contempt for "Gimo." In retrospect, his civil war analyses appear realistic, but he later conceded being naïve about the communists. Yet he could be tough, too. Joining the PPS in 1947, he wrote many of the hard-boiled slams at Mao in the *White Paper* and disliked Acheson's quest for accommodation with Beijing. When he came under heavy fire in 1950, State moved him to Germany and then faraway Lima, but in vain. He faced suspension in the summer of 1951. Though the department board cleared him, McCarran hauled him before his committee in 1952, resulting in repeated questions about his competence and trustworthiness. Under Dulles, a new department board using yet looser standards of proof ruled his retention incompatible "with the interests of the national security." Refusing an offer of his pension in exchange for resigning, he forced Dulles to fire him. Thereafter, he wandered the earth, from North Carolina to Spain to making furniture in Peru. Two distinguished books and the 1969 restoration of his security clearance refurbished his reputation, but he never resumed government work. Nor was he bitter, even at Dulles. Acheson never thought he did anything wrong. A "perfectly straight guy," he was condemned by a board that hadn't the "the faintest idea" what made a good foreign service officer.[5]

John Carter Vincent seemed least suited for martyrdom. Born in Kansas in 1900 and raised in a middle-class Baptist home in Georgia, he was no more a communist than "the angel Gabriel," writes author Robert P. Newman. Like Acheson, he sloughed the doctrinal trappings of his youth but "heartily clung to the Sermon on the Mount." After a long and distinguished foreign service career, including two decades in China, he became director of Far Eastern affairs in 1945. To keep him out of the China Lobby's line of fire, the department sent him to Switzerland as minister and to Tangier as diplomatic agent. But he was recalled in 1952 for investigation. Acheson, who had earlier rebutted charges against him, prized the talents of this "elegant, mustached," and courtly man. He was a conservative with a penchant for giving Acheson tough advice on Korea, but trouble began tracking him like Tuesday after Monday. McCarthy even sent a neurotic forgerer to Switzerland in search of dirt. Vincent took it in good cheer, saying, "If they don't like the cut of my trousers, I shall be perfectly willing to take some non-honorable but useful job."[6]

With Truman's firing of General Douglas MacArthur in the spring of 1951, cries grew louder for a state department purge. By August, McCarthy was railing against Vincent as another Hiss. McCarran was also sinking his teeth into him, and State's own loyalty and security board put him on its docket. Again to protect Acheson, Bohlen alerted others not to go out on a limb. Vincent's worst grilling came at the hands of the McCarran committee where, reported the horrified Alsop brothers, he was all but "beaten by a rubber hose." Three more department examinations of his record in 1952 resulted in clearances, but McCarran wanted him sent to a grand jury, and Hiram Bingham's higher board challenged the state department decisions. Now bolstered by Eugene Dooman, one of the losers in Acheson's 1945 purge of the Grew faction of Asianists, Bingham and company questioned Vincent for eight hours. In a close December 1952 vote, it negated the department's decision and recommended his ouster from the government on grounds of reasonable doubt of his loyalty.

On 15 December 1952, Acheson was forced to suspend him, but he was galvanized by what he deemed the rank injustice delivered by the Bingham board. Truman agreed and, using a legal technicality suggested by State's Adrian Fisher, formed a new independent commission headed by the fabled jurist Learned Hand to reexamine Vincent's record. This came just before Eisenhower's inauguration, causing McCarthyites to scream foul. Because the board had not finished when Dulles came into office, he seized control of the case. *He* would not follow St. Stephen and Acheson in being stoned to death! Though he too indirectly rejected Bingham's findings, he rated Vincent's record as below professional standards and, on 23 February, allowed him a quiet retirement with pension intact. Acheson was furious, but so were conservatives. A later Supreme Court decision brought imperfect vindication but no new diplomatic post, for Rusk again ignored friends' entreaties. Until Vincent's death in 1972, he lived in a scholars' world of research, lectures, and op-ed pieces. Politically estranged, he voted Socialist in 1968.[7]

As early as 1936, Acheson had castigated a Republican "red hunt" as a bigoted attack on FDR that would quash American liberties. As noted earlier, he spared neither himself nor the president in excoriating the federal loyalty-security program in retirement. In his 1955 book, *A Democrat Looks at His Party*, while acknowledging the threat of communists to internal security, he condemned the immoderate attempts to counter the threat and insisted there had been no need to establish a *loyalty* program as protection from *espionage*. Recreating on a beach in Antigua, Acheson wrote his old boss in 1953 lamenting how McCarthy's "bastardization" of American politics would actually weaken the fight against the "monolithic" communists.[8]

His own mistakes and resolve to cover Truman's back in a fouled political arena prevented him from making an effective defense of the China hands. Short of a pitched effort that would have made him even more vulnerable, he could probably have done little more. For in the wake of the Hiss affair and the Korean War, Acheson himself was suffering the most savage attack against a sitting cabinet officer in American history.

Hysteria's Detritus

By January of 1952, the FBI had conducted over 18,000 loyalty inquiries of federal employees. Over 4,000 resigned rather than face investigating boards, which had cashiered 580 workers while reinstating 220 on appeal. Thirty-three employees beat the state department board to the punch by resigning; seventeen more did so following board decisions against them. Acheson was little involved personally. He was not personally fearful of dissidents, but as Ernest R. May points out, it was only reasonable that in making personnel decisions he not put the president at risk or blatantly disregard public and congressional opinion. Though lion-like in the defense of core ideas and his own reputation, Acheson could be canny and even cold when cutting his losses. He would risk little for causes or people he considered negligible in significance. He took major risks for an unpopular China policy. He did the same for Donald Hiss and would have done the same for Jessup. He stuck his neck out for John Carter Vincent, but less so for Clubb and Davies, and even less for John Stewart Service.

Acheson considered it a mistake to treat homosexuals or drunks as criminals but was unprepared to block John Peurifoy's campaign to sweep them from the department. Lower-rank officials led this housecleaning, with Carl Humelsine boasting in 1953 that State had fired a homosexual "every three days." In the Acheson-Dulles era, the department fired or harried into resignation over four hundred homosexuals, far more than suspected "reds" or spies. None was found somehow to have assisted the USSR. Acheson's own language could take on the tinge of this assault on the sexually heterodox when he defended his associates as "clean-living" and the department as a "good, clean, loyal outfit." He glumly went along when Styles Bridges badgered him in a hearing to include "perversion" as a "security risk."9

Despite his publicly expressed concerns about racism's handicap in the conduct of U.S. foreign policy, in 1950 Acheson denounced William E. B. Du Bois's support of the Stockholm "peace pledge." He did nothing to stop harassment of nonconformist black entertainers. Diva Josephine Baker, who had long lived in France to escape discrimination, became a "smash hit" in Cuba in a tour of the western hemisphere. Because of her public criticisms of American racism while on tour, FBI agents and U.S. diplomats in Montevideo reported on her comings, goings, and sayings in a September 1952 swing through Uruguay. Already dismayed by the insistent rebukes of the notorious Paul Robeson, State revoked his passport after he criticized the Korean War effort and predicted that U.S. aggression would next extend to Africa.10

From the passport office, Ruth ("Ma") Shipley used her ironfisted control over travel rights to punish "communists" or anyone else who smelled fishy. Acheson would not stage a fight with conservatives over visas; if the laws on travel were bad, he said in 1950, "that was too bad, but that was the kind of country we had." In an April 1951 press conference he defended denying a visa to French singer Maurice Chevalier because he had signed the Stockholm pledge, raised money for a "Communist affiliate," and consorted with communists who would stick a knife "in his back" if he deserted them. Nor did he interfere with the decision to forbid future Nobel laureate Linus Pauling, a frequent critic of U.S. policies, to travel abroad. One of Shipley's few defeats came in 1952, when, gulled by a hoax, she alerted U.S. Customs to stop Owen Lattimore from decamping to

Moscow, only to have the FBI tell her he was not going anywhere, had not even bought a plane ticket. Truman ordered apologies to Lattimore and some handcuffs for Shipley. In September 1952, Acheson told Felix Frankfurter about trying to inject some sanity into Shipley's "Queendom of Passports" while confessing that it was "a hard struggle. These cases & the visa ones are the most distasteful part of this job." Late that year, when a House committee demanded to know who had vetted the appointment of an American communist discovered working for the UN secretariat, Acheson, thinking the person in question harmless, shot back that he would not "snatch the knotted cord from the hand of God and deal out murderous blows to my associates."[11]

A "Filthy Business" and "Sadistic Pogrom"

The worst of the attack on Acheson began in January 1950. Robert Taft—Mr. Republican—led the way with a claim over the radio that bipartisanship had "died when Dean Acheson became Secretary of State." In the Senate, he charged that left-wingers had taken over the state department, leading to the betrayal of Chiang Kai-shek. The *Chicago Tribune* called Acheson "another striped-pants" snob who ignored Asian peoples and betrayed "true Americanism to serve as a lackey of Wall Street bankers, British lords, and Communistic radicals from New York." In February, Bridges urged the Senate to censure Acheson and choke off funding for the state department. On 9 February, McCarthy's offensive began in Wheeling, West Virginia, where he accused Acheson of protecting 205 known state department communists (or, he later said, 57, or 81 in yet another version). McCarthy remained in full cry for months, describing Truman as a "son of a bitch" backed by "egg-sucking phony liberals" who sheltered "Communists and queers," "sold China into atheistic slavery," and stayed "drunk on bourbon and Benedictine." As to "the elegant and alien Acheson," he was "Russian as to heart, British as to manner"—"a pompous diplomat in striped pants with a phony British accent."[12]

A House member, piling on, referred to the "Hiss Survivors Association down at the State Department who wear upon their breasts the Cross of Yalta." Nebraska Senator Hugh Butler proclaimed: "I look at that fellow, I watch his smart-aleck manner and his British clothes and that New Dealism . . . and I want to shout, Get out, Get out." The attacks grew especially virulent after his statement on Hiss. He might have been better off, some thought, if he had a little "cow manure on his feet," or, as Dean Rusk put it, "a little hay" behind his ears, but "Acheson wouldn't do that." With Wherry convinced he was a "security risk," such playacting would probably have made no difference. Calls for his resignation came from a rainbow of political coloration, from China Lobby leader Walter Judd to Walter Lippmann. Arthur Krock had never seen a cabinet officer assaulted by so many and defended by so few. In an attack that was unlimited in its "ferocity," Acheson said later, the anti-communists struck at "the character and patriotism" of high policymakers and "gutted" the "house of government." According to one scholar's astonishing count, in Acheson's four years as secretary of state, Republicans made 1,268 antagonistic statements about him on the Senate floor and only seven that were favorable! No wonder he was stymied on China, seemed powerless to energize NATO, or fought in vain to gain popular support for policies in Asia. Lester Pearson in Ottawa thought it "dreadful to contemplate" Acheson's fall "in consequence of the insalubrious winds which are now blowing," a concern echoed in London.[13]

Apparently the only face-to-face meeting between Acheson and McCarthy came in a chance encounter on a Senate elevator in the spring of 1952. Smiling, McCarthy stuck out his hand with a loud, "Hi, Dean!" But Acheson ignored the man he considered "slovenly, lazy, and undisciplined." He was a "lazy, small-town bully, without sustaining purpose," a "thoroughly bad man," a "horrid little creature," and a "very cheap, low scoundrel." He was also a "tool" of the Taftite Republican conservatives and did "incalculable harm" to the nation.

In McCarthy's 1950–51 heyday—the "evil days," as Acheson remembered them—the state department fell to a defensive crouch, as opponents chose the times and places of battle. On the Monday after McCarthy's Wheeling speech, a jittery Peurifoy said that if any communists remained in the department, they would be "fired before sundown." Through February and March, Acheson found it necessary to deny recurrent reports of his resignation, defend the department against charges of disloyalty, and sit in painful silence as Peurifoy, in a joint congressional appearance, boasted further of his success in weeding out subversives. His humor returning, in a press conference Acheson joked about McCarthy's charge that Alice was aiding "purveyors to treason" by joining the Congress of American Women. As a San Francisco crowd gathered for one of his speeches, he said: "I hope you are not exposing yourselves to immediate danger by associating with me."[14]

Without fail, Truman defended Acheson and ridiculed his assailants. Others rallied, too, including an Acheson favorite, the tangy New Deal secretary of the interior, Harold Ickes, who wrote him that the attacks were as "twisted and dirty as a devious political mind can make them." Such "side-line cheers," Acheson replied, protected him from the "depressing effect" of McCarthy's "shabby performance." Henry Stimson rebutted McCarthy's barrages in a letter to the *Times*, and across the Atlantic, the *Economist* said the "outside world" considered Acheson the west's leader in containing Soviet aggression and the "best" U.S. secretary of state in "modern times." On 29 March 1950, as zephyrs fluttered his Florida shirttails in a press conference, Truman said Acheson would "go down in history as one of the great Secretaries of State." Then he "unmercifully denounced" McCarthy, Wherry, and Bridges as "saboteurs" and Moscow's "greatest asset." Wondering if reflective Republicans might have second thoughts, Reston wrote that Acheson was "one of the very few members of the

Truman Administration with any real intellectual stature" and had "a great appeal to the independent voters of America."[15]

That hardly mattered to Indiana's William Jenner, who cried on 2 April that every hour brought more proof that Acheson was double-talking the nation "deeper into Communist booby traps all over the world." Acheson, McCarthy told a GOP gathering in Milwaukee, had given communists "the guns, the whips, the blacksnakes, and clubs" needed to hold Poland's Christians "under Soviet discipline." When he did criticize communism, he did so "with a lace handkerchief, a silk glove, and with a Harvard accent." Acheson's most spirited verbal counterattack came in late April 1950, in a nationally broadcast speech to the American Society of Newspaper Editors. As he denounced attacks on his advisers as a "filthy business," a "mad and vicious operation" with which his audience had collaborated, a listener shouted, "Pour it on 'em, Mr. Secretary!" As he listened to the "ovation," Paul Hoffman thought McCarthyism was polishing rather than eroding Acheson's reputation. A *Times* headline described Acheson as on an "Offensive Against 'Mad' McCarthy Charges."[16]

It is a truism that the anti-communist offensive damaged state department morale for decades and injured Truman and Acheson, but it is also true that they continued to gain most of their objectives. The president, Reston wrote, managed to achieve all his large foreign policy and military goals "with very little opposition from the Congress or the press, and some of it without even asking the Congress." But the successes did not repeal the damage to the diplomatic corps, which worsened after Dulles's gutting. During the MacArthur hearings in June 1951, Acheson traced "reticence" from officers working in "highly controversial" areas to their growing belief they would get in "trouble" whatever they said. A year later, he told reporters this tendency might make him dependent on misinformation from intimidated underlings, exactly the problem producing mistakes in the Kremlin. Yet, perhaps inspired by Truman and Acheson's defiance, many other Foggy Bottom workers dug in to outlast McCarthy. Jessup had planned departing early in 1950 but refused "to leave under fire." "The outside enemy," recalled Luke Battle, increased department "cohesion," so that "there was very little ratting and running." Longtime assistant secretary Willard Thorp noted the many colleagues who had refused to give McCarthy the satisfaction of quitting under pressure, but he thought Acheson "was the one who really stuck it out."[17]

The vitriol grew worse with the disappointments of the Korean War, which Taft and McCarthy blamed on Acheson's "weak" Asian policies. In July and August 1950, the Veterans of Foreign Wars (VFW) demanded the heads of both Acheson and Louis Johnson for their "bungling." Richard Nixon, *Life* magazine, and the American Legion called for a new secretary of state, as did Wherry, who bleated that "the blood of our boys" was on Acheson's "shoulders." The November election, which coincided with the onset of China's shocking intervention, gained the GOP twenty-five additional seats in the House and five in the Senate. Many observers thought the state department was the election's biggest loser. Acheson, said McCarthy and his allies, ran a "crimson clique"; his "primary loyalty" was to "the British Labor Government, his secondary allegiance to the Kremlin." In December, forty-three Republican senators called for his resignation, including "moderates" in their first try at throwing mud. On the 15th, GOP majorities in both houses again demanded his resignation and a "thorough housecleaning" at State. Krock was already conjecturing about his successor, while Lippmann—who also advocated withdrawing from Korea—blamed Acheson for "disaster abroad and . . . disunity at home." Shortly thereafter, the Achesons encountered the Lippmanns at a dinner party. Seated next to the columnist, Alice demanded an explanation. "Well, now, Alice," Lippmann observed, "Dean has said some hard things to me in his time." "Yes, he has," she replied, "but not for money."[18]

The climax of Acheson's mugging came in the spring of 1951. In March, in a rare reference to Europe, McCarthy accused him of blocking German and Spanish contributions to western defense. MacArthur's sacking in April heightened fury over East Asia, where, in the words of Goodwin Knight, the lieutenant governor of California, the "American Neville Chamberlain" had "kow-towed to communism" in "nefarious and secret collusion" with America's "violent enemies." Using what amounted to a bill of attainder, House Republicans in May tried to eliminate appropriations for Acheson's salary to force him from office. Powerful Democrats wanted him gone, too, resentful of his know-it-all hauteur. Liberals Albert Gore and Paul Douglas hoped Truman would fire him, as did House Majority Whip, J. Percy Priest. Democratic leaders Tom Connally and Sam Rayburn teetered on the edge of opposition. Unfazed, Acheson enraged critics with his performance in the hearings on MacArthur's dismissal, probably because his testimony was so effective, though columnist William S. White called him "the most persuasive unpersuasive man in the Truman Administration." Nearly retiring the trophy for calumny, McCarthy called Acheson and George Marshall the leaders of a pro-Soviet conspiracy "so immense, an infamy so black, as to dwarf any in the previous history of man." The next Republican effort to excise Acheson's salary from the budget was so brazen, one House Republican said, the bill seemed to say, "No man with a mustache can serve in public office." This farce finally fell 171–81.[19]

All the while, White House and Foggy Bottom checked Acheson's pulse and prescribed remedies. One was to have substitutes for congressional testimony, and both General Omar Bradley and Marshall's successor at Defense, Robert Lovett, played this role. Jack McFall of congressional relations proposed a blue ribbon panel to inspect department internal security. Acheson took the idea to Truman, but it died in White House staff rooms. Partly because the 1947 Smith-Mundt Act barred spending to lobby Congress, the state department never came up with an orderly self-defense. In any case, Acheson complained to a journalist, it was impossible to fight on equal terms against someone who "did not abide by the rules which make it possible for society to function." Another public affairs officer in February 1951 wanted a campaign to recapture the "all in sorrow and not in anger" critics, including "the Alsops, Lippmann, Marquis Childs, Doris Fleeson, Clifton Utley, Raymond Swing and others." Aides at both State and the White House wanted Acheson to spend more time on the radio and meeting various groups and individuals, and when he snubbed a Denver speech invitation, an annoyed George Elsey said he had to "get out and fight." He should use his own words, not those of speechwriters who did "not know how to speak American."[20]

The harangues against Acheson hit their peak just as news from Korea bottomed out. Most critics then moved to other targets, while others entertained second thoughts about their past assaults. Echoes of those assaults still sounded, like unexploded ordnance on an old battlefield. VFW conventioneers in August 1951 cheered "wildly" when McCarthy called him the "Red Dean of Fashion." In 1952, freshman Republican senator Everett Dirksen thrust at "the Lavender lads" of the state department. In a final sally that October, McCarthy called him "one of the most dangerous men who ever has been in government." Drew Pearson told his diary Acheson was "too harassed, too tired, and too numb" to mobilize congressional backing. Just as Acheson began to wonder how Truman could afford to keep him on, his approval ratings in the polls began rising from a low mark of 20 percent. Democratic defenders reemerged, blinking, from their storm cellars. After such House liberals as Chet Holifield, Emanuel Cellar, and Richard Bolling spoke in his favor, shamed senators finally rallied, blocking GOP resolutions for his resignation by votes of 47–29 and 45–30. Truman stepped forward in a spunky 19 December 1951 press conference mostly devoted to Acheson. Eviscerating his critics as descendants of the cowards who calumniated William H. Seward because they were afraid to attack Abraham Lincoln, he said that if communists ever took over, Acheson "would be one of the first, if not the first, to be shot by the enemies of liberty and Christianity." A fascinated Krock thought McCarthyism was now uniting Democrats more than rallying Republicans. The "Republican tide of criticism" was "receding," according to Ambassador Oliver Franks.[21]

Defenders arose outside the government too. In the summer of 1950, Harvard had awarded Acheson an honorary degree and the Freedom House cited him for his "constructive" peace policy. Thomas Dewey's appeal for an end to partisan attacks softened terrible news from Korea at the end of the year. So did the appearance of old Cordell Hull, who had himself driven to the Foggy Bottom garage to tell Acheson he "wanted to be publicly counted" as a friend. January 1951 brought a pro-Acheson "manifesto" signed by nine hundred political scientists and historians—including Allan Nevins, Edward S. Mason, Louis Brownlow, V. O. Key, Samuel Eliot Morison, Crane Brinton, Foster R. Dulles, and the senior and junior Schlesingers. Elmer Davis scoffed at "The Crusade against Acheson" in *Harper's Magazine*. The enemies besieging this blameless

Christian gentleman and the finest secretary of state since Seward, said Davis, were the "Fascistoid" KKK and the Christian Front, the same "kind of people who gave Hitler his first mass support." In November 1951, the Jewish War Veterans awarded Acheson a medal for his defense against the Soviets and "distinguished services in uniting the free world for peace." He had already received a large boost in August and September 1951 during the televised Japanese peace treaty proceedings in San Francisco, where, as conference chair, he had hurled witty parliamentary counterstrokes against obstructionist Russians and Poles. "Through the miracle of television, just extended to the West Coast on the opening day of that conference," wrote journalist William H. Lawrence, "millions of Americans sitting in their homes were able to watch the 'soft' Mr. Acheson gavel Andrei Gromyko of Russia and his two satellite associates into silence and impotence."[22]

Democrats rediscovered their admiration of Acheson when polls showed 60 percent of the population wanting him to stay at his post, which is where Truman said he would stay "as long as I am President." Connecticut Democrat William Benton, the first to strike out at McCarthy from the Senate floor, defended Acheson and twitted still silent colleagues. At a department awards ceremony in October 1951, Acheson ripped into anti-communist critics, holding them responsible for a 50-percent decline in applications to the foreign service. University officials had told him that American youth were disinclined to face the kinds of "vicious personal attacks" being delivered against American diplomats. He blasted "Evil" and "reckless" partisans for damaging the national interest with "untrue attacks on the personal character and the personal loyalty and devotion of many among us." At year's end, after NATO and UN meetings in Canada and Europe, a *New York Times* headline read: "Acheson Position Stronger as Result of World Talks." And the administration continued to get its way. After a 9–0 committee vote sent Greek and Turkish membership in NATO to the Senate floor on 15 January 1952, the *Times* commented that "rarely had a high policy been decided with such speed."[23]

Acheson's revival must not be overstated. He had merely become less of a pariah as opponents found new grist for their mills in tax fraud charges against Attorney General J. Howard McGrath. Even those now championing Acheson's policies seldom gave him credit for them. But the change was welcome, and by the summer of 1952, Truman felt free to joke in a press conference about the American Legion's call for him to fire Acheson. Acheson told reporters in Paris in June that his position with Congress had "changed radically" for the better after San Francisco. Union members in Pittsburgh gave him a ten-minute ovation when he denounced "anti-Communists" of "strong voice and a weak conscience" who engaged in "indiscriminate denunciations and character assassinations."[24]

Despite the reappearance of supporters, being cast as the embodiment of one side of the communist–anti-communist clash took a toll. If the anti-communist atmosphere did not actually cause Acheson to do things he did not want to do, it held him back from those he did want to do. Though he denied it, the personal toll was probably worse than the effect on policy. He constantly had to deny plans to resign. He suffered mortifying displays of hostility. He heard about White House gossip treating him as an untouchable. As already described, Congress refused him the honor of addressing it in joint session. Such hostility was just part of his job, he explained—or claimed. His long experience with criticism, he told an ambassador in 1950, caused him to agree with "Plato's observation that government is the most difficult of all the arts." Admitting to reporters in January 1951 that he had not anticipated becoming so "unpopular," he waved it off as "an occupational hazzard [sic]." It was a burden he was "quite ready to bear," he said at the MacArthur hearings. The important thing, he wrote later, was that he and the president gained all the objects they had set their caps to until "the very eve of the campaign of 1952."[25]

However much he shrugged off the attacks on him, authorities worried for his safety. Four bodyguards followed the Acheson family around the clock, including weekends at Harewood. As nasty letters piled up in his home, he kept his country lathe hot making one piece of furniture after another as guards stood outside. In Washington, his matter-of-fact savoir faire impressed those who saw it. In Georgetown, the visiting Archibald MacLeish could hear him start his day by listening to his foes on the radio. "I remember him turning on the seven-thirty news while he shaved and listening to Fulton Lewis, all the while whistling away. It was during this period that Dean's intellectual arrogance became a great strength." He soldiered on, his demeanor free of dents. Drew Pearson saw him at the Norwegian embassy being "his usual smiling self." Early in 1951, Lovett told reporters: "He's no cookie pusher. He's a giant." Francis Russell from public affairs, who chatted with him often, said he never mentioned McCarthy. Instead, they talked about "fishing, farm problems, or God knows what, but there was never any wringing of hands or oaths, or talk about McCarthy." German special-ist Perry Laukhuff "never heard him complain" but believed "he suffered acutely." He was nonetheless "never anything but his collected, calm, urbane self."[26]

Astute observers were not so sure. His jokes about not resigning were strained, as after the fall 1950 elections when he said it was like being asked, "Is it true that you have leprosy?" Another time, he said he recognized a question about resigning "as an old friend." When introduced to high school students touring the Capitol, he expressed his delight "to expose them to the terror of looking at me." He would never admit how much he and Alice had suffered, Clark Clifford recalled, but *Alice* would, and said she was certain "McCarthy had shortened her husband's life by ten years." David Bruce thought the "torrent of abuse" must have "cruelly wounded" the spirit of this "superior" individual. As the "scapegoat for the failures and frustrations of his fellow-countrymen," his position was "as painful as the history of American public life can record." Acheson would not put up with any expressions of pity, believing with Francis Bacon that "the good things which belong to prosperity are to be wished, but the good things that belong to adversity are to be admired." "I am something of a stoic," he said, "both by nature and by inheritance. And I learned from the example of my father that the manner in which one endures what must be endured is more important than the thing that must be endured." "Being vilified," he said on another occasion, had "its stimulating aspects, and for all I know, it may even be good for the liver."[27]

But it was probably not particularly good for policymaking. As early as March 1950, Acheson told reporters on background that McCarthy's charges were chewing up his people, who spent hundreds of hours just defending themselves. He was not "crying about it," for apparently such things routinely happened in democracies. The CIA in May 1950 worried that Moscow's leaders would view American internal strife as a green light to act adventurously. It is almost certainly true, as many historians have observed, that in various areas, the administration acted with gratuitous belligerence to ward off attacks from the right. MacLeish warned Acheson not to "compete with" McCarthy "in scaring people about Russia. As long as you do that you are the kite-tail to his Holy War."[28]

He never considered quitting. Just as the lower-level officers who joked over coffee about who would next be accused, Acheson would not leave under fire. Truman might have made a fresh start if he had, but the president probably grasped that the McCarthyites would simply pocket Acheson and then attack any successor who failed to repudiate his policies—and Truman's. Apart from his loyalty, another reason Truman never hinted at making a change was Acheson's strength. As Truman's own popularity plummeted, he had to know that naming his fifth secretary of state in seven years would make him look even weaker, and inept to boot. Acheson's power depended on Truman's confidence, but he ironically gained more freedom to act under such a vulnerable chief executive than he might under a more popular president. Whatever its sources, Truman's backing was a consolation. Despite his troubles, Acheson wrote proudly, his state department served as Truman's "chief instrument for developing the foreign policy" that lasted for decades thereafter.[29]

Over the years, Acheson's recollections about McCarthyism would range from breezy to bleak. The somber assessment in his memoirs emphasized damage done by "this sadistic pogrom" to the civil and foreign service and universities' "China-studies programs." The McCarran-Bridges-Taft-McCarthy rampage, witlessly encouraged by the press, matched the post–World War I red scare; it was a "slaughter" carried out "in the night of the long knives." But sporadic signs of ordinary Americans' affection kept Acheson's merry spirit going. After a speech in Detroit in 1951, his hotel valet left him a note: "Mr. Acheson. It was a very good speech last night. Casey Presser. Valet Shop. Book Cadillac Hotel." Once as he climbed into a taxi, the driver asked: "Aren't you Dean Acheson?" "Yes I am," he answered, "do you want me to get out?" When McCarthy died in 1957, after telling reporters he had no comment, he recited some Latin to them and then translated: "Say nothing about the dead unless it is good." Badly scarred, at times he applied the same rule to his feelings about Congress, media, and American democracy itself.[30]

"A Race between Education and Irritation"

Acheson's bent for offending Congress has been exaggerated. He got along fine on the Hill in earlier years, and when he became secretary few predicted trouble ahead. His successes stemmed from an extraordinary grasp of important information, pragmatism, and an underrated ability to charm men unlike himself. As to the institution, whether Republican or Democratic, he thought Congress resembled the contumacious House of Commons in the years it tried blocking the statesmanship of Elizabeth I. Congress, he told friends in 1953, was "an unhappy, unnecessary, unconstructive evil which you have for the purpose of getting money and passing some legislation." Its members misunderstood the "intricacies" of the nation's problems, just as Elizabeth's Commons failed to grasp the necessities of dealing with France and Spain. The British parliament had grown in responsibility, but there was insufficient discipline in the United States for that to happen to Congress, which mimicked its constituents, "who don't know and don't care" about foreign policy. Members were "just generally raising hell around." When Acheson said "we and them," reporter Theodore H. White learned, he meant the United States versus the USSR; when he said "I and them," he spoke of himself and Congress. In old age, he yielded to his preference "for kicking fools" over "persuading them." Shortly before his death, he told an interviewer that, if better than the alternatives, democracy was not "worth a damn." He was asked whether Congress would improve if it were more representative. "I say the Congress is too damn representative," he scoffed. "It's just as stupid as the people are; just as uneducated, just as dumb, just as selfish."[31]

This was Acheson in one of his low, geriatric, and waspish moods, but such faulting of congressional behavior was nothing new. It was a view drawn from experience rather than study. Senators gave poor advice and were reluctant to consent to anything, but they were addicted to "the purgative quality of talk." Because authorization must precede appropriations, a plethora of committees crawled over legislation, causing him to spend a sixth of his "working days" traveling up and down the Hill to testify. The shirts of most senators, he said in retirement, were "stuffed with sawdust." Only "by pure chance" did they ever accomplish anything useful. He could nevertheless ride the Senate as he rode a horse, by showing no fear and riding it "into the bit." Even then, working with congressmen who were "more interested in rivers and harbors, and God knows what else" than in foreign policy was "a race between education and irritation." Alluding to Acheson's Hiss statement, Harry Vaughan in the White House thought he should "pay less attention to the Sermon on the Mount and more to the men on the Hill."[32]

Criticism of his relations with Congress, "like a bead in a rosary which each historian" must tell, irked him, since he managed to gain congressional approval of so many important measures. Perhaps, he conceded in 1971, he could have been more deferential, but he had "never really had any great yearning to be loved." Success was better, and he could "leave the love to somebody else." Despite all the congressional dislike of him, he told Eric Sevareid in 1969, Congress "usually did what they were asked to do." He may have been protesting too much, for he also liked recording exceptions to the rule. Senator Knowland, for example, was always "most courteous and friendly" to Acheson in private, and some of his worst congressional "enemies" were his "best friends."[33]

This is Pollyannaish, for it defies abundant evidence that many Senate and House members disliked Acheson. According to political scientist James Rosenau's analysis, "only" twenty-one senators of 121 serving during Acheson's tenure were "actively hostile" to him, but that seems like a large number to this reader. Moreover, those who were "indiscriminately" hostile formed a ring of influence—Robert Taft, John Bricker, Styles Bridges, William Jenner, Homer Capehart, Everett Dirksen, James Kem, William Langer, George Malone, Karl Mundt, Herman Welker, Kenneth Wherry, and Joseph McCarthy. Eight other "Discriminates" were nearly as antagonistic—Republicans Ralph Owen Brewster, Harry Cain, Forrest Donnell, Homer Ferguson, William Knowland, Wayne Morse, and Arthur Watkins of Utah, along with Democrat Patrick McCarran.[34]

Franks thought Acheson "got along very well" with such "gentleman" senators as Connally and Arthur Vandenberg, whose behavior and language came from the eighteenth century. In fact, his respect for the fatuous Connally was minimal, as it would be for anyone who, according to Reston, did not know the difference between "the Baltic States and the Balkans." Fellow Texan Hickerson, who liked Connally, concluded that there "was no love lost" between the senator and Acheson. He met often and cordially with Republican H. Alexander Smith of New Jersey (the "poor man's" Vandenberg), and though he found Alexander Wiley of Wisconsin "windy," he urged Truman to delete a harsh reference to him in his memoirs. The stentorian Vandenberg aroused both respect and contempt. He had a "rare capacity for instant indignation," but when he became mortally ill, Acheson visited him in hospital. In return, Vandenberg viewed Acheson as "the kind of lawyer a client would like to have if one were guilty as hell." Other senators were without qualification in Acheson's black book—Taft a prig, McCarthy's partner Wherry a bullyboy.[35]

Working the Working Press

In Acheson's uncomplicated view, reporters, newspapers, and radio and television networks were gnats. They swarmed around him, determined to force secrets out of him he wanted to keep secret. They were unable to understand why

silence might be golden. While he wanted closed doors to allow a touchy negotiation to germinate, they wanted full and instant disclosure. His motive was
statesmanship, theirs the profit margin. It was an "irrepressible conflict." Worse,
American reporters usually lacked the foundation to "understand what you're
talking about." Worst of all was their indiscretion. Their transgressions had
turned policymaking into playing "poker with a mirror behind you."[36]

But reporters could be pets as well as pests. Reston gibed that Acheson saw
no difference between "reporters and porters," thinking they should "carry whatever baggage he handed to us." Reporters were also conveyer belts for leaks. He
would tell an assistant when to leak, plan how he would express his outrage when
the leak occurred, and then order his underling to "go on" leaking. Despite all his
complaints, he mostly tried beguiling the Fourth Estate with candor and wit.
Elmer Davis thought he was both more honest and funny than any of his predecessors. Reston described his first secretarial press conference as "dotted
with pungent and flashing phrases." Instead of the "breezy" Byrnes or "abrupt"
Marshall, he conducted the session like a prosecutor seizing an "opportunity."
His "eyebrows and mustache are a little fierce," but his words, though seemingly
extemporaneous, were "about as unplanned as an international treaty." Reporters
sometimes found his entertainments patronizing. He once prefaced a legal and
moral disquisition on NATO commitments by remarking, "I really hate to do
this to nice fellows." When a department press officer chided him for being "too
severe," he explained in atonement he had only been acting on Lewis Carroll's
wisdom that a little boy sneezed only to "annoy because he knows how to sneeze."
"My whole relation with the press," he told friends, was one of "baiting them
and making up. Thanks to God. I thought they were spoiled; they thought I was
irritable; we're probably both right."[37]

Evasion was useful when wit failed. Asked during the Korean War if he was
harboring information he thought it inappropriate to disclose, he replied, "We
have some information"—period. Quips might work, too. When asked about
"the devaluation of the Russian ruble," he "turned with a weary smile to his big
black reference book," glanced at the reporter and asked: "How do I know what
I think until I hear what I say?" As a last resort, he was not above browbeating.
He complained directly to reporters about the conflict between their quest for
news and his interest in discretion. He was harsh in telling them they had been
gullible in swallowing McCarthy's slurs. In short, reporters were like members
of Congress—they knew too little and asked too much. He did not mind putting
"a little bit of the fear of God" into them. It was foolish to try to be friends with
"the press" and far better to be "respected."[38]

He far preferred the "working press" to columnists. Having seen his predecessors' faces redden as they read the morning columns, he decided "religiously"
to ignore them. Alice in contrast read the pundits daily and got in the habit of
telling him over breakfast what they said, leading to a "treaty" by which "she
would keep her indignation to herself." Columnists, he thought, cared little that

their wisdom might rotate a hundred eighty degrees from Tuesday to Friday, as long as they found something to offer to equally negligent readers. Arthur Krock always tried to cause "maximum mischief" by pitting different officials against one another, doubling "his score on that play." He used "acid" in his ink and was "far more dangerous as a friend than an enemy."

While never forgetting they worked different sides of the street, Acheson cultivated his tie to "Scotty" Reston as carefully as his dahlias. James Webb felt free to phone Reston, saying, "Dean's in trouble, give him a big boost." Just as rumors were spreading at the end of 1949 that Truman might name Reston an assistant secretary or appoint him to the policy planning staff, in fact he was writing both a flattering article on Acheson for the Sunday *Magazine* and a column taking him to task over State's complaints about the press. Acheson, he said, should remove a sign Reston spotted on a desk reading: "People Are No Damn Good." He described Acheson as "testy" after the Hiss press conference, but, though he would not tote Acheson's bags, Franks told London that Reston served as his "mouthpiece."

Acheson had a far more awkward relationship with fellow Grotonian Joseph Alsop, who shifted from supporter to harsh critic over China. Then, Alsop complained, Acheson "cut" him "dead" and eliminated his access to department sources. But even when the two men were no longer on speaking terms, the Alsop brothers vigorously backed Acheson in his struggle with Johnson at Defense. His least favorite columnist was Lippmann, whom he barred from his regular background sessions and called "that ambivalent Jeremiah" in his memoirs. Even more harshly, in a 1959 letter he put Lippmann down as a "fraud" who had "praised Hitler in May, 1933, and advocated a smaller [U.S.] Army on September 20, 1941. There is judgment for you."[39]

Annoyance at reporters and low-intensity warfare with columnists obscured a high-maintenance campaign to influence both. With no domestic constituents and no power to spend money to shape congressional views, the department could push its views only through the media, at the time almost exclusively radio and newspapers. Speeches were the main instrument, supplemented by background and off-the-record sessions, where Acheson adroitly fed reporters' appetites for information and analysis. He gritted his teeth at their sense of entitlement but met hundreds in groups of two, three, or a couple of dozen (over four hundred in one year by his own estimate). On background, he conducted forthright tours of the diplomatic horizon. He opened many classified files for Beverly Smith's "inside" article in the *Saturday Evening Post* on the start of the Korean War. As UN forces recovered from the Chinese intervention in January 1951, he met eight times in a week with reporters from magazines and both major and minor papers. His assistants stayed busy, too. Webb reported that in the last two weeks of July 1951 the department passed the thousand mark in "background conferences between ranking Department officials and correspondents." In the most recent session, number 1006, Hickerson talked to Beverly Smith about

Korea. In April 1952, Acheson spoke on background with Walter Cronkite and correspondents for ABC and the Mutual Broadcasting System. He saw reporters again on 2 and 12 May. In Paris in June, he lunched with writer Theodore White and two *Times* reporters. In July, he interrupted his only visit to Latin America for an off-the-record interchange in Rio de Janeiro. Humoring all these people peering at his poker hand seemed the best way to reach the minds of the American people who, for better or worse, would at least indirectly decide the fate of his policies.[40]

A Field of "Alien Knowledge"

It would be easy to find quotations depicting Acheson as scornful of the people's role in foreign affairs, or even as a disbeliever in democracy. An accurate portrait, however, must stress ambivalence. He thought his total diplomacy campaign was necessary precisely because he knew policy demanded popular support, even as he commented privately on deplorable public ignorance. Had he been one to pore over Gallup polls, he would have found it delectable to discover that only a third of the people knew he was secretary of state at the height of the campaign against him. These were the "Pee-pul" he referred to in a 1960 letter to Truman.[41]

On this issue, we must distinguish between Acheson's statements to confidants and his *actions*, for the latter usually reflected his knowledge that policy was doomed without popular and congressional sustenance. Successful policy, he said in a January 1950 speech, depended on "fundamental" popular views as articulated by the media, churches, businesses, unions, and "all the groupings of our national life." Both officials and the public benefited when the latter were well informed and able to criticize. A critical public increased chances to succeed "in this obscure and dangerous world where one must always act on premises imperfectly understood." At times he was delighted with the "intellectual level" of public debates, as in the 1950–51 "Great Debate."[42]

But the point is *ambivalence*, for the preceding paragraph overlooks the man who doubted if the people had enough sand and understanding for the times. They thought foreign policy was "strange," he wrote in his memoirs, "a field of 'alien knowledge.'" If "you truly had a democracy," he said more corrosively in the 1960s, "and did what the people wanted, you'd go wrong every time." He never recognized that popular anxiety and frustration grew partly from the administration's constant demand that they gird themselves for a seemingly permanent international contest. The cold war "will be with us for a very long time," he exhorted them in 1951. "If we will get that firmly in mind, we will begin to get over the impatience which leads people to try to find magic solutions."[43]

As he grew older, he became more disapproving, and it seemed more pressing than ever to educate the public, because popular ignorance created nearly insupportable problems. It was the people who had insisted on postwar demobilization, rejected universal military training, and hankered for UN hocus pocus instead of U.S. power in times of peril. When they did not meddle, they lapsed into lethargy. Even in power, some of his reflections had been pessimistic. In 1950, he worried about the impact of McCarthyism on the "simple-minded," and two years later he attributed dwindling support for the Korean effort to the wish of the *demos* for things to happen "quickly and decisively." In 1954, he teased Louis Halle for hoping Americans would "approach the spiritual and moral purity of Christ, Confucius, and Buddha rolled into one." Instead, they cared about "Senator McCarthy, the race track scandals in New York, and Chicago politics." A decade later, he mocked their "adolescent annoyance" with foreign policy, one reason he was justified to speak "clearer than truth."[44]

Thus, the people represented a problem in his total diplomacy campaign. One way he might have addressed it was through television, but the state department was still hesitant about using this new medium. Francis Russell in the public affairs office received offers from the young TV networks to help him reclaim "public trust" in the department. As already noted, Acheson and his assistants warily avoided the leading news show, "Meet the Press," because of moderator Lawrence Spivak's tough and conservative reputation. While thirty-three senators appeared on "Meet the Press" between 1950 and 1953, State sent only three ambassadors and the head of internal security. Russell urged Edward Barrett to figure out a way to use TV to "humanize" Acheson and "take him visually as well as audibly into the U.S. family circle." Finally, on 10 September 1950, he appeared on CBS's "Diplomatic Pouch," where Edward R. Murrow, Charles Collingwood, and Griffin Bancroft tossed him soft questions the department had scripted in advance. When Acheson mentioned Europe, a map of the continent flashed on the screen, replaced by an Asian map when he turned to East Asia. Acheson thought the show important and stole time from intense Big Three and NATO meetings in New York to get to the CBS studio. Three months later, with Chinese forces chasing U.S. armies and Republicans eagerly hunting down Acheson, he addressed the Broadcasters Advisory Council, a voluntary media body organized to cooperate with the administration. Despite doubts about the "Pee-pul," he knew he had to repair public relations.[45]

But he acted to do so only fitfully. In November 1950, Barrett reported from department polls two-thirds approval of its policies, possibly due in part to "Diplomatic Pouch." But as the Chinese intervention grew more serious, Acheson begged lack of time when asked to do more television. Touring the nation, Reston reported a gap in "understanding between the Department of State and the people it serves." Thinking it was futile to try changing the minds of hard-core Republicans, Barrett's office wanted the department to do a better job of convincing the "average American" of U.S. diplomatic achievements. A few weeks later, when the *Times'* Lester Markel told Acheson he needed to work harder to win over public opinion, he nodded in agreement but said he could not find time to do all the things that were "absolutely necessary."[46]

In reality, given the techniques of the time, the administration's efforts at public suasion were impressive. Acheson later recounted his own effort in a letter to Franks. In 1951, which he considered typical, department officials gave 2,432 speeches; held 15 background sessions with an average of 75 reporters attending; conducted "35 special meetings" for teachers, students, and veterans; organized 2 regional conferences for "the heads of private organizations"; assembled "national leaders" in 5 "consultative meetings"; and sent department officers to answer questions at 45 "national conventions or regional meetings." During Acheson's tenure, State issued 1,200 press releases, 20 documentary publications, 70 annual volumes of "current information," and "200 volumes a year, each running 20 to 500 pages, on treaties and international actions." But even as he wrote, he must have reflected that much of this labor had been futile.[47]

Failure to shape public opinion was not the crux of Acheson's predicament in 1950–51. Nor did popular ignorance or short attention spans cause it. The uncontrollable world itself was the chief source of Acheson's difficulties. Communism's advent in China, the Soviet atomic bomb, collapsing French authority in Indochina, European economic stagnation, and NATO's slowness to arm itself—all frustrated popular hopes for "normality" after two decades of sacrifice and crisis in depression and war. Conflict in Korea was the last straw. Rather than shrink from these challenges, Acheson typically pressed for ambitious involvement to cope with them. Only in China did he favor standing pat, hoping to win the pot through the opponent's overbidding. Otherwise, he sought aid for France in Southeast Asia, dollars and lower trade barriers for European economies, U.S. troops to man central European ramparts, and German forces to help them. In NSC-68, he urged a massive expansion of U.S. defense spending. Then he urged taking the fight to the aggressors in Korea. All his projects required more sacrifice, greater world entanglement, and an indefinite postponement of normality. This left many Americans frustrated or even furious.

The administration's fumbling of Soviet espionage caused the greatest damage, allowing critics in control of the issue to distort it beyond recognition. Acheson dismissed the matter with maddening insouciance. His daily speech and body language projected a belief that those disliking his remedies were fools. Though he considered himself patient, conservative Republicans and many Democrats found his scorn stinging. For the Republicans zealous to scrub Washington clean of Truman and of FDR's infestation of New Dealers, the lordly Acheson served nicely as a target. Many genuinely rejected his expansive view of the nation's duties abroad and were horrified at its cost. If no longer avowing isolationism, they attacked the symbol of the internationalism they hated and that person, "British in manner," so many detested anyway.

They unleashed the most vicious campaign of abuse and slander against political leaders in American history. Sectors of the media—particularly *Time* and the Chicago *Tribune*—deliberately abetted them. Many journalists and editors fortified the attack through slack reportage and unfiltered reprinting of every accusation passing McCarthy's lips. A fatigued public, not especially knowledge-able, read or heard these accusations, day after day. Many concluded that so much smoke pointed toward some fire. Acheson's growing distrust of the popular forces of American democracy was unsurprising. What was he to think when legislators preposterously charged him with treason? When the press uncritically parroted the same charges? And when the people believed them?

Part IV

19

TESTING GROUND—KOREA

"So Unlikely a Receptacle"

"Never has fate been secreted in so unlikely a receptacle as Korea appeared to be in 1943 in Cairo, or in 1945 at the Japanese surrender," Dean Acheson said in 1954. Viewing even that as "an understatement," he expressed wonder "that so much of the fate of the rest of the world was going to arise out of this place."[1]

At the end of the war against Japan, U.S. and Soviet armies moved into Korea, the former below and the latter above the 38th parallel, an abstract line that would critically intersect with Acheson's career. The first Korean War, which began with North Korean tanks rolling over the parallel, caused basic changes in U.S. cold war policies. In the second Korean War, U.S. forces threw back the invaders and headed north, above the 38th parallel. The third, which started with Chinese forces smashing the U.S. army and marines above the parallel, plunged the administration into crisis, stirred noxious new effusions of McCarthyism, and put Acheson's leadership powers to the test. For a year, he labored to prevent the crisis from derailing larger strategic goals. He also seized the occasion to establish new situations of strength by arming NATO and converting NSC-68's prescriptions to realities. Setbacks lay ahead, but, within the administration, no one seriously contested his foreign policy supremacy after June 1950.

The Korean War set off historic reverberations. The standoff in the mountains of the Hermit Kingdom and the limited military means used to achieve limited and unfamiliar ends so soon after the already idealized successes of

World War II undermined confidence in the administration and eased the way for the Republican victory in 1952. The insistence on limited war also led to a constitutional crisis when General Douglas MacArthur refused to abide by the limits placed on him. Unlike in earlier, European crises, Moscow now seemed prepared to use artillery and tanks to seize its objectives, even if through surrogates. Thus, in the Korean War the United States and its allies forsook its last hopes for an east-west accommodation. Washington shifted from subtle blends of economic aid and diplomacy to the straight whiskey of alliance expansion, industrial mobilization, and rearmament. Truman and Acheson blazed shortcuts toward the restoration of Germany and Japan. Keeping the west united meant an end to the ostracism of odious regimes in Spain, Formosa, and Argentina. What had seemed localized trouble spots in Asia now took shape as a major theater of the cold war, from Indochina and Indonesia in the west to Japan and Korea in the east. American policymakers would soon see connections between this theater and that of the Middle East as well. As they grew more militant, the forward strategy embodied in NSC-68 gained ascendancy. While an examination of the first weeks of war appears in the next chapter, here we focus on what preceded it and how the two Koreas, the Soviet Union, and the United States moved toward conflict.

Reading different U.S. historians' accounts of the origins of the Korean War is like walking through a revolving door. The view on the way in was of an utterly unprovoked and Soviet-ordered attack by Kim Il Sung. With slight changes, this remained the standard picture until Bruce Cumings's two volumes titled *The Origins of the Korean War* (1981–90) pivoted back out the door with a view of the war as a civil conflict. Using both U.S. and Korean sources, he emphasized the preceding years of mutual malice and military marauding across the border by both Koreas. Each side, one sponsored by the UN and the United States, the other guided by Moscow, ardently wished the other's destruction. Koreans of all persuasions rejected the nation's permanent division. Neither, Cumings held, was notably more culpable than the other when war came. The second volume appeared just in time to be outdated and for the reader to walk back through the door. Though Cumings's view might remain accurate in the eyes of the average Korean, from the perspective of international history, new works based on Soviet and Chinese archival records revived a more tangled version of the traditional account. The newest scholarship depicts the war as Kim's invention. He took the initiative and pressed the idea on Stalin. The Soviet ruler in turn—with the moral and material support of Mao Zedong—finally gave the go-ahead to a war he would have prohibited had he known how Washington would respond. Though U.S. officials worried about the bellicosity of South Korea's ruler, Syngman Rhee, they viewed the war's origins as an act of aggression by the north rather than a new stage of a civil war. Ideologically speaking, Stalin and Mao thought in terms of civil war but fully understood that the north started the fight.[2]

Russo-American skirmishes over Northeast Asia go back to the 1890s, but the seed of the Korean War was planted in the rush of events ending the Second World War. At Cairo in 1943, President Roosevelt and Prime Minister Churchill pledged "in due course" to restore Korean independence after forty years of Japanese rule. With the war's abrupt end, U.S. and Soviet troops rushed into Korea to round up surrendering Japanese soldiers. They accepted the 38th parallel as a temporary demarcation line to avoid accidental collisions between themselves, but over three years the parallel became a de facto boundary between American and Soviet-sponsored republics, equivalent to the "iron curtain" dividing Germany. While the Russians quickly established a government loyal to Moscow and the Korean Labor (communist) Party, Washington moved to put the southern republic on its feet only when efforts at reunification failed. When the north boycotted UN-sponsored elections, the international organization (and the United States) in August 1948 abandoned reunification and recognized the Republic of Korea (ROK) as Korea's only legitimate government. Americans soon found themselves joined at the hip to the unruly Syngman Rhee. (State department officials told his overseer, army general John R. Hodge, to keep both hands in his pockets and his "gun on the table" when dealing with Rhee.) With the Nationalists falling in China and the communists seeming menacing in North Korea, U.S. policymakers, especially in the state department, increasingly committed themselves to protecting the ROK. Washington sent modest amounts of economic and military assistance but refused any contractual commitments to South Korean security. Early on, Acheson saw South Korea as a potential trading partner for Japan, whose recovery he deemed vital for the resuscitation of Asia generally.[3]

The defense department wanted out of Korea as much as State wanted out of China. Cramped by Truman's budgets, the joint chiefs judged South Korea not worth a fight and eagerly awaited the scheduled withdrawal of foreign troops in 1948–49. In contrast, Under Secretary Acheson worried about the perception of a U.S. "strategic retreat" and considered South Korea, only a little over a hundred miles from Japan, worthy of Truman Doctrine protection. In May 1947, he unsuccessfully lobbied Congress for a large aid package to keep the north from making all of Korea "another satellite state." Using other sources, the administration poured $250 million into South Korea by the end of that year, nearly two-thirds of the amount spent for Greek-Turkish aid. While Pentagon leaders still favored withdrawal, General Albert C. Wedemeyer returned from an East Asian tour to tell Truman that if Russian troops remained in the north, withdrawal would represent a military defeat and certainly an "ideological retreat." This squared with State's conclusion in September 1947 that a policy of "scuttle and run" would seriously damage U.S. "prestige" in Asia "and the world at large."[4]

Largely from concern for Japan's security, Acheson in 1946 and 1947 had shown the most interest among high American officials in supporting South Korea. After he became secretary of state, he resumed his push for engagement.

Over the army's complaints, the CIA in February 1949 thought U.S. withdrawal might spark a communist revolt in the south and invasion from the north, destroying the ROK and eroding U.S. "security interests" in Asia. (In contrast, Stalin then mistakenly viewed U.S. withdrawal as a screen to give Rhee a free hand to attack the north.) With Truman's approval, Acheson prodded the NSC to the view that a communist takeover would be "a severe blow" to U.S. "prestige and influence." In the spring of 1949, Truman told Congress that South Korea was "a testing ground" of democracy. Acheson made similar remarks to House members, describing the U.S. presence in Korea as all that remained of efforts to contain the "Communist menace in Asia." The army withdrew in June anyway but in a compromise left behind a large advisory mission.5

South Korea's place in Washington's scheme of things remained ambiguous. The Pentagon steadily resisted any promises to defend it. Acheson did not press for that, either, then considering China, Japan, and Indochina as of more urgent concern. In May 1949, he rebuked Rhee's demand for concrete guarantees, telling him through U.S. Ambassador John Muccio that such lapses in "diplomatic courtesy" played poorly in Washington. In March, MacArthur publicly excluded all mainland territories in describing the U.S. "defense perimeter" in Asia, causing the South Korean ambassador to scurry to Foggy Bottom for a military guarantee. Acheson frostily told him it was "out of the question." He still hoped to hold South Korea in the western column without taking such risks, thinking that a steady supply of economic and military aid would be sufficient. In June, amidst clashes with congressional conservatives over China policy, he undertook what became a surprisingly arduous nine-month struggle to create a strong aid program.6

The "Defensive Perimeter"

Three weeks before U.S. troops left the peninsula, on 7 June 1949, the fight for South Korean aid opened with a presidential request for $150 million. The money would go to a wide range of development projects, from electrical power to fishing and fertilizer production, the last intended to enlarge rice output needed for trade with Japan. Primed by Acheson, Truman personally advised legislators of the bill's importance. Heavyweights from State testified on the Hill, Acheson telling House members that U.S. aid would give South Koreans a "fighting chance" to "take care of themselves." But the House Rules Committee dallied, aware of Pentagon doubts and angry about the failure to assist Chiang in like manner. Exasperated, Acheson grumbled in a letter that "the all-or-nothing boys refuse to do what is possible in Korea, because we will not attempt what is impossible in China." With his department itching to issue "a blast on the lack of Congressional action," he complained sarcastically (and off the record) to reporters in late July 1949 that duplicative authorization and appropriation hearings prepared one "for the life hereafter." Prospects brightened in the autumn, when the Senate finally passed the aid bill, 48–13. Both Senate and House also approved Mutual Defense appropriations and named South Korea as an eligible recipient. Acheson anxiously awaited House approval of the main bill but did not seek more ambitious payments or commitments. When Rhee fretted again about security, he told him "to appeal to the UN in the event of a North Korean attack."[7]

Here matters stood on the day, 12 January 1950, Acheson gave his supposedly infamous Press Club speech, long a staple of speculation in interpreting the origins of the Korean War. The notoriety of the speech stems from Acheson's omitting Korea and other continental territories when describing the U.S. "defensive perimeter" in Asia. In the wake of his ostensible victory over the chiefs on China and Formosa, his main purpose at the Press Club was to outline a post-Chiang policy that recognized the nationalist aspirations of Asia and advanced a Kennanesque rationale for U.S. restraint in the region. The passage so interesting to historians was almost an afterthought in a busy month, punctuated by fifteen scheduled meetings, seven appearances before committees, and eight other sessions on China, Formosa, Korea, conscription, budget and personnel issues, and "the All-American canal in the Southwest." As the day for the speech neared, Acheson received drafts from George Kennan, Dean Rusk, and others, but each seemed "worse" than the last. So he closeted himself on the morning of the speech, distilling what he wanted to say to a few notes. Talking off the cuff, he knew, might land him in "trouble," but he wanted to "put some life" in his remarks and argue, as if he were once again "in court." Unworried "about making a slip," he carried his slender notes to the luncheon. A colleague said he spoke without notes at all, but a reporter on the scene (jammed to the walls with "standing spectators") described him glancing at "a large notebook on the table before him" as he spoke impromptu in a "calm and urbane" voice.[8]

He uttered the word "Korea" exactly five times, once in the question and answer session, almost none referring to military defense. At a time when U.S. officials still equated "war" with World War III, he described U.S. military commitments in "the Pacific." The United States, he said, would defend all the "essential parts" behind a "defensive perimeter" that "runs along the Aleutians to Japan and then goes to the Ryukyus" and on to the Philippines. This passage went so quickly that a reporter spearing the last of his dessert might have missed its import. Stressing the limits of U.S. obligations, he was announcing the administration's intention to defend nothing on the Asian mainland. Offshore, it would defend the Aleutians, Philippines, Ryukyus, and Japan. For those beyond the perimeter, he counseled self-reliance and trust in the UN. If a continental nation comes under attack, its people must first defend themselves. Although Acheson personally had minimal respect for the UN, he presciently warned potential aggressors that their victims could rely "upon the commitments of the entire civilized world under the Charter of the United Nations," which had thus far "not proved a weak reed to lean on" in the defense of "independence against outside

aggression." (Army planners had earlier said nearly the same, adding prophetically that it might assist a UN-sanctioned "police action.") In describing U.S.
obligations, he compared Japan, where "we *have* direct responsibility" to act,
and Korea, where the same was true "to a lesser degree" and where "we *had*
direct responsibility" and where the United States "*did* act." Although using the
past tense, Acheson spoke more resolutely about Korea than any other extra-
perimeter area. Alluding to the continuing House stall on Korean aid, he declared
that interrupting what the United States had already done in Korea would be
"the most utter defeatism and utter madness." When a reporter asked about
the prospects of holding South Korea against North Korean military aggression,
Acheson referred him to the Pentagon. No one asked how faith in the UN
squared with Moscow's veto in the Security Council. By chance, the Soviet
boycott of the Security Council began the next day.[9]

Obviously, Acheson was in no position to make up his own "defensive perimeter." The one he outlined was identical to previously announced, official
formulations of the NSC and MacArthur. In 1951, after being accused of inviting
North Korea's attack, Acheson remarked that the words "defensive perimeter"
referred to "where you have your rights, your bases, your forces," that is—as he
put it yet again, in 1955—U.S. "outposts" where troops were "garrisoned." He
had been so certain he was repeating settled doctrine, he had not bothered to
check beforehand with the generals. His own "guess," he said in a Princeton
Seminar, was that his speech had changed nothing, since "acts and facts" rather
than speeches were what impressed communists. Nothing he said, he commented
obscurely in 1955, had "fooled the Russians one bit."[10]

More than a half century later, what seems remarkable is how few waves
Acheson's speech made at the time. Ambassador Oliver Franks thought it not
worth a comment to Whitehall. Newspapers focused on possible Sino-Soviet
tensions, but the "perimeter" received paltry attention. Reporters, first lacking
an official text, sometimes garbled it, as did the *Times*, which barely mentioned
the perimeter in the story's thirty-second paragraph, placing South Korea
inside the perimeter. In Seoul, Ambassador Muccio regarded it as a given that
South Korea's first resort would be the UN. Ignoring the "defensive perimeter"
altogether, James Reston praised the speech as one of Acheson's "best." Walter
Lippmann, too, bypassed the perimeter while lauding the effort to divert Chinese
animus toward the Soviet Union. A few hostile statements trickled out of North
Korea, which also misconstrued Acheson's meaning, condemning him for
putting South Korea *inside* the U.S. orbit of "subjugated countries."[11]

The Press Club remarks are not understandable without realizing that
Acheson had no premonition of war. He was far more worried about communist
exploitation of "social upheaval." Putting South Korea on the unsheltered side of
the perimeter made sense if he wanted to keep attention focused on Europe while
expecting no armed hostilities in Northeast Asia. Washington's conventional
wisdom then was that any war would be global, with the Soviet Union the enemy

and Europe the prize. South Korea, bordering both the USSR and PRC, would be too exposed and marginal to think about defending at first. Whatever Acheson thought, for days afterward he and aides tacked addenda to his speech, if not for public consumption. In secret testimony on the Hill, he expressed an unwarranted faith in Seoul's ability to defend itself against any attack launched solely by the north. He also said the United States in more dire circumstances could only combine with the UN to help, but since he considered UN action implausible in the face of a Soviet veto, this amounted to a forecast of no action. He was then unaware of how war itself would change his view, but Walton Butterworth, privy to his thinking, seemed to read his mind in advance. When South Korea's ambassador fretted about the Press Club speech on 20 January, Butterworth's consoling answer was that the UN's central role in creating his country gave it a singular status. It transcended "a definition of interest by a line drawn in any direction." Acheson's reaction five months later to the North Korean attack could not have surprised him.[12]

Drifting toward the Maw

Acheson realized he had taken some unnecessary chances in winging it with this speech and afterward tabbed Marshall Shulman from the UN delegation to be his full-time writer. He remained concerned about the desultory pace of Korean aid in the House and about Rhee's inflationary economic policies and saber-rattling in Korea. One reason the South Korean army took such a drubbing five months later was Washington's refusal to give Rhee arms he could use to take the offensive. The day after Acheson's speech, the CIA interpreted bristly noises north of the parallel as "defensive" measures offsetting "the growing strength of the offensively minded South Korean Army."[13]

A week after the Press Club speech, just as Truman earmarked nearly $11 million in Mutual Defense Assistance Program funds for South Korea, the House finally acted, but not as expected. It stunned the administration by rejecting the Korean aid bill, 192–191, the first congressional defeat of a major foreign policy measure in four years. Clearly, executive branch officials had been inattentive to the reasons for the long delay. Many who voted no, including sixty-one Democrats, were reacting to the administration disclaimer of future interest in Formosa two weeks earlier and, perhaps, to Chinese seizures of U.S. properties. Acheson, confounded, realized the administration had been "complaisant and inactive" and now had "a long road back." He urgently asked Truman in writing to make a new effort, emphasizing how other nations would view this abrogation of responsibility, which had "terrified nations in Europe." He also wanted to give public assurances that Washington was not writing off South Korea.

Truman released Acheson's letter and immediately went to work. He found support from several Republican senators, aghast at the House action, and from red-faced House members eager to redeem themselves. Assisted further by South

Korean promises of virtue, congressmen worked out a bipartisan compromise, restoring most of the requested funds in exchange for postponing the end of aid to Formosa from mid-February 1950 to the end of June. This again involved the United States in the Chinese civil war, mocking Truman's claim that he had disowned Formosa. The compromise passed on 9 February, 240–134. This ended the emergency, but not before Moscow, Beijing, and Pyongyang had all had a good look at the administration's struggle to help South Korea. Acheson always thought this fracas bulked "large" in triggering the June aggression. "The North Korean radio," he later wrote, "gave the action prominent attention" and specifically noted a House member's statement that he would not pour "money down a rat hole." But possibly of greatest interest to Kim Il Sung was Truman's austere military budgeting and the army's withdrawal from the peninsula.[14]

Acheson thought South Korea itself was still a mess. He pushed Rhee to fix his government's fiscal disorder and criticized his overbearing political tactics. He called Muccio home for consultations to illustrate his displeasure. In March, he told senators he thought the strategy of limited aid was working and in a speech warned hostile parties to keep their hands off with a veiled reference to the Truman Doctrine. His absorption with NATO and Germany makes it hard to gauge how optimistic he really was about Korea, but a report from Philip Jessup in April 1950 could not have made him sanguine. "There is constant fighting between the South Korean Army and bands that infiltrate the country from the North," Jessup wrote, "very real battles, involving perhaps one or two thousand men." South Korea would be helpless against an air attack. Butterworth feared Rhee was imitating Chiang Kai-shek's fate and urged quick action to prevent such an outcome. In early May, the joint chiefs, still dismissing the Seoul regime as unimportant, resisted state department proposals for more military aid. Tom Connally, chairman of the Foreign Relations Committee, caused a ruckus with a public prediction that both South Korea and Formosa would soon fall to the communists without a U.S. response. Rejoinders from State came immediately. In a 3 May press conference, Acheson asked Connally to recant but offered nothing concrete to stifle speculation. Though Washington still held back on any promises to defend South Korea, its presence in the country grew rapidly. Large missions supervised economic and military aid, and Muccio oversaw nearly two thousand workers in the largest U.S. embassy in the world, fitted with its own mortuary.[15]

But only Muccio really seemed worried. A CIA survey in mid-May 1950 detected no signs of communist aggression or other reasons to be anxious. In fact, belief that imminent elections would reduce Rhee's personal power, and thus the raw material for communist propaganda, made the CIA relatively optimistic—and the elections turned out as expected. The CIA, officials of the Economic Cooperation Administration, the state department, the White House—all of Washington, for that matter—and Muccio in Korea itself all seemed oblivious to what stared them in the face, a rapidly accelerating civil war. Kim Il Sung began moving forces closer to the 38th parallel, undetected by the CIA, which now omitted Korea from its list of trouble spots. On 19 June, it described the north as "a firmly controlled Soviet Satellite" capable of capturing Seoul, but the agency also believed Kim would not go beyond propaganda and the "infiltration" of guerrillas.[16]

As summer began, Dulles, now a member of the administration, was traveling in Asia. On 19 June, he stopped in Seoul to buck up Rhee and tell South Korea's legislators, "You are not alone." Three days later, accepting an honorary degree at Harvard, Acheson spoke of the Atlantic community and building western strength but mentioned Asia once. On the same day (23 June 1950 in Korea), Kim's troops were poised to attack. Endless border incidents had dulled observers' sense of danger. At the last moment, military officials received a trickle of intelligence warnings, but the past year had brought so much violence and so many reports about troop movements, the new warnings attracted little attention. Not quite nine years had passed since Pearl Harbor.[17]

Triangular Decision for War

Rhee was no innocent, and the United States was not immaculate in its decisions. The conversion of a civil war into a war of one state against another, however, occurred almost exclusively because of the north's combative expansionism and Moscow and Beijing's eagerness to blacken Washington's eye, using Kim as their fist. This summary excludes important wrinkles but is consistent with the findings of a cosmopolitan community of scholars examining documents released in the 1990s in Russia and China.[18]

It is unnecessary here to reckon with all the wrinkles in the new findings, but the views of Kim, Stalin, and Mao of the Press Club speech are intriguing. Inconclusive evidence, including the recollection of a retired North Korean general, suggests that Kim reacted excitedly to a description of Acheson's speech. Mao Zedong considered Truman's recent disclaimer on Formosa a stratagem to stimulate quarreling between Beijing and Moscow and, at Stalin's request, he pseudonymously attacked the speech in print. Historian William Stueck believes the speech and Acheson's flaccid reaction to Connally's pessimism prompted Stalin finally to give his permission for the attack to Kim, who had been relentlessly pressing the Soviet leader since 1948. On the other hand, nothing was said at all about Korea on 17 January 1950, when Andrei Vyshinsky, Vyacheslav Molotov, and Mao had a full conversation about Acheson's speech. Molotov gave Mao, who was in Moscow to negotiate the Sino-Soviet alliance, a full text for study, arguing that Acheson's claims of Soviet designs on Chinese territory were defamatory. Mao wondered if Acheson was laying down "a kind of smokescreen," behind which the imperialists would try to occupy *Formosa* while sowing Sino-Soviet "misunderstanding." In contrast, his intelligence chief apparently thought the defense perimeter definition might make occupying Formosa possible sooner rather than later.[19]

Three months later it was Kim's turn to visit Moscow. Only now, in April, did Stalin finally grant leave to attack South Korea, telling Kim the Americans were now less likely to try blocking communism's advance in Asia. As with Kim, what was far more likely to have influenced Stalin's judgment than Acheson's speech were Truman's defense cuts, the earlier withdrawal of troops from Korea, Washington's failure to rescue Chiang, and even the *China White Paper* itself. Stalin must have been encouraged by having the bomb, an alliance with Mao, and new confidence that Kim had consolidated his own regime. When Mao, who viewed Kim as Moscow's servant, met with him in Beijing in May, Stalin put in by telegram that "the present situation has changed from the situation in the past." Similarly, he was referring to Mao's triumph in China, the Soviet-Chinese alliance, and his own atomic bomb. Mao thought the Press Club speech opened the way to take Formosa, and Stalin thought the Chinese revolution itself had stayed the Americans' hand. Neither seemed to put any stock in Acheson's exclusion of South Korea from his perimeter discussion.

What if Acheson *had* categorically warned of an armed American response against any attack on South Korea? Stalin's quick rediscovery of prudence after Truman did send in forces suggests that such a forthright pledge could well have prevented the war, for Stalin gave Kim permission to go ahead only after concluding it would not produce a U.S. response. But the question is moot, because Acheson could not have made such a pledge. No one in Washington then even planned to send more troops to Europe, let alone fight in South Korea. He had neither authority nor inclination to make such a promise. Nor would it have made a difference if he had not mentioned the defense perimeter at all, for the communists had surely noticed MacArthur's earlier, almost identical statement. None of the Americans—Truman, Acheson, MacArthur, the joint chiefs—knew what they would do if South Korea were attacked, and none of them anticipated the attack itself.[20]

By June 1950, North Korea, the USSR, and the PRC had long been heading toward war, mostly because Kim pushed for it, Stalin allowed it, and Mao acquiesced. Neither Kim nor Rhee could start a war without his sponsor's approval. Since only he gained this consent, Kim has primary responsibility for the war, Stalin secondarily for overcoming reservations and granting permission to Kim. The United States also has some responsibility, because it did not act aggressively *enough* to deter Kim and Stalin. And some blame must go to South Korea, for as Kathryn Weathersby points out, Rhee's "bellicose statements strengthened Kim Il Sung's case before Stalin."

Pyongyang's claim, reiterated for fifty years, that the South Koreans had been the original aggressors is false. Kim deliberately started the war to create a unified, communist Korea and received Stalin's green light after sending him nearly fifty beseeching telegrams. Rhee would have loved uniting Korea under his rule, too, but lacked the necessary resources and sponsorship. When war came, Americans first thought it might be part of a broad onslaught against the west, but Stalin sought only a local triumph and a future check on Japan, and only after Kim persuaded him the United States would not answer with force, or in time. Kim was dogged. Stalin and Mao swung back and forth, cautious and enthusiastic in turn, one usually volunteering to hold the other's horse. Eager to consolidate his revolution and seize Formosa, Mao was the most cautious. The only way to prevent the Kim-Stalin team from acting was an unequivocal warning that Truman never thought of and the state department never dreamed of. With a half century's hindsight, we can see that had they promised a forcible defense of South Korea, there almost certainly would not have been a Korean War in 1950, changing history in incalculable ways.[21]

Washington Deciphers the Beginning of the War

The next chapter recounts the first days of the war. Here we consider the views that produced the U.S. response, the power and intensity of which surprised, even astounded, almost everyone, especially Stalin. A year after pulling its troops out of Korea, the United States sent them back, this time to fight. Five months after calling South Korea a secondary priority, U.S. leaders took extraordinary steps to prevent its loss. Though officially under UN aegis, an administration that normally acted collaboratively with allies acted alone in the first hours and was ready to continue alone if necessary. What caused such celerity and force? Or, why did U.S. officials suddenly redefine the "defensive perimeter"?

"Like glass fragments in a kaleidoscope," Acheson later said, North Korea's attack sparked "patterns" of meaning in his mind. He concluded first, and mistakenly, that the Soviet Union had almost certainly "mounted, supplied, and instigated" the assault. (In time, he would get it right, that is, that Stalin could have *prevented* the war.) He also viewed Kim's aggression as an "undisguised challenge" to America's role as South Korea's "protector." Failing to meet the challenge would breathe life into domestic isolationism, which would demoralize Europeans who thought the postwar U.S. commitment to internationalism was secure. Inaction in the face of the invasion, he believed, would cause communists also to seize Formosa, Indochina, and finally Japan. All Washington's recent diplomatic progress and "big, central ideas" would fall. Since Soviet obstructionism made collective security via the UN impossible, the United States would have to frame an alternative "international system" through a network of acts and treaties, building on the Marshall Plan, NATO, and MDAP. Unless it acted vigorously and immediately, the "whole system" would crumble, along with U.S. prestige, which as "the shadow cast by power" was "of great deterrent importance."[22]

The Soviets had made a conscious strategic choice in setting off this war, and however distant or seemingly negligible the theater, its effects would ripple through the world. In the view of Acheson and the Truman administration, the stakes in Korea "were not territorial in any immediate sense," writes Frank Ninkovich, but "symbolic chips that could later be cashed in for greater prizes."[23]

Most alarming was the new willingness in Moscow to take such high risks. If Stalin was ready to gamble using force in Asia, even by proxy, he might do the same in Yugoslavia or Berlin. To prevent that, the allies would have to convert NATO from a set of mutual promises to an authentic military alliance. That would require vast increases in spending, proving the soundness of NSC-68 and the error of Kennan and Charles Bohlen, who had minimized Moscow's menace. Stalin's drastic misjudgment of U.S. and western resolve greatly worried Acheson. If the Soviet leader did the same in Europe, the result might be World War III.[24]

Although no contemporary documents directly support the notion, Acheson's reaction to the events of June 1950 might also have been shaped by personal and political considerations. Later defensive statements that downplayed the pertinence of the Press Club speech may have camouflaged a concern that his ambiguous description of South Korea's place in U.S. considerations had been a terrible mistake. It is also true that advocating a tough and forward stance throughout Asia, as he did with the onset of war, put him back in sync with associates long urging him in that direction. And however willing to flout clamorous congressmen, with the department now under attack and Joseph McCarthy in full war paint, he may have found a sardonic pleasure in playing the militant and leading the charge. As Franks cabled London on 28 June, "Acheson and the State Department all of a sudden have a Far Eastern policy and one which receives general popular backing in America." This would give them "a degree of power and flexibility not possessed before."[25]

Leaving speculation aside, Acheson was highly conscious of the broader, historical meanings of this new war. So was Truman, who wrote Bess in Missouri on 26 June: "Haven't been so badly upset since Greece and Turkey fell into our lap." In his autobiography, the president traced how the path of communism in Korea followed the road of "Hitler, Mussolini, and the Japanese." Instead of replaying the ignominious "Manchuria" and "Munich," Truman and Acheson would replicate the exercise of strength in "Greece" and "Turkey," if possible without endangering their achievements in Europe. On the eve of the war, Acheson had told senators Asia had to be a "holding operation," because failure in Europe would mean "the whole business goes to pieces." Now South Korea did not look at all like a "holding operation." The large U.S. role assisting it financially, politically, and militarily had turned it into a virtual ward, putting U.S. prestige on the line. Both Truman and Acheson went to war in 1950 to defend U.S. prestige, a vital source of strength in conducting foreign policy. If they deserted their large South Korean investment, American shares would plummet on the international market. In effect, events and their perception of them forced a shift in the Asian defense perimeter.[26]

These events illustrate the difficulties involved in trying to mark a line of "containment" between places one will and will not defend. Tracing a watery "perimeter" through the western Pacific was easy enough. It was far harder to choose what to do if areas beyond it were threatened or attacked. Drawing the line itself implies an anterior decision to abandon those beyond the perimeter, but in a contested world order, this might guarantee worse choices down the road. In such a world, not only is the state beyond the perimeter at risk, so are supposedly "guaranteed" neighbors next door, within the perimeter. Doubting the assurances of the guarantor, they might decide to relax their connections to it and make accommodations to the power looming nearby. Nations watching— both those within and beyond the containment line—might wonder about the constancy of the guarantor. Thus, what looks like a prudent effort to delimit international commitments can lead to a grievous loss in prestige, Acheson's "shadow" of power. Nor is refusing to draw *any* line a solution, for the consequent appearance of weakness might cause even worse results.

The problems confronting the United States in the summer of 1950 were as old as history itself. Not unlike ancient Rome coping with the latest encroachments of Germans, Goths, and Illyrians on the frontiers of its ever-expanding empire, Washington faced the real meaning of lines drawn in the sand, or through the water. Could it permit enemies with impunity to hover just across the line? Or like Rome, must it push them farther back by promising to protect even more states and then making good on the promises?

"An Opportunity to Show Firmness and Determination"

Several other matters require notice before turning to the first weeks of the war. The first is the "feint" issue, the common belief among Americans that Stalin meant to trap them in Korea while outflanking them in Berlin, Yugoslavia, or Iran. It was a dangerous game, Acheson thought, for an insufficiently armed west to guess where the enemy would "come through the line." For weeks, alarmed intelligence officers had pointed all over the globe, except to Korea. When the war began, they were hunched over maps of the Balkans and monitoring Bulgarian troop movements menacing to Tito. Since Germany was divided artificially just like Korea, might a column of Soviet tanks slice its way through the Fulda Gap to Frankfurt? Defecting East German troops spoke of training for an invasion. Acheson also wondered, as he cabled Ernest Bevin on 10 July, if Korea might be the opening shot of a campaign spearheaded by China against Indochina, Burma, the Philippines, and Malaya, then, a little later, against "Hong Kong, Indonesia, Siam, India and Japan." Some of this smacks of panic. Once it subsided, Americans on close inspection realized Stalin was not taking such risks. For Truman and Acheson, in fact, confidence soon replaced dread. For they now realized the *United States* could take the offensive—and take greater risks.[27]

But first they had to determine the extent of Stalin's responsibility for the fighting in Korea. Acheson immediately tried divining Stalin's intentions, wanting to give him a chance to disclaim responsibility for the attack. He quickly answered Ambassador Alan Kirk's Moscow cable squarely blaming Stalin for the war with an order to get a disavowal of responsibility out of Foreign Minister Vyshinsky. Backed by David Bruce in Paris, Kirk protested, fearing such a démarche would corner the Soviets and directly engage their prestige. Acheson insisted, noting that Moscow had not yet committed itself in public and that Stalin might still retreat to the shadows. To help him, Acheson adopted Kirk's idea to blame the war on "communism" rather than the USSR, just as Washington had done in the 1947 Greek crisis. As he waited for a reply, he told a senator the Russians had probably "stimulated" the attack, but only North Korean troops seemed to be fighting. He was perturbed with Assistant Secretary Edward Barrett's reply when a reporter asked about Soviet responsibility: "Can you imagine Donald Duck going on a rampage without Walt Disney knowing about it?" Acheson told him to "hold [his] tongue."[28]

Ironically, the palpable reluctance in Washington to blame Stalin publicly moved him at first to rush more aid and words of encouragement to Kim, even as the CIA thought early U.S. actions would cause him to remain backstage. The CIA also saw no signs of Soviet troublemaking elsewhere. On 29 June, the reply from Moscow clattered over the state department teletype. Ignoring Andrei Gromyko's claim that South Korea had started the war, Acheson focused on a carefully parsed statement that Moscow's 1948 withdrawal of forces from Korea "confirmed" its "traditional principle of noninterference in the internal affairs of other states," to which it still adhered. When Kirk asked if this meant Moscow would help end the fighting, Gromyko said his statement was "complete" and should be examined "as a whole." Acheson viewed the message and the absence of "vitriol" in it to be a "good sign" of Stalin's intention "to disengage from this operation and at least not be caught publicly having anything to do with it." Bohlen agreed. Despite some concern about a concurrent call by Zhou Enlai for all Asians to rise in revolution against the west, so did Kennan, who concluded that the Russians intended to stay out of the war in Korea "but to embroil us to the maximum with their Korean and Chinese satellites."[29]

When Franks sent his cable to London about the state department finally having a clear Asian policy, he had apparently scented Acheson's eagerness for the fight ahead. Less than a week after North Korea's invasion, he no longer believed the cunning Soviets were trying to trap the United States in a remote Asian entanglement while it set another snare elsewhere. Keeping the door ajar for Stalin (and later Mao) to back off, Washington never disputed Stalin's mendacious denials that he had Soviet military personnel in Korea or Mao's claims that only Chinese "volunteers" joined the fight. Once Acheson put aside the fear that the war in Korea would mushroom into a world conflict, he ramped up his pursuit of ambitious goals. Stalin's recoil from open involvement, the Moscow embassy believed, gave the United States "an opportunity to show firmness and determination and, at the same time, to unmask important Soviet weaknesses to the eyes of the world and particularly in Asia." A forceful response in Korea, in Acheson's view, would reinforce Soviet caution. That would open the way to new American ventures in Europe. First, however, the United States must fight in Asia.[30]

20

IN THE COCKPIT

A Week in the Cockpit

WASHINGTON, D.C., SATURDAY, 24 JUNE 1950

In daylight savings season, the wristwatch on a person in Korea will read thirteen hours later than the watch on a man or woman in Washington, D.C. The war that began in Korea at 4 A.M. on Sunday, 25 June 1950, started at 3 P.M. on Saturday the 24th in the U.S. capital, where the thermometer approached 96 degrees. President Harry Truman was flying at that moment for his first weekend in Independence in six months after making a stop to dedicate Baltimore's new Friendship Airport. Army chief of staff, General Joseph Lawton ("Lightning Joe") Collins, was relaxing at his beach house on the Chesapeake. Both Secretary of the Air Force Thomas K. Finletter and Warren Austin, ambassador to the United Nations, were vacationing in New England. Louis Johnson of the defense department and General Omar Bradley, chairman of the joint chiefs of staff, had landed a few hours earlier from a tour of Asia, carrying General Douglas MacArthur's message on the need to keep Formosa out of communist hands. Dean Acheson, whom one historian would dub "The Commissar of the Cold War" for his leadership in the crisis about to occur, had left D.C.'s heat for the weekend at Harewood Farm in Maryland. There it was as quiet "as that haven could then be" when McCarthyite "crank mail" had led to around-the-clock shifts of guards pacing around his place. "The white telephone tied into the White House switchboard was used sparingly by considerate associates, but it was used," he wrote. "Even when evening came and the busy world was hushed and the fever of day was over, the movements of the security officers changing guard during the night echoed through that small house." The "weekend began well," however, and "after some hours of gardening and a good dinner I had turned in to read myself to sleep."[1]

In Korea, Ambassador Muccio and a United Press reporter almost simultaneously sent word of North Korean tanks and troops crossing the 38th parallel, violating both international law and the UN Charter. Each message reached Washington around 8:30 P.M., but because the reporter's arrived first, the first state department knowledge of the attack came from a UP reporter calling at 9:04 in search of confirmation. Just after the department sent Muccio an urgent query, his dispatch arrived, saying the attack appeared to be an "all out offensive." This news went at once to Johnson and army secretary Frank Pace, both already beset with curious reporters. Jack Hickerson, now in UN affairs and working the crisis shift with Philip Jessup, Dean Rusk, and others, roused Acheson from bed around ten o'clock. (He had also been at Harewood when Japan struck Pearl Harbor, picnicking with the MacLeishes.) He quickly approved what Hickerson called their "automatic" proposal to request an immediate cease-fire through the UN Security Council. Since Independence was not on daylight savings time, Truman was still up when Acheson called around 9:20 in Missouri. "Mr. President," he told him, "I have very serious news. The North Koreans have invaded South Korea." He received Truman's approval for the UN move and assurances of help in dismantling the communication barriers Johnson had built in his guerrilla war with the state department. He also dissuaded Truman from returning on a night flight. Next, Acheson called Ernest Gross, Austin's assistant in New York, and Senator Tom Connally. He then went back to bed, but the state department hummed through the night, drafting orders Truman might wish to issue, lining up the Security Council meeting (Hickerson alerted Secretary-General Trygve Lie at 3 A.M.), and monitoring sketchy reports from Korea.[2]

Over the next few days, Acheson repeatedly came to Truman primed with precise recommendations, which the president usually followed. Truman would send air and naval forces to help the retreating South Koreans and order elements of the Seventh Fleet from near the Philippines to steam the Formosa Straits, aiming to forestall fighting between Chiang and Mao's regimes. He would accelerate aid to France in Indochina. He would ask the Security Council to demand an end to North Korea's attack and summon UN members to South Korea's defense. And finally he would order MacArthur to lead U.S. troops into the fight on the ground. Acheson's swift move to seek cover through the UN gave international sanction to what the United States would have done anyway. It also enshrined the principle of multilateral action that allies preferred as a matter of principle and eventually supplied a forum where they could influence American actions.

SUNDAY, 25 JUNE 1950

Early in the morning in the department, Acheson found only bad news, including Muccio's report of North Korea's "naked aggression" and "absurd charges that ROK commenced invasion." The ROK army was fleeing ahead of North Korean tank columns headed straight for Seoul and the nearby Kimpo airport. When Acheson again called Independence, Truman said, "Dean, we've got to stop the sons of bitches no matter what." John Foster Dulles and John M. Allison, director of the office of Northeast Asian affairs, who had just left Korea on a swing through East Asia, recommended using U.S. forces if necessary, even at the risk of "Russian counter moves"; they thought failure to defend South Korea might even lead to "world war." After learning Muccio had ordered U.S. dependents to leave Seoul, Acheson, Rusk, Pace, James Webb, and others met again in the early afternoon. Bradley stuck to a scheduled appointment in Norfolk, Virginia, not appreciating the urgency of events. More anxious about Formosa, he was "confident" Rhee's forces could handle the problem and contemplated no U.S. action.

This left the lead to the state department. As it wanted, the Security Council almost verbatim passed a U.S.-sponsored resolution calling for "immediate cessation of hostilities" by both sides and a North Korean withdrawal to the 38th parallel. The resolution also urged all members to help achieve these goals. The vote was 9–0, with Moscow still boycotting because of the failure to seat the PRC; Yugoslavia abstained. After more meetings, Acheson urged Truman back to Washington. Evading reporters, the president took off early in the afternoon after telling Acheson to gather important advisers for a dinner meeting at Blair House, where he lived during White House renovations.[3]

A grim welcoming party of Acheson, Johnson, and Webb met the *Independence* when it landed early in the evening. In the limousine, Truman exclaimed: "By God, I am going to let them have it!" While airborne, he had instructed the Blair House kitchen to serve a "Very Important Dinner," setting off a culinary flurry to feed fourteen men with fruit, fried chicken, potatoes, asparagus, scalloped tomatoes, biscuits, salad, ice cream, and coffee. Before the dinner, Jessup heard him say: "We can't let the U.N. down! We can't let the U.N. down!" After a clearing of the mahogany dinner table, the conference, which included no one from Congress, lasted the rest of the evening. Sitting with the president from State were Acheson, Jessup, Webb, Rusk, and Hickerson. Johnson represented the armed forces with Generals Bradley and Collins, Air Force Chief of Staff General Hoyt Vandenberg, Chief of Naval Operations Admiral Forrest P. Sherman, and service secretaries Pace (army), Finletter (air force), and Francis P. Matthews (navy).

Asked by Truman to open, Acheson offered "a darkening report of great confusion." He recounted the latest news, all worse than the day before. He offered Truman "problems" to "consider," recommendations he had developed in concert with army officials in an earlier meeting, though not with Bradley or Johnson. MacArthur should begin sending materiel to the South Koreans. The president should give U.S. air units liberty to attack North Korean tanks and planes to cover the evacuation from Seoul. He should use the Seventh Fleet as a show of strength for Stalin and to block fighting between Formosa and mainland China. He should step up aid to Indochina. The old bureaucratic battle over Formosa hovered in the room along with cigarette smoke. In what Acheson called "an opening gun in a diversionary argument that Johnson wished to start with me," before dinner Bradley had read aloud MacArthur's memo on Formosa. Acheson opposed having MacArthur visit Formosa or any other new connection to "the Generalissimo." When he vaguely suggested the UN might determine Formosa's future status, Truman added that it might also be done through the peace treaty with Japan. Still, though Acheson's wish for a naval screen in the Formosa Straits aimed partly at preventing any "provocation" by Chiang, putting it there also represented an implicit end to his long fight to disentangle Washington from the KMT regime. No one took exception to his suggestions. Nor did anyone even hint at deserting South Korea. What Bradley called "an intense moral outrage" dominated conversation, which ended around 11:00.[4]

All the chicken and biscuits of this evening should not obscure the fact that Truman's actions were historic, though none yet ran counter to established U.S. policies. Some actions he ordered immediately without pause; some he acted on without waiting for the UN. He did not delay acting by talking first to Moscow. Nor, in the manner of William McKinley in 1898, did he throw the matter to Congress, hoping to spread responsibility for the results, though he would soon wish he had. Instead, as Acheson put it, Truman made decisions that everyone understood could "lead to far-reaching consequences." He ordered MacArthur to empty his Tokyo warehouses of ammunition for the South Koreans. In a unilateral rather than UN-sanctioned move, he started the Seventh Fleet northward while leaving open exactly what it would do when it arrived on station. No one had yet proposed using U.S. ground forces, but judgments already tilted in that direction. For the record, Johnson opposed "committing ground troops in Korea," but Admiral Sherman, seeing a "strategic threat to Japan" and saying "the Russians do not want war now but if they do they will have it," wanted to draw the line against communist expansion. So did the ailing Bradley.[5]

In an interesting moment in the Blair House session, after General Vandenberg claimed his air force could "knock out" Soviet air bases in the region "if we used A-Bombs," Truman as a matter of planning asked for preparations "to wipe out all Soviet air bases in the Far East." He wanted the state department's "best brains" to draft a statement he could give Congress on the 27th, which he never did. To Johnson's prescient suggestion that MacArthur's discretionary powers be minimized, Truman said he was not yet ready to make him "Commander-in-Chief in Korea." No one discussed China except in the Formosan context, which helped account for the meeting's unity. After telling everyone to keep the deliberations to themselves, the president retired. Many who exited Blair House's back door to dodge reporters had another night ahead of drafting orders and messages. In a live telegraphic communication ("teleconference"), the joint chiefs told MacArthur to expect new "high level decisions" as soon as "military and political situations develop."[6]

MONDAY, 26 JUNE 1950

Even bleaker reports arrived Monday morning. As Kim's tanks nosed into Seoul's suburbs, Muccio worried about falling into enemy hands. MacArthur said "complete collapse is imminent." Thinking Stalin had miscalculated Washington's readiness to respond, the CIA viewed the North Korean offensive as a "challenge" to U.S. world leadership. Truman publicly warned that the United States would not tolerate "such threats to the peace" or the flouting of the UN Charter. With a hand on his office globe, he told his assistant George Elsey that Korea was "the Greece of the Far East," and that if the United States acted as it had in Greece, it might stop further aggression. "But if we just stand by, they'll move into Iran and they'll take over the whole Middle East." Letting South Korea go without a fight would cause Moscow to "keep right on going and swallow up one piece of Asia after another." Then the Middle East "would collapse and no telling what would happen in Europe." Amid Republican denunciations of his foreign policy of "appeasement," Acheson testified on Capitol Hill and spent the afternoon assembling more suggestions for Truman. Then he escorted Seoul's teary ambassador to make a personal appeal for help in the Oval Office. Acheson also asked George Kennan to defer leaving the department for the duration of the crisis. After talking to military officials, he interrupted Truman's dinner to tell him that the wretched news from Korea called for another war council. It convened at Blair House at 9 P.M.[7]

    With few exceptions—for example, Webb was absent, in Truman's "dog house" for bringing up domestic politics the evening before—this group was the same as on the 25th. Truman obviously preferred such a setting to a formal meeting of the NSC. As his advisers gathered, Rhee and his cabinet were fleeing from Seoul. When Truman heard that Americans had shot down their first Soviet-built Yak fighter, he said he "hoped that it was not the last," but in allowing Acheson again to dominate the meeting, he signaled that civilians had primacy in this crisis. There was ready agreement when Acheson proposed lifting restraints on air and sea forces south of the 38th parallel, which he later said "was as far as anybody could see it at that time." He wanted more urgency in getting aid to the Philippines and Indochina, including a military advisory mission to the latter. With a recommended text in hand, he urged Truman to make a more comprehensive statement to the public and meet with congressional leaders. On this evening, Formosa evoked some curious contretemps, with Acheson essentially capitulating to the Pentagon. He advised Truman to go on with moving the

Seventh Fleet and warning both China and Formosa against military actions. Johnson was "pleased" with this development.

But Truman now caused Acheson distress by talking about "taking Formosa back as part of Japan and putting it under MacArthur's Command." Acheson stalled by suggesting further study. But the president barreled ahead, revealing that Chiang had written him, offering to step down and give MacArthur command of Nationalist forces to fight in Korea. Truman had again stuck peanuts up his nose, and Acheson argued that the "unpredictable" Generalissimo might "throw the ball game." After Acheson said it would be a serious mistake to get "mixed up in the question of the Chinese administration of the Island," Truman retreated. He would not "give the Chinese 'a nickel'" for anything, he now said, since Chiang had already taken everything Washington gave him and put it in "United States real estate." Through a discussion that now grew nomadic, Acheson's rearguard skirmishes could not disguise that both he and the president had retreated from the January declaration of neutrality in China's civil war. Acheson now stood where his colleagues had already arrived. The next day, he told the British that communist control of Formosa would threaten U.S. security in Asia. Its future could not be settled until "restoration" of security in the Pacific.[8]

Participants were of two minds about using U.S. ground forces. They would lean toward forcible intervention, then pull themselves back. General Collins, Acheson, and Truman himself came closest to the precipice. When Collins complained about the inadequacy of air strikes, Acheson urged stronger action even if it "were not successful." Truman mentioned calling up the National Guard, but with Bradley reluctant, he stepped back: "I don't want to go to war." When Collins restated the value of mobilization, Acheson also retreated, suggesting they hold mobilization "in reserve." Johnson hoped decisions already made would stop the war. No one was yet ready to wade into the Rubicon.[9]

TUESDAY, 27 JUNE 1950

Fourteen congressional leaders held a morning meeting in the cabinet room with the president, who asked Acheson to describe the crisis. He explained that one reason they had acted so vigorously was to stave off "jitters and panic" among Europeans who feared Washington might "take this lying down." After passing the baton back to Truman, an embarrassed Acheson listened to him describe UN issues he had entirely omitted. None of the guests thought Truman needed congressional consent for what he had done. As Acheson had advised, the president issued another public statement, condemning the movement of "communism" beyond "subversion" to "armed invasion and war" and summarizing his recent decisions. Not for the last time, references to the Formosa situation provoked umbrage in London. Reactions at home to Truman's remarks remained favorable. Thomas Dewey wrote supportive letters to Truman and Acheson, and the

House of Representatives rose in cheers on hearing the president's statement. Then the House extended the military draft by a vote of 315–4, with the Senate concurring 70–0 on Wednesday. Even Henry Wallace would soon rally to the flag. On this day, also, a new Security Council resolution asked members to offer South Korea help in repelling aggression. The resolution tacitly permitted crossings of the 38th parallel for tactical purposes. Soviet delegate Jacob Malik had already castigated Lie for allowing the first "illegal" vote, but if he had now returned to his Security Council seat, Gross said, "he would have buggered up everything."[10]

Rusk and Kennan began what became a habit of assembling NATO ambassadors to keep them abreast of war developments. Kennan told them fighting would probably be confined to Korea, but that the government recognized North Korea's aggression as having broad "strategic" significance. In an important bureaucratic moment, Averell Harriman returned to Washington from Paris, where he had overseen Marshall Plan aid, as special assistant to the president for national security. Truman warned Acheson that rumormongers would have Harriman angling for his job, but Acheson actually urged the return of his old rowing coach. Harriman would help guard Acheson's back from Johnson. With a reinvigorated Kennan helping at Foggy Bottom and a shrewd ally near Truman, he had girded himself for combat with not only the communists but any foes nearby.[11]

WEDNESDAY, 28 JUNE 1950

Senator Robert Taft lashed at the "bungling" and inconsistency he thought had brought on North Korea's attack. Truman had usurped "authority" over U.S. armed forces, and someone favoring the exercise of American strength in Asia should replace Acheson. Issuing a warning that would echo for years, Taft urged colleagues to either contest Truman's brazen use of power or accept the permanent loss of the Senate's constitutional powers over war. Acheson later described the speech as "bitterly partisan and ungracious, but basically honest," but he ignored it in a press conference, which he used to brand North Korea's invasion as "the most cynical, brutal, naked attack by armed forces upon an undefended country that could occur."[12]

The results of the attack continued to worsen. Returning from an inspection near the fighting, one of MacArthur's aides said he would need U.S. troops "to drive the invaders back to the 38th Parallel." As he reached Webb's office for a meeting, Acheson learned that both Seoul and Kimpo airfield had fallen. Harriman was as at the meeting, only twelve hours after Truman summoned him. Henceforth, Acheson let him read any cables and roam anywhere he wanted, including regular attendance in the 9:30 prayer meetings. At the afternoon NSC meeting, Truman—only now willing to preside regularly—wondered if Moscow was designing other attacks and asked for intelligence on Soviet intentions in Iran and Yugoslavia. On the military front, Acheson opposed raids against North Korean air bases. Truman was more flexible but agreed with Acheson's suggestion that operational command remain in Washington in case the Russians barged in. The issue was not MacArthur but the continuing assumption that U.S. forces would quickly quit Korea in a larger war. The state department was imploring allies for help. Britain and France were busy with their own fights in Malaysia and Indochina, but Acheson hoped at least Britain could help, which it quickly did with naval units. The more "outside" help, the more the operation would appear genuinely a UN affair.[13]

THURSDAY, 29 JUNE 1950

Australia, Canada, and the Netherlands offered military and naval units, and in other good news, the Senate, after months of dithering, approved legislation for the Mutual Defense Assistance Program. In a public statement, Truman said the United States intended only to restore South Korea to "its status prior to the invasion." In a press conference, after he said the country was "not at war," he answered "Yes" when a reporter asked if it was "correct to call this a police action." Whether he so intended, he had signaled the limited U.S. purposes in the war, but the phrase would plague him the rest of his term.[14]

In a late-afternoon session of the Blair House group (now formally constituted as the NSC), Truman remarked that "the Russians are going to let the Chinese do the fighting for them." Though breathing easier about Soviet intentions, officials were already worried about China. Truman kept emphasizing the need for restraint. Officials should be "damn careful" not to suggest a war with Moscow was imminent, and, while it was essential to throw back North Korea's aggression, he did not "want to get us over-committed to a whole lot of other things that could mean war." He authorized strikes against tactical targets above the 38th parallel, unaware that the willful, seventy-year-old MacArthur had already hit them, proof of the difficulty the president would face in limiting armed action. Skittish about Beijing, Acheson wanted it clear that Manchuria was off limits but strongly favored sending troops from Japan to protect emergency U.S. air bases in South Korea. At a time when slender budgets made any use of the army risky, this was a significant step toward sending it to combat. The chiefs also still hoped for a limited role but now believed it might be necessary to send forces into the breach. Otherwise, not only would South Korea be lost, but so would the reputation of the UN and allies' confidence in the United States. Returning from his own inspection in Korea, MacArthur cabled from Tokyo for more help. Acheson favored giving him "whatever he needs to stop disaster." Truman ordered the army to take on any noncombat duties and extended authority for air and naval operations above the parallel.[15]

Later in the evening, the state department received an offer from Chiang to send 33,000 of his troops to Korea. On informing the White House, Acheson was dismayed to find Truman eager to accept. But, Acheson answered, this would provoke Mao's intervention and leave Formosa exposed to attack. Unconvinced, Truman suggested they talk about it in the full war council on Friday. "Gimo" had again wormed his way between Truman and Acheson.[16]

Friday and Saturday, 30 June and 1 July 1950

In the middle of the night of 29–30 June, MacArthur sent an urgent message to Collins asking for combat troops, because the ROK army was crumbling and unable to defend itself. Even current defense lines would collapse without Americans defending them. After a 4:57 A.M. teleconference, army secretary Pace called the early-rising Truman, who at once approved dispatching a regimental combat team. He wanted another meeting before going further. MacArthur's shocking plea destroyed last hopes of getting off easy. Acheson had just received a desperate message from Muccio when the White House meeting began at 9:30. There Truman returned to Chiang's offer, which the military now first heard about. He still wanted to accept, hankering for a way to avoid sending American forces into the front lines. Acheson was emphatic: this might catapult the PRC into an expanding war and dissolve support at the United Nations. He was elated when the chiefs joined him, explaining that the poorly equipped KMT soldiers would do no better than Rhee's and that transporting them to Korea would divert resources needed to move Americans from Japan. Truman struggled, but was outnumbered and "accepted the position taken by practically everyone else at this meeting"; thus, he "politely declined" Chiang's offer. Then he quickly made his most important decision yet—MacArthur could send as many troops from Japan as he wanted. The orders went out rapidly, and GI's headed for the fight. Bradley also asked for an urgent request to Britain for troops. In a meeting Truman held with congressional leaders at 11:00 A.M., only Senator Kenneth Wherry raised objections. Shortly before receiving congressional authority to put National Guard and Reserve forces into federal service, the president publicly announced his decision to send Americans into the Korean fight.[17]

Despite his reputation for shooting from the hip, Truman had carefully deliberated with advisers for several days before making these first important troop decisions, partly because of lingering fears that perfidious Ivan had something else up his sleeve. He moved ahead as soon as he had firm recommendations in his hands. Advisers and foreign governments alike grasped the significance of his actions. The Norwegian ambassador told Acheson "the smaller nations of Europe were much heartened." Canadian ambassador Hume Wrong told his government that Truman's decisions "should obliterate" fears of American isolationism. Acheson believed the moment "was a turning-point in world history," but his surrender to the military on Formosa deeply disappointed the British. Ambassador Oliver Franks told London the action of the Seventh Fleet would "certainly deepen the rift between the U.S. and P.R.C." Days passed before GIs entered the fight, but the war now began to escalate steadily. On Saturday, 1 July, MacArthur was empowered to impose a naval blockade of all Korea. Fears grew in London that the Americans might be thinking about using nuclear weapons.[18]

Later, Acheson must have enjoyed looking again at the memo his chief spontaneously wrote and sent on 19 July "for your record." Referring to 24–25 June, Truman praised Acheson for moving to the Security Council even before telling him about it, thus ensuring that the United States did not "have to go into Korea alone." The first Blair House meeting had been his work, too, showing "that you are a great Secretary of State and a diplomat." His "handling of the situation since," he concluded, had "been superb." "That is a very sweet and typical action of the President," Acheson said in 1954. Astute, too, for Truman understood no one else in Washington could serve him so well. They both made mistakes in the months ahead, but Acheson's performance at the outset of the war set standards for intelligent and clear-sighted counsel in national crises that have seldom been surpassed.[19]

Slippage: Truman with Congress, Acheson with Formosa

At first the nation rallied behind the administration. When U.S. forces moved into combat, *Barron's* magazine exclaimed that "the citizens of Athens, Rome, and Britain would know what we are about." American troops were fighting "in an ancient and honorable task—to stop the barbarian at the gate." Truman should have capitalized on this climate of opinion by requesting some form of congressional sanction for his actions but did not. Prudence, politics, and a sense of constitutional niceties all called for resting his actions on something other than UN resolutions and his powers as commander-in-chief. A congressional resolution probably would not have immunized him against later jibes about his "police action," but without it, he stood naked when hard days ahead led to denunciations of "Truman's war." Acheson, too, was ambivalent on the issue, but the responsibility for not gaining congressional support lay with Truman.[20]

In their first briefing of congressional leaders, Acheson—with no dissent from Truman—opposed seeking a joint resolution, fearing that delay or a discordant debate might impede decision making and inhibit future presidents. He did not want a formal declaration of war, either, because it had ramifications in international law he preferred to avoid. Because the administration was the first after World War II to face this intermediate kind of conflict, uncertainty about how to gain legal authority for waging it is understandable and so was the state department's concern about a declaration of war, which might set off popular passions, extinguishing the chance to wage the limited war Acheson and his advisers favored.

Acheson soon rued the absence of a congressional sanction. Throughout July, much to the irritation of White House aides, he entreated Truman at least to address Congress, hoping to inspire a voluntary expression of congressional support. Even though that support was then Truman's for the asking, he hesitated. At first, he wanted to wait for better news from the front. As he tarried, he noticed that even Republican Styles Bridges was supportive and that Taft had commended his energetic response to aggression. Republican elders Dewey and Herbert Hoover were behind him as well. As we will see, all he finally did, after military lines stabilized in late July, was send a written message to Congress and give a radio speech to the public. His memoirs are both defensive and evasive on the issue. In 1950, his man Elsey blamed the inaction on confusion and excessive busyness. He also thought gaining congressional backing would have been impossible once Republicans started "sniping" at Truman. Acheson reexamined this episode in later years, sometimes assuming more personal blame than was warranted, but in a 1954 session at Princeton, Harriman placed the responsibility squarely on Truman: "You would have liked to have seen it happen, but the days rolled by; the President felt it was unwise to have a Joint Resolution because he didn't want in any way to have a precedent which might take away from the President's authority in the future." Acheson nonetheless blamed himself for not keeping the president out of this pickle. At first, he thought the lack of a congressional resolution did not matter, for the Republicans would have hit the administration anyway after the war soured. In time, he came to think that a voluntary congressional resolution "would have nipped in the bud all the statements about the Korean War being Mr. Truman's war." But in his last word on the subject, in *Present at the Creation*, he emphatically returned to the view that nothing would have stopped the partisan attacks on "Truman's war."[21]

The whole episode was a clinic in not shooting straight. While Acheson's dislike of a formal resolution nearly matched Truman's, he carried out a dismal scrimmage with the presidential staff over the issue. He had given Truman the speech draft requested of him on 25 June, but the president never used it. He apparently changed his mind about needing the speech once Connally told him that if a burglar broke into his house, "you can shoot at him without going down to the police station and getting permission." Connally thought Truman would run into an extended debate, "which would tie your hands completely. You have the right to do it as commander-in-chief and under the UN Charter." Truman thereafter blinded himself to the sniper fire already being directed at him by Wherry, William Jenner, and others. Taft explicitly questioned the president's authority to act on his own and declared his willingness to vote for a resolution if he asked for it. When Wherry demanded consultation before any new "large-scale actions," Truman said he would ask if he needed "Congressional action" but hoped to "get those bandits in Korea suppressed without that." The case of Senator William Knowland best illustrates the vulnerable position he had put himself into. First agreeing that the UN Charter and powers as commander-in-chief were all Truman needed, the Californian reversed course once China intervened. He then ripped the president for leading the nation into a war "without a declaration of the Congress of the United States."[22]

In a contentious meeting on Monday, 3 July, Acheson brought along another presidential speech written by Marshall Shulman, hoping for an accord on how to wangle Congress into voluntarily offering support. Aggressively pressing Truman to offer a personal "report" to Congress that Wednesday, he read aloud the text of a resolution that would commend the nation rather than its president and avoid controversial particulars. Present was Senate Majority Leader Scott Lucas, who liked the words but not the idea, because Congress might think Truman was actually asking for a declaration of war. He also disliked appeasing Taft and Wherry, whose "attitude" made him "sick." General Bradley, too, was opposed, fearing a debate that would open too many cans of worms. The upshot was to put the draft on ice. Acheson told his staff that Truman thought a resolution was unnecessary and damaging to the presidency. In support, Acheson had the department issue a memo listing eighty-five cases in which presidents had used military force without congressional sanction.[23]

Advised by Democratic congressional leaders a week later that the best time for a message had not yet arrived, Truman grew even more intransigent about the whole idea. And when Acheson continued to press, Elsey grew angry at his "highly offensive" badgering. In a 14 July cabinet meeting, Acheson also came close to insisting that Truman approve large increases in defense spending, in line with NSC-68. Perhaps enervated by weeks of dental work, the president relented (and Acheson stopped pushing for a congressional resolution). Then, Truman finally sent a written message to Congress and gave his radio and television address. He asked for a near doubling of military funding, announced larger draft calls, and summoned National Guard units to federal duty. Careful not to use the word "war," he hinted at expanding aims by endorsing UN efforts to give Koreans "an opportunity to choose their own form of government free from coercion." What he did not do was ask permission, that is, for a supportive resolution. The mood of Congress was hard to read. Centrist Republicans Henry Cabot Lodge, Jr., H. Alexander Smith, Alexander Wiley, and Bourke Hickenlooper backed Truman's decisions without criticizing him for past blunders, while Wherry reprimanded him for being insufficiently zealous in purging the administration's "alien-minded radicals and moral perverts."[24]

Aside from the resolution issue, Acheson enjoyed a remarkable ascendancy in the first weeks of the war. This is particularly notable considering that generals normally push diplomats aside at such times. Johnson's star now sank to the earth, for pundits blamed him rather than Truman for military unreadiness. Acheson's star seemed to shine even brighter when Truman, after a week of historic decisions, nearly disappeared, becoming, as Michael H. Hunt writes, "almost an invisible man, resistant to sitting down with his key advisers." With Acheson leading with new strength and energy, Canadian foreign minister Lester Pearson in July found him "inspired by the highest motives," with "no trace of warlike excitement or boastful imperialism in his attitude, but a sober and realistic determination to press along the path which he thought was the only one that could lead to peace." With the war as justification, he pressed harder for his objectives in Indochina, Europe, and defense spending. He showed up at key meetings knowing what he wanted, and usually got it. Especially after he retreated on Formosa, even Johnson and the chiefs deferred to the state department on the international politics of the war. Acheson's assistants rallied behind him. Congressmen seemed dazed if not awed. The UN itself usually did his bidding. Considering the beating he had just been enduring, this was an extraordinary comeback.[25]

Even with rekindled authority, China and Formosa remained his bête noire. Hopes of ignoring Chiang while forging relations with the PRC had crashed. The battle cruisers on station in the Straits were an iceberg freezing the U.S.-PRC relationship for a generation. He had not anticipated this, viewing the fleet-enforced quarantine as temporary, a way to stop an armed clash and prevent a Soviet takeover of Formosa in case of a general war. He had successfully opposed using Chiang's soldiers in Korea or basing U.S. planes on Formosa, but the Straits maneuver had incensed the men in Beijing, barring them from executing an already planned invasion. Acheson was no longer indifferent to Formosa's fate. Just as Kim Il Sung's attack instantly made territory beyond the "perimeter" look vital, communist encroachments elsewhere in Asia annulled Acheson's view of Formosa's marginal value. Now there were several reasons to secure the island. For one, it was the southern flank of a war theater. Its fall while South Korea was under attack would shake the Japanese. As he later told reporters, "The danger of Red Chinese action in Formosa at the exact moment that our forces were moving into Korea was so great that elementary military considerations required" using the fleet to counter such risks. Besides, the JCS wanted Formosa as an emergency landing point for U.S. warplanes hitting Korea from the Philippines.[26]

He never admitted that politics had anything to do with his change on Formosa. But he certainly knew that draping a U.S. mantle over the island would boost congressional backing on other issues and improve the administration's public standing. In July 1950, 58 percent of Americans favored "war with Russia" if the communists attacked Formosa. Yet Acheson cabled London on the 10th of that month with a claim that the Seventh Fleet decision had no political significance. Two weeks later in closed testimony, he gibed that Chiang was again "removing the generals who are any good and putting political generals in their places." In September, he chided his envoy in Taipei for letting "Gimo" think he could rely on U.S. sponsorship. Despite such flare-ups, however, he had lost his gambles on Formosa and the PRC.[27]

As proof, Beijing and Washington now reflexively abused one another, especially in word but also in deed. When U.S. citizens still living in China met mistreatment, Washington embargoed oil exports to the PRC. Later, when Mao's "volunteers" barged into the war, the United States blocked trade altogether and froze Chinese assets. In late July, MacArthur virtually ended chances of distancing Washington from the KMT regime with a controversial trip to Taipei, where he and Chiang heaped compliments on one another. In a 27 July NSC meeting, both Truman and Acheson generally endorsed the chiefs' views on Formosa but vetoed plans to use Chiang's air force against PRC troops massing across the Straits. In August, MacArthur cabled the VFW convention deprecating defeatists who thought Formosa indefensible. Acheson was furious. So was Truman, who was already tempted to fire MacArthur but for now simply ordered him to retract his message.

Nonetheless, the furies of war drew Acheson ever closer to Pentagon thinking and farther from that of European allies. Britain still tried to cash in on its diplomatic recognition of the PRC. France and India, too, resisted Washington's line. Acheson irritably spurned Anglo-Indian mediation initiatives he thought favored Beijing. By late July, with FDR's promise to return Formosa to "China" a distant memory, he told London that Formosa in communist hands would thrust a "dangerous enemy salient" among U.S. interests in Asia. Although Truman on 1 September once more said Washington had no long-term designs on Formosa and planned to withdraw the Seventh Fleet at the end of the war emergency, day-to-day events pushed him in the opposite direction. State was now represented in Taipei by a minister rather than a mere first secretary. Heavy doses of U.S. aid poured into the island. By June 1951, the onetime "wedge" strategy enthusiast considered the rulers of China "Moscow-trained" flunkeys and "co-conspirators in the aggression in Korea."[28]

The First Weeks of the War: Portents

As the first U.S. troops arrived in Korea, a new UN resolution authorized Americans to command a unified UN force and urged members to contribute forces. MacArthur told the JCS he faced a "critical" situation. Adding to the sense of crisis, newspapers printed stories on 11 July relating U.S. plans to move nuclear-capable bombers to air bases in the Pacific. The ragged U.S. combat companies in Korea were taking a licking, falling back steadily to the "Pusan perimeter" in the southeastern corner of the peninsula. As they regrouped and MacArthur contemplated a breakout, he sent bombers far north, where for the first of several times they struck Rashin, a port city seventeen miles from the USSR. These raids sometimes alarmed the president. They always alarmed Acheson, but when State expressed its concern about this first raid, Johnson told Acheson in a letter to mind his own business. Truman, however, told the JCS to impose stricter rules of air engagement. About to pull Inchon out of his hat, MacArthur barely noticed.[29]

Fears of a surprise Soviet strike elsewhere had dwindled but not dissolved. Allies remained especially worried, Attlee in particular about Indochina, Formosa, Malaya, Iran, or even Greece. In France, pessimists expected a war with the Soviets in three months, "optimists" in six. Truman and Acheson were concerned about Soviet naval maneuvers on the Black Sea and CIA reports in July that Albania or Hungary might start a proxy war in Europe. The agency also expected European communist parties to try sabotaging efforts to help South Korea. "Throughout the Soviet orbit," it reported in August, governments were preparing for war. If war with Moscow broke out, the chiefs recommended "full scale mobilization," a diminished commitment in Korea, and first steps toward executing general "war plans."[30]

What Stalin was actually doing was another story. His mood oscillated between timidity and temerity. After Washington's surprisingly strong response to North Korea's attack, he feared a *U.S.* surprise—for example, in Czechoslovakia—and wanted to minimize chances of a direct U.S.-Soviet military clash. In early July, he removed ships from exposed sea lanes near the war theater and barred Soviets of Korean descent from enlisting in Kim's forces. When MacArthur struck at Inchon, Stalin cut aid to Kim and increased it to Mao. Unannounced, he acted to defend the North Korean-Chinese border at the Yalu River, using Soviet planes with North Korean markings, flown by Soviet pilots in Chinese uniforms. Moscow's aid was sizable—and clandestine. Eventually, some 70,000 Soviets served in the war in some capacity. Beijing garnered enough Russian aid to equip sixty of its army divisions and a growing air force. Stalin's agents spread disinformation about starting a war in Europe, with the ironic result of accelerating Washington's interest in German rearmament. Before U.S. troops entered the war, he had wired his ambassador in Pyongyang that South Korea's quick "liberation" would negate chances of a U.S. intervention. Later, he pressed Mao to enter the war with nine army divisions if UN forces moved beyond the 38th parallel. He was being both cautious and aggressive when he sent troops to his own border with North Korea, where they would be ready should MacArthur's soldiers advance that far.[31]

As it became clear the Korean crisis would not be short-lived, Acheson, thinking again of converting weakness into strength, exhorted Truman to declare a state of emergency. Sensing the mood, Franks told London the administration was now "instinctively" carrying out the nation's "high" international "destiny." Bold decisions had relieved U.S. leaders "from doubt and tension." Perhaps, but on 14 July, Acheson told the cabinet the world was in a state of "extreme danger and tension." Aggressive new acts by Stalin or a major escalation in Korea could lead to a general war they were still unready to fight. Europeans, earlier elated by Washington's forwardness, were now "petrified," fearing that U.S. resources pledged for NATO would be dissipated on Asian battlefields. Japan too, Acheson believed, was wary of its close ties to the United States. The solution to all such doubts would be a forceful arms buildup by the entire western alliance. The United States should exploit its greatest comparative advantage in world affairs by ratcheting up its military production. Acheson pressed the president to "ask for money, and if it is a question of asking for too little or too much, he should ask for too much."

Now finally accepting Acheson's strategy, Truman on 19 July did ask Congress for the money needed for an alliance mobilization. The United States would counter international insecurity by stoking up its industrial capability. This would arouse fear in the Kremlin and quiet allies' fears and questions about U.S. leadership. Acheson rejected charges that this call to action was excessive or a cause of the ensuing U.S.-Soviet arms race. Material strength was what the doctor ordered for problems insusceptible to diplomacy's softer genius. Deciding how to cope with dangers facing the United States tapped his highest powers and spirit. This was public service at its most exciting and a never-ending diet of rare meat. That so many of his decisions were sound, Gaddis Smith writes, reinforced his "penchant for fast action" and near-contempt for "prolonged, reflective analysis."[32]

An example of fast action was the summons to other nations for help. Hickerson said the department might even accept "a camel corps from Yemen." The Dutch were the quickest to respond, offering a destroyer from a base in Indonesia. Except for France, from which he expected little, Acheson wanted help from all European allies and all of Washington's friends in Asia, the latter to give the lie to "communist propaganda that this is whites fighting Asiatics." Many soon found his prodding annoying. He pushed ahead anyway, delivering a blunt message to Canada's Pearson that the American people would write off allies who did not come through. On the other hand, in return for cooperation, the United States would provide allies with the military supplies they needed. With mutters of extortion, allies began paying dues to their protector. On 25 July, Britain offered an infantry brigade of seven thousand men. In August, the Canadians followed suit with a brigade. Australia anted up a battalion of infantry, New Zealand of artillery. Other offers came from Belgium, the Netherlands, Luxembourg, Turkey, the Philippines, Greece, and Thailand. Washington parried a French offer, because it would require pulling troops from NATO's lines. By mid-September, South African pilots and crews (if no planes) joined the roll, along with noncombat units from Denmark, Norway, and even neutral Sweden and India. A few troops came from Ethiopia and Colombia. Costa Rica, Bolivia, Panama, and Uruguay promised contributions they never sent. Others sent food and medicine. Pakistan refused Acheson's requests, hinting that help on Kashmir might change its mind. The assistance as Acheson expected had greater political than military import, but by late August, 9,000 non-U.S., non-ROK troops were fighting. Another 27,000 were on the way. Turkey dined out in America for decades on the prowess of its Korean War battalion.[33]

Whether they were helping or not, some allies persistently offered unwelcome advice on ending the war. Usually joined by New Delhi, London concocted formulas usually mixing a North Korean pullback to the 38th parallel and emoluments for China, including western recognition, a Formosa settlement satisfactory to Beijing, and title to the Chinese seat in the UN. These rankled the administration enough to cause fears in London they would "drive a wedge" between the British and Americans, or push the UK "into open hostility with the new China." Early in July 1950, Acheson's remarks to Franks about such intrusions dripped acid, and when Ernest Bevin urged one of these compromises on him, his response fell just short of acrimonious. A day later, Franks said Acheson "looked well but taut." There was no way to harmonize U.S. and British preferences, Acheson told Bevin, because Washington was unwilling to "pay appeasement prices." It might eventually support a PRC seat in the UN but not with a gun pointed at its head. The hospitalized Bevin was "a little taken aback," and, as Acheson wrote, "the correspondence clearly had no future, so we dropped it." These disagreements could arouse pique on both sides. Minister of State Kenneth Younger told Bevin that "military minds seem to have the upper hand in the United States at the moment," while Truman and Acheson wanted the British and Indians "straightened out." Indian brokering, Acheson told Australia's prime minister, was causing serious "damage." Only Canada's Wrong could see beyond the squabbling. "After all," he wrote Ottawa, the Americans had acted with great clarity and power less than a decade after Pearl Harbor and had "finally ended the widely prevalent belief that the United States could stand aloof from world affairs." For his money, this was "a very welcome and almost incredible change in the international scene."[34]

In fact, the communist side also held the Anglo-Indian peace initiatives in contempt. As U.S. fortunes in the war improved, Acheson and others were not thinking about what concessions Washington could make, but what new opportunities it might find. Very early, policymakers debated whether to drive beyond the 38th parallel if the chance arose. State department officials worried about the dangers of overextension in a secondary theater, but they also felt the lure of a great recovery and victory over expansionist communism. The idea first struck the joint chiefs as diversionary and a hazardous stretch of capabilities, but with Truman now supporting bigger budgets, they changed their mind once they sighted the possibility of an easy triumph. Details on this issue are in Chapter 23, but it is important to note here how quickly the temptation arose. Less than twenty days into the war, with U.S. and South Korean forces still retreating, Acheson commented on this "explosive" matter, and Truman said in public he had an open mind about it. The policy planning staff began studies, and on 17 July the president asked for the NSC's views. Twice in August, Warren Austin suggested that the UN should not stop short of Korean unification.[35]

*   *   *   *

Not long after the disturbance of his Harewood weekend, Acheson told reporters, "I do not recall any period of four weeks in the history of the United States when so much has been accomplished." The gadfly Kennan was less impressed. About to return to Princeton, he commented disdainfully on Washington's "poorly schooled minds," deaf to attempts "to infuse mutual understanding of concept, consistency of concept, and above all sophistication of concept." He wrote in his journal in August that Truman "doesn't understand"

U.S. policy. "Congress doesn't understand it; nor does the public, nor does the press. They all wander around in a labyrinth of ignorance and error and conjecture." Inevitably, he shared his downbeat views with Acheson in a farewell memo. In a searing critique of popular bellicosity and administration policy, he asserted that Washington's insistence on dominance in Japan—which he forgot having helped pioneer—had caused the war and provoked the Soviet Union's new and dangerous behavior. He argued for reestablishing productive U.S.-Soviet relations, regardless of congressional and public opinion, which he blithely dismissed as "not really my competence." With considerable self-knowledge, he added a personal note that Acheson would probably find his remarks "too remote from general thinking in the Government to be of much practical use." Acheson agreed, later describing the memorandum as "typical of its gifted author, beautifully expressed, sometimes contradictory." It was interspersed with "flashes of prophetic insight" and suggestions "of total impracticality."[36]

Acheson probably just filed this memo. But the nettlesome Kennan was the right man to warn him against complacency, for as Acheson admitted in 1953, the United States in August 1950 "was having a terrible time with a tenth rate satellite." The scene Kennan left was strewn with potentially uncontrollable impulses. Truman usually disliked Acheson's remonstrations about Chiang and Formosa. Right-wing Republicans thirsted for his humiliation. Some congressional leaders called for a preventive attack on the Soviet Union, as did Secretary of the Navy Francis Matthews, who paid the price of being sent to Ireland as ambassador. That MacArthur was a loose cannon had been a byword for a generation. The only manageable sector of Acheson's orbit was his own department. There, except on the 38th parallel issue, peace reigned because he had retreated on Formosa, because Kennan was on a new sabbatical, and because of the war itself.[37]

21

PRODDING EVOLUTION WITH ACTION: GERMAN REARMAMENT

Germany to the Foreground

Some of the loudest repercussions of the war in Korea came in Europe, where shrapnel punched holes in the still rickety walls of the western alliance. Before Korea, the U.S. government was unsure how best to defend western Europe and had only fitfully tried to overcome the fear and complacency blocking effective action by its allies. Americans thought the demonstration of Soviet willingness to use outright military aggression would activate the fear enough to eliminate the complacency. By now, virtually all U.S. leaders thought a large and long-term U.S. role in European defense was inescapable. But—again fitfully, and gradually —they also began to believe a West German renewal could lessen the American burden. In the middle of 1950, however, they did not yet see how to make this goal acceptable to both the Germans and their neighbors. Except for a few flinty military planners, Europeans shivered at the memory of jackbooted *Soldaten* in their midst.

The Kremlin's apparent readiness to risk using armies to reach its objectives unmasked the fatuity of planning in the barely year-old NATO. Based on what little had been achieved, a new war would probably replay the conflagration just five years past, with the Anglo-Americans liberating western Europe mile by mile after using nuclear weapons to batter the enemy and the territory he occupied. The only way to avoid such ruin was to push defensive lines from the Rhine to West Germany's eastern borders, filling the intervening space with enough soldiers to deter or defeat the Soviets. But Korea at first induced among Europeans a collective "What's the use?" shrug accompanied by a Faustian embrace of a U.S. nuclear defense. Acheson and other Americans preferred a conventional buildup of European armies, but many in allied nations feared this would cause a U.S. desertion of the continent, leaving them beholden to Adenauer's Germans. If Washington would not use its atomic bombs, the allies at least wanted its armored divisions, not an unshackled Germany, to man western defense lines.

It is impossible to exaggerate how high the stakes were in Germany. Having West Germany hang around Europe on its own, playing off eastern and western suitors in a manner that produced past wars, seemed extremely dangerous. To hold it for the west had come to seem vital regardless of how Moscow reacted. Moreover, adding a "lost" Germany to the "lost" China would be ruinous to the Truman administration. In short, controlling West Germany was both politically essential and worth a risk of war with the USSR.

Reports on Bonn's state of mind from U.S. High Commissioner John McCloy influenced Washington as it moved toward this position. When Paul Nitze and Averell Harriman swung from opposing to supporting German rearmament, their weight moved others, too. Weightier yet were the joint chiefs, who insisted on German rearmament after 25 June 1950. Acheson would finally shift as well. He had been privately thinking about German rearmament while publicly rejecting it. When he finally decided in its favor, he first muffled his views in public, and he never shed his anxiety about the risks involved. As detached as Truman was from the intricacies of policy choices, he played the most important role of all by keeping his mind open to all sides of the debate. Despite his reflexive disgust with the idea, he finally put himself fully behind rearming the Bonn republic. What finally convinced him—and others—was the hope of folding rearmed Germans within a "European" army. Through this act of what historian Wolfram F. Hanrieder calls "double containment," the west would check Moscow with a new *Wehrmacht* and keep the Germans from running amok by caging them inside supranational institutions.[1]

The Korean War, Acheson thought later, had made it impossible to solve the German problem through "evolution"; instead, it would have "to be helped along by action." Allies, especially the Scandinavians, Dutch, and the Germans themselves, could not accept war plans that assumed "defending" the west at the Rhine. So the alliance needed a "forward strategy" farther east to "have any chance whatever" in a war. "This made it absolutely clear," Acheson commented, "that Germany had to be connected with defense, not merely through military formations, but emotionally and politically," for if a war was fought on their soil, Germans "had to be on our side, and enthusiastically so."[2]

The discussions swirling around Germany illustrate how seriously American officials took the danger of Soviet military power. Through the summer of 1950, the CIA thought Kremlin leaders were feeling their oats and thinking the time might be ripe for attack. Just as they had told Kim Il Sung, they told East German leaders they might never have a better chance to grab what they wanted.

Communist sources had told the CIA a massive mobilization was under way—stockpiling, military conversion of industrial plants, and accumulation of aviation fuel—to put the USSR in "an advanced stage of readiness for war." Henry Byroade, whose German affairs office had resisted rearming Bonn, would change his mind with the outbreak of war in Korea and, at Acheson's orders, began preparing arguments for putting Germans back in military gray. As creative as he was debonair, Byroade would pioneer ideas for a "European defense force" that would assuage both European and Russian fears of a rearmed West Germany. Embracing this idea for its own purposes, France would succeed in delaying German rearmament until the Eisenhower administration.[3]

Who Wanted What

Large increases in Washington's spending would be necessary before it could send new divisions of GIs to Europe, which seemed to be the French precondition for agreeing to German rearmament. NATO had only sluggishly planned for a real war. Before Korea, Washington's, if not Acheson's, complacency flowed from faith in the A-Bomb, and Truman's budgets scarcely allowed anything else. Once the Americans decided to reverse course and launch a large military buildup, they found the Europeans instead determined to focus resources on social and economic reconstruction. Despite the accretion of Soviet strength, embodied in its new atomic bomb, European governments paled at the cost of raising armies to deter those to the east. It was difficult to estimate how many men the Soviet bloc had in place. Western officials claimed a high figure of 22–25 *Soviet* divisions, but whatever the real number, Russian and satellite forces dwarfed NATO's. Even before Kim's attack, Acheson was fighting off calls (and Truman's own impulses) for further *reductions* of western strength and for new UN arms control discussions, in which he was certain Moscow would cynically make "glittering" overtures. In the Pentagon, views of Soviet capabilities gave a desperate edge to successive war plans, which mostly varied in the path and pace leading to atomic paroxysm. In August 1950, the joint chiefs gave top priority to destroying the "Soviet capability to deliver atomic bombs." Amid fears of general war during the Chinese intervention in Korea in November, they adopted war plan "Reaper," calling for SAC to defend western Europe by unloading over a hundred atomic bombs on Soviet territory.[4]

Earlier, Acheson had hoped such half-measures as the Medium Term Defense Plan would be enough to keep the Russian finger off the trigger, which permitted him to ignore European diffidence about beefing up NATO. But his confidence had begun to fade even before North Korea attacked the south. East Germany was apparently rearming under Moscow's aegis by forming a 70,000-man "people's police." The Soviets themselves downed a U.S. plane over the Baltic Sea, threatened new trouble over Trieste and the Dardanelles, and, accompanied by virulent anti-American propaganda, started a "little" Berlin blockade.

With Congress stalled on military appropriations and the Germans and French wrangling over the Saar, his optimism receded from the peak reached at the promulgation of the Schuman Plan. The more he accepted the permanence of U.S. involvement in Europe, the more he would insist on cooperation and sacrifice from the allies. An instance of each was German rearmament.5

In retrospect, German rearmament seems overdetermined. It fixed a pivotal strategic problem while slashing a line even more decisively through a country that had made trouble for eighty years. By offering Bonn a shortened path to restored sovereignty, it helped smother a possible resurgence of militaristic nationalism. Before Korea, Acheson knew only that Washington needed something better than "Reaper" in countering Soviet military strength. The war and the emergent idea of a "European army" convinced him that arming the West Germans was the appropriate replacement. He would have preferred more time to bury German despotism and nationalism and for the Schuman Plan to get off the ground, but concerns about military weakness gave rearmament precedence. Putting rearmament ahead of all the plans and devices for ridding West Germany of its recent Nazi past, as Byroade recalled, meant trying "to start out with the military first, which is very, very difficult."

These difficulties had almost nothing to do with popular opinion, for the public appeared to pay little mind to Germany and was prone to accept whatever the administration proposed. Thus, while Walter Lippmann strenuously resisted a German army he feared would be bent on "revenge," polls in May favored the step by a 41–34 edge, a figure that jumped to 70 percent favorable by August, after the administration had gone public with its decision. Where popular resistance did play a role was among Germans themselves, especially the young, who were saying, "*ohne mich*" (without me). This distressed Adenauer but also gave him leverage for the day westerners came courting for German soldiers.6

Civilian leaders in Washington understood the delicacy involved in persuading the allies to accept German rearmament. The Low Countries and France wanted more *U.S.*, not German, troops. Not trained in delicacy, the joint chiefs were prepared to ignore the plaints of a wobbly France, where 25 percent of the public voted communist, to get soldiers from a West Germany that was 95 percent anti-communist. Most west Europeans had allowed the gradual restoration of the Federal Republic on the assumption it would remain unarmed. They feared that a reversal of that assumption would provoke a Soviet attack. At the *least*, they wanted the alliance to build enough strength to blunt such an attack on its own before risking German rearmament. This would give the allies enough power to defeat a new *Wehrmacht* if the Germans turned coat and their weapons westward.7

Britain, France, and West Germany each posed a distinctive problem for U.S. diplomacy. Churchill had long been shouting the virtues of German rearmament from his opposition bench. Though Washington resented the turbulence his statements caused in Germany, British military leaders stealthily leaned his way. It was far different across the Channel, where Charles Bohlen described opposition to German rearmament as "a natural pathologic Gallic reaction." In West Germany itself, Adenauer's now-brazen support for rearmament made Acheson determined to tread cautiously. He preferred that France support German rearmament before he supported it himself. In any case, he could not do so until Truman dropped his opposition.[8]

The more the Pentagon four-stars leaned on Acheson, the more he leaned on the World War I battery captain. On 5 May 1950, the chiefs insisted the secretary of state squeeze more divisions from NATO allies and effect the "appropriate and early arming of Germany." What France wanted was U.S. troops directly opposite the Red Army and, as a badge of Americans' seriousness, a prestigious U.S. general commanding NATO. The Pentagon answered: "Yes, but"—not until the Europeans rebuilt their own armies and let Germans do the same. Thus, the Pentagon arrived at a "single package": U.S. troops and commander, more continental and British forces, *and* German rearmament, all wrapped together. In May, Truman still thought these views "militaristic," and it would take months before he, Acheson, and the defense establishment achieved harmony on the question. Acheson and the joint chiefs would separately persuade the president. The secretary of state worried that giving too much to Bonn would encourage it to play east against west and that hasty rearmament would foreshorten the breathing spell needed to develop the Schuman Plan. Crucially, the French must also come to accept the rearming of their German neighbors. At Acheson's orders, Byroade talked with the generals trying to find a less explosive, integrative solution. As late as early August, however, Acheson agreed with Louis Johnson that NATO was "absolutely hopeless." Truman remained on the sidelines.[9]

Wrapping the Single Package

Even from the sidelines, Truman made his views felt, fuming shortly before the war began in Korea about British pressure to enlarge Bonn's police force. This, he told Acheson, would "break up western European unity" and give the French "a severe case of jitters." He opposed any moves toward building "a military machine" that might for some reason join with the Russians and bring ruin to everyone. Acheson replied in apparent agreement, condemning German rearmament as premature. Using a fourth of Bonn's budget to pay occupation costs was a preferable contribution to western defense, he held, while guns-and-soldiers rearmament would divide Europeans from Americans and both the Germans and Americans among themselves. American policy now sought protection against "a German menace" through democratizing the FRG and "anchoring" it "firmly into the West by ties of organization and of economic and political self-interest." The FRG still had to prove its assured "democratic Western orientation" before it could be armed, "perhaps as part of a 'balanced' western force." The level of rearmament that might now be allowed would be too little to make a real difference. In any case, Acheson told Truman, the allies must first further develop West Germany's organic connections to the west.[10]

Despite his earlier interest in German military contributions, Acheson was now deferring his own view to those of the president at home and France abroad. He also remained concerned about the rehabilitation of the Germans themselves. But what the Germans feared were the nearby Soviet armies. FRG officials begged McCloy for permission to carry sidearms. Bundestag members, said one, caused a run on cyanide with plans "to take their lives when the Communists come." McCloy told reporters the "puppet" government of East Germany posed the same peril as Kim's North Korean regime. Trying to cool nerves, on 3 July, Acheson told the NSC the same thing he had recently told Truman: rearmament was "premature." Both the French and "good" Germans needed more time. For now, the west should increase its own military strength and even make one more attempt to reunify Germany "before re-arming" it. Washington could best ease European fears by sending one of its own—everyone had Dwight Eisenhower in mind—to command a NATO force, even if it still lacked a command structure. After Truman accepted this idea, Acheson told Byroade: "You know, that little guy is truly amazing. I think he was conscious of the fact, that maybe by making this decision, he was creating a future President of the United States."[11]

Once Truman made the next, huge, step to German rearmament, Acheson would be ready to take the lead. On a crisp 6th of July, he gained NSC endorsement of secret discussions to that end. Reluctantly, Truman approved, claiming he had an open mind on the subject. A week later, Charles de Gaulle, out of power since 1946, fractured French unity by saying German rearmament was inevitable. At the same time, Acheson tried to keep his own country's government united by asking Johnson to "find out exactly what it was the soldiers wanted," remembering that political and financial costs must not be excessive. If not yet agreed, administration leaders were now all tilting toward some form of German rearmament. Nitze and even George Kennan in the state department now favored either a large FRG constabulary or steps toward a "powerful military force." Another convert, McCloy cabled Acheson on 18 July that Bonn would be lost "politically" unless given the chance "to fight in an emergency."[12]

Within just a few days, Acheson as well as Truman edged closer to this view. On 24 July 1950, the president asked Acheson to consider putting Germans in the U.S., British, or French armies fighting in Korea, thus using "German manpower" without creating "a German army." Probably with a mental roll of his eyes at the image of Germans rumbling through Korean canyons and hopeful of far better options, Acheson simply promised the department would work harder on the subject.

In a major development, Byroade within a week of Truman's request was speaking confidently of bringing about German rearmament within a western-Europe-wide defense force. As he and McCloy worked out the details, Acheson sold the general principle to the president in a freewheeling White House discussion. Acheson gave him a choice—either slip German forces inside a European army or inside a NATO force, either one acting under a central, non-German command. As if the premise were now already unchallengeable, he dismissed *whether* to rearm the Germans as no longer the issue. Rather it was *how* to rearm them without "disrupting" the alliance and allowing Germany "to act as the balance of power in Europe." After Truman gave him the go-ahead, Acheson set to work. His own "conversion," he wrote in his memoirs, had been "quick" ("sudden" would have been a far better word) because Korea had "speeded up evolution." Though he never liked bundling them together, he already agreed with the three elements of what became the Pentagon's "single package": new U.S. divisions as the spine of a true NATO armed force, an American in command, and a rearmed FRG confined within a European force under NATO's command.[13]

Acheson was now considering defense contributions from both Japan and Germany and pushing for the decision to send new divisions to Europe, the first nonoccupation U.S. forces ever sent abroad in "peacetime." Because France still thought it "unthinkable" to rearm the Germans before their "victims" could rearm, the administration knew it would have to offer large inducements. As Truman and his top advisers cruised the Potomac on the presidential yacht on 3 August, they reaffirmed the idea of offering new U.S. troops to Europe, conditioned on enlarged allied contributions. Allied High Commissioners had already approved a West German police force of 12,000. McCloy wrote Acheson that rearmament within a European force would complete Bonn's integration with the west, the "best possible insurance against further German aggression." On 11 August, the Council of Europe's Consultative Assembly, stimulated in part by the ebullient Churchill, ignored socialist leader Kurt Schumacher's protest and endorsed rearmament within a European army. Though without legal effect, this poll echoed across the Atlantic.[14]

Rushing the decision making were upcoming meetings of the Big Three and NATO Council in New York in mid-September. The pressure gave minimal time to clarify plans, prepare Congress, or educate the public. Leaks about conversations between Adenauer and McCloy—whose single "weakness," Acheson thought, was "he talked quite a lot"—interrupted efforts to communicate administration intentions. Deadpan, Acheson told reporters that the McCloy-Adenauer talks were insignificant. Then Adenauer went public, asking for authorization to create a 150,000-man security force. Asked by McCloy to make a formal request, on 29 August, Adenauer struck a loud chord—he wanted a paramilitary organization and then units for a European army. In notes to the Big Three, he also demanded a time certain to end the occupation and equal treatment of Germans in any European army. Even more brashly, he blamed shaky western resolve for outbursts of neutralism among his own people. McCloy took him to the woodshed at this point. Fretting over the rumors, Truman might have felt better if he had known that Jean Monnet in France now considered the

United States the alliance's "team leader." "Of all the countries of the West," Monnet wrote new premier René Pleven, "it is the readiest to accept change and listen to strong straight talk." It was not "imperialist" but "efficient."[15]

Despite their converging views, the officers and diplomats still had differences. In a sense, State's determination to achieve bureaucratic unity was responsible for the single package. Tactically, Acheson was eager to carry a clear U.S. position to New York, and the Pentagon's answer was the "single package." Although Acheson agreed with each part of it, he remained troubled about its rigidity and wanted more flexibility and more time for allies to come around. While he always stood ready to insist that the United States' great power was also its ticket to lead the entire western alliance, Acheson also always knew that the allies would find it easier to fall in line when—as a matter of principle— Washington showed a willingness to *restrain* its preponderant power. Making German rearmament "the first and the *sine qua non* of the rest" was "going about the project the hard way with a vengeance," but Johnson and the chiefs "stood united and immovable." Possibly at Acheson's urging, Truman on 26 August asked Defense and State to arrive at a set of unified recommendations. With the Pentagon immovable, the result was the single package. This would produce great tension with the allies in New York, much of it the result of Acheson's hard-charging diplomacy. Although in New York he was fully supportive of the individual contents of the single package, he later found it convenient to blame the resulting alliance discord on the defense establishment's "murderous tactics." In 1950, however, he acknowledged in talks with General Omar Bradley his fundamental agreement with the chiefs' objectives.[16]

Escorted by burly former Princeton guard and legal adviser, Adrian Fisher, on 30 August, Acheson appeared before a closed session of the Senate Appropriations Committee. In his testimony, he underscored how Moscow's new risk-taking had produced a world crisis. Typically, Republicans were unimpressed. In an "angry" and "table-pounding" attack, they accused him of trying to block German rearmament. Acheson fumed at their "careless talk" on Germany. Kenneth Wherry, who Acheson thought "totally lacked humor and possessed unlimited energy," wagged his finger across the narrow table at him. Possibly realizing, as William G. McAdoo once said, that it was "impossible to defeat an ignorant man in argument," Acheson instead blew his stack. He rose to his feet and told him "not to shake his 'dirty finger in my face.'" Wherry "bellowed that he would, and he did." When Acheson started a roundhouse swing at the Nebraskan, Fisher saved his skin, wrapping Acheson in his arms, pulling him down, and saying, "Take it easy, Boss; take it easy." Tennessean Kenneth McKellar gaveled the room to order with one hand and stifled guffaws with the other. MDAP specialist John H. Ohly witnessed the affair and recalled that had Fisher not caught Acheson's arm when he "tried to slug Wherry," he would have missed him "by about three feet and probably fallen flat on his face on the floor." On his way out, Acheson told a reporter he was "going home for a stiff drink."

Sheepish, the next day he apologized to McKellar. " 'Not at all, my boy, not at all,' he said, beating his cane on the floor. 'Funniest thing I've seen in thirty years on this Hill. I'll never forget Wherry's face when he saw the imperturbable Secretary aiming a haymaker at him. Do you know what I did after you left? I called Harry Truman and told him we could pay off the national debt by putting you two on the vaudeville circuit.' "[17]

This sideshow signified the rattled approach to the New York meetings. After Truman publicly denied plans to increase U.S. forces in Europe, Acheson contradicted him in an off-the-record session with reporters on 2 September. Suggesting that Europeans might not be willing to fight, he said U.S. troops were on their way, to be followed "as winter succeeding autumn" by an American commander. Pressure for action was coming from several quarters. The Dutch ambassador said smaller NATO states would rise from their "depression" if they had a "fifty per cent chance" to defend themselves. On arriving in New York for the alliance meetings, an exuberant McCloy irritated Acheson by telling journalists the Germans should have a chance to defend themselves. Truman was now ready to go ahead, no doubt in part because he thought fighting would soon be over in Korea. On 9 September, he made it official that he would send U.S. army units to Europe. This unprecedented U.S. commitment in time of peace was more remarkable, writes Michael Hogan, considering the "burden" Washington was already "shouldering as a result of the military-assistance program, the Marshall Plan, and the war in Korea."[18]

Contemporary events in the Korean War have undeservedly overshadowed these moves, in which Truman decisively put precedent behind him. The United States would now fight in the first day of any new large war. American army divisions would engage *permanently* in European defense and, in a future war, would *defend* rather than *liberate* western Europe. His move was partly the result of previous failure to convince allies that actions already taken were adequate for their protection. Europeans were aware, too, that each arriving GI meant one less German they had to accept. As long ago as 1914, the French had understood their needs when they negotiated with Britain about placing Tommys on the continent. Asked how many they wanted, a French diplomat reportedly said: "Just one, and if war comes, we will take care to see that he is killed." In New York, however, Acheson would refuse to play this game. He wanted German company on the defense frontiers. Truman's announcement left that matter unsettled, but he had sent a powerful message. The United States would directly back NATO's guarantees.[19]

In September 1950, Acheson still felt Europeans were unready to accept German rearmament. However skeptical of the single package, he was eager to infuse current positions of weakness with German (and Japanese) power. Since any mode of German rearmament required granting Bonn nearly full sovereignty, in New York he would intensify the effort to reduce the occupiers' powers, as Washington was doing in Japan. Korea had transformed the idea of integrating past enemies as allies from policy conjectures to the foundations of American strategy. Washington would bring its recent enemies into a security system strong enough to deter its former ally.

A Bomb at the Waldorf

The New York meetings lasted over two weeks, many held in Acheson's quarters at the Waldorf-Astoria hotel. He stayed in the city from 11 to 28 September—in one siege unable to escape the hotel for seventy-five hours—except for a quick day trip to Washington for Korean business. With him in New York were McCloy, Byroade, George Perkins, and Philip Jessup. The Pentagon sent "Rear Admiral Thomas H. Robbins, Jr., known as 'One Package' Robbins, to keep watch over me to see that I never wandered from the straight-and-narrow 'one package' path." Acheson addressed the General Assembly, solemnly received UN delegates, and in Big Three and NATO Council sessions discussed not only Germany but east-west trade, Yugoslavia, China, Formosa, the Korean War, and Turkish and Greek bids for NATO membership.[20]

Promises of more financial aid and troops met general enthusiasm. Having a U.S. commander for NATO was especially effective in diminishing fears that Washington would return to an isolationist cocoon. Improving matters for Acheson was Truman's decision to fire Louis Johnson, ending what the Alsop brothers called a "great subterranean struggle" between State and DOD for control of policy and for Truman's ear. Army generals had been in near revolt against Johnson's budget-minded "bullying." Unimpressed by Johnson's Korean War performance, Truman had been thinking of replacing him for weeks, and James Webb was doing his best to undermine him both in Congress and in the White House just as Johnson himself was scheming to have Harriman replace Acheson. As Margaret Asquith once said of David Lloyd George, Johnson "could not see a belt without hitting below it," but he also lacked the ability to realize when he had gone too far, for now a "whitefaced" Harriman took the tale of Johnson's scheming to Truman. The president promptly summoned Johnson and, overriding his tears, demanded his resignation. When word reached New York, Acheson poured "a few extra bourbons" in celebration. He was even happier when Truman lured General Marshall from his Virginia retirement to take Johnson's place. The chances for diplomatic-military cooperation rose sharply. In a punctilious observance of protocol, Marshall in cabinet meetings even insisted on deferring to Acheson as the senior cabinet officer. The secretary of state found it "harrowing" to be "treated so by a revered and beloved former chief."[21]

Big Three meetings began on 12 September and the larger, concurrent NATO Council talks three days later. The other Big Two, Bevin and Schuman, arrived on the 12th, each by sea. As a chagrined Acheson recalled, each had heard of what he would propose "about the time they left their cabins." Schuman had already warned Acheson he would resist any ideas of German rearmament. On his last legs and with only seven months to live, Bevin could barely stay awake in the discussions to come. But he was amenable to some form of German mobilization and would make a turn that materially advanced U.S. objectives. In one of the few recreational breaks, he also graciously treated the Achesons to a performance of the Sadler's Wells Ballet at the Metropolitan Opera.[22]

Developments in East Germany acted against French wishes. Attended by jingoistic talk, the satellite state's new "people's police" exposed the FRG's inability even to enforce internal order. Bevin, who harbored the same fears of Germany that had long wracked Truman, reacted to the East German force by advocating creation of a West German "gendarmerie" and hoped this would preclude the need for a West German army. For their own reasons, both the Americans and French disagreed. Acheson considered the idea diversionary and possibly dangerous, because it could lead to an independent German force outside the integrated structure he sought. For his part, Schuman opposed anything both armed and German.[23]

When the Big Three convened, Acheson was unusually aggressive. As if there could be no disagreement, he told Bevin and Schuman the only way to defend Europe was from German territory, and the only way to do that was involve the Germans themselves. Abandoning subtlety, he added that Congress might cut off MDAP funds otherwise. This combativeness was not the result of pressure from "One Package" Robbins but Acheson's own concern about NATO's skeletal character in the face of what he took as new Soviet belligerence. Because Moscow now had an atomic bomb, NATO needed enough armor, infantry, and artillery to offset the Soviets' prior advantage in ground warfare. Caught off balance in Korea and in Berlin in 1948, Acheson wanted no more rude surprises. He urgently demanded normalizing relations with Bonn and putting German military units within NATO but did not suggest alliance membership itself. Speaking from the single package script, he told Bevin and Schuman he was making "one proposal." It was a fixed menu, not a cafeteria choice. Europeans could make a "head start" in rearming but not stop the Germans from joining them.

The French called Acheson's combined proposals the "bomb in the Waldorf." Truman's offers of new divisions and more financial help did little to relieve the allies' sense of acting under duress. Acheson, Oliver Franks thought, was being unusually overbearing. Hervé Alphand, a French NATO deputy, told him: "Don't push Schuman so hard. He has to have time. We will work this out." With the chumminess he reserved for Acheson, an offended Bevin said, "You've got the right idea, me lad, but you're goin' about it the hard way." Though Acheson later told senators he might have been more tactful, in New York he was like steel, throwing one of Schuman's dissents in his face with the demand for "an answer now" on German rearmament.[24]

Europeans worried that the Americans were being careless about how Russia might react to their German initiative. Having just fomented an Asian war, an edgy Moscow might spark another to block the military buildup in the west and especially in Germany. In June, even McCloy had worried about the USSR taking "extreme countermeasures." After the New York talks, when Moscow officially declared it would "not acquiesce" to a revival of the Germans, O. Edmund Clubb informed Dean Rusk that this "straw in the wind" might not be "a bluff." But in the New York conference, a confident Acheson told Bevin U.S. nuclear power would stay the Soviets' hand. What might more likely set them off was the west's general gain in strength, regardless of the German issue. While acknowledging that the Soviets might go to war to prevent the west from becoming "strong enough to resist attack," he was ready to chance that.[25]

Possibly steeled by Acheson's resolve, Bevin on 13 September braved the displeasure of a cabinet already shaken by Churchill's trumpeting of German rearmament to join the U.S. position. Having obtained London's endorsement, his support became instrumental in achieving a compromise on Germany's role. For now, however, Schuman was terrified that Acheson's impetuosity would torpedo his own deliberate and economic path for reabsorbing the Germans, a process he thought would take decades. Schuman struck Acheson as like "a very active trout which has been well hooked and which puts up a terrific battle." He never categorically rejected a German role in "European" defense but insisted it come only after full maturation of NATO, complete with a U.S. commander. France's government and its people needed more time. More ardent in his opposition in private on the 14th, he invoked a standard Acheson deemed unattainable—Germany could rearm only after development of a European force, *minus* the Germans, that could stop a Russian attack. Wounded national pride generated Schuman's insistence that Bonn not be armed while "France itself was not armed."[26]

In the private discussions of 14 September, Bevin, no doubt ruminatively chewing the inside of his cheek, returned to his fear that the Soviets might attack at the mere mention of rearmament. Acheson rejected both these fears and the idea of ending the talks with an impossible plan to "defend Western Europe without German participation." The quicker western strength grew, the greater the chances the alliance could deter Soviet aggression. If he was so eager to use the Germans, Schuman countered, he should set them to work digging a "fortified defense line in Germany." Just hearing talk of a new army was making them insufferable. He and the still wobbly Bevin, Acheson wrote Truman, were ready "to accept what we offered" but not "to accept what we asked." On the 15th, Acheson told them Truman insisted at the least on an agreement in principle that a U.S. commander would have something to command. "By the time any young Germans were available for training," he assured Schuman, "the rearmament of the French" and others would be far advanced. He cabled Truman of his worry that France would put everyone back in the 1920s, "when we were adamant in not making any concessions to the Germans who were on our side, and then yielded under pressure to the Germans who were against us."[27]

His pressure won over smaller NATO members, even though, as future Bonn defense minister Franz Josef Strauss, quipped, they too wanted a German force strong enough to "deter the Russians but not scare the Belgians." But Schuman remained resistant to pressure. During a recess, all the delegations talked to their home governments. In London, despite irritation with Acheson, the cabinet approved Bevin's wish to join him. Taking advantage of Marshall's prestige, the Americans on 17 September invited all defense ministers to join the discussions. This turned out unexpectedly, for Britain's Emanuel Shinwell felt "terrorized" by Acheson's "blackmail," and France's Jules Moch seemed to hold a gun at Schuman's back. Ambassador David Bruce in Paris was urging Acheson to placate what a French official called "the delicacy of French opinion." In contrast, McCloy, saying that American public opinion was "getting damn delicate itself," wanted Acheson to block the possibility of Soviet soldiers pushing GIs back "without German troops to help them because of a French reluctance to face facts."

When talks resumed on 22 September 1950, Acheson mainly followed McCloy's advice. He declared that for Washington to take on such large defense responsibilities, it must do so "as far east as possible and must include Western Germany if German resources were to be denied to the Russians." Moch, who had lost five family members in concentration camps and his only son to Gestapo torturers, was even less willing to budge than Schuman. German rearmament would occur only "over his dead body." He accused the Americans of playing into the hands of French communists, whose expulsion from government he had helped engineer. The best Schuman could do was say, as he did on the 23d, that he had not "rejected" the idea of the "ultimate" military use of Germans.[28]

Acheson blinked first, accepting a delay in German rearmament while going ahead with the dispatch of U.S. divisions and a U.S. commander, thus untying the ribbon holding the single package together. In exchange, he insisted that the allies accept that Germany would somehow contribute to western European defense. They also gave conditional support to Adenauer's police force proposal and agreed to what London's high commissioner, Ivone Kirkpatrick, called spreading some "jam and butter" on West Germany's "bun,"—that is, to relax occupation controls. Should anyone in the Soviet bloc misunderstand, the conference communique also warned that NATO guarantees covered the FRG against any attack from the east.[29]

Acheson sent both personal and official communications to Truman throughout the conference. On the 15th, he told him that despite the obstinacy of Bevin and Schuman, he had blown some of their arguments "out of the water." He would yet carry the day, using NATO's smaller and supportive nations to make the British and French "uncomfortable on their seats." But as arguments blown out of the water kept resurfacing, Acheson grew soberer. The lesser powers, he reported on the 20th, were challenging the idea of denuding their own territory to send troops farther east. Sensing the Pleven Plan to come, he also

Dean Acheson on the ascent, probably late 1930s or early 1940s (Truman Library).

(*Above*): "This little pig stayed home": Acheson in light suit joins others in Secretary of State Edward Stettinius's lineup of assistant secretaries of state, December 1944 (Library of Congress); (*left*): Ernest Bevin arriving in Berlin for Potsdam conference, July 1945 (Truman Library).

White House conclave, 21 January 1947; Senators Arthur Vandenburg and Tom Connally.
Secretary of State George C. Marshal, President Harry Truman, and outgoing secretary of state,
James F. Byrnes (Truman Library).

Truman congratulates the new secretary of state, 21 January 1949 (Truman Library).

Meeting with Connally, Vandenberg, and Acheson's early alter ego, Ambassador at Large Philip Jessup, before 1949 CFM in Paris (Library of Congress).

Dean and Alice Acheson with "one of the most difficult men," Prime Minister Jawaharlal Nehru (with Indian ambassador, Vijayalakshmi (Nan) Pandit, and future prime minister Indira Gandhi), October 1949 (Truman Library).

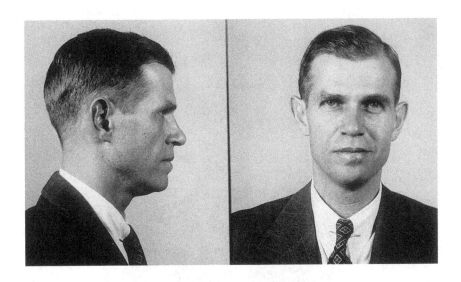

(*Above*): Alger Hiss (Library of Congress); (*below*): Joseph McCarthy with admirers, Wheeling, West Virginia, 8 February 1950 (Marquette University).

Acheson with foreign secretaries Robert Schuman (left) and Herbert Morrison (right), 1951 (Library of Congress).

(Facing page, top): Acheson's latter-day alter ego, Paul H. Nitze (Truman Library); *(bottom)*: Truman returns from Wake Island conference with MacArthur, 18 October 1950. Left to right: Marshall, Truman, Acheson, Secretary of the Treasury John Snyder (Jessup, over Acheson's shoulder) (Truman Library).

Acheson, Truman, and Marshall sending Harriman off to Tehran, 13 July 1951 (Truman Library).

(*Above*): Parlaying with Iranian prime minister, Muhammad Mosadeq, Walter Reed Hospital, October or November 1951 (Truman Library); (*below*): With Anthony Eden at UN General Assembly session in Paris, November 1951 (Truman Library).

Acheson and "my president" surrounded by photographers in Oval Office, 21 December 1951 (Truman Library).

Allies aboard the USS *Williamsburg*, January 1952. Seated, left to right: Eden, Winston Churchill, Truman, Acheson, Snyder, Secretary of Defense Robert Lovett. Standing, second from left, General Omar Bradley; third from left, UK Ambassador Oliver Franks; at far right, Harriman (Truman Library).

Eden, Acheson, Truman, Churchill, and cigar, aboard the presidential yacht, January 1952 (Truman Library).

George F. Kennan in Berlin, about to be declared persona non grata by Moscow, September 1952 (*Stars and Stripes*).

Acheson in his prime (Truman Library).

forecast that Paris would change its position within "weeks." How much these messages engaged Truman's attention is unclear. His automatic support for Acheson in New York made the latter think him a great president, but it was also a sign that Truman often simply waited for cues to do what his experts wanted. Thus, when Webb on 25 September summarized a study urging him "now" to name a NATO commander, he virtually recited Webb's phrasing in agreeing and the next day ordered a speedup of military deliveries to Europe.[30]

Those shipments symbolized the compromise involved in untying the single package. On paper, Acheson had accomplished nothing on German rearmament. In fact, U.S. policy had barely dodged a bullet when Marshall and Acheson tacitly agreed to throw the single package overboard, for otherwise they might have caused NATO to unravel. Though Acheson had not blown anyone out of the water, at a late moment he had prevented the foundering of the administration's European policies. On the positive side, his pressure for relaxed occupation controls had virtually changed West Germany from a "defeated" enemy to an "ally." Acheson himself thought the New York debates had been valuable. The foreign ministers had had a rousing but valuable argument. If not on a strict timetable, France had essentially committed itself to find a role for Germany in western defense. Paris understood it could not long appease Truman and Acheson with the patchwork of the New York conference. The French still dreaded the day when uniformed Germans would march again, but Schuman knew it was essential to deliver a plan to meet American concerns.[31]

The "Miasmic Cloud"

Defense ministers were scheduled to meet again soon in Washington. Backed by Marshall, Acheson warned Moch and Shinwell that the U.S. government would "review the whole thing" if they showed up unwilling to act on "German participation." The allies realized this meant taking a serious look at establishing Bonn itself as Washington's primary ally. The very possibility of this course would discourage stalling. As Acheson told Bevin privately, he planned to press France into "a sense of inevitability."[32]

Americans brooded about how the Germans were responding to this tug of war over their future, unaware that Adenauer himself preferred a French "initiative" on German rearmament. But the French were growing more disgruntled. Retaining cozy ties with the UK, the United States had persistently rebuffed their proposals to institutionalize a U.S.-UK-French NATO directorate, including a tripartite organization of military chiefs. So Moch had no particular reason to be gentle in telling Washington's representatives to think about the danger of arming people who would eventually turn coat, carting U.S. weaponry with them behind communist lines. Former prime minister Georges Bidault, soon to succeed Moch, told a British diplomat he resented U.S. "hustling." Having wanted to dismember Germany at Yalta, now the Americans wanted to "revive" its army.

"Where would it end?" In a speech, Schuman more mildly repeated his demand that France be "rearmed" before the Germans.[33]

As Acheson had predicted, a few weeks brought cooler heads in Paris. What he did not predict was how coolly adroit the French might be. Concocted like the Schuman Plan by Monnet (whom Acheson found "the only man he enjoyed being bribed by" because "he knew how to do it with understated flair"), the Pleven Plan seemed to offer a safe way to tuck German military power into a European army. Its obliging appearance, however, masked its true purpose to thwart that very object. Monnet and Pleven hoped to establish France rather than West Germany as Europe's dominant power, but without antagonizing Washington. Like a nuisance lawsuit, the Pleven Plan was just obscure and intricate enough to take years to negotiate and execute, by which time Paris might achieve continental military superiority. As we shall see, the plan would soon evolve into the European Defense Community (EDC), to be rejected in 1954 by the French Assembly itself. The Assembly's original support, Robert McGeehan has written, amounted to an instruction to Pleven to "fend off the American thrust" and seek "maximum delay."[34]

According to the Plan, Europeans would create an international army and then put it under the aegis of an ornate set of supranational institutions echoing the Schuman Plan. Members would consign their militaries to this force, but NATO would command it, led, France hoped, by Eisenhower. The general believed Germany's "vigorous" participation was essential to defend western Europe. The French plan would mix German forces with other armies in units no larger than battalions. West Germany's contribution could not exceed 20 percent of the whole, and Bonn would first have to ratify the Schuman Plan and renounce establishing either a defense ministry or general staff. Though attached to NATO, the EDC would report to a European defense minister answerable to a council of ministers and ultimately a new European parliament.[35]

Acheson could tell from an advance copy that, behind a facade of unity, this was a blueprint for delay, French preeminence, and permanent West German inferiority. Most Americans and Britons considered the scheme unworkable as well as politically obnoxious. Churchill foresaw "a bewildered French drill sergeant sweating over a platoon made up of a few Greeks, Italians, Germans, Turks, and Dutchmen," all confused by "the simplest orders." The Pleven Plan provided for no German air or naval units, and U.S. generals rejected the idea that its "army" could cope with the communists. Marshall called the plan a "miasmic cloud," while Shinwell thought it would "only excite laughter and ridicule" in Moscow. French officers confessed to Americans they had never been consulted on this "unsound" plan.

Acheson made positive sounds in public but privately called the plan "hopeless." Behind its terms, he told Franks on 25 October, lay a dank and pessimistic scheme. Suppose, the French seemed to be conjecturing, that the "Russian threat disappeared" over the next decade or so, leading to the withdrawal of U.S.

and British forces from the continent. The Pleven Plan would guarantee that whatever remained of NATO did not include a "complete" German army. Though Acheson did not know it, before the French cabinet, Schuman had already compared a Soviet threat that might "not loom as large over time" to a new "danger from across the Rhine." If the French "were not careful," Bevin thought, they might provoke "the Americans in exasperation to look to Germany rather than to France as the mainstay of Western Europe."[36]

Marshall said the United States would proceed with the arming of two German divisions by the end of 1951, but this obvious bluff simply exposed how thoroughly Paris had stymied Washington. The Pleven Plan also fomented enough anger in Germany to raise state department fears of a revival of both German nationalism and pacifism. Blocked by the French and worried by the Germans, Acheson thought about converting the EDC to advantage instead of starting a new and futile fight. With McCloy reporting French leaders accepting in principle some form of German contribution to western defense, in October Acheson resolved to "relax tensions." He would come to a December NATO conclave in Brussels determined to seem cooperative. But argumentative habits were hard to break. When Moch, whom Americans viewed as "complacent about the Russian threat," lambasted the Americans in a November press conference, a "very shocked" Acheson dressed down Ambassador Henri Bonnet in Washington.[37]

As westerners argued with one another, the possibilities for mischief must have seemed inexhaustible to Stalin. His government organs blared the evils of German rearmament and accused the west of all kinds of anti-Soviet perfidies. The eastern European satellites called for Germany to reunify, not rearm. When Moscow in early November asked for a new CFM meeting to discuss German "demilitarization," France swallowed the bait. Taking care to seem flexible, Acheson accentuated the negative in cables to his partners. Since Moscow's propagandistic purpose was to sow division among the allies and block the western buildup, he urged delay, noting that Russia commonly took "months" to reply to western overtures. But eventually they would have to respond that any CFM meeting must take up broader cold war issues and only after deputies' sessions to set an agenda and test Soviet seriousness. Britain agreed to this "No, unless" stance. Although France's preference was "Yes, but," it followed suit. With the replies sent to Moscow, the western partners began preparing for whatever might follow. Acheson stewed about Moscow's démarche all winter, expecting more trouble ahead. When the Chinese intervention in Korea produced pandemonium in Washington, Stalin ordered Molotov to "beat the iron while it is hot."[38]

By November, Acheson was engaged in his effort to push France into a salutary course by showing confidence in it, though he decided on this tactic reluctantly. Some of his actual impatience was on display when the Belgian government blamed communications problems for the current disagreement.

Acheson shot back that "virtually all" NATO members considered Paris's plan an utterly "unsound" solution to western military deficiencies. But, thinking that France acted from a deep-set fear of winding up a "poor fourth" to the United States, UK, and West Germany, he curbed his irritation in favor of a new approach. In Paris, as he saw it, concern about American staying power and British aloofness had revived the specter of facing revived German power alone. This is why Paris insisted on fully absorbing Bonn within a larger "European framework" before permitting rearmament. Acheson decided to boost France's hopes by demonstrating strong U.S. backing for its long-term objectives. Once more, he had decided that reassuring France was the formula for success.[39]

Adenauer's effrontery in criticizing the Pleven Plan also influenced his turn to France. Refusing to accept treatment as a second-class ally, the German leader publicly demanded equality in size of units, equipment, and policymaking. Acheson pointed to this "dangerous drift of German opinion" in making a "fresh personal approach" to Schuman on 29 November in a bid to end their own dispute. He entreated Schuman to embrace terms Charles Spofford was crafting as chair of NATO's Council of Deputies. Categorically abandoning the single package, Spofford recommended exchanging the new U.S. divisions and U.S. commander for a French commitment to the *principle* of German rearmament. But Paris would also have to accept the preliminary organization of German regimental combat teams (about half a division) that would report directly to the NATO command. In the meantime, negotiators would work out plans for a European defense force. Reminding Schuman of Washington's strong backing of European integration, Acheson asked him to take the lead in bringing it about. French leadership could create "a rallying point" for all Europe as it mobilized to defend fundamental values and traditions against "Communist nihilism and Soviet imperialism." Nothing could better guard against "another dangerous German aberration." Without committing himself, Schuman used the note to persuade his cabinet that Acheson would bend no further.[40]

Schuman was getting rougher signals from the British, who detested the Pleven Plan but whose partnership was vital to counterbalance West German power on the continent. The Labor government bridled at U.S. pressure to join all European groupings but decided not to fight "Pleven" head-on for fear the Americans would then quit Europe in disgust. In a need to appease both the United States and the UK, France accepted the Spofford plan in December 1950, though still hoping to postpone actual German rearmament.

The "Spofford Plan" was understood as a Franco-American compromise. Spofford's assistant, Theodore Achilles, considered it a two-track method to enlist the Germans militarily while accommodating French insistence on strong "political conditions." When Adenauer now criticized the Spofford Plan, Acheson wrote it down in his little black book and told Robert Lovett (returned to government as Marshall's under secretary) the time had come to "put the German matter in ice for a little while" and let the Germans "stew." It might take months to plan a unified military force and decide long-term NATO relations with Bonn. Bargaining simultaneously with Adenauer would cause "everything" to "go to pieces." The Big Three should first speak as one before offering anything concrete to the FRG.[41]

Acheson flew on 17 December to Brussels. Both British and French officials thought he looked "under strain." It was not because of politics at home but bad news from Korea and qualms about a new CFM. With Bevin counseling delay, Schuman doggedly sifted for flaws in "Spofford." Showing that U.S. leadership had not diminished because of problems in Korea, Acheson pressed hard for decision. After five days, the allies reaffirmed the Spofford Plan and procedures for implementing it through two parallel sets of talks. The high commissioners in Petersberg, overlooking the Rhine outside Bonn, would negotiate with Adenauer on establishing German military units. In Paris, France and other continental states, with the United States, UK, and Canada as observers, would work on the European defense force. In a bit of theater, the NATO Council asked Truman to name Dwight Eisenhower commander of whatever force was established. Acheson relayed the message to a waiting president, who announced the appointment as the promptbook said.[42]

Given the problems dividing the alliance, Brussels was a modest triumph, allowing Acheson's colleagues at Foggy Bottom to giggle when they heard Bevin had called him aside to say: "If they sack you, laddie, I've got a place for you." But everyone left Brussels seeing what they wanted to see. Americans thought they had a mandate to plan for German rearmament, while the French believed they saw further opportunities for delay. What they *had* clearly agreed to was the priority of military over economic and political issues. France immediately pledged three army divisions to Eisenhower's command, Adenauer began talking to the commissioners, and Truman announced a shift from civilian to military aid to Europe. Congress followed suit, closing down the Marshall Plan in favor of the Mutual Security Program. Economic aid to Europe plunged from around $1.4 billion in mid-1949 to $750 million two years later. Military assistance rose from zero to about $750 million in mid-1951, peaking at nearly $2 billion a year later.[43]

Though not gaining everything he wanted, Acheson had moved the alliance toward a strategy of armed strength, and allies had agreed to a centralized NATO headquarters. As in New York, Acheson had acted more bluntly than usual, applying pressure rather than massaging Europeans' sensitivities. Armaments and schemes to organize them into usable masses of force moved to the foreground of his vision as psychology receded. He acted on his belief, as he later put it, that "in the final analysis, the United States was the locomotive at the head of mankind, and the rest of the world was the caboose." (Ironically, before long, resentment of these tough tactics would supply another seed for European unification.) At home, Acheson moved against members of Truman's staff who wanted a new presidential initiative on arms control, which he considered ill timed. When Truman went ahead with plans for an arms control speech at the

UN in late October, "noisy objections" from State and Defense eviscerated all but an innocuous paragraph on the subject. The president himself invoked Acheson's mood in December, when he told British prime minister Clement Attlee that the French would "be gobbled up" if they did not cooperate in the face of the Soviets' "grave menace."[44]

* * * *

Did Washington overplay its hand promoting German rearmament? Did it help militarize the cold war in doing so? Did excessive eagerness for German arms give Adenauer too much bargaining power? Did pressure on allies needlessly broach an alliance crisis? All are legitimate questions. But if Bonn gained too much leverage, it was not wielded harmfully. Its eventual advent as a NATO partner was orderly and negotiated, agreed to during the Eisenhower administration by a France, freed of Indochina, that had thrown off many of its fears. Criticisms about excessive pressure are more just, though it is hard to envision the Europeans staging a serious military buildup otherwise. The Americans clearly understood that deterring the Soviets in the foreseeable future was primarily a task for U.S. power, nuclear in the short run and political and industrial in the long. Even so, Acheson had led the United States in provoking one of the roughest moments in NATO history by being so urgent about German rearmament. Despite his remark about "murderous tactics," he made no apologies for executing them. Though he later thought he might have acted more astutely in New York, he also believed "we did the right thing."[45]

His "mission accomplished," Acheson returned safely to Washington after a scary takeoff from a fog-enshrouded, ice-crusted Brussels runway. He would soon have similar takeoffs while rallying western allies. He knew creating "a position of power" would come neither quickly nor easily. "Constancy of purpose" was essential in building the alliance, he told an audience of African-American women in November 1950. It would take "year after year after year of effort" and of "being faithful to your allies and to our friends." It would take "the greatest patience, the greatest courage, the greatest determination, to carry this forward." Germany had strained Acheson's normal dexterity in the care and feeding of allies. Before long, so would Korea.[46]

22

ACCELERATION FROM A RUNNING START

Pedal to the Metal

Everything changed after Korea.

This is a hoary interpretive truism. The most prominent example usually given is Washington's hip-deep, first immersion in the Big Muddy of Indochina. The U.S. government brought a new urgency to the cold war. It was stimulated to rearm Germany. It supplanted economic with military aid, launched a large buildup of nuclear and conventional forces, enrolled Turkey and Greece in NATO, intensified economic warfare against its foes, shelved hopes for normal relations with China, and scurried to complete a peace treaty with Japan. Soon it made defense commitments to South Korea, Formosa, the Philippines, Australia, and New Zealand. It pressed cold war views on hemispheric governments and moved toward a military alliance with Pakistan. It became "increasingly necessary," wrote the state department's Jack McFall, to "pursue the cold war on all fronts."[1]

Yet in each case, policymakers were poised for these changes before the onset of war. They had crept toward German rearmament for a year and had anticipated phasing out the Marshall Plan since passage of the MDAP. Acheson had already surrendered his effort to forge ties with the PRC and was contesting the Pentagon over a Japanese peace treaty. The U.S. military buildup had been envisioned in NSC-68 and was begun late in 1949. Truman had already decided to make the H-Bomb, and Acheson was on the hustings early in 1950 propagating his message of "Total Diplomacy." The Korean War did not signal a radical turn in the cold war, but it finally enlisted Truman as a participant in a more mobilized approach to it. The war also brought about a more complete and conscious public backing of the mobilization. Having already acquired the keys to a speedier vehicle, Korea caused American leaders to put pedal to the metal.

Related events will appear in later chapters. Here we will examine this acceleration from a running start in connection with several military and economic issues, including the search for overseas bases that led to forging diplomatic ties with Francisco Franco's pariah regime in Spain.

"It Would Not Be Too Much"

Acheson said in 1953 that Korea "moved a great many things" from "theory" to reality and "urgency." Hopes of a cold war settlement through negotiations fell further by the wayside. His top priority was now to amass tangible signs of power, with economics and politics relegated to the new vehicle's backseat. He did not seem to be dismayed that this change in emphasis diminished the role of diplomacy, thus at least potentially trimming the influence of the state department. The president as a rule now attended NSC meetings. With Marshall as defense secretary, both Truman and Acheson worked more easily with the military, Douglas MacArthur excepted. Averell Harriman's presence in the White House bolstered Truman's confidence, too, as did the performance of his new CIA and AEC heads, Walter Bedell Smith and N. Gordon Dean. Acheson now shared his chief with more braves than earlier but liked the new shape of the administration and his improved ties with the Pentagon.[2]

These men and their chief knew their country still had at least ten times the 165 atomic warheads forecast for Moscow in 1953, and an air force to deliver them. If the NATO buildup worked, the alliance might eventually have enough ground forces to deter a Soviet invasion across the iron curtain. But now their optimism faded when they ran their fingers down columns comparing communist and western tanks, planes, and infantrymen. Anxiety still outweighed confidence among U.S. officials late in 1950. If Moscow had unwittingly started a world crisis in Korea, it might set off an even larger war by misreckoning western determination. The Chinese intervention in Korea deepened Washington's pessimism. Truman wrote in his diary: "It looks like World War III is here." The CIA thought the Soviets would pursue their militant strategy "regardless of the possibility that global war may result" and might already have "decided to precipitate" it. Even the increased military spending he was urging on the president, Acheson thought, might not avert a new world war.[3]

But, as he told reporters on background in January 1951, he did not think the situation so bad to justify the increasingly common and hallucinatory calls to have it out for good with the Russians in a preventive war. Even "victory," he warned, would be a "great tragedy." The commandant of the Air War College said in public his pilots could "break up Russia's five A-bomb nests in a week." As noted earlier, navy secretary Francis P. Matthews also expressed his preference for preventive war. The air force chief of staff summarily "retired" the commandant, and Truman and Acheson publicly chastised Matthews before exiling him to Ireland. "If we were going to have any kind of preventive war," Acheson recalled, it would be better to "have it with Ireland." The west, he held, should be working to nullify Soviet leaders' capacity for aggression rather than make a frenzied decision to whip the USSR now. Committed to patience by doctrine, they were unlikely to jeopardize their own regime with a risky attempt to preempt the western buildup. While Acheson thought the best way to meet Stalin's challenge was to amass power and wait him out, he also acknowledged that his favored strategy was risky, telling the Canadian ambassador several months later that "vigorous counteraction" could be the Soviet response to "any program of build-up."[4]

The buildup Acheson wanted was soon under way, with announcements on plans to double the size of American forces and requests for major MDAP increases. The nation hugely multiplied its stock of atomic and hydrogen bombs, as well as tactical nuclear weapons for stopping any Soviet invasion of West Germany. Among those applauding was Columbia University president Dwight Eisenhower. Convinced that Korea had confirmed NSC-68's "analysis" and proved its "thesis," Acheson at last gained Truman's endorsement of the paper. It was probably Paul Nitze, not Acheson, who said in a Princeton seminar, "Korea came along and saved us," but the secretary of state agreed and told Lester Pearson he thought Korea would draw enough public support to advance rearmament.[5]

But in fact, Truman's rearguard forays against an NSC-68 budget had not ended, and he slowed mobilization when victory in Korea seemed in sight. On 29 September, he approved the paper (now NSC-68/2) as a policy map for the next four to five years, but he still banned public talk about it or any mention of funds. (The paper itself evolved further into NSC-68/3, in which sweaty ideological passages gave way to cool blueprints on the destinations of new appropriations.) With Nitze pushing relentlessly for greater spending and a larger military, Acheson in Truman's presence faced off with the budget bureau and the still-timid chiefs on 23 November 1950. "It would not be too much," he said, "if we had all the troops that the military want. If we had all the things that our European allies want it would not be too much. If we had the equipment to call out the reserves it would not be too much. If we had a system for full mobilization it would not be too much." Encouraged by his economic adviser, Leon Keyserling, who thought the economy could sustain national mobilization, Truman on 14 December finally ordered NSC-68 implemented and two days later declared a national emergency. By June 1951, he had been thoroughly converted and told a press conference it would be a disaster to slow down the arms buildup because of new Korean peace talks. Americans, he added in September, should stick to their "knitting and go ahead with the defense program."[6]

Even after China intervened, the administration's worries were not about having enough resources for the fight in Korea. The grave danger facing the west was the Soviet Union's own buildup, now encompassing nuclear weapons. The authors of NSC-68 expected the point of "maximum danger"—that is, before the fruition of a western buildup—to come in 1954. Some thought it would come earlier. Through this period, the United States would be unready to "engage in global war." The "danger" in question was a Soviet miscalculation that it could cripple the U.S. military without inviting destruction in return. And Acheson in November 1950 thought current Soviet risk-taking demonstrated that Washington had less time "than we thought."[7]

Stalin entertained mirror-like fears of a U.S. attack in Europe. In late 1950, he alerted east European leaders to ready themselves for war by the end of 1952. Had he known that U.S. plans assumed he would hit first, he might have considered doing so. As he was telling his satellites in January 1951 "to prepare for an invasion of Western Europe," Washington's Joint Intelligence Committee filed a series of dolorous projections of an imminent war. With rearmament far from complete, General Omar Bradley thought the United States "would have a hell of a time winning" such a war. Until rearmament *was* fully under way, therefore, Acheson thought it vital to avoid incidents that could spark a "full-scale conflict." Meanwhile, Truman, still worried about too much spending, stretched out the planned increases in U.S. forces, justifying this and later postponements by moving the "maximum year of danger" further away.[8]

Stretched out or not, the buildup was huge, nearly quadrupling defense spending from 1950 to 1953. A defense budget already jacked up from $13.9 to $25 billion jumped another $17 billion after the Chinese intervention. Spending in 1951 rose to nearly $43 billion, boosting personnel in the military to 3.6 million. Including funds for the state department and other international affairs agencies and programs, disbursements rose from $17.7 to $35 billion in a single fiscal year. Draft calls doubled over two years, as did SAC personnel. Within a year of the declaration of the national emergency, the army grew from 10 to 18 divisions, naval vessels increased from 646 to 1,037, and air force combat wings from 48 to 87. In constant dollars, 1953 defense spending was the highest in the entire post-1945 era, as it was in dollars per capita and as a share of gross national product.[9]

All these dollars bought a generation of new tactical atomic weapons, air bases, allies' weapons, and a start toward German rearmament. The Pentagon overhauled the U.S. army to fit NSC-68's long-term demands rather than Korea's short-term emergency. Combined with allies, this new force probably came closer than believed to matching the Soviet bloc's, at least for defensive purposes. But while nearly all Soviet divisions hovered on the berm of western Europe, the United States had only five divisions there. The conventional buildup, therefore, never permitted an end to reliance on nuclear weapons. Going from 300 to 500-plus nuclear warheads ate up vast resources. By 1957, the

Atomic Energy Commission consumed one of fifteen kilowatts of electricity generated in the country. Washington's earlier inventive conversion of economic power to diplomatic purposes had set the stage for a switch to military solutions. With foreign aid shifting from social and civilian to military objectives, and the Mutual Security Program succeeding the Marshall Plan, economic aid to Europe shrank rapidly.[10]

Europeans followed the American example with some reluctance, even when financed lavishly by Congress. Complications arose from repeated congressional demands for more European sacrifice and snarls in actual weapons deliveries. Stubborn dollar shortages and inflation spurred by American war purchases worried allies about throttling their social and economic recovery, activating radical and neutralist sentiment. Acheson sympathized but had 531 masters to serve on Capitol Hill. With one face, he asked Congress for large appropriations and swore the allies would work harder; with the other, he told the allies to get on with it, but sometimes with crossed fingers. Still, Canadian and European military buildups nearly matched and sometimes exceeded that of the United States. From 1950 through 1953, the allies received $12 billion in U.S. aid, to which they added $32 billion from their own coffers. While American spending jumped 333 percent from 1950 to 1952, it rose 379 percent in Canada, 232 percent in France, 184 percent in the UK, and 148 percent in Italy. Allies lengthened terms of military service, and from 1950 to 1952, the number of men in uniform rose 27.3 percent in Britain and 52.9 percent in Canada.[11]

The vigorous U.S. response in Korea and bountiful aid to the allies ironically prompted some to pronounce the crisis past. Why overextend themselves when the spunky (and rich) Yanks were doing so well? As Acheson applied pressure, they pushed back. They did so wisely, for U.S. rearmament goals were excessive, causing another hiccup in economic recovery and spiking of inflation in Europe. The UK endured yet another financial crisis in 1951. Waves of anti-Americanism rolled through Europe. With even sober middle-class clerks scrawling "Go Home, Yankee" graffiti, their political leaders grumbled, too. British ambassador Oliver Franks complained that Americans were constantly trying "to impose their way of doing things" and were behaving "in Europe as if it belonged to them." Despite receiving over half of what some Americans called the "French Military Assistance Program," Paris channeled its resentment into the EDC. While bristling at such grievances, Acheson understood their causes. All the allies, he told anyone who would listen, deserved American patience and support. It would be foolhardy to confront the Soviet threat without them.[12]

Military, Peace, and Economic Offensives

Defense mobilization cost more than dollars. McCarthyism, which fed on the crisis atmosphere brought forth by mobilization, choked the avenues of mainstream political opinion. Unannounced, Truman abandoned Fair Deal domestic reform. Mobilization's reliance on private industry created the military-industrial complex. Rearmament stemmed the 1949 recession, but it also fostered the habit of stabilizing the economy through arms spending. It amplified presidential powers vis-à-vis both Congress and the states. These developments, as Michael Hogan and Aaron Friedberg show, did not produce a "garrison state," but they greatly expanded the dominion of national security agencies and their officials. On the other hand, as Douglas MacDonald points out, gearing up for the cold war could also stimulate progressivism. Seeking affiliation with nationalist reformers, Washington pushed for land reform and anti-corruption measures in the Philippines, Iran, and Formosa. It also sought accommodation with a nationalist revolution in Egypt and refused to act against revolutions in Iran, Guatemala, and Bolivia.[13]

Restraint in the face of radical revolutions unlikely to profit Moscow coexisted with a combative stance against communist-sponsored "peace" campaigns. The latest was scheduled to climax in a "World Peace Council" in East Berlin; the campaign called for a world peace pact negotiated by the Big Three, Moscow, and Beijing. It rattled European governments in February 1951, and Acheson wanted this "spurious Soviet peace propaganda" fought with "imagination." He instructed U.S. envoys to publicize communist felonies, which he itemized in a lengthy list. Moscow's propaganda, however, forced at least a show of interest in disarmament. After Soviet delegates had bolted UN arms control councils in 1950, Washington submitted warmed-over versions of the 1946 Baruch Plan to the Disarmament Committee of the General Assembly. The White House in late 1950 wanted to take the initiative, but a State speech draft was tailored to make the issue go away. In a design followed to the end of the Truman administration, Nitze also proposed a cap on the size of national military forces, a ban on bioloical and chemical weapons, and "disclosure and verification" of any agreements reached. Acheson looked cynically on the whole exercise, concerned only about a propaganda edge and avoiding damage in the unlikely case Moscow accepted U.S. proposals.[14]

Besides arms control, the state department also used a damage-control approach to congressional demands for tighter restrictions on trading in strategic goods with the eastern bloc. Acheson was loath to pressure allies who needed the sales and resources acquired in such trade, which relieved their dollar shortages. With both allies and Acheson resistant, economic warfare never worked as hoped by Congress, which, with the onset of war in Korea, grew more zealous in pushing for it. Through the Export Control Act of 1949, Washington had instituted restrictions on exports in two categories of strategic value (Lists 1A and 1B). Managing the lists was a multilateral Coordinating Committee (CoCom), founded in January 1950 and kept apart from NATO to shield the alliance from critics of commercial combat. At times the left hand of the state department enforced CoCom restrictions while the right hand loosened them, hoping to reduce allies' dependence on congressional aid dollars and the impact of West Germany's return to the marketplace. Acheson's light execution of CoCom did not prevent allies from feeling injured. It certainly did not dissuade Bradley, Louis Johnson (still defense chief at the time), and commerce secretary Charles W. Sawyer from agitating for tougher actions. Numerous appeals went to Truman, with Acheson arguing that it would be a blunder "to dragoon our friends." NSC debates in May 1950 ended in a standoff, with Acheson instructed to move the matter along in future NATO sessions. Allies generally agreed on List 1A, but U.S. embargo policy remained in disarray.[15]

Feeling the squeeze from Congress again, the administration had extended the embargoes to China and North Korea even before the onset of war. After 25 June 1950, requests turned into demands, accepted by some allies and defied by others. London was particularly intransigent, opposed to trade restrictions in principle and still thinking its economic ties to China would have a meliorating effect. The dispute in Washington continued, too. With Truman's apparent backing, Acheson in August 1950 held that current controls were working well enough, that allies trading outside them obtained essential and otherwise unavailable raw materials and foodstuffs, and that it would be an error to get tougher, especially when the United States was demanding sacrifices for rearmament. Because CoCom was secret, a Congress left in the dark sometimes made groundless complaints of allied noncooperation. As Acheson averted his gaze, his proxies fashioned ornate devices to circumvent congressional mandates and minimize damage to allies. A de facto compromise fell into place in late 1950 and early 1951. Washington offered moderation and new help for the alliance. Allies, worried about Korea and about U.S. attitudes (and having reduced needs for eastern goods), offered substantial compliance with the embargo.[16]

Then Congress suddenly bared its teeth. On 9 May 1951, a Senate agitated by the dismissal of General MacArthur and dissatisfied with allies' help in Korea, surprised the administration with the "Kem Amendment," named for Missouri Republican James Kem. Fastened to an appropriation bill, the amendment barred aid to any government selling goods to Moscow that U.S. citizens themselves could not legally sell. The administration tempered the effect of this move only by whipping allies into line. In June it gained Congress's permission for greater presidential discretion in enforcement. Congress also passed other legislation restricting commerce with the east and denying benefits to Soviet bloc states. Through the summer, State negotiated a higher level of allied conformity and abrogated old trade pacts with the Soviet Union, Bulgaria, and Romania. Under heavy pressure, neutral Sweden and Switzerland also accepted most of the trade regime.[17]

But in October, Congress replaced the Kem Amendment with the Battle Act, named for Democratic Representative Laurie Battle of Alabama. This act barred aid to countries who menaced U.S. security by trading with "enemies" but gave the president flexibility in "exceptional" cases. Though originating in continuing unhappiness with the allies on the Hill, the act was an administration victory over inflexibility. Though available as a threat, the Truman administration never invoked "Battle." When the Kem Amendment resurfaced in May 1952, it set off another quarrel and another state department turn of the screw to make allies look more obliging. The administration won another compromise measure after Acheson complained that the amendment would scuttle the foreign aid program. Despite all this hullabaloo, Washington never cut off a dollar of aid from allies over the issue. With Truman's acquiescence, Acheson continued to nod his approval of east-west trade when he thought it vital to an ally's interests.[18]

Not a Proper Regime

After war started in Korea, the United States lowered the bar on which people and what governments it would do business with, touring some global slums previously avoided. John McCloy in Germany handed out clemency judgments to those formerly in bad odor, causing a former executive of I. G. Farben, German munitions manufacturer, to note Americans' greater friendliness "now that they have Korea on their hands." Japanese war criminals also went free.[19]

The biggest beneficiary among states was Spain, the "great whale stranded on the shores of Europe." The administration had formerly inched toward better ties with Francisco Franco's fascist dictatorship, but with the Korean War, it leapt to the task. During the war, President Roosevelt considered Spain an enemy. Franco and his fascist Falange movement had won the Spanish civil war with Italian and German aid. In return, he sent 14,000 Spanish troops to fight with Hitler on the eastern front. Once Hitler looked a loser, Franco shifted to a semi-neutral policy barely acceptable to the allies, partly negotiated by Acheson, who held "sound" views on the pestilential regime. FDR had hoped to undermine the Falange government after the war. That Washington instead began to cozy up to Franco disgusted many. Adopting Germany, Italy, and Japan as allies was one thing, for democratic seedlings had replaced their repulsive wartime regimes, but Franco and his outcast system still stood.[20]

Truman despised Spain for many reasons, not least being its domination by Catholics and discrimination against Protestants. Franco's periodic actions against the president's beloved Masonic Order also affronted his Baptist soul. Though he regularly blew his top over efforts at normalized relations, in the end he gave way. Everyone in the administration felt the hot breath of congressional conservatives. In his own journey toward normalization, Acheson watched for reactions in Britain and France, where anti-Franco feelings remained high and officials blanched whenever Americans hinted they might "defend" Europe from behind the wall of the Spanish Pyrenees.[21]

At Yalta and Potsdam in 1945, the victorious allies had declared Spain unfit for UN membership. In a tripartite statement in March 1946, the U.S., British, and French governments condemned the Madrid government and urged the Spanish people to overthrow Franco. In an action similar to that against Juan

Perón's Argentina, the state department listed Franco's shortcomings in an official "Blue Book." But discord appeared in the administration as early as July 1946, when the JCS urged an effort to acquire Spanish air and naval bases. This was not likely while Washington was continuing to condemn Spain, as Under Secretary Acheson did in a November 1946 press conference, describing it as "not a proper [regime] to be in power because of its origin and activities." Shortly thereafter, the UN General Assembly reaffirmed the ban on Spanish UN membership. It also asked members to recall their ambassadors from Madrid, leaving chargés-d'affaires behind to do business. The United States reluctantly joined the General Assembly majority, and the UN injunction had only fleeting moral force. Perón defied it from the first, and others soon followed, including Egypt, the Philippines, and especially Latin American states.[22]

Members of Congress began taking junkets to Spain, where Franco and the infatuated solons heaped encomiums on each other. In August 1947, the Pentagon, its gaze fixed on vast plateaus and blue harbors apparently God-made for runways and anchorages, urged sending aid to Spain. But the administration moved cautiously. An effort to rescind the no-ambassador rule failed that November, but the ban was not reaffirmed, either. Under George Kennan's prodding, the NSC in December 1947 advocated restoring diplomatic relations, "irrespective of wartime ideological considerations or the character of the regime in power." Truman "concurred" rather than approved in January 1948. He felt more pressure when members of Congress threatened to torpedo friendly gestures toward Yugoslavia unless they were matched in Spain. Spurred by the Franco government's dexterous promotion, an effective "Spanish Lobby" sprang into action, led by such conservative Catholics as Patrick McCarran, Joseph McCarthy, and FDR's old postmaster-general, James Farley, and joined by ardent anti-communists, army and air force generals, and southern cotton exporters, all seeking closer U.S.-Spanish ties. As a private citizen, Acheson had remarked in congressional testimony that it was time to make Spain part of "Europe" rather than isolate it. The state department was divided when he became secretary in 1949. European affairs officers mostly opposed any change in Spain's status, but the department generally began to lean in the same direction as the lobby.[23]

Early in 1949, after Dean Rusk publicly argued that ostracism would only strengthen Franco, Acheson swiftly applied the brakes. He disliked moving too far ahead of allies in Europe, where anti-Franco feelings were far stronger than in the United States, where both the political left and interest in the Spanish civil war were waning. He also took into account those Americans who were still interested, most conspicuously Truman. In the UN delegation in April, with John Foster Dulles's support, Eleanor Roosevelt warned against any backsliding. Acheson told the Spanish chargé that NATO membership for Spain was not now in the cards. On 20 April, he conveyed Truman's orders to the UN delegation to abstain on any vote on the ambassadorial policy while supporting Spanish inclusion in UN agencies. But an Assembly debate in May brought no change.[24]

Acheson thought normal relations with Spain were only a matter of time. But he was also determined not to embarrass the president, whose contempt for Franco and "Catholic obscurantism in Spain" was quite familiar to him. Truman would share with anyone who listened his latest information on Spanish offenses against Masons and Baptists. On 5 May, Acheson had a stormy colloquy with senators about U.S.-Spanish relations in which he insisted on acting jointly with European allies. It was "dialectical" reasoning, he told reporters, to say that having a minister in Prague meant Washington must send an ambassador to Madrid. Spain was "fascist" and had no respect for human rights. Senator Robert Taft attacked Acheson's "Communist-front philosophy." C. L. Sulzberger of the *Times*, however, noticed under the heated debate Acheson's failure to bar private U.S. bank loans to Spain.[25]

Maneuvering continued through the rest of 1949. Members of Congress pushed for the Spanish connection. So did the military chiefs, who in Franco's phrase had "discovered the existence of the Pyrenees." Castigating Franco publicly, Truman twice in summer press conferences paraded his opposition to any loans or Marshall aid to Spain. Whenever his constancy appeared to falter, Eleanor Roosevelt was there to push him upright. Technically compliant to his wishes and nervous about European allies, the state department nonetheless prepared for rapprochement. It had to remain alert to Truman, who once walked into an NSC meeting and announced: "Item one on the agenda, I see, has to do with Spain and I would like to make it clear I consider Mr. Franco to have been a collaborator of Mr. Hitler's, and not the kind of a person that I propose we do business with. Therefore, I will not approve what I understand your recommendation is, and we will pass on to item two on the agenda." In September, he also disavowed Senator McCarran, in Spain discussing loans for Franco, and Acheson had blocked Johnson from accompanying the senator. Yet Truman's own navy had smoothed the way for McCarran when ships visited a Spanish port. Five admirals and two generals also made an authorized courtesy call on Franco. Acheson warned Ernest Bevin, who wanted to "let sleeping dogs lie," that he now preferred to leave the issue of representation to individual states. With Christmas decorations going up in Washington, pundits were still criticizing Acheson's double standard in courting Yugoslavia while rebuffing Spain's suit. Still resistant, Truman said that action in Madrid to protect "fundamental freedoms, particularly the freedom of worship" must precede any change. Though not blaming Truman, Acheson by now privately lamented the obstacles to normal relations.[26]

But he noticeably pushed the Spanish issue forward in January 1950, a full six months before the Korean War. Persuaded by the need for defense ties with Spain and unpersuaded that liberals at home would make a stink, he told Eleanor Roosevelt on 6 January of plans to move toward full diplomatic relations. In secret hearings on the 10th, he dilated on the error of using diplomatic ties as a moral yardstick, for neither recognition nor nonrecognition would influence a government's "internal operations." Washington could recognize Madrid while keeping it "at arms length." For that matter, the United States should keep ties open to all states, even when "you . . . hate their guts." But he also warned conservatives they were foolish to think Franco would ever be "a loyal and true ally." On 18 January, in a long letter vetted at the White House, he officially informed Senator Tom Connally—the Spanish lobby's "biggest catch"—of plans to restore relations. Since the UN ban had actually strengthened Franco, he argued, members of the international organization should soon be able to decide on their own about ties with Spain. More concerned about allied than domestic dissent, he added that Spain must develop better relations with its neighbors. To become eligible for U.S. aid, it must also liberalize its political regime and economy. He said nothing in the letter about bases or a Spanish role in European defense.[27]

Since in a March press conference, Truman said Franco's regime was the same as "the totalitarian Russian Government and the Hitler government," Acheson again sidestepped the issue. By May, however, the joint chiefs were itching to overcome Anglo-French objections. A week before war in Korea, Truman asked Acheson for advice. The response, a week into the war, threw cold water on the chiefs' hopes. Allies would be aghast if Washington looked to defend Europe in a distant Iberian redoubt. Interest in Spain might also signal that the Americans believed general war was imminent. Acheson also said that flouting both domestic and international revulsion for Spain would undermine U.S. world leadership. Reinforced by Acheson's words, the president at a 6 July NSC meeting said "it would take a lot of convincing to make him recognize Franco." And he meant it. On 1 August, when he signed a bill in which senators had inserted Marshall Plan credits for Spain, he remarked that they could insert what they liked, but *he* would decide whether to spend the funds. He said the same of a $62.5 million loan imbedded in an appropriations bill: he was not obliged to execute the loan. But this was nearly the last gasp of resistance. Strangely, just as the administration began employing McCarran's despised internal security act to deny visas to members of Franco's Falangist Party, its resistance to the Spanish lobby began to ebb.[28]

Though not decisive in policymaking, public opinion was rushing past both Truman and Acheson. A September 1950 Gallup Poll showed 69 percent support for Spanish membership in NATO. The venerated Marshall now spoke for such views at the Pentagon. By a 38–10 vote on 4 November, the UN General Assembly annulled the ban on ambassadors. The noise of these developments drowned out state department publication of documents revealing Spanish financial help to the Third Reich and another Truman remark to reporters that it would be a "long, long time" before he sent an ambassador to Spain. But on 16 November, he approved this very step after Acheson had made the case for it in a private meeting. Within days, Truman decided on sixty-three-year-old Stanton Griffis, a friend, New York financier, and entrepreneur who had already served in Egypt, Poland, and Argentina. Appointing him on 27 December and protesting that he had been "a little overruled and worn down" by the state department, Truman remained a skeptic about Griffis's mission. For, as he told reporters, Baptists in Spain were "buried in the middle of the night."[29]

In January 1951, a series of NSC papers on Spain supplied guidance for Griffis. Acheson wanted to prevent Spain from going "neutral," and he now wanted military bases. Citing evidence of alarming new Soviet risk-taking, he also wanted to include Madrid in NATO strategic planning, if not in the alliance itself. In time—once the bruises of German rearmament healed—he wanted to bring Spain under the aegis of NATO and the MDAP. As he began discussions, however, Griffis should not pay an "exorbitantly high price" for Franco's cooperation. On a parallel track, the state department would also encourage allies to improve their ties with Spain; but for strategic purposes, Acheson seemed willing to push ahead on Spain even if they objected, and Marshall was even more blunt about it. When Acheson found both London and Paris still disapproving, he ignored them. Early in their talks, Franco told Griffis he knew NATO membership was not imminent, but in return for U.S. aid, he was ready to promise support in any war with the Soviets, including north of what Griffis called the "Pyramids." He could accept U.S. air and naval bases, too, so long as they remained under ultimate Spanish sovereignty. The state department kept France and Britain only selectively informed of this dialogue; it especially omitted references to the bases, about which the UK would be especially sensitive given its Gibraltar holding and traditional influence in the Mediterranean.[30]

In approving Truman's decision to send new army divisions to Europe in April 1951, the Senate asked for inclusion of Spain in defense planning. Truman thanked Griffis for getting Franco to open some padlocked Protestant chapels and to make other promises about religious issues. In June, he approved an NSC paper on the impending U.S.-Spanish negotiations, to be headed by Chief of Naval Operations Admiral Forrest P. Sherman. Washington would seek the coveted bases and bring Madrid into western defense plans. If the British did not come along, Sherman should go ahead to gain a bilateral accord. Even after he put his signature on this document, Truman strayed from the NSC scenario, saying publicly in the middle of July that "I don't like Franco and I never will, but I won't let my personal feelings override the convictions of our military men."[31]

With London and Paris only vaguely informed of what lay ahead, Sherman and Griffis over their opposition sat down with Franco on 16 July to start what would be prolonged negotiations. Sherman's sudden death a few days later did not slow the pace of the rapprochement, but wrangling over details did. In August, Truman found new religious outrages to complain about, including Protestants having to bury their dead "in plowed fields" at night. "I've never been happy about sending an Ambassador to Spain," he told Acheson, "and I am not happy about it now." Acheson told colleagues to prepare themselves for "some kind of an explosion on this issue." Allies remained worrisome for other reasons. When one of the joint chiefs pointed to the eventual U.S. capacity to launch nuclear raids from Spanish bases as a reason for British exasperation, Acheson in effect had asked, why shouldn't they be exasperated? They were now only "the tail of the kite" and worried "about where the kite is going." As talks with Franco progressed, however, he disregarded British protests.[32]

The administration achieved little more in its last year. Pricked by the steady criticism of allies (and Truman), by the fall of 1951 Acheson was downplaying Spanish membership in NATO. Truman grumbled that Spain seemed "in a special sense his perennial problem." Acheson also worried that Pentagon nego-tiators envisaged a U.S. military presence too large for Spanish society to absorb. Spain, he was thinking in 1952, should be "more of an adjunct than a central factor" in western defense. When Griffis resigned his post, Acheson replaced him with Lincoln MacVeagh, a "school friend" and "adviser." MacVeagh had also been in the Athens embassy during the 1947 Greek crisis and Lisbon embassy when Portugal won its suit for NATO membership (a suit Franco quietly approved). Despite signs of progress in 1952, the two sides could not close a deal. British and French sniping and Truman's continuing irritation over religious issues held negotiators back. So did the fact that, in George Perkins's words, "the Spaniards were opening their mouths too wide." Finally, neither Truman nor Acheson had his heart in reconciling Washington with the Falangists.[33]

The 1952 campaign also reduced chances for settlement. Franco began counting on a better deal with the next president, and Acheson paid less attention. President Eisenhower replaced MacVeagh with career diplomat James Clement Dunn, who completed the Pact of Madrid in September 1953. It gave the United States the bases it wanted in return for large-scale U.S. aid and a virtual alliance with Franco. Franco awarded McCarran the Grand Cross of the Order of Isabella la Catolica. By 1958, nearly 20,000 Americans and their dependents worked in Spanish air bases.[34]

In 1955, Truman wrote Acheson that "Mr. Dull, Duller, Dullest" of Sullivan and Cromwell was undoubtedly generating "some fee for somebody" in his dealings "with that lousy totalitarian Franco." Acheson probably winced, then smiled. He too still found Franco a repulsive partner. Forging ties with him had required flouting the opinion of allies and promoting the objectives of many of Acheson's McCarthyite foes. It would have been worth the price of admission to see his expression when told of Senator McCarran's grand Spanish honor. These disclaimers aside, however, he and Truman had gone far toward the goals Eisenhower finally reached, demonstrating how far Korea and the militarization of the cold war had come to influence Acheson's policies.[35]

Prudence, Audacity, and Timing of the Most Exquisite Nature

By the time Acheson had committed himself to serious talks with Spain, armistice talks were under way in Korea, and MacArthur was in Coventry. The attacks on Acheson were about to diminish. The allies were trying to assemble the European

Defense Community, and a peace treaty with Japan was in the offing. In a pensive lecture at the National War College on 27 August 1951, Acheson paused to take stock and examine the long view. In the past year, crises had heated his language. To pump up support for his military-minded policies, he was quicker to invoke communist depravity. He commonly pointed to Stalin's efforts to build a "new world empire" while brusquely dismissing Kennan and Bohlen's cherished distinction between intentions and capabilities.[36]

Clarity of fundamental principles, he told his War College audience, would help them make the best tactical decisions in a world of "almost impossible choices." They should keep uppermost in mind the goal of creating a world that "at the very least is tolerable to the survival of our national values, and which at the best makes for the flourishing of those values." The conflict with the Soviet Union rested on profound differences in ideas and values. Grounded in a history of "secure insularity," American values had found constitutional embodiment: unity, justice based on a limited state, and a "domestic tranquility" permitting decision making through reasoned discussion and compromise. Working for the "general welfare" assumed a government that served rather than reigned. Finally, it was one of the greatest "blessings of liberty" that allowed each American the right "to make choices for himself." Soviet values in contrast originated in "profound insecurity," a "long history of invasion," and being an "outlander" in the eyes of western civilization. The result was an ideology of alienation and fear and a regime unchangeable through reason and negotiation. Kremlin rulers were an insecure "conspiracy" determined to perpetuate themselves in power by any means. They viewed any regime not "subject" to their own with hostility and especially hoped to subvert "the values which are represented in our union."

He told the students that U.S. policy should rest on two, basically separate suppositions. First, even if the hostile Soviet state had never existed, Americans must respond creatively to the storms of "emerging nationalism" erupting in Asia and the Middle East and persuade these "awakening" peoples to join the civilization and values "under which we live."

Contending with the Soviets was another matter altogether. This required mobilizing every element of the "free" world's strength. The United States had done this by shoring up its own power at the center of a western system, linking its power to the like-minded peoples of NATO. It had transformed its World War II enemies into parties of value in a common coalition for self-defense. All these efforts aimed at "a dependable preponderance of power on our side." The United States would use this power "eventually" to confront Moscow with circumstances it had "no choice but to accept." If necessary, there would be strength enough for defense against an armed Soviet attack.

The United States, Acheson warned, must never corner the Kremlin or force it "to fight or not fight on some particular issue." He conceded a deadly "paradox" involved in the buildup of western strength, for each step made the Soviets feel more insecure. Tension would "mount" further as the west fully incorporated

Germany and Japan on its side. To keep this tension from mushrooming into spasms of "world violence" would require combinations of "firmness and patience," along with "prudence and audacity" and "timing of the most exquisite nature." Washington would have to be like "steel" in its fundamental goals and utterly flexible in its means. Since there was "no room for error," mistakes would be "punishable by the most terrible disaster."

The communists were not the only source of danger, for America itself would face disaster if it fell into the hands of people of a "unitary" mind-set and an inclination to seek security through "preventive war." Equally dangerous were those seeking either a cynical "power deal" dividing the world into spheres of influence or a "world government on some magnificent scale."

Everyone had to be patient. There was "not one more river to cross" but "countless problems stretching into the future." To end the cold war, Americans must reconcile themselves to "limited objectives" and work in congress with others, for an essential part of American power was the "ability to evoke support from others—an ability quite as important as the capacity to compel." And when the cold war did end, Americans would have to deal with "the awakened masses of Africa," with a world of "dwindling supplies," and with their own "recklessness in running through them."

Acheson never used the word "hegemon," but this speech describes the elements of wisdom needed to use and preserve hegemonic power. The United States must manage its conflicts with the Soviet Union "so prudently that we do not, as great empires have done in the past, solve one great issue only to find ourselves weak, exhausted, powerless to deal with further problems." To lead the "free world," Americans must serve the interests of others as well as their own. To accept "responsibility" for other nations, Americans must "submit" to "standards and values" created by others. The bishop's son found his War College peroration in the Book of Common Prayer. "Grant us grace fearlessly to contend against evil and to make no peace with oppression; and, that we may reverently use our freedom, help us to employ it to maintain justice among men and nations." This high charge faithfully reflected his own mind and manner. It was subtle and discriminating. And it was wary of the overbearing use of power. He assumed without saying that the American people could sustain this balance of prudence and audacity, power and exquisite timing, for as long as became necessary to wage the cold war.[37]

Part V

23

IN THRALL: IRONIC
FAILURES IN KOREA

Introduction

NEVER DID AMERICAN PROSPECTS in a war shift so often as in 1950. The first fifty days were like the playing of an accordion. Nearly defeated, the tag end of the South Korean army and the first of the intervening U.S. force hung on in the Pusan perimeter, a patch of territory in the southeastern corner of Korea. Then, with General Douglas MacArthur's strike behind North Korean lines at Inchon, the UN force sprang northward, and the next sixty days resembled an accel-erated rendition of the Normandy breakout. MacArthur's forces rolled over a demoralized foe, seized Pyongyang, and neared the Yalu River and Chinese border. Finally, the accordion squeezed inward again when China's calamitous intervention in November and December threw UN forces back toward Pusan.

Dean Acheson was at his best in the first weeks of the war, embracing historic decisions and advancing his department's view of the conflict. With many others, however, he stumbled after the Pusan breakout. Discarding the original goal of restoring the status quo ante bellum, he upheld the dash across the 38th parallel. He neglected admittedly slim chances to negotiate an end to the war while U.S. forces remained near the parallel. He made no concerted effort to persuade either President Harry Truman or Secretary of Defense George Marshall to halt MacArthur's incautious sprint into the jaws of Mao Zedong's armies. He belittled the chances of a Chinese intervention and the ruinous outcome it might produce.

But these were ironic failures. Crossing the 38th parallel, the imaginary line astride Korea's waist, was an overdetermined decision. Given what Washington's leaders thought, knew, and thought they knew, deciding otherwise would have been nearly unbelievable. Chances for negotiations may have been illusive, depending on how far UN forces went beyond the parallel. Acheson later berated himself for not throwing himself in the breach against MacArthur's far northern march, but this was not primarily his responsibility. The failures of Truman, Marshall, and the joint chiefs were far greater. Given Mao's own expansive goals, the only certain way to forestall his intervention was to stop MacArthur immediately north of the 38th parallel. Some observers, then and later, believed Mao would also have held back if MacArthur had gone another sixty to eighty miles north and parked his army along the narrow Wonson-Pyongyang neck of North Korea. Even though this was some two hundred miles short of his ultimate advance, it is highly likely that even an advance to this point would have triggered all of Mao's aggressive urges, throwing China headlong into the war. Mao's price for *not* intervening at that point would have been nothing short of a U.S. withdrawal from Korea, desertion of Formosa, and grant of the Chinese seat in the United Nations.

In a final irony, after six of the worst weeks the U.S. government has ever endured, early in 1951 the fighting stabilized, lifting the crisis. Reasserting control over the "vast external realm," the administration scaled back its war aims. Rejecting London's calls for abject concessions in Asia, it reemphasized its own strategy of Europe first. It easily withstood a GOP challenge of plans to send new army divisions to NATO. If worse for the wear, by early February 1951, Truman and his deputies were still in command, their fundamental international goals and strategies intact.

Marching Beyond the Surveyor's Line

The choice posed by the 38th parallel was stark: whether to halt hostilities after restoring the status quo ante or chase the enemy beyond the line. A secondary choice involved how *far* to pursue the North Koreans. Although conclusions of the state department debate were slow in coming, the issues themselves seemed clear enough. Sending troops beyond the 1945 dividing line would arguably exceed the original UN mandate of restoring peace to the area. But stopping at the parallel would restore a condition now considered unsatisfactory, with South Korea's capital, Seoul, just south of the parallel, permanently exposed to attack. Marching a short distance beyond the 38th seemed a low-risk way to give South Korea a more defensible border—and avoid a break with Syngman Rhee. Moving yet farther offered the chance to administer a stinging defeat to "communism." Chasing North Korean forces all the way to the Yalu would liquidate a noxious Stalinist regime while discharging the UN's postwar goal of a united Korea. Additionally, the example set in Korea would surely discourage Stalin from trying to seize West Germany by force. On the other hand, going to the Yalu would magnify chances of a Chinese counterattack, as might even a shorter advance.

Any serious debate over the issue ended abruptly on 15 September when General MacArthur made his surprise invasion at Inchon, Seoul's working harbor twenty miles to the west and just south of the 38th parallel. With North Korean troops then both in front of MacArthur and to his rear, Washington thought it would be ludicrous to restore the parallel as a semi-legitimate boundary. The joint chiefs had always considered it without strategic meaning and did not want to be committed to a static defense of the parallel, which would drain resources without ending conflict between the two Koreas. MacArthur, Acheson wrote Paul Nitze in mid-July, could not be "expected to march up to a surveyor's line and just stop." Allies encouraged such forward thinking, with London markedly eager to cross the line. Fears that Moscow would respond dangerously dwindled when it reacted mildly to bombing raids on Rashin, less than twenty miles from Soviet territory. Policymakers thought the Chinese leaders were too embroiled in consolidating their rule to act and would probably be advised against action by the Russians, who then seemed notably passive. Instead of threatening to attack West Germany, Berlin, or Yugoslavia, as originally feared, Moscow was acting cautiously. This fact animated American leaders to take even greater risks.[1]

Nonetheless, the state department's first stabs at the 38th parallel issue were uncertain. Briefing NATO ambassadors in the first days of the war, department counselor George Kennan disavowed any plan to cross it. On 29 June, both Truman in an NSC meeting and Acheson in a speech said the U.S. objective was to restore peace at the border. Yet UN delegate Warren Austin alluded to unifying Korea, and MacArthur's early orders implied he was free to move beyond the parallel. Truman could theoretically have settled the issue—though not without inviting public debate—by forcefully declaring his sole mission to be reinstating the status quo ante, but the temptation to go farther was irresistible. Senator Robert Taft in early July urged the occupation of at least "the southern part of North Korea," a view soon endorsed by many in the administration.[2]

It nevertheless took nearly two months to decide the matter. Truman on 13 July publicly refused to rule out crossing what Rhee called an "obliterated" line and on the 17th asked for a judgment by the NSC. Debate in the state department pitted the cautious (Kennan and Paul Nitze's policy planning staff) against the adventurous (hawkish Asianists led by Dean Rusk). Rusk's assistant, John M. Allison, wanted to go "right on up to the Manchurian and Siberian border" and hold a "UN-supervised election for all of Korea." John Foster Dulles and old China hand John Paton Davies reinforced their view, as did Washington's political atmosphere. The FBI had just taken Julius Rosenberg into custody, and, pumped up in high accusatory mania, Joseph McCarthy was accusing Acheson of giving the USSR "a green light to grab whatever it could in China, Korea, and Formosa." A House Republican charged that state department leftists wanted "to cringe behind" the 38th parallel. Acheson wavered through July, confiding to senators on the 24th the "Russians or Chinese" might simply seize all of North

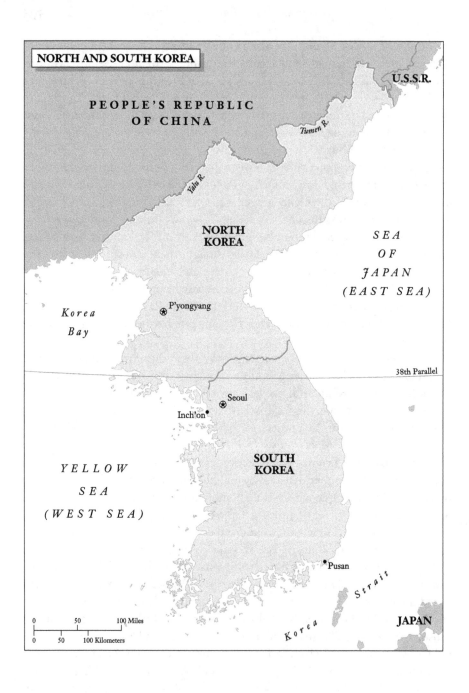

NORTH AND SOUTH KOREA

U.S.S.R.

PEOPLE'S REPUBLIC
OF CHINA

Tumen R.

Yalu R.

NORTH
KOREA

*SEA
OF
JAPAN
(EAST SEA)*

*Korea
Bay*

⊛ P'yongyang

38th Parallel

⊛ Seoul
Inch'on•

*YELLOW
SEA
(WEST SEA)*

SOUTH
KOREA

•Pusan

Strait

Korea

JAPAN

0   50   100 Miles

0   50   100 Kilometers

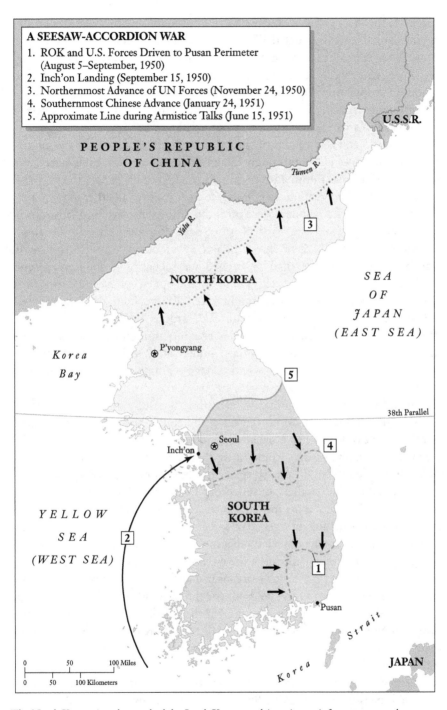

A SEESAW-ACCORDION WAR

1. ROK and U.S. Forces Driven to Pusan Perimeter
   (August 5–September, 1950)
2. Inch'on Landing (September 15, 1950)
3. Northernmost Advance of UN Forces (November 24, 1950)
4. Southernmost Chinese Advance (January 24, 1951)
5. Approximate Line during Armistice Talks (June 15, 1951)

U.S.S.R.

PEOPLE'S REPUBLIC
OF CHINA

Tumen R.

Yalu R.

NORTH KOREA

SEA
OF
JAPAN
(EAST SEA)

Korea
Bay

P'yongyang

38th Parallel

Seoul

Inch'on

YELLOW

SEA

(WEST SEA)

SOUTH
KOREA

Pusan

Korea Strait

JAPAN

0   50   100 Miles
0 50   100 Kilometers

The North Korean invaders pushed the South Korean and American reinforcements south to
Pusan. MacArthur landed at Inchon; UN forces counterattacked and drove toward the Chinese
border at the Yalu River. China came to the aid of the North Koreans and forced the allies back to
South Korea. Finally, another American and UN counteroffensive pushed the Chinese and North
Koreans north to the 38th parallel. Thus, the war ended about where it had begun.

Korea "on the theory that we were occupying the South and they were reoccupy-
ing the North." He worried that a further advance would be dangerous and
would damage his alliance-building carpentry in Europe. Not yet fully admitting
how Korea had shredded all hopes for a balanced China policy, he entertained
notions of propitiating the PRC, which would require restraint in Korea.[3]

In the quarrel still raking the department, Kennan and Nitze produced a
draft opposing a parallel crossing because it risked war. Allison tore into it as
"appeasement" and a surrender of "moral principles." At the end of the month,
the Pentagon wanted UN and congressional endorsements of a "united, free, and
independent" Korea. But in a proposal that smelled of blackmail, the JCS also
insisted the president guarantee enough resources to cover all other foreign obligations. They also said all bets were off if the Soviets intervened. With Allison
already studying how to reshape North Korea, Europeanists worried about
Acheson's loyalties. Charles Bohlen in Paris saw no one of "stature" to counsel
him except Kennan, who had postponed his sabbatical from government.
On 8 August, Kennan alerted Acheson to "watch out" when MacArthur gained
battlefield successes, because they might touch off interventions by the Soviets
or Chinese, or both. A week later, when U.S. troops finally halted the enemy
offensive in the south, Austin twice described Washington's goal as Korean
unification, but—Washington "sources" immediately insisted—only through
"negotiation." The CIA, which would change its mind several times, warned
that invading North Korea would present "grave risks," provoking entry by the
Soviets and a defense of the 38th parallel by the Chinese.[4]

Two significant events occurred on 1 September 1950. Truman declared
that the people of Korea had a "right to be free, independent, and united" without saying the United States would bring that about. Second, in what General
Omar Bradley considered "a masterpiece of obfuscation," the NSC seemed to
approve crossing the parallel. As self-protective as the Pentagon, the council
implied that UN forces must instantly retreat to positions below the parallel if
either Moscow or Beijing intervened or threatened to do so. In an off-the-record
session with reporters the next day, Acheson was still holding his options open,
saying that action would depend on the circumstances when MacArthur's force
reached the parallel. If the North Koreans had lost "their uniforms" and claimed
they had "been working in the fields all the time," South Korea could mop up.
But it would be quite "another situation" if the Russians seized control from a
destroyed North Korean state or if still-viable North Korean forces could stage
an attritional slugfest when MacArthur reached the parallel. He expressed no
preferences of his own.[5]

On 7 September 1950, an NSC meeting that could win no awards for clarity
addressed the issue. While asking State and Defense to find clearer language for
MacArthur's orders, in NSC-81/1 the council approved crossing the parallel but
ordered the general to consult Washington before doing so. If he succeeded in
destroying the North Korean army, all of Korea would be reunified following

free elections, with Rhee presumably gaining provisional power over the north. After adding an amendment to give MacArthur more flexibility, Truman signed the paper on 11 September. Acheson told senators that going north would be a UN decision and stressed the danger of having "Western troops fooling around" near the Soviet border. But he also squinted in another direction when he intimated that South Korean and U.S. forces could go all the way north if MacArthur found immediately beyond the 38th parallel "a whole lot of little bands skipping around and trying to get home" instead of a "unified force." Though Acheson ritualistically talked about preventing intervention by China, he condescended to Mao's nation. Referring to an accidental bombing of Chinese territory, he cracked that "the Chinese don't know the difference between a bomb and a rocket anyway. They both make an awfully big bang." The public knew nothing of these remarks, or of the NSC decision.[6]

On the fifth day of Acheson's "single package" negotiations in New York, MacArthur made his strike at Inchon in Operation CHROMITE. As North Korean forces collapsed and UN troops retook Seoul on 27 September, the decision on the parallel abruptly moved from hypothetical to urgent. From the Waldorf Hotel, Acheson agreed with instructions enlarging MacArthur's authority. That the orders came from Marshall, who had just taken over from the cashiered Louis Johnson, surely bolstered his confidence. If he had any doubts, he hid them in icily dismissing those of his personal assistant in what Lucius Battle called "the worst argument I ever had with Dean Acheson." With a "steely look," Acheson asked: "How old are you, Luke?" "Thirty." "And you are willing to pit your judgment against the entire JCS?" Soon, Marshall again cabled MacArthur, this time with language not vetted at State, language the administration would regret: "We want you to feel unhampered tactically and strategically to proceed north of 38th parallel."[7]

For five years, the administration had been on the defensive in Asia, internationally and domestically. But no more. In a state of euphoria after Inchon, it succumbed to a galloping optimism that nearly killed sober analysis of the risks lying ahead. In words it wanted MacArthur to use in broadcasting a call for North Korea's surrender, the state department presumed total victory. The UN would determine North Korea's future. In a cabinet meeting, Acheson cockily advocated ignoring the parallel to set the stage for using Korea as proof of "what Western Democracy can do to help the underprivileged countries of the world." In the UN session, Britain's Ernest Bevin called for reunifying Korea. Watching, James Reston in the *New York Times* referred to "the final crack-up of the Korean Communist army." (Even the Soviet Union's Andrei Vyshinsky was "talking privately about the Korean peace.") Bevin had crowed in a cable to Prime Minister Clement Attlee that the Soviets must be "made to realise that they are up against it." On 30 September, a day after restoring Rhee to power, MacArthur told the chiefs he considered "all of Korea open for our military operations." In the UN, Austin demanded that the aggressor must not have another chance to threaten world peace by gaining a "refuge behind an imaginary line." As he spoke, ROK units began heading north, and the next day MacArthur invited the North Koreans to surrender. Acheson on television said the war was "very close to an end." Moscow had signaled interest in negotiations ten days before, and on 2 October, Vyshinsky called for an immediate cease-fire and withdrawal of all foreign troops, coupled with internationally supervised elections. A few days later, Soviet personnel packed up and started leaving North Korea. In a complex game, Stalin was simultaneously urging Mao to save the communist cause by throwing his army into the breach.[8]

The sense of impending victory lasted into mid-October. By a vote of 47–5, the General Assembly resolved to establish a unified and democratic Korean government, with an increasingly otherwise-minded India opposed. Imbedded in the resolution's language was tacit ex post facto permission to cross the 38th parallel. On 23 October, after American units reached the North Korean capital of Pyongyang, Rhee proclaimed his "temporary civil control" of all Korea. South Koreans began arresting communists and other northern opponents of Rhee's regime. On the 24th, just as Acheson was musing about sending a mission to North Korea to see how "the communists *had* run that part of the country," MacArthur without reference home issued orders to "drive forward with all speed," abolishing previously ordered restraints. The five-star commander silenced his alarmed superiors by citing Marshall's earlier order to feel "unhampered tactically and strategically."[9]

Washington's inability to withstand its conquering hero was an important reason *he* crossed the 38th parallel, but it is impossible to compute the relative weight of the reasons Washington let him go. As indicated in historian Clay Blair's neat tally, they ran the gamut, from Washington's "new confidence in MacArthur" to the hope for a "smashing" win to sway other Asian peoples "flirting with communism." They included the convictions that Moscow feared a larger war and that Mao would not risk combat with the Americans. Washington was eager to dash Moscow's Asian pretensions and subvert its relations with Beijing. Unwilling to settle the war by negotiating with implacable enemies, Truman's government experienced an "overpowering urge to get rid of the 'Korean problem' once and for all." A final, powerful factor was the undeclared "impulse" to assert U.S. strength "worldwide and roll back communism." And, though unmentioned by Blair, nearly three-quarters of Americans polled favored this march into enemy territory, which began on the eve of off-year elections.[10]

To resist all this, Acheson would also have to resist his president. Most of his own advisers wanted to go forward, too, except for a covey of apostates in the PPS. One, Dorothy Fosdick, thought Acheson had betrayed his "better Atlanticist instincts" and played "right into Soviet hands." Kennan vigorously joined these critics, but Acheson found more wisdom in the views of Asianists Rusk and Allison, and even MacArthur, than the parting shots of a dreamer headed for Princeton's gothic towers. He seemed to agree with generals that sitting just south of a tactically irrelevant boundary would leave the ROK and all its defenders in permanent jeopardy.[11]

Besides, MacArthur's feats and the chance to wipe out Kim's regime were simply too exhilarating to resist. A clear-cut reduction in the acreage of world communism could do wonders to smother McCarthy and other Republicans. With each statement about Korean reunification and each approval of expanded military orders, Truman with Acheson's unvoiced approval closed the escape routes behind them, leaving only the chancy course northward.

Mao's zest for military adventure and striking a blow at the imperialists easily matched his enemy's and heavily influenced events to come. Communist records indicate the Chinese leader considered any crossing of the 38th parallel a huge provocation. Still, it is hard to imagine he would have gone all the way to the parallel to attack stationary UN forces. It is questionable but far more likely that he would have struck UN forces if they came to a full halt when they reached North Korea's capital. This would have left MacArthur not only controlling Pyongyang but 90 percent of Korea's population, even though still a substantial distance from Chinese or Soviet territory. But the war might have stopped there, stalemated, just as the youthful Luke Battle wanted—and would have been a UN victory. By accepting the status quo ante, or the status quo ante-plus, Truman could say he had rebuffed communism in Asia as he had in Greece and Turkey. He could have shown a face of power to the world while teaching Americans the wisdom of constraint in using such power. He could have escaped terrible battlefield defeats, the panic and gloom that followed, and other grave difficulties.[12]

Because we know about the difficulties to come, it is easy to condemn Truman and Acheson at this vital moment when they seized a chance to turn a point of weakness into strength and to silence if not slay their critics. But as Acheson later wrote, their goal of a "unified, independent, and democratic" Korea turned out to be nothing but "empty words."[13]

A moment's reflection clarifies why the circumspect alternative rejected by Truman must have looked as destructive as what actually happened. Had he halted MacArthur either at the 38th parallel, just above it, or even at Pyongyang *without* provoking Mao's onslaught, a large majority of Americans would almost surely have condemned him for letting the aggressors off the hook. He would have seemed fainthearted, if not worse, for not finishing them off. In other words, in this peninsula in which there were no truly good options, the "wisest" course might have led to a political disaster. So might the unwisest course, which Truman, longing for victory and vindication, chose when he sent MacArthur into the mouth of catastrophe. The ensuing Chinese intervention made Truman a deeply unpopular president. Acheson still toiled usefully to bolster western strength in Europe and to protect its interests in the Middle East, but more of his imaginative and constructive deeds now lay behind than ahead of him.

Military Romanticism Meets Self-Hypnosis

With few Chinese records yet released, it remains impossible to know exactly why Mao catapulted his "volunteers" into battle. But we know his primary motives, which were both defensive and offensive. MacArthur's advance not only roused concern about security—for China and Korea were "as close as the lips to the teeth"—but actuated all the circuits of Mao's deep-seated ache to drive the hated imperialists into the sea. He wanted to restore China's traditional sphere of power and to make its—and his—mark as the vanguard of revolution. He both feared Washington and wanted to humiliate it. Just as the Americans considered themselves in a struggle against an expansionist communist conspiracy, writes Michael Sheng, Mao believed they had targeted his regime "as one step toward the destruction of the 'revolutionary front' of the world." The Americans threatened China from Korea, and they had probably already killed his chance to seize Taiwan. They posed a danger to the very hope of an Asian anti-imperialist revolution. If possible, they had to be destroyed.[14]

Mao was a man of many manias who tried to industrialize China with backyard steel furnaces and revivify revolutionary ardor with recurrent purges and reeducation campaigns. American arms were just another contest, a goad to what Shu Guang Zhang calls his "military romanticism." He may even have decided to intervene *before* Inchon, though he probably would not have done so had the UN campaign stopped there. Nonetheless, by early August, he had mobilized a quarter million troops and put them along the Yalu, long before MacArthur posed any real threat to Chinese security. Immediately after Inchon, the insomniac, chain-smoking Mao instructed a subordinate to speed up plans for war, hoping "to win a glorious victory over the Americans." Once Mao's November intervention was under way and he had chalked up some successes, the British chiefs of staff concluded that his forces would now "go as far as they can." Chinese battle orders speak volumes on his grand objectives and imperviousness to U.S. assurances, both before and after MacArthur's last offensive. On 28 October 1950, he was planning for the "later annihilation of the enemy." Destroying "tens of thousands of the enemy's troops" would change the "whole international situation," he said on 18 November. On 11 December, after he had pushed the Americans back to the 38th parallel, he ordered his forces to cross it and beat them farther back so they could not "reorganize." Then would come a "final decisive campaign," during which his commander must refuse any cease-fire offers. On 26 December, he referred to his "long view of the war" that would destroy all enemy forces.[15]

That American leaders could not read Mao's mail does not acquit them of failing to read the danger of his zeal. In light of their misunderstanding of the situation, it would indeed have taken extraordinary restraint to surrender the opportunities MacArthur presented them. To prevent the fiasco to come, the joint chiefs would have to invoke nebulous fears to deny the urgent advice of a larger-than-life commander. They now bowed to him as a genius. Truman would have to refrain from delivering a smashing defeat to communism and pay no attention to the political explosions that would follow such self-abnegation. As Bruce Cumings writes, the victory at Inchon had created "the broadest coalition in Washington behind any Korean policy in the postwar period," from right to center-left, "healing breaches between internationalists and nationalists." Only Kennan among major American figures refused to board the bandwagon, a man not only not answerable to the public but who scoffed at its having any role in the making of foreign policy.[16]

As MacArthur's forces moved north, U.S. leaders satisfied themselves that Mao would not act. The best word to describe some of their reasoning is *weird*. Even as they reopened the foreign aid spigot for Chiang and bankrolled weapons purchases for Tibetan rebels, Acheson saw no reason for Beijing to feel threatened. Regarding the PRC as a Soviet puppet, Acheson and others concluded that since Moscow had not entered the war, neither would Beijing. They also concluded that since China had not intervened when it could have pushed the first arriving U.S. soldiers into the surf, it would not do so under harder conditions. Infiltrating these views were patronizing views of the Chinese and powerful tendencies to minimize them as nationalists, revolutionaries, and soldiers. Acheson did not grasp Mao's rage, his hostility to the capitalist west, or his fraternal feelings for the North Koreans who had fought with him to overthrow Chiang. Although an open channel between the United States and China might have made no difference, Acheson made no serious effort to create one.

Signs of a likely Chinese intervention appeared quite early. In the first days of the war, the JCS thought a half million Chinese troops stood in Manchuria but believed they had massed only for purposes of internal security. In early July, the state department discounted reports that MacArthur's forces had bumped into a smattering of Chinese soldiers or advisers. Only slightly concerned, on 24 July, Acheson told senators Beijing took its orders from Moscow, which was staying out of the fight. Soon afterward, he wrapped himself in a cloak of denial, deploring what would happen if China intervened, trying to reassure Beijing so it would not, and then convincing himself it *would* not. In late July, he told senators it would be "very bad" if the Chinese joined the war but added that with the help of go-betweens, State was assuring Beijing it had no reason to fight, stressing the lack of long-term American designs on Formosa.[17]

Unmistakable Chinese warnings began in August. The *People's Daily* parodied Acheson's defense perimeter speech as a "stretched-out snake" and bluntly warned that the PRC would not "supinely tolerate seeing their neighbors savagely invaded by imperialists." In the middle of the month, the CIA warned of a possible Soviet or Chinese intervention. The U.S. consul general in Hong

Kong in September twice exhorted Washington to take Chinese admonitions to heart. Acheson's reaction was obtuse at best. He claimed a major effort to detect China's intentions but showed minimal interest in assuaging its fears. With one hand in a 30 August press conference, he insisted Washington had done nothing to threaten China; with the other, he was stiffening allies' spines against offering it UN membership. Nor could he mask his condescension, as in his bombs and rockets remark, or repress his periodic blasts at Beijing as a Soviet puppet. It would be "sheer madness" for China to attack its traditional friends while ignoring the threat of "Russian penetration," he said on the eve of Inchon. With MacArthur's operation under way, State shrugged off reports tumbling into Washington via London, Moscow, and The Hague that China was steeling itself for combat. On 25 September in Beijing, Indian ambassador K. M. Panikkar heard that China would not "sit back with folded hands and let the Americans come up to the border." It would resist U.S. "aggression" even in the face of atomic bombs. Just as Truman issued orders to cross the parallel, London told the Americans not to credit the Indian warning and called Panikkar a "volatile and unreliable reporter."[18]

As MacArthur followed Japan's old attack route to Manchuria, Chinese leaders feared he might directly assault their country. On 3 October, Zhou Enlai told Panikkar the PRC might stay out if only ROK forces crossed the parallel, but any U.S. action in North Korea "would encounter Chinese resistance." This statement swiftly reached Washington, but instead of exploring Zhou's distinction, Acheson dismissed the report as the "mere vaporings of a panicky Panikar [sic]." Both the CIA and Ambassador Alan Kirk in Moscow abetted this attitude: Zhou was bluffing. And Washington knew Panikkar had earlier set off a false alarm with a predicted Chinese invasion of Formosa. If the Chinese did jump in, an equally unimpressed MacArthur told a British official, his air force would immediately smash Manchuria and northern China.[19]

Acheson discussed China's apparent fears and warnings with neither Beijing nor Moscow. He did nothing to exploit the Sino-Soviet cross-purposes in which he might still have believed. He warned aides against gloating over MacArthur's rout of Kim's force, but the only other caution Washington exercised came in a JCS note to MacArthur on 9 October saying he could not strike China itself in retaliation without consultation. Thinking the Chinese warnings a sham, Acheson also considered dithering riskier than driving forward. The very lack of Soviet outbursts justified ignoring those from Beijing. Contempt for Panikkar (Truman said he had "regularly" played Beijing's "game") boosted this sanguine view. So did State and CIA intelligence reports emphasizing Mao's fixation on solidifying his internal power. Acheson may also have been impressed by the advice of his trusted aide, John Carter Vincent, who from his Swiss exile advocated pushing ahead even if Zhou was *not* bluffing. Finally, squatting in the back of Acheson's mind may have been the fear that no one could stop MacArthur anyway.[20]

"Too Late Now to Stop This Process"

The literature detailing China's intervention in the Korean War is vast, multiplying, and contentious. Scholars poring over the same documents hold that Stalin did and did not renege on offers of Soviet air cover to Mao, that Mao did and did not decide to intervene only to pull back until he received Soviet help, and that Zhou did and did not misrepresent his talks with Stalin to serve his own veiled opposition to intervention. Although wildly optimistic that Washington would not come into the war and that he would wrap it up within a month, Kim wanted help. But he wanted only Soviet help and flatly turned down Mao's offers until MacArthur's offensive forced him to accept them. These perturbations, however, do not obscure the basic narrative. Mao did waver, partly because he was having trouble convincing colleagues of the need to intervene, but on the night of 1–2 October he made a first "final" decision to send troops across the Yalu "to fight the armies of the United States and the American lackey Syngman Rhee." According to a myth-like 1986 account, he made his conclusive decision on the 13th after he had "remained silent and did not shave for a whole week." The bearded revolutionary then ordered the attack that singed Acheson's mustache.[21]

Washington heard fragmentary reverberations of the arrhythmic Sino-Soviet-North Korean maneuvering in the first two weeks of October. There were also reports about military movements. Air Force Secretary Thomas Finletter grew "extremely worried" after air reconnaissance spotted tanks and artillery crossing from China to North Korea. Among those growing more concerned in the state department were U. Alexis Johnson, Livingston Merchant, and O. Edmund Clubb, who wanted to explore Indian negotiating proposals. Acheson told the British he would not seek Chinese participation in a UN discussion of Korea until after the November elections. If the Chinese wanted to play poker, they would "have to put more on the table." He still thought "showing hesitation and timidity" was riskier than marching north, where he figured the Chinese were probably bluffing. Though he agreed, Bevin wanted to make sure MacArthur would not strike China itself. Intelligence reports coming to Washington still considered a Chinese attack implausible, reinforcing Rusk's view that Beijing was too focused on internal dissent and disorganization to throw the dice for war. In Tokyo, MacArthur's intelligence corps failed to spot the first installment of a quarter million Chinese soldiers moving into North Korea.[22]

With mid-term elections two weeks away, Truman tried connecting himself to the warrior MacArthur by arranging a meeting on Wake Island. He also wanted some reassurance. He asked Acheson, Marshall, and the JCS to come along. All found excuses to say no, Acheson's that his presence would irritate the general. Besides, his job was to deal with "foreign powers and although MacArthur seemed often to be such I didn't think he ought to be recognized as that." No one remaining to advise the president—Averell Harriman, Secretary of the Army Frank Pace, Philip Jessup, and Rusk—had the stature to face down the beribboned commander. No one at Wake on 15 October subjected his prognoses to senior and weighty skepticism. MacArthur himself felt summoned "to the headmaster's study" but told Truman what he wanted to hear. The Chinese would almost certainly not intervene; if they did, he would grind them up in a great "slaughter"; and fighting would end by Thanksgiving. Truman returned home having failed to impress on MacArthur that he, not the general, established U.S. policies. Not only that, he had tacitly conspired to abrogate the chiefs' 30 September instructions to pause just above the 38th parallel before making further attacks. Later, MacArthur cited this and other signs of Truman's complaisance to defend himself against charges of disobedience.[23]

If the ill-fated Wake rendezvous had to occur, Acheson and especially Marshall should have been present to protect the president. But it is a large stretch to think that what the men at Wake said and did not say caused the imminent failure in Korea. For that, Truman, Marshall, Acheson, and the chiefs were all at least accessories. So was the CIA, which told Truman as he journeyed home the Chinese would give no more than covert help to their North Korean brethren. In late October, as Chinese forces encountered and even in some cases destroyed some ROK outfits, neither the Pentagon nor the agency took the clashes very seriously. In one of MacArthur's characteristically sinuous escapes from responsibility, he said it was Washington's job to assess the significance of Chinese warnings that, for himself, amounted to "blackmail." In the habit of overawing his superiors, he now again violated his orders, or at least elongated them. He placed U.S. forces out front in the march to the Yalu. Then, dividing them in two, with the army on the west and marines on the east (and with mountain ranges between), he charged into communist border country as Washington nervously acquiesced. Putting a stiff bridle on him at this point might have vitally affected the outcome, though by then, Mao planned to destroy all UN forces in a great communist victory. Over twelve days, about 130,000 "volunteers" entered North Korea without notice.[24]

As MacArthur was capturing Pyongyang on 19 October, the state department was seeing Chinese intervention as possible but "unlikely." Acheson worried about bombing raids far to the north, including a mistaken strike in clear weather against a Soviet airfield, but he was oblivious to the dangers posed by Mao's infantry. Far from wanting MacArthur to stop, or negotiate a buffer zone between UN forces and the Yalu, Mao was intentionally luring them north. As ROK troops reached an undefended sector of the Yalu on the 26th, neither MacArthur nor his Pentagon superiors seemed aware of the danger facing him. The day before, the PRC opened its first major attacks, soon backed by Soviet MIG fighters. Administration leaders stirred uneasily in a vague new sense of crisis, heightened by stories of Rhee's execution of political prisoners. On 1 November, Puerto Rican nationalists made a shocking attempt on Truman's life at the Blair House. Six months later, Acheson would single out 27 October as the date of his first realistic fear of a possible Chinese intervention, based on information from India. But even then, remarkably, his high-level advisers were writing brash directives on establishing a new united "Republic of Korea." Similarly, the Pentagon flooded MacArthur's in-box with orders on occupying North Korea in the name of the UN. "We can now be easy in our minds," said the *New York Times* on 29 October, "as to the military outcome" in Korea.[25]

The CIA seemed to bend over backward to ignore the plainest meaning of new information. Chinese units were now in Korea, it agreed on 30 October, but only in "small numbers"; they were probably trying to slow MacArthur by having "reports" made of their presence. Beijing only worried about its Yalu hydroelectric plants, said agency analysts. Marshall agreed, swallowing the theory whole. All the while, Acheson was meeting almost daily with defense officials, never with useful result. Just as the UN declared that MacArthur had no destructive designs on China's border or interests, Mao graciously released some U.S. prisoners and broke off his attack. His aim was to draw MacArthur even farther into his killing zone, a prospect Washington ignored. The scare caused by Mao's halfway attack might have shaped Democratic election defeats on 7 November, which expanded Republican congressional minorities, but a strained optimism revived with the pause in fighting. Puzzled, MacArthur wrote messages defending his own actions. "Here," Acheson remarked of one, was "a posterity paper if there ever was one," written to exculpate himself and put "maximum pressure on Washington to reverse itself and adopt his proposals for widening the war." Truman approved one such proposal—for new bombing raids on the Yalu area—over Acheson's objections.[26]

Acheson's memoirs serve as his posterity paper. Although unsparing in his criticism of MacArthur, he was nearly as severe in his criticism of all presidential advisers, including himself, for losing their "last chance to halt the march to disaster." They all knew "something was badly wrong" but "muffed" the chance to correct it. As the danger rose, they all became "deeply apprehensive" and were frank in speaking about it together but "not quite frank enough." Acheson felt unable to press military recommendations on the president that were opposed by the chiefs. They in turn slavishly adhered to traditional doctrines about a theater commander's autonomy. Acheson thought the United States might have avoided catastrophe had Marshall and the JCS proposed and Truman accepted falling back to the narrow "Pyongyang-Wonsan line" to form a "continuous defensive position." But that meant risking MacArthur's accusations "that they had denied him victory" and then firing him "under arguable circumstances." As a result, everyone stood transfixed until "the chance was lost." No one had acted improperly but none could have been "quite satisfied with himself afterward."[27]

"We Face an Entirely New War"

Washington was paralyzed from 6 to 9 November, riveted by premonitions of debacle. Washington's leaders could not understand how their own slackness had produced MacArthur's witless tactics, or how their ecstatic thirst for the destruction of a communist regime had imperiled their own army. Truman was receiving no effective advice from his counselors. Almost any decision now might bring dismal results. American forces could be ruined, or they might be preserved, through a huge expansion of the war or humiliating evacuation. Any of these could undermine NATO, halt the European defense buildup, drive a stake into the UN, set off searing domestic arguments, or even light the fuse of World War III.

Just as Mao's army went into temporary hiding, the CIA finally spotted it and changed its tune, now estimating a force large enough to halt MacArthur in his tracks, preserve Kim's regime, and sweep to victory. The communists had shown a "grave" willingness to risk "general war" and "a showdown with the West." In a cable to Bevin, Acheson noted ten possible motives for Beijing's action and finally admitted it must truly fear a U.S. attack. All he could then do was counsel against expanding the war, but he also wanted China punished. He kept a merry front and joked with reporters. When asked on 8 November to comment on Vyshinsky's claim that no regular Chinese units were in Korea, he told a story about the man who greeted Lord Curzon by saying, "Mr. Smith, I believe," to which Curzon replied: "My dear fellow, if you believe that, you will believe anything."[28]

In Moscow, Stalin was rubbing his hands at the drain of western resources that would follow a long Sino-U.S. struggle. In Washington, Truman's advisers met in his absence in a crucial NSC meeting on 9 November. On the table was MacArthur's mulish response to pleas for restraint, which he asserted would fatally compromise UN objectives. Having to patrol a static line of defense indefinitely would "destroy" his troops' morale. Everyone sitting around the table wanted negotiations but did nothing to promote them, and the meeting went nowhere. Acheson found no support for a 10-mile-wide buffer zone south of the Yalu, a pale version of the 60-to-120-mile strip London was championing. At one point, he joined Bradley in thinking "an election after reaching the Yalu" might end U.S. troubles. Polish peace feelers were surely unacceptable, requiring the departure of U.S. forces from Korea and the Seventh Fleet from the Straits, along with recognition of Chinese sovereignty over Formosa. No one thought of responding to find out if there was any give in the Polish positions. Nor did anyone advise ordering MacArthur to pause while they figured out what to do, let alone caution him. He remained free to do virtually anything except bomb Manchuria. On 10 November, the UN Security Council—which the Soviet representative had rejoined—reaffirmed respect for Chinese and North Korean borders and interests. With his orders unchanged and the Chinese hiatus four days old, MacArthur started off again.[29]

New warnings from Beijing came quickly. Zhou pointedly linked North Korea's independent existence to Chinese "security." Acheson reacted feebly, mixing halfhearted negotiating probes with more statements about China's safety not being in doubt. Finally, in the middle two weeks of November, he tried to contact Zhou, using Swedish, Indian, and Polish contacts, but with no result. On 15–16 November, Truman and Acheson issued reassuring statements describing U.S. intentions and disclaiming any designs on Manchuria or Chinese-owned facilities, north or south of the Yalu. Truman promised without qualification not to carry the war to Chinese territory. But neither man made approaching Beijing a top priority or asked themselves why China was chancing a showdown. This stemmed partly from continuing doubts that it *was*, doubts built on the fact that the latest Chinese warnings came through India, whose own head of external affairs said he had no confidence in Panikkar.[30]

If only subliminally, Washington now seemed to grasp its lack of credibility in Beijing. Following promises to remove itself from the Chinese civil war, the United States put the Seventh Fleet into the Formosa Straits. It jettisoned statements about fighting to restore the status quo ante bellum. It had first said only South Korean forces would move above the 38th parallel. Now the Americans again tried, but in vain, to allay China's suspicions. Acheson rejected British ideas of a broad buffer zone south of the Yalu, which he thought would be worthless if as he properly suspected Mao was fighting for a strategic victory. For now, he told Ambassador Oliver Franks, there was no choice but to let MacArthur proceed. An idea for disencumbering Washington from the Formosan government foundered when the U.S. delegation at the UN rebelled at leaving its fate in Security Council hands. Chinese broadcasts were excoriating all U.S. assurances as nefarious lies to cover MacArthur's plan to invade Manchuria. Moscow, using a Prague "Peace Congress," called for a worldwide conference to end the war, halt Japanese and German "militarization," eject the United States from Formosa, and prosecute U.S. citizens for war crimes. A stream of perplexing CIA estimates deepened anxiety in Washington. Because the estimates did not confidently identify Chinese intentions, officials refused to use them to halt MacArthur's offensive.[31]

Ignoring the writhing politicians he despised, MacArthur moved his twin but divided vanguards north, insensible to their peril. Scattered U.S. units reached the Yalu on the 21st, but the Chinese held back. Their number standing somewhere nearby was not the 60,000–70,000 estimated by MacArthur's intelligence officers but more than a quarter million, and their purpose was not to deter MacArthur but "annihilate" him. With Mao concealing his forces, fear now spread about his intentions. A newly alert Bevin protested MacArthur's talk of "hot pursuit" of the enemy into Manchuria. Knowing Acheson had "very little control" over him, Bevin cabled Zhou of the UN's lack of "hostile intent." The state department's Livingston Merchant wanted Truman to send a statement of benign intent directly to Mao—or Stalin. Now also fearful, Davies at the PPS urged stopping MacArthur and negotiating a demilitarized zone between Chinese and UN forces. The joint chiefs' General James H. Burns wanted his superiors to fly to Tokyo to talk to MacArthur about the growing emergency. He wrote Marshall that the United States ran "a serious risk of becoming involved in the world war we are trying to avoid." Yet Reston reported the administration still thought the Chinese were bluffing.[32]

Trailing assistants, Acheson on 21 November went to the Pentagon to see Marshall and the chiefs. The dialogue that ensued was lively but saturated with unwarranted optimism and bereft of concrete results. Acheson occasionally tried to pull the military away from the abyss but seemed unaware he had stepped into it himself. He wanted fighting confined to Korea to prevent a larger Chinese intervention but remained otherwise markedly ambitious, looking toward a new, UN-organized Korean government, a Chinese withdrawal, and "the surrender of North Korean remnants." He did not urge an end to MacArthur's offensive, gaining Marshall's gratitude for trying to be "useful" rather than to embarrass MacArthur. The chiefs' *idée de jour* was to unilaterally proclaim a slender buffer along the Yalu, from which soldiers on high ground could watch the river flats. Should this require negotiations, they demanded no cessation of MacArthur's offensive meanwhile. Army and air force leaders brushed off concern about how the Russians would react to having GIs patrol so close to their border, though Acheson, Harriman, and Admiral Forrest Sherman all expressed concern. The meeting closed with an informal consensus favoring some kind of demilitarized zone in the far north and against putting serious restraints on MacArthur. It was their last chance to confer before MacArthur kicked off his end-the-war offensive.[33]

On the 24th, the general declared that U.S. forces would be "home by Christmas." An early victim of his offensive was Mao Zedong's son, Mao Anying, killed in an air attack. MacArthur blithely thought he had cowed the Chinese, and the United States, said reporter Elmer Davis, was "warm with the certainty of victory." Raising imprudence to a new level, Acheson, after saying he did not know what the Chinese might do, wanted to *test* their seriousness by pushing ahead. The campaign, he told Bevin, would clarify "many matters which are now obscure." Sensing grave dangers, Attlee told his cabinet he might fly to Washington to talk to Truman.[34]

Two days after UN forces pushed out, the Chinese struck back with a shocking counterattack that produced the worst rout in U.S. military history, or, in Acheson's view, since Bull Run. Attacks "exploded" all round MacArthur's "many columns, in their front, on their flanks, and in their rear," Acheson wrote. United Nations forces, mainly American, took 11,000 casualties in seventy-two hours. Within days, communists again occupied Pyongyang. In a month, UN troops had again fallen below the 38th parallel and Seoul was about to fall, yet again. On 28 November, Washington received an agitated cable from its five-star commander: "We face an entirely new war."[35]

From the Frying Pan?

The next six weeks were the worst of Truman's presidency. MacArthur swayed from wanting to quit to starting another war against China. Of his advice to stop his foes by dropping atomic bombs into the Yalu, Bradley said, "I've never heard anything so preposterous in my life." Shocked Republicans demanded all restraints off MacArthur and the ouster of Acheson. Walter Lippmann called for a pullout and a clean sweep of the state department. Truman's approval ratings skidded to 36 percent, Acheson's to 20 percent of those who could identify him. Backlash spread, stirring opposition against sending new army divisions to Europe. Allies feared the outraged Americans would plunge into Asia, even start World War III with direct strikes against China, now equipped with a Soviet security pact. From their own avidity, China demanded UN censure of the United States and the removal of all foreign forces from Korea and Formosa.[36]

As Washington officials tried to regroup, the CIA still believed Mao would not act outside the Yalu basin. Worried that Europeans would doubt U.S. leadership, Acheson made his strangest attempt yet to calm the Chinese, directing their attention to the St. Lawrence and Rio Grande as proof of America's lamb-like intentions.

Administration leaders also began to devise an exonerative narrative of the crisis. Not yet ready to blame MacArthur publicly, they pointed to the immense preparation needed for China's offensive. Mao, they claimed with merit, had long plotted his attack irrespective of UN advances. Using a theory he would never relinquish, Acheson told Bevin the "two offensives ran into each other." Though exculpatory in purpose, this rationalization was not wildly off the mark, except that Acheson still considered Stalin the villain of the piece. Mao's necessary groundwork, he told senators, proved he planned "to destroy UN forces," not resist their northward progress. His refusal to accept blame for Washington was similar to his disclaimer of responsibility for Chiang's fall in the *China White Paper*. Urging PRC leaders not to be "dupes," on a radio broadcast he described MacArthur's offensive as no threat to their nation. Beijing's aggression, in contrast, was "premeditated," even more "unprovoked" and "immoral" than Pyongyang's original attack.[37]

On 28 November, he told senators in testimony that the danger of a larger war was "very close." The same day at the NSC, he predicted that the communists would use the Asian turmoil to apply new pressure on U.S. interests in Europe. Everyone at the meeting was anxious about MacArthur's next move and exasperated by his home-by-Christmas statement, but Marshall and the chiefs thought he could soon turn around and counterattack. Truman said no one should "pull the rug out from under him."

However deluded about the Chinese intervention, Acheson had already decided what the government should do in its wake: keep the war confined to Korea, maintain the NSC-68 buildup (aimed at Europe), and tell MacArthur he had to manage with the forces at hand. If not about MacArthur, both Acheson and Marshall had shed illusions about what the United States could achieve in Korea. They agreed too about the perils of overreaction or panic. Everyone must realize, Acheson said at the NSC gathering, that the war was "a world matter" and that pulling out would be ruinous to U.S. alliances. Without fighting on Chinese territory (or "playing with Chiang" again), they should covertly "stir up trouble" for Beijing and have China branded in the UN as an aggressor. Because they could do nothing about Moscow's hidden hand except through general war, they should not talk about it. Such talk, anyway, would frighten allies and expose U.S. weakness if unmatched by action. "Our great objective" now, he continued, must be "to terminate the fighting, to turn over some area to the Republic of Korea, and to *get out*"—but not "in a way that will lose face." Getting a Korean settlement would allow the United States to return to subduing French resistance to a European army. Moscow's risk-taking demonstrated that time "was shorter than we thought"—that the moment of maximum danger was already upon them. Acheson's powers of leadership seemed rejuvenated and his influence in the administration restored, even as he still harbored delusions about the war.[38]

Two days later, a frazzled Truman unwittingly deepened the crisis when he fell into a reporter's ambush. He seemed to say MacArthur could use nuclear weapons in Korea and that it was up to him whether to do so. Excited reporters gave him a chance to backtrack, but instead he added that the atomic bomb was just "one of our weapons." The commander in the field, he asserted, would "have charge of the use of the weapons, as he always has." As Acheson later recalled, afterward everyone "rushed round like chickens without heads and we put out a clarification." The result in Europe was tumult. Franks told Acheson of Britain's "very great" nervousness. Attlee, acting without the services of the ailing Bevin and ignoring Franks's advice not to take Truman's remarks literally, demanded an instant Washington audience.[39]

Truman's advisers went into virtually nonstop meetings to get on the same page for Attlee's unwanted descent on the Potomac. Acheson yielded the last scraps of hopes for a Sino-Soviet fissure but still considered it folly to react to the current crisis with a fight against Beijing's "second team." The "real enemy" was Moscow. As Attlee prepared for his flight, Washington officials agreed against withdrawal from Korea after many flirted with the idea, including Acheson. Still thinking of World War III, Army chief of staff General Lawton Collins said Korea was "not worth a nickel while the Russians hold Vladivostok and positions on the other flank." On 3 December, Rusk tipped the balance against evacuation, arguing that it would be far better to be pushed out than leave voluntarily. Convinced, and moved, Acheson told Truman: "We just can't let them do this to the United States." The nation would become one of "the greatest appeasers of all time," he told a meeting of State and Defense officials, "if we abandon the Koreans and they are slaughtered." Another "Dunkirk," would be a "disaster" but not a disgrace. If Attlee forced Truman into peace talks, Beijing would try to drive the United States out of Asia.[40]

Concerned about Soviet machinations and shaky domestic support, Acheson urged Truman to declare a national emergency, which he did two weeks later. No one yet openly criticized the UN commander, but Acheson had now "lost all faith in MacArthur's judgment." In meetings at the Pentagon on 1 December, he bewailed allies' "virtual state of panic," including signs that the crisis was inspiring neutralism in West Germany. The way to restore faith in U.S. leadership was not through spleen-venting raids on Manchuria, which could bring in the Russians and toss the United States "from the frying pan into the fire," but through winding up the war with a respectable peace settlement. The dispirited chiefs acquiesced, wanting as Acheson did to focus on holding "majority support" in the UN and restoring "a solid front among our allies." On the 2d, Acheson finished another long day at 10:30 P.M., when he "went wearily home to a famished wife for sustenance, spirituous and solid."[41]

In the emergency, Kennan volunteered to help, an offer Acheson jumped at. He returned from Princeton on Sunday, 3 December, and promptly associated himself with Rusk's case against bailing out. The worn out Acheson invited him home to dinner at day's end. Touched by the invitation, Kennan wrote later of his host's "characteristic spirit and wit, which no crisis and no weariness seemed ever to extinguish." Acheson undoubtedly mixed wicked anecdotes with dry martinis, but the humor-challenged Kennan remembered "a gentleman, the soul of honor, attempting to serve the interests of the country against the background of a Washington seething with anger, confusion and misunderstanding." He was burdened by "a dreadful situation he had not created" while enduring "the most vicious and unjust of personal attacks from the very men—the congressional claque and other admirers of General MacArthur—who, by their insistence on this adventurous and ill-advised march to the Yalu, had created it."

Kennan's memory slights Acheson's own culpability but nicely captures his buoyancy under fire. The next morning, he was off to greet Attlee at the airport. When he reached the department, he found a note from Kennan on his desk. What most counted now, Kennan wrote, was how Americans responded to this "major failure and disaster to our national fortunes." If they absorbed "its lessons" with honesty and dignity, if, as after Pearl Harbor, they fought back with new effort and intelligence, they could maintain the power, allies, and confidence needed for eventual negotiations with the Soviets. But if the government tried to hide "the full measure of our misfortune" or "seek relief" in "bluster or petulance or hysteria, we can easily find this crisis resolving itself into an irreparable deterioration of our world position—and of our confidence in ourselves." Stirred, Acheson read the note to those assembled in his office, including Kennan. He urged them to ignore the "spirit of defeatism emanating from headquarters in Tokyo," where MacArthur's contingent predicted a complete withdrawal, and set them to work repairing the damage and surmounting the pessimism rife at the Pentagon. He told Kennan he had been "greatly missed in the daily councils on the fifth floor." He telephoned Marshall to convey Kennan's wisdom, and in the days ahead repeatedly cited his view that the worst possible time for Washington to negotiate with the communist world was when its own armies were on the run.[42]

Goaded by the Soviet ambassador, Mao decided to go for broke. As his troops closed on the 38th parallel, he divulged his terms for peace. Washington must withdraw all troops from Korea, break ties to Formosa, and hand the China seat in the UN to the PRC. From Washington, Reston reported that "every official movement in the capital today, every official report from Tokyo, and every private estimate of the situation" signaled emergency and "alarm." Even during the first night of the war, the atmosphere had not been so "grim."[43]

Curious Quiescence

The fiasco in Korea was a famous defeat. MacArthur, Truman, Marshall, the joint chiefs, the CIA, and Acheson all deserve blame. As MacArthur drove north, political officials were unnerved by fear of the political right. They also feared letting a cold war triumph slip through their fingers. They were overawed by the man Acheson called the "Sorcerer of Inchon." Because the sorcerer moved so rapidly above the 38th parallel, and because Mao was so eager to smash the imperialists, by late November, almost nothing could have saved the hapless crew in Washington. Earlier restraint could have averted a Sino-American war. If political reality had made it impossible for Truman to order a halt at the 38th parallel, he might at least have taken his chances with stopping MacArthur from going much farther and still claim a UN victory without destroying the North Korean regime. In reality, of course, he and his aides applauded as MacArthur headed far beyond the parallel. What ushered them to defeat were assumptions of U.S. military superiority, hunger for a large win, and an aversion to negotiating with communists. Nearly every virus endemic to political debacles infected them, from sketchy information and poor judgment to lack of courage and will. In addition, there was Acheson's inability to challenge the sainted Marshall.[44]

Although we now know far more than previously about Chinese obduracy and militancy, American errors were breathtaking nonetheless. Specialists in the policy planning staff, John Melby recalled, "were just poo-poohing" the idea of Chinese intervention the moment signs of Mao's attack first surfaced. He was too overwhelmed with internal problems and would not fight "for years." Finding the fit of Mao's shoes uncomfortable, Acheson repeatedly insisted that U.S. "actions held no menace for anyone." A plague of intelligence failures confirmed policymakers' complacency. Even when reports on the Chinese buildup in Manchuria were accurate, CIA analyses were riddled with non sequiturs. MacArthur's own intelligence apparatus in Tokyo belittled PRC capabilities, while Washington underestimated China's stomach for war and the ability and courage of its soldiers. Western powers had gotten what they wanted in China for decades. Now the cultural blinders worn by Americans (*and* Chinese) created chasms of otherness neither Washington nor Beijing could span.[45]

Next to MacArthur, Truman and Marshall's failures were greatest, but Acheson's were great too, largely because of his inability to transcend that

Sino-American gulf. Like a man inexplicably relaxing on highway pavement, unaware of his danger until a truck's horns blasted until it was too late, Acheson could not grasp what impact MacArthur's advance on well-blazed Japanese invasion routes had on the Chinese. He thought they could barely put together a working state. He could not imagine why they worried less about Russian than American imperialism. A victim of cognitive dissonance, he believed both in the potential of great Sino-Soviet conflicts and that the Chinese communists were Soviet puppets. He pored over intelligence reports for signs that Moscow would push *China* into the war and found none. Dispatches from Kirk in Moscow and Loy Henderson in New Delhi underpinned his own prejudices. Even as Mao's troops began drawing blood, one of Acheson's favorites, John Paton Davies, said they would do no critical damage. And Acheson's disdain for India was a match for his contempt of China. Joseph Alsop recalled a dinner party in which, "in his most archly aristocratic form," he jeeringly referred to Ambassador "Pannicker." It did not help that Panikkar's source was Zhou Enlai, whom the state department had its own reasons to distrust.[46]

It was fatal not to curb MacArthur, and the man who might have done it, Marshall, refused. The city was full of people who knew MacArthur well enough to understand the necessity of taking extra precautions with him. None of them prodded Marshall to rein him in. This absorbed Acheson in 1967 as he sorted through papers in writing his memoirs. He asked Nitze if he could explain "Marshall's curious quiescence." Acheson personally recalled hearing Marshall claim that, since he was now a civilian, he could no longer treat MacArthur as if he were his chief of staff. "It seems to me," he wrote, "he overdid it." In vain, the memoirist also sought enlightenment from retired General Matthew B. Ridgway and from Marshall's biographer, Forrest C. Pogue. He would later assert that his own department could certainly not interfere in "a strategic military operation" or ask Truman "to intervene." He claimed that he had freely discussed "the utter madness and folly of what MacArthur was doing" with Marshall, but obviously to no effect. Almost certainly one reason they only *talked* was their continued hope that MacArthur would deliver them a huge cold war conquest.[47]

Acheson's assertion that his department could not thrust its oar into the currents of military strategy will not hold water. He did this all the time when Louis Johnson was secretary of defense. Because of his undue deference to Marshall, he devised elaborate reasons to explain why he did not challenge him to restrain his runaway five-star. With Nitze, Robert Oppenheimer, Herbert Feis, U. Alexis Johnson, and others listening around a Princeton table in 1954, he outlined the essentials of what he would repeat in *Present at the Creation*. He told his colleagues he could not blame either Marshall or Truman for not overriding this super-confident and "self-willed theater commander." MacArthur had constantly told them: "I know what I'm doing, boys, now don't you be nervous-nellies on this." He had a "grave" duty himself to complain to the joint chiefs but didn't, because he was a military "amateur." He also claimed he could not have gone to Truman and said, "Look, I don't know anything about soldiering, but for Heaven's sake this is very bad," because it would have put the president in a corner with a direct demand that he tackle "a situation which he could not solve." Responding to his pressure, Truman might have complained to the generals, and they in turn might have said that if he wanted to take over control of the 8th Army himself, he could have it, for "he was the Commander-in-Chief." Neither the president nor the chiefs, Acheson said at Princeton, could command that army "from Washington." Hamstrung by their view of a theater commander's role, the JCS did "the best they could." All Acheson might have accomplished by intervening was confront Truman "with the gravest sort of problem" to which he "could not offer any solution and nobody else could offer any solution. So I did not go."[48]

It almost certainly would have made no difference, anyway, after the 8th Army had moved beyond the northern neck of Korea, possibly even if it had stopped at the Wonson-Pyongyang line. Either of these, and surely the former, would have triggered an armed response by a hostile nation with a leader brimming with large ambitions. Ultimately, the clash between China and the United States was a failure of statesmanship on both sides. In the sense that their own flaws and errors brought ruin to both Americans and Chinese, it was also a tragedy. Recognizing at least the scale of the tragedy, Acheson described the Sino-American collision at the end of 1950 as "one of the most terrific disasters that had occurred to American foreign policy," which "did more to destroy that administration, and did more to undermine and destroy American foreign policy than anything." He finally blamed this "colossal" event on MacArthur's "desire to do what he felt was the right thing to do, and almost the complete impotence of the Government of the United States in any effective way to change or deal" with him. Because Acheson himself failed to "deal" with MacArthur, he finally refused to cast blame on others who didn't. He wondered if even George Washington could have: "I just don't know who would have."[49]

In 1952, McGeorge Bundy asked: "Could the United Nations and the United States have stopped in October, merely because of threats and fears?" He thought it "doubtful." The overdetermined decision to transit the 38th parallel and the inability of Washington to pull the "Stop" strap suggest the bleak wisdom of his answer. Its bleakness lies in the implication that a democratic government, led by generally admirable men, could not halt a calamitous train of events once it left the station, so paralyzed were they by the force of cold war passions and hemmed in by circumstances. Acheson found that the war brought an opportunity to substitute strength for weakness. He was in thrall to the same general of the army who rendered so many others helpless—but also to his own hopes.[50]

24

JOB'S COMFORTER AND
THE MAD SATRAP

The British Are Coming

The last two months of 1950 were "a dreadful passage for Truman," writes biographer David McCullough, in General Omar Bradley's view worse than the snow, mud, and blood of the Battle of the Bulge. They were awful for Dean Acheson, too. If having both enemies and "friends" crying for his head was not enough, now came the unwelcome visit of what Acheson called "a Job's comforter," Clement Attlee, ostensibly prompted by Truman's inept remarks about using atomic bombs in Korea. Coming just "as all our forces were going to pieces," this little summit might force inopportune peace talks and tear holes in the western alliance.[1]

The British prime minister talked with French leaders before leaving London and in some respects represented all of Washington's European allies. Although expecting less obeisance from neutrals in the wake of U.S. reversals, American leaders were distressed by the carping of allies, who seemed to believe the United States would imperil the world with a hubristic embrace of Mac-Arthurite ventures, dashing pell-mell into a broader Asian conflict and quitting its brief experiment in European leadership. In return, U.S. officials grumbled that communist bluster would cause the Europeans to faint dead away, deserting NATO's buildup in favor of appeasing the enemy with concessions that would convert hard problems into impossible ones.[2]

It was a dangerous moment, arousing allies to intrude and Americans to act on their own hook. Both sides were restive. In the middle of Attlee's visit, a false sighting of Soviet attack planes streaking for North America caused a full alert, with fighters scrambling from Canadian bases only to intercept flocks of geese. Moscow and Beijing were eager to exploit MacArthur's misfortunes. Soviet Foreign Minister Andrei Vyshinsky believed the "correlation of forces" now favored the communists. Mao Zedong wanted to force the enemy completely out of Korea. In a cabinet meeting, Acheson coupled complaints about Attlee's intrusion with invocations of "a week of prayer to produce the ammunition."[3]

Acheson routinely used his 9:30 staff meetings to prepare for such pilgrimages of foreign dignitaries. Planning for Attlee began at the same 4 December gathering at which Dean Rusk and George Kennan made their fervent pleas to hold fast in Korea. Hoping the Pentagon "would sing the same song," Acheson told his men to buck up the joint chiefs' morale while making sure "they did not bomb Manchuria." As the 9:30 meeting ended, Kennan told him the USSR would scent weakness in any Attlee-sponsored bid for a cease-fire. Now "was the poorest time possible for any negotiations with the Russians." Heartened by Rusk and Kennan's fortitude, Acheson went to the White House to tell the president "the Chinese simply must not be allowed to drive us out of Korea."[4]

Attlee's visit was as much about buttressing his own fading government as pulling Truman's hand off the nuclear button. The British might fear "annihilation without representation," but the prime minister knew better than to think Truman would go off half-cocked. Despite his later claims in the House of Commons about having a salutary effect on Truman, he told Canadians there had never been any danger of using the bomb in Korea. Coming to Washington gave him an excuse to request more financial help for Britain's arms buildup, but he was mainly out to stop the plan to condemn China in the UN as an "aggressor."

Acheson found the balding, dour, sixty-seven-year-old "persistently depressing." Countryman Harold Nicolson brushed him off as "so small, so chétif" and Winston Churchill as "a sheep in sheep's clothing." With his little Chaplinesque mustache, wrote Acheson, Attlee talked with the "passion of a woodchuck chewing a carrot." But Acheson's mounting irritation came not from personal dislike but faltering British confidence in U.S. leadership. The five days of talks that followed on 4–8 December left him with "a deep dislike and distrust" of all summits. "When a chief of state or head of government makes a fumble," he observed, "the goal line is open behind him." Yet he also found British fears useful to blunt bursts of Pentagon bellicosity and restrain Truman's longing to thrash the Chinese.[5]

In fact, Attlee quickly discovered the administration was already set on a moderate course, though in his judgment too harried by military defeat and domestic criticism to consider the more temperate possibilities he favored. Truman's government would neither expand the war nor call it quits. His advisers believed attacking China might draw in the Soviets, unshackle Chiang Kai-shek, and thus vastly expand the war, even to the point of a Chinese assault on Japan. Such a war would drain resources from a U.S. military still recouping from postwar demobilization, leave European allies exposed to a Soviet attack, and even cause them to seek cover in neutralism. Attlee learned that Acheson, at least, believed nothing in Asia was worth such a price.

But to end the fighting in Korea, the Briton still favored giving the PRC United Nations membership and cutting Formosa loose. In vigorous resistance, Acheson told him: "We must avoid rewarding the Chinese for their aggression and equally avoid putting an Army on the Chinese mainland and pulling in the Russian Airforce by all-out bombing of China." Attlee gained assurance the administration no longer hoped to take all of Korea, but Acheson, not about to let this visitor have a look at local dirty linen, rejected his insinuations that MacArthur's rashness had provoked Beijing's intervention. Only deserting South Korea altogether on 25 June, he told him, could have prevented the clash of two independently planned offensives.[6]

Acheson's largest concern was having allies force him to the peace table, which would badly compromise American foreign policy. In Asia, it would terrify the Philippines and probably scuttle peace talks with Japan. He accepted the hypothetical inevitability of negotiating with China but reproved Attlee—who thought Acheson "was obviously under heavy fire"—for his keenness for compromise. It was as unjustified as ill timed. When Attlee said nothing was "more important than retaining the good opinion of Asia," Acheson "remarked acidly that the security of the United States was more important." Bitter at China's betrayal of Americans who had "nursed" it through "50 years of friendliness," he answered Attlee's claim that conciliation would separate China from the USSR by cracking that he "had probably been more bloodied" for such views than anyone. Whatever the distant future might bring, he now saw no way to exploit any Sino-Soviet differences. "Satellites" or not, the Chinese were making trouble, and it made no sense to talk with them while U.S. forces were retreating. In a correct forecast of the months ahead, he hoped to reverse China's offensive and mete out severe and condign punishment of its armies before seeking peace talks. Correct strategic thinking, not the lack of good Chinese "table manners," drove his view. Since more hostility would harm the Chinese more than the Americans, it was time for them to "prove" they were friends, not the other way around. Neither diplomatic nor military circumstances required recognizing the PRC government, admitting it to the UN, or giving it Formosa. On 7 December, Truman blurted out another reason not to pay for peace. Giving China UN membership would be "political dynamite in the United States." Acheson quietly concurred: "This was true."[7]

Attlee must have noticed how China's intervention had hardened Washington's cold war attitudes. Truman told him the Chinese were and would remain "satellites of Russia." The only way to fight communism was "to eliminate it." Acheson described Mao's ruling group as "better pupils" of the Russians than the eastern Europeans. On the presidential yacht, *Williamsburg*, the president pointed out to Attlee "that we do not desert our friends when the going is rough."

Since the common danger was Soviet aggressiveness, Acheson remarked, all cold war issues were connected. Thus, the American people would consider it absurd to build strength in Europe while accepting weakness in Asia. Since Moscow now held all the high cards, the "moment for negotiations with the communist movement is the worst since 1917." The west should stick to building its own strength. What was going on in Korea, he presently told members of the Senate, was a pure power struggle between the United States and a united communist front "to see who is top dog."[8]

He showed no discomfort wielding a verbal bludgeon against Washington's staunchest ally and probably thought Attlee had it coming. Responsible Americans as opposed to "vociferous extremists" would react to any faintheartedness or allied efforts to undermine the U.S. position in Korea by rejecting plans to strengthen NATO. Bluntly pointing to the side on which the British had their bread buttered, he told Ambassador Oliver Franks that forcing an American "surrender" in Asia would cause "American opinion" to turn its back on "those who had brought about this collapse." In relief of Acheson's stern message, Truman and Attlee hit it off personally, and on the 6th Franks dissolved considerable tension with a gracefully hosted dinner at the British embassy. There "Captain Truman hammered out some Great War standards on the much-abused Embassy piano," and "Major Attlee sang along with tuneless gusto." Ignoring a few sour notes, the musicians and their scribes eventually reached broad agreement on which tune to play next. The Britons agreed with the decision to stay the course in Korea and with gritted teeth complied with the U.S. refusal to rush to negotiations with China. The Americans in turn implicitly agreed to keep the fighting confined to Korea and abandon any plans for Korean unification under pro-western aegis. The two sides agreed to seek a cease-fire through the UN and quickly assented when New Delhi sought approval of a project to help bring it about. Confidence rose when General Lawton Collins returned from a trip to Korea on the summit's last day to report that the retreat had ended, and so too had the mood of "hysteria." Attlee cabled Nehru that Truman, Acheson, and the Pentagon were acting "coolly and calmly" despite all their political troubles.[9]

The worst moment of this visit came near the very end, on 7 December. It was "one of those close calls that lurk in summit meetings," Acheson wrote, for, to his horror, Truman and Attlee met alone in a separate room. When they reemerged, both were smiling, but Truman failed to notice the feathers sticking in Attlee's mustache when he told their seconds about having agreed that the United States "would not consider the use of the bomb without consulting with the United Kingdom." Attlee had asked for a written statement, but Truman said it was impossible to improve on "a man's word." Swallowing hard and suffering from what Franks called "the equivalent of convulsions," Acheson waited a day to act amid discussions of a final communique. Then, along with two cabinet members and others, he maneuvered Truman into the Oval Office where he explained that his promise to Attlee violated U.S. law. Besides producing a congressional uproar, it would set off a "most vicious offensive against him and the British." Truman agreed instead to a broad pledge of close U.S.-UK contacts in *all* difficult world situations. Soon his special assistant for atomic energy, Gordon Arneson, had pen to paper trying to bridge the gap between "Mr. Attlee's brief and the consent decree." The new phrasing expressed Truman's hope "that world conditions would never call for the use of the atomic bomb" and his "desire to keep the Prime Minister at all times informed of developments which might bring about a change in the situation." "A little sadly," Attlee agreed. This seemed to be the end of the matter, and as far as the rest of the world knew, it was, but the two sides never agreed on a common record of their discussions. This left Attlee free later to claim victory in the Commons that the president had promised consultations and boast in cabinet that Truman had described the bomb as "in a sense a joint possession of the United States, United Kingdom, and Canada." According to a seasoned British reporter, Laborites long claimed that "Mr. Attlee stopped President Truman from actually using the atomic bomb." Though none of this was true, Acheson later remarked that "Churchill never asked, or got so much, as Attlee did."[10]

A Dreary Process

Acheson thereafter sought only what he considered moderate objectives in Korea. The United States should severely punish the Chinese army, contain the war to the peninsula, and not quit unless actually beaten militarily. He would consider sending bombers over China to answer any extreme provocation but was determined to give neither China nor Russia reason for expanding the war. Once the communists saw they could not seize South Korea by force, a cease-fire and talks for a creditable settlement would be permissible. (As with the Soviet Union, he always believed that the communists' recognition of reality would make negotiations possible.) But he would not pay an exorbitant price for settling—no phony national coalition government, no surrender of Formosa, and no seat for the PRC in the UN.[11]

Dislodged from his old position on Formosa, he now stood mostly in harmony with his advisers. Outside his department, he could see at least five threats to a sensible Korean strategy. First were governments wanting to propitiate the enemy—Asian neutrals, about whom he cared little, and European allies, about whom he did. At the other extreme was MacArthur, inclined to expand the war and thus estrange allies. Third were MacArthur's nominal military superiors, who remained stupefied by the wizardly conqueror of Nippon, and whose own itch for "victory" might encourage him to further belligerence. Fourth were a covey of conservative Republicans, who pushed in various directions, all endangering a policy of restraint. With two-thirds of the public agreeing, according to a January 1951 poll, Robert Taft's faction demanded a complete withdrawal from Korea. William Knowland and the old China Lobby called for attacking China but

agreed with Taft in scorning UN and European pusillanimity. They wanted
MacArthur unshackled, and they clamored for Acheson's dismissal. The fifth
"threat" was Truman. More politically vulnerable than ever, he despised the
Chinese communists and wanted them hurt.[12]

At the Pentagon, Marshall and Bradley had their hands full harnessing
MacArthur. In late December 1950, he had received JCS instructions to keep
fighting but not ignite a general war. In the message Acheson had called a "posterity paper," he demanded on 10 January to know how he could hold Korea and
Japan without the heavy reinforcements the chiefs were denying him. Fighting
on might be impossible, he intimated, because of low morale among the troops.
An angry Marshall snapped that when commanders begin bad-mouthing troop
morale, time had come to reexamine their own. Truman was "deeply disturbed"
to hear that decisions he had approved were "not feasible." The president and his
advisers fashioned a multipronged answer while Generals Collins and Hoyt
Vandenberg visited Korea to make their own appraisals. In a message Acheson
had not seen, the chiefs told MacArthur they were considering his requests
but reaffirmed past orders about the exercise of restraint. Yet they also listed
stronger measures he might take in an emergency. Truman added a personal
letter, praising MacArthur while reiterating the policy fundamentals he expected
him to follow. "If ever a message should have stirred the loyalty of a commander,
this one should have," wrote Acheson, who now viewed MacArthur as "incurably
recalcitrant and basically disloyal to the purposes of his Commander in Chief."[13]

When he learned of the actions that MacArthur now had conditional authority to take, on 17 January 1951 Acheson headed to the Pentagon to lodge strenuous objections. The conditional measures looked quite dangerous to a secretary
of state trying to prevent further expansion of the war, including a blockade
of China's coast, intrusive intelligence-gathering flights over its interior, the possibility of harassment of the mainland by Chiang, and support for guerrillas in
China itself. If the Chinese in response hit U.S. targets in Japan, MacArthur
could now argue he had the authority to launch both air and sea attacks on the
mainland. Whatever the UN thought, the generals and admirals told Acheson, it
was time "for unilateral action." Marshall and his former under secretary went at
it in an unvarnished exchange. The administration had to do something to silence
the domestic political uproar, Marshall declared. Well, countered Acheson, none
of the options the chiefs were handing MacArthur would accomplish that. What
they would do is rend America's alliances and destroy its support in the United
Nations. It was vital to keep the British with us. Perhaps rattled by the argument
with the colossal Marshall, Acheson ended with the odd entomological advice
that "we must go through a number of cocoons before we can get the British bug
out."[14]

With his top advisers in deadlock, Truman hesitated just long enough to
give Acheson a fragile victory, courtesy of MacArthur's new field commander,
Matthew B. Ridgway. With a grenade fixed to his shoulder strap, the vivid

Ridgway opened a counteroffensive with results that dispelled two months of pessimism. He had saved "the situation from disaster," Acheson recalled. With MacArthur briefly changing his tune, Truman recommitted himself to a limited war. In the Pentagon, respect for MacArthur finally began to ebb. Washington shortly settled on a brittle resolve to minimize strategic risks, strengthened by Acheson's renewed stature. "More than any other," Max Hastings writes, Acheson could "claim credit for having discouraged the President's most bellicose advisers." Without him, the administration almost surely would have taken more extreme measures. Acheson himself was still pushing an aggressive diplomatic option, to have China condemned as an "aggressor" in the UN General Assembly, an earlier resolution having fallen to a Soviet veto in the Security Council.[15]

Any comfort drawn in Britain from Attlee's Washington sojourn was short-lived, although Acheson was holding his "aggressor" resolution in reserve as London marketed ideas for a cease-fire and great-powers conference on the Far East. He wanted to calm down the British by letting them go ahead, reckoning that the Chinese would be too clumsy to exploit the opportunity. Directly after the December summit, he had engaged in a similar ploy. Then emboldened by better news from the front, he gained Truman's approval to placate both allies and neutrals by supporting an Indian-sponsored resolution to explore chances for a cease-fire. He was willing to face the certain domestic outrage because of his certainty that Beijing, scenting blood, would reject the resolution, disillusioning its sponsors and bolstering the U.S. position. Just as he expected in both instances, a caucus of Republicans cried for his resignation, and the PRC sneeringly denounced the resolution. He had been encouraged too by news from the UK, where Bevin told Attlee he must not risk causing the United States to "retire into a kind of armed isolation." Attlee must realize "what it would be like to live in a world with a hostile Communist bloc, an unco-operative America, a Commonwealth pulled in two directions and a disillusioned Europe," unable to call on U.S. help. Britain had no alternative but support the United States.[16]

Now Acheson again held his breath as the British cease-fire plan circulated, laden with concessions to China. It had been a "murderous" choice not to oppose it. Nor had it been easy to persuade Truman to instruct UN Ambassador Warren Austin to vote for it. This was a "shocking step," admonished Taft, but four days after it passed on 13 January, Beijing killed it as Acheson anticipated, making demands that were anathema to the General Assembly. Rusk and Jack Hickerson took a "battering" on the Hill for the U.S. vote. His maneuver, Acheson told Franks, had brought the administration "to the verge of destruction domestically."

Having won this gamble, he went on the offensive again, having Austin on 20 January 1951 table the resolution condemning China as an aggressor. Despite the fact that Washington was then secretly boosting arms aid to Tibetan guerrillas, Acheson also filed protests against Chinese actions in Tibet. Allies thought "condemning" China was gratuitous and mischievous, but Acheson, concerned about American public opinion, lobbied unapologetically for the resolution's passage. It was, he told a European ambassador on the 24th, a "dreary process" for Americans to slog it out in Korea at the price of heavy casualties and sharp criticism at home and then run into more of it from allies.

With the mortally ill Bevin now hors de combat, Britain remained a hard case. Seizing control of the UN process, they forced changes that would delay any of Acheson's requested "additional measures" against China following its condemnation. Acheson thought India's Nehru had bullied the London cabinet into playing the appeasers. When Indian ambassador Vijayalakshmi Pandit called on Acheson, he was in a scolding mood, complaining that her brother (Nehru) had caused him "a lot of trouble." He and Truman treated visiting Premier René Pleven to a scolding, too. All the pressure bore fruit on 1 February, as did Acheson's private assurance to London that the administration did not view the resolution as an excuse for war. The General Assembly resolution passed by a 44–7 vote, with nine states abstaining. In the end, the NATO contingent rallied. Among non-communist states, only India and Burma voted "nay." Besides condemning Beijing's aggression and reaffirming the UN defense of South Korea, the resolution demanded that China cease hostilities and withdraw its forces, formed a committee on "additional measures," and established an embryonic panel to seek a cease-fire. Acheson may have won, but, furious at his imperiousness, Britons would long pick at their scabs. Acheson himself three years later called the victory "hollow."[17]

First, Second, and Third Party: Secret Interlude

Remarkably, at a moment of both military and political volatility, Acheson had authorized assistants to carry out a secret probe to reverse Sino-American hostility and negotiate a Korean settlement. Because this ended without result, there is little need to rehearse the details, but the main lines of the story are intriguing. The probe began with a feeler from a representative of the PRC at the UN, conveyed through a Chinese student at American University in Washington. Charles Burton ("Burt") Marshall, known in the records as "First Party," replied for the state department and usually represented it in the contacts that followed, many by telephone. Those usually took the form of responses to statements of "Second Party," George A. Taylor, an Asianist scholar at the University of Washington. He in turn forwarded views of "Third Party" in China, a former employee of the U.S. army linked to the PRC government. He claimed to know Zhou Enlai but was not a party member. Gaining permission to proceed, Marshall carried out intense discussions on and off through January 1951, all through intermediaries. Marshall never actually met "Third Party" but in May sought fresh contacts in Hong Kong, home of the world's largest U.S. consulate. State closed the colloquy in June with nothing to show for the political risks entailed.[18]

The significance of this episode is its revelation that Acheson's department still sought to divide the PRC from its Soviet partner. Long after forswearing this tactic, Acheson authorized some interesting possible deals that were on "Third Party's" mind. Third Party represented himself as anti-Soviet and anti-Maoist, but he may have been an agent provocateur. Several times, he asked Marshall for assurances about U.S. reactions to either Mao's overthrow or, contrarily, Mao's offer of détente. Might recognition result? Despite how Washington continued to "vote and rant" about UN membership, would it consider a quiet end to its opposition and even offer economic aid? Most important, would it finally cut ties to Chiang? If Mao were overthrown, Third Party did not want "the kiss of death" of an ardent American embrace. His most urgent fear was that the looming resolution condemning Chinese aggression would end the dialogue.

The basic First Party response was that nearly anything could be worked out, including Formosa, *after* any Chinese government showed it was independent rather than a "servant of Moscow's interests" and did not seek war with the United States. United Nations membership remained impossible as long as Chinese armies fought in Korea. Washington would be "realistic" about internal policies, just as it was with Tito, who "did not have to be wheedled" to demonstrate his "independence from Moscow." Second and Third Parties warned that passage of the "aggressor" resolution could end the contacts, arousing suspicion in Foggy Bottom that they were a ruse to block it. As the vote neared, Marshall had clearance at the presidential level, transmitted through Averell Harriman's office, to keep up the talks. The policy planning staff agreed to send Marshall to Hong Kong to seek further contacts, and PPS director Paul Nitze suggested that Washington could prove its bona fides by not immediately pursuing the "additional measures" against China. When the resolution passed, Harriman demanded evidence that China was in earnest and that Third Party could speak for it.[19]

As mentioned, the dialogue petered out without result. Exchanges were desultory after passage of the UN resolution, which affronted Beijing. In Hong Kong, Marshall indicated he would talk to virtually anyone who had something to say. The department wanted Marshall to communicate both an interest in negotiations and contrarily a veiled nuclear threat. When only third-string Chinese sought him out, the clandestine initiative ended. "First Party" concluded that Beijing was "thoroughly locked into collaboration with Moscow," and that its high-handed methods had elevated Chiang's reputation on the mainland. Any Chinese "third force," he added, did "not amount to much."[20]

Moments of this dialogue suggest a startling flexibility in U.S. policy thinking, but the pliancy may only have been verbal. The department may have considered this episode simply a utilitarian attempt to gain intelligence while stirring a spoon in the cup of discord it thought affected Mao's circle. Knowing that any Chinese opposition was weak, the department surely did not expect a regime change. In light of domestic atmospherics, allowing the dialogue was risky. In the end, it echoed a familiar pattern: Acheson flirted with normalizing relations while recognizing that events had probably foreclosed such an option. This makes the episode something of a mystery, a risky dalliance he almost certainly did not intend to consummate.[21]

Cashiering "This Mad Satrap"

Meanwhile, Ridgway was working his magic, halting the most recent offensive despite the appearance in combat of units from the Soviet air force. By mid-January, he was back to within seventy-five miles of the 38th parallel, where he started his own offensive. This drive aroused a few new pipe dreams of liberationist triumph, but the administration was not smoking any. Acheson claimed that restoring the status quo ante bellum was a victory. He told his own diplomatic corps that defending South Korea had "gained valuable time" for the "free world" to build positions of strength. The "Great Debate" over sending non-occupation U.S. troops to Europe preoccupied Washington while Ridgway slugged it out on Korea's heartless terrain, and Acheson wanted no new Korean crises to disable efforts to balance Soviet power in Europe. He informed Rhee's government on 7 February 1951 that military unification of Korea was "no longer feasible." Though Ridgway was closing on the 38th parallel, the Pentagon agreed with the state department on limited-war advice for Truman. Some of the chiefs were ready to try an expanded war again but were pacified by George Marshall's prevailing moderation, reinforcing Acheson's. The united advice for Truman, therefore, was to avert a larger war that could suck in the Soviets and split the alliance, give up Korean unification, and pass the 38th parallel again only for tactical protection of UN forces. Moreover, Ridgway should flog Beijing's "volunteers" so *it* would adopt more abstemious goals. As a British observer noted, Ridgway's strategy was "homicidal not geographical." Once Washington succeeded in chastening the Chinese, it should seize the first opportunity to negotiate a Korean settlement, which was essential for restoring diplomatic focus on Europe. That moment arrived when Ridgway retook Seoul on 15 March, with most of South Korea again under his control.[22]

One obstacle now stood in the way of an effort to make peace, and he wore five stars on his shoulders. Despite Truman's recent personal message showing how a cautious strategy advanced larger objects elsewhere, MacArthur would have none of it. As Ridgway restored the military's reputation, his superior in Tokyo repeatedly defied *his* superiors in Washington. With remarkable empathy, Melvyn Leffler identifies the origins of his insubordination. He hated having the fruits of NSC-68 go to Europe, hated holding "a defensive position" with "limited manpower," and hated not being free to bomb Manchuria or use Chiang's troops "to help offset" Chinese superiority on the ground. And he worried that Truman's handcuffs would make it impossible to prevent Chinese air attacks on both his own Korean supply lines and Japanese airfields.[23]

Dissenting in public from Truman's goals is what ruined him in Washington. Twice, in February and March 1951, he grumbled to reporters about restraints that gave his foe "unprecedented military advantage" on the field. One story, possibly apocryphal, has the National Security Agency intercepting a conversation in which he boasted to European diplomats that he had plans to settle the "Chinese Communist Question" for good. If this was true, Truman could do nothing about it without exposing U.S. eavesdropping on allies' diplomatic traffic. MacArthur's defiance crested just as Washington policymakers were primed to move for a settlement. Acheson, Marshall, and the JCS painstakingly designed a statement Truman would issue as soon as Ridgway cleared the south of opposing forces. The statement would call for an immediate end to hostilities and start of talks for a Korean settlement. It would also signal U.S. willingness to discuss other issues with the PRC. The mutinous MacArthur usurped the administration plan on 24 March (nighttime of the 23d at home) with a bruising pronunciamento that ruled out discussing anything except a Chinese surrender. Insulting the PRC as a primitive state with an inferior army, he hinted that a new UN offensive would "doom" China, causing its "military collapse." Finally, he challenged his Chinese counterpart to meet him "in the field" to end the war.

Apart from everything else, this flagrant double cross of the president violated an earlier muzzling order against exactly such an announcement. MacArthur's disparaging tone would now make it impossible for Mao to accept Truman's planned summons to peace talks, as confirmed by the venom Radio Beijing now spewed at MacArthur and the Americans. Andrei Vyshinsky in Moscow also ripped into MacArthur as "a maniac, the principal culprit, the evil genius" of the war. It was, recalled Bradley, an "unforgivable and irretrievable act," or in Acheson's words, "a major act of sabotage of a Government operation."[24]

After news of this sabotage hit the capital, Acheson gathered defense under secretary Robert Lovett, Rusk, and others to his P Street home. They talked until one in the morning and concluded that MacArthur must be sent packing. Lovett, Acheson recalled, "was angrier than I had ever seen him" and wanted MacArthur dismissed immediately. At the UN, Britain's Gladwyn Jebb called him "this mad satrap," and his government nearly had seizures. The new foreign minister, Herbert Morrison, ordered Franks to tell Washington he expected no crossing of the 38th parallel and MacArthur reined in. The administration had stated that MacArthur's remarks went "beyond his responsibilities," which Franks reported even "the stupidest Western reader" could interpret as a repudiation. Wringing his hands, Rusk told Franks the administration was in turmoil but doing its best to cope. It would be difficult, because the attitude in Congress was "deplorable."[25]

An incensed Truman later claimed he then knew he had to sack MacArthur but could not yet act. He did not even discipline him. Instead, he quietly pigeonholed his plan for negotiations, realizing it could only sow confusion. Despite whispers to allies that MacArthur's edict had been "unauthorized and unexpected," Washington did not explicitly disown it. After their Georgetown conversation, Acheson, Lovett, and Rusk saw Truman, who "appeared to be in a state of mind that combined disbelief with controlled fury." The most severe action mentioned was to order MacArthur to silence again. From Truman down, however, anxiety grew about giving an out-of-control general the power to execute complicated and potentially provocative contingencies the administration had just agreed on. Some of these were a response to intelligence reports predicting a new Chinese offensive and identifying large numbers of Soviet aircraft in Manchuria, many capable of bombing Japan. Soviet submarines were on the prowl, too, and Moscow warned through India it would defend China against a U.S. attack. With its primary goal still being peace negotiations, the administration intended to balance any olive branch offered to China with a set of extremely severe actions Truman could choose to implement if Beijing refused the bid for peace, actions ranging from a show of naval force off the Chinese coast to air strikes against Manchurian bases. More than any other factor, the administration's refusal to allow MacArthur control over any of these options determined the timing of his dismissal.[26]

The particular event that tipped the scales came on 5 April, when Joseph W. Martin of Massachusetts, a Republican and minority leader, took to the floor of the House to read a two-week-old letter from MacArthur praising the representative's belligerent views on the war. MacArthur's letter derided the administration's fixation on Europe, paraded all his spurned war-winning suggestions, and trumpeted that "there is no substitute for victory." This outstripped even Truman's patience or his fears of Republican retribution for what he now must do. Outrage again struck London, which Franks said had a bad case of "MacArthuritis." Only heavy intervention by senior MPs quashed a House of Commons motion denouncing MacArthur. Other allies expressed their fears to Washington of having MacArthur anywhere around the fierce actions they knew might come. On cue, Truman ordered the atomic energy commission to release nine atomic bombs for shipment to Guam and Okinawa but kept them under the agency's control.[27]

Though the Martin letter was on his mind, Acheson disported himself at a dinner party Alice had planned. Then the Achesons attended a play with the Bill Bundys and the state department's Howland Sergeant and his wife, Myrna Loy, Acheson's favorite actress, followed by a late-evening conversation with Lovett. On the morning of 6 April, Acheson joined Marshall, Bradley, and Harriman to see Truman. The president's anger centered on the challenge to his authority and his foreign policy. MacArthur had damaged his administration and frayed relations with allies and the UN. Worst of all, he had challenged civilian control of the military. Acheson beforehand urged him not to reveal his own views until others had, so Truman quietly listened as the group talked for over an hour. Harriman quickly urged dismissal. Wanting more time to think, Marshall waffled, anxious about congressional anger and the fate of defense appropriations. Bradley wanted to "go slow" and have enough time to converse with individual service chiefs. Acheson advocated relieving MacArthur of all his commands, but only if the chiefs were firmly on board. And he warned the president: "If you relieve MacArthur, you will have the biggest fight of your administration." Truman had kept his counsel and set another meeting for the next morning. "I was careful," he wrote in his memoirs, "not to disclose that I had already reached a decision," but in his diary that night he wrote: "I've come to the conclusion that our Big General in the Far East must be recalled."[28]

After the White House meeting on the 6th, Acheson, Marshall, Bradley, and Harriman reconvened in Acheson's office, where the others quickly rejected Marshall's idea of merely calling MacArthur home for consultations, a disastrous idea in Acheson's view that would open the way for the general to exercise his "histrionic abilities on civilians" and again overawe the uniforms. When they met again with Truman on Saturday, the misery of Marshall and Bradley was so manifest that Acheson urged postponing a decision until Monday. He still wanted Truman served by a united front. He also wanted his advisers able to say Truman never expressed his own views until he had heard what his "civilian and military officers" had to say. The president himself was also talking to Speaker Sam Rayburn, Vice-President Alben Barkley, Secretary of the Treasury John Snyder, Chief Justice Fred Vinson, and maybe others. Meanwhile, a conservative magazine came out with yet another MacArthur statement, this one blaming civilians in Washington for not adequately supplying ROK units. In fact, keeping them on short rations was the result of his own low estimate of their abilities.[29]

After the Saturday session with Truman, the agonized Marshall and Bradley met alone. They tried drafting letters simply "telling MacArthur to shut up" but threw down their pens and gave it up. Besides their remnant awe of MacArthur, both worried about appearances. Marshall feared confirming World War II rumors he "had it in for" the general, while Bradley hoped to avoid the "kind of savage mauling" Marshall and Acheson were getting from "right-wing primitives." Both worried about accusations that Truman had politicized the joint chiefs. Following two hours of somber discussion, much of it sympathetic to MacArthur, they unanimously agreed to back firing him on purely "military" grounds. They also approved the new orders, which they would withhold until after MacArthur's dismissal. Eager to avoid their grave responsibilities, they hoped to give only views, not recommendations, to the president. "A sad and sober group," they went to Marshall with their decisions. He listened without giving his own views. Noël Annan exaggerated in believing his friend Acheson "got the Joint Chiefs" to recommend MacArthur's firing, but his patient pressure on Marshall and the chiefs was certainly important.[30]

The climactic White House meeting on the 9th went quickly. Bradley reported that the chiefs favored dismissing MacArthur and that he concurred. Marshall agreed. Acheson and Harriman did too, emphatically. Truman told them he had already decided MacArthur "had to go" when he scuttled the planned bid for peace talks on 24 March but first wanted full Pentagon backing. Now he wanted to know who should replace MacArthur in Tokyo. The popular choice was Ridgway, with General James A. Van Fleet assuming command on the battlefield. Truman instructed Bradley to have the necessary orders ready to execute on Tuesday. Thus, on 10 April 1951, he stripped MacArthur of all his commands, ending a career that began at West Point in 1898.[31]

Before the Oval Office meeting that day, Senators Pat McCarran and Styles Bridges both warned Acheson that MacArthur would drub Truman in any popularity contest. Knowing Truman's orders were being cut, Acheson merely promised to convey their message. The orders ran afoul of a farcical communications mix-up, causing MacArthur to learn of his firing on a news broadcast rather than through a personal audience with Secretary of the Army Frank Pace, as Truman had intended. Because the blunder caused the news to leak in the middle of the night, Acheson was up until dawn telephoning ambassadors and members of Congress. Among those he rousted from bed was John Foster Dulles, ordering him to Tokyo to reassure the Japanese. Asked to comment on MacArthur's dismissal at a cabinet meeting later in the week, Acheson told a shaggy story about a family with a lovely young daughter living near an army base. "The wife worried continually, and harassed her husband, over the dangers to which this exposed their daughter. One afternoon the husband found his wife red-eyed and weeping on the doorstep. The worst had happened, she informed him; their daughter was pregnant! Wiping his brow, he said, 'Thank God that's over!' "[32]

Over but not done. Now came the wrath of millions on Truman and Acheson's heads. Within weeks, however, the anger dissipated when channeled into congressional hearings. MacArthur's instincts about how to fight a war had a longer life. New attempts for an armistice soon followed his removal, but a visceral craving to savage the Chinese lasted to the end of the administration, felt by the very men who brought MacArthur down.

25

CAPTIVES OF WAR

Shooting MacArthur through the Heart

Besides a titanic contest between general and president, the MacArthur imbroglio was the last chapter of six years of tension between general and secretary of state. As Acheson said afterward: "It always seemed that whenever General MacArthur made a statement that embarrassed anybody I was the fellow who had to reply to it," a history begun in 1945 when he chided MacArthur for thinking he made his own Japanese policy. In a sign of how distant MacArthur was from what was going on back home, he had reacted to the news of Louis Johnson's firing in September 1950 by predicting that Acheson would topple next. When MacArthur himself fell, Acheson spoke discreetly for the record but described him in a letter as a victim of a "disastrous manic depressive tendency." In 1970, he switched to Truman-speak and called him a "jackass."[1]

When Truman explained his firing of MacArthur in a radio broadcast on 11 April, he said nothing about the foundations being laid for new and harsh measures he might order against the Chinese, orders he refused to let this ungovernable general execute. If such measures became necessary, Washington was telling London to come along if it knew what was good for it; Acheson believed time was ripe "for us to 'cash in'" on MacArthur's dismissal. On 27 April 1951, General Matthew Ridgway received official clearance to strike China directly in case of a severe air assault against his own forces. Atomic bombs were in transit to the Asian theater. Truman still held the on-off switch, but forces available to MacArthur's successor now had nuclear capability. Besides expecting Britain's backing in any military measures against China, Acheson wanted its help in surmounting UN "timidity" on economic sanctions against it and a "moratorium" on PRC membership. To make his point, he drew attention to "a strong wave of anti-British feeling in the United States." London had little choice but to close ranks.[2]

MacArthur's sacking had brought relief among allies, especially in the UK, where members of the House of Commons rose in cheers, some mistakenly thinking Prime Minister Attlee had forced Truman to the action. But the effect was mostly fear and dismay in Japan, Formosa, and the Philippines. In the United States, it was largely outrage. House Minority Leader Joseph Martin demanded Truman's resignation, while others cried for impeachment, and Senator Robert Taft condemned the state department as a branch of Downing Street. Criticism was still peaking when Secretary of Defense George Marshall greeted MacArthur's plane in San Francisco on the 18th. Martin and Senator Kenneth Wherry looked over his shoulder, bedazzled by their idol. (The symbol of GOP moderation, Arthur Vandenberg, died the same day.) As Truman's already low place in the polls fell like confetti, ticker-tape parades ushered MacArthur's progress toward Washington to address a joint session of Congress. The administration hunkered down, though Truman expected only "two or three weeks of hell." White House wits circulated a "Schedule for Welcoming General MacArthur":

12:30	Wades ashore from Snorkel submarine
12:31	Navy Band plays "Sparrow in the Treetop" and "I'll be Glad When You're Dead You Rascal You"
12:40	Parade to the Capitol with General MacArthur riding an elephant
12:47	Beheading of General Vaughan [Truman's military aide] at the rotunda
1:00	General MacArthur addresses members of Congress
1:30–1:49	Applause for General MacArthur
1:50	Burning of the Constitution
1:55	Lynching of Secretary Acheson
2:00	21-atomic bomb salute
2:30	Nude D.A.R.s leap from Washington Monument
3:00	Basket lunch, Monument Grounds

MacArthur's memorable speech, which roused GOP hawks, ended with the involuntarily correct prophecy that he would now simply "fade away." Truman snorted at "damn fool Congressmen crying like a bunch of women" over "nothing but a bunch of bullshit."[3]

As congressional hearings on MacArthur's dismissal approached, participants and observers alike took stock. While Acheson ordered aides not to crow about the general's downfall, a disgusted Republican critic, William Knowland, demanded the secretary's removal to restore a bipartisan foreign policy. Joseph McCarthy added that Acheson had already "become President" and was running "the military and everything else." Taft threw caution aside, urging all-out war against China, insisting that the people must choose between "Acheson or MacArthur." But the polls soon showed an up-tick for Truman, as disapproval of his action fell in May from 3–1 to 2–1.[4]

The armed forces and foreign relations committees of the Senate held the "MacArthur" hearings in May and June 1951. Most Republicans on the two panels were party moderates, and the administration benefited from rules calling for short, rotating question periods. All twenty-six senators would have repeated chances to take the stage but, as Acheson noted, an adroit witness could easily disrupt their continuity by talking "as long as he wanted in answering each question."

Democrats were ready for MacArthur when he appeared on 3 May. Over two days, Brien McMahon of Connecticut and the freshman senator from Texas, Lyndon B. Johnson, used his own words to reveal MacArthur as a person who denied responsibility for U.S. policy on a global scale while trespassing into areas he admitted were beyond his authority and expertise. After thundering a few vehement judgments about the administration's sins, he left in a huff, aware he had not helped himself. Neither had Ridgway helped him by rattling off a string of tactical victories as the hearings began.[5]

Then Pentagon leaders challenged MacArthur's version of the events leading to his ouster. With some fudging, they also denied ever supporting his views. They even stole his thunder by coupling their vigorous defense of the administration with dire warnings that China would rue the day if it again expanded the war. General Omar Bradley famously criticized MacArthur for trying to put the United States in "the wrong war, at the wrong place, at the wrong time, and with the wrong enemy." Taft (and columnist Walter Lippmann) sourly deplored this unholy alliance among the generals, admirals, White House, and state department, perhaps because the alliance worked. MacArthur's popularity went into a rapid slide, and mail to the White House turned sharply in Truman's favor. Millions of Americans switched off the hearings and began planning their summer vacations.[6]

Though coming near the end, Acheson's testimony was the longest. Starting on Friday morning, 1 June, with legal counselor Adrian ("Butch") Fisher at his side, he testified all but one day through Saturday the 9th, eight days compared to Marshall's seven and Bradley's six. Acheson's testimony came to 400,000 words and filled 624 pages of the published hearings. He joked with the press that Bradley had come in "a poor second" with 278,000 words. He had painstakingly prepared for three weeks, mostly at night, and prepared even more after each day of testifying. He scanned reams of memos, reports, and cables from his thirty months in office. With newspapers now headlining the defection of British spies Guy Burgess and Donald MacLean to the Soviet Union, he read all his own utterances on Alger Hiss. Supplying the documents and likely questions were Fisher, Dean Rusk, and Luke Battle. Preparing lists and "talking points," U. Alexis Johnson, a deputy assistant secretary, found Acheson "an extremely satisfying man to work for." In "dry run sessions" lasting deep "into the night," he "quickly seized what was crucial and remembered it precisely," translating the fabric of "pedestrian" material into the "weave" of a "very eloquent presentation."[7]

Surviving notes show Acheson's intent to underscore how MacArthur had taken the country to "the verge of the precipice" of war with the Soviets, and that his fatalistic attitude would have thrown the nation into the abyss, alienating allies and destroying the system of "collective security." He was wary of impromptu remarks and ready to answer any "$64 question." MacArthur's dismissal, he contended, was not about personalities but the Constitution and the foundations of U.S. foreign policy. He had also intended to disclose only the general outlines of the conversations leading to MacArthur's dismissal, but Truman in a 17 May press conference released him from any sense of confidentiality by telling reporters Acheson had originally been cautious for political reasons. Truman added that Acheson had also told him MacArthur's firing would cause a fuss—and it did.[8]

Saving Acheson for the end of the hearings was no accident. Fisher did a little "thimblerigging" with Johnson and Oklahoma's Robert Kerr to schedule him after the Pentagon chiefs had blasted MacArthur's military arguments. With the Senate chamber still smelling of cordite, Acheson settled into his witness chair at 10:02 A.M. on 1 June. On his best behavior and deftly exploiting his foes' hit-and-miss methods, he abided eight days of rambling and repetitive questioning. One administration critic, Senator Alexander Wiley, greeted him on the second day: "Well, Mr. Secretary, you're looking young and handsome this morning!" From the first, he pressed the view that UN forces had already chalked up "a powerful victory" by clearing South Korea of invaders, handing out "terrible defeats" to the enemy, and dashing "Communist imperialist aims in Asia." In short, U.S. strategy had worked, exposing MacArthur's folly. In a slip of the tongue—though faithful to official policy—he said Washington was content to end the fighting at the 38th parallel, which the Pentagon considered indefensible. Later truce talks briefly tripped on this discrepancy, with Chinese negotiators demanding adherence to Acheson's word. The soul of prudence before the senators, Acheson insisted that military adventures born of venom and vindictiveness would sunder the western alliance and destroy the chance to checkmate Soviet power in Europe.[9]

Answering Senate critics on the Chinese revolution, Acheson stuck to the *White Paper* view that deeds done or not done by Washington would have made no difference. Flagrantly dissembling on his last day of testimony, he denied having ever considered diplomatic recognition of the Beijing regime, a denial the *Times*'s James Reston described as "so unqualified" it suggested that the subject could never come up again "as long as Mr. Acheson remained Secretary of State," which *now* was true. As interest in the hearings faded and committee absenteeism grew, he forecast that like most wars, Korea would end in some kind of stalemate. Having already stopped communist "aggression," however, he viewed this as "honorable" and satisfactory.[10]

When he had finished, columnist Arthur Krock noted his "skill in enveloping himself in such a cloud of well-chosen words" the Republicans "could not locate his jugular." Though one muttered that his superior knowledge of the subject gave him an "unfair advantage" (!), most Republicans were forced to find his performance impressive. "You have had a long chore, sir," Wiley remarked, "and you have done a grand job for yourself, I would say, with that mind of yours." A less friendly newspaper critic suggested he could now "resign with honor." Asked how he would spend the weekend, he replied: "I have a plan that will test my capacity for the consumption of alcohol, and if another war erupts before I finish, it must be waged without my services," after which he began his research at the home of his good friend, Canadian Ambassador Hume Wrong.[11]

Acheson thought the hearings had proved MacArthur had "laid an egg" with the public. His disgrace had ended with a whimper. The committee must have thought so, for it never issued an official combined report. Unofficially, reaffirming that bipartisanship was near dead, angry Republicans shouted down the bromides issued by the majority, angrily reviling the administration and exonerating MacArthur to the end. McCarthy chose one of the days of Acheson's testimony to excoriate him and Marshall for nearly three hours on the Senate floor. Liberals were little happier at how far the administration had traveled to neutralize its critics. "If MacArthur's disastrous policies are to be followed," the *New Republic* held, "MacArthur should bear the responsibility as Secretary of State."[12]

Korea had indeed pushed Acheson farther than he wanted toward military solutions. But he now had renewed influence, the product of MacArthur's fall, Marshall's fatigue (he soon resigned), the Pentagon's gloom, and Truman's loyalty. But he never minimized the damage MacArthur had done, nearly ruining chances to prosecute the war rationally. MacArthur's defiance of the president had threatened "democratic government" and caused a grave constitutional crisis. As Acheson reviewed a draft of Truman's memoirs in 1955, he thought the ex-president had pulled his punches. "Emerson," he wrote, told the senior Holmes "after reading his critical essay on Plato—'If you strike at a king, you must kill him.' MacArthur can be shot right through the heart." His own memoirs described the damage caused by MacArthur's "willful insubordination and incredibly bad judgment" as impossible to exaggerate. He recounted how MacArthur had pressed "his will and his luck to a shattering defeat." Still absolving himself of blame for the Chinese intervention, he wrote instead of the damage done by MacArthur to the "prestige" of the United States and allies' confidence in American "judgment and leadership." MacArthur had "diminished" the "effectiveness" of U.S. diplomacy, stirred worldwide opposition to its policies, and handed Moscow new opportunities to make trouble.[13]

Looking for an Armistice, if Not Peace

Acheson now tried to repair the miscarried effort to open peace talks. Charles Bohlen in Paris had put out a feeler in April, only to have a Soviet diplomat tell him the communists expected victory. But with MacArthur removed, whispers of peace came from Moscow. Acheson asked George Kennan at Princeton to meet Jacob Malik, head of the Soviet UN delegation. That both Mao Zedong and Joseph Stalin seemed at least intermittently interested in negotiating seemed to signal some kind of weakness the U.S. government might have exploited with a new offensive, at least to win a taller stack of bargaining chips. Syngman Rhee thought so and insisted the war press on, but virtually no one in Washington had the stomach for that. When Chinese forces retreated behind the 38th parallel in the middle of the hearings, General James Van Fleet as ordered did not pursue them, setting the stage for an armistice.[14]

A few military leaders, like air force chief Hoyt Vandenberg, thought Van Fleet was "now hurting the Communists badly" and should keep it up. This is a mostly forgotten undercurrent of the war, but others also thought Washington was too eager for peace talks, blind to a new chance to pummel a reeling enemy. Historian Vojtech Mastny believes the United States could have gained a better settlement by hitting the Chinese harder in what would clearly have been a popular campaign. Chinese forces, Bernard Brodie wrote in the early 1970s, were "disintegrating," and Washington's "blunder" allowed them to recover, setting off two more years of misery, fruitless negotiations, and 12,000 more U.S. fatalities. Recently disclosed Soviet bloc documents show, writes Kathryn Weathersby, that the beating Van Fleet gave communist forces forced them to seek peace talks. But despite the vulnerability of Chinese forces, U.S. political and military leaders, including Ridgway in Tokyo, wanted an end to it. At best, Ridgway wrote, he might have seized "more real estate," but at the cost of shortening Mao's supply lines and stretching his own, inviting another accordion-like reversal of fortunes. Acheson agreed, and so did Truman, who had quietly recalled nuclear-capable B-29 bombers from Guam. No one could guarantee the success of another aggressive campaign, and the White House, Pentagon, and Foggy Bottom all knew it could cause a revolt at both the UN and NATO.[15]

The administration was moving in the other direction. As Kennan kept up his clandestine contacts with Malik into early June, Truman announced a willingness to settle for a boundary near the 38th parallel. The chiefs rejected Van Fleet's ideas for a new offensive and, on the Hill, Acheson conspicuously abandoned the goal of reunification—repelling "aggression" and reestablishing "peace and security" were victory enough. He did not want peace talks at "the worst of all places to conduct discussions," that is, the UN. The capricious Stalin apparently decided on no talks after all, goading Mao instead to resume the fight, giving his armies a chance "to study contemporary warfare" and rattle Washington. Mao briefly followed suit, thinking preliminary negotiations might serve to mask planning for a "larger operation." But when Malik abruptly asserted in a radio broadcast that the Soviet people wanted peace, Beijing, on 25 June, a year after the beginning of the war, endorsed the idea.[16]

In Moscow, Foreign Minister Andrei Gromyko suggested to the U.S. ambassador that Washington could finesse negotiations on political matters by having military officers run them. This was welcome to the state department, which hoped military responsibility for the talks would guard the state department from criticism for dealing with the communists. Despite the growing consensus for negotiations, Marshall, Charles Wilson (director of defense mobilization), and Acheson all worried that a truce might prove so relaxing it would choke off the NSC-68–inspired buildup. In Korea, Acheson told an audience in late June, Moscow had "presented a check which was drawn on the bank account of collective security," expecting it to "bounce," and was surprised when "the teller paid it." What had backed that check was American resolve, and he wanted to make certain it was there to cover future checks.[17]

More communists than Americans thought peace would come quickly, but no one realized it was two years off. After the Chinese accepted Ridgway's 30 June call for truce talks, formal discussions began on 10 July, first at Kaesong and then Panmunjom, both located just below the 38th parallel near Inchon. Even though Mao ordered his negotiators to be "obstreperous and rude," he expected an early agreement, and the two sides did agree on an agenda by the 26th. Then one deadlock after another delayed success until six months into the Eisenhower administration. The biggest barrier to a settlement was the disposition of prisoners, settled in 1953 on terms allowing POWs to refuse repatriation to the nations they fought for, the position taken by the U.S. government.[18]

Supposedly the ruling law on POWs was the 1949 Geneva Convention, which called for the return of all captives at the end of hostilities. Though the United States had not signed the convention until 1951 and had yet to ratify it, Washington declared that it would adhere to it, as did Pyongyang. In practice, all sides, but most notoriously both Koreas and China, violated many provisions. To different degrees, all the combatants also tried converting prisoners to their own ideology.

In a position that was arguably illegal but emotionally satisfying, Truman demanded that communist POWs have the right to refuse repatriation. He seemed sincere—and sincerely eager to mortify Beijing and Pyongyang when their countrymen refused to go "home." In partial justification of this position, many POWs held by UN forces were ex-Nationalist Chinese or captured ROK troops pressed into communist service. When they indicated they did not choose repatriation, the administration, to the beat of propaganda drums, would say they had chosen "freedom" over "communism." Truman and many other Americans were also thinking about their shame in 1945–46, when, with Britain, they forced the return of thousands of unwilling Soviet POWs from Nazi camps, many to be shot or imprisoned on returning to the USSR. But both Acheson and the military disliked Truman's position, the Pentagon especially, because the armed forces thought getting their own men back trumped all other issues. Despite his misgivings, Acheson loyally backed the president, and before long, the United States had tied its prestige to voluntary repatriation. As a result, talks at Panmunjom deadlocked.[19]

Acheson never mentioned his erstwhile opposition but described Truman's stance on POWs as "humanitarian." At first, however, he worked both sides of the fence. In August 1951, he favored paroling communist POWs who claimed their lives would be at risk if repatriated while opposing voluntary repatriation in principle. In fealty to Truman, however, by late January 1952 he was supporting the idea of a fait accompli in which the UN would unilaterally release all POWs not wanting to return to China or North Korea, to be followed by an all-for-all swap of the rest. This would give the communist governments a chance to finesse voluntary repatriation as a general proposition while accepting it "in fact." Coming down with both feet for Truman's position also squelched a growing and divisive debate on the subject in the department. The Pentagon remained unhappy enough to push the issue up to the White House in February 1952. The president at least momentarily shelved the fait accompli, but, aligning himself with the president, Acheson insisted that any relaxation on the issue would endanger the "psychological warfare position of the United States in its opposition to Communist tyranny." On 27 February, Ridgway asked for definitive guidance, unaware that Kim Il Sung, his regime grievously hurt by U.S. bombing, wanted a compromise to get out of the war. Truman's orders went out: no "forcible repatriation."[20]

Truman and Acheson knew this might be a deal-breaker, for, as Acheson told reporters, the enemy regimes could not admit "a possibility that any communist citizen might not want to return to communist territory." On 6 May, Washington issued its terms publicly along with Truman's declaration that "we will not buy an armistice by turning over human beings for slaughter or slavery."

Truman's decision remains controversial, for as U.S. negotiators fenced with the Chinese, U.S. troops fought up and down Porkchop Hill and Heartbreak Ridge, suffering nearly half of their casualties after the beginning of the now deadlocked armistice talks. Although the U.S. government never repudiated Truman's position, when its next war in Asia ended, Henry Kissinger demanded that each side promptly "return all captured persons" with no delays for "any reason."[21]

More Korean Frustrations

Deciding what to do about the prisoners was one thing—doing it was another. Over the last eighteen months of Truman's presidency, U.S. officers argued with the Chinese as artillery dueled nearby. The talks broke down several times. Because the POW issue threatened to end them for good, Washington had to consider its next course if they collapsed and Mao tried for total victory. Wanting the Chinese and Americans to be at each other as long as possible, Stalin urged Mao not to look too eager for peace. Still, after one rupture, negotiators in November 1951 agreed on a new boundary that slightly favored South Korea, leaving a demilitarized zone (DMZ) between north and south. On 2 January 1952, however, UN negotiators demanded the principle of voluntary repatriation of prisoners. This followed months of riots in South Korean POW camps that peaked in May 1952 with the temporary abduction of a U.S. general. All parties shared blame for the disorders, in which Chinese communists and former Nationalists fought each other and their guards to score political points.

Even the Americans screening POWs were stunned to learn in mid-April that only 31,231 of 106,376 Chinese and North Koreans sought repatriation to their home countries. The Chinese were even more shocked, causing another stalemate. Recounts in June showed 62,437 of 96,633 North Koreans and 6,500 of 20,750 Chinese wishing repatriation. Allowing for other factors and recounts, the UN eventually counted 83,722 POWs who would return to North Korea or China and 86,222 who would not, just about the total when the settlement was finally reached in 1953.[22]

Truman announced on 29 March against running for reelection, but this had no effect on his position on POWs, though U.S. positions bent just enough in July to make a compromise seem possible. Behind the scenes, increasingly severe disagreements among the communist states complicated negotiations. Kim wanted to end the war and Stalin to prolong it. Mao wanted both "peace" and to impress Moscow with his zeal. Chinese proposals relayed through India suggested settling the POW issue by avoiding matters of principle. They could either guarantee the return of certain numbers of Chinese or have the POWs decide for themselves after interviews with "neutral" officials and the Red Cross. Then Beijing repudiated its own proposal, leaving the Americans feeling ill used by New Delhi. Mexican president Miguel Aleman offered to play Alexander in cutting the Gordian Knot just as Zhou Enlai became unavailable, having gone to Moscow in August and September for five weeks of negotiations. Zhou wanted both arms and an end to the war for which Mao needed them, but Stalin was eager to fight to the last Chinese and American. China, he insisted, should not fear a nation of "merchants" whose soldiers fought only with "stockings, cigarettes, and other merchandise."[23]

Possibly bidding for a Nobel peace prize, Aleman in early September 1952 offered his intricate proposal at the UN's new Manhattan headquarters on Turtle

Bay. All POWs wanting to go home would gain immediate release. UN members would accept the rest as immigrants until the return of regional "normalcy" and determination of their permanent status. The state department liked the first but not the second part. Acheson had mild objections, but the Pentagon was vociferous and carried the day with Truman. In any case, the Soviets and Chinese buried the plan with their opposition. The administration then decided to offer revised proposals at Panmunjom and break off talks if the communists rejected them, turning matters back to Van Fleet. But the Chinese struck first, opening a new offensive on 6 October 1952 that caused the heaviest UN casualties in a year. The Americans left the negotiating table the next day.[24]

As early as April 1951, the administration had considered how to react if China took action in the wake of broken-down negotiations. Most of its plans seemed to be MacArthurism-without-MacArthur. Acheson tirelessly pressed Britain and France to join, at least in sharply warning the Chinese against any great escalation of the war, but in vain. He was also trying to keep Truman on an even keel, so key allies and other UN members could accept U.S. actions, whatever they would be. In December, he told Anthony Eden, foreign secretary in the new Churchill government, that the United States would meet any major Chinese offensive with a blockade and bombing of Chinese territory, and that it would act without seeking British permission. He also issued hollow threats to Paris about reducing U.S. aid in Indochina if the French were unhelpful. During a January 1952 summit in Washington, he told Churchill and Eden he expected an armistice soon, but if China then militarily violated a cease-fire, he wanted strong support for retaliatory measures. He still did not get any promises, even though he kept asking for them during spring negotiations with allies in Paris. By then particularly worried that China would send forces into Indochina, he asked at least for a Big Three statement of intentions. Without agreement on the military specifics, Eden refused even to discuss the principle of such a statement. So did France's Robert Schuman, who thought such a statement might itself provoke violence. Neither ally would hear of attacking China itself, and Acheson went home empty-handed.[25]

As if to bear out the allies' fears of the dangers lurking around the corner, on 13 June 1952 the Soviet Union downed a U.S. spy plane along its coast, with the loss of twelve crewmen. Ten days later, more than 500 U.S. bombers made their first attack on North Korean dams and power plants, including a Yalu River plant that generated electricity for Manchurian air bases. The raid darkened all of North Korea and parts of Manchuria for fifteen days. Americans cheered, but a British government caught by surprise was irate. British security leaks may explain why Washington had chested its cards, but Acheson, who by chance was in London, took his lumps. He apologized for the failure to consult but not for the raids. Outwardly placated, Eden later called Acheson "more Royalist than the King" in supporting the Pentagon chieftains. Neither Britain nor France ever agreed to Acheson's proposals for a warning to China. Nor did any nation ever deliver such a warning under Truman, whether unilateral, bilateral, or trilateral.[26]

Communist accusations of U.S. "germ" warfare surfaced in February 1952, just as Stalin in an anti-Semitic frenzy launched his last pogrom. Acheson issued an unalloyed denial, requesting an investigation by the international Red Cross. Worried by the American propaganda counteroffensive and prospects of Red Cross snooping, Moscow blocked an on-site inspection. Malik in the UN branded Acheson "an instigator, an advocate and one of the organizers of the use of bacteriological warfare" and called the Red Cross "a most vicious and shameless accomplice and lackey of American imperialism." Eventually the Red Cross had to end its "investigation," having never received replies from Beijing or Pyongyang. Documents revealed in 1998 highlight the "remarkable measures" all three communist governments took to "create false evidence," including purported "confessions" of U.S. pilots shot down in "germ bomb" raids on North Korea. Though transparently extorted, these statements forced Truman and Acheson to new denials. Finally, Moscow called off the campaign, seeing no future in it. On 2 May, the USSR informed Beijing the accusations were "based on false information" and pledged to punish any Soviet citizen involved in fabricating "the so-called 'proof.' "[27]

Washington's friend, Syngman Rhee, was sometimes worse than its enemies. Dissatisfied with anything short of Korean reunification under his rule, he repeatedly impeded armistice negotiations. His regime labored under runaway inflation, which swallowed most U.S. financial aid. In the late spring and early summer of 1952, Washington learned of a conspiracy from Rhee's own circle to throw him from power. Limited to one term unless reelected by the South Korean parliament, Rhee jailed fifty legislators to force his return. That failing, he declared martial law. The U.S. military was prone to give Rhee a blank check, and neither General Mark W. Clark (now in Tokyo, succeeding Ridgway) nor Van Fleet cared a whit about Seoul's constitutional niceties. State department officials were divided, and Acheson was averse to another fight with Defense without a successor to Rhee in sight. None of Truman's advisers ever presented the issue to him in a way requiring action. In May, after Rhee arrested the plotters and threatened to take even more extreme action, Washington finally took notice. Truman wrote him on 3 June of his shock, complaining that despotic methods would be a "tragic mockery" of American sacrifices. Instead of dissolving parliament, Rhee in a cynical reaction used emergency powers to eliminate high army officers he suspected of disloyalty. Now both the state and defense departments instructed Clark and Van Fleet to lean harder. They were nearly ready to arrest Rhee and turn the government over to the generals, but on 3 July, the National Assembly succumbed to his demand for constitutional changes. He then began emptying his jails, lifted martial law, and in August gained overwhelming reelection.[28]

"Very Soft on Principles"

The administration's power and ability to maneuver had decayed by the fall of 1952. Undercutting both, Republican presidential candidate Dwight Eisenhower promised in late October to go to Korea if elected (though for what purpose he did not specify). Acheson could sense the ebbing of his "authenticity" when he spoke for the government and, after Eisenhower's election in November, knew he could achieve little more. At the annual fall session of the UN, he had a major fight on his hand against various countries opposed to U.S. policy on POWs. Addressing the General Assembly, he likened forcible repatriation of prisoners to nineteenth-century U.S. fugitive slave laws. After he ticked off seventeen treaties signed by the USSR also opposing forcible repatriation, he "caustically" remarked: "Pretty good doctrine." At the conclusion of his speech, the audience "burst into one of the loudest rounds of applause heard in the United Nations for years."[29]

To put the suspended armistice negotiations back on track, he pushed for acceptance of voluntary repatriation through the Committee of 21 (the United States and twenty allies). Western unity quickly broke down, leading to nasty clashes with Britain and Canada. The immediate cause was a démarche captained by India's rancorous and austere delegate, V. K. Krishna Menon. Menon was trying to forge a compromise—a repatriation commission of "neutral" states—to attract backing from Latin America, the Commonwealth states, and a budding Arab-Asian bloc. China, with which Menon had channels of communication, hinted it might accept less than 100 percent return of its POWs. This seemed tempting to NATO allies, already bruised by U.S. pressure for German rearmament and defense spending and its failure to defend French rule in North Africa. The vexed Acheson entitled the pertinent chapter in his memoirs, "An Open Covenant Openly Connived Against," and the Indian subsection, "The Menon Cabal." Suspecting that Mao viewed Eisenhower as a softer target, Acheson tried converting Menon's sow's ear to silk.[30]

Americans first talked to Menon after Eisenhower's victory. Following an armistice (to be settled by the General Assembly rather than the Panmunjom negotiators), the repatriation commission would take custody of the POWs, classified according to their wishes and then set free to return to their "homelands," which the commission would "facilitate" but not force. Menon's commission would make decisions by majority vote, with an umpire to settle impasses. To the Americans' bafflement, Menon claimed his idea was compatible with the Geneva Convention, and to their annoyance, his "neutral" states included Czechoslovakia and Poland. Though he had earlier shown the text to the British and Canadians, for days he refused to show it to U.S. officials. His scheme did not mention "unrepatriates," he said, because he wanted to reassure China. A deeply suspicious Acheson thought Menon's "nebulous" proposal would repatriate those who agreed to return to China while holding the others as "prisoners until they did agree." Led by their acting ambassador, Ernest Gross, the Americans continued to seek elucidation, growing furious when they realized how fully London and Ottawa were backing Menon.[31]

As Ottawa's Lester Pearson noted, there were "no points of mental or spiritual contact between the practical, incisive, clear-headed Dean, and the vague, metaphysical, missionary Menon." After several days of U.S.-Indian talks, on 12 November, Menon swept aside Acheson's objections, fortified by his British and Canadian allies. Acheson found an effort to work separately through the British even more frustrating. Though British Minister of State Selwyn Lloyd thoroughly irritated him, Eden seemed worse, nodding at Acheson's points but supporting Menon anyway. Acheson acquired a heavier hammer by requesting and receiving new and tougher instructions from Truman. Gross waved these under Menon's nose on 13 November, and in a stormy session two days later Acheson warned Eden and Pearson they might find themselves voting only with the Arabs and Asians, for the Soviets thought Menon had not gone far enough in their favor. Acheson cabled Truman that the situation was "serious" and that while Menon's proposal gave "us the words," it gave the "other side the decision." With General Grant, he promised to "fight it out on this line if it takes all summer."[32]

Reaching for yet another hammer, he brought Lovett and General Bradley into the argument, but this changed nothing. The British and Canadians were resolved to back their Commonwealth partner, come what may. Over U.S. protests, Eden and Pearson on the Committee of 21 took Menon's paper as the basis of a final UN resolution. Acheson reacted by packing the drafting panel with many of his own people, knowing that officials who have written the discussion papers have an advantage over the "dissenters," who have "the burden of making changes." But he also used ruder tactics, and he and Gross both publicly treated Menon's efforts with contempt. More rankled every day, Acheson returned to Washington on the 18th for a cabinet meeting and a transition session with Eisenhower. He found both cabinet and Truman standing "firm," but Eisenhower was inscrutable. Not only did he not back the administration, he apparently told Eden it was all right with him if he backed Menon.[33]

The next day, 19 November 1952, produced nothing but bad news for the Americans, and Acheson put on a show that sullied his reputation. After a barely civil discussion, Eden's failure to budge convinced Acheson (back from Washington) that "we were not acting together, but at arm's length" and that he could no longer "trust anyone." A much worse encounter followed that evening, witnessed by Eden's private secretary, Evelyn Shuckburgh. Having just left a cocktail party and probably "a little tight," Acheson and Jack Hickerson suddenly showed up at Eden's Waldorf-Astoria suite. After asking for "a real martini" and pretending to be in good humor, Acheson badgered Lloyd as an untrustworthy "Welsh lawyer." The "astonished" Eden's eyebrows rose as his American friend threatened to scrap both NATO and "Anglo-American friendship" if

London stuck to Menon and that "empty glass of water," Pearson. He added that he was looking forward to tearing "the resolution apart" and "debagging that Swami." Afterward, Eden said he was "sad" to see the "temporary disintegration" of Acheson's "character." The loyal and appalled Shuckburgh said Acheson had acted like an "American tough guy shooting his way out of an awkward position and scattering his friends on every side." He was "just another tough guy."[34]

Though Acheson told the president the British, Canadians, and other allies were "very soft on principles," he remained hopeful he might stiffen them behind a worthy solution to the POW issue. In contrast, Shuckburgh thought Acheson now pretended "to like the Indian resolution" because his own position had "virtually collapsed." As newspapers drew attention to the Anglo-American squabble, he flew to Ottawa for a prearranged swan song. "High agitation reigned" in New York on his return, but a smiling Pearson, who had spent the weekend dealing with the disputatious Gross, seemed more obliging than before. Acheson and Gross continued to act as if planning to give no quarter, and their pressure on Nehru to make Menon see reason raised British hackles. Both the United States and Soviet Union, Schuckburgh thought, were "unwieldy, insensitive prehistoric monsters floundering about in mud." His colleagues fumed at press leaks engineered by Acheson and Gross highlighting disagreements that the British contingent claimed were fictional.[35]

Then inept Soviet diplomacy came to the rescue. On 24 November, Andrei Vyshinsky broadsided the Indian initiative, uniting all the former disputants and allowing Acheson to become statesmanlike again. According to his own poker-faced account, Acheson aired his "sorrow" at Vyshinsky's "disruptive attitude" and praised Eden and Menon's "statesmanship." A few trifling amendments, he said, would make Menon's draft acceptable. Beijing fiercely backed Vyshinsky, but it was too late. Temptations to accommodate the communists had wilted. The Latin American bloc rallied to Washington's cause. For another week, while "Eden went home and I wanted to," Acheson recalled, conferees hammered out final language. Having accepted the formerly unacceptable, Acheson now cajoled a distraught Menon from giving up because of the communists' attack on him. Now with the Americans at his side, he advanced a final draft, in which the final fate of "unrepatriate" POWs would be settled either in an international conference or by the UN itself. In place of a firm right to refuse repatriation, Acheson accepted a guarantee that final disposition of prisoners would be "strictly in accordance with international law." Once the Soviets had thrown in their "monkey wrenches," he wrote Truman, the United States was again "in pretty good shape." On 3 December 1952, the General Assembly voted for the mutated Indian resolution, 54–5, immediately rejected by China and North Korea.[36]

Thus, the western powers stuck together at the end, joined by the third world bloc after the communist assault on its putative Indian leader. Acheson had paid a price, however, for this struggle blocked efforts to push harsh new anti-Chinese actions through the "Additional Measures" committee. In retrospect, the POW squabble was mainly significant for exposing Chinese inflexibility. Stalemated but not defeated on the battlefield, Mao may still have hoped for a military break-through. He would not turn to peace again until after Eisenhower brandished new threats and, more important, Stalin died. By then, Truman and Acheson were out of power.[37]

Balancing the Books

One of Eisenhower's first actions was to "unleash" Chiang Kai-shek by remov-ing U.S. ships from the Formosa Straits. But Chiang's strongest weapons were rhetorical. A junketing Reston heard some of this in Taipei before trekking to Seoul, where Rhee cursed the truce talks and called for armed reunification of Korea. Neither Chiang nor Rhee had the power to affect large events, and shortly after Stalin's death on 5 March 1953, China accepted terms for the start of a prisoner exchange, and armistice talks resumed. In June, Rhee scooped the negotiators by freeing over 25,000 communist prisoners from his camps. This caused general reproach, but he had probably done everyone a favor. As General Collins would write, the drastic cut in numbers of nonrepatriate POWs gave the PRC "a face-saving alibi" for all the Chinese who refused repatriation. Beijing could claim Rhee had "kidnapped" them. The pace of negotiations then quick-ened, leading to a truce on 27 July 1953 (26 July in the United States). Eisenhower loyalists claimed his veiled threats of nuclear attacks moved China to settle, but the critical factor was the death in Moscow, for Stalin's absence from the counsels of war permitted Mao and Kim to make a kind of peace.[38]

Truman and Acheson had already proclaimed victory. In May 1952, Truman told his diary, "We knocked the socks off the communists in Korea." Apart from restoring the status quo ante, which gives his boast some merit, South Korea's stunning economic and political progress after 1950 makes the decision to go to war look both wise and prudent. Despite the Vietnam debacle to come, ensuring continuing U.S. power and influence in East Asia appears wise. Truman and Acheson were almost certainly correct to think that *not* defending South Korea would have wrecked the UN, though this was far from Acheson's main concern. But failing to defend South Korea would also have greatly diminished American influence and moral authority, and well beyond Asia. Moreover, defending a country Washington had not explicitly promised to defend must have discour-aged any thoughts Stalin entertained about encroaching on other states outside Washington's formal system of alliances.[39]

It was also right to confine the war to Korea. That said, the complacency of Truman's diary entry was ill placed given Rhee's record before the war and the administration's errors during the war. In addition, the struggle in Korea did nothing to produce the regional stability the United States sought or prevent the instability born of decolonization. Acheson remained puzzled by Asians' fierce anti-western feelings. Partly because so many of them doubted the U.S. "devotion to peace, lack of imperial ambition and interest in Asian freedom and progress," he wrote in August 1950, their governments refused to take a "clear stand" against "Soviet imperialism." The region defied most of Washington's efforts to impose order, let alone establish centers of western strength.[40]

Acheson never minimized the catastrophe that was the Chinese intervention. He wrote his former boss in 1955 that it "was an incalculable defeat to U.S. foreign policy and destroyed the Truman administration." It reinvigorated the McCarthyite attacks on Acheson and temporarily stalled his work in western Europe. The defeat at the hands of Mao's "volunteers" sounded for years, ricocheting in different directions. MacArthur's fiasco silenced the most fervent "rollback" advocates. A whole generation of army leaders hoped never again to fight on the Asian mainland. The attacks of the right against the Truman administration convinced Lyndon Johnson he could not retreat in Vietnam. Mao's intervention in Korea haunted him, too, causing tensions with military leaders who resented the restraints Johnson put on them to avoid another Chinese war. John Kennedy's election as president in 1960 resulted partly from a campaign claim that "communism" had been on the rise since Korea, to the disadvantage of the United States. Though this was a flawed perception, the USSR did seem to be growing in strength, and its North Korean protégé had survived. China had decisively reversed decades of western supremacy. It fought the United States to a draw on the battlefield, vastly expanding its prestige throughout the communist bloc, most of Asia, and much of Africa.[41]

But communist gains in Korea were mostly illusory, temporary, or offset by terrible losses. China sustained at least 400,000 casualties, perhaps many more, and at least 152,000 fatalities. North Korea, shattered by an underreported U.S. air war, took around three million casualties, mostly civilians. In contrast, around 37,000 Americans and 15,000 of its UN allies died in the war (with over 800,000 South Korean military casualties). Communist bloc political losses were more enduring. Although the economic sacrifices Mao made for war at first added to his dependence on Stalin, in stalemating the American imperialists, he had greatly raised the prestige of his revolution and nation. This magnified status helped convert arguments with Moscow into a historic fracture in relations, beginning in the late fifties.[42]

Most important, the Korean War led to the mobilization of western power Acheson had been seeking, a mobilization that fleshed out NATO and rearmed West Germany. Western nations became far better organized and wielded far greater military power than before. China faced an implacable foe resolved now to protect both South Korea and Formosa. The war in Korea also weakened the Soviet Union strategically. Because intensified cold war tensions undermined its grip on eastern Europe, Stalin's successors sought a respite from the east-west struggle. They abandoned the project to recapture Yugoslavia, toned down their "anti-imperialist" rhetoric, and gave new energy to develop Soviet bloc economies, though with little success. They intermittently sought improved diplomatic relations with the United States and the capitalist states of western Europe. The blunders of the United States had made the Korean War longer and costlier than necessary. The stalemate Washington achieved in Korea did not prevent future conflicts in Asia. But it went far to win the cold war in Europe.[43]

26

AT DIFFERENT ENDS OF THE
TRIANGLE: DOMESTIC DEBATES,
EUROPEAN ARMIES, BRITISH ALLIES

Doubts Abroad

New sources of tension developing in 1950 and early 1951 raised the height of Acheson's diplomatic hurdles. Disappointments in Korea and resentment at home of a Europe-first diplomacy brought a new spate of criticism, mostly from partisans of Chiang Kai-shek. A backlash in Europe, especially in France, resulted from concern about Washington's MacArthurism-without-MacArthur, resentment of U.S. domination of the alliance, and anger at its relentless pressure to rearm. Truman and Acheson readily faced down the domestic challenge. Resistance to American leadership in Europe was more significant, proving again that cold war policies were made in all alliance capitals, not only Washington.

Truman's boldness in Korea, which originally gave heart to the allies, also tempted them to let the United States do all the work instead of making the sacrifices needed to build their own armed forces. To them, a possible Korean armistice made a slowdown in military expansion seem sensible. So did economic trends, for heavy U.S. arms spending and stockpiling caused spikes of inflation that battered transatlantic treasuries. These currents enkindled protests and strikes in Europe and contributed to Labor's defeat in the British elections in October 1951. Moreover, the Pentagon's own ravenous consumption of weapons caused broken promises of weapons shipments to the allies.

Accompanying economic distress was an eruption of anti-Americanism, prompting General Bernard Montgomery to remark that America's unpopularity began when it "started handing out large gifts." French hackles rose as

Americans arrived on their soil to set up Eisenhower's command with "new air bases, rail lines, oil-storage depots, [and] extravagant headquarters." Resentments also streamed through cultural channels. The government in Paris temporarily blocked the sale of Coca-Cola, and French intellectuals bewailed New York's rise as a world art center and Hollywood's swamping of French cinema. By 1952, 43 percent of the French people preferred neutralism to the U.S. alliance.[1]

A Great Debate at Home: "More Critical than Serious"

The "Great Debate" resulted from Truman's decision to send fresh army divisions to Europe. This debate, which often ruled headlines from December 1950 to early April 1951 and fed off GOP victories in the recent off-year election, caught the administration off guard. Putting U.S. forces in harm's way in central Europe was no laughing matter, nor was Truman's robust claim to send them under his own authority, which disturbed some critics more than the decision itself. Republicans led the negative side in the debate, but luminaries of both parties appeared on both sides of the divide. John Foster Dulles, Thomas E. Dewey, Harold Stassen, Lucius Clay, and Senators Henry Cabot Lodge, Jr., and William Knowland all sided with the administration (with a mortally ill Senator Vandenberg on the sideline). Conservative Democrat Walter George and liberal Democrat Paul Douglas were among the critics. General Ridgway's counter-offensive in Korea took most of the air out of critics. At the debate's height, Acheson considered it a "smashing attack" against the commitment to internationalism, but once it fizzled, the administration's policies remained intact. It had been "more critical than serious," Acheson reflected, and no more challenges to his European policies occurred during the rest of his tenure.[2]

Inaugurating the debate through November and December 1950 were Senator Robert A. Taft, fresh from a glittering reelection with 57 percent of Ohio's vote, former President Herbert Hoover, and Joseph P. Kennedy, described by Acheson as not yet distinguished "through his progeny." Taft started with a bookish oration calling for an across-the-board reexamination of American foreign policy. Misreading the mood and Taft as an extremist, Acheson poked fun at him as a new breed of isolationist, a "reexaminist" farmer who planted crops one day and uprooted them the next to see how they were doing. Citing Holmes on Justice John Harlan, Acheson later wrote that because Taft's mind worked "like a vise, the jaws of which did not meet," he could hold only "the larger objects." The senator deserved better. In a 1951 book, he sensibly described the central issue as whether the president or the people (through Congress) could decide matters of war and peace. Although he eventually voted to send troops to Europe, he again spoke against it in a lengthy and scholarly January speech. Having caught "unshirted hell" for his first sally at Taft, Acheson was about to try conciliating him when Kennedy in mid-December recycled his defeatist appeasement of 1939–40 in a speech that ripped the UK as weak and unreliable. All

American forces should come home, for even if Reds overran Europe, it would matter little if the United States kept its strength mobilized in the western hemisphere. Hoover followed on Kennedy's heels. He approved MDAP aid but wanted the allies to defend themselves while the United States built an unassailable "fortress America." In the Senate, many Republicans garnished Taft's potatoes with their own parsley, agreeing on the need to defend Europe but not with U.S. ground forces. Instead, the United States should exploit its comparative advantage, relying on naval, air, and nuclear capacity to face down the communists.[3]

Though a GOP itch for a fight brought about this debate, critics' questions were important. Did the U.S. national interest require keeping western Europe out of communist hands? Did that mean sending troops to Germany? Would it be wiser to keep them home and rely on nuclear strength to deter a Soviet attack? Were the allies letting burdened American taxpayers bail them out while they enjoyed the fruits of peace and safety? And in his claims to executive authority, was Truman taking a dangerous step toward erecting a garrison state?

Acheson probably did not know that *Pravda* reprinted the statements of Kennedy and Hoover, but he was "shocked" by the hopelessness and "stench of spiritless defeat" emanating from them and other critics. He began to take them on at a 22 December 1950 press conference, charging that Hoover's "hemispheric defense" would mean either surrendering Europe or resorting "to the ultimate violence of nuclear weapons" for self-defense. Either would leave Moscow the master of the "entire Eurasian land mass" with resources "vastly superior" to those within U.S. reach, making it impossible to manage cold war issues except through war. Rejecting "quivering in a storm cellar waiting for whatever fate others may wish to prepare for us," he invoked the administration strategy of building strength "side by side with our allies." Six days later, Truman less ceremoniously dismissed Hoover's stance as nothing but "isolationism."[4]

The choleric Nebraskan, Kenneth Wherry, brought focus to the debate with Senate Resolution 8. This would authorize the sending of U.S. ground forces to Europe for NATO only with express congressional approval, a "barefaced attempt," Acheson said later, "to overthrow the basic conception of the constitution." Wherry's ploy was also the first instance of several in which the critics strayed from the core strategic issues, such as whether the Soviet danger in Europe justified the addition of U.S. forces, into a struggle between congressional and executive power, a contest almost always won by presidents. Nonetheless, Wherry also attracted backing from senators simply unhappy about rising defense spending.[5]

It was not long before Truman went after Wherry. In a combative press conference on 11 January, he ripped into him while defending his powers as president and commander-in-chief. "Of course," he would politely "consult" Congress, but he did not have to "ask their permission" to send troops wherever he liked. While he was cuffing Congress in the head, Acheson played good cop, trying to appease Senate nobles other than Taft and Wherry. In the face of bipartisan murmurings, by mid-January he was hinting at flexibility on how *many* troops Truman sent to Europe. Both Truman and Acheson tried mollifying Hoover, asking him to run an aid program for India, but the former president coolly declined. Despite friendly speeches by Lodge and Knowland and endorsements from a large group of social scientists, on 8 February, eighteen prominent Republicans including Hoover and Taft demanded the withdrawal of all U.S. troops from Europe. In the House, 118 Republicans called for an end to the administration's "tragic" and "costly" policies.[6]

In eleven days of hearings on S.R. 8, senators repeatedly pressed witnesses on presidential authority but barely nibbled at policy choices. War heroes Dwight Eisenhower, George Marshall, and Omar Bradley gained the administration considerable mileage in their testimony, while Matthew Ridgway helped offstage with his Korean counteroffensive. Though Eisenhower did not bowl over his interrogators, he contributed simply by not expressing his own misgivings about recent administration actions. Eisenhower, Marshall, and Acheson then all believed a U.S. troop presence in Europe would be temporary. On 15 February, Marshall's suggestion that the administration had only four new divisions in mind nearly disarmed Taft, who had already accepted the idea of "a few more."[7]

During his three hours of testimony on 16 February 1951, Acheson argued that U.S. forces could not wait for greater expansion of allies' armies for the simple reason that the Soviets needed deterring immediately. The Kremlin would be the first to notice if each of the allies said, "After you Alphonse." The receding advantage of the U.S. nuclear shield also made it essential to amass larger ground forces in a hurry. He reminded those who doubted that four more divisions would do the job—that the "primary" U.S. concern was to prevent, not win a war. He countered the case of "fortress America" by emphasizing America's "intangible ties" to Europe and the "cold, material facts" of the continent's fund of scientific knowledge, skilled laborers, raw materials, and ability to control the seas. The alliance with western Europe added "more than 200,000,000 free people" to the United States' side, a population that "under the heel of an aggressor" would represent "200,000,000 slaves" bent on destroying America "and the remainder of western civilization." If they fell to the Kremlin, Soviet "military might" would expand massively.[8]

Iowa's Bourke Hickenlooper gave him a hard time, noting that when asked in 1949 if Washington would send troops to Europe beyond those on occupation duty, Acheson had answered in a flat negative. Now the Iowan demanded expiation for this transgression. In an ineffective rejoinder, Acheson claimed he had meant to say that the Atlantic Pact did not *require* sending more. More candidly, he asserted that much had changed since 1949 and that the "danger in which we find ourselves" was now "much greater." Though Hickenlooper and Acheson continued their sandbox fight, featuring the kind of "You did too!"—"I did not!" rhetoric that left tempers "frayed," Hickenlooper never laid a glove on the substance of U.S. policy, only Truman's claims to authority.[9]

Nearly fifty other witnesses testified, some famous and some like a Thomas J. Reardon of Hartford, who declared himself "a sinner and whole citizen of the United States." What finally emerged on 4 April was the nonbinding Resolution 99, which passed the Democratic Senate by a vote of 69–21. It acclaimed Eisenhower's appointment to head NATO forces in Europe and vaguely endorsed Truman's authority while specifying that he could send "no ground forces" besides the already mentioned four divisions "without further congressional approval." Truman decided to neither acknowledge nor challenge the resolution. When the House of Representatives decided against making S.R. 99 a joint resolution, the Great Debate essentially ended. Suffering a mild case of complacency, Acheson on 9 April told the Belgian prime minister the best way for Europeans to neutralize congressional concerns was to act more vigorously in their own defense buildup.[10]

Thus ended a weak attempt to impeach both the troop decision and the administration case about the Soviet threat in Europe. The same Chinese intervention that had wounded the administration supported its views of external dangers. Despite the emotional allure of an America-first strategy, Congress had not supported it. The postwar sea change in world affairs had persuaded those Americans who paid attention that it was dangerous to allow Europe to fall uncontested to powerful enemies. Followed by the administration's successful weathering of MacArthur's dismissal, the Great Debate marked the relative weakness of the China Lobby Asia-firsters and those who had set off the debate. Two years later, Acheson remarked how awful it had been for the nation to psychoanalyze itself in front of an "amazed" world, but he no longer disputed the high level of the debate or the importance of its outcome. When Taft tried to renew the debate in 1952, the people essentially said they "were through with that." They already "knew the answers."[11]

Petersberg and Paris

Despite its easy win in the Great Debate, the administration found it harder to translate its European purposes into diplomatic progress with its partners. The Spofford Plan that emerged from the recent Brussels meetings put alliance members in two separate vehicles on courses to sideswipe one another. In Petersberg, outside Bonn, Konrad Adenauer's Federal Republic and the allied high commissioners would negotiate how to plug German "contingents" into NATO's defense of the continent. In Paris, the French-led Conférence pour l'Organisation de l' Armée Européenne would labor on the European Defense Community, or EDC. Even though the American Spofford contrived this twin procedure, it looked dubious to Washington. The French were still open to Soviet requests for Big Four talks on Germany, talks Acheson thought would be nothing but a "spoiling operation" intended to "cause trouble between us and our European friends and, more generally, to depict us to the world as warmongers."[12]

To simplify a little, Acheson's concerns about the three primary European allies were that the French were given to backsliding, the Germans to sulking, and the British to sticking their nose up at everything happening across the Channel. With these shortcomings in mind, he carefully shaped instructions for a tour by Eisenhower of his nascent NATO command. Because Acheson preferred edgy over bland temperaments, he was not "drawn to" the general and pulled no punches in his orders. Eisenhower should not repeat what he had said in the past about wishing to send some troops home to create a larger reserve. As in the past war, he should act as the embodiment of what the allies wanted—American "determination to proceed to the building of adequate strength." But he should also make clear that the allies in return must "do what is necessary."

Because it was necessary to do a little deflating of Adenauer's pretensions, Eisenhower should soft-pedal integrating German elements within his command. For now, Acheson was content with the slow pace at Petersberg, where Adenauer and the commissioners seemed to be writing blueprints as intricate and confusing as the despised Pleven Plan. Ex-general Hans Speidel, advising Adenauer, had warned that if Paris got its way in the EDC, "Bavarians would want sauerkraut and beer, French troops white bread and wine, and Italians spaghetti and Chianti." Adenauer was aiming heavy fire at anyone who hoped to use German forces "as cannon fodder." For such impudence, Acheson wanted to put rearmament on ice for a time. Still, the Big Three understood Bonn would have to approve any rearmament scheme, whether carrying a Paris or Petersberg trademark.[13]

Despite their insolence, Acheson still wanted to rearm the Germans and normalize relations in a hurry. He did not want to "push" them but to "follow as fast as they moved." John McCloy as U.S. High Commissioner was working to the same end in January 1951 when he commuted several death sentences from the Nuremberg war crimes trials and reduced others. By the "little revision" in early March, the allies reduced their authority over domestic law and authorized Bonn to establish a foreign office for dealings with states other than the victorious powers. Washington was receiving less help than usual from London in these efforts, especially after Ernest Bevin died in April. He left behind a government increasingly annoyed with Washington and skeptical about German rearmament. Like French leaders, Prime Minister Clement Attlee hoped the Russians might still offer an attractive alternative. Also like the French, he did not want German rearmament accomplished before others had restored their own military strength. This procrastination gave the U.S. Senate an alibi for delaying votes on military aid.[14]

Because Acheson thought that if France moved, the UK was likely to follow, he centered his attention on Paris. He told René Pleven forthrightly during a Washington visit in January that the United States would reject unsound outcomes from the Paris talks and not tolerate further delays in bringing in the Germans. Once Petersberg agreed on the configuration of German regimental combat teams, Washington would have to decide whether to integrate them as divisions in NATO or merge them in Paris's European force. He also told Pleven that "military requirements," not French views or German behavior, would determine the choice. Pleven surely noticed that Acheson did not rule out unilaterally rearming the Germans and putting them on the front lines if "Europe" failed to do so. In the early spring of 1951, Eisenhower opened Supreme Headquarters, Allied Powers, Europe (SHAPE), and continental governments concluded the European Coal and Steel Community treaty. But at the same time, a disintegrating UK government refused to come to grips with the "very painful subject" of German rearmament. Soon, Labor's health minister, Aneurin Bevan, would resign to protest heavy rearmament costs, throwing the cabinet into crisis.[15]

In June, "Petersberg" first came up with a plan, or rather a set of suggestions. These called for twelve German divisions backed by tanks and artillery, a light coastal naval force, and a tactical air force, all to merge directly into NATO. Because the Petersberg pattern subverted the Paris negotiations, France briskly rejected it. The Paris discussions themselves drifted, with the smaller powers bridling over the transparent French campaign to block a fair German role yet recoiling at the partial surrender of sovereignty imbedded in EDC. But the Paris talks were the only car left on the road, and Acheson later claimed in a great over-simplification that he climbed in as the "best way" to gain "an adequate German contribution." In fact, he was worried about losing German forces entirely. As negotiators piled proposals and amendments on one another, new U.S. soldiers began arriving, stripping Washington of a key bartering chip. Threatening to withdraw them—as Dulles would find out in a few years—would degrade the military balance they were supposed to help establish.[16]

Indeed, Paris's growing conviction that the Americans were in Europe to stay emboldened its resistance on Germany. As a result, its relations with the United States were about to suffer quite a rough patch. Paris complained about having to do the impossible all at once: rearm, reconstruct and modernize its economy, fight or placate rebels in Asia and North Africa, host a complex NATO infrastructure spreading over its soil, and accept hated schemes for German rearmament. Elections in June 1951 decimated centrist parties friendliest to the EDC, greatly adding to the representation of Gaullists and Communists. As Pleven took nearly two months to weave a new government, Acheson ventured extremely close to a radical shift in policy.[17]

"David Bruce's Devoted Mid-Wifery"

Usually when Acheson had trouble with Britain or Germany, he renewed his massaging of France. But because he would not wait on German rearmament indefinitely, in the early summer of 1951 he came to the verge of achieving that goal unilaterally. He was reined in only by the deft intervention of Ambassador David K. E. Bruce in Paris, who strongly favored the EDC over Petersberg. Acheson's idea was to use the provisional plans that had emerged from Petersberg to spoil the anti-German stew simmering in Paris. This would require a perilous finesse, loading German forces into NATO without a French say-so. Following Bruce's effective response, Acheson threw all the U.S. chips into the EDC.

His opening gambit appeared on 28 June in a telegram to Bruce written after consultation with McCloy, the joint chiefs, and European desk officers. To place admission of Germany to NATO on a fast track, he proposed ignoring the Paris talks. Using the Spofford Plan as a blueprint, he would put German divisions into Eisenhower's growing NATO force. Preferably, they would be mixed with other European units. Meanwhile, talks in Paris could proceed for a "long term approach," that is, the EDC. France aside, the United States was ready for "substantial" German equality and an early, "interim" attachment to NATO. This idea, he continued in a cheeky proposition, would simplify France's work by creating the "backbone" of a European force the EDC could join. Washington could no longer tolerate delay, he told Bruce, and there was no guarantee the Paris negotiations would succeed.[18]

Ironically, at this very time, Acheson gave a speech emphasizing the need for modesty in allied relations and not confusing "our own opinions with the will of God." In that spirit, Bruce believed the French could "be tactfully led but not driven." Five years Acheson's junior, Bruce was more than his equal socially. Born in privileged Virginia society, a familiar of F. Scott Fitzgerald and Edmund Wilson at Princeton, a collector of beautiful things and married to a Mellon heiress, he was ready to tackle Acheson over this issue and did so in a cable of 3 July. After generally lauding his boss's message, he tallied a list of particular objections. The U.S. government, he insisted, must assuage French fears about the German "national character." Nothing would be worse than to have the Germans irrevocably rearmed and then have to watch helplessly as all efforts at a combined force collapsed. This would leave a German army in the middle of the continent, able to do whatever it might. Believing the EDC the quickest path to a German contribution, he warned Acheson against provoking a dire alliance crisis by driving ahead in the face of French objections. On the other hand, by giving the EDC its unreserved support, the United States would have the right to insist on genuine inclusion of the Germans. They could not take that step in any case, Bruce wrote, until the allies ended occupation controls and arranged Bonn's new status through the "contractual" agreements, a chain of contracts on the allies' relations with Germany and a substitute for a peace treaty. But France would not sign the contractuals until it had gained its national security through the EDC.[19]

On 3 July, the same day Bruce answered Acheson, Eisenhower indirectly did the same by publicly declaring that Europe could achieve security only by trading in its "patchwork territorial forces" for a European army. This was quite remarkable, because Eisenhower had earlier considered the EDC the kind of "cockeyed idea" a "dope fiend" might invent. The author of Eisenhower's turnaround was Jean Monnet, the French guru of European unity. Moreover, Eisenhower was in no rush to add German troops. McCloy—also subject to Monnet's magic—not only joined Bruce's side but convinced Adenauer that Washington would insist on the EDC or something very much like it. If Eisenhower's switch was weighty, it was Bruce who turned Acheson around by neatly reversing McCloy's stratagem, convincing him that Adenauer was himself partial to the "European" structure.[20]

Cornered and quickly recognizing the "devoted mid-wifery" that had outmaneuvered him, Acheson decided to submit to "the hands of God and David Bruce." One reason was his acute awareness of Europeans' building restiveness under the pressure of his demands. In a memorandum of 6 July, he acknowledged that France would not budge until "the question of German sovereignty" had been settled, but the Germans would not be satisfied until they had been guaranteed sovereignty and equal treatment on European defense. Both France and Germany had to be satisfied "simultaneously." Though he still pushed hard against French delays, Acheson—and Marshall, too— committed themselves to the EDC. Nonetheless, in his 16 July response to Bruce, Acheson explained that it was essential for Bonn eventually to have forces in *NATO*. Other Europeans in the EDC might never "outweigh German influence," but NATO included the offshore weight of the United States, the UK, and Canada to keep Germany from tipping the scales. Though he never said so explicitly, his formula could work only if the United States surrendered hopes of staying in Europe only temporarily. Unlike Eisenhower, he now believed Americans must stay indefinitely to defend against both Soviet and German power in western Europe. Double containment was alive and healthy.[21]

On a prompt from Acheson, President Truman on 30 July 1951 signaled the tacit relinquishment of "Petersberg" for "Paris." In a modified version of the single package presented in New York the year before, the United States would support a "European Defense Force" enrolled under NATO *if* France accepted a "special plan for raising German contingents" and arrangements to restore "substantial German sovereignty." Acheson set November as a deadline for completing plans for the European force, German rearmament, and German contractuals.

Clearly, Bruce had not moved U.S. policy as far as he wanted. Acheson remained privately suspicious of the EDC and fearful that European integration projects would delay vital military decisions, and he issued a tattoo of public warnings against procrastination. Learning that officers in European military forces, including those of France, were skeptical of the EDC, on 9 August he reiterated to Schuman the U.S. terms for acceptance, also hinting that Bonn's membership in NATO was another American sine qua non for accepting the EDC. Schuman's unpromising reply three weeks later was as gracious as French attitudes permitted, but resistant nonetheless. The first German soldiers must wear *European* uniforms, he said, and it was inopportune even to talk about NATO membership before West Germany proved itself a good European citizen.[22]

Acheson knew he was firing blanks. Washington would have to make the best of what it could get. When Big Three defense ministers gathered in Washington in mid-September 1951, he vowed strenuous and "enthusiastic" support for the EDC. There would be "no turning back and no doubts." This gave new meaning to "no doubts" and marked another phase of stroking Paris, for Acheson now released all pressure about EDC arrangements. This seemed to make France a little more punctual and obliging, a little less peevish and defensive. Acheson told a National War College audience the United States could not stand over its friends "with a club" or overload them "with impossible demands."[23]

The limousine of the western buildup again seemed in the right lane. Later it would become clear that having the United States go "overboard" for the EDC aroused new suspicions in Paris of its own handiwork, as did other factors peculiar to French politics.[24]

"We Haven't Got Bleeding Hearts about Peace"

Early in 1951, the allies were also going through the motions of preparing for the talks on Germany requested by the Soviet government. In allied capitals there was considerable anxiety about Moscow's reactions to the goings-on in both Petersberg and Paris. In late January, a CIA estimate noted that German rearmament might trigger "global war." A month later, some of Acheson's colleagues worried about an East German attack on the western zones of Berlin. Acheson was skeptical about that particular case but had long said that western success in gaining military strength might cause a forcible Soviet response. Tangentially confirming his view, the CIA as late as May held that Soviet "consent" would be a prerequisite for rearming West Germany. Western nervousness stemmed largely from alarmist intelligence estimates of Soviet capabilities and exaggerated notions of how Stalin might use them. Washington worried about East German leader Otto Grotewohl's ability to fling 300,000 East Germans into battle on the side of the Russians. With MDAP deliveries lagging, Washington was relying on the SAC force even more than usual in war plans and threatening what Eisenhower and Dulles would later christen "massive retaliation." Truman stepped up production of nuclear materials, and U.S. generals began testing atomic bombs for use in land warfare.[25]

President Vincent Auriol in Paris wanted Germany left a disarmed, neutral "no-man's land," a view deriving from rattled nerves and an almost bottomless anti-German prejudice. French excitement about new four-power talks disgusted Acheson, who believed Moscow had simply seen that exploiting continental nerves might stop German rearmament in its tracks. Concerned that both Paris and London would give away too much in advance, he demanded that deputy-level negotiations must precede any conference and in a preemptive strike announced on 3 January 1951 that Washington refused to join discussions confined to Germany. He dreaded a seductive idea tossed up by the Russians, he told senators three weeks later, "such as that we all take our troops out of Germany, which means a 75-mile move for them and a very long one for us." He reminded Pleven a few days later that the west had successfully faced Vyshinsky down at the 1949 CFM. Only a Russian "change of heart" encompassing "a major reduction" in Soviet armed forces would justify any reconsideration of western policies. Hanging tough had worked before and still would.[26]

On 5 March 1951, the talks began in Paris's Palais Rose, at the deputy level as Acheson had insisted. He mainly wanted to make propaganda hay by exposing Soviet iniquity and was impervious to charges "that we haven't got bleeding hearts about peace." Philip Jessup drew the Palais Rose assignment, instructed to look willing to "talk anywhere at any time with anybody" but block anything that stopped the march toward western rearmament. By early May, Acheson thought Soviet delegate Andrei Gromyko had exposed himself as "an unreasonable bumpkin" in rejecting everything the Big Three offered. The British and French held firm against his challenges to German rearmament and NATO's very existence. On 21 June, after the French government survived national elections, the conference adjourned sine die. This more than any other conference of the era became a byword for cold war futility; the deputies had conducted seventy-four barren sessions without agreeing on an agenda for a Council of Foreign Ministers meeting. Despite widespread disappointment, Truman and Acheson were content. In 1949, they had frustrated Stalin's attempt to stop formation of a West German state; now they had blocked his effort to disrupt the campaign to energize NATO.[27]

Acheson's assurance that he was on the right path helped explain his nonchalance about a spitting match in the summer and fall of 1951 between Paul Nitze and Charles Bohlen over a new version of NSC-68. Backed in absentia by Kennan, Bohlen reasserted that protecting their own power dictated Soviet leaders' foreign policy and that Washington should meet Moscow halfway whenever it showed restraint. Acheson never thought any outsider could divine the Kremlin's motives and indulged Nitze in applying his own equally unknowable proposition that Stalin followed a master plan of hostility. Acheson was unworried about the details of the paper, only that it reassert the menace of the USSR. He and Nitze agreed the west still lacked "an adequate position of strength." As Acheson put it simply to Truman in mid-January 1952, since the Soviets were surely doing everything possible to strengthen themselves, it was incumbent on the Americans to be equally stalwart. When the old lion Winston Churchill told Acheson the Soviets feared "our friendship more than our enmity," Acheson quickly countered that growing western strength "would reverse this, so that the Soviets would fear our enmity more than our friendship and *would thus be led to seek our friendship*," which is how he wanted it.[28]

This mood matched current U.S.-USSR relations, which had steadily worsened, especially in the coarsening of language of exchanges. As always little concerned about "communism," Acheson instead berated the Soviets for their expansionism and misbehavior. In August 1951 he described the regime as a "conspiracy that walks like a state." For their part, Moscow agents that summer ratcheted up their harassment of U.S. diplomats. Czechoslovakia arrested American reporter William Oatis, ran him through an espionage show trial, and imprisoned him for two years. Besides publicly lashing out in response, Washington stripped Czechoslovakia of its most-favored-nation trade status and imposed other trade and travel restrictions. In a comic moment, the government of the District of Columbia drew the line when the state department proposed flunking all Soviet officials seeking driving permits.

Occasionally, Acheson tried defusing the mounting tension, hoping, for example, to tone down Truman's "shrill blasts at the Soviet Union" in speeches, but he was in the forefront of one of the more ludicrous moments of Soviet-American tension. Worsening relations had ended most of the ritualistic parties and receptions in which foes could suspend business and exchange pleasantries over a drink. Public insult was the order of the day, as in a vituperative attack against Truman by Moscow's new foreign minister, Andrei Vyshinsky, in a UN General Assembly meeting in Paris. At a dinner for delegates given by Auriol, Secretary-General Trygve Lie urged Acheson to speak to Vyshinsky. When he approached him, the Soviet delegate at the UN, Jacob Malik, accused him of slanderous remarks about Moscow's "slave camps." Acheson had no interest in Malik but turned to blister Vyshinsky for unnamed breaches of manners. When Malik interposed that the Russian word for "world" was the same as for "peace," Acheson retorted that he "was not interested in applesauce about words" and told Vyshinsky that if he "wanted to stop fooling around with doves and get on a twig, he would get on a twig with him and try to work out the problem." To which Vyshinsky said he "would get on the twig" if Acheson got off the ground. Inexplicably, Acheson proudly characterized this inane exchange to Luke Battle as "a rugged conversation" in which he had taken the initiative and "swapped blows with Mr. Vyshinsky." Two weeks later, a depressed Harold Ickes published a new word, "achinsky," defined as "discordance in managing negotiations between nations; hence, shouting down opposition in any negotiations; lack of artfulness in diplomacy."[29]

"We Were All at Different Ends of the Triangle"

The war in Korea contributed to such incivility, just as it caused Washington to reconsider who qualified as an ally. Though Acheson had barely bothered politeness when Greece and Turkey first requested membership in NATO, he now looked again. Their stock rose with each report of their soldiers' exploits in Korea. Acheson momentarily deferred to the joint chiefs, who shivered at the thought of adding responsibilities in the eastern Mediterranean, and he also worried that admitting Greece and Turkey would increase pressure for Spanish membership. But as early as September 1950, NATO "associated" itself with Greece and Turkey and invited them into Mediterranean planning. Now Acheson thought they should come fully into the alliance, persuaded by slowness of the defense buildup, new Soviet propaganda outbursts against Turkey, the lingering possibility of Turkish neutralism, and the need for more regional cooperation in the Middle East. Many senior state department diplomats favored admission, as did prominent outsiders. Thus, in March 1951, Acheson began working to break down Pentagon resistance. The possibility of gaining bases in Turkey helped, but historian Melvyn Leffler is probably correct that fear of Turkish neutralism was "decisive." Already enjoying bilateral ties with France and the UK, Turkey would now become a full NATO ally with the task of protecting its "eastern flank." Greece would tag along into the alliance.[30]

In May 1951, the U.S. government formally proposed inviting the two nations. "Sulky" opposition came from smaller states mortified to hear through press leaks that the Big Three had already decided on the move. Taking an amazed look at their maps, the Dutch and Danes had thought Italy bad enough as a "North Atlantic" ally, but now they might have to fight in the Levant. Nonetheless, the NATO Council in Ottawa agreed on the invitations in September, with final entry scheduled to occur at a NATO meeting in Lisbon in February 1952. Having long put behind him concerns that air bases on Turkish soil would provoke the Soviets, Acheson boasted to the Senate that adding the Greek and Turkish armies would allow NATO to form "a great semicircle which closes one-half of the Soviet Union from the eastern border." The Senate by voice vote gave its blessing on 29 January 1952. On demand for a roll call, the vote on 7 February was 73–2.[31]

Except for this issue, the "six days of long meetings, speeches, and boring formal social engagements" in Ottawa in September 1951 mainly fatigued Acheson. But two other noteworthy events occurred. The first was the formation of the Temporary Council Committee (soon the "TCC"), which would try to tailor defense spending for each ally according to rational cost-sharing criteria. Dubbed the "Wise Men," Monnet for France, Averell Harriman for the United States, and Chancellor of the Exchequer Hugh Gaitskell for Britain produced for the Lisbon conclave a 700-page report outlining a fifty-division force to cost nearly $50 billion over three years.

For Acheson, the other Ottawa moment of note had satirical rather than substantive significance. As we have seen, in an effort to emphasize NATO's social, economic, and cultural potential, the Canadians in 1949 had rammed through Article 2 over Acheson's objections. Now as the meeting's host, Foreign Minister Lester Pearson obtained a committee of Canada and four others to turn the article into reality. "With fitting justice," wrote Acheson, already annoyed at Canadian opposition to the admission of Turkey and Greece, Pearson chaired the committee. Its "labors," Acheson reported, "were prodigious but barren," colossal enough to draw a warning from Ambassador Hume Wrong in Washington that all the Canadian arm-flapping about Article 2 encouraged the rising sentiment of Americans that Canada spent too little time worrying about the "Soviet danger" and too much on "hazy ideas." Back in Washington, Acheson received Truman's hyperbolic compliment that he had done a "magnificent job." Such pats on the back were Truman's primary contribution to all the discussions in 1950 and 1951 on NATO, the EDC, and Germany. In European affairs especially, he routinely rubber-stamped what Acheson gave him, and dozens of pages of Princeton seminar transcripts covering recollections about Germany and NATO include not a single reference to Truman.[32]

The German hedgehog continued to leave quills in the hands of everyone touching it. Washington's decision to bet the farm on the EDC had solved little. Before going to Ottawa, Acheson had told senators the United States and France were "all at different ends of the triangle," with their opposing preferences "very effectively blocking one another and getting no place." As new governments found their sea legs in Britain and France in the fall of 1951, Acheson concentrated on the contractuals that would convert occupied West Germany to "an ally contributing by agreement to mutual defense." He wanted the wartime victors to reserve powers only on stationing troops in Germany, supervising Berlin, and setting terms for an ultimate peace treaty, including reunification and any "territorial questions." As always, he favored greasing the wheels of normalization through surrender of nonvitals. Because of arguments between his German bureau and the more cautious McCloy, he was also prepared to have the victors retain the right to use force against any effort to subvert West Germany's "liberal-democratic order." When Grotewohl in September 1951 stirred things up by ostensibly proffering talks on German reunification, Acheson swiftly ordered McCloy to do everything necessary to block them, for they would ruin the contractual agreements. He should tell Adenauer the United States favored "ultimate" reunification but "hammer hard" on the point that anything Grotewohl favored would jeopardize West German "freedom." Reunification must come through European "integration." Confirming his view of the cynicism of the East German announcement, Acheson learned that an East German official had said it did not take "a Columbus" to discover that Grotewohl was simply trying to wreck whatever the west was planning.[33]

When Acheson had his silly cocktail party argument with Vyshinsky, he was in the midst of a lengthy stay in Paris for sessions of the UN General Assembly. As a sign of the times, his party, which arrived "in waves" to the City of Light, numbered eighty, "representatives, alternates, advisers, congressional staff advisers, assistants, and information officers." Bruce hosted the Achesons at the ambassadorial residence. When street noise made it impossible for Acheson to sleep, Jessup's wife corrected the problem with "a box of pills." Though Acheson and Eden often disagreed, these meetings first laid the foundation of their friendship, especially after Acheson learned how to avoid hurting the feelings of the new British foreign minister. Acheson struck Eden as brilliant, with a mind that "never dawdles," though his inability to "suffer fools gladly" was a weakness, since diplomats frequently had to work with fools. Because of a vague physical resemblance, others often confused Acheson with Eden. A U.S. naval officer once accosted Eden in an airplane with a note reading: "You are either Dean Acheson or Anthony Eden. Whichever you are, will you autograph my book?"[34]

The alliance made history on 21 November, when Adenauer joined the Big Three discussions, an event Acheson thought overshadowed any other in this long Paris session. Hoping to complete a clutch of treaties and agreements before the U.S. presidential election campaign set in, Acheson urged Adenauer to act quickly on the EDC. Hoping to wean the chancellor from any thoughts of an exclusive bilateral connection with the Americans, the French courted him, too, appearing ready to approve the main lines of the contractual agreements and nearly full-sized German divisions for the European army. Planners then envisioned an EDC force of about forty-three divisions, twelve each supplied by Germany and Italy. Only France, with fourteen, could place forces outside the Community. The grand Franco-German bargain would be ready when Bonn agreed to these terms, the contractuals, and the Schuman Plan. Acheson was doubtful, for the Paris government was also battling another financial crisis that could be "disastrous" to what he flattered Truman by calling "your great design in Europe."[35]

As he anticipated, progress was sluggish rather than swift, almost causing the cancellation of NATO meetings in Rome at the end of the month and early December. Plagued by pleurisy, in Rome Acheson staggered through sessions in an atmosphere "heavy almost to the point of pessimism." With the EDC conference mired in debate over minutiae, no TCC report ready, and the Europeans wrestling with problems made more difficult by their intensified defense efforts, he urged the president to imitate his own stoicism. Some of the allies were lapsing into naivete about Moscow's intentions, a problem exacerbated by a "hair-raising" briefing by General Alfred Gruenther that left many feeling impotent to do anything. Acheson resisted pressures for some way to guarantee the preservation of West German democracy. Instead of hectoring the Germans, allies should be confident about the web of circumstances now enmeshing Bonn, the imminent blending of its army with others, and NATO troops on its soil. Moreover, the nearly completed peace treaty with Japan made no such ideological demands. It was far better, he advised Truman, to unhandcuff the Germans and invite them "in every possible way" to associate freely with their new allies. But most of those allies were not so sanguine, and Acheson was now certain his hoped-for German settlement would remain incomplete at the end of the year.[36]

A brief Roman holiday provided a little renewal, as Acheson strolled with Alice along the stones of ancient Roman roads. On 4 December, they boarded the *SS Independence* in Naples for a leisurely voyage home. At home again, Acheson was upbeat for public consumption. Eisenhower was already in business at SHAPE, four new U.S. divisions manned the defense lines, and the "Wise Men" were at work. Great progress was under way renewing German sovereignty and establishing both the Schuman Plan and EDC. With his own aides, however, he was far less optimistic. Both French and British attitudes troubled him. "The French tend to blame us for all their troubles," while British leaders were "like people who have been asleep for five years and suddenly awaken and seemed to have little realization that a great deal has gone on." Adenauer worried that they would "make a deal" with Moscow and sell the "Germans down the river."[37]

The British are Coming II

Amid all the meetings, Acheson worked on a set of staff changes. James Webb, wracked with migraines, excluded from policymaking, and unable to stop Nitze from restoring PPS's place of privilege, resigned as under secretary. (He reappeared a decade later as administrator of the National Aeronautics and Space Administration [NASA] under John Kennedy and Lyndon Johnson.) Acheson was delighted to put the vital fifty-three-year-old Bruce in his place. Though he still consulted on Japan for several months, Dean Rusk left Washington to head the Rockefeller Foundation. (He too resurfaced in 1961, as secretary of state.) The new assistant secretary for Near Eastern and South Asian affairs was Henry Byroade, replacing George McGhee, who became ambassador to Turkey. Robert Murphy would soon move his ambassadorial shingle from Brussels to Tokyo. Loy Henderson moved from New Delhi to Tehran, replaced by Democratic politico, Chester Bowles. Truman needed a new ambassador to replace an exhausted Alan Kirk in Moscow. Although Acheson had zestfully defended Kennan against critics in a January 1951 speech, he also told reporters the new envoy to Moscow "wouldn't be Chip Bohlen or George Kennan but someone with the same temperament as Admiral Kirk, who didn't think he had a mission to settle all our problems overnight." After changing his mind, he sold Truman on Kennan and then persuaded the latter to end his sabbatical to take the post.[38]

None of his new men would take issue with his scorn for gimmicky approaches to international relations. He was scarcely polite in February 1951 when Senator Hubert Humphrey introduced him to a psychologist from UCLA who was peddling a plan to deter Soviet attacks through Voice of America psychodramas. His eyebrows must have risen ever higher as he heard about flooding the airwaves with "archaic" Russian music to evoke Russians' ancestral impulses and a VOA "soap opera" about Americans living in a Soviet city who befriended neighbors over objections of the "block commissar." Acheson wondered if playing "old Russian church music" would not limit the program's appeal to the elderly. And what about the soap opera premise, whose plot he likened to achieving "an understanding between the colonial settlers and the Indians" after the Indians had "scalped Aunt Bessie"? He was more openly sour about publicity-driven schemes of former advertising executive William Benton, now senator from Connecticut, who implied, as Acheson put it, that a more effective diplomacy consisted of "simply plastering the American flag around the world."[39]

At year's end, he encountered something else he abhorred, a Churchillian vision of summitry and Anglo-American amity. Eden had said in Rome the restored prime minister would like an invitation from President Truman for a state visit in January. Churchill also hankered for a summit with Stalin (a là Tehran and Yalta), disliked ideas of European federation, and was openly contemptuous of the "sludgy amalgam" of the EDC, to which the Americans had converted. Acheson reluctantly made the arrangements. When he came to the New World, the prime minister sandwiched a trip to Ottawa between two sets of negotiations in Washington, capped by an address to Congress.[40]

On 5 January 1952, the seventy-seven-year-old World War II hero docked in Brooklyn on the *Queen Mary*. If he hoped to be welcomed in Washington with something like FDR's florid deference to the Former Naval Person, he was disappointed. Eden's party understood this. A new slippage in Britain's trade balance, under secretary Roger Makins wrote, put it "back in the breadline," with troubles in "Persia and Egypt" giving Americans the impression "the British Empire is in liquidation." Whitehall and Foggy Bottom were also in rising discord over the pace of progress in Europe. Truman, still angry about London's policies in China, wanted a clearly defined agenda, with no private tête-à-têtes and his advisers always "present." Acheson urged him to make the visit pleasant and let Churchill do "all of the fighting and make all of the disagreeable statements." Despite Truman's ease in making Churchill feel at home, the change in tone was clear. Eden's right-hand man Evelyn Shuckburgh told his diary: "It was impossible not to be conscious that we are playing second fiddle."[41]

Alice "idolized" the doughty wartime leader, and in 1969 Dean Acheson said Churchill was "the most outstanding man I've ever met." If in 1952 he was "weakening," he still seemed "formidable and quite magnificent." Acheson's best oenophiles were "ransacking New York and Washington" to make sure the prime minister would have the wine and brandy he relished. At the beginning of the summit, Truman hosted a large Potomac party on the *Williamsburg*. Bedecked in naval blue jacket and brass buttons, Churchill had Lord Cherwell, his scientific adviser, "get out his slide rule and compute the depth of the inundation which would take place in the dining-room if all the champagne Mr. Churchill had drunk in his life were poured into it. The results were disappointing to the Old Man. He had expected that we would all be swimming like goldfish in a bowl whereas it would hardly come up to our knees."[42]

Sixteen times over nine days in the two-stage summit, Acheson met with Churchill, Eden, or both. Preferring Bevin's "my boy," when Eden called him "my dear," he was alarmed that "some rugged member of the press" might hear, but his liking for Eden grew. Both on the Potomac and on shore, Acheson argued that the greatest current peril was not an attack by the Red Army but "creeping actions" by satellites aimed at exhausting the west. Though concerned about overstraining European polities, he pushed for a defense buildup large enough to make any Soviet aggression in Europe "too dangerous to be attempted." He hoped the allies could settle the EDC and contractuals within sixty days, as well as adopt the Wise Men's counsel in financing the "O" in NATO. Though Churchill detested the "bucket of wood pulp" that was the EDC, he said he would politely do nothing to kill it—"Let the communiqué sing out that we are all in favor of the European Army." Eden agreed when Acheson asked for help in bringing the Benelux states along, who feared approval of the EDC would give Washington an excuse to desert the continent, leaving them "alone with France and Germany, and perhaps Italy." In fact, both Acheson and Eden warned them that without the EDC they would face a national German army unattached to a larger European framework.[43]

After alternately amusing his Ottawa hosts with his prodigious consumption of champagne and criticisms of their departures from standards of the British empire, Churchill returned to Washington to address Congress. Afterward, "with all the pomp and glitter we could muster," the Achesons feted Churchill with a reception and dinner. The following day, however, brought a full-blown argument in the White House's cabinet room against Truman's insistence on U.S. possession of the North Atlantic Naval Command. After reading a supposedly agreed-on draft, Churchill tore it to ribbons and threw the pieces in the air. "Hurricane warnings along the Potomac," uttered a British admiral. Then came a bombastic recitation of British naval courage in sheltering Europe from tyrants. "As the majestic speech rolled to its conclusion," Oliver Franks passed Acheson a note warning him to be "very, very careful." After huddling with others, Acheson emerged with a finesse. Truman would withdraw a request that Churchill "accept" Washington's view of the Atlantic Command and, as work went ahead to establish it, Churchill could continue his public objections, reserving the right to suggest changes later. "For an interminable minute," Churchill read the draft communique. Then, "looking across at the President, he said, 'I accept every word of it.'" Later he received the small potatoes of the Channel Command. Never enamored of Acheson's situations of strength strategy, at the very end he half-heartedly argued for a new summit with the Russians. The Americans said no.[44]

Coda: To London and Lisbon

The next NATO meeting was to begin in Lisbon on 20 February 1952. On the death of King George VI two weeks beforehand, the Big Three foreign ministers decided to hold a preliminary conclave while hundreds of world figures came to London for the funeral. Success at Lisbon was suddenly in doubt, leaving Acheson "depressed and discouraged." Ancient enmities threatened to suffocate the new European order in which he had invested so much. France had unexpectedly appointed an "ambassador" to the Saar, the border region long disputed with Germany, even though the prevailing understanding was that the area would eventually go to Bonn. Irate, Adenauer threatened to withhold German units from the EDC. Then Acheson received a shocking letter from Schuman full of demands for security guarantees and libels against Germany. In Acheson's response on 2 February, he praised Schuman's past deeds before appealing for more patience and wisdom. It was pointless, he wrote, to "solve a difficult question" by injecting an "insoluble" one. "Lisbon," he wrote later, would be "the supreme gamble upon which we would stake our whole prestige, skill, and power."[45]

The greatest obstacles now to his European goals lurked in the relations among the traditional great powers. Either French nationalism, German resentment, or British diffidence could cripple European defense. He sought to prevent losing western Europe to either a Soviet attack or methods of intimidation that would be effective if Europeans felt vulnerable to attack. If war came, he wanted the capabilities to win it. Never fastidious about ways and means and lacking other alternatives, he had made a "no-turning-back" commitment to gain the needed strength through the EDC. The United States had made the French Idea its own. West Germany would find restoration in a European community. Defense of the community would come through the supranational absorption of the Federal Republic. And success for the French Idea would mean a more secure United States.

The French had been right in 1950 to think German rearmament was a year or two premature. And Churchill, like the Americans originally, was right to consider the EDC a military monstrosity. The greatest irony in a story full of them would come in 1954, with Paris's act of infanticide, killing the EDC in what was a good deed for everyone. What occurred afterward would deliciously mock earlier struggles, for it was a burst of diplomatic creativity in 1955 by the formerly aloof Britain that brokered West Germany's full emergence as a sovereign state and member of NATO. In retirement, Acheson surely smiled when he saw the admirable Eden rather than the deplorable Dulles doing the final work of attaching Bonn to NATO.

Part VI

27

COMMAND IN JAPAN

Japan: A Preview and Overview

Dean Acheson was in his element when engaged in European affairs, with the Soviet Union as his target. By his own accounting, the Japanese peace treaty of 1951 was his single triumph in Asia. Washington held all the high cards in Japan; otherwise, creating situations of strength in Asia was a daunting task. The treaty capped a long-term goal of linking this latent powerhouse to the western coalition. Japan stood strategically off the Asian land mass, heavily populated with an educated and industrious people. A historically proven power in war, Japan could now become invaluable in hosting U.S. military bases. Unlike MacArthur's Formosa, it was a truly unsinkable aircraft carrier. In Theodore Roosevelt's time, it was the first Asian nation to garner the real respect of American statesmen. In Acheson's time, he was among the first U.S. officials to fasten on its importance, but George Marshall and especially George Kennan paved the way toward restoring Japan for the western, anti-Soviet coalition in Truman's first term. Acheson's sponsorship for the next steps was essential, but to keep the issue out of conservatives' line of fire, John Foster Dulles received the job to make the treaty itself.

On issues he regarded as vital to U.S. security, only here did Acheson stay mainly in the background. In other areas he deemed secondary, he would hover on the periphery, taking control only if events endangered his European pursuits. On Indochina, he was the account manager from the outset because it linked so crucially with French and European affairs. He would assume leadership on

Egypt and Iran because of their nexus with another NATO pillar, Great Britain. No European ally was significantly involved in Latin America, where he left primary responsibility to subordinates.

In Truman's second administration, a curious quartet of the president himself, General Douglas MacArthur, Acheson, and Special Representative (formerly the "Consultant") Dulles led the way to a Japanese peace treaty. All four favored a quick and nonpunitive settlement. They wanted Japan's economy on their side, with its historic links to China and Southeast Asia, one reason the United States in the Eisenhower administration would override allies' misgivings to include Japan in the General Agreement on Tariffs and Trade (GATT). As to its military potential, some Americans were already entertaining second thoughts about the pacifist constitution MacArthur had imposed on it.

Easily overlooked in the story of the Japanese peace treaty were two conflicts that accompanied every step toward its fruition, that between the state and defense departments in the United States, and that between Washington and London. Reasons to hold on to Japan were abundant, and administration leaders favored liberality over vindictiveness to realize that goal. This reflected the remarkable speed with which many Americans sloughed the passions of the Pacific War. The more lasting outrage of Japan's close neighbors only highlights the importance of U.S. leadership in restoring Japan to the international community as an ally rather than an outcast. Even Britain harbored vengeful impulses. The Pentagon's views were different. Military leaders became quite annoying to Acheson and the state department on this issue, for the Pentagon wanted to delay any settlement until after securing control of bases for use in future wars. Part of the chiefs' bullheadedness came from old resentments. The state department had gotten its way on Korea (hanging on against the military's wish to leave) and China (wanting to get out when the generals hoped at least to encourage *Chiang* to hang on). The determined admirals and generals at home and victimized neighbors of Japan abroad formed a potentially formidable coalition against a liberal concordat.

When war struck Korea, parties on all sides grew more alert to Japan's importance, including Stalin, who feared future Japanese aggression. Dulles and Kennan believed budding U.S. dominance of Japan accounted for the timing of North Korea's attack. In the war itself, bases on the island state became indispensable to U.S. operations. Through 1954, over $3 billion of U.S. war spending in Japan finally galvanized its economy, erasing American fears of permanent dependence. The war significantly accelerated the reversal of the MacArthur revolution in Japan, including U.S.-inspired crackdowns on leftist parties and unions. MacArthur quickly if ruefully started the machinery to create a 75,000-man Japanese "self-defense" force.

Contention between the state and defense departments over Japan was well under way by the middle of 1950. The communists, Acheson wrote, were far less trouble than the Pentagon. Besides fearing loss of military bases and a critical jumping off point for other East Asian military forays, the joint chiefs claimed to fear that writing a peace treaty without participation of the Soviets would incite them to attack, perhaps in the guise of sending their own "occupation" forces. Nonetheless, that September, Truman announced a decision to go ahead with a treaty. The shaky consensus permitting his declaration, however, crumbled as soon as Mao entered the Korean War. This made a quick treaty more imperative in State's eyes while adding to Defense's motives for delay. At that time, the state department also decided, though with no enthusiasm, that Japan's nervous neighbors would have to receive some kind of U.S. security guarantees.[1]

Acheson and Dulles wanted a simple treaty that ended the state of war and occupation, excluded crippling reparations payments, and possibly allowed for rearmament. Washington would separately agree to security pacts with nearby states. As it worked out, the United States also concluded a security pact with Japan that preserved U.S. military and basing rights on its territory. Officially, the UK would negotiate alongside the United States, but in reality, Washington dominated the process and was intent throughout on complete control. It would not invoke the four-power Council of Foreign Ministers or two other organizations established after the war, the Allied Council and Far Eastern Commission. Dulles would end up negotiating with Japan and other states, one government at a time. The peace conference would simply ratify a fait accompli. By the spring of 1951, Dulles's methods (justified by approved U.S. policy) put the Anglo-American connection under considerable strain. Reversing earlier leanings toward speed and mercy, Britain would bristle at how Washington overlooked its views and interests, and those of India and other Commonwealth partners.

Acheson and Dulles in Tandem

That the debonair Acheson and devout Dulles cooperated so capably is an ironist's delight, for they detested one another. While the starchy Dulles was too correct to make nasty cracks about Acheson, even ten years after the Republican's death, Acheson referred to him as a "psalm-singing Presbyterian Wall Street lawyer." Their differences, thought journalist Joseph C. Harsch, went back to the English civil wars, pitting "the cavalier and king's man" against "the pious Cromwellian roundhead." Dulles was the grandson of one secretary of state (John Watson Foster) and nephew of another (Robert Lansing), and Acheson knew he expected to supplant him. Yet they managed an efficient division of labor. Acheson kept Truman informed and shielded from Pentagon wiles. Both men worked on the generals and admirals. Dulles kept MacArthur in his corner, broke through the Fabian tactics of Japanese prime minister, Shigeru Yoshida, and held the hands of Senate Republicans. A veteran of Versailles, he preached to Australians and New Zealanders that harsh "peace" treaties were folly. Truman's vital role was to back them up, which Acheson recalled he did "with very great firmness." When the Pentagon rattled Dulles's nerves, Truman told him to "go right ahead," and "I'll tell the military just to get out of this thing." Even the president, however, could not discourage the chiefs.[2]

Because Washington hoped to divert attention from its hanging on to dozens of U.S. bases and keeping thousands of GIs on Japanese soil, the treaty would be silent on the subject. A parallel security pact would give Japan guarantees in return for this military bounty. The separate security treaties with the Philippines, Australia, and New Zealand—each, Acheson wrote, "wanted one with us but no one else"—meant Dulles could avoid loading down the peace treaty with security provisions for Japan's former victims. Acheson wanted to move even more quickly when he learned the Japanese were losing "respect for the quality and character" of U.S. forces after young draftees began replacing the postwar GIs. It was impossible to have "junior officers" ensconced in the "residences of the traditional leaders of Japan" while the leaders lived "in the garage."[3]

Other than an army general who served as Dulles's minder for the Pentagon, his chief aide was John M. Allison, a future ambassador to Tokyo. Allison kept MacArthur closely informed, helping cool his resentment at not having Dulles's job. With drafters already working on the treaty, Dulles began intense negotiations with Yoshida in Japan, ironing out most of their differences by early February 1951. On the 10th, Dulles had an audience with Emperor Hirohito. He then took his movable feast to Manila, Canberra, and Wellington before returning late in the month to Washington to report to Truman, Acheson, and the American public. When State's Henry Byroade complained about inconsistencies between peace plans for Germany and Japan, Dulles told him to live with them. He was back in Tokyo in April to reassure the Japanese about the firing of MacArthur, who left the day Dulles arrived. Because of tireless pressure from the Philippines, he also brought news that Japan must pay reparations in some form, but the working draft still said nothing on the subject. Joining Manila in demanding Japanese paybacks were Formosa, Burma, Australia, and New Zealand. Less interested in financial indemnification, India insisted on Formosa's outright cession to the PRC, including the offshore Pescadores. Nehru's railing against U.S. retention of Okinawa and Japanese military bases washed over Dulles's back.[4]

The British connection was both more important and more difficult. Neither Dulles nor Acheson was willing to lose control of the negotiations or submit to Britain's penchant for penalties, and London was vulnerable to U.S. insistence on control. Young foreign office candidates might no longer answer questions about life's three most important things by saying, "God, love, and Anglo-American relations," but their leaders wished to protect the tie with Washington. But they were also determined to defend their tenuous ties to the PRC and insisted that Japan forge its future Chinese relations with Beijing rather than Taipei. In an airing of differences beginning in March 1951, Dulles objected to inviting Beijing to the peace conference and argued against Britain's hope to include punitive treaty provisions, including a "war guilt" clause. Every time the British pushed on this subject, the Americans found it hard to believe their indifference to Japan's value as a cold war ally. Allison's solution to the argument over which "China" to invite was to invite neither. While Britain's new foreign minister, Herbert Morrison, became more accommodating on some issues, he remained firm on the relationship between Japan and China. Dulles in turn complained about British "delaying tactics." When Ambassador Oliver Franks defended his government with references to its queasiness about MacArthur, Acheson told him bluntly that only the Americans and Japanese would hence-forth be wielding power in the Far East, and he would refuse to let British complaints stand in the way of U.S. objectives. Dulles similarly, and ominously, warned that all the "very large rocks" London had put "on the road to progress" tempted Washington to "make a unilateral agreement with Japan." On cue, Yoshida on 20 April 1951 reproached British proposals as the equivalent of "an imposed peace."[5]

Prolonged sessions in London in the first half of June managed to close differences enough to produce a joint treaty draft. While Dulles spurned British desires to strip Japan of its gold stocks, he agreed to reparations in the form of services negotiated with individual states. Japan would renounce all special rights in China, but neither "China" would receive an invitation to the conference. Over strong objections, the British accepted Dulles's insistence that a sovereign Japan could decide what ties to form with Beijing and Taipei. Deeply concerned about Britain's future in Asia, Morrison wretchedly admitted defeat to col-leagues. He mistakenly believed, however, he had extracted a pledge from Dulles not to force a Tokyo-Taipei connection or rule out one between Tokyo and Beijing. Allison carried the joint draft treaty for inspection in Paris and then to various Asian and Pacific capitals. Dulles's failure to consult Nehru personally confirmed the Indian's deepest suspicions of the Americans.[6]

"An Operator's License and an Operator but Not an Automobile"

Keeping Great Britain on the reservation was hard enough, but nearly a year of difficult talks between Washington's diplomats and generals preceded the conclusion of Dulles's negotiations in London. MacArthur in Tokyo was not a problem, and the state department expected him to be its queen against the Pentagon's ever-ready ranks of rooks and knights, but the chiefs were uncowed and rejected State's early formulations. Once more refusing to accept responsi-bility for their views, they seemed to plan on lodging objections until Truman forced them to stop. But in July 1950, after the onset of war, Omar Bradley as chief of the chiefs decided he could trust Dulles to protect the military's interests. Ultimately, he told Acheson, the military would be supportive, a statement allow-ing the September 1950 presidential announcement of negotiations.[7]

But the four-stars almost never stuck to their word when it came to Japan. Marshall's replacement of Johnson improved prospects, but Washington's national security bureaucracy was still divided. Truman accompanied his public announcement that negotiations lay ahead with instructions to the state department that gave it what Acheson called "an operator's license and an operator but not an automobile." They would have to make that by themselves. Dulles was the operator and would become the prime manufacturer. The collision between U.S. and Chinese armies in Korea, however, almost totaled his vehicle. Disheartened state department officials wondered about living with no peace treaty. China's intervention made Acheson more urgent and he went on the attack, insisting to Marshall on 13 December 1950 that it was now senseless to postpone the treaty, especially because the Pentagon would surely realize most of its goals through Dulles's negotiations. The bureaucracy roiled with indecision. Marshall gave in to Acheson, the brass pulled him back, and then the pro-treaty forces outflanked the chiefs. With Acheson and Marshall at last in accord, Truman on 10 January 1951 gave final approval to negotiations. He officially named Dulles Special Representative of the President, with ambassadorial rank, to attach Japan to the "free nations of the world" and enlist its services against "the further expansion of communist imperialism." Deferring to the chiefs' concerns, however, the next month he also ordered two infantry divisions to Japan, not for transit to Korea but for the defense of Japan.[8]

Through February and March 1951, Dulles traveled to Japan and the Pacific and consulted with congressional committees, Truman, and the state department. Just as he returned to Japan in April after the sacking of MacArthur, for whom he had foreseen a major role in gaining congressional and public approval, he discovered that the chiefs were again backsliding. They would no sooner salute a presidential decision than the smoldering embers of their contumacy would reignite. Now they demanded no treaty until they could finish the war, though Bradley made the pharisaical comment that the chiefs played a "purely advisory role" and that "their military advice did not have to be accepted." In June, the military came up with another variation, now opposing *execution* of any treaty until after U.S. ratification. Acheson surmised that Marshall would not man the barricades to defend this "Pentagon's Last Stand." Telling Truman that Dulles's hard-won London treaty draft already included a provision delaying execution until nine months after Japanese ratification, he asked him to overrule the chiefs' demand for a "perpetual" veto. On 29 June 1951, at a climactic White House gathering in Marshall's absence, Truman asked Robert Lovett what his boss thought. He answered that the state department's "advice should be pretty nearly controlling," that Dulles had largely met military needs, and that trying now to renegotiate "might do harm." Nodding, the president took the side of the state department. Yet more military nagging lay ahead.[9]

Perhaps the communists caused less trouble than the Pentagon because they didn't try hard enough. With its "volunteers" fighting Americans through most of the treaty process, Beijing confined itself to propaganda flare-ups. Dulles was meticulous about keeping the Soviet Union informed. Telling Jacob Malik at the UN in late October 1950 he hoped Moscow would sign his treaty, he tendered as a reward the quick return of South Sakhalin and the Kuriles. He denied that U.S. policy posed any "offensive threat" to Moscow but made clear he would proceed whatever its reaction. He personally believed Moscow's acceptance of the treaty was "most unlikely." Because Stalin did not cooperate, he forfeited the chance for a quick retrieval of lost Soviet territories, but he was probably more concerned about U.S. retention of a large military presence in Northeast Asia. In the final treaty, Japan would simply renounce sovereignty over the lost Russian territories. In May 1951, the Soviet government issued a series of complaints, demanded that all foreign troops get out of Japan, and called for the abortion of Dulles's whole project in favor of a new four-power Council of Foreign Ministers consisting of the USSR, PRC, UK, and USA. When the state department briskly if legalistically said no, Acheson received a little note from the White House: "Dean: This document is a jewel. HST."[10]

Washington worried far more about the contention with Britain, which clung to quixotic hopes of friendly ties with the PRC and flaunted its contempt for Chiang's regime. It also still hoped to redirect Japanese commercial energy toward China rather than Commonwealth sterling markets. Dulles would not satisfy any of its concerns. On 12 January 1951, he told Franks the United States ruled out any PRC role on the Japanese settlement as long as its soldiers "were killing Americans in Korea." If Acheson had his Adenauer in integrating Bonn into the Western alliance, Dulles would have his Yoshida. With Yoshida dutifully standing in his corner, Dulles gradually wore London down. On 19 May, in a prearranged response to a state department note, Yoshida announced his anticipation of peaceful ties with Formosa's KMT government. On 19 June, Attlee's government capitulated, agreeing to have both "Chinas" excluded from the conference (which outraged Chiang) and let Japan decide on ties with the China of its choice. The Americans decided to leave nothing to chance, inducing a letter from Yoshida to Dulles in August stating that his government "most definitely" had "no intention to conclude a bilateral treaty with the Communist regime." When Whitehall on 9 August asked if Japan would be *barred* from a Beijing relationship, Dulles flipped the switch of his fog machine, saying it was impossible "to give any categorical answer." But there would be more arguments over this issue.[11]

"This Arch of Defense"

In early July 1951, the administration scheduled the "Conference for Conclusion and Signature of a Treaty of Peace with Japan" at the San Francisco Opera House, site of the UN's founding. The Pentagon sniped all the way to the Golden Gate, demanding a host of familiar guarantees, and Acheson, gritting his teeth, furnished them. Also all the way to San Francisco, the Philippines confirmed Josh Billings's adage that "the wheel that squeaks the loudest is the one that gets the grease." Manila pummeled Washington with claims, especially for war reparations. At one point, it tugged and pulled at the treaty text for weeks. The reward for its labors was its bilateral security pact with the United States, signed on 30 August by Acheson and Philippines foreign minister, Carlos Romulo. Manila's persistence left a major imprint, for it forced inclusion of reparations in the treaty. Similar pressure generated the ANZUS pact with Australia and New Zealand (described in Chapter 29). Only in July did Acheson snuff out Chiang's hopes for a similar agreement, but Dulles would make it right for "Gimo" in 1954.[12]

As the conference neared, invitees pored over the circulating treaty draft, including the article requiring Japan to negotiate "services" reparations with individual states. "Never," Acheson later quipped, "was so good a peace treaty so little loved by so many of its participants." Of the fifty nations invited, Burma and Yugoslavia declined to attend. So did India, and not content with that, Nehru attacked the treaty itself, abhorring its snub of Soviet and PRC interests and the continued U.S. military presence in Japan. Japan would be a formal participant only after the signing, when Yoshida would receive an invitation to speak. When Moscow surprised Dulles by responding positively to his R.S.V.P., he felt some alarm at facing this "wrecking crew." Yet another major power who spurned an invitation was MacArthur, now in exalted exile in Suite 37-A of New York's Waldorf Hotel. Offered the chance to make a state department-vetted speech, he thundered through aides that the text was "totally unacceptable." He refused to attend unless invited by "the Allied Powers as a whole," which he never was, to Dulles's obvious relief.[13]

On 27 August 1951, shortly before participants convened in San Francisco, Acheson spoke about the treaty's import at the War College in Washington. By bringing a self-respecting Japan into the "community of nations," the United States would go far toward creating an "interdependent" defense system as in Europe, one in which "no one nation can pull loose from the others and return to freedom to make war aggressively." The combination of peace treaty and security pacts would "bring into full reality in the Western Pacific this arch of defense into which each nation will be so tied into the efforts of every other nation that fear between them will not exist and no one nation can conduct an independent military course." The danger, he warned his audience (and Truman a few days later), was that reviving Japan would raise tensions, when the Soviet Union realized it was losing more ground. He anticipated Soviet " 'shock' tactics" in San Francisco aimed at stirring popular Japanese resistance, at delaying the signing, or at bullying delegations from signing. Whatever might happen, including a new Korean offensive to broadcast communist power and Japanese vulnerability, he advised Truman to stick to his course. The U.S. delegation, he assured him, would be ready to use its "overwhelming" backing from "the free nations" to conclude the treaty.[14]

And they did. The peace treaty of 8 September and the U.S.-Japanese security pact must be viewed together. The treaty divested Japan of its territorial gains and relinquished Japanese claims to Formosa without identifying its rightful rulers. Japan surrendered the offshore Pescadores standing between Formosa and the mainland, parts of the Kurile Islands and the southern part of Sakhalin, and all its post–World War I mandates in the Pacific. The treaty recognized Korea's independence and granted continued U.S. rights to Okinawa in the Ryukyus, south of Japan, and to the Bonin Islands farther east. Though no war-guilt clause weighted the treaty, Japan promised to act against its war criminals. As a foundation of the security pact, a treaty provision allowed Japan to make collective security arrangements with partners of its choice and host foreign troops on its soil. The peace treaty also provided reparations, but only to those who claimed them through negotiations. (Burma boycotted San Francisco but in 1954 was the first to sign such an agreement, followed by the Philippines, Indonesia, and South Vietnam.) Japan was also required to offer most-favored-nation trading terms to those who reciprocated. The treaty said nothing about the domestic character of the Japanese regime. Extraordinarily, it was silent on China, where its armies had done their worst, except to renounce its former "special rights and interests."

The separate security pact allowed U.S. forces to remain for the duration of the Korean War, granted them long-term basing rights, and barred Japan from manufacturing armaments that might menace the peace. Acheson's failure to press for Japanese rearmament reflected the sensible view that this former nation of warriors should remain militarily weak.[15]

Just four months after House Republicans had tried garnishing Acheson's salary, San Francisco was an undiluted coup for him. Using the security pact as an excuse, he loaded his delegation with members of Congress likely to help later, including such a steady opponent as Iowa's Burt Hickenlooper, "who went along and was very interested in what there was to do, brought his wife, had a good time, got to know everybody, and understood the treaty so that when it came before the Senate he went along very well." Republican H. Alexander Smith, in contrast, was already crowding Yoshida to establish relations with Formosa. Once Acheson had arrived in San Francisco, he and Dulles advised the Japanese leader to adopt "an attitude of friendly calm and confidence" toward other Asian delegations, not to utter a word that would reopen treaty terms to debate, to be "responsive" on reparations, and be quiet about the security pact. If asked about ties with China, he should "say something to the effect" that such a weighty problem required serious "study and that no decision has as yet been reached."[16]

As Acheson made his rounds, posing for pictures with other foreign ministers, he informed them of the rules he would enforce as presiding officer. "Having now done all," he was "content, like Oliver Cromwell, to leave the issue in the hands of the Lord of Battles." Then ptomaine poisoning felled him. "If I have ever felt worse, the memory of it mercifully escapes me." Luke Battle quickly told Truman, busy entertaining at a reception. He immediately "abandoned his piano, marched across the room, and vociferously ordered his Secretary of State off to bed, as if he were a small boy up past his bedtime."

Mended overnight, Acheson opened the proceedings on 5 September by gaveling down Andrei Gromyko's motion to invite Beijing to the conference. Out of order, he proclaimed, as Americans watched the nation's first coast-to-coast television production. Acheson having permitted a pair of short speeches to debate his ruling, Poland's Stefan Wierblowski took up the cudgels for Gromyko. When he hit the five-minute deadline, Acheson dropped his gavel again, recognizing the UK's Kenneth Younger to replace him at the yellow podium. Wierblowski, perhaps deafened by simultaneous-translation earphones, kept talking. Because "the situation was rapidly moving from the amusing to the critical, as the Pole quite openly defied me," Acheson began approaching Wierblowski, intending to escort him personally to his seat. On the east coast, a Long Island mechanic flagged down Lovett driving through Locust Valley, inviting him to join the crowd at his TV set, where "your friend Acheson is going to take a swing at a Pole!" As Lovett watched, "Wierblowski backed away from the rostrum, his voice fading from the air. Younger darted into the vacant place" while Acheson "stood guard to prevent a counterattack." The Locust Valley citizens cheered, "and for the first time in village history a Secretary of State became a local hero." Gromyko and company then contested the conference rules and election of permanent officers, including Acheson. In response, backed by the "kind of majority parliamentarians dream about" (from 36–3 to 47–3), he raised and lowered his new hammer. Egged on by Latin Americans, whose eagerness to serve U.S. ends embarrassed even state department regulars, Acheson routed the opposition. It was a great show, not unlike wrestling, as forty-five delighted millions watched from California to Maine.[17]

From the first, Acheson's men had designed the conference as a "political convention, run by bosses," with votes for the treaty, up or down, and no reservations or amendments allowed. The United States as the "principal occupying Power" would get what it wanted. As Dean Rusk recalled, once the procedural rules were adopted, "discussions of substance were out of order because questions of substance had been decided in the rules of procedure." "We really screwed the Russians," he confessed. At the time, a British observer sniffed at Acheson's "irregular" squelching of Gromyko, but Rusk gloated in a cable to Foggy Bottom at the "grand slam" votes they were getting to overwhelm any opposition. He predicted that forty to forty-eight delegations would sign the treaty, and forty-eight it turned out to be. After the debates and voting ended, and after Acheson had seen to the rewriting of most of Yoshida's speech, the Japanese prime minister delivered it to a reduced audience, for the Russians and their friends had walked out. "I don't blame them," a tardily contrite Rusk said years later. "Those rules of procedure were outrageous, and I blush to think of my own role in those parliamentary maneuvers." But in 1951 he was part of a happy evening crowd in Acheson's suite "for mutual congratulations and gossip." On 8 September, when delegates queued to sign the treaty, Acheson led the way for the United States, followed by Dulles and Senators John Sparkman (Democrat) and Alexander

Wiley (Republican). At another table, Acheson, Dulles, Wiley, and Republican Styles Bridges put their pens to the security pact.[18]

Even some of the British, who disliked Acheson's parliamentary thrusts, considered the conference "a great personal triumph" for him. To put Gromyko and the eastern European communists in their places, remarked Acheson's young friend, Noël Annan, "did him much good." Even Republicans were elated, including H. Alexander Smith, who spoke of Acheson's "commendable and brilliant" handling of the conference. His old California adversary William Knowland declared it "outstanding."

Acheson was to close the conference with an address and at Alice's suggestion (and Rusk's) spurned a staff draft to speak his mind. Holding a few notes at the podium and referring affectingly to "reconciliation," he gently counseled "our Japanese friends" and Yoshida that "a great broad highway to a position of equality, of honor, of friendship in the world" lay open to them. When he finished "to a hushed audience," Wiley rose shouting, "Everybody up!" While the ovation "was going on," Acheson wrote, "a television man on the floor near my wife called to a cameraman in the gallery, 'Get Acheson!' My wife, amused, said to the wife of one of our Republican delegates beside her, 'Even at a time like this they still want to "get" him.' To which she got the comforting reply, 'I don't think they meant it that way, my dear.'"[19]

The Yoshida Letter

Acheson knew his new popularity would be evanescent, and he may not have been surprised, either, by the contention that still bedeviled the Japanese story for some months. Most revolved around Dulles's effort to have Yoshida open ties with Formosa rather than the PRC. Bickering on the subject, which started in 1950, reappeared as Dulles and Morrison flew together to Washington from San Francisco. Though Morrison would not exactly say so, London wanted Tokyo to recognize the Beijing government. Dulles, while claiming an association with the KMT would be Japan's "natural desire," denied he had made any secret deals on the matter. Morrison warned that preemptive acts would cause opponents at home to accuse Attlee's government of being "deceived by the United States."

From there, it was downhill. Dulles told James Webb the next day he expected Yoshida to say publicly that his government would not "deal with the Chinese Communists." On 12 September 1951, Truman received a letter from Knowland, signed by fifty-six senators, including liberal Democrats, warning that "recognition of Communist China by Japan or the negotiating of a bilateral treaty with the Communist Chinese regime" would damage both Japanese and U.S. interests. Six days later, Zhou Enlai denounced the San Francisco treaty as "illegal and invalid."[20]

Other issues also remained, including the pacing of ratification. Politics made it an easy call to have Dulles carry the ball in the Senate, and in late October he agreed to take on the task if Truman would promptly submit the treaty when the Senate reconvened in January. Dulles also warned that in an election year, Truman and Acheson might hear baseless charges of his infidelity. Everyone foresaw further trouble from the military. In unaccustomed humor, Dulles told Truman that "getting the colonels out of their Japanese villas" would be the greatest U.S. victory in Japan since Pearl Harbor.[21]

When Livingston Merchant flew to London to find common ground on the Formosa-PRC issue, the new foreign minister, Anthony Eden, not only rejected his formulas but said the British representative in Tokyo was urging Yoshida against recognition of Formosa. This was a lost cause, however, for the Americans were in a mood to poke fingers in London's eyes and were quite prepared to exercise U.S. preponderance over both ally and former foe. Dulles descended anew on Tokyo, escorted by a gaggle of senators. For days he crossed swords with Eden's Sir Esler Dening as he pressed Yoshida to do something that would satisfy the legislators. Eden protested through Franks and ordered Dening to stop talking to the incorrigible Dulles, an instruction he ignored. Franks also hit a brick wall, and in Tokyo, Yoshida did Washington's bidding. After establishing the equivalent of an embassy in Taipei, on 24 December he signed the "Yoshida Letter." Drafted by Dulles, it recited Japan's intent to sign a peace treaty with Formosa.

Returned to Washington, on 7 January 1952 Dulles received the still secret missive by diplomatic pouch just before the arrival of the Churchill summit party. Though the letter perfectly suited Senate wishes, Yoshida's biographer says he had never intended to recognize the communist regime. Anticipating the still unreleased letter, on 8 January he announced that "so long as China is a communist country and disturbs the peace and order of foreign countries," Japan could not "hold intercourse with her" but it could with states such as Formosa that left its "internal peace" undisturbed. He had already closed the door on early Sino-Japanese commercial relations by joining U.S. economic sanctions against the PRC and endorsing the Battle Act.[22]

Acheson's part in this heavy-handed stratagem again shows he was no anglophile. More trouble lay over the horizon because of disputes over who saw Yoshida's letter and when. Acheson later claimed that the mistake of not gaining British approval of the letter during Churchill's visit came "not from sharp practice" but, he said with studied vagueness, "clumsy action based on what seemed to be a true reading of one another's minds." He certainly did not regret the policy behind the letter, which he defended with unaccustomed heat to Eden and Churchill. Any Japanese move to redirect its "military virtues and industrial capacity" toward the communists, he told them, would cause a "great shift in the world power situation." In a reversal of his own past views, he also chided British apathy on trade with Beijing, arguing that a newly sovereign state lacking a clear ideological identity might fall into China's orbit simply from a desire for profits. Nor would he any longer brook any chance of Formosa slipping into communist hands, which would cause "terror" in both Japan and the Philippines. "The heart of the matter in the Far East," he asserted, "was to build up sufficient strength so as to hold Japan on the side of the West."[23]

Unlike Eden, Sir Winston was not fixated on the Yoshida letter and came far closer to Washington's view of the PRC. But the episode caused hurt feelings and bruises that lasted years. Eden asked prospective presidential candidate Eisenhower not to make the "tricky" Dulles his secretary of state, and when his own career crashed over the Suez affair in 1956, many Britons blamed Dulles's faithlessness, though Dulles always denied he had violated any promises to Morrison. During the January 1952 summit, probably at Churchill's prompting, Eden seemed finally to drop the matter but made clear to Acheson that London would not admit to any change in its own policy.[24]

As the British departed on 15 January, the state department publicly released Yoshida's letter and Truman sent the treaty to the Senate, leaving the impression that the British had just approved the letter. Acheson admitted this was an unqualified and "inexcusable bungle" that embarrassed the entire Churchill cabinet. Eden landed in London both to news about the letter and Acheson's letter of apology. Sowing further confusion, Franks had never told Eden how much he knew of the letter, which caused him chagrin when it was released as Eden flew over the Atlantic. With his mortified plea that Dulles say nothing that changed the "technical" fact that Eden and Acheson had ever discussed the Yoshida letter, the story neared its end. A new twist came in late January, when the Alsop brothers published a column, "Row over Formosa," that reportedly shattered the "equanimity" of former foreign secretary Morrison, leading to nasty interparty arguments in Britain. Then, to the abashed Acheson's gratification, the dispute ended.[25]

Adopting a Friendly Policy

On 5 February 1952, the Senate Foreign Relations Committee unanimously sent the peace treaty to the Senate floor. Five days later, Tokyo and Taipei began negotiating their new ties. Washington and Tokyo still had not finished the "Administrative Agreement" on U.S. forces in Japan, which Yoshida had wanted treated outside the peace treaty. Rusk as "Ambassador" went to Japan to negotiate, though he was now president of the Rockefeller Foundation. The Pentagon swiftly entangled him with new demands to maximize U.S. rights and to complete negotiations before Senate ratification. Outraged officials at State considered this an attempt to reinstate occupation "under another name." Only Acheson's personal intercession stopped Lovett from going to Truman with the chiefs' new claims, which centered on what U.S. forces could do and how much they would consult with the Japanese government in case another war broke out in the region. Rusk was confident that Foggy Bottom and the White House combined would face down the Pentagon pests. In a month of nonstop talks, he hammered out an accord satisfying both countries. It took effect at the end of April, after ratification of the treaty.[26]

Dulles had defended the treaty in hearings while Acheson lay low. Management of the treaty in the full Senate went to Knowland, whose ideological credentials handcuffed the conservatives. Approval came on 20 March in a 66–10 vote; the security treaty gained a 58–9 tally. Nine Republicans and one Democrat voted against the treaty after a reservation declaring that "China" in the text must mean "Formosa" lost 29–48. Not unreasonably, Dulles thought the Yoshida letter had carried the day. Urged to move quickly by Acheson, Truman on 15 April signed the Japanese accords along with the ANZUS and Philippines security pacts. The peace treaty went into formal effect on 28 April 1952.[27]

That was a busy day. The occupation ended, and Japan and Chiang's Republic of China signed their own treaty. The previous October, Truman had gone through the motions of offering the Tokyo ambassadorship to Dulles. After receiving the expected demurral, he named Robert Murphy, Acheson's constant counsel on Germany. "I had never even set eyes on the Pacific Ocean," Murphy remembered, commenting that it "was not flattering" when briefers said Truman chose him precisely because he was "an ignoramus about the Orient." He would breeze through the Senate, Acheson said, because his record on Asia was blank. As Murphy headed to his new post, Dulles vacated his and began defaming the administration's foreign policy. Acheson meanwhile was mending fences with Eden. On 11 April 1952, Acheson's fifty-ninth birthday, he wrote Eden denying press reports about their alleged "clash of personalities." His own personality, "as my wife and daughters frequently point out, is a most defective one. But it would take a worse one than mine to clash with you from whom I have always received kindness and friendship. The opinion attributed to me, I do not hold; the facts stated are false; and the attempted psychoanalysis was done by a plumber."[28]

In its remaining months, the Truman administration halfheartedly pressed rearmament on Yoshida, which he effectively resisted, blaming public opinion. The U.S. military gradually relaxed, though Bradley still muttered about not having total control of Japan's outlying islands. In September 1952, Japan joined the secret western grouping, CHINCOM, for limiting strategic exports to China. Yoshida joined in part so he could blame loss of the China market on the cold war. Acheson's satisfaction over Japan was palpable. In a session with Walter Cronkite and other TV journalists in early April, he remarked on Japan's ability to help stabilize revolutionary situations in Asia. A month later, he told others about placing Japan so "it could play a major role in Pacific affairs" while hoping the United States had not created a new "menace" in doing so. The stakes were high. If Washington fashioned a lasting friendship with Tokyo, Japan would become "a strong stabilizing influence" in the region. But this would take "time and patience," with the latter always in short supply among Americans.[29]

*   *   *   *

Beginning in his pre-Marshall Plan 1947 speech in Mississippi, where he advocated absorbing its "workshop" within the western coalition, Acheson regarded Japan as the most vital U.S. concern in Asia. This seemed a far more intelligent use of resources than propping up Chiang or the hopeless task of contesting communist control of the Chinese mainland. Analyses of his January 1950 Press Club speech usually skip past how firmly he tucked Japan *within* the defense perimeter. Dulles did the day-to-day work of negotiating the peace treaty, but Acheson's prints were all over it. With World War II behind them, Acheson more quickly than most understood that the United States, Germany, and Japan had far more mutual than conflicting interests and acted on that perception. As with Germany, he pressed steadily for a quick, generous, and uncluttered Japanese peace treaty, certain that Washington could not effectively oppose its current Soviet adversary by repressing its former enemies. Holding Japan to the side of the west through liberality and persuasion was only one instrument available to the United States, however, for like his Pentagon colleagues he sought U.S. military supremacy off the Chinese coast. He also thought it imperative to impress Japan with U.S. strength and seriousness by acting forcefully in Korea.

Despite their dislike of one another, Acheson and Dulles, the fifty-first and fifty-second secretaries of state, could take satisfaction in their work to transform Japan from a point of vulnerability to an unquestioned position of strength. They did not foresee the economic powerhouse (and nuisance) it would become. Because of the work of the Truman administration, and especially that of MacArthur, Acheson, and Dulles, by 1952, just seven years after Iwo Jima and Hiroshima, it would have taken extraordinary negligence to lose this valuable ally.

28

FAILURE IN INDOCHINA AND CHINA

Slouching Toward the Big Muddy[1]

Well before the start of the Korean War, the American commitment in Southeast Asia grew apace. As already described in Chapter 16, a string of diplomatic junkets marked signs of things to come. Following Philip Jessup's 1949–50 sweep through Asia came Allen Griffin touring on the issue of economic aid, David Bell on Philippine reform, and John Melby on military aid. Melby returned warning against deeper involvement. But belief that Japanese economic recovery depended on stability in Southeast Asia further prodded Washington toward intervention in Indochina. Acheson like most of his colleagues was convinced the United States could improve on France's performance. Second thoughts came when Ho Chi Minh's forces smacked French armies about in the fall of 1950, but instead of giving up, the Americans looked for new solutions. At first, Washington just wrote larger checks to Paris. Acheson claimed to believe the "Associated States" established by France, with Vietnam headed by Emperor Bao Dai, were virtually sovereign, but the Asian states he sought to enlist to the same view were unpersuaded.

His own claims for the Indochinese states were suspect. When Bao Dai sent a shopping list of aid requests in the fall of 1950, Acheson brusquely told him to channel them to Paris in the future. French efforts to raise "national" armies in 1951 stirred hopes, but the Vietnamese people rallied tepidly, with only 38,000 of a promised 115,000 in uniform by the end of the year. The flow of dollars continued, now reaching the half billion mark (some $3.7 billion in 2005 values).

Partly because of scare talk out of Paris, Acheson feared a Korean truce might free Mao Zedong to apply the coup de grâce in Vietnam with his armies.

Many of his worries about Indochina were linked to his concern about the European Defense Community. He gradually came to realize France might quickly and fully support the EDC if it *abandoned* Indochina, since its army's return to the continent would lessen fears of being outmatched by the Germans. But this was hardly how he wanted to strengthen the EDC, for as the governing NSC paper stated, holding on in Indochina was "essential to the security of the free world." Trying to fix France, European defense, and Indochina simultaneously, he fell into a series of incoherent improvisations. Repeatedly, he pushed the French on Monday and gave way to them on Tuesday. He demanded France give the Associated States more independence but cosseted it with inducements to stay in the region. France begrudgingly allowed U.S. envoys to talk to pro-independence nationalists in French North Africa but not in Southeast Asia, where the Americans in any case did not distinguish between nationalists and communists. Acheson told one of his ambassadors in June 1952 that Paris "would like to get out" but "could not find a way," which was "very fortunate for us." He told the French themselves they could not count on U.S. ground forces for help—Washington would not fight "another Korea"—but by May of 1952 he was pledging "naval and air support."[2]

Retrospectively, the galloping commitment to France in Indochina seems futile on its face. But at the time, high American officials seem never to have paused to rethink what they were doing. It was nearly another two decades, when Acheson advised another president, before he thought it time to cut American losses in Indochina. Earlier, as secretary of state he invoked virtually every rationale for staying on that U.S. governments ever articulated. To defend Indochina was to defend vital "security interests." Foreshadowing Eisenhower's dominoes, in August 1952 he told ANZUS officials that Thailand "would not last" if "Indochina fell." In an eerie augur of future rhetoric, he inserted the quotation marks himself when he said that establishing an indigenous Vietnamese army would supply the "light at the end of the tunnel."[3]

But no Vietnamese light shone that far. When France incurred more defeats, Acheson advocated another $150 million in aid. He turned the other cheek when Paris bristled at U.S. intrusions or its prime minister dressed down an American ambassador in public for inquiring about how the French were using U.S. aid. All the while, he worried about the EDC, and thus NATO, for the thought went "round and round and round and round in the French mind" that strength lost in Indochina would mean superior German might in Europe. Because France would not allow a European force to be dominated by West Germany, the very success of NATO might depend on success in the paddies of Indochina. France's skill, and obstinacy, in playing its hand in Indochina profoundly frustrated Acheson. Although American aid funded nearly half the cost of the war, "to hear the French talk," he told Anthony Eden, "one would think that his Government were only supplying them with the odd revolver or two." By his own standards, his Indochina policies failed. It was far worse for a humiliated France, which suffered 90,000 casualties in the war and spent double what Washington had given it in the Marshall Plan. When a new government headed by Pierre Mendès-France gained power in 1954, it quit Indochina and killed the European Defense Community with one stroke.4

Thigh Deep: "Having Put Our Hand to the Plow, We Would Not Look Back"

Acheson was in a large company in knowing little about Indochina. He had heard but dismissed reports of traditional animosity between Vietnamese and Chinese peoples. As far as he was concerned, Ho was a puppet in a plan to conquer Southeast Asia with Mao Zedong's backing. In reality, Mao moved first one way and then another, depending on his most recent calculation of interests. Soon after routing Chiang, he sent weapons, medicine, clothes, and food across the border to help Ho. Within two months of the beginning of war in Korea, contingents of his People's Liberation Army (PLA) were fighting with Ho's forces in the north of Vietnam. But at other times, he was circumspect, hoping Washington would not deepen its involvement in Indochina. In mid-1952, instead of sending requested troops to Ho, Mao sent PLA contingents to the border in a "gesture of support."5

The U.S. position in Indochina was a lonely one. The Indian government criticized the United States for supporting Bao Dai, but U.S. disagreement with Britain was more serious, despite similar thinking in London. The UK was actually quicker to picture dominoes toppling all the way to the British colony of Malaya. The communist threat in Indochina might make Australia and New Zealand feel more dependent on Washington for protection and less willing to man Commonwealth obligations in the Middle East. The British also feared a communist-dominated Indochina would make Japan more dependent economically on the PRC. But their insistence on ruling out the use of force to contain any Indochina-related Chinese adventurism caused friction with the United States. By the spring of 1952, London's greatest concern was of a unilateral U.S. military strike against Chinese actions in Indochina. Attitudes in Washington, a British official complained, were "inspired not by cool strategic reasoning but by vengeful petulance."6

Even though the Truman administration considered Indochina primarily a French responsibility, tensions with Paris grew as U.S. trucks offloaded their aid and Americans like Melby began flying in and out of Saigon, waving Treasury checkbooks. Indirectly financing the French national budget, Washington in effect held a mortgage on Indochina. What Paris really wanted was sympathy. It deeply resented American meddling and pampering of the locals. And as Americans' criticism of French management of Vietnam compounded, so did their certainty they could do a better job. Acheson thought success depended on more bona fide independence for the Associated States, expeditious reforms to undercut communism's appeal, and an end to French interference in U.S. efforts to reach these goals. His growing skepticism of the French effort did not bring with it larger respect for the Vietnamese, who seemed too immature to resist communist efforts to manipulate them.[7]

Warnings bubbled to the surface from lower rungs of the state department. Bureau information officer Charlton Ogburn, a veteran of "Merrill's Marauders" in Burma and a midwife of Indonesian independence, worried about the direction of U.S. policy but had no power to shape it. He presciently outlined Washington's available choices in a 1950 memo to Dean Rusk as either "to wash our hands of the country and allow the Communists to overrun it" or "continue to pour treasure (and perhaps eventually lives) into a hopeless cause" and alienate "vital segments of Asian public opinion." Before returning to Princeton, the more influential George Kennan used a memo to tell Acheson he opposed "guaranteeing the French in an undertaking which neither they nor we, nor both of us together, can win." It was better, he wrote, to let the internal dynamics of Vietnam work out a resolution, even if it was some kind of communist victory. It is hard to imagine such an aggressive actor as Acheson accepting this counsel of passivity, especially after 25 June 1950. By then, he was concentrating on the short-term question of whether Beijing planned to throw PLA divisions into the fray. Two months later, he thought Chinese intervention improbable, as did the British, but the French considered it "likely."[8]

Acheson wanted more decisive action to move the "vast majority" of Vietnamese off the fence they now sat on, "trying to spot who is going to win." The best motivator would be a "national" army. It would help, too, if Bao Dai showed some spirit and acted like a real leader. The good news, he told journalists on 2 September 1950, was that a homegrown military force would free seasoned French noncoms to be instructors in newly minted NATO divisions. Though Ambassador David Bruce in Paris warned that Washington might have to pay highly for a "national" Vietnamese army, Acheson seemed ready to pay for whatever might stop the Soviets, Chinese, and Ho's Vietnamese from grabbing Indochina. At the important New York meetings a few days later, he hinted at much greater aid if France did the right thing in Southeast Asia.[9]

Just afterward, with PLA help in planning, the Viet Minh struck serious blows along the Chinese border. Luckily for the French, Beijing restrained Ho from pushing farther, because North Korea was then in trouble after MacArthur's invasion at Inchon. In October, Washington announced large new infusions of aid for the Indochina war, including old bombers Acheson and defense secretary George Marshall had insisted on over the chiefs' objections. Despite French complaints that the aid was insufficient, Acheson thought later it had been more than they could "absorb." On 18 October 1950, he fired off a message to Saigon criticizing Bao Dai for having just spent three months frolicking on the

French Riviera. By early November, he was pondering alternatives to the playboy emperor, who was puzzled at Americans' inability to understand that his imperial style awed the Vietnamese people.[10]

The Chinese intervention in Korea made all of Asia seem urgently important. Rusk's deputy, Livingston Merchant, exuding premonitions of defeat and preparing an alibi, declared Indochina a "French responsibility" and proposed a "second line of defense" from Thailand to the Philippines. Grasping even shorter straws, Jessup also considered diverting attention to the campaign against the rebel "Huks" in the Philippines. Horrified at the prospect of American diplomats being seized, as Angus Ward had been in China, Acheson ordered a quick exit for the U.S. consul in case Viet Minh forces took Hanoi. Still hoping to sway the fence sitters, he also demanded that Bao get off his throne and do some serious government work. He wanted Paris to issue a schedule for full independence to the Associated States. Offered instead a vague announcement of a vague equivalent, Foggy Bottom nonetheless gushed that Indochina's "independence" within the French Union was near at hand.[11]

Amid the crisis in Korea, on 20 November 1950, John Ohly, deputy director of mutual security aid, warned Merchant (and Acheson) that the growing commitment in Indochina would lead inexorably to a tragic end, with the United States taking on the losing liability for French imperialism. At the least, it should review why it was there. Merchant ignored Ohly, telling him the horse was out of the barn. Writing near the 1960s climax of the U.S. intervention in Vietnam, Acheson observed that the dangers Ohly noted had taken years to materialize, but "materialize they did." In 1950, however, he had decided "that having put our hand to the plow, we would not look back." He made that decision in the face of evidence that Washington's aid programs and diplomatic admonishments were making little if any difference. The joint chiefs insisted that, if China struck in Vietnam, the United States should avoid any "general war" and send no forces to Indochina. France hoped to banish some of this American glumness on 8 December by agreeing to a Vietnamese national army. Three weeks later, it signed the "Pau Accords," giving the Associated States a large dose of economic sovereignty. On 23 January 1951, the United States, France, and Associated States concluded a mutual defense agreement, and more U.S. military aid flowed.[12]

When the Korean War began souring, Chinese and Soviet leaders had urged Ho to start another offensive, which he did on 26 December 1950 with a large-scale, Chinese-supplied attack along the Red River delta near Hanoi. Communist gains set off groans through the west. The CIA thought the Chinese themselves might strike "at any time." Help arrived early in 1951 in the person of the general with two surnames, Jean de Lattre de Tassigny, who crushed his foes in several battles. But most news from Vietnam remained discouraging. In a late January visit to Washington, Premier René Pleven hinted at negotiating with the communists in case of a Chinese intervention, causing the Americans to promise more aid. Any sense of progress or a U.S.-French accord faded a few weeks later when Pleven's government fell. A new coalition under Henri Queuille would not form until 10 March, confirming Queuille's belief that "politics is the art of postponing decisions until they are no longer relevant."[13]

To U.S. officials wanting to be convinced, Vietnam took on the look of a national state. In early February, the minister in Saigon, Donald Heath, pronounced it "90%" independent. But this was beside the point if it could not command popular loyalty. Heath himself thought not "one figure" in Bao's circle could inspire "public enthusiasm" and that Ho remained the "only Viet who enjoys any measure of national prestige." As Robert J. McMahon writes, despite the Pau Accords, Paris's retention of real power made the Associated States' independence "a sham." Meanwhile, with each shipment of U.S. materiel arriving in response to Paris's latest importuning, the French in Saigon saw a new American plot to supplant them.[14]

Few Americans were paying attention to the drab story of U.S. policies going nowhere strategically. The failure was evident in a May 1951 NSC paper on Asia that screeched with dissonance. Its authors wrote that U.S. interests in Indochina were limited to such matters as protecting minerals for the strategic stockpile, but they declared the region of major long-range significance. Looking in one direction, NSC-48/5 said the United States could not "guarantee" stopping communists from seizing Southeast Asia. Looking in the other, it reaffirmed intentions to answer any armed Chinese intervention with an asymmetric but unspecified assault on China, the very option London and Paris had repeatedly rejected. In June, with Cambodia now queuing outside the U.S. treasury, Truman shifted nearly $80 million in aid funds to Indochina from European accounts. Even as U.S. spending spiraled throughout Asia, Acheson claimed in congressional testimony that France and Britain were doing their part in Malaya and Indochina.[15]

French resentment of Americans looking over their shoulders grew almost directly proportional to the size of the mushrooming U.S. aid mission in Indochina. Heath said the crowd in the Special Technical and Economic Missions (STEM), by throwing their weight around, was undoing his efforts to calm the French, who were also infuriated by "sly" Vietnamese efforts to widen the disputes. In Washington for consultations in September, Heath joined talks in which Acheson promised Robert Schuman that Indochina was Washington's first priority in dispensing military aid. Along with Schuman came de Lattre. If only temporarily, Merchant thought de Lattre's "flamboyance, vigor and Napoleonic character and personality" reawakened American optimism. Wherever he went—including the Pentagon, which Lovett told him to consider "comme chez vous"—he stuck to France's message. Bao Dai was a statesman and was moving fast on the national army; Korea and Vietnam were "one war," and de Lattre was winning the latter. He condemned STEM's "missionary zeal," complained about slow deliveries of aid, and imperiously demanded more. Raising the specter of communism spreading from Indochina to the Suez, he told the National Press Club that Hanoi was "the Berlin of Southeast Asia." However impressed, officials deflected his one-war arguments by emphasizing their own focus on Europe, asked hard questions about the national army, denied his requests for jet aircraft, and offered alibis about the slow deliveries.[16]

In the fall of 1951, the army chief, General J. Lawton Collins, established the first permanent U.S. military mission in Vietnam. By mid-November, he was confident the French and Vietnamese could hold on "indefinitely," short of a full and direct Chinese intervention. The estimate was consistent with the chiefs' adamant opposition to using U.S. forces in Indochina, especially on the ground. At year's end, the state department was more pessimistic than the Pentagon about the future of the larger region if Vietnam fell, while the brass were more cautious about how to prevent such an event. With no help coming from either Paris or London, both State and Defense were stumped about what to do if China acted through infiltration and subversion. When they heard de Lattre was stricken with cancer, they saw no one to fill his shoes. Collins grumbled, "The French always say, 'We can't do anything, you can, so if you don't do anything that's your responsibility.' "[17]

Long before President Lyndon Johnson's administration did the same thing, Truman's absorbed months of bad news about Indochina without ever saying: "Enough! Let's do something different!" On 27 December 1951, Acheson said everyone knew the French were "trying to find a way to drop the problem in our lap." Glum sketches came from Bruce in Paris. The French would simply like to call off a war that had already killed eight hundred graduates of St. Cyr. Fifty percent of all French officers were in Indochina and almost two-thirds of France's best noncoms. As Bruce outlined them on 26 December, Washington had only ghastly options. No wonder Mendès-France looked good to the dispirited French! In January 1952, de Lattre succumbed to cancer, shattering nerves in both Paris and Saigon. Heath cabled that with the French physically and morally exhausted, the best they could achieve was a standoff. Washington had nothing to offer but more money and exhortations. When de Lattre died, the United States was paying a third of French war costs. By the end of 1952, it paid two-thirds.[18]

By January 1952, the failure of U.S. policy in Indochina was too obvious to deny. Acheson could think of nothing "effective" to do, he said during the Churchill summit. British officers took alarm at U.S. contingency plans calling for the bombing and blockading of China to retaliate for any major Vietnamese intervention. It was hard for Washington to chart out sensible options when, on the one hand, Paul Nitze could foresee the stakes of Indochina leading to all-out war with the USSR while General Collins imagined losing nothing more than "some rice" if the communists seized "Indochina, Siam, and Burma." Acheson both sneered at Bao Dai's demands for wider authority and conceded his "indispensability." He wanted to tell the Chinese they would be "pasted" if they attacked yet admitted that allies refused to permit such warnings. He was certain the struggle in Indochina was a China-led "bleeding" operation but admitted bafflement on how to stop the hemorrhage. While doubting Bao's regime had enough time to win on political and economic grounds, he denied the conflict could be resolved with guns. As the Vietnamese sat "on the fence, waiting to see who is going to win," the French might quit, leaving Americans holding the bag.[19]

In Lisbon in February 1952, he promised France another $200 million in arms aid. But just as he did so, his fears seemed confirmed when the minister for the Associated States, Jean Letourneau, hinted at negotiating with the Viet Minh at a Saigon press conference. Despite a raft of clarifications and emendations, including from Letourneau, U.S. officials believed he had planted the seeds of betrayal. Washington seemed to be pushing the French so hard, Acheson soon told House members, they were about to collapse "from the strain of it." On 8 March, Antoine Pinay formed the eighth and penultimate French government of Acheson's tenure. In all the games of musical chairs of shifting coalitions, Schuman always sat at the foreign minister's place, but his presence did nothing to dampen suspicions of France's design to talk itself out of Vietnam, even as From-the-USA aid still poured in. When Senator Brien McMahon remarked in a hearing that half of all American aid to France actually went to Indochina, Acheson corrected him—it was more than half and "a terrible problem." J. William Fulbright asked: What if France jumped ship? "Well, I just can't answer that," said Acheson. "I don't know."[20]

Unable to change events in France or Indochina, in a meeting of Acheson and Marshall's deputies on the morning of 5 March, the Americans proved they could still fight each other. Preparing for an afternoon NSC session, Charles Bohlen and Nitze took the offensive for State, reproaching the military for refusing to say what they might accomplish in Indochina. The chiefs as usual declined to discuss specifics until State unequivocally said the United States must defend Southeast Asia and detailed what allies would or would not do. They also turned a deaf ear when Nitze begged at least for estimates of what they could do in Indochina with what they had. Finally, air force chief Hoyt Vandenberg showed his hand, demanding the unachievable: a huge budget increase "at the expense of the civilian economy" and promises that France and Britain would "go whole hog with us" in bombing and blockading China. And use Chiang's army too. In other words, Bohlen and Nitze countered, they were consigning Indochina to the communists even as they still wanted to "punish" the PRC out of spite. A laconic Collins said that was about it. The meeting ended as Nitze promised to come up with a draft of the political assumptions the chiefs insisted on before the afternoon meeting, over which Truman would preside.[21]

Acheson was incredulous when he heard of the morning debacle. After getting the NSC meeting delayed, he and Lovett joined the A.M. gladiators. Each side accused the other of demanding decisions without knowing what the *other* wanted. No one, however, commented on the utter lack of guidance from Truman. He seemed uninformed, and both sides may have thought him uneducable. It seems a fair judgment that while Acheson at least had a glimmer of what he wanted, the military did not, except to avoid trouble. When Lovett urged just giving the French much more money as being far "cheaper than an all-out war against Communist China," he tacitly joined Acheson in appealing for more sensitivity to allies' concerns. The chiefs should make plans using Nitze's draft of (familiar) assumptions. Now that they had wrung this list from the state department, Admiral William Fechteler insisted on rewriting it! Acheson managed not to explode but insisted the chiefs follow his own understanding of the situation, especially of where France stood. The NSC must calculate the relative importance of U.S. interests in Indochina and NATO, because if France plunged deeper into Southeast Asia, it might be unacceptably weakened in Europe, especially as compared to West Germany. The meeting ended inconclusively. Truman appears to have remained silent throughout.[22]

Slogging

Little changed during the last nine months of the Truman administration. Intelligence officers speculated about China's intrusion into Indochina while diplomats felt Paris's pulse for symptoms of panic or resignation. In the very picture of futility, Acheson still sought allied support for possible reprisals against Beijing but still in vain. And he still both demanded more autonomy for Vietnam and deprecated Bao Dai. And despite vague agreement on essentials, the state and defense departments remained in contention.

A key reason for the bickering was Truman's failure to do anything to stop it or offer direction. Left free to squabble, the chiefs felt they were being forever asked if they could do x or y without being told what political ground they stood on. Acheson and his advisers thought them irredeemably irresponsible. Drawing a red line between "military" and "political," the chiefs disowned any obligation to consider political conditions. Their wariness was understandable, and now it is clear they were closer to reality than the state department by insisting on non-involvement in Indochina except in ideal circumstances. In Korea, they had to fight a terrible war that had not gone as expected, and the civilians had saddled them with negotiating an armistice. They had to accept the odious business of firing MacArthur. As they argued with Acheson and his assistants, they knew Eisenhower might replace Truman as commander-in-chief. All the policymakers were stuck in the same boat, plunging through strong currents without motor, oars, or rudder. Because they could not foresee what either China or France would actually do, they could not see the rapids ahead. Knowing little about the nations and peoples of Indochina, boxed in by an expanding cold war consensus, and lacking the imagination to free themselves, the administration failed to read clear evidence that the endeavor in Indochina was futile. Nobody could see how to change weakness into strength.

The tension and irritation drearily played out to Eisenhower's inauguration. Without fresh ideas, Acheson grew more irritable with Paris, where he had meetings in the spring of 1952, and where Pinay told him the French people were "weary and tired of the Indo-China war." Washington spent more money on aid in Vietnam than anywhere but Korea, but equipment stacked up in Saigon warehouses for lack of good ways to use it. Acheson told reporters France "would like to get out but could not find a way, and it was very fortunate for us that this was the case." In Washington discussions in June, he was ready to approve use of U.S. air and seapower to assist the French and strike at the Chinese periphery but only after reaching the very political understandings with allies he could never achieve. He probably took little comfort from French promises not to open negotiations "of any kind" with the enemy without "prior notice." For their part, the British began examining ideas of a large regional security pact resembling the later Eisenhower-Dulles invention, the Southeast Asia Treaty Organization (SEATO).[23]

After the Pentagon had sufficient time to absorb Nitze's statement of political and diplomatic assumptions, the Americans finally if temporarily agreed among themselves on NSC-124/2, signed by Truman on 25 June 1952. It was ritualistic in invoking Southeast Asia's importance to U.S. security. It was also sickeningly familiar in urging more aid, better propaganda, more autonomy for the indigenous states, and a more earnest effort from Paris. It posited a readiness to act unilaterally, though there was little evidence anyone really meant that. Finally, NSC-124/2 included more textured descriptions of how to hit back against the bogey of Chinese intervention. But they were too couched with contingencies to offer sure guidance to policymakers.[24]

The day Truman signed this document, Acheson was in London for more talks but also to receive an honorary Doctorate in Civil Law from Oxford University. The president insisted he fly in the *Independence* and escorted his party to the airport. Though Acheson used a light touch in describing the ceremony in a letter to Truman, the honor pleased and moved him. The talks with Eden and Schuman, however, failed to get past the old story on Indochina. He again wanted to gear up for action against China, and his partners again demurred. The only fruit harvested was a new committee—with Nitze as the U.S. representative—to outline possible actions against China and the assumptions behind them being demanded by the armed forces of all three countries. The chance that deputies would find agreement where their superiors did not seemed remote.[25]

A new internecine struggle started in the middle of July 1952 when the chiefs discovered Nitze had been trimming his sails to find agreement with allies. In a session that grew progressively more peevish, Nitze claimed London and Paris would eventually come Washington's way and castigated the chiefs' relentless recital of grievances. Bohlen pounced when they again balked at writing plans unless the White House and state department gave them signed and sealed political directives. When Nitze noted the concern among allies that the United States might use atomic bombs against China, the chiefs' chairman, General Omar Bradley, retorted that since Washington had spent "billions" on these bombs, it seemed a shame to leave them "in storage." The administration remained divided, and the news from Indochina remained bleak. In September, Acheson said in the NSC that Ho's blows to France's "prestige and power" could eliminate its value as an ally, in Asia and Europe.[26]

In late October, the Viet Minh dealt the French and its "nationals" a stunning defeat at Nghia-Lo, northwest of Hanoi. The timing was terrible, coming just after the United States had agreed that the UN should discuss French colonialism in North Africa. Paris was indignant. On 27 October, President Vincent Auriol expressed "grief" to see the inventor of "the rights of man" being "put on trial." British observers thought every political party in France was openly searching out the quickest exit from Indochina. Six days after Eisenhower's election, Ambassador James Dunn in Paris reported that the Paris government demanded Washington treat its role in Indochina as that of defending the "free world" rather than waging a "colonial war." Acheson also heard from other sources that France was looking for international backing in negotiating its way out of Indochina.[27]

Tunnels, Dominoes, and Next Moves

In a briefing shortly after the election, Acheson told Eisenhower much of France was ready to give up and that the Vietnamese people seemed unwilling to "come down on one side or another." Chilly if not churlish, Eisenhower barely seemed to listen.[28]

Lame duck or not, Acheson wanted a better accounting of how France was spending U.S. money. Near the end of his last NATO Council meeting in December 1952, in Paris, the French suddenly made new appeals for support. Already "tired, hungry, and exasperated," he blew up, complaining about the information France gave him. A few days later, Pinay's government fell. When René Mayer succeeded him on 7 January 1953, the old Gaullist Georges Bidault took over the Quai d'Orsay. This time, Schuman too had fallen. The last of the old Acheson-Bevin-Schuman team left office two weeks later.[29]

Acheson later denied his Indochinese policy had been a "muddled hodge-podge." He also claimed that not to help France would only have accomplished ousting the "colonial power"; "doing nothing" would be unfit for "the leader of a great alliance." He had decided to help France in Asia to build its confidence in Europe, but in fact that confidence had plummeted by the time he left office. As he long feared, France then abandoned Indochina, and when the United States moved to replace it, Eisenhower-Dulles used the same Truman-Acheson formula: money, military missions, and vows to do better.

Scholar William Duiker condemns the Truman-Acheson policy as "essentially without optimism and without ideas," but its real problem was misplaced optimism and too many bad ideas. Acheson never came close to converting weakness in Indochina into strength. He had to work through France to achieve

American ends. He kibitzed from the corner, hoping the fighter could get off the ropes and land a knockout punch. In the abstract, he understood that a Vietnamese regime beholden to its former masters stood no chance against popular revolutionaries, but he could hardly act on this theory, especially through a resentful ally. In reality, it is hard to say he understood what was happening, considering his governing underestimation of Asian leaders and soldiers.[30]

Although he knew his policies were not working, he never considered joining Paris in seeking a negotiated end to war in Indochina. Besides the overriding fact that he hoped to save Indochina rather than negotiate it away, other circumstances blocked such a course. Had he remained secretary in 1954, he might have joined an approach to China, but only to put draping over a western defeat and only with French cooperation. In 1951–52, gaining a negotiated settlement would have meant trampling on French wishes in a repellent display of alliance hegemony. Even if France had been agreeable, talking to the Soviet Union would have seemed beside the point, for Americans knew it was not directly involved in Indochina. And in his post-wedge configuration, Acheson would object to an open negotiation with China, for it would have legitimated Mao's regime and its role in Southeast Asia.

Popular opinion would certainly not have forced Acheson to such a negotiation, for Indochina had then barely dented public consciousness. Far more important, he was not then of a mind to concede a contested cold war battlefield. His persistence did not originate from an inflated notion of the intrinsic value of Southeast Asian territory, but a growing zero-sum consciousness that made surrendering any western position to the communists seem intolerable. Moreover, though he rarely articulated the connection, he seemed to believe the yet to be disproved idea that the prosperity, stability, and western orientation of Japan depended on continuing control of Indochina. In short, so long as a chance remained to win the fight in Indochina, Acheson (and the Truman administration) would stay the course, even if fresh out of ideas.[31]

Marking Time

The Chinese intervention in Korea finally pushed Acheson to accept Marshall's judgment that the hostile seizure of Formosa would gouge a grave "wedge" in the offshore line of Pacific defense. By then, supporters of Formosa had gained many of their objectives, including the defense of Chiang's government and UN seat. Washington had raised an array of economic sanctions against the PRC. Acheson was skeptical about these but went along to keep his people from getting "kicked around on the Hill." As evidence that he had not changed his mind about Chiang, he laughed with reporters in February 1951 at the thought of the Nationalists and Communists invading each other at the same time. If the administration "released" Formosa to hit the mainland, he quipped, Chiang's soldiers "probably wouldn't go" but would say: "Thanks, boys, we are going to see our families." He had not totally given up hope of inciting divisions or "mass defections among the peoples and military leaders of Communist China," a hope that would go smash if Washington tied itself irretrievably to Chiang. That it would be an uphill battle to avoid the connection, however, became clear in the autumn of 1951 when Truman failed to get Philip Jessup's appointment to the UN delegation through the Senate, forcing him instead to use a temporary recess appointment.[32]

Always more aggressive on China, Dean Rusk the previous spring had made it harder for Acheson to maintain any kind of balance on the China-Formosa issue. In a speech to the China Institute of New York on 18 May 1951, Rusk had launched a withering and sarcastic attack on the communist regime as a "colonial Russian government," a "Slavic Manchukuo[33] on a large scale" that failed even the "first test" of being "Chinese." This ideological blast overlapped the last gasps of Burt Marshall's Hong Kong–based peace feelers and preparations for Korean truce talks. The *Times* thought Rusk's gaseous oration aimed at inspiring an internal revolt against the CCP. Whatever its intent, it certainly offended allies, especially Britain. Foreign secretary Herbert Morrison felt obliged to file an official complaint. Called on the carpet by an angry Acheson, Rusk claimed he had said nothing inconsistent with current policy. In the future, Acheson told aides, he "wanted all the speeches on controversial subjects cleared with him personally." Reporters had learned through leaks that he had "roundly scolded" Rusk, but he tried to put a good face on the hubbub in public. When asked at a press conference if Rusk had properly chosen his words, he said he did not "want to criticize the literary composition of my colleagues." Rusk escaped with a mere wrist tapping, perhaps benefiting from sympathy for his current health problems.[34]

Rusk had tapped into the vehemence against China sweeping through Washington. The administration imposed an embargo on Chinese trade, banning U.S. merchant ships from Chinese ports or from loading cargo in home ports bound for China. In May under U.S. prodding, the United Nations called for a ban on commerce in strategic goods with China and North Korea. Having already organized CoCom, regulating allies' trade to the Soviet Union and its satellites, the administration in 1952 arranged its even more restrictive fraternal twin, CHINCOM, against China. Over Acheson's objections, Truman again pondered having Chiang attack the mainland and send troops to Korea. In early 1951, without informing Acheson, he had authorized forays into China by KMT forces stranded in Burma after the civil war. At the same time, through the CIA, the United States was trying to frustrate Beijing's effort to impose its will on Tibet. At a Paris UN session in November 1951, Acheson had contributed to the rhetorical heat by describing Beijing's behavior as "so low that it would take considerable improvement to raise it to the general level of barbarism."[35]

State and the Pentagon sparred over China and Formosa to the end of the Truman administration. The offspring of the military's frustrations in Korea were fantasies about attacking China. Throughout 1952, navy department personnel caused Acheson concern. On April Fool's Day in Tokyo, more than two years after Truman punished a previous navy secretary for advocating preventive war, his successor, Dan Kimball, told a reporter the Seventh Fleet would "cheer" from the "sidelines" if Chiang invaded the mainland. Although the state department soon regarded the incident closed, in July came news that a hundred jets from a U.S. carrier task force had swept just outside the PRC's territorial limits to give it something "to think about." Acheson forced a disgusted Lovett (who thought the action "sophomoric—just crazy") to rap the navy's knuckles. Asked in Manila the next day about the jets, a grinning navy chief William Fechteler returned the question to a reporter: "They sure look good, don't they?" If he could add "baby atom bombs" to their arsenal, he added, his fliers could hit Korea, too. Lovett immediately cabled him to "keep quiet." As incident piled on incident, Acheson jammed his phone line to Lovett demanding restraints on the blue-water desperados, but to little effect. On 24 July, in Chicago and supposedly off the record, Kimball said the navy would fly over Chinese cities next time instead of just fooling around its coastline. "If anything does happen now," Acheson told Lovett, "we will really be in trouble with our Allies."[36]

The Chinese Failure

Because nothing terrible did happen, Acheson spent most of his last weeks in office on Egypt and Iran. After Eisenhower's election, he wistfully told reporter Herbert Matthews that a second time around he might just go along with popular sentiment on China and Formosa to avoid crucifixion by Republicans. In office, Eisenhower "unleashed" Chiang, but KMT troops were in no shape to threaten the mainland. The action actually exposed Chiang's vulnerability, leading in 1954 to a U.S. security guarantee to Formosa.[37]

American policy toward both China and Indochina in this period was strongly shaped by ignorance of Asian peoples and history, profound cultural differences, and a brand of imperial arrogance. Acheson, though far less than his opponents, underestimated the new communist rulers of China. The failure to understand the tectonic shift of this Asian revolution and the deep historical resentment against the west driving China's impetus for autonomy reduced already slim chances of reaching an understanding with it. Had there been an accommodation with this China, the United States might have averted the ruinous encounter with Mao's armies in Korea and maybe the Korean War itself.

But the evidence strongly suggests such an understanding was simply not in the cards. Just as Americans could not see their way to accommodating China, the reverse was more true. Paranoid about the United States and heavily dependent on Moscow, Mao showed no interest in any deal from Washington except one in which he would sweep every chip from the table. Contrary to what Acheson originally thought, Mao did not then seek to separate himself from Stalin or crave economic sustenance from the United States. He thought rough rather than smooth relations with the United States strengthened both his party and state. American backing of Chiang confirmed Mao's disbelief in Washington's claimed benignity.

While Truman had few personal ideas about foreign policy, among them was a deep animus toward the Chinese communists stemming from primal differences in belief and a lasting outrage over the Angus Ward case and Mao's intervention in Korea. Both Truman and Acheson knew defying the growing national fury against the PRC would touch off firestorms of criticism. By 1951, if not earlier, Acheson had tacitly decided that such continued defiance would ruin his diplomacy in Europe, which he would not risk.

Thus, he ended up supporting Formosa and taking the same stance toward China he had earlier adopted toward the USSR, opposing any negotiations until he was certain they would bear positive results. To reach such certainty first required the building of strength. But except in Japan—and marginally in the Philippines—western strength in Asia remained notable for its absence. Eisenhower inherited a fixed refusal to recognize the People's Republic, a tacit commitment to protect Chiang's Formosa fortress, an adamant opposition to UN membership for the PRC, and refusal to discuss any of these. Two decades and four administrations would pass before Richard Nixon and Henry Kissinger would break the logjam in Sino-American relations. When it occurred, Acheson approved.

29

RAZOR EDGE SENSIBILITIES: ANZUS AND INDIA

Accommodating Kangaroos and Kiwi

The drive to make peace with Japan reflected the sole Asian priority Acheson took on willingly and with conviction. He was also an early proponent of a significant American role in South Korea, of course, but with no premonitions of how events there would dominate U.S. foreign policy. His preference would have been to pursue a fundamentally passive approach to China and Formosa. The fateful plunge into Indochina, as we have just seen, resulted partly from the growing Asian crisis but stemmed mainly from views of France's role in Europe, not Southeast Asia, and secondarily from his concern for the future economic development of Japan. With issues related to foreign aid dominating, the United States tried to accommodate Indonesian ruler Sukarno's nationalism while keeping him out of the communist camp, but Acheson mostly oversaw rather than conducted that diplomacy.

Because at the beginning of his tenure he saw U.S. security centered in Europe, that was where he focused in building situations of strength. Asia became a theater of crisis when the new Chinese regime challenged western interests and as European defense prospects seemed linked to the armed struggle in Indochina. In time, especially because of Korea, all of Asia came to seem a perilous field of weakness, independent of events in Europe. Although Acheson's responses were largely ineffective and ungainly, most enlarged U.S. responsibilities.

In an impromptu 1952 press conference, he tried to place Asia in the broader stream of the postwar revolutions in U.S. foreign policy. After World War II, the administration had worked to strengthen the "free world," mainly in Europe, through the Marshall Plan, NATO, and MDAP. But actual fighting surprisingly broke out in Korea, Indochina, and the Philippines. This made it clearer than ever that the fundamental prerequisite for "free world" strength anywhere was "strength at the center," that is, the United States itself. A now three-year-old rearmament program had made it possible to repulse enemies in Korea and funnel large amounts of aid to the fight against Indochinese and Philippine insurgencies. In the wake of the Korean War, the treaties and agreements with Japan, Philippines, and ANZUS nations aimed to establish "centers of strength and security in the Pacific." Building strength had become a global strategy. "We are at work," he said, "in every part of the world, on every problem—for one purpose, which is to get strength at every point where there was weakness," the only way to "lay the foundation" for settling and ending the east-west contest.[1]

The Japanese peace treaty was a major part of this work, and, as Acheson saw them, the pacts with the Philippines, Australia, and New Zealand were the grudgingly paid tolls on the turnpike to the San Francisco peace conference. In the interest of husbanding strategic resources, he had formerly spurned Asian security pacts, especially those involving only "white" nations. But Korea and the necessities of the Japan peace treaty changed his mind. Because Australia and New Zealand, too, faced a new international order—the return of Japan as a regional factor, the communist victory in Beijing, Indonesia's latent expansionism, and Britain's ebbing power—they wanted new guarantees from the United States. Both felt anxious about their exclusion from Acheson's 1950 defense perimeter speech and fell into near panic with the outbreak of war in Korea. When Washington opened the door for Turkey and Greece to join NATO, Canberra and Wellington jammed their feet across the threshold, too.

Shortly after the shooting started in Korea, Robert Menzies, beginning seventeen years as Australian prime minister, came to Washington via London. Cool to U.S. defense ties and deferential to British strategic interests, he hoped to dampen the keenness of his minister for external affairs, Percy Spender, to send help to Korea. Menzies boarded the *Queen Mary* for Washington thinking Britain would also stay out of Korea. But back in Australia, Spender learned London *would* send troops and announced on his own authority that Australia would too, actually beating Britain to the punch. The Americans made an unhappy Menzies feel better with their lavish attention. He had lunches with Truman and Acheson and received a $250 million loan from the World Bank. He addressed Congress, and the Pentagon gave him the Legion of Merit. Six weeks later, when Spender bent Acheson's ear at the UN about an alliance, he heard the same message the secretary was then giving the Turks and Greeks, that the campaign to rebuild Europe's strength would boost Australia, too, and that no formal guarantee was necessary, for the United States would surely rush to Australia's help if attacked. He was "as closed as an oyster" when Spender kept pressing for an official commitment. The British were displeased at Spender's maneuvers, but

in Washington in September 1950 he lobbied both Truman and leading members of Congress for security ties. A month later, he again importuned Acheson
and Jack Hickerson in the state department. Acheson began claiming he had an
open mind on the subject when John Foster Dulles told him such a pact might be
necessary to gain Australian approval of the Japanese treaty. Hoping to satisfy
Spender with symbols of participation, Foggy Bottom offered to set up an
Australian military mission in Washington. But he was not so easily placated.
Back in New York on 30 October, Spender again approached Acheson, now
emphasizing Australian vulnerability to a restored Japan.[2]

London was disturbed as soon as it noticed Spender's courtship, wanting
Australia to help in Malaya and keep up its traditional Commonwealth role
in Middle Eastern defense. (This was not a misplaced concern, for although
Australia's future pact with the Americans ostensibly freed it to shift military
resources to Malta and Cyprus, and it briefly did, Canberra ended its Middle
Eastern role in 1954.) If Britain could not stop the courtship, it wanted a part in
the honeymoon, but Acheson would not consider it, already disliking how much
ANZUS would look like a white man's club in the middle of Asia. Besides, though
he never said so, he thought the days had passed when Britons could tell parts of
the old empire what to do. A Canadian jibed that "all roads in the Commonwealth
lead to Washington." In any case, with Menzies now supporting, Spender told
Dulles in February 1951 that his country and New Zealand could not sign the
Japanese treaty unless they had their own security arrangement. Using an
argument the French used about West Germany, he claimed to worry that Tokyo
would do a "flip-flop" after pretending to join the west. Acheson was finally
convinced of the futility of resisting, and told Secretary of Defense George
Marshall on 5 April the pact was unavoidable. Grumbling all the way, the JCS
warned they would nevertheless block any efforts to intrude on their own strate-
gizing. London, too, finally made a grudging peace with the U.S.-Australian tie.[3]

The "made in Australia" ANZUS pact was signed in Washington on
1 September 1951. Although the treaty parties merely pledged to consult in case
they came under attack, neither State nor Defense would have freely chosen such
an arrangement. But Acheson dutifully told senators in March 1952 he hoped the
cluster of new treaties would begin "the development of an effective system of
regional security in the Pacific." ANZUS gained Senate consent that month;
Truman filed his ratification in April.[4]

Acheson was torn by the Pentagon's effort to frustrate the new partners'
hopes of joining the inner sanctum of western defense planning. Partially sympa-
thizing with the military, if not its "tantrum of negation," he wanted to keep faith
with allies making robust contributions in Korea and the Middle East. When
he proposed periodic meetings of an ANZUS council of foreign ministers or
deputies, complete with military committee, the chiefs resisted. Admiral William
Fechteler groaned, "Oh, no!" on hearing the ANZUS partners hoped to send
liaison officers to Pearl Harbor. After the Pentagon finally agreed to a version of

Acheson's proposal, ANZUS scheduled its first Council to meet in Hawaii in August 1952. While claiming no desire to "crash" the party, Anthony Eden claimed a right as a "Pacific power" to send an observer, but Acheson threw "cold water" on the idea. The Australians would resent any such "chaperonage"; besides, if Britain came, then the French and Filipinos would also want to attend. But he also rebuffed the efforts of Spender, now ambassador in Washington, to link ANZUS to NATO and European affairs. On the eve of the Hawaiian sessions, Acheson wrote Truman that "despite the tendency of Australia and New Zealand to magnify the importance of the treaty," he was trying hard to keep it from looking to Asians like "a future NATO for the Pacific" or a "white man's treaty."[5]

The three-day meeting at an Oahu marine air base was anticlimactic. Now waited on by Jeffrey Kitchen, with Luke Battle hidden from McCarthyites in another post, Acheson stepped from his plane onto the Honolulu tarmac. He smiled queasily when comely greeters ringed his neck with leis. Since they concealed "small crawling creatures that find their way down a shirt collar," he took "an opportunity for delousing and suitable refreshment" before buttering up his new partners. His operating theory was that feeling "remote, uninformed and worried by the unknown," more than anything they wanted a chance to talk and be taken seriously. After bluntly explaining to Australian Foreign Minister Richard Casey why ANZUS could not be a NATO equivalent, he gave candid and astute *tours d'horizon* on world affairs. His duty done, he cabled Truman on 7 August that he and Pacific commander Admiral Arthur Radford had "decided that instead of starving the Australians and New Zealanders we would give them indigestion." This made them "happy as clams." Off the clock, he tumbled in the Hawaiian surf while Alice sketched the local flora. To the end of his term, he was fielding British complaints about not being in ANZUS. When Casey told him of Churchill's accusation that Australia was "an apostate to the Empire," he could only offer sympathy.[6]

Making Sense of the Subcontinent

Awareness of Britain's diminishing influence impelled the United States toward a more forward role in the Asian subcontinent. The area challenged Acheson, for as he noted in a 1950 speech, it contained enough "differences in race, in ideas, in language and religion and culture" to make Europe seem "homogeneous." The policies overseen by Truman and implemented by Acheson established patterns in U.S. relations with the area that continued for many years. Dealings with India were usually troubled, featuring arguments over Kashmir, the Korean War, and famine relief. When not focused on Kashmir, relations with Pakistan usually revolved around military issues, on which most Americans found the Pakistanis more simpatico than Indians. A wide cultural and religious gap separated the United States from both nations.[7]

The most comprehensive effort at defining policy toward South Asia came in a February–March 1951 assemblage of U.S. envoys in Ceylon, chaired by Assistant Secretary for Near Eastern and South Asian Affairs George McGhee. Underlining how Korea had toughened Washington's outlook, McGhee stressed the need to identify America's real friends and enemies. Minerals important for U.S. defense technology partly accounted for South Asia's rising significance, but he emphasized geopolitics. Without India and Pakistan in the western camp, all Asia could be lost. He laid down a series of tangible objectives, from mineral acquisition and open commercial markets to gaining access to military bases in India and Pakistan in case of a general war. Like Acheson, however, McGhee was struck by the obstacles to reaching these goals, including ferociously antagonistic Indo-Pakistani relations, Indian naivete about communism, primitive economies, insufficient U.S. resources for producing economic change in the area, the anti-Americanism of the "highly emotional, stubborn" Jawaharlal Nehru, and a growing sentiment in Congress to give Nehru tit for tat.[8]

In a manner that became more evident after Acheson left office, democratic and mostly secular Indians and devout and Muslim Pakistanis vied for America's special attention. Hoping to maintain a balance of power on the subcontinent (and still cherishing lingering hopes for British leadership), the United States sought neutrality in disputes between the two. Washington tended to send economic aid to India and military assistance to Pakistan, satisfying neither. The Indians resented the war-making hardware going to Pakistan because it endangered the local military balance, while the Pakistanis, for all their anti-communist enthusiasm, felt unappreciated as a cold war ally. While Nehru openly lambasted American foreign policy, Pakistani skill at appearing deferential won over Americans' favor. Progressively viewing Pakistan as "more Western than Eastern-minded," Washington grew interested in its ability to help advance Middle Eastern goals. Gradually, writes Dennis Kux, Washington and Karachi became "friends" if not "allies." What mainly accounted for the sentiments of U.S. policymakers, remarked British Ambassador Oliver Franks in 1950, was that they "had no doubts about where Pakistan stood in the Cold War."[9]

Pakistani Prime Minister Liaquat Ali Khan came to Washington in May 1950 to balance Nehru's earlier visit and, the Americans hoped, to advance a Kashmir settlement. He probably received little pleasure from his welcome, however, for he had no presidential tête à tête, and a schedule mix-up killed an intended private session with Acheson. Though he met Pentagon leaders, he did not get the arms shipments he wanted. But Americans generally got a good impression of this whiskey-drinking monotheist who threw an opulent reception at the Pakistani embassy and danced with Bess Truman. It is unknown what he thought about a businessman at a Los Angeles lunch who asked him if "the blank space between the two parts of Pakistan as shown on the menu card was Africa."[10]

Admiring Karachi's energetic backing of U.S. resolutions against China in the UN, the administration continued paying court. A small arms aid package in

December 1950 was followed by Point Four assistance. Small loans and grants helped correct wheat shortages, and by the spring of 1951, U.S. policymakers wondered if Pakistan might supply military bases useful in case of war with the USSR. Liaquat waltzed with the U.S. government as dexterously as with the first lady, petitioning for quid pro quos in the form of guarantees against India. In May 1951, however, he refused new Pakistani units for Korea unless Washington satisfied him on Kashmir, which it was unable to do. After his assassination five months later, the United States continued a modest stream of aid to his successor, Khwaja Nazimuddin. No important changes occurred in the U.S.-Pakistani association in the last year and a half of Truman's presidency. Later efforts by Eisenhower and Dulles to involve Pakistan in Middle Eastern defense accomplished little except to further the U.S. takeover of the role traditionally filled by Great Britain in the Middle East and South Asia.[11]

"Razor Edge Sensibilities" All Around

Besides the disputed border region of Kashmir, the nearby Buddhist kingdom of Tibet became an important facet of U.S.-Indian relations in the period of Acheson's secretaryship. His personal involvement in both was minimal. When Britain left in 1947, the subcontinent was divided between India and Pakistan, with the understanding that "princely" states could attach themselves to either, though virtually everyone expected those that were predominantly Muslim to join Pakistan, which they did. Unfortunately, the princely state of Kashmir straddled the putative Indian-Pakistani border and concentrations of Hindu and Muslim peoples. Fighting over it began almost instantly, but the United Nations arranged a cease-fire in January 1949, drawing a kind of boundary (the "line of control") that left India holding about two-thirds of the territory. A final settlement was supposed to follow a UN-sponsored plebiscite, but the vote never occurred, more from Indian resistance than Pakistani. Neither state ever removed its troops from the disputed area.

Washington made several efforts from 1948 through the end of Truman's administrations to settle the issue within a UN framework, hoping all the while for British leadership. In turn, the UK hoped the powerful Americans would find a rabbit in *their* hat. Over the years, both India and Pakistan gauged much of their view of U.S. policy in terms of the Kashmir dispute. New Delhi remained in an almost steady state of irritation because of its conviction of a U.S. bias toward Pakistan. In fact, Americans at first leaned toward India, but shrewd Pakistani gestures and tactless Indian behavior quickly alienated them. On several occasions, the UN made calls for settlements, appointed mediators, or urged combinations of demilitarization and mediation. Pakistan almost routinely accepted the proposals, leaving it to India, uniformly, to reject them. Among Americans who were heavily involved, the most prominent was Frank Graham, onetime North Carolina senator and university president and a veteran of the UN Good Offices

Committee on Indonesia. For years, he served as UN mediator but was never able to end the conflict. After Liaquat's assassination, Acheson told Truman his successor might face a major war over Kashmir.[12]

After mostly avoiding this issue, Moscow in January 1952 abruptly cast its line into the troubled waters on India's side, reviling U.S. and British proposals and calling Graham the Pentagon's "secret agent." Realizing he had nothing to gain from such crudities, Nehru dissociated India from the charges. Shortly afterward, Graham managed to get India and Pakistan around the same table in New York. Optimism surged in June when Pakistan made a major concession on the number of troops it would withdraw from Kashmir, but Nehru refused to reciprocate. In August and September, talks shifted to Geneva, with Graham still trying to broker a breakthrough. That not working, the UN Security Council at the end of the year passed yet another resolution that Nehru repudiated. More ministerial-level talks early in 1953 came to nothing, as did all others for a half century.[13]

Dislike of China's consolidation of control of Tibet, on India's northeast border, united the United States and India during Truman's second administration, but Acheson had little to do with this, and nothing either country did had much effect. Before the 1949 Nationalist defeat, Acheson briefly considered military help for the Tibetans, but with Mao's victory over the Nationalists, Washington could only be sympathetic, thinking it could achieve nothing better unless a cooperating UK and India led the way. As the first PRC troops entered Tibet in March 1950, Washington remained officially silent, partly because Chiang's Nationalists also considered Tibet part of China, as had the United States for that matter. Three months later, with Tibet buying Indian weapons secretly paid for by Washington and with Tibetan agents talking to U.S. officers in India about more help, Acheson told Ambassador Loy Henderson he hoped to encourage resistance through cooperation with the UK. But when London backed off, Americans told the Tibetans they could help, if at all, only with India's full cooperation. Nehru, however, was interested in befriending the new Chinese rulers. Washington appeared mostly to be going through the motions, because the state department must have understood that India could not meet the condition of full cooperation.[14]

On 5 October 1950, eighty thousand Chinese troops poured into Tibet, just days before their brothers plunged into Korea. Now Nehru wanted even more restraint, and Washington did nothing more than back Tibetans' request for a UN discussion. Even this commitment was weak, for the U.S. delegation soon joined the British in postponing debate, effectively killing any chances for UN succor. Following inconclusive discussions about U.S. help in staging his rescue, the Dalai Lama fled from Lhasa toward the Indian border. With American intermediaries talking only fitfully and vaguely about helping, Tibetan leaders instead began thinking about how to settle with Beijing.[15]

In the spring of 1951, Washington joined its ongoing rhetorical assaults on China's intervention in Korea to a vigorous condemnation of its actions in Tibet.

Though Truman authorized CIA training of Tibetans, they agreed under duress to China's "peaceful liberation" of their homeland in May. In discussions, low-level U.S. officials were clear that Washington would not risk major exposure on the issue, but they still urged the Tibetans to resist. Acheson was cautious, urging the same on Henderson after noticing the nauseated tone of his report on India's "philosophic acquiescence" to the PRC takeover. Unwilling to offer asylum for the fifteen-year-old god-king, Acheson could do nothing when the youth returned to Lhasa in July. Tibet's "constitutional" bodies officially consented to China's terms on 28 September 1951. This nearly ended the story for the state department, for some time in 1952 control of the matter passed to the CIA. By that summer, probably without Acheson's full knowledge, agents were working with resistance groups who used surplus U.S. goods routed through India. Much of the CIA activity remains murky, but it clearly had little effect. After a fruitless decade seeking better terms for his nation and people, in 1959 the Dalai Lama put himself in the hands of U.S. agents for safe delivery to exile in northern India.[16]

The main lines of Indo-U.S. relations might have taken a different course had Mao Zedong's revolution not engendered a U.S. fixation on Beijing's threat rather than the promise of a democratic and independent New Delhi. Personalities were important, too, but even had Nehru not been prime minister or Acheson secretary of state, the relations between the two states would surely have been strained. Such is the power of geography, history, and long-term interests in international relations. Almost any Indian leader would have criticized U.S. policies in the Korean War—called by an Indian historian "a disaster for the U.S. relationship with India"—and other Indians echoed Nehru's criticisms of America's "anti-Communist hysteria, war psychology, and fear complex."[17]

If Nehru's person was not exactly at the center of troubled U.S.-Indian relations, his aversion for western capitalism and his self-importance, which he saw confirmed in his growing stature in the eyes of other newly emerging peoples, combined to make Washington consider Indian foreign policy particularly irritating and pretentious. Bilateral ties were in the hands of men hugely different in character and personality. In New Delhi was the prickly and moralizing prime minister, said by a friend to be "flattered" by Britons and Canadians to think himself the "only living statesman" who could carry the "banner for those seeking world peace." In Washington sat the ironic bon vivant, four years Nehru's junior, who belittled moralist poseurs and believed U.S. power more than anything else kept the peace. Because of India's potential, he tried to close his eyes to its anti-imperialist sanctimony and offer aid when droughts exposed India's failure to feed its own people. He made no bones about finding Nehru deeply irksome, though this animus was more about personalities than philosophies. Nehru, he told colleagues in 1952, was an "irresponsible person." Seven years later, he wrote a friend that "India rather appals [sic] me." He "liked some" Indians, but "by and large they and their country give me the creeps." In 1961, when India forcibly seized the offshore Portuguese enclave of Goa, he wrote of the "elegance" and "saintliness, with which Mr. Nehru could cut a purse or slit a throat and cover the operation with the new legitimacy of the Third World."[18]

Economic aid issues dominated U.S.-Indian relations, and virtually every time the two nations made contact, it rubbed Acheson the wrong way. In the spring of 1950, in a painful attempt to protect its dignity, India denied it had a food emergency in the same breath it condemned Washington for not opening its treasury to relieve it. At best, Acheson thought, this was "mental compartmentalism." A master of bad timing in dealing with Americans, Nehru publicly aired some of his anti-U.S. complaints in 1951 just as Truman was asking Congress to send large amounts of food. As shipments first arrived, Nehru damned the Japanese peace treaty and U.S. policies toward Formosa and the Ryukyus. When China intervened in Korea, he mostly said, "I told you so." With its image of India congealing as feeble and irresponsible, Washington's deeper embrace of Pakistan caused Nehru to throw more stones at American windows. By then, the U.S. ambassador was a pro-Indian enthusiast, Chester Bowles, who helped smooth relations. Acheson praised his "colossal" work but clearly doubted his judgment. As Emerson once said of another, Acheson believed that "the louder" Nehru "talks of honour, the faster we count our spoons."[19]

The "relentlessly didactic" Bowles (as John Kenneth Galbraith called him) had succeeded Henderson in Delhi's "maximum hardship" post. Acheson considered Bowles mainly a pest, but he was certain to form better ties with Nehru than the crusty Henderson, who had to overcome prejudice against his avidly anti-communist Latvian wife. Fresh from two years as governor of Connecticut, the fifty-year-old Bowles brought a charming and sociable spouse with him. Truman was "appalled" when he accepted India over other available posts. "Well," the president said, "I thought India was pretty jammed with poor people and cows wandering around streets, witch doctors and people sitting on hot coals and bathing in the Ganges, and so on, but I did not realize that anyone thought it was important." Bowles was a veteran of various economic posts under FDR, had served as a delegate to a UNESCO conference in Paris, and chaired the National Convention of UNESCO in the United States. He had worked with the UN's Trygve Lie and helped shape the Point Four program. Truman sent him off with idiosyncratic instructions. Referring to Nehru's 1949 visit to the White House, he told Bowles: "The first thing you've got to do is find out if Nehru is a Communist. He sat right in that chair and talked just like a Communist."[20]

Citing his racial-cultural sensitivity and resistance to "imperious behavior," Andrew Rotter calls Bowles the best U.S. ambassador sent to India in the Nehru era. Eleanor Roosevelt praised him to the skies, and Truman once said he was a fine ambassador because he was a professional politician. He was surely Nehru's favorite, but he fell short in Acheson and State's view. He and Acheson shared a native state and Yale degree but little else. Bowles's years in advertising, Acheson wrote in 1958, had left him with "a permanent deformity like the Chinese habit of footbinding." Though occasionally rewarding him with tactical praise, he abhorred the dewy-eyed liberalism that made Bowles both a founder of Americans for Democratic Action and enthusiast for India. His worse sin, however, was a case of diplomatic localitis, what Brits call "going native." As Fraser Wilkins, a veteran foreign service officer on his staff recalled, Bowles rode his bicycle to work and sent his children to Indian schools. But Indians soon thought they had "him in their pocket." Consequently, Washington ignored him, which the Indians also figured out. When Acheson failed to deliver the large boosts in aid Bowles favored, the ambassador's response was insurrectionary. Refusing to credit either the budgetary or political liabilities foreign aid advocates faced, he rebelled against Acheson's instructions and tried going over his head to Truman. Even when dutifully reporting negative information about Nehru, he remained an uncritical devotee of his rule.[21]

Since he did not present his credentials until November 1951, Bowles missed some of the nastier moments in U.S.-Indian relations that occurred on Henderson's watch, most arising from Indian criticisms of U.S. policy toward China, the Korean War, and its role in the cold war generally. Though New Delhi voted for the first Security Council resolution to halt North Korean aggression, it abstained on the UN resolution asking members to help, a vote Nehru unblinkingly claimed was a bureaucratic error. India also opposed resolutions in 1950 and 1951 on Korea's reunification and censure of China. Then, as we have seen, it fought Acheson on the prisoner of war issue and rejected the Japanese peace treaty. Acheson's ostentatious praise of Pakistan's participation in the San Francisco conference was no accident. In the spring of 1950, Henderson's embassy had reported pervasive "resentment towards America" stemming from Kashmir, the failure to offer Marshall Plan-size aid, and a deep distaste for freewheeling American capitalism. In Bowles's time, foreign aid would provide the locus of tension, aggravated by India's shame at receiving charity from this powerful, white, and capitalist state.[22]

When India's food crisis broke in the summer of 1950, McGhee quickly proposed an assistance program to which both Acheson and Truman were amenable. As the crisis grew patently more severe, Vijayalakshmi Pandit, Nehru sibling and the Indian ambassador in Washington, formally requested two million tons of American food grains to avert a famine. A Point Four agreement seemed also in the works. Acheson told Madame Pandit the administration was sympathetic and already looking for available domestic grain stores. But after Chinese armies hit the Americans in Korea, he demanded advance assurance of a positive Indian reception before he would sound out Congress. He personally favored a grant over a loan, "since a dollar debt would embitter relations between the two countries." No U.S. official demanded a quid pro quo, though Acheson told Pandit the "people on the Hill would be favorably impressed" by a more obliging Kashmir policy and greater Indian understanding of the world situation in which the United States found itself.[23]

Outside of Congress, being generous attracted wide support at home. Besides Roosevelt, supporters included Pearl Buck, Walter White of the NAACP, the YMCA, the National Council of Churches, and leading newspapers. To stimulate more of the same, Acheson asked Pandit for photos and other information dramatizing the severity of the crisis. But the material latently depicted Indians as beggars, and such other compassionate gestures as "Herblock" cartoons depicting India as "a famished supplicant" mortified Indian officials, who refused to offer estimates of starvation fatalities. While Senator Tom Connally and other congressional leaders remained unenthusiastic, in late January 1951, a concurrent resolution favoring aid attracted adherents, and a bipartisan group of twenty-five members came out in favor of loans. In early February, Acheson urged Truman to "make a big play" for a two-year $180 million grant that would buy two million tons of grain, tied to a few strings about distribution. Summoning congressional leaders, Truman emphasized India's inability to pay, the need for bipartisan support, and the benefits of having aid legislation originate in Congress rather than the White House. Although former president Herbert Hoover politely declined to administer the aid, he boosted supporters by telling reporters on leaving the White House that Americans must open their hands to people in such straits. "This doesn't fall into the category of politics," he insisted, but "into the category of Christianity."[24]

On 12 February 1951, Truman officially asked Congress to grant India two million tons of grain. Despite widespread public support, the congressional debate eventually turned wrathful, with members denouncing Indian neutralism and anti-Americanism. This naturally further poisoned relations with India. McGhee's conference of U.S. diplomats in Ceylon (India having refused a site for the meeting) also flayed New Delhi's blindness to the "communist danger" and efforts to form a neutralist bloc in the UN. The assembled diplomats urged the state department to challenge India "vigorously, both at home and abroad through the press, radio, and other media" whenever it acted against U.S. interests or misrepresented its policies.[25]

At first confident of success, the administration had cheered when the House foreign affairs committee approved its proposal on 1 March, but then the legislative process stalled. Indian attitudes were not the only problem, for though the tensest moments of the "Great Debate" were over, Truman and Acheson had underestimated senators' views of their prerogatives. They had also grown complacent at the unexpected news that Robert Taft, William Knowland, and even Joseph McCarthy all endorsed Indian aid. But the Senate's ire erupted anew when an Indian UN delegate in a Texas lecture identified his nation's "chief enemy" as "not communism but Western imperialism." New Delhi apologized, but immediately afterward Nehru whined anew about delays caused by the "insulting and outrageous" United States. On 30 March, the Soviets and Chinese jumped in with grain offers. Acheson stifled his resentment at the "very stubborn" Indians; it was fundamentally important to prevent starvation, whatever Nehru said. But the prime minister kept drawing on his fund of bitterness, now because U.S. officials insisted on overseeing distribution of the grain, a standard provision of U.S. aid programs. As Henderson warned about the Indians' "razor edge sensibilities," a resolute administration pressed its case. As spring neared, the Senate was moving crablike toward grant aid, as the administration recommended, while a grudging House favored a loan, repayable in part in important strategic minerals.[26]

It took another six weeks to overcome the raw feelings and get a bill to Truman. At the end of April, Nehru declared his country not "so down and out" it had to accept dictates that sullied India's "honor." On 1 May, he took to the airwaves to denounce foreign aid "strings." To respond, members of Congress studiedly twiddled their thumbs. In New Delhi, Henderson spoke of Nehru's genuine "idealism," intellectual powers, and "warm heart," but worried about the effects of his "vanity" and "petty snobberies." In a personal letter on 7 May, Henderson told McGhee that Nehru was "trying to find some way to back track so that he can accept aid under the terms of the Senate Bill without losing too much face." Yet three days later, Nehru told his parliament he preferred the "simpler" House bill, implying he would reject a grant. This offended the Senate, which had gone along with Acheson's preferences for a grant. Even those kindly disposed now deemed Nehru an ingrate. Acheson cabled Henderson threatening to block any aid unless Nehru accepted U.S. terms. Before he could carry out his threat, the legislative holdup ended, and the House bill passed on 24 May. Nehru made a "slightly wry face" when Henderson showed him the provision about advertising the U.S. source of the aid, but he consented to all conditions. The Senate bill followed on the 26th—now a loan, too—and on 6 June the compromise India Emergency Food Aid Act went to Truman, who signed it on the 15th. As Rotter writes, however, a generous legislative act, repeatedly tweaked to meet Indian feelings, "marked a low point in Indo-U.S. relations." As if in proof, Henderson soon told the department to expect no gratitude. Nor would Nehru change any policies that so goaded Washington.[27]

By August, stevedores were offloading midwestern grain at Indian ports, and by December, Acheson thought U.S.-Indian ties much improved. By early February 1952, he was lobbying Averell Harriman to channel more mutual security aid to both India and Pakistan. It was urgent to advance economic development, rather than distribute weaponry or form alliances, to block radical solutions to the subcontinent's state of crisis. Citing the rise of the PRC and Communist Party gains in India's state and federal elections, Acheson told Harriman the west must promptly and decisively prove that chances of eradicating social misery lay with democratic over authoritarian regimes. If India fell victim to "subversion," its neighbors would be left "in almost untenable positions," hastening "the day when all of the Asian land-mass, with more than a billion people, would fall into the Soviet bloc." Factionalism and disorder, as well as possible communist aggression, threatened Pakistan, "strategically athwart the historic invasion route to the subcontinent." The essential point was to assist it in making "progress in the economic sphere."[28]

These proposals may well have shown Bowles's new influence, even as his importunities made the department squirm. According to the colorful recollection of economic officer Leroy Stinebower, when told during a home leave that his aid plans were impracticable, Bowles left the department "in a towering rage, went over to the White House for lunch, and started complaining loudly with no end to the President," at which point Truman said "'Ah, go to hell Chester,' and that was the last we ever heard of it."

In fact, despite Acheson's own hopes for ambitious aid projects, he and the president by then thought their chances close to nil. In early 1952, he told Truman that asking for too much would risk a congressional rebuff, reversing "Bowles's remarkably successful efforts in improving Indian-American relations." Muffling the blow with lavish praise for his labors, he told Bowles "it looked like a massacre to go to Congress for more money now." He shot down Bowles's suggestion that Truman make a 4th of July speech proclaiming American fealty to the "struggle for independence by dependent peoples." This would only blight Acheson's effort to balance support for a debate over Tunisian independence in the UN with continued loyalty to France. The snubbed Bowles complained that having stopped the communists cold at Europe's "front door," Washington now left the Asian "back door unlatched." Beleaguered by similar messages, on 24 July Acheson sent Bowles a gently worded cable of unmistakable meaning: that's enough.[29]

But at the end of the administration, the unflagging Bowles resumed his hectoring with what Robert McMahon calls "near apocalyptic" protests against chumming up with Pakistan. With this torrent still in full flow, Acheson on 8 January 1953 answered in a long "Dear Chet" message. He praised his efforts but in a patient explanation of political realities slammed the door on yet more proposals. He was not about to end his state department days worrying about a rapprochement with India, the country that had fought him to a standstill on Korean POWs and was now pushing hard for a UN seat for Beijing in hopes of giving a Security Council veto to the "Arab-Asian bloc."[30]

Under Eisenhower, friction between the United States and India became more visible, but except for Dulles's more severe strictures against cold war neutralism, the issues dividing the two nations remained the same. Aside from setting modest precedents in using U.S. agricultural abundance to assist a third world country in need, Acheson had achieved little in the region, but he had made no egregious mistakes, either. Though not his deliberate intention, his approach to the subcontinent accelerated the substitution of American for British influence in the region. Never regarding the subcontinent as a bridgehead for western power, his limited record in India and Pakistan actually reflected his conviction that NATO, Germany, Korea, and Indochina were all more strategically important.

30

FALLING BETWEEN TWO STOOLS: THE MIDDLE EAST, NORTH AFRICA, AND AFRICA

Sources of Discontent

At first, the United States in the early cold war period preferred avoiding any major Middle Eastern involvement, but as time passed, Washington decided it wanted the area on its side in the contest against the Soviet Union. Americans, therefore, would have to do what they could to resolve area disputes between Arabs and Israelis, between the British and Egyptians, and between the British again and Iranians.

The Middle East and all of Africa sprawled over a vast area of the world. For Dean Acheson, these territories had two things in common. First, much remained under the colonial rule of Washington's NATO allies, especially in North African and sub-Saharan Africa. To protect their economic and political strength, and to avoid hollowing out barriers against Soviet expansion, he would not deliberately act to quicken the demise of European colonialism, even though he knew its time was past. Besides having ties to western Europe, Africa and the Middle East seemed of only marginal significance. Second, therefore, until 1951 and 1952 Acheson viewed dealing with them a nuisance and where he could left it to others.

States of the Middle East, whether of ancient (Egypt) or recent (Saudi Arabia, Israel) lineage, mostly stood outside the story of colonialism and decolonization, and an often indifferent Acheson hoped to minimize his personal involvement with them too. There is no question he was Eurocentric and, he thought, for good, rational, and strategic reasons. How much was that

Eurocentrism shaped by racist prejudice? In the absence of specific declarations in the documentary record, one must infer the answer, but his attitudes toward this part of the world are not obscure. He had little or no interest in or prejudice against either Arabs or Islam and was immune to anti-Semitism. Nonetheless, Arabs and the Jews of Israel profoundly aggravated him.

As to blacks, he understood the damage domestic racial practices posed for U.S. foreign policy, and while correcting these was hardly the job of the state department, he made modest gestures in that direction. If representing *freedom* in the cold war was to be more than a pretense, he knew the United States and its allies had many blemishes in need of correction, and in the United States the most damaging was certainly racism. As under secretary in 1946, he had addressed the Fair Employment Practices Commission on the "adverse effect" of racial discrimination on U.S. foreign relations. As secretary in 1952, he filed an amicus curiae brief in *Brown v. Board of Education* listing the "alarming" number of countries—goaded by Soviet propaganda—that railed at the "hypocrisy" of U.S. claims "to be the champion of democracy while permitting practices of racial discrimination here in this country." The rhetoric is clear enough, but Acheson and the state department did virtually nothing to contest racist practices in South Africa or European colonies. In the spring of 1950, he urged a group of black college students journeying to Europe to speak the truth about American racial issues, tell Europeans what they were doing about "those problems," and express their "faith in the democratic process." But he moved in a world drenched in racist views of Africans (and African-Americans), and even in the absence of damning racist statements or declarations, it is safe to assume he held ordinary, contemporary views of black Africa. As an older man and former secretary of state, his attitudes became retrograde, and he did make damning and public racist statements.[1]

For nearly a century, Great Britain had dominated Egypt and points northeast and ruled a number of sub-Saharan colonies. Britain's need for safe sea routes from the Mediterranean to Queen Victoria's crown jewel of India had supplied the impetus behind controlling the Suez Canal and imposing protectorates on Egypt and Sudan. Defending its grip on Iranian petroleum explained much of its sway in other nearby locales. The UK had military bases in more than a half dozen Middle Eastern territories, and its holdings in the region included petroleum, banking and insurance, commercial air routes, and mining. Yet it was in the Middle East, as an Acheson aide put it, where Americans first saw the British empire begin to "fold up."

By 1945, the United States was already the dominant outside oil power in Saudi Arabia, but it still preferred to play second fiddle in the region at large. Washington lavished foreign aid on western Europe but made few disbursements in the Middle East. A focus on Europe and Korea, inexperience in the Middle East, and old habits of deference to London left the state department little inclined to give detailed guidance to its diplomats in the field. Barring crises of large magnitude, supervision at first belonged to Assistant Secretary for the Near East, South Asia, and Africa, George McGhee, and later to the sleek Henry Byroade. For Arab-Israeli troubles, Acheson could rely on that perennial volunteer for hard tasks, Dean Rusk. But in 1951–52, Egypt fastened Acheson's personal attention just when nationalist agitation against French rule in North Africa also thrust him into controversies in the UN that jeopardized relations with a vital NATO ally. He had hoped the old metropole powers could keep the lid on in the region while being supple enough to forestall rebellions attractive to the communists. The Europeans' failure to do this led to a stutter-step expansion of U.S. involvement and responsibility, and Acheson's.[2]

Although nowhere as close as in later years, the U.S.-Israeli connection was already close enough to arouse Arab suspicion. Acheson always had to keep a finger on the presidential pulse as he tried to counter such suspicion. This required greater personal attention than in other regional matters, where he could leave others to sift through daily dispatches. He considered the Arab-Israeli clash irrational and after leaving government did not disguise his distaste for the area. Its importance centered on Suez and the need to "keep the oil flowing," not its "few people." Domestic politics, he told colleagues at Princeton in 1954, made Arab-Israeli disputes impossible to resolve. Insofar as he could maneuver through the political minefield, he thought his top priority was to keep "friendly ties with Britain." Compared to the U.S.-Soviet conflict, he did not care whether Jordan or Syria were real countries or "little fragments" the Europeans had "created for their own convenience." Their problems would probably go unresolved for many years, giving people the chance to "have colloquia about them and meetings and seminars."[3]

Reminiscing at the Princeton seminar, he expressed "dissatisfaction" at "everything we did" in Africa and the Middle East. To keep third world states and nascent states out of communist hands, he had used combinations of political, economic, and military methods, hoping the new states would advance along liberal Western lines but "in their own way." But promoting liberalism and autonomy caused collisions with resentful allies, making him "stop, look, and listen." This bothered the reformers—Chester Bowles, Justice William Douglas, labor leader Walter Reuther—who wanted unremitting U.S. pressure aimed at "raising people's standards of living, and proclaiming liberty, and throwing off chains." He was certain this would not work, but neither would coercion by force, which could only "overcome other force," its "only achievement." Looking back in 1954, he considered his mix of moderate instruments no match for "nationalism, xenophobia, and the conflicts between the Western powers and the Middle Eastern powers." Weakness was impossible to convert into strength in the face of the region's "fanatical xenophobia."[4]

Acheson's retrospection was simultaneously too hard and too soft on himself and State. In fact, over time they acquired nuanced notions of developments in Africa and the Middle East and of what ideally should be done. It is equally true they never stopped approaching the region with insular pictures of Arabs and Africans in their mind and never stopped listening to self-serving advice from Europeans. Having visited his sprawling mandate, in October 1950, McGhee expressed certainty that few of its peoples could rule themselves and that France could indefinitely keep control of the volatile territories in the Maghreb. Deaf to the dissonance of his own language, he remarked: "We have the good-will of the native people and we should make every effort to maintain it and at the same time not alienate the French." Hazily aware of the region's new importance, State sent its first consul to Kuwait in March 1951 and bumped legations up to embassies in Lebanon, Syria, and Jordan the next year. A cold war–generated preoccupation with "stability," not knowledge of regional circumstances, dictated U.S. reactions to such events as the July 1951 assassination of Jordan's King Abdullah and a coup in Damascus later that year. The Korean War reinforced the tendency and raised new concerns about exposed oil supplies. Though Acheson well knew the role of U.S.-Israeli ties in generating Arab anger, he occasionally blamed it on "communists," warning Arab states in May 1951 not to parrot Russian criticisms of U.S. aid programs. The closer he paid attention to regional realities in his diplomacy toward North Africa and the Middle East, the closer he came to solutions, though never to the solutions themselves.[5]

"They Seemed to Do the Wrong Things"

Endless rows over arms sales and Palestinian refugees always threatened to undercut Acheson's standing with Truman and, he thought, open the door for Soviet intrigue. The state department under George Marshall had very much gotten on the president's wrong side on Israel. Whatever the role anti-Semitism played in the department (accusations of which Acheson always rejected), officials believed creation of the Israeli state from Arab territory defied the principle of self-determination and planted seeds of war. Both Jews and Arabs clamored for arms, and in August 1949, shortly after a truce ended the first Arab-Israeli conflict, the UN lifted its ban on Middle Eastern arms sales. With the British again free to sell arms to its clients in Jordan, Iraq, and Egypt, the department announced it would approve sales only for self-defense. As weapons seeped into the region, from communists states (mainly to Israel) as well, Acheson, already being criticized for spurning one Israeli bid for arms, acted to stabilize the issue through great power cooperation. The result was the ambiguous U.S.-British-French Tripartite Declaration of 15 May 1950, a pronouncement appearing to withhold arms from states that would not renounce "aggression" while permitting sales that contributed to regional "balance." In pledging action if one state transgressed another's border or armistice lines, the declaration tacitly guaranteed Israeli territorial integrity. It also apparently legitimized boundaries others were still hoping to change, by force if necessary. The Tripartite Declaration served important if short-term international ends, but its main value for Acheson was to halt the parade of pro-Israeli congressmen into his office. War in Korea soon overtook the issue, and two years passed before the three powers organized the coordinating committee to execute declaration goals. In time, Arab-Israeli enmity and the fact that the Americans, British, and French had bigger fish to fry overwhelmed this early effort at establishing mutual security in the area. First France, then other states soon turned the area into an arms bazaar.[6]

The state department mostly wanted the Israeli conflict to go away. Prone to blame the Israelis anyway, the department found Israel's cold war neutrality and recognition of the PRC irritating. When Truman conveyed his own "indignation" about Israel's "silence" on Korea, it acted and on 2 July 1950 accepted U.S. policies at the UN. It did not send the troops Acheson requested but did dispatch ambulances and medical supplies. It also offered to build U.S. bases in the Negev desert, blend its military with American forces in any regional security system, and proposed sites for pre-positioned supplies to use in a war with the Soviets. Acheson shrugged off this new enthusiasm but thought it much better than having Israel buy eastern European arms. He also still held back on selling the Israelis new arms, including a requested purchase of obsolete tanks from the Philippines. In turn, Israel worried that Moscow might now take action against Soviet Jews.[7]

The steadiest irritant in U.S.-Israeli relations was the plight of some 700,000 Palestinian refugees. Washington criticized the seizure of their property and refusal to readmit them to Israeli territory and funneled aid to the refugees. In October 1950, Acheson took Ambassador Abba Eban and Israeli Foreign Minister Moshe Sharett to task, telling them that whenever Israelis or Arabs had the chance "to do the right thing," instead "they seemed to do the wrong things." Nothing came of his demand for help to the refugees, and, though only Jordan among Arab states had admitted Palestinians, anti-Americanism surged among Arabs, less because of the treatment of Palestinians than a kind of angry pessimism about Israel's development and its backing from the United States. In the NSC on 12 October, Acheson insisted that the administration's obvious pro-Israeli bias was the fundamental cause of poor relations with the Arabs, noting their complaint that "our position in the UN was against aggression except when it was committed by Israel." But he had nothing more radical in mind than helping Arab governments "develop projects" attractive to lenders.[8]

Arabs found much to seethe about, including U.S. sponsorship for an Israeli seat in the UN. Their complaint about bias in foreign aid programs, however, was misplaced, for grant aid to Israel remained modest under Truman. At times, Congress outbid even the president in Israeli aid expenditures, sometimes in response to Eban's deft lobbying. With "benevolent irony," Acheson thanked him for his courtesy in keeping him informed of Israel's wants. Eban occasionally tangled with the "complex and subtle" secretary of state but admired him. "His outer elegance," he wrote, though "a little too careful and refined, was the reflection of a precise intellect rather than a dandified pose." He did not tolerate "excess in rhetoric or emotion," preferring "balance" and "the lowest audible key." Like others, Eban spotted Acheson's "excessive" faith in reason "as a determining factor in the life of mankind. He sought shelter from the gusts of sentiment, passion and prejudice, by pretending that they were not blowing at all, or alternatively, that they would soon subside."9

Over time, Truman's definition of "balance" in the ratio of Israeli to Arab assistance wore Acheson down. An aide, Leroy Stinebower, recalled the time the White House returned a draft aid budget "with just one mark on it": an HST comment that State had not followed his rule of Middle Eastern impartiality. A puzzled Stinebower took it to Acheson: "I can't understand this. What does he mean?" "Don't you understand?" was the reply: "Take the aid that you're going to give to the whole Middle East, give 50 percent to Israel, and divide the rest up." That was "impartial."10

Eban was moved by Acheson's "fidelity to Truman," especially considering his "superior intellect," but the Arabs could hardly agree. The state department was never able to persuade them how hard it tried to find a middle ground. Nor were they likely to appreciate Acheson's victory over Eban and his domestic allies in refusing formal recognition of Jerusalem as sovereign Israeli territory or as Israel's capital. (Acheson yielded partially in February 1951 to make it easier for U.S. diplomats to do business with Israeli agencies.) In January 1950, when U.S. ambassador to Cairo, Jefferson Caffery, pleaded for moderation toward Israel, Egypt's irate foreign minister, Mohammed Salaheddin, defined his policy "in a few words":

1. Egypt would never attack Israel. . . .
2. Egypt would never make peace with Israel.
3. Egypt would never recognize Israel.
4. Egypt would never collaborate with Israel.

Shortly thereafter, just before the Arab League barred all negotiations with Israel, a Saudi official told McGhee that an expansionist Israel had plans to seize Syria, Jordan, and other territories. Since they had no aggressive designs of their own, Arabs would treat Israel as if a wall "surrounded it." If that was not enough territory for the Israelis, they could all board ships "to London and Paris." In April, a bomb exploded near the U.S. legation in Damascus, igniting a diatribe against both Americans and Israelis by a high Syrian official. Acheson urged Truman to make a public statement to help offset such hostility. Though he refused, after another appeal in April, the president promised to curb other anti-Arab statements coming out of the executive branch.11

In March 1951, Acheson resisted when Israel said it wanted Truman to invite its sixty-five-year-old prime minister, David Ben-Gurion, to Washington. The president was too busy, he said, but the trip came off anyway in early May, complete with official dinners and talks with Truman and Acheson. Then

Ben-Gurion toured the American diaspora, raising cash. Thinking Israel accounted for Middle Eastern turmoil, Acheson did not react when the Polish-born prime minister told him only Turkey and Israel could stage a regional defense against the Russians. The Arabs, he averred, "had an historic inability to stand up" to any major challenge. It was futile, he argued, to try appeasing Arabs by withholding aid to his country, for, he implied, Arab sentiments came from irrational impulses. Aid to Israel, moreover, would have the nice effect of destroying Arab hopes of an Israeli "economic collapse." Having seen almost $70 million go to Israel in the 1952 budget, Acheson made the case to Truman for restraint in fiscal 1953. Even modest aid should be conditioned on reversing what Ben-Gurion had told Acheson was his first priority, attracting 600,000 more immigrants within three years, justifying all the Arabs' suspicions of Israeli expansionism. Arabs would mock U.S. claims it was trying to stabilize current "armistice frontiers" through the Tripartite Declaration.[12]

Acheson was not pro-Arab, but he was certainly not pro-Israeli, either. He urged Egypt to keep Suez open to traffic to Israel and to make oil available to it but seemed commonly ready to drop the matter when Cairo resisted. He rejected Israeli claims that Anglo-American plans for Middle Eastern defense schemes were simply the latest example of Britain's appeasement of the sheikhs. The plight of Palestinian refugees, Acheson thought, was an "incubus on peace prospects" and, combined with Israel's very existence, caused cold war neutralism among Arabs, a judgment Truman did not quarrel with. A novel source of discord arose when Eban in 1951 protested the movement toward rearmament of the Germans as rewarding their "evil doing." Acheson then had his turn to grouse when Tel Aviv started negotiations with Bonn for reparations, since the U.S. treasury would eventually foot the bill. But he changed his mind after a poignant appeal from Eban, clearing the way for a 1952 German-Israeli accord. Acheson also assented that year to making Israel eligible for aid from the Mutual Defense Assistance Program. Despite its first intentions, by the end of the Truman administration, Israel found itself almost fully absorbed within the western coalition in the cold war.[13]

In April 1952, with Truman in attendance, Acheson told an NSC meeting that the Middle East was "perhaps our worst problem area," partly because U.S. interests often conflicted with British and French concerns, but mostly because of the "violent" Arab reaction to the U.S. bias toward Israel. The British and French were rankled at "our obvious sympathy" for the area's "nationalist aspirations," all adding up to "a very tough problem for American policy-makers." This meeting adopted an NSC paper that urged using "all feasible and appropriate means" to resolve the issues causing tensions with the Arab states, a truism, Acheson surely thought, about as useful as praying for rain in the Sahara. When he left office, he thought the Arab-Israeli dispute beyond solution—or at least American solution. "Unhappily," he wrote, all his "time and effort" on the conflict produced only "a long record of failure." This may be excessive. After all, he had striven for the evenhandedness that would eventually allow both sides to believe they might rely on American impartiality in finally settling their conflict.[14]

"Hard Enough to Annoy But Not Hard Enough to Succeed": Morocco and Tunisia

Had he been blessed with complete freedom of choice, Acheson would have ignored the growing nationalist unrest in French Morocco and Tunisia in North Africa, in his eyes a marginal region. The agitation posed a threat to France and U.S.-French relations, and it played out in the United Nations General Assembly, where small states often succeeded in forcing debate on explosive subjects, a key reason for Acheson's detestation of the organization.

Previous interest in the region came from U.S. interest in possible sites for air bases in Libya and Morocco. Although the threat seemed remote even in the U.S. capital, policymakers also thought North Africa could be a target for Moscow's expansionism. (Ironically, as demonstrated by Yahia Zoubir, the USSR hoped a determined France would block a U.S. sphere of influence.) Americans at first trusted their European allies to take the lead and hold the lid on any strife. With the disappointment of this hope, the United States tried leading but ended in a policy straddle unacceptable to either nationalists seeking independence or allies demanding uncritical allegiance. Both similarities and differences between the U.S. experience in North Africa and French Indochina were soon evident. Here, U.S. diplomats wooed nationalists instead of avoiding them as pariahs, but here, too, fear of communist infiltration and concern about reinforcing Paris's role in Europe led Washington to compromise its anti-colonialism. Instead, it pinned its hopes on a benign French "tutelage" and "orderly" progress toward independence. When sparks flew over Morocco and Tunisia in the United Nations, France first took refuge in delay and obstructionism and then in denials of UN jurisdiction. Knowing the indefinite perpetuation of French colonialism was impossible, Acheson was not prepared fully to placate the Paris government. But fear of communist expansionism and concern about the French part in NATO barred him from openly supporting Moroccans and Tunisians seeking independence, whether or not they found support from communists.[15]

Acheson developed textured understandings of the tensions with France arising from the struggles in the UN. French "repression and hanging on" was the product of a general national agony. Plagued too by the struggle in Indochina, the Paris government worried about inflation, about Charles de Gaulle awaiting the people's summons back to power, about the French Communist Party, and about siren songs periodically heard in Moscow. Fearful and suspicious, the French found a nice target in the Americans, with their pressure for rearmament and emancipation of West Germany. France's stubbornness about North Africa was symptomatic of fears of Germany's return to European affairs. Whatever his criticisms of French conduct, Acheson disliked picking at the scabs in public. On Morocco, which he deemed utterly unready for independence, he backed France almost without stint. Tunisia was another matter. Its claims for independence were stronger, and its supporters sat in his own UN mission, particularly Eleanor Roosevelt.[16]

Acheson did not act simply from his personal preferences but in rhythm with McGhee's Near Eastern Affairs office (NE). In October 1950, the assistant secretary held another of his diplomats' conferences in Tangier, Morocco, where he articulated the now standard Washington shuffle, that it must "generally" support "independence" while giving Europeans "the benefit of the doubt" on how to attain it. His audience thought using cold war excuses to back France would dry up America's "reservoir of goodwill." They pointed to the prestige enjoyed by the United States in Libya. Yet, like McGhee, they could think of nothing better than coaxing the French (and Spanish) to be more flexible and humane toward nationalists. They also suggested aid programs for social improvements in the French colonies, even though those wanting independence would consider them props for the status quo and the French a stimulus to rebellion. McGhee's own bottom line was blunt—the drive for self-government might "get out of hand," in which case the United States must stand with France.[17]

The United States had indeed joined a UN majority in establishing independence for Libya, conquered by Italy earlier in the century and freed by British and American armies during the war. Mainly interested in air base rights, Washington carried on secret negotiations with Libya even as it was still moving toward legal independence. By November 1950, SAC aircraft with a mission to bomb the USSR had arrived at Wheelus air base, and while the strategic rationale changed over time, American flyers remained at Wheelus until 1970.

Greater trouble impended to the west in Tunisia and Morocco. Yielding to *force majeure*, they had become French protectorates (in 1881 and 1912, respectively) rather than formal colonial possessions. According to the 1946 French constitution, they were therefore eligible to become overseas departments of metropolitan France, but, as in Vietnam, Paris instead gave them semi-autonomous status in the French Union. Morocco's Istiqlal (Freedom) party under Sultan Muhammed V and Tunisia's Néo-Destour (New Constitutional) movement under Habib Bourguiba demanded the better alternative of independence and knocked at the door of the UN for help. This imposed a hard choice on Washington, which had bases in Morocco on French sufferance, and Paris counted on categorical U.S. backing. Divided between NE anticolonialists and EUR desk officers, the department wrung its hands, hoping to support France *and* eventual independence. In short, Acheson faced wretched alternatives and clashing counsel. In Morocco, he thought, France was "trying to make a modern democratic state" against the resistance of "a reactionary Sultan" and "medieval" Berbers, but the choice seemed harder in Tunisia. Finally he made what he called the "understandable, but possibly the worst, decision," pushing France "hard enough to annoy but not hard enough to succeed."[18]

Though Washington came closest to slaking French thirst for approval in Morocco, a sense of what was right plus outside pressures caused Acheson to push for a measured movement toward self-rule. Responding in January 1951, Paris asked the United States to disavow all interest in Moroccan "internal affairs." Washington's refusal stirred anti-Americanism among the French settlers, or *colons*, while the French commander raked Acheson's diplomats for talking to Tunisians. He also put U.S. consular officials under surveillance. Paris was incensed when Moroccans and Tunisians reached directly to Washington and London and to their UN missions for support. Standing as firm as he could for his old partner, Acheson told Robert Schuman on 11 September 1951 that U.S. and French interests in Morocco were "identical" and promised to use his "limited influence" to prevent even a discussion of Moroccan independence in the UN.[19]

He even advised Schuman how to circumvent the UN troubles. But he was also readying a retreat. In Paris in October 1951 for the General Assembly meetings, Acheson made clear he could not block a debate on Morocco. He explained to Schuman that he was powerless to combat congressional, media, and public opinion and the proclivities of his own delegates, who viewed the Assembly as the "Town Meeting of the World." Whether complaints of oppression were true or not, Americans traditionally rallied to those claiming to be oppressed. Still, with the help of all its western friends, France managed in a 28–23 vote (with 7 abstentions) to postpone the Moroccan discussion "for the time being." The compromising tactics used to gain this temporary respite caused chagrin on all sides. Acheson had a problem, he told senators in February 1952, for "if we start telling the French we think they had better run the whole country differently they are likely to say, 'I guess we don't need your bases here.'" Nearly a year later, in October 1952, Washington abandoned all its European allies in the General Assembly Political and Security Committee and joined a 34–20 majority that put both Morocco and Tunisia on the agenda. McGhee's successor, Henry Byroade, had advised sticking to France while insisting it make progressive reforms, but having already driven that potholed path in Indochina, Acheson would not do so again. With no Ho Chi Minh present, with both Moscow and Beijing far away, with both his own delegation and U.S. opinion demanding at least a chance to discuss what Americans declared on their own in 1776, and with only weeks left in his tenure, he chose to defy Washington's closest continental ally.[20]

He thought Tunisia's Bourguiba "by far the most moderate of the North African Arab leaders," but moderation is in the eye of the beholder. Aware of how Indonesia gained independence, the French-educated and repeatedly jailed Tunisian leader, then in his late forties, infuriated Paris with his bids for UN intervention. The state department again fell between two stools in March 1950 by advocating the gradual grant of autonomy. Bourguiba wanted independence, not autonomy, and now, not later. Paris said it was none of Washington's business in the first place. The French resident general in Tunis told McGhee only a few isolated intellectuals backed Bourguiba. Allowed to return to Tunisia from his most recent exile in September 1951, he first toured the world, rounding up support in Arab capitals especially. Over vigorous French objections, he talked to low-level desk officers in Washington, telling them that earlier French promises for eventual independence might have averted a crisis, but now the *colons* had blocked all reforms. In November, John D. Jernegan, the U.S. consul general in Tunis, urged the department to pressure France to make large preemptive concessions to the Néo-Destour. But, with James Webb as his conduit, Acheson replied that France was already on the "right track" and that Tunisians should stop trying to exploit Middle Eastern turmoil for their own purposes.[21]

His hopes of quietly nudging France toward a more progressive policy without ever publicly opposing it proved unworkable after January 1952, when the French banned Bourguiba from holding a Néo-Destour congress, placed him under house arrest, and then again deported him. These acts sparked violent street protests and reprisals that took two hundred lives. By March, Jernegan was calling leaders of a puppet "nationalist" administration "stooges." With Tunisians again approaching the UN, Washington could no longer act backstage, which Acheson thought dramatically cut chances for good results. At home, the American Federation of Labor (AFL) executive council called for Tunisian "home rule," NBC radio seemed to report French misdeeds in North Africa daily, and an unusually attentive press pilloried the *colons*. In March, Acheson told Ambassador Henri Bonnet that to forestall even worse events, France must release arrested Tunisians, tell the world it would negotiate, and do so in good faith. The fuming Bonnet "would have none of it," invoking not only the mantra that Tunisia was a domestic issue but what Acheson called "Gallic logic"—to wit, stubbornly asserting "an erroneous conclusion deduced from an erroneous premise."[22]

Already worried about "the rise of the Islamic movement," Acheson was near his limits of patience with Paris. And Eleanor Roosevelt would not let him off the hook, scheduling personal meetings with him and Truman in April 1952 to press her case. She had been compliant on Morocco but insisted that going the wrong way on Tunisia would estrange the Asian-Arab bloc and further destabilize North Africa. On 8 April, she came out for the independence of Asian and African colonies publicly, just as Acheson was being "hit around-the-ears" on Tunisia. Telling Truman it was "one of the most difficult decisions" he had ever made, he decided it was impossible to keep Tunisia off the Security Council agenda. He rejected British pressure to take an unstinting stand for France. He had told Truman of putting secret pressure on Paris to expedite a "serious" reform clearly ending in "self-government." At the same time, he believed French standing as a Great Power made it essential to preserve some kind of primacy in North Africa. Awkwardly moving from one stool to another, he planned somehow to demand Tunisian autonomy without wounding Paris. On 14 April, a vote to put Tunisia on the Security Council agenda failed to gain a majority, with a U.S. abstention displeasing all sides—and Roosevelt. Bitter at being pushed into public contention on the issue, in a press conference on 16 April, Acheson complained about how any UN member who had it in mind could damage U.S. relations with its friends by demanding public votes. It was just as bad at home, for his "domestic critics," he jabbed, "seemed to believe that a fight was always desirable and always had a right side—theirs."[23]

As he vainly searched for a middle course, he sparked escalating French anger, Asian and Arab disappointment, and his own delegate's irritation. He hoped for some kind of solution before May, when he would attend both UN and bilateral meetings in Paris. But on 2 May, his ambassador, James C. Dunn, received a tongue-lashing from a Quai d'Orsay official who expressed wonder at Washington's inability to grasp France's problems or the current government's precarious tenure. Regardless of American public opinion, the French embassy in the United States said that "rightly or wrongly" France would resist all inter-ference on North Africa. It might even be necessary to pull out of Indochina, or even abandon NATO, to gain enough military force to hold on in Morocco and Tunisia. If sufficiently wronged, France might leave the UN itself. These were hardly credible threats, but they shook American officials. Preparing for his Paris sojourn, Acheson told Bonnet on 15 April that the current situation was worse "than a vicious circle," because there was "no movement at all." Home for con-sultations, Jernegan said the newest French resident general based his preference for beating "the opposition into submission" before offering them "a carrot" on a philosophy of "brutality for Arabs."[24]

With Acheson's position at home already "almost untenable," he faced a torrent of anger on 28 April, early in the bilateral Paris talks. The grim French contingent told him Tunisia was solely their concern and protested the absence of complete U.S. backing. Amid ominous hints about U.S. bases in Morocco, they asked where exactly they could count on Washington. If necessary, Schuman declared, France would simply pursue its own interests, which were "those of Western civilization." Acheson countered by demanding the kind of prudence that would allow him to resist inflamed media and opinion at home. His countrymen might know little about North Africa, but their instincts favoring those demanding a voice were sound. Though he could not change such senti-ments, he might "canalize" them if Paris gave him something to work with. A debate on whether to *have* a debate on Tunisia was unavoidable. He would have to move even further from what Schuman wanted if Paris did not act quickly, creatively, and sincerely toward greater autonomy for the peoples of North Africa. The problem, said the French, according to Acheson's remarks to reporters, was they had no one left to negotiate with because they had already "thrown the friendliest" Tunisians "in jail." On his return home, he told other reporters that Truman's lame duck administration was ready if necessary to "defy public opinion" in support of France, and on 2 June told members of Congress that U.S. and French interests in North Africa were identical. This was brave talk, but by the arrival of New York's autumn session of the UN, he was resigned to canalizing both American and international opinion. France must accept a debate on Tunisia and take the offensive with a bulletproof reform program.[25]

The French claimed the Tunisians would not respond to a moderate program because they were relying on U.S. support for immediate independence. Acheson wanted to reassure Paris, but his own people goaded him to support a Tunisian agenda item, and on 26 September 1952, he informed France his delegation would vote for a debate. Paris remained inflexible. It would fight without quarter against the UN's "competence" to consider North African issues and any attempt to inscribe them on the agenda. If their resistance failed, Dunn reported to Acheson, they claimed they would walk out of any substantive debate. By 13 October, Acheson feared Paris might find itself forced to choose "between its interests in NATO and its interests in North Africa."[26]

When the General Assembly opened, Acheson and Philip Jessup vigorously lobbied Asian and Arab delegates, hoping for their support on the irksome Korean POW issue and for a chance to deflect, or co-opt, their mounting ambitions. Acheson pressed the Arabs particularly not to make a stink over Tunisia. On 22 October, his delegation took the lead in a 34–20 committee decision to put Tunisia and Morocco on the agenda, voting with the Soviets and against all its European allies. Though long warned this would occur, the French, both in Paris and New York, were beside themselves. Paris newspapers, Dunn reported, expressed "bewilderment and indignation." Acheson took out his frustration with a prickly lecture to his own delegation, telling the thirty-second president's widow and her colleagues they must protect NATO and America's "strategic" interests in North Africa. Without North Africa, the French would not consider themselves a "power."[27]

On 25 October, he wrote the president about how adroitly the Arabs and Asians were jamming him up. Prevailing anti-colonialism and anti-racism had snared the United States in the middle, and the Soviets were doing their best to divide the west and stir Arab-Asian resentment. Nor were the Latin Americans their normally helpful selves. Europeans were in a sour, doomed, rearguard fight to retain the residues of empire. His own effort to "make a virtue" of the U.S. "predicament," charting paths to moderate results, enraged the French, who faced "an unstable and inflamed political situation at home." But they had loyally helped him on the POW matter, and he hoped his "personal spade work" with Latin Americans and Arabs would hold U.S. "friends and allies together in the face of a determined Soviet effort to drive wedges between us."[28]

Riding such a wedge, French President Vincent Auriol ripped into Washington in a speech two days later. Acheson was trying through messages to Schuman to repair the broken "harmony." Though he used tried and true flattery about Paris's record in Southeast Asia and the "Europe of tomorrow," Paris was not buying any. Arrived in New York, Schuman complained that friends had failed to protect French "dignity." He might speak in a plenary session but would refuse to appear in any venue making him look like the "accused in the dock," that is, the committee deciding on agenda items. When Acheson said the Arabs and Asians would consider this an "affront," Schuman waved them off as "extremists" and "parties not qualified to condemn and criticize" despite all their "inflammatory harangues." What he wanted from Acheson was evidence of Washington's "confidence in France." He could not act as France's lawyer, Acheson told him, only its friend.[29]

The French sense of betrayal was huge. David Bruce, now under secretary and always tuned to French thinking, thought Paris would "bolt" the organization if the UN dared sent a study commission to North Africa. On 12 December, the Political Committee on a 44–3 vote (including a U.S. "yea") called for urgent bilateral talks leading to Tunisian independence while expressing false confidence that France agreed. Acheson's party, in other words, had succeeded in getting a resolution that only promoted Franco-Tunisian discussions, not a UN debate, and did nothing to lessen French control of Tunisia. It also did nothing to ease pressure on France. Acheson's domestic critics seemed satisfied, but he also hoped for some credit from third world groups. Shortly before he left office, however, a National Intelligence Estimate held that U.S. standing in the Middle East was crumbling, harmed by close ties to the UK, France, and Israel.[30]

In 1956, after several more years of mayhem, both Morocco and Tunisia gained independence, two years after France left Vietnam. In the Suez crisis of the same year, Eisenhower and Dulles went much further than Truman and Acheson in breaking with the colonial powers, but at grave cost to the alliance— and with Democratic activist Acheson carping sharply from the sidelines. A half century later, it is clear that neither Truman-Acheson nor Eisenhower-Dulles found a way to please old friends while enlisting new ones in North Africa and the Middle East.

Flirting with the Spirit of '76

As a "Europeanist," George Ball once said, Acheson "cared nothing for Africa." His record on sub-Saharan Africa is much what one would expect of an elite, white American of his time. Out of office, it became worse. In his seventies, when he had become keen to stick his thumb in liberals' eyes, he canvassed against the UN campaign to end white rule in Rhodesia (along with that other "Europeanist," George Kennan), trumpeted his esteem for Antonio Salazar's orderly state in Portugal, and defended the latter's African colonies against "outside" meddling. There had been earlier hints. Sounding like a "realist," he had asserted in a 1950 speech that it was "escapism in dealing with the world" to go "from state to state with political litmus paper testing them for true-blue democracy." He disliked dealings with rulers of new nations, preferring to do business with their ex-masters. As to colonial Africa below the Maghreb, a department policy paper in April 1950 described it as "the largest remaining backward area in the world."

Although his messages, memoranda, and speeches as secretary of state contain no explicitly racist smoking guns, his attitude was consistent with a well-mannered variety of old school American racism. In office, he and his aides sometimes showed they could be moved by both a residual, traditional anti-colonialism and, as in the case of South Africa, more immediate needs to stockpile uranium and gather allies for the Korean War. At some unknown price to their consciences, they mostly acted on the latter impulse.[31]

In 1949, Europe's imperial colors, especially those of Britain, France, Belgium, and Portugal, splashed across maps of Africa, which then contained only four sovereign nations: ancient Egypt and Ethiopia, Liberia, and white-ruled South Africa. Acheson limited most of his notice to the Belgian Congo, site of a large reserve of scarce uranium ore, and South Africa, where a mild search for a middle way resembled the Tunisian case, with slimmer results. Before State set up a separate bureau for African affairs late in Eisenhower's presidency, they fell to the NE bureau. In practice, men from the European desks, all partisans for "their" NATO partners, shaped many of the decisions. With more foreign service officers working on West Germany than all of Africa, those toiling in that vineyard were spread thin. The U.S. consul general at Dakar in Senegal was also accountable for Dahomey, Guinea, Ivory Coast, Mauritania, Niger, Sudan, the Upper Volta, all French possessions, and the trust territory of Togoland. The Leopoldville consul in the Congo oversaw Chad, Gabon, Ubangi-Shari (Central African Republic), and the Cameroons as well. Because Liberia was founded by the American Colonization Society and settled by freed American slaves, by tradition it was handled separately. The United States envoy was Edward R. Dudley, the state department's first African-American at the rank of ambassador. Only $700 million of nearly $91 billion in foreign aid from 1946 through 1961 reached black Africa, including $400 million from the Marshall Plan, much of which helped European partners strengthen rule over their colonies. Point Four had the same effect. Designed to buttress west European recovery, no ECA aid went to places like Liberia.[32]

Because the administration's "concerns about communism and strategic minerals" nearly always "outweighed principles such as self-determination and majority rule," James H. Meriwether writes, it is all the more remarkable that better American anti-imperialist principles still popped up now and then, causing Europeans and South Africans a steady state of chagrin. American diplomats working in Africa always had Europeans on their mind; and, conversely, the Europeans found reason to worry when Yanks suddenly showed up in these unfamiliar surroundings. But in the end, the Americans mostly marched in step with London, Paris, and Lisbon, even as awareness grew that embracing imperialists was a poor way to gain African allegiance in any contest with "international communism."[33]

Washington found that it was extremely easy to set the Europeans on edge, as McGhee did in an 8 May 1950 speech in Oklahoma City simply by applauding "the progressive development" toward self-rule of "the dependent peoples of Africa." This set off weeks of vicious criticism from France. A micro event two years later in Southern Rhodesia also illustrates the point. When U.S. Consul John P. Hoover sought help getting acquainted with "natives," a bristling British police official demanded to know why. When told it was to learn something about their thinking, the Briton exclaimed that if Hoover "wanted to know what the Africans were thinking, he could tell me exactly and at any time." Hoover then went to the secretary for native affairs, who was both "suspicious" and nonplused, saying that Hoover's approach was "the first time that any foreign government official has ever asked such a thing of me." He promised to be helpful if Hoover was "discreet and did not give the Africans any false ideas." In 1949, Washington had voted in the UN for a World Court advisory opinion on the status of South West Africa (Namibia), still held by Pretoria from an interwar League of Nations mandate. When South Africa protested, Foggy Bottom accused it of acting injudiciously in light of "the new and powerful forces now emerging in the world." A 1951 state department pronouncement on the Congo about "the rights and privileges due the dignity of man" would have amused the ghost of King Leopold but not the Belgian government. Britain, too, suffered a few anti-imperialist pinpricks when Washington greeted the future ruler of independent Ghana (then Gold Coast) in a private visit in 1951.[34]

Such timorous moves and statements swiftly declined when the transformative Korean War altered U.S. priorities. Americans became more interested in military help than making a good impression on local Africans, as in Acheson's pursuit of combat forces. Courteously declining an offer from Liberia, he said yes to Ethiopia, which sent three battalions to Korea, one after another. Ethiopia in return became eligible for U.S. military aid. Officials muted any disapproval of South African apartheid, and McGhee grew alarmed about Africa as a "fertile field for communism." The African peoples, he said in a 1951 speech, should not be fooled by inducements from communists, who would give them "a dark future of political and cultural enslavement" rather than independence. While not utterly stilling liberal sentiments, after 25 June 1950, Americans said far less than before about human rights or even eventual independence.[35]

"A Dog with a Green Tail"

The state department hardly flicked an eye at Belgium's disgraceful rule in the Congo, where the United States obtained most of its uranium for nuclear weapons. Belgians reportedly had "an almost morbid hypersensitivity" to any expressions of American interest in the Congo, but they need not have worried. Washington valued Belgium as a NATO member and owner of the coveted uranium ore, whose "uninterrupted flow" the department considered the highest priority in relations with Brussels, which cannily wrung considerable funds in return, both for the home country and Congo. Nervousness in 1951 at how rising African anti-colonialism might affect the ore supply reduced any temptation to interfere in Congo's internal rule, and Foggy Bottom was ready to resist any such efforts in the UN.[36]

Well before Korea, in November 1948, the state department had exhibited both unease about South Africa's racial practices and satisfaction at its reliable cold war record. Besides, South Africa was another uranium source, and good bilateral relations were of "great importance," Acheson said in December 1951 while instructing his UN delegation to avoid alienating South Africans with charged references to human rights. Although unwilling to lift a hand to change the character of the South African regime, policymakers hoped it could find a quiet way to preserve itself without outraging the world or throwing the large, nonfranchised black majority into the hands of the communists. McGhee's own Texas background, he testified, engendered "sympathy" for South Africans' "extremely difficult racial problem."[37]

A diminishing supply of Congolese uranium raised the value of South Africa's lode. Pretoria also sent fighter pilots to Korea and paid its lend-lease debt. India reviled the South African regime and, in the fall of 1950, when it raised South African treatment of Indian workers and immigrants in the UN, the U.S. delegation tried to act as conciliator. The Americans also needed India's votes on Korea, and, trying a few weeks later to gain its support against Chinese intervention, supported an Indian resolution urging an end to the apartheid system established by Pretoria after its 1948 elections. Acheson told the South Africans he had no choice, given the "critical situation in Asia." As an offset, he offered eligibility for military aid within the MDAP program.[38]

Growing awareness of South Africa's racial "repression" failed to outweigh U.S. appreciation of cold war loyalty, Pretoria's mineral supplies, and its "strategic position in time of war." In December 1951, Acheson fretted about problems in chrome and manganese shipments and was probably unaware of an earlier report from the embassy on a meeting with angry black South Africans. Denying they were communists, they asserted that Moscow rather than Washington sided with "their struggle against oppression." They expected little from "a broken power" like Britain but did from "the great western exponent of freedom." But in 1951–52, Washington's priorities remained chrome, manganese, and uranium, and there was little bite in Acheson's advice to adopt more humane racial policies. The U.S. delegation continued to cushion South Africa from attacks in the UN. At a Princeton seminar in 1954, Acheson denied there was any "possibility" of taking "any useful action" on South Africa.[39]

Some of this pessimism came from his last months in office, when EUR's George Perkins told him South Africa's "extreme measures" against blacks might lead to a constitutional crisis, and that "serious disturbances" would menace access to strategic minerals as well as damage U.S.-South African relations.

Pretoria was clearly "heading for serious trouble." In the same month, an asser-tive NAACP convention at home demanded an end to backing South Africa's "cruel and barbaric white supremacy doctrine," as well as its "cold-blooded" design to swallow other territories, including South West Africa. Washington was again caught between protecting hard things like manganese and getting on the right side of history. The synthesis, emerging in the late summer of 1952 when Brazil advanced a resolution on South West Africa, was an irresolute call for delay.[40]

This was hard to repeat in September 1952, when India more aggressively determined to shine a UN spotlight on apartheid. It seemed not to occur to American officials that this brand of racial totalitarianism was no improvement on the "socialist" brand in the USSR. India's initiative, coinciding with the tumult over French North Africa, drew widespread support. As might be expected, Acheson straddled, supporting some kind of resolution while urging New Delhi not to exacerbate South Africa's human rights situation with blunt solu-tions. He instructed his delegation to allow discussion of apartheid but block efforts to make South Africa answerable to the UN. The result was another innocuous endorsement of racial equality that did not even mention South Africa. Concerned about a precedent that might bite back at U.S. racial practices, he wanted any resolution to be so minute in particulars that, unlike all other cases, it could "be described as if it involved a dog with a green tail and pink eyes and blue legs." He told South Africa's ambassador he had done his best amid hostile domestic and international opinion. But he again chided his delegates for swoon-ing over "glowing principles" and "dropping" the ball in defending concrete U.S. interests.[41]

By 1954, he feared "anti-western" revolutionary impulses might explode throughout Africa and deplored how little attention foreign offices paid to the coming crisis. This seemed a revisionist concern of a retired statesman, con-sidering how little his own foreign office had done. Under his watch, prevailing American racial views and preoccupation with supporting allies pushed policy far from supposed national historical principles. In later years, he wandered even farther. As he journeyed to the right, he cultivated a growing relish at condemn-ing the United Nations, whose fixed institutional habits he thought had caused most of the conflicts with friends over such distant and insignificant places as Morocco, Tunisia, and South Africa.[42]

Personally Free of the Slightest Suspicion of Paternity

President Truman was unsentimental about the United Nations but said many of the right things to encourage its development and used it effectively to national advantage. Acheson, in contrast, hardly cared who knew of his contempt for the organization. Since he never held high expectations for the UN, he was unsur-prised at its flaws. It was an intellectual error, he always thought, to think of it as a body apart. The UN's only strength came from "those who belong to it and are willing to back it up." He would use the UN when necessary to advance U.S. policies, but otherwise, as in the Truman Doctrine, he made no bones about ignoring it. He snorted at the foundational principle of one-state, one-vote. As a rationalist, he honored reasoned debate, but he considered such debates valuable only when they occurred among those already in agreement on fundamentals. In any case, especially when debates occurred in an open forum, they did not settle world disputes. A vital deficiency of the UN was that members with no stakes in major controversies had equal claim to orate on them to an attentive audience, forcing responses from those who did have their security on the line. His experience told him that solutions to international problems originated not in debate but in vigilant statecraft backed by economic, political, and military power. The marshaling of such power conquered the Axis, quelled the Greek crisis, and charted the path to European recovery. NATO, a politico-military alliance rather than a conversational forum, ensured that recovery and gave Soviet leaders reason to act prudently. Swift use of force averted a ruinous loss of repute in Korea. The most intractable problems arose where it was impossible to apply such strength, in China, Indochina, and most of the Middle East.

The controversies of 1951–52 strongly reinforced already negative views of the UN. Overlooking his own use of the General Assembly in the Korean War to circumvent Soviet vetoes in the Security Council, he condemned the power artificially given to miniature states and diminutive duchies to force public debates in the Assembly on any question they fancied, even when millions of words had no chance to actually affect the situations addressed. It was "intolerable," he wrote in 1961, to force the United States "to vote on every resolution, however theoretical, however hostile to one of its allies, which any country may regard as useful in a propaganda campaign." It had also been a mistake to put UN headquarters in Manhattan, because it cast a specially glaring spotlight on the United States. He scorned enthusiasts whose hearts fluttered at the thought of universal harmony and the UN's promise to end war and conflict to the end of time. He believed, David McLellan writes, that "people who could not face the truth about human nature were for the UN; people who fairly squished with the juice of human kindness but who had a pretty soggy brain were also for the UN; people who preferred to preserve their illusions intact favored the UN."[43]

At the time he became secretary of state, the *New York Times* expected Acheson to give the UN little more than "perfunctory support." This was true enough, but he also used its annual sessions to advantage, huddling with allies for important work and lobbying others. In State's 1949 reorganization, the U.S. delegation came under the bureau of United Nations affairs. The first officer of note with responsibility for UN matters, Rusk was aghast at the mission's size, nearly 250 people. On learning that Turkey managed with one and Britain with seven, he cut his force to 150, getting "more work done because we spent less time reading each other's papers." The nominative head of the UN mission in

Acheson's tenure was Republican Warren Austin, whom he considered equal to Arthur Vandenberg in his "hyperbolic sincerity." Though loyal, Austin was never inside the rooms where officials made important diplomatic calculations. As infirmities overtook him, his deputy Ernest Gross became a virtual acting ambassador.[44]

From the first, Acheson had little use for Secretary-General Trygve Lie, once a Norwegian foreign minister, and even less after Lie's spring 1950 "peace campaign." Beginning with a Washington speech (almost in chorus with the Stockholm Peace Appeal for the Prohibition of the Atomic Weapon), Lie conducted a whirlwind "let's make peace" tour of London, Paris, and Moscow touting a "twenty-year peace plan." On 20 April, in an audience with Truman and Acheson, he waxed eloquent on the UN's stellar role in Greece, Korea, and Indonesia. Acheson, who thought his peace plan "sounded very much like appeasement," bit his tongue instead of saying that U.S. policy and power had done most of the work. After Lie made another round of capitals to offer his plan, the White House snubbed him, Truman saying "his schedule was pretty full." More bluntly, on 7 June 1950, Acheson remarked publicly that the Soviets were the authors of current world tensions and disputed Lie's suggestions that cold war conflicts could be negotiated away. Instead, "we must carry forward in our own determination to create situations of strength in the free world, because this is the only basis on which lasting agreement with the Soviet Government is possible."[45]

But how quickly the contemptible can become the estimable! After North Korea sent its tanks south and the UN became South Korea's official defenders, Lie rallied to the flag. When his original Soviet sponsors wanted to discard him, Acheson sprang to his defense. India was ready to nominate a replacement as Lie's term neared its end, but Acheson asked Ernest Bevin to help scotch the effort. In an argument that lasted weeks, the Security Council's five permanent members failed to agree on a candidate, and new contenders sprang up in Mexico, Lebanon, India, and the Philippines. The Soviets wanted a Pole but hinted they could support any Latin Americans. When Britain and France said they favored Lie but would not veto another choice, Austin cracked the whip—it was Lie or nothing. Then Acheson cracked his whip on the Latin Americans, threatening to veto any choice but Lie. He would not endure having the Soviets punish Lie or let them "get away" with an assault prejudicing "our victory in Korea." He instructed his mission to "pull no punches" but could not prevent the USSR from stopping Lie's formal reelection by the Security Council. Instead, on 1 November 1950, Washington managed to get his term extended three years with a 46–5 vote in the General Assembly, following which Acheson allowed an empty discussion of Lie's "peace plan." Two years later, Lie resigned. American McCarthyites disliked him, and the Soviets never recognized his second-term authority. In 1953, after Acheson's departure, Swedish economist Dag Hammarskjöld succeeded Lie.[46]

Acheson was always alert to the UN's uses and opposed members of Congress who wanted Moscow's membership stripped, which, he explained, would simply free it from Charter obligations and eliminate "almost the only remaining forum in which the free world" could talk to the Russians. But he never forgave the UN for giving power to petty states to embarrass the United States before a world audience. Arabs and Latin Americans, he told Canadians in 1952, had "contributed little or nothing" to collective security, and the debates they generated, he added years later, were "usually rude" and full of insulting exchanges. Another defect was the UN's built-in dedication to the status quo. Opposing all wars because "change" always led to instability was a "very dangerous" view, he said in 1954, noting that such views would have blocked the American revolution. In fact, wars often resulted in "a great deal of progress."

Most of his criticisms were less philosophical and more derisive, as in a reference to FDR's keenness for "that delusive phrase 'the United Nations.'" When Gross told him the deputy UN job attracted him for its "potentialities," Acheson "practically ordered me to go to a psychiatrist" and "thought I ought to have my head examined." Acheson's friend George Ball became UN ambassador in the 1960s, prompting a letter from P Street: "I always thought you were one of the brightest guys in town, but now I'm reserving a room for you at St. Elizabeth's." The UN, he agreed, was "certainly an American contribution to a troubled world," but he was personally "free of the slightest suspicion of paternity." In his curmudgeonly years of indiscretion, he claimed to believe the United States had corrupted diplomacy with its "damned moralism, beginning with Woodrow Wilson's self-determination and ending with that little rat Leo Pasvolsky's United Nations."[47]

Interviewed by an obituarist in 1970, Acheson said he "never thought the U.N. was worth a damn. To a lot of people it was a Holy Grail, and those who set store by it had the misfortune to believe their own bunk." This was shooting from the hip, but much of Acheson's critique deserves consideration. Insofar as the UN had succeeded, he remarked in 1951 to a room of magazine and book publishers, it was because of "the strength of the United States, its economic strength, its military strength." Thus, it had similarities to NATO. The only reason either organization achieved results was that American strength and power were present "at the heart."

Acheson spent hundreds of hours sustaining and working with allies, but a so-called universal organization was another matter, intrinsically inhospitable to great power guidance. The UN's champions lauded it as a forum for weak nations and powerless peoples and a safety valve for venting accumulated injustices. He thought letting off steam was hardly a form of diplomacy and likely to scald those nearby. United Nations paladins praised the egalitarianism of the General Assembly, while Acheson sneered at the illusion of national equality in international affairs. Defenders believed the UN allowed a more virtuous diplomacy than that practiced behind closed doors. Acheson, who in a 1962 public appearance remarked that he had always thought "the very conception of a door is that it might be closed," would have laughed and pointed to the General Assembly itself, rife with cynical trading of votes from one bloc to another. And UN advocates might insist that, other shortcomings aside, special UN agencies on hunger, women, children, and drug addiction did neglected and invaluable work. A disbelieving Acheson would have poured water on this tribute in the same spirit with which he wrote off NATO's Article 2, which embodied "every worthy aspiration that ever occurred to any human being." Truman was proud of the UN's American origins and oversaw its founding. Acheson, his greatest secretary of state, worked with it because he must, but he was not its friend.[48]

31

PICKING UP STICKS IN
EGYPT AND IRAN

Introduction

It is virtually impossible to change one part of the world without causing dangerous shifts in others, and in this, actors in world politics are sometimes like wallpaper hangers. As soon as they get one corner of the roll to stick, another unrolls, and they have to start over. Hanging new wallpaper—trying to make something close to what the world formerly looked like—while trying to get into the swing of new rhythms is especially hard, if not impossible. This is what American officials tried to do in the colonial and ex-colonial world of the 1940s and 1950s.

World War II dealt fatal blows to the British, French, and Dutch empires, and though postwar friction first emerged in Europe, Washington knew it would also materialize in the debris of those empires. The prospect posed two key questions. How could the United States assure that strategically important colonies, ex-colonies, or soon-to-be-ex-colonies would stay with the "west" and free of communist domination? And how could the United States secure them for the west without wrecking its relations with either the former European colonial rulers or those they formerly ruled? To put it another way, how could the United States, newly convinced it had interests to protect throughout the world, sort through empire's wreckage without inadvertently stirring up new trouble that communists might exploit? As in the child's game, Pick-Up Sticks, when players have first dropped their sticks, bits and pieces of old European possessions and protectorates lay strewn all over the floor, precariously piled in Asia, Africa, and the Middle East. Americans sorted through them, hoping to avoid missteps causing further derangement. They could use several kinds of sticks in their sorting: conventional diplomacy, trade and economic assistance, military force, or the Black Sticks of clandestine operations added by the Eisenhower administration.[1]

Work on the third world pile continually produced confirmation of the law of unintended consequences. Trying to co-opt revolutionaries seeking independence and national identity with methods that would assuage allies usually antagonized both. When Americans backed France in Indochina, the French became more dependent and the Vietnamese nationalists and revolutionaries grew more resentful and determined. Pressing Paris on colonial questions incensed the French, with ripple effects hurtful to NATO and German rearmament. Refusing unqualified support for anti-colonialists in the UN made the United States look, to them, like the European colonialists. Americans found no middle ground to stand on, no way to pick up one stick without stirring others—not from ineptitude or stupidity but because it was impossible to be close friends of both imperial states and those resisting their rule.

These diplomatic straddles dominated U.S. efforts to referee or defuse conflicts between Britain and two increasingly combustible nations in the Middle East. The first was Egypt, a British protectorate in a system begun in 1882 and now run under a 1936 treaty. The second was Iran, which private British interests, strongly backed by the government, had made a virtual oil fiefdom. Acheson's expenditure of time in 1951–52 on these conflicts was extraordinary. As he picked his way along, this so-called anglophile repeatedly clashed with London. Yet when ultimately forced to choose between anti-colonial revolutionaries and Washington's prime ally, he predictably opted for the latter. He did it, however, with sufficient balance that, when he left office, neither Egyptians nor Iranians considered the United States their foe. That would quickly change, especially in Iran, where Eisenhower's CIA overthrew the government in 1953, leaving in its trail a land mine that exploded a quarter century later in the mullahs' rage against the "Great Satan."[2]

Egyptian and Iranian leaders in 1951–52 did not connive to defy Britain in chorus, but they did act at the same time. Because Acheson was seeking a middle ground in both these theaters of tension, they require examination in parallel in this and the following chapter. The British, like the French, demanded loyalty from Washington. The Americans pleaded for concessions and flexibility to achieve a larger good.

Setting Some Scenes

For years, the oil and its by-products that kept automobiles humming, tool-and-die machines running, tanks moving, and cruisers cruising had become a locus of interest in the Middle East. Americans first paid close attention in the 1920s, when the United States became a net importer of oil. In the late 1940s, it wanted to keep Middle Eastern oil out of Soviet hands and available to a recovering western Europe. Other U.S. economic interests in the Middle East were far less important, whether imports for civilians (figs, oriental rugs) or soldiers (copper, molybdenum). The need to secure the Trans-Arabian Pipeline (TAPLINE), built by the Arabian American Oil Company (Aramco), to the Mediterranean, shaped relations with Syria, Lebanon, and Saudi Arabia.

While Raymond Hare, the new U.S. ambassador in Riyadh in 1950, negotiated with the Saudis for an air base, the privately owned Aramco did its own negotiating. Touchy about how its subjects would react to the alien Americans, and aware of the wartime U.S. decision to split oil profits evenly with Venezuela, the Saudi royal family wanted and got better deals on both oil and the air base. First in December 1950 came the oil bargain, by which Aramco paid half its net operating income to the Saudis. Then came a new five-year agreement, which the royals wanted kept quiet, on the Dhahran air base and packages of military and Point Four aid. Hare worried that U.S. support for Israel and the presence of infidel Americans would disturb future relations. Scouting for ways to gain the Saudis' trust, early in 1952 Washington sent Truman's physician to treat King Ibn Saud, who had once told a junketing U.S. general that if he "could find a Communist in Saudi Arabia, I will hand you his head."

London resented the growing U.S. influence in its old stomping ground, but Acheson and his colleagues in fact hoped the British could continue to play a large role in the region. Yet it soon became evident the two nations had divergent goals. London aimed to protect concrete economic and territorial interests. Washington, seeking to shore up the defense of Europe with Middle Eastern assets, looked for obliging local nationalists who could help block Soviet expansion. Though Great Britain was a natural U.S. ally, by 1951 Assistant Secretary George McGhee thought it was also a strategic millstone. Acheson demanded a "more affirmative" policy to protect "vital" U.S. "security interests in the Middle East."[3]

As Korea and rearmament in Europe made possession of oil more vital, the link grew between Europe and defense of the Middle East, increasing the leverage of nations sitting atop the oil reserves. Britain was trying to renew outmoded agreements on oil and military bases with Egypt, Iran, and Iraq. With its imperial sway waning from India to Palestine, with an eye on commerce and its influence in Asia and Australasia, London grew more anxious to affirm its prewar authority. In many respects, both Arab nationalists and Americans seemed more worrisome to it than the Russians. Iranians demanded an Aramco-like deal from the Anglo-Iran Oil Company (AIOC), the giant British firm holding Iranian oil concessions. Cairo wanted control of Sudan for itself. It also wanted the departure of British troops, who guarded the Suez Canal and enforced London's Egyptian protectorate. Iraq blasted its 1930 treaty with Britain as "outdated and incompatible with current world developments." Only in Jordan, widely considered Britain's lackey, did its power seem intact.[4]

Washington had an embassy in Cairo but, since Egypt had long been a dependency of either the Ottomans or British, seldom treated it as a sovereign state. In contrast, Persia ("Iran" since 1935) had always been independent. The United States opened diplomatic relations with Persia in 1856 but showed scant interest in it until the 1920s. After the early cold war crisis of 1946 passed, Washington worried only intermittently about Soviet threats to Iran. It almost never worried about a direct communist design on Egypt, but it did fear that in a general war the Soviets might vault over the "Northern Tier" (along a Turkey-Iraq-Iran line) to seize oil supplies, capture the Suez bastion, and destroy or neutralize SAC bases. Partly because Britain then had far more military and naval resources in the region, Acheson looked to U.S.-UK cooperation "to create strength in the area." As Washington focused on general cold war threats and London concentrated on shoring up its eroding imperial holdings and communications, both tried enlisting Egypt at the center of its system in efforts that generated much wheel spinning but little else.[5]

We will see more about these defense schemes below, but here a brief foreshadowing is desirable. American officials thought that if they could draw links between the Northern Tier and its European allies, Arab and Turkish armies in a war could delay Soviet invaders as Anglo-Americans fell back on Suez to stage a counterattack. The need to organize this rear trench caused grudging U.S. support for British plans to fashion security on an "Arab foundation." In addition, London had in mind having a British officer atop NATO's Mediterranean command. The first British design centered on Egypt and was called the Middle East Command, or MEC. At various times, British and Americans considered France, Turkey, Australia, New Zealand, South Africa, Pakistan, other Arab states, and even Israel, as candidates for the MEC, all possibly linked to NATO. Besides anti-Soviet defense, the British hoped the MEC would resolve tensions with Egypt, preserving their grip on Suez. Though often quite skeptically, the Americans were mainly interested in a method for deterring or defending against Soviet aggression in a secondary theater.[6]

But Acheson's interest went beyond military concerns, thinking that a modernized Egypt might be just the ticket for establishing a Middle Eastern position of strength. Since *modernized* might mean *revolutionary*, or at least *anti-imperialist*, this idea would surely not make Britain happy. Acheson himself was ambivalent about such a prospect, but his interest in co-opting Egypt for the west powered his support for the MEC. In any event, both Britons and Americans would be shocked when all Arab states said no to the MEC. Under McGhee's pressure, Acheson persuaded himself that a Pakistani involvement would make the idea more palatable to Cairo. Even as, by fits and starts, he would grow skeptical about the MEC, his aides and the British made strenuous efforts to gain Egypt's adherence. But some of Egypt's "modernizers" would think instead the time had come to throw the British out altogether and the Egyptian government that tolerated them.[7]

The Iranian story also warrants a preview. In 1949, Acheson had resisted Iran's efforts to milk large assistance from Washington. His retrospective judgment that State's approach to Iran then had lacked "decisiveness and vigor" seems excessive, considering that Iran was six thousand miles away and bordered on a Russia that had always considered its neighbor a matter of vital interest. Moreover, Britain held Iran's oil and refineries, and Americans did not have the benefit of inside connections with the regime of Shah Mohammed Reza Pahlavi. In a period of rocky U.S.-Iranian relations, Tehran stayed neutral in Korea and shut down Voice of America transmitters on its soil. It also exhibited noticeable ingratitude for military aid shipments, prompting Acheson to warn the Shah against trying to extort more aid by playing a Soviet card.[8]

Before long, Muhammad Mosadeq would supersede the youthful Shah as the focal point of Acheson's attention. As prime minister, this magnetic leader would directly challenge AIOC, the British behemoth that, unlike most regional oil enterprises, produced a raft of valuable refined petroleum products. The London government held the majority of stock in AIOC, its largest foreign investment. AIOC was a vital source of hard currency and of the petroleum powering the Royal Navy. Centered at the Abadan refinery in the delta of the Shatt al-Arab river near the Persian Gulf, AIOC had long dominated the Iranian economy. Abadan was the world's largest, most complex, and versatile refinery, and, writes Howard M. Sachar, "an economic heritage of all but measureless value." While Iranians did the dirty work, Britons held the top jobs and took all the profits home, paying British rather than Iranian taxes. AIOC charged high prices in Iran for its products and bought Iranian politicians at low prices.[9]

Americans had been urging London to make better terms since 1948. They grew more fretful when the war in Korea turned a world oil surplus into a perceived shortage, but AIOC responded with huge production increases that left cash-poor Iran more frustrated than ever, especially after learning it was receiving less than half in annual royalties what the company paid the UK government in *taxes*. AIOC even withheld these royalties in reprisal for Tehran's failure to ratify a "supplemental agreement" negotiated in 1949, supposedly an improvement for Iran over a 1933 accord. Iranians, Acheson wrote, felt "a sense of grievance that a vast natural resource was being extracted by foreigners under arrangements thought unfair to those living on the surface." The "unusual and persistent stupidity" of AIOC and the British cabinet aggravated the controversy. But most Americans thought it near impossible to work with the Iranians, too, "like eating soup with a fork," said McGhee. In Acheson's view the crisis opened "rare opportunities for Communist propaganda," leading possibly to "a Communist *coup d' état*" or Britain's expulsion. Even more than in Egypt, Washington was impatient with Britain while reluctant to undercut it.[10]

Harbingers of Crises

Before the onset of the AIOC affair, U.S. concerns in Iran mostly fixed on its exposure to the Soviet Union. Acheson still thought the regime of the Shah was like the Chiang gang on Formosa: corrupt at heart and unsalvageable by U.S. aid. He warned the Shah that his serial coquetting with Moscow would have the "worst possible effect" on U.S. public opinion. With respect to the AIOC, however, he believed Iran's demands were reasonable and wanted a settlement allowing it to pay its own way in the world. Because he wanted a fresh start and thought the current U.S. ambassador, John Cooper Wiley, had succumbed to localitis, in the spring of 1950 Acheson replaced him with Henry Grady. This veteran had successfully navigated worrisome missions to India, Palestine, and Greece but was the wrong man to dampen the monarch's ambitions. The Shah soon decided the liberal Grady, an expansive Irish-American of anglophobic leanings, was just the one to open the American cornucopia. Grady held a doctorate in economics and misread Acheson's bolstering of the embassy economic staff as a commitment to an ambitious aid program.[11]

Anti-foreign militants greeted Grady's arrival with riots. By the time he unpacked, Washington was already scolding London on the AIOC affair. Iran's new prime minister, Ali Razmara, said his government would not ratify the supplemental agreement until AIOC put more Iranians at management desks and opened its books (Iran was a 20 percent shareholder). He also wanted AIOC to tie Iranian prices for refined products to local costs rather than world prices. He did not threaten nationalization. Acheson urged him to eschew any more drastic nostrums and held aid hostage to making progress toward resolution of the conflict. But he also accused AIOC of a narrow-minded disregard for the diplomatic impact of its actions. Ironically, he put more pressure on London than Tehran because the British were easier to "talk to." This apparent bias alarmed Clement Attlee's government. The state department thought it far more likely the Iranian government might collapse at the hands of the outlawed and subversive Tudeh (Masses) Party, but Truman worried about Soviet efforts to court Tehran and Razmara's apparently welcoming embrace.[12]

Grady had confidence in the "reasonable" Razmara but not the "irrational, nationalist" Majlis, the popular branch of the Iranian legislature. With both Iran and Britain aware of the impending Aramco deal, by mid-September 1950 the state department grew concerned about Iran's rising "hatred" of Britain. McGhee, a onetime oil geophysicist with years of contacts with AIOC, flew to London to talk sense to both the government and company. They were shocked at his "bombshell" of classified information on the Aramco contract and unhappy when he direly warned that if they rejected Razmara's requests, AIOC could "forget" about any chances for compromise as soon as the Iranians heard of the Saudi deal. Right now Razmara still opposed nationalization, McGhee noted, but he would have to act vigorously in behalf of Iranian interests to maintain his position.

A past Oxford student and future chairman of the English-Speaking Union, McGhee admired things British, but his brazen sermons outraged London officials, who viewed him as an "infant prodigy" fronting for U.S. oil companies. By his own account, AIOC board members told him "to mind my own business" and insisted they knew how to handle the Iranians, who would "take a mile" if "given an inch." AIOC's determination to hang tough convinced him it was essential for the government to seize policymaking from the company. In fact, the cabinet already had such power but found it convenient to deflect U.S. and Iranian anger to AIOC.[13]

As in Indochina and North Africa, these attempts to discover a middle road riled both sides. For weeks after China's intervention in Korea, Washington feared a general war, underlining the need for secure oil supplies. If Iran slid into Moscow's hands, the west would lose prestige as well as petroleum. If Britain tarried in offering compromises to alleviate Iran's economic and political disorder, it would invite a renewed surge of hypernationalism that could throw the government into Tudeh hands. On the other hand, putting too much pressure on the British to compromise could cause damage, too. The CIA near the end of 1950 estimated that a loss of AIOC assets would wreak havoc in Britain's economy, with wide repercussions, including the possibility of deranging European finances and stopping the western military buildup in its tracks. In such a scenario, the United States at the least would have to reopen its treasury so Britain and the Europeans could make ends meet.

Acheson still thought the burden was on Britain to act flexibly, but he hoped to persuade it to do so without making Iran think about playing the two powers against one another or simply grow more unyielding. This helps explain why Washington never executed a $25 million Export-Import Bank loan for Iran and why the administration did not press the World Bank to approve a $10 million loan for Tehran. As relations with Iran spiraled downward at the end of 1950, Razmara, convinced he faced an Anglo-American conspiracy, made a trade agreement with Moscow, spurned small U.S. loans, canceled VOA and BBC relay station rights, and apparently connived in the escape of imprisoned members of Tudeh.[14]

In November 1950, Acheson implored the ailing Ernest Bevin to end the oil quagmire, alerting him to the likely impact of the imminent Aramco deal. Most U.S. officials disliked Razmara in the first place; if he tried selling Iranian oil to the Soviet bloc, he might activate the Battle Act, cutting off all U.S. aid and forcing withdrawal of the small U.S. military mission in Iran. It was not Acheson's aim, but western subversion of Razmara was in the wind as a solution. Washington had already begun a covert program to reduce Soviet and Tudeh influence in 1948, and early in 1951 the administration became aware of British attempts to undermine Razmara. At the same time, it became increasingly evident that AIOC's behavior in Iran was egregious. While selling oil to the British military at huge discounts, it made profits of £100 million in 1950 alone, though it had paid Iran only £50 million in royalties over five years. It offered no management jobs to Iranians but recruited Indians for unskilled jobs. The ember setting off all this dry tinder was Razmara's assassination on 7 March 1951.[15]

The issues in Egypt were different but the pattern similar, including a new ambassador in the person of the sixty-three-year-old Louisianan, Jefferson Caffery, the U.S. diplomatic corps' senior envoy. He had first headed an embassy in 1926 and most recently been ambassador to France. Now Caffery, his wife, and his valet debarked in Alexandria from the *S.S. Excambion*. Presenting his credentials in September 1949, he quickly became a kind of American "viceroy." His work was cut out for him, for the CIA considered King Farouk's goals—from expulsion of the British to the destruction of Israel—as hostile. London may have seen Caffery's appointment to mean Acheson would move independently in Egypt. At first, in fact, he hoped Caffery could nudge Farouk toward a new agreement with the UK.[16]

The impulse toward Anglo-American accord came as Washington was still deferring to London in the region and had given little thought to Egypt. As late as July 1950, McGhee viewed the quarrel over the stationing of British troops at Suez as a bilateral matter of no interest to his own government. The more Americans paid attention, however, the more they grew wary of British policies, a case in point being Sudan. Though once described by General Charles "Gordon of Khartoum" as "a useless possession, ever was and ever will be," Sudan had long been the object of Anglo-Egyptian competition. The two nations had jointly ruled there since 1899, but Cairo now wanted sole control, for Sudan contained the source of the Nile, and its northern reaches had been part of Egypt for twenty-seven centuries.[17]

Nor were Americans much interested in British ideas about Middle Eastern defense until Korea forced greater attention to all military issues. As the Sixth Fleet moved from Suez's approaches to Europe's southern flank, the state department grew more concerned about preserving the British presence in Egypt. Acheson therefore was unhappy when the visiting Egyptian foreign minister, Mohammed Salaheddin, told him in October 1950 that his country would not cooperate in any regional defense ideas until Britain left. If Washington supplied arms, the Arab states could protect the Middle East themselves. Not planning to go quietly, London spun out new ideas for an independent or autonomous Sudan and a joint British-Egyptian defense apparatus. Now viewing Egypt not as a stopping off point on the transit to India but a cold war asset, Bevin was determined to maintain the Suez complex, Britain's most important foreign base.[18]

With Caffery saying U.S. influence in Egypt was "higher than it has been for years," the state department rummaged for ways to do even better, readier than before to move independently of Britain in the eastern Mediterranean basin. For months, McGhee had tried enlisting Acheson against the Pentagon toward a larger U.S. role. Thinking about why the war began in Korea, he wanted ringing declarations of U.S. interest to deter any attack on the Middle East. When the joint chiefs resisted with pleas of scarce resources, he quoted to them from an NSC-68 annex, to the effect that one should not let large commitments in one area "jeopardize capabilities to act" in others. Since Britain no longer had the power to defend its old treaty rights, he wanted them surrendered in "Egypt, Jordan and Iraq."[19]

This diminishing British ability to apply military power in the area opened McGhee to cooperative regional schemes. Along the same course of thought, on 27 January 1951 Acheson warily asked the defense department for ideas about fortifying western positions on an arc from South Asia to the Middle East. He understood that a large role for the United States would make it a target for Arabs' multiple grievances. Since in the Moscow embassy's view the Soviets might also be thinking about cultivating the "relatively quiet and neglected Near East garden," he began pressing for unprecedented U.S. involvement. But in a 30 January meeting, the Pentagon resisted, still licking its wounds from China's onslaught in Korea. The chiefs dismissed the Middle East as an inferior theater and insisted on funneling scarce resources to NATO and Korea. McGhee was "kidding" himself and dealing "in illusions," thought General Lawton Collins. After meetings in Istanbul, however, McGhee was even more certain the British approach in Egypt endangered western interests and must change.[20]

Tentative Opposition to "Victorian Paternalism" and the "Big Stick"

Proof that constructive change came too slowly was abundant throughout 1951, as Britain's relations with both Egypt and Iran careened toward breakdown. Ongoing discussions about Middle Eastern defense organizations that would center on Egypt were like Alice's conversations in Wonderland, completely ignoring evidence of Egypt's stiff rejection of all of them. In another unreal moment, McGhee in April 1951 marketed a Pentagon idea in London that would defend the "Northern Tier" with forces from Pakistan, India, Iran, and Iraq but include no Americans. In May, Washington accepted the different British notion of a Middle East Command (MEC) linked to NATO and headed by a British admiral (partially compensating for Churchill's failure to get a countryman on top of NATO's Mediterranean Command). Besides Egypt, the Americans now wanted a role for Pakistan in the MEC, for quite unclear reasons.[21]

Meanwhile, the British were hurtling toward conflict with Egypt. The Egyptians were demanding evacuation of UK forces, while the Americans were insisting on a negotiated settlement, but the teetering Labor government in London was defiant and, McGhee reported in the first week of April, ready to use force. In May, members of the Egyptian parliament ripped into the British as "dogs," called for a "non-aggression treaty with Russia," "melodramatically tore up a copy of the 1936 Treaty to tumultuous applause," and berated Washington for sticking with the offending imperialists. With Egypt's rejection of MEC now clear beyond a doubt, other potential participants—Turkey, Iran,

Greece—voiced reservations. In Britain, former Tory foreign secretary Anthony Eden trumpeted that use of the "big stick" would silence Egypt (a view he wanted "his friend, Dean Acheson" to hear). The Labor ministers, meantime, had run out of ideas.[22]

At one point, Salaheddin told McGhee to consider events in Iran a "practical lesson to us, to you, and to the British." While still blaming London for those events, Washington urged restraint on the Iranians, a hope challenged on 7 March 1951 when Prime Minister Razmara died at the hands of a Fedayan-e Eslam assassin, triggering riots and strikes in both Tehran and Abadan. The Shah named another middle-road opponent of nationalization to succeed Razmara over opposition of the Majlis. Led by a minority of the recently organized National Front, the legislators resolved to seize control of the nation's petroleum and began making plans to that end. Ironically, Washington's stingy aid policy and insistence on economic self-reliance helped propel this drive for more sweeping measures.[23]

Since the Labor government had nationalized the coal, electricity, and railroad industries in the UK, it could hardly object in principle to Tehran's nationalizing the AIOC. Instead, it claimed Iran in this particular case could not do it, citing a 1933 agreement purportedly waiving the right. This riled Acheson, who urged both sides to negotiate a settlement. Although he was already stepping back from any embrace of the Anglo cousins, he was not quite ready to reach out to an increasingly unruly Tehran, and he barred sending it emergency economic aid for fear of encouraging other countries to stage similar crises. Hardly noticing his circumspection, the British were in a steady state of umbrage because of their dealings with the thirty-nine-year-old McGhee. Only realization that Acheson's views were identical kept them from an official protest of McGhee's advice.[24]

This stage of the Anglo-Iranian crisis came to a head in April 1951. The new Iranian premier resigned, and National Front activists demanded a replacement favoring nationalization. One of its own advisers thought AIOC was then "confused, hidebound, small-minded and blind." The U.S. and British governments could not agree on what to do. Acheson warned against trying to manipulate the choice of a new prime minister and even more against any thoughts of a military intervention. A discouraged Franks, who had been McGhee's "moral tutor" at Oxford, told Acheson in confidence that settlement depended on the cabinet's pulling the negotiations out of the hands of AIOC officers, whose "Victorian paternalism," Grady predicted from Tehran, would lead to "outright confiscation." Acheson tried to mask differences with Britain to prevent their exploitation by Iran, an effort not noticed in London, which charged him with appeasement. On 28 April, the Majlis passed a nationalization bill. Though denying its legality, the UK seemed to act temperately by appealing to the International Court of Justice for arbitration. In reality, the British were spoiling for a fight and drawing up plans for airborne drops to seize Abadan. Already the presumptive owners of the subsoil petroleum, Iranians now intended to seize the rest of the profit-making apparatus in a revolutionary bid to achieve national identity and independence. On the 29th, the Shah, who had no love for Britain, acquiesced in the Majlis bill and named the sixty-nine-year-old Mosadeq prime minister.[25]

With Bevin's death two weeks earlier, Acheson was rapidly losing hope Britain would abandon its pigheaded Iranian diplomacy. "Never had so few lost so much so stupidly and so fast," he wrote later. Britain had forfeited a chance to do as Aramco in Saudi Arabia, "graciously" surrendering "what it no longer had the power to withhold," and thus now "had to use the Iranian vocabulary." What he now feared was the derangement of relations with other "oil-producing states" and the creation of "rare opportunities for Communist propaganda." British actions "might drive Iran to a Communist *coup d'état*, or Iran might drive Britain out of the country. Either would be a major disaster. We were deeply concerned," he recalled.[26]

The government in London was also impaired by an ailing Attlee, the mortal illness of its chancellor of the exchequer, and the resignation of Aneurin Bevan, the popular founder of the state health system, with the result that the remnant cabinet had become even more intransigent. Acheson considered the new foreign secretary, sixty-three-year-old Herbert Morrison (whose wife was also gravely ill), simply ignorant. In contrast, the British thought the Americans were replaying London's own errors of appeasement in the 1930s. It was a peculiar reversal of arguments over China, where Washington found London too timid in the face of Beijing's outrages. What Attlee's government failed to grasp was Acheson's own ambivalence. The United States, for example, denounced Iran's unilateralism, and Acheson was firm about blocking U.S. oil companies from any "concession jumping" harmful to the AIOC. This was unlikely anyway, for despite alarms about "shortages," the world was awash in oil, not a good omen for Tehran. The state department also encouraged U.S. companies to make sales to AIOC's traditional customers, stealing a high card from Mosadeq's hand.[27]

With the CIA now sniffing around Iran and Britain staging military exercises, Mosadeq gave notice that any shooting would start World War III. Between 10 and 18 May, Acheson warned London at least five times against military action. The only justifications for using force, he declared, would be in response to Tehran's invitation (presumably the Shah's), to protect evacuating British nationals, or to resist either Soviet intervention or a communist coup. Although in the NSC he denounced possible British military intervention as "sheer madness," he accepted that Mosadeq's actions might justify "extraordinary" *political* moves to prevent Iran's loss to "the free world." Although a department statement on 18 May 1951 challenged the legality of unilateral nationalization— setting off fierce cries in Iranian newspapers—Britons considered the statement hectoring and excessively neutral. Future prime minister Harold Macmillan told his diary that Washington had addressed Britain and Iran "as if we were two Balkan countries being lectured in 1911 by Sir Edward Grey." Some Americans were also dissatisfied. On 21 May, *Life* magazine demanded Acheson's dismissal for the imminent "loss" of Iran.[28]

Uneasy about the parallel crises in Egypt and Iran, on 23 May, Acheson told his new ambassador in London, Republican business executive Walter Gifford, that Britain must show "infinite restraint." In reinforcement, Truman talked publicly about how many nations hated foreign oil companies. For good measure, he added that Mexico had been "right" to nationalize U.S.-owned oil properties in the 1930s.[29]

Britain's Positions Crumble

Through the summer of 1951, the two crises threatened to lurch out of control. "As a result of events in Iran, Egypt became ebullient," Eden wrote. While the Americans fretted daily about Iran, Egypt grabbed their attention a little less often. In each, Washington's efforts to cultivate friendly ties with the Middle Eastern state frayed its alliance with Britain. Because an outright breach was too awful to contemplate, the U.S.-UK connection held, leaving leaders in Tehran and Cairo dissatisfied with the Americans.[30]

The Iranian crisis was comparatively easy to understand, and the key question for Washington was how far to go against an ally trying to retain its own Persian situation of strength. In contrast, the breakdown in Egypt was surreally mixed with each western power's pursuit of the ignis fatuus of "Middle Eastern defense." To Acheson's horror, by the early fall of 1951, excruciating choices were rapidly becoming unavoidable, all seemingly unfriendly to Britain. He put little credit in a recent concession on "some form of nationalization," coupled as it was with vigorous denials of Tehran's right to carry it out unilaterally. At his suggestion, Truman appealed for conciliation in letters to Attlee and Mosadeq. Taking nationalization as a given, the president told Attlee that Iran was ready to make some kind of settlement, while he pleaded with Mosadeq to try "friendly negotiation." Neither party gave ground. Meanwhile, Mosadeq ordered payments for AIOC products directed to National Iranian Oil Company, and when shippers and other parties refused, by the end of June 1951, the oil flow ebbed to a trickle. In State's view, London expected a collapse in the Iranian effort to run the oil fields and refinery, followed by disorder and a new and acceptable government. When Tehran snubbed AIOC's first negotiating offer, Acheson nudged London to be more flexible but avoided giving further "gratuitous advice," wishing to avert charges of "appeasement." Far from it, for in trying to assure enough oil for Korea, the United States was helping reroute oil shipments in a way reinforcing London's embargo of Iranian oil.[31]

London never realized how far Acheson leaned in its favor, including his 27 June statement criticizing Iranian tactics. But in Morrison's mind, a true ally would show the fleet in the Persian Gulf. Opposition leader Winston Churchill described "Mussy Duck" in a letter to Truman as "an elderly lunatic bent on wrecking his country and handing it over to communism." Acheson grew gloomy as Mosadeq, armed with new laws for harassing British technicians, ached to expel all the British from the country, and an irresolute Shah lacked the "nerve" to "act." Though still fearing Soviet intervention, the administration jacked up levels of "military, economic and technical" support to Mosadeq as the only leader available. But it was ready to act with London if it saw signs of "communist subversion" of Iran. In a speech on 29 June, Acheson worried aloud about na-tionalist impulses "turning people almost crazy." Instead of "seeking their own real interests," people like the unnamed Mosadeq were letting passions drive them toward self-destruction.[32]

One reason Mosadeq acted with such confidence was his false belief that British workers would obey his orders and U.S. companies line up to buy his nationalized petroleum. Such illusions began to make Acheson, like the British, see the causes of the crisis in the *nature* of Iranians, especially Mosadeq. They were imbued with the "fanatical idea," he wrote a senator, of throwing "the British out even if it wrecks the country." But even as he cultivated a "wild men in Persia" image, he saw the British as mulish and deluded. In Tehran, Grady blamed the British almost exclusively for making Mosadeq "a world figure and a symbolic champion" of "downtrodden" countries. State department aides worked nights figuring out how to avoid drawing the Soviets into the crisis. Most of their ideas involved substituting a new multinational company for the AIOC to keep the oil flowing, preserve an iota of British pride, and safeguard Iranian revenue and sovereignty. The administration also discarded mere "good offices" for something very much like mediation, with Harriman as mediator.[33]

On the 4th of July, Acheson, Nitze, McGhee, Doc Matthews, and Franks met at Harriman's "hilltop veranda" above the Potomac. They did not spare Franks in their two hours of talk, but it spoke volumes that they gathered in his company without saying a word to Iran's envoy, former president of the UN General Assembly Nasrollah Entezam. To "stop the drift" toward military inter-vention, Acheson suggested that Harriman go to Tehran to get "negotiations started again." Only the "reluctant bride" disagreed but acquiesced when Truman approved the idea. With the unenthusiastic consent of both sides, Harriman arrived in Tehran on 14 July 1951 just in time to witness new protests that left twenty dead. It was not a good sign, and despite untiring shuttling between Tehran and London, he ended his effort after six weeks, having achieved nothing except prevent further escalation. The British, he said, were "arbitrary and unyielding," Mosadeq, "rigid and adamant." When a Harriman assistant told Mosadeq the conflict could only harm Iran, Mosadeq "would roll his eyes and reply simply, 'Tant pis pour nous.' " Both the UK and Iran, Acheson concluded, preferred conflict on a "nonnegotiable issue" to settlement. Mosadeq's success at stirring revolutionary dreams had imprisoned him in a cell of radicalism. Attlee, on the other hand, battered by pre-election Conservative jingoism, had turned obdurate for King and country.[34]

Despite Acheson's powerful instinct to back Mosadeq, in a kind of two-steps-forward-one-step-back manner, he began moving closer to the UK. Several things accounted for this movement—London's unrelenting importuning, its supposed acceptance of the principle of nationalization, the failure of Harriman's mission, and the growing conviction that, however colorful, Mosadeq was insufferable. But this sidling was fitful, never stable, and always accompanied by complaints about British unreason.

Midway in Harriman's stay in Tehran, Britain moved ships to the Persian Gulf and paratroopers to Crete in the early workings of Plan "Buccaneer." After stern U.S. protests in late July, the force stood down but British truculence did not. If we're firm, blustered the chairman of AIOC, the Iranians would "crawl on their bellies and accept what we offered them." Such statements convinced Washington that British policy toward Iran—a nation no high London official had visited since the war—was outmoded, fed by an incorrigible colonial outlook. As late as 8 August, even as British negotiators flew into Tehran, destroyers with Union Jacks fluttering appeared off Abadan, just over the horizon. On 31 August, this belligerence drew a promise from Truman (sent at Acheson and Harriman's urging) to Attlee that the United States felt free to act independently. He also warned the prime minister against any violations of "the legitimate aspirations of the Iranian people."[35]

Acheson now traded Grady in for a new ambassador. Already nettled by a string of irritants, he decided Grady had to go after receiving implicit criticism of himself in cables urging a break with Britain. Grady had said he would serve only a year, but he would surely have stayed if permitted. In February 1952, when queried in Congress if he had fired Grady, Acheson replied: "He quit. He wanted to quit. We thought that he had gotten so excitable that it probably was a good thing." Grady's fixation on economic development, unrelated to the Abadan crisis, had badly missed the point. Replacing him was Acheson's old friend and Truman Doctrine co-conspirator, Loy Henderson, shifted from New Delhi.[36]

Unable to pay either government or oil workers, Mosadeq in early September ordered British technicians out of the country as he prepared to seize Abadan. In retaliation, AIOC halted all payments to Iranian workers, forcing him to dip into dwindling state funds. The government in London warned of reprisals against anyone purchasing Mosadeq's oil, banned exports to Iran, and froze its sterling assets in Britain, all in the expectation that the Shah would react now and oust Mosadeq. The United States (and U.S. oil companies) cooperated with British sanctions, with Acheson executing a benevolent neutrality twisted in London's favor. Washington also supplied credits to help Britain with crisis-induced short-falls while dragging its feet in sending aid to Tehran. One reason for such cooperation may have been Acheson's realization that his repeated warnings against military intervention had indeed thwarted an attack. Because of his pressure, the British could frighten Mosadeq with their highly visible ships and troops but not pull the trigger. In fact, it may all have been a bluff, for, aside from Morrison, most cabinet members resisted using military force.[37]

In executive testimony in late September, Acheson described the Iranian situation as "just about as bad as it can be." Both sides were being "childish," "foolish," and emotional. Domestic politics dictated London's behavior. With Churchill "roaring like a lion and saying that nobody can shove him around," Attlee had retorted: "Well, nobody can shove me around either." The fact was both were "going to be shoved around, and the question is, by whom?" It would be better if friends did the shoving. With events moving their way, Acheson thought, the Soviets would probably just watch and wait. In London, meanwhile, Attlee had told colleagues, "I am handling Persia," and in one of his first moves tried again on 26 September to enlist Truman to his side. Still hoping the Shah would fire Mosadeq, he implored the president to help keep the British and Americans marching "together." A British deputy, Roger Makins, was thoroughly tired of lectures from a supposed ally that refused to join ranks. With Britain about to take the conflict to the UN Security Council (where Mosadeq planned to defend Iran personally), he fumed at Acheson's plans to talk to the Iranian leader in New York.[38]

On 27 September as expected, Mosadeq seized the Abadan complex. Henderson begged for forceful steps to halt London from committing "armed aggression" and got what he wanted when Acheson told London that any "obvious" outside attempt to topple Mosadeq would only strengthen him, eliminating any chance for a new oil accord. Military intervention could even lead to the overthrow of the Shah, the "last element in Iran on which the Western world can rely," a view with a life of seven presidencies. Britain, he again urged, should study the Saudi Arabian deal to find a way out. Though facing likely defeat in the upcoming election, Attlee's government caved in, concluding that it "could not afford to break with the United States on an issue of this kind."[39]

Mosadeq was stronger than ever, and the Shah told Henderson he was "helpless" to do anything about him. In the UN Security Council, Mosadeq would fight a British resolution asking for enforcement of an interim injunction against him from the International Court of Justice. Unhappy that Attlee had gone to the UN without consultations, and disliking his resolution, Foggy Bottom sought alternatives. Just as delegates began gathering in New York on 8 October 1951, Egypt chimed in by denouncing its 1936 treaty with Britain. Reacting more to Iran than the Egyptian events, the British press vociferously if inconsistently attacked Attlee's government for either "bullying" or "excessive meekness."

Thus burdened, his delegation also fared badly in the Security Council. In a learned tour de force, the charismatic David from Iran propelled one stone after another against Goliath. A "petulant" Morrison in London told the U.S. embassy that his own countrymen were "saints," Mosadeq a "naughty boy," and Acheson a "defeatist." Ernest Gross in the UN likened British efforts to answer Mosadeq to "singing the last act of 'The Twilight of the Gods' in a burning theater." Meanwhile, he added, the Soviet delegate smiled "like a Cheshire cat." Short of votes, the red-faced Britons withdrew their resolution, hoping instead for relief at the International Court. Deepening the insult, Truman invited Mosadeq to Washington for high-level talks. He would come down, he joked, as soon as he got out of the jail the Security Council planned to toss him in.[40]

Britain was also staggering toward debacle in Egypt and, Morrison thought, a possible repetition of the "Persian situation." The Americans, he thought, were a "lap behind us," but Britain, he declared on 15 October 1951, would stand fast. Morrison's achievements had all come in domestic affairs, and Attlee later admitted his appointment was a "bad mistake": he had "no idea he was so ignorant." In Washington, Acheson took control of Egyptian matters, which still revolved around "Middle Eastern defense," all essentially aimed at giving Britain an excuse to keep its forces near Suez. Truman accepted Acheson's idea of converting Suez to "allied" bases under formal Egyptian control but ultimately subject to allied direction. To get Egypt to agree, Acheson warned, Truman would have to dampen his ardor for Israel. A spin-off of this latest tack was NATO membership for Turkey, Ankara's price for cooperation. Washington's price for cooperating with Britain in Middle Eastern defense was London's assent to NATO membership for both Turkey and Greece. Acheson certainly did not want to lose Egypt, but his approval of this miscellany of defense schemes seemed perfunctory. In secret testimony in September, he had told senators he saw "no sense in getting a guarantee that Turkey would go to the defense of Egypt, or Israel would go to the defense of Saudi Arabia." The whole idea was a chimera, as he would learn when Egypt not only rejected a role in MEC but abrogated its 1936 treaty. "If ever there was a political stillbirth," Acheson wrote, MEC "was it."[41]

Its failure would be quickly forgotten, but not Egypt's break with Britain. Oblivious to the nationalist sentiment that moved even King Farouk and learning nothing from Mosadeq's expulsion of AIOC, Britain made a series of demands in the UN against Egypt. On 8 October, outraged members of the Cairo parliament introduced legislation looking to abrogate both the 1936 treaty and 1899 Sudan condominium, slashing British rights in Egypt, and recognizing Farouk as Sudan's king. Frenzied crowds snaked through the streets waving banners reading, "Long Live King of Egypt and the Sudan," "Get Out of Our Country," *and* "Long Live Mossadeq." Hardly noticed in the hubbub was Acheson's declaration two days later that Egypt's unilateral abrogation of the British treaty had no legal standing.[42]

Though still with faint hopes for a jerry-rigged settlement, Washington now considered less orthodox methods, creating an interagency committee chaired by the CIA's Kermit Roosevelt to study the option of a coup, perhaps led by "new" men friendly to western interests. Acheson thought neither nationalism nor Farouk was the problem, but the party dominating Cairo politics, the Wafd (Delegation), an elitist nationalist group that had gained power denouncing Perfidious Albion. As Roosevelt's unit went into its brown study, in yet another trademarked gasconade, Morrison promised to hold on to Suez "on behalf of the free world." On 16 October, British troops killed five demonstrators attacking British dependents at Ismailia along the Canal. Acheson urged London to act with enough "restraint" to hold "world opinion" to its side while the Egyptians upbraided Caffery for Washington's pro-British statements and heaped ridicule on the MEC.

On 25 October, Churchill's Conservatives defeated Attlee's government at the polls. Two days later, Caffery told Acheson the Egyptians were following a "blindly fatalistic policy" of "do or die." They deeply resented the British and were beginning to think ill of all westerners, some ranting about making "friends" with the USSR. Yet he hoped Washington had enough credit in London to force a moderation of its conduct before the British lost all *their* credit in Cairo. Egyptians, he believed, still hoped Washington could "do something to save them from the mess which they are in." This was thin gruel but better than nothing. Caffery had identified the path Acheson would follow for the next fifteen months. Regional defense would take a backseat to a vigorous effort to preserve Egyptian goodwill.[43]

32

JOUSTING WITH MOSADEQ, WAITING FOR NASSER

Jousting with Mosadeq

Muhammad Mosadeq led the endeavor to free Iran of outsiders' domination. Often ailing and given to fainting and weeping spells, he habitually lay in hotel or hospital beds, robed and beslippered, talking to diplomats or reporters. Such eccentric conduct was misleading, for this Persian was a man of parts. Not London's hated lunatic, he was a formidable leader feared by Mohammed Reza Shah Pahlavi. Born in 1882 in a landholding family, he studied in France, took a doctorate in law in Switzerland, and returned to Iran imbued with both rationalist and nationalist values. Serving as both a finance and foreign minister and helping establish the National Front in 1949 was part of his hope to bring Iran into a modern age, but these did not stop the Shah's father, Reza Shah Pahlavi, from briefly throwing him in prison. First as legislator and then as prime minister, he pursued an ambitious agenda to improve ordinary Iranians' lives and develop democratic and constitutional institutions at the Shah's expense. He hated British imperialism, and Britons in turn despised him. But Americans often took pleasure in his company. George McGhee talked to him twenty odd times and thought him "a delightful fellow," spending half their time "laughing at his jokes." But he also thought Mosadeq was unrealistic about how far the United States would go to retain Iranian oil for the west.[1]

In a playful profile in his memoirs, Acheson described Mosadeq as "small and frail with not a shred of hair on his billiard-ball head." He had a "thin face" and "a long beak of a nose flanked by two bright, shoe-button eyes." Amused by his "pixie quality," he described meeting Mosadeq at Washington's Union Station: "I watched a bent old man hobble down the platform supporting himself with a stick and an arm through his son's. Spotting me at the gate, he dropped the stick, broke away from his party, and came skipping along ahead of the others to greet us." In discussions, he had "a delightfully childlike way of sitting in a chair with his legs tucked under him," but his "passions" drove him into a corner where he could act only on "extreme solutions." In time, Acheson came to see him as "essentially a rich, reactionary, feudal-minded Persian inspired by a fanatical hatred of the British and a desire to expel them and all their works from the country regardless of cost." He was "a great actor and a great gambler." Ranting and weeping in the Majlis, he was a "unique" leader who "sowed the wind and reaped the whirlwind."[2]

These recollections point to a common tendency to underestimate Mosadeq as a child or jester. His six weeks in the United States in the autumn of 1951 produced a remarkable if fleeting celebrity. *Time* named him "Man of the Year," but not out of admiration, and ranting, fainting, and weeping pervaded press coverage. Through some eighty hours of talks with U.S. officials, McGhee was usually his interlocutor, accompanied by interpreter Vernon Walters, previously with Averell Harriman in Tehran, who translated from Mosadeq's French. In New York, the Americans met Mosadeq in both hospital and hotel rooms, negotiating as they sat at the foot of his beds. As Mosadeq laughed at his own "countless jokes," McGhee tried instructing him in the basics of "the international oil business," to which Mosadeq, who appeared to think Britain needed him more than vice versa, would smile and say, "I don't care about that. You don't understand. It's a political problem." Once the Americans understood that Mosadeq had not nationalized the Abadan complex itself, they worked hard with him on a plan to have a neutral agency run Abadan and allow AIOC to acquire oil for its customers through another, broker-like agency and share profits 50–50 with Iran.

This and many other ideas foundered on disputes over pricing. The Americans claimed the problem was Mosadeq's demand to receive the equivalent of retail rather than wholesale prices. For Mosadeq, however, purging the country of the British trumped everything else. All the westerners were probably alarmed at the very thought of the Iranian state entering the international oil business. When Henry Byroade encouraged him to leave enough British technicians at Abadan to keep the oil flowing, Mosadeq replied: "Well, if you're a Moslem and you're against drinking alcohol, one drop is as bad as a gallon, so not even one Britisher can stay." Acheson told Truman on 10 October 1951 that a settlement might depend on a U.S.-backed "threat" to boycott Iranian oil. But Mosadeq vastly strengthened his position by winning the Security Council debate against the British. The withdrawal of the UK resolution for enforcing an International Court injunction against Iran was a stunning moral defeat for the UK. "Overnight," Acheson wrote, Mosadeq had become "a television star, quite outshining the British representative."[3]

Afterward, the victorious Mosadeq journeyed to Washington for medical treatment, staying in Walter Reed Hospital's presidential suite, where he held many of his talks over the next thirty days, including sessions with Truman and Acheson. On 23 October, however, he lunched with U.S. principals at Blair House. As Acheson later recalled, at one point, Mosadeq, sitting "in a chair with his feet tucked under him," took on a "terribly pathetic" appearance, "leaned over toward the President and said, 'Mr. President, I am speaking for a very poor country—a country that is all desert, just sand, a few camels, a few sheep.'" Acheson asked: "Rather like Texas?" Mosadeq "burst into a laugh," dropped his "gambit," and pleaded for large amounts of aid. We will not fund an anti-British campaign, Truman replied, but would stand ready to help at signs of a settlement. Russia, the president added, "was sitting like a vulture on the fence waiting to pounce" on Iran's oil. Mosadeq was unable to divide Acheson from Truman, the latter telling him he should "speak with Mr. Acheson just as though he were speaking to the President himself."[4]

Acheson joined hours of the talks at Walter Reed and the Shoreham. Everyone "petted and took care" of Mosadeq at the hospital, where he "held court in pajamas and bathrobe." Acheson attributed the failure to make progress to Mosadeq's stubbornness on pricing yet seemed fairly optimistic about the discussions as he left for UN meetings in Paris in early November. In Britain, Winston Churchill resumed power with a House of Commons margin of 321–295 just as Mosadeq agreed to have a Dutch company purchase the Abadan refinery from AIOC and run it on a fee basis. In turn, AIOC could buy crude at "attractive" prices and create a new company to market it. The whole package depended on prior agreement on prices. Because the terms looked hard for the British, the state department argued with London that it was the best they could get—it was impossible to return to the status quo ante. Acheson worried that Churchill would not accept such a deal, having come to power bellowing for tougher treatment of the Iranians.[5]

On 4 November in Paris, his thinning optimism vanished when he ran into a buzzsaw in what Eden called "disagreeable" discussions. Eden refused to accept that AIOC was finished and rejected Acheson's alarmist view that "Communism" was the only alternative to Mosadeq. (In truth, Moscow considered him a tool of the "American monopolies.") One evening, with several "dry martinis" again freeing his tongue, Acheson told Eden to "learn to live in the world as it is." But Eden said no to Washington's putative Dutch-company finesse; he would rather lose all the oil than Britain's world standing, especially in the Middle East. On the 7th, when he complained about Mosadeq's success in dividing Washington from London, Acheson retorted that a different appraisal of the situation, not Mosadeq, was the problem. Acheson's reports from Paris prompted Mosadeq's interlocutors in Washington to tell him he might as well go home. The department, however, was still looking for ways to offer him financial aid, hoping to keep the door open for a settlement and elevate U.S. over British influence in

Tehran. After Acheson urged Nitze to find a way out of the crisis, he joined McGhee and Walters at the Shoreham on 9 November. McGhee and Nitze played good-cop, bad-cop, but in the absence of progress in Paris, all present agreed they could then accomplish nothing more.[6]

Before leaving, Mosadeq made an urgent request to Truman for financial help. The Churchill government was turning headlong toward belligerence, especially concerned about the loss of face but also about going bankrupt from the loss of taxes on Iranian oil. Acheson oscillated between impatience and sympathy: asking the British to let the Dutch supplant the AIOC in Iran, he commented, was like "asking us to step aside in favor of Guatemala." Churchill's government, he thought, had no idea they were in the middle of the twentieth century, differing from their predecessors only in their "truculent braggadocio." On 14 November, he told Eden AIOC's failure to negotiate in good faith made it impossible for Washington to strengthen the Shah vis-à-vis Mosadeq. However much it damaged alliance "solidarity," he added, the United States in "a last extremity" would follow its "own interest" in keeping Tehran afloat. In confidence to a reporter, he said the British were unrepentant colonialists whose urge to punish Iran might end up shoving it "behind the Iron Curtain." In Washington, a dejected McGhee told Mosadeq that Truman had not decided on his financial request. Britain was being inflexible, he and Nitze told Mosadeq, but so was he. Acheson's own view was that the British were the guiltier party, spoiling for "a fight to the finish." As he wrote in 1969, though Mosadeq might again "have danced away," Acheson still regretted the absence of a supple British diplomacy that would have given him reason to push Mosadeq to accept a genuinely fair settlement. But in 1951 this U.S. démarche had ended.[7]

Waiting for Nasser

The British dug ever deeper holes for themselves in Egypt, and the Egyptians were observant enough to notice that Washington had barred them from using military force against Mosadeq. If the Iranian sometimes seemed sphinx-like as he chatted away, King Farouk and the ruling Wafd Party were straightforward enough when they denounced the Anglo-Egyptian treaty of 1936. In a land Americans associated with camels and pyramids, Britons and Egyptians were now shooting each other. Mobs ran the streets, some targeting Farouk for his tepid nationalism. Laborers walked off their Canal jobs, and London slashed fuel oil shipments to retaliate. Churchill nearly doubled the British troop presence to over 60,000, with more coming. And Acheson straddled two stools again, satisfying neither side. The middle-way solutions he sought appear imaginary a half century later, a now-familiar dilemma. As with the Chinese, Indochinese, or Iranians, the only way Washington could gain the Egyptians' favor was by breaking with a close ally. Acheson might have done better had he made this or that different choice, but it is unimaginable in the international circumstances he faced that he would have broken with Britain. The advice from Jefferson Caffery, his ambassador in Cairo, to walk the "tightrope" between helping the Egyptians without "deserting our British friends" was useless.[8]

As Acheson moved to take direct control of Egyptian issues, McGhee went to Turkey as ambassador, replaced temporarily by Burton Y. Berry and then by Henry Byroade. Criticizing Egypt because he thought it was inciting Arab unrest, Acheson criticized the UK more strenuously, upbraiding Eden for cutting off Egypt's oil during NATO meetings in Rome late in 1951. The UK ambassador in Cairo, Ralph Stevenson, told Caffery he expected an Egyptian "explosion" followed by British "reoccupation" and then Britain's permanent expulsion. Only Washington's "still considerable prestige," Caffery advised, would keep Egypt from falling "like an overripe plum" into Moscow's hands. In an inspection trip, Berry not only observed a "general and intense" loathing of the British, but a mushrooming population, a "largely illiterate" and ignorant society, and a widening gap between rich and poor, all ruled by "the most corrupt party" ever to govern Egypt. With the British itching for a fight, he urged recognizing Farouk as king of Sudan and recasting the MEC to tickle "Egyptian vanity." The Soviets, he said, were acting "circumspectly," and Egypt's elites feared them far less than the assassins of their own "Moslem brotherhood."[9]

From Washington on 14 December 1951, Acheson lectured Eden that bluster and gunboats, while efficacious in the 1880s, were no longer acceptable to "world opinion." Anticipating a visit from Churchill, he proposed a package combining recognition of Farouk as "King of Egypt and the Sudan" with a referendum in which the Sudanese would choose their own future, along with Egyptian agreement to join MEC. Egypt's nationalists did not much like it, but the British beat them to the punch in rejection, as they did other variations over the next two months. Just as in Iran, Acheson told aides, the UK's swaggering and anachronistic actions endangered vital western interests. But fresh ideas were scarce. The MEC, he now thought, was "pretty barren." Eager to avoid the Egyptian mess, the Pentagon proposed shifting Middle Eastern defense northward, from the Nile delta to the line between Turkey (now in NATO) and Pakistan. This would lessen the significance of Egypt and the Suez bases, already vulnerable to Soviet atomic attack. The Pakistan variant, however, remained a no-sale in London, and in Karachi, too, as long as Kashmir remained unsettled.[10]

There was no progress at the January 1952 U.S.-UK summit in Washington, which was straightaway followed by violence in Egypt. Both Egypt and Iran emerged as irritants shortly after Churchill's party arrived. On 6 January, as the group sailed the Potomac on the president's yacht, Acheson asked for something better than "merely sitting tight." Even perfect cooperation between Britain and the United States would now leave them "like two people locked in loving embrace in a rowboat which was about to go over Niagara Falls." He hoped Churchill and Truman could "break the embrace and take to the oars." Churchill, who considered the Egyptian uproar a "bastard child of the Iranian situation," chuckled at the image but was indifferent to the message. While both sides underestimated Farouk's nationalism, thinking he might solve their problem by ousting the troublesome Wafd government, efforts to find a common ground were also barren. Having failed to get his way with Truman, in an address to Congress on 17 January, Churchill unwisely went over his head by urging dispatch of "token" U.S. forces to Suez. When the "agitated" Egyptian ambassador protested, Acheson observed that the idea was British, not American. When directly asked if there *would* be U.S. military action, Acheson's own note-taker portrayed his response "as masterful double-talk without telling him yes or no."[11]

The double-talk did nothing to stop resumption of the violence, as British tanks and artillery struck Egyptian police at Ismailia, killing forty. On 26 January 1952, "Black Saturday," after a summary U.S. rebuff of Eden's plea for military support, rioters swarmed through Cairo, torching hundreds of buildings, from the Badiya Belly Dance Hall to the renowned Shepheard's Hotel and Turf Club. Twelve British subjects were burned alive and more than five hundred westerners injured. The next day as Caffery coached Farouk over two-way radio, he sacked the Wafd government. Acheson telephoned Oliver Franks with a jab about the failure of London's "splutter of musketry." In a break in the violence a day later, he mixed metaphors in writing Eden that "we have had a very close shave" but were "far from being out of the woods." Churchill now expected more sympathy from Washington, but more discord lay ahead.[12]

Acheson was in Europe much of February 1952, consulting almost daily with Eden. Cairo all but asked for his mediation, but "the last thing" he wanted was getting "in the middle." He "needled" Eden to be more flexible but accepted his excuse that Churchill and the cabinet were the inflexible ones. Disliking this kid-gloves treatment of Eden, Caffery wanted a sharp line drawn against British *policy*. Teddy Roosevelt's grandson, Kermit Roosevelt, was meeting clandestinely with the men soon to be called the Free Officers, a disparate group of mostly junior army officers led by Lieutenant Colonel Gamal Abdel Nasser. Plotting to oust Farouk, they hoped the Americans would prevent a rescue or British intervention. Acheson understood that they considered Britain, not the United States, their enemy.[13]

He was squeezing Britain on both Egypt and Iran precisely as he did the same to France on Tunisia, with similar results. In an NSC meeting in April, he agonized about being trapped between Islamic and Arab hatred, on one hand, and French and British displeasure, on the other. Lacking any novel ideas, he seemed to draw vague confidence from thinking about a military coup in Cairo. In the state department, only Nitze was ready to discard MEC and look for fresh ideas. Having already lost all moral standing in the region, he thought, Britain would be the only beneficiary from Middle Eastern defense contraptions. But no one else backed his ambitious idea of protecting Iran, if not Egypt, by putting it under the mantle of the Truman Doctrine. By May, therefore, Nitze's planning staff was again on the search for a workable MEC formula, eliminating all the reluctant Arab states and replacing them with Turkey and Pakistan and such "Middle Eastern" stalwarts as Australia, New Zealand, and South Africa. MEC now became MEDO (Middle East Defense Organization), described as a mere "planning board" to reduce Arab suspicions. Washington never considered putting its own forces into any of these schemes. Only partly for that reason, as Peter L. Hahn writes, they all "languished."[14]

Caffery was right about Acheson's favoritism toward Eden, though it might have been unconscious. Having formed a durable friendship, he seemed less willing to deliver hard truths to him than his predecessor, Herbert Morrison. Even so, Eden would not bend in spring meetings in Paris. Informing Acheson of London's anger at Washington, he vowed he would never "sell the Sudanese down the river" or help the Egyptians by "feeding the Sudanese to them," even though they had been "naughty" (Morrison's word for Mosadeq). Within a month, Acheson had grown pessimistic, even fatalistic. Outlining a kind of domino theory, he told Eden the whole region might be lost if Egypt slipped out of control.[15]

Egypt did just that as two prime ministers consecutively fell from power. While Farouk scuffled, Roosevelt's men assiduously ascertained the likely leaders of a new order. In a Brazil press conference in July 1952, Acheson criticized Eden for being unwilling to travel to Egypt in the name of peace. On returning to Washington, he found his department expecting another volley of British musketry any minute. As the transatlantic discord sharpened, he complained that the UK "wails for full support from the US but what it wants is support for doing nothing."

On 22 July, while Farouk and his retinue were in Alexandria, the Free Officers seized Cairo, 225 kilometers away. Americans on the scene apparently anticipated this coup and seemed keen to deal with its ringleaders, but it was still unclear how they would, or could, exploit the new circumstances.[16]

"An Independent American Solution over British Opposition Was . . . More Easily Said than Done"

The British position was also sinking in Iran. Linking the two situations, Mosadeq on his return from the United States visited Cairo to urge solidarity against London. When a U.S official had observed as Mosadeq left Washington that he was going home empty-handed, the smiling prime minister said that was far better than returning "with an agreement which I would have to sell to my fanatics." Britain now played into his hand by freezing Iranian dollars held in London and threatening lawsuits against anyone who might buy oil through Iran's new nationalized company. The UK further dried up Tehran's revenue stream by finding new petroleum sources for its own factories and military. Mosadeq considered breaking Britain's boycott by selling to communist states, which disquieted Washington, again (see the previous chapter) because it would violate the Battle Act and thus eliminate the chance to give him economic assistance. Moscow, however, was not interested. At this point, Acheson thought, the Anglo-Iranian struggle resembled "static trench warfare."[17]

Like Caffery in Egypt, Loy Henderson in Iran urged Acheson to break with a Britain that had "lost touch," but the secretary of state had different priorities, wanting to protect the U.S -UK partnership no matter how much London tested his patience. But it was discouraging that discussions on Iran in the Churchill summit were no better than on Egypt. In a cantankerous moment, Churchill heaped contempt on the timid Attlee and boasted that *he* would have used a "splutter of musquetry" rather than be booted out of Abadan. After he bemoaned the lack of U.S support, Acheson in a return dig noted that Iran was the only oil-producing state in the world causing problems. Nonetheless, London rejected a lengthy menu of state department plans for compensating AIOC for Iran's nationalization. The British not only considered all of them inadequate but sneered that they were the product of Washington's "fidgety and theoretical" temper. While Americans thought the issue urgent, according to Franks the cabinet in London was unperturbed, since previous Persian conflicts had never gone "over the cliff." Acheson simply said Washington saw it differently.[18]

In the middle of Churchill's January visit, Acheson had traveled to Capitol Hill for secret testimony in both houses of Congress. Pessimism now punctuated his usual and refreshing candor. He thought Mosadeq was "not a liberal," or "reformer," or "radical," or "Communist," or even a "Socialist," but had the attitude of "a rich old landowner." Rich or not, since his youth he had been dead set to throw the British out of his country. Now having painted himself in a corner, he was vulnerable to ouster by Iran's communists. The Soviets, "sitting pretty," had no need to intervene. Because of Britain's "great decline," it was common enough that troubles frequently arose in the Middle East, but now Mosadeq had turned troubles into a crisis. Cornered by his own violence, he was like an "animal at bay," biting and butting "at anybody who comes near him with any sort of a plan." It was a "desperate" situation and Acheson was "at wit's end to know what in the world one can do." He might possibly influence Mosadeq through use of Mutual Security aid, but his audience of congressmen had made this difficult with onerous, formalistic demands that every recipient stand up and declare himself part of the "free world." Mosadeq governed an ancient nation, with the world's longest border on the USSR, and he was not about to stand up and say, "I am your boy." Acheson was still "fishing," trying to "hook" him but (switching images) complained again that Congress was demanding that Mosadeq march down the aisle and say, "I have salvation." Mosadeq's refusal to debase himself made it impossible to run a legal military mission in Iran. As to the AIOC dispute, Acheson still blamed Mosadeq for thinking he was running a "filling station" instead of a refinery. Had he been raising cattle, he would be trying to sell them "at the butcher shop price."[19]

Nitze had replaced Philip Jessup as Acheson's key troubleshooter with foreign powers, and now in London he was looking for the common ground that eluded everyone during Churchill's visit. The situation had worsened, for Mosadeq had expelled British diplomats while Churchill was in Washington. Henderson was urging Acheson to save Mosadeq from himself and Iran for the "west." All Acheson had for such a strategy was a commonplace mix of carrot and stick, including a small Point Four agreement that went into effect on 17 January. As Nitze closeted himself with deputies in London, Acheson pressed Churchill and Eden with words. He also tried pressuring Mosadeq by holding up a World Bank loan and refusing requests for direct budgetary support. Iran, he informed its leader, would have cash aplenty when it made a sensible settlement. Blocked by the British-engineered boycott from selling oil, Iran's situation would soon grow acute, pushing Acheson a few inches closer to Britain.[20]

Another discouraging development was the collapse of a plan to have the World Bank (IBRD, or International Bank for Reconstruction and Development) run Iran's petroleum operations as a trustee while Tehran and London negotiated a final settlement. The scheme failed because of its own Byzantine complexity, Mosadeq's prickliness, IBRD technocrats' lack of empathy for Iranian nationalism, and a host of arcane financial complications. For now, the collapse of yet another plan destroyed the last shreds of Acheson's hopes. On 27 March 1952, he told reporters that Mosadeq had to find a way to get out of the box he had put himself in through zeal, pride, refusal to let British technicians work the oil fields, and his wrongheaded attitude toward oil prices.[21]

But in April, Mosadeq did agree to a formula for accepting U.S. military aid that stressed Iran's readiness to defend the UN Charter rather than the "free world." Eden complained testily that this move, on which he had not been consulted, would give the Iranian rascal new life just when London had worn him down. (Moscow also protested, claiming a violation of a 1921 treaty with Iran.) The British were now quite eager to simply get rid of Mosadeq.

In the United States, while the state department was trying to settle with him, another group sought ways to pull him down. Originally, the less savory options now concocted in both the UK and United States aimed at weakening his National Front movement, but some CIA officials planned even stronger measures, and did so without telling Truman, Acheson, the NSC, or, probably, the CIA director. Henderson's willingness to listen silently while the Shah talked hypothetically about firing Mosadeq may have persuaded him that Washington would applaud if he somehow drove Mosadeq out of office. Americans increasingly embraced Britain's view of Mosadeq, and the state department was thinking of arranging a liberal offer to any successor, spending the last half of 1952 working on one after another. At each stage, state department officials came closer to British preferences, though London was irritated that they still had any interest in saving Mosadeq. Acheson had virtually given up, growing more exasperated by the day with all varieties of third world nationalists. They seemed to believe, he told reporters in July 1952, that, once they had tossed off their colonial shackles, they could "accomplish overnight" what others had taken "a hundred years" to do.[22]

Disputes over control of Iran's army widened the differences between the Shah and Mosadeq. Just as observers thought the Shah might act against him, Mosadeq dramatically resigned on 16 July. The monarch immediately replaced him with Ahmad Qavam, who had gotten in Washington's hair in 1946. Americans now deemed him malleable, however, and moved to reward him with $26 million in aid. But Mosadeq was far from done. He appealed to the public, and thousands poured into the streets in answer, setting off five days of riots, often energized by Islamicists' anger at Qavam's wish to separate religion from politics. He resigned and a traumatized Shah on 21 July reappointed Mosadeq, who promptly purged the army of officers planning his ouster.[23]

In response to these stunning events, Acheson urged international mediation. One day after Mosadeq returned to power in Iran, the Free Officers staged their coup in Egypt, and in a further rebuff to London the International Court denied it had jurisdiction over nationalization of AIOC. Mosadeq was stronger than ever—vis-à vis the Majlis, the Shah, and the British—but probably weaker in the eyes of Iranian radicals. If he fell again, Acheson thought Tudeh leftists would take over. Washington had pulled back the aid offered Qavam, and on 28 July, Henderson faced an angry Mosadeq in the beginning of another long spate of negotiations. Their exchanges took weeks, swinging from calm to fierce, but ended without result. Henderson's reports sharpened the U.S. propensity to identify Mosadeq with mania. Acheson still preferred bolstering to overthrowing him but was also still moving more in tune with the British, if not the AIOC. Late in July, the state department offered dollar aid, methods to sell Iranian oil to the UK, and international arbitration while London and Tehran negotiated a permanent settlement. As Washington waited for a reply, Mosadeq fought for his political life in the midst of a struggle to make the Iranian state a constitutional monarchy. Bitter at their rush to help Qavam, he seemed far more wary than before of Americans.[24]

In August, only a round of letters between Truman and Churchill prevented a new ratcheting up of U.S.-UK tensions. At one point, when Eden rejected yet another démarche, Acheson complained that as described in Eden's note, it resembled the one he had sent only in being made "by means of a typewriter." Perhaps, he jabbed at Franks, the AIOC had written Eden's reply. In fact, abdominal surgery now sidelined Eden, spurring Churchill to take command and send what Acheson considered an unusually elastic note to the president. Truman's response both indicated his hopes for unity and warned Churchill that nationalization in Iran was now as "sacred" as the Koran.

Surprisingly, within six days the two agreed on a joint tender. Though not unlike other proposals, each component now depended on acceptance of the others. Washington would give Iran $10 million in aid, the International

Court would arbitrate compensation, and AIOC-Iranian talks would determine a final settlement. With rumors flying in Tehran that Mosadeq would break diplomatic relations with the UK, the British chargé d'affaires, George H. Middleton, joined Henderson in informally presenting the package to him. Churchill called Mosadeq's vituperative response "the drivellings of this old man in bed." Both Whitehall and Foggy Bottom reacted by issuing propaganda barrages, not against Mosadeq, but the Majlis they thought was pushing him. On 30 August, Middleton and Henderson forced Mosadeq to commit himself by making the joint proposal official. In a summary oral rejection, Mosadeq said fake "professions of friendliness" could no longer trick Iranians, who "were not donkeys." On 16–17 September, both Majlis and the Iranian Senate ardently supported him, and Mosadeq rejected the Anglo-American proffer in writing a week later. His message infuriated London for its palpable effort to split the allies.[25]

Acheson now thought of having U.S. companies buy Iranian oil, a problematic idea that ran flush into a current justice department antitrust suit against the very firms he had in mind. Truman opposed the suit but felt bound to observe legal niceties. With his encouragement, State, Defense, the CIA, Commerce, and Interior all set their teeth against Justice's "police dogs" and what Acheson called its intolerance of "the mammon of unrighteousness." (The American people were a problem, too, for equating antitrust with the "Ten Commandments.")

But the companies themselves resisted. They did not need Mosadeq's oil and did not relish doing business with him. Even so, the administration pressed ahead, insensible to the irony that a crisis starting with a socialist government in Britain that refused to coerce the AIOC might end with a capitalist government that muscled private companies for state ends. Acheson again sent Nitze to London, but Churchill and a recuperating Eden weren't having any. Subordinates wanted Acheson to pull out all stops, but he thought "an independent American solution over British opposition was . . . more easily said than done." As the administration tried solving the antitrust conundrum, a "much worried" Mosadeq on 4 October tearfully told Middleton "Persia would soon be dead" without emergency financial aid, and there would be no point in "negotiating with a dead man." As he faltered, Washington came up with yet another plan. American oil companies not currently doing Middle Eastern business would establish a *new* firm that would contract to sell Iran's petroleum products to AIOC for fifteen years; London would end its boycott; and Tehran would compensate the AIOC over a six-year period with some $300 million in petroleum. It hardly mattered that Truman disliked the plan, because Justice liked it even less: No.[26]

Almost nothing short of total betrayal of the British might have saved the situation, and that might not have done it, either. Mosadeq probably no longer wanted an agreement, since disagreement better served his interests. Perched uneasily on a xenophobic tiger, he implied in a 16 October broadcast that he might break diplomatic relations with Britain. Six days later, he did.[27]

"We Have to Fly Wing to Wing"

Nearly organic ties with Britain held back opportunities for the United States to achieve truly close relations with revolutionary Egypt. After the Free Officers toppled the Cairo government on the night of 22–23 July 1952, Americans who had already courted the coup leaders moved quickly, hoping to cut through old colonial grievances. Washington, not London, was now the outside power of moment in Egypt. But whether U.S. officials liked it or not, muscular connections to the UK implicated them in the legacy of European imperialism. This was not lost on army general Muhammad Naguib, Egypt's new leader, or the thirty-three-year-old Gamal Abdel Nasser, biding his time backstage.

As in Southeast Asia, there was something bleak and inexorable about the U.S. pursuit of the middle road in the Middle East. But Washington hoped friendly ties to the Free Officers might keep them with the west, contribute to regional defense, and even help reconcile Egypt to the UK—and Israel. Truman provisionally authorized Acheson to offer weapons to the new regime. This greatly irritated London, already angry that Acheson had publicly extolled the new leadership. At home, the Pentagon claimed the state department had not justified arms transfers with "an approved strategic plan and force requirements for the area." This "attitude," Acheson wrote, "made one want to shake the Joint Chiefs of Staff until their ribbons fell off." Israel was skeptical, too. In the end, a short calendar and British cries of "appeasement" frustrated Acheson's plans. So did Truman.[28]

At first, State's optimism looked warranted. Junta officers quickly told Caffery they might join in regional defense and they would certainly stamp out any Egyptian communists. Denying any political ambitions of their own, they installed Ali Maher as prime minister. The rebels forced Farouk's abdication with only a few shots fired, and Caffery helped the monarch leave the country without alienating them. With Acheson's congratulations in his pocket, he briefly took on exceptional influence, blocking the replacement of Maher with a former signer of the Stockholm Peace Appeal and the appointment of a "commie" land reform expert. He applauded and helped engineer Naguib's ascension as prime minister in September. Their path smoothed, CIA officers were soon training a new Egyptian intelligence service.[29]

More overtly, U.S. diplomats moved as fast as they could to win over the new regime, encouraged when Naguib made further claims of interest in Middle Eastern defense and none at all in harming Israel. The nettled British kibitzed, condemning any friendly gestures not conditioned on acceptance of their Suez base and resenting the likely loss of an arms sales market. Acheson intended to reciprocate any Egyptian cooperation, though he was mindful of Caffery's advice not to embrace Egypt too warmly. It was best not to have his more radical colleagues worry about where the "moderate" Naguib might go. The apparent success of this courtship caused Soviet intelligence to conclude that Washington had inspired the Free Officers' coup to recruit Egypt to MEDO.[30]

To combat the socioeconomic decay that seemed a greater threat than anything dreamed up in Moscow, the state department began funneling economic and technical aid to Naguib's government. It aroused more British carping about appeasement by backing an ambitious land reform program. It even discouraged Naguib from being too friendly to Israel, fearing he would lose standing with other Arabs. As U.S. influence grew, Acheson wondered if Britain could any longer play any role outside Europe; Byroade thought both Britain and France were "through" in the Middle East. But Acheson was still uneasy enough to ask Caffery on 30 September for more assurances from the new government. Cairo did not have to be obvious, but he needed more. Naguib complied with a broadcast statement that Egypt expected no new war with Israel and a conspicuous Yom Kippur appearance at Cairo's foremost synagogue, complete with newspaper photos of Naguib talking to the Grand Rabbi. By early October, Acheson was ready to start serious negotiations to give Egypt foreign aid and incorporate it in MEDO.[31]

In mid-October 1952, the half-Sudanese Naguib suddenly outmaneuvered Britain by dropping claims to Sudan and negotiating with Sudanese factions on their future. Caffery actually saw these proposals as a British victory, since they sheltered Sudan from Egyptian ambition, but they also deprived London of a club used to criticize U.S. policies. Now the protector of Sudan's independence, Egypt announced plans for a plebiscite in which people could choose association with Cairo or full independence—a far better gesture than showing up at a synagogue. Having made "one gesture after the other," the Egyptians now wanted something "convincing" in return. A lack of time and a resistant president would prevent Acheson from providing them.[32]

On the Iranian case, Acheson had decided he would not break with "our closest ally" and the "most important element of strength in the Western alliance outside of the United States." The Atlantic partners had to work together "just like pigeons." When one turned, "the others do it too. We have to fly wing to wing." But even if he would not peel off from Britain's path, he still pushed to redirect it. His determination to act in concert with London reduced his room for maneuver, but the antitrust issue was even more troublesome. With plenty of oil available, American executives showed little inclination to cooperate, hardly surprising since Acheson's men were essentially trying to erect a large petroleum cartel. Nor did the businessmen want to act like poachers, face AIOC lawsuits, or ally themselves with Mosadeq's repugnant principles. General Omar Bradley turned "purple with rage" at the fervor of Justice's trustbusters. Finally, Truman ordered the attorney general to substitute a civil case for the criminal suit, releasing some pressure on the companies but not while Acheson was still in office. While he was, he tried yet again with a complex notion by which U.S. oil companies would buy and market Iranian oil, while the United States kept Iran financially afloat with funds diverted from NATO. Mosadeq rejected the plan, however, partly in Nitze's view because of a flawed calculation that he could get something better from the incoming President Eisenhower.[33]

On 18 November, Acheson told Eisenhower the stalemate was a case of Iranians being "unreasonable" and the British too thick to accommodate such emotions. Even with a string of failed ventures behind him, he pushed to the very last for a path to the center of the AIOC maze. At UN sessions in New York in November and December 1952, he told Eden there was "not enough cheese" in a new British proposal. Back in Washington, he talked yet again with U.S. oil firms, while Nitze held Eden's hand in London. In early December, Mosadeq received a personal message from Henderson (in Washington for consultations) appealing to his statesmanship and entreating him to offer a plan the AIOC and Britain could accept. Mosadeq was mistakenly certain the British had "instigated" this letter.

Even with maximum rather than minimal goodwill all round, at this late date there were too many snags and loose ends to overcome. Oil companies and oil-producing states had already adjusted to the Iranian boycott. American companies were terrified of the justice department. The facilities at Abadan were rapidly deteriorating. Pricing and currency issues and shifts in the international market spawned new obstacles. London held fast to a "legalistic" negotiating stance. And Mosadeq, now "more inflamed, more suspicious" than earlier, was more vulnerable at home, especially with petroleum exports falling to a trickle.34

Trilateral talks continued into January. In one of their last discussions during the Truman administration, Henderson, back in Tehran, found Mosadeq full of "suspicion, pettiness, and overcaution." He sat at his bedside "for eight consecutive hours" explaining the latest U.S. proposal. On 9 January, Truman announced the switch from a criminal to civil suit in the antitrust matter. Though this was better than nothing, the state department had hoped Justice would drop the action altogether. The three governments came close to narrowing the gaps among them, but people do not win cigars by getting close. As time ebbed, Truman grew sensibly averse to saddling Eisenhower with something not his own doing, and the British anticipated more sympathy from him. Unlike Mosadeq, who believed the same, the British knew their man.35

Eisenhower's election also threw a wrench into Acheson's last efforts on Egypt. Truman, however, was the main spoiler, for Acheson's strategy challenged his solicitous regard for Israel. MEDO remained entangled with his efforts to the end. On the principle that Egypt must be MEDO's first Arab member, on 5 November 1952, Acheson again urged Britain to negotiate its differences over the Suez base. London tried, and a provisional decision to move its area headquarters to the crown colony of Cyprus might have been a break-through, but a string of setbacks frustrated the effort. Shortly after Caffery concluded an arrangement making Egypt eligible for MDAP funds, Acheson realized that a powerful ventriloquist in the Oval Office was behind all the officials the department ran into who insisted on new aid to Israel as the price for Egyptian funding. In a conversation with Acheson on 6 January 1953, Truman was superficially obliging but barred any aggressive effort to win over Egypt.

Approving only modest arms *purchases*, he insisted on leaving the rest to Eisenhower. The chiefs backed him. Truman also put strings on a small economic aid program Acheson wanted for Egypt, refusing to permit anything more extensive unless Israel received the same and Egypt first signed a peace treaty. Acheson caught the drift. Throwing up his hands, he told Israeli Ambassador Abba Eban: "Well, I don't see why we shouldn't bequeath some headaches to our successors."[36]

Retrospectively, he disparaged all his work in the Middle East. He tardily regretted trying to engross Arabs into western security arrangements. In whatever guise, MEC-MEDO was a "rather fanciful" idea with no "defensive capacity." By 1954, he seemed also to regret attempting to build up either Iran or Egypt with aid. It might have been best, he mused at Princeton, simply to amass U.S. military power in a region that had too little basis for reliable military strength of its own. In hindsight, it also seemed to him almost immaterial if Iran had fallen into communist hands so long as Washington did what was necessary to force everyone's recognition of U.S. primacy. These musings were remarkably off target, for, in fact, while still in office, he had moved the United States in the right direction in Egypt. Though it would take another generation, eventually under Anwar Sadat, Egypt made peace with Israel, cut loose from the Soviet Union, and opted out of pan-Arab and Islamicist enthusiasms.[37]

By the time Acheson had gathered all his revisionist wool at Princeton, Nasser had ousted Naguib, whose record had not been inconsequential. In February 1953, Britain and Egypt agreed to end their dual administrative control of Sudan and then quickly agreed to grant Sudan's independence in three years if approved in a plebiscite. In 1956 Sudan's parliament simply declared its independence, an act in which both Egypt and the UK acquiesced. Washington and London finally agreed to shift the focus for regional defense northward. With U.S. strategic bombers coming on line, and the Suez bastion dwindling in significance, Cairo and London agreed in July 1954 on the base's evacuation in two years.

Egypt's new ruler, Nasser, however, was an ardent nationalist and hostile to the west, a hostility certainly reinforced by Truman's favoritism toward Israel. Even Acheson was surprised, however, when he followed the departure of British troops in 1956 by nationalizing and seizing the Suez Canal. Although Acheson had long deprecated Britain's saber rattling and predicted it would ultimately lose Suez, he was outraged when Eisenhower and Dulles turned against the British in the Suez crisis. This occasioned his first coming-out as a retiree, and he flung notably partisan criticisms about being indifferent to the "alliance" that comprised a vital American position of strength. Conveniently forgetting his former disgust with British belligerence, he now thought London and Paris should have attacked Egypt instantly following Nasser's seizure of the Canal. Joining the Soviet Union to condemn NATO allies in the UN was unforgivable.[38]

After Acheson left government, Washington and London's covert agencies settled matters in Iran with a coup, the CIA's maiden voyage in overthrowing governments. He would surely have opposed this venture despite the fact that in the waning days of the administration, the NSC had approved language opening the door to such an operation. As Acheson, Nitze, and Henderson had been trying to salvage U.S.-Iranian relations, CIA operatives, consulting with the British, had been planning how to end the Mosadeq nonsense. In November 1952, Roosevelt told British counterparts they must await Eisenhower's advent to act, because Acheson unfortunately "was absolutely fascinated" by Mosadeq and "in fact sympathetic to him." In contrast, John Foster Dulles and his brother, Allen, CIA deputy director, wanted to oust Mosadeq. Roosevelt and the Dulles brothers even screened their plans from Truman, although in 1948 he had approved covert actions to prevent communist seizure of Italy and did the same later for similar reasons in the Philippines. As we will see in Chapter 33, he was also mightily tempted to overthrow a standing government in Guatemala, only to have Acheson halt him.

Had they been in office in 1953 or 1954, Truman and Acheson might conceivably have given the nod to action against Mosadeq, but Acheson's approval of such a coup seems unlikely, and no direct evidence indicates that either he or Truman approved such a thing. In 1961, Acheson privately denounced the Bay of Pigs disaster and proudly wrote Truman that he had told friends "how you and I had turned down similar suggestions for Iran and Guatemala."[39]

As Roosevelt expected, Eisenhower quickly endorsed the Mosadeq intrigue. Five days after the dancing ended at the inaugural balls, the Dulles brothers (with Allen now heading the CIA) met Roosevelt on eliminating "that madman Mossadegh." In August 1953, they accomplished their goal in Operation Ajax, described by Douglas Little as "proposed by Whitehall, rejected by Truman, and resurrected by Eisenhower." When it was done, it became clearer why Britain had so vigorously resisted Acheson's diplomacy. Ironically, however, the petroleum settlement the new Iranian government accepted strongly resembled what Acheson had pressed for at the end. Iran held legal ownership of the producing wells and refinery, but U.S. and British firms managed the industry. In an expanded echo of Acheson's intent, Eisenhower then poured in aid, $60 million in 1953, double that in 1954.[40]

Later, Acheson not only emphasized the family resemblance of the 1954 settlement to the ones he had proposed. He also underscored Mosadeq's "craziness." He came later to doubt that either his own ideas or Eisenhower's would prevent future nationalist outbursts. He never retracted his view of British pigheadedness, and though he became a great friend of Eden, he described him as someone who thought one 1930s visit to Iran gave him enough knowledge to deduce that Mosadeq and his followers were mere "rug dealers." However unreliable, Mosadeq represented a "very deep revolution, nationalist in character, which was sweeping not only Iran but the whole Middle East."

He sensed and understood many of the truths of the 1951–52 Iranian story, but not that his own struggle to ply a middle course had exacerbated the British-Iranian crisis. Pushing Iran to settle and withholding aid until it did fueled Eden's intransigence. It also forced Mosadeq to look for support from Iran's own radicals. His attack on AIOC sometimes looked more like a looting than nationalization and may have been spurred by the niggardliness of U.S. aid. Acheson's insistence on British rearmament also intensified Britain's resolve to preserve its valuable Iranian holdings. Acheson fully understood about being caught between parties with irreconcilable goals. Being the moderate in such cases almost never brings rewards, applause, or success. He made both London and Tehran suspicious of his diplomacy, which is the common recompense for a mediator. Once he left office, Egypt too would grow suspicious of the Americans. While Acheson was secretary of state, however, Britain remained a close ally and neither Iran nor Egypt an enemy.[41]

33

LATIN AMERICA: CRITICAL BUT NOT SERIOUS

Spanish Verbs

Compared to Europe, the Latin American record made by President Truman and Dean Acheson is marked by ignorance and neglect as neither of them knew much about the nations to the south. The president once greeted a Bolivian diplomat with the cheery remark, "I remember you; you are the man who plays a piano and whose country needs an outlet to the sea," and saw nothing amiss in sending a trinket maker to a Latin American state as ambassador. When Americans had shown great interest in Latin America—as was the case, for instance, with John Quincy Adams and, more recently, Cordell Hull—it was primarily to block meddling by European interlopers and secondarily to open up the hemisphere for U.S. trade. Some momentary concerns in the early cold war led to the 1947 Rio Pact, in which hemispheric nations promised to consider an attack against one an attack on all. But this was more a kind of leftover hiccup from World War II than a well-defined policy of the cold war. Because Washington then saw no threat to itself from elsewhere in the hemisphere, its policy toward the "neighboring" republics was shifting and often ill defined.[1] As late as 1949, former ambassador to Brazil, Adolf A. Berle, remarked: "We have simply forgotten about Latin America." In Europe and Asia, U.S. officials used aid programs to counter the strategic threat posed by communists and their Soviet ringmasters. Since they discerned no communist infection nearby, they were deaf to Latin Americans' appeals for economic programs of their own.[2]

In the 1940s and 1950s, Americans commonly saw Latin America and its peoples through powerful cultural prisms. The man from Middletown was no exception and linked commotions in the hemisphere to "Hispano-Indian culture—or lack of it," which "had been piling up its problems for centuries." In his memoirs, Acheson wrote that the region's problems were caused by the lack of "population control," "archaic" societies, "primitive politics, massive ignorance, illiteracy, and poverty." To perpetuate their own power, the "small, reactionary ruling class" of most countries resisted much-needed foreign capital, just as they had done "since Columbus and the Conquistadores." Accurate or not, this is the only analytical remark about Latin America in nearly eight hundred pages in *Present at the Creation*. The sixty-plus references in its index to post-1948 Latin America refer mostly to passages about who did or did not support U.S. positions on cold war issues. A five-page narrative of Acheson's 1952 visit to Brazil is little better than a banal travelogue. Never pretending to know much about the area, he cited "experts in these matters" when he discussed hemispheric issues. Just as he asked aides for tuition on Germany in 1949, he threw questions to his staff a year later about Latin American states. Were they "richer or poorer, going Communist, Fascist or what?" He seldom met with Latin American ambassadors. He left it to Truman to make junketing Latin American presidents feel they were in his league.[3]

For day-to-day diplomacy, he relied on Edward G. ("Eddie") Miller, Jr., Assistant Secretary for American Republic Affairs. Like Acheson a graduate of Yale and Harvard Law School, the thirty-eight-year-old Miller was already a seasoned Wall Street lawyer when appointed in June 1949. Given even more running room than George McGhee in the Middle East, he shook up a dispirited bureau that had gone two years without a leader. With an eye for public relations, he goaded Acheson to give a major speech on Latin America and Truman to give more audiences to visiting envoys. Not wanting his new clients to feel neglected, he often trekked through the region, visiting eight Latin American capitals in his first six months in office. Fluent in Spanish since growing up in Puerto Rico and Cuba, he recruited more Spanish and Portuguese speakers to his reorganized staff. The U.S. ambassador to Argentina, Stanton Griffis, considered him the perfect "diplomat for Latin-American relationships, born with a silver spoon full of Spanish verbs in his mouth." Capable of offering a natural-looking "abrazo" to Latin American counterparts, Miller filled his colorful memoranda with some of the spiciest and most caffeinated language available in an often pallid official record. "Like the figure on Keats' Grecian Urn," he once wrote, "the United States would always be pursuing and the Latin Americans would always play the role of the flirtatious maidens, always beckoning and never giving in." His verve and lively pen probably explain why Acheson refused his resignation in December 1951. In a letter three years later, an amused Acheson recalled when Miller told him a situation in Bolivia had been "critical but not serious." His animation left the secretary of state free to be inattentive. In Latin American affairs, Acheson became Miller's Truman; when the attorney offered counsel, client Acheson went along.[4]

"Much Less in Need of Them Than They Are in Need of Us"

Acheson's first speech made at Miller's behest was for the Pan American Society of the United States in September 1949. Mostly boilerplate, it emphasized Washington's Good Neighborly commitment to noninterventionism and the Rio Treaty commitment to collective security. Despite Washington's unhappiness about recurrent coups d'état in the area, he implied that hemispheric nations were responsible for their own future. He answered complaints about the lack of a regional Marshall Plan by urging Latin Americans to seek assistance from Point Four, the World and Export-Import Banks, and private investment. If the language was bland, it was partly because Acheson could not say aloud that the United States was more dominant in the hemisphere than ever but fundamentally indifferent to it, since it stood outside the boundaries of the contest with the Soviet Union. Key U.S. officials showed little sign they considered "communism" a hemispheric threat. They were far more concerned about nationalism, especially its economic variety, and the threat this posed to private U.S. investments.[5]

The assumption of American supremacy led to attitudes bordering on the contemptuous. Columnist Drew Pearson heard that during the war Acheson had "made sneering remarks in meetings about Latin Americans"—since they "were going to be with us anyway, why bother to help them?" Agreeing, George Kennan insisted in 1950 that Latin Americans should always understand "that we are by and large much less in need of them than they are in need of us." The United States should seek respect rather than friendship from them. With Miller's approval, Louis Halle of the policy planning staff expressed a large "impatience" over Latin America's "failures of democracy." In "On a Certain Impatience with Latin America," published under the signature "Y" in *Foreign Affairs* in July 1950, he wrote that the region must further evolve before one could tell the differences between its "sheep" and "goats."[6]

When U.S. officials snapped their fingers, they usually expected hemispheric governments to stand to attention, as for example in the fight over Trygve Lie's new term as secretary-general of the UN. As Acheson recalled in 1954, he gave advance briefings on his strategy in the Japanese peace conference to Latin American delegates, swearing them to secrecy, "whereupon they went around and leaked a good deal of this to some of their brethren, mostly on the view that it was their own suggestion!" So reflex-like were Latin American votes in the UN supportive of the United States that Acheson once thought some occasional dissent might be better. Equally reflexive were North Americans' images of their southern neighbors. In a press conference, Miller spoke of events "down there" in Panama. Acheson, who thought Latin Americans loved to make "broad sweeping statements, which they have no intention whatever, or capacity, to carry out," said in House testimony in 1952 that Mexicans and Uruguayans understood "orderly government," but in Nicaragua and Peru, "you have reaction rampant, and there is stability there because there is not a chance for anyone to be unstable." Generally the "situation" in the hemisphere was acceptable; economic problems were "brewing," but Washington could "keep that on an even keel."[7]

Kennan had no match in slurring the Latins. Following a month's study trip to Latin America in February and March 1950, he submitted a report thick with deprecation, racism, and heated stereotypes. The combination of "nature and human behavior," he wrote, had generated an "unhappy and hopeless background for the conduct of human life." Resorting to a version of the traditional Black Legend that demonized Spanish rule, he blamed the "extensive intermarriage" of Spanish, Indians, and African slaves that had inscribed "handicaps to progress" in "human blood." Consequently, a typical Latin American wrapped himself in his own "cocoon" and lived by "a species of make-believe." An aghast Miller intercepted this inflammatory treatise and persuaded Acheson to lock it up. But he should not have been so shocked, for in 1949 a department study compared the United States and Latin America using "% white population" as a key variable. Other officials spoke casually about Latin American "breeds." They saw Costa Ricans, Michael Krenn observes, as illogical people with "short memories"; Guatemalans suffered from "mental deviousness and difficulty of thinking in a straight line."[8]

Though the crooked-thinking Guatemalans would soon provide an exception, the state department seldom brooded over hemispheric communists. Far more worrisome were economic nationalists—protectionists and opponents of American investments. Of these, communists seemed just another brand rather than Moscow's agents. Acheson rarely got his tail tied in a knot over anything happening in Latin America, but protectionism and hostility to U.S. capital were more likely to supply annoyance than anything else. He nonetheless never wavered from a mildly sanguine view of the U.S. position in Latin America, which, he told senators in January 1952, was "in pretty good shape." Though he had "a little concern" about Chile and "a few noisy groups in Brazil," they posed "no real problem." Even in Argentina and Guatemala, it was best just "to live through" a situation where "we have vociferous anti-American people in the saddle."[9]

As had been true for a half century, American leaders also worried about Latin American "instability," which early in Acheson's tenure mainly infected the Caribbean and Central America. A "Caribbean Legion" of exiled democrats sponsored by the presidents of Guatemala and Costa Rica tried to topple dictatorial regimes in the Dominican Republic and Nicaragua. With Washington cutting off arms sales to its sponsors, the crusade eventually petered out. Worrying more about the Legion than its targets suggested that the Truman administration was ready to tolerate authoritarian rulers as long as they did not contribute to chaos. Ironically, dictatorships flourished partly because they were planted in the rich soil of the Good Neighbor Policy, with its commitment to nonintervention. In reality, the U.S. government in Acheson's time did not expect better from the area and its emotional peoples. They would fight over anything, said Willard L. Beaulac, ambassador to Colombia. In certain countries, he thought, they "would fight with tanks and cannon, or with pistols and machetes, or with sticks and stones." Miller himself had "no patience whatsoever" for the "soft and mushy thinking in our country regarding dictatorships in Latin America."[10]

Latin American states of all stripes craved not only the kind of economic aid going to Europe but higher prices and open U.S. markets for the commodities they mined and planted. The state department, however, repulsed such demands at the 1948 Bogotá inter-American conference, preached laissez-faire, and wished its hemispheric neighbors well. Belgium and Luxembourg received more grant aid than all of Latin America from 1945 to 1950. Since it had not suffered war damage, Latin America did not qualify for Marshall Plan spending. What assistance it received usually came in small packages of technical aid, credits, and loans at market rates of interest. In September 1950, however, with Point Four about to shift to weapons aid, even the hard-bitten Miller shook his head at how new aid packages to India and Pakistan would offend Latin Americans. Arms aid or purchases were another matter. As under secretary, Acheson had opposed arms sales, concerned they would augment dictators' powers and destabilize the hemisphere, but he changed his mind during the Greek-Turkish crises, partly because others might sell them anyway. Heavy weapons sales in the region soon followed, accompanied by programs to train, co-opt, and perhaps temper the nationalism of Latin American officers. His last doubts fell by the wayside with the onset of war in Korea, after which Latin America became eligible for grants from the Mutual Defense Assistance Program. By the end of the Truman administration, a flood of military agreements and weapons reinforced armies throughout the region.[11]

The Korean War, which opened the gates for arms, also brought Acheson's requests for help on the battlefield. Only Colombia's response—an infantry battalion and a naval frigate—satisfied him. Other Latin American governments resisted, still miffed at how little reward they had received for helping in the last war. The Pentagon was not much interested anyway, distracted by symbolic contributions, including "single airplanes, surgical teams," and a few ambulances. To make them feel more appreciated, Acheson also saw to the convening of a meeting of the Organization of American States in Washington in March and April 1951. After an initial greeting from Truman, Acheson called for a free world "partnership" against the "mortal threat" of Soviet communism, which, surely with tongue in cheek, he described as the greatest menace in the hemisphere's history. Little action followed, but Miller was happy, thinking the conference had "surpassed all expectations."[12]

Miller's Mandate

It would be superfluous to record Washington's relations with various Latin American states when Acheson was secretary of state, because he usually did little more than stick his head in Miller's office to see how things were going. For most countries in the hemisphere, Miller, desk officers, and envoys in the field did the work. Oddly, however, it was Truman who led the way in relations toward Mexico. He pushed hard to give aid to the state-owned oil company, Petróleos Mexicanos S.A., or Pemex, but state department professionals mostly frustrated his wishes. His interest came from a populist dislike of the U.S. oil companies whose assets Mexico had expropriated years before. As to Cuba, he readily accepted Acheson's recommendation to extend formal recognition following the 10 March 1952 coup staged by General Fulgencio Batista Zaldívar. While a sign of Washington's broad tolerance for authoritarianism, recognizing Batista probably comported with the views of ordinary Cubans, long tired of the corrupt and inefficient regime he ousted. Ten American republics had already offered recognition when Washington acted. A few days later, Batista severed relations with the USSR.[13]

Except for Guatemala, even Miller had little time for most of Central America, saying near the end of the administration he had spent less than an hour on Honduras. But the area's recidivist instability kept his assistants scurrying, especially concerning Costa Rica, which gave up on the Caribbean Legion at Washington's insistence, and Nicaragua, ruled by the notoriously brutal Anastasio Somoza García. Of all the tolerated Latin dictatorships, this was the nastiest, but Somoza's votes always backed the United States in the UN, and both Miller and General Harry Vaughan, Truman's lax military aide, had a personal weakness for the Nicaraguan. So did Truman, who publicly mentioned that his and Somoza's daughters were schoolmates at Gunston School. In the spring of 1952, when Somoza was in the United States, Truman asked Acheson if he should ask the Nicaraguan to lunch at the White House. He was "vain and egocentric" and given to feathering his own nest, Acheson replied, but he was "energetic" and had "restored order to Nicaragua." After breaking bread with Truman, Somoza traveled to Boston to have gallstones removed, greeted by flowers from the president.[14]

Low-level arguments about economic aid, conducted by Miller on the U.S. side, dominated relations with Brazil. With the exception of an overnight stay in Trinidad, Acheson visited only this Latin American country. His July 1952 sojourn, following weeks of harrowing negotiations in Europe, was mostly about rest, recreation, and minimal attention to business. He did address both houses of the Brazilian legislature and listened when Brazil's finance minister said he had conquered the hearts of "Brazilian women." The weeklong stay made a large impression on him, related in a giddy letter to Felix Frankfurter. Like the United States in the middle of the nineteenth century, Brazil was "undisciplined, as full of energy as a colt, rich, vulgar, cultivated, poor, technically competent, naive, administratively hopeless. . . . I am in love with it."[15]

Washington mostly quarreled with Argentina in the Truman years, but Acheson, who as under secretary had settled a departmental fight over Argentina by firing both gladiators (Spruille Braden and George Messersmith), was quite content to let Miller minister to the squabbling. Washington had long disliked Argentina's ruler, Juan Domingo Perón, who gloried in rubbing Americans the wrong way, showed undue sympathy to Hitler, and had been late to join the war against him. But with his dirigiste economy weakening, he had lost most of his power to annoy by 1949, and Miller worked to normalize relations. He never fully accomplished this goal, for Perón periodically trumpeted devotion to his "Third Position" between east and west. Over time, however, by refusing either to meet Perón's peremptory demands for aid or rise to his bait, Miller both quieted the relationship and undermined Perón's appeal to others in the region. Relations improved enough in March 1950 to justify a visit to Buenos Aires. When Miller afterward wrote of the arrival of a "United States-Argentina honeymoon," Acheson asked: "Which is the bride and which is the groom?" The question was justified, for the relationship remained troubled. A failed military uprising in the fall of 1951 left Perón touchier than ever about American slights. Miller thought he really wanted "to be accepted as one of the boys" but was unwilling to give him that satisfaction. Nor would Acheson, who in January 1952 in House testimony described as "childlike" Perón's complaint that he and his wife Eva had never received a presidential invitation to the United States. When Argentina cracked down on U.S. journalistic outlets, Acheson and Miller ended anything remotely resembling courtship of the regime. In July 1952, Perón's powerful thirty-three-year-old wife, "Evita," died of cancer. As if nothing had happened, her husband signed a treaty with the Soviet Union ten days later, but his regime was now on its last legs, and the military threw him out of power in 1955.[16]

Danger Zones

Acheson's largest Latin American involvement emerged in response to revolutionary politics in Bolivia and, especially, Guatemala. It would be a mistake to assume that he might have advanced democracy, promoted economic justice, and driven dictators from the hemisphere by showing much more interest and faithfully siding with the angels. Nor were indifference and the low cold war priority given to Latin America the main reasons for the perpetuation of the regional status quo. The Good Neighbor legacy was partly responsible, however. Despotic rule proliferated more under its rubric than in the interventionist decades preceding the FDR era. Even if Acheson and his colleagues had been of a mind to move the region off dead center, local nationalism and suspicion of gringos would have constrained them. Considering the supercharged anti-communist mood of the time, what is remarkable is Truman and Acheson's composure when revolutionaries did rattle the cages of archaic Latin American regimes. Two cases in point were Bolivia and Guatemala. Both reflected the low rating given Latin American states in Acheson's diplomacy and his relaxed attitude toward homegrown radical change.

Washington's reaction to the Bolivian revolution of 1952 was both tranquil and obliging. Rather than feeling threatened, the state department spotted a chance to help (and moderate) the Bolivian upheaval. A landlocked and destitute nation resting high in the Andes, Bolivia has long been ruled by Europeans or mestizos, though mostly populated by indigenous peoples who were voteless before the revolution. The 1952 turnover, writes Cole Blasier, was "the only genuine social revolution to which the United States provided early and sustained support." Virtually all grant aid sent to Latin America in the 1950s went to the revolution Truman accepted in Bolivia and the government Eisenhower inserted in Guatemala.[17]

Bolivia's fortunes were unluckily tied to the mining and selling of tin, mostly to a dwindling U.S. market. Paltry investment, years of intensive mining of low-grade ore, and falling prices set off a series of economic crises. These climaxed in strikes and a massacre in the Cataví area in May 1949. The murder of two American citizens caught Acheson's attention, and he chafed for months at La Paz's slowness in punishing the guilty parties. The tin trade was a subject of bilateral negotiation, in which Washington resisted demands for higher prices, especially after they had doubled during the Korean War. It also protested what it deemed Bolivia's adverse investment climate and confiscatory currency laws aimed at the mining companies. When La Paz tried boosting prices even higher, Washington drove them down by opening its strategic stockpile of tin. Bolivia then cut off its nose to spite its face, throwing its economy into a tailspin by embargoing all tin exports, half intended for the United States. This was hardly what the state department wanted when it stood for building "strength rather than weakness in the free world." But a settlement remained out of reach. Negotiations stalemated in the spring of 1952, just before the revolution.[18]

The Movimiento Nacionalista Revolucionario (MNR) led the revolution in April and made Víctor Paz Estenssoro president. A founder of the MNR, Paz Estenssoro would eventually serve three terms as president. Though his movement had taken on fascist coloration during the war, it now acted for workers and peasants. The preceding regime, with the army's help, had prevented Paz Estenssoro's election in 1951, accusing the MNR of being a communist front. Acheson had quickly recognized the army junta, citing the MNR's past undemocratic record and dalliances with communists. As the 1952 revolution's leaders settled in, they rushed to persuade Washington they were no longer either fascists or communists. Fearing worse if the revolution failed, Acheson and Miller moved toward a speedy accommodation. Miller concluded that the MNR and Paz Estenssoro controlled Bolivian territory and enjoyed wide popular support.

He was impressed by their disavowal of communism and promises to respect international obligations, and he knew more obstreperous MNR cadres stood ready to grab power if they had the chance. Paz Estenssoro promised just compensation to the owners if Bolivia nationalized the mines. Miller advised recognition in May amid the circumstances that elicited his "critical but not serious" comment. With other hemispheric republics already extending diplomatic recognition, Acheson advised Truman to do the same, which he did in early June.[19]

Recognition did not mean approval, and Washington kept up its guard. In October, Acheson acknowledged that nationalization was legal but warned that it would discourage new foreign investment. The MNR government went ahead anyway. Besides nationalization, it instituted universal suffrage and extensive land reform and slashed the army's powers, all the while keeping Bolivia's communists at arm's length. Having succeeded in keeping Washington friendly, MNR leaders began receiving the benefits of sizable U.S. aid programs. Though the Truman administration never wrapped up a new tin agreement, Eisenhower did in July 1953, at a price closer to U.S. than Bolivian wishes. The Eisenhower administration then promptly sent $5 million in food aid. By the end of 1953, Bolivia had received $100 million in aid, making it the largest per capita beneficiary of U.S. assistance. Bolivians soon faced a new kind of problem, becoming less dependent on Americans' tin purchases but perilously reliant on the whims of those in Congress, the state department, and the White House who calibrated the flow of American assistance.[20]

A farce that would turn to tragedy loomed in the Central American republic of Guatemala, the only Latin American country, Kennan said in his suppressed report, likely to succumb to organized communists, and where Juan José Arévalo's reformist government, elected in 1944, had already caused qualms in Washington. A humanitarian practitioner of "spiritual socialism" and a nimble politico, Arévalo toiled to improve the lives of the poor and elevate workers' rights against mainly U.S.-owned firms. Seeking freedom from the shadow of North America, he confronted Guatemala's Moby-Dick, the U.S.-owned United Fruit Company (UFCO) and its subsidiary, International Railways of Central America (IRCA). Standing in his corner was the nationalist army colonel, Jacobo Arbenz Guzmán. Egged on by his ideological wife, Arbenz dreamily wondered about applying Marx's teachings to his impoverished country. When he succeeded Arévalo in 1951, CIA officials began scouting for coadjutors in the state department who would help bring him down. Unknown to Acheson, they struck paydirt instead at the "highest level," snaring Truman. In due course, when leaks from this colander-like plot dripped on Acheson's desk, he would persuade Truman to halt it. Acheson himself played economic hardball with Arbenz, but his main impulse toward Guatemala was that of live and let live. Eisenhower and Dulles obeyed different impulses and ousted Arbenz in a coup in 1954, setting off four decades of military rule and repression.[21]

Except perhaps for the original "banana republic" of Honduras, no Central American society was more under the heel of outside interests. Businessmen in stateside office towers ran Guatemala's transportation, telephone, and electrical systems. United Fruit owned over half a million acres of banana plantations, three-quarters of them lying fallow. Travelers from the capital, Guatemala City, to the Atlantic coast had to board the UFCO-owned IRCA, which gave sweetheart rates to UFCO itself to ship bananas to the sea. UFCO also owned all the port operations in Puerto Barrios and most of the ships coming in and out. Directly or indirectly, the livelihood of 40,000 Guatemalans depended on United Fruit.[22]

The primary reform established by Arévalo that came to set American teeth on edge was a Labor Code immediately reviled by UFCO but first viewed by the administration as enlightened. As Acheson took office, the department was weathering UFCO demands for action, pondering ways to check Arévalo's power, and putting in place a ban on U.S. weapons purchases. In June of 1949, the ambassador in Guatemala City protested years of harassment against American firms and displays of "pro-Soviet propaganda and attitudes."

The ambassador was sixty-three-year-old businessman Richard C. Patterson, Jr., last seen offending Tito in Yugoslavia (Chapter 9). Foreign service officers sneered at the indiscreet and monolingual Patterson, who openly solicited complaints from UFCO. Following a career at RCA and RKO, the well-heeled Patterson had been a regular at Democratic conventions, and under FDR he served as an assistant secretary of commerce and trustee of the Export-Import Bank. Impressed by a campaign donation of $100 thousand for radio broadcasts, Truman forgave his making a fist of the Yugoslav assignment and gave him the Guatemalan post over Secretary of State George Marshall's objections.[23]

The assassination in July 1949 of Colonel Francisco Arana, head of the armed forces and Arbenz's rival, further divided Guatemalan society. On one side were communists and those like Arévalo and Arbenz, who did not worry about mounting communist influence. On the other were landowners, merchants, and many army officers. Unrest and violence followed Arana's murder, which Arbenz might have arranged, casting doubt on a prevailing Foggy Bottom opinion that Arbenz was a mere "opportunist." But the department did not panic, despite pressure from UFCO and congressional conservatives. Nor did Miller, though he had formerly served the law firm representing UFCO's interests. He instructed Patterson to complain about the treatment of U.S. business interests but opposed any harsh sanctions. At the most, he and Acheson preferred a quiet termination of discretionary aid projects. In Guatemala City, however, Patterson started one argument after another over such issues as the failure to play the "Star-Spangled Banner" at the dedication of a new wing of Hospital Roosevelt. He became such an irritant that Arévalo remarked to Samuel Guy Inman: "You do not have an Ambassador of the United States here, but a representative of United Fruit."[24]

When Patterson began talking to the opposition and demanding the sacking of seventeen government officials he figured were communists, Arévalo had seen enough. He wanted Patterson removed without formally declaring him persona non grata. The state department had seen enough too and on 25 March 1950 told Patterson to get out on the next plane. While the department publicly made implausible excuses about his health, Patterson was urging UFCO to start an "all-out" campaign to persuade senators of its ill treatment by the Guatemalans. Amazingly, Truman gave him yet another posting, as ambassador to Switzerland, but not before Patterson achieved notoriety by inventing the "duck test." He knew that a creature looking and swimming and quacking like a duck *was* a duck, and he was equally confident about his ability to identify communists. Nonetheless, in the wake of this imbroglio, one of Acheson's aides told reporters "we are very calm and collected" about Guatemala.[25]

Acheson was soon spreading the message not to confuse homegrown radicals with Soviet-connected communists. He wanted Arévalo persuaded that Americans wished only to help generate prosperity and "liberal democracy" and told the U.S. chargé d'affaires to be patient instead of jumping on every provocation. Miller, who was preparing to visit Guatemala, was critical of UFCO and even friendlier to Arévalo when he proclaimed his solidarity with Washington in the Korean War and ratified the Rio Treaty. Even without Patterson, however, there were other officials finding reasons to worry. In May 1950, Deputy Assistant Secretary Thomas C. Mann took Guatemala's ambassador to task because of Arévalo's habit of criticizing right-wing governments while giving leftists a pass. Following Acheson's tactic of passive discord, the administration blocked World Bank and Exim loans and withheld help from Point Four, which Guatemala had denounced as a tool of imperialism. From 1949 to the eve of the coup in 1954, U.S. aid fell from a pocket-sized $2.9 million to a skimpy $200 thousand. State would not acknowledge this cold shoulder, letting Arévalo figure it out himself. Had anyone asked, Acheson could justifiably say Washington had no obligation to give discretionary aid to anyone.[26]

Before his July 1950 visit to Guatemala City, Miller had decided to delay sending a replacement for Patterson, wanting the Guatemalans to "stew in their own juice for a while." In the visit itself, he reassured Arévalo of Washington's commitment to nonintervention but chided him for the anti-American propaganda spewed by "extremists" in the coterie around him. Arévalo dismissed them as unimportant and said he knew it would be "stupid" to substitute Soviet for American friendship. While the state department remained calm in the wake of Miller's trip, others were quite exercised. Former New Deal fixer Tommy Corcoran, who served as a UFCO lobbyist, had already told woeful tales about Arévalo's agrarian reform laws to CIA deputy director Allen Dulles. Dulles at first was unimpressed, but if he happened to change his mind, the CIA was growing in its ability to act, its staff growing from 300 in 1949 to 6,000 in 1952. Mann gave Corcoran no encouragement, either, but told him all bets were off if Guatemala fell "under the totalitarian control of Communist elements." In August 1950, CIA agents began slipping into the country. They had the approval of Truman, who had not informed the state department of his decision.[27]

As Arbenz's accession to power neared, Miller forecast that he would lean hard to the left yet be an improvement over Arévalo. The latter was an academic and an ideologue, while, Washington mistakenly thought, Arbenz was a cynic or opportunist, with no axe to grind against United Fruit. After Arbenz won the November 1950 election, U.S. officials expected a centrist agenda, sprinkled with enough anti-yanqui rhetoric to hold radicals' loyalty. Once inaugurated in March 1951, Arbenz appointed only a few communists to office, but they received such key ministries as transportation, agriculture, and social security. Annoyed at the cut-off of U.S. aid and absence of a U.S. ambassador, he surprised Washington with quick moves to build state-owned power plants, carve out a highway to compete with IRCA, accelerate land reform, and slap limits on foreign oil investments. He was also shopping around the eastern bloc for weapons. The state department finally sent a career officer as the new ambassador, who continued executing the muted tactic of unpublicized pressure, hoping to divide Arbenz from his communist *compañeros*. This quietist approach became harder to sustain because of growing controversies between Guatemala and other hemispheric governments. Evidence of Guatemalan expansionism and interference in the internal affairs of other states—which had begun under Arévalo—led half a dozen governments to noisily break relations with Guatemala City.[28]

By June of 1951, when U.S. officials realized Arbenz was not the cynical, temporizing leader they expected, Acheson laid out a more stringent approach, but it still favored refusal to grant favors over reprisals. The United States shaved economic privileges, put aid on ice for the Guatemalan leg of the Inter-American Highway, and said no to new assistance. Already modest aid programs in education, health, and sanitation declined sharply. Miller now called Guatemala a communist "danger zone" and complained in August that "extremist labor demands" were persecuting U.S. businesses. In September, Under Secretary James Webb ominously noted that the department could not abide seeing "communists gain control." But on 14 November 1951, in discussion with UFCO officials, Miller and Mann did not even hint at using irregular methods. Mann advised finding a model for Guatemalan problems in the 50–50 oil deal with Venezuela.[29]

In the same spirit in January 1952, Acheson in executive testimony took a calm if inexpert view of Guatemala's people and politics, leaving the impression that the whole business was unworthy of his time. After all, what was Eddie Miller for? Communists, Acheson said, were causing some trouble, but there were only "three or four hundred" of them. The rest of "the vast Indian population" had no more "idea about Communism than they have about aviation." House Majority Leader John W. McCormack of Massachusetts disagreed, rumbling in February that Guatemala had become a "Soviet beachhead." United Fruit bemoaned the failure to enforce the Monroe Doctrine, which caused the historiographically challenged Miller to say that Monroe had multilateral diplomacy in mind. Only uncontested evidence of an armed Soviet intrusion would warrant unilateral action.[30]

"Covert ops" people in the CIA were already plotting, but as late as March 1952, the agency's intelligence branch mirrored State's analysis. Although more pessimistic a month later, analysts were still encouraged by communists' failure to penetrate the army. Then, in June, Arbenz issued Decree 900, which promised to revolutionize Guatemalan agriculture. Oligarchical landowners howled, not the least because the decree might unleash the land hunger of Guatemala's Indians. Next door, Somoza denounced the decree, too. But American aid officials contentedly observed that the decree was "constructive and democratic," similar to programs carried out in Japan and Formosa. The state department was less sanguine, observing that Decree 900 would force UFCO to surrender some 200,000 acres in return for $1.2 million, paid in bonds over twenty-five years. Hoist on its own petard because it had given lowball property evaluations for past tax returns, UFCO now roared that Arbenz had no right to use the same figures in calculating compensation. The state department suggested $16.5 million instead.[31]

In November 1951, more than a year after sending in their first covert agents, CIA officials began having serious discussions and looking for approval higher up. In January 1952, they gave Truman evidence of Guatemala's felonies, accompanied by blackly pessimistic forecasts about the future. Three separate exile groups were working against the regime and thus eligible for CIA help, one headed by Colonel Castillo Armas, code-named "Rufus." By late March, the agency was computing costs of bribing Guatemalan officials and army officers, while looking for help in other countries. Somoza visited Washington in May, escorted by a fawning General Vaughan, and reportedly told the state department that with a few more weapons, he and "Rufus" could get rid of Arbenz. (One account says he boasted to Truman at lunch "that with 600 pieces of hardware he would 'knock off' A.") The Dominican Republic and UFCO would help with financing. A member of the U.S. embassy staff in Managua later related a thirdhand story that Somoza had also sought to convey his view to Truman through Miller and Acheson. This might have occurred, for Acheson surely had Somoza in mind in a 1953 recollection when he commented that someone had tried "to get me to give him the wink to clean out communism in Guatemala." When Somoza returned home, Vaughan's assistant, Colonel Cornelius ("Neil") Mara, accompanied him. As we will see, Mara pushed for drastic action on his return to Washington. Miller got wind of it and, mistaking the Vaughan-Mara nexus to mean the scheme originated in the army, sent word to Somoza that any clandestine action would violate both the Organization of American States and UN charters.[32]

CIA director Walter Bedell Smith had already named Colonel J. C. King to head PBFORTUNE, or "Operation Fortune." The agency was expecting funding from the Dominican Republic, Venezuela, Nicaragua, and Honduras. Through Corcoran, King asked UFCO for ships for sending men and arms to Castillo Armas, who was in Nicaragua but about to move to Honduras. Castillo Armas would make a multipronged attack from the sea and across three international borders. But first, he needed Uncle Sam's nod, a few more CIA agents, and cash. All this took months.

The denial of an export license in early July 1952 for a shipment ready to leave the port of New Orleans exposed part of the plan to the state department. Miller and Under Secretary David Bruce reaffirmed denial of the license and ordered a shocked CIA officer "not to spark any revolutionary movement." Taken aback, Dulles and CIA inspector general Stuart Hedden saw Miller and Mann on 10 July. The CIA men asked three questions: "Would the State Department like to see a different government in Guatemala?" Would it oppose change brought about by force? Did it want the CIA "to take steps" to overthrow the government? Miller and Mann replied "positively" to the first question, "negatively" to the second, and, according to a CIA account, "by implication, positively" to the third. Miller later contradicted this account, saying he did not mind sending money but opposed arms shipments as too risky. Yet he did tell Dulles and Hedden that U.S. companies needed protection in Latin America. Whatever he and Mann said was too fuzzy for Smith, who phoned Bruce for clarification. Bruce seemed satisfied by the conversation. A day later, Colonel Mara in three crisp memos offered Truman a plan for robust measures against Arbenz, though he had in mind a state department project. The president received the memos a day after his regular Thursday appointment with Acheson. A penciled gloss on one by an unidentified writer recapped Somoza's view that he "could clean up the Guatemala regime with 10,000 rifles and one million rounds," with no U.S. involvement. Still not informing Acheson, Truman apparently ordered Smith to carry out the plan. Eleven days later, Dulles ordered the CIA's Frank Wisner to create "a cover story" and "a place on the Eastern Seaboard available to freighters and manifest clearings for the inventory to be made available."33

The first published account of this affair, by *New York Times* reporter Herbert Matthews, was based on an interview with Miller. While Matthews captured the story's essentials, he misstated its chronology. Miller said the export license incident prompted Acheson to see Truman immediately, with the result that the ship was diverted to the Panama Canal Zone. Doubtless Acheson did meet the president at some point about the scheme, but when is unclear. Truman's official calendar shows no meeting with Acheson between 10 and 21 July 1952. Thus, there was wide opportunity for the plot to thicken at a time of unusually thin communication between president and secretary of state. Acheson had been in Europe and Brazil through most of June and July. In August, he went to Honolulu for conversations with ANZUS allies. Throughout the summer, he was preoccupied with Egypt, Iran, Korean POWs, and, then in mid-September, with a small crisis when Moscow declared Ambassador George Kennan persona non grata. Truman, meanwhile, was also on the road, especially in September. As others maneuvered, Truman and Acheson were usually in different cities. How much Acheson knew of the maneuvers themselves remains unclear.34

According to a CIA postmortem, "on or about" 13 August, Dulles said "the Agency had the green light to go ahead on the project." But it was not until 9 September that Smith gave his formal approval. On 26 September, Somoza's ambassador, Guillermo Sevilla-Sacasa, visited Miller. He drew on his "brimful of secret information" in telling Miller about "Central American plots" and Nicaragua's hope to "cut out the cancerous growth in Guatemala." "Mr. Miller said nothing" in response. On the same day, Sevilla-Sacasa also spoke to Mann about how a "military group" would overthrow Arbenz. Mann warned against expecting U.S. military support, but Sevilla-Sacasa was justified to think both Foggy Bottom officials had just winked at him.

Yet two days later, when this Nicaraguan troubadour returned with more, Mann sat him down, told him that he (Mann) spoke "officially," and reiterated the full U.S. adherence to OAS and UN principles. It was unwise, he told the ambassador, "to speak of military adventure against Guatemala participated in by a group of American States." Either Miller, Bruce, or possibly Acheson must have intervened, for now Mann sternly denounced the coup plans as "reckless" and almost certain to leak. Worse, the United States could hardly "fight aggression in Korea and be a party to it in this hemisphere." A few days later in Panama, Miller gave the same message to Somoza's younger son, "Tachito." On 3 October, in a comprehensive attempt to set the record straight (or get on the right side of it), Mann sent Acheson a narrative of recent events. Mostly blaming Mara for misleading the Nicaraguans, he unequivocally insisted he and Miller had told Sevilla-Sacasa that Washington "could never condone military intervention on the part of an American State against one of its neighbors." Intriguingly, he also said the ambassador for the Dominican Republic claimed that his president, Rafael Leónidas Trujillo Molina, and President Truman had an "understanding" about "anti-communist activities in the Caribbean and particularly in Guatemala."35

On 4 October, CIA Director Smith ordered Wisner to "get the show on the road." Almost immediately, an unraveling of discipline and secrecy extinguished CIA plans. On 7 October, an agent in Managua asked U.S. Ambassador Thomas Whelan to transmit a "verbal message" to Somoza, purportedly from the White House. He was not to tell the state department. Whelan asked: Was this the president's order? When the agent refused to say, Whelan refused to carry the message, saying he "was signed up for the season and playing full time on the one ball club." When "Tachito" in Panama asked if the "machinery" was on the way, Miller was finally convinced the myriad plotters had blown their cover.36

Using evidence available in the early 1990s, Nick Cullather writes that having "caught wind of the operation," Acheson on 8 October told Smith "to call it off," because a "blown" operation would "destroy the remnants of the Good Neighbor policy" and erode support for U.S. policies in the United Nations. Once "Fortune" was "blown," Cullather concludes, Miller "wasted no time terminating it." Although close to the target, this analysis is slightly off, especially on the role of Truman, who nowhere in this tale showed any concern about the UN. Nor could Acheson have summoned Smith on 8 October, a day he was attending a General Assembly session in New York. Nor did Miller "promptly" terminate anything.

What did occur on the 8th was a fascinating four P.M. meeting between Wisner and King of the CIA and, from the state department, Bruce, Miller, Mann, and Doc Matthews. It was here, according to a CIA document, that "State stops the show." On Smith's behalf, Wisner said the agency thought it had State's approval, but now a "question had apparently risen" that it disapproved. CIA officers had said little about the plan, Wisner explained, because they thought State probably preferred not to know. The state department, he avowed, had "primary responsibility" for diplomatic objectives, while the CIA was merely an "executive organization" to help implement them. Thus, if State disliked "this particular project," the CIA would "take immediate steps" to halt all its "objectionable" phases.

Why, asked the state department group, did Somoza claim he had U.S. approval? Once the CIA contingent denied having anything to do with *that*, everyone "agreed" the problem originated in the "White House staff." Wisner and King in fact had not given up and urged state department reconsideration. Arbenz headed a villainous regime that someone would try overthrowing, "whether we support it or not," but a failed attempt would prejudice U.S. policy. Acheson's subordinates would not be moved. No successful coup, they said, could be kept quiet, and there must be "no question" that Washington had "a hand" in any attempt. Bruce added that he did not object if the CIA raised anti-Arbenz monies, for the state department knew it was "constantly passing money for purposes which the Department could not approve of and must do this in order to operate." But it must be done "securely." By implication, he rejected any U.S. involvement in gathering and shipping arms. Later in the day, he described the meeting in his journal as concerning a "Latin American project that had been the subject of considerable study by us." The conferees had "agreed it would not be undertaken." His biographer thinks Bruce then "convinced Acheson the operation was illegitimate and persuaded him to ask the president to cancel it."[37]

Whenever Acheson did this persuading, the event did not make it to Truman's calendar. They might have met on 12 October, when Truman flew into Washington from a west coast campaign trip; or they might have conferred by telephone during the trip. Whenever the conversation occurred, we are forced to imagine how it went. Acheson would have been the soul of tact, though it surely tested his serenity at this late date to see Truman stuffing peanuts up his nose again. He would not conceivably have dressed Truman down or made a histrionic threat to resign unless the president reined in his Nicaraguan dogs. Instead, he would act as if Truman was as dismayed as he was by this madcap conspiracy. He would have told him about the multiplying gaffes and leaks, looked him in the eye, and said something like, "Well, this just shows how sensible you have been not to let things like this happen in your administration. Just give me the word, and I'll put an end to it." Caught, Truman would be grateful for the chance to pretend he knew nothing about it.

In contrast, ample records document exactly when the CIA knew the jig was up. On 9 October 1952, the day after the climactic Foggy Bottom meeting, King told his crew that because of a state department "policy decision" opposing the "shipment of machinery as planned, this decision being precipitated by indiscretions of Somoza, all of the action planned in support of the opposition was off." He blamed "Tachito's" approach to Miller in Panama and the Dominican and Nicaraguan ambassadors' indiscretions in their visits to Mann. This all proved, he added wearily, that "no Latin American can be trusted to keep his mouth shut." He nonetheless planned to keep "Rufus" in reserve, financing him with those funds Bruce did not want to know about. Soon, Bedell Smith chastely declared his loyalty to state department policy. But in an allusion to Eisenhower's likely election as president, he also remarked that "the explosive situation in the Caribbean" might mean an early change of heart at State. King cabled Castillo Armas that the operation was off but also told him: "Our group is now considering the next step." The Somocistas found it hard to believe their venture had been scotched. At a stag dinner in Managua for his father on 13 October, Tachito took Whelan outside to tell him: "For god's sake Tommie tell Eddie [Miller] to get me those arms" and that "things are bad." Whelan commented: "The boy is worried." But he would not be for long.[38]

Coda

The importance of this episode depends on whether one is considering Acheson, Truman, or U.S. diplomacy generally. A few historians think Acheson shut "Fortune" down only when he feared exposure of the U.S. hand.[39] This seems incorrect. While Acheson never mentions Guatemala in his memoirs, at a Princeton seminar just a year after the events in question, he related an anecdote about a conversation with Somoza during his visit to the United States. After telling Acheson they called him "the Dean" in Nicaragua, Somoza said he had told Whelan: "If the Dean would just tip me the wink, there won't be any more communists in Guatemala." This, Acheson said at Princeton, "scared the daylights out of me." "No, we can't do that," he says he replied, since violating international legal norms, including the UN Charter, would cause all kinds of trouble. "Oh," Somoza countered, "it won't cause you any trouble at all." At home, he tossed "communists" in a lake full of sharks. When he made similar remarks at the White House, Truman "began to laugh, and said, 'I guess you have got a point.'" Somoza was "off to the races," peddling "all sorts of schemes." In a letter already referred to, written in 1961 after the Bay of Pigs fiasco, Acheson told Truman of telling his European friends that he and the president had "turned down similar suggestions for Iran and Guatemala."[40]

His reasons for opposing this 1952 design do not include reluctance to bruise Latin Americans' tender sensitivities, and he held no brief for the Arbenz government. His approach to Guatemala was both nuanced and opportunistic but did not encompass ousting a freely elected president. More aware than the CIA of the damaging ripples a covert operation would spread, he would surely want to quash a plot leaking from all corners. But his opposition to the scheme was more than practical. Along with Bruce, he was probably one of the administration's last holdouts against black operations against other governments, however malodorous. At the very time he cut off "Fortune," he also blocked CIA hopes to overthrow Mosadeq in Iran. He may have scorned the UN, but this international lawyer did not approve flouting its charter or other tenets of international law, and PBFORTUNE was blatantly illegal. Most important, he never doubted for a minute that his most vital responsibilities lay in Europe, and that nothing in Latin America merited taking major risks, especially illegal ones.

That "Fortune" almost came off nonetheless suggests more continuity between Truman and Eisenhower on covert operations than many partisans of either have admitted. Had Acheson been in office as relations with Guatemala continued worsening, he might have found it hard to withstand taking another shot at Arbenz. Relations did continue to fail in his last weeks. In mid-November 1952, when Guatemala's UN ambassador accosted him protesting "vicious" propaganda against his government in the U.S. press, Acheson retorted that he might consider instead what Guatemalan actions accounted for such criticism. On 12 December, CIA's Smith wrote Bruce that Guatemala had stepped up its pro-communist and anti-American campaigns. He also carefully observed that the CIA had nothing to do with groups he knew were mobilizing internally against Arbenz. But Miller still believed Guatemala (and Bolivia) posed nationalist rather than communist challenges and that Soviet influence in the hemisphere was minimal. Acheson agreed.[41]

In 1953, Allen Dulles became the head of the CIA. Again taking up the cause, the agency found in President Eisenhower and Secretary of State John Foster Dulles men with fewer scruples and less skepticism about covert actions. Arbenz seemed blind to the threat, expropriating some 234,000 acres of fallow UFCO lands in March 1953 and another 173,000 in 1954. In October 1953, Acheson's old security director, John Peurifoy, arrived in Guatemala City as ambassador, quickly earning his wife's nickname for him, "pistol packing Peurifoy." Using a previously ignored technique, he isolated Guatemala at the 1954 Inter-American Conference in Caracas by ramming through a strident declaration against hemispheric communism. In June, the CIA and "Rufus" overthrew Arbenz's government. In Mexican exile three years later, the former Guatemalan president joined the Communist Party.[42]

Dean Acheson never thought the cold war was centered on East Asia, let alone North Africa or the Middle East, and least of all Latin America. The fate of the free world, as Americans were beginning to call it, depended on events in Europe. More precisely, it depended on the future of Germany *in* Europe. For other events, Acheson assigned men he trusted to keep watch, Dean Rusk in Asia, George McGhee in the Middle East, and Eddie Miller in Latin America. When trouble spots in these regions seemed ready to boil over, and seemed to implicate the Kremlin, he took personal command. No such circumstances appeared in Latin America in Truman's presidency. Only during the 1962 Cuban missile crisis, when Acheson would briefly advise President John F. Kennedy, did he think hemispheric events deserved first-priority attention, but not because of anything about Cuba or the Caribbean as such. It was because Nikita Khrushchev had put nuclear weapons in Cuba in an effort to force Washington to abandon its position of strength in *Germany*. Thus, we must return to Acheson's 1952 efforts to secure that position—in league with America's European allies.

Part VII

34

LISBON TO LETDOWN: THE FATE OF THE EDC

Forward Power in Europe

On European matters, Acheson greeted 1952 with a mixture of hope and unease. In February, NATO Council and Big Three meetings would gather in Portugal's capital, where he hoped the allies could complete work on the European Defense Community. He also expected to finish its necessary twin, the "contractuals" that would virtually reinstate the sovereignty of the Federal Republic of Germany (FRG) and were the equivalent of a peace treaty between the FRG and the western occupying powers. He expected the two tasks to take another thirty to sixty days. France still insisted on sewing Germany into the pan-European fabric of the EDC before actually allowing it to rearm. In Bonn, Konrad Adenauer would not give the European Defense Community a single soldier until the occupation ended. Satisfying both would allow the west to establish enough forward-based forces to worry if not defeat the Red Army. But even as a climactic settlement seemed imminent, France, Germany, and Britain were all throwing sand into the gears of this vital position of strength.

Paris had forced Acheson to defer to its sensitivities and accept the EDC, but he had not swerved in wanting to get "Germany into the defense." While he saw in these European accords ways to fortify western Europe against Russian aggression, many Europeans saw them as ways to cement arrangements that would prevent them from having to face either an expansionist USSR or resurgent Germany alone. Britain wanted a stronger defense system it would not have to join directly, retaining its special link to the United States. France's eventual goal, Acheson understood, was to shed its dependence on Washington, but he nonetheless encouraged development of European unity, since elevating European (and French) confidence and strength was good for U.S. security. Though already aware of the high price Washington would pay for France's cooperation, he lavished praise on it as the avant garde of western security. In January 1952, he told House members that despite being "completely hopeless in their internal life," the French had "shown extraordinary vitality and leadership" unsurpassed "in 500 years." Now there were only a few more hurdles to leap in creating the necessary "forward power in Europe" to deter Soviet aggression. These accomplishments would ultimately make it possible to end the cold war.[1]

London: Keeping "The Great Objective in Mind"

Both economic and election cycles jeopardized these goals. By draining European dollar supplies, rearmament and Korean War purchases again caused a stuttering in economic recovery and sparked inflation, depleting resources needed for either rearmament or social renewal. Declining exports set off another British hard currency crisis. Washington's pressure to rearm, restore Germany, and condemn Chinese aggression set off anti-American fulminations in 1951–52. French politics had listed to the right in June 1951, when Charles de Gaulle's *Rassemblement du Peuple Français* took 21 percent of the seats in the National Assembly, shaking the reformist Christian Democratic coalition headed by the MRP (*Movement Républicaine Populaire*). Premier René Pleven fell from office on 18 January, succeeded by Edgar Faure. Soon Italian provincial elections would give leftist and rightist parties large gains at the expense of the center. And at home, on 29 March 1952, Truman announced he would not seek reelection, stunning Acheson and undercutting his authority with other nations. With the American hunting season open, John Foster Dulles, no longer in Truman's chicken coop, pecked at his policies as weak and passive. Republican Senator Henry Cabot Lodge, Jr., announced that Eisenhower would be on the ballot in the New Hampshire primary, spurring the five-star general to affirm he was indeed a Republican and would do his duty if called.[2]

As noted in Chapter 26, just as Acheson thought his European goals were in sight, French foreign minister Robert Schuman on 29 January 1952 sent him a surprise note full of new complaints and demands. Acheson's favorite continental statesman averred that the EDC would impose "very heavy sacrifices of a moral kind" on France, accused Bonn of conniving to receive special favors, and predicted that letting Germany into NATO would transform it into a revanchist alliance. This was a return to positions Acheson thought already disposed of. Schuman also insisted on barring West Germany from NATO and from manufacturing either artillery or gunpowder. He would not countenance having more German than French troops in the EDC. Further, the United States and Britain must guarantee that the West Germans would never leave the EDC. Most disappointing to Acheson, he insisted on an economic union between France and the disputed Saar territory. In yet another provocation, he wanted Adenauer excluded from meetings in London that would precede those in Lisbon.

From Paris, Ambassador David Bruce saw in this note fear that France would lose European political dominance to Germany as long as its own armies fought in Indochina. From Bonn in contrast, High Commissioner John McCloy reported Germans' hysterics over French efforts to treat them as inferiors in the EDC. Complaining that Schuman had adopted divisive tactics at just the wrong moment, Acheson's response on 4 February was flattering as usual but dominated by firmness. He sharply reminded Schuman of the many ways the United States had already helped France and Europe. He warned that Paris's current approach might disgust the American public. Fearing that the Saar issue could "make or break decisions of vast importance," he wanted it set aside for future settlement. German membership in NATO, too, was an issue for the future, but he vigorously disagreed with Schuman's assertion that it would conflict with obligations to the EDC.[3]

This interchange revealed the depth of allies' dislike of a hurried timetable on Germany. With a true peace treaty foreclosed, because it would require participation by a unified Germany and the Soviet Union, Acheson saw the contractuals as the quickest way to end the occupation and convert the FRG into an ally. He had overcome his dislike to accept the EDC as a way to link Bonn to NATO, and Schuman's letter plunged him into gloom.

The death of Britain's King George VI caused a rescheduling of both the London and Lisbon meetings, with funeral proceedings to begin on 13 February now attracting all kinds of leaders to London, where Acheson would serve as Truman's representative. In the days immediately preceding his departure, mixed news arrived from Europe. On 7 February, Schuman replied to Acheson with a note that was both civil and stiff, tenaciously holding his ground on every point of dispute. Warning that the National Assembly might reject all the past year's work, he demanded Big Three unity in the face of West German pressure for "concessions." A day later, Adenauer's Bundestag endorsed, 214–156, the principle of joining a European army but also passed resolutions barring acceptance of a second-class role. Finally, the French National Assembly approved the EDC in a 327–287 vote. But it too attached bothersome riders, these pronouncing against German membership in NATO and demanding a guarantee from Washington and London that Germans would permanently stay in the EDC and Anglo-American forces remain on the continent "as long as seems necessary."[4]

In London, Acheson stayed at the embassy residence near Hyde Park. After walking by the bier in Westminster Hall, he signed "the books" at Buckingham Palace and other royal residences. He had an audience with the young Queen Elizabeth and her prince. The 15th of February was a hard day, starting a little past eight in the fog and "patches of drizzle" that followed "one another across the Thames." The mourning diplomats waited in the cold for an hour, but his "ever-solicitous" secretary Barbara Evans had supplied Acheson with long underwear "and a small container of alcoholic restorative." It was his toughest experience ever, he later told Congress, adding that anyone wanting to "represent the President at a royal funeral can have the job." After standing in one spot for ninety minutes, the mourners took three hours to walk a mere three miles. "You try doing that, and doing this slow business, with a drum booming, so that even if you do not want to keep step, you cannot help it, because that drum goes 'wham, wham.'" Ahead of him was Moscow's "bundled up" representative, Jacob Malik, who moved "with the inevitability of a Sherman tank." Then they all boarded a train to Windsor Castle. Wartime Canadian and British friends shared food and drink before a march to St. George's Chapel for the final rites. Finally, back in the embassy, Acheson imbibed more of "Miss Evans' restorative" before soothing his "aching muscles" in "a long, hot bath."5

The bath did nothing to wash away disagreements with the allies. Those with France stemmed not just from the issues already mentioned but from a fundamental clash over the likelihood of war. Thus, immediately before the London meetings began, Truman announced the existence of a "very real" chance of war with the USSR while Schuman remarked that it was not "imminent or inevitable." Britain seemed tempted to join Paris's demands for U.S. assurances of future German virtue. Acheson admonished both to cease insulting a nation they knew would soon be a full-fledged partner; they must realize that, without the EDC, they might face their worst nightmare, an independent German army. Paris and London were also insisting that Bonn make a greater financial contribution to western defense and forswear manufacturing any dangerous weapons or explosives, despite current shortfalls in allied production. Acheson might have laughed at a James Reston article trumpeting his ability to slip Germany directly into NATO and threaten an end to congressional funding for either NATO or the EDC if the Europeans did not cooperate. He had threatened the first for months without effect, and the second would be a self-destructive bluff. Instead of empty threats, therefore, he tried amid the London drizzle to persuade Churchill, Eden, and Schuman to greet Adenauer as a true ally. A combined U.S.-UK promise to find a recipe forbidding German secession from the EDC caused a more tranquil Schuman to agree Adenauer could at least join the talks.6

The U.S.-UK promise reflected Acheson's growing comfort with Eden. Americans seeing them pictured together in newspapers often mistook one lanky, sartorially splendid, and mustachioed foreign minister for the other. Because they came to think so much alike, they began cooking up scenes of contention to persuade Schuman they were not ganging up on him. Nonetheless, the "guarantee" against German secession was challenging. Because Acheson thought the impending U.S. presidential campaign ruled out a new treaty or congressional resolution, he proposed a presidential declaration to accompany either the signing of the EDC treaty or submission of the contractuals to the Senate. Truman and Acheson's assistants began drafting words to pledge U.S. action "against anyone who breaks out of the ring," whether Germany, a Gaullist France, or an Italy captured by communists. Such a statement, he hoped, would get Schuman "over his neurotic obsession with a guarantee." He counted on Eden for a stout UK guarantee to precede any statement from Truman.[7]

Once Adenauer joined the discussions on 18 February, Acheson receded to the background, encouraging Schuman to learn how to trust the German leader. The Big Three had already agreed that restrictions on German production— the "security controls"—would consist of self-denying vows by Bonn itself not to manufacture "atomic, biological, and chemical weapons," military aircraft, "guided missiles," or large naval vessels. Acheson also thought he had struck "gun barrels" and explosives from the *verboten* list, but more arguments on these would follow. He remained concerned that giving way to demands by Adenauer rather than voluntarily displaying trust of the FRG might provoke the very insolence Schuman and Eden worried about. They should "keep the great objective in mind" rather than smack Adenauer on the knuckles about trivia. As Adenauer put it, "It was an odd partner who, on joining an enterprise, was required to say three times over that he expected to be a well-behaved member." As he and Schuman began huddling together, often speaking in German, neither Acheson nor Eden interrupted, or even asked for translation. At one point, Adenauer and Schuman the Alsatian began laughing about the meaning of *Rechtskraft*. With Adenauer succeeding in reducing their fears, Schuman and Eden finally agreed to delete repeated references to Germany's "pacific intentions." At that point, Acheson cut in to say he saw "a large area of agreement." Even so, Schuman would not fully agree on the negotiated "security controls" until late in the following Lisbon conference.[8]

Not only that, regression set in on the last day of the London meetings, which ended with a painful exchange between a newly mistrustful Schuman and a now exasperated Adenauer, who finally exploded: "Have confidence!" Acheson then flew to Lisbon. His lengthy cable to Truman from Lisbon indicated among other things just how little supervision he received from the White House. He approached Lisbon with "hope," he told the president, but also reported that Schuman was wracked by doubts. Aware of Gaullist and Communist opposition to the EDC, Acheson feared the French Socialists might desert the MRP coalition, which would kill the European projects for good. The dwindling of support, as Reston noted, signaled Europeans' realization that the Korean War would not lead to World War III, shaking their belief in the necessity of the buildup favored in Washington. Ironically, Acheson's campaign to stiffen NATO had succeeded sufficiently to shrink fears of the Soviet Union, spawning a complacency that worked against his "sudden-diplomacy." "And when the old confidence revives in Germany and France," Reston concluded, "the old enmities rise with it—which is what Mr. Acheson now is trying to deal with at the Lisbon meeting."[9]

Lisbon: "Something Pretty Close to a Grand Slam"?

Even if Stalin did not intend to invade western Europe, by 1952 he had transformed his large occupation army in East Germany into a force designed for offensive operations. Regardless of rising confidence in western Europe, NATO as a true force was still a dream. It was certainly no threat to any legitimate Soviet interests. With western Europe still fundamentally defenseless in case of general hostilities, Acheson's hope as he moved from the banks of the Thames to the Tagus was to reverse Schuman's proclivity to treat Bonn "as both ally and enemy." With U.S. forces engaged in Korea, French in Indochina, and British guarding the Suez Canal, he wanted to plug NATO's gaps with the suppressed military power of West Germany.

To do so would require overcoming different kinds of resistance from France and Great Britain. So long as fighting in Southeast Asia pinned down eight of France's best divisions and consumed more officers than emerged from its service schools, Paris could not muster the forces Washington wanted for Europe and therefore would not permit a German force outmatching its own on European soil. This concern explains Schuman's prickliness, along with the Saar dispute, suspicions of Anglo-American collusion, and anger at lack of U.S. support for Paris in North Africa.

British policy was far more in tune with but not identical to Acheson's. Having overridden Churchill's disdain for the EDC, Eden was feeling his oats and seemed ready to emerge from his long apprenticeship. His willingness to join Washington in providing guarantees against German secession affirmed that the UK could act in the alliance vanguard while staying out of the EDC. This would preserve its special connection to Washington and offshore role as the head of a non-European Commonwealth. In Lisbon, he would work at his own project of triple containment: keep Germany inhibited, Britain detached, and the United States joined at the hip.[10]

Acheson reveled in Lisbon's "glorious sunshine" on the first day, 20 February 1952, "a most welcome change from the rain and fog of London." While Alice ventured from the embassy residence in old Lisbon, attracting the locals' admiration as she moved about the city to paint, her husband attended five plenary NATO Council meetings, a series of caucuses with Eden, Schuman, and Benelux ministers on Germany and the EDC, separate Big Three engagements, and audiences with Portuguese ruler António de Oliveira Salazar. As foreign ministers met in one room, defense and finance ministers met in others. Acheson thought his Lisbon labors strongly aided by Director of Mutual Security Averell Harriman, Secretary of Defense Robert Lovett, and Secretary of the Treasury John Snyder. They worked as a team on the "constant flow of telegrams" to Truman. At home, the president smothered burbles of interference in their momentarily leaderless departments.[11]

Many of the goals decided on at Lisbon never saw life, but Acheson thought it the "most productive" conference he ever attended. Greece and Turkey formally entered NATO, which created the new post of secretary-general and agreed to Acheson's proposal to move its headquarters from its temporary London home to Paris. The NATO Council adopted the weighty report on cost sharing offered by the "Wise Men" committee of deputies, and, as Acheson, Eden, and Schuman talked almost continuously, Adenauer in Bonn promised to forego production of warships, guided missiles, or anything nuclear. Thus assured, the Lisbon conferees adopted the "contractuals" for normalizing relations with Bonn, which in turn made the EDC appear ready for approval in the spring. Pacified by these promises and agreements on Germany's financial contributions to western defense, France also gained Acheson's promise of more dollar aid. Most notably, the allies agreed on a massive military buildup, solemnly swearing by the end of 1952 to field a 50-division army (12 of them German, attached to the EDC), 4,000 aircraft, and a "strong naval force." As the conference neared its end, Acheson, though exhausted after working twenty hours a day for four days, cabled Truman in a moment of euphoria: "We have something pretty close to a grand slam."[12]

All this work had begun agreeably enough, with Acheson and Schuman having a "very pleasant, friendly, and amusing" chat at a tea hosted by Acheson. Schuman seemed ready to accept his assurances and to see Adenauer as a "European" like himself. On 22 February, Acheson met Salazar, who much impressed him—Plato if not modern civil libertarians, he said later, would have seen his virtues. On 22–23 February, the Council ratified deputies' spadework on the German contractuals, endorsed a European army tied to NATO, and adopted the Wise Men's report. When Canada's Lester Pearson declined the post of NATO secretary-general, Acheson and Eden began eying Oliver Franks. Things seemed to be going well, prompting an unbelieving Acheson to cable Truman: "Life is never as clean as this."[13]

Monday, 25 February, produced a marathon, beginning with a French squall against the fourteen divisions assigned to them by the Wise Men. Leaking of Faure's efforts to fashion a compromise on this issue aroused accusations of a "sellout" from Charles de Gaulle. Then Franks snubbed Eden's bungled proffer of the secretary-generalship and, in his "iciest tones," rebuffed Acheson's plea to reconsider. Although the NATO Council did much work, it also adjourned before settling Germany's financial payments for defense, on which other nations' contributions depended.

Thus, with their assistants trailing behind, Acheson, Schuman, and Eden gathered at the British embassy at ten P.M. to ponder proposals from a committee of the German high commissioners. The abstruse issues involved in squaring German and French financial figures do not warrant retelling, but Acheson's account of the ensuing all-nighter does. Before long, "quibbling arguments broke out, which confused an exhausted Schuman and bored Eden, who was catching cold." Acheson hoped "midnight weariness" would produce a settlement, and sure enough, Schuman left for bed, expecting a working committee of deputies to unravel the last knots. Instead, the committee erupted in discord, with the French and Anglo-Saxons finding different meaning in identical instructions. Eden "exploded in a most spectacular and satisfying pyrotechnical display, accompanied by animadversions upon French national deficiencies." "Every time a crisis occurs in the world," he bellowed, "some damn Frenchman goes to bed!" This "shocked everybody into the necessary state of fright," and when Eden said he would personally shake Schuman from his sleep, the latter's aides dashed to his bedside themselves. "Puzzled," Schuman fell back to his pillow after supporting the Anglo-Saxon version of events and telling his assistants to accept their word on other such disagreements. Then the fuming, ill, and "fed up" Eden retired, but not before giving his proxy to Acheson, who complained that "at every crisis some damn Englishman goes to bed." "So I stayed in the living room until 4 o'clock that morning and every dispute that came up, if it was a French dispute I was Mr. Schuman; if it was a British one, I was Mr. Eden; and if our people raised any fuss, I was myself, speaking for Harriman, Lovett, Snyder, everybody else."[14]

The haggard ministers reassembled Tuesday the 26th at the French embassy. A long day of discussion failed to bring final accord on German "security controls," but the three men made progress on a synchronized signing of the EDC treaty and German contractuals. Acheson hankered to have the EDC signing at The Hague but agreed to Paris instead. He briefly demanded Strasbourg for signing the German contractuals, not for its pâté de foie gras but its emblematic significance as the base of the fledgling European Union. Again, he gave way to the obvious and preferred choice of Bonn. After the final Lisbon communique, he ended his "grand slam" message to Truman by reporting that he and John Snyder, as "the last of the Four Musketeers, leave tonight."[15]

Many parts of the grand slam never came to pass in reality, most notably the ambitious NATO buildup. The Europeans knew they had promised more than their voters would allow, and only Acheson, Reston thought, would gain easy support at home. "For once," he wrote, his "homecoming promises to be tranquil." He had carried out a virtual revolution in German policy without stirring a major public debate, acting the "cupid" in gaining German and French promises "to kiss and make up." Although a member of Congress thought Acheson had taken "time by the forelock and brought home the bacon," Reston, on second thought, believed his greatest achievement in Lisbon might have been to prevent repudiation of the EDC by either Paris or Bonn. C. L. Sulzberger, Reston's colleague, warned that "the German people, apathetic and surly, neither wish to arm nor to finance such a privilege. The majority of Frenchmen still detest the Germans and mistrust them—above all with a gun in their hands." Though seemingly confident about Lisbon's achievements in a radio and television broadcast on 29 February, Acheson added: "The days of danger are still with us."[16]

Even with some goals unrealized, Lisbon remains a signal success in what Acheson called a "chain of achievement." In a mere seventeen months after the September 1950 Waldorf Hotel meetings, NATO had added Turkey, Greece, and (indirectly) the Federal Republic of Germany as members, created new institutions for running the alliance, and dispatched a World War II hero and fresh U.S. army divisions to make it a military reality. On 28 March 1952, Acheson wrote that the alliance had become a "far stronger, broader and more mature organization," the result of what he termed "the supreme gamble upon which we would stake our whole prestige, skill, and power." In Lisbon, he harvested promises to create a force that could deter or stop a Soviet attack, which guaranteed the continuation of heavy congressional arms subsidies for the allies. In line with NSC-68, Lisbon was also a valiant effort to keep any future war nonnuclear. Since 1947, U.S. promotion and pressure had moved western Europe to unprecedented acts of cooperation and "integration." Acheson's ministrations to the FRG established what Wolfram F. Hanrieder calls "a remarkably stable German-American relationship," with strong public support in both countries. Although Acheson did not say it, he also understood that U.S. actions since 1947 had made it western Europe's leader.[17]

"Signed and Sealed But . . ."

The "grand slam" was the high watermark of American optimism about NATO. Just as Acheson was claiming a historic achievement of European unity, "a cold wind" across the Atlantic brought word that Faure's government had fallen over the defense spending increases promised at Lisbon. Acheson came to believe the large military expansion of NATO and the EDC fell victim to U.S. elections, unforeseen congressional cuts in foreign aid, and deepening French disenchantment over Indochina. Hopes for détente also played a role, first emerging when Stalin offered a deal on Germany in March 1952 (see the next chapter) and then reemerging when he died the next year. Even at Lisbon, some of the Europeans may have been playacting, giving Acheson paper victories they did not plan to carry out. Many not only did not want to pay the financial and political costs of military expansion but did not believe the U.S. estimates of Soviet military prowess that justified them. They had already begun hoping that American tactical nuclear weapons would blunt any Soviet threat, an outcome Acheson deplored.[18]

Business on the EDC and contractuals oscillated between advances and retreats into the spring. Acheson fretted about the dangerous prolongation of the western occupation of Germany, the "first-class mess" Stalin's German proposals might cause, and the possible collapse of the EDC, leading to an Anglo-American retirement from Europe and thus the "disaster" of a "neutral Germany." On 11 April, his fifty-ninth birthday, he told Schuman tardy progress on the EDC was "gravely imperiling all our plans." But suddenly after "nightmarish weeks" of immobility, the logjam broke, and on 22 May Acheson again flew to Europe for his "most critical" mission. The EDC and contractuals—intertwined and negotiated in unison—were virtually ready, owing mainly in his view to Adenauer's "European" statesmanship. In Bonn, Acheson devised new treatments for French fears of German secession from the EDC while sweet-talking Schuman through nonstop talks on the last wrinkles of the contractuals. In Paris, police cracked heads of rioters protesting the arrival of General Matthew Ridgway to replace Eisenhower. As his countrymen shivered with concern, old Socialist Party leader Edouard Herriot begged the "slightly naïve" American idealists not to "drag us" into repeating the 1920s effort to trust the Germans. With a moping Schuman appearing to lose control of his own ministry, Adenauer begged Acheson to buck him up. Both Adenauer and Acheson feared a French failure of nerve would strand Germany in the center of Europe, where it might play what Adenauer called "its own game between the two great powers."[19]

At two A.M. on 25 May, negotiators in Bonn tied the knots between NATO and the EDC. Each group would consider an attack against it as an attack on the other. With the "security controls" settled, the last difficulty was the guarantee against German secession from the EDC. Eden promised a treaty pledging that as long as Britain was in NATO, it would use force supporting any endangered EDC member. Philip Jessup invented the U.S. counterpart, accepted in the wee hours by France. Since NATO's Article 4 required consultations should any member think its security endangered, President Truman and the Churchill government would promise action against any threat to the EDC's "integrity or unity" as if it were a threat to "their own security." For good measure, the Americans promised to keep forces in Europe, meaning Germany. In the afternoon of the 25th, the Bonn negotiators learned that a ham-fisted Soviet threat against Bonn had backfired, solidifying German support of the late-night measures and nullifying the previous day's charge by Kurt Schumacher, West Germany's mortally ill opposition leader, that anyone signing the contractuals could not be a true German.

The reward for the delegates' success was a splendid dinner in a former archbishop's palace overlooking the Rhine. The next morning, 26 May 1952, a "smiling and relaxed" Schuman joined others in signing one agreement, four conventions, a clutch of annexes, and "a score" of exchanged letters. Despite this hillock of contractuals, the Big Three reserved the power to intercede in protecting the still not fully sovereign FRG from either external attack or internal subversion. They also forbade unilateral German action to negotiate a peace treaty with Moscow, alter its borders, expel western forces, or cut off access to Berlin. At the signing ceremony, Acheson made a ringing endorsement of liberty as an essential part of a legitimate political system. One of the west's "great aims," he declared, "one of the great themes of its culture, and one of the great achievements of its people, has been freedom." Although West Germany and Berlin would now enjoy freedom, one of the "great aims" was incomplete until "all Germans—east and west" were "reunited in freedom."[20]

Then it was off to the Clock Room of Paris's Quai d'Orsay to sign the 132 articles and 12 associated protocols of the fifty-year EDC treaty. The "dazzling" Acheson and Eden sat "at either end of a long table with representatives of the other NATO nations along one side," symbolizing, thought the *New York Times* writer, that French, German, Italian, and Low Country EDC members would be "flanked by the superior power of the United States and Britain." Acheson and Eden signed their commitments to the EDC, that of the United States amended at the last minute but consistent with Jessup's design. Because of all the spilled ink and crosscutting pacts, Germans and Americans would now defend the others' security despite the failure to insert Bonn in NATO. It was, Acheson told senators, a "subterfuge": "Twelve nations give a guarantee to 6 nations, and 6 nations give it to 12," even though all but one of the 6 was part of the 12!

Within hours of the ceremonies, French leaders began throwing mud on all the recent achievements. Defense minister René Pleven predicted that EDC would never get past the Assembly while France bled in Indochina, and the obdurate President Vincent Auriol, imprisoned by the Nazis for three years, dismissed the anti-secession guarantees as hollow "du blabla." Soon, de Gaulle characterized the EDC as a *"mélange apatride"* (stateless mixture), created so "Germany would be reputed not to have an Army while at the same time reconstituting a military force." As Eden later wrote, "all was signed and sealed, but far from delivered."[21]

Ebbing

Like great waves, American diplomacy first crashed on European shores in 1947 with the Truman Doctrine and the Marshall Plan, again in 1949 with NATO, and finally, from the fall of 1950 to spring of 1952, with the push for German rearmament and the EDC. Then the surf of what Acheson called the "high moment of renewed energy and hope" subsided, chased by rip tides of apathy and resistance. Euphoria eddied away as one government after another reneged on its Lisbon pledges. Eager for success, Acheson had accepted cheap promises the allies soon ignored. In November, along with the Democrats' thrashing in an acidic election campaign, came a diplomatic freeze on Germany and the EDC. Executives, representatives, and the people they represented scuffled at cross-purposes. In both France and Germany, many favored delaying approval of both the Bonn-Paris agreements and Schuman Plan. In the UK, too, growing numbers clamored for more independence of the Americans and détente with the Russians.[22]

In what turned out to be a piece of unwarranted optimism, Acheson told the national security council not to expect French ratification of the EDC until October. Obsessed with the German "menace" and "almost completely unaware of the Soviet threat," French cabinet ministers, he told reporters while still in Paris, claimed they could not get the EDC through the Assembly without more U.S. help in Indochina and more understanding on North Africa. Even though the Senate ratified his European handiwork on 1 July, Acheson's ability to shape events was wilting. In Europe, he had neither Eisenhower nor the retired John McCloy working their magic. Bursts of anti-Americanism in France caused the state department to believe Paris would ratify nothing. Equally discouraging were British and French media reports, "allegedly quoting high govt sources," blaming Washington for the slippage in the Lisbon goals.[23]

Linking Germany's revival under U.S. sponsorship to its own perceived decline, France allowed its relations to the United States to sink to new lows from the Clock Room signings to the abandonment of Indochina and the Assembly's defeat of the EDC in 1954. The French came to realize the EDC would eliminate both an independent German army and an independent *French* army. In the summer of 1952, one of the worst U.S.-French arguments came over Paris's demands that Washington repair France's dollar shortages by purchasing its defense products. As ingratiating as fingernails on a blackboard, Ambassador Henri Bonnet alleged in a foul meeting with a U.S. defense official that Washington, not Paris, was torpedoing the Lisbon goals by welshing on promised aid. By early September, Acheson found himself exhorting his ambassador, James C. Dunn, to stamp out the view that Washington was "forcing a reluctant France to accept EDC." In October, after listening to the reading of a message from Acheson detailing the ways Washington had helped France, its new premier, Antoine Pinay, ripped into Dunn and refused to accept the note. Convinced that U.S. positions on North Africa had the most corrosive effects on U.S.-French relations, Dunn only grudgingly accepted denials that Pinay's government was conducting secret talks with the Russians.[24]

Though Pinay in late October briefly tried charming instead of insulting Dunn, in a speech on the 27th, President Auriol complained bitterly about rearmament costs, Indochina, and North Africa. Relations with France, Dunn opined, had not been so bad since 1946. A dismayed Acheson replied that European (and U.S.) security relied on France *and* Germany, not one or the other. For over two years, he had been trying to gain French acceptance of the Germans. Concerned about their sensitivity, he had not prodded them to ratify the EDC. The problem was that the United States agreed with France only 90 rather than 100 percent of the time. Though sorely tempted, he had discarded the option of saying to hell with Paris and tying U.S. fortunes to Bonn's. Near the end of the year, René Mayer, a shuttlecock on the EDC, succeeded Pinay as prime minister, and shortly before Acheson's retirement, Schuman finally lost the foreign ministry to the old Gaullist Georges Bidault. Both were bad omens for the EDC. Not long before the Assembly rejected it in 1954, Acheson described France as the Achilles heel of the alliance, making "the future of the coalition almost hopeless." Its paralysis in Indochina and inability to reconcile with Germany "paralyzed" everything else in Europe, since a Franco-German rapprochement was "central" to creating "a strong NATO, a strong EDC," even "a strong Western European civilization" able to withstand "totalitarianism." In both Europe and Asia, "almost every problem you come up against brings you to the inability of France to decide and act."[25]

Washington was so preoccupied with France, it was caught by surprise when the EDC suddenly hit the wall in *Germany*. McCloy's successor, Walter J.

Donnelly, said Adenauer's growing bitterness at French resistance made him again prefer equal membership in NATO. When other Germans questioned whether the EDC treaty was at odds with the Federal Republic's constitution and eventual hopes for reunification, Adenauer withdrew it from the legislature. After Bonn's highest court declared the pact constitutional, he finally resubmitted it in March 1953, but not before giving alibis to other jittery governments to defer their own days of decision.[26]

Britain was also a source of frustration. Its ongoing refusal to join any continental undertaking was a key reason for French attitudes. It led the parade of those claiming the need to "stretch out" their military buildup. In early September, Acheson told Pearson he not only had "no sympathy" for Britain's excuses, he considered its claim to prefer air power and nuclear weapons (strategic and tactical) a mere cover for cuts Churchill made for "political reasons." Pearson, unpersuaded, thought U.S. rearmament pressure made Europeans think "there is just about as much to be feared from U.S. rashness as from Soviet aggression." In Pearson's capital of Ottawa for a neighborly farewell in November, Acheson referred aridly to the arrest of Lisbon's momentum. "Grave problems" now faced NATO, and "*rapprochement* between France and Germany" looked "more remote than ever." Plans for European defense had been "checked," and he was "full of foreboding about the future." Briefing Eisenhower a few days earlier, he pronounced French ratification of the EDC "uncertain" and could not predict early German approval anytime soon, either.[27]

He was "very deeply depressed about the whole thing." With Europe hanging "by the thin threads of the lives of Adenauer and Schuman," in his last Paris meetings in late December, he tried putting a whip to NATO's haunch. Old friends smiled and clapped their hands when he made a vigorous speech about their accomplishments, but they treated his lame duck delegation "with the gentle and affectionate solicitude that one might show to the dying." In private, he shared his deepest pessimism with France's Jean Monnet. From a summer of high "momentum," they had moved to a season of "retrogression," and now the west might be heading toward "complete disaster." For five years, the United States had come an "amazing distance" in response to "brilliant" and pathbreaking "European initiatives," but if European unity now failed, none of it would last and the "basis of American policy would begin to disintegrate." If its partners "gave up the struggle," it would be "quite quixotic," as well as politically impossible, for U.S. forces to stay in Europe in such large numbers. As the "unfaltering paladin of European interests," John L. Harper writes, Acheson's own "conscience was clean." In vast understatement, he cabled Truman from Paris that the "atmosphere" was "quite different" from Lisbon's.[28]

The "Disease" of the Grand Alliance

In January 1953, when Acheson left office, no one had ratified the EDC treaty. The convention regularizing relations with West Germany lay still in the water, though in March, the Germans ratified the EDC and contractuals. In Acheson's farewell appearance before the Senate's foreign relations committee, he admitted NATO's forces were not up to "Lisbon standards," and that State's calendar for making them ready to fight kept slipping. Well into that year, no more than fifteen NATO divisions, few in topflight condition, stood opposite the Red Army.

Still, the effort to create a European situation of strength had come far. NATO did not exist when Acheson entered office. Only three years after its founding, it had established an array of commands and committees and a sophisticated headquarters organization, also Lisbon's handiwork. Bulldozers scraped the ground in France and Belgium for bases and "infrastructure." A multinational force gradually spread over hundreds of miles of the central European landscape. In the view of Britain's Hastings Lionel (Lord) Ismay, who became secretary-general after Pearson and Franks declined the job, this force was ready to fight "from the North Cape to the Caucus." But it was hard to maintain momentum. No sooner had Stalin died than the U.S. government itself suggested stretching out the attainment of higher force levels. Before long, Eisenhower and Dulles wanted only thirty "standing" divisions along NATO's central front. Ominously, this meant a far greater role for tactical nuclear weapons.[29]

French weakness in Indochina and fear of Germany were the fundamental reasons for the EDC's death in 1954. Acheson had French vulnerability in mind when he wrote Truman in October 1953 about "the disease from which our Grand Alliance has suffered." With France's defeat at Dien Bien Phu, a new coalition government headed by the Radical Party's Pierre Mendes-France threw in the towel in Southeast Asia. Knowing the outcome, it finally submitted the EDC to the Assembly, which administered its coup de grâce by a vote of 319–264 on 30 August 1954. With Acheson watching grumpily from his law office, Britain's reluctant Europeans came to the rescue, using a revived Western European Union (WEU) as its instrument, formed in 1948 but neglected after creation of NATO. France had always insisted on some kind of British partnership in helping contain a rearmed Germany, and the WEU enjoyed the vital element of British membership. In a most ingenious achievement, Eden jumped on a moment of new French vulnerability. A large electoral victory in the fall of 1953 expanded Adenauer's bargaining power, while Eisenhower and Dulles, like Acheson before, were itching to arm the Germans with or without the French. With a new promise to keep U.S. forces on the continent in his pocket, Eden with Mendes-France's tacit understanding brokered a new set of agreements, concluded in October 1954. These welcomed the FRG (and Italy) to the WEU and, through a new set of contractuals, restored West German sovereignty. Bonn reconfirmed its acts of self-denial on nuclear and chemical weapons and gave guarantees against any adventure for "lost" territories. It could now rearm by joining its forces with those of other Union states, all assigned to NATO. As 1954 ended, the French Assembly approved Eden's package 287–260.

Now assured of British participation, France took the last, inescapable step in May 1955, permitting West Germany's entry into NATO, with its entire military expressly allotted to NATO duties. With exquisite irony, Paris in the end accepted Acheson's first choice, putting a new German *Bundeswehr* directly in NATO. London's vow to keep its own forces in Europe for the life of the Brussels pact helped subdue the French fear of having the Germans overwhelm them. It had finally dawned on Paris that the Germans could not perpetrate any mischief within NATO, hemmed in by Britain and the transatlantic American superpower. Soon a new, more relaxed French generation accepted the dedication of the Germans to "Europe" as equal to their own. In yet another irony, it was de Gaulle's France, not a revanchist Germany, that "seceded" from NATO forces in the 1960s.[30]

Coda

In his drive to turn weakness into strength by rearming Germany, Acheson had not fully grasped what the allies really wanted from NATO and what they would abide in a German revival. Even more than robust armies in the field, they wanted a "permanent" U.S. commitment to their future and involvement in European security. None favored including West Germany in European security unless the United States led the way in defending western Europe. It is odd that Acheson, so attuned to allies' needs, had a tin ear on the German issue, half understanding but minimizing the vital questions that worried them. He was justly impatient with the avarice behind Anglo-French efforts to weaken German export capabilities by sidetracking Bonn into producing low-level weaponry. But other concerns deserved more sympathetic consideration. France's ambassador to the UK, René Massigli, drew on phantasmal fears in predicting that a rearmed Germany would immediately drag NATO into a war for "lost territories," but it was careless not to address Schuman's more realistic fears. Many European leaders had personally heard the jackboots of German armies in two wars, mercilessly destroying the best *armées* France could hurl against them. To scoff at such cold sweats provoked Europeans' anger, paralyzing U.S.-French relations and stirring anti-Americanism through the continent. Europe was not ready for German rearmament in 1951 and 1952. It was in 1954–55, when Eden pulled the WEU rabbit from his hat. By then, Europeans had made enough progress in rebuilding their armies, economies, and morale to make Adenauer's *Bundeswehr* palatable. And Paris no longer had to send its best to Indochina.[31]

Although France did not see the world as Acheson did, it was always at the center of his concerns. Unlike Washington, Paris had not reconciled itself to a lasting cold war or rid itself of dreams of building an east-west bridge to Moscow. If France succeeded in excluding the United States from continental leadership, however, West Germany would hold the whip hand, which was far worse. Solving the problem by enfolding it within a web of supranational institutions was a brilliant solution, but without a vital European connection to the UK and United States, the FRG would remain in a position to dominate western Europe.

Acheson grasped French anxieties without being willing to surrender to them. He never utterly gave up the idea of forcing Paris to accept a central German role in western defense. Though he never acted on it, his attraction to unilaterally arming the Germans over French objections was visible to others. His pertinacity and impatience on the issue (in part a response to Pentagon pressure) rubbed wounds already sore from France's recent inglorious experience in war and its fear of national decline. Given his overall strategy, the logic of this stance was unassailable but not Acheson's sense of timing. He provoked tension by insisting on actions France and others were unready to take willingly. The very distinction between German rearmament now and a little later opened unnecessary rifts.

Lawrence S. Kaplan criticizes the eager embrace of the FRG for helping "insure a division of Germany for a generation," but surely the key word is *helping*. Acheson's worries about Stalin's intentions, which were neither benign nor transparent, did not arise from a fevered imagination. The failure to genuinely test the Soviet bid for a German settlement described in the following chapter might conceivably have prolonged Germany's division, but Acheson was correct to prefer division to reunification. Neither cold war bloc suffered from postponing reunification until 1990. On the other hand, both might have come to harm had an armed, reunified, and unanchored Germany materialized in the early 1950s. Moreover, Germans of the FRG unquestionably benefited politically and economically from decades of living in the embrace of NATO and what became the European Union. Acheson's policies went far to advance West German economic and social recovery, acceptance by its western neighbors, and, finally, rearmament. In detail, these comprise the very definition of a "position of strength." In realpolitik terms, he had done much to restore a favorable European balance of power.[32]

In helping Bonn become a strong and "normal" state, and then affirming it as a friend, Acheson laid the foundation for a close U.S.-German association that hastened the FRG's acceptance by western Europeans. The beginning of France's acceptance of a new West German reality came with the Schuman Plan, and even the EDC represented a retreat from fear. The true turning point came years later when the restored Charles de Gaulle put an alliance with Germany at the center of his foreign policy. That he used the alliance to challenge U.S. supremacy in Europe does not gainsay that peace and comity had finally become the Franco-German norm. McCloy justly claimed that the American policies Acheson so tenaciously pursued had helped make another great European war "unthinkable" and "ended one of history's longest threats to peace." To be sure, Acheson's insistence engendered resistance but it also exposed the futility of Germanophobia and quickened the advent of European unity. Prosperous societies found the assurance to banish anxieties that had been frustrating their recovery, allowing them to move toward a grander union than Schuman ever dreamed of. This European triumph occurred under the umbrella of U.S. power and within the NATO strengthened under Acheson's leadership in the wake of the Korean War. He had made a huge contribution toward building the strength needed to neutralize any Soviet designs against western Europe, unite its governments, join them to West Germany's future, and bind Washington lastingly to the continent. At the root of his design was a spacious view that identified the security and interests of the United States with those of a strong, united, and healthy western Europe.

35

APPLES OF DISCORD: GERMANY
AND THE SOVIET UNION, 1952

A "Spoiling Operation"

Many early cold war events might have happened differently, and leaders might have made different decisions. What if FDR had not died in 1945? What if U.S. armies in 1950 had called a halt at the 38th parallel in Korea? And what would have happened if the western powers had given a true test to the Soviet diplomatic proposals on Germany in March 1952 instead of deflecting them? Did they abort a chance to remove Germany as the center of east-west conflict? Did their aversion to a hazardous negotiation consign East Germans to forty more years of repression? Might a different course have enhanced U.S. security? Would the next decades have produced a more prosperous and democratic Europe?

Even if we could know what Josef Stalin's intentions were, we could not definitively answer these questions, but available evidence strongly indicates that a comprehensive negotiation on Germany in 1952 would have ended in failure. Stalin was not serious, as soon became clear. And in 1955 Moscow itself, though technically holding its offer open, categorically repudiated the very idea of German reunification proposed in 1952.

The 1952 Kremlin action came because Soviet leaders agreed the United States had made its grand slam bid at Lisbon. Although Moscow accurately surmised the west could not implement its ambitious objectives, it worried nonetheless. The imperialists would now absorb, and arm, the Federal Republic of Germany, perhaps adding a half million troops to their alliance. The Soviets had meager hopes of blocking the EDC and German contractuals. Thus, only weeks after the Lisbon conference, on 10 March 1952, Moscow sent notes to the Big Three calling for a Big-Four German settlement. The centerpiece of the proposal was a peace treaty that would reunify and neutralize Germany. Once all foreign troops had left its soil, it could field its own national army. Both the CIA and NATO thought something like this proposal was imminent, and as mentioned in a previous chapter, East German Prime Minister Otto Grotewohl had issued his own plan for reunification in September 1951. The most stringent of conditions the west had put on consideration of Grotewohl's proposal was an election through all of Germany, certified as genuinely free by a UN commission. As expected (and as Acheson had hoped), the communists found this unaccept-able. After the UN actually formed such a commission, it was barred entry to both East Germany and East Berlin. Later, Grotewohl made other, similar proposals, but nothing came of them either.[1]

In its new note, Moscow warned of the necessity of foiling a revived German "militarism" and stipulated that all foreign armies must dismantle their bases and leave within a year. Moscow used standard communist definitions of what groups in Germany might legitimately hold power, elective or not. Banning all but "anti-fascist" organizations, for example, would mean disqualifying all but the commu-nists and their co-opted "friends." Such boilerplate did not surprise the west, but seemingly clashing proposals to return Nazis and former military officers to their full political rights did. The new Germany, according to the Kremlin's draft peace treaty, could join the UN but no organization defined as hostile to any of the Big Four—namely, NATO. The reunified state would have to accept borders "established" at Potsdam. The most staggering provision would have let Germany build its own "national armed forces" and manufacture any weapon not banned by the peace treaty. As Big Three analysts pored over these terms, in Moscow, the deputy foreign minister, Andrei Gromyko, revealed the Kremlin's real aims by bragging to Stalin that the 10 March note would expose the imperialists' "aggres-sive intentions" and advance the fight against West Germany's "remilitariza-tion." Moscow's immediate publication of the note suggested that a propaganda campaign rather than serious negotiations lay ahead.[2]

Despite some backsliding to come, western leaders judged that Stalin's real end in offering "something for all elements in Germany" was to splinter Konrad Adenauer's Christian Democratic parliamentary majority. They opposed return-ing to the Potsdam arrangements cherished by Moscow. Big Four oversight over the neutrality of a reunified Germany would give the Soviet Union many oppor-tunities to make trouble, including diversion of Ruhr basin resources from the European Coal and Steel Community to reparations for itself.

Acheson mainly read the Soviet note as a wily attempt to stir western discord and prevent inserting the West German keystone into the arch of NATO. He also considered it a sign of weakness and thus proof that the strategy of building situations of strength worked. He hoped to sweep the note aside and exploit the vulnerability underlying it. Lengthy negotiations would awaken pacifist sentiment, stalling the drive to strengthen defenses, but to sustain popular support for that drive, the allies must look willing to negotiate. Stalin's maneuver had exposed the ambiguity in Acheson's strategy. If the defense buildup aimed at eventual negotiations from strength, had not the moment arrived to cash in the west's chips, using Soviet fear of Germany to end the European cold war? Acheson still thought western strength deficient for such a gamble, even if he thought the Soviet proposals genuine and serious, which he did not. For proof, he pointed to Moscow's continuing refusal to make a settlement on Austria. No, this was a "spoiling operation," an attack on Adenauer's policies and an effort to shatter west European unity. The operation would attract the "timid" and the "wishful thinkers," the Frenchmen who feared the Bonn republic and hankered for a "'satisfied' Soviet Union," and the Germans who cared for reunification over all else.[3]

Even if the Soviets *were* serious, Acheson did not want to talk to them. The result might be irresolution in the alliance and damage to German morale. Besides, while Soviet troops would have to move only a few kilometers back into Poland, GIs might have to go all the way home. NATO would lose both West Germany and the most advantageous starting line in an east-west war. "Here American diplomacy had finally put together a plan for the defense of Europe," Adam Ulam writes, unerringly capturing Acheson's attitude, and had managed to overcome "American neo-isolationism, British apprehensions, French suspicions, and German touchiness," and now the "wretched Russians" had presented "another beguiling plan, again hinting obscurely that under certain conditions they just might throw their East German regime to the wolves." Ongoing tension instead of negotiations, Acheson always thought, was more valuable in fighting Soviet power.[4]

The pacifist or fatigued public opinion he worried about was in Europe, not at home. While an alert minority of Americans expressed their wishes on Korea and China, with the exception of the "Great Debate" described earlier, in European affairs he usually operated in a virtual vacuum of public opinion. In fact, apathy about Europe sometimes produced yawns in Congress when he was seeking needed appropriations. Otherwise, public inattention to NATO, Germany, and the EDC allowed a large and free space for his diplomacy. His negative reaction to Stalin's note had nothing to do with domestic politics.

Sir Anthony Eden, who also saw Moscow's note as a snare, took the lead through the next weeks in sculpting an allied response. The allies quickly agreed any negotiations must pivot on strict guarantees that a reunified and neutral Germany would have a genuinely democratic government. Needing to appear open to negotiations, both Eden and Acheson dreaded that the Soviets might look even more reasonable in return, setting off endless talks and a cessation to progress on the contractuals and the EDC. If pressed to deliver a settlement, Eden feared western governments might be forced to remove their troops before actually getting a peace treaty. If the Soviets then stalled, the evacuated armies would leave behind them embittered Germans under a weak government, all easy prey to Moscow's manipulation. The Soviets, for example, might offer Germans open export and import markets in all of eastern Europe and Russia. In sum, the worst nightmare was that public opinion–driven talks would hatch a rearmed Germany dependent on Soviet goodwill for the last steps of normalization. The west must react to the Soviet note without inspiring an inopportune Soviet answer or destruction of the steadfast Adenauer by a wrathful German public.[5]

The reaction of the French ran from wary to petrified. The note had put a blazing light on how much better off they were in the company of malleable and friendly allies than overshadowed by a revived, Soviet-sponsored Reich. Paris officials did not believe Germany could be truly neutral with Red divisions looming across its borders. Instead, it would eventually become the greatest of all Soviet satellites, beyond any French capacity to manage, even with troops returned from Indochina. The Quai d'Orsay also feared Stalin might actually accept bona fide elections, discarding Grotewohl's tatterdemalion regime for a chance to make off with the whole country. The more temperate the USSR seemed, the more awful the prospects.[6]

Many Germans seized news of Moscow's démarche with hope. Socialists pondered jumping the traces, but the allies were correctly confident about Adenauer's holding firm. He thought negotiations with the Soviets would be appropriate only "when the West is stronger." Any settlement must reunify Germany and emancipate eastern Europe, too. Still horrified at what a neutral Germany would mean for all Europe, he feared even asking for clarification of Stalin's note. The proposal, he told the allies, was a "stratagem" designed to make them think ill of the Germans. Rebuking the willingness of Kurt Schumacher, his Socialist rival, to accept neutralization, he later wrote that Moscow's real intention was to "use Germany's neutrality to draw it" into the Soviet orbit. The EDC and contractuals offered far better prospects, and "we had to choose."[7]

The Soviet offer had come far too late to tempt any of the allies, who now worked to elude what they unanimously viewed as a trap.

The Battle of the Notes

Taking in the sun in Key West, Truman read Acheson's letter of 11 March saying the state department had long anticipated a move like Stalin's. Containing "the usual apparent hooks," it was too crafty to rebuff "out of hand." Though intrigued by the possibility that Moscow might now be hurting enough to pay a "bigger price" than before, Acheson wanted a hard-hitting answer that led nowhere but was crafted to blame Stalin for that outcome. To stymie Moscow's "obvious purpose" of disrupting plans for the contractuals and the EDC, he thought the common allied answer should ignore all the details of the Soviet message. Though not one of its addressees, Adenauer's granitic reaction became critical to how the allies responded. Believing the Soviet note a sign of desperation

and scorning its various attempts to woo German opinion, he despised the offer
to create a national army and opposed a free-floating German force as much
as the French. His refusal to renounce the "lost territories" was probably a piece
of politicking, for absorption of the largely Protestant east would adulterate
the strength of his Christian (and Catholic) Democrats in the west. While
public opinion required the Big Three to appear forthcoming in their response,
Adenauer was dead set against any conference. He was "more American than the
Americans," said his minister for inter-German affairs, Jakob Kaiser. Thus, the
allies had no reason to be obliging on Bonn's account.[8]

Although Eden, working with the French, was supposedly in charge of
fashioning the Big Three answer to Moscow, the state department was working
too. Acheson chafed over differences that emerged between the two sides of the
Atlantic, but a united position was not long in coming. The Europeans insisted
that public opinion required offering specific replies to particular Soviet propositions. The Americans insisted on tying these to another UN commission for
attesting to the electoral integrity of any new German government. The same
government should be free to act independently prior to the conclusion of a peace
treaty. A united German government, the allies agreed, must also be free to join
any international grouping not banned by the UN Charter. Disputing Moscow's
version of Potsdam, they also insisted that a final boundary settlement come
after the peace treaty. This was the gist of the messages the Big Three ambassadors individually delivered to the Soviet foreign ministry on 25 March. With
a "customary merrily malicious twinkle in his eye," Andrei Vyshinsky promised
an early answer but instantly rejected the electoral commission, German
membership in NATO, or any change in the Potsdam borders.[9]

As Washington waited for an answer, Acheson ruminated on the broader
ramifications of the exchange on background with reporters and in a private
letter to Herbert Bayard Swope. He thought any genuine settlement demanded
pushing Soviet armies "back beyond the marshes," that is, from all of eastern
Europe. Moscow might possibly agree to the free elections the west called for,
but under current arrangements, they could then march right back into Germany
to overturn the results. The west could not relax while the Red Army stood
only "100 miles from the Rhine," for Stalin had not "given up the idea that all
Europe might be sovietized." Once the west had gained enough strength, it could
insist on this Soviet retreat while persuading Moscow to agree by addressing
its valid security concerns with arms control and other measures. The cold
war, however, would continue so long as the Soviet regime remained in power,
for it depended on the sense of external threat to legitimize its hold on power.
As to Stalin's current proposals, Acheson wondered whether he would permit
industries in East Germany to return to private ownership, which was a vital
matter because truly free elections were impossible if all the voters worked
for state-owned enterprises. What could be done about the "secret police"
ready to send "people who voted the wrong way" to Siberia? Stalin's insistence on

four-power authority over German neutrality and ban on NATO membership were obvious signs that he was setting a trap. Whatever happened in the exchange of diplomatic notes, the west should continue its effort to integrate "Germany into Western Europe." Thinking he could not advance his point of view through candid public remarks, Acheson fed documents on the Soviet proposals to reporters instead.[10]

Buried in the 10 March Soviet note was an implication that Stalin might be willing to sacrifice his German satellite. He had never been enamored of a separate east German state and had not yet overhauled it along Soviet lines, as he had done in other satellites. But instead of preparing to surrender East Germany, he was doing the opposite even as his underlings pieced together a reply to the west. He told the East German president, Wilhelm Pieck, to set his regime in order. In fact, Stalin was unafraid of the EDC and German contractuals. He seemed only mildly interested in the flurry set off by his own démarche, which he was sure the Big Three would reject, because the Americans "need their army in West Germany to hold Western Europe in their hands." The United States would rearm the West Germans and put them in NATO, and since an independent West German state already existed, he admonished Pieck to get his "own state" mobilized. Two days later, on 9 April, the next Soviet note came out of Moscow. Though restrained in tone, it demanded four-power rather than UN oversight of elections, again barred Germany from being associated with any organization hostile to "peace-loving" states, held to the Potsdam boundaries, and reaffirmed Germans' right to a national army.[11]

A relieved Adenauer thought this clumsy rehash would convince nobody. Acheson was also surprised at its staleness but saw danger in its superficial courtesy. He momentarily favored offering discussions at the deputy level to satisfy German public opinion, confining the agenda to marginal matters in the knowledge that talks would come to naught and the allies could meanwhile complete the EDC and contractuals. But these negotiating tactics aside, he was now becoming increasingly combative. Convinced that Stalin acted from a consciousness of weakness, he wanted to press even harder for advantage, rebuilding the strength of western Europe until the USSR could be pushed entirely from Europe. Once the Soviets saw they could not reverse western Europe's rising power and strength without a ruinous war, they would be ready for a settlement satisfactory to the west, either through actual negotiations or, more likely, a tacit acceptance of the facts on the ground. (Several weeks later, on 2 May, he told reporters no *deal* would ever get the Soviets out of the middle of Europe.) It was time to accelerate rather than brake. "If the Soviets are willing to make small concessions now," Acheson wrote John McCloy on 12 April, they should "be willing to make even more as Western strength grows." For public consumption in a speech a week later, he accented Moscow's felonious goals and tactics. The Soviet notes were "apples" thrown over the iron curtain in hopes of tempting West Germans to bite, killing off the EDC. Any West Germans who were tempted could "see what the Soviet Union means by freedom" simply by looking "across the curtain at their brothers in East Germany."[12]

New concern among the allies about risking any negotiations caused Acheson to drop his idea about deputy-level talks. Adenauer became unmovable on the subject shortly after a statement of East Germany's Socialist Unity Party (SED) described Germany as still unliberated, with the Red Army still needing to remove "the yoke of American imperialism." In France, Robert Schuman insisted on more rigorous preconditions than ever for negotiations. On 13 May, the Big Three independently sent replies, the most novel features of which were specific refutations of tangible points in the Soviet notes, including a denial that assimilating the FRG within pan-European bodies posed any menace to the Soviet Union. Despite the appearance of a soupçon of flexibility, the west designed its robust answers to end the exchange. In reaction, Stalin began a new course of harassment, hassling U.S. military police in Berlin, flushing out unreliables in the German Democratic Republic (GDR), and inciting riots in the West German city of Essen. On 22 May, a few days before completion of the German contractuals in Bonn, McCloy thought Stalin would try an attack on western "nerves" with more shock tactics, "border incidents, plane incidents and troop concentrations or maneuvers."[13]

Moscow's third note, issued on 24 May, was stuffed with heated sectarian rhetoric and probably written by "hacks," according to George Kennan, now ambassador in Moscow. Following the note came show trials in the GDR, which also cracked the whip against property holders. Acheson was surprised that this hackneyed dispatch caused tremors of nerves among his allies. The unexpected discord between Europeans, who now wanted to appear more accommodating, and the Americans, determined to hold firm, caused weeks to go by before they could agree on a response. During this hiatus, Acheson jabbed at Eden for having already boasted that the west had won "the battle of the notes." Washington thought Schuman's cold feet were the main cause of the delay, but it was more likely that, with the EDC and contractuals now in the bag, he was confident that talks with the Soviets carried no risks. Holding them would increase chances for National Assembly approval of the defense community and contractuals. Eden seemed to agree for similar reasons—but not Adenauer. None of it made sense to Acheson. With Adenauer in his corner, he twice called in and belabored the British and French ambassadors, insisting that any east-west talks would throw German politics into turmoil and smash Adenauer's chances to secure the contractuals and the EDC.[14]

The squabbling lasted until late June but ended suddenly on Acheson's arrival in the UK on 23 June 1952 to receive his honorary degree at Oxford. With processionals interrupted by palavering huddles and repeated telephone calls to see what Adenauer could accept, over several days the allies found harmony. As details of the note took shape, Acheson happily wired home that its "whole tenor" made a positive Soviet response "unlikely" while almost guaranteeing that Moscow would have to bear the "onus" for the negotiation's failure. The note actually went to Moscow on 10 July 1952, four months after the first Russian bid.[15]

As evidence that the allies had invested too much psychic energy on this fray, Stalin lost interest as soon as he saw he could stop neither the EDC nor the contractuals. On 25 July, he told visiting Italian Socialist Party leader Pietro Nenni the exchange had been "completely phony and futile." Moscow took six weeks before sending another answer on 23 August. This time, Stalin's factotums were lackadaisical as well as hackneyed, mostly repeating themselves. The state department thought the Soviets had simply accepted the EDC and contractuals as a fait accompli. Kennan wanted a quick stop to this tiresome correspondence, urging that Washington use secret talks to see what Moscow *might* accept in Germany (Acheson wrote, "Later," on the margin). An almost equally formulaic western response went to the Soviets on 23 September, which Moscow never answered. The battle of the notes was indeed over. Eden had overseen much of the drafting of allied dispatches; Schuman had carefully balanced what he thought prudent with what French legislators would accept; Adenauer had not budged in his resistance to anything threatening to sell his budding state down the river. Throughout, Acheson looked for ways to exploit the Kremlin's vulnerability.[16]

Another Lost Chance?

How earnest Stalin was in his 1952 proposals was something of a mystery, perhaps even to himself. It is at least possible he wanted a settlement. Besides being a monster, he was an opportunist, and under certain circumstances he might genuinely have accepted the reunified, neutral, and armed Germany his notes offered. Owning a minuscule nuclear armory, he might have thought he could block the EDC and German contractuals by tossing over the puppet East German regime. All this is possible but not probable. It strains credulity to believe he really thought a new and independent German army was preferable to a force hemmed in by NATO allies. He might have risked such an outcome only if he thought a settlement ridding the continent of U.S. troops would give him the opportunity to seize control of all Germany.[17]

Still, one could see how he might have been ready to take some major risks in the spring of 1952. In Europe, events had gone badly for the USSR since the Marshall Plan, and now Stalin faced the prospect of a powerfully reinforced NATO and restored West German state with an army allied to the imperialists. The Americans still enjoyed overwhelming nuclear supremacy. Having made no new gains on the continent since the end of the war, the Soviet ruler might have considered a desperate shot at a diplomatic revolution. By jettisoning the pawn of the ersatz East German regime—not yet fully "Stalinized" or recognized as a state—he might have thought he could capture Europe's queen, that is, *all* of

Germany. Soviet records suggest that in their most romantic Marxist-Leninist moods, he and other Politburo members believed they could even win Germany for socialism through democratic elections. Less quixotically, he might have hoped that returning to a four-power, sphere of influence system ("Potsdam") would end the cold war in favor of "peaceful coexistence," with Germany serving as a buffer state. This would remove the sharpest point of friction with the Americans, left cheek by jowl with the Russians in the heart of Europe at the end of the war.

Again, it is possible, or even plausible, but improbable that Stalin so intended. Historians critical of U.S. policy in the early cold war usually emphasize his conservatism and caution, but this gamble would hardly be cautious. Far more likely, he planned to *conserve* what he already held. In Vyacheslav Molotov's opinion, his boss "would never have abandoned" his socialist conquest of East Germany. Diplomat Vladimir Semyonov recalled that before authorizing the 10 March note, Stalin not only asked those in the foreign ministry if they were certain the Americans would reject it, but also hinted that evil things would befall these minions if they did not. His real intent, according to Soviet records examined by Gerhard Wettig, was to mobilize the "German 'masses'" and Moscow-controlled communists in West Germany "in an intense effort to oust Adenauer's government and to force the Western powers out of Germany." Kremlin leaders, Wettig concludes, did not expect a positive western response or even consider it "desirable." They never even discussed it as a goal. "It was the general public, particularly in Germany, to whom the message was directed."[18]

Moscow's actions in East Germany provide the most compelling evidence of the USSR's actual expectations. As the exchange of notes proceeded, both Soviet and East German officials "took it for granted" nothing would block the new impetus toward making the GDR a good collectivist state. Quickly realizing he had not seduced the Bonn Germans, Stalin told Pieck the EDC was not anti-Soviet but an assertion of U.S. power in Europe. He reacted to the first western response, on 7 April 1952, by ordering a mobilization of the GDR. Stalin told Pieck to raise a real army and soon appointed Soviet generals to head it. In July, after years of delay, his East German servants finally set about socializing their satellite outpost. A drive to collectivize private estates caused twenty thousand farmers to flee to the west, but East German leaders betrayed no fear that Stalin was about to sacrifice their regime on the altar of realpolitik. They shored up their power, cracked down on Christian churches, and purged their party of possible malcontents. The result was economic decline and social unrest. More East Germans fled to the west, and after Stalin's death, uprisings rattled East Berlin.[19]

Western governments were only partly aware of these events and acted from their own needs. They would have been in grave trouble had Adenauer been receptive to Stalin's bid, which exposed the Soviets' sole ability to untie the ribbons on presents coveted by many Germans: reunification and "lost" territories. But Adenauer was so "European," a genuinely forthcoming Big Three response to Moscow would have required defying his wishes. Far too much water had coursed over the dam, far too much had been accomplished in partnership with Adenauer for the allies to pursue a scheme that could have destabilized central Europe. Acheson wanted to preserve the western muscle he was convinced had shaken these notes out of Moscow. He was certain a long east-west negotiation would erode this strength and that western leaders might never again find the right circumstances to rally their people to the large ends they had almost achieved. Worst of all, "successful" talks would subtract Germany's weight from the armies needed to reach beyond the Rhine. Accepting a neutral Germany, James L. Richardson writes, was "too great a gamble" and "a violation of the maxims of prudence in diplomacy."[20]

Not all in the west agreed. Churchill found Stalin's gambit enticing, hoping to finish his overextended career as a peacemaker. Among many Germans lamenting this alleged *verpaßte Gelegenheit* (wasted opportunity) was Social Democratic leader Willy Brandt. Historians too have criticized the Big Three choice. Adam Ulam believed Washington's refusal to risk thorny negotiations with unguaranteed results showed its failure to understand "the truth that patience and a sense of timing are major ingredients of the art of diplomacy." Richard J. Barnet thought the Truman administration feared negotiations "more than confrontation."

Though intended as a criticism, this is on the mark, but Acheson, who considered prudence a vital part of statesmanship, would have said it was foolish to take needless risks and common sense to tolerate bearable tensions to avoid even worse. When one wins a sizable pot, it is prudent to stand pat rather than go double or nothing. By the spring and summer of 1952, the Big Three knew they had made striking progress. They had averted economic collapse, resisted ejection from Berlin, instigated a Franco-German rapprochement on the foundations of European integration, constructed a grand alliance, and gone far toward arming it with real teeth. And—though some Europeans regretted this—allied diplomacy had now almost finished bringing the Bonn republic into the NATO system.[21]

Events in 1953 suggest Acheson and his colleagues had been right. When the ruling group succeeding Stalin discredited and shot secret police chief Lavrentia Beria, they used trumped-up charges that he had conspired to abandon the socialist state of East Germany for a reunified and bourgeois Germany. As early as May 1953, the budding Khrushchev-Bulganin regime had decided to discard Stalin's 1952 charade.[22]

Kennan Agonistes

One of the lowest points in U.S.-Soviet relations came in the last months of 1952. It is no accident that Acheson acquired his repute as a cold war militant during some of the most desolate years of Soviet rule. In his last months, Stalin slid into a phobic abyss, suspicious of his own Politburo servants, of Jews, and of any "cosmopolitan" who had spent time in the west. Foreign diplomats in Moscow, shadowed by secret police, worked in a "sublimely malevolent" environment, one reason Acheson never ceased thinking of the USSR as a malign force, "a rigid autocracy ruled by police power." The unity of communism, he had said in a speech in April 1952, was "the unity of the cemetery." Even if it moved "on carpet slippers instead of hobnailed boots," he warned in a rare campaign speech that fall, Soviet military strength would continue to mount. Critics, he told ANZUS allies in August, said "we were trying to hold a ring around Soviet Russia," but what Acheson really wanted was assurance that "freedom of choice rested with us, not the Russians."

Such freedom was a product of strength, enshrined in an update of NSC-68 (NSC 135/3). This legacy paper of Acheson's stewardship, again shaped by Paul Nitze, considered western strength great enough to do whatever was necessary to wage the cold war, and for as long as was necessary. Even more assertive than the original NSC-68, the new paper promoted aggressive use of propaganda against the communist world and efforts to "induce a retraction of the Kremlin's control and influence" in that world. American policy should foster "the seeds of destruction within the Soviet system," which would finally force the "Soviet bloc" to conform its behavior to "generally accepted international standards." No "time limit" was set for achieving American purposes. The point, as Nitze wrote a colleague, was that pushing ahead with western goals in a way that did not cause war required "clearly preponderant power," likely "more power than to win military victory in the *event* of war." Acheson agreed.[23]

Sadly, as the state department became more committed to policies Kennan no longer found sympathetic, this illustrious Soviet expert was driven out of Moscow and his first posting as ambassador. Of fifty-nine U.S. chiefs of mission who had preceded him in Moscow, he was the first ever declared persona non grata. He later wrote, in a relentlessly candid appraisal, that he had not been "wholly fitted for the task," despite all his training and experience. Though he complained that Acheson had given him insufficient direction and support, he confessed he was "probably too highly strung emotionally, too imaginative, too sensitive, and too impressed with the importance of [his] own opinions, to sit quietly on that particular seat." Already estranged from Washington, in Moscow he quickly fell out with his own staff, at one point giving a future ambassador, Malcolm Toon, an unjustly negative fitness report. Even worse was to come.[24]

His assignment began as inauspiciously as it ended. Truman named him to the post in February 1952. Confirmed in March, he began his preparations in Washington on 1 April. When he called on the president, he received "no instructions of any kind." At the state department, his objections to U.S. German policy, about which he seemed poorly informed, made no impression on Acheson. He resented not receiving "real instructions" from either president or secretary of state and felt feebly briefed in the department. He was shocked to learn that Acheson did not want him to explore Moscow's attitudes on Germany, writing in his diary that the secretary expected large diplomatic gains "without making any concessions whatsoever to the views and interests of our adversaries." His mission would be to "play a game" he "could not possibly win," then accept "the onus of whatever overt failures were involved."[25]

Thus abandoned by his friends, he landed in the capital of his enemies on 5 May, forced in his "instructionless state" to write his own letter of credence for Vyshinsky. No one in Moscow wanted to talk to him, either, but he sought a meeting with Vyshinsky to lodge protests about a propaganda campaign featuring anti-American rhetoric unmatched in "viciousness" and "shamelessness." Tepidly concurring, Acheson more or less urged him not to get his nose out of joint, and Kennan decided the time was not ripe for a protest. Instead, in reference to Moscow's fury over a congressional discussion of its culpability in the Katyn massacre, he implied in a cable that U.S. behavior must change to improve relations. Acheson ignored this, but he probably shared Kennan's alarm at the unsubtle activities of U.S. intelligence officers attached to the embassy. With the propaganda onslaught unabated, in May, Kennan asked that Truman publicly condemn the "incredible torrent of abuse and falsehood" spewed by the Kremlin. Acheson softly brushed this and like suggestions aside, commenting that the "hate-America" campaign was probably aimed at dividing the allies and that a presidential declaration would "play into Sov hands."[26]

But on 6 June, Acheson lit into the outgoing Soviet ambassador (and KGB station chief), Alexander Panyushkin, for Moscow's violent rhetoric. With daunting mendacity, Panyushkin denied the truth of the Katyn massacre (in which he may have been involved) and avowed that the Soviet government had no control over the "free" Soviet press. In the late 1940s, the lengthy letters of the U.S. ambassador to Argentina, George Messersmith, had won him the sobriquet, "Forty-Page George." Now, Kennan sent home a stream of painfully self-absorbed dispatches that were so long, department veterans might have been tempted to bring the slur against Messersmith out of retirement. Kennan registered nearly every public lie in *Pravda* or *Izvestia* as a private affront and became convinced his own appointment was the cause of this rhetorical assault. Each time Acheson ignored him, the bruises caused at the hands of the apparatchiks deepened in purple. Acheson finally urged him to protest the hate campaign, and he did so on 19 June, just six days after a U.S. spy plane was shot down off the Soviet coast. In a long autobiographical cable, Kennan said the discussions had gone well, complete with signs of Soviet respect for him and his "opinion." He urged Washington to do nothing in response to the libels, which continued.[27]

Kennan left Moscow on 19 September for a meeting of European chiefs of mission in London. During a layover at Berlin's Templehof airport, with reporters gathered round, pencils poised on notebooks, he poured out months of frustration and mortification at Soviet abuse of westerners. The behavior of the Soviet leviathan, he said, was like that of the Third Reich. When Moscow erupted in fury at these remarks, he claimed he had not "volunteered" them but only answered reporters' questions about the treatment of diplomats in Moscow. He had spoken candidly because it was no secret the Soviets treated them abominably. Besides, it was "essential" for the people of the United States and the world to know the facts.[28]

Then he spent time in the London conference disparaging U.S. policy. The initial purpose of the western military buildup was to make a broad U.S.-Soviet settlement feasible. Since the current atmosphere made this impossible, he vaguely implied it was incumbent on Washington to adopt a more modest but unspecified approach to bring the Soviets to reason. Containment, he suggested, was too costly to sustain. Removing the differences at the heart of the Soviet-American confrontation—Japan, Germany, and Austria—was the only hope for "avoiding a war," but he did not say how to do this. Acheson's views notwithstanding, it was impossible "to stand still indefinitely with no war, no peace." Disappointed by Acheson's absence at the conference, he faulted his core strategy of "mobilizing in order to talk on equal terms," which he said was not working. While still in London on the night of 25 September, Kennan wrote in his diary of how miserable he would feel returning to Moscow and living "through further weeks and months of exposure to foul, malicious, and insulting propaganda." War was a real possibility because Washington was pursuing "the false logic that would lead" to it.[29]

The next day *Pravda* launched a scathing personal attack, charging Kennan with lying "ecstatically" at Templehof. Shocked, Kennan's comment to the department was almost wholly personal—the Soviets resented *him*, not the United States or its policy. He should be ordered home for consultations, with his absence from Moscow being "prolonged as long as might be deemed desirable." He felt a "loneliness greater than" he had "ever conceived," he wrote in his diary. In a letter to Bohlen, he said he wished never to return to Moscow.[30]

On 3 October, just after he flew to Geneva to visit his daughter, the other shoe dropped. Vyshinsky called the U.S. chargé d'affaires on the carpet and handed him a note denouncing Kennan. He then declared him persona non grata, and demanded his recall for "slanderous attacks hostile to the Soviet Union in a rude violation of generally recognized norms of international law." Acheson's swift and wholesale rejection of the charges was a formality, but Kennan thanked him for "magnificent support" exceeding what he "personally deserved." Senator William Knowland demanded that Washington go tit for tat, expelling the new Soviet ambassador, breaking relations, and withdrawing recognition of the USSR. Acheson ignored all such effusions. But at a time he hoped for Soviet help in breaking the Korean POW impasse, he was far from happy with Kennan. He ordered him to take "compassionate leave" in Germany, found him a comfortable house near Bonn, and made him stay there until the election at home was over. As U.S.-Russian relations nose-dived, the Soviets on 7 October downed a B-29 bomber in the area of the Kuriles. Angry at the repeated displays of Soviet vulnerability to American air incursions, Moscow sent provocative flights over Japan. Ten days after it did so, U.S. planes carried out massive and unmolested sweeps over the territory of the eastern Soviet Union. Tit for tat.[31]

*   *   *   *

Kennan's ordeal came at a markedly frigid moment in the history of U.S.-Soviet relations. That he was expelled from the Soviet Union for comments about the vile treatment allotted all aliens in Moscow said more about Stalin's insensate regime than Kennan's lack of ballast. It said little to nothing about whether the Soviet Union posed a real threat to the west. Acheson had no doubt it did, and offensive conduct like that Kennan had protested reinforced his view that no one could soon "settle" the cold war. Even before Stalin died in March 1953, many Americans and Europeans hoped the new American president, Eisenhower, would somehow achieve a détente. By then, Acheson had no say in the matter, but he was sure such hopes were premature. Building situations of strength should go on. This meant that the cold war would go on, too, to no certain end, a condition dispiriting to others but never to Acheson.

36

SCOPE FOR THE EXERCISE OF
EVERY VITAL POWER

Farewells

The tension that produced George Kennan's ignominy bred support for Acheson's projects, but he was dismayed that relations with Moscow had turned so sour. Dreary, teeth-gritting antagonism eliminated all civil diplomatic discourse or any chance the USSR might help resolve the Korean POW dispute. Worse, coupled with the languishing of the European Defense Community and "Lisbon," tensions pushed defense strategy farther down the nuclear roadway. Eisenhower's "New Look" sat on top of the Truman administration's growing dependence on atomic arms, delays in the NATO buildup, and the relative cheapness of nuclear weapons. In February 1952, the United States tested its first tactical nuclear weapons. Shipments to Europe of these projectiles in the spring caused the British to be even less eager to fulfill their Lisbon obligations. Aware that a conventional European deterrent was some time off, Acheson gave tempered support to greater nuclear weapons production.[1]

Another source of gloom was the presidential campaign. Traditionally, secretaries of state stayed out of campaigns, but Acheson was a favorite Republican target. Already thinking Democratic contender Adlai Stevenson lacked "the stuff of command," he grew even more critical when the Stevenson campaign asked Truman to fire Acheson to boost the Illinoisan's chances. But of course Truman declined, leaving Eisenhower running mate Richard Nixon free to label Stevenson a graduate of Acheson's "Cowardly College of Communist Containment." Aghast at Eisenhower's coddling of McCarthy, stagy pledges to go to Korea, and promise to "liberate" eastern Europe, Acheson took to the hustings. Noticing how stunned some friends were when Eisenhower won an overwhelming victory, however, he told them they had to accept that the time had come for GOP rule the same way they must some day "accept growing old."[2]

The administration's last days coincided with the hydrogen bomb's first. At its Pacific test site on 1 November, the United States exploded its first hydrogen "device" with terrifying results, yielding a thousand times the power of the Hiroshima bomb and obliterating one of the Marshall Islands. The government soon revealed the barebones facts of the test, but Truman thought he should say more. Acheson was opposed, worried that public "handwringing" would stir popular guilt feelings and panicky demands for disarmament. But with test data already leaking to the press, Truman went ahead, making bleak statements in his final State of the Union message in January 1953. A war with hydrogen bombs, he said, would "dig the grave" of both the United States and the USSR. Since it was impossible to constrain technological progress, future wars could "extinguish" civilization itself.[3]

By then Republicans were eyeing corner offices in Washington and buying houses in the suburbs. When Kennan met with Truman and Acheson in November, he saw "in their eyes the faraway look of men" about to take "malicious pleasure in reserving their most bitter problems for those who are about to displace them." In a farewell dinner tribute in Paris, Anthony Eden credited Acheson with inventing "the theory of creating 'positions of strength.'"

Friends thought he was "worn out," and Acheson later wrote that "wear and tear" had made "a rest not unwelcome." Even if he and Truman could have had another round in office, "neither of us could have gone on with the same energy and zest. Probably our judgment would have reflected the decline. To leave positions of great responsibility and authority is to die a little, but the time comes when that must be faced." His worn look in his last press conference on 14 January 1953 prompted a rookie reporter to wonder if he always had that "hurt look." He was actually feeling elegiac. He quoted Shakespeare about the "sweet sorrow" of "parting" and another poet about being "happier than those he leaves behind." And he thanked Truman for his "complete" loyalty.[4]

After his press conference, he and Alice hosted a dinner on P Street for Truman and other administration loyalists. He resigned early on the 15th, allowing him to duck signing the commission of John Foster Dulles, whose people seemed "like Cossacks quartered in a grand city hall, burning the paneling to cook with." Before a ceremonial crowd of several thousand on the lawn behind the state department building, aides presented his cabinet chair to him. He told his admirers to rely on the strength of American values to overcome the defamation they were enduring from the "primitives." "Fools and self-seeking blackguards" had vilified them, but he had no doubt they had created "the best foreign office and service in the world." Afterward, streams of men and women came to his office for a last handshake and "a word of farewell." The *Washington Post* said he left Foggy Bottom knowing he had "made a remarkable dent on his times." He was his "good right hand," wrote Truman in accepting his resignation. No one had done more to strengthen the will of the "people of the free world." He could now "take a good long rest," knowing he was one of America's greatest secretaries of state, for neither "Jefferson nor Seward showed more cool courage and steadfast judgment." The Moscow press, naturally, disagreed, describing him with malicious wit as a "dandy," a "wily hypocrite," and an "ambitious fish in Wall Street's Foggy Bottom, who imagined himself an ocean shark."5

After the inauguration rites, the Achesons gave a farewell luncheon for the Truman family, White House staffers, and cabinet members. The street was jammed with well-wishers, who cheered as each guest entered the P Street home. When they chanted, "we want Harry!" Acheson brought Truman outdoors for a quick wave and smile. At dusk, sixty-three months after the under secretary and party of one had fixed his bond to a lonely president by greeting him at Union Station, they returned to the site. The special train pulled out, and Truman waved "from the rear platform as the crowd roared its farewell." With echoes of "Auld Lang Syne" in the air, Acheson told a reporter: "There's the best friend in the world."6

"The Most Active, Interesting and Pugnacious Character in Town"

Acheson believed that "command, or, if one prefers, supreme leadership, demands and gives scope for the exercise of every vital power a man has in the direction of excellence." Acting as a public servant matched the joy he experienced in wielding power. After twelve years as one of the leading figures in what he called the "vast external realm" of world politics, he was now suddenly deprived of both pleasures. After buttonholing compatriots in Washington and negotiating with allies in European conference rooms, he would now rusticate for eight years. When Democrats returned to office, they were eager for his counsel. Once again, though never as a nine-to-five appointee, he could exercise his vital powers. Although his efforts to shape policy often did not conclude as he wished, he enjoyed himself enough to say yes when even his old enemy Richard Nixon asked for help.7

Nearly all of his retirement advice ran in the same groove he had worked as secretary. Kennedy, Johnson, and Nixon all wanted his assistance on NATO. The reason the transatlantic alliance remained at the top of his priorities to his death was his belief that Europe was the cold war's great prize. Though it was obvious he remained a "Europeanist," some observers missed his view that if Europe was the center of the world, *Germany* was the center of Europe. Making the Federal Republic part of the "west" made it possible to block Soviet domination of Europe. Whatever the unique controversies of the moment, he would always advocate strengthening U.S. ties to West Germany, not the least because the special connection fostered U.S. leadership of the whole western alliance.

He never stopped believing in the necessity of working closely with NATO partners—or, with equal fervor, in the necessity of *leading* the alliance.

His stewardship of American foreign policy was of lasting historic importance because of his relentless insistence that it rest on foundations of strength. In 1949–53, he was preoccupied with reestablishing *military* strength because it seemed most wanting. Economic strength was another vital mode of power, something he seldom worried about in an era in which U.S. economic dominance remained unchallenged. In manifold ways, he sought to bring *political* strength to bear and, though with mixed success, had worked to preserve domestic backing of U.S. foreign policy. Far more successfully, he nurtured ties with friends and allies abroad. But he also unashamedly strove to have the United States *lead* those friends.

Dean Acheson was among the boldest of men and one of the most aggressive and assertive to serve a twentieth-century president. No longer having politically to protect Truman's administration, he grew even more assertive in retirement, saying things he surely would not have said in office. Most he aimed against Washington's new powers that be. Unintimidated, he clashed with all the chief executives he advised. When he died in 1971, James Reston described his peculiar talent for telling presidents "what he truly believed about the realities of power in the world and not what they wanted to hear." His talent for straight talk gradually deteriorated into a bent for the offensive and even cruel—and by choice rather than chance. To the end of his life, he remained outrageous, but now reactionary and obnoxious too.[8]

For some time after Dulles took over the state department, Acheson simply relaxed. With Archibald and Ada MacLeish, he and Alice spent two months on Antigua, then little known in the United States and still waving the cross of St. George. By the 1960s, expeditions to Antigua, Barbados, and other islands became an annual habit, shared sometimes with the MacLeishes or Edens. On his Harewood grounds in Maryland, he ran his lathe, wrote letters, and joined Alice in tilling "rival flower plots." In the city, when something special appeared on television, he invited himself to a friend's home, for he never owned a "boob-tube." In Alice's absence—as when she traveled to Europe in 1962—he lived a bachelor's "solitary life," accepting dinner invitations and carrying all kinds of things to bed to read "without being accused of slumping into senility." He drove his car to Pennsylvania to give a lecture at the Army War College, and he traveled to New York to lecture international students. "Soldiers are suckers for my line, and foreign students, I fear, will take a dim view of it. Soldiers like dogmatism, even when it isn't their dogmatism. Foreign students, so far as I have been able to discover, don't like anything." In the late 1950s, he was in large demand as a lecturer. Besides two months at Cambridge University in 1958, he appeared a hundred-odd times in assorted forums. Offered a glass of white wine before a late-afternoon lecture at the Brookings Institution, he demanded a dry martini. "The Brookings people," Arthur Schlesinger, Jr., records, "politely said that spirits were not available. 'No martini,' said Acheson, 'no lecture.' (He got the martini.)"9

With or without Alice at home, he grew lonely, until the "exceptional and delightful creature," Paul Nitze, noticed he was no longer showing up at the usual dining spots. After Nitze drew him back, inviting him to the Metropolitan Club, Acheson told him: "You know, you are the first person in Washington who has asked me to have lunch since I was Secretary of State." Also owning a farm in Maryland, Nitze now became a boon companion. In his wake came others, including Louis Halle, the onetime resident philosopher of the policy planning staff. The Princeton Seminars, hosted by Robert Oppenheimer just as the government pulled his security clearance, surrounded him with even more old friends. He mended fences with Joseph Alsop, but intractable disagreements over Germany had killed his friendship with James Warburg, surely the only person who called Acheson "Deano." He made young new friends, too, like writer Michael Janeway. Another, twenty-three years his junior, was Noël (later Baron) Annan, former British intelligence officer, author, and academic politician. When they saw *Dr. Strangelove* together, "Mr. Acheson fell about laughing." His most treasured senior friend remained Felix Frankfurter, finally forced from the high court by poor health. In 1962, Acheson tried to boost his morale with "a shaker of martinis," which he claimed the doctor said had produced a "remarkable therapeutic effect." When the justice died in 1965, the crestfallen Acheson organized a memorial service in Frankfurter's apartment. Until Acheson was sixty-eight, he attended to other friendships serving on the Yale Corporation. A devoted Eli who would blissfully belt out "For God, for Country, and for Yale" on a moment's notice, he composed the citation for the honorary degree Yale gave to Cole Porter in 1960. When MacLeish tempted him with a faculty post at Harvard, Acheson reminded him that "the train to Boston goes through New Haven."10

His finances were not as comfortable as people living in an age of overpriced lawyers might imagine. Having to work, he rejoined Covington, Burling as something of a "pensioner." Because Republican businessmen were slow to enlist the talents of this controversial Truman man, at first he "stared at the wall." Though he never reestablished his reputation as a leading attorney, in due course international clients came around, and in the early sixties, he represented Cambodia against Thailand at the International Court of Justice at The Hague. But the law seemed tedious and, in contrast to his days at State, again illustrated what Frankfurter called the difference between "French cooking and hardtack." Practicing law made him feel "stale," and he "hated" working "to get more money for people who don't need it or deserve it."

Worst of all was the loss of power, which felt like "the end of a love affair." Because public service drew on "vital powers," he explained in a 1957 letter, returning to private life left him "feeling flat and empty." At fifty-nine, he had lost the happiness that ancient Greeks understood came through "the limitless scope of governmental responsibilities." He seemed, a journalist observed in 1962, "lonely for the power he once had, lonely for the days when, for good or ill, he and his friend Harry had the fate of what in those days was called 'the free world' in their hands, almost alone in their hands."[11]

In the Eisenhower years, he first tried reentering his preferred world of responsibilities through lectures and writings, interpreting events through the prism of his own experiences. Battering Eisenhower and Dulles for overreliance on nuclear weapons and rejection of "limited war," he insisted that such wars were the "only kind that we or anyone else can afford." Still skeptical of "containment," he challenged Truman in 1958 for saying publicly that Washington must respond "whenever and wherever we are challenged by the Communists." "Opposition to Russia," he reminded him, was "a dangerous business which requires lots of sense and coolness in making decisions of where and how." As more years passed, he felt content with his own record, writing publisher John Cowles in 1963 that winning the cold war required plugging "away at the policies I have advocated since the end of the war." The "one sure way to lose the cold war" was "to lose Germany." Power, he told C. L. Sulzberger in a sober mood a year before his death, was "a dangerous thing" when used excessively, "as when we totally destroyed Germany and Japan in World War II and upset the entire world balance." With nuclear weapons much more of a factor than when he ran the state department, he thought there was no choice but to exercise power and negotiate simultaneously, "keeping Moscow informed" to avoid the dangers of "escalation."[12]

As time passed, his body weakened—abdominal ailments, failing thyroid, weakened eyesight—but, except for some bouts of melancholy, his spirit rarely flagged. In 1964, the *New York Times* called him "America's leading iconoclast," and two years later its correspondent, Reston, found "The Gentleman from Sandy Spring" in fine fettle, "now almost 73, going on 50." Having then regained renown from stints of service for John F. Kennedy and Lyndon B. Johnson, he seemed "the most active, interesting and pugnacious character in town—a poet among the mechanics, a believer among the skeptics, and almost the last of our contemporaries who believes that history and power have a future." The boldest mind in Washington and its most "savage" critic, he was one of the city's last "free spirits" who said what he thought "with clarity, ardor and style." If presidents rejected Acheson's counsel, now "beyond ambition," he was content to return to his law office, his lathe, "his dahlias and his writing." Having "come to terms with life," he had reconciled "his professional and his private life, as few do." There was "no more thoughtful friend, no better public servant, no better talker or writer, and no more eloquent critic" in Washington.[13]

But his criticism of others and their policies grew less eloquent and more savage as he moved in stages from waspish to occasionally loutish. He reserved much of his vitriol for the United Nations, aka the "department of emotion," "Mother of Nonsense," or "international orphan asylum." In a private letter in

1966, he called Secretary-General U Thant "a contemptible little rat." As early as 1957, David K. E. Bruce found him "devastating, clever, bitter and not constructive." He was "overfull of bile and it is sad." Two years later while dining at Acheson's farm, the faithful Sulzberger described him as "charming, suave, witty" but also deeply cynical, telling "one story after another terminating, 'Balls, balls, balls.'" By 1961, he had grown resentful of his Cassandra's reputation, correct on the issues but "destined never to be believed." Increasingly, he counted on Barbara Evans to carve out the more odious effusions from his speeches and papers, though in a 1967 letter to Barbara Tuchman he confessed he still preferred "to kick fools" to "persuading them."[14]

Blowing off Steam

Aside from Nitze, his most important tie in retirement was Harry Truman, "the best friend in the world." But he did not scruple from telling Citizen Truman when he thought he was wrong, even in letters addressed, "Dear Mr. President" or "Dear Boss." He helped raise nearly $2 million for the Truman Library in Independence, shaking cash from the wallets of a number of his old colleagues. He also helped HST with his memoirs, trekking to Missouri for interviews and poring through the ghostwriters' drafts. As noted earlier, he thought Truman had been too easy on MacArthur and took umbrage at smears of "striped pants boys in the State Department." He also served as a sounding board on contemporary affairs: "Whenever you want to blow off steam, we claim priority on being blowee, as the lawyers would say." This led to a few rifts, as in 1957, when he scolded Truman for being too soft on Eisenhower and Dulles, and in 1958, when he told him he had been "gravely wrong" to support them in the crisis over the offshore islands of Quemoy and Matsu. "Please, Mr. President," he pleaded, "do not continue this line," for it neutralized criticism from the Democratic opposition.[15]

With only a short pause, he began expressing his opinion as a member of that opposition. Eisenhower had never impressed him, but Dulles, whom he loathed, was his favorite target, especially after he mistreated the old China hands Acheson had tried to protect. He called him a "psalm-singing Presbyterian Wall Street lawyer" long after his death. The evening Dulles died, Acheson stunned a dinner party by exclaiming: "Thank God Foster is underground."

The first issue that catapulted Acheson from his post-inauguration blues was the "New Look," Eisenhower's repudiation of the conventional buildup sanctioned by NSC-68 and Lisbon, coupled with Dulles's oath to answer any aggressor with "massive retaliation." In his 1955 book, *A Democrat Looks at His Party*, he also battled talk about "limited" nuclear war and tactical nuclear weapons. While the United States must be ready for nuclear war, even more it must hope for reasonable men to prevent its occurrence. It was mad to embrace "disaster in order to escape anxiety." But just as Dulles's brandishing of violence aroused his contempt, so did Eisenhower's efforts at détente. Rather than parlay with Nikita Khrushchev in Geneva, he should be applying intensive pressure to break down Moscow's creaky economy. The Suez crisis of 1956 deeply affected Acheson, when the British, French, and Israelis combined to punish Egypt for nationalization of the Suez Canal, only to have a U.S.-Soviet condominium in the UN stop them. The British surrender in the face of Khrushchev's nuclear threats proved the bankruptcy of the New Look. He was even more exercised by the abandonment of key allies. The reason the UK and France had acted without consulting the United States was their mistrust of "Foster," for which he did not blame them, for he "didn't trust him either."[16]

After Eisenhower's reelection in 1956, Acheson assumed chairmanship of the foreign policy section of the new Democratic Advisory Council (DAC), a post he used less to boost the party than his own line and to curb the influence of such "woolyheaded [*sic*] liberals" as Stevenson and Chester Bowles. His diplomatic obiter dicta estranged numerous fellow Democrats, and he offended others with his bossiness and sarcasm in committee meetings. Responding to the wooing of Lyndon Johnson, one of the DAC's original sponsors, Acheson offered counsel on both domestic and foreign affairs and favored Johnson's nomination for president in 1960. Johnson had "thousands of faults," he told Truman, but was "a giant among pigmies." He could not resign himself to "Fat Boy" Stevenson unless he could "usher in a golden age before the twilight, like the 30 years of the Antonines," but "this paunchy quipster is no Marcus Aurelius."[17]

Acheson's most momentous polemic was an indirect product of his DAC duties, coming after the BBC's 1957 Reith Lectures, in which Kennan had proposed disengaging all foreign armies from central Europe. Kennan cringed "with horror and remorse" in advance of Acheson's expected attack but was staggered by its ferocity. With a number of Democratic luminaries, including Truman, backing him, Acheson in early 1958 said in a statement that Kennan had "never grasped the realities" of "power relationships," to which he brought a "rather mystical attitude." His ideas had been "rejected" a decade earlier (at the same time Acheson was dallying with Kennan's Plan A on Germany) because they would have destroyed western deterrence. In a press conference, he added that Kennan's ideas were indistinguishable from isolationism, and "I'm against it." Delighted at the fracas, Reston observed that next to seeing "the Lincoln Memorial in moonlight, the sight of Mr. Dean G. Acheson blowing his top is without doubt the most impressive view in the capital." Having recently jabbed at Dulles and even whacked some "Democratic colleagues," he had now thrown "a murderous haymaker at George Kennan." When the *Washington Post* called his attack "savage," Acheson wrote a friend: "I felt savage about it." Dulles sent a generous note praising his swordplay, causing Acheson to report that Alice, "already suspicious," interpreted the letter as reason to leave him.[18]

After the initial round, Kennan and Acheson inspected the damage to their thorny friendship. It had been unpleasant to clash "with an old friend," Acheson wrote CBS's Richard Hottelet, but his ideas were "dangerous in the extreme and called for some antidote." For his part, Kennan was perplexed that the disagreement had turned "personal" and ugly. Acheson sent proofs of his next salvo ("The Illusion of Disengagement," for the April 1958 *Foreign Affairs*), almost taunting Kennan even as he claimed still to treasure their relationship. While Kennan replied sadly about Acheson's wounding remarks in connection with their 1949 disagreements, Acheson gaily alerted friends that his next sally might be even "more cruel." Kennan had been ill, but it was unfair to "do as much damage as George has done and then rush off to immunity in the hospital." Knowing their "brawl" dismayed mutual friends, Acheson told a chagrined Philip Jessup: "George always engenders more solicitude in others than he shows for others." Nor did he care that Joe Alsop called him "brutal."[19]

For those in the chorus, "The Illusion of Disengagement" blew Kennan out of the water. Lying behind an introductory bouquet to "a man of the highest character and reputation" lay the fist of Acheson's argument. Like the "America First" isolationists, Kennan wanted to "crawl back into the cocoon of history." Disengagement was born of "monasticism and the diplomacy of earlier centuries." Carrying it out would forfeit all "the most valuable fruit" of the policy of strength and produce either a state dominated by the Soviets or a neutral Germany playing one power system against the other, just as it had done before two previous wars. Instead, the west should continue building its conventional military power until it could negotiate away the incubus of nuclear weapons. With Stalin's death, possibilities of ending the cold war had grown, but only because the west had stayed strong, while Kennan was proposing a self-imposed weakness. On receiving the proofs, Kennan had genially written Acheson that he had seldom "seen error so gracefully and respectably clothed," errors he addressed in the same journal in January 1959. There he charged Acheson with thinking Moscow would some day "give us all we want" without the United States "making any compromises" or paying "any price."[20]

Acheson now defended a modified version of the early cold war views of Kennan, who now was their critic. After the appearance of Acheson's article, the two men ran into each other in London, chatting agreeably and trading promises to put the controversy behind them. Publicly they did, but Acheson always put Kennan down in private thereafter, saying when Kennedy made Kennan ambassador to Yugoslavia that Tito would "have a field day playing with poor George's marshmallow mind."[21]

In Service to Kennedy

Kennedy and Johnson liberated Acheson from his law office to become minister without portfolio, laboring mostly on NATO. He always had mixed views of Kennedy, starting inauspiciously when he censured the young senator's 1957 speech attacking French colonialism in Algeria as a case of snapping "impatient fingers at a people who were great before our nation was dreamt of." When he shortly encountered Jacqueline Kennedy at New York's Penn Station, she launched into criticism of his speech as they waited for the same train, causing him to point "out to her that we were likely to be spending some hours together" and could "either spend this time fighting or we could be pleasant. And she said, 'all right, let's be pleasant.' "22

JFK had always been "extremely deferential" toward the senior statesman, even knowing Acheson would not favor his election. Acheson thought Kennedy would defeat Nixon in 1960 but worried he would hand the state department to J. W. Fulbright or Bowles. "I do not mention myself," the sixty-seven-year-old wrote in a private letter, "not because of modesty, but because I will not be asked to participate, a situation which is not distasteful to me." In a Georgetown fortuity, Clark Clifford represented the Kennedys when they sold their home, while Acheson acted for the purchaser. As president-elect, Kennedy called on Acheson in the same neighborhood three weeks after his election for advice on major appointments. He talked in Acheson's living room for ninety minutes after turning down a drink from a host who "never trusted a man who wouldn't have a drink with him." Acheson nudged him away from the "dilettante" Fulbright. Assured that Bowles would not get the job, either, he suggested Bruce with Nitze as under secretary, thinking he could elevate the latter to the top a year or two later when he became better known. After Kennedy said no to that idea, and to the notion of appointing a Republican (John McCloy), Acheson suggested Dean Rusk, underscoring his loyalty and willingness to take on thankless tasks. But he warned that good lieutenants did not always make good generals. In a gesture that could have had several meanings, Kennedy asked Acheson to become ambassador to NATO, but he declined, saying he was "too old to go home every three months to answer my cables."23

At the very beginning of the administration, when Kennedy in a Rose Garden stroll told Acheson about the plans that led to the Bay of Pigs fiasco, his alarmed companion said he hoped he was not "serious"; one needn't call in Price, Waterhouse "to discover that 1500 Cubans weren't as good as 25,000 Cubans." He soon had more reasons for disenchantment, for Kennedy seemed far too preoccupied with his own and the national "image." Publicly the Kennedy circle attracted plaudits for "crisis management," but Acheson was beginning to see them as a "group of young men who regard themselves as intellectuals" but were "capable of less coherent thought than we have had since Coolidge." (Near the end of his life, he pronounced the martyred Kennedy charming but "out of his depth" and given to "high-school thought.") Rusk gravely disappointed him, and he wrote Truman in May 1961 that State's morale had "about struck bottom." Asked if it was hard to guess what Rusk was thinking, he growled: "Did it ever occur to you that he wasn't thinking?" Pointing to Rusk's eclipse by NSC adviser McGeorge Bundy, someone asked Acheson what he would do if he were Rusk, to which he replied: "Resign." After it was bruited about that Acheson was calling Rusk "the little dean" around town, Rusk loyalists started calling Acheson "the big mustache." In November 1961, after Bowles's ouster as under secretary in a Kennedy-arranged *petit* massacre, Acheson ran into one of his least favorite Kennedy men, G. Mennen (Soapy) Williams, assistant secretary for African affairs. Pointing to his own waist, Acheson told him: "Soapy, yours will be the next scalp on my belt."[24]

What started Acheson working in the Kennedy administration was the Berlin crisis, first triggered in the Eisenhower presidency when Khrushchev threatened to give East Germany control of access to the city. The crisis raised the frightful possibility of nuclear war, Acheson believed, because of Washington's neglect of conventional forces. Though he thought Berlin did not warrant the use of nuclear weapons, his conviction of the necessity of staring down an attempt to dominate Europe made him ready to advise the kind of Dullesian "brinkmanship" he publicly disparaged. Kennedy put him in the thick of deliberations on Berlin and NATO, impressed by his "intimidating seniority," once Acheson had again refused the NATO post. He wanted no title or salary that would force him to drop any of his private jobs. He headed an advisory body, working closely with Nitze and defense secretary Robert McNamara. Once more in harness, he acted like "a man with a mission," thought Barbara Evans, crisscrossing the Atlantic and looking "better and younger" than she had "seen him in years." Warned by Bundy that Acheson saw "the Atlantic as the center of everything," Kennedy would eventually cool to his counsel.[25]

Before that cooling, Acheson pressed for daring gambles with a verve, certainty, and authority that either electrified or petrified those around Kennedy. Thinking the president should go to the brink to reinforce western credibility, he offered the same advice he had given Truman in 1950, to stage a massive conventional arms buildup and declare a national emergency. Anything less might shatter West Berlin's resolve and panic allies worldwide. In case the communists blockaded Berlin, he should order brigades up the autobahn. When he assured Chancellor Adenauer of U.S. steadfastness, *Der Alte* said: "You have lifted a stone from my heart." Kennedy asked him in the summer of 1961 what he should do if Khrushchev called for a summit. Acheson advised deputies' discussions, where the allies could make it up as they went along. "Plenty of elderly, unemployed people" were available who could "converse indefinitely without negotiating at all." He could easily do it himself "for three months on end."[26]

Both John and Robert Kennedy found Acheson intimidating but not Bundy or Rusk. Acheson loved "popping off," Bundy said, and Rusk recalled him arriving at a meeting "with a scowl on his face, as if he smelled a dead dog." In due course, JFK chose a more tempered approach to the Berlin affair, electing to accept negotiations if the right moment came. After the crisis ended with Soviet erection of the Berlin Wall, Acheson grew disgusted with what he considered the administration's weakness. The Wall "would have come down in a day if Harry Truman had been President," he said privately. He blamed Stevenson and

Walter Lippmann, "the archangel of appeasement," for emasculating Kennedy's resolve. By September 1961, he feared that NATO defeatism would produce a "humiliating defeat." Since the "First Amendment protects silence as well as speech," he had decided to go "underground."[27]

But not for long. In 1962–63, he advised the administration on relations with France and Britain. He also raised Cain about U.S.-British ties while lecturing at the U.S. Military Academy on 5 December 1962. Despite his admiration for individual Britons, their country had long been slipping in his esteem because of its resistance to European unity and idiocy in the Middle East. Soon, he said privately, it would become "a slightly more world-conscious Sweden." He exhorted Kennedy to stop all talk of a "special relationship." He claimed he had no plans to ignite any fireworks in response to West Point's speaking invitation, and most of the lecture was indeed innocuous. But with his gift for the provocative phrase, he managed also to remark that Britain had "lost an empire" and not yet found a new "role." Its effort to stand apart from Europe and stick to its special ties to the Commonwealth and the United States had "about played out." Similar observations were a commonplace in Britain, but it was wicked for an outsider to make them. Rancorous responses indicated that he had touched a nerve. He had also frightened the administration, which promptly issued versions of "he wasn't speaking for us!" Prime Minister Harold Macmillan gave Acheson the back of his hand. By taking John Bull too lightly, he had fallen into "an error which has been made by quite a lot of people in the course of the last 400 years, including Philip of Spain, Louis XIV, Napoleon, the Kaiser and Hitler." The British cultivated their outrage for months and never let Acheson forget his transgression. Churchill, nearly ninety, was deeply resentful. At home, only Henry Kissinger defended him. Acheson himself remained uncontrite about affronting that "bewildered country," though he admitted in 1970 that perhaps he had been too "epigrammatic," proving that the "first requirement of a statesman is that he be dull."[28]

Acheson was no more impressed by the handling of the Cuban missile crisis, in which he had played a marginal role shortly before the West Point speech. The only member of Kennedy's historic executive committee (ExComm) without a government title, he quickly turned up his nose at all the freewheeling talk. His hawkish advice ignored, he decided his presence was inappropriate and retreated to Harewood to mulch flowerbeds. Rusk's failure to lead had disheartened him. When Rusk suffered a weepy near breakdown, Acheson shot out: "Pull yourself together, Dean, you're the only Secretary of State we have." Robert Kennedy, too, raised his bile by arguing that air strikes on the missiles would be another Pearl Harbor. But when presidents called, Acheson answered and soon abandoned his flowers for a transatlantic flight to brief the allies. At a London stop, he passed along information for Macmillan in exchange for Ambassador Bruce's bracer of Scotch. In Paris, de Gaulle moved him by saying: "Your President has done me great honor by sending so distinguished an emissary." Looking like "a pear on top of two toothpicks," he waved aside proffered photographs of missile emplacements with the remark that "a great nation like yours would not act if there were any doubt about the evidence."[29]

Kennedy, Acheson thought, had been "too eager to liquidate this thing" when he had a chance to tighten "the thumbscrew on Khrushchev," but for the record, he sent a warm letter of congratulations. The firm riposte to Khrushchev's gamble, he surmised, would deter such ploys in the future. He nonetheless thought it was time for truth telling in the wake of Robert Kennedy's posthumous crisis memoir, published in a nation awash with Camelot nostalgia. In an article for *Esquire*, he assigned U.S. success to "plain dumb luck." Actually, John Kennedy might have agreed. And despite Acheson's bristles, Kennedy had considered him a "titan." He "would have made a helluva Supreme Court justice," the president told Ben Bradlee of the *Washington Post*, but had been too old "when I had my first vacancy."[30]

Johnson

Some of Acheson's first work with Lyndon Johnson came in 1957 on the Senate majority leader's landmark achievement in gaining passage of a civil rights bill. Though Johnson made an excellent first impression on him, Acheson soon learned what an operator he was. Later he said Johnson "could meet himself coming around four corners, before you could get around one." In turn, Bundy warned LBJ of some of the barnacles on Acheson's hide. He had "little patience for less developed countries, the U.N., Adlai Stevenson, George Kennan, etc."[31]

Despite the warning, Johnson returned Acheson to his European labors, now mainly resisting de Gaulle's undermining of NATO and keeping Adenauer in a U.S. rather than French embrace. By the time de Gaulle invited U.S. forces to leave France in 1966, Acheson, seventy-three, was operating as LBJ's NATO adviser, with a staff and office on the seventh floor of the state department. However ensconced at Foggy Bottom, he had a shaky relationship to the administration and felt hamstrung in his "Gallic war" by State's defects and the "screwballs" on Fulbright's Senate foreign relations committee. "Everything is different," he wrote Truman, "from when you-know-who was in the White House and in the State Department." He had a "love-hate affair" with Johnson himself, finally blowing up in a meeting in which he accused the White House of organizing machinations against himself and his circle of advisers, including George Ball and John McCloy. "The old wolf can still bite," he told Eden. He grew ever more disenchanted with Rusk, who "as number one" at State, had "been no good at all."[32]

In a break from these Washington struggles, he spent most of the summer of 1964 in Geneva, attempting a mediation of the Greek-Turkish conflict over Cyprus, freed from British rule in 1960. Sent partly because of his Truman Doctrine reputation in both contending countries, he devised a plan for effectively partitioning the island between the two NATO allies. This was blocked by Mihail Christodolou Mouskos (Archbishop Makarios III), president of the Republic of Cyprus, who wanted union with Greece alone. Makarios would do nothing to oblige Acheson, whom he disliked. Although the mediation failed, Acheson's visibly pro-Turkish recommendations shaped Washington's approach to Cyprus for a generation. He also steeped himself in the atmosphere of the Swiss city and, as Alice painted, wrote *Fragments of My Fleece*. Back home, he told Luke Battle that had the Greeks not toadied to Makarios, he "might have cropped the Archbishop's whiskers and solved the idiotic problem."[33]

Acheson's most significant service in the Johnson administration came in leading a group of foreign policy elders who moved from backing the dispiriting Vietnam War to persuading the president the time had come to get out of it. His own conversion from "hawk" to "dove" had been both hard and slow. In 1965, despite Acheson's own role in deepening U.S. involvement in Vietnam, his friend George Ball, Rusk's under secretary, enlisted his help in trying to push LBJ toward negotiating an end to the war. Acheson helped but was not yet convinced of the wisdom of Ball's counsel. When Ball veered sharply against the war later that year, in a counterthrust Johnson pitted him against a Senior Advisory Group on Vietnam—quickly dubbed the "wise men"—who backed the president. Bundy observed that "the mustache was voluble" in sustaining Johnson's hard line, but when LBJ bleated about all the criticism he received from people he thought would "love" him, the mustache, more pirate-like now in retirement, answered: "Mr. President, it's simple. You're not a very lovable person."[34]

By the summer of 1967, prospects for victory had faded. The administration looked unnerved to Acheson, and the more he saw Johnson in action, the more he admired Truman. But he had not yet given up the ghost in Vietnam. Thinking the communists would simply "give up" if Americans succeeded on the battlefield, he opposed negotiations and trashed Fulbright's "lousy" Senate committee and Fulbright as "a dilettante fool." Like millions of others, however, the communists' Tet Offensive, beginning at the end of January 1968, shook him. Prodded by Averell Harriman, he switched sides, saying the war was worse than immoral—it was "a mistake." Johnson again mustered the "wise men," hoping for their support, but Acheson demanded and received thorough briefings by a covey of mid-level officials spanning diplomatic, military, and intelligence perspectives. Convinced that a military victory, by any definition, was impossible, he opposed further escalation and the dispatch of more troops.[35]

On 15 March 1968, three days after LBJ nearly lost the New Hampshire Democratic primary to antiwar candidate Eugene McCarthy, Acheson sat alone with the president for lunch and said the military was deceiving him. He had to find a way out, for "winning" would take at least five years and a limitless drain of resources. On 25–26 March, after Robert Kennedy joined the presidential sweepstakes, the fourteen "wise men" gathered at the White House, most notably Acheson, McCloy, Omar Bradley, Matthew Ridgway, and two who had recently left the administration, Ball and Bundy. Acheson had once called such groups the "sons of bitches from out of town," but now they bore down on Johnson in favor of disengagement, with Acheson leading the way in arguing that victory was out of reach. When the chairman of the joint chiefs, General Earle Wheeler, interjected that U.S. forces were not *trying* for a victory, a fuming Acheson asked: "Then what in the name of God are five hundred thousand men out there doing—chasing girls?" If they were not there "to gain a military solution, then words have lost all meaning."[36]

Within a week, Johnson halted the bombing of North Vietnam, called for peace talks, and withdrew from the presidential campaign. The "establishment" had turned its back on the war as part of a broader erosion of the cold war consensus molded in the Truman years, but Acheson thought he had been loyal to his own bedrock assumptions. Through 1950–52, he had done much to commit the United States to South Vietnam, though often with clenched teeth. In 1968, he believed hanging on would cost more in U.S. credibility than it would lose by letting go. He was still the Atlanticist who issued the *China White Paper* and tried to disentangle the United States from Chiang to concentrate on vital matters in Europe. At Joe Alsop's one evening in 1969, he got in a shouting match with LBJ adviser Walt W. Rostow, who asked: If Asia meant so little to Acheson, why had he rushed to defend South Korea? "To validate NATO," Acheson replied.[37]

Nixon and Kissinger

Lyndon Johnson was a volatile but sometimes forgiving man and he reacted benignly to Acheson's wise man role. In 1964, he had already awarded him the Presidential Medal of Freedom and now, eleven days after pulling out of the presidential campaign, wrote him a touching personal letter. "You and I both know," Johnson wrote, "there have been a number of times when I did not like the advice you gave me. I am aware that you were aware that I would not like it when you gave it to me—and I am also aware that as you define your duty, my dislike was, and had to be, an irrelevancy."[38]

Acheson's connection with Nixon was mostly about NATO and the U.S. role in Europe. It also had much to do with ego and an old man's vanity. The matchmaker of the connection was Kissinger, who first became Acheson's friend after praising his attack on Kennan's BBC lecture. They had first met in 1953 when graduate student Kissinger tracked Acheson down for an interview. Acheson graciously endured his weighty, Germanic questions, sometimes answering "acerbically." Everything was fine, Kissinger recalled, "until I inquired into his reaction to one of MacArthur's particularly muscular dispatches. 'You mean before or after I peed in my pants?' asked this paragon of old-world diplomacy." It was not long before he was reading Kissinger's books and receiving "numerous flattering (if not fawning) letters" from him. The two men talked diplomacy at P Street breakfasts.

In 1968, Acheson had backed Hubert Humphrey's losing presidential run but hoped that if elected, Nixon could extract the United States from Vietnam as Eisenhower had settled the Korean War without political punishment. Nixon's national security adviser, Kissinger admired Acheson more than any other secretary of state of "the postwar generation" and urged the president to make an overture to him. It was Acheson, however, who moved first in March 1969 at Washington's annual Gridiron Club dinner. An Oval Office meeting between the two quickly followed, with Kissinger sitting in. Afterward, Acheson complaisantly confessed he was not immune to Nixon's switch from "abusive hostility to respect," with "a dash of flattery" thrown in.[39]

Nixon's attention coincided with positive reviews of Acheson's memoirs and sparked a modest public rebirth and a torrent of his op-ed pieces and letters to the editor. He wrote Eden: "I find the pleasure of being listened to seductive." Interviewed by the *New York Times* in October 1969, he let fly at those trying to "destroy" Nixon and declared "England bankrupt, France divided, Nationalist China finished," the Soviet Union "frightened," and Italy "hardly a country." Though he quietly objected to Nixon's incursion into Cambodia in 1970, the administration's opening to China deeply impressed him, enough that David Acheson thinks his father would have voted for Nixon's reelection had he been living in 1972. Less lenient, Alice shook her head at the idea of granting amnesty to her husband's former tormenter.[40]

Acheson's greatest value to Nixon was in helping repel uprisings by formerly internationalist Democrats grown disaffected by Vietnam. Resolutions emerged annually from the Senate to remove U.S. troops from Europe, usually from the desk of Montana's Mike Mansfield. Democrats also fought Nixon's decision to create an anti-ballistic-missile system as a bargaining counter for arms control negotiations. Acheson fought all these outbreaks, usually in league with other elders, including Nitze, McCloy, Robert Lovett, and Lucius Clay. But youngsters also worked with him, including Richard Perle, Peter Wilson, Paul Wolfowitz, and Edward Luttwak, whom Acheson proudly called "our four musketeers." His last hurrah came in the spring of 1971, when he rallied yet another bipartisan array of reputation against Mansfield. Flanked by the others after a White House meeting on 13 May, he told the press that Nixon was resolutely against Mansfield's "asinine" amendment. When a reporter asked why their meeting had taken so long, he said, "we are all old, and we are all eloquent." Down went Mansfield's amendment, and Kissinger wrote Acheson: "You were magnificent, as usual, and you deserve a substantial part of the credit for the successful outcome." To Acheson, it had been "great fun" resulting "in a most satisfying victory."[41]

Present at the Writing

If the law could not satisfy Acheson in retirement, writing could, and he turned out to have a great talent for it. Generating more income was one reason to write as much as he did, but so was re-exercising his vital powers. Starting with shorter pieces in the mid-fifties and writing everything by hand on legal pads—because "you write better and think more carefully when you do it with your own hand"— he churned out a stream of articles and books. The latter ranged from policy advocacy to memoir, including three posthumously published miscellanies. A long hiatus occurred between his first plans to write his memoirs and the day he actually started writing. Hundreds of sometimes rambling pages of Princeton Seminars transcripts were important in the effort. Though formidable in texture, they had gathered dust for a decade as he avoided this task and tried his hand at others, including short stories. When Sally Reston wrote to praise one of his first books, he claimed it had been "written by a close relative of the same name who showed great and early promise but who, unfortunately, took to drink." The first books grew from lectures, *A Citizen Looks at Congress*, at the University of Virginia, and *Power and Diplomacy*, at the Fletcher School of Law and Diplomacy. *Morning and Noon*, a pre–state department memoir dedicated to Frankfurter, drew praise from reviewers. One noted that scenes in Acheson's earlier *Sketches from Life of Men I Have Known* confirmed his repute for "a temper rich in thermal units."[42]

   Present at the Creation was the last book published in Acheson's life. In the late fifties, he had dropped the idea of writing it, but, as noted earlier, he changed his mind, David Acheson claims, after being threatened with the idea that his bane, Adolf Berle, might write it. Kissinger gave the project a large boost in 1964 by matching Acheson with excellent research assistants who sifted through the documentary record for him. Beginning in 1966, Acheson wrote most of the book either at Harewood or in the West Indies, often in breaks from service to LBJ. When Barbara Evans received the longhand pages, she deciphered Acheson's "exotic calligraphy" and tracked down "the serpent of error." "Writing is not easy," he told an interviewer, and requires overcoming the "old Adam of laziness." In March 1967 he told Reston he had "written about 130,000 words" and had "between 250–300 thousand more to go—a bit less than a third done." He was enjoying himself in a "masochistic sort of way."[43]

   W. W. Norton published *Present at the Creation: My Years in the State Department* in 1969. Starting with an epigraph credited to Alphonso X, the Learned (1252–84), King of Spain—"Had I been present at the creation I would have given some useful hints for the better ordering of the universe"—Acheson took readers from 1941 to 1953 in 778 pages. By any measure, it was a sterling effort. Apart from Kissinger's own prodigious recollections, Acheson's memoir easily outshines in interest and literary quality those of any other secretary of state. Memoirs by nature are self-serving, but in this, Acheson was no match for Kissinger in his cunning. He omits some scenes in which he acted badly—the martini-drenched wrangle over Korean POWs with the British at the UN comes to mind—yet often tells the reader enough to suggest why he might have misbe- haved. Historians would be rash to rely only on *Present*, but strangers to his life would find both knowledge and entertainment in it. The official and unofficial Acheson voices are virtually identical; the memoir writer differs from the letter writer mostly in being more tactful. The finest parts of the book are the profiles of Acheson's diplomatic partners, especially Bevin, Schuman, and Adenauer. Despite an occasional penchant for the orotund (shared with Kissinger), the narrative drives with a zest that helps explain the book's many years in print. More candid than most public men, in settling old scores Acheson usually skewers with understatement. Like his president, he abhorred looking back after deciding to go forward, and the memoir fails to reflect on paths not taken. It abounds with plaudits to its dedicatee: "To Harry S. Truman, 'The captain with the mighty heart.'"

He was not shocked when the left poked hard at the volume (Ronald Steel's review in the *New York Review of Books* was titled, "Commissar of the Cold War"), but he *was* surprised to receive a generous letter of praise from Kennan. In May 1970, shortly after Acheson suffered a stroke, his book received the Pulitzer Prize for history, inspiring another wave of praise. Lovett warned that he might "collect an Oscar, an Emmy," too, "and anything else that is not nailed down." The Pulitzer, Acheson wrote Lawrence S. Eagleburger, had been "a great boon to my rather sagging spirits, and they have been further lifted by notes from my friends telling me of their approval of the book and the prize."[44]

"The Great Barbarian Take-Over"

It is a wonder that Acheson could write such a lively, droll, and astute book, one free of acrimony, at a time his own personality had soured as much as it had. By 1969, his manner was often scathing, his viewpoint retrograde. In private, especially when making observations on the unruly society around him, he was particularly disapproving. Some friendships fell casualty to this acridity, but he remained a devoted family man. At a lunch in 1970, Sulzberger found him "exceptionally friendly, an erect, distinguished, and elegant figure in a white suit Mark Twain might have envied." A year later, his daughter Mary Bundy told David Lilienthal she and her father were "really good adult friends. It is a joy to have such a friend." His mind still purred smoothly when advising presidents, and that part of his brain that wrote his memoir escaped the corrosion of spirit with which he faulted the world around him. His sourness was surely partly a product of age but also an overstated expression of his old self. He used words as knives, loved to shock others, and was often found pawing for a fight. As the Democratic Party, in shock from Vietnam, listed to the left, Acheson moved to the right. Far younger men curdled in response to the whirlwinds of the late sixties, but Acheson at times seemed to think the young and rebellious were deliberately choosing to flout the standards by which he had grown up and that he still honored. One Acheson now clashed with another. He was a friend to his family, a clearheaded writer, and an ever nastier polemicist.[45]

He directed some of his venom at things he had long disliked, including (in 1956) a press that "misinforms us, and our complacent, ignorant and fat-headed, fat bellied fellow citizens." This was small change compared to his 1959 remark to Cabell Phillips that "we are reliving the ordeal of the Roman Empire and the great barbarian take-over." In his most inglorious form, the late Acheson was overtly racist and ready to defend tyrannical white regimes in Africa. Side by side with racism stood decent if patronizing personal relations with blacks he knew, including a former employee he defended against charges of drunkenness and resisting arrest. After gaining his freedom, the employee accepted a ride home from Acheson. He said he could pay him only with a bottle of Wild Turkey, which he offered from his pocket. "Is it a new bottle?" "Well, it is practically new; I done hardly tasted it." Already worried that African-Americans were unduly "impatient," he worried when black migrants from the south began voting in blocs. The United States, he fretted in 1971, faced "black urban government" linked to "white exodus." "Blacks, women, and inflation" all shook the nation's foundations, with women's new role "large and disturbing." According to David Acheson, his father thought "violence, crime, and disorder had gotten entirely out of control."[46]

The most "basic relationships of the last 200 years," he thought, were dissolving before his eyes, the result of unprecedented "affluence" and advances in science, along with the new "position of women." Well, a BBC interviewer inanely wondered in 1970, apart from all that, wasn't he hopeful about the future? "I am afraid that I must say that I am not very hopeful," came the reply. All governments labored under the glare of television and the demands of the "egalitarian principle," which caused people to believe they were free not to think and that "anyone's ideas are just as good as anyone else's ideas." This was a formula to destroy discipline, the "long-term" view, and the ability to accommodate "our own prejudices with nations who have different prejudices." Out-of-control egalitarianism made "us all believe that we are little gods outside our own universe, directing it instead of little ganglia within." He did not want to see "how it all comes out." "Mediocrities" were everywhere, he told Sulzberger. Even eighteen-year-olds had the vote—a terrible idea. "People have opinions but no knowledge, and leaders are made in the image of the masses. Democracy is only tolerable because no other governmental system is."[47]

He even grew crabby in the Caribbean. He scowled at the restlessness and "growing incivility" of black workers. The unrest was the by-product of the "poverty" created by British rule in these "largely unproductive and over populated islands," and it was "naive" to expect "cooperation from the Noble Savage." He could foresee the day when resentful "servants" would "drive away tourism" and then win their freedom "to enjoy the pleasures of canabalism [sic]." To the sometimes equally querulous George Ball he wrote: "Keep on making sense; you have the field to yourself."[48]

Reverting to "Primitive Tribalism"

Acheson's soft spot for white rule in Africa went back at least to his admiration of Portugal's António de Oliveira Salazar, the recipient too of Kennan's blessing. One of Acheson's first fights with Kennedy came after the young president made cautious efforts to distance the United States from Portuguese rule in Angola. It was no good to say such a change brought Washington more in line with the UN, Acheson held, for that body was dominated by puny states dedicated to forcing unpleasant choices on great powers and independence on people unready for it. In another affront to Soapy Williams, who carried Kennedy's message to Africa, Acheson said that just because Williams hailed from "the dark city of Detroit" did not mean he should "pander to the dark and delirious continent of Africa." Colonialism had seen its day, he said in a 1963 lecture, "not because it is wicked" or because the downtrodden peoples of the world could "govern themselves," but because rule had slipped "from the enfeebled hands of the imperial powers of Europe." "Unable to govern themselves," new states now found themselves "in a most precarious and difficult situation."[49]

Africa was much on his mind in his last years, and he found allies in his rejection of knee-jerk anti-colonialism in two old colleagues, Kennan and Charles Burton Marshall. Acheson, whose health stopped him from traveling in 1969 to South Africa on the ticket of a foundation lobbying against South African sanctions, vigorously defended its rule in South-West Africa (Namibia) in a 1971 op-ed article. From 1965 on, he fired rhetorical rockets at the UN for contesting white-ruled Rhodesia's declaration of independence and at the Washington and London governments for supporting third world "juvenile delinquents" and the "Black Mafia" of African delegates at Turtle Bay. In 1966, he engaged in a yearlong row over the issue with the U.S. ambassador to the UN, "that ass [Arthur] Goldberg."[50]

He pounded at the issue to the end of Johnson's administration. The "Children's Crusade" against Rhodesia could "throw all southern Africa into chaos" and came from states not practicing universal suffrage themselves. He aimed his prickliest barbs at Britain's "mad policy" and Harold Wilson, its "loony" prime minister (Wilson gibed that Acheson had "lost a State Department and not yet found himself a new role"). Littering his statements were aspersions against African blacks, as in his reference to Rhodesians as "still in a state of primitive neolithic culture." As Kissinger labored to split the difference between African liberation and the entrenchment represented by Acheson, the latter (and Marshall) testified in November 1969 before the House subcommittee on Africa, chaired by African-American congressman Charles Diggs. The continent's best hopes, Acheson insisted, lay with the "competent, highly-developed people who ruled southern Africa," not those who had reverted to "primitive tribalism."[51]

Friends and family members drew back in dismay at a dotage dominated by defending Rhodesia. Harriman in 1970 pronounced Acheson's attitude "atrocious," proving that he was altogether "a European man" rather than a "universal statesman" who had "transcended time." Even his daughters, "natural and by marriage," Acheson grumbled in 1971, "think I am an old reactionary." He seemed unperturbed that his contemporary allies included the likes of Barry Goldwater, James Eastland, Strom Thurmond, George Wallace, Patrick Buchanan, William F. Buckley, and assorted members of the John Birch Society.[52]

In his last public appearance, in June 1971, he again testified in the Senate in defense of Ian Smith's regime and was again planning a trip to southern Africa he would never take. He had looked forward to meeting Roy Welensky, former Rhodesian prime minister and now one of his favorite correspondents. In late July, Welensky, who had lived his entire life "where the Whites have been outnumbered," wrote that "the Black man" was preoccupied with "dignity and face-saving." On 7 October, Acheson wrote back: "I still cling to Bret Harte's aphorism, 'That for ways that are dark And for tricks that are vain The Heathen Chinese is peculiar.' But no more so than the heathen Japanese."[53]

*   *   *   *

On a mild 12th of October, five days after quoting Harte, Acheson spent several hours laboring in his Harewood flowerbeds. Then he started a letter to Eden in his study, where at six o'clock in the evening, a servant found him "slumped over a desk." Summoned to the scene, a family doctor pronounced him dead. A massive stroke had killed him at age seventy-eight. As memorial planning went forward, Schlesinger wrote in the *Times* that "in a city of gray and anonymous men, Dean Acheson stood out like a noble monument from another and more vivid era." He was "an independent, unintimidated figure to the end," declared the *Washington Post*. It was an unforgettable experience, wrote one of its reporters, to meet "one of the most fascinating, intelligent, witty, critical, eloquent and controversial figures on the Washington and world scene for a generation." His old friend David Lilienthal took to his diary in tribute. "What a remarkable man," he wrote, "and what an extraordinary part he played in the history of the world. With his delightful quality of wryness, he couldn't be called a cynic, not a full-blown one. There must have been in him an infrastructure of hope to sustain him through the trials and exhausting and often hopeless struggles of his public service." Nixon ordered U.S. flags lowered to half-staff. Hundreds crowded the memorial service at the National Cathedral, after which Acheson was buried "on a sparkling warm Indian summer in Georgetown."[54]

Five years later, with Kissinger presiding, the state department renamed the West Auditorium for Acheson. It was fitting homage to a great secretary of state, even though, as his son believed, Acheson in his retirement years had "allowed himself too much fun and brushed the edges of the outrageous, savoring the freedom from official constraints that went with his private status." "Brushed the edges" are charitable words for some of the directions Acheson took at the end. But however distasteful, they did not erase his earlier achievements.[55]

37

CONCLUSION: POWER FOR
A PURPOSE

A "Spacious Environment"

Modern American strategy emerged with the dawn of the cold war more than a half century ago. It involved both new instruments and new uses of power. Power allows one nation to get another to do its wishes, whether enemy or ally. It comes from many sources—geography and natural resources, an ingenious and relatively large population, allies among other states, and large and effective military forces. Using this power to achieve one's purposes is what strategy is about. After 1945, Americans' objective was to found and uphold a world order compatible with their own values and institutions.

American leaders thought the actions needed to carry out these purposes benefited the world at large. They welded power to purpose in an insistent and self-aware manner that had almost no precedent in U.S. history. Mostly, they were successful, producing the International Monetary Fund and World Bank, the Truman Doctrine and Berlin airlift, the Marshall Plan and North Atlantic Treaty Organization, the beginnings of European integration, and, with varied results, the intervention in Korea. In transfiguring the Japanese empire and most of Nazi Germany into democratic and peaceable states, reviving their economies, and absorbing them within the "western" alliance, they effected one of the most notable diplomatic feats in recent history, which went far to assure how the cold war would end. Asked by Henry Kissinger to name his proudest achievement, Harry S Truman replied: "We completely defeated our enemies and made them surrender. And then we helped them to recover, to become democratic, and to rejoin the community of nations."[1]

All this was accomplished under Truman as president, a doughty man better known for courage and loyalty to subordinates than strategic thinking. But he had an eye for good people in military and diplomatic affairs. Men with exceptional skill, temper, and judgment stood at his side, officers like Omar Bradley, George Marshall, and Dwight Eisenhower, and civilians like Clark Clifford, Robert Lovett, and Averell Harriman. The deputy with the steadiest strategic outlook was Dean G. Acheson. Some of his most constructive achievements came while acting as under secretary for Marshall. Then, from January 1949 to January 1953, he guided the use of American power as Truman's fourth secretary of state. These men sought nothing less than to create a world in which societies with free institutions and liberal economies could succeed. In the immediate aftermath of World War II, this was a strategy without an enemy. The object was not to fight the Soviet Union, seen as troublesome but not yet a strategic antagonist, but to build a liberal world order and prevent another world war. Washington would reshape these objectives when it identified Moscow's urges as a serious threat to this world. Truman and his aides knew the capable use of power abroad was crucial to safeguarding America's own ideals, institutions, and traditions.

One of their more notable feats was the forthright creation and application of strength to carry out their international goals in a country traditionally suspicious of the open exercise of governmental power. Impressed by the limits of what the voters would allow them, earlier leaders had muffled the link between diplomatic means and ends. Theodore Roosevelt was an aficionado of national power, whose building of the U.S. navy reflected a strong awareness of the connection, but he mostly rationed himself to disciplining the Caribbean and working on the margin to influence events elsewhere. Woodrow Wilson was hugely ambitious in wanting to change the very nature of international affairs but was in denial about using national power to do so. As a pragmatist and master of legerdemain, Franklin Roosevelt masked the significance of both power and principle, forfeiting strategic clarity as he shrouded his purposes. But the New Deal and especially World War II acclimated the people to a strong state, paralleling the expansion of the United States' international power and sense of its vital national interests. The Truman administration stumbled at first but then candidly wed power to purpose in pursuit of its ambitious objectives. With momentary exceptions, Truman's successors followed his lead to the end of the cold war.

Both as under secretary and secretary of state, Acheson made the strongest record in European and military-strategic affairs. Though doomed to failure, the Acheson-Lilienthal Plan was a genuine attempt to block a nuclear arms race before it began. Once he had definitively joined the cold war consensus, he guided the rejoinder to Russia's apparent threat against Turkey, forged the Truman Doctrine, and with others invented the Marshall Plan, maybe the most dazzling deed of the cold war. As secretary of state, he assured the adoption of NATO and led the way to give it reality. He helped bring Britain as far into European association as it would go and played a large role in ending Franco-German enmity. Through "double containment," he answered Soviet expansionism by adding West Germany's power to the west while containing it within NATO and other institutions. In sponsoring NSC-68, he launched a vigorous campaign for rearmament and attempted to reduce strategic dependence on nuclear weapons.

Outside Europe, his record was ambiguous. Overseeing Japan's reemergence as a robust, pro-western state was a clear-cut and historic victory. His steering of the decision making after North Korea's invasion of South Korea, however, led to mixed results. His most notable failures, for which he shared liability with others, included not making clear before 1950 that the United States would rise to South Korea's defense. Worse was failing to stop General MacArthur from provoking the Chinese intervention, which turned a major victory into impasse. The primary liability for this debacle lay at Truman and Marshall's feet. Acheson, however, was in the vanguard in leading the United States into Indochina's Big Muddy. His ultimate loyalty to NATO partners Britain and France blocked his spirited efforts to gain the trust of Iranian and Egyptian nationalists. Seeing no threats to vital interests or resources in South and Central America, he consigned it all to subordinates. In retirement, he sullied an already sparse record in sub-Saharan Africa with a shrill defense of surviving white regimes.

There were two prongs to Acheson's strategy. One, stressing the needs of American society, governed the early postwar period, when most U.S. officials considered the USSR a friend or at least a conventional competitor. The second prong emphasized the outer projection of American power and dominated policy after Washington identified Moscow as a source of peril. But even when this became the dominant thrust of Acheson's foreign policy, his goal of protecting American values and social, economic, and political habits remained its foundation.

As World War II closed, Acheson said the goals of U.S. policy were to create "a world situation in which this great experience in liberty that we call America can survive and flourish." The United States sought to promote "as spacious an environment as possible" so that other societies might thrive as well. A return to the economic combat of the 1920s and depression years would imperil these goals, dry up commerce, slash living standards, and spark conflicts when nations jostled for security "over the backs of its neighbors." It would lead, in one nation after another, to the imposition of "arbitrary and absolutist controls" by governments, and possibly their destruction in increasingly ferocious contests between left and right. These internal struggles would suck in the "great powers," seeking advantage by throwing their weight behind one faction or another.[2]

In 1945, Acheson thought the main hurdle to an open and "energetic" world was the demand of war-weary, stricken peoples that their governments use all their powers to relieve their distress. The result would be authoritarian regimes, whether of the left or right, colliding in ideological trajectory with liberal American principles. In self-defense, the United States might find itself going down the same road. Liberty and a limited state could give way to bureaucracies regulating everything in sight, nonstop mobilization of military power to ward off foreign aggression, and a narrow scrutiny of internal dissent and nonconformity. Once Acheson identified the Soviet Union as a menace, he still feared that widespread social disorganization would lure frightened Germans and Japanese into the hands of Moscow's disciplinarians. This would effectively annul America's war-time victories and push it deeper into regimented, insecure isolation.

In defense of American institutions and traditions, the United States in the Truman and Acheson years used its new strength to reverse the ruin and chaos in western Europe. First trying loans, it advanced to the Marshall Plan, in effect granting to Europe the fruits of America's own farms and factories. This was an act of great liberality and a spectacular case of doing well by doing good. Because the Treasury paid U.S. producers to supply the largesse, Europeans were again able to buy American goods. By restoring western Europe to a semblance of liberal order, the American people were able to protect what they had fought for in World War II.

But there was a large fly in this analgesic ointment. Still seeking to expand its influence in Europe, the USSR tried to break up the Marshall Plan and block western recuperation, using propaganda, verbal bullying, subversion, and labor strikes wherever communists could pull them off, especially in France, Italy, and Belgium. East-west friction aroused feelings of military insecurity, diverting west Europeans from concentrating on recovery. American leaders would not repeat the errors of the 1920s and decided they must offer further, tangible pledges of lasting U.S. support and involvement. The most important vehicle of commitment was the North Atlantic Treaty Organization, which at first aimed more at easing psychological than military insecurity.

What kind of threat did Acheson think the Soviets posed? The primary problem for him was not what communists did to economies or the peoples they ruled, but, he had declared in 1950, how the Soviets, driven and justified by an ideology defining virtually all other states as hostile, jeopardized western security and civilization itself. The USSR seemed a terrible threat because it assembled military power far beyond what it might credibly need for its own defense. The impulse to amass such power fed on the fear that the free societies to the west, by their nature, comprised a threat to Moscow's control of the east.

Acheson did not think Soviet forces—grown from 2.8 to 5.7 million men between 1948 and 1953—would maraud by design across western Europe, but feared that unexpected east-west friction would degenerate into a crisis that flung the United States into a war for which it was unprepared. A more plausible danger was that Moscow would gain a free victory because the west would be afraid to act in the face of Kremlin intimidation. He conceded that some Soviet decisions and actions stemmed from genuine fears. But he worried far more about western military weakness than how correcting that problem might alarm the communists. Armed with the atomic bomb, Josef Stalin might try to push his empire farther west, petrifying still recovering societies and triggering a war the west lacked the armed forces to fight successfully. The very appearance of this weakness might tempt Moscow to act recklessly.[3]

Having ascertained that economic resources alone could not guard U.S. interests or calm allied fears, Acheson adopted an uncomplicated strategy of amassing countervailing power. The first task, for which he had minimal responsibility, was to put America's (and the west's) own house in order, sustaining economic growth and a liberal society that could justly represent the forces of freedom. The next step was to gather and *use* other forms of power. As Nicolo Machiavelli knew, a society without power was an insecure society, "and without security," writes Paul Kennedy, "all of mankind's other achievements—the arts and sciences, literature, economic progress, civil society—are constantly at risk." Acheson agreed but also appreciated the limits of power, which accounted for his concern that adherence to pell-mell "containment" would undermine rather than fortify American power. Rather than "contain" the Soviets at all particular points, the west should match and preferably outmatch its power generally.

He wanted to *win* the cold war, which meant blocking any Soviet expansionism long enough to envelop Germany and Japan within the western system, thus overriding Soviet geopolitical strength. This meant building large enough military forces to convince the Soviets they would suffer intolerable damage in any war, forces gained through NATO, U.S. and European rearmament, and the Mutual Defense Assistance Program. These would limit Moscow to political maneuvers in attempts to shape Europe according to its own strategic and ideological blueprints, a contest Acheson thought the west could not lose.[4]

This was the strategy of building situations of strength, which could countermand virtually every cold war danger. It would restrain the USSR and would free western Europeans to get on with economic rehabilitation. It would stiffen NATO with planes and tanks and end West Germany's doubts about casting its lot with the west. It would discourage new military exploits by China and supply a shield behind which Washington could complete its design for Japan's future. Building situations of strength might also silence conservative militants at home.

The purpose of building positions of strength was to create power rather than discuss and settle differences. Acheson's commitment to permanent U.S. engagement abroad, especially in Europe, only nominally sought a negotiated settlement with the Soviets, for he hoped to compel a de facto acceptance of western strength, negotiations or not. The west would resolve cold war conflicts on its own by removing all possible "areas of weakness" rather than through accords with Kremlin miscreants, at least until they turned a new leaf. Should they not budge, his unstated intent was to persevere until western strength was unassailable. Then the Soviets would have to yield. He would not surrender western strong points in east-west talks, and when the cold war finally ended, they remained intact.⁵

Protection from Predators

What is Acheson's standing in the history of the cold war? How does his record in pursuit of the strategy of strength hold up? British biographer Roy (Lord) Jenkins said the Truman years were "as dangerous as they were creative" and Acheson's "nerve as good as his vision." Acheson's contemporary, Theodore H. White, wrote that "if any man offered himself as personal silhouette of American supremacy in the postwar world, it was Dean Acheson, Secretary of State." "At the height of his power abroad," White judges, he "had no counterpart. He was like the sun god or a Benjamin Franklin with thunderbolts." Truman and Acheson, "the greatest Secretary of State in the twentieth century," together "ushered in the most creative period in the history of American foreign policy," writes Henry Kissinger. Discounting White's hyperbole, these judgments seem apt, and while it is tricky to compare men working generations apart, there seems little reason to limit Kissinger's accolade to the twentieth century, for only John Quincy Adams and William H. Seward from earlier times might rate higher.⁶

Many see Acheson otherwise, especially those repelled by his hauteur and gusto for cold war diplomacy. Critics have argued that the Truman Doctrine was overwrought, Acheson's role in the Marshall Plan secondary, and that he was a Johnny-come-lately in founding NATO. They have judged the *China White Paper* and Alger Hiss affairs as political debacles. They view the mounting embroilment in Indochina as an awful mistake and the miscarriages in Korea as offsetting any of his just accomplishments.

Much of this dispraise falls on inspection. The rhetoric of the Truman Doctrine pales next to John Kennedy's promise to "pay any price, bear any burden, meet any hardship, support any friend, oppose any foe to assure the survival and the success of liberty." Besides armoring the administration against conservatives at home, the Truman Doctrine rallied the spirits of Europeans fearing another era of American isolationism. The Marshall Plan had many parents, but Acheson was at least primus inter pares in laying its foundation. Others indeed took the first steps with the Atlantic treaty, but Acheson kneaded the senatorial egos necessary to gain wide approval of this tradition-breaking pact. Far more than others, he made it a reality through deft handling of European allies and the Germans. No doubt the *White Paper* was a fiasco, but it was not the cause of Chiang Kai-shek's failure in China or Mao Zedong's success. Acheson's inability to grasp the truth about Hiss—widely shared—injured his (and Truman's) standing. But their political troubles and plummeting poll ratings failed to stop them from reaching most of their goals. When they did fail, it was not through domestic resistance but because other world actors had designs of their own and effectively pursued them. Acheson had much to answer for in China's plunge into the Korean War, but considerably less than MacArthur, Truman, and Marshall. And it bears repeating that the west greatly profited from the war. Western mobilization and rearmament were at the heart of establishing western preponderance. In human and material losses, and in alliance fissures opened, the biggest losers by far in Korea were the North Koreans, Chinese, and Soviets.

In gauging Acheson's deeds, one must compare what happened on his watch to what could have happened. Merely because historic events are commonly known does not mean they were bound to occur. Sixty years after the close of World War II, this is especially important in considering Germany and Japan. Remembering that American "reconstruction" after the Civil War took more than a century, that the easy vanquishment of Spain in 1898 led directly to a dirty and misnamed "small" war in the Philippines that lasted years, and that the Versailles "peace" soon gave way to Hitler, the nonviolent acceptance of defeat by West Germany and Japan and their swift conversion into peaceable and democratic western allies is breathtaking. Among Americans, Acheson played a larger role in this story than anyone else, with vital help from Lucius Clay and John McCloy in Germany and John Foster Dulles and Douglas MacArthur in Japan, and always from Truman, the ultimately responsible party. When Acheson worked to reintegrate West Germany and Japan into the system of "western" strength, they were still occupied nations. It was primarily his drive that made it possible for them to become independent actors again. Japan returned to full sovereignty under his aegis and the Federal Republic of Germany nearly did so.

NATO's growth from phrases on paper to a potent military combine was mostly Acheson's deed too, working alongside his diplomatic companions, Ernest Bevin and Robert Schuman. All the efforts to renew western Europe's economies and its confidence, from the British loan to the Mutual Defense Assistance Program, produced decades of goodwill for the United States in Europe. They also provided a spark for European unity, for it was at Washington's insistence, starting with the Marshall Plan, that Europeans threw over hypernationalism for mutuality. The impulse bridged the Atlantic, with the United States and Canada joining an association of nations remarkably united in international goals and democratic sympathies. With a growing sense of purpose and energy, the United States spearheaded the drive to strengthen the west, capped by adding the denatured West Germans to the strategic partnership. Much friction occurred along the way, and pieces of the new structure would come unstuck when France abandoned its military role in NATO, but the effort to build a strong and united western Europe was a spectacular success. It led eventually, and peacefully, to an end of the cold war when a new Kremlin generation led by Mikhail Gorbachev realized the futility of past practices and the Soviet Union's urgent need to participate in the modernity and prosperity achieved in the west.

None of this was predestined. Less than a decade after FDR ran its gauntlet, a reborn isolationism might have defeated the Atlantic pact and the Marshall

Plan. Had this occurred, western European states might have scrambled for their own modes of security while the United States drifted away, a development Stalin may have expected. All of Scandinavia would probably have succumbed to the semi-satellite status of "Finlandization." Without NATO's defensive mantle, Italy's Communists might have taken power through free elections. Besides being exposed to Soviet designs, Greece and Turkey would have lacked the referee to keep them from fighting each another. Worst of all, France would surely have sought Soviet help for protection against Germany. At the mercy of a Franco-Soviet squeeze, it is unlikely West Germans would have taken the course to liberalism, democracy, and peace that Washington effectively urged upon them. Even *with* the Marshall Plan and NATO, Great Britain preferred an offshore role, and without them, British isolationism would surely have been magnified. In these cases, the United States would have had trouble avoiding the protectionist economy and even the garrison state Acheson feared. Americans would have enjoyed far less security and prosperity. But none of these things happened, largely because of a creative American internationalism working in brilliant cooperation with Europeans.[7]

Lessons learned led to cold war accomplishments. Chiefly, Americans had learned isolationism did not work and supported the Marshall Plan and NATO. This allowed their government to help end seventy-five years of Franco-German enmity. Europeans, too, had learned the necessity of avoiding the errors of the 1920s and 1930s. Americans encouraged this reversal of fortunes because they had learned *theirs*. Because lessons take time to sink in, it took a generation of statesmanship to accomplish these feats. On the American side, an astonishing amount of this labor occurred in the eight years of Harry Truman's presidency, much of it done by Dean Acheson at Foggy Bottom.

His own skills and persona account for his record. He kept sane hours but was one of Washington's liveliest and brainiest officials. He drew on energy, cerebral dexterity, poise, and high spirits. Though a proud-crested man, he had a critical sense of other people's needs, most pertinently Truman's. His radar arced around Washington, tracking the president's political constraints. Acheson's insistence that subordinates accept his judgment of what Truman would accept explained why the White House trusted him, a trust that expanded his influence and autonomy, and that of the department. The influence also expanded to Congress, for the stereotype of Acheson as an archon of arrogance slighting congressional inferiors is incorrect. He held scores of candid interchanges on the Hill, peppering his remarks with graphic analogies and illustrations. In the state department, he enjoyed working above all with Paul Nitze, Philip Jessup, and David Bruce, and, despite their frayed relations, he also picked the crop of George Kennan's creativity. No other secretary so vivaciously led his department or engaged in such fertile discussion with its professionals. With Europeans, he usually converted conflict into concord, even when they felt he was leaning on them. Where differences or conflicting interests persisted, he sometimes insisted on Washington's objectives but was as likely to give way or good-naturedly steer round differences.

Labels commonly used in the study of international relations do not fit Acheson well. The cliché "pragmatist" is all right, if all the word means is being practical day-to-day, taking up problems as they appear, and not worrying overmuch about how to move from point A to B. In all these points, he was of course pragmatic, but so are most officials. Does a strategy of building situations of strength make him a "realist"? He was usually "realistic" when tying objectives to accessible power, and NSC-68 was designed to make a correction when American goals badly outstripped the ability to achieve them. Unlike strict "realists," he did not think other nations' internal affairs were off limits and was certain the cold war would not end until something profound changed in the nature of the Soviet Union. American policy under his leadership continually intruded on the internal arrangements of allies. With its sharp rules about budgeting and the spending of aid dollars, the Marshall Plan is a prime example. The Truman Doctrine explicitly promised to offer help in response to *internal* subversion. It was not a narrow-bore realist who defined the national interest as the maintenance of "as spacious an environment as possible in which free states might exist and flourish." He was too "realistic" and hard-nosed for the label "Wilsonian" to fit him, and he expressly rejected it. Parallels with Ronald Reagan are most tempting, for, like Acheson, the president who presided over the beginning of the end of the cold war believed in winning that contest. Both also believed the most important means toward that end was strength. Rather than settle on a label, however, it is probably best to accept Acheson's own description of his intent, to work in league with "like-minded states to secure and enrich the environment and to protect one another from predators through mutual aid and joint effort."[8]

Another of his strengths was his bent for collaboration and his calculus on the junction between power and mutuality. The key to building situations of strength, he believed, lay in the expansion of U.S. and allied military, economic, political, and moral power. Because of its greater strength and large responsibilities, he thought the United States had a perfect right to lead, believing as noted earlier that it was "the locomotive at the head of mankind, and the rest of the world was the caboose."

But it could not act alone, which he regularly reminded those who grumbled about foreign aid disbursements. His emphasis on collaboration was not the product of a sentimental attachment to "multilateralism" but a realization that the moral legitimacy of the world's greatest power was intricately connected to its ability to minister to other nations' needs and to exercise restraint in pursuit of its own interests. In contrast, unilateralism would thwart U.S. objectives and undercut its security by alienating its own allies. It was both "pragmatic" and "realistic" to gain their consent to the protection the United States provided them. That consent was the more willingly given when the United States accepted restraints on its own power. It was "idealistic" to identify America's interests as reaching out to a greater community, by which Acheson never meant the United Nations. As Josef Joffe writes, the "genius of American diplomacy" in the latter part of the twentieth century "was building institutions that would advance American interests by serving others."9

"Designs and Ambitions" in a Changed World

It is misleading to impose the standards of the early twenty-first century on men acting in the middle of the previous century. We must pay attention to the setting in which Truman and Acheson acted and to the foe they faced. Unlike their immediate successors but like officials after the close of the cold war, they performed on an unfamiliar stage depopulated by the demolition of empires and the decline of once great powers. The new setting permitted room only for two remnant superpowers, both unaccustomed to being in the spotlight and to engaging with the other. In 1945, many nations' leaders, whether seeking stability or revolution, groped to discover the nature of this postwar world and how to act in it. No one knew how much nuclear weapons would transform it. Leaders were certain to stumble as they felt their way through a dimly seen new international "system." Truman's first two years of muddle were as much the result of the radically altered landscape he faced than of his inexperience.

Countering the flux of a new international system was the uniformly malignant Soviet state ruled by Josef Stalin. American leaders made most of their hard-line decisions on the assumption that the regime and leader they opposed rivaled the Third Reich and Hitler in contempt for decency. If they exaggerated the Soviet "threat," so did millions of Europeans, and they were correct in thinking the USSR was a malevolent power. Soviet leaders, writes Martin Malia, "were anarchist in order to pulverize the old, capitalist world, and dictatorial in order to build a new, socialist world." Yugoslav dissident communist, Milovan Djilas, wrote that "Stalin was a monster who, while adhering to abstract, absolute, and fundamentally utopian ideas, in practice recognized and could recognize, only success—violence, physical and spiritual extermination." Washington knew Stalin had slain millions through purges and the forcible collectivization of agriculture and had flung other millions into the Gulag. It knew the Soviets had betrayed socialists and republicans alike in the Spanish civil war and exterminated the Polish elite in the Katyn forest. FDR had hoped against hope that Stalin would fulfill promises for free elections in eastern Europe. Truman knew that instead he had locked down the satellite states under regimes constructed in his image.10

Stalin always had security for the Soviet state in his mind, but Marxism-Leninism, supplemented by an aggrieved nationalism, supplied him with strong motives for hostility to states and regimes he did not control. As early as 1931, long before he had the power to commit aggression or "peacefully" wring concessions from neighbors, he complained bitterly about how the old czarist regime had been constantly "beaten" by others, ticking off those who had humiliated the homeland, the "Mongol khans," the "Turkish beys," the "Polish and Lithuanian gentry," the "British and French capitalists," and the "Japanese barons." Only Russia's long-standing weakness caused it to be beaten so easily and often. He would correct that, building the instruments with which his regime could disturb and dominate others. At the least, he wanted security for the Soviet socialist experiment, and he was dissatisfied with anything less than absolute security.[11]

Yet although Stalin was a disturber of the peace, in the wake of World War II he acted with caution after seizing the states needed to form a corridor between the Soviet Union and Germany. He monitored Anglo-American responses to his ventures and often pulled back when pressed hard. American actions in Germany and Japan frustrated but did not portend aggression against him. In fact, he had nothing to fear from western states except their challenge to his hopes for additional expansion.

It was nonetheless quite appropriate for U.S. leaders to consider him a menace, especially after he tried killing the Marshall Plan. They could not know what else he might attempt with the Red Army at his disposal, along with the atomic bomb and subservient communists in western countries. Since historians today are still unsure what he was up to, it is no wonder U.S. leaders then planned for the worst. Although they probably overrated his threat to western Europe, they actually underestimated his danger to his own people, unaware that the Gulag teemed with more victims than ever in the Truman years and that Stalin was at his most psychotic at the very end of his life. When Nikita Khrushchev denounced Stalin in 1956, he thought historians would "break their teeth" flushing out the whole story. Russian historian Vladislav Zubok says that Soviet records reveal a leadership in 1945 "full of jingoist fervor and determination to maximize war gains," adding that American leaders were justified to fear Stalin's "designs and ambitions." Though the USSR itself was hungry and exhausted, Djilas writes, its "armies and marshals, heavy with fat and medals and drunk with vodka and victory, had already trampled half of Europe under foot." Stalin was sure they "would trample over the other half in the next round." In short, writes Tony Judt with little care for historiographical niceties, the "wishful search for evidence that the US bore primary responsibility for the origin and pursuit of the Cold War is now a dead duck." Stalin's Soviet Union was a lethal state, and when Acheson rejected the idea of calculating policy according to Soviet "intentions" rather than "capabilities," he had in mind that Stalin's incalculable intentions might be as dark as Soviet capabilities could make them.[12]

Conundrums

Especially after the Korean War opened the way for the NSC-68 buildup, the strategy of developing strength seemed effective. But a nagging question suggests itself years later. The view of Soviet military power as a live threat supported the strategy, but, given the continuing U.S. preponderance in nuclear weapons, did it make sense to "build strength" indefinitely? Would it have been better to pause once it seemed reasonably safe and make a vigorous effort to end east-west tension? Acheson always tacitly assumed time was on the American side, but it is clear now that the Soviets would certainly try to match the U.S. buildup. Would it have been better, therefore, to negotiate and preempt such a tit-for-tat arms race?

Though the archives do not answer this question definitively, we can imagine how Acheson might have reacted to the idea. Germany would surely be at the heart of any negotiations, and he could argue persuasively against risking any U.S. gains there. Braking the train of mobilization, he would hold, would signal Americans and allies alike to relax the very pressure that impelled Moscow to come to the table. We cannot say for certain whether he was right or wrong, but in his support is the fact that Stalin at this time gave no sign he was willing to negotiate sincerely about anything important. It remains true that Acheson did not quite know what to do with the power he helped amass. He never said whether the United States was preparing for a short- or long-term danger, but by default he appeared to opt for the latter. As Melvyn Leffler has written, the failure of both sides to make a concerted effort to achieve a settlement guaranteed an extended arms race, along with "constant anxiety, eternal vigilance, and a protracted cold war."[13]

These reflections suggest a different question altogether. Were Acheson and the United States not aggressive *enough*? In 1952, just as Stalin's rule neared an end, the U.S. bombing offensive was ripping apart North Korea's factories, roads, and dikes, bleeding Soviet resources and Chinese manpower. With Moscow stymied in Korea and helpless to stop the western alliance from absorbing the Bonn Republic, cold war scholar Vojtech Mastny believes the moment had come to demand the removal of Russian forces from East Germany and the rest of eastern Europe. Whether or not a concerted push to achieve this goal would have been more effective after Stalin died in 1953, this was the "right time to wage the right war (to dispose of the tyrannical system once and for all) in the right place (Europe)." Mastny does not mean a soldier's war, but a political and diplomatic campaign to force the Soviets to submit to western demands "without fighting a battle." The situation required "a vigorous diplomatic offensive from the position of strength that Dulles insisted so much the United States was in, backed by the implied threat of force." In 1952, Acheson, who did much to assemble this strength, rather than avoid negotiations, should have used Stalin's note on Germany to demand reunification through free elections. Stalin would likely have rejected such demands, leaving it to the next U.S. administration to make "comprehensive demands" of Stalin's successors, demands backed by "superior" power the Kremlin "could not ignore." These were the "optimal preconditions" for omnibus negotiations, settling the German issue, ending the Korean War, and even resolving Sino-American disputes. Afterward, Moscow would have found it virtually impossible to hold the lid on the satellites, ending its rule in eastern Europe long before 1989–91.[14]

This fascinating speculation flies in the face of 1952 realities. The United States was also stymied in Korea and quarreling with Britain and France over POWs, Indochina, Germany, Iran, and Egypt. It is difficult to imagine a weary administration in these circumstances risking any such initiative. Mastny's scheme would have scared the allies to death. The great difficulty Washington had holding the allies to its side as they figured out how to *avoid* real negotiations suggests how much more difficult it would have been to unite behind a strategy to *embrace* them. Eisenhower and Dulles were no more ready to take such risks than Truman and Acheson, as witness their passivity in reaction to the uprisings and near uprisings soon to occur in East Germany, Poland, and Hungary.

"You Cannot Avoid Difficulty"

At the heart of Acheson's statesmanship, especially in Europe, was the link between American purpose and strength. The strength resulted from clear strategy, political resolve, healthy economies, and military forces, or as he once put it, "common sense and a little organization and a gun or two around in a critical moment." Acheson personified this strength, inspiring the state department to a brief moment of policy primacy before it fell to the ravages of McCarthyism, Dulles's neglect of professionals, and, before long, the imperialism of NSC advisers. Acheson's power rested on Truman's, drawn directly from the sovereign authority of American voters. A vital reason for Acheson's achievements was his success at helping change Truman from a man at sea in diplomacy to a confident leader who knew his secretary of state to be loyal, able, and valued abroad. Acheson's mastery of his department and manifest ability to speak for Truman translated directly into influence with American allies, making him one of the most trusted U.S. secretaries of state abroad.

Absent in Acheson's approach was the ability to promise either Americans or Europeans when an end would come to the sacrifices he asked them to make. He was not a dealer in hope, or able to see to the far shore. The best he could offer was that at some indeterminate moment in the future, the Soviet Union would recognize realities, ending the cold war. His repeated exhortations for patience suggest he realized that others would find an endless struggle insupportable. As it turned out, of course, the cold war ended much as he said it would, but it remains significant that Acheson did not seem to care how long it lasted. To the end of his days, he was writing "build strength" on his prescription pad.

Building situations of strength was fatiguing, but except for a few years in the Nixon-Ford-Carter era when Washington sought détente with Moscow, most of Truman and Acheson's successors followed the main lines of their strategy. The worst failures lying ahead involved lapses in relating power to purpose, as in the

Vietnam War, which most Americans finally considered impractical, immoral, or both, and thus corrupt in purpose.

The sharp polarization of the world between communist and "free" accounted for much of the durability of Acheson's strategy, but when the communist world broke down, so did the coherence of American foreign policy. This calls to mind the resemblance between the years immediately after the end of the cold war and after World War II. In 1945, Americans encountered a fundamentally changed world order, just as they did after the collapse of the Soviet Union. In 1945—and in 1989–91—U.S. officials were unsure if their country would now face dangerous new enemies. As Acheson wrote, the future seemed "clouded" and the "significance of events . . . shrouded in ambiguity." The Truman-Acheson generation soon enough identified their foes as the Soviet Union and People's Republic of China in particular and "communism" in general. Their successors a half century later began to think the "enemy" might be radical Islam. Otherwise, the times had changed greatly. Makers of foreign policy in the 1990s and 2000s faced issues barely known in Acheson's times, from nuclear proliferation and ecological decay to drug running and terrorism.[15]

However novel today's difficulties, vital truths from the past are still germane. It is still true that liberty and opportunity thrive in the United States when its power helps enlarge the freedom and opportunities of others. Truman and Acheson intuitively knew democracies do not make war on one another and believed their own country could protect weaker nations as they fostered the economies, civil societies, and cooperative values that made democracy possible. (For *pragmatic* and *realistic* reasons, they also supported regimes with no intentions of practicing democracy.) They knew the United States would profit from joining rather than bullying others. The ability to lead, Acheson wrote, is preceded by gaining the trust of those led. As he explained in a 1951 speech, allies will offer that trust when they think Americans will "embrace" the allies' interests even as they pursue their own. If the United States took "the attitude that we will coerce nations, we are so right that if they do not do exactly what we want them to do we will withhold economic aid, we will withhold military aid, we will do this, we will do that. If we take that attitude, then we are indistinguishable from the relationship which exists between the Soviet Union and countries which are associated with it." Americans should act in confidence that they "are the leader." But for others to accept this leadership, they must believe "that the pattern of responsibility within which we operate is a responsibility of interests which are broader than our own and that we look to the sort of thing that Thomas Jefferson was talking about when he spoke of the need of paying a decent respect to the opinions of mankind."[16]

Using the elements of a nation's power to attain its purposes abroad requires art, skill, and wisdom. Truman and Acheson understood it also required courage. They wasted little time pondering "exit strategies." They served with no guarantees and without offering them to the people. They knew the more daunting the difficulties, the more important it was they do their best. It is "utterly confusing," Acheson declared, to think problems can be solved easily. "You cannot avoid difficulty," he told the War College in 1948. "Therefore, what you must do is to make the best decision you can to meet that situation and not slink from it." Those "charged with the formulation and execution of policy have got to be sure they don't slink from problems, they must do the very best they can in meeting them and get on."[17]

A NOTE TO THE READER

Second and later citations of published sources refer only to their authors except in cases when they are associated with more than one cited work, in which case abbreviated versions of titles will be used (for example, Chace, 25, 34; David Acheson, 33–34, 49, 75). Instead of placing a note after every statement of fact or interpretation, or every quotation, I have normally put a single note at the end of a paragraph, sometimes after two or even three related paragraphs. The order of citations within a note corresponds generally to the structure of the paragraph itself. Thus, the first source listed will refer to the beginning of the paragraph, the last to the end. But I have always placed page numbers of a single printed source from lowest to highest and multiple citations to newspapers in chronological order; these sometimes do not correspond to the order of data in the paragraph.

I use the following abbreviations in the notes:

1941–1947 microfilm—Papers of Dean Acheson: Files as Assistant Secretary of State, 1941–1945 and as Under Secretary of State, 1945–1947, Harry S. Truman Library, Independence, Missouri, March 1978, microfilm

1955 Acheson Oral History, A.M. or P.M.—Acheson Oral History, 17 February 1955, A.M., Truman Papers, Truman Library

Acheson Oral History 1971, TL—Dean Acheson, Oral History Interview, 30 June 1971 (Independence, MO: The Harry S. Truman Library, May 1986)

Acheson Oral History, JFKL—Dean Acheson, recorded interview by Lucius D. Battle, 27 April 1964, John F. Kennedy Library Oral History Program

Among Friends—David S. McLellan and David C. Acheson, eds., *Among Friends: Personal Letters of Dean Acheson* (New York: Dodd, Mead, 1980)

Assignment of Ground Forces—*Assignment of Ground Forces of the United States to Duty in the European Area: Hearings before the Committee on Foreign Relations and the Committee on Armed Services, United States Senate, Eighty-Second Congress, First Session, on S. Con. Res. 8: A Concurrent Resolution Relative to the Assignment of Ground Forces of the United*

> *States to Duty in the European Area, February 1, 15, 16, 19, 20, 21, 22, 23, 24, 26, 27, and 28, 1951* (Washington: Government Printing Office, 1951)

China White Paper—United States Relations with China: With Special Reference to the Period 1944–1949, Based on the Files of the Department of State (Washington: Government Printing Office, 1949)

CWIHPB—Cold War International History Project Bulletin

Daily Meetings—Minutes of Secretary's Daily Meetings, 1949–1952, 29 June 1949, Office of Executive Secretariat, Box 1, RG59, U.S. National Archives

"Dean Acheson, a Remembrance"—"Dean Acheson, a Remembrance," Cosmos Club, Washington, DC, 6 April 1989, 34, James Reston Papers, Box 12, Subject Files, University of Illinois Archives

Documents on British Policy—Roger Bullen and M. E. Pelly, eds., *Documents on British Policy Overseas*, Series I, Volume 3 (London: Her Majesty's Stationery Office, 1986)

Executive Sessions of the Senate Foreign Relations Committee . . . 1947–1948—Executive Sessions of the Senate Foreign Relations Committee (Historical Series). Volume I: Eightieth Congress, First and Second Sessions, 1947–1948 (Washington: U.S. Government Printing Office, 1976)

Executive Sessions of the Senate Foreign Relations Committee . . . 1949–1950 —Executive Sessions of the Senate Foreign Relations Committee (Historical Series). Volume II: Eighty-First Congress, First and Second Sessions, 1949–1950 (Washington: U.S. Government Printing Office, 1976)

Executive Sessions of the Senate Foreign Relations Committee . . . 1951—U.S. Congress, Senate, Committee on Foreign Relations, *Executive Sessions of the Senate Foreign Relations Committee (Historical Series). Volume III. Part 1: Eighty-Second Congress, First Session, 1951* (Washington: Government Printing Office, 1976)

Executive Sessions of the Senate Foreign Relations Committee . . . 1952—Executive Sessions of the Senate Foreign Relations Committee (Historical Series). Volume IV: Eighty-Second Congress, Second Session, 1952 (Washington: Government Printing Office, 1976)

For the Press, January 12, 1950—For the Press, January 12, 1950, No. 34, James Webb Papers, Box 20, Dept. of State . . . Acheson, Dean Folder, Truman Library

FRUS—U.S., Department of State, *Foreign Relations of the United States*

Guatemala, 1952–1954—www.state.gov/r/pa/ho/frus/ike/guat/

Hamburger, "Mr. Secretary—I"—Philip Hamburger, "Profiles: Mr. Secretary—I," *New Yorker*, 12 November 1949

Hamburger, "Mr. Secretary—II"—Philip Hamburger, "Profiles: Mr. Secretary—II," *New Yorker*, 19 November 1949

The International Scene—The International Scene [a War College Speech] by The Honorable Dean G. Acheson, 27 August 1951, 25, Acheson Papers, Box 69, Press Conf. 1949–1953, Classified Off the Record Speeches Folder, Truman Library

JL—Lyndon Baines Johnson Library

Jones, "Secretary's Harvard Speech"—Memorandum for the Files RE: The Secretary's Harvard Speech of June 5, 1947, Joseph Jones Papers, Box 2, Truman Library

Memoranda of Conversations [with the document's date, sometimes but not always with a topic title]—John P. Glennon, Evans Gerakas, and William F. Sanford, Jr., eds., *Foreign Relations of the United States: Memoranda of Conversations of the Secretary of State, 1947–1952, Microfiche Publication* (Washington: Department of State, 1988)

Memoranda of the Secretary of State [and, when available the document's date, topic title, and fiche number on which the document is located]—John P. Glennon, Editor in Chief, and Evans Gerakas, Editor, *Foreign Relations of the United States: Memoranda of the Secretary of State, 1949–1951, and Meetings and Visits of Foreign Dignitaries, 1949–1952, Microfiche Publication* (Washington: Department of State, 1988)

Meeting, Lindsay Hoban, 5–12–52—Meeting, Lindsay Hoban, 5–12–52, Acheson Papers, Box 69, Press Conf. 1949–1953, Jan. 1952–Jan. 1953 Folder, Truman Library

Military Assistance Program—U.S. Congress, Senate Committee on Foreign Relations, *Military Assistance Program, 1949; Held in Executive Session before the Committee on Foreign Relations and the Committee on Armed Services, United States Senate, Eighty-first Congress, First Session on S.2388*, introduction, Richard D. Challener (Washington: Government Printing Office, 1974)

Military Situation in the Far East—U.S. Congress, Senate Committee on Foreign Relations, *Military Situation in the Far East: Hearings before the Committee on Armed Services and the Committee on Foreign Relations, United States Senate, Eighty-Second Congress, First Session, to Conduct an Inquiry into the Military Situation in the Far East and the Facts Surrounding the Relief of General of the Army Douglas MacArthur from His Assignments in That Area* (Washington: Government Printing Office, 1951)

Nelson, *PPS Papers*—*The State Department Policy Planning Staff Papers, 1947–1949*, introduction, Anna Kasten Nelson, foreword, George F. Kennan, 3 vols. (New York: Garland Publishing, Inc., 1983)

Nomination of Dean G. Acheson—*Nomination of Dean G. Acheson: Hearing before the Committee on Foreign Relations, United States Senate, Eighty-First Congress, First Session . . . January 13, 1949*, George M. Elsey Papers, Box 61, Truman Library

Off the Record Press Conference, August 26, 1949—Secretary's Off the Record Press Conference, August 26, 1949, Acheson Papers, Box 68, Press Conf. 1949–53, July–Dec. 1949 Folder, Truman Library, 5–7

PAC—Dean Acheson, *Present at the Creation* (New York: W. W. Norton, 1969)

Pattern of Responsibility—McGeorge Bundy, ed., *The Pattern of Responsibility*, intro. Douglas Southall Freeman (Boston: Houghton Mifflin, 1952)

Princeton Seminars—Princeton Seminars, Princeton University Library, various dates, Microfilm

Project 1517—Office of the Historian, "Historical Research Project No. 1517: History of the National Security Council" (unpublished; Washington: United States Department of State, Bureau of Public Affairs, June 1987)

PSF—Truman Papers, President's Secretary's Files, Truman Library

Remarks at the National War College, 21 December 1949—National War College Lecture, Washington, D.C., 21 December 1949, Remarks at the National War College by the Honorable Dean Acheson, James Webb Papers, Box 20, Truman Library

Review of the World Situation, CIA, 17 May 1950—Review of the World Situation, CIA 5–50, 17 May 1950, Truman Papers (PSF), Box 208, N.S.C. Meeting No. 57 Folder, Truman Library

Reviews of the World Situation—*Reviews of the World Situation, 1949–1950*, Volume 8 of *The Legislative Origins of American Foreign Policy: The Senate Foreign Relations Committee in Executive Session, 1913–1933; 1947–1950*, ed. Richard D. Challener (New York: Garland, 1979)

Round Table—"Record of Round-Table Discussion by Twenty-Five Far East Experts with the Department of State on 'American Policy Toward China,' October 6, 7, and 8, 1949," Truman Papers (PSF), Box 174, 3, China—Record of Roundtable Folder, Truman Library

Selected Executive Session Hearings of the Committee, 1943–1950—U.S. Congress, House Committee on International Relations, *Selected Executive Session Hearings of the Committee, 1943–1950: Historical Series. Volume IV: Foreign Economic Assistance Programs, Part 2* (Washington: Government Printing Office, 1976)

Selected Executive Session Hearings of the Committee, 1951–1956—U.S., Congress, House Committee on Foreign Affairs, *Selected Executive Session Hearings of the Committee,*

1951–1956. Historical Series. Vol. 15, European Problems (Washington: Government Printing Office, 1980)

Service, "State Department Duty"—"John S. Service, State Department Duty in China, the McCarthy Era, and After, 1933–1977: An Interview Conducted by Rosemary Levenson, 1977–1978, with an introduction by John K. Fairbank" (Berkeley: University of California Regional Oral History Office, China Series: John S. and Caroline Service Oral History Project, 1981)

SMOF—Truman Papers, Staff Member office file, Truman Library

Snyder Oral History 1967–69, TL—John W. Snyder Oral History Interview, 8 November 1967–3 September 1969 (Independence, MO: The Harry S. Truman Library, September 1970)

Snyder Oral History 1976, TL—John W. Snyder, Oral History Interview, 18 March 1976 (Independence, MO: The Harry S. Truman Library, December 1985)

Snyder Oral History 1980, TL—John W. Snyder, Oral History Interview, 15 March 1980 (Independence, MO.: The Harry S. Truman Library, November 1982)

Sudoplatov—Pavel Sudoplatov and Anatoli Sudoplatov, with Jerrold and Leona P. Schecter, *Special Tasks: The Memoirs of an Unwanted Witness—A Soviet Spymaster* (Boston: Little, Brown, 1994)

TL—Truman Library

UIA—University of Illinois Archives

United States Foreign Policy for a Post-War Recovery Program—U.S. Congress, House Committee on Foreign Affairs, *Hearings. United States Foreign Policy for a Post-War Recovery Program, 80th Congress, 1st and 2nd Session* (Washington: Government Printing Office, 1948)

War College Speech—War College Speech, 16 September 1948, Acheson Papers, Box 69, Press Conf. 1949–1953, Classified Off the Record Speeches Folder, Truman Library

YUL—Yale University Library

NOTES

Chapter 1

1 See, for example, the excerpt from Arthur M. Schlesinger, Jr., "Rating the Presidents: Washington to Clinton," *Political Science Quarterly* 11 (Summer 1997): 179–90, at www.pbs.org/wgbh/pages/frontline/shows/choice2004/leadership/schlesinger.html (viewed 4/26/05). Throughout this book, I repeatedly refer to "American" foreign policy, and to officials and other citizens of the United States as "Americans," aware that other hemispheric peoples view themselves as "Americans" as well. The cumbersomeness of alternative phrasing explains why "Americans" rarely describe themselves as "citizens of the United States."

2 Borrowing from William James's remark about George Santayana. Walter Isaacson and Evan Thomas, *The Wise Men: Six Friends and the World They Made: Acheson, Bohlen, Harriman, Kennan, Lovett, McCloy* (New York: Simon & Schuster, 1986), 131.

3 James Chace, *Acheson: The Secretary of State Who Created the American World* (New York: Simon & Schuster, 1998); Douglas Brinkley, *Dean Acheson: The Cold War Years, 1953–71* (New Haven: Yale University Press, 1992).

4 (New York: W. W. Norton, 1969). Hereafter cited as *PAC*.

5 Chace cited above; Gaddis Smith, *Dean Acheson* (New York: Cooper Square, 1972), vol. 16 of *American Secretaries of State and Their Diplomacy*, ed., Robert H. Ferrell and Samuel Flagg Bemis; David S. McLellan, *Dean Acheson: The State Department Years* (New York: Dodd, Mead, 1976). Speaking of interpretive disagreements, while I have tried making the case for my own interpretations in this book and have cited important secondary sources with which I might not agree, with a few exceptions, I devote little space to historiographical disputes on the assumption they would weary most readers.

Chapter 2

1 Gooderham is pronounced GOOD-rum. Neither parent became a U.S. citizen. As Acheson wrote in *Morning and Noon* (Boston: Houghton Mifflin, 1965), 8, referring to a time

before the birth of his younger brother, "my sister and I were by constitutional right citizens of the United States," while his parents were "subjects of the Queen-Empress, Victoria, Defender of the Faith." Later, Acheson described his national lineage as a "mundane inheritance from the Scots Lowlands, by way of Ulster, and the South of England." *New York Times*, 18 January 1958. His father, born in 1857, died in 1934; his mother died at eighty-seven in Washington in 1958. Younger brother Edward (Ted) Acheson, once a journalist, writer of detective stories, and wartime member of the Office of Strategic Services (OSS), took a doctorate at the London School of Economics before a long career as a popular economics professor at George Washington University. He died in 1966. The "flamboyant, glamorous, beautiful" redheaded Margot (born "Margaret") died in 1959. *New York Times*, 30 September 1966; David C. Acheson, *Acheson Country: A Memoir* (New York: W. W. Norton, 1993), 30, 51, 99–100. John T. McNay, *Acheson and Empire: The British Accent in American Foreign Policy* (Columbia: University of Missouri Press, 2001), makes too much of the Ulster background. See review by John L. Harper, *Journal of American History* 89 (September 2002): 709.

2 Isaacson and Thomas, 52–53; Chace, 25, 34; *New York Times*, 26 July 1958 and 18 April 1950; David Acheson, 33–34, 49, 75.

3 Acheson to Marshall Shulman, 14 October 1954, Acheson Papers, Box 28, Folder 366, Yale University Library (hereafter YUL); Isaacson and Thomas, 55; David Acheson, 40–41, 64, 218; David Fromkin, *In the Time of the Americans: FDR, Truman, Eisenhower, Marshall, MacArthur—The Generation That Changed America's Role in the World* (New York: Alfred A. Knopf, 1995), 35; Evan Thomas, *The Very Best Men: Four Who Dared: The Early Years of the CIA* (New York: Simon & Schuster, 1995), 90; Chace, 28; Acheson to Alexander Zabriskie, 5 April 1949, Acheson Papers, Box 43, Secretary of State, 1949–53, Alph.–Z Folder, Truman Library (hereafter TL), Independence, Missouri; McLellan, *State Department Years*, 4, 8–9.

4 Acheson, *Morning and Noon*, 37.

5 Philip Hamburger, "Profiles: Mr. Secretary—II," *New Yorker*, 19 November 1949, 40–41 (which followed "Profiles: Mr. Secretary—I," printed 12 November 1949) (hereafter referred to as Hamburger, "Mr. Secretary—I" and "Mr. Secretary—II"); David Acheson, 168; Noël Annan, "Dean of the Cold War," *New York Review of Books*, 19 November 1998, 17; Isaacson and Thomas, 85–86; Gaddis Smith, *Dean Acheson*, 5; McLellan, *State Department Years*, 10.

6 Chace, 35–37; Isaacson and Thomas, 87.

7 Dean Acheson, *Grapes from Thorns* (New York: W. W. Norton, 1972), 39; Chace, 39; Smith, *Dean Acheson*, 7; McLellan, *State Department Years*, 13, 20; Acheson, *Morning and Noon*, 123; Douglas Brinkley, "Dean Acheson and Jean Monnet: On the Path of Atlantic Partnership," in Clifford P. Hackett, ed., *Monnet and the Americans: The Father of a United Europe and His U.S. Supporters* (Washington: Jean Monnet Council, 1995), 74; Hamburger, "Mr. Secretary—II," 44. Alice Acheson's paintings hang in Washington's Phillips Collection and the National Museum of Women in the Arts. She died in 1996 at age 100. *New York Times*, 22 January 1996. Jane Acheson married Dudley Brown, a Milwaukee utilities executive; Mary, William Bundy, associated with Acheson's law firm before becoming an important policymaker in his own right. After stints at Groton, Yale, wartime naval service, and Harvard Law School, David Campion Acheson became a corporate lawyer and public servant. He married author and prep school history teacher Patricia Castles. President Bill Clinton named their daughter Eleanor Dean Acheson assistant attorney general in 1993.

8 David Acheson, 21, 44, 59; personal communication from Elisabeth Griffith.

9 Dean Acheson, *A Democrat Looks at His Party* (New York: Harper & Brothers, 1955), 47; idem, *Morning and Noon*, 43, 47, 54, 124, 162; McLellan, *State Department Years*, 23; David Acheson, 40; Howard C. Westwood, *Covington & Burling, 1919–1984* ([Washington]: Privately Printed, 1986), 55; Brinkley, "Acheson and Monnet," 74. As a nonvoting nineteen-year-old,

his enthusiasm for Theodore Roosevelt's Bull Moose Progressive candidacy had led to the break with his Republican father.

10 James P. Warburg, *The Long Road Home: The Autobiography of a Maverick* (Garden City, NY: Doubleday, 1964), 120, 150, 163, 190; Acheson, *Morning and Noon*, 160, 160–65; Drew Pearson Papers, American University, column of 22 September 1933; Richard A. Loss, "Secretary of State Dean Acheson as Political Executive: Administrator of Personnel Security," *Public Administration Review* 34 (July 1974): 352; Arthur M. Schlesinger, *The Age of Roosevelt: The Crisis of the Old Order, 1919–1933* (Boston: Houghton Mifflin, 1957), 240–42; McLellan, *State Department Years*, 24–27; Herbert Feis, *1933: Characters in Crisis* (Boston: Little, Brown, 1966), 285–88; Isaacson and Thomas, 135; Princeton Seminars, Princeton University Library, 2 July 1953, Microfilm (cited hereafter as Princeton Seminars, with date of particular seminar session, e.g., Princeton Seminars, 2 July 1953); Hamburger, "Mr. Secretary—II," 46.

11 Princeton Seminars, 2 July 1953; Acheson to Truman, 5 February 1954, Acheson Papers, Box 30, Folder 392, YUL.

12 McLellan, *State Department Years*, 29, 31–32; Chace, 34, 68; Princeton Seminars, 2 July and 10 October 1953; David Acheson, 207; Isaacson and Thomas, 135, 137–38; George W. Ball, *The Past Has Another Pattern: Memoirs* (New York: W. W. Norton, 1982), 19; Acheson, *Morning and Noon*, 212–14.

13 David Acheson, 92; Chace, 56; Brinkley, "Acheson and Monnet," 74.

14 Much of the text of the Yale speech is in *Nomination of Dean G. Acheson: Hearing before the Committee on Foreign Relations, United States Senate, Eighty-First Congress, First Session . . . January 13, 1949*, 19–21, George M. Elsey Papers, Box 61, TL (hereafter referred to as *Nomination of Dean G. Acheson*); and see McLellan, *State Department Years*, 38.

15 Princeton Seminars, 2 July 1953; McLellan, *State Department Years*, 43. Whether intended or not, the sexual slur is obvious.

16 I am following usage of official state department personnel guides in using the term "under secretary" rather than "undersecretary." See *Principal Officers of the Department of State and United States Chiefs of Mission, 1778–1790* (Washington: Department of State Publication 9825, Office of the Historian, Bureau of Public Affairs, January 1991). All information about department job titles and terms of office come from this invaluable volume.

17 *PAC*, 22–23; John Morton Blum, *From the Morgenthau Diaries: Years of Urgency, 1938–1941* (Boston: Houghton Mifflin, 1965), 214, 336; Fred L. Israel, ed., *The War Diary of Breckinridge Long: Selections from the Years 1939–1944* (Lincoln: University of Nebraska Press, 1966), 196 (emphasis in original); Jonathan G. Utley, "Upstairs, Downstairs at Foggy Bottom: Oil Exports and Japan, 1940–41," *Prologue* 8 (Spring 1976): 24, 26–28; Irvine H. Anderson, Jr., "The 1941 *De Facto* Embargo on Oil to Japan: A Bureaucratic Reflex," *Pacific Historical Review* 44 (May 1975): 217–23; *PAC*, 26; Waldo Heinrichs, *Threshold of War: Franklin D. Roosevelt and American Entry into World War II* (New York: Oxford University Press, 1988), 177, 246–47n.

18 *PAC*, 3, 15–16; SR71-125, Dean Acheson Interviewed by Eric Sevareid, 8 November 1969, Recording, Part II, TL; Dean Acheson, *This Vast External Realm* (New York: W. W. Norton, 1973), 288–89; Acheson to Felix Frankfurter, 19 December 1958, Acheson Papers, Box 11, Folder 147, YUL; Merle Miller, *Plain Speaking: An Oral Biography of Harry S. Truman* (New York: Berkley, 1973), 377; Acheson, *Morning and Noon*, 165; Robert Bendiner, *The Riddle of the State Department* (New York: Farrar & Rinehart, 1942), ix, 109; Oliver Franks in "Dean Acheson, A Remembrance," Cosmos Club, Washington, DC, 6 April 1989, 34, James Reston Papers, Box 12, Subject Files, University of Illinois Archives (hereafter UIA) (hereafter "Dean Acheson, A Remembrance"), 19.

19 *PAC*, 9, 12, 14–15, 18, 38; Dean Acheson, *Fragments of My Fleece* (New York: W. W. Norton, 1971), 129–30; Acheson to Hans J. Morgenthau, 3 January 1957, Acheson Papers, Box 23, Folder 289, YUL; Acheson, *Vast External Realm*, 281–82; Jordan A. Schwarz,

Liberal: Adolf A. Berle and the Vision of an American Era (New York: Free Press, 1987), 17, 134, 144; James Reston, *Deadline: A Memoir* (New York: Random House, 1991), 101, 466; John Lamberton Harper, *American Visions of Europe: Franklin D. Roosevelt, George F. Kennan, and Dean G. Acheson* (New York: Cambridge University Press, 1994), 260; Steven Schwartzberg, *Democracy and U.S. Policy in Latin America during the Truman Years* (Gainesville: University Press of Florida, 2003), 232n . For the "Welles Affair," see Irwin F. Gellman, *Secret Affairs: Franklin D. Roosevelt, Cordell Hull, and Sumner Welles* (Baltimore: Johns Hopkins University Press, 1995). In the 1960s, Acheson learned why FDR returned him to government when reading the 3 January 1941 diary entry of another assistant secretary, Breckinridge Long: "The Secretary sent for me and handed me a little pencilled memorandum written on a White House memorandum pad and signed 'F.D.R.' It read that . . . he wanted Dean Acheson to fill the vacancy [Henry F.] Grady left." Israel, 169.

20 *PAC*, 14, 22, 28–29, 38, 111, 133–34; Blum, *Morgenthau Diaries . . . 1938–1941*, 133, 136; Randall Bennett Woods, *A Changing of the Guard: Anglo-American Relations, 1941–1946* (Chapel Hill: University of North Carolina Press, 1990), 130; Acheson to Hull and Stettinius, 28 January 1944, Acheson Papers, Box 27, TL; document, author unidentified, 8 December 1945, and copy of 20 May 1944 Drew Pearson article in the *Philadelphia Record*, Papers of Dean Acheson: Files as Assistant Secretary of State, 1941–1945 and as Under Secretary of State, 1945–1947, Harry S. Truman Library, Independence, Missouri, March 1978, microfilm, made available to me by Walter LaFeber (cited hereafter as 1941–1947 microfilm); *New York Times*, 11 December 1945; Bruce Robellet Kuniholm, *The Origins of the Cold War in the Near East: Great Power Conflict and Diplomacy in Iran, Turkey, and Greece* (Princeton: Princeton University Press, 1980), 168–71; Acheson, *Grapes from Thorns*, 20.

21 *PAC*, 64, 88; Richardson Dougall, "The U.S. Department of State: From Hull to Acheson," in Gordon A. Craig and Francis L. Loewenheim, eds., *The Diplomats, 1939–1979* (Princeton: Princeton University Press, 1994), 45; [Harley Notter], *Postwar Foreign Policy Preparation, 1939–1945* (Washington: Department of State, 1950), 135–36, 140, 209–10.

22 *PAC*, 17, 50–57, 59; Acheson, *Vast External Realm*, 175–76; Gregory A. Fossedal, *Our Finest Hour: Will Clayton, the Marshall Plan, and the Triumph of Democracy* (Stanford: Hoover Institution Press, 1993), 79; James W. Cortada, *United States-Spanish Relations, Wolfram and World War II* (Barcelona: Manuel Pareja, 1971), 93–94; *U.S. and Allied Efforts to Recover and Restore Gold and Other Assets Stolen or Hidden by Germany during World War II: Preliminary Study*, Coordinated by Stuart E. Eizenstat, Under Secretary of Commerce for International Trade, Special Envoy of the Department of State on Property Restitution in Central and Eastern Europe, Prepared by William Z. Slany, The Historian, Department of State (Washington, May 1997), vi–ix, 187–88.

23 Acheson, *Grapes from Thorns*, 20.

24 *PAC*, 28, 30–34; George C. Herring, Jr., *Aid to Russia, 1941–1946: Strategy, Diplomacy, The Origins of the Cold War* (New York: Columbia University Press, 1973), 157–59; Leon Martel, *Lend-Lease, Loans, and the Coming of the Cold War: A Study of the Implementation of Foreign Policy* (Boulder: Westview Press, 1979), 76–78; Hugh De Santis, *The Diplomacy of Silence: The American Foreign Service, the Soviet Union, and the Cold War, 1933–1947* (Chicago: University of Chicago Press, 1980), 128; McNay, 43–44; U.S., Department of State, *Foreign Relations of the United States 1941*, vol. 3, pp. 12, 43–45, 104 (henceforth, *FRUS*, with volume and page numbers indicated [thus: *FRUS 1941* 3: 12, 43–45, 104]); *FRUS 1942* 1: 533–34; Michael F. Hopkins, *Oliver Franks and the Truman Administration: Anglo-American Relations, 1948–1952* (Portland, OR: Frank Cass, 2003), 17; Woods, 99; John Morton Blum, *From the Morgenthau Diaries: Years of War, 1941–1945* (Boston: Houghton Mifflin, 1967), 125–26; idem, *Morgenthau Diaries . . . 1938–1941*, 243–44; Robert Skidelsky, *John Maynard Keynes. Volume Three. Fighting for Freedom, 1937–1946* (New York: Viking, 2001), 126–31.

25 *PAC*, 88; Acheson to Mary Acheson Bundy, 23 May 1945, in David S. McLellan and David C. Acheson, eds., *Among Friends: Personal Letters of Dean Acheson* (New York: Dodd, Mead, 1980), 55 (hereafter cited as *Among Friends*); Richard L. Walker, "E. R. Stettinius, Jr.," in vol. 14 of *American Secretaries of State and Their Diplomacy*, ed., Robert H. Ferrell and Samuel Flagg Bemis (New York: Cooper Square, 1965), 21; William D. Hassett, *Off the Record with F.D.R. 1942–1945*, intro., Jonathan Daniels (New Brunswick: Rutgers University Press, 1958), 304; John Lewis Gaddis, *The United States and the Origins of the Cold War, 1941–1947* (New York: Columbia University Press, 1972), 155.

26 Dougall, 46–47; Acheson to Roy Welensky, 28 August 1969, Acheson Papers, Box 33, Folder 430, YUL; David Acheson, 71; *PAC*, 89–91; *Washington Post*, 22 December 1944; http://lcweb2.loc.gov/pp/ mdbquery.html (search: "Dean Acheson") (viewed 4/29/05); *Executive Sessions of the Senate Foreign Relations Committee (Historical Series). Volume II: Eighty-First Congress, First and Second Sessions, 1949–1950* (Washington: U.S. Government Printing Office, 1976) 2: 105 (henceforth *Executive Sessions of the Senate Foreign Relations Committee . . . 1949–1950*).

27 Chace, 106; *PAC*, 107–9; Acheson Letters to Mary Bundy, 9 May and 13 June 1945, Acheson Papers, Box 4, Folder 52, pp. 2, 22, YUL. Rabble rousing she might have been, but as Acheson had divined, Jesse Sumner was a witty and accomplished woman, educated at the University of Chicago, Oxford, and Columbia. When told that UNRRA, which she opposed, was "humanitarian," she responded: "So is keeping a gigolo." *New York Times*, 15 August 1994.

28 Under convertibility, a British businessman could exchange pounds sterling for dollars for purchases in the United States, whose merchants would therefore receive payment in dollars. Holders of sterling in the British Commonwealth could make similar exchanges to buy American goods.

29 *PAC*, 68, 81–84; Blum, *Morgenthau Diaries . . . 1941–1945*, 248, 260–62, 274–75; Leroy Stinebower, Oral History Interview, 9 June 1974 (Independence, MO: The Harry S. Truman Library, July 1979), 7–8, 14; Armand van Dormael, *Bretton Woods: Birth of a Monetary System* (New York: Holmes and Meier, 1978), 199–200, 203; Alfred E. Eckes, Jr., *A Search for Solvency: Bretton Woods and the International Monetary System, 1941–1971* (Austin: University of Texas Press, 1975), 157, 161; Robert A. Pollard, "Economic Security and the Origins of the Cold War: Bretton Woods, the Marshall Plan, and American Rearmament, 1944–50," *Diplomatic History* 9 (Summer 1985): 274–76; U.S. Congress, House of Representatives (78th Congress, 2d session), *Hearings Before the Special Committee on Post-war Economic Policy and Planning of the House of Representatives* (Washington: Government Printing Office, 1945), 1071–98.

30 John S. Hill, "American Efforts to Aid French Reconstruction between Lend-Lease and the Marshall Plan," *Journal of Modern History* 64 (September 1992): 502; *New York Times*, 25 February 1945; U.S., House, Committee on Banking and Currency, *Bretton Woods Agreements Act*, 79th Cong., 1st Sess., 1945, 35; *PAC*, xvii, 122.

31 Clifford C. Matlock, Oral History Interview, 29 October 1973 and 6 June 1974 (Independence, MO: The Harry S. Truman Library, February 1976), 9. Similar negotiations with France resulted in an Export-Import Bank credit of $650 million in May 1946, also in exchange for promises about liberalizing its economy.

32 Roger Bullen and M. E. Pelly, eds., *Documents on British Policy Overseas*, Series I, Volume 3 (London: Her Majesty's Stationery Office, 1986), 388 (hereafter *Documents on British Policy*, with series and volume number [e.g., I–3]); Lord Oliver Franks, Oral History Interview, 27 June 1964 (Independence, MO: The Harry S. Truman Library, 1971), 8; Summary of Mr. Acheson's Remarks to the American Platform Guild Conference, State Department, January 3, 1946, and Jerome Davis to Acheson, 5 January 1946, 1941–1947 microfilm; Melvyn P. Leffler, *A Preponderance of Power: National Security, the Truman Administration, and the*

Cold War (Stanford: Stanford University Press, 1992), 101; *New York Times,* 19 March and 9 December 1946; Melvyn P. Leffler, "Negotiating from Strength: Acheson, the Russians, and American Power," in Douglas Brinkley, ed., *Dean Acheson and the Making of U.S. Foreign Policy* (New York: St. Martin's Press, 1993), 182; McLellan, *State Department Years,* 94–95; Martin Weil, *A Pretty Good Club: The Founding Fathers of the U.S. Foreign Service* (New York: W. W. Norton, 1978), 256.

33 Robert L. Messer, *The End of an Alliance: James F. Byrnes, Roosevelt, Truman, and the Origins of the Cold War* (Chapel Hill: University of North Carolina Press, 1982), 76 and passim; Geoffrey Roberts, "Sexing up the Cold War: New Evidence on the Molotov–Truman Talks of April 1945," *Cold War History* 4 (April 2004): 105–25. Thanks to Melvyn Leffler for drawing my attention to the Roberts article.

34 Acheson to David C. Acheson, 30 April 1945, Acheson Papers, Box 1, Folder 4, YUL; *Among Friends,* 55.

35 *PAC,* 112–13. Even later, Acheson partly recanted his recantation. *Among Friends,* 330. Thanks to Marc Gallicchio for drawing my attention to this.

36 *Among Friends,* 55; Acheson to David C. Acheson, 30 April, 1945, Acheson Papers, Box 1, Folder 4, YUL; Acheson memorandum, 6 May 1957, Acheson Papers, Box 11, Folder 147, YUL; Acheson to Mary Bundy, 1 July and 20 July 1945, Acheson Papers, Box 4, Folder 52, YUL; *PAC,* 106, 110–11, 113–15, 119–20; *New York Times,* 19 August 1945. Evidence is mixed on whether, in 1945, Acheson still wanted the solicitor's job. The 2005 equivalent of $9,000 was $97,650. http://woodrow.mpls.frb.fed.us/research/data/us/calc/. (Viewed 4/28/05).

37 Alonzo L. Hamby, *Beyond the New Deal: Harry S. Truman and American Liberalism* (New York: Columbia University Press, 1973), 89; *New York Times,* 17 and 19 August and 20, 21, 23, and 25 September 1945; *PAC,* 120–21, 126–27; Howard B. Schonberger, *Aftermath of War: Americans and the Remaking of Japan, 1945–1952* (Kent: Kent State University Press, 1989), 49. MacArthur nonetheless gave Acheson a souvenir Japanese sabre in March 1946; Acheson Papers, Box 21, Folder 259, YUL.

38 Princeton Seminars, 2 July 1953; Schonberger, *Aftermath of War,* 36; Weil, 238; Messer, *End of an Alliance,* 179; *PAC,* 123; Leffler, *Preponderance of Power,* 41–44, 104–5.

39 Francis Russell, Oral History Interview, 13 July 1973 (Independence, MO: The Harry S. Truman Library, August 1976), 15–16; *PAC,* 135–36, 163, 746; *FRUS 1945* 2: 609–10; McLellan, *State Department Years,* 75–77.

40 R. Gordon Arneson, Oral History Interview, 21 June 1989 (Independence, MO: The Harry S. Truman Library, October 1990), 27–29; Richard Rhodes, *Dark Sun: The Making of the Hydrogen Bomb* (New York: Simon & Schuster, 1995), 300. For a detailed account, see Septimus H. Paul, *Nuclear Rivals: Anglo-American Atomic Relations, 1941–1952* (Columbus: Ohio State University Press, 2000).

41 *PAC,* 191–92; Leffler, *Preponderance of Power,* 139.

42 Robert H. Ferrell, ed., *Off the Record: The Private Papers of Harry S. Truman* (New York: Harper & Row, 1980), 49; idem, ed., *Dear Bess: The Letters from Harry to Bess Truman, 1910–1959* (New York: W. W. Norton, 1983), 530; *PAC,* 210; Isaacson and Thomas, 372; James F. Byrnes, *Speaking Frankly* (New York: Harper & Brothers, 1947), 245; Messer, *End of an Alliance,* 200; Harvey H. Bundy and James Grafton Rogers, *The Organization of the Government for the Conduct of Foreign Affairs, Prepared for The Commission on Organization of the Executive Branch of the Government* (Washington: Government Printing Office, 1949), 77; Deborah Welch Larson, *Origins of Containment: A Psychological Explanation* (Princeton: Princeton University Press, 1985), 243.

43 *PAC,* 200. At the time, Acheson wrote Frankfurter that "as he expected, there was not a soul there to meet him." Joseph P. Lash, assisted by Jonathan Lash, *From the Diaries of Felix Frankfurter* (New York: W. W. Norton, 1975), 293.

Chapter 3

1 Parts of this chapter appeared earlier as "Patterns of Peril: Dean Acheson Joins the Cold Warriors, 1945–46," *Diplomatic History* 20 (Summer 1996): 321–55.

2 Acheson to Mary Bundy, 12 May 1945, Acheson Papers, Box 4, Folder 52, YUL; Herring, 246; Fossedal, 179; Robert A. Pollard, *Economic Security and the Origins of the Cold War, 1945–1950* (New York: Columbia University Press, 1985), 52–53, 278n.; Larson, *Origins of Containment*, 278–79, 331; Frank Ninkovich, *Germany and the United States: The Transformation of the German Question since 1945* (Boston: Twayne, 1988), 55–56; Barry Rubin, *The Great Powers in the Middle East 1941–1947: The Road to the Cold War* (London: Oxford University Press, 1980), 180.

3 *PAC*, 194; Acheson to Truman, 5 February 1954, Acheson Papers, Box 30, Folder 392, YUL.

4 Address by the Honorable Dean Acheson, Under Secretary of State, at a Rally Sponsored by the National Council of American-Soviet Friendship, at Madison Square Garden, New York City, November 14, 1945, at 9:00 P.M., E.S.T., Acheson Papers, Box 89, TL; *PAC*, 130–31; *New York Times*, 15 November 1945. During his 1949 confirmation hearings as secretary of state, he cited the speech in support of his anti-communist credentials but complained that he was "continually criticized" for appearing at such a gathering. *Nomination of Dean G. Acheson*, 22–23.

5 *FRUS 1945* 4: 493; Gaddis Smith, *Acheson*, 29; Odd Arne Westad, *Cold War and Revolution: Soviet-American Rivalry and the Origins of the Chinese Civil War, 1944–1946* (New York: Columbia University Press, 1993), 116; Robert J. Donovan, *Conflict and Crisis: The Presidency of Harry S Truman, 1945–1948* (New York: W. W. Norton, 1977), 152, 249. In Romanizing Chinese words, I have compromised between the PRC's official "pinyin" system (not accepted in Taiwan), and spellings more familiar to western readers: thus, Kuomintang instead of Guomindang and Chiang Kai-shek instead of Jiang Shi, but Mao Zedong rather than Mao Tse-tung.

6 Albert Resis, ed., *Molotov Remembers: Inside Kremlin Politics: Conversations with Felix Chuev* (Chicago: Ivan R. Dee, 1993), 8. Melvyn Leffler first drew my attention to this source.

7 Kuniholm, *Origins of the Cold War in the Near East*, 285; Fraser J. Harbutt, *The Iron Curtain: Churchill, America, and the Origins of the Cold War* (New York: Oxford University Press, 1986), 148; Louise L'Estrange Fawcett, *Iran and the Cold War: The Azerbaijan Crisis of 1946* (Cambridge, UK: Cambridge University Press, 1992), 125–26; "Plenum Transcripts, 1955–1957," *Cold War International History Project Bulletin* (Issue 10, March 1998): 59 (hereafter *CWIHPB*).

8 Kuniholm, *Origins of the Cold War in the Near East*, 285; War College Speech, 16 September 1948, Acheson Papers, Box 69, Press Conf. 1949–1953, Classified Off the Record Speeches Folder, TL, 26–27 (hereafter War College Speech, 16 September 1948).

9 Acheson to Mary Bundy, 6 August 1945, Box 4, Folder 52, and to John Cowles, 8 October 1957, Acheson Papers, Box 6, Folder 82, YUL; Barton J. Bernstein, "The Quest for Security: American Foreign Policy and International Control of Atomic Energy, 1942–1946," *Journal of American History* 60 (March 1974): 1017–19; Pavel Sudoplatov and Anatoli Sudoplatov, with Jerrold and Leona P. Schecter, *Special Tasks: The Memoirs of an Unwanted Witness—A Soviet Spymaster* (Boston: Little, Brown, 1994), 181 (hereafter cited as Sudoplatov); Rhodes, 203–4; Joseph I. Lieberman, *The Scorpion and the Tarantula: The Struggle to Control Atomic Weapons, 1945–1949* (Boston: Houghton Mifflin, 1970), 143; *PAC*, 123–24; Atomic Bomb, 21 September 1945, Truman Papers, President's Secretary's Files (henceforth PSF), Box 199, TL; Walter Millis, ed., with the collaboration of E. S. Duffield, *The Forrestal Diaries* (New York: Viking, 1951), 94–96.

10 Rhodes, 204; Donovan, *Conflict and Crisis*, 131; *PAC*, 124; Memorandum Requested by the President. Subject: U.S. Policy Regarding Secrecy of Scientific Knowledge about Atomic Bomb and Atomic Energy, Truman Papers (PSF), Box 199, TL; Sudoplatov, 197, 201.

11 *PAC*, 125, 743–4; Gregg Herken, *The Winning Weapon: The Atomic Bomb in the Cold War, 1945–1950* (New York: Alfred A. Knopf, 1980), 35; Gaddis, *U.S. and the Origins of the Cold War*, 268; Robert L. Messer, "Acheson, the Bomb, and the Cold War," in Brinkley, *Acheson and . . . U.S. Foreign Policy*, 59.

12 Joseph Manzione, " 'Amusing and Amazing and Practical and Military': The Legacy of Scientific Internationalism in American Foreign Policy, 1945–1963," *Diplomatic History* 24 (Winter 2000): 35n.; Bernstein, "Quest for Security," 1029; David E. Lilienthal, *The Journals of David E. Lilienthal. Vol. 2: The Atomic Energy Years, 1945–1950* (New York: Harper & Row, 1964), 10; *PAC*, 153.

13 David Lilienthal, 27; Richard G. Hewlett and Oscar E. Anderson, Jr., *A History of the United States Atomic Energy Commission. Volume I. The New World, 1939–1946* (University Park: Pennsylvania State University Press, 1962), 541; James F. Byrnes, 269.

14 Rhodes, 355; Hewlett and Anderson, 558; Bernstein, "Quest for Security," 1031.

15 *PAC*, 154; Feis, 208–9, 216, 218, 222, 226, 229, 252; Jordan A. Schwarz, *The Speculator: Bernard M. Baruch in Washington, 1917–1965* (Chapel Hill: University of North Carolina Press, 1981), 492.

16 Jordan A. Schwarz, *Speculator*, 492, 495; *In the Matter of J. Robert Oppenheimer: Transcript of Hearing before Personnel Security Board and Texts of Principal Documents and Letters*, foreword, Philip M. Stern (Cambridge: MIT Press, 1970), 36–37; Walter LaFeber, *America, Russia, and the Cold War, 1945–1992*, 7th ed. (New York: McGraw-Hill, 1993), 41; *PAC*, 156; Bernard M. Baruch, *Baruch: The Public Years* (New York: Holt, Rinehart and Winston, 1960), 361; Arnold A. Offner, *Another Such Victory: President Truman and the Cold War, 1945–1953* (Stanford: Stanford University Press, 2002), 148; David Lilienthal, 41, 59, 131; Hewlett and Anderson, 565, 570, 572–74.

17 Vladislav Zubok and Constantine Pleshakov, *Inside the Kremlin's Cold War: From Stalin to Khrushchev* (Cambridge: Harvard University Press, 1996), 78; Samuel R. Williamson, Jr., and Steven L. Rearden, *The Origins of U.S. Nuclear Strategy, 1945–1953* (New York: St. Martin's Press, 1993), 39; Gaddis, *U.S. and the Origins of the Cold War*, 335; Arneson Oral History, TL, 29; Jordan A. Schwarz, *Speculator*, 500–501; Messer, "Acheson, the Bomb . . . ," 63; Steven L. Rearden, *The Formative Years, 1947–1950* (Washington: Historical Office, Office of the Secretary of Defense, 1984), vol. I of *History of the Office of the Secretary of Defense*, ed. Alfred Goldberg, 439.

18 Larry G. Gerber, "The Baruch Plan and the Origins of the Cold War," *Diplomatic History* 6 (Winter 1982): 92–93; Jordan A. Schwarz, *Speculator*, 504n.; *PAC*, 155; Messer, "Acheson, the Bomb . . . ," 64; David Holloway, *Stalin and the Bomb: The Soviet Union and Atomic Energy* (New Haven: Yale University Press, 1994). In 1972 in a letter to historian Robert H. Ferrell, Acheson's secretary Barbara Evans fought suspicions that her boss cynically designed the Acheson-Lilienthal Plan to guarantee Soviet rejection. "I well remember," she wrote, Acheson's "jubilant (for a time at least) conviction there was a way to deal with international control of atomic energy and can remember and see him coming into the outer office at the State Department aglow with enthusiasm for the Acheson-Lilienthal staff proposals. I also know his really deep disappointment that the proposals were (probably) mishandled and that they came to naught, realizing ultimately that they would have, regardless of any correct handling." Robert H. Ferrell, *Harry S. Truman: A Life* (Columbia: University of Missouri Press, 1994), 445n.

19 Millis, 134; David McCullough, *Truman* (New York: Simon & Schuster, 1992), 486. Some Soviet leaders were "appalled" by the western reaction and made attempts to allay the fears it prompted. Albert Resis, *Stalin, the Politburo, and the Onset of the Cold War, 1945–1946*

(Pittsburgh: University of Pittsburgh Press, 1988), 16–17, 21–23, 25. Relying on Acheson's memoirs, Resis mistakenly lumps him with Walter Lippmann in considering the speech "belligerent" at the time of its delivery.

20 Rhodes, 233; Larson, *Origins of Containment*, 253–55; Charles R. Morris, *Iron Destinies, Lost Opportunities: The Arms Race between the U.S.A. and the U.S.S.R., 1945–1987* (New York: Harper & Row, 1988), 25; Strobe Talbott, *The Master of the Game: Paul Nitze and the Nuclear Peace* (New York: Alfred A. Knopf, 1988), 43; Scott Lucas, *Freedom's War: The American Crusade against the Soviet Union* (New York: New York University Press, 1999), 15; Paul H. Nitze, with Ann M. Smith and Steven L. Rearden, *From Hiroshima to Glasnost: At the Center of Decision: A Memoir* (New York: Grove Weidenfeld, 1990), 78; George F. Kennan, *Memoirs 1925–1950* (New York: Pantheon Books, 1967), 292–93; David Mayers, *The Ambassadors and America's Soviet Policy* (New York: Oxford University Press, 1995), 161; *FRUS 1946* 6: 696n.

21 "Moscow Embassy Telegram #511, 'The Long Telegram,'" 22 February 1946, in Thomas H. Etzold and John Lewis Gaddis, eds., *Containment: Documents on American Policy and Strategy, 1945–1950* (New York: Columbia University Press, 1978), 50–63; *PAC*, 151.

22 McCullough, 488; Thomas G. Paterson, ed., *Major Problems in American Foreign Policy.* Vol. 2: *Since 1914*, 3d ed. (Lexington, MA: D. C. Heath, 1989), 288–92.

23 Gaddis, *U.S. and the Origins of the Cold War*, 296; McCullough, 490; Harbutt, 197, 218, 227; *Khrushchev Remembers: The Glasnost Tapes*, trans. and ed., Jerrold L. Schecter with Vyacheslav V. Luchkov (Boston: Little, Brown, 1990), 355; John Baylis, *The Diplomacy of Pragmatism: Britain and the Formation of NATO, 1942–1949* (Kent: Kent State University Press, 1993), 43; Kuross A. Samii, *Involvement by Invitation: American Strategies of Containment in Iran* (University Park: Pennsylvania State University Press, 1987), 76.

24 Richard Gid Powers, *Not Without Honor: The History of American Anticommunism* (New York: Free Press, 1995), 194; Weil, 256; Woods, 299; W. W. Rostow, *The Division of Europe after World War II: 1946* (Austin: University of Texas Press, 1981), 3–5, 127; Edward Rice-Maximin, "The United States and the French Left, 1945–1949: The View from the State Department," *Journal of Contemporary History* 19 (October 1984): 732–33; Joyce and Gabriel Kolko, *The Limits of Power: The World and United States Foreign Policy, 1945–1954* (New York: Harper & Row, 1972), 156; Michael M. Boll, *Cold War in the Balkans: American Foreign Policy and the Emergence of Communist Bulgaria, 1943–1947* (Lexington: University Press of Kentucky, 1984), 174–75; John Gillingham, "From Morgenthau Plan to Schuman Plan: America and the Organization of Europe," in Jeffry M. Diefendorf, Axel Frohn, and Hermann-Josef Rupieper, eds., *American Policy and the Reconstruction of West Germany, 1945–1955* (Washington: German Historical Institute, and New York: Cambridge University Press, 1993), 116–17.

25 Eduard M. Mark, "The War Scare of 1946 and Its Consequences," *Diplomatic History* 21 (Summer 1997), 392–93, 405n (I have relied heavily on this important article in the pages that follow); Larson, *Origins of Containment*, 282 (emphasis in original).

26 Mark, "War Scare of 1946," 401; Acheson Oral History, 17 February 1955, A.M., Truman Papers, TL, 2–3 (hereafter cited as 1955 Acheson Oral History, A.M. or P.M.); Terry H. Anderson, *The United States, Great Britain, and the Cold War 1944–1947* (Columbia, MO: University of Missouri Press, 1981), 137; *FRUS 1946* 7: 840–43, 847–48; Larson, *Origins of Containment*, 282–83; Millis, 192.

27 David Lilienthal, 215; Jonathan Knight, "American Statecraft and the 1946 Black Sea Straits Controversy," *Political Science Quarterly* 90 (Fall 1975): 470–73.

28 Mark, "War Scare of 1946," 387, 404–6, and passim; Leffler, *Preponderance of Power*, 123–25; idem, "Strategy, Diplomacy, and the Cold War: The United States, Turkey, and NATO, 1945–1952," *Journal of American History* 71 (March 1985): 807–25; Larson, *Origins of Containment*, 280–81; Resis, *Molotov Remembers*, 73–74.

29 Mark, "War Scare of 1946," 387, 397–98.

30 Ibid., 384, 386–87, 394–96, 399, 402–03, 405, 408, 412; Michael Warner, ed., *CIA Cold War Records: The CIA under Harry Truman* (Washington: History Staff, Center for the Study of Intelligence, Central Intelligence Agency, 1994), 72, 81; Chester J. Pach, Jr., *Arming the Free World: The Origins of the United States Military Assistance Program, 1945–1950* (Chapel Hill: University of North Carolina Press, 1991), 100; Bruce Robellet Kuniholm, "Loy Henderson, Dean Acheson, and the Origins of the Truman Doctrine," in Brinkley, *Acheson and . . . U.S. Foreign Policy*, 93.

31 Mark, "War Scare of 1946," 399–400; Larson, *Origins of Containment*, 280, 283–84; Pach, *Arming the Free World*, 99; Secretary of War to Secretary of State, 8 July 1945, RG145, U.S. National Archives (document given to me by Melvyn P. Leffler); Leffler, "Strategy, Diplomacy, and the Cold War," passim; *PAC*, 195.

32 *PAC*, 196; Reston, "The No. 1 No. 2 Man in Washington," *New York Times Magazine*, 25 August 1946, 8, 44. Emphasis added. I want to thank Chester Pach for the idea of cold war moments and cold war outlook.

33 Weil, 258; *PAC*, 360.

34 I wish to thank Robert Kagan for the need to highlight the factor of British decline.

35 Walter L. Hixson, *George F. Kennan: Cold War Iconoclast* (New York: Columbia University Press, 1989), 34; *FRUS 1946* 8: 66–69, 77; Fawcett, 106–7, 135, 138; McLellan, *State Department Years*, 110–11; Kuniholm, *Origins of the Cold War in the Near East*, 394n; 1955 Acheson Oral History, A.M., 8; www.historyguide.org/europe/kennan.html (viewed 4/20/05).

36 *New York Times*, 9 December, 12 December, 3 September, and 17 October 1946; *FRUS 1946* 1: 985; Robert L. Messer, "Roosevelt, Truman, and China: An Overview," in *Sino-American Relations, 1945–1955*, ed. Harry Harding and Yuan Ming (Wilmington, DE: Scholarly Resources, 1989), 73; Sheldon R. Anderson, *A Dollar to Poland Is a Dollar to Russia: U.S. Economic Policy toward Poland, 1945–1952* (New York: Garland, 1993), 73.

37 *New York Times*, 16, 19, 21, and 23 February 1947; Larson, *Origins of Containment*, 306.

Chapter 4

1 Leffler, *Preponderance of Power*, 39–40; *PAC*, 192–93; Dean Acheson, *Sketches from Life of Men I Have Known* (New York: Harper & Brothers, 1961), 153.

2 *PAC*, 140, 143–44; Acheson, *Sketches from Life*, 150–51.

3 *New York Times*, 3 May 1946; Leffler, *Preponderance of Power*, 169.

4 www.trumanlibrary.org/diary/page3.htm (and pages 6 and 7) (viewed 5/2/05).

5 Acheson, *Sketches from Life*, 147; David Lilienthal, 158–59; *New York Times*, 25 January 1947.

6 *New York Times*, 23 February 1947; *PAC*, 213; McCullough, 560; Willard L. Thorp, Oral History Interview, 10 July 1971 (Independence, MO: The Harry S. Truman Library, January 1978), 173.

7 Louis J. Halle, *The Cold War as History* (New York: Harper Colophon Books, 1967), 116; Dean Acheson, "The Eclipse of the State Department," *Foreign Affairs* 49 (July 1971): 601; idem, *Vast External Realm*, 290; *PAC*, 213–14; Ed Cray, *General of the Army: George C. Marshall: Soldier and Statesman* (New York: W. W. Norton, 1990), 589–90; *New York Times*, 14 January 1945.

8 *PAC*, 29, 237; Princeton Seminars, 2 July 1953; Fraser Wilkins, Oral History Interview, 20 June 1975 (Independence, MO: The Harry S. Truman Library, December 1979), 19.

9 Clark M. Clifford, Oral History Interview, 23 March, 13 and 19 April, 10 May, and 26 July 1971, 16 March 1972, and 14 February 1973 (Independence, MO: The Harry S. Truman Library, April 1977), 158; McGeorge Bundy, ed., *The Pattern of Responsibility*, intro. Douglas Southall Freeman (Boston: Houghton Mifflin, 1952), 16–18 (hereafter cited as *Pattern of Responsibility*); *New York Times*, 5 June 1946.

10 Harry S. Truman, *Memoirs. Volume Two: Years of Trial and Hope* (Garden City: Doubleday, 1956), 106.

11 *PAC*, 195; Howard Jones, *"A New Kind of War": America's Global Strategy and the Truman Doctrine in Greece* (New York: Oxford University Press, 1989), 28; Lash, 278. George II died 1 April 1947, succeeded by his brother Paul I.

12 *FRUS 1949* 3: 174–75; Kuniholm, "Loy Henderson," 94; Donovan, *Conflict and Crisis*, 251.

13 Acheson, *Sketches from Life*, 107; Stephen G. Xydis, *Greece and the Great Powers, 1944–1947: Prelude to the "Truman Doctrine"* (Thessalonica: Institute for Balkan Studies, 1963), 9, 447; Pollard, *Economic Security*, 117; *FRUS 1946* 7: 263; Leffler, *Preponderance of Power*, 127; Woodrow J. Kuhns, ed., *Assessing the Soviet Threat: The Early Cold War Years* (Washington, DC: Center for the Study of Intelligence, Central Intelligence Agency, 1997), 101; *FRUS 1947* 5: 24–25, 28–29; Thanasis D. Sfikas, "War and Peace in the Strategy of the Communist Party of Greece, 1945–1949," *Journal of Cold War Studies* 3 (Fall 2001): 13.

14 *New York Times*, 2 October 1946; *FRUS 1947* 5: 2–3.

15 John D. Iatrides, "Revolution or Self-Defense? Communist Goals, Strategy, and Tactics in the Greek Civil War," *Journal of Cold War Studies* 7 (Summer 2005): 24–25; Peter J. Stavrakis, *Moscow and Greek Communism, 1944–1949* (Ithaca: Cornell University Press, 1989), 214–15; Vojtech Mastny, *The Cold War and Soviet Insecurity: The Stalin Years* (New York: Oxford University Press, 1996), 26; Princeton Seminars, 9 July 1953.

16 Joseph Marion Jones, *The Fifteen Weeks (February 21–June 5, 1947)* (New York: Viking Press, 1955), 3–4; *PAC*, 217; *FRUS 1947* 5: 32; Denis Smith, *Diplomacy of Fear: Canada and the Cold War, 1941–1948* (Toronto: University of Toronto Press, 1988), 265n; Kuniholm, "Loy Henderson," 97–98; George C. McGhee, Oral History Interview, 11 June 1975 (Independence, MO: The Harry S. Truman Library, December 1977), 20–21.

17 Acheson, *Fragments*, 42; Truman, *Years of Trial and Hope*, 100; Lawrence S. Wittner, *American Intervention in Greece, 1943–1949* (New York: Columbia University Press, 1982), 67; McCullough, 541; H. W. Brands, *Inside the Cold War: Loy Henderson and the Rise of the American Empire, 1918–1961* (New York: Oxford University Press, 1991), 155–56; Cray, 594; Howard Jones, 33; *PAC*, 218.

18 Paul H. Nitze, Oral History Interview, 11 and 17 June, 4–6 August 1975 (Independence, MO: The Harry S. Truman Library, July 1990), 226.

19 *FRUS 1947* 5: 45; Pollard, "Economic Security and the Origins of the Cold War," 279–80.

20 Gaddis, *U.S. and the Origins of the Cold War*, 344–45.

21 Clark Clifford, with Richard Holbrooke, *Counsel to the President: A Memoir* (New York: Random House, 1991), 132; Larson, *Origins of Containment*, 303–4; Nitze Oral History, TL, 226.

22 *New York Times*, 28 February 1947; Denis Smith, 185; Forrest C. Pogue, *George C. Marshall: Statesman 1945–1959* (New York: Viking Press, 1987), 164; Cray, 595; J. M. Jones, 139.

23 Denis Smith, 185; Isaacson and Thomas, 365. Most of this account comes from *PAC*, 219, and a fuller version in J. M. Jones, 139–41. For skepticism about the centrality of Acheson's role, see Pogue, *Marshall: Statesman*, 165. Some accounts have Vandenberg telling Truman, "the only way you are ever going to get this is to make a speech and scare the hell out of the country." Recited in numerous histories over many years, this quotation appears to originate in the unfootnoted Eric F. Goldman, *The Crucial Decade—and After: America, 1945–1960* (New York: Vintage Books, 1961), 59.

24 Denis Smith, 186–87; Arthur H. Vandenberg, Jr., with the collaboration of Joe Alex Morris, ed., *The Private Papers of Senator Vandenberg* (Boston: Houghton Mifflin, 1952), 340–41.

25 Loy W. Henderson, Oral History Interview, 14 June and 5 July 1973 (Independence, MO: The Harry S. Truman Library, January 1976), 89; Wittner, *Intervention in Greece*, 73; J. M. Jones, 76–77; *Washington Post*, 7 March 1947.

26 Memorandum for the File: The Drafting of the President's Message to Congress on the Greek Situation, Delivered before a Joint Session of Congress, 12 March 1947, Joseph M. Jones Papers, TL; Larson, *Origins of Containment*, 308; J. M. Jones, vii.

27 Henderson Oral History, TL, 86; *PAC*, 220; Memorandum for the File: The Drafting of the President's Message to Congress on the Greek Situation, Delivered before a Joint Session of Congress, 12 March 1947, Joseph M. Jones Papers, TL; J. M. Jones, 155–57, 159–60, 166; LaFeber, *America, Russia, and the Cold War*, 54; Fossedal, 213; Howard Jones, 41–42; Terry Anderson, 169; Wittner, *Intervention in Greece*, 68–69.

28 Kennan, *Memoirs, 1925–1956*, 315–16; Charles E. Bohlen, *Witness to History: 1929–1969* (New York: W. W. Norton., 1973), 261; David Lilienthal, 159; Draft 3–10–47, George M. Elsey Papers, Box 17, TL; Clifford, *Counsel to the President*, 137; Memorandum for the File: The Drafting of the President's Message to Congress on the Greek Situation, Delivered before a Joint Session of Congress, 12 March 1947, Joseph M. Jones Papers, TL; Elsey to Clifford, 7 March 1947, George M. Elsey Papers, Box 17, TL; Donovan, *Conflict and Crisis*, 282; *In the Matter of J. Robert Oppenheimer*, 41; C. H. Humelsine, Memorandum for Commander Elsey, 10 March 1947, George M. Elsey Papers, Box 17, TL; Kuniholm, "Loy Henderson," 75; John J. Iselin, "The Truman Doctrine: A Study in the Relationship between Crisis and Foreign Policy-Making" (Ph.D. Dissertation, Harvard University, 1964), 298ff., especially 345; Warren I. Cohen, *Dean Rusk. Volume XIX of the American Secretaries of State and Their Diplomacy*, eds., Samuel Flagg Bemis and Robert H. Ferrell (Totowa, N.J.: Cooper Square Publishers, 1980), 11; *PAC*, 220. The U.S. ambassador to the UN, Warren R. Austin, was not even informed of the impending policy announcement until the day before its delivery in Congress, which Acheson called a "fortunate error." *PAC*, 223.

29 *PAC*, 221–22; Howard Jones, 30; Arthur M. Schlesinger, Jr., ed., *The Dynamics of World Power: A Documentary History of United States Foreign Policy 1945–1973*, Vol. II, Part I: *Eastern Europe and the Soviet Union*, ed., Walter LaFeber (New York: Chelsea House, 1989), 309–13.

30 Frank A. Ninkovich, *Modernity and Power: A History of the Domino Theory in the Twentieth Century* (Chicago: University of Chicago Press, 1994), 369n.

31 Howard Jones, 41, 43–45; Wittner, *Intervention in Greece*, 80–83; McLellan, *State Department Years*, 120; Denis Smith, 189, 191.

32 Wittner, *Intervention in Greece*, 80; *FRUS 1947* 5: 108.

33 *New York Times*, 14 March 1947; Acheson, *Sketches from Life*, 131. The Senate confirmed Lilienthal 50–31 on 9 April.

34 Dean Acheson, Oral History Interview, 30 June 1971 (Independence, MO: The Harry S. Truman Library, May 1986), 12 (hereafter referred to as Acheson Oral History 1971, TL); Thomas G. Paterson, *Soviet-American Confrontation: Postwar Reconstruction and the Origins of the Cold War* (Baltimore: Johns Hopkins University Press, 1973), 200; *New York Times*, 21–23 March 1947.

35 Thomas G. Paterson, "If Europe, Why Not China? The Containment Doctrine, 1947–1949," *Prologue* 13 (Spring 1981): 19; *New York Times*, 21–23 March 1947; Daniel Yergin, *Shattered Peace: The Origins of the Cold War and the National Security State* (Boston: Houghton Mifflin, 1977), 295; Donovan, *Conflict and Crisis*, 286.

36 Michael Warner, 100–101, 103; Howard Jones, 53; J. M. Jones, 196.

37 *PAC*, 224; J. M. Jones, 175–76; Howard Jones, 55.

38 Mastny, *Cold War and Soviet Insecurity*, 35, 38–39; Offner, 206–7; Christopher M. Woodhouse, *The Struggle for Greece 1941–1949* (London: Hart-Davis, MacGibbon, 1976), 285.

39 Ronald Steel, *Walter Lippmann and the American Century* (Boston: An Atlantic Monthly Press Book, Little, Brown, 1980), 438–40.

40 John Lewis Gaddis, *Russia, the Soviet Union, and the United States: An Interpretive History* (New York: John Wiley and Sons, 1978), 186.

41 *New York Times*, 16 January 1952.

Chapter 5

1 Hill, 501; Isaacson and Thomas, 386.

2 Henry Lucien Bonnet, Oral History Interview, 29 June 1970 (Independence, MO: The Harry S. Truman Library, June 1987), 17; Fred L. Block, *The Origins of International Economic Disorder: A Study of United States International Monetary Policy from World War II to the Present* (Berkeley: University of California Press, 1977), 73.

3 Leffler, *Preponderance of Power*, 160–61.

4 Ibid.; idem, "Negotiating from Strength," 184.

5 Philip Zelikow, "George C. Marshall and the Moscow CFM Meeting of 1947," *Diplomacy & Statecraft* 8 (July 1997): 99, 109, 111–12; Robert H. Ferrell, *George C. Marshall* (New York: Cooper Square, 1966), 71 (vol. 15 of *American Secretaries of State and Their Diplomacy*, ed., Robert H. Ferrell and Samuel Flagg Bemis); Anne Deighton, *The Impossible Peace: Britain, the Division of Germany and the Origins of the Cold War* (Oxford: Clarendon Press, 1990), 156–57; Dennis L. Bark and David R. Gress, *A History of West Germany. Volume 1: From Shadow to Substance, 1945–1963* (Oxford: Basil Blackwell, 1989), 188.

6 John Lewis Gaddis, "Perpetuating the Cold War: The German Question" (unpublished paper, September 1994), 5; Deighton, *Impossible Peace*, 100 and passim, especially chapter 4; Josef Foschepoth, "British Interest in the Division of Germany after the Second World War," *Journal of Contemporary History* 21 (July 1986): 392, 404; Marc Trachtenberg, *A Constructed Peace: The Making of the European Settlement, 1945–1963* (Princeton: Princeton University Press, 1999), 56–65.

7 Leffler, *Preponderance of Power*, 151; *FRUS 1947* 3: 222; Kolko and Kolko, 139; Bark and Gress, 131; Louis Galambos, *The Papers of Dwight David Eisenhower: The Chief of Staff, VII* (Baltimore: Johns Hopkins University Press, 1978), 676n.; Jean Edward Smith, ed., *The Papers of General Lucius D. Clay: Germany 1945–1949* (Bloomington, 1974) 1:184; Lucius D. Clay, Oral History Interview, 16 July 1974 (Independence, MO: The Harry S. Truman Library, July 1979), 22.

8 Ninkovich, *Germany and the United States*, 50; *New York Times*, 23 March 1947.

9 Fossedal, 214; Leffler, *Preponderance of Power*, 151; Takeshi Igarashi, "Dean Acheson and the Japanese Peace Treaty," in Brinkley, *Acheson and . . . U.S. Foreign Policy*, 135.

10 *New York Times*, 1 October 1947 and 24 September 1948; Elbridge Durbrow, Oral History Interview, 31 May 1973 (Independence, MO: The Harry S. Truman Library, April 1978), 82; William Curti Wohlforth, *The Elusive Balance: Power and Perceptions during the Cold War* (Ithaca: Cornell University Press, 1993), 133; Wilson D. Miscamble, C.S.C., *George F. Kennan and the Making of American Foreign Policy, 1947–1950* (Princeton: Princeton University Press, 1992), 53–74; Scott Jackson, "Prologue to the Marshall Plan: The Origins of the American Commitment for a European Recovery Program," *Journal of American History* 65 (March 1974): 1066; Kennan, *Memoirs, 1925–1950*, 326.

11 David Lilienthal, 215; Millis, 350–51.

12 *New York Times*, 14 March 1947; *PAC*, 227–28; Princeton Seminars, 2 July 1953; J. M. Jones, 27, 211.

13 "My notes discussed with Acheson first time Mississippi speech considered," Joseph Jones Papers, TL; *PAC*, 228; Georg Schild, *Bretton Woods and Dumbarton Oaks: American Economic and Political Postwar Planning in the Summer of 1944* (New York: St. Martin's Press, 1995), 131.

14 Address Made Off the Record Before the American Society of Newspaper Editors by the Honorable Dean Acheson, Acting Secretary of State, Washington, D. C., April 18, 1947, Acheson Papers, Box 69, TL.

15 *PAC*, 228–29; Durbrow Oral History, TL, 83–84; Miscamble, *Kennan and the Making of American Foreign Policy*, 47; Clifford Oral History, TL, 162.

16 Hamburger, "Mr. Secretary—II," 54; J. M. Jones, 274–81.

17 Michael Wala, *The Council on Foreign Relations and American Foreign Policy in the Early Cold War* (Providence: Berghahn Books, 1994), 110; *New York Times*, 9 and 10 May 1947; Leonard Miall, Oral History Interview, 17 June 1974, www.trumanlibrary.org/oralhist/ miall.htm, 5–8 (viewed 5/4/05); Warburg to Acheson, 9 May 1947, Acheson Papers, Box 33, Folder 426, YUL; Sir Roger Makins (now Lord Sheffield), Oral History Interview, 15 June 1964 (Independence, MO: The Harry S. Truman Library, January 1966), 2–3.

18 *FRUS 1947* 3: 223–30, 232; Leffler, *Preponderance of Power*, 159; *PAC*, 230–31; Memorandum for the Files RE: The Secretary's Harvard Speech of June 5, 1947, Joseph Jones Papers, Box 2, TL (hereafter referred to as Jones, "Secretary's Harvard Speech"). Emphasis in original.

19 *FRUS 1947* 3: 235; *PAC*, 232; Princeton Seminars, 2 July 1953.

20 Jones, "Secretary's Harvard Speech"; *PAC*, 233–34; McCullough, 562–63; *FRUS 1947* 3: 237–39.

21 Baylis, *Diplomacy of Pragmatism*, 64; John Saville, "Ernest Bevin and the Cold War, 1945–1950," *Socialist Register* (1984): 92; Deighton, *Impossible Peace*, 187; Halvard M. Lange, Oral History Interview, 22 May 1964 (Independence, MO: The Harry S. Truman Library, January 1966), 3–4; John Killick, *The United States and European Reconstruction, 1945–1960* (Edinburgh: Keele University Press, 1997), 89; James W. Riddleberger, Oral History Interview, 6 and 26 April 1972 (Independence, MO: The Harry S. Truman Library, January 1975), 98.

22 Wala, *Council on Foreign Relations*, 182–83; Denis Smith, 195; *New York Times*, 19 July 1947; Michael Wala, "Selling the Marshall Plan at Home: The Committee for the Marshall Plan to Aid European Recovery," *Diplomatic History* 10 (Summer 1986): 247–48, 252, 257–58, 263. Wala persuasively demonstrates the error of Acheson's claim that the Committee was thoroughly private in origin and independent of the government. *PAC*, 240.

23 Wala, *Council on Foreign Relations*, 206; *Town Meeting*, 14 October 1947, 5–7, Acheson Papers, Box 4, TL; Acheson to John Ferguson, 17 December 1947, Acheson Papers, Box 3, Com. for the Marshall Plan corresp. 1947–8, Folder 1, TL; *New York Times*, 16 June and 29 November 1947, 22 January 1948; Address by the Honorable Dean Acheson Before the National-American Wholesale Grocers' Association, Atlantic City, January 21, 1948 (Reading Copy and Notes), Acheson Papers, Box 4, TL. Acheson attributed "Liquor doesn't affect me" to Bohlen. Press Conference, 2 August 1950, Acheson Papers, Box 68, TL.

24 Block, 84; Abraham Boxhoorn, *The Cold War and the Rift in the Governments of National Unity: Belgium, France and Italy in the Spring of 1947: A Comparison* (Amsterdam: Historisch Seminarium van de Universiteit van Amsterdam, 1993), 245–46, 248; Deborah Kisatsky, "The United States, the French Right, and American Power in Europe, 1946–1958," *The Historian* 65 (Spring 2003): 621.

25 U.S. Congress, House Committee on Foreign Affairs, *Hearings. United States Foreign Policy for a Post-War Recovery Program, 80th Congress, 1st and 2nd Session* (Washington: Government Printing Office, 1948), 694–98, 700–702, 734, 738. Henceforth *United States Foreign Policy for a Post-War Recovery Program*.

26 John Gillingham, *Coal, Steel, and the Rebirth of Europe, 1945–1955: The Germans and French from Ruhr Conflict to Economic Community* (Cambridge, UK: Cambridge University Press, 1991), 118; Block, 89, 91, 240n; Hill, 524; Leffler, *Preponderance of Power*, 164–65.

27 Acheson, *Sketches from Life*, 200; Block, 83; Bernard W. Poirer, "The European Recovery Program and Truman and MacArthur: Interview with Governor W. Averell Harriman," 10 January 1980, Washington, DC (Fairfax, VA: Iroquois Research Institute, n.d.), 2; Michael J. Hogan, "American Marshall Planners and the Search for a European Neocapitalism," *American Historical Review* 90 (February 1985): 45.

28 Alfred Grosser, *The Western Alliance: European-American Relations since 1945*, trans., Michael Shaw, foreword, Stanley Hoffmann (New York: Continuum, 1980), 74; Matlock Oral History, TL, 39; Henry A. Kissinger, *Years of Upheaval* (Boston: Little, Brown, 1982), 911.

29 Alan S. Milward, *The Reconstruction of Western Europe 1945–51* (London: Methuen, 1984), 465–66 and passim; E. Allan Lightner, Jr., Oral History Interview, 26 October 1973 (Independence, MO: The Harry S. Truman Library, March 1982), 89; Warburg to Acheson, 6 February 1948, Acheson Papers, Box 3, TL; Charles S. Maier, "The Two Postwar Eras and the Conditions for Stability in Twentieth-Century West Europe," *American Historical Review* 86 (April 1981): 341–42; Diane B. Kunz, *Butter and Guns: America's Cold War Economic Diplomacy* (New York: Free Press, 1997), 52–54; Killick, 3, 10–11, 15, 89, 94, 96.

30 Vojtech Mastny, "NATO in the Beholder's Eye: Soviet Perceptions and Policies, 1949–56" (Washington: Cold War International History Project, Woodrow Wilson International Center for Scholars, Working Paper No. 35, March 2002), 20; Don Cook, *Forging the Alliance: NATO, 1945–1950* (New York: Arbor House/William Morrow, 1989), 96; Mastny, *Cold War and Soviet Insecurity*, 27, 31–33, 35, 40, 43.

31 James Reston, "A New Role for a New State Department," *New York Times Magazine*, 25 May 1947, 64, 65; *New York Times*, 12 May 1947; Hamburger, "Mr. Secretary—II," 48; Cook, 159; *PAC*, 236.

32 David Acheson, 56; James Reston, "Secretary Acheson: A First-Year Audit," *New York Times Magazine*, 22 January 1950, 8; *PAC*, 239; Gaddis Smith, *Acheson*, 51.

33 *Among Friends*, 665; *PAC*, 239.

34 *New York Times*, 8 October 1947; William E. Pemberton, *Bureaucratic Politics: Executive Reorganization during the Truman Administration* (Columbia: University of Missouri Press, 1979), 91–92; Richard Norton Smith, *An Uncommon Man: The Triumph of Herbert Hoover* (New York: Simon & Schuster, 1984), 376; *PAC*, 241–45; David Lilienthal, 329; Alonzo L. Hamby, *Man of the People: A Life of Harry S. Truman* (New York: Oxford University Press, 1995), 403; Vandenberg, 393–94; Hogan, "American Marshall Planners," 56.

35 Summary of Remarks to Be Made by the Honorable Dean Acheson at the 1948 Oberlin Symposia, Oberlin, Ohio, April 9, 1948, and pencil notes for the same, Acheson Papers, Box 4, TL.

36 War College Speech, 16 September 1948.

37 Princeton Seminars, no date, stamped " '48 Address"; *New York Times*, 1 October 1948.

38 Edward L. Schapsmeier and Frederick H. Schapsmeier, *Prophet in Politics: Henry A. Wallace and the War Years, 1940–1965* (Ames: Iowa State University Press, 1970), 190.

39 Isaacson and Thomas, 462. The friend and partner was Gerhard Gesell, later a prominent federal judge.

40 Mark A. Stoler, *George C. Marshall: Soldier-Statesman of the American Century* (Boston: Twayne, 1989), 173; Vandenberg, 462; Acheson to Edward G. Miller, Jr., 16 November 1948, Acheson Papers, Box 23, Folder 285, YUL; Acheson, *Vast External Realm*, 246–47; *PAC*, 249; Isaacson and Thomas, 462–64; Princeton Seminars, Rewrite, Record 3, page 1; *Conversations with Eric Sevareid* (Washington: Public Affairs Press, 1976), 75.

41 *New York Times*, 8 and 9 January 1949; Hamby, *Beyond the New Deal*, 356; Hopkins, 107; Robert W. Merry, *Taking on the World: Joseph and Stewart Alsop—Guardians of the American Century* (New York: Viking, 1996), 181.

Chapter 6

1 *New York Times*, 14 January 1949; Senator Tom Connally, as told to Alfred Steinberg, *My Name Is Tom Connally* (New York: Thomas Y. Crowell, 1954), 332; Telegram, Adolf A. Berle, Jr., to Honorable Tom Connally, January 12, 1949, Reston Papers, Box 30, Working Files, UIA; Berle, 586–87; *Pattern of Responsibility*, 6; *PAC*, 252–53; *Nomination of Dean G. Acheson*, 2–17, 19–25; *Executive Sessions of the Senate Foreign Relations Committee . . . 1949–1950* 2: 26–27. On 18 January, Acheson resigned from his firm, which became Covington, Burling, Rublee, O'Brian & Shorb. Westwood, 111.

2 Alex Danchev, *Oliver Franks: Founding Father* (Oxford: Clarendon Press, 1993), 117; David Acheson, 25, 103; Noël Annan, "Dean Acheson," *Yale Review* 77 (October 1988): 468; Hamburger, "Mr. Secretary—II," 38–41; *New York Times*, 31 July 1949; Gaddis Smith, *Acheson*, 85; Henry Brandon, *Special Relationships: A Foreign Correspondent's Memoirs from Roosevelt to Reagan* (New York: Atheneum, 1988), 64.

3 Hamburger, "Mr. Secretary—I," 41–42; David Acheson, 25–26; Reston, *Deadline*, 147; McCullough, 753.

4 David Acheson, 108–9; Annan, "Dean of the Cold War," 11; Hamburger, "Mr. Secretary—I," 41; Acheson, *Morning and Noon*, 144; "Dean Acheson, a Remembrance," 37.

5 *New York Times*, 4 September 1951; David Acheson, 113–14. In 1961, Jean Monnet bought Acheson "a flashy Hawaiian-style necktie, the kind Acheson loved to wear while drinking martinis." Brinkley, "Acheson and Monnet," 91.

6 Hamburger, "Mr. Secretary—I," 39.

7 Byron, *Don Juan* (12th Canto) (1823); *New York Times*, 10 March 1949.

8 Gaddis Smith, *Acheson*, 410; Brinkley, "Acheson and Monnet," 78; Paul H. Nitze, "Introduction," in *Acheson and . . . U.S. Foreign Policy*, xxiii; Dean Acheson, "Thoughts about Thought in High Places," *New York Times Magazine*, 11 October 1959, 90; Hamburger, "Mr. Secretary—II," 55; idem, "Mr. Secretary—I," 42.

9 David Acheson, 25, 27–28, 50, 62, 64, 69, 125, 128; Danchev, *Franks*, 116; "Dear Boss: Unpublished Letters from Dean Acheson to Ex-President Harry Truman," *American Heritage* 31 (February–March 1980): 46; Scott Donaldson, with R. H. Winnick, *Archibald MacLeish: An American Life* (Boston: Houghton Mifflin, 1992), 261, 389.

10 David Acheson, 79, 129, 151–53, 160, 162, 164–65, 184, 187; Isaacson and Thomas, 549; Kai Bird, *The Chairman: John J. McCloy, the Making of the American Establishment* (New York: Simon & Schuster, 1992), 99; Chace, 73; Acheson, *Sketches from Life*, 33–34; www.nytimes.com/books/first/m/mordden-roses.html (viewed 5/6/05); Honoré Catudal, *Kennedy and the Berlin Wall Crisis: A Case Study in U.S. Decision Making*, foreword, Martin J. Hillenbrand (Berlin: Verlag, 1980), 57; Acheson to Konrad Adenauer, 28 June 1961, Acheson Papers, Box 85, TL.

11 Annan, "Dean Acheson," 469; Reston, *Deadline*, 153; David Acheson, 142–44; Charles S. Murphy, Oral History Interview, 2 May, 3 June, 24 July 1963, 21 May, 24 June, 15 July and 25 July 1969, 19 May 1970 (Independence, MO: The Harry S. Truman Library, May 1971), 508; *PAC*, 731. Kennan, too, and many years later, Secretary of State George P. Schultz, habitually used gardening metaphors. Kenneth W. Thompson, *Masters of International Thought: Major Twentieth-Century Theorists and the World Crisis* (Baton Rouge: Louisiana State University Press, 1980), 155; private communication from Robert Kagan.

12 David Acheson, 212; Reston, "First-Year Audit," 7.

13 *New York Times*, 24 September 1948 and 13 January 1950; David Acheson, 90, 156; Department of State, For the Press, January 12, 1950, No. 34, James Webb Papers, Box 20, TL.

14 Reston, *Deadline*, 154; Perry Laukhuff, Oral History Interview, 23 July 1974 (Independence, MO: The Harry S. Truman Library, March 1979), 151; Thomas D. Cabot, Oral History Interview, 6 June 1975 (Independence, MO: The Harry S. Truman Library, July

1979), 22–23; Princeton Seminars, 2 July 1953; Reston to Louis M. Lyons, 26 January 1950, Reston Papers, Box 30—Working Files, UIA.

15 Franks Oral History, TL, 26–28, 30; "Dean Acheson, a Remembrance," 21; Hamburger, "Mr. Secretary—II," 47; "Dear Boss," 46. In 1950, the French financial minister told Acheson: "You have the outside of the Englishman, but you think like a Frenchman." *PAC*, 458.

16 Acheson to David K. E. Bruce, 17 February 1954, Acheson Papers, Box 4, Folder 50, YUL; David K. E. Bruce, Oral History Interview, 1 March 1972 (Independence, MO: The Harry S. Truman Library, May 1974), 26–32; Hamburger, "Mr. Secretary—II," 51; Gillingham, *Coal, Steel, and the Rebirth of Europe*, 131; Dr. Walter H. Judd, Oral History Interview, 13 April 1970, www.trumanlibrary.org/oralhist/judd, 117 (viewed 5/6/05); *FRUS 1952–1954* 5, Pt. 1: 21.

17 William S. McFeely, *Grant: A Biography* (New York: W. W. Norton, 1981), 516; Acheson to Philip H. Watts, 9 December 1957, in *Among Friends*, 133; Isaacson and Thomas, 697; David Acheson, 208.

18 Jonathan Mirsky, "On Noel Annan (1916–2000)," *New York Review of Books*, 13 April 2000, 8; David Acheson, 47; *Conversations with Eric Sevareid*, 69.

19 David Acheson, 101, 156–57; McCullough, 756; Halle, *Cold War as History*, 114; *New York Times*, 9 December 1946 and 20 January 1949; Clifford, *Counsel to the President*, 141.

20 Laukhuff Oral History, TL, 148–50; Nelson D. Lankford, *The Last American Aristocrat: The Biography of David K. E. Bruce, 1898–1977* (Boston: Little, Brown, 1966), 251; David Acheson, 66–67, 105; *Strengthening the Forces of Freedom: Selected Speeches and Statements of Secretary of State Acheson, February 1949–April 1950* (Washington: Department of State, United States Government Printing Office, 1950), 133; *New York Times*, 16 April 1958; David Acheson, 211–12.

21 Acheson, *Morning and Noon*, 5; Elmer Davis, "The Crusade against Acheson," *Harper's Magazine* (March 1951): 28; Reston, *Deadline*, 144; *New York Times*, 26 November 1950; *PAC*, 216; Reston, "The No. 1 No. 2 Man in Washington," 8; Reston to Dean Acheson, 4 February 1949, Reston Papers, Box 29, TV Folder, UIA; *New York Times*, 28 April 1949.

22 1955 Acheson Oral History, A.M., 4. Truman attended the Kansas City, MO, school of law, 1923–1925.

23 Katie Louchheim, ed., *The Making of the New Deal: Insiders Speak* (Cambridge: Harvard University Press, 1983), 231; Ellis O. Briggs, *Farewell to Foggy Bottom: The Recollections of a Career Diplomat* (New York: David McKay, 1964), 295; John L. Harper, 250; U. Alexis Johnson, with Jef Olivarius McAllister, *The Right Hand of Power* (New York: Prentice-Hall, 1984), 118; Stanley W. Black, *A Levite among the Priests: Edward M. Bernstein and the Origins of the Bretton Woods System* (Boulder: Westview Press, 1991), 53; *Town Meeting*, 14 October 1947, 5, Acheson Papers, Box 4, TL; Franks Oral History, TL, 32; "Dean Acheson, a Remembrance," 19.

24 Dean Acheson, "Fifty Years After," *Yale Review* 51 (October 1961): 1–2; Acheson, *Democrat*, 53; Bendiner, 180; Acheson to Camille Gutt, 12 December 1961, Acheson Papers, Box 85, TL; Helen M. Lilienthal, ed., *The Journals of David E. Lilienthal. Volume II: Unfinished Business 1968–1981* (New York: Harper & Row, 1983), 144.

25 Noël Annan, *The Dons: Mentors, Eccentrics and Geniuses* (Chicago: University of Chicago Press, 1999), 18–19; Acheson to Alan Bullock, 27 April 1955, Acheson Papers, Box 4, Folder 51, YUL; Department of State, For the Press, January 12, 1950, No. 34, James Webb Papers, Box 20, TL; National War College Lecture, Washington, DC, 21 December 1949, Remarks at the National War College by the Honorable Dean Acheson, James Webb Papers, Box 20, TL (hereafter cited as Remarks at the National War College, 21 December 1949), 4.

26 *Conversations with Eric Sevareid*, 72; War College Speech, 16 September 1948, Acheson Papers, Box 69, TL, 4, 26, 28, 31, 38–39.

27 Michael H. Cardozo, Oral History Interview, 29 May 1975 (Independence, MO: The Harry S. Truman Library, October 1978), 53; *New York Times*, 5 March 1950; Acheson to Hans J. Morgenthau, 3 January 1957, Acheson Papers, Box 23, Folder 289, YUL; Princeton Seminars, 10 October 1953.

28 *PAC*, 302; Franks Oral History, TL, 30, 27.

29 Acheson, *Morning and Noon*, 65; Acheson to Michael Janeway, 24 May 1960, in *Among Friends*, 182; Acheson to Truman, 14 July 1961, Acheson Papers, Box 31, Folder 398, YUL; Acheson to John Cowles, 5 August 1963, Acheson Papers, Box 6, Folder 83, YUL; War College Speech, 16 September 1948; Excerpt from Off-the-Record Speech by the Secretary of State on March 17, 1949, Acheson Papers, Box 43, TL; Acheson to John W. Sparkman, 28 July 1952, Acheson Papers, Box 43, TL; Acheson, Memorandum, 20 February 1963, Acheson Papers, Box 86, TL; Acheson to Eelco Van Kleffans, 6 September 1961, Acheson Papers, Box 85, State Department & White House Advisor 1961 September Folder, TL.

30 Isaacson and Thomas, 132, 324; *FRUS 1952–1954* 6, Pt. 1: 825; Acheson, *Sketches from Life*, 156; Acheson to Alan Bullock, 27 April 1955, Acheson Papers, Box 4, Folder 51, YUL; Princeton Seminars, 13 December 1953; Remarks at the National War College, 21 December 1949, 2–3.

31 Acheson, *Sketches from Life*, 156; Edward W. Barrett, Oral History Interview, 9 July 1974 (Independence, MO: The Harry S. Truman Library, August 1980), 33–34; Acheson to Stanton Griffis, 18 January 1950, Stanton Griffis Papers, Box 9, TL; Abraham F. Lowenthal, "Yes, We Can Avoid a New Latin War," *Washington Post*, 3 June 1984; Reston, *Deadline*, 145.

32 Acheson to David L. Cunniff, 3 November 1949, Acheson Papers, Box 43, TL; David Acheson, 213–14; Laukhuff Oral History, TL, 152–53; *New York Times*, 15 January 1950; Acheson, *Sketches from Life*, 23; Clifford, *Counsel to the President*, 142; Acheson, *Morning and Noon*, 87; McLellan, *State Department Years*, 19; Dean Acheson, "Homage to General Marshall," *The Reporter* 21 (26 November 1959): 25; "Dear Boss," 47; 1955 Acheson Oral History, P.M., 18.

33 Thomas J. Schoenbaum, *Waging Peace and War: Dean Rusk in the Truman, Kennedy, and Johnson Years* (New York: Simon & Schuster, 1988), 14, 193; Dean Acheson, "Morality, Moralism, and Diplomacy," *Yale Review* 47 (June 1958): 483, 492–93.

Chapter 7

1 Reston, "New Role," 8; *New York Times*, 9 January 1947; Reston, "First-Year Audit," 38; Brookings Institution, International Studies Group, *The Administration of Foreign Affairs and Overseas Operations: A Report Prepared for the Bureau of the Budget, Executive Office of the President* (Washington: Brookings Institution, 1951), 248, 250; John Franklin Campbell, *The Foreign Affairs Fudge Factory* (New York: Basic Books, 1971), 38; Bundy and Rogers, 41; William J. McWilliams memorandum, 21 April 1950, James Webb Papers, Box 23, Folder 1, TL.

2 Acheson, "Eclipse of the State Department," 596; idem, "The President and the Secretary of State," in Don K. Price, ed., *The Secretary of State* (Englewood Cliffs, N.J.: Prentice-Hall, 1960), 37; Roger Hilsman, *The Politics of Policymaking in Defense and Foreign Affairs* (New York: Harper & Row, 1971), 168.

3 Princeton Seminars, 16 July 1953; Nitze Oral History, TL, 218; *Memoranda of the Secretary of State* 50:667, 1 September 1950; Notes on Talk with Mr. Acheson, 26 February 1951, Truman Papers (PSF), Box 160, Subj. File–Cabinet, State, Secy, Acheson Folder, TL.

4 Michael T. Benson, *Harry S. Truman and the Founding of Israel*, foreword, Stan A. Taylor (Westport: Praeger, 1997), 182; Laukhuff Oral History, TL, 154, 157; Francis H. Heller, ed., *The Truman White House: The Administration of the Presidency, 1945–1953* (Lawrence: Regents

Press of Kansas, 1980), 151; Diane S. Clemens, "Averell Harriman, John Deane, the Joint Chiefs of Staff, and the 'Reversal of Co-Operation' with the Soviet Union in April 1945," *International History Review* 14 (May 1992): 386.

5 J. M. Jones, 111; Robert J. Donovan, *Tumultuous Years: The Presidency of Harry S. Truman 1949–1953* (New York: W. W. Norton, 1982), 35; *PAC*, 237; Benson, 182.

6 C. S. Murphy Oral History, TL, 535; Clifford Oral History, TL, 169–70; Princeton Seminars, 13 February 1954, 16 July 1953.

7 C. S. Murphy Oral History, TL, 109–10.

8 Walter LaFeber, *The American Age: United States Foreign Policy at Home and Abroad*, 2d ed. (New York: W. W. Norton, 1994), 444; Weil, 258; *FRUS 1952–1954* 10 *(Iran 1951–1954)*: 244.

9 Acheson, *Morning and Noon*, 191; Merle Miller, 378; Michael Charlton, "The President's Men at the NSC. Part II. The Struggle under Carter," *The National Interest* 21 (Fall 1990): 103.

10 *PAC*, v, 354; Benson, 43; *Among Friends*, 94.

11 McCullough, in preface to Brinkley, *Acheson and . . . U.S. Foreign Policy*, xiv; Hickerson Oral History, TL, 77; John W. Snyder, Oral History Interview, 15 March 1980 (Independence, MO: The Harry S. Truman Library, November 1982), 70, 80 (hereafter Snyder Oral History 1980, TL); John W. Snyder, Oral History Interview, 18 March 1976 (Independence, MO: The Harry S. Truman Library, December 1985), 79 (hereafter referred to as Snyder Oral History 1976, TL); Admiral Robert L. Dennison, Oral History Interview, 10 September, 6 October, and 2 November 1971 (Independence, MO: The Harry S. Truman Library, June 1972), 96, 144; *Conversations with Eric Sevareid*, 73; Robert H. Ferrell, "Truman: On and Off the Record," in George W. Egerton, ed., *Political Memoir: Essays on the Politics of Memory* (London: Frank Cass, 1994), 275; McCullough, 755.

12 Hamburger, "Mr. Secretary—I," 50; McCullough, 754–55; Lucius D. Battle, Oral History Interview, 23 June 1971 (Independence, MO: The Harry S. Truman Library, September 1980), 9; Hamby, *Man of the People*, 543.

13 "No yearning to be loved—Dean Acheson talks to Kenneth Harris," *The Listener* (8 April 1971): 442; McCullough, 752; Edward Weintal and Charles Bartlett, *Facing the Brink: An Intimate Study of Crisis Diplomacy* (New York: Charles Scribner's Sons, 1967), 140; Princeton Seminars, 11 December 1953. Acheson recommended Republican Walter S. Gifford (1885–1966), AT&T's president and board chairman for twenty-five years, who served to the conclusion of the Truman administration.

14 Acheson, "Eclipse of the State Department," 604; Nitze Oral History, TL, 218; Princeton Seminars, 2, 9, and 15 July 1953; *Public Papers of the Presidents of the United States: Harry S. Truman, 1950* (Washington: Government Printing Office, 1965), 151; *PAC*, 282; Reston, "First Year Audit," 38.

15 Truman Papers (PSF), Box 225, March–April 1950 Folder, TL; *New York Times*, 13 December 1951, 23 December 1951, and 23 June 1952; www.trumanlibrary.org/calendar/ (viewed 5/7/05).

16 *PAC*, 276; Princeton Seminars, 2 and 15 July 1953; *Memoranda of the Secretary of State* 51:136, 23 March 1951; Laukhuff Oral History, TL, 154–55; Durward V. Sandifer, Oral History Interview, 15 March and 29 May 1973 (Independence, MO: The Harry S. Truman Library, September 1975), 89; Chace, 198.

17 *PAC*, 137; J. Graham Parsons, Oral History Interview, 1 July 1974 (Independence, MO: The Harry S. Truman Library, March 1978), 99–100; Laukhuff Oral History, TL, 155.

18 Arnold Beichman, *The "Other" State Department: The United States Mission to the United Nations—Its Role in the Making of Foreign Policy* (New York: Basic Books, 1968), 202; *New York Times*, 26 February 1949; Hopkins, 50–51; James E. Webb, "U.S. Organization for the

Conduct of Foreign Affairs," *Department of State Bulletin* 24 (February 1951): 274–75; Princeton Seminars, 2 July 1953; *Executive Sessions of the Senate Foreign Relations Committee . . . 1949–1950* 2: 98–99.

19 J. M. Jones, 113; *PAC*, 718; Dean Acheson, *A Citizen Looks at Congress* (New York: Harper & Brothers, 1957), 65; Hamburger, "Mr. Secretary—II," 54; Brands, *Inside the Cold War*, 296.

20 Reston, "First-Year Audit," 7, 9, 35; Princeton Seminars, 2 July and 10 October 1953; Ben Hill Brown, Oral History Interview, 24 May 1975 (Independence, MO: The Harry S. Truman Library, July 1979), 54; I. M. Destler, *Presidents, Bureaucrats, and Foreign Policy: The Politics of Organizational Reform* (Princeton: Princeton University Press, 1972), 54; Acheson, "Thoughts about Thought," 86–87; 1955 Acheson Oral History, A.M., 46; *PAC*, 21–22; Press Conference, 1–24–51, Acheson Papers, Box 68, Press Conferences-1951 Folder, 6, Press Conferences–1951 Folder, TL.

21 B. H. Brown Oral History, TL, 54–55; Reston, "First-Year Audit," 35; Princeton Seminars, 2 July 1953.

22 Thorp Oral History, TL, 177; Dean Acheson, "Legislative-Executive Relations," *Yale Review* 45 (June 1956): 490; *PAC*, 15; Princeton Seminars, 2 July 1953; *Pattern of Responsibility*, 238; Jack K. McFall, Oral History Interview, 24 June 1970 (Independence, MO: The Harry S. Truman Library, December 1970), 35.

23 Acheson, "Legislative-Executive Relations," 491; Princeton Seminars, 8 July 1953; *New York Times*, 11 January 1950.

24 Miscamble, *Kennan and the Making of American Foreign Policy*, 292n.; *FRUS 1952–1954* 9, Pt. 2: 1808; Chace, 200; Marshall Shulman remarks in May 1994 Shepardson Fellowship Seminar, Council on Foreign Relations, New York; Nitze, *From Hiroshima to Glasnost*, 86–87; idem, "Introduction," xxi; H. Freeman Matthews, Oral History Interview, 7 June 1973 (Independence, MO: The Harry S. Truman Library, January 1976), 31–32; Elbert G. Mathews, Oral History Interview, 13 June 1975 (Independence, MO: The Harry S. Truman Library, December 1979), 50; *New York Times*, 16 August 1951.

25 *New York Times*, 9 November 1951; Memorandum of Conversation, 11 February 1949, Final Visit of Norwegian Foreign Minister, Truman Papers (PSF), Box 183, TL; Laukhuff Oral History, TL, 146–48; Princeton Seminars, 2 and 9 July 1953; Reston, "First-Year Audit," 9, 35; Chace, 198; T. D. Cabot Oral History, TL, 21; Hamburger, "Mr. Secretary—I," 46.

26 Princeton Seminars, 2 July 1953; www.trumanlibrary.org/oralhist/howe.htm, 28 (viewed 5/8/05); John P. Glennon, editor in chief, and Evans Gerakas, editor, *Foreign Relations of the United States: Memoranda of the Secretary of State, 1949–1951, and Meetings and Visits of Foreign Dignitaries, 1949–1952, Microfiche Publication* (Washington: Department of State, 1988): 49:1003 ("Conversation with the President"), 17 November 1949, and 49:1072 ("Meeting with the President"), 20 December 1949, hereafter cited as *Memoranda of the Secretary of State*, and, when available the document's date, topic title, and fiche number on which the document is located. I am grateful to Walter LaFeber for sharing microfilm excerpts of this collection with me.

27 Reston, "New Role," 7; Hamburger, "Mr. Secretary—I," 42, 46, 48; Laukhuff Oral History, TL, 161–63; *Washington Post*, 13 October 1971; 31 July 1995 telephone conversation with George D. Moffett of the *Christian Science Monitor*.

28 Princeton Seminars, 2 and 9 July 1953; Acheson, "Thoughts about Thought," 89; Chace, 200; Laukhuff Oral History, TL, 151; Reston, "First-Year Audit," 9; John D. Hickerson, Oral History Interview, Washington, DC, 10 November 1972, 26 January and 5 June 1973 (Harry S. Truman Library, September 1976), 91; Herbert L. Matthews, *A World in Revolution: A Newspaperman's Memoir* (New York: Charles Scribner's Sons, 1971), 402.

29 Acheson, *Vast External Realm*, 272; *PAC*, 162–63; *New York Times*, 8 January 1949.

30 Vijaya Lakshmi Pandit, *The Scope of Happiness: A Personal Memoir* (New York: Crown, 1979), 251; Russell Oral History, TL, 30; www.trumanlibrary.org/oralhist/andrewss.htm, 31 (viewed 5/8/05). Alsop's animadversions appear in a draft of his memoirs (Joseph W. Alsop Papers, Library of Congress) but not the published version, Joseph W. Alsop, with Adam Platt, *"I've Seen the Best of It": Memoirs* (New York: W. W. Norton, 1992). Thanks to Bruce Craig for sharing the LC document.

31 Stanley Meisler, *United Nations: The First Fifty Years* (New York: Atlantic Monthly Press, 1995), 54; Brian Urquhart, *Ralph Bunche: An American Life* (New York: W. W. Norton, 1993), 225; Jake C. Miller, *The Black Presence in American Foreign Affairs* (Washington: University Press of America, 1978), 58, 64, 90, 111, 296; Brenda Gayle Plummer, *Rising Wind: Black Americans and U.S. Foreign Affairs, 1935–1960* (Chapel Hill: University of North Carolina Press, 1996), 272; Michael L. Krenn, *Black Diplomacy: African Americans and the State Department, 1945–1969* (Armonk, NY: M. E. Sharpe, 1999), chapters 1–3; Dougall, 44; Carol Anderson, *Eyes off the Prize: The United Nations and the African American Struggle for Human Rights, 1944–1955* (New York: Cambridge University Press, 2003), 204; Lankford, 248; Stanley I. Kutler, *The American Inquisition: Justice and Injustice in the Cold War* (New York: Hill and Wang, 1982), 257n; *Dictionary of American Biography, Supplement 8, 1966–1970* (New York: Charles Scribner's Sons, 1988), 589–91.

32 *FRUS 1949* 5: 771; *PAC*, 256; Princeton Seminars, 2 July 1953; Laukhuff Oral History, TL, 155; "Dean Acheson, A Remembrance," 25; McFall Oral History, TL, 95; Lucius D. Battle, Oral History Interview, 23 June 1971 (Independence, MO: The Harry S. Truman Library, September 1980), 10; Chace, 198. Near the end of his term, Acheson moved Battle to a foreign post to help his career, taking on Jeffrey Kitchen in his place. *PAC*, 256, 687; Lucius Battle Oral History, Lyndon Baines Johnson Library (hereafter JL), Austin, Texas.

33 Princeton Seminars, 9 July 1953; W. Henry Lambright, "James Webb and the Uses of Administrative Power," in Jameson W. Doig and Erwin C. Hargrove, eds., *Leadership and Innovation: A Biographical Perspective on Entrepreneurs in Government* (Baltimore: Johns Hopkins University Press, 1987), 176–78, 180–81; T. D. Cabot Oral History, TL, 8–9; "Record of Round-Table Discussion by Twenty-Five Far East Experts with the Department of State on 'American Policy Toward China' October 6, 7, and 8, 1949" (hereafter Round Table), Truman Papers (PSF), Box 174, 3, China–Record of Roundtable Folder, TL; W. Henry Lambright, *Powering Apollo: James E. Webb of NASA* (Baltimore: Johns Hopkins University Press, 1995), 52; Brandon, 73; Acheson to Frankfurter, 19 December 1958, Acheson Papers, Box 11, Folder 147, YUL.

34 Unlike the other regional offices, this position dates back to a division of Latin American affairs formed in 1909.

35 Greece, Turkey, and Iran were then all under this office.

36 *PAC*, 54, 144; Thorp Oral History, TL, 7; Mathews Oral History, TL, 50–51; Philip D. Sprouse Oral History Interview, 11 February 1974 (Independence, MO: The Harry S. Truman Library, March 1977), 11–12; John F. Melby, Oral History Interview, 7, 14, 21, and 28 November 1986 (Independence, MO: The Harry S. Truman Library, October 1988), 232; W. Walton Butterworth Oral History Interview, 6 July 1971 (Independence, MO: The Harry S. Truman Library, May 1983), 53; Arthur R. Ringwalt Oral History Interview, 5 June 1974 (Independence, MO: The Harry S. Truman Library, January 1976), 21–22; *New York Times*, 7 August 1949. In 1949, assistant secretaries were salaried at $10,300 (about $84,500 in 2005 dollars), with congressional plans to boost compensation to $16,000. Congress approved a raise to $15,000 in the same bill raising cabinet secretaries' salaries (including Acheson's) from $15,000 to $22,500 (2005 equivalent: $184,600). *New York Times*, 12 and 15 October 1949; *Executive Sessions of the Senate Foreign Relations Committee . . . 1949–1950* 2: 111, 116.

37 Donald C. Blaisdell, Oral History Interview, 29 October 1973 and 27 June 1975 (Independence, MO: The Harry S. Truman Library, April 1977), 90; Hamburger, "Mr.

Secretary—I," 44; Frederick E. Nolting, Jr., Oral History Interview, 30 June 1975 (Independence, MO: The Harry S. Truman Library, February 1985), 26; Cardozo Oral History, TL, 52; Gary May, *China Scapegoat: The Diplomatic Ordeal of John Carter Vincent*, introduction, John K. Fairbank (Washington: New Republic Books, 1979), 211; *PAC*, 17, 588; Princeton Seminars, 2 July 1953; Adrian Fisher Oral History, JL; Nancy E. Bernhard, "Clearer than Truth: Public Affairs Television and the State Department's Domestic Information Campaigns, 1947–1952," *Diplomatic History* 21 (Fall 1997): 550, 554n.; Lambright, *Powering Apollo*, 51; Thorp Oral History, TL, 7.

38 Bird, *Chairman*, 340; Byroade Oral History, TL, 3, 54, 62–64; Geoffrey W. Lewis Oral History Interview, 15 July 1974 (Independence, MO: The Harry S. Truman Library, October 1978), 64; Laukhuff Oral History, TL, 111, 137.

39 Frank A. Mayer, "George Crews McGhee," in Cathal J. Nolan, ed., *Notable U.S. Ambassadors since 1775* (Westport: Greenwood Press, 1997), 257–58; Matlock Oral History, TL, 116; Danchev, *Franks*, 122; Henry L. Deimel, Oral History Interview, 5 June 1975 (Independence, MO: The Harry S. Truman Library, February 1982), 57–58; Acheson to John Cowles, 2 October 1969, Acheson Papers, Box 7, Folder 85, YUL; *Memoranda of the Secretary of State* 51:307, 18 May 1951.

40 *PAC*, 17, 84; *New York Times*, 24 September 1948.

41 Keith Eagles, "Charles Eustis Bohlen (1904–1974)," in Nolan, 20; Acheson to Bill Tyler, 31 May 1960, Acheson Papers, Box 32, Folder 405, YUL; Frank Pace, Jr., Oral History Interview, 17, 22 January, 17, 25 February, 26 June 1972 (Independence, MO: The Harry S. Truman Library, June 1974), 113.

42 Yergin, *Shattered Peace*, 27; Matthews Oral History, TL, 31–32.

43 Brinkley, *Dean Acheson*, 92; Chace, 273; Lambright, *Powering Apollo*, 52–53; Martin Mayer, *The Diplomats* (Garden City, New York: Doubleday, 1983), 212; Miscamble, *Kennan and the Making of American Foreign Policy*, 157; Hixson, 86–87, 90; Kennan, *Memoirs 1925–1950*, 443, 465; Nitze, *Hiroshima to Glasnost*, 86.

44 Kennan, *Memoirs, 1925–1950*, 426–27; Richard B. Finn, *Winners in Peace: MacArthur, Yoshida, and Postwar Japan* (Berkeley: University of California Press, 1992), 246; John L. Harper, 217–18; Acheson to John P. Frank, n.d. [1967], Acheson Papers, Box 11, Folder 137, YUL; Joint Oral History Interview: The Truman White House. Participants: Charles Murphy, Richard Neustadt, David Stowe, James Webb, by Hugh Heclo and Anna Nelson, 20 February 1980, Washington D.C. (Independence, MO: Harry S. Truman Library, n.d.), 84.

45 Kennan, *Memoirs, 1925–1950*, 426; Remarks at the National War College, 21 December 1949, 7–8; *Executive Sessions of the Senate Foreign Relations Committee . . . 1949–1950*, 2: 104; Miscamble, *Kennan and the Making of American Foreign Policy*, 296; *New York Times*, 28 January 1951; David Callahan, *Dangerous Capabilities: Paul Nitze and the Cold War* (New York: An Edward Burlingame Book, 1990), 70–71. See also my "The Secretary, the Spy, and the Sage," *Diplomatic History* 27 (January 2003): 1–14.

46 Nitze Oral History, TL, 151, 217–18; Chace, 273; Hixson, 52; Talbott, 50; Lambright, *Powering Apollo*, 54; Nitze, *Hiroshima to Glasnost*, 86; John H. Ohly, Oral History Interview, 30 November 1971 (Independence, MO: The Harry S. Truman Library, June 1984), 102–5; Ronald McGlothlen, *Controlling the Waves: Dean Acheson and U.S. Foreign Policy in Asia* (New York: W. W. Norton, 1993), 36; "Dean Acheson, A Remembrance," 2.

47 Dean Rusk, as told to Richard Rusk, ed., Daniel S. Papp, *As I Saw It* (New York: W. W. Norton, 1990), 154; Princeton Seminars, 14 March 1954; Philip D. Sprouse Oral History Interview, 11 February 1974 (Independence, MO: The Harry S. Truman Library, March 1977), 233; Warren I. Cohen, *Dean Rusk*, 34; Rusk, 177.

48 Princeton Seminars, 22 July and 10 October 1953; Dean Acheson, "Philip C. Jessup, Diplomatist," in Wolfgang Friedmann, Louis Henkin, and Oliver Lissitzyn, eds., *Transnational Law in a Changing Society* (New York: Columbia University Press, 1972), 6, 8; Arlene

Lazarowitz, "Philip Caryl Jessup," in Nolan, 195–200; Justus D. Doenecke, *Not to the Swift: The Old Isolationists in the Cold War Era* (Lewisburg: Bucknell University Press, 1979), 215; Allen Weinstein, *Perjury: The Hiss-Chambers Case* (updated edition, New York: Random House, 1997), 16, 338; Alistair Cooke, *A Generation on Trial: U.S.A. v. Alger Hiss* (New York: Alfred A. Knopf, 1950), 302; Princeton Seminars, 10 October 1953; Notes on the President's Meeting with Under Secretary of State James Webb–March 26, 1950–Little White House, Truman Papers (PSF), Box 159, Subj. File–Cabinet, State, Secretary–Misc Folder, TL.

49 Rusk, 160; Chace, 79; Notes on the President's Meeting with Under Secretary of State James Webb–March 26, 1950–Little White House, Truman Papers (PSF), Box 159, Subj. File–Cabinet, State, Secretary–Misc Folder, TL; Princeton Seminars, 14 March 1954. Someone wrote on a January 1949 document on new department appointments: "Warren Austin must go. Phil. Jessup." The unidentified author is presumably reporting Jessup's view. Acheson Papers, Box 58, TL.

50 James S. Pacy and Daniel B. Henderson, "Career Versus Political: A Statistical Overview of Presidential Appointments of United States Chiefs of Mission since 1915," *Diplomacy & Statecraft* 3 (November 1992): 382–403; Nancy Bernkopf Tucker, *Patterns in the Dust: Chinese-American Relations and the Recognition Controversy, 1949–1950* (New York: Columbia University Press, 1983), 159; Lanxin Xiang, *Recasting the Imperial Far East: Britain and America in China, 1945–1950* (Armonk, NY: M. E. Sharpe, 1995), 172; Acheson to Lucius Battle, 7 December 1964, Acheson Papers, Box 2, Folder 26, YUL; *PAC*, 549; Kuniholm, *Origins of the Cold War in the Near East*, 240n.

51 *New York Times*, 23 April 1950.

52 *PAC*, 214; George M. Elsey, Oral History Interview, 10 and 17 February, 9 March 1964, 10 and 17 July 1969, 7 and 10 July 1970 (Independence, MO: The Harry S. Truman Library, May 1974) 2: 319; Leffler, *Preponderance*, 270, 272; Williamson and Rearden, 133; Anna K. Nelson, "Turf Wars: Implementing the National Security Act of 1947" (unpublished paper, 1997), 17.

53 *PAC*, 243; Acheson, "Eclipse of the State Department," 603; Princeton Seminars, 2 July 1953, 10 October 1953; Dean Acheson, recorded interview by Lucius D. Battle, 27 April 1964, p. 23, John F. Kennedy Library Oral History Program (henceforth cited as Acheson Oral History, JFKL); T. D. Cabot Oral History, TL, 44–45.

54 Joseph Alsop and Stewart Alsop, "How Our Foreign Policy Is Made," *Saturday Evening Post*, 30 April 1949, 115; Alsop, *"I've Seen the Best of It,"* 301; Princeton Seminars, 8 July and 10 October 1953; Lambright, *Powering Apollo*, 54–55; *PAC*, 364, 441; Anna Kasten Nelson, "President Truman and the Evolution of the National Security Council," *Journal of American History* 72 (September 1985): 374; Mark A. Stoler, *George C. Marshall: Soldier-Statesman of the American Century* (Boston: Twayne, 1989), 184; Melby Oral History, TL, 213.

55 Princeton Seminars, 8 July 1953; Franks Oral History, TL, 9–10; Matthew J. Connelly, Oral History Interview, 28 and 30 November 1967, 21 August 1968 (Independence, MO: The Harry S. Truman Library, May 1969), 53; *PAC*, 570; John W. Snyder Oral History Interview, 8 November 1967–3 September 1969 (Independence, MO: The Harry S. Truman Library, September 1970), 1016 (hereafter referred to as Snyder Oral History 1967–69, TL); Milton Katz, Oral History Interview, 25 July 1975 (Independence, MO: The Harry S. Truman Library, November 1978), 78.

56 www.trumanlibrary.org/oralhist/howe.htm, 11, 21 (viewed 5/8/05); McGhee Oral History, TL, 17; Battle Oral History, TL, 36–37, 39.

57 Nelson, "Truman and the Evolution of the National Security Council," 365–66, 368, 371–72; Office of the Historian, "Historical Research Project No. 1517: History of the National Security Council" (unpublished; Washington: United States Department of State, Bureau of Public Affairs, June 1987), 5 (hereafter referred to as Project 1517); Millis, 315; Minutes of Secretary's Daily Meetings, 1949–1952, 29 June 1949, Office of Executive

Secretariat, Box 1, RG59, U.S. National Archives, henceforth referred to as Daily Meetings (again thanks to Walter LaFeber for making available a large file of these documents on microfilm); Alsop and Alsop, "How Our Foreign Policy Is Made," 116; Anna K. Nelson, "Reshaping U.S. National Security Policy: NSC 68 as a Case Study" (unpublished paper, 2000), 7–8; Princeton Seminars, 2 July 1953.

58 Interview between Under Secretary of State James E. Webb and Mr. Frank Shea, *Time Magazine*, assisted by Mr. Lloyd Lehrbas, Special Assistant to the Under Secretary, May 4, 1950–11:45 A.M., 12, James Webb Papers, Box 23, TL.

59 Truman to David H. Morgan, 28 January 1952, and to Maury Maverick, 2 July 1952, Ferrell, *Off the Record*, 235, 258; "Dear Boss," 47; *PAC*, 733; Princeton Seminars, 16 July 1953.

60 Battle Oral History, TL, 4; Martin Mayer, 249–50; *PAC*, 105; Elsey Oral History, TL, 1: 1, 7–8, 124; Memorandum for Mr. Murphy: Subject: Secretary Acheson and the Denver Conference, May 24, 14 May 1951, George M. Elsey Papers, Box 101, Personal Correspondence–Acheson Folder, TL; Memorandum for Mr. Murphy: Subject: Proposed Presidential Commission to review U.S. position on international control of atomic energy, 19 April 1950, George M. Elsey Papers, Box 88, National Defense–Atomic, 1950 Folder 2, TL.

61 Rudy Abramson, *Spanning the Century: The Life of W. Averell Harriman, 1891–1986* (New York: William Morrow, 1992), 446; Hamburger, "Mr. Secretary—I," 50; Marshall Shulman remarks in May 1994 Shepardson Fellowship Seminar, Council on Foreign Relations, New York; Princeton Seminars, 2 July 1953; Weintal and Bartlett, 96; Acheson to Anthony Eden, January 1965 (?), Acheson Papers, Box 9, Folder 117, YUL; Heller, *Truman White House*, 40.

62 Acheson to Truman, 12 April 1951, Truman Papers (PSF), Box 160, Subj. File–Cabinet, State, Secy, Acheson Folder, TL.

Chapter 8

1 Acheson to Truman, 18 July 1955, Acheson Papers, Box 31, Folder 394, YUL.

2 Alan K. Henrikson, "The Creation of the North Atlantic Alliance, 1948–1952," *Naval War College Review* 32 (May–June 1980): 11.

3 John P. Glennon, Evans Gerakas, and William F. Sanford, Jr., eds., *Foreign Relations of the United States: Memoranda of Conversations of the Secretary of State, 1947–1952, Microfiche Publication* (Washington: Department of State, 1988), 30 April 1948 (hereafter cited as *Memoranda of Conversations*, with the document's date, sometimes but not always with a topic title); Leffler, *Preponderance of Power*, 215–16; Arthur M. Schlesinger, ed., *The Dynamics of World Power: A Documentary History of United States Foreign Policy, 1945–1973*, Vol. 1, Part 1: *Western Europe*, ed. Robert Dallek (New York: Chelsea House, 1983), 133; Theodore Achilles, Oral History Interview, 13 November and 18 December 1972 (Independence, MO: The Harry S. Truman Library, March 1976), 8–9, 36.

4 Escott Reid, *Time of Fear and Hope: The Making of the North Atlantic Treaty 1947–1949* (Toronto: McClelland and Stewart, 1977), 63; Pollard, "Economic Security and the Origins of the Cold War," 284; Ottavio Barié, "The Final Stage of Negotiations: December 1948 to April 1949," and Gaddis Smith, "The Atlantic Pact as a Problem of U.S. Diplomacy," in Ennio Di Nolfo, ed., *The Atlantic Pact Forty Years Later: A Historical Reappraisal* (New York: Walter de Gruyter, 1991), 56, 68; Tony Judt, "New Germany, Old NATO," *New York Review of Books*, 29 May 1997, 44; G. John Ikenberry, *After Victory: Institutions, Strategic Restraint, and the Rebuilding of Order after Major Wars* (Princeton: Princeton University Press, 2001), 207.

5 *Pattern of Responsibility*, 60; *Memoranda of Conversations*, 1 April 1949, North Atlantic Treaty; Notes on Meeting in Secretary's Office on MacArthur Testimony May 16, 1951, Acheson Papers, Box 63, MacArthur Testimony Folder, TL; *FRUS 1949* 6: 448.

6 Theodore Achilles, Oral History Interview, 13 November and 18 December 1972 (Independence, MO: The Harry S. Truman Library, March 1976), 36; *FRUS 1949* 3: 507–8; Princeton Seminars, 15 July 1953; Sir Nicholas Henderson, *The Birth of NATO* (Boulder: Westview Press, 1983), 83; *FRUS 1949* 4: 85–86; R. D. Cuff and J. L. Granatstein, *Canadian-American Relations in Wartime: From the Great War to the Cold War* (Toronto: Hakkert, 1975), 126–27; Reid, 167, 172, 178; Danchev, *Franks*, 102; idem, "Taking the Pledge: Oliver Franks and the Negotiation of the North Atlantic Treaty," *Diplomatic History* 15 (Spring 1991): 199–219; Baylis, *Diplomacy of Pragmatism*, 111–12; Alan K. Henrikson, "Ottawa, Washington, and the Founding of NATO," in Joel J. Sokolsky and Joseph T. Jockel, eds., *Fifty Years of Canada–United States Defense Cooperation: The Road from Ogdensburg* (Lewiston, NY: Edwin Mellen Press, 1992), 111; *Documents on Canadian External Relations. Volume 15: 1949*, ed., Hector Mackenzie (Ottawa: Department of Foreign Affairs and International Trade, 1995), 517, 527, 547; Lester B. Pearson, *Mike: The Memoirs of The Right Honourable Lester B. Pearson, PC, CC, OM, OBE, MA, LLD: Volume 2: 1948–1957*, ed. John A. Munro and Alex. I. Inglis (Toronto: University of Toronto Press, 1973), 68; Hopkins, 248; *PAC*, 70, 277.

7 Henderson, *Birth of NATO*, 91; Baylis, *Diplomacy of Pragmatism*, 109; Hermann-Josef Rupieper, "American Policy toward German Unification, 1949–1955," in Diefendorf, Frohn, and Rupieper, 48; *Documents on Canadian External Relations* 15: 532; *PAC*, 282.

8 Hopkins, 19–20, 51, 88, 249; Danchev, *Franks*, 103–4, 116, 118–19; idem, "In the back room: Anglo-American defence cooperation, 1945–51," in Richard J. Aldrich, ed., *British Intelligence, Strategy, and the Cold War, 1945–1951* (London: Routledge, 1992): 217; Franks Oral History, TL, 1–2, 27; *New York Times*, 18 October 1992; *PAC*, 288, 323; Gaddis Smith, *Acheson*, 144; Brandon, 75; Henrikson, "Ottawa, Washington," 92. Paris would have been badly wounded had it known of the Acheson-Franks meetings. Franks also had easy access to Jessup, Nitze, Rusk, and Kennan. Danchev, "In the back room," 218. He later served as chairman of Lloyds Bank and headed a life insurance company before returning to academic life. His last public service was to head a study of the 1982 Falklands War. Knighted in 1945, he was elevated to the peerage in 1962 and died in 1992.

9 *FRUS 1949* 4: 117; Danchev, *Franks*, 104–5; Baylis, *Diplomacy of Pragmatism*, 214; Hopkins, 111; Cook, 214; Schlesinger, *Dynamics of World Power*, Vol. I, Part 1, 141; *Documents on Canadian External Relations* 15: 521; John W. Young, *France, the Cold War, and the Western Alliance, 1944–49: French Foreign Policy and Post-war Europe* (New York: St. Martin's Press, 1990), 217.

10 Lange Oral History, TL, 11; Henderson, *Birth of NATO*, 42, 85; *PAC*, 278–79; Danchev, *Franks*, 105–6; *FRUS 1949* 4: 123, 125–35, 141–42; Cees Wiebes and Bert Zeeman, "United States' 'Big Stick' Diplomacy: The Netherlands between Decolonization and Alignment, 1945–1949," *International History Review* 14 (February 1992): 55; Klaus Schwabe, "The Origins of the United States' Engagement in Europe," Irwin M. Wall, "France and the North Atlantic Alliance," and E. Timothy Smith, "United States Security and the Integration of Italy into the Western Bloc, 1947–1949," in Heller and Gillingham, 52–53, 87–89, 175; *Memoranda of the Secretary of State* 49:124, 2 March 1949; Daily Meetings, 2 March 1949; E. Timothy Smith, "The Fear of Subversion: The United States and the Inclusion of Italy in the North Atlantic Treaty," *Diplomatic History* 7 (Spring 1983): 139–55.

11 Leffler, *Preponderance of Power*, 281; Baylis, *Diplomacy of Pragmatism*, 114; Lawrence S. Kaplan, *The Long Entanglement: NATO's First Fifty Years* (Westport: Praeger, 1999), 33; idem, "Dean Acheson and the Atlantic Community," in Brinkley, *Acheson and . . . U.S. Foreign Policy*, 45–46; Grosser, 86; Valur Ingimundarson, "Between Solidarity and Neutrality: The Nordic Countries and the Cold War, 1945–1991," *CWIHPB* (Issues 11, Winter 1998): 272.

12 *PAC*, 277; Reid, 93; Hickerson Oral History, TL, 78–79; Daily Meetings, 9 March 1949. Emphasis in original.

13 Marshall D. Shulman, *Stalin's Foreign Policy Reappraised* (Cambridge: Harvard University Press, 1963), 63; *Memoranda of the Secretary of State* 49:139 (Memorandum by the Director of the Executive Secretariat [Humelsine] to the Secretary of State's Special Assistant [Battle]), 9 March 1949; *Memoranda of the Secretary of State* 49:159, 21 March 1949; *New York Times*, 26 February 1949; Luc De Vos, "A Little 'Fish' in a Big Political 'Pool'—Belgium's Cautious Contribution to the Rise of Military Integration in Western Europe," in Norbert Wiggershaus and Roland G. Foerster, eds., assisted by Birgit Schulz and Winfried Heinemann, *The Western Security Community, 1948–1950: Common Problems and Conflicting National Interests during the Foundation Phase of the North Atlantic Alliance* (Oxford: Berg, 1993): 102; Vojtech Mastny, "The New History of Cold War Alliances," *Journal of Cold War Studies* 4 (Spring 2002): 61.

14 Press and Radio News Conference on North Atlantic Pact, Friday, March 18, 1949–9 A.M., Acheson Papers, Box 68, Press Conf. 1949–53, Jan.–June 1949 Folder, TL, 1, 15–17, 22–23; *Strengthening the Forces of Freedom*, 80–87; *FRUS 1949* 4: 244.

15 Pearson, 60; *PAC*, 283–84; Truman, *Years of Trial and Hope*, 253; Henderson, *Birth of NATO*, 112; Young, *France, the Cold War, and the Western Alliance*, 220; Reid, 63.

16 B. H. Brown Oral History, TL, 10–11; Henry Byroade, Oral History Interview, 19 and 21 September 1988 (Independence, MO: The Harry S. Truman Library, November 1989), 67; Hixson, 82; *Memoranda of Conversations*, 9 March 1949, Policy with respect to Germany.

17 Pollard, "Economic Security and the Origins of the Cold War," 278; Lightner Oral History, TL, 90–91; Norman M. Naimark, "'To Know Everything and to Report Everything Worth Knowing': Building the East German Police State, 1945–1949" (Washington: Cold War International History Project, Woodrow Wilson International Center for Scholars, Working Paper No. 10, August 1994), 3.

18 William I. Hitchcock, "France, the Western Alliance, and the Origins of the Schuman Plan, 1948–1950," *Diplomatic History* 21 (Fall 1997): 616–17n.; Leffler, "Negotiating from Strength," 189.

19 *New York Times*, 3 September 1946; Leffler, *Preponderance of Power*, 230–31; Princeton Seminars, 9 July 1953; Acheson to Robert S. McNamara, 19 September 1963, Acheson Papers, YUL.

20 *PAC*, 267–70, 272–74; Princeton Seminars, 9 July 1953; *FRUS 1949* 3: 156–58, 666–67, 694–95, 705–13, 717–18, 721; Acheson, "Philip C. Jessup," 7; Clay Oral History, TL, 41–42; Gaddis Smith, *Acheson*, 82–90; *Memoranda of Conversations*, 31 March 1949, Conversation with Mr. Bevin; Philip C. Jessup, "Park Avenue Diplomacy—Ending the Berlin Blockade," *Political Science Quarterly* 87 (September 1972): 377–400.

21 Reston, "First-Year Audit," 36; Melvyn P. Leffler, "The United States and the Strategic Dimensions of the Marshall Plan," *Diplomatic History* 12 (Summer 1988): 296; Wilson D. Miscamble, "Deciding to Divide Germany: American Policymaking in 1949," *Diplomacy & Statecraft* 2 (July 1991): 315n.; Byroade Oral History, TL, 61; Princeton Seminars, 9 July 1953.

22 *FRUS 1949* 3: 51–53, 84–88, 113, 547–48, 561, 563, 573; Princeton Seminars, 9 July 1953; Memo for Pres. 1–27–49, Truman Papers (PSF), Box 220, NSC Meetings . . . Discussions (1949) Folder, TL; Digest of Meeting of the NSC Sub-Committee on Germany held on Friday, January 28, 1949, at 9:00 A.M. in the Cabinet Room of the White House, Truman Papers (PSF), Box 219, NSC Meetings . . . Regular . . . Data Folder, TL.

23 Kennan, *Memoirs 1925–1950*, 443; Nitze Oral History, TL, 208; *FRUS 1949* 3: 90–93; Miscamble, *Kennan and the Making of American Foreign Policy*, 149–54, 160–61, 166–71, 174, 193, 282, 283.

24 Princeton Seminars, 9 July 1953; *PAC*, 286; Acheson Talk, Thursday, Dec. 22, 1949, Reston Papers, Box 30, Working Files, UIA; Reston, "First-Year Audit," 36; Jean Edward Smith, *Lucius D. Clay: An American Life* (New York: Henry Holt, 1990), 536; *Memoranda of Conversations*, 9 March 1949, Policy with respect to Germany; Trachtenberg, *Constructed Peace*, 105n.

25 Daily Meetings, 15 March 1949; *FRUS 1949* 3: 106–13, 118–37; *Memoranda of the Secretary of State* 49:157, 21 March 1949; J. E. Smith, *Lucius D. Clay*, 537; Annan, "Dean of the Cold War," 13.

26 Princeton Seminars, 9 July 1953; Thomas A. Schwartz, *America's Germany: John J. McCloy and the Federal Republic of Germany* (Cambridge: Harvard University Press, 1991), 37–38; *FRUS 1949* 3: 137–38, 140–42, 861; Miscamble, "Deciding to Divide Germany," 303; Miscamble, *Kennan and the Making of American Foreign Policy*, 164.

27 *FRUS 1949* 3: 158–71, 173–76, 233–35; Hitchcock, "France, the Western Alliance," 617; *PAC*, 272; Schwartz, *America's Germany*, 38–39; Miscamble, *Kennan and the Making of American Foreign Policy*, 165; *New York Times*, 8 and 9 April 1949.

28 Schwartz, *America's Germany*, 41–42; Carolyn Woods Eisenberg, *Drawing the Line: The American Decision to Divide Germany, 1944–1949* (Cambridge, UK: Cambridge University Press, 1996), 70; Acheson, *Sketches from Life*, 22; Riddleberger Oral History, TL, 42; Lewis Oral History, TL, 63.

29 *FRUS 1949* 3: 249, 730, 859–61; Terence Prittie, *Konrad Adenauer 1876–1967* (London: Tom Stacey, 1972), 138; Notes on 5–6/49 CFM: Preparations, Germany, Sov. arms, etc., Princeton Seminars; Princeton Seminars, 16 July 1953; Reston, "First-Year Audit," 35; *Memoranda of the Secretary of State* 49:300, 29 April 1949; Miscamble, *Kennan and the Making of American Foreign Policy*, 166–67; Daily Meetings, 21 April 1949.

30 Dean Acheson, *The Current Situation in Germany* (Washington: Office of Public Affairs, Department of State, 1949), 1–2, 4; *New York Times*, 29 and 30 April 1949; *FRUS 1949* 3: 749–50.

31 In German, *Grundgesetz*.

32 *FRUS 1949* 3: 865–67; Miscamble, *Kennan and the Making of American Foreign Policy*, 166–68; E-mail of Stephen A. Schuker to author, 1 October 1998.

33 *Memoranda of the Secretary of State* 49:351–53 (An Approach to the CFM), 9 March 1949; *PAC*, 291; Kennan, *Memoirs 1925–1950*, 444.

34 Reston, *Deadline*, 323; Bohlen, 285–86; Miscamble, *Kennan and the Making of American Foreign Policy*, 169–71; Schwartz, *America's Germany*, 39–40; Princeton Seminars, 16 July 1953; *FRUS 1949* 3: 875–76, 884–85; Kennan, *Memoirs 1925–1950*, 444; Notes on 5–6/49 CFM: Preparations, Germany, Sov. arms, etc., Princeton Seminars; Leffler, *Preponderance of Power*, 281; Memorandum for the President, May 18, 1949, Truman Papers (PSF), Box 220, NSC Meetings . . . Discussions (1949) Folder, TL.

35 Secretary's Off the Record Press Conference, August 26, 1949, Acheson Papers, Box 68, Press Conf. 1949–53, July–Dec. 1949 Folder, TL, 5–7 (hereafter Off the Record Press Conference, August 26, 1949); *Reviews of the World Situation, 1949–1950*, Volume 8 of *The Legislative Origins of American Foreign Policy: The Senate Foreign Relations Committee in Executive Session, 1913–1933; 1947–1950*, ed. Richard D. Challener (New York: Garland Publishing, Inc., 1979), 5, 11, 14, 20; henceforth *Reviews of the World Situation*.

36 Norman A. Graebner, "Dean G. Acheson, 1949–1953," in Graebner, ed., *An Uncertain Tradition: American Secretaries of State in the Twentieth Century* (New York: McGraw-Hill, 1961), 273; *Reviews of the World Situation*, 16–17; *Strengthening the Forces of Freedom*, 123; Vandenberg, 485. Though Acheson and Truman had invited Vandenberg and Connally to join the Paris delegation, all then agreed they would better serve at home advancing ratification of the NATO pact. *New York Times*, 10 May 1949.

37 *FRUS 1949* 3: 887–90.

38 *PAC*, 293; Leffler, "Strategic Dimensions of the Marshall Plan," 297; Nitze, *Hiroshima to Glasnost*, 72.

39 *PAC*, 293–94; McLellan, *State Department Years*, 156, 248–50.

40 Nicholas Henderson, *Inside the Private Office: Memoirs of the Secretary to British Foreign Ministers* (Chicago: Academy Chicago, 1987), 21, 32, 51; Offner, 87; Donald Neff, *Fallen Pillars:*

U.S. Policy towards Palestine and Israel since 1945 (Washington: Institute for Palestine Studies, 1995), 45; Acheson, *Sketches from Life*, 1–3, 8; Saville, 96; Robin Edmonds, *Setting the Mould: The United States and Britain 1945–1949* (Oxford: Oxford University Press, 1986), 184; Brandon, 74; Anthony Eden, *The Memoirs of Anthony Eden: Full Circle* (Boston: Houghton Mifflin, 1960), 221; *PAC*, 270–71; Cook, 75; Princeton Seminars, 9 July 1953; Eben A. Ayers, Oral History Interview, 12 January 1967–30 June 1970 (Independence, MO: The Harry S. Truman Library, August 1972), 56; *FRUS 1949* 9: 50.

41 *PAC*, 271–72; Acheson, *Sketches from Life*, 31–32, 34; Princeton Seminars, 9 July 1953.

42 Remarks at the National War College, 21 December 1949, 7; Georges Bidault, *Resistance: The Political Autobiography of Georges Bidault*, trans., Marianne Sinclair (New York: Frederick A. Praeger, 1967), 131; *Memoranda of Conversations*, 2 May 1952; Henderson, *Inside the Private Office*, 46; *PAC*, 34, 294; Princeton Seminars, 16 July 1953; C. L. Sulzberger, *A Long Row of Candles: Memoirs and Diaries [1934–1954]* (Toronto: Macmillan, 1969), 446.

43 *Memoranda of the Secretary of State* M-12, 21 May 1949; *FRUS 1949* 3: 818, 892–94; Nitze, *Hiroshima to Glasnost*, 72.

44 *PAC*, 295, 297; Acheson, *Sketches from Life*, 8; Henderson, *Inside the Private Office*, 44; *FRUS 1949* 3: 918–20, 923, 925; Notes on 5–6/49 CFM: Comment on Sov. German proposal, Princeton Seminars; *Reviews of the World Situation*, 26; *New York Times*, 25–26 May 1949; Theodore H. White, *In Search of History: A Personal Adventure* (New York: Harper & Row, 1978), 344; *Memoranda of the Secretary of State* 49:402, 26 May 1949.

45 Isaac Kramnick and Barry Sheerman, *Harold Laski: A Life on the Left* (New York: Allen Lane, Penguin Press, 1993), 348; Mark Wilkinson, ed., with Timothy C. Dowling, *The Cold War: Opening Shots, 1945–1950* (Lexington, VA: Virginia Military Institute, 2003), 60; *FRUS 1949* 3: 928–31; *PAC*, 297.

46 *FRUS 1949* 3: 934–56; Notes on 5–6/49 CFM: Vyshinsky-Bevin exchange re sleep (6/2/49), Princeton Seminars; *PAC*, 297–98; *New York Times*, 5 June 1949; Hans W. Gatzke, *Germany and the United States: A "Special Relationship?"* (Cambridge: Harvard University Press, 1980), 164.

47 *FRUS 1949* 3: 957–63, 965–66, 970–75, 977–83; Notes on 5–6/49 CFM: Vyshinsky-Bevin exchange re sleep (6/2/49), Princeton Seminars; Notes on 5–6/49 CFM: 6/7/49: DA "cracks" at Vyshinsky, Princeton Seminars; *Documents on Canadian External Relations* 15: 75; *Memoranda of the Secretary of State* 49:471, 9 June 1949; LaFeber, *American Age*, 494.

48 Theodore H. White, 344; *New York Times*, 12 and 13 June 1949; Remarks at the National War College, 21 December 1949, 6; *PAC*, 300; Acheson, *Sketches from Life*, 88; *FRUS 1949* 3: 983–92, 997–1007; Princeton Seminars, 16 July 1953; *Memoranda of the Secretary of State*, M-74, M-75, 14 June 1949. Both contemporary and scholarly usage alternate between MAP (Mutual Assistance Program) and MDAP (Mutual Defense Assistance Program). I mostly use the latter.

49 *FRUS 1949* 3: 1009–39; *Reviews of the World Situation*, 33; Rolf Steininger, "1955: The Austrian State Treaty and the German Question," *Diplomacy & Statecraft* 3 (November 1992): 495; *PAC*, 300–301.

50 *PAC*, 301; *New York Times*, 24 June and 1 July 1949; *Strengthening the Forces of Freedom*, 5, 124–27; Milovan Djilas, *Conversations with Stalin*, trans., Michael B. Petrovich (New York: Harcourt, Brace & World, Inc., 1962), 153; Norman M. Naimark, *The Russians in Germany: A History of the Soviet Zone of Occupation, 1945–1949* (Cambridge: Belknap Press of Harvard University Press, 1995), 9; Mastny, *Cold War and Soviet Insecurity*, 25, 79, 193.

51 Hamby, *Beyond the New Deal*, 364; *Reviews of the World Situation*, 23–25, 27–28, 31, 33–34, 38–41, 43–44, 46; Nitze, *Hiroshima to Glasnost*, 72.

52 See McLellan, *State Department Years*, 163, for another view.

53 Notes on 5–6/49 CFM: Wrapup, significance of CFM ("p. 15"), Princeton Seminars; Princeton Seminars, 9 and 16 July 1953; Acheson to Truman, 21 July 1953, Acheson Papers,

Box 30, Folder 391, YUL; Acheson to Bullock, 25 February 1955, Acheson Papers, Box 4, Folder 51, YUL.

Chapter 9

1 Acheson, *Vast External Realm*, 7; *PAC*, 726; Acheson, "Fifty Years After," 3–5; *Pattern of Responsibility*, 42; U.S. Congress, House Committee on International Relations, *Selected Executive Session Hearings of the Committee, 1943–1950: Historical Series. Volume IV: Foreign Economic Assistance Programs, Part 2* (Washington: Government Printing Office, 1976): 38 (hereafter *Selected Executive Session Hearings of the Committee, 1943–1950*); Ninkovich, *Modernity and Power*, 193; Acheson, *Democrat*, 62. The phrase "vast external realm," which Acheson repeatedly quoted, appears in Justice George Sutherland's opinion in the 1936 Supreme Court case, *United States v. Curtiss-Wright Export Corporation*.

2 Reston, *Deadline*, 146; Rusk, 532; *PAC*, 923; Brandon, 96; Acheson to Truman, 4 December 1956, Acheson Papers, Box 31, Folder 395, YUL; Princeton Seminars, 15 May 1954.

3 *PAC*, 727; *Selected Executive Session Hearings of the Committee, 1943–1950*, 38–39; Acheson, "Fifty Years After," 7.

4 *Patterns of Responsibility*, 19, 21–23, 30, 240; SR71–125, Dean Acheson Interviewed by Eric Sevareid, 8 November 1969, Recording, Part I, TL; *FRUS 1951* 3, Pt. 1: 657; *PAC*, 376; Acheson, *Sketches from Life*, 103; Schlesinger, *Dynamics of World Power*, Vol. II, Part 1, 411; *New York Times*, 10 October 1969; *FRUS 1952–1954* 12, Pt. 1: 181; Address Made Off the Record before the American Society of Newspaper Editors by the Honorable Dean Acheson, Acting Secretary of State, Washington, D.C., April 18, 1947, 2, Acheson Papers, Box 69, TL; *The Presidential Documents Series: Official Conversations and Meetings of Dean Acheson* [1949–53], microfilm (Frederick, MD: University Press of America, 1980), reel 1; Thomas G. Paterson, *Meeting the Communist Threat: Truman to Reagan* (New York: Oxford University Press, 1988), 44; *FRUS 1950* 3: 1722; Acheson to Clark Clifford, 17 January 1949, Clark Clifford Papers, Box 39, Inaugural Address, Folder 1, TL. Emphasis in original.

5 1955 Acheson Oral History, A.M., 6–7; *FRUS 1949* 5: 603–4, 1: 612–17; Acheson, *Democrat*, 196–97.

6 Acheson, "Fifty Years After," 3–5; *Selected Executive Session Hearings of the Committee, 1943–1950*, 38–40; Princeton Seminars, 2 July 1953; *Memoranda of Conversations*, 19 November April 1951, Various Matters Raised . . . ; *Strengthening the Forces of Freedom*, 84.

7 Acheson to Truman, 5 February 1954, Box 30, Folder 392, and 17 September 1958, Box 31, Folder 397, Acheson Papers, YUL; Princeton Seminars, 11 October 1953; "Mr. Acheson Answers Some Questions," *New York Times Book Review*, 12 October 1969, 2; "Hard Words from the veteran American statesman Dean Acheson, in conversation with William Hardcastle," *The Listener*, 18 June 1970, 827.

8 *United States Foreign Policy for a Post-War Recovery Program*, 703, 737; Press-Radio 4/8/49, Acheson Papers, Box 68, Press Conf. 1949–53, Jan.–June 1949 Folder, TL; U.S., Congress, House Committee on Foreign Affairs, *Selected Executive Session Hearings of the Committee, 1951–1956. Historical Series. Vol. 15, European Problems* (Washington: Government Printing Office, 1980), 161 (hereafter *Selected Executive Session Hearings of the Committee, 1951–1956*); "Essentials of Peace," February 8, 1950, No. 124, Reston Papers, Box 30, Working Files, UIA.

9 Acheson to Truman, 5 February 1954, Acheson Papers, Box 30, Folder 392, YUL; *Pattern of Responsibility*, 24; McLellan, *State Department Years*, 162, 181; "Mr. Acheson Answers Some Questions," 31. Wilson D. Miscamble has also found the architect metaphor useful, arguing that George F. Kennan was the "rejected architect" of the western postwar system, while Acheson was its "master builder." "Rejected Architect and Master Builder: George

Kennan, Dean Acheson, and Postwar Europe," *Review of Politics* 58 (Summer 1996): especially 457–62.

10 *New York Times*, 3 February 1949; *FRUS 1949* 5: 637; Walter LaFeber, "NATO and the Korean War: A Context," in Lawrence S. Kaplan, ed., *American Historians and the Atlantic Alliance* (Kent: Kent State University Press, 1991), 40–41.

11 *Pattern of Responsibility*, 52–53; *FRUS 1949* 3: 748; *New York Times*, 9 April and 9 August 1949; Princeton Seminars, 16 July 1953; *FRUS 1949* 5: 627; Off the Record Press Conference, August 26, 1949.

12 John Lewis Gaddis, *Strategies of Containment: A Critical Appraisal of Postwar American National Security Policy* (New York: Oxford University Press, 1982), 62–63; *Strengthening the Forces of Freedom*, 88–90; *PAC*, 285; Princeton Seminars, 16 July 1953; *New York Times*, 24 June 1949; Achilles Oral History, TL, 75.

13 E. Timothy Smith, *The United States, Italy and NATO, 1947–52* (New York: St. Martin's Press, 1991), 110; Helen Leigh-Phippard, *Congress and US Military Aid to Britain* (London: St. Martin's Press, 1995), 29; *PAC*, 307; Outline on "Defense of Europe," Princeton Seminars; Paris to Secretary of State, 27 May 1949, Truman Papers (PSF), Box 163, Subj. File—Conferences, Paris Conf. May '49 Folder, TL; *FRUS 1949* 1: 288; David R. Kepley, *The Collapse of the Middle Way: Senate Republicans and the Bipartisan Foreign Policy, 1948–1952* (Westport: Greenwood Press, 1988), 27; *Memoranda of the Secretary of State* 49:50 (Subject: Discussion with Senators Connally and Vandenberg), 15 June 1949.

14 Schlesinger, *Dynamics of World Power*, Vol. I, Part I, 144; *PAC*, 307–12; Pach, *Arming the Free World*, 222; U.S. Congress, Senate Committee on Foreign Relations, *Military Assistance Program, 1949; Held in Executive Session before the Committee on Foreign Relations and the Committee on Armed Services, United States Senate, Eighty-first Congress, First Session on S.2388*, introduction, Richard D. Challener (Washington: Government Printing Office, 1974), vi (hereafter *Military Assistance Program*), 22; Lawrence S. Kaplan, *The United States and NATO: The Formative Years* (Lexington: University Press of Kentucky, 1984), 126; Daily Meetings, 3 August 1949. The requested appropriation was the equivalent of $11.5 billion in 2004 dollars.

15 *New York Times*, 29 July 1949; *Strengthening the Forces*, 91–100; *PAC*, 312.

16 Kaplan, *Long Entanglement*, 52; idem, *United States and NATO*, 126; *PAC*, 307, 309; Thomas J. Christensen, *Useful Adversaries: Grand Strategy, Domestic Mobilization, and Sino-American Conflict, 1947–1958* (Princeton: Princeton University Press, 1996), 96; *Military Assistance Program*, vi; *Memoranda of Conversations*, 16 September 1949, Visit of Norwegian Foreign Minister; Outline on "Defense of Europe," Princeton Seminars.

17 *FRUS 1949* 6: 449; E. Timothy Smith, *US, Italy and NATO*, 99; Princeton Seminars, 10 October 1953; *FRUS 1949* 4: 353ff.

18 Guy de Carmoy, *The Foreign Policies of France, 1944–1968*, trans., Elaine P. Halperin (Chicago: University of Chicago Press, 1970), 27; Press and Radio News Conference, Friday, August 12, 1949—12:20 P.M., Acheson Papers, Box 68, Press Conf. 1949–53, July–Dec. 1949 Folder, TL; *Strengthening the Forces of Freedom*, 128–29; Emerg. of W. Germany, Synopses, Princeton Seminars.

19 Gatzke, 181; *New York Times*, 16 September and 13 October 1949; Hitchcock, "France, the Western Alliance," 618; *FRUS 1949* 3: 381, 385, 533; Emerg. of W. Germany, Synopses, Princeton Seminars.

20 Emerg. of W. Germany, Synopses, Princeton Seminars; David Clay Large, *Germans to the Front: West German Rearmament in the Adenauer Era* (Chapel Hill: University of North Carolina Press, 1996), 39; Conversation with the President, Item 2, Rearmament of Germany, 17 November 1949, Acheson Papers, Box 64, TL. I am grateful to Arnold Offner for use of a number of documents he had copied at the Truman Library.

21 *FRUS 1949* 3: 597, 599–603, 618ff.; *Memoranda of Conversations*, 15 September 1949; Emerg. of W. Germany, Synopses, Princeton Seminars; Bird, *Chairman*, 324.

22 Princeton Seminars, 16 July 1953; Scott Newton, "The 1949 sterling crisis and British policy towards European integration," *Review of International Studies* 11 (July 1985): 172, 180; Acheson to Alastair Buchan, n.d. (1963?), Acheson Papers, Box 4, Folder 50, YUL; *Pattern of Responsibility*, 296; Block, 240n.

23 Leffler, *Preponderance of Power*, 312, 321; Hogan, "American Marshall Planners," 48–49.

24 Leffler, *Preponderance of Power*, 315–16; Hitchcock, "France, the Western Alliance," 620–21; *Memoranda of Conversations*, 15 September 1949. Acheson worried as little about the ideology of French Socialists as about the British Laborites, and for the same reason—they were usually good diplomatic partners. Kisatsky, 625.

25 Leffler, "Strategic Dimensions of the Marshall Plan," 298; Daily Meetings, 18 October 1949; Saki Dockrill, *Britain's Policy for West German Rearmament, 1950–1955* (Cambridge: Cambridge University Press, 1991), 19; Leffler, *Preponderance of Power*, 285, 320; Schwartz, *America's Germany*, 103; François Duchêne, *Jean Monnet: The First Statesman of Interdependence* (New York: W. W. Norton, 1994), 190; Hitchcock, "France, the Western Alliance," 619; *FRUS 1949* 3: 420, and 4: 469–70; Michael J. Hogan, "The Rise and Fall of Economic Diplomacy: Dean Acheson and the Marshall Plan," in Brinkley, *Acheson and . . . U.S. Foreign Policy*, 11; Roy Rempel, "The Anglo-Saxon Powers and the German Rearmament Question: 1950–1954" (unpublished paper, 1994), 12; J. L. Harper, 219–20.

26 Franks Oral History, TL, 21; Press-Radio 2–9–49, Acheson Papers, Box 68, Press Conf. 1949–53, Jan.–June 1949 Folder, TL, 7; *Memoranda of Conversations*, 3 April 1949; Block, 99; Miscamble, *Kennan and the Making of American Foreign Policy*, 290–91; *Memoranda of Conversations*, 3 November 1949, ECA Administrator Hoffman's forthcoming trip to Europe; Princeton Seminars, 9 July 1953; *FRUS 1949* 4: 346, 348–49.

27 Off the Record Press Conference, August 26, 1949; Franks Oral History, TL, 8; Dougall, 42; Andrew J. Rotter, *The Path to Vietnam: Origins of the American Commitment to Southeast Asia* (Ithaca: Cornell University Press, 1987), 145–46; *Strengthening the Forces of Freedom*, 51–60; *Memoranda of the Secretary of State* 49:1033, 3 December 1949.

28 Merry, 182; Michael J. Hogan, *The Marshall Plan: America, Britain, and the Reconstruction of Western Europe, 1947–1952* (Cambridge: Cambridge University Press, 1987), 249; Hopkins, 119–31.

29 Hopkins, 132–35; Hogan, *Marshall Plan*, 262; Franks Oral History, TL, 9–10; Hogan, "Rise and Fall of Economic Diplomacy," 12; Leffler, *Preponderance of Power*, 317; Miscamble, *Kennan and the Making of American Foreign Policy*, 287; *FRUS 1949* 4: 338–39, 847–48; *FRUS 1949* 3: 461; Gillingham, *Coal, Steel, and the Rebirth of Europe*, 171; Ninkovich, *Modernity and Power*, 181.

30 *United States Foreign Policy for a Post-War Recovery Program*, 739.

31 Nathaniel P. Davis, *Few Dull Moments: A Foreign Service Career* (Philadelphia: Dunlap Printing, 1967), 140; *FRUS 1949* 5: 21; McLellan, *State Department Years*, 256; Mastny, *Cold War and Soviet Insecurity*, 72; Acheson to Norman A. Graebner, 29 May 1959, Acheson Papers, Box 13, Folder 170, YUL.

32 *FRUS 1949* 6: 415, 438; 2, Pt. 1: 294; and 5: 235, 239, 241, 247, 368; *A Decade of American Foreign Policy: Basic Documents, 1941–1949*, rev. ed. (Washington: Department of State, 1985), 516; Joseph F. Harrington and Bruce J. Courtney, *Tweaking the Nose of the Russians: Fifty Years of American-Romanian Relations, 1940–1990* (Boulder: East European Monographs, distributed by Columbia University Press, 1991), 73; Lorraine M. Lees, *Keeping Tito Afloat: The United States, Yugoslavia, and the Cold War* (University Park: Pennsylvania State University Press, 1997), 99; *New York Times*, 25 February 1950 and 21 July 1949; *Strengthening the Forces of Freedom*, 112–13; Acheson to Bela Varga, 22 August 1950, Acheson Papers, Box 43, Secretary of State, 1949–53, Alph.—V Folder, TL; Mastny, *Cold War and Soviet Insecurity*, 83; *FRUS 1951* 4, Pt. 2: 1350.

33 *FRUS 1949* 5: 314–16, 318–19, 873–74, 957, and 6: 438; *FRUS 1950* 4: 363; Mastny, *Cold War and Soviet Insecurity*, 80–81; Thomas Powers, *The Man Who Kept the Secrets: Richard Helms & the CIA* (New York: Alfred A. Knopf, 1979), 44–45; William Blum, *The CIA: A Forgotten History: US Global Interventions since World War 2* (London: Zed Books, 1986), 56; John Prados, *Presidents' Secret Wars: CIA and Pentagon Covert Operations since World War II* (New York: William Morrow, 1986), 48; Bruce Page, David Leach, and Philip Knightley, *The Philby Conspiracy* (New York: Ballantine Books, 1981), 178–84; Nicholas Bethell, *The Great Betrayal: The Untold Story of Kim Philby's Biggest Coup* (London: Hodder and Stoughton, 1984), 111. Soviet forces helped liberate Belgrade in 1945 (and then left Yugoslavia), but Tito's partisan army did the main job of expelling Germany and its Axis partners.

34 Jussi Hanhimäki, "Self-Restraint as Containment: United States' Economic Policy, Finland, and the Soviet Union, 1945–1953," *International History Review* 17 (May 1995): 287, 290; Mastny, *Cold War and Soviet Insecurity*, 44; Jussi Hanhimäki, *Containing Coexistence: America, Russia, and the "Finnish Solution"* (Kent: Kent State University Press, 1997), 93; *FRUS 1950* 4: 575; *FRUS 1952–1954* 8: 755.

35 *PAC*, 332.

36 Hanhimäki, *Containing Coexistence*, 52; Mastny, *Cold War and Soviet Insecurity*, 34–35; John M. Cabot, Oral Reminiscence, 18 July 1973 (Independence, MO: The Harry S. Truman Library, July 1977), 50; Ayers Oral History, TL, 139–89; De Santis, 149, 165.

37 *PAC*, 332; Beatrice Heuser, *Western "Containment" Policies in the Cold War: The Yugoslav Case* (London: Routledge, 1989), 87; E-mail of Stephen A. Schuker to author, 30 September 1998; *FRUS 1949* 5: 860–61, 873–74, 903–4, 909–10, 915ff.; A Report to the President by the National Security Council on Economic Relations between the United States and Yugoslavia, February 17, 1949, Truman Papers (PSF), Box 205, N.S.C. Meeting No. 34 Folder, TL; Wittner, *Intervention in Greece*, 272–73, 277–78; Lees, 68–70; Charles Sawyer, foreword, John Wesley Snyder and Dean Acheson, *Concerns of a Conservative Democrat* (Carbondale: Southern Illinois University Press, 1968), 185.

38 *FRUS 1949* 5: 219, 916, 920, 936, 938, 956–57, 972; Off the Record Press Conference, August 26, 1949; *New York Times*, 30 August 1949.

39 *FRUS 1949* 3: 20, 5: 972–75, 983; Meeting of Ambassadors, 10-22-49, Truman Papers (PSF), Box 163, Subj. File—Conferences, Paris Conf. (Oct.–Nov. 1949) Folder, TL; Perkins to Acheson, Meetings of Ambassadors in London and Paris, 7 November 1949, Truman Papers (PSF), Box 163, Subj. File—Conferences, Paris Conf. (Oct.–Nov. 1949) Folder, TL.

40 Lees, 75, 83–84, 91; *FRUS 1949* 5: 980–81; Ferrell, *Truman in the White House*, 328; Reston, "First-Year Audit," 36; Lawrence S. Kaplan, *A Community of Interests: NATO and the Military Assistance Program, 1948–1951* (Washington: Office of the Secretary of Defense Historical Office, 1980), 118; Daily Meetings, 6 February 1950; Press Conference 2-24-50, Acheson Papers, Box 68, Press Conf. 1949–53, Jan.–Dec. 1950 Folder, TL; Review of the World Situation, CIA 5–50, 17 May 1950, Truman Papers (PSF), Box 208, N.S.C. Meeting No. 57 Folder, TL (hereafter Review of the World Situation, CIA, 17 May 1950); *Memoranda of Conversations*, 19 June 1950, Call of the Yugoslav Ambassador.

41 John C. Campbell, Oral History Interview, 24 June 1974 (Independence, MO: The Harry S. Truman Library, November 1979), 151; Lees, 86, 88–92, 100; U.S. Congress, Senate, Committee on Foreign Relations, *Executive Sessions of the Senate Foreign Relations Committee (Historical Series). Volume III. Part 1: Eighty-Second Congress, First Session, 1951* (Washington: Government Printing Office, 1976), 23 (henceforth *Executive Sessions of the Senate Foreign Relations Committee ... 1951*); Background Press Meeting, February 8, 4:30 P.M., February 9, 1951, Acheson Papers, Box 68, Press Conferences—1951 Folder, TL; Memo for the Files ... 9 February 1951 ... Hightower, Acheson Papers, Box 68, TL; *New York Times*, 15 February 1951; Leffler, *Preponderance of Power*, 418.

42 Mastny, *Cold War and Soviet Insecurity*, 117–19; Lees, 92, 94, 97, 105, 109–12; *FRUS 1951* 4, Pt. 2: 1694; *New York Times*, 18 May 1951. One of Italy's arguments about its need for Trieste was population pressure. Acheson later wrote: "It seemed to me that if Italy wished to regard birth control from the medieval point of view of what was then Vatican policy, she had only herself to blame." *PAC*, 573.

43 Lees, 117; *New York Times*, 12 September 1952.

Chapter 10

1 English translation of a common Chinese term for the United States. See David L. Shambaugh, *Beautiful Imperialist: China Perceives America, 1972–1990* (Princeton: Princeton University Press, 1991).

2 "Taiwan" is of Chinese derivation, "Formosa" (meaning "beautiful") from Portuguese explorers. Except when "Taiwan" appears in quotations, I have used "Formosa" throughout the book because that was the common usage in the United States in the 1940s and 1950s.

3 *Memoranda of Conversations*, 28 (?) November 1948, Memorandum for the Under Secretary; Robert M. Blum, *Drawing the Line: The Origin of the American Containment Policy in East Asia* (New York: W. W. Norton, 1982), 28.

4 McGlothlen, *Controlling the Waves*, 210n; Rotter, *Path to Vietnam*, 5–7.

5 *PAC*, 257; Rotter, *Path to Vietnam*, 116; William S. Borden, *The Pacific Alliance: United States Foreign Economic Policy and Japanese Trade Recovery, 1947–1955* (Madison: University of Wisconsin Press, 1984), 196; *Reviews of the World Situation*, 135.

6 Ronald McGlothlen, "Acheson, Economics, and the American Commitment in Korea," *Pacific Historical Review* 58 (February 1989): 30n; Edwin W. Martin, Oral History Interview, 3 June 1975 (Independence, MO: The Harry S. Truman Library, February 1977), 114; Lanxin Xiang, 172; Rusk, 422.

7 On the "lost chance" issue, pro and con, see John W. Garver, "Polemics, Paradigms, Responsibility, and the Origins of the U.S.-PRC Confrontation of the 1950s," *Journal of American-East Asian Relations* 3 (Spring 1994): 1–34; Michael Sheng, "The United States, the Chinese Communist Party, and the Soviet Union, 1948–1950: A Reappraisal," *Pacific Historical Review* 63 (November 1994): 527; Niu Jun, "The Origins of Mao Zedong's Thinking on International Affairs (1916–1949)," in Michael H. Hunt and Niu Jun, eds., *Toward a History of Chinese Communist Foreign Relations, 1920s–1960s: Personalities and Interpretive Approaches* (Washington: Woodrow Wilson Center Asia Program, n.d.), 19; Steven M. Goldstein, "Chinese Communist Policy toward the United States: Opportunities and Constraints, 1944–1950," in Dorothy Borg and Waldo H. Heinrichs, eds., *Uncertain Years: Chinese-American Relations, 1947–1950* (New York: Columbia University Press, 1980), 235–36, 254–60; Judith Munro-Leighton, "A Postrevisionist Scrutiny of America's Role in the Cold War in Asia, 1945–1950," *Journal of American-East Asian Relations* 1 (Spring 1992): 77; Yang Kuisong, "The Soviet Factor and the CCP's Policy toward the United States in the 1940s," *Chinese Historians* 5 (Spring 1992): 30; Michael Sheng, "Chinese Communist Policy toward the United States and the Myth of the 'Lost Chance,' 1948–1950," *Modern Asian Studies* 28 (July 1994): 475–502; and five articles in the Winter 1997 issue of *Diplomatic History* (volume 21): Warren I. Cohen, "Introduction: Was There a 'Lost Chance' in China?" (71–75); Chen Jian, "The Myth of America's 'Lost Chance' in China: A Chinese Perspective in Light of New Evidence" (77–86); Garver, "Little Chance" (87–94); Michael Sheng, "The Triumph of Internationalism: CCP-Moscow Relations before 1949" (95–104); and Odd Arne Westad, "Losses, Chances, and Myths: The United States and the Creation of the Sino-Soviet Alliance, 1945–1950," *Diplomatic History* 21 (Winter 1997): 105–15.

8 Paterson, "If Europe," 27; Messer, "Roosevelt, Truman, and China," 72–73; Gaddis Smith, *Acheson*, 110; Acheson, Memorandum, February 20, 1963, Acheson Papers, Box 86,

State Department & White House Advisor 1963, Jan.–Dec. Folder, TL; Edwin W. Martin Oral History, TL, 46–49, 66.

9 Chen Jian, *China's Road to the Korean War: The Making of the Sino-American Confrontation* (New York: Columbia University Press, 1994), 73–74; Qiang Zhai, *The Dragon, the Lion, & the Eagle: Chinese-British-American Relations, 1949–1958* (Kent: Kent State University Press, 1994), 43. Soviet policy was far more complicated than imagined in the west. Skeptical of Mao's chances in the civil war, fearful he would become an "Asian Tito," and concerned about clashing with Washington, in 1948 Stalin also attempted a mediation and discouraged Mao from moving south of the Yangtze, advice that could leave China divided and dependent on Moscow. Besides Chen Jian and Qiang Zhia, see Brian Murray, "Stalin, the Cold War, and the Division of China: A Multi-Archival Mystery" (Washington: Cold War International History Project, Woodrow Wilson International Center for Scholars, Working Paper No. 12, June 1995), 7, 9, 16; and Westad, "Losses, Chances, and Myths," 111–12.

10 Melby Oral History, TL, 165; *PAC*, 257.

11 Shu Guang Zhang, *Deterrence and Strategic Culture: Chinese-American Confrontations, 1949–1958* (Ithaca: Cornell University Press, 1992), 15–16; idem, " 'Preparedness Eliminates Mishaps': The CCP's Security Concerns in 1949–1950 and the Origins of Sino-American Confrontation," *Journal of American-East Asian Relations* 1 (Spring 1992): 49.

12 *FRUS 1949* 8: 88, 90, 105, 160, 240, 671; J. W. Jones Oral History, TL, 82–83; *The State Department Policy Planning Staff Papers, 1947–1949*, introduction, Anna Kasten Nelson, foreword, George F. Kennan, 3 vols. (New York: Garland, 1983): 3: 26 (henceforth Nelson, *PPS Papers*); Douglas J. Macdonald, "Communist Bloc Expansion in the Early Cold War: Challenging Realism, Refuting Revisionism," *International Security* 20 (Winter 1995/96): 169; Zhang Baijia, "Zhou Enlai—The Shaper and Founder of China's Diplomacy," in Hunt and Niu Jun, 79.

13 Record of Actions by the National Security Council at its Thirty-Third Meeting, February 3, 1949, Truman Papers (PSF), Box 191, Subj. File–NSC Actions . . . 1947–1949 Folder, TL; Sidney W. Souers, Memorandum for the President, February 3, 1949, Truman Papers (PSF), Box 205, N.S.C. Meeting No. 33 Folder, TL; Memorandum for the President, February 4, 1949, Truman Papers (PSF), Box 220, NSC Meetings . . . Discussions (1949) Folder, TL; Sidney W. Souers, Memorandum for the President, February 17, 1949, Truman Papers (PSF), Box 205, N.S.C. Meeting No. 33 Folder, TL; *Memoranda of the Secretary of State* 49:61, 7 February 1949. Shortly thereafter, the Nationalists themselves asked for a suspension to keep U.S. arms out of Mao's hands, thus in Acheson's words solving Washington's "dilemma." Memorandum for the President, March 4, 1949, Truman Papers (PSF), Box 220, NSC Meetings . . . Discussions (1949) Folder, TL.

14 Acheson Talk, Thursday, Dec. 22, 1949, Reston Papers, Box 30, Working Files, UIA; *Selected Executive Session Hearings of the Committee, 1943–1950*, 43, 49.

15 *FRUS 1949* 8: 123, 132; Secretary's Notes for meeting with Republican Congressmen at the House Ways and Means Committee on the letter they addressed to the Secretary re China policy; Meeting 2/24/49, Acheson Papers, Box 64, TL; *New York Times*, 25 February 1949; Princeton Seminars, 22 July 1953; *PAC*, 306. Acheson recalled four and a half years later that he had begun by saying that China was "like the situation where the great oak falls, you can't see clearly until the dust settles." Princeton Seminars, 22 July 1953.

16 *FRUS 1949* 8: 65, 108, 110, 120, 141–42, 559, 665–66.

17 McGlothlen, *Controlling the Waves*, 141–42; Chen Jian, *China's Road to the Korean War*, 12–13; NSC-41: A Report to the National Security Council by the Secretary of State on United States Policy Regarding Trade with China, February 28, 1949, Truman Papers (PSF), Box 205, N.S.C. Meeting No. 35 Folder, TL; Blum, *Drawing the Line*, 31–32; Shu Guang Zhang, *Deterrence and Strategic Culture*, 36; *FRUS 1949* 9: 291–92; Statement by the Secretary of State at the 35th Meeting of the National Security Council on the Formosan Problem, Truman

Papers (PSF), Box 205, N.S.C. Meeting No. 35 Folder, TL; Memorandum for the President, March 4, 1949, Truman Papers (PSF), Box 220, NSC Meetings . . . Discussions (1949) Folder, TL.

18 Statement by the Secretary of State at the 35th Meeting of the National Security Council on the Formosan Problem, Truman Papers (PSF), Box 205, N.S.C. Meeting No. 35 Folder, TL; Daily Meetings, 8 March 1949; Qiang Zhai, *Dragon*, 90; *FRUS 1949* 9: 337–41, 608.

19 Nick Cullather, " 'Fuel for the Good Dragon': The United States and Industrial Policy in Taiwan, 1950–1965," *Diplomatic History* 20 (Winter 1996): 7; *FRUS 1949* 8: 193, 950; Zhang Baijia, 80.

20 John C. Brewer and Kenneth W. Rea, "Dr. John Leighton Stuart and U.S. Policy toward China, 1946–1949," and Margaret B. Denning, "The American Missionary and U.S. China Policy during World War II," both in Patricia Neils, ed., *United States Attitudes and Policies toward China: The Impact of Missionaries* (Armonk, N.Y.: M. E. Sharpe, 1990), 195–210, 230–44; *FRUS 1949* 8: 665; Odd Arne Westad, *Decisive Encounters: The Chinese Civil War, 1946–1950* (Stanford: Stanford University Press, 2003), 306.

21 *FRUS 1949* 8: 173–74, 230–31, 278, 677–79, 682–83, 724; Yu-Ming Shaw, *An American Missionary in China: John Leighton Stuart and Chinese-American Relations* (Cambridge: Harvard University Press for Council on East Asian Studies, Harvard University, 1992), 243; John Leighton Stuart, *Fifty Years in China: The Memoirs of John Leighton Stuart, Missionary and Ambassador* (New York: Random House, 1954), 239. Stuart made unauthorized contacts with the communists while Acheson was contemplating his reply. Yang Kuisong, 32; Chen Jian, "Myth of America's 'Lost Chance,' " 80, 83–84. Mao immediately informed Stalin while telling him that "we will be happy to see that the embassies of all capitalist countries get out of China."

22 William J. Duiker, *U.S. Containment Policy and the Conflict in Indochina* (Stanford: Stanford University Press, 1994), 73; *FRUS 1949* 7, Pt. 2: 1140, and 8: 294; *New York Times*, 15 April 1949; McLellan, *State Department Years*, 189; Douglas J. Macdonald, *Adventures in Chaos: American Intervention for Reform in the Third World* (Cambridge: Harvard University Press, 1992), 24; Daily Meetings, 3 May 1949.

23 "Commies" was not ideological venting but telegraphic shorthand aimed at reducing the cost of diplomatic traffic; one cannot help wondering, however, about the long-term impact of its use on state department thinking.

24 *FRUS 1949* 9: 22–23, 32, and 8: 250–51.

25 Cullather, " 'Fuel for the Good Dragon,' " 9; *Memoranda of the Secretary of State* 49:301, 28 April 1949.

26 *FRUS 1949* 9: 12–13; Thomas J. Christensen, "A 'Lost Chance' for What? Rethinking the Origins of U.S.-PRC Confrontation," *Journal of American-East Asian Relations* 4 (Fall 1995): 253; Sheng, "Triumph of Internationalism," 482n, 498–99; Yang Kuisong, 32; John Lewis Gaddis, *We Now Know: Rethinking Cold War History* (New York: Oxford University Press, 1997), 54; Shu Guang Zhang, *Deterrence and Strategic Culture*, 51; McGlothlen, *Controlling the Waves*, 99; Nick Cullather, *Illusions of Influence: The Political Economy of United States-Philippines Relations, 1942–1960* (Stanford: Stanford University Press, 1994), 79.

27 *FRUS 1949* 8: 356–60, 363–64, 368–69, 371–72, 384–85, 388, 392–94, 397–98; Yang Kuisong, 34; Edwin W. Martin, "The Chou Demarche: Did the US and Britain Miss a Chance to Change Postwar History in Asia?" *Foreign Service Journal* 58 (November 1981):13–16, 32; Sheng, "Chinese Communist Policy toward the United States," 487; Kuhns, 318.

28 *Memoranda of the Secretary of State* M-51, 8 June 1949, M-83[?], 16 June 1949; *New York Times*, 22 June 1949; *FRUS 1949* 8: 400, 702; *Memoranda of the Secretary of State* 49:869, 1 October 1949; William Stueck, *The Road to Confrontation: American Policy toward China and Korea, 1947–1950* (Chapel Hill: University of North Carolina Press, 1981), 123; Blum, *Drawing the Line*, 79.

29 Sergei Goncharov, "Stalin's Dialogue with Mao Zedong: Ivan Vladimirovich Kovalev, personal representative of Joseph Stalin to Mao Zedong, answers the questions of Historian-sinologist S. N. Goncharov," trans., Craig Seibert, *Journal of Northeast Asian Studies* 10 (Winter 1991–1992): 67; *FRUS 1949* 8: 766–67; Shaw, 252.

30 Michael H. Hunt, "Mao Tse-tung and the Issue of Accommodation with the United States, 1948–1950," in Borg and Heinrichs, *Uncertain Years*, 207–9; Warren I. Cohen, "Conversations with Chinese Friends: Zhou Enlai's Associates Reflect on Chinese-American Relations in the 1940s and the Korean War," *Diplomatic History* 11 (Summer 1987): 287–88; Shu Guang Zhang, "'Preparedness Eliminates Mishaps'," 51; idem, *Deterrence and Strategic Culture*, 77; *FRUS 1949* 8: 768–69; J. M. Cabot Oral History, TL, 64, 83–84; Livingston Merchant, Oral History Interview, 27 May 1975 (Independence, MO: The Harry S. Truman Library, December 1979), 28–30. It is extremely odd that Stuart omits any reference to this episode in his 1954 memoir, *Fifty Years in China*.

31 Blum, *Drawing the Line*, 63; Warren I. Cohen, "Acheson, His Advisers, and China, 1949–1950," in Borg and Heinrichs, *Uncertain Years*, 37; *FRUS 1949* 8: 780–81, 791–94; Shaw, 255; Douglas Macdonald, "Communist Bloc Expansion," 177.

32 Sheng, "The United States, the Chinese Communist Party, and the Soviet Union," 529; *FRUS 1949* 8: 436–40, 1222; *FRUS 1949* 9: 50–52; Daily Meetings, 15 July 1949.

33 McLellan, *State Department Years*, 189–90; Princeton Seminars, 22 July 1953; *Memoranda of Conversations*, 18 July 1949, Memorandum for Ambassador Jessup; *New York Times*, 28 July 1949; Michael Schaller, *The American Occupation of Japan: The Origins of the Cold War in Asia* (New York: Oxford University Press, 1985), 200.

34 Melby Oral History, TL, 168–69, 172–74; SR71–125, Dean Acheson Interviewed by Eric Sevareid, 8 November 1969, Recording, Part I, TL; Lanxin Xiang, 163; Warren I. Cohen, "Acheson, His Advisers, and China," 20–21, 24–25; Daily Meetings, 30 June 1949; Princeton Seminars, 22 July 1953; Sprouse Oral History, TL, 48; "John S. Service, State Department Duty in China, the McCarthy Era, and After, 1933–1977: An Interview Conducted by Rosemary Levenson, 1977–1978, with an introduction by John K. Fairbank" (Berkeley: University of California Regional Oral History Office, China Series: John S. and Caroline Service Oral History Project, 1981), 353–54 (henceforth Service, "State Department Duty").

35 *Memoranda of the Secretary of State* 49:425, 28 [29?] June 1949, 49:484, 15 June 1949, 49:639, 25 July 1949, 49:581, 11 July 1949; Princeton Seminars, 22 July 1953; Alan D. Harper, *The Politics of Loyalty: The White House and the Communist Issue, 1946–1952* (Westport: Greenwood Press, 1969), 115; David M. Finkelstein, *Washington's Taiwan Dilemma, 1949–1950: From Abandonment to Salvation* (Fairfax, VA: George Mason University Press, 1993), 167; *FRUS 1949* 8: 780, 782; *United States Relations with China: With Special Reference to the Period 1944–1949, Based on the Files of the Department of State* (Washington: Government Printing Office, 1949) (hereafter referred to as *China White Paper*), iii–iv, vii–vii, x–xi, xv–xvi; Robert P. Newman, "The Self-Inflicted Wound: The China White Paper of 1949," *Prologue* 14 (Fall 1982): 144.

36 *China White Paper*, xvi–xvii; Blum, *Drawing the Line*, 95; *New York Times*, 16 August 1949; Michael H. Hunt, *The Genesis of Chinese Communist Foreign Policy* (New York: Cambridge University Press, 1996), 195; He Di, "The Most Respected Enemy: Mao Zedong's Perception of the United States," in Hunt and Niu, 31; Chen Jian, *China's Road to the Korean War*, 76–77; J. H. Kalicki, *The Pattern of Sino-American Crises: Political-Military Interactions in the 1950s* (New York: Cambridge University Press, 1975), 13–14.

37 *FRUS 1949* 9: 1389; *PAC*, 302–3; Princeton Seminars, 22 July 1953; Press and Radio News Conference of Phillip [*sic*] C. Jessup, Wednesday, August 4, 1949 – 5:30 P.M., Acheson Papers, Box 68, Press Conf. 1949–53, July–Dec. 1949 Folder, TL; *Strengthening the Forces of Freedom*, 142–44.

38 *New York Times*, 7 and 21 August 1949; Blum, *Drawing the Line*, 99; Nancy Bernkopf Tucker, *Patterns in the Dust*, 156; Kepley, *Collapse of the Middle Way*, 46; Steel, *Walter Lippmann*, 466; Donovan, *Tumultuous Years*, 84; *PAC*, 375; Rosemary Foot, *The Wrong War: American Policy and the Dimensions of the Korean Conflict, 1950–1953* (Ithaca: Cornell University Press, 1985), 48.

39 Press and Radio News Conference, Friday, August 12, 1949 – 12:20 P.M., Acheson Papers, Box 68, Press Conf. 1949–53, July–Dec. 1949 Folder, TL; Off the Record Press Conference, August 26, 1949. In 1955 he described his statement about getting "another Secretary of State" as "rather violent." Princeton Seminars, 22 July 1953.

40 Princeton Seminars, 16 July 1953; Melby Oral History, TL, 166–68; John S. Service, *The Amerasia Papers: Some Problems in the History of US-China Relations* (Berkeley: Center for Chinese Studies, China Research Monographs, University of California, 1971), 134.

Chapter 11

1 1955 Acheson Oral History, A.M., 36.

2 Warren I. Cohen, *Dean Rusk*, 41; Daily Meetings, 31 August 1949; Miscamble, *Kennan and the Making of American Foreign Policy*, 237; McGlothlen, *Controlling the Waves*, 157; *PAC*, 328; Blum, *Drawing the Line*, 23; Stueck, *Road to Confrontation*, 132.

3 See, for example, McGlothlen, *Controlling the Waves*, 102–3.

4 Sergei N. Goncharov, John W. Lewis, and Xue Litai, *Uncertain Partners: Stalin, Mao and the Korean War* (Stanford: Stanford University Press, 1993), 79; Shu Guang Zhang, *Deterrence and Strategic Culture*, 69; Daily Meetings, 11 (?) July 1949; Miscamble, *Kennan and the Making of American Foreign Policy*, 234–36; Finkelstein, 172; *FRUS 1949* 9: 358, 361, 363; Ritchie Ovendale, "Britain, the United States, and Recognition of Communist China," *The Historical Journal* 26 (March 1983): 144; Lanxin Xiang, 183.

5 *Memoranda of the Secretary of State* 49:869, 1 October 1949, 49:877, 3 October 1949; *FRUS 1949* 9: 128–29; James Tuck-Hong Tang, *Britain's Encounter with Revolutionary China, 1949–54* (New York: St. Martin's Press, 1992), 56–57. Worried about Indochina, France too found Britain's de facto recognition of the PRC irritating and did not offer recognition until 1964. *Documents on British Policy* IV-2: 134.

6 *FRUS 1949* 9: 81–85, 90; Tang, 56.

7 Round Table, introductory page, 1–2 (original citation in Chapter 7); Christensen, *Useful Adversaries*, 100n; Miscamble, *Kennan and the Making of American Foreign Policy*, 238–39.

8 Round Table, 4–12, 20–26, 35–36, 71, 76–79, 111–14. David S. Patterson, then of the State Department Historical Office, first helped me identify DuBois.

9 Round Table, 28, 31–33, 47–51, 54–57, 67, 69, 82, 87–90, 94, 108, 119–20, 124, 126, 132, 138–44, 147, 150–51, 153, 157–58; Owen Lattimore, *Ordeal by Slander* (Boston: Little, Brown, 1950), 66; Shaw, 186.

10 Round Table, 29, 40–47, 50–53, 60–63, 70–71, 123; Robert P. Newman, *Owen Lattimore and the "Loss" of China* (Berkeley: University of California Press, 1992), 202.

11 *Reviews of the World Situation*, 94–101; Blum, *Drawing the Line*, 141.

12 *FRUS 1949* 9: 67, 107, 124–25, 128–29, 132; *Public Papers of the Presidents . . . 1949*, 520; *Strengthening the Forces of Freedom*, 191; Duiker, 79; Blum, *Drawing the Line*, 155.

13 Chen Jian, *China's Road to the Korean War*, 33–38, 55, 60; Shu Guang Zhang, "In the Shadow of Mao: Zhou Enlai and New China's Diplomacy," in Craig and Loewenheim, 346; Sheng, "Chinese Communist Policy Toward the United States," 478; Yang Kuisong, 33–34; Princeton Seminars, 22 July 1953; *Memoranda of the Secretary of State* 49:949 (Meeting with the President, Monday, October 31), 31 October 1949 (Meeting with the President, Monday, November 14), 14 November 1949; Chen Jian, "The Ward Case and the Emergence of Sino-

American Confrontation, 1948–1950," *Australian Journal of Chinese Affairs* 30 (July 1993): 151–54, 164–67; *FRUS 1949* 8: 1003, 1007, 1011–13, 1015–18, 1039; *Public Papers of the Presidents . . . 1949*, 568. A naval intelligence program *was* operated from Ward's consulate. Nancy Bernkopf Tucker, ed., *China Confidential: American Diplomats and Sino-American Relations, 1945–1996* (New York: Columbia University Press, 2001), 41, 506n.

14 McGlothlen, *Controlling the Waves*, 153; *PAC*, 340, 344; Chen Jian, "The Ward Case," 167; *Memoranda of the Secretary of State* 49:949 (Meeting with the President, Monday, October 31), 31 October 1949; *FRUS 1949* 8: 1008 and 9: 402; *Memoranda of the Secretary of State* 49:1013, 21 November 1949; *New York Times*, 9 November 1949.

15 Christensen, *Useful Adversaries*, 97, 97n; United States Interests in China, Truman Papers (PSF), Box 173, China–1949 PSF Subj. File Folder, TL.

16 For years American officials indicated their hostility to the PRC regime through conspicuous references to "Peiping" (often pronounced "Bay-ping") rather then "Peking" (or the later transliteration, "Beijing") because the Chinese characters for "Peking" mean "northern capital," whose existence under the communists Washington did not want to acknowledge. In private letters from the mid-fifties through the early sixties, Acheson shifted from "Peiping" to "Peking."

17 *FRUS 1949* 9: 160–61, 168–70; Gordon H. Chang, *Friends and Enemies: The United States, China, and the Soviet Union, 1948–1972* (Stanford: Stanford University Press, 1990), 56; Rotter, *Path to Vietnam*, 106; Press Conference 11–16–49, Acheson Papers, Box 68, Press Conf. 1949–53, July–Dec. 1949 Folder, TL; *New York Times*, 17 November 1949; Qiang Zhai, *Dragon*, 43; McGlothlen, *Controlling the Waves*, 152–53; Shu Guang Zhang, *Deterrence and Strategic Culture*, 53. For Johnson's role, see Keith D. McFarland and David L. Roll, *Louis Johnson and the Arming of America: The Roosevelt and Truman Years* (Bloomington: Indiana University Press, 2005), 253–61.

18 *Memoranda of the Secretary of State* 49:997 (Conversation with the President), 17 November 1949; Schaller, *American Occupation*, 205; *FRUS 1949* 9: 195, 429.

19 *FRUS 1949* 9: 173, 205–8; Finkelstein, 221, 245.

20 Sheng, "Triumph of Internationalism," 104; Westad, "Losses, Chances, and Myths," 115.

21 *FRUS 1949* 8: 618, 632–36; *FRUS 1950* 6: 294; Lanxin Xiang, 212; Odd Arne Westad, "Unwrapping the Stalin-Mao Talks: Setting the Record Straight," *CWIHPB* (Issues 6–7, Winter 1995/1996): 23–24; Warren I. Cohen, "Acheson, His Advisers, and China," 41; Wang Jisi, "An Appraisal of U.S. Policy toward China, 1945–1955, and Its Aftermath," in Harding and Yuan Ming, 291; *FRUS 1949* 8: 618, 632–36; Vladislav Zubok, " 'To hell with Yalta!'—Stalin Opts for a New Status Quo," *CWIHPB* (Issues 6–7, Winter 1995/1996): 25.

22 Princeton Seminars, 23 July 1953; Recognition of Chinese Communist Regime, 6 December 1949, Acheson Papers, Box 64, TL; *FRUS 1949* 9: 219–20, 225, 241–43, 248, 443; Peter Lowe, *Containing the Cold War in East Asia: British Policies towards Japan, China and Korea, 1948–53* (Manchester, UK: Manchester University Press, 1997), 117; Miscamble, *Kennan and the Making of American Foreign Policy*, 241; Stueck, *Road to Confrontation*, 134.

23 Princeton Seminars, 23 July 1953; Ronald W. Pruessen, *John Foster Dulles: The Road to Power* (New York: Free Press, 1982), 434; *FRUS 1949* 8: 717–19 and 9: 223; U.S. Congress, Senate Committee on Foreign Relations, *Military Situation in the Far East: Hearings before the Committee on Armed Services and the Committee on Foreign Relations, United States Senate, Eighty-Second Congress, First Session, to Conduct an Inquiry into the Military Situation in the Far East and the Facts Surrounding the Relief of General of the Army Douglas MacArthur from His Assignments in That Area* (Washington: Government Printing Office, 1951), 1667–69 (henceforth, *Military Situation in the Far East*); McGlothlen, *Controlling the Waves*, 106; Daily Meetings, 24 December 1949; Acheson Talk, Thursday, Dec. 22, 1949, Reston Papers, Box 30, Working Files, UIA.

24 *FRUS 1949* 9: 463–67; *PAC*, 350. Acheson, who normally worked well with Bradley, later claimed they had agreed to prohibit the phrases "from a purely military point of view" or "purely political or diplomatic point of view" from their conversations. Acheson, *Sketches from Life*, 163.

25 Memorandum for the President, 30 December 1949, Truman Papers (PSF), Box 220, NSC Meetings . . . Discussions (1949) Folder, TL. As it turned out, Johnson did not attend this meeting; when he thought he would lose, he usually absented himself.

26 Note by the Executive Secretary on *The Position of the United States with Respect to Asia*, Reference: NSC 48/1, 30 December 1949, Truman Papers (PSF), N.S.C. Meeting No. 50 Folder, TL.

27 *FRUS 1949* 8: 636–37, 647–50; "Stalin's Conversations with Chinese Leaders: Talks with Mao Zedong, December 1949–January 1950, and with Zhou Enlai, August–September 1952," with commentaries by Chen Jian, Vojtech Mastny, Odd Arne Westad, and Vladislav Zubok, *CWIHPB* (Issues 6–7, Winter 1995/1996): 6; Mastny, *Cold War and Soviet Insecurity*, 89; Nancy Bernkopf Tucker, *Patterns in the Dust*, 152; Bruce Cumings, *The Origins of the Korean War. Volume II: The Roaring of the Cataract, 1947–1950* (Princeton: Princeton University Press, 1990), 416; Sulzberger, *Long Row of Candles*, 492; Su Ge, "The Making of American Policy towards Taiwan, 1948–1955," *Journal of Oriental Studies* 3 (1992): 31; Stueck, *Road to Confrontation*, 141; *New York Times*, 8 January 1950; Princeton Seminars, 2 July 1953; Kepley, *Collapse of the Middle Way*, 63; *PAC*, 350; Acheson, *Among Friends*, 68. The "red haired girl" does not originate with *Peanuts* but with an 1893 poem by Albert Bigelow Paine, "That Red-Haired Girl."

28 *PAC*, 350–51; Daily Meetings, 3, 4, 5 January 1950.

29 *PAC*, 351; Blum, *Drawing the Line*, 180–81; Meeting with the President, 5 January 1950, Acheson Papers, Box 65, TL; Memorandum: Concerning Statement by the President on January 5, 1950, concerning China, George M. Elsey Papers, Box 59, Foreign Relations . . . Formosa Folder, TL; *Memoranda of the Secretary of State* 50:24, 6 January 1950; Princeton Seminars, 23 July 1953; *Public Papers of the Presidents . . . 1950*, 11; *New York Times*, 6 January 1950; *Strengthening the Forces of Freedom*, 170–73.

30 LDB (Luke D. Battle) to Acheson, 1 June 1951, Acheson Papers, Box 65, TL.

31 Franks thought Acheson had anticipated the 6 January UK recognition and deliberately timed the presidential statement on the 5th to deflect American anger against Britain. Hopkins, 145. Canadian recognition of the PRC did not come until 1970, blocked, as was Acheson, by the Korean War.

32 *New York Times*, 6 January 1950; Christensen, *Useful Adversaries*, 110n; Rosemary Foot, *The Practice of Power: US Relations with China since 1949* (Oxford: Clarendon Press, 1995), 85; Blum, *Drawing the Line*, 184; Chen Jian, "The Ward Case," 169; Odd Arne Westad, "Fighting for Friendship: Mao, Stalin, and the Sino-Soviet Treaty of 1950," *CWIHPB* (Issues 8–9, Winter 1996/1997): 233–34.

33 Hopkins, 146; Robert Accinelli, *United States Policy toward Taiwan, 1950–1955* (Chapel Hill: University of North Carolina Press, 1996), 15 (emphasis in original); Nancy Bernkopf Tucker, "American Policy toward Sino-Japanese Trade in the Postwar Years: Politics and Prosperity," *Diplomatic History* 8 (Summer 1984): 205–6.

34 Unless otherwise noted, all remaining references in this chapter are from 1955 Acheson Oral History, A.M., especially 10–17, 19–20, 27–30, 35–38, 41–43.

35 Trygve Lie, *In the Cause of Peace: Seven Years with the United Nations* (New York: Macmillan, 1954), 255.

36 Acheson to Hans J. Morgenthau, 16 January 1957, Acheson Papers, Box 23, Folder 289, YUL.

37 Princeton Seminars, 23 July 1953.

Chapter 12

1 Miscamble, *Kennan and the Making of American Foreign Policy*, Chapters 7–8; *Documents on Canadian External Relations* 15: 97.

2 Richard J. Barnet, *The Alliance: America, Europe, Japan: Makers of the Postwar World* (New York: Simon & Schuster, 1983), 114; Paul H. Nitze, "Military Power: A Strategic View," *The Fletcher Forum* 5 (Winter 1981): 160.

3 McGlothlen, *Controlling the Waves*, 32; Princeton Seminars, 14 March 1954; John Dower, "Occupied Japan and the Cold War in Asia," in Michael J. Lacey, ed., *The Truman Presidency* (Cambridge, UK: Cambridge University Press, 1989), 375; *FRUS 1949* 7, Pt. 2: 714. Like "Commies" (see Chapter 10), the telegraphic "Japs" might have had incalculable effects on those using it.

4 *FRUS 1949* 7, Pt. 2: 927–28.

5 McGlothlen, *Controlling the Waves*, 41–43; Schonberger, *Aftermath of War*, 247; Leffler, *Preponderance of Power*, 335; Princeton Seminars, 14 March 1954; Peter Lowe, "Challenge and Readjustment: Anglo-American Exchanges over East Asia, 1949–53," in T. G. Fraser and Peter Lowe, eds., *Conflict and Amity in East Asia: Essays in Honour of Ian Nish* (Houndmills: Macmillan Academic and Professional, 1992), 149.

6 *New York Times*, 2 March and 17 April 1949; Schonberger, *Aftermath of War*, 85; NSC-41: A Report to the National Security Council by the Secretary of State on United States Policy Regarding Trade with China, February 28, 1949, Truman Papers (PSF), Box 205, N.S.C. Meeting No. 35 Folder, TL; McGlothlen, *Controlling the Waves*, 38–39, 42, 218n; Rotter, *Path to Vietnam*, 42, 45; Schaller, *American Occupation*, 168; Schonberger, *Aftermath of War*, 242; Round Table, 82–83, 120–22, 124–26, 169–74.

7 Schonberger, *Aftermath of War*, 243; Schaller, *American Occupation*, 176; Japanese Peace Treaty, 24 February 1949, Acheson Papers, Box 64, TL; Memorandum for the President, 30 December 1949, Truman Papers (PSF), Box 220, NSC Meetings . . . Discussions (1949) Folder, TL.

8 For the Press, January 12, 1950, No. 34, James Webb Papers, Box 20, Dept. of State . . . Acheson, Dean Folder, TL (hereafter For the Press, January 12, 1950); Meeting, The White House, 4 February 1950, Acheson Papers, Box 65, TL; Daily Meetings, 2, 3 February 1950; Memorandum of Conversation with the President, 20 February 1950, Acheson Papers, Box 64B, February 1950 Conversations File, TL.

9 McGlothlen, *Controlling the Waves*, 44, 219n; Lambright, *Powering Apollo*, 59; Notes on the President's Meeting with Under Secretary of State James Webb–March 26, 1950–Little White House, Truman Papers (PSF), Box 159, Subj. File–Cabinet, State, Secretary–Misc Folder, TL; Kepley, *Collapse of the Middle Way*, 79–80; Princeton Seminars, 14 March 1954; David W. McIntyre, *Background to the Anzus Pact: Policy-Making, Strategy and Diplomacy, 1945–55* (Christchurch, N.Z.: St. Martin's Press, 1995), 53.

10 Princeton Seminars, 14 March 1954; Nicholas E. Sarantakes, "John Allison," in Nolan, 7; McIntyre, 48; Michael Schaller, *Altered States: The United States and Japan since the Occupation* (New York: Oxford University Press, 1997), 26; John Lewis Gaddis, "The American 'Wedge' Strategy, 1949–1955," in Harding and Yuan Ming, 163.

11 William Safire in *New York Times*, 26 April 1998.

12 Dirk U. Stikker, *Men of Responsibility: A Memoir* (New York: Harper & Row, 1966), 333; McLellan, *State Department Years*, 239; *Selected Executive Session Hearings of the Committee, 1943–1950*, 41–42; Dean Acheson, "Fifty Years After," *Yale Review* 51 (October 1961): 7.

13 *FRUS 1950* 2: 436; Princeton Seminars, 15 May 1954.

14 H. W. Brands, *The Specter of Neutralism: The United States and the Emergence of the Third World, 1947–1960* (New York: Columbia University Press, 1989), 313; Princeton Seminars, 14 March 1954; George McGhee, *Envoy to the Middle World: Adventures in Diplomacy*, foreword

by Dean Rusk (New York: Harper & Row, 1983), 373; Sara Wilson, "Pomp and Circumstance: The Creation of the Bureau of African Affairs" (unpublished paper, 1996).

15 Donovan, *Tumultuous Years*, 28–29; Stanley Andrews, Oral History Interview, 31 October 1970 (Independence, MO: The Harry S. Truman Library, September 1981), 1–4, 30, 43; Achilles Oral History, TL, 66–67, 135; Nitze Oral History, TL, 221–22; Elsey Oral History, TL, 1: 145–48; Robert Freeman Smith, "United States Policy-Making for Latin America during the Truman Administration: The Conflict of Personalities, Priorities, and Perceptions," *Continuity* 16 (Fall 1992): 99.

16 Andrews Oral History, TL, 4; Princeton Seminars, 9 July 1953; B. H. Brown Oral History, TL, 40; *PAC*, 254, 363–66; Acheson to Herbert Feis, 9 July 1963, Acheson Papers, Box 10, Folder 132, YUL; Acheson to Clark Clifford, 17 January 1949, Clark Clifford Papers, Box 39, TL; *New York Times*, 27 January 1949; Clifford Oral History, TL, 363–66; Lloyd C. Gardner, "Economic Foreign Policy and the Quest for Security," in Norman A. Graebner, ed., *The National Security: Its Theory and Practice, 1945–1960* (New York: Oxford University Press, 1986), 92; Acheson Oral History 1971, TL, 6–7.

17 Thomas G. Paterson, "Foreign Aid under Wraps: The Point Four Program," *Wisconsin Magazine of History* 56 (Winter 1972–1973): 122, 124; *Strengthening the Forces of Freedom*, 61–62, 67; Cary Reich, *The Life of Nelson A. Rockefeller: Worlds to Conquer, 1908–1958* (New York: Doubleday, 1996), 447; *PAC*, 265; Daily Meetings, 24 June 1949; Andrews Oral History, TL, 12–14, 22, 43.

18 *Memoranda of Conversations*, 1 August 1947, Visit of Nokrasky Pasha, E's P.M., 3 September 1947, Egyptian request; Fred H. Lawson, "The Truman Administration and the Palestinians," in Michael W. Suleiman, ed., *U.S. Policy on Palestine from Wilson to Clinton* (Normal, IL: Association of Arab-American University Graduates, Inc., 1995), 66–67; Peter L. Hahn, *Caught in the Middle East: U.S. Policy toward the Arab-Israeli Conflict, 1945–1961* (Chapel Hill: University of North Carolina Press, 2004), 68; *PAC*, 562; Amikam Nachmani, " 'It Is a Matter of Getting the Mixture Right': Britain's Post-War Relations with America in the Middle East," *Journal of Contemporary History* 18 (January 1983): 117–40.

19 Princeton Seminars, 15 May 1954; Walter LaFeber, *Inevitable Revolutions: The United States in Central America*, 2d ed. (New York: W. W. Norton, 1993), 15.

20 Douglas Little, "Pipeline Politics: America, TAPLINE, and the Arabs," *Business History Review* 64 (Summer 1990): 255–57, 278–81; Irene L. Gendzier, *Notes from the Minefield: United States Intervention in Lebanon and the Middle East, 1945–1958* (New York: Columbia University Press, 1997), 98; Fred H. Lawson, "The Iranian Crisis of 1945–1946 and the Spiral Model of International Conflict," *International Journal of Middle East Studies* 21 (August 1989): 314, 317–20.

21 Edwin A. Locke, Jr., Oral History Interview, 5 April 1967 (Independence, MO: The Harry S. Truman Library, October 1967), 132–33; Warren I. Cohen, *Dean Rusk*, 34; Princeton Seminars, 15 May 1954.

22 *PAC*, 169–71; Reston, *Deadline*, 390–91; George T. Mazuzan, *Warren R. Austin at the U.N. 1946–1953* (Kent: Kent State University Press, 1977), 99; Acheson to Truman, 18 July 1955, Acheson Papers, Box 31, Folder 394, YUL; Peter L. Hahn, private e-mail message, 28 September 1998.

23 Daily Meetings, 28 March and 15 April 1949; Fred H. Lawson, "The Truman Administration and the Palestinians," *Arab Studies Quarterly* 12 (Winter/Spring 1990): 59–61; *Memoranda of the Secretary of State* 49:56, 5 February 1949; Princeton Seminars, 15 July 1953; *Memoranda of Conversations*, 5 April 1949; *FRUS 1949* 6: 959; Lawson, "The Truman Administration and the Palestinians," in Suleiman, 64–65.

24 Neff, 96; Peter L. Hahn, "The View from Jerusalem: Revelations about U.S. Diplomacy from the Archives of Israel," *Diplomatic History* 22 (Fall 1998): 514–15; Daily Meetings, 8 June 1949, 26 August 1949; *FRUS 1949* 6: 1110; Leffler, *Preponderance of Power*,

288; Hahn, *Caught in the Middle East*, 137; A Report to the National Security Council by the Secretary of State on United States Policy toward Israel and the Arab States, September 1, 1949, NSC 47/1, Truman Papers (PSF), Box 193, Subj. File–NSC Memo. Approvals–253 Folder, TL; Peter L. Hahn, "Alignment by Coincidence: Israel, the United States, and the Partition of Jerusalem, 1949–1953," *International History Review* 21 (September 1999): 689. Hahn's *Caught in the Middle East* is full of information on Niles's activities.

25 *FRUS 1949* 6: 1341–42; Hahn, *Caught in the Middle East*, 74.

26 Dennis Kux, *Estranged Democracies: India and the United States 1941–1991*, introduction, Daniel P. Moynihan (New Delhi: Sage, 1993), 50; *PAC*, 420; *Selected Executive Session Hearings of the Committee, 1943–1950*, 159; *FRUS 1949* 2, Pt. 1: 239; M. Srinivas Chary, *The Eagle and the Peacock: U.S. Foreign Policy toward India since Independence*, foreword, Norman A. Graebner (Westport: Greenwood Press, 1995), vii, 24; Pandit, 250; H. W. Brands, "India and Pakistan in American Strategic Planning, 1947–54: The Commonwealth as Collaborator," *Journal of Imperial and Commonwealth History* 15 (October 1986): 46; *FRUS 1950* 5: 1404.

27 *FRUS 1949* 6: 53; Dennis Merrill, *Bread and the Ballot: The United States and India's Economic Development, 1947–1963* (Chapel Hill: University of North Carolina Press, 1990), 39; Off the Record Press Conference, August 26, 1949; Brands, "India and Pakistan," 45; *Memoranda of Conversations*, 30 August 1949, Presentation of a Copy of the President's Appeal to the Prime Minister of India; Robert J. McMahon, *The Cold War on the Periphery: The United States, India, and Pakistan* (New York: Columbia University Press, 1994), 54–55.

28 Chary, 74; Mathews Oral History, TL, 56–59; *PAC*, 335–36; *Memoranda of Conversations*, 9 February 1950, Interview with Walter White; Judd Oral History, TL, 45; Brands, *Inside the Cold War*, 205; McMahon, *Cold War on the Periphery*, 55, 57.

29 McMahon, *Cold War on the Periphery*, 71–72.

30 *New York Times*, 24 March 1949; Linda Wills Qaimmaqami, "The Catalyst of Nationalization: Max Thornburg and the Failure of Private Sector Developmentalism in Iran, 1947–1951," *Diplomatic History* 19 (Winter 1995): 11–12.

31 Princeton Seminars, 15 May 1954; Daily Meetings, 16 November 1949; McGhee, *Envoy to the Middle World*, 65; *Memoranda of Conversations*, 18 November 1949, Exchange of Views Between the Shah of Iran and the Secretary; *Memoranda of the Secretary of State* 49:1007, 18 November 1949; *FRUS 1949* 4: 62; *Memoranda of Conversations*, 18 November 1949, Iranian Desire for Greater Security Assurances; *FRUS 1950* 5: 505.

Chapter 13

1 *New York Times*, 4 December 1949.

2 R. C. Raack, "Stalin Plans His Post-War Germany," *Journal of Contemporary History* 28 (January 1993): 56; Mastny, *Cold War and Soviet Insecurity*, 84; Philip A. Karber and Jerald A. Combs, "The United States, NATO, and the Soviet Threat to Western Europe: Military Estimates and Policy Options, 1945–1963," *Diplomatic History* 22 (Summer 1998): 410, 412, 415; Jerald A. Combs, "Gardner Cold War Essay," 20 October 1997, http://h-net.msu.edu/cgi-bin/logbrowse.pl?trx=vx&list=H-Diplo&month=9710&week=c&msg=SgVp9xsSOsoIybaoZeHuwA&user=&pw= (viewed 9/20/04); idem, "Cold War Historiography," 9 September 1998, http://h-net.msu.edu/cgi-bin/logbrowse.pl?trx=vx&list=H-Diplo&month=9809& week=b&msg= UeICocuNlokEoh2CKAdb9Q&user=&pw= (viewed 9/20/04); Eduard M. Mark, "Gardner Cold War Essay," 19 October 1997, http://h-net.msu.edu/cgi-bin/logbrowse.pl?trx=vx&list=H-Diplo&month=9710&week=c&msg=ONwKHRh3MpqoNo7YutBRRA&user=&pw= (viewed, 9/20/04).

3 Mark, "Gardner Cold War Essay"; Karber and Combs, 402; Combs, "Gardner Cold War Essay"; *Memoranda of Conversations*, 21 January 1952, Netherlands Views on European Defense; *FRUS 1949* 5: 627.

4 Mastny, *Cold War and Soviet Insecurity*, 78; Michael Warner, 319; Wohlforth, *Elusive Balance*, 110; Leffler, "Strategic Dimensions of the Marshall Plan," 299.

5 Gaddis, *Strategies of Containment*, 148; Allan R. Millett and Peter Maslowski, *For the Common Defense: A Military History of the United States of America* (New York: Free Press, 1984), 477; Harry R. Borowski, *A Hollow Threat: Strategic Air Power and Containment before Korea* (Westport: Greenwood Press, 1982); Lawrence S. Wittner, *One World or None: A History of the World Nuclear Disarmament Movement through 1953* (Stanford: Stanford University Press, 1993), 255; Rhodes, 320; Ronald E. Powaski, *March to Armageddon: The United States and the Nuclear Arms Race, 1939 to the Present* (New York: Oxford University Press, 1987), 51; Leffler, *Preponderance of Power*, 276; David Alan Rosenberg, "U.S. Nuclear Stockpile, 1945 to 1950," *The Bulletin of the Atomic Scientists* 38 (May 1982): 25–30; idem, "The Origins of Overkill: Nuclear Weapons and American Strategy, 1945–1960," *International Security* 7 (Spring 1983): 3–71.

6 *FRUS 1949* 1: 415–16; Leffler, *Preponderance of Power*, 275; Alan S. Milward, "NATO, OEEC, and the Integration of Europe," in Heller and Gillingham, 248; David Alan Rosenberg, "American Atomic Strategy and the Hydrogen Bomb Decision," *Journal of American History* 66 (June 1979): 72; *FRUS 1949* 1: 415–16; *Public Papers of the Presidents . . . 1949*, 511n; Rosenberg, "Origins of Overkill," 21–22.

7 Kaplan, *United States and NATO*, 113, 143; Lord Ismay, *NATO: The First Five Years, 1949–1954* (Utrecht: Bosch-Utrecht, 1954), 30.

8 *FRUS 1949* 1: 402; *PAC*, 308; *Reviews of the World Situation*, 42–43.

9 *Reviews of the World Situation*, 189.

10 *Memoranda of the Secretary of State* 49:1016 (Memorandum by Conversation with the President, Item No. 4), 21 November 1949; 1955 Acheson Oral History, P.M., 6; S. Nelson Drew, ed., *NSC-68: Forging the Strategy of Containment, with Analyses by Paul H. Nitze* (Washington: National Defense University, Fort Lesley J. McNair, 1994), 33; Project 1517, Appendix, 1.

11 Williamson and Rearden, 133; *PAC*, 345; Paul Nitze, "The Development of NSC 68," *International Security* 4 (Spring 1980): 172; Gregory Mitrovich, *Undermining the Kremlin: America's Strategy to Subvert the Soviet Bloc, 1947–1956* (Ithaca: Cornell University Press, 2000), 49.

12 Holloway, *Stalin and the Bomb*, 295–99; Miscamble, *Kennan and the Making of American Foreign Policy*, 308; Rhodes, 207, 280, 470; *In the Matter of J. Robert Oppenheimer*, 76; *PAC*, 345.

13 Paul Y. Hammond, "NSC-68: Prologue to Rearmament," in Warner R. Schilling, Paul Y. Hammond, and Glenn H. Snyder, *Strategy, Politics, and Defense Budgets* (New York: Columbia University Press, 1962), 291; Williamson and Rearden, 123; Richard G. Hewlett and Francis Duncan, *A History of the United States Atomic Energy Commission. Volume II. Atomic Shield, 1947–1952* (University Park: Pennsylvania State University Press, 1969), 395; 1955 Acheson Oral History, P.M., 6–7; Rhodes, 407; *In the Matter of J. Robert Oppenheimer*, 77, 80; R. Gordon Arneson, "The H-Bomb Decision [I]," *Foreign Service Journal* 46 (May 1969): 29; *PAC*, 345–47; David Lilienthal, 583–84; Arneson Oral History, TL, 62–63.

14 *FRUS 1949* 1: 574–77, 591; Miscamble, *Kennan and the Making of American Foreign Policy*, 303; McCullough, 756–57; *PAC*, 346. By "eventually," he meant within 18–30 months.

15 *FRUS 1949* 1: 599–600.

16 Timothy J. Botti, *Ace in the Hole: Why the United States Did Not Use Nuclear Weapons in the Cold War, 1945 to 1965* (Westport: Greenwood Press, 1996), 19; Miscamble, *Kennan and the Making of American Foreign Policy*, 304–6; Callahan, 83; *FRUS 1949* 1: 612–17; *FRUS 1951* 1: 878–80.

17 Arneson, "H-Bomb Decision [I]," 29; idem, "H-Bomb Decision [II]," *Foreign Service Journal* 46 (June 1969); 24; *PAC*, 348; Rhodes, 406–407; Samuel F. Wells, Jr., "Sounding the Tocsin: NSC 68 and the Soviet Threat," *International Security* 4 (Fall 1979): 120; Rosenberg, "American Atomic Strategy," 82.

18 Steven L. Rearden, "Frustrating the Kremlin Design: Acheson and NSC 68," in Brinkley, *Acheson and . . . U.S. Foreign Policy*, 165; Rhodes, 417. Acheson denied the significance of the Fuchs case in 1955. 1955 Acheson Oral History, P.M., 12.

19 Arneson, "H-Bomb Decision [II]," 26–27; idem, "H-Bomb Decision [I]," 27; Declassified Version of Mr. Lilienthal's Memorandum of January 31, 1950, Acheson Papers, Box 87, Chronological File of State Dept. memos, TL; *PAC*, 348–49.

20 *PAC*, 349; Arneson, "H-Bomb Decision [I]," 27; Hewlett and Duncan, 408.

21 1955 Acheson Oral History, P.M., 10.

22 *PAC*, 346, 753n; Miscamble, "Rejected Architect and Master Builder," 451n.; 1955 Acheson Oral History, P.M., 8–9, 13; *New York Times*, 10 October 1969; Isaacson and Thomas, 489; Miscamble, *Kennan and the Making of American Foreign Policy*, 306; Kennan, *Memoirs, 1925–1950*, 474; idem, *Memoirs 1950–1963* (Boston: Little, Brown, 1972), 65; Acheson, *Vast External Realm*, 135–36. For more on this Acheson-Kennan contretemps, see my "The Secretary, the Spy, and the Sage."

23 Leffler, *Preponderance of Power*, 330; pencil note, George Elsey Papers, Box 88, National Defense–Atomic, 1950 Folder 1, TL; Wells, 119; *PAC*, 377–78; Philip M. Stern, with Harold P. Green, *The Oppenheimer Case: Security on Trial* (New York: Harper & Row, 1969), 154–55, 158; *New York Times*, 17 and 5 February 1950.

24 Daily Meetings, 6 February 1950; *Strengthening the Forces of Freedom*, 10–14, 16; *PAC*, 379; *New York Times*, 14 February 1950.

25 McCullough, 761; Raymond P. Ojserkis, *Beginnings of the Cold War Arms Race: The Truman Administration and the U.S. Arms Build-Up* (Westport, CT: Praeger, 2003), 64; Rosenberg, "American Atomic Strategy," 85; Secretary Acheson's Background Press Conference, March 13, 1950, Acheson Papers, Box 68, Press Conf. 1949–53, Jan.–Dec. 1950 Folder, TL; Williamson and Rearden, 132; *FRUS 1950* 2: 352–53; Leffler, *Preponderance of Power*, 369–70.

26 Roger Dingman, "Atomic Diplomacy during the Korean War," *International Security* 13 (Winter 1988/89): 69.

Chapter 14

1 Acheson, *Sketches from Life*, 162; Princeton Seminars, 10 October 1953; Michael J. Hogan, *A Cross of Iron: Harry S. Truman and the Origins of the National Security State, 1945–1954* (New York: Cambridge University Press, 1998), 198–99.

2 Aaron L. Friedberg, *In the Shadow of the Garrison State: America's Anti–Statism and Its Cold War Grand Strategy* (Princeton: Princeton University Press, 2000), 97; Warner R. Schilling, "The Politics of National Defense: Fiscal 1950," in Schilling, Hammond, and Snyder, 29, 113, 209–12, 220. In 2005 dollars, the fiscal 1951 allotment came to $97 billion. Except for special Korean War levies, there were no general tax increases in the Truman presidency.

3 *PAC*, 345, 374, 377; Sec Acheson's Denver 8–2–52, Acheson Papers, Box 69, Press Conf. 1949–1953, Jan. 1952–Jan. 1953 Folder, TL; Hammond, 342; Wells, 124; Hogan, *Cross of Iron*, 104, 292; Larry I. Bland, ed., *George C. Marshall: Interviews and Reminiscences for Forrest C. Pogue*, rev. ed., introduction by Dr. Pogue (Lexington, VA: George C. Marshall Foundation, 1991), 327–28.

4 *PAC*, 347–48; Wells, 125n, 129–30; Ernest R. May, ed., *American Cold War Strategy: Interpreting NSC 68* (Boston: Bedford Books of St. Martin's Press, 1993), 10–11, 13; *In the Matter of J. Robert Oppenheimer*, 86. "NSC-68" superseded NSC-20/4 (1948) as a general guide to U.S. policy. Truman received the original version on 7 April 1950. Others appeared through mid-December 1950. The last of these, NSC-68/4, signed on 14 December, was followed on

the 16th by a presidential proclamation (no. 2914) declaring the state of national emergency that paved the way for the NSC-68–designed security and military program.

5 *PAC*, 371; Recent Soviet Moves, Truman Papers (PSF), Box 187, Russia 1949–1952 Folder, TL; Wells, 125–27; *FRUS 1950* 1: 145–47, 185–87, 196–98, 200–201, 254; Drew, 4.

6 *PAC*, 373–74; *FRUS 1950* 1: 204–6; Note on a meeting at the State Department Wednesday, March 23, 1950, Sidney Souers Papers, Box 1, Souers–White House Counsel, 1950–53 Folder, TL; Benjamin O. Fordham, *Building the Cold War Consensus: The Political Economy of U.S. National Security Policy, 1949–51* (Ann Arbor: University of Michigan Press, 1998), 51; Omar N. Bradley and Clay Blair, *A General's Life: An Autobiography by General of the Army Omar N. Bradley* (New York: Simon & Schuster, 1983), 519; Hammond, 326.

7 *FRUS 1950* 1: 213–26; Ernest R. May, *Interpreting NSC 68*, 13; Wells, 135–37; Fordham, 58.

8 George M. Elsey, Memorandum for Mr. Murphy, Meeting with Undersecretary Webb, April 7, 1950, George M. Elsey Papers, Box 88, National Defense–Atomic, 1950 Folder 1, TL; Ernest R. May, *Interpreting NSC 68*, 14; *FRUS 1950* 1: 234; Drew, 35; Hammond, 333; Wells, 131n.; Lucas, *Freedom's War*, 87.

9 All quotations from NSC-68 are from *FRUS 1950* 1: 235–92.

10 *PAC*, 374, 377; Drew, 13; Hammond, 319; Princeton Seminars, 10 October 1953. In 2005, the budget estimate would run to $217–362 billion.

11 Princeton Seminars, 10 October 1953. Emphasis mine.

12 *PAC*, 753n; *Pattern of Responsibility*, 22; Summary of Secretary's Remarks before the Advertising Council, February 16, 1950, Acheson Papers, Box 69, Press Conf. 1949–1953, Classified Off the Record Speeches Folder, TL. Chapters 5–7 of Drew provide a handy compilation of commentaries on NSC-68.

13 Princeton Seminars, 10 October 1953; Martin Malia, "The August Revolt," *New York Review of Books*, 26 September 1991, 22; *PAC*, 375.

14 *PAC*, 374–75.

15 The phrase, "Upper Volta with rockets," has been attributed to many prominent public figures but seems to have originated with Xan Smiley of London's *Telegraph*. http://www.cdi.org/russia/johnson/3059.html##6 (viewed 5/29/2005).

16 Acheson, *Grapes from Thorns*, 147; Daily Meetings, 24 January 1950; Princeton Seminars, 10 October 1953; Hamby, *Man of the People*, 525; Memorandum for the President, 5 May 1950, Truman Papers (PSF), Box 220, NSC Meetings . . . Discussions (1950) Folder, TL.

17 *Assignment of Ground Forces of the United States to Duty in the European Area: Hearings before the Committee on Foreign Relations and the Committee on Armed Services, United States Senate, Eighty–Second Congress, First Session, on S. Con. Res. 8: A Concurrent Resolution Relative to the Assignment of Ground Forces of the United States to Duty in the European Area, February 1, 15, 16, 19, 20, 21, 22, 23, 24, 26, 27, and 28, 1951* (Washington: Government Printing Office, 1951), 107. Hereafter cited as *Assignment of Ground Forces*.

18 Summary of Secretary's Remarks Before The Advertising Council, February 16, 1950, Acheson Papers, Box 69, Press Conf. 1949–1953, Classified Off the Record Speeches Folder, TL; *Strengthening the Forces of Freedom*, 77; *New York Times*, 22 February 1950.

19 Michael Nelson, *War of the Black Heavens: The Battles of Western Broadcasting in the Cold War* (Syracuse: Syracuse University Press, 1997), 37; Princeton Seminars, 10 October 1953; Warner, xlv; Memorandum for the President, 21 April 1950, Truman Papers (PSF), Box 220, NSC Meetings . . . Discussions (1950) Folder, TL; Daily Meetings, 4 May 1950.

20 Ojserkis, 75; *Memoranda of the Secretary of State* 50:348 (Memorandum of Conversation with the President: The President's Speeches on His Western Tour), 1 May 1950; Princeton Seminars, 10 October 1953; Ernest R. May, "The American Commitment to Germany, 1949–55," *Diplomatic History* 13 (Fall 1989): 439; *New York Times*, 7 May and 3 June 1950;

706 Notes to Pages 246–254

Review of the World Situation, CIA, 17 May 1950; For Webb from Acheson, ACTEL 15, 19 May 1950, Truman Papers (PSF), Box 163, Subj. File–Conferences, London Conf.–NATO May '50 Folder, TL; James I. Matray, "America's Reluctant Crusade: Truman's Commitment of Combat Troops in the Korean War," *The Historian* 42 (May 1980): 441; *Memoranda of the Secretary of State* 50:421 (Memo telcon DA–Johnson), 5 June 1950; Daily Meetings, 8 June 1950; Warner, 332.

21 Record of Actions by the National Security Council at its Sixty–Eighth Meeting, September 29, 1950, Truman Papers (PSF), Box 191, Subj. File–NSC Actions, records 1950 Folder, TL; Hammond, 351, 356, 358; *Memoranda of the Secretary of State* 50:738, 29 September 1950, 50:840, 27 November 1950.

22 SR62–199, Presentation of Bust of Dean Acheson at Truman Library, 31 March 1962, Recording, TL; Nelson, *Black Heavens*, 37; Acheson, *Vast External Realm*, 125–26.

23 Thomas G. Paterson, "Presidential Foreign Policy, Public Opinion, and Congress: The Truman Years," *Diplomatic History* 3 (Winter 1979): 1–18; Acheson, "Legislative–Executive Relations," 491; Acheson to Hans J. Morgenthau, 3 January 1957, Acheson Papers, Box 23, Folder 289, YUL; Elmer Davis, 28; *U.S. News & World Report*, 24 March 1950, 15; For the Press, January 12, 1950; Acheson to Louis Halle, 17 March 1955, Acheson Papers, Box 15, Folder 189, YUL.

24 Press–Radio 2–25–49, Acheson Papers, Box 68, Press Conf. 1949–53, Jan.–June 1949 Folder, TL; Bernhard, "Clearer than Truth," 546, 560; Daily Meetings, 4 February 1950, 25 February 1949; Russell Oral History, TL, 13; *Memoranda of the Secretary of State* 50:106, 7 February 1950; Secretary Acheson's Background Press Conference, March 13, 1950, Acheson Papers, Box 68, Press Conf. 1949–53, Jan.–Dec. 1950 Folder, TL.

25 David F. Krugler, *The Voice of America and the Domestic Propaganda Battles, 1945–1953* (Columbia: University of Missouri Press, 2000), 96–97, 111, 113; *Memoranda of the Secretary of State* 50:140 (Battle memo to Lehrbas), 16 February 1950; Summary of Secretary's Remarks Before The Advertising Council, February 16, 1950, Acheson Papers, Box 69, Press Conf. 1949–1953, Classified Off the Record Speeches Folder, TL.

26 *FRUS 1950* 4: 276–77; *New York Times*, 10 and 12 March 1950.

27 *Strengthening the Forces of Freedom*, 151; Secretary Acheson's Background Press Conference, March 13, 1950, Acheson Papers, Box 68, Press Conf. 1949–53, Jan.–Dec. 1950 Folder, TL.

28 *PAC*, 375, 380–81; Conversation with the President, California Speaking Commitments, 9 March 1950, Acheson Papers, Box 65, TL; *Strengthening the Forces of Freedom*, 20–28.

29 *New York Times*, 17–19 March 1950; *Khrushchev Remembers*, 356. Zhou Enlai also denounced the speech.

30 *Memoranda of the Secretary of State* 50:287 (Battle to Brown), 12 April 1950; Hamby, *Beyond the New Deal*, 375–76; *PAC*, 379; *New York Times*, 22 April 1950; Coral Bell, *Negotiation from Strength: A Study in the Politics of Power* (New York: Alfred A. Knopf, 1963), 17.

31 *New York Times*, 23 and 30 April 1950; Bernhard, "Clearer than Truth," 562–63; Lucas, *Freedom's War*, 84–85.

32 *New York Times*, 28 May and 21 June 1950; *PAC*, 376–77.

Chapter 15

1 Trachtenberg, *Constructed Peace*, 102.

2 *FRUS 1949* 6: 449, 1652.

3 Meeting of Ambassadors, 10–22–49, Truman Papers (PSF), Box 163, Subj. File–Conferences, Paris Conf. (Oct.–Nov. 1949) Folder, TL; *FRUS 1949* 4: 469–72, 475, 478, 483–86, 488–93. Regional ambassadorial conferences were Under Secretary James Webb's idea.

4 *FRUS 1949* 3: 296, 629; Bird, *Chairman*, 328.

5 Hamburger, "Mr. Secretary—II," 55; Schwartz, *America's Germany*, 75–76; *FRUS 1949* 3: 429, 490, 618–25, 628.

6 Acheson to Alan Bullock, 27 April 1955, Acheson Papers, Box 4, Folder 51, YUL; Emerg. of W. Germany, Synopses, Princeton Seminars; Princeton Seminars, 10 October 1953; Schwartz, *America's Germany*, 77, 80–83; *FRUS 1949* 3: 541, 545, 632–38; Hitchcock, "France, the Western Alliance," 619; Bird, *Chairman*, 326; Bark and Gress, 274; Emerg. of W. Germany, Roll 1, Synopses, 1–4, 7–8, Princeton Seminars; *New York Times*, 10 November 1949.

7 *FRUS 1949* 3: 309–310, 312–14, 629; Hans-Peter Schwarz, *Konrad Adenauer: A German Politician and Statesman in a Period of War, Revolution and Reconstruction. Volume I: From the German Empire to the Federal Republic, 1876–1952*, trans., Louise Willmot (Providence and Oxford: Berghahn Books, 1995), 485; *New York Times*, 14 November 1949; Lightner Oral History, TL, 89; *PAC*, 340–42; Bird, *Chairman*, 325; Schwartz, *America's Germany*, 78–80; Acheson, *Sketches from Life*, 167, 172–73; Princeton Seminars, 10 October 1953. Schumacher too referred to Americans as "the best Europeans." *FRUS 1949* 3: 309.

8 *PAC*, 342–43; Princeton Seminars, 10 October 1953; *New York Times*, 15 November 1949.

9 Acheson, *Sketches from Life*, 170; Princeton Seminars, 10 October 1953; Acheson to Robert S. McNamara, 16 September 1963, Acheson Papers, Box 86, State Department & White House Advisor 1963, Jan.–Dec. Folder, TL; European Recovery Program Interview with Dr. Konrad Adenauer, 10 June 1964 (Independence, MO: The Harry S. Truman Library, January 1966), 13; *FRUS 1949* 3: 314–15, 639.

10 Emerg. of W. Germany, Synopses, Princeton Seminars; *Memoranda of Conversations*, 13 November 1949, Review of Discussions . . . in Bonn; *FRUS 1949* 3: 318, 325, 340–42; Press Conference 11–16–49, Acheson Papers, Box 68, Press Conf. 1949–53, July–Dec. 1949 Folder, TL; Conversation with the President, Item 2, Rearmament of Germany, 17 November 1949, Acheson Papers, Box 64, TL; *Public Papers of the Presidents . . . 1949*, 570; Hitchcock, "France, the Western Alliance," 623n.; Bark and Gress, 277; *Memoranda of the Secretary of State* 49:1029, 29 November 1949; Daily Meetings, 30 November 1949; *Memoranda of the Secretary of State* 49:1030, 30 November 1949.

11 *Memoranda of Conversations*, 1 December 1949; Konrad Adenauer, *Memoirs 1945–53*, trans., Beate Ruhm von Oppen (Chicago: Henry Regnery, 1965), 199; Emerg. of W. Germany, Synopses, Princeton Seminars; Kaplan, *United States and NATO*, 155; *New York Times*, 4 December 1949; Press Conference 12–14–49, Acheson Papers, Box 68, Press Conf. 1949–53, July–Dec. 1949 Folder, TL; Bark and Gress, 277.

12 Douglas G. Brinkley, "Dean Acheson and European Unity," in Heller and Gillingham, 179; *Memorandum of Conversation*, 18 January 1950, Acheson Papers, Box 65, TL.

13 *New York Times*, 22 December 1949; *Memoranda of the Secretary of State* 49:1033, 3 December 1949; Summary of Secretary's Remarks Before The Advertising Council, February 16, 1950, Acheson Papers, Box 69, Press Conf. 1949–1953, Classified Off the Record Speeches Folder, TL; Acheson, Memorandum for the President, 16 February 1950, Truman Papers (WHCF), Box 41, State Department Corres 1950 [2 of 5] Folder, TL; *Memoranda of the Secretary of State* 50:196 (Secretary's Comments on Draft of Economic Speech), 7 March 1950; Notes on the President's Meeting with Under Secretary of State James Webb–March 26, 1950–Little White House, Truman Papers (PSF), Box 159, Subj. File–Cabinet, State, Secretary–Misc Folder, TL.

14 London to Secretary of State, Rec'd January 7, 1950, 11:45 A.M., Telegrams–London, Winant, Truman Papers (PSF), Box 189, Telegrams–London, Winant, Folder, TL; Geoffrey Warner, "Ernest Bevin and British Foreign Policy, 1945–1951," in Craig and Loewenheim, 119; John L. Harper, 296; Schwartz, *America's Germany*, 93; Thomas A. Schwartz, "The Transnational Partnership: Jean Monnet and Jack McCloy," in Hackett, 182.

15 *PAC*, 352–53; Princeton Seminars, 10 October 1953; Lawrence S. Kaplan, "Western Union and European Military Integration 1948–1950—An American Perspective," in Wiggershaus and Foerster, 55; Baylis, *Diplomacy of Pragmatism*, 89; Kaplan, *Community of Interests*, 77.

16 *New York Times*, 14 January 1950; Rempel, 7; Daily Meetings, 27 February 1950; Kennan, *Memoirs 1925–1950*, 448; *PAC*, 437.

17 Laukhuff Oral History, TL, 146–47; Edwin McCammon Martin, Oral History Interview, 6 July 1970 (Independence, MO: The Harry S. Truman Library, September 1981), 24; Byroade Oral History, TL, 73; Hogan, *Marshall Plan*, 311; idem, "Rise and Fall of Economic Diplomacy," 17; Schwartz, *America's Germany*, 119; Harriman to Acheson, 13 March 1950, Acheson Papers, Box 65, TL; Bark and Gress, 277; Large, *Germans to the Front*, 41.

18 *FRUS 1950* 3: 641, 652, 816; Hitchcock, "France, the Western Alliance," 624; Saki Dockrill, 17; Press Conference 4–5–50, Acheson Papers, Box 68, Press Conf. 1949–53, Jan.–Dec. 1950 Folder, TL; *Documents on British Policy* II-2: 187; Leffler, "Strategic Dimensions of the Marshall Plan," 300; *Reviews of the World Situation*, 291.

19 Schwartz, *America's Germany*, 122–23; Memorandum for the President, 5 May 1950, Truman Papers (PSF), Box 220, NSC Meetings . . . Discussions (1950) Folder, TL; Ninkovich, *Germany and the United States*, 84.

20 Princeton Seminars, 10 October 1953; Daily Meetings, 7 and 31 March 1950; *Documents on British Policy* II-2: 17.

21 Kepley, *Collapse of the Middle Way*, 75, 81–82; Truman to Styles Bridges, 26 March 1950, Truman Papers (PSF), Box 228, Foreign Policy–Bipartisan Policy Folder, TL; *Memoranda of Conversations*, 27 April 1950; Acheson to Truman, 5 April 1950, Truman Papers (PSF), Box 160, Subj. File–Cabinet, State, Secy, Acheson Folder, TL; Richard J. Ellis, *Presidential Lightning Rods: The Politics of Blame Avoidance* (Lawrence: University Press of Kansas, 1994), 87; *New York Times*, 2 April and 7 May 1950.

22 Princeton Seminars, 10 October 1953.

23 *PAC*, 382, 384; Princeton Seminars, 10 October 1953; Hitchcock, "France, the Western Alliance," 603; Scott Newton, 179; Mastny, "NATO in the Beholder's Eye," 17.

24 Danchev, "In the back room," 216–17; Princeton Seminars, 10 October 1953; *PAC*, 387–88.

25 *PAC*, 384–88, 392–93; *Documents on British Policy* II-2: 293; *New York Times*, 10 May 1950; Schwartz, *America's Germany*, 95.

26 Outline on "Defense of Europe," Princeton Seminars; Anne Deighton, " 'Arming the Key Battleground': German Rearmament, 1950–55," *Diplomacy & Statecraft* 3 (July 1992): 345; *Documents on Canadian External Relations* 16; 867; Saki Dockrill, 18; *New York Times*, 10 May 1950; Princeton Seminars, 10 October 1953; *FRUS 1950* 3: 1015; *PAC*, 395, 399; Schwabe, 180.

27 *New York Times*, 20, 21, and 28 May 1950; For Webb from Acheson, ACTEL 15, 19 May 1950, Truman Papers (PSF), Box 163, Subj. File–Conferences, London Conf.–NATO May '50 Folder, TL; Princeton Seminars, 10 October 1953; Situation Just Prior to Korea, Roll 1, Synopses, 12, Germany, Princeton Seminars; *PAC*, 400–401.

28 Ismay, 30; Cook, 239; Viebke Sørensen, "Economic Recovery versus Containment: The Anglo-American Controversy over East-West Trade, 1947–51," *Cooperation and Conflict* 24 (no. 2, 1989): 79; Review of the World Situation, CIA, 17 May 1950; Outline on "Defense of Europe," Princeton Seminars.

29 *New York Times*, 3 and 8 June 1950; Press Conference 6–7–50, Acheson Papers, Box 68, Press Conf. 1949–53, Jan.–Dec. 1950 Folder, TL; Marc Trachtenberg, "A 'Wasting Asset': American Strategy and the Shifting Nuclear Balance, 1949–1954," *International Security* 13 (Winter 1988/89): 48; *FRUS 1950* 4: 688–69; Ferrell, *Harry S. Truman*, 357.

Chapter 16

1 William Adams Brown, Jr., and Redvers Opie, *American Foreign Assistance* (Washington: The Brookings Institution, 1953), 412; Qiang Zhia, *Dragon*, 53.

2 For the Press, January 12, 1950; *PAC*, 355–56.

3 Robert J. McMahon, *The Limits of Empire: The United States and Southeast Asia since World War II* (New York: Columbia University Press, 1999), 44–45; *Reviews of the World Situation*, 266.

4 *FRUS 1949* 7 Pt. 2: 1128–33; Schaller, *American Occupation*, 158–59; Nelson, *PPS Papers* 3: 39, 48, 52; David W. Mabon, "Elusive Agreements: The Pacific Pact Proposals of 1949–1951," *Pacific Historical Review* 57 (May 1988): 151–55.

5 *PAC*, 671–72; "Mr. Acheson Answers Some Questions," 30; Martin Thomas, *The French North African Crisis: Colonial Breakdown and Anglo–French Relations, 1945–62* (Houndmills, Basingstoke, Hampshire: Macmillan Press, 2000), 41.

6 Mark Atwood Lawrence, "Transnational Coalition–Building and the Making of the Cold War in Indochina, 1947–1949," *Diplomatic History* 26 (Summer 2002): 468; *FRUS 1949* 7, Pt. 1: 8, 22–25, 28–29, 36–46, 56–57, 65–66; Duiker, 69–71, 75–76.

7 Off the Record Press Conference, August 26, 1949; Round Table, 84–85, 88–91; *Presidential Documents Series*, Reel 1; Chary, viii; *Reviews of the World Situation*, 90; Duiker, 81.

8 *Memorandum of Conversation, Checking Communism in South East Asia*, 8 July 1949, Acheson Papers, Box 64, TL; *FRUS 1949* 7, Pt. 1: 83–88, 101–102; Blum, *Drawing the Line*, 154–58.

9 *FRUS 1949* 7, Pt. 1: 29, 74, 200–203; Chen Jian, *China's Road to the Korean War*, 102–103; Douglas Macdonald, "Communist Bloc Expansion," 182–84; *New York Times*, 5 February 1950; Schaller, *Altered States*, 19–20; Garver, "Little Chance," 93; Central Intelligence Agency, 7 October 1949, Intelligence Memorandum No. 231, Subject: Consequences of Communist Control of French Indochina, Truman Papers, Staff Member office file (hereafter SMOF), Box 2, NSC/CIA (5–11) Intel. Memoranda. Dec. 48–Dec. 49 Folder, TL; *Reviews of the World Situation*, 159–60; Garver, "Polemics, Paradigms, Responsibility," 24–25; Shu Guang Zhang, *Deterrence and Strategic Culture*, 172; Rotter, *Path to Vietnam*, 169.

10 Princeton Seminars, 15 May 1954; Service, "State Department Duty," 357; Melby Oral History, TL, 212; Robert Buzzanco, "Prologue to Tragedy: U.S. Military Opposition to Intervention in Vietnam, 1950–1954," *Diplomatic History* 17 (Spring 1993): 204–205.

11 *FRUS 1950* 6: 691–92, 703, 711, 716–17, 720–22; Donovan, *Tumultuous Years*, 145; Leffler, *Preponderance of Power*, 341; Press Conference 2–24–50, Acheson Papers, Box 68, Press Conf. 1949–53, Jan.–Dec. 1950 Folder, TL; For the Press, January 12, 1950; *Memorandum of Conversation*, 3 February 1950, Acheson Papers, Box 65, TL; Meeting, The White House, 4 February 1950, Acheson Papers, Box 65, TL.

12 *Memoranda of the Secretary of State* 50:131 (McWilliams memo of conversation with Acheson), 14 February 1950; *FRUS 1950* 6: 730–33, 740.

13 Hogan, *Marshall Plan*, 311; Brown and Opie, 407; Col. R. Allen Griffin, Oral History Interview, 15 February 1974, www.trumanlibrary.org/oralhist/griffinr.htm, 52–53, 61 (viewed 9/20/04); *FRUS 1950* 6: 24–25; *Memorandum of Conversation with the President*, 20 February 1950, Acheson Papers, Box 66, TL; Melby Oral History, TL, 211–13; Samuel P. Hayes, ed., *The Beginning of American Aid to Southeast Asia: The Griffin Mission of 1950* (Lexington, MA: Heath Lexington Books, 1971), xi, 11.

14 Daily Meetings, 11 April 1950; McGlothlen, *Controlling the Waves*, 116; *Pattern of Responsibility*, 54; Kepley, *Collapse of the Middle Way*, 81–82.

15 *New York Times*, 20 March 1950; *FRUS 1950* 6: 69–76, 88–91, 766–67; Lanxin Xiang, 217; *PAC*, 673.

16 *FRUS 1950* 6: 780–86, 812; Chen Jian, *China's Road to the Korean War*, 115; Memorandum for the President, 5 May 1950, Truman Papers (PSF), Box 220, NSC Meetings ... Discussions (1950) Folder, TL; *New York Times*, 5 and 9 May 1950; *FRUS 1950* 3: 1038.

17 Review of the World Situation, CIA, 17 May 1950; Alessandro Brogi, *A Question of Self-Esteem: The United States and the Cold War Choices in France and Italy, 1944–1958* (Westport: Praeger, 2002), 117; *FRUS 1950* 6: 819; *Reviews of the World Situation*, 267.

18 David Mayers, *Cracking the Monolith: U.S. Policy against the Sino–Soviet Alliance, 1949–1955* (Baton Rouge: Louisiana State University Press, 1986), 73.

19 Finkelstein, 273; Princeton Seminars, 23 July 1953; Kepley, *Collapse of the Middle Way*, 65; *New York Times*, 14 January 1950; *PAC*, 355; For the Press, January 12, 1950; *Reviews of the World Situation*, 184; Shu Guang Zhang, *Deterrence and Strategic Culture*, 57; *Memoranda of the Secretary of State* 50:36, 13 January 1950; Meeting, The White House, 4 February 1950, Acheson Papers, Box 65, TL.

20 He Di, "The Most Respected Enemy," 34; Schaller, *American Occupation*, 215; Yuan Ming, "The Failure of Perception: America's China Policy, 1949–50," in Harding and Yuan Ming, 150; Chen Jian, *China's Road to the Korean War*, 61. Chen Jian updated previous work on the ideological motivations of CCP–PRC anti–Americanism in *Mao's China and the Cold War* (Chapel Hill: University of North Carolina Press, 2001).

21 Sheng, "The United States, the Chinese Communist Party, and the Soviet Union," 534; Qiang Zhai, *Dragon*, 101; McGlothlen, *Controlling the Waves*, 155; *Memoranda of Conversations*, 29 May 1950, Trygve Lie's Visit to Moscow, 21 January 1950, Meeting in the Secretary's office; *FRUS 1950* 2: 224, 243.

22 Kuhns, 353; *Reviews of the World Situation*, 126–27, 133–34, 164.

23 Glenn D. Paige, *The Korean Decision [June 24–30, 1950]* (New York: The Free Press, 1968), 47; *FRUS 1950* 6: 313n, 339; Daily Meetings, 2 March 1950.

24 *FRUS 1950* 6: 294–96, 308–11; Finkelstein, 288; McGlothlen, *Controlling the Waves*, 158; *New York Times*, 16 February 1950; Garver, "Polemics, Paradigms, Responsibility," 8–11.

25 McGlothlen, *Controlling the Waves*, 155; Nancy Bernkopf Tucker, *Patterns in the Dust*, 192; *Strengthening the Forces of Freedom*, 149; *FRUS 1950* 6: 321–22; *Reviews of the World Situation*, 251–54, 265, 271–76; Chen Jian, *China's Road to the Korean War*, 61.

26 Michael Schaller, "Consul General O. Edmund Clubb, John P. Davies, and the 'Inevitability' of Conflict between the United States and China, 1949–50: A Comment and New Documentation," *Diplomatic History* 9 (Spring 1985): 155.

27 *New York Times*, 6 April 1950; Finkelstein, 296; *Memoranda of Conversations*, 24 March 1950, Conversation between the Secretary & Rep. Herter; *FRUS 1950* 1: 206–209.

28 Shu Guang Zhang, " 'Preparedness Eliminates Mishaps,' " 63, 68, 71; *FRUS 1950* 6: 327–29; Christensen, *Useful Adversaries*, 161; Shu Guang Zhang, *Deterrence and Strategic Culture*, 72–73; McGlothlen, *Controlling the Waves*, 119; Nancy Bernkopf Tucker, "China's Place in the Cold War: the Acheson Plan," in Brinkley, *Acheson and . . . U.S. Foreign Policy*, 115.

29 Nitze was also pressuring Acheson about Formosa. Accinelli, 19.

30 Qiang Zhai, *Dragon*, 37; Douglas Macdonald, *Adventures in Chaos*, 13.

31 Nitze Oral History, TL, 250–51; Schonberger, *Aftermath of War*, 246; Christensen, *Useful Adversaries*, 127–28, 130–31; McGlothlen, *Controlling the Waves*, 120, 209n; Stueck, *Road to Confrontation*, 146; *FRUS 1950* 6: 90, 339 and 2: 244, 247; Accinelli, 17, 19.

32 *FRUS 1950* 2: 379–84, and 6: 347–51; *Memoranda of Conversations*, 29 May 1950, Conversation between the President and the Hon Trygve Lie; Lie, 271; Chen Jian, *China's Road to the Korean War*, 118; Su Ge, 33; McGlothlen, *Controlling the Waves*, 123.

33 *FRUS 1950* 6: 347; McGlothlen, *Controlling the Waves*, 124; Foot, *Practice of Power*, 87; Cumings, *Roaring of the Cataract*, 538; Lowe, "Challenge and Readjustment," 145; William M. Leary and William Stueck, "The Chennault Plan to Save China: U.S. Containment in Asia and

the Origins of the CIA's Aerial Empire, 1949–1950," *Diplomatic History* 8 (Fall 1984): 362; Christensen, *Useful Adversaries*, 129–30.

34 Warren I. Cohen, "Ambassador Philip D. Sprouse on the Question of Recognition of the People's Republic of China in 1949 and 1950," *Diplomatic History* 2 (Spring 1978): 214; Chen Jian, *China's Road to the Korean War*, 118–19; Christensen, *Useful Adversaries*, 136; McGlothlen, *Controlling the Waves*, 155; *Memoranda of Conversations*, 23 June 1950, Visit of Secretary of Foreign Affairs and Ambassador of the Philippines; *New York Times*, 25 June 1950.

35 Nancy Bernkopf Tucker, *Taiwan, Hong Kong, and the United States, 1945–1992: Uncertain Friendships* (New York: Twayne, 1994), 32; Notes on Meeting in Secretary's Office on MacArthur Testimony May 16, 1951, Acheson Papers, Box 63, MacArthur Testimony Folder, TL.

Chapter 17

1 Weinstein, *Perjury*, 508–12; Sam Tanenhaus, *Whittaker Chambers: A Biography* (New York: Random House, 1997), 519–20; Tony Hiss, *The View from Alger's Window: A Son's Memoir* (New York: Alfred A. Knopf, 1999); Eduard Mark, "Who Was 'Venona's' 'Ales'? Cryptanalysis and the Hiss Case," *Intelligence and National Security* 18 (Autumn 2003): 45–72. Other important works relating to the Hiss case—many employing post–cold war disclosures of both U.S. intelligence and Soviet records—are Robert Louis Benson and Michael Warner, eds., *Venona: Soviet Espionage and the American Response, 1939–1957* (Washington: National Security Agency, Central Intelligence Agency, 1996); John Earl Haynes and Harvey Klehr, *Venona: Decoding Soviet Espionage in America* (New Haven: Yale University Press, 1999); idem, *In Denial: Historians, Communism & Espionage* (San Francisco: Encounter Books, 2003); Harvey Klehr, John Earl Haynes, and Fridrikh Igorevich Firsov, eds., *The Secret World of American Communism*, Russian documents trans., Timothy D. Sergay (New Haven: Yale University Press, 1995); Thomas C. Reeves, *The Life and Times of Joe McCarthy: A Biography* (Lanham, MD: Madison Books, 1997), originally published in 1982; Allen Weinstein and Alexander Vassiliev, *The Haunted Wood: Soviet Espionage in America—the Stalin Era* (New York: Random House, 1999); G. Edward White, *Alger Hiss's Looking-Glass Wars: The Covert Life of a Soviet Spy* (New York: Oxford University Press, 2004); and the previously cited works of Kutler and Richard Gid Powers. General Dmitri A. Volkogonov had sifted through selected KGB files, but Hiss worked for the GRU, Soviet army intelligence. Among those rallying to Hiss's defense after Volkogonov's "findings" were John Chabot Smith, his biographer, and John Lowenthal, who had made a film in his favor. *New York Times*, 13 November and 17 December 1992, and 15 October 1993. For the "hard right," see Ann H. Coulter, *Treason: Liberal Treachery from the Cold War to the War on Terrorism* (New York: Crown Forum, 2003). For Truman's disbelief as late as November 1953 in the realities of communist espionage, see Katherine A. S. Sibley, *Red Spies in America: Stolen Secrets and the Dawn of the Cold War* (Lawrence: University Press of Kansas, 2004), 311n.

2 Klehr, Haynes, and Firsov, 326; Sudoplatov, 215; Weinstein and Vassiliev, 68, 231; "Preface: Soviet Espionage and the American Response, 1939–1957," in Benson and Warner, vii–xxxiii; David Holloway, "Sources for *Stalin and the Bomb*," *CWIHPB* (Issue 4, Fall 1994): 8n.

3 Merle Miller, 382; *PAC*, 251; Tanenhaus, *Whittaker Chambers*, 226; Benson and Warner, 423; Weinstein and Vassiliev, 7, 341; G. Edward White, xvii, 29; Ted Morgan, *Reds: McCarthyism in Twentieth-Century America* (New York: Random House, 2003), 155.

4 Denis Smith, 96, 98–101, 129, 132; Bruce Craig, "Alger Hiss, Harry Dexter White and the Canadian Connection: A Reassessment" (unpublished paper, first draft, November 1992, in author's possession), 20, 23–25, 26, 28; James Barros, "Alger Hiss and Harry Dexter White: The Canadian Connection," *Orbis* 21 (Fall 1977): 595–96; Gregg Herken, " 'A Most Deadly Illusion': The Atomic Secret and American Nuclear Weapons Policy, 1945–1950," *Pacific*

Historical Review 49 (February 1980): 63; Truman to Byrnes, 17 November 1945, and Truman to William Lyon Mackenzie King, 20 November 1945, Truman Papers (PSF), Box 172, TL; J. W. Pickersgill and D. F. Forster, *The Mackenzie King Record. Volume 3: 1945–1946* (Toronto: University of Toronto Press, 1970), 37, 39, 42–44, 47–48, 58–59; Haynes and Klehr, 15; Benson and Warner, xxiv; Tanenhaus, *Whittaker Chambers*, 205; Acheson to Truman, 22 December 1945, Truman Papers (PSF), Box 172, TL. Readers should see Craig's later *Treasonable Doubt: The Harry Dexter White Spy Case* (Lawrence: University Press of Kansas, 2004). My thanks to Benedict Z. Zobrist of the Truman Library for locating the Truman letters and memoranda and to Denis Smith for identifying them in his files.

5 Athan G. Theoharis and John Stuart Cox, *The Boss: J. Edgar Hoover and the Great American Inquisition* (Philadelphia: Temple University Press, 1988), 239–40; Joseph C. Grew, *Turbulent Era: A Diplomatic Record of Forty Years, 1904–1945*, ed., Walter Johnson, assisted by Nancy Harvison Hooker (Boston: Houghton Mifflin, 1952): 2: 1452; Service, "State Department Duty," 319, 332, 370; Newman, *Lattimore*, 141; Richard Gid Powers, 195; *Nomination of Dean G. Acheson*, 27–28; David McKean, *Tommy the Cork: Washington's Ultimate Insider from Roosevelt to Reagan* (South Royalton, VT: Steerforth Press, 2004), 180–82; Tanenhaus, *Whittaker Chambers*, 204–5.

6 G. Edward White, 46, Bendiner, 173; Tanenhaus, *Whittaker Chambers*, 160–63; Beatrice Bishop Berle and Travis Beal Jacobs, eds., *Navigating the Rapids, 1918–1971: From the Papers of Adolf A. Berle*, introduction, Max Ascoli (New York: Harcourt Brace Jovanovich, 1973), 582–87; Weinstein and Vassiliev, 48; Isaac Don Levine, *Eyewitness to History: Memoirs and Reflections of a Foreign Correspondent for Half a Century* (New York: Hawthorn Books, 1973), 193–95; Whittaker Chambers, *Witness* (New York: Random House, 1952), 464, 469; Loy Henderson to James Barros, 24 March 1978, Loy Henderson Papers, Box, 2, Library of Congress. My thanks to Stephen A. Schuker for a copy of this letter.

7 Levine, 198; Tanenhaus, *Whittaker Chambers*, 169–70, 203–4; Haynes and Klehr, 91–92; Berle and Jacobs, 582–83.

8 Tanenhaus, *Whittaker Chambers*, 203, 206, 231, 247; Weinstein and Vassiliev, 267–69; Henderson to Barros, 24 March 1978; Weinstein, *Perjury*, 316–17; Haynes and Klehr, 138–43, 146, 149–50. Italics in original.

9 Athan G. Theoharis, "Unanswered Questions: Chambers, Nixon, the FBI and the Hiss Case," in Theoharis, ed., *Beyond the Hiss Case: The FBI, Congress, and the Cold War* (Philadelphia: Temple University Press, 1978), 268–69; Barros, "Alger Hiss and Harry Dexter White," 602–3; Richard Gid Powers, 221; Weinstein, *Perjury*, 317–19, 323–24; Christopher Andrew, *For the President's Eyes Only: Secret Intelligence and the American Presidency from Washington to Bush* (New York: HarperCollins, 1995), 167.

10 J. Edgar Hoover to George E. Allen, 29 May 1946, Truman Papers (PSF), Box 167, Subj. File–FBI Atomic Bomb Folder, TL; Weinstein, *Perjury*, 312; *New York Times*, 3 July 1946.

11 Barros, "Alger Hiss and Harry Dexter White," 603; Henderson to Barros, 24 March 1978; G. Edward White, 50; Weinstein, *Perjury*, 327–29. In an undocumented, imprecisely dated story probably gilded by hindsight, Hiss, according to his biographer, recalled a sharp confrontation with Acheson around this time in which he complained that Acheson's speeches were "scaring hell out of Congress, and making people think there was real danger of a Russian invasion of Western Europe, when the Russians were clearly too exhausted by the war to do anything of the sort." " 'If you don't scare Congress, they'll go fishing,' Acheson replied." John Chabot Smith, *Alger Hiss: The True Story* (New York: Holt, Rinehart and Winston, 1976), 139. When Smith interviewed Hiss, the "scaring the hell out of Congress" phrase had become a standard part of the Truman Doctrine story. On the other hand, Acheson's "they'll go fishing" rings true.

12 Gary May, *China Scapegoat*, 197; *New York Times*, 9 March 1952; Service, "State Department Duty," 366.

13 Irwin F. Gellman, *The Contender: Richard Nixon: The Congress Years, 1946–1952* (New York: The Free Press, 1999), 409; Acheson, *Democrat*, 127; *PAC*, 711; 1955 Acheson Oral History, P.M., 20, 24–27.

14 James Warburg to Dean Acheson, 6 February 1948, Acheson Papers, Box 3, Com. for the Marshall Plan corresp. 1947–8, Folder 2, TL; Acheson to John Ferguson, 17 December 1947, Acheson Papers, Box 3, Com. for the Marshall Plan corresp. 1947–8, Folder 1, TL; Pruessen, *Dulles: Road to Power*, 371; Cooke, 85; Tanenhaus, *Whittaker Chambers*, 223–24; Chambers, 469, 543, 569–70, 576–77.

15 Tanenhaus, *Whittaker Chambers*, 224, 240–42, 247, 329–31; McCullough, 652; Weinstein, *Perjury*, 16, 19; Pruessen, *Dulles: Road to Power*, 372, 401; Gellman, *Contender*, 245; Weinstein and Vassiliev, 2, 4, 19; Haynes and Klehr, 202–3.

16 Benson and Warner, 117, 119; Tanenhaus, *Whittaker Chambers*, 264, 277, 283, 299–305, 317; Weinstein, *Perjury*, 243, 249–51, 266, 268–69.

17 *PAC*, 251; Westwood, 102; Acheson to Louis Halle, 13 September 1963, Acheson Papers, Box 15, Folder 190, YUL; George W. Ball, "Present after the Creation," *New York Review of Books*, 17 December 1992, 11; Chambers, 45.

18 Draft of memoirs, Joseph Alsop Papers, Library of Congress; Alsop to George A. Eddy, 26 November 1979, Alsop Papers, LC (thanks to Bruce Craig for sharing these documents); Weinstein, *Perjury*, 9, 38, 147–48, 170, 337, 535n; *Washington Post* clipping, 20 August 1951, George M. Elsey Papers, Box 101, Personal Correspondence–Acheson Folder, TL. Acheson's memoirs say nothing about counseling the Hisses or representing Currie. Weinstein claims (170, 572) that in 1949, Secretary of State Acheson might have given the Hiss team department documents helpful to their case. Aside from a December 1948 defense attorney letter expressing hope for such help, he cites only a vague statement that "some officials at State complained to the FBI the following year about such practices by the Secretary." This would have been highly implausible behavior for someone who followed department rules in not taking documents home for evening work, left his own papers behind at retirement, and who as an experienced attorney understood how damaging exposure of such pilfering would be to him and to the administration. It is nearly unimaginable that he would have secreted department security files to lawyers fighting charges brought by the justice department of the administration of which he was the leading cabinet member.

19 All information about and quotations from the open hearing of the 13th are from *Nomination of Dean G. Acheson*, a 31-page document.

20 Arthur M. Schlesinger, *A Life in the Twentieth Century: Innocent Beginnings, 1917–1950* (Boston: Houghton Mifflin, 2000), 495–97.

21 *Nomination of Dean G. Acheson*, 5–8, 11–13; "Notes on telephone conversation between DA and Justice Frankfurter," undated but probably ca. 12 September 1953, Acheson Papers, Box 11, TL.

22 Acheson's executive testimony appears in *Executive Sessions of the Senate Foreign Relations Committee . . . 1949–1950* 2: 5–34, about 21 pages of which are dominated by the Hiss issue, especially pp. 5–22. This quotation is from *PAC*, 252.

23 "Acheson's suspicions became a bit clearer when he evaded giving direct answers to several questions about the possibility" that Hiss's wife, Priscilla, "had stolen the papers." Weinstein, *Perjury*, 345. Weinstein is probably seeing too much between the lines. Acheson's testimony seems confused but not so cunning.

24 *Executive Sessions of the Senate Foreign Relations Committee . . . 1949–1950* 2: 4–6, 8–16, 19–20, 22, 31–32.

25 James Rowe, Jr., to Acheson, 14 January 1949, Acheson Papers, Box 27, Folder 339, Abe Fortas to Acheson, 14 January 1949, Box 11, Folder 137, and Acheson to Fortas, 19 January 1949, Box 11, Folder 137, YUL.

26 Tanenhaus, *Whittaker Chambers*, 97, 237, 312, 420; G. Edward White, 45, 47, 260n; Chambers, 569; Richard Breitman and Alan M. Kraut, *American Refugee Policy and European Jewry, 1933–1945* (Bloomington: Indiana University Press, 1987), 188; David S. Wyman, *The Abandonment of the Jews: America and the Holocaust, 1941–1945* (New York: Pantheon Books, 1984), 186.

27 Weinstein, *Perjury*, 572n. In 1953, McCarthy accused Acheson's son-in-law, William P. Bundy, of transgressions connected to Donald Hiss. Also a member of the law firm, Bundy had contributed $400 to Alger's defense fund because of ties with Donald. When Nixon and Dulles backed Bundy, McCarthy dropped the matter. *New York Times*, 7 October 2000; Ted Morgan, 450.

28 Weinstein, *Perjury*, 572n; *PAC*, 354, 359; James R. Dickenson, "Cold Warrior with a Tart Tongue," *The National Observer*, 23 October 1971, 6; Kramnick and Sheerman, 572. Acheson borrowed from a London *Times* writer, who described the McCarthyite attack as "a revolt of the primitives against intelligence." Elmer Davis, 24.

29 Berle and Jacobs, 584; Loy Henderson to James Barros, 24 March 1978, Loy Henderson Papers, Box, 2, Library of Congress.

30 *FRUS 1949* 5: 806–8, 812; *New York Times*, 17 September 1949; Robbie Lieberman, "'Does That Make Peace a Bad Word?' American Responses to the Communist Peace Offensive, 1949–1950," *Peace & Change* 17 (April 1992): 203–11.

31 Cooke, 182, 212, 261n, 302; Tanenhaus, *Whittaker Chambers*, 374, 383n; Weinstein, *Perjury*, 337–38, 345, 399–400, 459; Daily Meetings, 11 March 1949; Chambers, 741n; *New York Times*, 26 January 1950.

32 Brinkley, *Acheson and . . . U.S. Foreign Policy*, xxi–xxii; Paul H. Nitze, *Tension between Opposites: Reflections on the Practice and Theory of Politics* (New York: Charles Scribner's Sons, 1993), 140; Isaacson and Thomas, 491; Chace, 226–27; *PAC*, 360; Lisle A. Rose, *The Cold War Comes to Main Street: America in 1950* (Lawrence: University Press of Kansas, 1999), 117; Press Conference 1-25-50, Acheson Papers, Box 68, Press Conf. 1949–53, Jan.–Dec. 1950 Folder, TL; Tanenhaus, *Whittaker Chambers*, 436–37; McCullough, 760.

33 Isaacson and Thomas, 493; *PAC*, 359–60; 1955 Acheson Oral History, P.M., 19; Chace, 226; Brinkley, *Acheson and . . . U.S. Foreign Policy*, xxii; Tanenhaus, *Whittaker Chambers*, 438; *Public Papers of the Presidents . . . 1950*, 133; Donovan, *Tumultuous Years*, 133.

34 *Public Papers of the Presidents . . . 1949*, 510; Chambers, 777; Weinstein, *Perjury*, 450; McCullough, 760; Reston, *Deadline*, 153; Reston letters to Archibald MacLeish, 24 January 1950, Harold Phelps Stokes, 26 January 1950, and Louis M. Lyons, 26 January 1950, Reston Papers, Box 30, Working Files, UIA.

35 Tanenhaus, *Whittaker Chambers*, 433, 438–39; James P. Warburg to Acheson, 26 January 1950, Box 33, Folder 427, YUL; Weinstein, *Perjury*, 450; *PAC*, 360–61, 365; *New York Times*, 26 and 27 January and 1 February 1950; Public Comment on Secretary Acheson's January 25 Remarks about Alger Hiss, George M. Elsey Papers, Box 61, Summary of Press . . . Statement on Hiss Folder, TL.

36 Rose, 118–19; "I have been asked to explain the statement . . . ," undated, Acheson Papers, Box 89, Atomic Bomb and Atomic Energy Folder, TL; *New York Times*, 1 March 1950; Steel, *Walter Lippmann*, 468–69. My emphasis.

37 Matthews, 402; Princeton Seminars, 10 October 1953; 1955 Acheson Oral History, P.M., 16–18.

38 *Conversations with Eric Sevareid*, 77; "Hard Words," 827.

39 Chambers, 616.

40 *PAC*, 251.

41 Webb—Handed to the Secretary by Mr. Clark in NY, Mar. 12, 1951, Acheson Papers, Box 68, Press Conferences—1951 Folder, TL; *New York Times*, 13 March 1951.

Chapter 18

1 Weinstein and Vassiliev, 299; Reeves, 356.

2 Truman to Acheson, 31 March 1950, Truman Papers (PSF), Box 160, Subj. File–Cabinet, State, Secy, Acheson Folder, TL; *New York Times*, 24 December 1999; Sprouse Oral History, TL, 11–12; Melby Oral History, TL, 173; *FRUS 1949* 8: 310; Conrad E. Snow, Oral History Interview, 2 July 1973 (Independence, MO: Harry S. Truman Library, February 1976), 29–30.

3 *New York Times*, 14 July 1951, 6 and 9 March 1952, and 11 May 1980; Chambers, 270–71n; O. Edmund Clubb, Oral History Interview, 26 June 1974, www.trumanlibrary.org/ oralhist/clubb.htm, 3 (viewed 6/8/05); Edwin W. Martin Oral History, TL, 87–88; Nathaniel P. Davis to Acheson, 6 March 1952, Nathaniel P. Davis Papers, Box 1, Clubb . . . Corres., 1952 Folder, TL; Nathaniel P. Davis, 155–56; *PAC*, 633, 760–62.

4 *Lexington* (Ky.) *Herald-Leader*, 5 February 1999; Service, "State Department Duty," 353, 359, 362, 367a, 368–69, 375, 378, 380–81, 384, 386–87, 391–92, 392b, 393–94, 401, 406, 434a, 434c, 455, 472–73, 531; Reeves, 300–305, 323–25; Harvey Klehr and Ronald Radosh, *The Amerasia Spy Case: Prelude to McCarthyism* (Chapel Hill: University of North Carolina Press, 1996), 210; 1955 Acheson Oral History, P.M., 21 (emphasis added); Armistead M. Lee letter, *Washington Post*, 31 July 1995; Affidavit of Dean Acheson, Secretary of State, *John S. Service v. Hiram Bingham, et al.*, John Service Papers, Box 1, Court Case–John S. Service Folder, TL; T. J. Schoenbaum, 200. Unlike Clubb, Service could not claim his retirement benefits.

5 James Fetzer, "The Case of John Paton Davies, Jr.," *Foreign Service Journal* 54 (November 1977): 15, 18, 20, 22, 32; Theodore H. White, 181; *New York Times*, 14 July 1951 and 24 December 1999; 1955 Acheson Oral History, A.M., 41, P.M., 15; Byroade Oral History, TL, 41–42.

6 Newman, *Lattimore*, 362; May, *China Scapegoat*, 24–28, 181–86, 291; *PAC*, 304; *Executive Sessions of the Senate Foreign Relations Committee (Historical Series). Volume I: Eightieth Congress, First and Second Sessions, 1947–1948* (Washington: U.S. Government Printing Office, 1976), 1: 55, 315–21 (henceforth *Executive Sessions of the Senate Foreign Relations Committee . . . 1947–1948*); Bevin Alexander, *The Strange Connection: U.S. Intervention in China, 1944–1972* (Westport: Greenwood Press, 1992), 71; Cumings, *Roaring of the Cataract*, 712; Reeves, 364–69.

7 May, *China Scapegoat*, 187, 190–205, 224–31, 235–41, 247–60, 263–65, 267–89; Ernest R. May, "The China Hands in Perspective: Ethics, Diplomacy, and Statecraft," in Paul Gordon Lauren, ed., *The China Hands' Legacy: Ethics and Diplomacy* (Boulder: Westview Press, 1987), 105; *PAC*, 710–13, 767–69; FRUS 1952–1954 1, Pt. 1: 33; *New York Times*, 4 January 1953; *Public Papers of the Presidents . . . 1952–53*, 1110–11; Reeves, 461. Both Service and Davies died in 1999, Clubb in 1989.

8 Loss, 354; Acheson, *Democrat*, 120–22, 127–28, 137–40; Acheson to Truman, 2 March 1953, Acheson Papers, Box 30, Folder 391, YUL.

9 Gellman, *Contender*, 409; Loss, 355; Ernest R. May, "China Hands in Perspective," 104; Robert Dean, "Masculinity as Ideology," 12 March 1998, http://h-net.msu .edu/cgi-bin/logbrowse.pl?trx=vx&list=H-Diplo&month=9803&week=b&msg= bhnnqskbjuJIbgjRgDi5lg&user=&pw=, and 23 March 1998, http://h-net.msu.edu/cgi-bin/ logbrowse.pl?trx=vx&list=H-Diplo&month=9803&week=d&msg=d57juwf BwyqnFHcJmvd7EQ&user=&pw= (viewed 9/20/04); Robert D. Dean, *Imperial Brotherhood: Gender and the Making of Cold War Foreign Policy* (Amherst: University of Massachusetts Press, 2001), 66, 76; David K. Johnson, *The Lavender Scare: The Cold War Persecution of Gays and Lesbians in the Federal Government* (Chicago: University of Chicago Press, 2004), 7, 17, 71–72.

10 Gerald Horne, *Black and Red: W.E.B. Du Bois and the Afro-American Response to the Cold War, 1944–1963* (Albany: State University of New York Press, 1986), 131–32; Mary L.

Dudziak, "Josephine Baker, Racial Protest, and the Cold War," *Journal of American History* 81 (September 1994): 548, 552, 566.

11 *FRUS 1950* 2: 72; Press and Radio News Conference, Wednesday, April 25, 1951, 11:30 a.m., Acheson Papers, Box 68, Press Conferences–1951 Folder, TL; *New York Times*, 22 May 1952, 30 December 1952, and 1 January 1953; Kutler, 89–92; Newman, *Lattimore*, 355; *PAC*, 16; Acheson to Felix Frankfurter, 9 September 1952, Acheson Papers, Box 11, Folder 145, YUL.

12 *New York Times*, 9 and 14 January 1950; Campbell, *Foreign Affairs Fudge Factory*, 117; Princeton Seminars, 23 July 1953; Blum, *CIA*, 18; Reston, *Deadline*, 217; Michael Kazin, *The Populist Persuasion: An American History*, rev. ed. (Ithaca: Cornell University Press, 1998), 185; Brandon, 96.

13 *PAC*, 364; Melvin Small, *Democracy and Diplomacy: The Impact of Domestic Politics on U.S. Foreign Policy, 1789–1994* (Baltimore: Johns Hopkins University Press, 1996), 94; Campbell, *Foreign Affairs Fudge Factory*, 117; *New York Times*, 5, 11, 18, 19, and 22 March 1950; Michael D. Pearlman, *Warmaking and American Democracy: The Struggle over Military Strategy, 1700 to the Present* (Lawrence: University Press of Kansas, 1999), 305; Yergin, *Shattered Peace*, 278; Steel, *Walter Lippmann*, 468–69; Acheson, *Democrat*, 65–66; Ellis, 86, citing Glen H. Stassen, "Individual Preference versus Role-Constraint in Policy-Making: Senatorial Response to Secretaries Acheson and Dulles," *World Politics* 25 (October 1972): 96–119; *Documents on Canadian External Relations* 16: 358; *Documents on British Policy* II-2: 45.

14 Reeves, 231, 401; *PAC*, 362–63, 370; "No yearning to be loved," 443; *New York Times*, 16 February 1950, 1, 9, and 16 March 1950, and 13 October 1971; Acheson to Michael Janeway, 3 April 1962, Acheson Papers, Box 16, Folder 209, YUL; Weinstein, *Perjury*, 451; Press Conference 3–8–50, Acheson Papers, Box 68, Press Conf. 1949–53, Jan.–Dec. 1950 Folder, TL.

15 *Public Papers of the Presidents . . . 1952–53*, 223; Chace, 83; Harold L. Ickes to Acheson, 22 March 1950, and Acheson to Ickes, 3 April 1950, Acheson Papers, Box 16, Folder 204, YUL; *New York Times*, 26, 27, and 31 March 1950; *Public Papers of the Presidents . . . 1950*, 234–36; Acheson to Henry L. Stimson, 27 March 1950, Acheson Papers, Box 43, Secretary of State, 1949–53, Alph.–Sta–Sz Folder, TL; Notes on the President's Meeting with Under Secretary of State James Webb–March 26, 1950–Little White House, Truman Papers (PSF), Box 159, Subj. File–Cabinet, State, Secretary–Misc Folder, TL; Truman to Styles Bridges, 26 March 1950, Truman Papers (PSF), Box 228, Foreign Policy–Bipartisan Policy Folder, TL; *Memoranda of Conversations*, 27 April 1950, Truman Papers (PSF), Box 225, March–April 1950 Folder, TL.

16 James N. Rosenau, "Senate Attitudes toward a Secretary of State," in John C. Wahlke and Heinz Eulau, eds., *Legislative Behavior: A Reader in Theory and Research* (Glencoe: Free Press, 1959), 339; *Memoranda of the Secretary of State* 50:129, 13 February 1950; Reeves, 299; *Pattern of Responsibility*, 233–43; *PAC*, 366–67; *New York Times*, 23 and 24 April 1950; Bernhard, "Clearer than Truth," 562–63; Paul G. Hoffman to Don Hoffman, 25 April 1950, Paul Hoffman Papers, Box 2, Chronological File 1950–April–June Folder, TL.

17 *New York Times*, 26 November 1950; James Reston, *The Artillery of the Press: Its Influence on American Foreign Policy* (New York: Harper & Brothers, 1967), 46; *Military Situation in the Far East*, 1683; Secretary, Drummond, Kuh, 3–27–52, Acheson Papers, Box 69, Press Conf. 1949–1953, Jan. 1952–Jan. 1953 Folder, TL; The Secretary, Bryson Rash . . . George de Carvalho . . . Holmes Alexander . . . Lloyd Lehrbas, Acheson Papers, Box 69, Press Conf. 1949–1953, Jan. 1952–Jan. 1953 Folder, TL; Notes on the President's Meeting with Under Secretary of State James Webb–March 26, 1950–Little White House, Truman Papers (PSF), Box 159, Subj. File–Cabinet, State, Secretary–Misc Folder, TL; Battle Oral History, TL, 13; Thorp Oral History, TL, 26, 168, 181.

18 *New York Times*, 3 and 14 July, 17, 18, and 31 August, 9 October, and 7, 12, and 16 December 1950; Gellman, *Contender*, 316; Joseph C. Goulden, *Korea: The Untold Story of*

the War (New York: Times Books, 1982), 389; Foot, *The Wrong War*, 107; David Caute, *The Great Fear: The Anti-Communist Purge under Truman and Eisenhower* (New York: Simon & Schuster, 1978), 43; Steel, *Walter Lippmann*, 474; Annan, "Dean Acheson," 473.

19 Large, *Germans to the Front*, 124; *New York Times*, 4, 20, and 27 May, 1, 3, 7, 15, 17, and 28 June, 11, 26, 27, and 29 July, and 20 August 1951; Graebner, "Dean G. Acheson," 285.

20 Pace Oral History, TL, 128; *Memoranda of the Secretary of State* 51:677 (Memorandum of Telephone Conversation), 17 October 1951; McFall Oral History, TL, 44–49; Memorandum for the Files: The Secretary, Lester Markel, *New York Times*, January 23, 1951, Acheson Papers, Box 68, Press Conferences–1951 Folder, TL; Mr. Barrett, F. H. Russell, The Secretary and Current Public Opinion, 2/2/51, Truman Papers (WHCF), Box 42, State Department Corres 1951–52 [2 of 6] Folder, TL; Memorandum for Mr. Murphy: Subject: Secretary Acheson and the Denver Conference, May 24, 14 May 1951, George M. Elsey Papers, Box 101, Personal Correspondence–Acheson Folder, TL.

21 William Stueck, *Rethinking the Korean War: A New Diplomatic and Strategic History* (Princeton: Princeton University Press, 2002), 226; *New York Times*, 8, 10, and 19 December 1950, 30 August 1951, 10 August and 6 October 1952; Barry Rubin, *Secrets of State: The State Department and the Struggle over U.S. Foreign Policy* (New York: Oxford University Press, 1985), 72; Max Hastings, *The Korean War* (New York: Simon & Schuster, 1987), 184; McLellan, *State Department Years*, 301; Franklin D. Mitchell, *Harry S. Truman and the News Media: Contentious Relations, Belated Respect* (Columbia: University of Missouri Press, 1998), 230; Press and Radio Conference #247, December 19, 1950, Truman Papers (PSF), Box 225, TL; *Documents on British Policy* IV-2: 258n.

22 *New York Times*, 19 July and 10 December 1950, 29 January, 16 September, 30 November, and 31 December 1951; *PAC*, 88; Elmer Davis, 23–29.

23 Ted Morgan, 394; Ellis, 89; *New York Times*, 14 September 1951, 19 October 1951, 13 December 1951, and 16 January 1952; Reeves, 378; Acheson, *Grapes from Thorns*, 96; Daily Meetings, 1 December 1950.

24 The President's Press and Radio Conference #314, August 28, 1952, Truman Papers (PSF), Box 226; *New York Times*, 16 March and 7 October 1952; *Memoranda of Conversations*, 2 June 1952, Luncheon.

25 Acheson, "Legislative-Executive Relations," 491, 493; Princeton Seminars, 10 October 1953; *Memoranda of Conversations*, 29 December 1950; Memorandum for the Files: Secretary Acheson, Ed Milne . . . Paul Martin . . . Al Warner, January 18, 1951, Acheson Papers, Box 68, Press Conferences–1951 Folder, TL; *New York Times*, 8 June 1951.

26 McLellan, *State Department Years*, 228; Verne W. Newton, *The Cambridge Spies: The Untold Story of Maclean, Philby, and Burgess in America* (Lanham, MD: Madison Books, 1991), 257; McCullough, 766; *Memoranda of Conversations*, 6 February 1951; Tyler Abell, ed., *Drew Pearson Diaries, 1949–1959* (New York: Holt, Rinehart and Winston, 1974), 162; Isaacson and Thomas, 546; Russell Oral History, TL, 39; Laukhuff Oral History, TL, 150.

27 Memorandum of the Press and Radio News Conference, Wednesday, November 8, 1950, Acheson Papers, Box 68, Press Conf. 1949–53, Jan.–Dec. 1950 Folder, TL; *New York Times*, 10 December 1950 and 17 May 1951; Memo of Press Conference, 5–16–51, Acheson Papers, Box 68, Press Conferences–1951 Folder, TL; Clifford, *Counsel to the President*, 142; Lankford, 250; Merle Miller, 268–69, 307.

28 Secretary Acheson's Background Press Conference, March 13, 1950, Acheson Papers, Box 68, Press Conf. 1949–53, Jan.–Dec. 1950 Folder, TL; Review of the World Situation, CIA, 17 May 1950; Donaldson, 426.

29 *PAC*, 345.

30 Ibid., 369–70; *Memoranda of the Secretary of State* 51:499 (Memorandum for S/S), 25 July 1951; Peter Duignan and L. H. Gann, *The Rebirth of the West: The Americanization of the Democratic World, 1945–1958* (Cambridge, MA: Blackwell, 1992), 114; Reeves, 673.

31 Princeton Seminars, 10 October 1953; Acheson to Barbara Tuchman, 1 June 1967, Acheson Papers, Box 31, Folder 401, YUL; Theodore H. White, 346; Acheson Oral History, TL 1971, 9.

32 Acheson, "Legislative-Executive Relations," 484–85; *PAC*, 266; War College Speech, 16 September 1948, 25; Acheson to William S. White, 28 December 1956, Acheson Papers, Box 34, Folder 434, YUL; *Memoranda of Conversations*, 20 June 1951, Miscellaneous Matters; Princeton Seminars, 2 July, 9 July, 22 July, and 10 October 1953; T. D. Cabot Oral History, TL, 47; Benson, 36.

33 Acheson to Harold Stein, 23 August 1957, Acheson Papers, Box 29, Folder 371, YUL; "No yearning to be loved," 443; *PAC*, 101; *New York Times*, 13 October 1971.

34 Rosenau, 336–37, 346n.

35 Franks Oral History, TL, 28; "Dean Acheson, A Remembrance," 32; Princeton Seminars, 2 and 15 July 1953; Acheson Oral History, TL 1971, 18; Hickerson Oral History, TL, 86–87; Acheson to Truman, 5 April 1950, Truman Papers (PSF), Box 160, Subj. File–Cabinet, State, Secy, Acheson Folder, TL; Ellis, 87; Acheson to Truman, 21 June 1955, Acheson Papers, Box 30, Folder 393, YUL; *PAC*, 71; David Robertson, *Sly and Able: A Political Biography of James F. Byrnes* (New York: W. W. Norton, 1994), 428; Kepley, *Collapse of the Middle Way*, 38; Acheson, *Sketches from Life*, 123–32.

36 War College Speech, 16 September 1948, 22–26; Princeton Seminars, 2 July 1953; Memorandum for the Files: Secretary Acheson, Ed Milne . . . Paul Martin . . . Al Warner, January 18, 1951, Acheson Papers, Box 68, Press Conferences–1951 Folder, TL.

37 Reston in "Dean Acheson, a Remembrance," 31; Brandon, 65; Elmer Davis, 28; *New York Times*, 3 February 1949; Press and Radio News Conference on North Atlantic Pact, Friday, March 18, 1949–9 A.M., Acheson Papers, Box 68, Press Conf. 1949–53, Jan.–June 1949 Folder, TL; Princeton Seminars, 22 July 1953.

38 Press Conference 11–16–49, Acheson Papers, Box 68, Press Conf. 1949–53, July–Dec. 1949 Folder, TL; Press-Radio 4–20–49, Acheson Papers, Box 68, Press Conf. 1949–53, Jan.–June 1949 Folder, TL; *New York Times*, 24 April and 7 May 1950; Press-Radio 2–16–49, Acheson Papers, Box 68, Press Conf. 1949–53, Jan.–June 1949 Folder, TL; Princeton Seminars, 22 July 1953.

39 Gaddis Smith, *Dean Acheson*, 410–11; Princeton Seminars, 9 and 16 July and 10 October 1953; War College Speech, 16 September 1948, 2; Acheson to James Webb, stamped Sep 28 1949, James Webb Papers, Box 22, Folder 3, TL; Daily Meetings, 7 March and 15 December 1949, and 6 February 1950; *New York Times*, 15 January 1950; Reston to C. L. Sulzberger, 17 February 1950, and to David H. Holbrook, 17 February 1950, Reston Papers, Box 30, Working Files, UIA; Cumings, *Roaring of the Cataract*, 417; Alsop, *I've Seen the Best of It*, 303, 346; Merry, 183–84; *PAC*, 223; Acheson to Ernest A. Gross, 2 November 1959, Box 14, Folder 178, YUL.

40 Princeton Seminars, 9 and 23 July 1953, and 13 February 1954; *Memoranda of the Secretary of State* 50:140, 16 February 1950, Battle memo to Lehrbas; Memorandum for File, June 30, 1951: Subject: Blair House Meeting–June 27, 1950, George M. Elsey Papers, Box 71, Korea–June 27, 1950 Folder, TL; *Memoranda of Conversations*, 22 January 1951; Memorandum for the Files: Secretary Acheson, Joseph Harsch . . . Carlton Kent . . . Herbert Ellison, January 22, 1951, Acheson Papers, Box 68, Press Conferences–1951 Folder, TL; Background Press Meeting, February 8, 4:30 P.M., February 9, 1951, Acheson Papers, Box 68, Press Conferences–1951 Folder, TL; *Memoranda of Conversations*, 13 February 1951, Memorandum for the Files; Mr. Webb, July 23, 1951, Department of State: Notes and briefing, James Webb Papers, Box 23, Folder 1, TL; Secretary, Drummond, Kuh, 3–27–52, Acheson Papers, Box 69, Press Conf. 1949–1953, Jan. 1952 – Jan. 1953 Folder, TL; *Memoranda of Conversations*, 27 March, 11 April, 2 May, and 2 June 1952; The Secretary, Bryson Rash . . . George de Carvalho . . . Holmes Alexander . . . Lloyd Lehrbas, Acheson Papers, Box 69, Press Conf. 1949–1953, Jan.

1952–Jan. 1953 Folder, TL; Meeting, Lindsay Hoban, 5–12–52, Acheson Papers, Box 69, Press Conf. 1949–1953, Jan. 1952–Jan. 1953 Folder, TL (henceforth Meeting, Lindsay Hoban, 5–12–52); Memo, Press Conf., Salazar's, 7–5–52, Acheson Papers, Box 69, Press Conf. 1949–1953, Jan. 1952–Jan. 1953 Folder, TL.

41 Elmer Davis, 28; Acheson to Truman, 28 June 1960, Acheson Papers, Box 31, Folder 398, YUL.

42 For the Press, January 12, 1950; Acheson, *Vast External Realm*, 125–26.

43 *PAC*, 719; Wesley T. Wooley, Jr., *Alternatives to Anarchy: American Supranationalism since World War II* (Bloomington: Indiana University Press, 1988), 119; Walter LaFeber, "American Policy-Makers, Public Opinion, and the Outbreak of the Cold War, 1945–50," in Yonosuke Nagai and Akira Iriye, eds., *The Origins of the Cold War in Asia* (New York: Columbia University Press, 1977), 49, 60; *Pattern of Responsibility*, 293.

44 Princeton Seminars, 12 December and 11 October 1953; Acheson to Truman, 12 April 1951, Truman Papers (PSF), Box 160, Subj. File–Cabinet, State, Secy, Acheson Folder, TL; *FRUS 1949* 5: 812; *Memoranda of Conversations*, 11 April 1952; Meeting, Lindsay Hoban, 5–12–52; Acheson to Louis Halle, 5 March 1954, Acheson Papers, Box 15, Folder 189, YUL; Acheson to Patrick Devlin, 2 April 1964, Box 8, Folder 97, YUL.

45 Bernhard, "Clearer than Truth," 546, 559; idem, *U.S. Television News and Cold War Propaganda, 1947–1960* (New York: Cambridge University Press, 1999), 69, 75–78, 81–82, 88–89, 113.

46 Daily Meetings, 6 November 1950; *New York Times*, 9 November 1950; Situation as of December 14 with respect to the standing of the Secretary and the State Department with the American Public, 12/15/50, George M. Elsey Papers, Box 58, Foreign Relations–General 1950–51, Folder 1, TL; *Memoranda of Conversations*, 23 January 1951; Memorandum for the Files: The Secretary, Lester Markel, *New York Times*, January 23, 1951, Acheson Papers, Box 68, Press Conferences–1951 Folder, TL.

47 Acheson to Oliver Franks, 7 July 1954, Acheson Papers, Box 12, Folder 150, YUL.

Chapter 19

1 Princeton Seminars, 13 February 1954.

2 Cumings's first volume is subtitled *Liberation and the Emergence of Separate Regimes, 1945–1947*; the second, already cited, is *The Roaring of the Cataract, 1947–1950* (both published by Princeton University Press). Preceding Cumings by nearly twenty years, I. F. Stone described North Korea's attack as a response to belligerent southern probes across the 38th parallel, a view echoing the propagandistic explanations of communist states in the 1950s. *The Hidden History of the Korean War*, 2d ed. (New York: Monthly Review Press, 1972), originally published in 1952.

3 Erik van Ree, *Socialism in One Zone: Stalin's Policy in Korea, 1945–1947* (Oxford: Berg, 1989), 10, 199; Xiaoyuan Liu, "Sino-American Diplomacy over Korea during World War II," *Journal of American–East Asian Relations* 1 (Summer 1992): 223–64; Stueck, *Rethinking*, 47.

4 McGlothlen, *Controlling the Waves*, 54; Cumings, *Roaring of the Cataract*, 45–46, 52; *Executive Sessions of the Senate Foreign Relations Committee . . . 1947–1948* 1: 54; Truman, *Years of Trial and Hope*, 326; John Lewis Gaddis, "The Strategic Perspective: The Rise and Fall of the 'Defensive Perimeter' Concept, 1947–1951," in Borg and Heinrichs, *Uncertain Years*, 104.

5 Michael Warner, 268, 274; Kathryn Weathersby, " 'Should We Fear This?': Stalin and the Danger of War with America" (Washington: Cold War International History Project, Woodrow Wilson International Center for Scholars, Working Paper No. 39, July 2002), 4–5; Donovan, *Tumultuous Years*, 96; McGlothlen, *Controlling the Waves*, 67; Lee, 31; James I.

Matray, *The Reluctant Crusade: American Foreign Policy in Korea, 1941–1950* (Honolulu: University of Hawaii Press, 1985), 198, 204; Cumings, *Roaring of the Cataract*, 385.

6 Matray, *Reluctant Crusade*, 191; Memorandum of Conversation: Korea, Military Assistance and Related Matters, July 11, 1949, *Presidential Documents Series*, Reel 1.

7 Memo to Pres., Meeting with Cong. Leadership, 6–18–49, Truman Papers (PSF), Box 159, Subj. File–Cabinet, State, Secy Folder (Folder 2), TL; McGlothlen, *Controlling the Waves*, 69–73, 78; Princeton Seminars, 13 February 1954 (where Acheson conflates the 1949 and 1950 contests over Korean aid); Bruce Cumings, "Introduction: The Course of Korean-American Relations, 1943–1953," in Cumings, ed., *Child of Conflict: The Korean-American Relationship, 1943–1953* (Seattle: University of Washington Press, 1983), 33; Daily Meetings, 24 August 1949; Off the Record Press Conference, August 26, 1949; Round Table, 130.

8 Acheson, "Legislative-Executive Relations," 487; Lucius Battle, in "From Where I Stood: A Panel," Francis H. Heller, ed., *The Korean War: A 25-Year Perspective* (Lawrence: The Regents Press of Kansas, 1977), 12; Russell Oral History, TL, 12; 1955 Acheson Oral History, A.M., 45–46; *New York Times*, 15 January 1950.

9 For the Press, January 12, 1950; *PAC*, 355–57. James F. Schnabel and Robert J. Watson, *The History of the Joint Chiefs of Staff: The Joint Chiefs of Staff and National Policy. Volume III: The Korean War, Part I*, introduction, Terrence J. Gough (Wilmington, DE: Michael Glazier, 1979), 26. The presence of a department stenographer accounts for the availability of a text of this ad-libbed speech. Princeton Seminars, 13 February 1954. Emphasis mine, reconstructing how I believe he actually vocalized these words.

10 *New York Times*, 2 March 1949; *PAC*, 357; Notes on Meeting in Secretary's Office on MacArthur Testimony May 16, 1951, Acheson Papers, Box 63, MacArthur Testimony Folder, TL; Princeton Seminars, 13 February 1954; 1955 Acheson Oral History, A.M., 44–45.

11 Hopkins, 159; Princeton Seminars, 13 February 1954; *New York Times*, 13 and 15 January 1950; Ambassador John J. Muccio, Oral History Interview, 10 and 18 February 1971 (Independence, MO: The Harry S. Truman Library, January 1972), 16; Finkelstein, 278; Cumings, *Roaring of the Cataract*, 424–25.

12 *Reviews of the World Situation*, 184, 191; Gye-Dong Kim, "Who Initiated the Korean War?" in James Cotton and Ian Neary, eds., *The Korean War in History* (Atlantic Highlands, NJ: Humanities, 1989), 40.

13 Marshall Shulman remarks in May 1994 Shepardson Fellowship Seminar, Council on Foreign Relations, New York; *FRUS 1950* 7: 8; Kuhns, 349.

14 McGlothlen, *Controlling the Waves*, 74–75, 78; *Congressional Record*, 81st Congress, 2d Sess., 19 January 1950, 656; *New York Times*, 20 and 21 January and 10 February 1950; *PAC*, 358; Acheson to Truman, 20 January 1950, Truman Papers (PSF), Box 243, Korea data–general PSF–Korean War File, TL; Cumings, *Roaring of the Cataract*, 425; Christensen, *Useful Adversaries*, 116; Princeton Seminars, Synopsis A, 9–10; Acheson, "Legislative-Executive Relations," 494; idem, *Citizen Looks at Congress*, 83–84.

15 *FRUS 1950* 7: 28, 35–36, 42, 64–66; *FRUS 1950* 6: 69–70; Blum, *CIA*, 45; Daily Meetings, 5 April 1950; Matray, "America's Reluctant Crusade," 442; Press and Radio News Conference, Wednesday, May 3, 1950, 11:00 A.M., EST, Acheson Papers, Box 68, Press Conf. 1949–53, Jan.–Dec. 1950 Folder, TL; Cumings, *Roaring of the Cataract*, 466; Ninkovich, *Modernity and Power*, 193.

16 Review of the World Situation, CIA, 17 May 1950; *FRUS 1950* 7: 88–89, 109–10, 120; Matray, "America's Reluctant Crusade," 443; Kathryn Weathersby, "New Russian Documents on the Korean War," *CWIHPB* (Issues 6–7, Winter 1995/1996): 39; J. Lawton Collins, *War in Peacetime: The History and Lessons of Korea* (Boston: Houghton Mifflin, 1969), 42–43.

17 Paige, 74; James G. Hershberg, *James B. Conant: Harvard to Hiroshima and the Making of the Nuclear Age* (New York: Alfred A. Knopf, 1993), 492; *New York Times*, 23 June 1950; Weathersby, "New Russian Documents," 39; Millett, 200.

18 At this writing, the most important groundbreaking work appears in a series of articles by Kathryn Weathersby: "Korea, 1949–50: To Attack, or Not to Attack? Stalin, Kim Il Sun, and the Prelude to War," *CWIHPB* (Issue 5, Spring 1995): 1–9; "New Findings on the Korean War: Translation and Commentary," *CWIHPB* (Issue 3, Fall 1993): 1, 14–18; "New Russian Documents on the Korean War," *CWIHPB* (Issues 6–7, Winter 1995/1996): 30–84; "Soviet Aims in Korea and the Origins of the Korean War, 1949–1950: New Evidence from the Russian Archives" (Washington: Cold War International History Project, Woodrow Wilson International Center for Scholars, Working Paper No. 8, 1993); and "The Soviet Role in the Early Phase of the Korean War: New Documentary Evidence," *Journal of American-East Asian Relations* 2 (Winter 1993): 425–58. Other important works, listed alphabetically by author, are Evgueni Bajanov, "Assessing the Politics of the Korean War, 1949–51," *CWIHPB* (Issues 6–7, Winter 1995/1996): 54, 87–91; Chen Jian, "China's Changing Aims during the Korean War, 1950–1951," *Journal of American-East Asian Relations* 1 (Spring 1992): 8–41; idem, *China's Road to the Korean War*, previously cited; idem, "The Sino-Soviet Alliance and China's Entry into the Korean War" (Washington: Cold War International History Project, Woodrow Wilson International Center for Scholars, Working Paper No. 1, June 1992); Thomas J. Christensen, "Threats, Assurances, and the Last Chance for Peace: The Lessons of Mao's Korean War Telegrams," *International Security* 17 (Summer 1992): 122–54; idem, *Useful Adversaries*, previously cited; "Documentation," *CWIHPB* (Issue 4, Fall 1994): 60–85; Garver, "Polemics, Paradigms, Responsibility," previously cited; Goncharov, Lewis, and Xue Litai, previously cited; Hyun-Su Jeon, with Gyoo Kahng, "The Shtykov Diaries: New Evidence on Soviet Policy in Korea," *CWIHPB* (Issues 6–7, Winter 1995/1996): 69, 92–93; Li Xiaobing, Wang Xi, and Chen Jian, trans., "Mao's Dispatch of Chinese Troops to Korea: Forty-Six Telegrams, July–October 1950," *Chinese Historians* 5 (Spring 1992): 63–86; Alexandre Y. Mansourov, "Stalin, Mao, Kim, and China's Decision to Enter the Korean War, September 16–October 15 1950: New Evidence from the Russian Archives," *CWIHPB* (Issues 6–7, Winter 1995/1996): 94–119; Mastny, *The Cold War and Soviet Insecurity*, previously cited; Qiang Zhai, *Dragon*, previously cited; Shen Zhihua, "Sino-Soviet Relations and the Origins of the Korean War: Stalin's Strategic Goals in the Far East," *Journal of Cold War Studies* 2 (Spring 2000): 44–68; William W. Stueck, Jr., *The Korean War: An International History* (Princeton: Princeton University Press, 1995); Robert C. Tucker, "The Cold War in Stalin's Time: What the New Sources Reveal," *Diplomatic History* 21 (Spring 1997): 273–81; Westad, "Fighting for Friendship," previously cited, 224–36; idem, "Secrets of the Second World: The Russian Archives and the Reinterpretation of Cold War History," *Diplomatic History* 21 (Spring 1997): 259–71; Vladislav M. Zubok, "CPSU Plenums, Leadership Struggles, and Soviet Cold War Politics," *CWIHPB* (Issue 10, March 1998): 28–33; and idem, "Stalin's Plans," previously cited. Though differing on details, these works all assign primary responsibility for the Korean War to communist states.

19 John Merrill, *Korea: The Peninsular Origins of the War* (Newark: University of Delaware Press, 1989), 167; Weathersby, "Soviet Aims in Korea," 26; He Di, "The Most Respected Enemy," 34; William Stueck, "Acheson and the Korean War," 31 March 1997, http://h-net.msu.edu/cgi-bin/logbrowse.pl?trx=vx&list=H-Diplo&month=9703&week=e&msg=jC%2bj%2b78cBPk6mAtqNDrhUw&user=&pw=, and 1 April 1997, http://h-net.msu.edu/cgi-bin/logbrowse.pl?trx=vx&list=H-Diplo&month=9704&week=a&msg=KXGAGNYJlONEqhnOzwhubw&user=&pw= (viewed 9/20/04); Westad, "Fighting for Friendship," 225–26, 232–33.

20 Westad, *Decisive Encounters*, 318; James I. Matray, "Acheson's Press Club Speech Reexamined (unpublished paper, June 2000), 28 (later published as "Dean Acheson's Press Club Speech Reexamined," *Journal of Conflict Studies* 22 (Spring 2002): 28–55; "Documentation," 61; Weathersby, " 'Should We Fear This?'," 9–11; Goncharov, Lewis, and Xue Litai, 101. For the contrary view that Acheson's "well-intentioned but carelessly worded

speech" was crucial in causing Stalin to give Kim Il Sung his approval for the war, see Gaddis, *We Now Know*, 72–75.

21 Kathryn Weathersby, "Origins of the Korean War," 18 February 1997, http://h-net.msu.edu/cgi-bin/logbrowse.pl?trx=vx&list=H-Diplo& month=9702&week=c&msg=uYYpdkpjIb7rJjhz8YFi%2bg&user=&pw= (viewed 9/20/04); idem, "Soviet Role," 428–30; idem, "New Russian Documents," 31–32; idem, "New Findings," 14. For more on North Korea's inability to act independently, see idem, "New Russian Documents," 27, 31, 36; Douglas Macdonald, "Communist Bloc Expansion," 180–81; Weathersby, "Korea, 1949–50," 2–4, 9n; Hyun-Su Jeon, 92; Kuhns, 390; Chen Jian, "Sino-Soviet Alliance," 20–21; Bajanov, 54, 87; Robert C. Tucker, "Cold War in Stalin's Time," 277–78; "Cumings and Weathersby—An Exchange on Korean War Origins," *CWIHPB* (Issues 6–7, Winter 1995/1996): 122; Weathersby, "Soviet Aims in Korea," 29, 31; and idem, "Soviet Role," 439. For a picture of a super-shrewd Stalin maneuvering Mao into war that he then deliberately contrives to *lose* to prolong Sino-American tensions, see Richard C. Thornton, *Odd Man Out: Truman, Stalin, Mao, and the Origins of the Korean War* (Washington, DC: Brassey's, 2000), in which virtually all documents are read for what might appear between the lines rather than the lines themselves.

22 *PAC*, 405; Glen St. J. Barclay, "A Chill Wind from Guam: Perceptions of United States-Allied Relations," *Australian Journal of Politics and History* 29 (1983): 279; Notes on Meeting in Secretary's Office, Tuesday, May 29, 1951–re Statement to precede testimony, Acheson Papers, Box 63, TL.

23 Ninkovich, *Modernity and Power*, 19.

24 Princeton Seminars, 11 October 1953.

25 *Documents on British Policy* IV-2: 17n.

26 Ferrell, *Dear Bess*, 562; Truman, *Years of Trial and Hope*, 333; Gaddis, *Strategies of Containment*, 114.

27 Princeton Seminars, 11 October 1953, 13 February 1954; Cumings, *Roaring of the Cataract*, 611; Trachtenberg, *Constructed Peace*, 99; *FRUS 1950* 7: 349.

28 *FRUS 1950* 7: 139–41, 148, 169, 174, 176–77; Mastny, *Cold War and Soviet Insecurity*, 98; *New York Times*, 26 June 1950; *Memoranda of the Secretary of State* 50:467, 26 June 1950; Barrett Oral History, TL, 39–40; Edward W. Barrett, *Truth Is Our Weapon* (New York: Funk & Wagnalls, 1953), 156–57.

29 Weathersby, "'Should We Fear This?'," 16; Central Intelligence Agency, 28 June 1950, Intelligence Memorandum No. 300, Subject: The USSR and the Korean Invasion, Truman Papers, SMOF, Box 2, NSC/CIA (5–11) Intel. Memoranda (1950–June '51) Folder, TL; Record of Actions by the National Security Council, Record 308, 6–28–50, Truman Papers (PSF), Box 191, Subj. File-NSC Actions, records 1950 Folder, TL; *FRUS 1950* 7: 229–30; Merle Miller, 281; Paige, 247–48; Princeton Seminars, 13 February 1954.

30 Matray, "America's Reluctant Crusade," 450; Notes on Meeting, George M. Elsey Papers, Box 71, TL; *Memoranda of Conversations*, 30 June 1950, Korean Crisis; Rosemary Foot, "The Sino-American Conflict in Korea: The US Assessment of China's Ability to Intervene in the War," *Asian Affairs* 14 (June 1983): 166; Kuhns, 391.

Chapter 20

1 Beverly Smith, "Why We Went to War in Korea," *Saturday Evening Post*, 10 November 1951, 22, 76; Ronald Steel, "Commissar of the Cold War," *New York Review of Books*, 12 February 1970; Schnabel and Watson, 1: 58–59; *PAC*, 402.

2 *FRUS 1950* 7: 125–27, 131; Schnabel and Watson, 1: 61–63, 66; *PAC*, 403–4; Chace, 87; McCullough, 774–75; Hickerson Oral History, TL, 91–92; Merle Miller, 270; T. J. Schoenbaum, 210–11; Connally, 345.

3 *FRUS 1950* 7: 132, 140–41, 155–56; *PAC*, 404–5; Merle Miller, 273; Beverly Smith, 76; Schnabel and Watson, 1: 67, 69–73; Omar Bradley, *A General's Life*, 532. In Tokyo, MacArthur too initially underestimated the seriousness of events in Korea, criticizing Muccio's evacuation order.

4 Notes on Meeting in Secretary's Office in Re Testimony on MacArthur Hearings, 15 May 1951, Acheson Papers, Box 63, TL; Donovan, *Tumultuous Years*, 197; Margaret Truman, *Harry S. Truman* (New York: William Morrow, 1973), 457; Princeton Seminars, 13 February 1954; Richard F. Haynes, *The Awesome Power: Harry S. Truman as Commander in Chief* (Baton Rouge: Louisiana State University Press, 1973), 167; *FRUS 1950* 7: 157–58; *PAC*, 405–6; Omar Bradley, *A General's Life*, 535, 537.

5 Princeton Seminars, 13 February 1954; Notes on Meeting in Secretary's Office in Re Testimony on MacArthur Hearings, 15 May 1951, Acheson Papers, Box 63, TL; Acheson to Louis Halle, 17 March 1955, Acheson Papers, Box 15, Folder 189, YUL; *PAC*, 406; *FRUS 1950* 7: 157–61; McCullough, 778; Matray, "America's Reluctant Crusade," 447. On 27 June, Bradley was ordered to bed for forty-eight hours.

6 *FRUS 1950* 7: 158–60; *PAC*, 406; Pace Oral History, 78, TL; McCullough, 778–79; Omar Bradley, *A General's Life*, 536; Schnabel and Watson, 1: 81–82. Truman appointed MacArthur commander of Korean military activities on the 27th. Collins, 15.

7 Schnabel and Watson, 1: 84, 89; *FRUS 1950* 7: 170, 172–73; Kuhns, 391; Donovan, *Tumultuous Years*, 204–5; Ralph E. Weber, ed., *Talking with Harry: Candid Conversations with President Harry S. Truman* (Wilmington, DE: Scholarly Resources, 2001), 321; June 26, 1950–Monday: Subject: President Truman's conversations with George M. Elsey, George M. Elsey Papers, Box 71, Korea–June 26, 1950 Folder, TL; Leffler, *Preponderance of Power*, 366; *PAC*, 407; Kennan, *Memoirs 1925–1950*, 486; Beverly Smith, 80.

8 Paige, 73; *FRUS 1950* 7: 178–83, 187; Omar Bradley, *A General's Life*, 536; Notes on Meeting in Secretary's Office in Re Testimony on MacArthur Hearings, 15 May 1951, Acheson Papers, Box 63, TL.

9 *FRUS 1950* 7: 182–83.

10 Ibid., 200–203; Beverly Smith, 82; Su Ge, 44n; Margaret Truman, 464; Princeton Seminars, 16 July 1953; Donovan, *Tumultuous Years*, 209; *PAC*, 410; Peter Lowe, "An Ally and a Recalcitrant General: Great Britain, Douglas MacArthur and the Korean War, 1950–1," *English Historical Review* 105 (November 1990): 630; McCullough, 782; Schnabel and Watson, 1: 95; Beichman, 185.

11 *PAC*, 410–11; *Documents on Canadian External Relations* 16: 25; "HST ordered Av. H. back," pencil note, George M. Elsey Papers, Box 71, Korea–June 27, 1950 Folder, TL; Isaacson and Thomas, 509–11; Princeton Seminars, 13 February 1954.

12 Princeton Seminars, Synopsis B, page 7; *PAC*, 410; *New York Times*, 29 June 1950.

13 Schnabel and Watson, 1: 97, 102–3, 142; *FRUS 1950* 7: 212–13; Princeton Seminars, 13 February 1954; *Memoranda of Conversations*, 28 June 1950, Meeting of the NSC in the Cabinet Room; Matray, "America's Reluctant Crusade," 449; Acheson to Paris Embassy, 28 June 1950, Truman Papers (PSF), Box 243, Korea–Foreign telegrams–DoS Folder, TL.

14 *Pattern of Responsibility*, 248; Leland M. Goodrich, *Korea: A Study of U.S. Policy in the United Nations* (New York: Council on Foreign Relations, 1956), 113; Princeton Seminars, Synopsis B, page 7; *Public Papers of the Presidents . . . 1950*, 504; Beverly Smith, 86.

15 Schnabel and Watson, 1: 104, 124, 143; *Memoranda of Conversations*, 29 June 1950, Meeting of the NSC in the Cabinet Room at the White House; Princeton Seminars, Synopsis B, page 7; Donovan, *Tumultuous Years*, 211–13; *FRUS 1950* 7: 240–41; Collins, 18.

16 *FRUS 1950* 7: 239; *PAC*, 412; Princeton Seminars, Synopsis B, page 10.

17 Collins, 20, 98; *FRUS 1950* 7: 248–50, 250–54, 263; Donovan, *Tumultuous Years*, 215; Notes on Meeting in Secretary's Office in Re Testimony on MacArthur Hearings, 15 May 1951, Acheson Papers, Box 63, TL; *PAC*, 412; Schnabel and Watson, 1: 117–20; Truman, *Years*

of Trial and Hope, 343; M. L. Dockrill, "The Foreign Office, Anglo-American relations and the Korean war, June 1950–June 1951," *International Affairs* 62 (Summer 1986): 460.

18 Ferrell, *Off the Record*, 185; *FRUS 1950* 7: 258, 271; *Memoranda of Conversations*, 30 June 1950, Korean Crisis; Laura Belmonte, "Anglo-American Relations and the Dismissal of MacArthur," *Diplomatic History* 19 (Fall 1995): 64; Schnabel and Watson, 1: 123; M. L. Dockrill, 460.

19 Margaret Truman, 471; Princeton Seminars, 13 February 1954. McCullough, 783, dates Truman's memo 11 July, but Acheson actually read the text aloud in the Princeton seminar, including the date of 19 July.

20 Ninkovich, *Modernity and Power*, 373.

21 *Military Situation in the Far East*, 2014; Kepley, *Collapse of the Middle Way*, 87–88; Truman, *Years of Trial and Hope*, 453; July 1950, Subject: Congressional Action, George M. Elsey Papers, Box 71, Korea–July 1950 Folder, TL; Memorandum for Mr. Smith: Subject: Congressional Resolution, July 16, 1951, George M. Elsey Papers, Box 71, Korea–July 1950 Folder, TL; Princeton Seminars, 16 July and 11 October 1953, 14 February 1954; Acheson to Harold Stein, 23 August 1957, Acheson Papers, Box 29, Folder 371, YUL; Merle Miller, 280–84; *PAC*, 414–15.

22 *FRUS 1950* 7: 160; Connally, 346; Kepley, *Collapse of the Middle Way*, 87–89; David J. Weinstein, "The Korean Conflict: Congress Reacts to the President's Decision" (unpublished paper, April 1994), 5; Donovan, *Tumultuous Years*, 222; David S. McLellan, "The Role of Political Style: A Study of Dean Acheson," in Roger Hilsman and Robert C. Good, eds., *Foreign Policy in the Sixties: The Issues and the Instruments: Essays in Honor of Arnold Wolfers* (Baltimore: Johns Hopkins University Press, 1965), 241.

23 Memorandum for File: Subject: Preparation of President's Message to Congress on Korea, July 19, 1950, George M. Elsey Papers, Box 71, Korea–July 19, 1950 Message Folder, TL; http://www.gwu.edu/~nsarchiv/coldwar/interviews/episode-5/battle2.html (viewed 9/22/04); *FRUS 1950* 7: 283, 286–91.

24 *Memoranda of the Secretary of State* 50:502, 10 July 1950; Memorandum for File: Subject: Preparation of President's Message to Congress on Korea, July 19, 1950, George M. Elsey Papers, Box 71, Korea–July 19, 1950 Message Folder, TL; McCullough, 790–91; Mastny, *Cold War and Soviet Insecurity*, 101; *FRUS 1950* 7: 430; Foot, *The Wrong War*, 71; Kepley, *Collapse of the Middle Way*, 94–95.

25 Michael H. Hunt, "Beijing and the Korean Crisis, June 1950–June 1951," *Political Science Quarterly* 107 (Fall 1992): 473; Pearson, 154.

26 Chen Jian, *China's Road to the Korean War*, 101; Hunt, "Beijing and the Korean Crisis," 457n; Qiang Zhai, *Dragon*, 97; Accinelli, 31; Memorandum for the Files: Secretary Acheson, Ed Milne . . . Paul Martin . . . Al Warner, January 18, 1951, Acheson Papers, Box 68, Press Conferences–1951 Folder, TL; Princeton Seminars, 13 February 1954.

27 Acheson to Louis Halle, 17 March 1955, Acheson Papers, Box 15, Folder 189, YUL; *FRUS 1950* 7: 350; Christensen, *Useful Adversaries*, 128; *Reviews of the World Situation*, 316; Nancy Bernkopf Tucker, *Patterns in the Dust*, 200.

28 Lowe, "Ally and a Recalcitrant General," 630n; *FRUS 1950* 6: 396, 398, 402–4; Omar Bradley, *A General's Life*, 548; Lanxin Xiang, 220; Accinelli, 36, 46, 67; Qiang Zhai, *Dragon*, 97; *Military Situation in the Far East*, 1738; *FRUS 1950* 2: 17.

29 Collins, 34; Schnabel and Watson, 1: 184; Mastny, *Cold War and Soviet Insecurity*, 101; Minutes of Meeting on MacArthur Testimony (Question of what he says when asked about Conferences with President), 15 May 1951, Acheson Papers, Box 63, TL; Botti, *Ace in the Hole*, 28; Foot, *The Wrong War*, 76; *FRUS 1950* 7: 721–22.

30 Message from Mr. Attlee to the President, undated, Truman Papers (PSF), Box 170, Attlee, Clement–Misc. PSF Subj. File Folder, TL; Jules Moch, Oral History Interview, 29 April

1970 (Independence, MO: The Harry S. Truman Library, March 1982), 22–23; *Memoranda of the Secretary of State* 50:481, 3 July 1950; Trevor Barnes, "The Secret Cold War: The C.I.A. and American Foreign Policy in Europe, 1946–1956, Pt. 2," *Historical Journal* 25 (September 1982): 652; Bradley, Memorandum for the Secretary of Defense, 10 July 1950, http://www.gwu.edu/~nsarchiv/NSAEBB/index.html (viewed 7/2000).

31 Mastny, *Cold War and Soviet Insecurity*, 100, 102; Weathersby, "Soviet Aims in Korea," 26–27; Shu Guang Zhang, *Deterrence and Strategic Culture*, 98; Douglas Macdonald, "Communist Bloc Expansion," 181; Eduard Mark, "Korean War," 19 October 1997, http://h-net.msu.edu/cgi-bin/logbrowse.pl?trx=vx&list=H-Diplo&month=9710&week=c&msg=ONwKHRh3MpqoNo7YutBRRA&user=&pw= (viewed 1/8/2005); Yufan Hao and Zhai Zhihai, "China's Decision to Enter the Korean War: History Revisited," *China Quarterly* (March 1990): 112; Weathersby, "New Russian Documents," 40, 43.

32 Ra Jong-Yil, "Special Relationship at War: The Anglo-American Relationship during the Korean War," *Journal of Strategic Studies* 7 (September 1984): 309; Schnabel and Watson, 1: 186; Lee, 86–87; *PAC*, 420–21; Donovan, *Tumultuous Years*, 242–43; Gaddis Smith, *Dean Acheson*, 189.

33 *Documents on Canadian External Relations* 16: 64; Schnabel and Watson, 1: 145, 151–52, 163, 166, 169, 171–72, 174–75; Daily Meetings, 11 July 1950; Lee, 87; Stueck, *Korean War*, 73, 138.

34 M. L. Dockrill, 460–61; Tang, 87; *FRUS 1950* 7: 329–31, 347–51; Hopkins, 161; *Documents on British Policy* IV-2: 42–44, 48; *PAC*, 418; Geoffrey Warner, 121; *Memoranda of the Secretary of State* 50:501, 10 July 1950; Christensen, *Useful Adversaries*, 178; *Memoranda of Conversations*, 28 July 1950, Conversation with Australian Prime Minister; Lee, 83.

35 *FRUS 1950* 7: 387; Foot, *The Wrong War*, 68–69.

36 Gaddis Smith, "A History Teacher's Reflections on the Korean War," *Ventures* 8 (No. 1, 1968), 61; Kennan, *Memoirs 1925–1950*, 500; Kennan to Mr. Secretary, 21 and 23 August 1950, Acheson Papers, Box 65, TL; *PAC*, 445–46.

37 Princeton Seminars, 11 October 1953; Schnabel and Watson, 1: 260.

Chapter 21

1 Schwartz, *America's Germany*, 127–29; "double containment," quoted in idem, "The United States and Germany after 1945: Alliances, Transnational Relations, and the Legacy of the Cold War," *Diplomatic History* 19 (Fall 1995): 558.

2 Princeton Seminars, 11 October 1953; *Documents on Canadian External Relations* 16: 1013.

3 Trachtenberg, *Constructed Peace*, 98–99; Byroade Oral History, TL, 73, 80; Laukhuff Oral History, TL, 111–12.

4 John S. Duffield, "The Soviet Military Threat to Western Europe: US Estimates in the 1950s and 1960s," *Journal of Strategic Studies* 15 (June 1992): 209–16, 221–22; *FRUS 1950* 1: 65–66; Rosenberg, "Origins of Overkill," 17; Mastny, *Cold War and Soviet Insecurity*, 107–8; Review of the World Situation, CIA, 17 May 1950.

5 James L. Richardson, *Germany and the Atlantic Alliance: The Interaction of Strategy and Politics* (Cambridge: Harvard University Press, 1966), 20; Princeton Seminars, 10 October 1953.

6 Bird, *Chairman*, 342; Acheson to Alan Bullock, 25 February 1955, Acheson Papers, Box 4, Folder 51, YUL; Laukhuff Oral History, TL, 110–11; Byroade Oral History, TL, 89; Steel, *Walter Lippmann*, 476–77; Schwartz, *America's Germany*, 348n; Cook, 249.

7 Grosser, 122; Trachtenberg, *Constructed Peace*, 111.

8 Harriman to Acheson, 13 March 1950, Acheson Papers, Box 65, TL; Ninkovich, *Germany and the United States*, 86; Byroade Oral History, TL, 78–80.

9 Ninkovich, *Germany and the United States*, 84–85; Walter LaFeber, "NATO and the Korean War: A Context," *Diplomatic History* 13 (Fall 1989): 465; Cook, 245; *FRUS 1950* 3: 652; Byroade Oral History, TL, 83; *Memoranda of the Secretary of State*, 50:562, 3 August 1950.

10 From Frankfort to Secretary of State, 13 June 1950, Truman Papers (PSF), Box 178, Germany Folder, TL; Truman to Acheson, 16 June 1950, Truman Papers (PSF), Box 178, Germany Folder, TL; Acheson to Truman, 30 June 1950, Truman Papers (PSF), Box 208, N.S.C. Meeting No. 60 Folder, TL; *Documents on British Policy* II-2: 331.

11 Bird, *Chairman*, 339; A Report to the National Security Council by the Secretary of State on the Rearmament of Western Germany, July 3, 1950, Truman Papers (PSF), Box 208, N.S.C. Meeting No. 60 Folder, TL; Byroade Oral History, TL, 85–86.

12 http://www.weatherpages.com/wxhistory.html (viewed 10/11/04); Record of Actions by the National Security Council, Records 310–316, 7-6-50, Truman Papers (PSF), Box 191, Subj. File–NSC Actions, records 1950 Folder, TL; Memorandum for the President, 7 July 1950, Truman Papers (PSF), Box 220, NSC Meetings . . . Discussions (1950) Folder, TL; Bark and Gress, 278; *Memoranda of the Secretary of State*, 50:506, 12 July 1950; Daily Meetings, 18 July 1950; Bird, *Chairman*, 340.

13 *Memoranda of the Secretary of State*, 50:526, 24 July 1950; Schwartz, *America's Germany*, 129–30; *FRUS 1950* 3: 167–68; *PAC*, 437; Marc Trachtenberg and Christopher Gehrz, "America, Europe, and German Rearmament, August–September 1950: A Critique of a Myth," *Journal of European Integration* 6 (no. 2, 2000): 9–35.

14 Bird, *Chairman*, 340–41; Laurence W. Martin, "The American Decision to Rearm Germany," in Harold Stein, ed., *American Civil-Military Decisions: A Book of Case Studies* ([University, Alabama]: Published in cooperation with the Inter-University Case Program by University of Alabama Press, 1963), 654; Large, *Germans to the Front*, 84; Leffler, *Preponderance of Power*, 385, 387; Bark and Gress, 279; Saki Dockrill, 23; Richardson, 19; Memorandum of Conversation with the President, 10 August 1950, Item No. 2, Mr. Spofford's Return and Report, Acheson Papers, Box 65, TL.

15 Princeton Seminars, 11 October 1953; Princeton Seminars, The Impact of Korea, pp. 5, 7; Norbert Wiggershaus, "The Problem of West German Military Integration, 1948–1950," in Wiggershaus and Foerster, 387–88; Ninkovich, *Germany and the United States*, 88; Saki Dockrill, 22; *Memoranda of the Secretary of State* 50:619 (Termination of State of War with Germany), 21 August 1950; Duchêne, 228.

16 *PAC*, 437–38; Large, *Germans to the Front*, 84; Truman to Acheson, 26 August 1950, Truman Papers (PSF), Box 163, Subj. File–Conferences, Conf. of For. Min., NATO 9/50 Folder, TL; Laurence W. Martin, 656–57; *Memoranda of the Secretary of State* 50:660 (Memorandum for S/S), 30 August 1950. For a different—and tempting—interpretation of Acheson's role in forming the "single package," see Trachtenberg and Gehrz, 11, 14, 16, 18, as well as 26–27.

17 *FRUS 1950* 1: 393–95; *New York Times*, 31 August 1950; *Washington Post*, 31 August 1950; *PAC*, 439; Acheson, *Sketches from Life*, 133–35; http://www.quotationspage.com/quote/23566.html (viewed 6/25/05); Ohly Oral History, TL, 133–34. Later Acheson twice claimed he had deliberately fired up his temper for the outburst against Wherry. *Sketches from Life*, 133–34; Princeton Seminars, 11 October 1953.

18 Princeton Seminars, The Impact of Korea, p. 7; "Yesterday afternoon the Secretary received and talked OFF THE RECORD . . . ," 2 September 1950, Acheson Papers, Box 62, Personal Correspondence, Co-Cz Folder, TL; *Memoranda of Conversations*, 9 September 1950, First Call of the Ambassador-designate of the Netherlands; Princeton Seminars, 11 October 1953; Bird, *Chairman*, 341; *PAC*, 439–40; Hogan, *Marshall Plan*, 375.

19 Hilsman, *Politics of Policymaking*, 187.

20 *PAC*, 442.

21 Joseph Alsop and Stewart Alsop, *The Reporter's Trade* (New York: Reynal, 1958), 148–49; http://www.australianpolitics. com/words/quotations/019.shtml (viewed 4/25/05); Lambright, *Powering Apollo*, 61–62; Robert H. Ferrell, ed., *Truman in the White House: The Diary of Eben A. Ayers* (Columbia: University of Missouri Press, 1991), 358, 361; Franks Oral History, TL, 18; Achilles Oral History, TL, 93; *PAC*, 441.

22 *PAC*, 440; *New York Times*, 16 and 17 September 1950; Princeton Seminars, 11 October 1953; *FRUS 1950* 3: 1187; Large, *Germans to the Front*, 85; *Documents on British Policy* II-3: 86.

23 Bark and Gress, 278; Rempel, 10; Schwartz, *America's Germany*, 119; Princeton Seminars, 11 October 1953; USUN, New York, to Secretary of State, Department of the Army Staff Communications Office, 16 September 1950, Truman Papers (PSF), Box 163, Subj. File–Conferences, Conf. of For. Min., NATO 9/50 Folder, TL (see *FRUS 1950* 3: 1190 for the nature of this document); *Memoranda of Conversations*, 12 September 1950; *PAC*, 442; Schwabe, 182; Spencer Mawby, *Containing Germany: Britain and the Arming of the Federal Republic* (Houndmills, Basingstoke, Hampshire: Macmillan Press, 1999), 3, 34.

24 Acheson to Alan Bullock, 27 April 1955, Acheson Papers, Box 4, Folder 51, YUL; *Selected Executive Session Hearings of the Committee, 1951–1956*, 263; Franks Oral History, TL, 19–20; Princeton Seminars, 11 October 1953; Achilles Oral History, TL, 93; Acheson, *Sketches from Life*, 27, 42; Schwartz, *America's Germany*, 135; *FRUS 1950* 3: 313–14, 1192, 1208; *Executive Sessions of the Senate Foreign Relations Committee . . . 1951* 3, Pt. 2: 567.

25 Trachtenberg, *Constructed Peace*, 111; Beate Ruhm von Oppen, ed., *Documents on Germany under Occupation, 1945–1954* (London: Oxford University Press, 1955), 520–21; *FRUS 1950* 1: 479; *Memoranda of Conversations*, 12 September 1950; *FRUS 1950* 3: 320.

26 Franks Oral History, TL, 18; Saki Dockrill, 34; *FRUS 1950* 3: 287, 299, 306, 598, 1200; Acheson to Alan Bullock, 25 February 1955, Acheson Papers, Box 4, Folder 51, YUL; Princeton Seminars, 11 October 1953. A rush of MDAP funds soon made France unquestionably more militarily powerful than West Germany.

27 Henderson, *Inside the Private Office*, 40; *FRUS 1950* 3: 299, 312–13, 337, 1230; *Documents on British Policy* II-3: 49, 62.

28 *PAC*, 442; Large, *Germans to the Front*, 85–88; Trachtenberg and Gehrz, 28n; Trachtenberg, *Constructed Peace*, 109; *FRUS 1950* 3: 303–4, 314, 338, 342, 1392, 1443; *Documents on British Policy* II-3: 90, 93, 135; Achilles Oral History, TL, 93–94; Moch Oral History, TL, 26; Schwartz, *America's Germany*, 138.

29 *FRUS 1950* 3: 352, 1214, 1288–89, 1295–98.

30 Ibid., 301–2, 334–35; 1229–31, 1245–46; Laurence W. Martin, 646.

31 *PAC*, 443–45.

32 Acheson to Alan Bullock, 27 April 1955, Acheson Papers, Box 4, Folder 51, YUL; *FRUS 1950* 3: 1393. The Washington meetings of defense ministers were rendered anticlimactic by Paris's announcement of the Pleven Plan.

33 Trachtenberg and Gehrz, 4; *FRUS 1950* 3: 384; Irwin M. Wall, *The United States and the Making of Postwar France, 1945–1954* (New York: Cambridge University Press, 1991), 144; *Documents on British Policy* II-3: 137, 156n.

34 Brinkley, "Acheson and Monnet," 74, 91; Duchêne, 63, 130; Hackett, 36; Robert McGeehan, *The German Rearmament Question: American Diplomacy and European Defense After World War II* (Urbana: University of Illinois Press, 1971), 65–66.

35 *PAC*, 458; Stephen E. Ambrose, *Eisenhower. Volume One: Soldier, General of the Army, President-Elect, 1890–1952* (New York: Simon & Schuster, 1983), 496–97.

36 *PAC*, 458–59, 598; Trachtenberg, *Constructed Peace*, 110; Large, *Germans to the Front*, 94; *FRUS 1950* 3: 439; *Documents on British Policy* II-3: 212, 216; Mark S. Sheetz, "France and

the German Question: Avant-garde or Rearguard? Comment on Creswell and Trachtenberg," *Journal of Cold War Studies* 5 (Summer 2003): 44.

37 *PAC*, 457–59; *Memoranda of Conversations*, 3 November 1950, German Rearmament; *FRUS 1950* 3: 1409; *Documents on British Policy* II-3: 228–29.

38 *FRUS 1951* 3, Pt. 1: 1048; *FRUS 1950* 4: 904, 911; Notes on Meeting in Secretary's Office, 6 November 1950, Acheson Papers, Box 65, TL; *Memorandum of Conversation, German Participation in Western European Defense and Korean Situation*, 7 November 1950, Acheson Papers, Box 65, TL; *PAC*, 483; *FRUS 1950* 3: 1441; Mastny, *Cold War and Soviet Insecurity*, 111.

39 *Memorandum of Conversation, German Participation in Western European Defense and Korean Situation*, 7 November 1950, Acheson Papers, Box 65, TL; *FRUS 1950* 3: 439, 451.

40 McGeehan, 72; *FRUS 1950* 3: 496–98, 605–6; Schwartz, *America's Germany*, 151.

41 Trachtenberg, *Constructed Peace*, 112–13, 117; Wall, *United States and the Making of Postwar France*, 203; *Documents on British Policy* II-3: 275; Schwartz, *America's Germany*, 152; *FRUS 1950* 3: 578–80; *Memoranda of the Secretary of State* 50:893, 15 December 1950; *FRUS 1950* 4: 801.

42 *Documents on British Policy* II-3: 397; *PAC*, 486–88; Deighton, "'Arming the Key Battleground,'" 347; Michael Creswell, "The United States, France and German Rearmament, 1950–1954" (unpublished paper, 1994), 16; Schwartz, *America's Germany*, 153; Large, *Germans to the Front*, 106; *FRUS 1950* 3: 591–93, 606.

43 *New York Times*, 22 December 1950; *FRUS 1950* 3: 600; figures extrapolated from table in Kaplan, *Community of Interests*, 103.

44 Lloyd C. Gardner, "Harry Hopkins with Hand Grenades? McGeorge Bundy in the Kennedy and Johnson Years," in Thomas J. McCormick and Walter LaFeber, eds., *Behind the Throne: Servants to Power to Imperial Presidents, 1898–1968* (Madison: University of Wisconsin Press, 1993), 205; *Memoranda of the Secretary of State* 50:747–48, 9 October 1950; November 10, 1950, Memorandum Concerning the President's Address to the United Nations, October 24, 1950, George M. Elsey Papers, Box 88, National Defense–Atomic . . . McMahon Resolution Folder, TL; *FRUS 1950* 3: 1747.

45 Princeton Seminars, 11 October 1953.

46 *PAC*, 488; Princeton Seminars, 16 July 1953; *Pattern of Responsibility*, 88.

Chapter 22

1 *Memoranda of the Secretary of State* 50:518, 12 July 1950.

2 Princeton Seminars, 11 October 1953; Leffler, *Preponderance of Power*, 363.

3 John S. Duffield, "Soviet Military Threat," 216; Ferrell, *Off the Record*, 204; *FRUS 1950* 7: 1309–10.

4 Memorandum for the Files: Secretary Acheson, Ed Milne . . . Paul Martin . . . Al Warner, January 18, 1951, Acheson Papers, Box 68, Press Conferences–1951 Folder, TL; *PAC*, 478; Tami Davis Biddle, "Handling the Soviet Threat: 'Project Control' and the Debate on American Strategy in the Early Cold War Years," *Journal of Strategic Studies* 12 (September 1989): 277; Schnabel and Watson, 1: 260. *FRUS 1951* 1: 847.

5 Wells, 145; Pearson, 152; Princeton Seminars, 11 October, 9 July, and 10 October 1953; Princeton Seminars, Summary of Synopses; Princeton Seminars, The Impact of Korea, Roll 1, Synopses. The transcript for the seminar (9 July 1953) containing "Korea came along and saved us" shows the statement coming from "Q," that is, the person "questioning" Acheson, and the context suggests strongly that "Q" was Nitze. Among the many historians to attribute the statement to Acheson is Bruce Cumings, *Roaring of the Cataract*, 761.

6 Paul G. Pierpaoli, Jr., "Mobilizing for the Cold War: The Korean Conflict and the Birth of the National Security State, June–December 1950," *Essays in Economic and Business History* 12

(1994): 108; Daily Meetings, 26 September 1950; Record of Actions by the National Security Council at its Sixty-Eighth Meeting, September 29, 1950, Truman Papers (PSF), Box 191, Subj. File–NSC Actions, records 1950 Folder, TL; *Memoranda of the Secretary of State* 50:738, 29 September 1950; Callahan, 134; Leffler, *Preponderance of Power*, 373; Nelson, "Reshaping U.S. National Security Policy," 22–23; *FRUS 1950* 1: 427–29; Memorandum for the President, 15 December 1950, Truman Papers (PSF), Box 220, NSC Meetings . . . Discussions (1950) Folder, TL; Leffler, "Negotiating from Strength," 196; *Public Papers of the Presidents . . . 1951*, 366–67, 528.

7 Trachtenberg, "Wasting Asset," 17, 24, 26; Mastny, *Cold War and Soviet Insecurity*, 109; Daily Meetings, 10 October 1950.

8 Mastny, *Cold War and Soviet Insecurity*, 113–14; Mark, "Gardner Cold War Essay"; Francis J. Gavin, "Politics, Power, and U.S. Policy in Iran, 1950–1953," *Journal of Cold War Studies* 1 (Winter 1999): 64; *Memoranda of Conversations*, 11 April 1951, Observations Made by . . . Parker.

9 Christensen, "Threats, Assurances," 130n; Hogan, *Cross of Iron*, 311 Leffler, *Preponderance of Power*, 444; John Baylis, *Anglo-American Defence Relations 1939–1979: The Special Relationship* (New York: St. Martin's, 1981), 41; Friedberg, *Shadow of the Garrison State*, 83; idem, "Why Didn't the United States Become a Garrison State?" *International Security* 16 (Spring 1992): 113n; *Washington Post*, 13 August 1998.

10 Wells, 140; David T. Fautua, "The 'Long Pull' Army: NSC 68, the Korean War, and the Creation of the Cold War U.S. Army," *Journal of Military History* 61 (January 1997): 110–11; Mastny, *Cold War and Soviet Insecurity*, 110; Leffler, *Preponderance of Power*, 369; Rhodes, 561; Daily Meetings, 22 March 1949.

11 Leffler, *Preponderance of Power*, 412; Lee, 84–85; Baylis, *Anglo-American Defence Relations*, 41. Kaplan, *Community of Interests*, passim, is indispensable reading on Europeans' efforts.

12 Brandon, 160.

13 Hogan, *Cross of Iron*; Friedberg, *Shadow of the Garrison State*; Paul G. Pierpaoli, Jr., *Truman and Korea: The Political Culture of the Early Cold War* (Columbia: University of Missouri Press, 1999), 12, 233–35; Douglas Macdonald, *Adventures in Chaos*, 41.

14 *FRUS 1951* 4, Pt. 2: 1246, 1255–56; *Memoranda of the Secretary of State* 51:72, 2 February 1951; Callahan, 141–43; *FRUS 1951* 1: 470.

15 Michael Mastanduno, "Trade as a Strategic Weapon: American and Alliance Export Control Policy in the Early Postwar Period," *International Organization* 42 (Winter 1988): 132–33, 136; *New York Times*, 1 June 1949; *Reviews of the World Situation*, 45; Sørensen, 79; Helen Leigh-Phippard, "US Strategic Export Controls and Aid to Britain, 1949–58," *Diplomacy & Statecraft* 6 (November 1995): 723; Memorandum for the President, 5 May 1950, Truman Papers (PSF), Box 220, NSC Meetings . . . Discussions (1950) Folder, TL.

16 Sørensen, 70, 72, 80–81, 84–85; Memorandum for the President, 25 August 1950, Truman Papers (PSF), Box 220, NSC Meetings . . . Discussions (1950) Folder, TL; *FRUS 1951* 1: 1074, 1185; Mastanduno, 136–41.

17 Sørensen, 86–89; *FRUS 1951* 1: 1183.

18 Sørensen, 71, 89; idem, "Defense without Tears: U.S. Embargo Policy and Economic Security in Western Europe, 1947–1951," in Heller and Gillingham, 274; Leigh-Phippard, "US Strategic Export Controls," 735, 739–40; Mastanduno, 122–23, 130; *FRUS 1952–1954* 1, Pt. 1, 470–41, and Pt. 2, 848; Ian Jackson, *The Economic Cold War: America, Britain and East-West Trade, 1948–63* (Houndmills, Basingstoke, Hampshire: Palgrave, 2001), 82–83.

19 Bird, *Chairman*, 368.

20 *PAC*, 62; David F. Schmitz, *Thank God They're on Our Side: The United States and Right-Wing Dictatorships, 1921–1965* (Chapel Hill: University of North Carolina Press, 1999), 157–58. The whale is Edmund Burke's figure.

21 Offner, 16; Theodore J. Lowi, "Bases in Spain," in Stein, 669–70.

22 Schmitz, 162; Boris N. Liedtke, *Embracing a Dictatorship: US Relations with Spain, 1945–53* (New York: St. Martin's Press, 1998), 29, 31; *New York Times*, 16 November 1946; Bond Oral History, TL, 17; Lowi, 687.

23 Liedtke, 39–41, 46; Lowi, 669, 672, 675–76, 679; Jill Edwards, *Anglo-American Relations and the Franco Question 1945–1955* (Oxford: Clarendon Press, 1999), 97–98, 116 (and Chapter 10 on the "cotton lobby"); Schmitz, 165; Lees, 95; J. M. Cabot Oral History, TL, 55–56; *Memoranda of Conversations*, 1948, Attitude in the U.S. Towards Normal Diplomatic Relations with Spain; *United States Foreign Policy for a Post-War Recovery Program*, 707; Mark S. Byrnes, "'Overruled and Worn Down': Truman Sends an Ambassador to Spain," *Presidential Studies Quarterly* 29 (June 1999): 264.

24 *Memoranda of the Secretary of State* 49:158, 21 March 1949; Warren I. Cohen, *Dean Rusk*, 38–39; *FRUS 1949* 4: 734–40; Edwards, 138.

25 *PAC*, 169; *Memoranda of the Secretary of State* 49:342, 9 May 1949; Lowi, 677, 683–84; *Strengthening the Forces of Freedom*, 132–35; *New York Times*, 12 and 15 May 1949.

26 Edwards, 124–25; Liedtke, 71; *Public Papers of the Presidents . . . 1949*, 113, 155; Mark S. Byrnes, 270; *Memoranda of the Secretary of State* 49:590 (mid-July 1949?); McLellan, *State Department Years*, 195–96; Nitze Oral History, TL, 364; Lowi, 678–79; *Memoranda of Conversations*, 14 September 1949, Conversations with Mr. Bevin on Spain; *FRUS 1949* 4: 758; *New York Times*, 4 December 1949; *Memoranda of the Secretary of State* 49:1081 (20 December 1949); Daily Meetings, 16 December 1949.

27 *New York Times*, 21 January 1950; *Memoranda of the Secretary of State* 50:25 (6 January 1950); Daily Meetings, 9 January 1950; *Reviews of the World Situation*, 126–27; Mark S. Byrnes, 267, 272–71; Edwards, 170; *FRUS 1950* 3: 1549–55.

28 *Public Papers of the Presidents . . . 1950*, 234–35, 680; *FRUS 1950* 3: 1560–62; *New York Times*, 1 June 1950; Memorandum for the President, Subject: The Joint Chiefs' Proposals on Spain, June 10, 1950, Truman Papers (PSF), Box 208, N.S.C. Meeting No. 60 Folder, TL; Memorandum for the President, 7 July 1950, Truman Papers (PSF), Box 220, NSC Meetings . . . Discussions (1950) Folder, TL; Walter S. Poole, *History of the Joint Chiefs of Staff. The Joint Chiefs of Staff and National Policy. Volume IV, 1950–1952* (Washington: Office of Joint History, Office of the Chairman of the Joint Chiefs of Staff, 1998), 164; Liedtke, 83–84; Lowi, 681; *New York Times*, 7 September 1950.

29 Edwards, 218; Lowi, 681, 688; *Public Papers of the Presidents . . . 1950*, 697, 712, 762; Press and Radio Conference #245, November 16, 1950, 4.00 P.M., George M. Elsey Papers, Box 64, Foreign Relations–Spain Folder, TL; *Memoranda of the Secretary of State* 50:821, 16 November 1950; Mark S. Byrnes, 274; Stanton Griffis, *Lying in State* (Garden City, NY: Doubleday, 1952), 155–56, 269.

30 A Report to the National Security Council by the Secretary of State on United States Policy toward Spain, January 15, 1951, Truman Papers (PSF), Box 211, NSC Meeting No. 82 Folder, TL; Liedtke, 93; Griffis, 250–51; National Security Council Progress Report by the Under Secretary of State on the Implementation of United States Policy toward Spain (NSC 72/4), June 5, 1951, Truman Papers (PSF), Box 213, NSC Meeting No. 95 Folder, TL; Lowi, 685; Large, *Germans to the Front*, 124.

31 Lowi, 685; Griffis, 289; Griffis Address to American Chamber of Commerce in Spain, May 8, 1951, Stanton Griffis Papers, Scrapbook Files, General File, Box 9, TL; Daily Meetings, 5 June 1951; National Security Council Progress Report by the Under Secretary of State on the implementation of United States Policy toward Spain (NSC 72/4), June 5, 1951, Truman Papers (PSF), Box 213, NSC Meeting No. 95 Folder, TL; A Report to the President by the National Security Council on United States Policy toward Spain, June 27, 1951, Truman Papers (PSF), Box 213, NSC Meeting No. 95 Folder, TL; Liedtke, 106.

32 National Security Council Progress Report by the Acting Secretary of State on the implementation of United States Policy toward Spain (NSC 72/6), September 7, 1951, Truman Papers (PSF), Box 214, NSC Meeting No. 103 Folder, TL; Edwards, 234–35; Memorandum for the Secretary of State from the President, August 2, 1951, Truman Papers (PSF), Box 188, Spain Folder, TL; Daily Meetings, 3 August 1951; *FRUS 1951* 1: 878.

33 *Memoranda of Conversations*, 16 September 1951, Meeting with Mr. Lange; Edwards, 252; *Executive Sessions of the Senate Foreign Relations Committee (Historical Series). Volume IV: Eighty-Second Congress, Second Session, 1952* (Washington: Government Printing Office, 1976) (henceforth *Executive Sessions of the Senate Foreign Relations Committee . . . 1952*) 4: 15, 39; Liedtke, 141, 147; *PAC*, 622; *New York Times*, 13 March 1952; Schmitz, 167; Edwards, 253.

34 Lowi, 696–98; Liedtke, 204–6; Schmitz, 168; Edwards, 258.

35 Truman to Acheson, 10 November 1955, Acheson Papers, Box 31, Folder 394, YUL. Sullivan and Cromwell was Dulles's New York law firm.

36 *FRUS 1950* 3: 200; *Memoranda of Conversations*, 14 August 1950, North Atlantic Union and Related Matters; *FRUS 1950* 5: 1469.

37 The International Scene [a War College Speech] by The Honorable Dean G. Acheson, 27 August 1951, 25, Acheson Papers, Box 69, Press Conf. 1949–1953, Classified Off the Record Speeches Folder, TL (hereafter cited as The International Scene, 27 August 1951).

Chapter 23

1 Notes on Meeting in Secretary's Office in Re Testimony on MacArthur Hearings, 15 May 1951, Acheson Papers, Box 63, TL; Isaacson and Thomas, 530; Christensen, "Threats, Assurances," 130n; Lowe, "Challenge and Readjustment," 157; Lee, 74; Foot, "Sino-American Conflict," 163–64; Trachtenberg, "Wasting Asset," 28.

2 Princeton Seminars, 13 February 1954; Schnabel and Watson, 1: 221; U. Alexis Johnson, Oral History Interview, 19 June 1975 (Independence, MO: The Harry S. Truman Library, August 1978), 49–50; Richard E. Neustadt and Ernest R. May, *Thinking in Time: The Uses of History for Decision-Makers* (New York: Free Press, 1986), 45–46; Shu Guang Zhang, *Deterrence and Strategic Culture*, 87.

3 Foot, *The Wrong War*, 68–69; *FRUS 1950* 7: 272, 387; *PAC*, 451; Isaacson and Thomas, 530; *Reviews of the World Situation*, 317. For more on Allison's aggressive stand, see William Stueck, "The March to the Yalu: The Perspective from Washington," in Cumings, *Child of Conflict*, 197.

4 *FRUS 1950* 7: 386–87, 430, 449–54, 460, 600–603; Foot, *The Wrong War*, 71; Schnabel and Watson, 1: 222–23; Kennan, *Memoirs 1925–1950*, 488; Princeton Seminars, 14 February 1954; *PAC*, 451; Lee, 104; Michael T. Ruddy, *The Cautious Diplomat: Charles E. Bohlen and the Soviet Union, 1929–1969* (Kent: Kent State University Press, 1986), 103; Kennan, *Memoirs 1950–1963*, 24; Donovan, *Tumultuous Years*, 271.

5 Truman, *Years of Trial and Hope*, 358–59; *PAC*, 452; Omar Bradley, *A General's Life*, 559; "Yesterday afternoon the Secretary received and talked OFF THE RECORD . . . ," 2 September 1950, Acheson Papers, Box 62, Personal Correspondence, Co-Cz Folder, TL.

6 NSC Meeting, September 7, 1950, Acheson Papers, Box 65, TL; Memorandum for the President, 8 September 1950, Truman Papers (PSF), Box 220, NSC Meetings . . . Discussions (1950) Folder, TL; Omar Bradley, *A General's Life*, 560–61; Schnabel and Watson, 1: 227; *Reviews of the World Situation*, 350–54.

7 Brandon, 88–89; Schnabel and Watson, 1: 228; http://www.gwu.edu/~nsarchiv/coldwar/interviews/episode-5/battle2.html (viewed 9/22/04); *FRUS 1950* 7: 826.

8 Memorandum for the President. Subject: Suggested Broadcast of Surrender Terms to North Koreans, September 27, 1950, Truman Papers (PSF), Box 159, Subj. File–Cabinet, State, Secretary–Misc Folder, TL; Shu Guang Zhang, *Deterrence and Strategic Culture*, 87; *New York Times*, 28 September 1950; *Documents on British Policy* IV-2: 152; John W. Spanier, *The Truman-MacArthur Controversy and the Korean War* (New York: W. W. Norton, 1965), 102; Mansourov, 99–100, 106n; Acheson Papers, Box 62, TL; Stueck, "March to the Yalu," 207; Mastny, *Cold War and Soviet Insecurity*, 105.

9 Princeton Seminars, 13 February 1954; Mansourov, 101, 103; Schnabel and Watson, 1: 244–45; *PAC*, 462; Martin Lichterman, "To the Yalu and Back," in Stein, 600. My italics.

10 Clay Blair, *The Forgotten War: America in Korea, 1950–1953* (New York: Times Books, 1988), 237, 325–27; Robert S. Prince, "The Limits of Constraint: Canadian-American Relations and the Korean War, 1950–51," *Journal of Canadian Studies/Revue d'études canadiennes* 27 (Winter 1992–1993): 141–42.

11 Callahan, 129; Gaddis, "Strategic Perspective," 108–9.

12 Henry A. Kissinger, *Diplomacy* (New York: Simon & Schuster, 1994), 480.

13 *PAC*, 445.

14 Xiaoyuan Liu, 256; Weathersby, "New Russian Documents," 34; idem, "New Findings," 16; Michael Sheng, "The Psychology of the Korean War: The Role of Ideology and Perception in China's Entry into the War," *Journal of Conflict Studies* 22 (Spring 2002): 66.

15 Eliot A. Cohen, "'Only Half the Battle': American Intelligence and the Chinese Intervention in Korea, 1950," *Intelligence and National Security* 5 (January 1990): 140; Goncharov, Lewis, and Xue Litai, 174; Hunt, "Beijing and the Korean Crisis," 464; Chen Jian, *China's Road to the Korean War*, 158; idem, "China's Changing Aims," 40–41; *Documents on British Policy* IV-2: 227; "Mao's Telegrams during the Korean War, October–December 1950," trans., Li Xiaobing and Glenn Tracy, *Chinese Historians* 5 (Fall 1992): 66, 73, 75, 82–83, 85.

16 Cumings, *Roaring of the Cataract*, 709.

17 Schnabel and Watson, 1: 257; *FRUS 1950* 6: 397; *FRUS 1950* 7: 852.

18 Hastings, 133; Lichterman, 590; *FRUS 1950* 7: 600, 814; *New York Times*, 31 August 1950; *PAC*, 452; *Pattern of Responsibility*, 265; Gaddis Smith, *Acheson*, 201–2; Peter G. Boyle, "Britain, America and the Transition from Economic to Military Assistance, 1948–51," *Journal of Contemporary History* 22 (July 1987): 531; Shu Guang Zhang, *Deterrence and Strategic Culture*, 94–95; Goncharov, Lewis, and Xue Litai, 170–71.

19 Steel, *Walter Lippmann*, 472; Kuhns, 443–48; Stueck, *Korean War*, 95, 105.

20 Stueck, "March to the Yalu," 214; Truman, *Years of Trial and Hope*, 362; Cumings, *Roaring of the Cataract*, 712.

21 Shen Zhihua, "Sino-North Korean Conflict and Its Resolution during the Korean War," trans., Dong Gil Kim and Jeffrey Becker, *CWIHPB* (Issue 14/15, Winter 2003–Spring 2004): 9–11; Weathersby, "'Should We Fear This?'," 10; "Russian Documents on the Korean War, 1950–53," intro., James G. Hershberg, trans., Vladislav Zubok, *CWIHPB* (Issue 14/15, Winter 2003–Spring 2004): 370–71, 76; Christensen, *Useful Adversaries*, 156, 159–160; Chen Jian, "Sino-Soviet Alliance," 27–32; idem, "China's Changing Aims," 17; idem, *China's Road to the Korean War*, 186–87; Hunt, "Beijing and the Korean Crisis," 459, 461–62; Mansourov, 95, 98–107, 114, 116, 118–19; Robert C. Tucker, "Cold War in Stalin's Time," 277–78; Bajanov, 89; Goncharov, Lewis, and Xue Litai, 176; Westad, *Decisive Encounters*, 322; Shen Zhihua, trans., Chen Jian, "The Discrepancy between the Russian and Chinese Versions of Mao's 2 October 1950 Message to Stalin on Chinese Entry into the Korean War: A Chinese Scholar's Reply," *CWIHPB* (Issues 8–9, Winter 1996/1997): 237–41; Li Xiaobing, Wang Xi, and Chen Jian, 67–69, 71–72, 74; Mastny, *Cold War and Soviet Insecurity*, 105–6; Shu Guang Zhang, *Deterrence and Strategic Culture*, 95, 97–99; Jonathan D. Pollack, "The Korean War and Sino-American Relations," in Harding and Yuan Ming, 219.

22 Stueck, *Korean War*, 94; Lichterman, 595; Goulden, 282; *FRUS 1950* 7: 848, 864–66, 868–69; Peter N. Farrar, "Britain's Proposal for a Buffer Zone South of the Yalu in November 1950: Was It a Neglected Opportunity to End the Fighting in Korea?" *Journal of Contemporary History* 18 (April 1983): 330; *Documents on British Policy* IV-2: 165n; Callum A. MacDonald, *Korea: The War before Vietnam* (New York: Free Press, 1987), 67; Memorandum to Deputy Secretary of Defense, Subject: Summary of Intelligence Estimates on Intervention by Chinese Communists in the Korean War (12 October–24 November 1950), Truman Papers (PSF), Box 182, Korea Folder, TL; Michael Warner, 351–53; *FRUS 1950* 7: 934; Kuhns, 450–51; Harry G. Summers, Jr., "The Korean War, Fresh Perspective," www.thehistorynet.com/mh/blthekoreanwar/index.html (viewed 9/20/04).

23 Truman, *Years of Trial and Hope*, 365–67; C. S. Murphy Oral History, TL, 190–91; Elsey Oral History, TL, 2: 278; Matthews Oral History, TL, 21; Princeton Seminars, 13 February 1954; *FRUS 1950* 7: 948–60; "Substance of Statements Made at Wake Island Conference on October 15, 1950, Compiled from Notes Kept by the Conferees from Washington," attached to Pace Oral History, TL, 128; Ferrell, *Off the Record*, 200. While it is probably true Acheson expressed strong reservations about the Wake conference, when Truman formally asked for his approval, he gave it. *Memoranda of the Secretary of State* 50: 746 (Meeting with the President, Subject: President's Proposed Trip to Hawaii [sic]), 9 October 1950.

24 Eliot A. Cohen, "'Only Half the Battle,'" 138; Kuhns, 455–56; Schnabel and Watson, 1: 262, 280–82; Mastny, *Cold War and Soviet Insecurity*, 107.

25 Princeton Seminars, 13 February 1950; Daily Meetings, 21 October 1950; *FRUS 1950* 7: 987; Goncharov, Lewis, and Xue Litai, 199–200; Li Xiaobing, Wang Xi, and Chen Jian, 76, 78; Eliot A. Cohen, "'Only Half the Battle,'" 136, 140; Notes on Meeting in Secretary's Office in Re Testimony on MacArthur Hearings, 15 May 1951, Acheson Papers, Box 63, TL; Melby Oral History, TL, 126; Directive for the Occupation of North Korea, October 28, 1950, Truman Papers (PSF), Box 210, NSC Meeting No. 72 Folder, TL; *Documents on British Policy* IV-2: 188n; Farrar, "Britain's Proposal," 331; *New York Times*, 29 October 1950.

26 Kuhns, 458–63; Eliot A. Cohen, "'Only Half the Battle,'" 140; Schnabel and Watson, 1: 289–95; Christensen, "'Lost Chance,'" 267; Mark Perry, *Four Stars* (Boston: Houghton Mifflin, 1989), 33; *PAC*, 463–64; Truman, *Years of Trial and Hope*, 374–76; Memorandum of Conference between Secretary Acheson, Under Secretary of Defense Lovett and Mr. Dean Rusk, November 6, 1950, Acheson Papers, Box 65, TL, and Omar Bradley, *A General's Life*, 584, 587. Later the myth arose that Marshall and the chiefs urged Acheson at this point to use his influence with Truman to rein in MacArthur, only to have him refuse. Lichterman, 602; *PAC*, 754n; Schnabel and Watson, 1: 323n; Collins, 202n.

27 *PAC*, 465–66, 468.

28 Memorandum to Deputy Secretary of Defense, Subject: Summary of Intelligence Estimates on Intervention by Chinese Communists in the Korean War (12 October–24 November 1950), Truman Papers (PSF), Box 182, Korea Folder, TL; *FRUS 1950* 7: 1051–53; Daily Meetings, 6 November 1950; Memorandum of the Press and Radio News Conference, Wednesday, November 8, 1950, Acheson Papers, Box 68, Press Conf. 1949–53, Jan.–Dec. 1950 Folder, TL.

29 Schnabel and Watson, 1: 301–2; Memorandum for the President, 10 November 1950, Truman Papers (PSF), Box 220, NSC Meetings . . . Discussions (1950) Folder, TL; *FRUS 1950* 7: 1126–27; Foot, *The Wrong War*, 94–95; Accinelli, 52; Stueck, *Korean War*, 116; Farrar, "Britain's Proposal," 333–34, 339.

30 Peter N. Farrar, "A Pause for Peace Negotiations: The British Buffer Zone Plan of November 1950," in Cotton and Neary, 70; *FRUS 1950* 7: 1158; Blair, 423; Kuhns, 464; Callum MacDonald, *Korea*, 53.

31 Farrar, "Pause for Peace Negotiations," 66; idem, "Britain's Proposal," 336; McGlothlen, *Controlling the Waves*, 131; Accinelli, 52–53; Schnabel and Watson, 1: 314; Mastny, *Cold War and Soviet Insecurity*, 108–9; Foot, "Sino-American Conflict," 164–65; Eliot A. Cohen, "'Only Half the Battle,'" 141; Kuhns, 466.

32 Eliot A. Cohen, "'Only Half the Battle,'" 136; Christensen, "Threats, Assurances," 140–41; M. L. Dockrill, 464; Lee, 100; Farrar, "Pause for Peace Negotiations," 71; *FRUS 1950* 7: 1165, 1181–83; Schnabel and Watson, 1: 309, 316–17; *New York Times*, 16 November 1950.

33 *FRUS 1950* 7: 1204–8; *Documents on British Policy* IV-2: 208–14.

34 Goncharov, Lewis, and Xue Litai, 342n; Elmer Davis, 27; *FRUS 1950* 7: 1228–29; M. L. Dockrill, 464.

35 *PAC*, 469; SR71–125, Dean Acheson Interviewed by Eric Sevareid, 8 November 1969, Recording, Part I, TL; *FRUS 1950* 7: 1237.

36 Powaski, *March to Armageddon*, 59.

37 Eliot A. Cohen, "'Only Half the Battle,'" 143–44; Gaddis, "Strategic Perspective," 112n; *FRUS 1950* 7: 1250; *Pattern of Responsibility*, 263, 269; *FRUS 1950* 7: 1259; *PAC*, 477; *New York Times*, 30 November 1950; Tang, 100.

38 *Reviews of the World Situation*, 372, 374; NSC Meeting, 28 November 1950, Truman Papers (PSF), Box 171, Subj. File–For. Affairs, Attlee Meeting–Dec. '50 Folder, TL; Memorandum for the President, 28 November 1950, Truman Papers (PSF), Box 220, NSC Meetings . . . Discussions (1950) Folder, TL; and *FRUS 1950* 7: 1242–49; *PAC*, 469, 471; Truman, *Years of Trial and Hope*, 385–88. Emphasis in original.

39 Reston, *Artillery of the Press*, 33–34; *Public Papers of the Presidents . . . 1950*, 727; "No yearning to be loved," 442; *Memoranda of the Secretary of State* 50:850, 1 December 1950; *Documents on British Policy* IV-2: 223n. It was a bad week for Truman. On 5 December, a day after Attlee arrived in Washington, his friend and press spokesman, Charlie Ross, died of a heart attack, and the next day he wrote the notorious letter to the *Washington Post* music critic, Paul Hume, who dared criticize Margaret Truman's singing. Ferrell, *Off the Record*, 204.

40 Meeting of the President with Congressional Leaders, 11 A.M., Friday, December 1, 1950, Truman Papers (PSF), Box 171, Subj. File–For. Affairs, Attlee Meeting–Dec. '50 Folder, TL; Truman, *Years of Trial and Hope*, 390–91; *FRUS 1950* 7: 1279, 1309, 1324–26; T. J. Schoenbaum, 219–20; *Memoranda of the Secretary of State* 50: 862–63 (Meeting in Mr. Matthews' office, at approximately 12:00 Noon, re Korea), 3 December 1950.

41 *PAC*, 472–75; *FRUS 1950* 7: 1276–82, 1302.

42 Kennan, *Memoirs 1950–1963*, 26–27, 30; Miscamble, "Rejected Architect and Master Builder" 456–58; Miscamble, *Kennan and the Making of American Foreign Policy*, 329; *Documents on British Policy* IV-2: 286; *PAC*, 476–77; Chace, 308.

43 Mastny, *Cold War and Soviet Insecurity*, 111; Christensen, *Useful Adversaries*, 172; Hunt, "Beijing and the Korean Crisis," 466; Goulden, 405.

44 Isaacson and Thomas, 537.

45 Melby Oral History, TL, 125, 242; *Memoranda of the Secretary of State* 50: 747, October 1950; Eliot A. Cohen, "'Only Half the Battle,'" 133, 139; David S. McLellan, "Dean Acheson and the Korean War," *Political Science Quarterly* 83 (March 1968): 36.

46 McLellan, "Acheson and the Korean War," 21; Shu Guang Zhang, *Deterrence and Strategic Culture*, 85–87, 102–3; Foot, "Sino-American Conflict," 161–64; Princeton Seminars, 13 February 1954; Alsop, *I've Seen the Best of It*, 325.

47 Nitze Oral History, TL, 268; Acheson to Paul Nitze, 1 November 1967, Acheson Papers, Box 23, Folder 295, YUL; R. A. Winnacker, Memorandum for Mr. Nitze, Subject: General Marshall and Korea, November 1950, 27 November 1967, Acheson Papers, Box 23, Folder 295, YUL; Acheson to Matthew B. Ridgway, 17 October 1967, Acheson Papers, Box 26, Folder 328, YUL; Acheson to Forrest C. Pogue, 23 October 1967, Acheson Papers, Box 25, Folder 317; Princeton Seminars, 10 October 1953, 13 February 1954.

48 Princeton Seminars, 13 February 1954.

49 Ibid.

50 *Pattern of Responsibility*, 266.

Chapter 24

1 McCullough, 813; *PAC*, 478; Princeton Seminars, 13 February 1954. See Job 16:2.

2 Stueck, *Korean War*, 131.

3 *New York Times*, 22 July 1959; *PAC*, 479–80; Kathryn Weathersby, "Stalin, Mao, and the End of the Korean War," in Odd Arne Westad, ed., *Brothers in Arms: The Rise and Fall of the Sino-Soviet Alliance* (Washington, DC, and Stanford, CA: Woodrow Wilson Center Press and Stanford University Press, 1998), 93; Mastny, *Cold War and Soviet Insecurity*, 111–12; Stueck, *Korean War*, 143; Notes on Cabinet Meeting, 5 December 1950, George M. Elsey Papers, Box 73, TL.

4 Princeton Seminars, 2 July 1953; Memorandum for the Secretary, December 4, 1950, Acheson Papers, Box 65, TL; Miscamble, *Kennan and the Making of American Foreign Policy*, 329–30; Kennan, *Memoirs 1950–1963*, 32; Rusk, 170.

5 *Documents on Canadian External Relations* 16: 298–99; *PAC*, 478, 480; Danchev, "In the back room," 228; Kenneth Harris, *Attlee* (New York: W. W. Norton, 1982), 300; M. L. Dockrill, 464–65; Rosemary Foot, "Anglo-American Relations in the Korean Crisis: The British Effort to Avert an Expanded War, December 1950–January 1951," *Diplomatic History* 10 (Winter 1986): 49.

6 *FRUS 1950* 7: 1376, 1383, 1431–32; *Memoranda of the Secretary of State* 50:868, 7 December 1950; Kenneth Harris, 464.

7 *Documents on British Policy* IV-2: 254; *FRUS 1950* 7: 1366–67, 1376, 1392, 1401–2, 1451–52; *PAC*, 481; Truman, *Years of Trial and Hope*, 399.

8 *FRUS 1950* 7: 1367–68, 1375, 1383, 1395; *Reviews of the World Situation*, 411; Kennan, *Memoirs 1950–1963*, 29; *PAC*, 482.

9 *FRUS 1950* 7: 1374, 1469–70; Danchev, *Franks*, 130; *PAC*, 480–81; Schnabel and Watson, 1: 379; Stueck, *Korean War*, 140.

10 *FRUS 1950* 7: 1462–64, 1473–75, 1479; *FRUS 1951* 1: 875–76; *PAC*, 484–85; Arneson Oral History, TL, 70–72; McIntyre, 33; "No Yearning to Be Loved," 442; Hopkins, 190; Thomas Risse-Kappen, *Cooperation among Democracies: The European Influence on U.S. Foreign Policy* (Princeton: Princeton University Press, 1995), 60; Miall Oral History, TL, 40; *Documents on Canadian External Relations* 16: 306; *Documents on British Policy* IV-2: 239–50, 254–58.

11 Shu Guang Zhang, *Deterrence and Strategic Culture*, 114–15; *FRUS 1950* 7: 1445–46, 1588–89, 1600–1604.

12 Kepley, *Collapse of the Middle Way*, 119–21; Leffler, *Preponderance of Power*, 403; Foot, *Wrong War*, 122–25.

13 Schnabel and Watson, 1: 410–12; Truman, *Years of Trial and Hope*, 434–36; *PAC*, 514–17.

14 Memorandum for the President, 18 January 1951, Truman Papers (PSF), Box 220, NSC Meetings . . . Discussions (1951) Folder, TL; Foot, *The Wrong War*, 119–20; *PAC*, 516.

15 *PAC*, 515; Hastings, 186; *FRUS 1951* 7, Pt. 1: 27.

16 *FRUS 1951* 7, Pt. 1: 28; *Documents on Canadian External Relations* 16: 306; *Documents on British Policy* IV-2: 253; Foot, "Anglo-American Relations," 54; Stueck, *Korean War*, 139–42; *PAC*, 513; "Mao's Telegrams," 124.

17 *Documents on British Policy* IV-2: 289, 310n, 326n; *FRUS 1951* 7, Pt. 1: 92–93, 98, 108–9; Stueck, *Korean War*, 151–57; *PAC*, 513; Daily Meetings, 23 January 1951; *Memoranda of Conversations*, 24 January 1951, Korea; Callum MacDonald, *Korea*, 86; Foot, "Anglo-

American Relations," 55–56; *Memoranda of Conversations*, 27 January 1951, Indian Ambassador's Call; *Memoranda of the Secretary of State* M-283, 29 January 1951; Princeton Seminars, 14 February 1954.

18 For the discussions and all relevant quotations below, see *FRUS 1951* 7, Pt. 2: 1478, 1481–82, 1485–86, 1488, 1491, 1493–94, 1499–1502, 1530–31, 1534, 1545, 1551, 1561, 1653, 1697–98, and 1716. Information on Second and Third Party is in *FRUS 1951* 7, Pt. 2: 1476; Dingman, "Atomic Diplomacy," 76n; Stueck, *Korean War*, 157; Nitze, *Hiroshima to Glasnost*, 112; and Goulden, 548. Born in England, Taylor studied and taught in China before World War II, taught at Washington from 1939 to 1974, and died in 2000. A political target for his views in the 1950s, he testified against Owen Lattimore and university employees. Mark Selden, "Introduction" to "Asia, Asian Studies and the National Security State: A Symposium," *Bulletin of Concerned Asian Scholars* 29 (January–March 1997).

19 No such assurance was offered. One reason may have been the impossibility of carrying out a proffer suggested by Marshall, freeing a certain American jailed in China for espionage. Unbeknownst to Washington, China had already executed him. Goulden, 549.

20 Princeton Seminars, 14 March 1954; Dingman, "Atomic Diplomacy," 76. As described by Dingman, the veil may have been more evident than the threat, which consisted of declarations that China should not misinterpret the firing of MacArthur, exaggerate U.S. patience, or forget that Washington had the power "to set [China's] development back for decades."

21 Central Intelligence Agency, Memorandum for the Senior NSC Staff, Subject: Position of the United States with Respect to Communist China, 11 January 1951, Truman Papers (PSF), Box 198, Senior NSC Staff – Miscellaneous Folder, TL.

22 *FRUS 1951* 7, Pt. 1: 85, 159, 172–77, 188–94, 202–6; Pt. 2: 1567–68; Accinelli, 59; Callum MacDonald, *Korea*, 91; Trachtenberg, "Wasting Asset," 27; Schnabel and Watson, 1: 460–62, 467–68, 477–82; *PAC*, 517; Stueck, *Korean War*, 168.

23 Leffler, *Preponderance of Power*, 404–5.

24 Lichterman, 626–28; Princeton Seminars, 14 February 1954; Truman, *Years of Trial and Hope*, 439–41; William Manchester, *American Caesar: Douglas MacArthur, 1880–1964* (Boston: Little, Brown, 1978), 634–35; Omar Bradley, *A General's Life*, 627–28; *PAC*, 518. For the NSA-intercept story, see Goulden, 477; Cray, *General of the Army*, 708; Stanley Weintraub, *MacArthur's War: Korea and the Undoing of an American Hero* (New York: Free Press, 2000), 315–16; and Nitze Oral History, TL, 268. For doubts, see Michael Schaller, *Douglas MacArthur: The Far Eastern General* (New York: Oxford University Press, 1989), 294n.

25 *PAC*, 518–19; M. L. Dockrill, 472; Belmonte, 659; Lowe, "Ally and a Recalcitrant General," 647n; *Documents on British Policy* IV-2: 384.

26 Stueck, *Korean War*, 175; *PAC*, 519; Truman, *Years of Trial and Hope*, 442–43; Belmonte, 661, 666; Callum MacDonald, *Korea*, 187; Rhodes, 449.

27 Schaller, *Douglas MacArthur*, 234–35; Stueck, *Korean War*, 181–82; Belmonte, 662–63; Omar Bradley, *A General's Life*, 629–30; Roger M. Anders, "The Atomic Bomb and the Korean War: Gordon Dean and the Issue of Civilian Control," *Military Affairs* 52 (January 1988): 1–6.

28 Chace, 313; McLellan, *State Department Years*, 313; Truman, *Years of Trial and Hope*, 447–48; *PAC*, 521; Omar Bradley, *A General's Life*, 632–33; Ferrell, *Off the Record*, 210–11.

29 *PAC*, 521–22; Omar Bradley, *A General's Life*, 632–33, 635, who places the Acheson-Marshall-Bradley-Harriman meeting in Marshall's office.

30 Omar Bradley, *A General's Life*, 633–35; Stueck, *Korean War*, 180; Belmonte, 663; Schnabel and Watson, 1: 540; Truman, *Years of Trial and Hope*, 448; Annan, "Dean of the Cold War," 14.

31 Truman, *Years of Trial and Hope*, 448; *PAC*, 522; Omar Bradley, *A General's Life*, 635.

32 *PAC*, 522–24; Truman, *Years of Trial and Hope*, 448–49; *FRUS 1951* 6, Pt. 1: 972; Callum MacDonald, *Korea*, 98; Hopkins, 203; *Memoranda of the Secretary of State* 51:214, 11 April 1951; *Documents on British Policy* IV-2: 406.

Chapter 25

1 Princeton Seminars, 14 March 1954; Weintraub, 133; Ferrell, *Harry S. Truman*, 333; *New York Times*, 13 October 1971.

2 Belmonte, 641–42, 660–63, 665–66; Callum A. MacDonald, "The Atomic Bomb and the Korean War, 1950–53," in Dick Richardson and Glyn Stone, eds., *Decisions and Diplomacy: Essays in Twentieth Century International History: In Memory of George Grün and Esmonde Robertson* (London: Routledge, 1995), 188–89; *FRUS 1951* 7 Pt. 1: 309, 352; Schnabel and Watson, 1: 487–88, 490; Victor S. Kaufman, *Confronting Communism: U.S. and British Policies toward China* (Columbia: University of Missouri Press, 2001), 57.

3 Stueck, *Korean War*, 184–85; John P. Rossi, "The British View of the 1952 Presidential Election," *Mid-America* 76 (Winter 1994): 72n; *New York Times*, 13, 17, and 24 April 1951; Kepley, *Collapse of the Middle Way*, 124–25; *FRUS 1951* 7, Pt. 1: 369; Barrett Oral History, TL, 45; Schaller, *Douglas MacArthur*, 242–43; Hershberg, *James B. Conant*, 528.

4 *Memoranda of the Secretary of State* 51:228, 16 April 1951; *New York Times*, 23 and 28 April 1951.

5 Omar Bradley, *A General's Life*, 639, 723n; *PAC*, 524; *Military Situation in the Far East*, passim; Manchester, 667.

6 Manchester, 675; Dingman, "Atomic Diplomacy," 77; *Pattern of Responsibility*, 278.

7 Meeting with magazine and book publishers, June 29, 1951, Old State Building, Reston Papers, Box 30, Working Files, 3, UIA; *Pattern of Responsibility*, 276; Acheson, *Citizen Looks at Congress*, 66; U. Alexis Johnson, 118; *Memoranda of the Secretary of State* 51:327, 29 May 1951.

8 Secretary's Dictation on His Ideas, 5–10–51, Acheson Papers, Box 63, MacArthur Testimony Folder, TL; Notes on Meeting in Secretary's Office in Re Testimony on MacArthur Hearings, 15 May 1951, Acheson Papers, Box 63, TL; Notes on Meeting in Secretary's Office in Re Testimony on MacArthur Hearings–May 15, 1951, Acheson Papers, Box 63, MacArthur Testimony Folder, TL; Notes on Meeting in Secretary's Office on MacArthur Testimony May 16, 1951, Acheson Papers, Box 63, MacArthur Testimony Folder, TL; Minutes of Meeting, 5–22–51, Acheson Papers, Box 63, MacArthur Testimony Folder, TL; Notes on Meeting in Secretary's Office, Tuesday, May 29, 1951—re Statement to precede testimony, Acheson Papers, Box 63, TL; Minutes of Meeting on MacArthur Testimony (Question of what he says when asked about Conferences with President), 15 May 1951, Acheson Papers, Box 63, TL; Truman statement in Truman Papers (PSF), Box 225, May–June 1951 Folder, TL.

9 Fisher Oral History, JL, 12–15; *New York Times*, 3 June 1951; *Military Situation in the Far East*, 1716, 1718, 1946.

10 *Military Situation in the Far East*, 1717, 1776; *New York Times*, 7, 10, and 11 June 1951.

11 *New York Times*, 5 July 1951; Goulden, 544–45; *Pattern of Responsibility*, 288; Foot, *Wrong War*, 139; Hamby, *Man of the People*, 563; *PAC*, 525–26.

12 Princeton Seminars, 12 December 1953; Schnabel and Watson, 1: 557–58; Kepley, *Collapse of the Middle Way*, 130–31; Cray, 721; Hamby, *Beyond the New Deal*, 427.

13 Princeton Seminars, 14 February 1954; Acheson to Truman, 25 July 1955, Acheson Papers, Box 30, Folder 393, YUL; *PAC*, 526–28.

14 *FRUS 1950* 7, Pt. 1: 483–86, 507–11; Stueck, *Korean War*, 176; *PAC*, 532; Miscamble, *Kennan and the Making of American Foreign Policy*, 332–33; Mastny, *Cold War and Soviet Insecurity*, 124–26; *New York Times*, 3 June 1951.

15 Callum MacDonald, *Korea*, 116; Mastny, *Cold War and Soviet Insecurity*, 123; Bernard Brodie, *War and Politics* (New York: Macmillan, 1973), 94–97, 105; Weathersby, "Stalin, Mao," 109; Matthew B. Ridgway, as told to Harold H. Martin, *Soldier: The Memoirs of Matthew B. Ridgway* (New York: Harper & Row, 1956), 219; *PAC*, 529; Risse-Kappen, 61.

16 *PAC*, 532–34; Kennan, *Memoirs 1950–1963*, 36–37; *Pattern of Responsibility*, 284–85; Robert C. Tucker, "Cold War in Stalin's Time," 277–78; Weathersby, "New Russian Documents," 60–61, 64–65; idem, "Stalin, Mao," 97, 99; *FRUS 1951* 7, Pt. 1: 538; James F. Schnabel and Robert J. Watson, *The History of the Joint Chiefs of Staff: The Joint Chiefs of Staff and National Policy. Volume III: The Korean War, Part II* (Wilmington, DE: Michael Glazier, 1979), 565.

17 *New York Times*, 27 June 1951; *FRUS 1951* 7, Pt. 1: 551–54, 560–61, 567–68; *Pattern of Responsibility*, 254.

18 Mastny, *Cold War and Soviet Insecurity*, 126; *FRUS 1951* 7, Pt. 1: 699–700. Over 20,000 North Korean and Chinese prisoners, mostly the latter, eventually refused repatriation, as against 21 Americans, 1 Briton, and 325 South Koreans. Burton I. Kaufman, *The Korean War: Challenges in Crisis, Credibility, and Command* (New York: Alfred A. Knopf, 1986), 341.

19 Stueck, *Rethinking*, 160; Callum A. MacDonald, " 'Heroes behind Barbed Wire'— The United States, Britain and the POW Issue in the Korean War," in Cotton and Neary, 135–50; Acheson, *Sketches from Life*, 101; Stueck, *Korean War*, 244–45, 250–52; James I. Matray, "Introduction," *Journal of Conflict Studies* 22 (Spring 2002), 12; Memorandum for the President. Subject: Suggested Broadcast of Surrender Terms to North Koreans, September 27, 1950, Truman Papers (PSF), Box 159, Subj. File–Cabinet, State, Secretary–Misc Folder, TL; Johnson Oral History, TL, 71–73.

20 *PAC*, 653; Princeton Seminars, 14 March 1954; Callum MacDonald, *Korea*, 139; *FRUS 1951* 7, Pt. 1: 857; Nitze Oral History, TL, 276; Shen Zhihua, "Sino-North Korean Conflict," 19; *FRUS 1952–1952* 15, Pt. 1: 40–45, 68–69.

21 Secretary, Drummond, Kuh, 3–27–52, Acheson Papers, Box 69, Press Conf. 1949–1953, Jan. 1952–Jan. 1953 Folder, TL; Truman, *Years of Trial and Hope*, 460–61; William Roskey, "Korea's Costliest Battle: The POW Impasse," *Parameters* 23 (Summer 1993): 102, 105; Princeton Seminars, Korea—Synopsis H, pp. 5–9.

22 Weathersby, "Stalin, Mao," 102, 109; idem, "New Russian Documents," 72; Schnabel and Watson, 2: 735–39, 748–49, 758–60, 768–74, 837, 868; Stueck, *Korean War*, 261–64, 268–69.

23 Shen Zhihua, "Sino-North Korean Conflict," 19–20; "Russian Documents on the Korean War, 1950–53," 371; Schnabel and Watson, 2: 863–65; *FRUS 1951* 7, Pt. 1: 586; Mastny, *Cold War and Soviet Insecurity*, 147–48; Weathersby, "Stalin, Mao," 104; "Stalin's Conversations with Chinese Leaders," 13.

24 Pearson, 318; *FRUS 1952–1954* 15, Pt. 1: 475–83, 485–89, 492–99, 512–25, 532–40; Stueck, *Korean War*, 286–87, 290; Schnabel and Watson, 2: 887–907; Weathersby, "New Russian Documents," 79.

25 *New York Times*, 28 June 1951; Central Intelligence Agency, 2 July 1951, Meeting of Chinese Communist Leaders and Soviets on 4 June, Truman Papers, SMOF, Box 3, NSC/CIA. Memos for Pres. Apr.–Aug. '51 Folder, TL; Schnabel and Watson, 2: 641–42; *FRUS 1951* 7, Pt. 1: 1332, 1463; Memorandum of Conversation at Dinner at British Embassy, Sunday, January 6, 1952, Acheson Papers, Box 67, TL; V. S. Kaufman, 57; Kevin Ruane, " 'Containing America': Aspects of British Foreign Policy and the Cold War in South-East Asia, 1951–54," *Diplomacy & Statecraft* 7 (March 1996): 149; Leffler, *Preponderance of Power*, 473; Duiker, 125; *FRUS 1952–1954* 13, Pt. 1: 163; *FRUS 1952–1954* 12, Pt. 1: 102; *PAC*, 648.

26 *Washington Post*, 20 October 1995; Qiang Zhai, *Dragon*, 121; Stueck, *Korean War*, 279, 283; *PAC*, 656–57; Foot, *The Wrong War*, 185; Russell D. Buhite, *Soviet-American Relations in Asia, 1945–1954* (Norman: University of Oklahoma Press, 1981), 213; *FRUS 1952–1954* 12, Pt. 1: 113, 137; Ruane, "'Containing America,'" 150.

27 Milton Leitenberg, "New Russian Evidence on the Korean War Bacteriological Warfare Allegations: Background and Analysis," *CWIHPB* (Issue 11, Winter 1998), 189–90; Kathryn Weathersby, "Deceiving the Deceivers: Moscow, Beijing, Pyongyang, and the Allegations of Bacteriological Weapons Use in Korea," ibid., 177–79, 183–84; Schnabel and Watson, 2: 810, 815; Acheson to President Truman, 11 March 1952, Acheson Papers, Box 67, TL; *New York Times*, 27 March 1952.

28 Muccio Oral History, TL, 30, 33–35; Edward C. Keefer, "The Truman Administration and the South Korean Political Crisis of 1952: Democracy's Failure?" *Pacific Historical Review* 60 (May 1991): 145–68; Lightner Oral History, TL, 114–15, 117–21; Stueck, *Korean War*, 277–78; Schnabel and Watson, 2: 790–96; *FRUS 1952–1954* 15, Pt. 2: 228–31, 252–56, 264–70, 279–86, 290–95, 301–8, 316–17, 324–43, 349–51, 354–55, 361–64, 376–79, 402–4.

29 *PAC*, 699; *New York Times*, 25 October 1952.

30 Message for the President from the Secretary of State, October 25, 1952, Truman Papers (PSF), Box 149, Subj. File–Agencies, Un. Nations–Misc. Folder, TL; *PAC*, 696, 700. This account draws heavily on Stueck, *Korean War*, 292–306.

31 *FRUS 1952–1954* 15, Pt. 1: 24, 585–89, 595–97; *PAC*, 700; Pearson, 323; Eden, 24.

32 Pearson, 324; Anita Inder Singh, *The Limits of British Influence: South Asia and the Anglo-American Relationship, 1947–56* (London: Pinter Publishers, 1993), 101; *FRUS 1952–1954* 15, Pt. 1: 611–13, 615–16, 629, 633; *PAC*, 701–2.

33 *PAC*, 701–2; *FRUS 1952–1954* 15, Pt. 1: 637–46, 654–55; *Documents on Canadian External Relations. Volume 18: 1952*, ed., Donald Barry (Ottawa: External Affairs and International Trade Canada, 1990), 207; Stueck, *Korean War*, 299; *FRUS 1952–1954* 1, Pt. 1: 25; Frederic C. Mosher, W. David Clinton, and Daniel G. Lang, *Presidential Transitions and Foreign Affairs* (Baton Rouge: Louisiana State University Press, 1987), 144.

34 *FRUS 1952–1954* 15, Pt. 1: 657–60; *PAC*, 703; Evelyn Shuckburgh, *Descent to Suez: Diaries 1951–56*, selected for publication by John Charmley (London: Weidenfeld and Nicolson, 1986), 54, 56–57; Callum MacDonald, *Korea*, 171.

35 *FRUS 1952–1954* 15, Pt. 1: 662–63, 670, 677; *New York Times*, 23 November 1952; Shuckburgh, 54–55, 59; *PAC*, 704; Pearson, 184–85, 315–35.

36 *PAC*, 705; *FRUS 1952–1954* 15, Pt. 1: 677–86, 689, 694–98, 700–705; *New York Times*, 25 November 1952; Stueck, *Korean War*, 301.

37 Stueck, *Korean War*, 302.

38 Reston, *Deadline*, 200; Roskey, 103–5; Collins, 356–57; Weathersby, "New Findings," 15; Dingman, "Atomic Diplomacy," passim; Rosemary Foot, "Nuclear Coercion and the Ending of the Korean Conflict," *International Security* 13 (Winter 1988–1989): 92–112.

39 Ferrell, *Off the Record*, 250.

40 *FRUS 1950* 5: 1468.

41 *Among Friends*, 103; Goncharov, Lewis, and Xue Litai, 202; Stueck, *Korean War*, 362–63.

42 Westad, *Decisive Encounters*, 323–24.

43 J. Chester Cheng, "The Korean War through Chinese Eyes: China Crosses the Rubicon," *Journal of Oriental Studies* 31 (1993): 1; Stueck, *Korean War*, 6, 350, 352–53, 361–64, 367–68.

Chapter 26

1 Klaus Larres to the author, summer 2000; John L. Harper, 305; Frank C. Costigliola, *France and the United States: The Cold Alliance since World War II* (New York: Twayne, 1992), 83.

2 Ted Galen Carpenter, "United States' NATO Policy at the Crossroads: The 'Great Debate' of 1950–1951," *International History Review* 8 (August 1986): 399–401, 401n; *PAC*, 489–96.

3 http://dewine.senate.gov/Election%20Pages/election_data/1950.htm (viewed 7/5/05); *PAC*, 491; David R. Kepley, "The Senate and the Great Debate of 1951," *Prologue* 14 (Winter 1982): 215, 218; Phil Williams, *The Senate and US Troops in Europe* (London: Macmillan, 1985), 55; Princeton Seminars, 11 December 1953; Senator Robert A. Taft, *A Foreign Policy for Americans* (Garden City: Doubleday, 1951), 21–23; Ronald E. Powaski, *The Entangling Alliance: The United States and European Security, 1950–1993* (Westport: Greenwood Press, 1994), 14; *New York Times*, 30 November 1950, and 24 December 1950; Press clipping from 21 December 1950 *Washington Evening Star*, George M. Elsey Papers, Box 66, Foreign Relations–Western Union Folder, TL.

4 *New York Times*, 24 December 1950; Kepley, "Senate and the Great Debate," 218; Princeton Seminars, Great Debate, Synopses; Donald J. Mrozek, "Progressive Dissenter: Herbert Hoover's Opposition to Truman's Overseas Military Policy," *Annals of Iowa* 43 (Spring 1976): 275–91.

5 *FRUS 1951* 3, Pt. 1: 22; Kepley, "Senate and the Great Debate," 213; Princeton Seminars, 12 December 1953.

6 *Public Papers of the Presidents . . . 1951*, 20; Daily Meetings, 30 January 1951, and 5 February 1951; *New York Times*, 18 January 1951; Carpenter, 406; *PAC*, 494.

7 All testimony is in *Assignment of Ground Forces*, already cited.

8 Ibid., 77–125 (quotations from 78–79, 81, 85, 113–14); *New York Times*, 18 February 1951.

9 *Assignment of Ground Forces*, 108, 114; Princeton Seminars, 16 July 1953.

10 *Assignment of Ground Forces*, 267, 432–33; *FRUS 1951* 3, Pt. 1: 24; Kaplan, *Community of Interests*, 153; Powaski, *Entangling Alliance*, 17; *Memoranda of Conversations*, 9 April 1951, Conversation with Belgian Prime Minister. This would be the last of the confrontations with Senator Wherry, who died the following December.

11 Kepley, "Senate and the Great Debate," 225–26; Kaplan, *Community of Interests*, 153; Carpenter, 413; Princeton Seminars, 12 December 1953.

12 *FRUS 1951* 3, Pt. 1: 802; *PAC*, 551.

13 *PAC*, 493; *FRUS 1951* 3, Pt. 1: 396–400; Hitchcock, *France Restored*, 153; McGeehan, 72; Schwartz, *America's Germany*, 212; *FRUS 1950* 3: 579.

14 Daily Meetings, 6 February 1951; Schwartz, *America's Germany*, Chapter 6; *PAC*, 552; Manfred Jonas, *The United States and Germany: A Diplomatic History* (Ithaca: Cornell University Press, 1984), 290–91; Geoffrey Warner, 119; Saki Dockrill, 56, 68; Mawby, 6, 41, 54, 67, 70.

15 Integrated Forces and European Army, Truman Papers (PSF), Box 165, Subj. File–Conferences, Truman-Pleven Talks Background Material Folder, TL; *PAC*, 559; Danchev, *Franks*, 120.

16 Powaski, *Entangling Alliance*, 18; Edward Fursdon, *The European Defence Community: A History* (New York: St. Martin's Press, 1980), 115; Creswell, 18; Hitchcock, *France Restored*, 154; *PAC*, 557; Henrikson, "Creation of the North Atlantic Alliance," 6.

17 *PAC*, 552; Creswell, 18–19; Hitchcock, *France Restored*, 160.

18 *FRUS 1951* 3, Pt. 1: 801–5. See also Martin F. Herz, *David Bruce's "Long Telegram" of July 3, 1951*, foreword, Ellsworth Bunker (Washington: Institute for the Study of Diplomacy, Edmund A. Walsh School of Foreign Service, Georgetown University, 1978), 5–7.

19 *Pattern of Responsibility*, 296–98; McLellan, *State Department Years*, 347–49; Theodore H. White, 283; Costigliola, *France and the United States*, 75; *FRUS 1951* 3, Pt. 1: 805–12; John L. Harper, 309.

20 *Assignment of Ground Forces*, 21; Powaski, *Entangling Alliance*, 22; Thomas A. Schwartz, "The 'Skeleton Key'—American Foreign Policy, European Unity, and German Rearmament, 1949–54," *Central European History* 19 (December 1986): 380; idem, "Dual Containment: John J. McCloy, the American High Commission, and European Integration, 1949–1952," in Heller and Gillingham, 206; David Clay Large, "Grand Illusions: The United States, the Federal Republic of Germany, and the European Defense Community, 1950–1954," in Diefendorf, Frohn, and Rupieper, 383; Bark and Gress, 289; Saki Dockrill, 70.

21 Princeton Seminars, Outline of Discussion for the October 9–10 Meetings, The Defense of Europe; Princeton Seminars, 12 December 1953; *FRUS 1951* 3, Pt. 1: 813–19, 832–36, 850.

22 Herz, 22; Creswell, 19; *FRUS 1951* 3, Pt. 1: 849–52, 1164–67, 1188–90; *PAC*, 558; *Memoranda of Conversations*, 2 August 1951, Secretary's Conversation with General Gruenther.

23 *FRUS 1951* 3, Pt. 1: 1270; The International Scene, 27 August 1951.

24 Princeton Seminars, 11 and 12 December 1953.

25 Memorandum for the President, 25 January 1951, Truman Papers (PSF), Box 220, NSC Meetings . . . Discussions (1951) Folder, TL; *Memoranda of Conversations*, 13 February 1951, Memorandum for the Files; Frank Schumacher, "Propaganda, Ideology, and Alliance Management: The United States and West Germany, 1949–1955" (unpublished paper, June 2000), 6; Mastny, *Cold War and Soviet Insecurity*, 126; John S. Duffield, "Soviet Military Threat," 216, 218; Rearden, "Frustrating the Kremlin Design," 172; George H. Quester, *Nuclear Diplomacy: The First Twenty-five Years* (New York: Dunellen, 1970), 77; Rosenberg, "Origins of Overkill," 22–23.

26 Hitchcock, *France Restored*, 161; *PAC*, 553–54; *New York Times*, 4 January 1951; *Executive Sessions of the Senate Foreign Relations Committee . . . 1951* 3, Pt 1: 13; *Memoranda of the Secretary of State* M-293-94, 314, 30 January 1951; *FRUS 1951* 4, Pt. 1: 318, 325, 327.

27 *PAC*, 554–55; *Memoranda of the Secretary of State* 51: 65, 7 February 1951, 51: 310, 21 May 1951, and 51: 333, 7 June 1951; *Memoranda of Conversations*, 5 February 1951, Talk with a Correspondent; Mawby, 64; Princeton Seminars, 12 December 1953; Poole, 132.

28 *FRUS 1951* 1: 107, 165, 170, 173–75, 191, 234–35; Mitrovich, 88–89, 97; Callahan, 135–38; Memorandum for the President, January 17, 1952, Truman Papers (PSF), Box 200, NSC–Atomic Energy–Expansion of the Atomic Energy Program Folder, TL; *FRUS 1952–1954* 8: 962. Emphasis mine.

29 The International Scene, 27 August 1951; Daily Meetings, 20 September 1951; *FRUS 1951* 4, Pt. 2: 1276–81, 1672–73; Igor Lukes, "Changing Patterns of Power in Cold War Politics: The Mysterious Case of Vladimír Komárek," *Journal of Cold War Studies* 3 (Winter 2001): 69; *New York Times*, 18 November 1951; Victor H. Rothwell, *Anthony Eden: A Political Biography 1931–57* (Manchester: Manchester University Press, 1992), 113; Acheson, *Sketches from Life*, 99; *FRUS 1951* 4, Pt. 2: 1671–73; *PAC*, 582; Hamby, *Beyond the New Deal*, 439.

30 *Documents on Canadian External Relations* 16: 975; Princeton Seminars, 11 October 1953; *Memoranda of Conversations*, 19 September 1950, Turkish Membership in NATO; *PAC*, 563; *New York Times*, 17 February 1951; Ekavi Athanassopoulou, *Turkey-Anglo-American Security Interests, 1945–1952: The First Enlargement of NATO* (Portland, OR: Frank Cass, 1999), 200; Michael J. Cohen, *Fighting World War Three from the Middle East: Allied Contingency Plans, 1945–1954* (Portland, OR: Frank Cass, 1997), 59; Leffler, "Strategy, Diplomacy, and the Cold War," 823; idem, *Preponderance of Power*, 424; George S. Harris, *Troubled Alliance: Turkish-American Problems in Historical Perspective, 1945–1971* (Washington: American Enterprise Institute and Hoover Institution on War, Revolution and Peace, 1972), 823.

31 *PAC*, 569–70; *Executive Sessions of the Senate Foreign Relations Committee . . . 1951* 3, Pt. 2: 450–51; Michael J. Cohen, *Fighting World War Three*, 57; *Selected Executive Session Hearings of the Committee, 1951–1956*, 171; *New York Times*, 16 January 1952.

32 *PAC*, 569–71; Hitchcock, *France Restored*, 158; Kaplan, *United States and NATO*, 171; Abramson, 463–64; Pearson, 63–64, 85; *Documents on Canadian External Relations. Volume 17: 1951*, ed., Greg Donaghy (Ottawa: Department of Foreign Affairs and International Trade, 1996), 934.

33 *Executive Sessions of the Senate Foreign Relations Committee . . . 1951* 3, Pt. 2: 467; *PAC*, 558; *FRUS 1951* 3, Pt. 1: 852; Schwartz, *America's Germany*, 244–46; Bird, *Chairman*, 380; Byroade Oral History, TL, 104–5; *FRUS 1951* 3, Pt. 2: 1789; Ninkovich, *Germany and the United States*, 96.

34 *PAC*, 578; Eden, 221; *New York Times*, 7 November 1951; Hopkins, 234.

35 *PAC*, 583–87; Ruud van Dijk, "The Stalin-Note: Last Chance for Unification?" (unpublished paper, June 1994), 55n; Adenauer, 400; *FRUS 1951* 3, Pt. 2: 1610; Powaski, *Entangling Alliance*, 23; Paris to Secretary of State (Acheson to Truman), 20 November 1951, Truman Papers (PSF), Box 165, Subj. File–Conferences Sec. State–Rome, Italy, etc., Folder, TL.

36 *FRUS 1951* 3, Pt. 1: 749–50, 752, 754; *FRUS 1951* 3, Pt. 2: 1730–32.

37 *PAC*, 591–93; Daily Meetings, 13 December 1951.

38 Lambright, *Powering Apollo*, 65–68; *PAC*, 588–89; *New York Times*, 28 January, 30 November, 6–7, 10, and 13 December 1951, and 29 July 1952; Warren I. Cohen, *Dean Rusk*, 75; *Principal Officers of the Department of State*; *Memoranda of Conversations*, 5 February 1951, Talk with a Correspondent; Miscamble, *Kennan and the Making of American Foreign Policy*, 334–35. When Nitze confessed that he had urged Webb to resign, Acheson retorted: "If you are not careful who you fire when I am away, you may be next!"

39 *Memoranda of Conversations*, 15 February 1951; *Memoranda of the Secretary of State* 51: 116–18, 16 March 1951.

40 Rempel, 26.

41 Hopkins, 230; *Memoranda of the Secretary of State* 51: 712–13, 12 December 1951; Daily Meetings, 5 January 1952; Jan Melissen, *The Struggle for Nuclear Partnership: Britain, The United States and the Making of an Ambiguous Alliance, 1952–1959* (Groningen: Styx, 1993), 10.

42 Lester B. (Mike) Pearson to Acheson, 15 January 1952, and Acheson to Pearson, 23 January 1952, Acheson Papers, Box 67, TL. Much of the narrative of Churchill's visit to Washington and Ottawa stems from these two remarkable letters. The other key sources are *PAC*, 594–603; SR71-125, Dean Acheson Interviewed by Eric Sevareid, 8 November 1969, Recording, Part II, TL; *Memoranda of Conversations*, 6 January 1952; and *FRUS 1952–1954* 6, Pt. 1: 737 (for the full range of the summit, 730–857).

43 Hopkins, 227; *FRUS 1952–1954* 6, Pt. 1: 800; John W. Young, *Winston Churchill's Last Campaign: Britain and the Cold War, 1951–5* (Oxford: Clarendon Press, 1996), 76, 81, 86; Lester B. (Mike) Pearson to Acheson, 15 January 1952, and Acheson to Pearson, 23 January 1952, Acheson Papers, Box 67, TL; *Memoranda of the Secretary of State* M-558, 7 January 1952; *Memoranda of Conversations*, 7 January 1952, Meeting in Secretary's Office, and 10 January 1952, EDC; Saki Dockrill, 94.

44 Lester B. (Mike) Pearson to Acheson, 15 January 1952, and Acheson to Pearson, 23 January 1952, Acheson Papers, Box 67, TL; *FRUS 1952–1954* 6, Pt. 1: 846–51, 856–57; *PAC*, 601; Kaplan, *Long Entanglement*, 62.

45 *PAC*, 608–9; *FRUS 1952–1954* 5, Pt. 1: 19–20.

Chapter 27

1 *PAC*, 428.

2 *New York Times*, 12 October 1969; Joseph C. Harsch, *At the Hinge of History: A Reporter's Story* (Athens: University of Georgia Press, 1993), 137; *FRUS 1951* 6, Pt. 1: 161; Princeton Seminars, 14 March 1954.

3 *PAC*, 432–33, 540; Princeton Seminars, 14 March 1954.

4 *PAC*, 434, 540; Lowe, "Challenge and Readjustment," 149; Robert T. Fearey, "Summary of Negotiations Leading up to the Conclusion of the Treaty with Japan," in Thomas W. Burkman, ed., *The Occupation of Japan: The International Context* (Norfolk, VA: MacArthur Memorial Foundation, 1984), 283, 285; Roger V. Dingman, "The Diplomacy of Dependency: The Philippines and Peacemaking with Japan, 1945–52," *Journal of Southeast Asian Studies* 17 (September 1986): 316; *FRUS 1951* 6, Pt. 1: 779, 827–30, 873–74, 880–87, 930, 985–89.

5 Inder Singh, 1; Chihiro Hosoya, "Japan, China, the United States and the United Kingdom, 1951–2: The Case of the 'Yoshida Letter,' " *International Affairs* 60 (Spring 1984): 250; *FRUS 1950* 6: 1297–1303; Aaron Forsberg, *America and the Japanese Miracle: The Cold War Context of Japan's Postwar Economic Revival, 1950–1960* (Chapel Hill: University of North Carolina Press, 2000), 71, 74; Howard B. Schonberger, "Peacemaking in Asia: The United States, Great Britain, and the Japanese Decision to Recognize Nationalist China, 1951–52," *Diplomatic History* 10 (Winter 1986): 62–63; *Memoranda of Conversations*, 9 April 1951, Conversation with Belgian Prime Minister; *FRUS 1951* 6, Pt. 1: 909–26, 962–67, 1003; Lowe, *Containing the Cold War*, 41.

6 *FRUS 1951* 6, Pt. 1: 1105–6, 1110–16, 1118–33; Fearey, 287–88; Hopkins, 216; Forsberg, 71, 74; Blair, 54.

7 *FRUS 1950* 6: 1175–82; *PAC*, 434.

8 Dean Acheson and Louis Johnson, Memorandum for the President, 7 September 1950, Truman Papers (PSF), Box 182, Japanese Peace Treaty Folder, TL; *PAC*, 435, 539; Daily Meetings, 7 December 1950; McIntyre, 292; *FRUS 1950* 6: 1363–64, 1383–85, 1388–89; *Memoranda of Conversations*, 27 December 1950; *FRUS 1951* 6, Pt. 1: 782–83, 788–89; Poole, 230.

9 *FRUS 1951* 6, Pt. 1: 790–92, 969–71, 991, 1019–21, 1156, 1159–64; Omar N. Bradley, Memorandum for the Secretary of Defense, Subject: Japanese Peace Treaty, 26 June 1951, Truman Papers (PSF), Box 182, Japanese Peace Treaty Folder, TL; *PAC*, 435, 541; Marshall to Acheson, 28 June 1951, Truman Papers (PSF), Box 182, Japanese Peace Treaty Folder, TL; Dean Acheson, Memorandum for the President, 28 June 1951, Truman Papers (PSF), Box 182, Japanese Peace Treaty Folder, TL.

10 Qiang Zhai, *Dragon*, 71; *FRUS 1950* 6: 1332–36, 1350–51; Fearey, 282; Mastny, *Cold War and Soviet Insecurity*, 125; Fearey, 286–87; *PAC*, 540–41.

11 *FRUS 1951* 6, Pt. 1: 794, 1135, 1236, 1242, 1249; *FRUS 1952–1954* 14, Pt. 2: 1071; Blair, 52.

12 *FRUS 1951* 6, Pt. 1: 1223–24, 1256–61, 1313–14; *PAC*, 541; Dingman, "Diplomacy of Dependency," 307–8; *FRUS 1951* 7, Pt. 2: 1764.

13 *PAC*, 541–42; *FRUS 1951* 6, Pt. 1: 1266–67, 1275–77, 1289–91, 1297, 1299, 1307.

14 *FRUS 1951* 6, Pt. 1: 1266; Forsberg, 44; The International Scene, 27 August 1951; Dean Acheson, Memorandum for the President, 29 August 1951, Truman Papers (PSF), Box 165, Subj. File–Conferences, Jap. Peace Treaty–San Francisco, Sept. '51 Folder, TL.

15 Fred L. Israel, ed., *Major Peace Treaties of Modern History: 1648–1967* (New York: Chelsea House, 1967): 4: 2641–56; Finn, 304–5; Forsberg, 69, 72.

16 Princeton Seminars, 14 March 1954 and 12 December 1953; *PAC*, 544–45; *FRUS 1951* 6, Pt. 1: 1315–20, 1326–27.

17 *PAC*, 545–47; McGlothlen, *Controlling the Waves*, 47; Finn, 302.

18 Princeton Seminars, 14 March 1954; Lowe, *Containing the Cold War*, 70, *FRUS 1951* 6, Pt. 1: 1334–35; Schaller, *Altered States*, 40; J. W. Dower, *Empire and Aftermath: Yoshida Shigeru and the Japanese Experience, 1878–1954* (Cambridge: Council on East Asian Studies, Harvard University, distributed by Harvard University Press, 1979), 408; Rusk, 177; *PAC*, 547–48. Nikita Khrushchev records his strong disapproval of Stalin's decision against signing the treaty:

"All we had to do was sign, and everything would have fallen into place . . . [and] have restored peaceful relations with Japan." *Khrushchev Remembers*, 83–84.

19 *Pattern of Responsibility*, 262; Lowe, *Containing the Cold War*, 71; Annan, "Dean of the Cold War," 14; *New York Times*, 11 September 1951; Rosenau, 336; Princeton Seminars, 14 March 1954; *PAC*, 548–49.

20 *FRUS 1951* 6, Pt. 1: 1343–44, 1347; *PAC*, 603; Dower, *Empire and Aftermath*, 405; Qiang Zhai, *Dragon*, 109.

21 *FRUS 1951* 6, Pt. 1: 1372–73; 1378–80.

22 Ibid., 1389–90, 1431, 1436–38, 1443–50, 1466–70, 1472, 1477; Hosoya, 249, 251–57; *FRUS 1952–1954* 14, Pt. 2: 1063–64, 1073–75; *PAC*, 603; Forsberg, 73; Schaller, *Altered States*, 42; Dower, *Empire and Aftermath*, 401, 403, 406; Accinelli, 86.

23 *PAC*, 603–5; *FRUS 1952–1954* 14, Pt. 1: 783.

24 V. S. Kaufman, 58; Hopkins, 237; Lester B. (Mike) Pearson to Acheson, 15 January 1952, and Acheson to Pearson, 23 January 1952, Acheson Papers, Box 67, TL; *FRUS 1952–1954* 14, Pt. 2: 1075–80.

25 *FRUS 1952–1954* 14, Pt. 2: 1083, 1088, 1093, 1128; *PAC*, 604–5; Lester B. (Mike) Pearson to Acheson, 15 January 1952, and Acheson to Pearson, 23 January 1952, Acheson Papers, Box 67, TL; Princeton Seminars, 14 March 1954.

26 Walter LaFeber, *The Clash: U.S.-Japanese Relations throughout History* (New York: W. W. Norton, 1997), 291; *FRUS 1952–1954* 14, Pt. 2: 1121–22, 1133–34, 1144–45, 1194, 1207.

27 Bernard C. Cohen, *The Political Process and Foreign Policy: The Making of the Japanese Peace Settlement* (Princeton: Princeton University Press, 1957), 155; Kepley, *Collapse of the Middle Way*, 138; *FRUS 1952–1954* 14, Pt. 2: 1217, 1228–30, 1240n.

28 *FRUS 1952–1954* 14, Pt. 2: 1248n, 1254–55; Robert Murphy, *Diplomat among Warriors* (New York: Pyramid Books, 1964), 378; Richard D. Challener, "The Moralist as Pragmatist: John Foster Dulles as Cold War Strategist," in Craig and Loewenheim, 141; *PAC*, 605–6.

29 H. W. Brands, "The United States and the Reemergence of Independent Japan," *Pacific Affairs* 59 (Fall 1986): 390–92; *FRUS 1952–1954* 14, Pt. 2: 1332, 1354; Forsberg, 104; *Memoranda of Conversations*, 11 April 1952; The Secretary, Bryson Rash . . . George de Carvalho . . . Holmes Alexander . . . Lloyd Lehrbas, Acheson Papers, Box 69, Press Conf. 1949–1953, Jan. 1952–Jan. 1953 Folder, TL.

Chapter 28

1 With apologies to Pete Seeger ("Waist Deep in the Big Muddy," 1967) and the memory of Richard H. Rovere (*Waist Deep in the Big Muddy: Personal Reflections on 1968*, 1968).

2 Wall, *United States and the Making of Postwar France*, 233–34, 239; *FRUS 1951* 6, Pt. 1: 563; Grosser, 131; *FRUS 1952–1954* 11, Pt. 2: 1649; *FRUS 1952–1954* 13, Pt. 1: 143.

3 *FRUS 1952–1954* 12, Pt. 1: 137, 191, 193; Russell H. Fifield, *Americans in Southeast Asia: The Roots of Commitment* (New York: Thomas Y. Crowell, 1973), 181.

4 Princeton Seminars, 9 July 1953; Eden, 93; Stanley Karnow, *Vietnam: A History* (New York: Viking Press, 1983), 188.

5 *FRUS 1950* 6: 854; Chen Jian, "China's Changing Aims," 11; Qiang Zhai, *China and the Vietnam Wars, 1950–1975* (Chapel Hill: University of North Carolina Press, 2000), 20–21, 37; Westad, *Decisive Encounters*, 318; Shu Guang Zhang, " 'Preparedness Eliminates Mishaps,' " 67–68.

6 *FRUS 1950* 5: 1480; Kevin Ruane, "Refusing to Pay the Price: British Foreign Policy and the Pursuit of Victory in Vietnam, 1952–4," *English Historical Review* 110 (February 1995): 74; idem, " 'Containing America,' " 145, 147–49.

7 Mark Philip Bradley, *Imagining Vietnam and America: The Making of Postcolonial Vietnam, 1919–1950* (Chapel Hill: University of North Carolina Press, 2000), 147.

8 *FRUS 1950* 6: 136, 863; Kennan to Mr. Secretary, 21 and 23 August 1950, Acheson Papers, Box 65, TL; *Memoranda of Conversations*, 23 August 1950, French Memoranda on Defense Program.

9 *FRUS 1950* 6: 868–70, 876; "Yesterday afternoon the Secretary received and talked OFF THE RECORD . . . ," 2 September 1950, Acheson Papers, Box 62, Personal Correspondence, Co-Cz Folder, TL; Leffler, *Preponderance of Power*, 382; *Memoranda of Conversations*, 12 September 1950; *PAC*, 673.

10 Poole, 213; Duiker, 102, 104; Shu Guang Zhang, *Mao's Military Romanticism: China and the Korean War, 1950–1953* (Lawrence: University Press of Kansas, 1995), 70; *PAC*, 674; *FRUS 1950* 6: 893, 898–99, 913.

11 *FRUS 1950* 6: 901–2, 909, 913, 920, 938; *Memoranda of the Secretary of State* 50:766, 20 October 1950.

12 Wall, *United States and the Making of Postwar France*, 239; *PAC*, 674; *FRUS 1950* 6: 924–30, 949–53; *FRUS 1952–1954* 13, Pt. 1: 30n; Poole, 215.

13 Shulman, 164; Chen Jian, *China's Road to the Korean War*, 133; *FRUS 1950* 6: 958–63; *Executive Sessions of the Senate Foreign Relations Committee . . . 1951* 3, Pt. 1: 26; *FRUS 1951* 6, Pt. 1: 368–69; www.wist. info/authors/q.html (viewed 9/20/04) (Queuille).

14 *FRUS 1951* 6, Pt. 1: 377, 384–85, 395–96; McMahon, *Limits of Empire*, 60; Kenton J. Clymer, "Cambodia: The View from the United States, 1945–1954," *Journal of American-East Asian Relations* 6 (Summer–Fall 1997): 110.

15 *FRUS 1951* 6, Pt. 1: 33–71, 423; Clymer, 105; *Pattern of Responsibility*, 286.

16 *FRUS 1951* 6, Pt. 1: 425–28, 433–39, 447–52, 455–59, 462–66, 492, 499–504, 506–21; Buzzanco, 209; Lloyd C. Gardner, *Approaching Vietnam: From World War II through Dienbienphu, 1941–1954* (New York: W. W. Norton, 1988), 102.

17 *FRUS 1951* 6, Pt. 1: 545, 568–70; Ruane, " 'Containing America,' " 146.

18 Daily Meetings, 27 December 1951; *FRUS 1951* 6, Pt. 1: 571; *FRUS 1952–1954* 13, Pt. 1: 18–19; Wall, *United States and Making of Postwar France*, 45–54, 246, 248.

19 *FRUS 1952–1954* 13, Pt. 1: 15–16, 27–28; McIntyre, 369; Ruane, " 'Containing America,' " 146–47; *Executive Sessions of the Senate Foreign Relations Committee . . . 1952* 4: 151, 153–54, 160; *FRUS 1952–1954* 12, Pt. 1: 22–36; Daily Meetings, 1 and 8 February 1952; William Conrad Gibbons, *The U.S. Government and the Vietnam War: Executive and Legislative Roles and Relationships. Part I: 1945–1960* (Princeton: Princeton University Press, 1986), 107.

20 *FRUS 1952–1954* 13, Pt. 1, 38–39, 54–55, 61; *PAC*, 675; *Selected Executive Session Hearings of the Committee, 1951–1956*, 261; *Executive Sessions of the Senate Foreign Relations Committee . . . 1952* 4: 177–78.

21 *FRUS 1952–1954*, 12, Pt. 1: 55–69.

22 Ibid., 69–75; *FRUS 1952–1954* 13, Pt. 1: 61–62.

23 *FRUS 1952–1954* 12, Pt. 1: 96–97, 112–14; *FRUS 1952–1954* 13, Pt. 1: 203–8; *Memoranda of Conversations*, 2 June 1952, Luncheon, and 9 June 1952, Report on India.

24 *FRUS 1952–1954* 12, Pt. 1: 125–34; *FRUS 1952–1954* 13, Pt. 1: 208.

25 Hopkins, 240; *FRUS 1952–1954* 6, Pt. 2: 1547; *PAC*, 658–61, 676, 763; Leffler, *Preponderance of Power*, 473–74; Duiker, 127; *FRUS 1952–1954* 13, Pt. 1: 210–13.

26 *FRUS 1952–1954* 12, Pt. 1: 143–56; *FRUS 1952–1954* 2, Pt. 1: 137, 146.

27 Leffler, *Preponderance of Power*, 474; Wall, *United States and Making of Postwar France*, 231; Ruane, "Refusing to Pay the Price," 78; *FRUS 1952–1954* 13, Pt. 1: 278, 301.

28 Robert D. Schulzinger, *A Time for War: The United States and Vietnam, 1941–1975* (New York: Oxford University Press, 1997), 56; Truman, *Years of Trial and Hope*, 521.

29 *PAC*, 677; *FRUS 1952–1954* 13, Pt. 1: 319–21, 323–25, 331n.

30 *PAC*, 673, 678; Duiker, 128.

31 The matter is complex, but Japanese prosperity turned out not to rely on Indochinese market ties but on massive exports to the United States, which took their first postwar leap because of Korean War purchases. Later, Japan profited heavily in sales to the United States in Vietnam and the Vietnamese in the 1960s. Thanks to Walter LaFeber for this latter point.

32 *FRUS 1950* 7: 1405; ACTION IN THE NSC, December 14, 14 December 1950, Acheson Papers, Box 65, TL; Memorandum for the President, 15 December 1950, Truman Papers (PSF), Box 220, NSC Meetings . . . Discussions (1950) Folder, TL; *Memoranda of Conversations*, 5 February 1951, Talk with a Correspondent; *Memorandum of Conversation*, February 6, 1951, Acheson Papers, Box 68, Press Conferences–1951 Folder, TL; Memorandum for the President, 3 May 1951, Truman Papers (PSF), Box 220, NSC Meetings . . . Discussions (1951) Folder, TL; *New York Times*, 5–6 October and 8–10 October 1951.

33 The name given to the Japanese puppet state of Manchuria in the 1930s.

34 *FRUS 1952–1954* 7, Pt. 2: 1671–72; Accinelli, 72–73; Warren I. Cohen, *Dean Rusk*, 63–64; Callum MacDonald, *Korea*, 107; Lee, 164; T. J. Schoenbaum, 224; Daily Meetings, 21 May 1951; Press Conference, 5–23–51, Acheson Papers, Box 68, Press Conferences – 1951 Folder, TL; *New York Times*, 24 May 1951; *Memoranda of the Secretary of State* 51:235 (4/18/51 memo to Barrett); Rusk, 173.

35 Foot, *Practice of Power*, 53; Mayers, *Cracking the Monolith*, 101; *New York Times*, 14 November 1951; *FRUS 1951* 6, Pt. 2: 1864; Leonard A. Kusnitz, *Public Opinion and Foreign Policy: America's China Policy, 1949–1979* (Westport, CT: Greenwood Press, 1984), 49; Mark A. Ryan, *Chinese Attitudes toward Nuclear Weapons: China and the United States during the Korean War* (Armonk, New York: M. E. Sharpe, 1989), 93. On trade restrictions, see chapters 2–5 of Shu Guang Zhang, *Economic Cold War: America's Embargo against China and the Sino-Soviet Alliance, 1949–1963* (Washington: Woodrow Wilson Center Press, 2001).

36 *FRUS 1952–1954* 14, Pt. 1: 45, 79–84.

37 Matthews, 402.

Chapter 29

1 Sec Acheson's–Denver 8–2–52, Acheson Papers, Box 69, Press Conf. 1949–1953, Jan. 1952–Jan. 1953 Folder, TL.

2 R. J. O'Neill, "The Korean War and the Origins of ANZUS," in Carl Bridge, ed., *Munich to Vietnam: Australia's Relations with Britain and the United States since the 1930s* (Carlton: Melbourne University Press, 1991), 104–6, 108–9; National Archives of Australia, 1950 Cabinet Notebooks, www.naa.gov.au/The_Collection/Cabinet/1950_Cabinet_Notebooks/1950_Note books/A11099_1-1_1950.doc (viewed 9/20/04); *FRUS 1950* 6: 148–52, 200–201, 212–17, 222–25; Percy Claude Spender, *Exercises in Diplomacy: The ANZUS Treaty and the Colombo Plan* (New York: New York University Press, 1970), 44.

3 Magnus Persson, *Great Britain, the United States, and the Security of the Middle East: The Formation of the Baghdad Pact* (Lund: Lund University Press, 1998), 85–86; *FRUS 1952–1954* 12, Pt. 1: 160; Anne Orde, *The Eclipse of Great Britain: The United States and British Imperial Decline, 1895–1956* (New York: St. Martin's Press, 1996), 184; LaFeber, *America, Russia, and the Cold War*, 120; *FRUS 1951* 6, Pt. 1: 150, 154, 156–58, 183–87, 192–202, 207, 220–22; *FRUS 1950* 6: 225–28; O'Neill, 110–12; McIntyre, 336.

4 *FRUS 1951* 6, Pt. 1: 222–23, 232–33, 250–51; *PAC*, 541; Geir Lundestad, " 'Empire by Invitation' in the American Century," *Diplomatic History* 23 (Spring 1999): 207; J. G. Starke, *The ANZUS Treaty Alliance* (Melbourne: Melbourne University Press, 1965), 73.

5 *PAC*, 637, 662; *FRUS 1952–1954* 12, Pt. 1: 75–77, 86–87, 117–19, 142, 158, 160.

6 *PAC*, 686–89; *FRUS 1952–1954* 12, Pt. 1: 170–83, 186–202, 213–14, 229.

7 Department of State, For the Press, January 12, 1950, No. 34, James Webb Papers, Box 20, TL.

8 Andrew J. Rotter, *Comrades at Odds: The United States and India, 1947–1964* (Ithaca: Cornell University Press, 2000), 78, 98; South Asia Regional Conference of United States Diplomatic and Consular Officers, Nuwara Eliya, Ceylon, February 26–March 3, 1951, George McGhee Papers, Box 2, Dept. of State, South Asia . . . 1951, Feb . . . Folder, TL.

9 Robert J. McMahon, "United States Cold War Strategy in South Asia: Making a Military Commitment to Pakistan, 1947–1954," *Journal of American History* 75 (December 1988): 821–22; Inder Singh, 116; Kux, *United States and Pakistan*, 49.

10 *FRUS 1950* 5: 1492, 1498n; Kux, *United States and Pakistan*, 34–37; Andrew J. Rotter, "Christians, Muslims, and Hindus: Religion and U.S.-South Asian Relations, 1947–1954," *Diplomatic History* 24 (Fall 2000): 607; McMahon, *Cold War on the Periphery*, 74–77.

11 Sultana Afroz, "American Economic Aid to Pakistan, 1947–1960: A Reassessment," *Journal of South Asian and Middle Eastern Studies* 15 (Summer 1992): 29; Chary, 95; *FRUS 1951* 6, Pt. 2: 2203–5; Inder Singh, 118; *FRUS 1952–1954* 11, Pt. 2: 1818; Rotter, *Comrades at Odds*, 61.

12 Mahmudul Huque, *The Role of the United States in the India-Pakistan Conflict, 1947–1971: Quest for Stability* (Dhaka: Academic Publishers, 1992), 28; A. M. M. Saifuddin Khaled, "The United States and the Failed Attempts at U.N. Mediation in Kashmir, 1949–1953," *Journal of the Pakistan Historical Society* 47 (July–September 1999): 11, 15–17; Rotter, *Comrades at Odds*, 140–44; Dennis Kux, *The United States and Pakistan, 1947–2000* (Washington: Woodrow Wilson Center Press, 2001), 30–31; *FRUS 1951* 6, Pt. 2: 2224–25.

13 Huque, 44; Khaled, 17–18.

14 A. Tom Grunfeld, *The Making of Modern Tibet*, rev. ed. (Armonk, NY: M. E. Sharpe, 1996), 94, 96, 99; Warren W. Smith, Jr., *Tibetan Nation: A History of Tibetan Nationalism and Sino-Tibetan Relations* (Boulder: Westview Press, 1996), 272, 276; S. Mahmud Ali, *Cold War in the High Himalayas: The USA, China and South Asia in the 1950s* (New York: St. Martin's Press, 1999), 16.

15 Warren Smith, 277, 282, 284, 284n, 285–86; Ali, 20, 29–30; Grunfeld, 94, 97.

16 Warren Smith, 278–79n; 292–308, 315, 319; Ali, 31, 33, 41; *FRUS 1951* 7, Pt. 2: 1691, 1693–96, 1712; Grunfeld, 97–98, 100, 104; Inder Singh, 62, 255. For more on the CIA, see James Conboy and James Morrison, *The CIA's Secret War in Tibet* (Lawrence: University Press of Kansas, 2002); Thomas Laird, *Into Tibet: The CIA's First Atomic Spy and His Secret Expedition to Lhasa* (New York: Grove Press, 2002); John Kenneth Knaus, *Orphans of the Cold War: America and the Tibetan Struggle for Survival* (New York: PublicAffairs, 1999); and idem, "Official Policies and Covert Programs: The U.S. State Department, the CIA, and the Tibetan Resistance," *Journal of Cold War Studies* 5 (Summer 2003): 54–79.

17 Chary, 85; *FRUS 1950* 5: 1472.

18 *FRUS 1951* 6, Pt. 2: 2091; *FRUS 1952–1954* 3: 46; McNay, 26; Dean Acheson, "Foreword" to Franco Nogueira, *The Third World* (London: Johnson, 1967), 14.

19 *FRUS 1950* 5: 1464–66; *Executive Sessions of the Senate Foreign Relations Committee . . . 1951* 3, Pt. 1: 365; Robert J. McMahon, "Toward a Post-colonial Order: Truman Administration Policies toward South and Southeast Asia," in Lacey, 358; Brands, *Specter of Neutralism*, 66; *FRUS 1952–1954* 11, Pt. 2: 1649–50; www.cancellieri.org/aphorisms_english.htm (viewed 7/18/05).

20 John Kenneth Galbraith, *Name-Dropping: From F.D.R. On* (Boston: Houghton Mifflin, 1999), 132, 164; Rotter, *Comrades at Odds*, 20; idem, "Gender Relations, Foreign Relations: The United States and South Asia, 1947–1964," *Journal of American History* 81 (September 1994): 520; Chester Bowles, *Ambassador's Report* (New York: Harper & Row, 1954), 5; Howard B. Schaffer, *Chester Bowles: New Dealer in the Cold War* (Cambridge: Harvard University Press, 1993), 37.

21 Steve Neal, ed., *Eleanor and Harry: The Correspondence of Eleanor Roosevelt and Harry S. Truman* (New York: Scribner, 2002), 211–12; Rotter, *Comrades at Odds*, 278–80; *Among Friends*, 143; Wilkins Oral History Interview, TL, 77–78.

22 *FRUS 1950* 5: 1461–63; McMahon, *Cold War on the Periphery*, 82–83; Surendra K. Gupta, *Stalin's Policy towards India, 1946–1953* (New Delhi: New Asian Publishers, 1988), 221.

23 Robert J. McMahon, "Food as a Diplomatic Weapon: The India Wheat Loan of 1951," *Pacific Historical Review* 56 (August 1987): 354–57; *Memoranda of Conversations*, 29 December 1950, Factors Entering into Consideration of Indian Request for Food Grain; Inder Singh, 93.

24 McMahon, "Food as a Diplomatic Weapon," 359–64; Andrew J. Rotter, "Feeding Beggars: Class, Caste, and Status in Indo-US Relations, 1947–1964," in Christian G. Appy, *Cold War Constructions: The Political Culture of United States Imperialism, 1945–1966* (Amherst: University of Massachusetts Press, 2000), 69–70; Daily Meetings, 30 January and 5 February 1951; *FRUS 1951* 6, Pt. 2: 2095–2113.

25 *FRUS 1951* 6, Pt. 2: 1664–88, 2113; Brands, *Specter of Neutralism*, 66; McMahon, "Food as a Diplomatic Weapon," 349–50, 365; South Asia Regional Conference of United States Diplomatic and Consular Officers, Nuwara Eliya, Ceylon, February 26–March 3, 1951, George McGhee Papers, Box 2, Dept. of State, South Asia . . . 1951, Feb . . . Folder, TL.

26 McMahon, "Food as a Diplomatic Weapon," 366–72; *FRUS 1951* 6, Pt. 2: 2118, 2133, 2139, 2142–50; *Executive Sessions of the Senate Foreign Relations Committee . . . 1951* 3, Pt. 1: 361, 365; Rotter, *Comrades at Odds*, 78, 98, 100.

27 McMahon, "Food as a Diplomatic Weapon," 372–74; Knaus, 72; *FRUS 1951* 6, Pt. 2: 2153, 2158, 2161–64, 2168; Rotter, *Comrades at Odds*, 271, 274.

28 *Memoranda of Conversations*, 21 December 1951, US-Indian Relations; Acheson to Harriman, 8 February 1952, Truman Papers (PSF), Box 180, India-China-Bowles Folder, TL.

29 New Delhi to Secretary of State, 5 July 1952, Truman Papers (PSF), Box 180, India Folder, TL; Stinebower Oral History Interview, TL, 82–83; *FRUS 1952–1954* 11, Pt. 2: 1646–52, 1654–57; *Memoranda of Conversations*, 9 June 1952, Report on India.

30 *FRUS 1952–1954* 11, Pt. 2: 1668–77, 1682–84; McMahon, "United States Cold War Strategy," 829; *FRUS 1952–1954* 3: 633.

Chapter 30

1 Dudziak, 544–46, 555; Plummer, 198.

2 Gendzier, *Notes from the Minefield*, 25; Byroade Oral History, TL, 77; Lawson, "The Truman Administration and the Palestinians," *Arab Studies Quarterly*, 54; McNay, 49; Warren I. Cohen, *Dean Rusk*, 34.

3 Princeton Seminars, 15 May 1954.

4 Ibid., 15 and 16 May 1954; SR62–199, Presentation of Bust of Dean Acheson at Truman Library, 31 March 1962, Recording, TL.

5 *FRUS 1950* 5: 215–27; *FRUS 1951* 5: 151–52, 258, 999; Gendzier, *Notes from the Minefield*, 38; Stueck, *Korean War*, 81.

6 Peter L. Hahn, "Discord or partnership? British and American policy toward Egypt, 1942–56," in Michael J. Cohen and Martin Kolinsky, eds., *Demise of the British Empire in the Middle East: Britain's Responses to Nationalist Movements 1943–55* (Portland, OR: Frank Cass, 1998), 168; *PAC*, 396; Peter L. Hahn, *The United States, Great Britain, and Egypt, 1945–1956: Strategy and Diplomacy in the Early Cold War* (Chapel Hill: University of North Carolina Press, 1991), 101; Scott Lucas and Ray Takeyh, "Alliance and Balance: The Anglo-American Relationship and Egyptian Nationalism, 1950–57," *Diplomacy & Statecraft* 7 (November 1996): 635.

7 Herbert Druks, *The Uncertain Friendship: The U.S. and Israel from Roosevelt to Kennedy* (Westport, CT: Greenwood Press, 2001), 145–47; Hahn, "View from Jerusalem," 212, 234.

8 *FRUS 1950* 5: 1003–5, 1034–35; Memorandum for the President, 13 October 1950, Truman Papers (PSF), Box 220, NSC Meetings . . . Discussions (1950) Folder, TL.

9 Yaacov Bar-Siman-Tov, "The United States and Israel since 1948: A 'Special Relationship'?" *Diplomatic History*, 22 (Spring 1998): 234; *Memoranda of Conversations*, 5 April 1951, Grant-aid to Israel; Hahn, "View from Jerusalem," 519; *FRUS 1951* 5: 971; Abba Eban, *Personal Witness: Israel Through My Eyes* (New York: G. P. Putnam's Sons, 1992), 223; idem, *Abba Eban: An Autobiography* (New York: Random House, 1977), 159.

10 Stinebower Oral History Interview, TL, 83–84.

11 Eban, *Personal Witness*, 16; Hahn, *Caught in the Middle East*, 112, 117–18; Neff, 135–36; *FRUS 1950* 5: 667, 702, 817, 839, 895–99, 947, 1211–12.

12 *Memoranda of Conversations*, 22 March 1951; *FRUS 1951* 5: 636, 667–70, 972.

13 Hahn, *Caught in the Middle East*, 125, 128; Michael J. Cohen, *Fighting World War Three*, 225; *FRUS 1951* 5: 141, 186–87, 878; *Memoranda of Conversations*, 30 January 1951, Visit of the Israel Ambassador; *Memoranda of Conversations*, 19 November 1951, General Matters of Interest to US and Israel; Eban, *Personal Witness*, 222; *FRUS 1952–1954* 9, Pt. 1: 959, 999.

14 *Selected Executive Session Hearings of the Committee, 1951–1956*, 182; Memorandum for the President, 24 April 1952, Truman Papers (PSF), Box 220, NSC Meetings . . . Discussions (1952–53) Folder, TL; *FRUS 1952–1954* 9, Pt. 1, 225; *PAC*, 259.

15 Martin Thomas, "Defending a Lost Cause? France and the United States Vision of Imperial Rule in French North Africa, 1945–1956," *Diplomatic History* 26 (Spring 2002): 218, 222; Yahia Zoubir, "The United States, the Soviet Union and the Decolonization of the Maghreb, 1945–62," *Middle Eastern Studies* 31 (January 1995): 59; Wall, *United States and Making of Postwar France*, 234; Martin Thomas, "France Accused: French North Africa before the United Nations, 1952–1962," *Contemporary European History* 10 (2001): 95.

16 *PAC*, 638, 641.

17 North African Regional Conference of U.S. Diplomatic and Consular Officers, Tangier, Morocco, October 2–7, 1950, George McGhee Papers, Box 1, Department of State, North African . . . Folder 1, TL; *FRUS 1952–1954* 11, Pt. 1: 563; *FRUS 1950* 5: 1569–80.

18 *FRUS 1949* 4: 529, 532–45; *FRUS 1951* 5: 1346; *FRUS 1952–1954* 11, Pt. 1: 550–51; *PAC*, 561.

19 *FRUS 1950* 5: 1738, 1746; *FRUS 1951* 5: 1368–69, 1387–89; Martin Thomas, "Defending a Lost Cause," 228; idem, *French North African Crisis*, 38.

20 *Memoranda of Conversations*, 9 October 1951, Moroccan Situation; *FRUS 1951* 2: 145–46; *Memoranda of Conversations*, 4 November 1951, Con with British For Min; *Memoranda of Conversations*, 6 November 1951, Tripartite Ministerial Meeting; Princeton Seminars, 14 March 1954; *FRUS 1952–1954* 3: 32–33; *Executive Sessions of the Senate Foreign Relations Committee . . . 1952* 4: 156; *FRUS 1952–1954* 11, Pt. 1: 128; *New York Times*, 23 October 1952.

21 *PAC*, 638; *FRUS 1950* 5: 1774, 1787, 1792; *FRUS 1951* 5: 1405–10, 1414–16, 1419–24. Washington rebuffed French protests of Bourguiba's talks in Washington and his broadcast of a speech on the Voice of America.

22 Wall, *United States and Making of Postwar France*, 246; Martin Thomas, "Defending a Lost Cause," 229, 232; idem, "France Accused," 98; *FRUS 1952–1954* 11, Pt. 1: 665–68, 685–86, 691; *PAC*, 638.

23 Secretary, Drummond, Kuh, 3-27-52, Acheson Papers, Box 69, Press Conf. 1949–1953, Jan. 1952–Jan. 1953 Folder, TL; *PAC*, 638–69; *FRUS 1952–1954* 11, Pt. 1: 700, 703, 709, 717–20, 722, 724–26, 733; Daily Meetings, 9 April 1952; Acheson, Memorandum for the President, Your Conversation with Mrs. Roosevelt on Tunisia, April 9, 1952, Truman P (PSF), Box 188, Folder T, TL.

24 Martin Thomas, *French North African Crisis*, 47 (see 40 for the impact of French internal politics); *FRUS 1952–1954* 11, Pt. 1: 736–37, 742–43, 745, 751–54, 758–63.

25 Paris to Sec. of State, 27 May 1952, Truman Papers (PSF), Box 159, Subj. File–Cabinet, State, Secy, Misc Conference Folder, TL; *FRUS 1952–1954* 11, Pt. 1: 766–71, 784, 787, 797–98, 805–6; Theodore H. White, 346; *Memoranda of Conversations*, 2 June 1952, Luncheon; *Executive Sessions of the Senate Foreign Relations Committee . . . 1952* 4: 492, 494.

26 *FRUS 1952–1954* 11, Pt. 1: 801–2, 807, 813–14, 818, 946.

27 *Memoranda of Conversations*, 21 October 1952, Secretary A's Conversations with Foreign Ministers of the NEA Area; Stueck, *Korean War*, 291; *FRUS 1952–1954* 11, Pt. 1: 826–33.

28 Message for the President from the Secretary of State, October 25, 1952, Truman Papers (PSF), Box 149, Subj. File–Agencies, Un. Nations–Misc. Folder, TL.

29 Wall, *United States and Making of Postwar France*, 231; *FRUS 1952–1954* 11, Pt. 1: 837–48.

30 Abell, 228–29; *FRUS 1952–1954* 11, Pt. 1: 848–49, 854n; *FRUS 1952–1954* 9, Pt. 1: 338; Martin Thomas, *French North African Crisis*, 52.

31 Thomas J. Noer, *Cold War and Black Liberation: The United States and White Rule in Africa, 1948–1968* (Columbia: University of Missouri Press, 1985), 65; *PAC*, 379; *FRUS 1950* 5: 1525.

32 Jonathan E. Helmreich, *United States Relations with Belgium and the Congo, 1940–1960* (Newark: University of Delaware Press, 1998), 154; *FRUS 1952–1954* 11, Pt. 1: 233; www.state.gov/r/pa/ho/faq/ (viewed 3/11/05); Peter Duignan and L. H. Gann, *The United States and Africa: A History* (New York: Cambridge University Press, 1984), 315; David N. Gibbs, "Political Parties and International Relations: The United States and Decolonization of Sub-Saharan Africa," *International History Review* 17 (May 1995): 313; Statement of the Department's Position on Arguments Advanced by Mr. Grew, Truman papers (PSF), Box 182, Folder L, TL. For the difficulties of Afro-American diplomats to find assignments out of the "Liberia-Azores-Canary Islands-Madagascar circuit," see Krenn, *Black Diplomacy*, 50–55. State department officials claimed the greatest obstacle to making black appointments elsewhere was the racism of host countries, especially in the Middle East and Latin America. Ibid., 52.

33 James H. Meriwether, *Proudly We Can Be Africans: Black Americans and Africa, 1935–1961* (Chapel Hill: University of North Carolina Press, 2002), 72.

34 Clipping, George C. McGhee, "American Aims in Africa," *The Forum*, June 3, 1950, George McGhee Papers, Box 2, Department of State, Correspondence, 1950, June–December Folder, TL; *FRUS 1950* 5: 316, 1540–45, 1547–49; Thomas J. Noer, "Truman, Eisenhower, and South Africa: The 'Middle Road' and Apartheid," *Journal of Ethnic Studies* 11 (Spring 1983): 82–83; Helmreich, 155; *FRUS 1951* 5: 1269–70.

35 Stueck, *Korean War*, 74; www.geocities.com/lmak27455/Ethiopian_Korean_War_Veterans/(viewed 7/20/05); www.korean-war.com/ethiopia. html (viewed 7/19/05); Meriwether, 130; *FRUS 1951* 5: 1223–24.

36 Hewlett and Duncan, 426; Helmreich, 128, 151, 153, 155–57.

37 *FRUS 1951* 2: 853; Noer, "Truman, Eisenhower, and South Africa," 80; McGhee, *Envoy to the Middle World*, 131.

38 Hewlett and Duncan, 426; *Memoranda of Conversations*, 24 July 1950, Active Assistance for Korea; Thomas Borstelmann, *Apartheid's Reluctant Uncle: The United States and Southern Africa in the Early Cold War* (New York: Oxford University Press, 1993), 143, 164; Noer, *Cold War and Black Liberation*, 28–29; *FRUS 1950* 2: 563–64, 575; *FRUS 1951* 5: 1427.

39 *FRUS 1951* 5: 1433–42, 1448–49; Borstelmann, *Apartheid's Reluctant Uncle*, 185, 187; Princeton Seminars, 14 March 1954.

40 *FRUS 1952–1954* 11, Pt. 1: 920; Meriwether, 117; *FRUS 1952–1954* 3: 1146–47; Noer, "Truman, Eisenhower, and South Africa," 86.

41 *FRUS 1952–1954* 11, Pt. 1: 806, 924–27, 936, 947–49, 963, 975–77; *Memoranda of the Secretary of State* M-591, 14 October 1952; Noer, "Truman, Eisenhower, and South Africa," 85; Thomas Borstelmann, *The Cold War and the Color Line: American Race Relations in the Global Arena* (Cambridge: Harvard University Press, 2001), 73. I am indebted to Borstelmann for the totalitarianism reference.

42 Princeton Seminars, 15 May 1954.

43 The International Scene, 27 August 1951; Acheson, "Fifty Years After," 9; *PAC*, 112; McLellan, *State Department Years*, 51.

44 *New York Times*, 24 January 1949; Beichman, xviii, 78, 89; *PAC*, 224; Gary B. Ostrower, *The United Nations and the United States* (New York: Twayne, 1998), 46.

45 Andrew W. Cordier and Wilder Foote, eds., *Public Papers of the Secretaries-General of the United Nations. Volume 1: Trygve Lie, 1946–1953* (New York: Columbia University Press, 1969), 18–19; *PAC*, 378; *FRUS 1950* 2: 372–73, 378–84, 389–90; *Memoranda of Conversations*, 29 May 1950, Conversation between the President and The Hon Trygve Lie; Lie, 271, 314–16; *New York Times*, 8 June 1950.

46 *FRUS 1950* 2: 146–50, 156, 158–60, 162, 165–70, 395–96; *Memoranda of Conversations*, 24 October 1950, Secretary-General; Paul Gordon Lauren, "The Diplomats and Diplomacy of the United Nations," in Craig and Loewenheim, 466–67.

47 Acheson to Gerard Swope, 11 February 1952, Acheson Papers, Box 43, Secretary of State, 1949–53, Alph.-Sta –Sz Folder, TL; *FRUS 1952–1954* 6, Pt. 2: 2060–61; Douglas Brinkley and G. E. Thomas, "Dean Acheson's Opposition to African Liberation," *Transafrica Forum* 5 (Summer 1988): 70; Princeton Seminars, 15 May 1954; Acheson, *Grapes from Thorns*, 20; Linda M. Fasulo, *Representing America: Experiences of U.S. Diplomats at the UN* (New York: Praeger, 1984), 45; Beichman, 177–78; Ball, *Past Has Another Pattern*, 437; Princeton Seminars, p. 4, Acheson Papers, TL; Acheson to Charles Burton Marshall, 30 October 1967, Acheson Papers, Box 22, Folder 279, YUL. The reference is to St. Elizabeth's Hospital for the Insane in Washington, D.C. See Chapter 2 for Pasvolsky.

48 *New York Times*, 13 October 1971; *Pattern of Responsibility*, 296; SR62–199, Presentation of bust of Dean Acheson at Truman Library, 31 March 1962, Recording, TL.

Chapter 31

1 For the rules of Pick-Up Sticks, see www.woodentoys-uk.co.uk/wooden-games6-mikado-rules.html (viewed 7/21/05).

2 See McNay, 3 (and passim) for a very different interpretation of the ultimate course of Acheson's policy in Egypt and Iran, emphasizing his addiction to an anglophilic, nineteenth-century "imperial-style" rule.

3 Gendzier, *Notes from the Minefield*, 31, 43, 51, 68, 107; Little, "Pipeline Politics," 280; Paul J. Hare, *Diplomatic Chronicles of the Middle East: A Biography of Ambassador Raymond A. Hare* (Lanham, MD: University Press of America, 1993), 88, 90–95; *FRUS 1950* 5: 61–62, 83; *FRUS 1951* 5: 22, 114, 258, 1050–51, 1072; *FRUS 1952–1952* 9, Pt. 2: 2410; Inder Singh, 115; Princeton Seminars, 15 May 1954. Aramco was a condominium of the Standard Oil Companies of California and New Jersey, Socony-Vacuum, and Texas Oil Company. Its deal with Saudi Arabia included the "golden gimmick," by which it paid half its net operating income to Riyadh as an income tax, declared fully tax deductible for U.S. tax purposes. Burton I. Kaufman, "Mideast Multinational Oil, U.S. Foreign Policy, and Antitrust: The 1950s," *Journal of American History* 63 (March 1977): 945.

4 Poole, 172.

5 Irene L. Gendzier, "The United States, the USSR and the Arab World in NSC Reports of the 1950s," *Arab-American Affairs* 28 (Spring 1989): 22–29; *Memoranda of the Secretary of State* M-367, 30 March 1951.

6 Hahn, *Caught in the Middle East*, 76; idem, "National Security Concerns in U.S. Policy toward Egypt, 1949–1956," in David W. Lesch, ed., *The Middle East and the United States: A Historical and Political Reassessment* (Boulder: Westview Press, 1996), 93.

7 Matthew F. Holland, *America and Egypt: From Roosevelt to Eisenhower* (Westport, CT: Praeger, 1996), viii; Ayesha Jalal, "Towards the Baghdad Pact: South Asia and Middle East Defence in the Cold War, 1947–1955," *International History Review* 11 (August 1989): 418.

8 *PAC*, 502; *FRUS 1952–1954* 10 (*Iran 1951–1954*): 3.

9 Samii, 125–26; Orde, 188; Mark J. Gasiorowski, *U.S. Foreign Policy and the Shah: Building a Client State in Iran* (Ithaca: Cornell University Press, 1991), 59; *PAC*, 499–501; Howard M. Sachar, *Europe Leaves the Middle East, 1936–1954* (New York: Alfred A. Knopf, 1972), 388–89. "Mosadeq" is how the Iranian leader himself spelled his name in writing French or English, though in doing so he violated most of the important principles of transliteration. E-mail from James Goode, 13 March 2005. Other common transliterations include Mossadegh, Mossadeq, Musaddiq, Mosaddeq, and Mussadiq.

10 Ritchie Ovendale, *Britain, the United States, and the Transfer of Power in the Middle East, 1945–1962* (London: Leicester University Press, 1996), 33; *PAC*, 499–501, 506; letter of Linda Wills Qaimmaqami to author, 26 July 1991.

11 *FRUS 1950* 5: 470–71, 483, 505, 531; Qaimmaqami, "Catalyst of Nationalization," 16; *PAC*, 502; Richard W. Cottam, *Iran and the United States: A Cold War Case Study* (Pittsburgh: University of Pittsburgh Press, 1988), 89; Mary Ann Heiss, *Empire and Nationhood: The United States, Great Britain, and Iranian Oil, 1950–1954* (New York: Columbia University Press, 1997), 28; Princeton Seminars, 15 May 1954.

12 Stephen Kinzer, *All the Shah's Men: An American Coup and the Roots of Middle East Terror* (Hoboken, NJ: John Wiley, 2003), 73; *FRUS 1950* 5: 569, 571, 576–77; *PAC*, 503; Princeton Seminars, 15 May 1954; Heiss, 32; Stueck, *Korean War*, 82; Mark J. Gasiorowski, "U.S. Foreign Policy toward Iran during the Mussadiq Era," in Lesch, 54; idem, *U.S. Foreign Policy*, 48.

13 *FRUS 1950* 5: 581–85, 593–600; Princeton Seminars, 15 May 1954; McGhee, *Envoy to the Middle World*, 100–102; Kinzer, 87; Daniel Yergin, *The Prize: The Epic Quest for Oil, Money, and Power* (New York: Simon & Schuster, 1991), 453; Holland, 12; Steve Marsh, *Anglo-American Relations and Cold War Oil: Crisis in Iran* (New York: Palgrave Macmillan, 2003), 4.

14 Heiss, 46; Gavin, 66; Qaimmaqami, "Catalyst of Nationalization," 22–23; *FRUS 1950* 5: 614–15; McNay, 149–51; Henry F. Grady, "What Went Wrong in Iran?" *Saturday Evening Post*, 5 January 1952, 57; George C. McGhee, *Envoy to the Middle World*, 54.

15 *FRUS 1950* 5: 616–18; Linda Wills Qaimmaqami, "Max Thornburg and the Failure of Private Sector Developmentalism in Iran, 1947–1951" (unpublished paper, 1991), 24; Leffler, *Preponderance of Power*, 479; Mark J. Gasiorowski, "The 1953 Coup D'Etat in Iran," *International Journal of Middle East Studies* 19 (August 1987): 267–68; Zachary Karabell, *Architects of Intervention: The United States, the Third World, and the Cold War, 1946–1962* (Baton Rouge: Louisiana State University Press, 1999), 55; Heiss, 12–13; Princeton Seminars, 15 May 1954.

16 Holland, 2–3.

17 *FRUS 1950* 5: 293–94; Holland, 6; Notes on the President's Meeting with Under Secretary of State James Webb–March 26, 1950–Little White House, Truman Papers (PSF), Box 159, Subj. File–Cabinet, State, Secretary–Misc Folder, TL; Edward Hoagland, *African Calliope: A Journey to the Sudan* (New York: Random House, 1979), 71; 60.

18 Philip F. Dur, *Jefferson Caffery of Louisiana: Ambassador of Revolutions: An Outline of His Career* (Lafayette: University of Southwestern Louisiana Libraries, 1982), 61; *FRUS 1950* 5: 236, 305, 310–11; Michael J. Cohen, "The Strategic Role of the Middle East after the War," in Michael J. Cohen and Kolinsky, 25. Mohammed Salaheddin was sometimes rendered Salah El Din in U.S. documents.

19 *FRUS 1950* 5: 5–10, 322–24, 329; Michael J. Cohen, *Fighting World War Three*, 248–49.

20 National Security Council Progress Report by the Department of State on the Implementation of United States Policy toward Arms Shipments to the Near East (NSC 65/3), January 24, 1951, Truman Papers (PSF), Box 211, NSC Meeting No. 82 Folder, TL; *PAC*, 562; *FRUS 1951* 5: 22, 27–42; McGhee, *Envoy to the Middle World*, 23; Hahn, *United States, Great Britain, and Egypt*, 110–11; Michael J. Cohen, *Fighting World War Three*, 249–53, 256.

21 *FRUS 1951* 5: 353–55; Inder Singh, 117–18; Hahn, "Discord or Partnership," 170; idem, "Containment and Egyptian Nationalism: The Unsuccessful Effort to Establish the Middle East Command, 1950–53," *Diplomatic History* 11 (Winter 1987): 28.

22 McNay, 173; James Cable, *Intervention at Abadan: Plan Buccaneer* (New York: St. Martin's Press, 1991), 47; *FRUS 1951* 5: 352–61, 365, 679.

23 *FRUS 1951* 5: 71; Gasiorowski, *U.S. Foreign Policy*, 49–50; Heiss, 55; Qaimmaqami, "Catalyst of Nationalization," 18–20.

24 *FRUS 1952–1954* 10 (*Iran 1951–1954*): 25, 29; *FRUS 1951* 5: 296–97; Wm. Roger Louis, *The British Empire in the Middle East 1945–1951: Arab Nationalism, the United States, and Postwar Imperialism* (Oxford, UK: Clarendon Press, 1984), 656.

25 Danchev, *Franks*, 123; George C. McGhee, *On the Frontline in the Cold War: An Ambassador Reports* (Westport, CT: Praeger, 1997), 108; Daily Meetings, 9 and 16 April 1951; Heiss, 60, 69; *FRUS 1952–1954* 10 (*Iran 1951–1954*): 36, 43–44; Karabell, 56, 58; Gavin, 71.

26 *PAC*, 504, 506.

27 Heiss, 70; Gasiorowski, "U.S. Foreign Policy toward Iran," 55–56.

28 Louis Galambos, ed., *The Papers of Dwight David Eisenhower: NATO and the Campaign of 1952: XII* (Baltimore: Johns Hopkins University Press, 1989), 226n.; *PAC*, 506–7; *FRUS 1952–1954* 10 (*Iran 1951–1954*): 50, 52, 56; James F. Goode, *The United States and Iran: In the Shadow of Musaddiq* (New York: St. Martin's Press, 1997), 30, 34; Princeton Seminars, 15 May 1954; Cable, 49; John Foran, "Discursive Subversions: *Time* Magazine, the CIA Overthrow of Musaddiq, and the Installation of the Shah," in Appy, 167.

29 *FRUS 1951* 5: 366–67, 698; James A. Bill, *The Eagle and the Lion: The Tragedy of American-Iranian Relations* (New Haven: Yale University Press, 1988), 78.

30 Eden, 217.

31 Heiss, 73; *FRUS 1952–1954* 10 (*Iran 1951–1954*): 59–63, 68; Daily Meetings, 21 June 1951.

32 Gavin, 71; Marsh, *Anglo-American Relations*, 84; *FRUS 1952–1954* 10 (*Iran 1951–1954*): 69–79; Goode, *In the Shadow of Musaddiq*, 34–35; Memorandum for the President, 28 June 1951, Truman Papers (PSF), Box 220, NSC Meetings . . . Discussions (1951) Folder, TL; 1955 Acheson Oral History, A.M., 8; Meeting with magazine and book publishers, June 29, 1951, Old State Building, Reston Papers, Box 30, Working Files, UIA, 14–15.

33 Goode, *In the Shadow of Musaddiq*, 35; Princeton Seminars, 15 May 1954; Grady, 58; *FRUS 1952–1954* 10 (*Iran 1951–1954*): 79–81; *PAC*, 506.

34 *PAC*, 507–9; *FRUS 1952–1954* 10 (*Iran 1951–1954*): 84–88, 92–94, 97–98, 101–3, 105–7, 112–15, 123, 127–28, 131–34, 145, 150–55; Heiss, 82, 87, 92; Goode, *In the Shadow of Musaddiq*, 37, 43; Karabell, 59–60; Daily Meetings, 13 August 1951; Gasiorowski, "U.S. Foreign Policy toward Iran," 55; Kinzer, 104; Princeton Seminars, 15 May 1954.

35 *FRUS 1952–1954* 10 (*Iran 1951–1954*): 82–84, 127–28, 131–34, 151–52, 154–55; Cable, ix, 80; Princeton Seminars, 15 May 1954; McGhee, *On the Frontline*, 111; Goode, *In the Shadow of Musaddiq*, 43.

36 *FRUS 1952–1954* 10 (*Iran 1951–1954*): 88, 150, 162n; *Executive Sessions of the Senate Foreign Relations Committee* (. . . 1952) 4: 159.

37 Heiss, 93, 96; McGhee, *On the Frontline*, 112; Leffler, *Preponderance of Power*, 479; Gasiorowski, "The 1953 Coup," 263; Kenneth Harris, 482–83.

38 *FRUS 1952–1954* 10 (*Iran 1951–1954*): 167–70; *FRUS 1951* 4, Pt. 1: 686; *Executive Sessions of the Senate Foreign Relations Committee . . . 1951* 3, Pt. 2: 452, 456–58; Kenneth Harris, 482; Goode, *In the Shadow of Musaddiq*, 52.

39 *FRUS 1952–1954* 10 (*Iran 1951–1954*): 173, 177–78, 181–83, 257; Karabell, 61, Heiss, 97.

40 *FRUS 1952–1954* 10 (*Iran 1951–1954*): 185–89, 191, 205–8, 211n; Marsh, *Anglo-American Relations*, 79; Kenneth Harris, 483; Heiss, 97–99; Cable, 104; Bernard Donoughue and G. W. Jones, *Herbert Morrison: Portrait of a Politician* (London: Weidenfeld and Nicolson, 1973), 505; Karabell, 65.

41 Holland, 15; McNay, 174–75; *FRUS 1951* 5: 372–76, 381; Cable, 23; *Executive Sessions of the Senate Foreign Relations Committee . . . 1951* 3, Pt. 2: 452; *PAC*, 563–65.

42 *PAC*, 563; *FRUS 1951* 5: 389, 397–98; Michael J. Cohen, *Fighting World War III*, 284, 286; McNay, 176–77.

43 Lucas and Takeyh, 637; Holland, 22; Miles Copeland, *The Game of Nations: The Amorality of Power Politics* (London: Weidenfeld and Nicolson, 1969), 48; Michael J. Cohen, *Fighting World War III*, 286–87; *FRUS 1951* 5: 230–31, 398–400, 402–5, 411–12; McNay, 178; *New York Times*, 18 October 1951.

Chapter 32

1 Richard W. Cottam, *Iran and the United States: A Cold War Case Study* (Pittsburgh: University of Pittsburgh Press, 1988), 94; Gasiorowski, *U.S. Foreign Policy*, 61; Heiss, 17–18; McGhee Oral History, TL, 52.

2 *PAC*, 503–4.

3 *FRUS 1952–1954* 10 (*Iran 1951–1954*): 211–18, 224–36; Vernon A. Walters, *Silent Missions* (Garden City: Doubleday, 1978), Chapter 13; McGhee, *On the Frontline*, 113–14; Heiss, 100–102; Goode, *In the Shadow of Musaddiq*, 55–56; Byroade Oral History, TL, 125; *PAC*, 510.

4 *FRUS 1952–1954* 10 (*Iran 1951–1954*): 241–44; Princeton Seminars, 15 May 1954; *PAC*, 504.

5 McGhee, *On the Frontline*, 114; *PAC*, 510; *FRUS 1952–1954* 10 (*Iran 1951–1954*): 244–55.

6 Young, *Winston Churchill's Last Campaign*, 58; *FRUS 1952–1954* 10 (*Iran 1951–1954*): 256–60, 265–72; Edwards, 252; Vladislav Zubok, "Soviet Intelligence and the Cold War: The 'Small' Committee of Information, 1952–53," *Diplomatic History* 19 (Summer 1995): 466–67; Selwyn Lloyd, *Suez 1956: A Personal Account* (New York: Mayflower Books, 1978), 7; Destler, 227; Nitze Oral History, TL, 215, 328–29.

7 *FRUS 1952–1954* 10 (*Iran 1951–1954*): 281, 283; Paris to Secretary of State, 10 November 1951, Truman Papers (PSF), Box 180, Iran Folder, TL; Paris to Secretary of State, 14 November 1951, Truman Papers (PSF), Box 180, Iran Folder, TL; *PAC*, 511.

8 Michael J. Cohen, *Fighting World War Three*, 288; idem, "The Strategic Role of the Middle East," 33; J. Wesley Adams, Oral History Interview, 18 December 1972 (Independence, MO: The Harry S. Truman Library, January 1976), 54–56; *FRUS 1951* 5: 413.

9 *FRUS 1951* 5: 424–49, 435–37; Paris to Secretary of State (Acheson to Truman), 20 November 1951, Truman Papers (PSF), Box 165, Subj. File–Conferences Sec. State–Rome, Italy, etc., Folder, TL.

10 *FRUS 1951* 5: 438–39; Hahn, *United States, Great Britain, and Egypt*, 136–38; Daily Meetings, 14 December 1951; Hahn, "National Security Concerns," 95; Kux, *United States and Pakistan*, 47.

11 *Memoranda of the Secretary of State* M-54, 6 January 1952; *PAC*, 565, 600; Heiss, 114; *FRUS 1952–1954* 9, Pt. 1: 171–76; *FRUS 1952–1952* 9, Pt. 2: 1746–49; Eden, 89; *PAC*, 565; Daily Meetings, 22 January 1952.

12 *PAC*, 565–66; Michael J. Cohen, *Fighting World War Three*, 290–91; Adams Oral History, TL, 58–59; *FRUS 1952–1954* 9, Pt. 2: 1755, 1757–59; Hopkins, 233.

13 *Memoranda of Conversations*, 15 February 1952, Egypt and the Sudan; *FRUS 1952–1954* 5, Pt. 1: 97; *FRUS 1952–1954* 9, Pt. 2: 1765, 1773–76; Holland, 27; Miles Copeland, *The Game Player: Confessions of the CIA's Original Political Operative* (London: Aurum Press, 1989), 153–56; see also idem, *Game of Nations*, 51–53, 59, 63.

14 Secretary, Drummond, Kuh, 3–27–52, Acheson Papers, Box 69, Press Conf. 1949–1953, Jan. 1952–Jan. 1953 Folder, TL; *FRUS 1952–1954* 9, Pt. 2, 1778–86, 1790–93, 1800; Memorandum for the President, 24 April 1952, Truman Papers (PSF), Box 220, NSC Meetings . . . Discussions (1952–53) Folder, TL; *FRUS 1952–1954* 9, Pt. 1: 218–21, 223–25, 233–34, 238–47, 249–51; Hahn, *Caught in the Middle East*, 78.

15 *FRUS 1952–1954* 9, Pt. 2, 1808–13; Eden, 260.

16 Holland, 22; *FRUS 1952–1954* 9, Pt. 2: 1824–43; Memo, Press Conf., Salazar's, 7–5–52, Acheson Papers, Box 69, Press Conf. 1949–1953, Jan. 1952–Jan. 1953 Folder, TL; Daily Meetings, 18 July 1952; Joel Gordon, *Nasser's Blessed Movement: Egypt's Free Officers and the July Revolution* (New York: Oxford University Press, 1992), 163; Scott Lucas, "The Limits of Ideology: US Foreign Policy and Arab Nationalism in the Early Cold War," in David Ryan and Victor Pungong, eds., *The United States and Decolonization: Power and Freedom* (New York: St. Martin's Press, 2000), 145–46.

17 Heiss, 104–5, 107, 109–10; *FRUS 1952–1954* 10: 285; Daniel Yergin, *The Prize: The Epic Quest for Oil, Money, and Power* (New York: Simon & Schuster, 1991), 466; Leffler, *Preponderance of Power*, 478; *PAC*, 679.

18 *FRUS 1952–1954* 10: 304–5, 311–20; Memorandum of Conversation at Dinner at British Embassy, Sunday, January 6, 1952, Acheson Papers, Box 67, TL; *FRUS 1952–1954* 9, Pt. 1: 175–76; Princeton Seminars, 15 May 1954; Heiss, 116.

19 *Executive Sessions of the Senate Foreign Relations Committee . . . 1952* 4: 18, 20–21; *Selected Executive Session Hearings of the Committee, 1951–1956*, 179, 182–85. Mosadeq's attitude toward military aid also came from a reluctance to build up a military mainly loyal to the Shah. Karabell, 70.

20 *FRUS 1952–1954* 10: 323–27; Heiss, 113, 117–18.

21 *FRUS 1952–1954* 10: 366–69, 371; David S. Painter, *Oil and the American Century: The Political Economy of U.S. Foreign Oil Policy, 1941–1954* (Baltimore: Johns Hopkins University Press, 1986), 184; Heiss, 109, 119; Amy L. S. Staples, "Seeing Diplomacy through Bankers' Eyes: The World Bank, the Anglo-Iranian Oil Crisis, and the Aswan High Dam," *Diplomatic History* 26 (Summer 2002): 401–9.

22 *FRUS 1952–1954* 10: 371–77, 379n, 382–86, 407–8; Daily Meetings, 21 May 1952; Gasiorowski, "The 1953 Coup," 265, 269, 283n; Daily Meetings, 16 May 1952; Memo, Press Conf., Salazar's, 7–5–52, Acheson Papers, Box 69, Press Conf. 1949–1953, Jan. 1952–Jan. 1953 Folder, TL.

23 Heiss, 131–33.

24 *PAC*, 679–80; *FRUS 1952–1954* 10: 414–25, 427–30; Henderson Oral History, TL, 227; Karabell, 78–79; Acheson to Truman, 30 July 1952, Truman Papers (PSF), Box 159, Subj. File–Cabinet, State, Secretary–Misc Folder, TL; Heiss, 137, 139; *Memorandum of Conversation, Iran*, 31 July 1952, Acheson Papers, Box 67a, TL.

25 Heiss, 138–46; *FRUS 1952–1954* 10: 433–37, 439–43, 445–51, 455–79; *PAC*, 680–81; Princeton Seminars, 15 May 1954; Goode, *In the Shadow of Musaddiq*, 88.

26 Heiss, 146, 152–53; *PAC*, 682; *Memoranda of Conversations*, 10 September 1952, Visit of Dr. Luns; Stephen D. Krasner, "A Statist Interpretation of American Oil Policy toward the Middle East," *Political Science Quarterly* 94 (Spring 1979): 88–89; Gasiorowski, "The 1953 Coup," 275; Nitze Oral History, TL, 324; *FRUS 1952–1954* 10: 482–92; Muhammad Musaddiq to Acheson, [7 October 1952], Truman Papers, Box 159, Subj. File–Cabinet, State, Secretary–

Misc Folder, TL; Burton I. Kaufman, *The Oil Cartel Case: A Documentary Study of Antitrust Activity in the Cold War Era* (Westport, CT: Greenwood Press, 1978), 44.

27 *FRUS 1952–1954* 10: 498, 504.

28 Lucas, "Limits of Ideology," 146; *FRUS 1952–1954* 9, Pt. 2: 1863; *PAC*, 567.

29 *PAC*, 566; Daily Meetings, 23 July 1952; Gordon, 165, 167–78; Acheson to Truman, 30 July 1952, Truman Papers (PSF), Box 159, Subj. File–Cabinet, State, Secretary–Misc Folder, TL; Dur, 65–66; Holland, 29.

30 *FRUS 1952–1954* 9, Pt. 2: 1857–61; Persson, 84–85; Gordon, 168; Zubok, "Soviet Intelligence and the Cold War," 459.

31 Sachar, 603; Holland, 30, 32; Hahn, *Caught in the Middle East*, 92–93; *FRUS 1952–1954* 3: 63; *FRUS 1952–1954* 9, Pt. 2: 1863–65.

32 *FRUS 1952–1954* 9, Pt. 2: 1877; Gordon, 168; Holland, 32.

33 *FRUS 1952–1954* 10: 510–13, 518–21, 539; Goode, *In the Shadow of Musaddiq*, 92; Byroade Oral History, TL, 125–26; Nitze Oral History, TL, 325–27, 329; Heiss, 154, 157–58; *PAC*, 683–84; Princeton Seminars, 15 May 1954; Samii, 131–32; B. I. Kaufman, *Oil Cartel Case*, 45.

34 *FRUS 1952–1954* 1, Pt. 1: 25; *FRUS 1952–1954* 10: 540–42; Shuckburgh, 55–56; Princeton Seminars, 15 May 1954.

35 *FRUS 1952–1954* 10: 544–46, 552, 555–61, 563–65, 580–81; Heiss, 158, 160–63; *PAC*, 684; Princeton Seminars, 15 May 1954; Henderson Oral History, TL, 226–27; Byroade Oral History, TL, 124; Mosher, et al., 148; *FRUS 1952–1954* 9, Pt. 1: 655–56; B. I. Kaufman, *Oil Cartel Case*, 46–47.

36 Holland, 32–33; *FRUS 1952–1954* 9, Pt. 1: 311–13, 1092; *FRUS 1952–1954* 9, Pt. 2: 1889–91, 1907, 1927–28, 1954–55, 1961, 1964–65; *PAC*, 567; Poole, 180; Hahn, *Caught in the Middle East*, 82; Rami Ginat, *The Soviet Union and Egypt, 1945–1955* (London: Frank Cass, 1993), 159; Hahn, *United States, Great Britain, and Egypt*, 151; Eban, *Autobiography*, 172.

37 Princeton Seminars, 15 May 1954.

38 *PAC*, 567; C. L. Sulzberger, *The Last of the Giants* (New York: Macmillan, 1970), 331; Acheson to Truman, 4 December 1956, Acheson Papers, Box 31, Folder 395, YUL.

39 Gavin, 78–81; Blum, *CIA*, 68; James A. Bill, "America, Iran, and the Politics of Intervention, 1951–1953," in James A. Bill and William Roger Louis, eds., *Musaddiq, Iranian Nationalism, and Oil* (Austin: University of Texas Press, 1988), 279; Gasiorowski, "U.S. Foreign Policy toward Iran," 59–60; Gendzier, *Notes from the Minefield*, 147–48; Gasiorowski, "The 1953 Coup," 270, 282n; Acheson to Truman, 3 May 1961, Acheson Papers, Box 31, Folder 398, YUL. In December 1952, Charles Bohlen instructed Byroade to contact and cooperate (whatever that meant) with Kermit Roosevelt. Gavin, 80.

40 Peter Grose, *Gentleman Spy: The Life of Allen Dulles* (Boston: Houghton Mifflin, 1994), 364; Douglas Little, "Gideon's Band: America and the Middle East since 1945," *Diplomatic History* 18 (Fall 1994): 520; Kinzer, 164; Mosher, et al., 150; B. I. Kaufman, "Mideast Multinational Oil," 954. Mosadeq died in 1967 after fourteen years of imprisonment and house arrest. Steve Marsh believes that, given more time to be frustrated with Mosadeq, Truman and Acheson would have approved his ouster by covert means. "Continuity and Change: Reinterpreting the Policies of the Truman and Eisenhower Administrations toward Iran," *Journal of Cold War Studies* 7 (Summer 2005): 79–123.

41 *PAC*, 685; Princeton Seminars, 15 May 1954; Goode, *In the Shadow of Musaddiq*, 45, 96.

Chapter 33

1 "Neighboring" is a matter of perception. Washington, D.C., is almost the same distance from Moscow as from Rio de Janeiro; London is over a thousand miles closer to D.C. than Rio.

2 McFall Oral History, TL, 72; Agrément for Appointment of Víctor Andrade as Ambassador of Bolivia, 23 June 1952, Miller Lot Files (53), Box 2, D26, National Archives (courtesy of Christopher Welch); Peter H. Smith, *Talons of the Eagle: Dynamics of U.S.-Latin American Relations*, 2d ed. (New York: Oxford University Press, 2000), 125. Thanks to Philip Brenner for the Berle quotation. See footnote 1, Chapter 1, on calling citizens of the United States "Americans."

3 *PAC*, 257–58, 497; Daily Meetings, 3 January 1950.

4 R. F. Smith, "United States Policy-Making for Latin America," 100–101; *New York Times*, 16 August 1951; *FRUS 1950* 2: 590, 700; *FRUS 1951* 2: 930n, 1102, 1108, 1139; Griffis, 254; Acheson to Marshall Shulman, 14 October 1954, Acheson Papers, Box 28, Folder 366, YUL. Miller may have been echoing the once common remark of Austrians that the condition of the Austro-Hungarian Empire was "critical but not serious."

5 Speech by the Honorable Dean Acheson, Secretary of State, before the Pan American Society of the United States, at the Roosevelt Hotel, New York City, Monday, September 19, 1949, at 9:30 P.M., E.D.T., Clark Clifford Papers, Box 43, TL; *PAC*, 330.

6 Abell, 10; *FRUS 1950* 2: 622; Leslie Bethell, "From the Second World War to the Cold War: 1944–1954," in Abraham F. Lowenthal, ed., *Exporting Democracy: The United States and Latin America* (Baltimore: Johns Hopkins University Press, 1991), 64; "Y," "On a Certain Impatience with Latin America," *Foreign Affairs* 28 (July 1950): 565–79.

7 Princeton Seminars, 14 March 1954 and 9 July 1953; *Memoranda of Conversations*, 2 November 1951, General Assembly; *Selected Executive Session Hearings of the Committee*, *1951–1956*, 181.

8 Miscamble, *Kennan and the Making of American Foreign Policy*, 314–15, 317; *FRUS 1950* 2: 600–602, 624, 767n; Kennan, *Memoirs 1925–1950*, 480; Michael L. Krenn, *The Chains of Interdependence: U.S. Policy toward Central America, 1945–1954* (Armonk, NY: M. E. Sharpe, 1996), 43–44.

9 *FRUS 1950* 2: 592–93; Stephen G. Rabe, "The Elusive Conference: United States Economic Relations with Latin America, 1945–1952," *Diplomatic History* 2 (Summer 1978): 290–91; *Executive Sessions of the Senate Foreign Relations Committee . . . 1952*, 4: 28; Morris H. Morley, *Imperial State and Revolution: The United States and Cuba, 1952–1986* (New York: Cambridge University Press, 1988), 41.

10 Charles D. Ameringer, *The Caribbean Legion: Patriots, Politicians, and Soldiers of Fortune, 1946–1950* (University Park: Penn State University Press, 1996), passim; John H. Coatsworth, *Central America and the United States: The Clients and the Colossus* (New York: Twayne Publishers, 1994), 60; *FRUS 1949* 2: 604; Edward G. Miller, Jr., to Willard L. Beaulac, 12 December 1950, Edward G. Miller Papers, Box 1, Assistant Secretary Correspondence, B, Folder 1, TL.

11 Rabe, "Elusive Conference," 292; *FRUS 1950* 2: 686–87; Chester J. Pach, Jr., "The Containment of U.S. Military Aid to Latin America, 1944–49," *Diplomatic History* 6 (Summer 1982): 232–33, 235, 239; idem, *Arming the Free World*, 43–44, 51–53; Schwartzberg, 80; Christopher Welch, "Heads of Wheat and Heads of Pins: A Narrative Account of U.S.-Argentine Relations, 1945–1946" (unpublished paper, 1992), 10–11; *FRUS 1949* 2: 606; Stephen G. Rabe, "Inter-American Military Cooperation, 1944–1951," *World Affairs* 137 (Fall 1974): 142.

12 John Child, *Unequal Alliance: The Inter-American Military System, 1938–1978* (Boulder: Westview Press, 1980), 116; *FRUS 1951* 2: 925–28, 960, 969; Acheson, Memorandum for the President, Subject: Meeting of Consultation of Ministers of Foreign Affairs of American States, December 16, 1950, Truman Papers (PSF), Box 159, Subj. File–Cabinet, State, Secretary–Misc Folder, TL.

13 Secretary of State Acheson to the President of the United States, Memorandum for the President, Subject: Continuation of Diplomatic Relations with Cuba, 24 March 1952, Truman Papers (PSF), Box 159, Subj. File–Cabinet, State, Secy, Misc Conference Folder, TL;

F. Parkinson, *Latin America, The Cold War, & The World Powers, 1945–1973* (Beverly Hills: Sage, 1974), 28.

14 Krenn, *Chains of Interdependence*, 84, 160; Princeton Seminars, 22 July 1953; Karl Bermann, *Under the Big Stick: Nicaragua and the United States since 1848* (Boston: South End Press, 1986), 239; *Public Papers of the Presidents . . . 1952*; Memorandum for the President, Subject: Visit of General Anastasio Somoza, President of Nicaragua, May 1, 1952, Truman Papers (PSF), Box 183, Nicaragua, TL; A. Somoza to the President, Truman Papers (PSF), Box 183, Nicaragua, TL.

15 *PAC*, 666–70; *FRUS 1952–1954* 4: 592; *Among Friends*, 73–74.

16 Joseph S. Tulchin, *Argentina and the United States: A Conflicted Relationship* (Boston: Twayne, 1990), 100, 107; Glenn J. Dorn, " 'Bruce Plan' and Marshall Plan: The United States's Disguised Intervention against Peronism in Argentina, 1947–1950," *International History Review* 21 (June 1999): 351; *FRUS 1951* 2: 1085n, 1086n, 1139; *Selected Executive Session Hearings of the Committee, 1951–1956*, 181.

17 Cole Blasier, "The United States and Revolution," in James M. Malloy and Richard S. Thorn, eds., *Beyond the Revolution: Bolivia since 1952* (Pittsburgh: University of Pittsburgh Press, 1971), 53; James F. Siekmeier, *Aid, Nationalism, and Inter-American Relations: Guatemala, Bolivia, and the United States, 1945–1961* (Lewiston, NY: Edwin Mellen Press, 1999), 5–6.

18 James W. Wilkie, *The Bolivian Revolution and U.S. Aid since 1952: Financial Background and Context of Political Decisions* (Los Angeles: Latin American Center, University of California, Los Angeles, 1969), 30–31; Herbert S. Klein, *A Concise History of Bolivia* (New York: Cambridge University Press, 2003), 207, 211; *FRUS 1949* 2: 525, 543n; *FRUS 1950* 2: 745, 750–51, 753; *FRUS 1951* 2: 1152–54, 1158, 1166n; Siekmeier, *Aid, Nationalism, and Inter-American Relations*, 231–32; James L. McDonald, "Overriding Interests: Subversion as an Instrument of U.S. Foreign Policy" (Ph.D. Dissertation, American University, 1998), 304–5; *FRUS 1952–1954* 4: 485.

19 McDonald, 303, 320–22; *FRUS 1951* 2: 1150–51; G. Earl Sanders, "The Quiet Experiment in American Diplomacy: An Interpretative Essay on United States Aid to the Bolivian Revolution," *Americas* 33 (July 1976): 32–35; Siekmeier, *Aid, Nationalism, and Inter-American Relations*, 22, 236; Blasier, 63–64; Bryce Wood, *The Dismantling of the Good Neighbor Policy* (Austin: University of Texas Press, 1985), 146–47; *FRUS 1952–1954* 4: 490–93n.

20 *Memoranda of Conversations*, 7 October 1952, Call of the Vice President of Bolivia; Siekmeier, *Aid, Nationalism, and Inter-American Relations*, 238; idem, " '[T]he Most Generous Assistance': U.S. Economic Aid to Guatemala and Bolivia, 1944–1959," *Journal of American and Canadian Studies* 11 (March 1994): 26–27; Wood, 146–47; Blasier, 65; Sanders, 33; *FRUS 1952–1954* 4: 493n, 510; McDonald, 310, 314–15; Klein, 214, 217–18.

21 *FRUS 1950* 2: 603; Nicholas Cullather, *Operation PBSUCCESS: The United States and Guatemala, 1952–1954* (Washington: History Staff, Center for the Study of Intelligence, Central Intelligence Agency, 1994), 17. A more readily available edition of Cullather's book is titled *Secret History: The CIA's Classified Account of Its Operations in Guatemala, 1952–1954* (Stanford: Stanford University Press, 1999).

22 Kenneth D. Lehman, "Revolutions and Attributions: Making Sense of Eisenhower Administration Policies in Bolivia and Guatemala," *Diplomatic History* 21 (Spring 1997): 196; Coatsworth, 67; Ronald Schneider, *Communism in Guatemala, 1944–1954* (New York: Praeger, 1958), 48.

23 *FRUS 1949* 2: 654–55; Gaddis Smith, *The Last Years of the Monroe Doctrine, 1945–1993* (New York: Hill & Wang, 1994), 75; *Executive Sessions of the Senate Foreign Relations Committee . . . 1951* 3, Pt. 1: 358; Ayers Oral History, TL, 139.

24 McDonald, 259; Richard H. Immerman, *The CIA in Guatemala: The Foreign Policy of Intervention* (Austin: University of Texas Press, 1982), 97, 99, 118; Wood, 154; *FRUS 1949* 2: 656–58.

25 *FRUS 1950* 2: 869–74, 876–80, 901, 907; Immerman, 99–100; Wood, 155; Stephen Schlesinger and Stephen Kinzer, *Bitter Fruit: The Untold Story of the American Coup in Guatemala* (Garden City, NY: Doubleday, 1982), 85–86; Coatsworth, 69; LaFeber, *Inevitable Revolutions*, 116. In 1999 Harvard University Press issued an "expanded edition" of Schlesinger and Kinzer's book.

26 *FRUS 1950* 2: 885–86, 902, 917; Immerman, 94, 109–10; Wood, 143; Krenn, *Chains of Interdependence*, 179, 181; Siekmeier, "Most Generous Assistance," 7; idem, *Aid, Nationalism, and Inter-American Relations*, 18n.

27 *FRUS 1950* 2: 888–89, 904–7; McDonald, 256; Michael W. Dravis, "Storming Fortress Albania: American Covert Operations in Microcosm, 1949–54," *Intelligence and National Security* 7 (October 1992): 426; Cullather, *Operation PBSUCCESS*, 10.

28 Immerman, 61, 106; Karabell, 100; Stephen M. Streeter, "Interpreting the 1954 U.S. Intervention in Guatemala: Realist, Revisionist, and Postrevisionist Perspectives," *History Teacher* 34 (November 2000): 67; *FRUS 1950* 2: 922, 922n; Cullather, *Operation PBSUCCESS*, 11–12; *Executive Sessions of the Senate Foreign Relations Committee . . . 1951* 3, Pt. 1: 345; Siekmeier, *Aid, Nationalism, and Inter-American Relations*, 17, 217; *FRUS 1951* 2: 1418–19, 1430; Schneider, 297; Sharon I. Meers, "The British Connection: How the United States Covered Its Tracks in the 1954 Coup in Guatemala," *Diplomatic History* 16 (Summer 1992): 412.

29 *FRUS 1951* 2: 1436–44, 1446–48; Cullather, *Operation PBSUCCESS*, 12; Siekmeier, *Aid, Nationalism, and Inter-American Relations*, 218; Krenn, *Chains of Interdependence*, 64, 173; *Memoranda of Conversations*, 14 September 1951, Development of Land and Zinc properties in Guatemala.

30 *Executive Sessions of the Senate Foreign Relations Committee . . . 1952* 4: 28; Immerman, 117; McDonald, 265; Wood, 141.

31 *FRUS 1952–1954* 4: 1031–37; McDonald, 260; Cullather, *Operation PBSUCCESS*, 13; Karabell, 103; Siekmeier, *Aid, Nationalism, and Inter-American Relations*, 220–21; Coatsworth, 71.

32 www.state.gov/r/pa/ho/frus/ike/guat/ (viewed 7/29/05) (henceforth referred to as *Guatemala, 1952–1954*), Editorial Note, Document 8, Editorial Note, Documents 14, 31; Central Intelligence Agency, Office of the Director, Memorandum for Rear Admiral Robert L. Dennison, Naval Aide to the President, Subject: Estimate of Situation in Guatemala, 14 January 1952, Truman Papers (PSF), Box 178, G–PSF Subject File, TL; Cullather, *Operation PBSUCCESS*, 17–18; Princeton Seminars, 22 July 1953; McDonald, 269–71; Brigadier General Cornelius J. Mara, Oral History Interview, 7 and 9 June 1971, 75–76, www.trumanlibrary.org/oralhist/maracorn.htm (viewed 7/29/05).

33 McDonald, 270–71; *Guatemala, 1952–1954*, Editorial Note, Documents 10, 12, 17, 21, 23; Schlesinger and Kinzer, 92; Piero Gleijeses, *Shattered Hope: The Guatemalan Revolution and the United States, 1944–1954* (Princeton: Princeton University Press, 1991), 228–30; Immerman, 120–21; Matthews, 262–63; Cullather, *Operation PBSUCCESS*, 18; C. J. Mara, Memorandum for the President, 11 July 1952, Truman Papers (PSF), Box 178, G–PSF Subject File, TL; C. J. Mara, Memorandum for the President, 11 July 1952, Truman Papers (PSF), Box 178, G–PSF Subject File, TL; C. J. Mara, Memorandum for the President, 11 July 1952, and Pencil Notes, Truman Papers (PSF), Box 178, G–PSF Subject File, TL. "PB" was cryptospeak for Guatemala (thanks to Nick Cullather).

34 Matthews, 264; www.trumanlibrary.org/calendar/index.html (viewed 7/29/5).

35 *Guatemala, 1952–1954*, Documents 17, 23, Editorial Note 19; *Memorandum of Conversation, Central American Plots and Plans*, 26 September 1952, Miller Lot Files (53), Box 8, D26, National Archives; *Memorandum of Conversation, Action against Guatemala*, 26 September 1952, National Archives; *Memorandum of Conversation, Nicaragua's Desire for Arms*, 29 September 1952, National Archives; *FRUS 1952–1954* 4: 1041–42. Thanks to Christopher Welch for the Sevilla-Sacasa memoranda. While CIA documents identify Mara at this time as a colonel, Mann on 3 October describes him as "Brigadier General Mara."

36 *Guatemala, 1952–1954*, Document 20; Whelan to Mann, 13 October 1952, Lot Files, RG 59, Nicaragua, National Archives (courtesy of Christopher Welch).

37 Cullather, *Operation PBSUCCESS*, 19; *Guatemala, 1952–1954*, Document 23; Burton Hersh, *The Old Boys: The American Elite and the Origins of the CIA* (New York: Charles Scribner's Sons, 1992), 338–39; Lankford, 249.

38 *Guatemala, 1952–1954*, Editorial Note 19, Documents 23–25; Whelan to Mann, 13 October 1952, Lot Files, RG 59, Nicaragua, National Archives (courtesy of Christopher Welch). "Tachito"—Anastasio Somoza Debayle—was Nicaragua's president 1967–72 and 1974–79.

39 For three examples, see Coatsworth, 72; John E. Findling, *Close Neighbors, Distant Friends: United States-Central American Relations* (Westport: Greenwood Press, 1987), 112; and Karabell, 104.

40 Princeton Seminars, 22 July 1953; Acheson to Truman, 3 May 1961, Acheson Papers, Box 31, Folder 398, YUL.

41 *Memoranda of the Secretary of State* M-692-94 (US-Guatemalan Relations), 17 November 1952; *Memoranda of the Secretary of State* M-705-07 (Talk with Guatemalan Ambassador), 1 December 1952; *FRUS 1952–1954* 4: 1055–56; Lehman, 186.

42 Coatsworth, 70–71; www.greekworks.com/english/politics/2003/0401_kitroeff.php (viewed 7/29/05). Arbenz's exile was torturous, leading him from Mexico to Switzerland to France to Czechoslovakia to the Soviet Union to Uruguay to Cuba and finally again to Mexico, where he drowned in his own bathtub in 1971. His body was exhumed from a cemetery in El Salvador and reburied in Guatemala in 1995.

Chapter 34

1 *Memoranda of Conversations*, 7 January 1952, Meeting in Secretary's Office; *Selected Executive Session Hearings of the Committee, 1951–1956*, 170.

2 *FRUS 1952–1954* 6, Pt. 2: 1577; Rolf Steininger, *The German Question: The Stalin Note of 1952 and the Problem of Reunification*, ed., Marc Cioc, trans., Jane T. Hedges (New York: Columbia University Press, 1990), 25; *PAC*, 632.

3 *Documents on British Policy* II-2: 197; *FRUS 1952–1954* 5, Pt. 1: 7–8, 10, 12–13, 15, 17–24; *FRUS 1952–1954* 6, Pt. 2: 1144–45. French efforts to attach the Saar failed; the local population in a 1956 referendum chose to join the FRG, which it did on 1 January 1957 as the Saarland.

4 *New York Times*, 7 and 9 February 1952; *FRUS 1952–1954* 5, Pt. 1: 26–28; Bark and Gress, 290; Poole, 149–50.

5 *Selected Executive Session Hearings of the Committee, 1951–1956*, 176, 241–42; *PAC*, 612–14.

6 McGeehan, 177; *FRUS 1952–1954* 5, Pt. 1: 68; Princeton Seminars, 13 December 1953; *New York Times*, 13 February 1952; *PAC*, 611.

7 *PAC*, 616; *FRUS 1952–1954* 5, Pt. 1: 40–43, 45–52; Rothwell, 109; London to Secretary of State (Acheson to Truman), 16 February 1952, Truman Papers (PSF), Box 165, Subj. File–Conferences Sec. State–Rome, Italy, etc., Folder, TL.

8 *PAC*, 615–19; *FRUS 1952–1954* 5, Pt. 1: 53–71; *New York Times*, 19 February 1952; *Selected Executive Session Hearings of the Committee, 1951–1956*, 243, 245. One translation of *Rechtskraft* would be "legal force."

9 *PAC*, 619–21; *FRUS 1952–1954* 5, Pt. 1: 72–78, 80–86; *New York Times*, 20 February 1952.

10 *PAC*, 600, 608; Mawby, 73.

11 Acheson, *Sketches from Life*, 47, 110; *PAC*, 622; Princeton Seminars, 14 March 1954; *Selected Executive Session Hearings of the Committee, 1951–1956*, 252.

12 *PAC*, 622–23; *Selected Executive Session Hearings of the Committee, 1951–1956*, 251; *FRUS 1952–1954* 5, Pt. 1: 176.

13 *FRUS 1952–1954* 5, Pt. 1: 129–31, 134–35, 155, 174–75, 251–55; *PAC*, 624–28; Poole, 151. Salazar deflected Acheson's interest in purchasing uranium mined in Portugal.

14 *FRUS 1952–1954* 5, Pt. 1: 142–45, 158–60; *PAC*, 623–26; Princeton Seminars, 14 February and 14 March 1954; Hopkins, 239, 244n.

15 *FRUS 1952–1954* 5, Pt. 1: 165–68, 170, 175–79, 260.

16 Ibid., 174; *New York Times*, 24, 26, and 28 February, and 1 March 1952; *PAC*, 627; *Selected Executive Session Hearings of the Committee, 1951–1956*, 248–49, 253.

17 *FRUS 1952–1954* 5, Pt. 1: 174, 259; Acheson to Charles M. Spofford, 28 March 1952, Acheson Papers, Box 43, Secretary of State, '49–53, Alph., Spaak-Srebnick Folder, TL; Wolfram F. Hanrieder, *Germany, America, Europe: Forty Years of German Foreign Policy* (New Haven: Yale University Press, 1989), 243.

18 McGeehan, 197; Princeton Seminars, 14 March 1954; *PAC*, 627, 709; Williamson and Rearden, 175.

19 Memo, Press Conf., 4-16-52, Acheson Papers, Box 69, Press Conf. 1949–1953, Jan. 1952–Jan. 1953 Folder, TL; *FRUS 1952–1954* 7, Pt. 1: 24–25, 87–88; *Memoranda of Conversations*, 10 April 1952, Discussion of Items of General Interest to the Dutch; *FRUS 1952–1954* 5, Pt. 1: 641, 683; Princeton Seminars, Outline of Discussion for the October 9–10 Meetings, the Defense of Europe, and 12 December 1953; *Memoranda of Conversations*, 6 May 1952, Indochina, North Africa . . . ; *PAC*, 623, 641–44; *FRUS 1952–1954* 6, Pt. 2: 1214–15, 1215n; Mastny, *Cold War and Soviet Insecurity*, 143; Prittie, 168; Steininger, *German Question*, 98.

20 *PAC*, 644–46; *FRUS 1952–1954* 7, Pt. 1: 96–102, 105–18, 142–65; *Executive Sessions of the Senate Foreign Relations Committee . . . 1952* 4: 469; Leffler, *Preponderance of Power*, 458–59.

21 Theodore H. White, 325; *PAC*, 647; *New York Times*, 28 May 1952; Leffler, *Preponderance of Power*, 459; Ruane, "Refusing to Pay the Price," 75; Hans-Peter Schwarz, 685; Charles G. Cogan, *Oldest Allies, Guarded Friends: The United States and France since 1940*, foreword, Stanley Hoffmann (Westport: Praeger, 1994), 83; Eden, 52.

22 *PAC*, 709; *New York Times*, 21 June 1952.

23 *FRUS 1952–1954* 7, Pt. 2: 1260; *Memoranda of Conversations*, 2 June 1952, Luncheon; *FRUS 1952–1954* 6, Pt. 1: 142; *FRUS 1952–1954* 5, Pt. 1: 313; Kisatsky, 637.

24 Wall, *United States and Making of Postwar France*, 190; Kevin Ruane, *The Rise and Fall of the European Defence Community: Anglo-American Relations and the Crisis of European Defence, 1950–55* (Houndmills, Basingstoke, Hampshire: Macmillan Press, 2000), 35; *FRUS 1952–1954* 6, Pt. 2: 1229–31, 1248–52, 1256–59.

25 *FRUS 1952–1954* 6, Pt. 2: 1266–67, 1277–78, 1289; Wall, *United States and Making of Postwar France*, 231; Hitchcock, *France Restored*, 177; Princeton Seminars, 14 March and 16 May 1954.

26 *FRUS 1952–1954* 6, Pt. 1: 649; John W. Young, "German Rearmament and the European Defence Community," in Young, ed., *The Foreign Policy of Churchill's Peacetime Administration 1951–1955* (Leicester: Leicester University Press, 1988), 87.

27 *FRUS 1952–1954* 6, Pt. 1: 651–52; *Documents on Canadian External Relations* 18: 715–16, 721; *FRUS 1952–1954* 6, Pt. 2: 2062; *FRUS 1952–1954* 1, Pt. 1: 11, 27.

28 Shuckburgh, 51; U.S. Congress, Senate, Committee on Foreign Relations, *Executive Sessions of the Senate Foreign Relations Committee (Historical Series). Volume V: Eighty-Third Congress, First Session, 1953* (Washington: Government Printing Office, 1976), 13; Text of Secretary Acheson's Statement to the North Atlantic Council, Thurs, 18 December 1952, George M. Elsey Papers, Box 101, Personal Correspondence–Acheson Folder, TL; *PAC*, 707–10; *Memoranda of Conversations*, 14 December 1952; John L. Harper, 325; *FRUS 1952–1954* 5, Pt. 1: 352.

29 *Executive Sessions of the Senate Foreign Relations Committee . . . 1953* 5: 7; Ismay, 38; Powaski, *Entangling Alliance*, 25; Hanrieder, 41.

30 Acheson to Truman, 8 October 1953, Acheson Papers, Box 30, Folder 391; Wall, *United States and Making of Postwar France*, 45–54, 235, 264–65; Cogan, 75, 93; Edward Fursdon, "The Role of the European Defense Community in European Integration," in Heller and Gillingham, 236; Michael Creswell and Marc Trachtenberg, "France and the German Question, 1945–1955," *Journal of Cold War Studies* 5 (Summer 2003): 23; Ruane, *Rise and Fall*, 6–7.

31 *Documents on British Policy* II-3: 84–85.

32 Kaplan, *Community of Interests*, 175.

Chapter 35

1 *FRUS 1952–1954* 5, Pt. 1: 46n, 282; Evan Luard, *A History of the United Nations. Volume 1: The Years of Western Domination, 1945–1955* (New York: St. Martin's Press, 1982), 226–28.

2 *FRUS 1952–1954* 7, Pt. 1: 169–72; Mastny, *Cold War and Soviet Insecurity*, 135–36.

3 *PAC*, 630; Mastny, *Cold War and Soviet Insecurity*, 136–37; Kissinger, *Diplomacy*, 501; *Memoranda of Conversations*, 13 March 1952, Prohibition of Production of Influence Mines in Germany, Reply to Soviet note.

4 W. R. Smyser, *From Yalta to Berlin: The Cold War Struggle over Germany* (New York: St. Martin's Press, 1999), 115; Adam Ulam, *Expansion and Coexistence: The History of Soviet Foreign Policy, 1917–67* (New York: Praeger, 1968), 535.

5 *PAC*, 631; Steininger, *German Question*, 53.

6 Steininger, *German Question*, 52–53; Smyser, 115; Young, *Winston Churchill's Last Campaign*, 95; *PAC*, 630.

7 Ninkovich, *Germany and the United States*, 95; Bird, *Chairman*, 380; Steininger, *German Question*, 10, 23, 72.

8 Acheson to President Truman, 11 March 1952, Acheson Papers, Box 67, TL; *FRUS 1952–1954* 7, Pt. 1: 182, 184; van Dijk, 6, 27, 27n; Steininger, *German Question*, 21n, 25, 29, 55, 57; *Memoranda of Conversations*, 13 March 1952, Prohibition of Production of Influence Mines in Germany, Reply to Soviet note; Smyser, 116.

9 *FRUS 1952–1954* 7, Pt. 1: 174, 183–92; Acheson to President Truman, 19 March 1952, Acheson Papers, Box 67, TL; Hanrieder, 153; Steininger, *German Question*, 61; *PAC*, 631.

10 *New York Times*, 27 March 1952; Secretary, Drummond, Kuh, 3–27–52, Acheson Papers, Box 69, Press Conf. 1949–1953, Jan. 1952–Jan. 1953 Folder, TL; Acheson to Herbert Bayard Swope, 31 March 1952, Acheson Papers, Box 43, Secretary of State, 1949–53, Alpha.–Sta–Sz Folder, TL.

11 "Stalin and the SED Leadership, 7 April 1952: 'You Must Organize Your Own State,'" *CWIHPB* (Issue 4, Fall 1994): 48; *FRUS 1952–1954* 7, Pt. 1: 199–202.

12 *FRUS 1952–1954* 7, Pt. 1: 204–8, 210–12; *Memoranda of Conversations*, 10 April 1952, Discussion of Items of General Interest to the Dutch; *Memoranda of Conversations*, 11 April 1952; Memo, Press Conf., 4–16–52, Acheson Papers, Box 69, Press Conf. 1949–1953, Jan. 1952–Jan. 1953 Folder, TL; The Secretary, Bryson Rash . . . George de Carvalho . . . Holmes Alexander . . . Lloyd Lehrbas, Acheson Papers, Box 69, Press Conf. 1949–1953, Jan. 1952–Jan. 1953 Folder, TL; *New York Times*, 20 April 1952.

13 *FRUS 1952–1954* 7, Pt. 1: 223–47, 339, 342, 345; Steininger, *German Question*, 81.

14 *FRUS 1952–1954* 7, Pt. 1: 247–56, 258–65, 267–73; Mastny, *Cold War and Soviet Insecurity*, 139; *New York Times*, 25 May 1952; Steininger, *German Question*, 87–88; Ninkovich, *Modernity and Power*, 296.

15 *FRUS 1952–1954* 7, Pt. 1: 274–81, 287–91.

16 Ibid., 292–98, 301–4, 323–26; *FRUS 1952–1954* 6, Pt. 2: 1585–86; Steininger, *German Question*, 92.

17 Richardson, 35.

18 Resis, *Molotov Remembers*, 36; Gaddis, *We Now Know*, 127; Gerhard Wettig, "Stalin and German Reunification: Archival Evidence on Soviet Foreign Policy in the Spring of 1952," *Historical Journal* 37 (June 1994): 415, 417, 418.

19 Mastny, *Cold War and Soviet Insecurity*, 135–36; van Dijk, 23; "'You Must Organize Your Own State,'" *CWIHPB* (Issue 4, Fall 1994): 48; Naimark, *Russians in Germany*, 166; Mark Kramer, "The Early Post-Stalin Succession Struggle and Upheavals in East-Central Europe: Internal-External Linkages in Soviet Policy Making (Part 3)," *Journal of Cold War Studies* 1 (Fall 1999): 11–12; Wettig, 418; Steininger, *German Question*, 146; Christian F. Ostermann, "The United States, the East German Uprising of 1953, and the Limits of Rollback" (Washington: Cold War International History Project, Woodrow Wilson International Center for Scholars, Working Paper No. 11, December 1994): 4; *FRUS 1952–1954* 7, Pt. 2: 1555–57; "'This Is Not a Politburo, But a Madhouse': The Post-Stalin Succession Struggle, Soviet Deutschlandpolitik and the SED: New Evidence from Russian, German, and Hungarian Archives," introduced and annotated by Christian F. Ostermann, *CWIHPB* (Issue 10, March 1998): 62; James Richter, "Reexamining Soviet Policy towards Germany during the Beria Interregnum" (Washington: Cold War International History Project, Woodrow Wilson International Center for Scholars, Working Paper No. 3, June 1992): 8–9.

20 Richardson, 36–37.

21 Young, *Winston Churchill's Last Campaign*, 97; Barnet, 138; Ulam, 537.

22 Richter, 25.

23 *New York Times*, 21 February, 20 April, and 7 October 1952; Leffler, *Preponderance of Power*, 488; Gaddis, *Strategies of Containment*, 124; *FRUS 1952–1954* 2, Pt. 1: 58–59, 144, 147–48, 156. My emphasis.

24 Kennan, *Memoirs 1950–1963*, 166; David Mayers, "George Frost Kennan (1904–)," in Nolan, 213–14.

25 *FRUS 1952–1954* 8: 962n, 967–68; Miscamble, "Rejected Architect and Master Builder" 456–57; Kennan, *Memoirs 1950–1963*, 107–11.

26 *FRUS 1952–1954* 8: 970–79, 979n; 981–84; Kennan, *Memoirs 1950–1963*, 120–21.

27 *FRUS 1952–1954* 8: 985–1000, 1011–13, 1021–38, 1042–43; *Washington Post*, 20 October 1995.

28 Kennan, *Memoirs 1950–1963*, 158–59; *FRUS 1952–1954* 8: 1049.

29 *FRUS 1952–1954* 6, Pt. 1: 644–46, 658–61.

30 Kennan, *Memoirs 1950–1963*, 162; *FRUS 1952–1954* 8: 1048–51.

31 Kennan, *Memoirs 1950–1963*, 163–64; *FRUS 1952–1954* 8: 1053–57, 1058n, 1058–59; Peter Grose, *Operation Rollback: America's Secret War behind the Iron Curtain* (Boston: Houghton Mifflin, 2000), 209; www.afa.org/magazine/june2001/0601overfly.asp (viewed 11 August 2005). Because Dulles gave Kennan no new assignment, he again left the foreign service in the spring of 1953. Miscamble, "Rejected Architect and Master Builder," 461.

Chapter 36

1 *FRUS 1952–1954* 2, Pt. 2: 934.

2 PAC, 686–93; McCullough, 907; *New York Times*, 17 October 1952; Brinkley, *Dean Acheson*, 9–10.

3 Rhodes, 502; *FRUS 1952–1954* 2, Pt. 2: 1051–52, 1055; *New York Times*, 14 January 1993; Paul Boyer, "'Some Sort of Peace': President Truman, the American People, and the Atomic Bomb," in Lacey, 201.

4 Kennan, *Memoirs 1950–1963*, 170; Shuckburgh, 69; *New York Times*, 2 November 1952; Acheson, "Legislative-Executive Relations," 495; *PAC*, 633; *New York Times*, 15 January 1953; *PAC*, 716–17. The "other poet" was Californian Edward Pollock (1823–58), the poem, "The Parting Hour."

5 *Among Friends*, 89; Brinkley, *Dean Acheson*, 11; *PAC*, 717–20; *New York Times*, 17 January 1953; Graebner, "Dean G. Acheson," 287–88; Truman to Acheson, 16 January 1953, Acheson Papers, Box 30, Folder 391, YUL; K. P. S. Menon, *The Flying Troika: Extracts from a Diary by K. P. S. Menon, India's Ambassador to Russia 1952–61* (London: Oxford University Press, 1963), 21.

6 *PAC*, 721; Chace, 363.

7 *New York Times*, 2 February 1958.

8 Brinkley, *Dean Acheson*, 330.

9 Chace, 367; Donaldson, 418; Douglas Brinkley, "Dean Acheson and the 'Special Relationship': The West Point Speech of December 1962," *Historical Journal* 33 (September 1990): 599; Acheson to Sir Roy Welensky, 11 July 1968, Acheson Papers, Box 33, Folder 430, YUL; Cabell Phillips, "Dean Acheson Ten Years Later," *New York Times Magazine*, 18 January 1959, 60; Brinkley, *Dean Acheson*, 264; Acheson to Michael Janeway, 23 April 1962, Acheson Papers, Box 16, Folder 209, YUL; Phillips, "Ten Years Later," 10, 60; Schlesinger, *Life in the Twentieth Century*, 443.

10 Nitze Oral History, TL, 361–62; Acheson to Henry Byroade, 21 August 1956, Box 4, Folder 55, and to C. B. (Burt) Marshall, 27 April 1955, Box 22, Folder 278, Acheson Papers, YUL; Brinkley, *Dean Acheson*, 18, 226; Acheson to Louis Halle, 17 March 1955, Box 15, Folder 189, and to Michael Janeway, 23 April 1962, Box 16, Folder 209, Acheson Papers, YUL; Merry, 355, 417; Annan, "Dean Acheson," 473, 476–77; William McBrien, *Cole Porter: A Biography* (New York: Alfred A. Knopf, 1998), 377; Brinkley, *Dean Acheson*, 339n.

11 David Acheson, 58; *New York Times*, 2 February 1958 and 8 April 1961; Acheson Oral History, JFKL, 13; Brinkley, *Dean Acheson*, 18; Chace, 369; Reston in "Dean Acheson, a Remembrance," 35; Reston, *Deadline*, 153; Henry A. Kissinger, *Years of Renewal* (New York: Simon & Schuster, 1999), 1062; *Among Friends*, 133; Merle Miller, 375.

12 Bell, 154–55; Acheson to Truman, 17 September 1958, Box 31, Folder 397, YUL; Chace, 408; C. L. Sulzberger, *An Age of Mediocrity: Memoirs and Diaries, 1963–1972* (New York: Macmillan, 1973), 658–60.

13 Brinkley, *Dean Acheson*, 226; *New York Times*, 6 April 1966.

14 James A. Bill, *George Ball: Behind the Scenes in U.S. Foreign Policy* (New Haven: Yale University Press, 1997), 140; Acheson to Roy Wilensky, 26 January 1971, Box 34, Folder 432, to Alastair Buchan, late June 1963, Box 4, Folder 50, to Barbara Tuchman, 1 June 1967, Box 31, Folder 401, to Noël G. Annan, 21 December 1959, Box 1, Folder 8, and to Michael Janeway, 5 March 1963, Box 16, Folder 209, Acheson Papers, YUL; Brinkley, "Acheson and European Unity," 150; idem, *Dean Acheson*, 4; Sulzberger, *Giants*, 575.

15 Acheson to Truman, 8 October 1953, Box 30, Folder 391, Acheson Papers, YUL; Monte M. Poen, ed., *Letters Home* (New York: Putnam, 1984), 246; Francis H. Heller, "Harry S Truman: The Writing of His Memoirs," in Egerton, 266, 268; Acheson to Truman, 21 June 1955, Box 30, Folder 393, to Truman, 18 July 1955, Box 31, Folder 394, to Truman, 5 February, 1954, Box 30, Folder 392, to Truman, 15 January 1957, Box 31, Folder 396, and to Truman, 16 and 17 September 1958, Box 31, Folder 397, Acheson Papers, YUL.

16 *New York Times Book Review*, 12 October 1969, 30; *PAC*, 712–13; David Acheson, 201; Brinkley, *Dean Acheson*, 19, 34, 67; Dean Acheson, "Instant Retaliation: The Debate Continued," *New York Times*, 28 March 1954; Acheson, *Democrat*, 70–71, 74, 79; Acheson to Henry Byroade, 21 August 1956, Box 4, Folder 55, and to Truman, 4 December 1956, Box 31, Folder 395, Acheson Papers, YUL; Sulzberger, *Age of Mediocrity*, 659.

17 Brinkley, *Dean Acheson*, 56, 58; Brinkley and Thomas, 67; Arthur M. Schlesinger, *A Thousand Days: John F. Kennedy in the White House* (Boston: Houghton Mifflin, 1965), 280–81; Bill, *Ball*, 140; Acheson to Truman, 31 August 1959, Box 31, Folder 397, Acheson Papers, YUL.

18 Miscamble, "Rejected Architect and Master Builder," 464; Kennan, *Memoirs 1950–1963*, 250; Brinkley, *Dean Acheson*, 80–84; *New York Times*, 12, 13, and 19 January 1958; Hixson, 181; John L. Harper, 327; John Foster Dulles to Acheson, 13 January 1958, Box 9, Folder 111, Acheson Papers, YUL.

19 Douglas Brinkley, "Kennan-Acheson: The Disengagement Debate," *The Atlantic Community Quarterly* 25 (Winter 1987–1988): 418; Miscamble, "Rejected Architect and Master Builder," 463, 464–65; George Kennan to Acheson, 20 March 1958, Box 17, Folder 222, Acheson Papers, YUL; *Among Friends*, 137; Acheson to Philip Jessup, 25 March 1958, Box 17, Folder 212, Acheson Papers, YUL.

20 Acheson, "Illusion of Disengagement," 371–82; Kennan to Acheson, 20 March 1958, Box 17, Folder 222, Acheson Papers, YUL; Hixson, 183; Miscamble, "Rejected Architect and Master Builder," 465.

21 Brinkley, *Dean Acheson*, 91.

22 Ronald J. Nurse, "Critic of Colonialism: JFK and Algerian Independence," *Historian* 39 (February 1977): 314, 318; Acheson Oral History, JFKL, 2.

23 Acheson Oral History, JFKL, 2, 6–9; Acheson to Dirk Stikker and Mme. Stikker, 1 November 1960, Acheson Papers, Box 29, Folder 375, YUL; Clifford, *Counsel to the President*, 362; Brinkley, *Dean Acheson*, 113–16; Acheson Oral History, JFKL, 6–9; Martin Mayer, *Diplomats*, 75.

24 Acheson Oral History, JFKL, 13–14; Acheson to Truman, 3 May, 14 July, and 21 September 1961, Box 31, Folder 398, Acheson to John Davies, 18 April 1963, Box 7, Folder 93, Acheson Papers, YUL; "No yearning to be loved," 444; Weintal and Bartlett, 162; Michael R. Beschloss, *Crisis Years: Kennedy and Khrushchev, 1960–1963* (New York: Edward Burlingame Books, 1991), 249; Brinkley, *Dean Acheson*, 309.

25 Kaplan, "Dean Acheson and the Atlantic Community," 49; Dean Acheson, "Wishing Won't Hold Berlin," *Saturday Evening Post*, 7 March 1959, 82, 85–86; Brinkley, *Dean Acheson*, 2; McGeorge Bundy, *Danger and Survival: Choices about the Bomb in the First Fifty Years* (New York: Random House, 1988), 372; Acheson Oral History, JFKL, 10–11; Nitze, *Hiroshima to Glasnost*, 197; Beschloss, 242; Brinkley, "Acheson and Monnet," 94; Nancy Bernkopf Tucker, "China's Place in the Cold War," 125n; Trachtenberg, *Constructed Peace*, 298.

26 Acheson, Notes to Henry Owen, Acheson Papers, Box 85, State Department & White House Advisor 1961 Folder, TL; Acheson Oral History, JFKL, 17, 19; Catudal, 143–47; Beschloss, 244.

27 Kai Bird, *The Color of Truth: McGeorge Bundy and William Bundy, Brothers in Arms: A Biography* (New York: Simon & Schuster, 1998), 210, 212; T. J. Schoenbaum, 338; Beschloss, 257; Acheson to Eelco Van Kleffans, 6 September 1961, Acheson Papers, Box 85, State Department & White House Advisor 1961 September Folder, TL; Acheson to Truman, 21 September 1961, Box 31, Folder 398, Acheson Papers, YUL.

28 Dean Acheson, "Our Atlantic Alliance: The Political and Economic Strands," *Vital Speeches of the Day*, January 1, 1963: 163–64; Douglas Brinkley, "Dean Acheson and the 'Special Relationship': The West Point Speech of December 1962," *Historical Journal* 33 (September 1990): 604, 607; Lankford, 310; *New York Times*, 8 December 1962; Klaus Larres, *Churchill's Cold War: The Politics of Personal Diplomacy* (New Haven: Yale University Press, 2002), 176; Brinkley, *Dean Acheson*, 320; "Hard Words," 827.

29 Isaacson and Thomas, 620–22, 625; Acheson Oral History, JFKL, 24, 26–27; T. J. Schoenbaum, 321; James A. Nathan, "The Heyday of the New Strategy: The Cuban Missile

Crisis and the Confirmation of Coercive Diplomacy," *Diplomacy & Statecraft* 3 (July 1992): 320; James G. Blight and David A. Welch, *On the Brink: Americans and Soviets Reexamine the Cuban Missile Crisis*, foreword, McGeorge Bundy (New York: Hill and Wang, 1989), 352; Neustadt and May, 7; Ball, *Past Has Another Pattern*, 294; Brinkley, *Dean Acheson*, 164; "No yearning to be loved," 443; Lankford, 307–8.

30 Beschloss, 521; Brinkley, *Dean Acheson*, 170; Theodore C. Sorensen, *Kennedy* (New York: Harper & Row, 1965), 810; "Dean Acheson's Version of Robert Kennedy's Version of the Cuban Missile Affair: Homage to Plain Dumb Luck," *Esquire* (February 1969): 76–78, 94, 96.

31 Lucius Battle Oral History, JL, 2; Brinkley, *Dean Acheson*, 205, 207; "Dean Acheson," in Publishers Weekly Editors and Contributors, *The Author Speaks: Selected PW Interviews, 1967–1976* (New York: R. R. Bowker, 1977), 416.

32 Weintal and Bartlett, 103–4; Acheson to Desmond Donnelly, 11 April 1966, Acheson Papers, Box 88, State Department & White House Advisor 1965–68, Folder 4, TL; Brinkley, *Dean Acheson*, 235; Acheson to Jane Acheson Brown, 18 April 1966, Box 4, Folder 48, to Anthony Eden, 29 June 1966, Box 9, Folder 117, Acheson to Truman, 3 October 1966, Box 31, Folder 400, and Acheson to Anthony Eden, 30 December 1967, Box 9, Folder 118, Acheson Papers, YUL; Acheson to Dick (Lord) Casey, 15 August 1966, Acheson Papers, Box 88, State Department & White House Advisor 1965–68, Folder 5, TL; Acheson to Truman, 28 June 1966, Acheson Papers, Box 88, State Department & White House Advisor 1965–68, Folder 5, TL.

33 Claude Nicolet, *United States Policy Towards Cyprus, 1954–1974: Removing the Greek-Turkish Bone of Contention* (Bibliopolis: Mannheim und Möhnesee, 2001), 251–89; Ball, "Present after the Creation," 14; *New York Times*, 5 September 1964; Acheson to Lucius D. Battle, 7 December 1964, Box 2, Folder 26, Acheson Papers, YUL.

34 George Ball Oral History, JL, 3–4, 8; Bird, *Chairman*, 578; Isaacson and Thomas, 651; Bill, *George Ball*, 80.

35 Acheson to John Cowles, 21 August 1967, Box 7, Folder 84, Acheson Papers, YUL; Walt W. Rostow to LBJ, 20 October 1967, National Security File, Box 95–96: Vietnam, JL; Memorandum to Johnson, 2 November 1967, Meeting Notes File, Box 2, JL; Jim Jones to the President, [2 November 1967], Meeting Notes File, Box 2, JL; Jim Jones to the President, [2 November 1967], Meeting with Foreign Policy Advisors, Thurs, November 2, 1967, Meeting Notes File, Box 2, JL; Isaacson and Thomas, 692; www.citizinemag.com/commentary/commentary-0308_iraqdebate.htm (viewed 8/14/05); Acheson to John Cowles, 14 March 1968, Acheson Papers, Box 88, State Department & White House Advisor 1965–68, Far East, Nuclear Proliferation, Gold Crisis Folder, TL. In 1804, Boulay de la Meurthe, hearing of a duke's execution, proclaimed: "C'est pire qu'un crime, c'st une faute."

36 Townsend Hoopes, *The Limits of Intervention: An Inside Account of How the Johnson Policy of Escalation in Vietnam Was Reversed* (New York: David McKay, 1969), 205; Brinkley, *Dean Acheson*, 260–62; Rusk, 480; Clifford, *Counsel to the President*, 517–18.

37 Isaacson and Thomas, 697–98.

38 Brinkley, *Dean Acheson*, 220, 262.

39 Henry A. Kissinger, *White House Years* (Boston: Little, Brown, 1979), 942; Evan Thomas, "Why Were We in Vietnam? He'll Tell You," *New York Times Book Review*, 23 March 2003, 10; Acheson to Henry Kissinger, 15 December 1964, Box 18, Folder 226, and to Sir Roy Welensky, 11 July 1968, Box 33, Folder 430, Acheson Papers, YUL; Kissinger, *Years of Renewal*, 190; Gregory T. D'Auria, "Present at the Rejuvenation: The Association of Dean Acheson and Richard Nixon," *Presidential Studies Quarterly* 18 (Spring 1988): 394–96.

40 D'Auria, 399–400, 403; *New York Times*, 10 October 1969; Schulzinger, 93; Acheson to Lord Avon (Anthony Eden), 9 September 1971, Box 9, Folder 119, Acheson Papers, YUL; Brinkley, *Dean Acheson*, 301; Isaacson and Thomas, 717.

41 Jay Winik, *On the Brink: The Dramatic, Behind-the-Scenes Saga of the Reagan Era and the Men and Women Who Won the Cold War* (New York: Simon & Schuster, 1996), 52–53; D'Auria, 402–3; Kissinger to Acheson, 21 May 1971, Box 18, Folder 226, Acheson Papers, YUL; Williams, 179–80, 184; Kissinger, *White House Years*, 945.

42 SR62-199, Presentation of bust of Dean Acheson at Truman Library, 31 March 1962, Recording, TL; Reston in "Dean Acheson: A Remembrance," 35–36; Acheson to Truman, 8 October 1953, Box 30, Folder 391, and 5 February 1954, Box 30, Folder 392, Acheson Papers, YUL; Princeton Seminars, 14 March 1954; *New York Times Book Review*, 23 May 1961, 37.

43 Brinkley, *Dean Acheson*, 266; "Acknowledgments" in *PAC*; *Author Speaks*, 416; Acheson to James Reston, 8 March 1967, Reston Papers, Box 30–Working Files, UIA.

44 *New York Times Book Review*, 12 October 1969, 8; Brinkley, *Dean Acheson*, 277.

45 Sulzberger, *Age of Mediocrity*, 657; Helen Lilienthal, 214. With no supporting evidence, Charles W. Yost pegs the late Acheson to hardening of the arteries. *The Conduct and Misconduct of Foreign Affairs* (New York: Random House, 1972), 66.

46 Truman to Acheson, 4 December 1956, Box 31, Folder 395, Acheson Papers, YUL; Phillips, "Ten Years Later," 10; Westwood, 351–52; Brinkley and Thomas, 71–72; Acheson to Roy Welensky, 30 June 1970, Box 33, Folder 431, Acheson Papers, YUL; David Acheson, 154.

47 "Hard Words," 827–28; Acheson to Lord Avon (Anthony Eden), 9 September 1971, Box 9, Folder 119, Acheson Papers, YUL: Sulzberger, *Age of Mediocrity*, 658–60.

48 Acheson to Roy Wilensky, 26 January 1971, Box 34, Folder 432, and to Lord Avon (Anthony Eden), 9 September 1971, Box 9, Folder 119, Acheson Papers, YUL; Bill, *George Ball*, xvii.

49 Richard D. Mahoney, *JFK: Ordeal in Africa* (New York: Oxford University Press, 1983), 216; Acheson, "Foreword," 15; Acheson, Oral History, JFKL, 14–15, 18; Acheson to Eelco Van Kleffans, 7 August 1961, Acheson Papers, Box 85, State Department & White House Advisor 1961 August Folder, TL; Barbara Evans to Acheson, n.d., Box 41, Folder 38, Acheson Papers, YUL; Brinkley, *Dean Acheson*, 389n; McNay, 36–37, 198–99.

50 Miscamble, "Rejected Architect and Master Builder," 466; Chace, 433; Acheson to Lewis Douglas, 26 October 1969, Box 9, Folder 110, to Sir William Elliott, 2 January 1967, Box 9, Folder 122, and to Ranald McDonald, 20 November 1969, Box 34, Folder 264, Acheson Papers, YUL; *New York Times*, 21 April 1971; *Washington Post*, 11 December 1966; Anthony Lake, *The "Tar Baby" Option: American Policy toward Southern Rhodesia* (New York: Columbia University Press, 1976), 112–13; Brinkley, *Dean Acheson*, 316–18; Dean Acheson, *Dean Acheson on the Rhodesian Question* (Washington, DC: Rhodesian Information Office, n.d. [1969?]), 3, 5.

51 Acheson, *Rhodesian Question*, 7–9, 22, 27–28; Brinkley, *Dean Acheson*, 317–23; Lake, 115, 128n; Acheson to Sir Roy Welensky, 11 July 1968, Acheson Papers, Box 33, Folder 430, YUL; D'Auria, 405.

52 Brinkley, *Dean Acheson*, 318, 326–27; Acheson to John Cowles, 29 May 1971, Box 7, Folder 86, Acheson Papers, YUL.

53 Andrew J. DeRoche, *Black, White, and Chrome: The United States and Zimbabwe, 1953 to 1998* (Trenton, NJ: African World Press, 2000), 172; Brinkley and Thomas, 71; Brinkley, *Dean Acheson*, 326; Gerald Horne, "Race from Power: U.S. Foreign Policy and the General Crisis of 'White Supremacy,'" *Diplomatic History* 23 (Summer 1999): 457. While anti-Chinese sentiment in California helped account for the popularity of Harte's "The Heathen Chinee," or "Plain Language from Truthful James" (1870), the intent of the verses may have been satirical or ironical.

54 Chace, 437; *New York Times*, 13 and 17 October 1971; *Washington Post*, 13 October 1971; Helen Lilienthal, 237; *Public Papers of the Presidents . . . 1971*, 1041; Brinkley, *Dean Acheson*, 330.

55 "History of the Dean Acheson Auditorium," Office of the Historian, U.S. Department of State, July 2003.

Chapter 37

1 Kissinger, *Years of Renewal*, 599.

2 See chapters 2 and 9 for much of the language (and connecting citations) in this and the following paragraph.

3 Acheson, Oral History, JFKL, 13; *Pattern of Responsibility*, 19, 21–23, 41; Friedberg, *Shadow of the Garrison State*, 76.

4 Paul Kennedy, "The Modern Machiavelli," *New York Review of Books*, 7 November 2002, 52.

5 *Pattern of Responsibility*, 32–33; *PAC*, 380.

6 http://64.233.161.104/search?q=cache:HtFGMoXFWMwJ:dosfan.lib.uic.edu/ERC/briefing/dossec/1993/9304/930421dossec.html++%22as+dangerous+as+they+were+creative%22&hl=en (viewed 8/17/05); Theodore H. White, 343–44; *New York Times*, 27 October 1976; Weil, 268.

7 See the highly suggestive exercise in "counterfactual history" in Kaplan, *Long Entanglement*, 221–37.

8 *PAC*, 727.

9 Josef Joffe, "How America Does It," *Foreign Affairs* 76 (September/October 1997): 27.

10 Martin Malia, *The Soviet Tragedy: A History of Socialism in Russia, 1917–1991* (New York: Free Press, 1994), 122; Djilas, 191.

11 Michael Dobbs, "Plane Incident Illustrates Historic Soviet Insecurity," *Washington Post*, 19 September 1983, quoting Seweryn Bialer, *Stalin and His Generals: Soviet Military Memoirs of World War II* (New York: Pegasus, 1969).

12 Anne Applebaum, "The Worst of the Terror," *New York Review of Books*, 17 July 2003, 16; Vladislav Zubok, "Stalin's Plans and Russian Archives," *Diplomatic History* 21 (Spring 1997): 296–97, 305; Djilas, 106; Tony Judt, "Why the Cold War Worked," *New York Review of Books*, 9 October 1997, 42.

13 Leffler, *Preponderance of Power*, 445.

14 Mastny, *Cold War and Soviet Insecurity*, 164–66.

15 *PAC*, 3.

16 Acheson, *Democrat*, 96–97; Meeting with magazine and book publishers, 29 June 1951, Old State Building, Reston Papers, Box 30, Working Files, 24, UIA.

17 War College Speech, 16 September 1948, Acheson Papers, Box 69, TL.

INDEX

Nitze, Paul H. (*cont'd*):
Formosa, 278; and Franks, 685n. 8;
and German reconstruction, 357, 361,
458; and the Hiss case, 294, 295; and
Indochina, 490, 491–92, 493; and
interagency meetings, 122; and Iran, 546,
554, 559, 561, 563, 564, 566; and Kennan,
118; and the Kennedy administration,
629, 630; and Korea, 395, 398, 415, 425;
and the Marshall Plan, 55; and NSC-68,
119–20, 239, 240, 241–42, 243, 244, 246;
and nuclear weapons, 229, 230, 231, 233,
235; social life, 624; and Turkey, 42; and
Webb resignation, 463, 742n. 38
Nixon, Richard: on Acheson's death, 640;
Acheson's service to, 622; and China
relations, 498; and the Hiss case, 282,
287–88, 296; and McCarthyism, 307; and
presidential campaign, 620; and Vietnam,
635
Nobel Peace Prize, 114
Nordic Pact, 133
North Africa, 39, 132, 512, 519–25, 594,
599, 600. *See also specific countries*
North Atlantic Naval Command, 465
North Atlantic Treaty Organization
(NATO): Acheson's emphasis on, 88, 157,
622; and Acheson's legacy, 644, 645, 647,
648; and the ANZUS pact, 502; and the
CFM, 141, 147, 148, 149; and China, 183;
and the cold war, 376, 622–23, 646, 649;
and defense spending, 236; and the EDC,
589–97, 598, 599–603; and Egypt, 549,
555; and European reconstruction,
257–58, 261–64; and export controls, 380;
and German reconstruction, 161, 356,
358, 360, 362, 364–66, 368–69, 369–74,
453–58, 460–61, 466; and the "Great
Debate," 450; and Indochina, 485, 487,
492, 535; and Iran, 563; and the Johnson
administration, 632–33; and Kennan, 118;
and Kennedy, 628–29; and Korea, 330,
333, 334, 344, 352, 420, 424, 446, 459–60,
634; Lisbon meeting, 465–66; and Louis
Johnson, 123; and the Marshall Plan,
78; and McCarthyism, 310; and MDAP
assistance, 158, 159; and Mediterranean
issues, 160; and the Middle East, 514,
537, 542; and military aid, 252; and the
National War College speech, 388; and
Nixon, 634; and North Africa, 523, 524;
and NSC-68, 244; and nuclear weapons,

223, 224, 225, 227, 231; origins of,
128–34; and postwar foreign policy, 500;
ratification efforts, 687n. 36; and Soviet
peace plans, 607, 608, 610, 611; and Spain,
385, 386, 387; and sub-Saharan Africa,
526, 527; and trade policy, 164; and the
Truman Doctrine, 49; and the UN, 532,
533; UN contrasted with, 530; and
Vietnam, 269, 270; and West Germany,
603; and Yugoslavia, 168
North Korea: and Acheson's legacy, 644;
and China, 204; and export controls, 381;
and German reconstruction, 361; impact
of War on, 648; and Indochina, 487; and
prisoners of war, 437–38, 439, 444; push
for war, 332; Soviet influence in, 446; and
the 38th parallel, 719n. 2; and "total
diplomacy," 250; war damage, 653.
See also Korean War
North Vietnam, 169
Norway, 132, 133, 202, 346, 353
NSC-34-2, 180
NSC-41, 180, 198
NSC-48-2, 197, 199
NSC-48-5, 489
NSC-68: and Acheson's legacy, 644; analysis
of, 243–44; and the cold war, 616; creation
of, 238–41; and defense spending, 377;
and the EDC, 597; and Eisenhower,
626; and European reconstruction, 252,
264, 265, 458; and hydrogen bomb
development, 228; and interagency
meetings, 122; and Kennan, 118; and
Korea, 323–24, 334, 349, 411, 426, 437,
652–53; and the Middle East, 542; and
military strength, 244–45, 375; and the
National Security Act, 123; and Nitze,
119–20; and nuclear weapons, 224, 225,
232, 235; origins of, 237–38; policy
recommendations, 241–43; and public
opinion, 245–46, 247–48, 319; and
realism, 650; and "total diplomacy,"
248–51; and Truman, 704–5n. 4
NSC-81-1, 398
NSC-124-2, 493
NSC-135-3, 616
nuclear weapons: and the Acheson-
Lilienthal Plan, 31–35, 38, 643, 668n. 18;
Acheson's comments on, 108; Acheson's
evolution on, 45; and the balance of
power, 154; and the Berlin crisis, 630;
and the cold war, 1, 377, 646, 651; and

CPSIA information can be obtained
at www.ICGtesting.com
Printed in the USA
LVHW050604151220
674181LV00004B/9